D0773238

THE AGRARIAN
HISTORY OF ENGLAND
AND WALES

THE AGRARIAN HISTORY OF ENGLAND AND WALES

GENERAL EDITOR
JOAN THIRSK

M.A., PH.D., HON.D.LITT., F.B.A., F.R.HIST.S.

*Sometime Reader in Economic History
in the University of Oxford*

III

1348–1500

THE AGRARIAN
HISTORY OF ENGLAND
AND WALES

VOLUME III 1348–1500

EDITED BY
EDWARD MILLER

M.A., HON.D.LITT., F.B.A., F.R.HIST.S.

Sometime Master of Fitzwilliam College, University of Cambridge

Mills College Library
Withdrawn

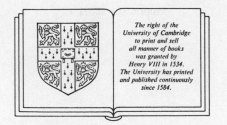

The right of the
University of Cambridge
to print and sell
all manner of books
was granted by
Henry VIII in 1534.
The University has printed
and published continuously
since 1584.

CAMBRIDGE UNIVERSITY PRESS

CAMBRIDGE
NEW YORK   PORT CHESTER
MELBOURNE   SYDNEY

Published by the Press Syndicate of the University of Cambridge
The Pitt Building, Trumpington Street, Cambridge CB2 1RP
40 West 20th Street, New York, NY 10011, USA
10 Stamford Road, Oakleigh, Melbourne 3166, Australia

© Cambridge University Press 1991

First published 1991

Printed in Great Britain at the University Press, Cambridge

British Library cataloguing in publication data
The agrarian history of England and Wales.
Vol. 3: 1348–1500
1. England. Agricultural industries, history
1. Miller, Edward, 1915–
338.1'0942
Library of Congress catalogue card number: 66-19763

ISBN 0 521 20074 1

333.0942
A 277
v. 3

CONTENTS

CHAPTER 1

Introduction: Land and People

By EDWARD MILLER

CHAPTER 2

The Occupation of the Land

vii

Mills College Library
Withdrawn
MILLS COLLEGE LIBRARY

CHAPTER 3

Farming Practice and Techniques

CHAPTER 4

Marketing the Produce of the Countryside,
1200–1500

By DAVID L. FARMER, M.A., D.PHIL., F.R.HIST.S.,
Professor and Head of the History Department, St Thomas More College,
University of Saskatchewan

Mills College Library
Withdrawn

CHAPTER 5

Prices and Wages, 1350–1500

By David L. Farmer

CHAPTER 6

Landlords

By J. M. W. Bean, M.A., D.PHIL., F.R.HIST.S.,
Professor of Medieval History, Columbia University in the City of New York

CHAPTER 7

Tenant Farming and Tenant Farmers

CHAPTER 8

Peasant Rebellion and Peasant Discontents

By E. B. FRYDE, M.A., D.PHIL., F.B.A., F.R.HIST.S.,
Professor of History, University College of Wales, Aberystwyth,
and NATALIE FRYDE

CHAPTER 9

Rural Building in England and Wales

ENGLAND

By H. E. J. LE PATOUREL, B.A., F.S.A.

WALES 891

By L. A. S. BUTLER, M.A., PH.D., F.S.A., M.I.F.A.,
Senior Lecturer in Medieval Archaeology, University of York

PLATES

Between pp. 838 and 839

FIGURES

TABLES

Statistical supplement

PREFACE

BY THE GENERAL EDITOR

With the publication of this volume, covering one and a half centuries between 1350 and 1500, a significant period in the agrarian history of England and Wales, encompassing the aftermath of the Black Death, is surveyed, and the gap between volume II, published in 1988, and volume IV, published in 1967, is now bridged. At the same time, the series as a whole has taken a considerable step towards completion, for the only volume remaining unpublished is volume VII, spanning the years 1850–1914, which should appear in 1992–3.

The time taken to complete the different volumes has reflected not only the problems of an enterprise involving many different authors, but also the broadening of the subject, and hence the expansion of ambition, since the scheme was first drawn up in 1956. Starting with some sense of the distinctiveness of the agricultural regions of the kingdom, the editors of volumes II, III, IV, and V strove to exploit the remarkable archives of our local record offices, and to delineate more exactly the separate histories of the regions, in order to arrive at a new synthesis of knowledge and understanding of our varied agricultural, economic, and social experience. The task has proved laborious but richly rewarding, for it has opened up unexpected vistas. As a result, these scholars at the cutting edge of new research would have liked to be able to accommodate at once all their fresh insights in this book, but the overall plan for the series has placed constraints on the desire for infinite flexibility. The present volume is, therefore, a compromise between our view of the subject around 1960 and the panorama, more clearly visible to us in some directions than in others, in 1990.

Any large survey, however, offers new perspectives, and this work has a double reason for that success. Not only does it assemble new knowledge, it also surveys the multifarious regions of England and Wales simultaneously, and so enhances the clarity of strong contrasts. These at once call for deeper layers of explanation to be explored. So we owe a debt of gratitude to Dr Edward Miller and his authors, who have thus placed a new benchmark along the path of the agrarian historian. May it serve the same function as the other volumes already published, of stimulating a fresh bout of research.

In 1967 Professor H. P. R. Finberg, the original editor and planner of
this series of volumes, paid tribute to the small group of scholars from
the 1880s onwards who 'made an epoch' in the writing of agrarian
history – Frederic Seebohm, J. E. Thorold Rogers, Paul Vinogradoff,
and F. W. Maitland. A century later, we can count a larger band of
labourers in a better-tilled countryside. Fewer wastes lie totally
unexplored, although that also means that the eye can now focus on
detail that once went unnoticed. So the unanswered questions multiply,
but the hope is also strengthened that this volume will recruit more
toilers in the field.

Every generation, of course, brings original insights, as it views old
scenes anew. The angle of our vision, however, does not often undergo
such a dramatic shift as has occurred in the late 1980s, consequent upon
the new directions planned for the future of agriculture. Thus we may
expect to benefit from some fresh perspectives on the past, and in
constructing at this time a new framework for the period 1350–1500,
and on a grander scale than any hitherto, Dr Miller and his authors can
take pride in a timely achievement. From its heights we have the chance
to view with broader understanding a traumatic period of agricultural
adaptation in the late Middle Ages, and not least because it contains
features which are not totally alien to our present experience.

PREFACE

This volume of *The Agrarian History of England and Wales* was originally planned, in consultation with the late Professor H. P. R. Finberg and Professor H. E. Hallam, some twenty years ago, and its arrangement was designed to complement that of volume II which Professor Hallam was planning at that time. That intention has been maintained, but inevitably, as a co-operative work completed over an extended period, it has taken some directions of its own; and equally inevitably, although there is a substantial unanimity of approach, not every contributor has viewed the circumstances and developments of the later middle ages in an absolutely identical way. Such divergences, as well as some differences of approach, serve to underline the fact that many matters are still debatable and will continue to be debated. To that extent this survey of the late medieval countryside may perhaps principally be regarded as a contribution to an on-going discussion.

As was the case with volume II, the length of time between the initial planning of volume III and its completion arose from the fact in some cases that suitable contributors could not immediately be found and in others that arrangements made failed to produce results. Some contributors had already submitted drafts by the late 1970s, and while all have availed themselves of the opportunity to revise their contributions in 1988–9, Professor Fryde's chapter on peasant rebellions and discontents and Dr Owen's portions of Chapters 2, 3, and 7 are largely in the form in which they were submitted and revised at the earlier date. Other contributions have been extensively or wholly rewritten, some more than once, and yet others had to be recommissioned at a relatively late date. I found it necessary to assume responsibility for those parts of Chapters 2, 3, and 7 dealing with the southern counties when arrangements to cover that region broke down; and I am greatly indebted to three authors for stepping into similar breaches at very short notice: to Mrs Jean Le Patourel for agreeing to undertake the chapter on rural buildings in England; to Professor Mavis Mate for providing the sections of Chapters 2, 3, and 7 relating to south-east England, and above all to Professor David

Farmer. He not only undertook to provide a chapter on the marketing of agricultural produce, but also agreed to extend its scope backwards to *c.* 1200 in order to compensate in part for the fact that it had proved impossible to provide a chapter on marketing in volume II. Finally, in one respect the present volume differs from volumes published earlier in that Dr Butler decided to provide no illustrations of Welsh rural buildings in his contribution to Chapter 9 since all the relevant illustrative material is available in the 1988 edition of P. Smith's *Houses of the Welsh Countryside*, to which full references are given.

Many obligations have inevitably been incurred in the composition of this volume. In addition to those specifically acknowledged by individual authors, contributors collectively are indebted to the staffs of numerous libraries and record repositories – private, local, university, and national. We are grateful to the following for permission to use and reproduce their photographs: to the Royal Commission on the Historical Monuments of England in Plates Ib, IIb, IIIa, IIIb, IV, Va, VIa, VIb, VIIa, IXa, Xa, Xb, and XIIa; to the Cambridge University Collection of air photographs in Plates IIa, VIIIa, VIIIb and XIIb; to *Country Life* in Plate Vb; and to the British Library in Plate XIb. Dr King also gratefully acknowledges the support he received for his work on the East Midland region from the Huntington Library, San Marino, California; from the USA–UK Educational Commission; and from the British Academy's Small Grants Research Fund in the Humanities. As editor and contributor I owe a special debt to Professor David Farmer for generously furnishing material relating to the southern counties garnered in the course of his own researches, especially in the Winchester and Glastonbury records; to the late Professor Finberg for his guidance in the early days and, more recently, to Dr Joan Thirsk for her encouragement and advice; and to the staff of the Cambridge University Press, most particularly to Mr William Davies and Mrs Margaret Sharman, for their patience, assistance and support.

Midsummer Day, 1989   EDWARD MILLER

ABBREVIATIONS

AA	*Archaeologia Aeliana*
Add.	Additional
AHEW	*The Agrarian History of England and Wales*, II, ed. H. E. Hallam; IV and V, ed. Joan Thirsk
AHR	*Agricultural History Review*
Anglesey Antiq. Soc.	*Transactions of the Anglesey Antiquarian Society and Field Club*
Annales ESC	*Annales: Economies, Sociétés, Civilisations*
Arch. and N.H. Soc.	Archaeological and Natural History Society
Arch. Camb.	*Archaeologia Cambrensis*
Arch. Cant.	*Archaeologia Cantiana*
Arch. Jnl	*Archaeological Journal*
B. Acad.	British Academy
BL	British Library
Bull. BCS	*Bulletin of the Board of Celtic Studies*
Bull. IHR	*Bulletin of the Institute of Historical Research*
Bull. JRL	*Bulletin of the John Rylands Library*
Cal. Inq. Misc.	*Calendar of Miscellaneous Inquisitions*
CBA	Council for British Archaeology
CC	Cambridge University Collection of Air Photographs
CChR	*Calendar of Charter Rolls*
CCR	*Calendar of Close Rolls*
CEcH	*Cambridge Economic History of Europe*, I, ed. M. M. Postan; II, ed. M. M. Postan and Edward Miller; IV, ed. E. E. Rich and C. H. Wilson
CIPM	*Calendar of Inquisitions Post Mortem*
Complete Peerage	G. E. Cockayne, *The Complete Peerage of England, Scotland, Ireland,*

xxiii

	Great Britain and the United Kingdom, revised edn
CPR	*Calendar of Patent Rolls*
CWAAS	*Transactions of the Cumberland and Westmorland Antiquarian and Archaeological Society*
EcHR	*Economic History Review*
EETS	Early English Text Society
EHR	*English Historical Review*
EPNS	English Place Name Society
GAD	Glastonbury Abbey Documents, Longleat House, Wiltshire
Glamorgan Inventory	Royal Commission on Ancient and Historical Monuments of Wales, *An Inventory of the Ancient Monuments in Glamorgan*, in progress
Gras, *English Village*	N. S. B. Gras and E. C. Gras, *The Economic and Social History of an English Village: Crawley, Hampshire*
Harl.	Harleian
HMC	Historical Manuscripts Commission
HMSO	Her Majesty's Stationery Office
Hon. Soc. Cymmr.	*Transactions of the Honourable Society of Cymmrodorion*
i.p.m.	inquisitions *post mortem*
J, Jnl	*Journal*
JMHRS	*Journal of the Merioneth History and Record Society*
Jones Pierce, *MWS*	T. Jones Pierce, *Medieval Welsh Society: Selected Essays*
Leland, *Itinerary*	L. Toulmin Smith, ed., *The Itinerary of John Leland in or about the years 1535–1543*
MCR	Merton College Rolls, Merton College, Oxford
Med. Arch.	*Medieval Archaeology*
Mid. Hist.	*Midland History*
N. & Q.	*Notes and Queries*
NBR	National Buildings Record, Royal Commission on the Historical Monuments of England
NCH	E. Bateson *et al.*, eds., *A History of Northumberland*

NLW	National Library of Wales
North. Hist.	*Northern History*
NS	New Series
OS	Old Series
PP	*Past and Present*
PRO	Public Record Office
RCHM, England	Royal Commission on the Historical Monuments of England
RCHM, Wales	Royal Commission on the Ancient and Historical Monuments of Wales
Rec. Comm.	Record Commission
Rec. Ser.	Record Series
RHS	*Transactions of the Royal Historical Society*
RO	Record Office
Rot. Parl.	*Rotuli Parliamentorum*
RS	Rolls Series
Scriptores Tres, ed. Raine	J. Raine, ed., *Historiae Dunelmensis Scriptores Tres*
Smith, *Houses*	P. Smith, *Houses of the Welsh Countryside*
SR	*Statutes of the Realm*, ed. A. Luders *et al.*
Sussex Arch. Colls.	*Sussex Archaeological Collections*
UCNW	University College of North Wales, Bangor
VCH	*The Victoria History of the Counties of England*
WAM	Westminster Abbey Muniments
WNFC	*Transactions of the Woolhope Naturalists' Field Club*
WPR	Winchester Pipe Rolls, Hampshire Record Office, Eccl. Comm. 2
Yorks. Deeds	W. Brown *et al.*, eds., *Yorkshire Deeds*

CHAPTER 1

INTRODUCTION: LAND AND PEOPLE

Amongst the changes which took place during the last century and a half of the middle ages was a reversal of the demographic tendencies which had prevailed at least since the late twelfth century. The population of the country not only ceased to grow: it became markedly smaller and even in the early sixteenth century it stood at a much lower level than in 1300. The numbers of potential producers, consumers, tenants, and labourers were all drastically reduced. These were circumstances necessarily calling for agrarian readjustment. They conditioned, even where they did not cause, a wide-ranging revision of patterns of estate organization which had dominated the English countryside during the preceding centuries; and they provided the context for major alterations in the relations between landlords and tenants, in the social structure of village populations, and in the coherence of manorial communities which had derived part of their solidarity from the fact that they owed common obligations to a common lord. Some general aspects of these changes will be the concern of this introduction: their diverse manifestations in the various regions of late medieval England and Wales will receive more particular treatment in some of the chapters which follow.

A. PEOPLE

Just how many people there were at different points in time may be regarded as the obvious point of departure for this investigation, but it is one which immediately runs into problems presented by the available evidence. It is possible in the fourteenth and fifteenth centuries occasionally to count taxpayers, sometimes for the country as a whole, or for particular places to establish the number of tenants or of participants in the affairs of manorial courts; in some instances the data provided by court rolls may even allow a degree of family reconstitution to be attempted; but any certainty that all the people have been accounted for, or about the proportion of them accounted

I

for, is much more elusive. There do appear to be indications, however, that in some places the down-turn of the population curve came well before the middle years of the fourteenth century. Nor does this seem only to have been the case in special areas like the northern Borders where Scottish raids had destroyed some agricultural outposts and even farmlands down-country. It has also been persuasively argued that the subsistence crises of the early decades of the fourteenth century reflect a situation in which the land from which an over-populated countryside sought to win its daily bread was, at least in some places, yielding less generously, putting the very lives of the multitude of very small cultivators at risk whenever harvests were poor.[1] These conclusions were drawn from evidence relating to the old-settled parts of southern England and there must be doubt whether anything like this degree of over-population prevailed generally; but on some of the southern estates of the bishops of Winchester the famines of 1315–17 do appear to have been a turning point after which a population that had been rising began to fall back, and on various Essex manors high mortality occasioned by these famines was followed by three decades of demographic decline.[2] On the other hand, the population of Halesowen (Worcs.), although it was significantly reduced by the subsistence crises of the early fourteenth century, was increasing once more in the two or three decades before the Black Death, though at a somewhat slower rate than in the later thirteenth century. In this respect Halesowen may have been at least as typical as Essex or Winchester manors; and in some parts of East Anglia continued population growth down to 1349 seems to have been made possible by exceptionally intensive methods of husbandry and the development of by-employments. The balance between success and failure during the early fourteenth century in meeting the challenge of multiplying people has still to be exactly determined.[3]

There is much less doubt about the long-term demographic trend during the century and a half after 1349, although putting figures to it, explaining it and charting its chronology have generated many debates. This is no place for a study in depth of epidemics in late medieval England, but clearly they were recurrent and of varying sorts. That they also affected population levels seems equally evident so that, in this

---

[1] *AHEW*, II, pp. 258–9; M. M. Postan, in *CEcH*, I, 2nd edn, pp. 556–9; *idem, Essays on Medieval Agriculture*, pp. 150–74.

[2] J. Z. Titow, 'Some evidence of thirteenth-century population increase', *EcHR*, 2nd ser. XIV, 1961, p. 220; L. R. Poos, 'The rural population of Essex in the later middle ages', *EcHR*, 2nd ser. XXXVIII, 1985, p. 521.

[3] Z. Razi, *Life, Marriage and Death in a Medieval Parish*, esp. p. 45; R. M. Smith, ed., *Land, Kinship and Life-Cycle*, pp. 26–7, 90; B. M. S. Campbell, 'Agricultural progress in medieval England: some evidence from eastern Norfolk', *EcHR*, 2nd ser. XXXVI, 1983, pp. 26–46.

respect, the first major plague visitation in 1348–9 was a turning point. One historian of the population of Europe describes it as "probably the greatest single event in the demographic history of the middle ages after the plague of Justinian" and a strong case can be made against those who are inclined to minimize the mortality it occasioned.[4] Indications of its impact, its generality and its severity are numerous. In the Bedfordshire village of Milbrook, for example, the lord of the manor, and then his son and heir and all the bondmen and cottars were said to have died; and the lord of Glensfield (Leics.), his son and his elder grandson all perished, leaving as heir to the manor a second grandson aged only four. 1349 was remembered as a year of pestilence in Cornwall as well as in Bedfordshire; in Essex and Hertfordshire the pestilence was said to be "common", which may not unfairly be interpreted as universal; in Staffordshire and Worcestershire the plague was said to be "deadly"; in Suffolk the abbey of Bury St Edmunds found itself short of monk-priests and plague deaths as well as the sea contributed to the destruction of Dunwich; and even in remote Northumberland the cemetery at Belford had to accommodate the dead of half a dozen adjacent hamlets. The comments of contemporaries were doubtless coloured by the fact that the visitation of 1348–9 was something totally outside their experience, but this does not mean that their impression of its severity and generality must be dismissed as mere exaggeration.[5]

More important from the long-term point of view, however, was the fact that the epidemic of 1348–9 could be described as the "first pestilence" in Huntingdonshire in 1363, in Middlesex in 1373, in Oxfordshire in 1376, in Northumberland in 1377.[6] It was followed by others, possibly somewhat less lethal but almost as widespread, in both England and Wales in 1361–2 (referred to in 1377 in Sussex as the "middle pestilence"), in 1369, in 1375, in 1390.[7] Nor did epidemics end with the fourteenth century. Ely priory had a "monstrous mortality" in 1458–9; in 1421 pestilence was said to have raged in Northumberland, Cumberland and Westmorland for the past three years; a systematic study of death rates among the Canterbury monks has

---

[4] K. F. Helleiner, in *CEcH*, IV, p. 5; and Christopher Morris, review of J. F. D. Shrewsbury, *A History of Bubonic Plague in the British Isles*, in *Historical J.*, XIV, 1971, pp. 209–10.

[5] *VCH Beds.*, III, p. 318; *VCH Worcs.*, IV, p. 448; *CIPM*, IX, nos. 151, 264, 404, and X, nos. 32, 534, 537; *CPR*, 1349–54, p. 105; *CCR*, 1349–54, p. 620; C. Richie, 'The Black Death at St Edmund's abbey', *Suffolk Inst. of Arch.*, XXVII, 1955–7, pp. 47–50; *NCH*, I, pp. 385–6.

[6] *CIPM*, XI, no. 550 and XIII, no. 167; *Cal. Inq. Misc.*, III, no. 992; *NCH*, IX, p. 312.

[7] *CIPM*, XIV, no. 344; J. M. W. Bean, 'Plague, population and economic decline in England in the later middle ages', *EcHR*, 2nd ser. XV, 1963, pp. 427–30; W. Rees, 'The Black Death in Wales', *RHS*, 4th ser. III, 1920, pp. 123–5.

revealed fairly frequent but relatively moderate surges of mortality in the first half of the fifteenth century followed, in its second half, by less frequent but steeper increases of deaths which were often specifically attributed to epidemic disease; and an analysis of literary and testamentary sources relating to East Anglia concludes that epidemic diseases were the most important influence upon mortality rates and that their most important feature was their frequency rather than their virulence.[8] There were still visitations which were more or less country-wide, although most were probably now local or regional in their incidence and towns may have suffered more than the rural areas. It seems hard to deny, however, that these repeated peaks of mortality must have represented a "continual sapping of human resources" over these generations.[9]

At the same time the periodic enhancement of death rates may not, by itself, be the sole explanation of long-term demographic trends. Everything suggests that mortality in 1348–9 was generally far heavier than that caused by any subsequent epidemic; but what has become increasingly evident, since the pioneering work on the effects of the Black Death on the Winchester manors carried out more than seventy years ago, is the rapidity and relative completeness of recovery from a totally unprecedented natural catastrophe.[10] Inevitably there was short-term dislocation; but most (though not quite all) the land which dead tenants had held was fairly soon taken up again, often on terms which had only been marginally modified. Further, although labourers often demanded higher wages and some customary tenants displayed a growing reluctance to perform the services they owed, agricultural price levels were high enough to make the 1350s and 1360s something like an "Indian summer of demesne farming".[11] It is impossible to measure with any degree of accuracy the overall reduction of population, although in one Norfolk village plague in a single year achieved a demographic reversal which seventy years of recurrent famine had failed to accomplish. There must have been variations in its toll from place to place, but the estimate that it was in the range of 30–45 per cent seems reasonable and finds more recent support in estimated losses of 42 per cent among tenants on the lands of the bishop

[8] *VCH Cambs.*, IV, p. 34; *NCH*, III, pp. 42–3; *Rot. Parl.*, IV, p. 143; J. Hatcher, 'Mortality in the fifteenth century: some new evidence', *EcHR*, 2nd ser. XXXIX, 1986, pp. 28–9; R. S. Gottfried, *Epidemic Disease in Fifteenth-Century England*, p. 225.

[9] J. Saltmarsh, 'Plague and economic decline in England', *Cambridge Historical J.*, VII, 1941, p. 40; Bean, 'Plague, population and economic decline', pp. 423, 427–31.

[10] A. E. Levett, *The Black Death on the Estates of the See of Winchester*, esp. pp. 142–60; and compare *idem*, *Studies in Manorial History*, pp. 248–52 and table II, for the St Albans estates.

[11] A. R. Bridbury, 'The Black Death', *EcHR*, 2nd ser. XXVI, 1973, pp. 583–4; C. Dyer, *Lords and Peasants in a Changing Society*, pp. 113–18.

of Worcester, of 41–59 per cent among Durham priory's tenants in south-east Durham, and of 40–46 per cent at Halesowen (four times the level of mortality there in a famine year like 1317).[12]

That the agricultural routine of the countryside was frequently so quickly restored after 1349 must surely reflect first and foremost the reserves of population existing there in 1348 – reserves large enough in many places to constitute a measure of over-population. There may, however, be some indications that population levels recovered somewhat, in the Essex countryside for instance, in the post-plague decade, possibly because the turnover of holdings and the greater availability of land made for earlier and perhaps more fruitful marriages. On the other hand, there is little sign of this recovery at Coltishall (Norfolk), although there and elsewhere it is very difficult to make adequate allowance for the effects of movement of population into and out of particular communities.[13] In any case recovery, if it took place, was probably temporary and there is little sign generally that it was sufficient to lead to a recurrence of over-population in the 1370s.[14] Even in Essex the new wave of epidemics in the 1360s initiated two generations of gently declining population lasting until the early fifteenth century, followed thereafter by stagnation for the rest of that century.

The mortality occasioned by the national epidemics in 1361–2, 1369, and 1375 was much less than that caused by the Black Death in 1348–9: at Halesowen, for instance, it has been calculated that, in each of these three visitations the death rate among males over twenty was only about one-third or less of the 1349 rate, although it was still $4\frac{1}{2}$ to $6\frac{1}{2}$ times the average death rate in the first half of the fourteenth century. Admittedly these peak years were offset by much lower rates in years that were free of epidemics, so that in the period 1350–1400 as a whole the death rate at 2.04 per cent per annum on average was lower than it had been (at 2.48 per cent) over the period 1300–1348; but even so, a population severely diminished by the Black Death was again reduced by the mortalities of the 1360s and 1375, and it continued to fall for

[12] B. M. S. Campbell, 'Population pressure, inheritance and the land market in a fourteenth-century peasant community', in R. M. Smith, ed., Land, Kinship and Life-Cycle, p. 127; J. Hatcher, Plague, Population and the English Economy, 1348–1530, pp. 21–5 with reference to the literature to 1977; Dyer, Lords and Peasants, p. 239; T. Lomas, 'South-east Durham: late fourteenth and fifteenth centuries', in P. D. A. Harvey, ed., The Peasant Land Market in Medieval England, p. 259; Razi, Life, Marriage and Death, p. 103.

[13] Bridbury, 'The Black Death', pp. 589–91; Poos, 'The rural population of Essex', pp. 524–5, 527; Campbell, 'Population pressure, inheritance and the land market', p. 99.

[14] As suggested by I. Blanchard in R. M. Smith, ed., Land, Kinship and Life-Cycle, p. 227 and note.

much of the rest of the century. Nor was Halesowen's experience in any way unusual. Epidemic outbreaks continued in the later fourteenth, the fifteenth, and even into the sixteenth century. In Leicestershire, indeed, it seems to have been the visitation of 1390 which was regarded as the "great pestilence"; and in the West Midlands, as in Kent and East Anglia, both national and more localized epidemics made bouts of high mortality a regular feature in most decades, generating demographic decline or at best the stagnation of most village populations for the rest of the middle ages.[15]

It is a much more difficult matter to convert calculations of the populations of individual parishes (themselves approximations based upon many assumptions) into aggregates for the country as a whole. These have to be based upon records which were drawn up with no demographic end in view, principally the taxation records of 1377 and the tax returns and muster rolls of the 1520s. A rehearsal of the complexities of the calculations involved, or of the debates they have occasioned, would be out of place here; but the present state of discussion suggests that a pre-plague population somewhere in the range of 4.5–6 m had by 1377 been reduced to 2.5–3 m (though some would put the figure as low as 2.2 m) and by the mid-fifteenth century to 2–2.5 m (one estimate for c. 1430 is only 2.1 m). Recovery, moreover, had not gone far by the 1520s, when the most elaborate calculation gives a result of 2.3 m, although it has been suggested that this figure may be on the low side and that a range of 2.5–2.75 m might be preferable.[16] The approximate character of these estimates is obvious enough, but given the evidence available they are the best that can be achieved; and if they can be allowed some validity, they do point to the late middle ages as being "the longest period of declining and stagnant population in recorded English history", a period in which, by the mid-fifteenth century, the inhabitants of the country had been reduced to a level barely if at all higher than that of Domesday England.[17]

It is, of course, over-simple to regard population trends in these generations as no more than a direct response to recurrent peaks of mortality. Some districts and places faced special problems: Scottish raids in the north and French raids in the south, for instance, erosion, and the flooding of sea marshes in many coastal districts, or Glyndŵr's

[15] Razi, *Life, Marriage and Death*, pp. 117, 125–8, 130; *VCH Leics.*, III, pp. 136–7; Dyer, *Lords and Peasants*, pp. 223–5.

[16] Hatcher, *Plague, Population and the English Economy*, pp. 68–70; J. Cornwall, 'English population in the early sixteenth century', *EcHR*, 2nd ser. XXIII, 1970, pp. 32–44; J. C. Russell, *British Medieval Population*, p. 146; W. G. Hoskins, *The Age of Plunder*, London, 1976, p. 4.

[17] Hatcher, *Plague, Population and the English Economy*, pp. 11, 69.

rebellion in Wales and the marches. There might also be other adverse influences. There was land in some Lincolnshire parishes that was sandy and stony and too barren to be let to farm, as well as land that was liable to flooding. Arable at Wilton in Hockwold (Norfolk), on the other hand, was valueless because of the damage done by rabbits from the Duchy of Lancaster warren, while at Enfield (Middx.) and some of the hamlets in Caus forest (Salop) the damage came from deer, and deer as well as plague mortality contributed to the early depopulation of Hale (Northants.).[18] These adverse circumstances, however, merely supplemented a general tendency of population to fall or encouraged people to move to districts which were less unfortunate or more inviting. Yet it is the general downward trend that is in some senses paradoxical since periodic high mortality rates might have been expected to create some of the circumstances favouring a recovery of population levels: land that was more readily available and cheaper to buy or rent, wages that were higher than they had been, a population which in general was probably better fed, all conditions which may have made possible earlier and perhaps more fruitful marriages.

What seems to have happened in fact, however, was that population declined everywhere or almost everywhere (and not merely in places suffering exceptional adversity or poorly endowed by nature) for two or three generations and had still shown little significant recovery by the time of the first Tudor ruler. It is another matter to regard these trends as a simple reflection of periodically high mortality without further qualification. It is possible, for instance, that some epidemics may have been age specific. Plague mortality in 1348–9 may have risen with age, and the fact that the survivors might be in a position to succeed young and marry early could help to explain some signs of a slight recovery of population levels during the following decade.[19] The 1361–2 epidemic, on the other hand, was called "the mortality of children", and a like description may have applied to that of 1369 and perhaps to some later outbreaks. If it is apt, while the life expectancy of adults may have improved somewhat in the later fourteenth century (and there are some indications that it did), that of infants and children is likely to have fallen, creating a rural age structure heavily biased towards the middle-aged and elderly. This might explain why, in circumstances which might be assumed to favour early and fertile marriages, at Halesowen families were smaller in the second half of the fourteenth century than they had been in the first, and other

---

[18] *CIPM*, x, no. 248; xi, no. 183; xiii, nos. 20, 167, 204, 239, 508; xv, no. 27; xvi, nos. 613, 710; K. J. Allison et al., *The Deserted Villages of Northamptonshire*, p. 41.

[19] Razi, *Life, Marriage and Death*, p. 109.

investigators have noticed with some surprise how small families were elsewhere in the later part of that century.[20] Even infant mortality, however, may not be the sole explanation of this phenomenon: it has been suggested that, in some circumstances, it might reflect deliberate delay in marrying or deliberate limits upon fertility; but these are matters upon which fourteenth-century evidence sheds no certain light and that for the fifteenth century is even less explicit and less explored.[21] At the same time it is possible that a tendency for epidemics to take a heavier and more frequent toll of urban than rural populations, by creating vacancies and opportunities in the ranks of townsfolk, had the effect of encouraging migration from country to town, thus draining people from villages into communities in which they were more vulnerable and militating against a general recovery of population levels. Demographic questions of this sort will probably never be answerable with any assurance, given the evidence which is available; but a falling population during the century or so after the Black Death, and no particular signs of an up-turn during the ensuing half century, do appear to be reasonably well established. They were by no means the only causes of agrarian developments over these generations, but as conditioning influences they need constantly to be kept in mind.

B. PEOPLE AND LAND

Falling population obviously altered the balance between the supply of land and the demand for it. The consequences will occupy much space in many of the chapters which follow, but two of them were in general terms a tendency for rent levels to fall over the long term and for the less acceptable incidents of tenures (and of villein tenure in particular) to be whittled away. What happened at Forncett (Norfolk) was in no way exceptional. Much of the bondland by the 1370s and nearly all of it by 1406 was let for money rent rather than services; and there was a progressive fall in the average rent per acre from about $10\frac{3}{4}$d. in 1376–8 to 9d. in 1401–10 and then to $6\frac{1}{2}$–8d. for the rest of the fifteenth century. The Leicester abbey rent roll, too, in 1477 was only two-thirds of what it had been in 1341. At the same time, as the numbers of

[20] *Anonimalle Chronicle, 1333–1381*, ed. V. H. Galbraith, Manchester, 1927, p. 50; A. Gransden, 'A fourteenth-century chronicle from the Grey Friars of Lynn', *EHR*, LXII, 1957, pp. 275–7; Razi, *Life, Marriage and Death*, pp. 130–1, 139–43, 150–1; Helleiner, in *CEcH*, IV, pp. 10–11; Russell, *British Medieval Population*, pp. 230–1, 260–70. For small families, also Dyer, *Lords and Peasants*, pp. 232–4.

[21] Dyer, *Lords and Peasants*, p. 234; Campbell, 'Population pressure, inheritance and the land market', pp. 127–8; J. Hatcher's study of the Canterbury monks, 'Mortality in the fifteenth century', inevitably throws little light on these matters.

villagers decreased, there was more tenant land potentially available to each of them and this was further augmented as landlords jettisoned demesne acres, allowing both the landless and smallholding peasants to add modestly to their minuscule holdings, the middling farmer to add enough to his holdings to afford better support for a family, and entrepreneurs to build up farms in the more modern sense by engrossing holdings, taking up demesne land, or both. Some villagers, of course, at least for some part of their life-cycles, might still have little or no land for, alike in the fourteenth-century poll-tax returns and the Tudor tax rolls, labourers were still a substantial element in the village populations. On the other hand the tendency for tenant numbers to fall was especially marked among tenants with the smallest holdings; and as time passed there were also apt to be rather more tenants with above, and often markedly above, average holdings as an ampler land supply gave greater scope to the ambitious and enterprising. It comes as no surprise to find some wealthy tenants in the Durham priory manors in south-east Durham in 1496, for by that time only 115 tenants held the land that had been in the hands of 176 in 1382.[22]

Land use as well as the social structure of villages was affected by the new circumstances, especially where in the thirteenth and early fourteenth centuries arable cultivation had moved onto terrain yielding less than generous returns when used for that purpose.[23] From the second half of the fourteenth century onwards, as demand for land became less insistent, it became harder to let arable land on the old terms and, if it was poor or stony or sandy or "weak", even to let it at all. The outcome might be, at Overton (Hants.) in 1447, merely to depress rents for land that "could not be demised more dearly"; but at Highclere (Hants.) in 1430–1 no rent at all came either from a virgate or from a fair-sized enclosure (perhaps an intake from the down) because no one wished to rent them, and at least the latter had been absorbed into the common. In Cornwall, too, where the rural economy displayed considerable resilience, poorer land especially in the west proved increasingly difficult to let after c. 1420, pushing down rents and causing almost half the land at Helston-in-Kerrier to lapse from cultivation by Edward IV's reign. Likewise in Cheshire, at Ashton-juxta-Mondrem in 1360, it was a matter of doubt whether 40 acres of demesne could be let as arable or merely used for herbage, and

[22] Davenport, *Economic Development of a Norfolk Manor*, pp. 52, 78; *VCH Leics.*, II, pp. 184–7; R. H. Hilton, *The Economic Development of some Leicestershire Estates*, p. 100; T. Lomas, 'South-east Durham', p. 310.

[23] On this matter M. M. Postan's observations remain highly relevant: *Essays on Medieval Agriculture*, pp. 214–48 and in *CEcH*, I, 2nd edn, pp. 548–59.

at Oulton Lowe in 1370 a series of demesne fields were valued only for herbage. Neither the downward movement of rents nor the conversion of some arable to pasture need to be treated as symptoms of an agrarian crisis: rents perhaps reflected a lesser degree of desperation than they had sometimes done formerly; and some rolling back of the "frontier between corn and hoof", which in previous generations had "moved very far, indeed too far, cornwards", was probably a move towards better land-use.[24]

The most extreme manifestation of that move was the depopulation of villages and their conversion to pasture. In the country as a whole, however, depopulating enclosure was still not all that common in the late middle ages; where it did take place it was usually the end product of a protracted process of shrinkage, and its significance in the changing use of land may sometimes have been exaggerated. Only a modest proportion of the villages that were ultimately deserted were definitively killed by 1500. On the other hand, their ultimate fate was often determined by the fact that they were in any case small communities, frequently located on the poorer soils. In many places hamlet settlements (some of them secondary settlements on the frontiers of village territories) were shrinking into isolated farms and, in general, the picture emerging from the West Midlands in the century after the Black Death is not untypical of many parts of the country: of tenants deserting poorer and declining settlements in a search, far likelier to be successful than in earlier times, for better land and easier landlords. Even in Norfolk, where the amount of early depopulation was not very large, where it did happen it was mainly on the light soils in the west of the county.[25]

At this stage, on the other hand, the predominant impression is of "a piecemeal reduction in the number of tenants and in the cultivated land of villages", by no means restricted to places which would subsequently be deserted. Depopulating enclosure might even be the last resort of a landlord who, like Sir Edward Belknap at Burton Dassett (War.), found that "arable land was in such abundance that men could not get tenants to occupy their lands".[26] A turning point may have come around 1450, after which it was not so much a matter of dissatisfied tenants deserting villages as of landlords seeking to turn arable into

[24] WPR 159439, 159449; J. Hatcher, *Rural Economy and Society in the Duchy of Cornwall*, pp. 132, 156–9, 161–3; PRO Chester 3/4/3, 3/7/17 (I am indebted to P. H. W. Booth for these references); Postan, *Essays on Medieval Agriculture*, p. 247.

[25] C. Dyer, 'Deserted medieval villages in the West Midlands', *EcHR*, 2nd ser. XXXV, 1982, pp. 23–5; M. W. Beresford, *Lost Villages of England*, pp. 160–3; K. J. Allison, 'The lost villages of Norfolk', *Norfolk Archaeology*, XXXI, 1957, pp. 138–9.

[26] Dyer, 'Deserted medieval villages in the West Midlands', pp. 25, 27; *idem, Lords and Peasants*, pp. 257–63.

pasture, if only to salvage some returns from declining assets. After long years of seeking to attract or retain tenants by concessions, some of them had recourse to a policy of converting run-down villages into sheep runs, which at least had the advantage of needing relatively few labourers. This may well have seemed the best available option at a time when demand for land remained slack. Demesne leaseholders may also have been attracted to a like policy in some cases for a similar reason, and also some small landowners, who might in any case continue to exploit some of their land directly if only because, as rents fell, they lacked estates large enough to live on as rentiers.[27]

The balance of supply and demand affected labour as well as land. The great majority of English villagers, of course, relied principally upon resources within the family to satisfy their needs for labour, although these resources might be somewhat reduced as the readier availability of tenancies permitted an earlier escape from the family circle, and as the demand for labour itself tempted some (not excluding young women) to look for better employment prospects away from their native place. At all times, however, there were "servants", including "servants in husbandry", full-time workers commonly engaged by the year, amongst villagers in numbers which in Leicestershire have been estimated at not far short of 30 per cent of taxpayers both in 1381 and the 1520s. In addition, small landholders often arranged to work for each other as part of that village network "in which goods, labour and produce were exchanged without much use of cash", and which the sources are apt to reveal only obliquely; and some of them with the smallest holdings must either have relied upon earnings from part-time employment to supplement what they won from the soil or have taken up some small parcel of land to supplement what they got in wages for work that was not continuous throughout the year.[28]

It does appear, none the less, that the ranks of the very smallest landholders were seriously thinned by the heavy mortalities during the second half of the fourteenth century; and the submerged landless class, apparently so numerous in English villages at the opening of the fourteenth century, must almost certainly have been similarly reduced in numbers. The pool of available full-time and part-time labour, in other words, became smaller as part of a general reduction of

[27] Allison et al., *Deserted Villages of Northamptonshire*, p. 11; Dyer, 'Deserted medieval villages in the West Midlands', pp. 28–9; idem, *Standards of Living in the Later Middle Ages*, pp. 42–3 and the references there.

[28] R. H. Hilton, in *VCH Leics.*, II, p. 187; idem, *The English Peasantry in the Later Middle Ages*, pp. 49–53; Dyer, *Standards of Living*, p. 185.

population, but also because young men and women found opportunities available outside the family holding and, with tenancies in good supply, even the landless found social promotion within their grasp.[29] How many chances of betterment there were is shown by the extent to which holdings soon found tenants even after the mortality of 1348–9; and how much wider the choices available to sons and heirs were is suggested by the frequency with which the traditional bond between a particular family and a particular holding was broken during the later middle ages.[30] There are, it is true, signs that this bond was recovering some of its strength towards the end of the middle ages, perhaps indicating the achievement of a new equilibrium; but in the meantime, especially for the lords of manorial demesnes, the difficulty of mobilizing wage labour had been compounded by the growing unwillingness of servile tenants to accept holdings from which traditional labour services were due. Not surprisingly the wages paid to casual workers and at least the money wages paid to full-time workers had increased sharply.[31]

Rising wage levels, on the other hand, were offset at first even for manorial lords by the fact that for most of the third quarter of the fourteenth century markets for their principal products were relatively favourable. Wheat prices were well above any level they had reached since the bad harvests in the second decade of the century; and if wool prices were not especially high, demand was good as wool exports reached levels higher than those in the years before the outbreak of the Hundred Years' War, and an increasing amount of wool was also being exported in the form of cloth manufactured in England. Indeed, the sheep flock needed in the 1350s and 1360s to supply wool and cloth exports, and to replace dwindling cloth imports, may have been even larger than that which provided the peak exports of wool in the early years of the century.[32] At least down to the second plague of 1361–2, moreover, possibly helped by the labour legislation, wages seem also to have been brought under some sort of control. These were the conditions making an "Indian summer of demesne farming" possible.

Like most Indian summers, however, it was of limited duration. Its continuance was ultimately incompatible with the long-term depression of producer prices from the 1370s onwards, together with the

---

[29] Postan, *Essays on Medieval Agriculture*, p. 211.

[30] R. Faith, 'Peasant families and inheritance customs in medieval England', *AHR*, XIV, 1966, pp. 86–91; Dyer, *Lords and Peasants*, p. 302; *idem*, 'Changes in the link between families and land in the West Midlands in the fourteenth and fifteenth centuries', in R. M. Smith, ed., *Land, Kinship and Life-Cycle*, pp. 305–11; but see also Z. Razi's qualifications: 'The erosion of the family–land bond in the late fourteenth and fifteenth centuries', *ibid.*, pp. 295–304.

[31] Below, ch. 5.

[32] T. H. Lloyd, *The Movement of Wool Prices in Medieval England*, pp. 19, 66 (Fig. 2).

perpetuation of high wage levels and tenant resistance to labour services, the direct or indirect consequences of the continuing fall and subsequent stagnation of population. In the event, by 1400 arable production, with its heavy labour requirements, was being abandoned on all but the more conservative larger estates; and on virtually all of them it had been given up before the fifteenth century had proceeded very far. Where pasture was available, pastoral, and especially sheep, farming was often continued on some scale by landlords for much longer, particularly because it called for much less labour than corn-growing: the changing emphasis is clearly manifest at Forncett where the eight demesne ploughmen and other *famuli* of the late thirteenth century had been reduced, by 1376, to a single shepherd and a warrener. Many lords, however, had also abandoned sheep farming before, and often well before, the end of the fifteenth century. Much of the wool their flocks produced supplied international markets for wool and cloth, the behaviour of which rural producers could neither foresee nor control; and especially in the middle years of the fifteenth century they had to face something of a collapse of the cloth export market in combination with a failure of wool exports to recover anything like their level in the early years of the century. The sagging prices of this period must have eaten into the profits of sheep farmers, which in any case, especially on high-cost large estates, were probably modest. The fact that wool prices were relatively low through much of the fifteenth century possibly also reflects a situation in which more wool was being produced than could easily be absorbed by the export market for wool and the native textile industry. Not surprisingly, therefore, when they could, large proprietors were apt to abandon their sheep to lessees as they had already abandoned their arable.[33]

The leasing of demesne ploughlands, pastures and flocks enlarged still further the resources available to tenant farmers. The archbishop of Canterbury in the fifteenth century was sometimes compelled, although usually only for a few years, to let his demesnes piecemeal; but much more commonly they were held by a single individual or by two or three friends or kinsmen. Much the same was true in Wiltshire generally and on the bishop of Worcester's West Midlands estate, while on Westminster abbey's manors leases of demesnes *en bloc* to farmers after 1350 contrast with its earlier policy of piecemeal leases (although leasing of parcels of demesne might still take place as long as any substantial amount of direct exploitation by the abbey continued). On the estates of Durham priory and Leicester abbey, too, there was a

---

[33] Davenport, *Economic Development of a Norfolk Manor*, pp. 24, 50; Lloyd, *Movement of Wool Prices*, pp. 24–7; J. N. Hare, 'The Wiltshire Rising of 1450', *Southern History*, IV, 1982, pp. 16–18.

similar transition from leases of small parcels of demesnes on a short-term basis to the concession of whole demesnes to a single lessee or to a small group of partners.[34] There are some signs that, as time passed, the length of leases was increasing, with tenants themselves often perpetuating their hold on their acquisitions by negotiating reversions in favour of their heirs. The new "farmers", cultivating on a scale rare among tenants in earlier generations, were becoming a permanent part of the rural scene. Towards the close of the middle ages, moreover, multiple holdings of customary land, which earlier had been apt to be broken up on the death of the tenant who accumulated them, also were more likely to pass intact to heirs as part of a revived concern to keep in the family inheritances which were developing into farms in the modern sense of that word.[35]

Demesne lessees and tenants who built up multiple holdings were men of divers sorts. The latter, it is true, for the most part emerged from the ranks of the peasantry, although in the late middle ages increased peasant mobility made their opportunities for advancement less localized than they might once have been and, in Bedfordshire for example, by the end of the fifteenth century merchants and even gentlemen were dealing in the customary land market.[36] Demesne lessees were more diversified even from an earlier date. Gentlemen lessees were somewhat commoner on the Canterbury manors than elsewhere, perhaps because the London market made commercial farming in its vicinity particularly profitable; but there were some of them everywhere even if, as on the Worcester estate, they sometimes sublet the land they took on lease. In general, too, lessees of this rank become more numerous towards the end of the fifteenth century. The same may also have been true of merchants, but estate officials appear at every stage in the development of demesne leasehold. Always and everywhere, however, most lessees were drawn from the ranks of husbandmen and yeomen, and especially from those "working farmers...although not of the smallest sort" who had been the reeves, rent collectors and so forth of manorial lords. This was one good reason

---

[34] F. R. H. Du Boulay, 'Who were farming the English demesnes at the end of the middle ages?', *EcHR*, 2nd ser. XVII, 1965, pp. 444–6; B. F. Harvey, 'The leasing of the abbot of Westminster's demesnes in the later middle ages', *EcHR*, 2nd ser. XXII, 1969, p. 19; *idem*, *Westminster Abbey and its Estates*, p. 151; J. N. Hare, 'Demesne lessees of fifteenth-century Wiltshire', *AHR*, XXIX, 1981, p. 2; T. Lomas, 'South-east Durham', pp. 302–3; Hilton, *Leicestershire Estates*, pp. 90–1.

[35] Dyer, *Lords and Peasants*, pp. 210–11; *idem*, 'Changes in the size of peasant holdings in some West Midland villages', in R. M. Smith, ed., *Land, Kinship and Life-Cycle*, p. 292; B. Harvey, *Westminster Abbey and its Estates*, pp. 154–5; T. Lomas, 'South-east Durham', p. 299.

[36] P. D. A. Harvey, ed., *The Peasant Land Market*, pp. 251, 339–40.

why some serf lessees are still to be found in Wiltshire well into the fifteenth century.[37]

Is the conclusion, therefore, that "in the end...the peasants...entered into their own"? It would perhaps be more accurate to say that a minority of them, no doubt by the exercise of conspicuous enterprise, entered upon what had been their landlords' own, often supplemented by what had been the possessions of their neighbours. In their new positions, raised well above the average standing of the peasantry, they might be joined by other men of enterprise – lawyers, merchants, and gentlemen among them. Once established, moreover, such men were no more exempt than the lords of manors from what John Rous called "the plague of avarice [which] infects these times". So in 1517 leaseholders were returned as the enclosers and depopulators at, for example, Milton (Berks.) and Middle Claydon (Bucks.), as well as many other places. This was perhaps one demonstration of their enterprise, and the taking up of a lease might be the first crucial step upon a course of social promotion, like that which took the Knatchbulls, Romney Marsh yeomen who came to farm nearly two thousand acres at Willop and Cheyne (Kent), to a seventeenth-century baronetcy and a nineteenth-century peerage.[38] Such conspicuous manifestations of peasant social promotion during the late middle ages, on the other hand, are likely to have made a smaller aggregate contribution to enhanced rural standards of living than the much more limited increments added to the holdings of more modest villagers, whose happiness might be very directly linked to having fuller stomachs. There were still years, of course, when harvests were poor (1438 was a case in point); but the small gains of land made by many of the rank and file of villagers may have been their principal shield against the recurrence of dearths like those which had afflicted them in the late thirteenth and early fourteenth centuries.

At the same time, the context of landlord and tenant relationships in the late middle ages involved more than fluctuations in the supply of and demand for land. On the one hand very many villagers were *nativi de sanguine*, born to servility, over whom their lords had extensive powers of command and control; on the other, many of them were also bound to tenurial conditions which empowered their lord to demand some share of their family labour and, at least from time to

[37] See esp. B. Harvey, 'The leasing of the abbot of Westminster's demesnes', pp. 20–1; Hare, 'Demesne lessees of fifteenth-century Wiltshire', p. 5.

[38] A. R. Bridbury, *Economic Growth: England in the Later Middle Ages*, Hassocks, 1975, p. 92; M. W. Beresford, *Lost Villages of England*, p. 81; I. S. Leadam, ed., *The Domesday of Enclosures*, II, pp. 506–7, 572–3; Du Boulay, 'Who were farming the English demesnes at the end of the middle ages?', pp. 153–4.

time, some share of their produce, livestock and chattels, as well as cash rents, entry fines, and penalties imposed by manorial courts. The erosion of many of these attributes of lordship is discussed in many parts of this volume, and was something to which peasant resistance to seigneurial demands made a significant contribution. In the more dramatic episodes of resistance, like the revolt of 1381, discontents other than those aimed at landlords were involved; but one ingredient in that rising was undoubtedly an attempt to call a halt to the endeavours of lords to preserve or even to reimpose their traditional authority and rights in circumstances in which a shortage of tenants made it more and more difficult to sustain them. The dramatic character of this episode, moreover, made it more difficult in the future for lords to press their demands too hard, particularly since the downward trend of population weakened still further their bargaining power.[39] The "truculence of tenants", in fact, continued through the difficult middle years of the fifteenth century right through to its end and even beyond. One Monmouthshire tenant of the duke of Buckingham in 1503 gave up his holding rather than pay more rent and, a few years later, another in Northamptonshire had "gone out of the town and hath took another farm".[40]

The ultimate result was a profound modification of village society. Distinctions of status still basic in many manorial communities in 1348 had largely gone by 1500, together with labour services and other manifestations of servility. On the Westminster abbey estate, for instance, by the mid-fifteenth century or soon after, "words with a servile meaning or implication fell out of use in the context of land tenure".[41] There were still tenurial distinctions – between copyhold, leasehold, tenure at will, freehold – although the differences between them were often less than precise; but villein tenure in its traditional sense had virtually vanished. This did not mean, of course, that village society was marked by a greater equality: on the contrary, a sense that inequalities may even have increased is perhaps suggested by the distinction contemporaries sometimes drew between yeomen and husbandmen, to say nothing of mere labourers, although here again the lines between classes are anything but hard and fast. Essentially, however, what distinguished one villager from another was no longer status, but rather the amount of land an individual held, the grazing rights which went with it, the livestock and other goods he possessed.

[39] On 1381, below, ch. 8 and C. Dyer, 'The social and economic background of the rural revolt of 1381', in R. H. Hilton and T. H. Aston, eds., *The English Rising of 1381*, pp. 9–42.

[40] Dyer, *Lords and Peasants*, pp. 188–9, 275–7; B. J. Harris, 'Landlords and tenants in England in the later middle ages', *PP*, no. 43, 1969, pp. 146–50.

[41] B. F. Harvey, *Westminster Abbey and its Estates*, p. 275.

Some terms of tenure might be more favourable to tenants than others, but so long as tenants were hard to come by the least favourable implications were the less likely to be pressed. After all, the tenant had the ultimate sanction: he might go out of town and take another farm.

Another characteristic of the times was significant in this connection and that was the increased mobility of country people. There may be an element of truth in the judgement that, in the mid-fourteenth century, "the immobility of labour ... is still a very weighty reality", although in fact villagers had always moved: to other villages, to towns, to areas of industrial development or of agricultural reclamation. Lords, of course, often sought to limit movement to safeguard their supplies of labour and the services which were owed to them; and tenants themselves, in the conditions of growing land scarcity in the late thirteenth and early fourteenth centuries, might find fewer opportunities beckoning them to better themselves elsewhere. After 1349, however, lords like the abbots of Ramsey may have tried initially to inhibit emigration by tenants and to bring back those who had left, but in fact there appears to have been no significant reduction of the number of tenants leaving manors during the second half of the fourteenth century, and after about 1390 the outflow became a veritable flood. In the West Midlands, too, intensified mobility is very evident in the late fourteenth and throughout the fifteenth centuries, resulting in the change-over of something like three-quarters of the surnames in many villages in every 40–60 years. Some countryfolk give an impression of something like perpetual motion, like the man from Holywell (Hunts.) who at various times between 1403 and 1437 turns up at Colne (Hunts.), Soham (Cambs.), Ely (Cambs.), Ramsey (Hunts.), and Ely once more. There were women who were hardly less footloose, like one from Graveley (Cambs.) who seems to have lived for some time in Kent before turning up somewhere in Norfolk in 1433.[42]

Much of this movement was merely to neighbouring villages, perhaps where better land might be available, or land on better terms, or both. Tenant mobility, in other words, helped to push down rents and modify services on the one hand and, on the other, to concentrate cultivation on the better soils. At Halesowen incomers were often enabled to establish themselves in the parish through marriage to a Halesowen woman with land of her own, as doubtless often happened elsewhere. Not everyone who moved, of course, did so with the immediate intention of securing a holding. Some simply sought better paid employment, like the Forncett bondman who in 1394 had

---

[42] Levett, *The Black Death*, p. 81; J. A. Raftis, *Tenure and Mobility*, pp. 144–57, 170, 178, 180; Dyer, *Lords and Peasants*, pp. 366–7.

withdrawn from the manor "for the purpose of getting greater gain in the autumn season"; others are found as servants, apprentices and village craftsmen; and yet others found their way to developing industrial communities. The clothiers of fifteenth-century Castle Combe, for example, seem mostly to be incomers and their servants included Welshmen and even an Irishman; and in the fifteenth century at least three people moved to the growing Suffolk town of Lavenham from the Huntingdonshire village of Warboys.[43] There might also, however, be movement the other way: in Cornwall, for instance, some tin miners, at a time when their industry was depressed after 1349, may have helped to fill gaps in the ranks of agricultural tenants. Rural industrialization, on the other hand, had not gone far enough by the mid-fourteenth century to make this last sort of migration economically significant in most parts of the country; but in the last century and a half of the middle ages there was probably a net outflow of migrants into rural industrial employments, whether full-time or part-time, to supplement migration of a more traditional sort from agricultural communities to craft or other service occupations in other agricultural villages. In Huntingdonshire, for instance, one Houghton man became a tailor at Hemingford Abbots and another a tailor at Upwood, while a brewer's son from Weston seems to have become the abbot of Ramsey's brewer at the abbey. Even where no major industrial development took place there were opportunities in the countryside for craftsmen as well as agriculturalists.[44]

The relationship of families, as well as tenants, to the land was influenced by the changing circumstances of the later middle ages. Before 1349 the operations of the land market were governed in many particulars by the interest of lords in preserving tenemental structures which were a framework for tenant obligations and also by the reluctance of tenants to surrender any of their land upon which they depended for a sometimes precarious subsistence. For these reasons the bond between particular families and particular holdings had been very strong, so that the assumption was that any given holding would pass intact to the member of a specific family whom local custom designated as heir only when death, old age or "impotence" made it impossible for a sitting tenant to carry on its cultivation. If there were exceptions to this rule (in districts where partible inheritance applied at least to some tenancies, for instance), in general *inter vivos* transactions

[43] Razi, *Life, Marriage and Death*, pp. 121–2; Davenport, *Economic Development of a Norfolk Manor*, p. 72; E. M. Carus-Wilson, 'Evidences of industrial growth on some fifteenth-century manors', *EcHR*, 2nd ser. XII, 1959, p. 202; D. Dymond and A. Betterton, *Lavenham: 700 Years of Textile Making*, Woodbridge, 1982, p. 26.

[44] Hatcher, *Duchy of Cornwall*, pp. 119, 146–7; Raftis, *Tenure and Mobility*, pp. 177–8.

between tenants tended to be subordinate to *post mortem* inheritance of holdings, except perhaps in the densely populated areas of East Anglia, where sales of parcels of land in bad years to buy food created a "crisis-determined" land market.[45] Falling population during the post-1349 generations altered this situation. An heir might find a holding available to him well before he was due to come into his inheritance, perhaps in another village if not in his own; and the likelihood that sons excluded by customary rules from the family patrimony might be able to obtain a tenement was much improved. The results were a great increase in *inter vivos* transactions and, in many cases, disregard for customary rules of descent by blood. Lords of manors, even though initially they made what use they could of their powers to compel members of unfree families to take up vacant unfree holdings, were sufficiently anxious to recruit tenants not to turn away those without a family connection with a particular tenure; and, as the traditional regime of services was dismantled, their interest in preserving the tenemental framework intact was weakened. The consequence was a still more active land market, both for whole tenements and for smaller parcels of land.[46]

It is possible that, in some degree, the continuing force of the hereditary principle is concealed by records which do not enable us to recognize some of those who took up holdings as simply more distant relatives (often in the female line) of previous tenants than had earlier been common; even so, there can be little doubt about the weakening of the bond between a particular holding and a particular nuclear family during the later middle ages.[47] Because incoming tenants were less frequently the heirs designated by custom to succeed on customary terms, the conditions of tenure that tenants would accept even to take up standard holdings were more and more apt to be subject to negotiation. The outcome is clear on an estate so "heroically indifferent" to changed economic circumstances as Westminster abbey's: as late as the second half of the fifteenth century the monks offered by no means ineffective resistance to the fragmentation of holdings, but more and more tenancies were of a contractual rather than the traditional customary sort. Even on these manors, however, a more active land market both for standard holdings and for supplementary parcels of land gave a new fluidity to landholding in the

[45] R. M. Smith, ed., *Land, Kinship and Life-Cycle*, pp. 18–21, 113–20; P. D. A. Harvey, ed., *The Peasant Land Market*, pp. 102–3, 120.

[46] R. Faith, 'Peasant families and inheritance customs', pp. 86–7; *idem*, 'Berkshire: fourteenth and fifteenth centuries', in P. D. A. Harvey, ed., *The Peasant Land Market*, pp. 110, 120–1.

[47] See the debate between Z. Razi and C. Dyer in R. M. Smith, ed., *Land, Kinship and Life-Cycle*, pp. 298–304, 305–11.

late middle ages. If the limited resources of large sections of medieval peasantry restricted their dealings to small plots of land, an expanding range of opportunities was available to a small minority of entrepreneurs who, as dealers in peasant land as well as lessees of demesnes, were emerging as farmers on a scale very different from that of traditional peasant agriculturalists.[48]

Another feature of the fluidity of landholding, however, was the impermanence of the gains of individual entrepreneurs. On the Westminster estates some larger holdings were apt to dissolve again into their constituent virgates and other parcels; on the bishop of Worcester's lands for much of the fifteenth century there was a tendency for composite holdings to break up during a tenant's later life or at his death; in Berkshire the emerging yeomanry of the late middle ages was soon supplanted by new men in Tudor times; and in fifteenth-century Bedfordshire, "gradual piecemeal accumulation and dispersal" was the typical story at Leighton Buzzard.[49] Only towards the end of the fifteenth century, perhaps as long-term adjustments in land use and management reached some degree of completeness, and possibly in some cases because tenants were beginning to feel the need of protection against intrusive speculators and entrepreneurs, are there signs of significant change. By then, peasant families in Berkshire were once again finding heritable tenures (reversions, leaseholds for lives, copyholds by inheritance) privileges worth paying for; there was also an increase at this time in land passing within the family in south-east Durham; and at least some multiple holdings in the West Midlands achieved a degree of stability which enabled them to be transmitted entire from generation to generation. These new attitudes possibly mark something like a term to the long and painful process of adaptation to the demographic changes of the later middle ages.[50]

C. LIMITING INFLUENCES

The long period of time which adaptation required is an indication that many of the implications of a changing situation were neither readily perceived nor easily accepted. Circumstances in the immediate wake of the unprecedented mortality in 1348–9 explain why that should have been so initially: the reserves of population in the English countryside

---

[48] B. F. Harvey, *Westminster Abbey and its Estates*, pp. 244–6, 308–11, 316–17.

[49] *Ibid.*, pp. 289–90; Dyer, *Lords and Peasants*, p. 312; P. D. A. Harvey, ed., *The Peasant Land Market*, pp. 176–7, 248.

[50] P. D. A. Harvey, ed., *The Peasant Land Market*, pp. 120–1, 251, 261; Dyer, 'Changes in the size of peasant holdings in some West Midland villages', p. 292; *idem, Standards of Living*, pp. 142–3.

were so great that gaps in tenant ranks could be filled relatively quickly in most cases; and good prices or favourable markets enabled a great deal of demesne production to continue on something like the traditional pattern despite rising wages. Only the continued downward trend of population and a long period of low or even very low agricultural prices of almost every sort made that traditional pattern in the end unsustainable.

This still does not mean that adjustment to change came readily, for custom and usage might stand in the way. Labourers, with the fewest customary rights to cling to, were perhaps the first to grasp at the advantages implicit in their new situation: thus the sharpest rise of money wages occurred in the two decades immediately following the Black Death, although a gentler upward trend continued long after that. One result may have been to persuade landlords still cultivating their demesnes to prefer servants in husbandry hired by the year, most of whom were partly paid in kind, to dearer casual labour. In some instances, to this end, they supplemented the backing for annual contracts provided by the labour legislation by an exercise of their seigneurial power to compel villeins to work full-time for wages in lieu of performing their labour services. The bishop of Wells made precisely that arrangement with two fardel holders in 1382–3 and thirty years earlier at Farleigh Hungerford (Somerset), even though most services had been commuted, one customer was excused his works because he was acting as the lord's ploughman. Custom, however, still had some influence in stabilizing the rewards of manorial *famuli*. On the Hampshire manor of Crawley ploughmen got the same money wages and liveries in kind in the second decade of the fifteenth century as they had in the 1350s; and even when money wages improved, liveries in kind often remained at their traditional levels, thus declining in value as grain prices fell. Their recipients, on the other hand, were probably more concerned with the sufficiency of these payments in grain to fill their stomachs than with their value in the market place, and they may have set some store by regular employment and remuneration as contrasted with the hazards of casual employment. Whatever the forces of inertia operating, however, wages moved up as population levels fell and fewer labourers might also mean that casual workers had a better chance of more regular employment.[51] These were matters which helped to shape the policies both of landlord demesnes and tenant holdings.

[51] D. Farmer, 'Crop yields, prices and wages in medieval England', *Studies in Medieval and Renaissance History*, NS VI, 1983, Fig. 1 and pp. 145–6; *Somerset and Dorset N. & Q.*, XI, 1908–9, pp. 238, 243; PRO SC 6/970/14; Gras, *English Village*, pp. 272, 275, 301, 310; R. M. Smith, ed., *Land, Kinship and Life-Cycle*, pp. 35–8.

The factor of inertia was also reflected in the relation of landlords and tenants. Immediately after the Black Death many tenants seem to have been willing to accept reasonable land on the traditional terms. When an heir and an heiress at Wakefield in January 1350 took up 25 acres and 10 acres respectively "to hold according to the custom of the manor", we cannot be quite sure that what they owed for these holdings was unchanged; but that was quite specific when, about the same time, a cottage holding at Fordington (Dorset) was conceded to a man and his wife for the due and accustomed rent and services.[52] Of course tenants, sometimes sooner rather than later, learned to bargain about what they would give for land as demand for holdings fell with falling population or when adverse economic circumstances affected returns from them. In the depression years of the mid-fifteenth century, for example, rents were forced still lower and many tenants refused to pay those they owed, at least in full, so that arrears piled up. These attitudes, moreover, did not only apply to rents in the narrow sense: the tenants at Norton (Worcs.) in 1450 were said to "refuse the customs" due from them, and their contemporaries on the bishop of Worcester's manors rejected servile obligations and many manifestations of the bishop's lordship as well as rents they deemed excessive. Quite apart from reducing the revenue the bishop got from his tenants, peasant resistance was helping to narrow his lordship to a more strictly economic character.[53]

These changes, however, took time and only gained real momentum from about 1390; but by the late fifteenth century a renewed stability had been achieved in many places, as the revised rent levels themselves became customary, tenancies were tending to lengthen, and links between family and holding were strengthened once more. The relative slowness in reaching a new equilibrium, if it owed something to a willingness of some tenants to accept for a time terms of tenure that were customary, owed even more to the unwillingness of landlords to acknowledge that their changed situation in relation to their tenants was definitive. Lords, or their expert advisers, were in no way incapable of making reasoned judgements, as the Duchy of Lancaster auditors did in 1388 when they recommended, "because the produce from Higham Ferrers and Raunds is of no value beyond its costs, which are so great each year that the said produce involves a great loss to the lord", that the demesnes of these two Northamptonshire manors should be leased. These were truths, however, which had been masked for two decades or more after the Black Death by good agricultural prices, which persuaded many lords that they faced no more than "mediocre years"

[52] H. M. Jewell, ed., *Wakefield Court Rolls, 1348–1350*, p. 165; PRO SC 2/169/29.

[53] Dyer, *Lords and Peasants*, pp. 179–89; *idem*, 'A redistribution of incomes in fifteenth-century England', *PP*, no. 39, 1968, pp. 24, 32–3.

and that in due course better times would return.[54] That hope explains why some landlords, like the monks of Westminster, could be "heroically indifferent" to economic change, having recourse to various temporary forms of tenure in order to get customary land off their hands; and why much land was let at a low rent because it could not be let more dearly, but in the obvious anticipation that some day dearer lettings would once again be possible. Ultimately, of course, economic realities and the prolonged, but only occasionally explosive, resistance of the peasantry combined to lower rents, dismantle much of the traditional manorial regime, and narrow the scope of traditional manorial lordship. Defence of their customary expectations by lords had often delayed, but did not prevent, change; and the revival of custom at the end of the middle ages in many respects confirmed and entrenched the gains made by tenants and the new terms on which their land was held.

Other influences retarded change as well as the unwillingness of landlords to accept it, including a propensity to regard land as a source of subsistence rather than as an economic investment. Even though, by 1500, most of the larger landlords received the greater part of their incomes in the form of cash, not all of them had totally jettisoned the idea that a landed estate might also be a source of supplies. Even Henry VI's royal household was supplied with rabbits from the warren at Aldbourne (Wilts.) and down to the end of the fourteenth century, and often well beyond that date, many of the great monastic houses continued to draw heavily upon their own lands for necessary provisions. Much of the meat consumed at Battle abbey in the fourteenth century came from its own manors and when Marley (Sussex), a principal supply manor, was finally leased late in the century much of its rent was paid in kind, as it still was in the 1450s and as some of it still was in the early sixteenth century. Selby abbey, too, still depended heavily in the early fifteenth century upon the produce and tithes of its manors and parishes for wheat for bread-making, malt for brewing, and beans, peas and oats for pottage; but also, to add diversity to monastic living, for milk and cheese from the dairy at Stainer and, from a diversity of places, for cattle, sheep, swans, rabbits, pheasants, partridges, herons, geese, ducks, cockerels, pigeons, and eggs.[55]

[54] G. A. Holmes, *The Estates of the Higher Nobility in XIVth Century England*, pp. 126–7; PRO DL 29/465/7604, quoted below, p. 46.

[55] Dyer, *Standards of Living*, p. 69; PRO DL 29/683/11068; *Cellarers' Rolls of Battle Abbey, 1217–1513*, eds. E. Searle and B. Ross, Sussex Rec. Soc., LXV, 1967, pp. 18–19; E. Searle, *Lordship and Community*, pp. 326–7; J. H. Tillotson, ed., *Monastery and Society in the Later Middle Ages: Selected Account Rolls from Selby Abbey, Yorkshire, 1398–1537*, Woodbridge, 1988, pp. 141–8, 178–93.

Smaller landlords were perhaps even more apt to rely upon self-supply and may often have continued at least some demesne cultivation when greater men abandoned it. At Farleigh Hungerford in 1386 the milk from the single cow was reserved for the lord's children; the lady of Porlock in the early fifteenth century used the home manor to supply the grain (and especially the wheat) she needed, oxen, sheep, capons and other livestock and poultry for her larder, and even wool to make cloth and horses to ride; and in the 1490s an East Anglian dowager took part of the rent from Yoxford (Suffolk) in the form of dairy produce, eggs, chickens, geese, and malt. Some smaller monasteries showed a similar concern for supplies. In early sixteenth-century Suffolk, Sibton abbey's North Grange provided the monks with milk, cheese, butter, calves, bullocks, "bacon hogs", hens, geese, and capons; and other estates contributed grain, and also sixty-four wethers which were duly prepared for the kitchen in "Le Slaughter-hous". These are merely a few illustrations of the reluctance of landlords to relinquish lands which contributed so directly to their day-to-day needs; and even when direct exploitation of their manorial demesnes was given up, some of them, like the Battle monks, fixed rents from them which continued to serve those needs.[56]

There is much less direct information about what tenants got from their land, although some of them must have had an even sharper concern than their betters about its contribution to their subsistence. One calculation, inevitably and admittedly an approximation, suggests that a man with 30 acres of open-field land in about 1300 might need a third to a half of his grain crop to feed himself and his family, together with half the dairy produce supplied by his cows and whatever could be got from his pigs and his poultry. A tenant with half that amount of land (and such tenants were much more numerous in the thirteenth century than holders of 30 acres) would have had little grain left over after his family was fed and was quite likely to have fewer livestock; and the very numerous smallholding tenants would need to work for wages in order to supplement the produce of their scraps of land if they and their families were to eat.[57] This background conditioned the attitudes of villagers in the new circumstances after 1349. Demands for higher wages were perhaps one of the more immediate means by which the poorer amongst them sought to improve their living standards, but more adequate holdings might seem to offer a better guarantee of more adequate subsistence. In the early post-plague years the customary burdens to which manorial tenements were subject might appear

[56] PRO SC 6/970/21; C. E. H. Chadwyck Healey, *History of Part of West Somerset*, pp. 425–7; C. Richmond, *John Hopton: a Fifteenth-Century Suffolk Gentleman*, pp. 72–3; A. Denney, *The Sibton Abbey Estates*, pp. 141–6. [57] Dyer, *Standards of Living*, pp. 110–18.

acceptable in order to get more land, although in due course those burdens would appear excessive. Where the increments tenants acquired took the form of pastoral rights they might be enabled to supplement the bread, ale, and pottage provided by their cornlands with more generous amounts of butter, cheese, and bacon; and as average holdings grew somewhat larger and rents and other charges became somewhat lighter they might have had more money in their pockets to increase the amounts of meat and fish they consumed. In the land markets of the late middle ages this was the sort of consideration that was probably paramount in the minds of the great majority of villagers. What they aimed at was a living that was both rather better and less precarious than in the pre-1349 generations.

A policy of acquisition that went beyond these limits gave rise to difficulties. In the first place there soon came a point at which an enlarged holding exceeded the capacity of a tenant family to provide the labour needed to cultivate it, especially during the peak periods of the farming year. Larger holdings, therefore, quickly ran into some of those problems of escalating costs which helped to persuade landlords to abandon demesne cultivation. This limiting influence was perhaps especially strong during years of depressed prices in the mid-fifteenth century and may help to explain why the larger composite tenancies at that time showed so little signs of permanence. Larger holdings, moreover, called for more investment as well as more labour. Any tenant with a reasonable amount of arable needed implements to plough and harrow it, a cart to lead away the harvest, hand tools for the many tasks of cultivation, and draught animals to plough and cart and harrow. The cost of these requisites, apart from that of draught animals, was not perhaps very high, but a tenant taking up land might also need to acquire additional livestock to make the most of his common rights and supply manure for his arable. The reeve of Cuxham (Oxon.), who died in 1349 and was no doubt one of the more substantial tenants of that manor, had 56 ewes, 11 lambs, a sow and young pigs, 2 cows, a heifer, a calf, and some poultry. To build up that sort of stock from scratch would have involved considerable expenditure, although once acquired (except in years of serious livestock epidemics) it might be more or less self-replacing as well as a source of a modest income. The fact that most tenant farmers were mixed farmers, however, needing to invest in both arable equipment and livestock, tended to impose limits upon the scale of operations of many of them; and it might well be beyond the resources of an ordinary villager to stock even pastoral holdings of any size. This may be one reason why Cotswold sheep pastures were often acquired by wool merchants and why merchants and butchers were not uncommon among Wiltshire lessees. In that county, after all, when the Duchy of Lancaster's stockman leased Collingbourne and Everley, he had to find £77 to buy up the sheep flock: this was no small sum to raise at that time.[58]

In the case of demesne leaseholds, the problem of finding the capital to stock and equip a farm of substantial size was in some cases made easier by the action of the lessor. Some landlords assisted tenants with the cost of manorial buildings, as Leicester abbey did by providing "great timber" for repairs at Kirkby Mallory. Others did much more than that. When Durham priory leased Bellasis in 1373 the stock went with the demesne; and the rector of Cuxham, when he leased the Merton manor there in 1361, clearly got both the livestock and the "dead stock", since he covenanted to return them at the end of the lease as they had been when he received it. In like manner Westminster abbey initially provided almost every lessee with some livestock and other requisites, making it easier for the abbey to find tenants and perhaps also indicating that hope had not yet quite been lost that one day the "mediocre years" would end, enabling the abbey to resume demesnes which were fully equipped. By the 1420s and 1430s, however, that hope was dying and the practice of providing lessees with stock was gradually abandoned on the abbot's lands, although it persisted on the convent's manors until the dissolution. In the meantime it had helped to make possible the creation of what may not improperly be described as "embryonic capitalist farms".[59]

In one other respect change may have been checked rather than furthered by the post-1350 situation. By 1300 Norfolk, for example, was tackling the problem of accommodating a growing population on a cultivable area which had reached somewhere near its maximum limits, resulting in an extreme subdivision of holdings, at least in part by markedly intensive methods of husbandry. The amount of arable fallowed was reduced, seeding rates were heavy and crops were carefully weeded, legumes were sown on a large scale both to enrich the soil and provide fodder for livestock, and the manure the latter supplied was supplemented by marling and its application regulated by systematic folding. It has been suggested that similar production methods were adopted in Kent and probably in other densely

[58] *Manorial Records of Cuxham*, ed. P. D. A. Harvey, p. 153; Dyer, *Lords and Peasants*, pp. 214–15; Hare, 'Demesne lessees of fifteenth-century Wiltshire', pp. 9–10.

[59] Hilton, *Leicestershire Estates*, p. 129; T. Lomas, 'South-east Durham', p. 304; *Manorial Records of Cuxham*, ed. P. D. A. Harvey, pp. 101–3; B. F. Harvey, 'The leasing of the abbot of Westminster's demesnes', pp. 21–2; *idem, Westminster Abbey and its Estates*, pp. 153–4; Dyer, *Lords and Peasants*, p. 217.

populated areas, and even in the late fourteenth century Battle abbey was getting consistently high grain yields for its manors, again as a result of heavy seeding, heavy manuring, and large sowings of legumes, with a consequent virtual elimination of fallow in some cases.[60] Better yields achieved by these means, however, were obviously expensive both in terms of the investment (in seed, livestock and so forth) and of the labour required to achieve them. High labour costs might be a disincentive, therefore, to adopting or continuing intensive arable cultivation, particularly when grain prices were anything but favourable. Even in Norfolk in the fifteenth century, when the population pressure had been sufficiently reduced to replace the fragmentation of holdings by consolidation and engrossing, labour inputs had been much reduced; and on some Sussex manors the high seeding rates of the previous century had been diminished. There are even signs in some places that improved yields were sought not by more but by less intensive cultivation, land being cropped only at intervals with periods under grass between. These forms of convertible husbandry became practicable as the pressure of people upon the land was relaxed.[61]

Some influences external to agriculture, on the other hand, may have accelerated rural change, and particularly industrial development in the countryside. Mining, exploitation of the still considerable tracts of woodland, processing of some minerals which miners won from the ground, the making of leather and turning it into consumer goods, brewing, spinning and weaving wool both for the home and the expanding export markets for cloth, called for many skills which were indigenous in the countryside. Rural crafts, therefore, were capable of being expanded to offer not only full-time employment but also part-time work for countryfolk and their families, and especially for smallholders who, given the seasonal character of the demand for labour in agriculture, might have time available for some non-agricultural employment. The history of medieval rural industry in the country as a whole has yet to be adequately studied, but its influence upon the agrarian history of the fourteenth and fifteenth centuries is clear enough in general terms. Mining and cloth-making particularly had direct consequences for the rural environments in which they were conducted. In the south-west, for example, increased mining activity in the second half of the fifteenth century in Mendip created an

---

[60] B. M. S. Campbell, 'Agricultural progress in medieval England: some evidence from eastern Norfolk', *EcHR*, 2nd ser. XXXVI, 1983, pp. 27–42; P. F. Brandon, 'Cereal yields on the Sussex estates of Battle abbey during the later middle ages', *EcHR*, 2nd ser. XXV, 1972, pp. 403–20.

[61] Campbell, 'Agricultural progress in medieval England', pp. 38–9, 44; *idem*, 'Population pressure, inheritance and the land market', pp. 125–6; below, p. 276.

integrated string of industrial villages, mainly inhabited by miner-peasants, stretching from Hinton Charterhouse to Priddy (Somerset); and further west, high tin output in Cornwall, especially in the period 1385–1420, and the substantially increased output of the Devon mines in the late fifteenth and early sixteenth centuries, created both demands for labour and a market for foodstuffs to feed an increased industrial population. Mining, in brief, offered alternative or supplementary employment opportunities and the chance to dispose of agricultural surpluses to customers close at hand.[62]

In the meantime, in this same region, cloth production along both sides of the Devon–Cornwall border was also expanding as export figures for the south-western ports indicate. They increased notably in the 1430s and 1440s, and again, after something of a set-back, in the years 1480–1510: in the 1490s they were five times their level in the 1360s. The expansion of cloth-making in the country as a whole in the century and a half after 1350, much of it taking place in villages and small country towns, virtually drove imported textiles from English markets and at the same time supplied average annual exports which increased from about 10,000 broad cloths in 1351–70 to nearly 30,000 in the opening decades of the fifteenth century and then to almost 57,000 in the last two decades of that century. Development on this scale obviously meant expanded employment opportunities, often as in mining enabling some industrial work to be combined with agriculture, and at the same time it created new local markets for wool and for the foodstuffs which industrializing communities needed to supplement what they could produce themselves. In the clothing areas, too, by the beginning of the sixteenth century interlinked industrial villages had appeared, like those around Lavenham (Suffolk), where the well-known family of clothiers, the Springs, had a network of employees and suppliers in near-by villages like Cockfield and Preston and even further afield in Glemsford and Stoke-by-Clare. There were comparable developments in many other parts of the country, and especially in the southern Cotswolds, in Somerset and Wiltshire, along the Stour valley in Essex, around Worstead in Norfolk, and in West Yorkshire from Leeds as far west as Huddersfield and Halifax. These, moreover, were merely the principal centres of a textile industry which was much more widely disseminated; and miners were at work in many parts other than the south-west – including eastern Derbyshire,

[62] I. Blanchard, 'Industrial employment and the rural land market, 1380–1520', in R. M. Smith, ed., *Land, Kinship and Life-Cycle*, pp. 237–41, 263; W. G. Hoskins and H. P. R. Finberg, eds., *Devonshire Studies*, London, 1952, pp. 241–6; J. Hatcher, *Duchy of Cornwall*, pp. 146–7, 169–70; *idem, English Tin Production and Trade before 1550*, Oxford, 1973, pp. 156–9.

the Weald, Swaledale and, despite the restrictive attitudes of ecclesiastical property owners, even Tyneside. The prosperity of the countryside was conditioned by industry as well as by agriculture.[63]

For that reason industrial development and changes in the location of industry exercised an important influence upon regional prosperity in a land that was still preponderantly agricultural. Almost everywhere the rural population was lower than before 1348; and high costs and low prices during much of the late middle ages, despite the fact that land was cheaper, made many villagers unwilling to go far beyond the point where their families provided their needs for labour, hardly a context favouring major agricultural advances. Yet the uniformities in this situation ought not to be exaggerated. Early sixteenth-century taxation records suggest that some parts of the country were much more densely populated than others, something which had always been true and which did not necessarily reflect recent circumstances. On the other hand the changes which had taken place in the regional distribution of taxable wealth between the early fourteenth and the early sixteenth centuries may, in this connection, be much more significant. From this point of view certain areas do appear to stand out as localities the relative wealth of which had increased to a marked extent in the course of the later middle ages; the most important are the south-west (including the textile districts of Gloucestershire and Wiltshire), the clothing districts of East Anglia, parts of the West Riding of Yorkshire, the environs of London, and the peat fens of Cambridgeshire and Huntingdonshire (though in this last case improvement was not sufficient to make these fens anything but a relatively poor area). On the whole, however, rural industrialization does appear to have been an influence raising general, including agricultural, levels of prosperity in some parts of the country by comparison with others, just as the demand of London and its suburbs was a continuing stimulus to farming in the capital's environs.[64]

The influences which governed the changing distribution of wealth did not, of course, necessarily operate continuously and uniformly over the century and a half following the Black Death. It now seems likely that even London, once assumed to have gone on growing, may, like other towns, have suffered a reduction of population in the fifteenth

[63] E. M. Carus-Wilson and O. Coleman, *England's Export Trade, 1275–1547*, table of cloth exports; A. R. Bridbury, *Medieval English Clothmaking*, London, 1982, App. E; Dymond and Betterton, *Lavenham*, pp. 13–14, 25; E. M. Carus-Wilson, in *CEcH*, II, 2nd edn, pp. 678–81.

[64] J. Sheail, 'The distribution of taxable population and wealth in England during the early sixteenth century', *Institute of British Geographers*, LV, 1972, pp. 11–26; H. C. Darby et al., 'The changing geographical distribution of wealth in England, 1086–1334–1525', *J. of Historical Geography*, 5, 1979, pp. 247–62; G. Astill and A. Grant, eds., *The Countryside of Medieval England*, pp. 201–2.

century, only partly offset by suburban growth in that century's later years. Falling urban populations elsewhere may go back to a somewhat earlier date. Towns are generally thought to have been less populous in 1377 than they had been in 1348, an assumption which may well frequently be justified. The inhabitants of York and Colchester, on the other hand, appear to have become more numerous during the second half of the fourteenth century, principally through immigration made possible by the enhanced mobility of countryfolk; but if these towns were draining men and women from the countryside, they also afforded a growing market for rural produce.[65] The fifteenth century, however, does seem to have witnessed a fall in the populations of most established towns, with a parallel contraction of the markets they offered to country producers and the range of opportunities available to country people. Even so, cloth-making was turning places like Castle Combe and Lavenham from villages into towns, although these and other industrializing areas periodically suffered hard times when growth was checked. When that happened, as it did in the clothing districts of Wiltshire in the mid-fifteenth century, the agricultural communities from which they drew supplies were also inevitably affected. Overall the numbers of townsfolk probably fell between 1348 and the opening of the sixteenth century roughly in proportion to the fall in the population of the country as a whole; but there was a good deal of variation from place to place and areas developing industrially could support more towns, more villages growing into towns, and more villages in which there was significant non-agricultural activity. In such areas, too, the market opportunities open to farmers might well expand, at least periodically if not continuously, stimulating a measure of agricultural change in order to meet changing demand, while at the same time the reduction of the pressure of population on the land made it more possible for particular areas to specialize to a greater degree in the products to which they were best suited. A degree of regional agricultural specialization became increasingly evident.[66]

The extent and pace of change, however, must not be exaggerated. Much English farming was still carried on in traditional ways within a traditional context: the interlocking of the rights of individuals with those of their neighbours made that almost inevitable. In many villages, too, social structure was not all that different from what it had been in the early fourteenth century. Of course there were differences. People

[65] J. A. F. Thomson, ed., *Towns and Townspeople in the Fifteenth Century*, Gloucester, 1988, pp. 55–6; R. H. Britnell, *Growth and Decline in Colchester*, pp. 95–7; *VCH City of York*, pp. 84–6.

[66] Hare, 'The Wiltshire Rising of 1450', pp. 17–19; D. M. Palliser, 'Urban decay revisited', in Thomson, ed., *Towns and Townspeople*, pp. 15–18; Astill and Grant, eds., *Countryside of Medieval England*, p. 227.

were fewer; even small and middling tenants might have somewhat enlarged their holdings; and most of them held on easier terms. More decisive was the passing of traditional demesne cultivation, of labour rents, of many of the powers lords had exercised over the persons of their tenants, and of the presumption that a large proportion of countryfolk were born to unfreedom. Most landlords by the end of the fifteenth century were primarily rentiers, and most tenants were primarily payers of money rents with occasional increments like fines for entry. In these respects the tide had run by and large in the favour of tenants, but what they had gained was by no means totally underwritten by guarantees. It is probably fair to say that the tenurial picture at the end of the middle ages was an "extraordinary muddle", that the terms used to describe tenures lacked technical connotation, and that their interpretation depended upon the specific custom of the manor in which they were used. Further, lords retained in their manor courts jurisdiction over their customary tenants (and particularly over the large and diverse class of copyholders) and their landholding; for, despite some debate among the judges and a good deal of protective action by chancery and the conciliar courts, copyholders do not seem to have enjoyed any clear right to common law protection of their titles until Elizabethan times. Finally, even when a measure of security of title had been gained, custom might offer no shield against the enhancement of entry fines, something which might negate whatever security of tenure a tenant enjoyed. As long as tenants were at a premium, as they had been during most of the later middle ages, these were not very relevant considerations; but, under changed circumstances in the future, the apparent rights and expectations of tenants might seem very much less secure.[67]

Insecurity, of course, might arise from economic conditions as well as from the tenant's standing at law. Small and middling farmers, because they owed rents and had to save money to pay fines for entry and reversions, of necessity had to produce for the market as well as for their family's sustenance. They might be largely insulated, because they depended principally on family labour, from the effects of rising labour costs, and they were favoured by reductions of rents and other charges; but they could not be totally unaffected by the rising prices of some agricultural requisites or by periods of low agricultural prices, the effects of which must have been all the greater because their margins were so narrow. In many places, on the other hand, they might enjoy more generous grazing rights than in the past as lords withdrew from

[67] P. D. A. Harvey, ed., *The Peasant Land Market*, pp. 328–30; C. M. Gray, *Copyhold, Equity and Common Law*, Cambridge, Mass., 1963, pp. 61–6; *The Reports of Sir John Spelman*, ed. J. H. Baker, II, Selden Soc., XCIV, 1978, pp. 184–7.

active farming, the arable frontier retreated and tenant numbers were reduced; although once again the collapse of markets or the ravages of animal diseases might on occasion turn profit into loss. In general, however, and for much of the time, things were almost certainly easier for this majority element amongst villagers in the late middle ages. It is doubtless going much too far to regard that period as a "golden age" for the peasant farmer, for the balance between coping and failing to cope in changing circumstances was inevitably a fine one; but for many it may have seemed enough that they had more to eat for more of the time than had always been the case in times past.

At the same time, side by side with men cultivating on this sort of modest scale, a minority of tenant farmers had emerged operating on a much larger scale than most of their neighbours. These were men who had accumulated tenant holdings, taken over demesnes from landlords, or both, and who evidently farmed principally for the market. They were, as we have seen, men of many sorts, but many of them came from the ranks of the peasantry, and especially from the ranks of the wealthier villagers, with the resources (as well as the necessary enterprise) to face the costs of cultivation on a still larger scale. In this sense there was a progressive tendency for the gap between wealthier and poorer in village society to grow wider as time passed.[68] Those who achieved this degree of economic promotion, however, shared some of the vulnerability to changing economic circumstances which had persuaded most landlords to abandon their demesnes: labour shortages, high labour costs and periods of depressed prices, as well as periodic visitations of animal disease demanding heavy investment to replace flocks and herds. As producers of grain, wool and other agricultural products they may well have been more cost-effective than landlords exploiting their demesnes directly had been, especially if they had ready access to industrial or urban markets or extraneous customers like the ships that needed provisioning in the south-west or the Calais garrison seeking provisioning from the south-east. On the other hand, because they farmed mainly for the market, the fact that wool prices in the mid-fifteenth century were only half what they had been in the 1370s, and that wheat prices stood at only two-thirds of their 1360s level, makes it hardly surprising that the consolidation of the new yeoman class was achieved so slowly or that it attained a measure of stability only at the very end of the fifteenth century.

In the meantime some landlords, and not merely the smaller gentry like John Hopton in Suffolk, who "slipped in and out of direct management as need required", had returned to active farming.[69]

[68] Razi, *Life, Marriage and Death*, pp. 147–50.
[69] Dyer, *Standards of Living*, p. 43; also Richmond, *John Hopton*, ch. 2.

Some who did so were new men, investing capital derived from other activities (the law, administration, commerce), others men who concluded that despite low prices stock farming offered a better return from land than anything they could get from rent, and others again men who decided that tenants were so hard to come by that their only recourse was to take the land in question into hand. The Spencers of Althorp (Northants.) were descended from Warwickshire graziers who had learned in their native county that sheep rearing could be made profitable and that depopulation could be turned to their advantage. At the beginning of the sixteenth century they bought their way into good Northamptonshire sheep land and continued to support themselves in part as sheep-farming gentlemen for a century or more thereafter. By the opening of the sixteenth century, too, some leading gentry families in Norfolk were sheep farmers. Sir Roger Townshend of East Rainham had 7,911 sheep in 1479 and he had over 9,000 ten years later. He sold some wool to King's Lynn merchants, perhaps for export, and wethers to King's Lynn butchers, but most of his wool went to the merchants supplying the local cloth industry.[70] Gentlemen entrepreneurs like the Spencers and the Townshends may always have been exceptional and where their enterprise was successful it no doubt helped if, like the Townshends, they had a local textile industry for their flocks to supply, or if, like some of the gentlemen who took leases of some of the Canterbury demesnes, they were within reach of the London market. At the same time the reappearance of gentlemen producers and the emergence of other producers on a largish scale who were rising into gentility, and who probably directed their production more deliberately and more exclusively at the market than the old demesnes had done, may be regarded as one more indication of the success of late medieval society in adapting to the changing balance between land and people which was initiated in 1349 and worked out during the generations which followed.

[70] M. E. Finch, *The Wealth of Five Northamptonshire Families, 1540–1640*, Northants. Rec. Soc., XIX, 1955, pp. 38–9; K. J. Allison, 'Flock management in the sixteenth and seventeenth centuries', *EcHR*, 2nd ser. XI, 1958, pp. 100, 107–8.

CHAPTER 2

THE OCCUPATION OF THE LAND

A. THE NORTHERN BORDERS

In the northern region, as in the other regions of England, the expansion of cultivated land had reached its limits by the early fourteenth century. The extension of cultivation and of settlement took the forms familiar further south. New settlements were established, often on the margins of existing vills, such as Newton-on-the-Moor on the western edge of the township of Shilbottle in Northumberland. Land at high altitude was ploughed up, for instance at Slaley and Sweethope in Northumberland, both over 700 feet, and the uplands throughout the region were extensively colonized as grazing land for cattle and sheep: the moorlands of Kidland (Northumb.), for example, were developed both as sheep runs and as summer pasturing for cattle on the initiative of the monks of Newminster abbey. Towards the end of the thirteenth century there were signs in the north, as elsewhere in England, of pressure on available resources of land. When the prior of Durham brought part of Spennymoor into cultivation in the 1290s he was opposed by the tenants of Tudhoe and Hart, who feared that the prior's action would extinguish their right of common pasture on the moor of Spennymoor; and four landowners who disputed grazing rights on Chatton Moor in Northumberland thought it necessary to demarcate their respective shares with boundary stones. The northern region appears to have participated fully in the expansion of both pastoral and arable farming that characterized the thirteenth century elsewhere in England, and by 1300 the north was feeling the same pressures that were becoming apparent further south.[1]

In the later middle ages, the reversal of the pattern of growth and expansion is at least as marked in the four northern counties as further south, and in some parts of Northumberland and Cumberland the

[1] R. Newton, *The Northumberland Landscape*, London, 1972, pp. 89–93; A. J. L. Winchester, *Landscape and Society in Medieval Cumbria*, pp. 39–42; *Newminster Cartulary*, ed. J. T. Fowler, Surtees Soc., LXVI, 1876, pp. 73–83, 163–5; *NCH*, VI, p. 350; XIV, p. 226; R. B. Dobson, *Durham Priory 1400–1450*, p. 275, citing *Scriptores Tres*, ed. Raine, p. 74.

reversal of the trend was even sharper. The war with Scotland, which began in 1296 and lasted intermittently until the Scottish Reformation, has been given a major share of the blame for the contraction of the northern agrarian economy. The numerous occasions on which Northumberland, Cumberland, and Westmorland were relieved of the burden of taxation, and the detailed evidence of many petitions and manorial documents, leave no doubt that the Scottish raids, especially in Edward II's reign, brought widespread destruction to the north. In some of the more exposed and vulnerable parts of north Northumberland, such as the manor of Wark-on-Tweed, the war with Scotland brought about a virtual cessation of arable farming in the first two decades of the fourteenth century, and in both north Northumberland and north Cumberland damage to churches and to capital installations such as mills was widespread. But in the more southerly, and in the more remote, parts of the region destruction was less severe. Durham suffered less than Northumberland, partly because of its geographical position and its topography, and partly because its communities were able to band together to raise money to buy off the raiders. In Cumberland, the more upland, and the more southerly, districts suffered less than the low-lying northern parts exposed to the full force of Scottish invasion. Evidence for damage to churches in the diocese of Carlisle during the period of Scottish raids suggests that destruction was much less widespread in the southern deaneries of the diocese than in the deanery of Carlisle itself.[2]

On the other hand war was not the only disaster which northern rural society had to face in the early fourteenth century. I. Kershaw has drawn attention to the widespread incidence of livestock disease throughout England between 1315 and 1322, and the pastoral economy of the north suffered severely. A. J. L. Winchester has suggested that murrain of sheep "may have become endemic" in the early fourteenth century, and in Northumberland disease probably inflicted rather more devastating losses than the Scots were capable of: in 1319, for example, Hexham abbey lost all its oxen and dairy cattle from murrain.[3]

Scottish raids were at their most frequent and destructive between 1314 and 1322, and after the conclusion of the Treaty of Edinburgh in 1328 there are signs that the northern rural economy was beginning to recover from the damage inflicted by Robert I and his lieutenants. The rents which Holy Island priory received from its property on the mainland, for example, had returned by the 1330s to levels not substantially lower than those prevailing in the 1290s, and similar signs

[2] J. A. Tuck, 'War and society in the medieval North', *North. Hist.*, XXI, 1985, pp. 33–52.

[3] I. Kershaw, 'The great famine and agrarian crisis in England, 1315–22', *PP*, no. 59, 1973, pp. 3–50; Winchester, *Medieval Cumbria*, pp. 46–7.

of recovery and resilience have been observed in Berwickshire. But although the raids may have diminished in frequency and ferocity, they did not cease altogether: at no time in the later fourteenth and fifteenth centuries was the fear of invasion entirely lifted from the inhabitants of the northern counties, and in particular those of Northumberland and Cumberland. Winchester has shown how severely the Scottish invasion of 1345 affected the townships of the Eden valley and north-east Cumberland, while in 1388 the earl of Fife's army cut a swathe of destruction up the Eden valley as far as Appleby and in the east the earl of Douglas's force penetrated as far south as Brancepeth in County Durham.[4] These natural and man-made disasters in the course of the fourteenth century manifestly damaged the northern rural economy, but it is questionable how far the long-term decline in revenues from agriculture, which is apparent on many northern estates by the middle of the fifteenth century, was accentuated by these disasters. J. M. W. Bean has stressed the serious nature of the decline in income from rents and farms on the Percy estates in both Cumberland and Northumberland in the first half of the fifteenth century, and Durham priory's receipts from its churches in Northumberland and Durham declined by almost a half between 1348 and 1464. But this long-term decline is paralleled in other parts of England which did not experience invasion from Scotland, and the demographic decline induced by the plagues of the later fourteenth century is almost certainly the principal reason. In 1485–6 the bailiff of Alnwick put the decay of rents in the barony down to "war and pestilence long ago", and there is nothing in such a succinct generalization with which a modern historian would wish seriously to disagree.[5]

The decline in population and consequent shrinkage in cultivation in the century after 1348 can be discerned in every part of the region and on every type of land. The incidence of mortality from the plague varied, of course, from district to district. The number of deaths from the 1348–9 plague amongst the tenants-at-will in twenty-nine of Durham priory's vills is recorded. On the prior's vills in south-east Durham mortality seems to have been high, perhaps as much as 40–50 per cent of the population; but in the absence of any estimates for the total population of the prior's vills other than those in south-east Durham it is impossible to know what proportion of the population

---

[4] Tuck, 'War and society in the medieval North', pp. 33–52; Winchester, *Medieval Cumbria*, pp. 44–7; R. B. Dobson, 'The last English monks on Scottish soil', *Scottish Hist. Rev.*, XLVI, 1967, p. 3.

[5] J. M. W. Bean, *The Estates of the Percy Family*, pp. 24–7, 29–35; Dobson, *Durham Priory*, p. 271; *Scriptores Tres*, ed. Raine, pp. ccxlviii–cclii; Alnwick Castle Mss. C VI 4a. I am grateful to His Grace the Duke of Northumberland for allowing me access to the manuscripts at Alnwick.

these mortality figures represent. In the northern region, however, as elsewhere in England, the plague of 1348–9 seems to have been followed by a recovery, with landlords finding tenants for vacant holdings, but from the 1360s, as the cumulative effect of successive outbreaks of plague brought about a demographic crisis, demand for land fell away and a long-term contraction in the occupancy of the land set in. Unfortunately there is no evidence from Durham estates for mortality in the plagues of 1361 and 1369 comparable to that for 1348–9, but there is some reason to believe that the diocese of Carlisle suffered particularly heavily in the plague of 1361. In 1362 the number of wills proved before the bishop of Carlisle was 50, whereas the average in previous and succeeding years was 3.66; and the number of presentations to benefices vacant through death was fifteen, whereas the usual annual number was no more than two or three. None the less, the long-term effects of plague were everywhere apparent. In the predominantly pastoral district of Inglewood Forest in Cumberland, Thomas de Hutton had to give new land to maintain a chantry at Bramwra in 1361 because the chantry's ancient endowment had been bereft of tenants and cultivators by the plague and now lay sterile and waste. In the bishop of Durham's corn-growing vills in the south and east of the bishopric, land was in the lord's hand through lack of tenants by 1365; in the barony of Embleton on the Northumbrian coastal plain the same tendency was apparent, and in the upland country of Redesdale, tofts and crofts lay untenanted in the early fifteenth century.[6]

In certain districts, the Scottish war made the contraction all the more intense and prolonged. The vill of Ord, near Berwick, owned by Holy Island priory, never recovered from the damage inflicted upon it by the Scots in Bruce's reign, and it had been written off by 1350. The vill of Antechester, high up in the Cheviots in the parish of Kirknewton, was wasted by the Scots in the fourteenth century, and, in the words of Bowes's 1541 survey, since then "hath lyen waste unplenyshed"; while by the sixteenth century the shielings on Kidlandlee had been abandoned because of the danger from Scottish incursions. Further away from the border, destruction by the Scots was an occasional hazard for which allowance was made against the farms owed by tenants when it occurred, but the threat of invasion and devastation was ever present in men's minds and created a psychological climate in which men were unwilling to take land or capital installations at farm

[6] VCH Durham, ii, pp. 258–9; T. Lomas, 'South-east Durham', in P. D. A. Harvey, ed., The Peasant Land Market, pp. 257–61; Carlisle RO, Register of Bishop Wetton; ibid., Records of the Hulton Family, D/Van Hulton 2; PRO DL 29/354/5837; The Priory of Hexham, ed. J. Raine, ii, 21.

"propter metu Scottorum". In bringing about a decline in the rural economy, this psychological climate was, in the long run, probably more important than actual destruction and inhibited agricultural activity even at times of formal truce or peace between the two kingdoms.[7]

The shrinkage of cultivated land within vills was accompanied, throughout the region, by a retreat from the margins. High land which had been ploughed up in the thirteenth century was now abandoned, and the cultivation of the more marginal lowlands was also discontinued. In bringing about the abandonment of farming at high altitude, climatic change may have played a part. A fall of 1° in the average summer temperature is sufficient to prevent corn ripening in such places as Sweethope in Northumberland. Most authorities agree that a change of this kind occurred in the fourteenth century, but it is unlikely that any long-term change in the climate would have greatly affected farming at lower levels. The Scottish wars may explain why some marginal land was abandoned: it is significant, for example, that Ord, the only one of Holy Island's vills that never recovered from the Scottish raids, lay on poor land and was one of the least productive of the priory's estates. But the principal reason for the abandonment of marginal land was almost certainly the relaxation of the population pressure that had made the extreme extension of arable land necessary by the end of the thirteenth century.[8]

The decline in cultivation and the retreat from the margins does not, however, seem to have brought about the desertion of substantial numbers of villages in the region. In Cumberland eight deserted villages have so far been identified, six of them in the Irthing valley, and in Westmorland only two are known. In view of the dispersed pattern of settlement in the upland parts of those two counties a large number of deserted sites should not be expected, but there is evidence for the abandonment of upland farmsteads as well as for the diminution in size of lowland villages. In Northumberland 165 deserted village sites are known, but evidence for late medieval desertion is sparse. Dewley near Newburn was returned as a separate vill in 1296 but was described as waste in 1367, and the vill of West Backworth, on poor land in Tynemouthshire, was deserted sometime between 1339 and 1538 and its lands converted into pasture. The Scottish war led to the

[7] Tuck, 'War and society in the medieval North'; *AA*, 2nd ser. XIV, 1891, p. 32; *Newminster Cartulary*, ed. Fowler, p. 307; *NCH*, XI, p. 188; XV, pp. 450–1; B. Harbottle and R. A. S. Cowper, 'An excavation at Memmerkirk', *AA*, 4th ser. XLI, 1963, pp. 45–63; Alnwick Castle Mss. C VIII 1e; PRO DL 29/354/5840, 5842, 5844; PRO SC 6/952/6.

[8] For some discussion of climatic change see S. M. Wright, 'Barton Blount: climatic or economic change?', *Med. Arch.*, XX, 1976, pp. 148–52.

abandonment of some settlements in the pastoral uplands around the Cheviot, but generally in Northumberland the desertion of villages appears to have been the result of the activities of improving landowners in the sixteenth and eighteenth centuries. It has sometimes been suggested that the need for manpower to defend the border made deliberate depopulation inadvisable; but more probably the abundance of readily available grazing land even in the mainly arable vills made it unnecessary deliberately to remove villagers to turn their lands into pasture.[9]

In County Durham, 29 deserted village sites had been identified by 1968, and others have come to light since. Some, such as Woodham and Newhouses, may have been deserted in the early fifteenth century, but much research remains to be done on the scale and chronology of desertion in the county. However, neither the cathedral nor the priory of Durham appear to have adopted depopulation as a deliberate policy on their lands, and in Durham, as in other counties of the region, shrinkage rather than desertion was probably the fate of the majority of rural settlements in the century and a half after the Black Death.[10]

In the arable vills of the eastern coastal plain and the Eden valley, the abandonment of holdings allowed the surviving tenants-at-will to take over more land. At Heworth in 1373 each tenant held three tenements, and in the large arable vill of Billingham an increase in the number of holdings in the hands of each tenant is also apparent. On the land of the barony of Morpeth in the Wansbeck valley, the tenants of the vill of Angerton took at farm the waste husbandlands and cottages in the neighbouring vill of Hartburn; while in the vills of Hexham abbey and in the arable vills of the Eden valley certain bond tenants were able substantially to increase their holdings by taking over abandoned land and so enhancing their standing within their vills. Even so, the supply of vacant land outran demand, and on the estates of the bishop and prior of Durham and of the earls of Northumberland land remained waste and untenanted throughout the fifteenth century.[11]

In many parts of the region, the uncultivated land was converted into

[9] M. W. Beresford and J. G. Hurst, eds., *Deserted Medieval Villages*, pp. 185, 198–200, 206; *The Northumberland Lay Subsidy Roll of 1296*, ed. C. M. Fraser, Newcastle, 1968, p. 65; *The Percy Chartulary*, ed. M. T. Martin, Surtees Soc., CXVII, 1909, p. 434; *NCH*, IX, p. 39; XV, pp. 467–8; Newton, *The Northumberland Landscape*, pp. 104–6; Harbottle and Cowper, 'An excavation at Memmerkirk', pp. 55–6.

[10] Beresford and Hurst, eds., *Deserted Medieval Villages*, pp. 186–7; N. McCord, *Durham History from the Air*, Durham, 1971, p. 24; B. K. Roberts, 'Village plans in County Durham: a preliminary statement', *Med. Arch.*, XVI, 1972, pp. 33–57; Winchester, *Medieval Cumbria*, pp. 47–8.

[11] *Halmota Prioratus Dunelmensis*, eds. W. H. Longstaff and J. Booth, pp. 121, 135; T. Lomas, 'South-east Durham', p. 309; Alnwick Castle Mss. C VI 2b, 2c; C VIII 1a; E II 1a m.2; PRO SC

pasture. In certain districts, more especially in the west but also in some of the poorer and more upland parts of Northumberland, there was no rigid distinction in any case between arable and pasture; but in the vills of the eastern coastal plain, which had been predominantly arable before 1348, pasture farming became increasingly important. In north Northumberland the decline in the garbal tithe income of Holy Island priory suggests substantial conversion of arable to pasture, and here the Scottish war may provide part of the explanation. Stock could be moved to the safety of higher ground or protected within pele towers or bastles, whereas standing corn was an obvious and tempting target to raiders from across the border. In the vills of Lesbury, Alnham, Longhoughton and Acklington in the barony of Alnwick between one-fifth and one-half of the bondages had been converted to pasture by 1369, while further south at Langley in the barony of Prudhoe 100 acres of demesne and seven out of twenty husbandlands were worth nothing more than their herbage in 1366. The same was true in the good grain-growing land of south-east Durham: at Easington, for instance, the land of sixteen cottagers had been converted to pasture by the time of Bishop Hatfield's survey. Further west, at West Thickley, a vill lying at an altitude of 600 feet, 74 acres had gone out of cultivation and at the time of Hatfield's survey were occupied by the farmer of Midridge Grange, presumably as pasture.[12]

In south-east Northumberland, however, conversion of arable to pasture appears to have been more widespread than in any other part of the region. On the estates of Tynemouth priory virtually all the arable demesne had been turned into pasture by the dissolution and was in the hands of the tenants: only in the vills of Tynemouth itself and Preston did arable demesne still exist by 1539. Furthermore, many bondage holdings had fallen into the prior's hands during the second half of the fourteenth century for want of tenants, and these too were converted into pasture. At Monkseaton, for example, over 500 acres of arable land, including all the demesne land of the priory, had been converted into pasture, and conversion on a similar scale took place in the neighbouring vill of Backworth. One influence on the priors of Tynemouth in converting their demesnes into pastoral holdings may have been the demand from Newcastle, the major urban centre in north-east England, for meat and dairy produce. Tynemouth's policy of converting arable demesne to pasture contrasts sharply with the policy of the priors of Durham towards their demesnes in the south-east

11/156; *Priory of Hexham*, ed. Raine, II, pp. 5–10; *Bishop Hatfield's Survey*, ed. W. Greenwell, pp. 131–2; *Scriptores Tres*, ed. Raine, pp. ccxcvi–ccc.

[12] Tuck, 'War and society in the medieval north'; PRO C 135/185, 202; *Bishop Hatfield's Survey*, ed. Greenwell, pp. 27, 131–2.

of County Durham, where in most cases they were able to lease their demesnes to farmers who continued arable farming. Despite the conversion of some land to pasture, cereal growing remained the basis of agriculture in south-east Durham, whereas on the lands of Tynemouth priory a fundamental change took place. The conversion of arable to pasture in Tynemouthshire may reflect a deliberate policy on the part of the priors, based on a belief that a higher return was possible by going over to pasture farming. Not only the former arable demesnes, but the large quantity of freehold land acquired during the fourteenth century, and bondage holdings that had fallen to the priors for lack of tenants, were converted into pasture and passed into the hands of the tenants in the late fourteenth and fifteenth centuries.[13]

Changes in land use in the later middle ages might therefore vary from estate to estate depending upon the policy of particular lords, though variations in local conditions also provide part of the explanation. Perhaps the boulder clays overlying the coal measures in south-east Northumberland made arable farming a less attractive proposition than in south-east Durham, or perhaps the danger of Scottish raids was thought to be much greater and men were thus unwilling to take the risk of continuing arable farming on the prior's demesnes: at one point in the fifteenth century fear of Scottish attack was sufficient to prevent corn being sown for four years in succession on some of the tenant land of Tynemouth.[14]

In Cumberland and Westmorland the evidence for land use in the later middle ages is sparser. Throughout the middle ages in most of these two counties pastoral farming was more important than arable, and certain of the towns and great religious houses depended for their corn supplies on imports from Ireland. Only in the Eden valley, in the Irthing valley, and on the coastal plain did arable farming predominate. Sixteenth-century evidence for field systems makes it possible to say that arable farming continued in the Irthing valley throughout the later middle ages, and the same was true on the Percy lands of the honour of Cockermouth and in the Eden valley vills; but it is not possible to determine the extent to which arable contracted and was replaced by pasture. In the Eden valley vills of Penrith, Scotby, Salkeld, Carlatton, Langwathby, and Sowerby the demesne lands were still under cultivation in 1371, and it is therefore perhaps possible to suggest that there was no wholesale conversion to pasture such as took place in Tynemouthshire. Taking the region as a whole, Tynemouthshire appears to be exceptional in the degree to which pasture replaced arable

[13] *NCH*, VIII, pp. 115–17, 229, 405–6; IX, p. 39.
[14] BL Cott. Nero D VII f.51v. The 1296 Lay Subsidy Roll suggests that the Liberty of Tynemouth was the least wealthy district of Northumberland.

land; elsewhere there was undoubtedly an increase in pasture at the expense of arable, but except in Tynemouthshire the balance does not appear to have shifted decisively away from arable. In south-east Durham and in the vills of the north Northumbrian coastal plain, cereal farming was still the predominant activity at least until the sixteenth century.[15]

B. YORKSHIRE AND LANCASHIRE

At the opening of the fourteenth century, even after vigorous expansion in preceding generations, Yorkshire and Lancashire were still relatively poor counties. In terms of the ratio of taxable wealth to acreage, if the four northernmost counties are ignored, only Devon and Cornwall ranked lower than the West Riding; Lancashire and the North Riding were the West Riding's near neighbours in the order; and, while the East Riding came higher in the list, it was still somewhat below the middle point. This relative poverty reflected a terrain and climate which restricted the options open to farmers, so that the natural landscape had been less radically modified here than in many parts of England. Much of it was moorland: and not merely in the Yorkshire Moors and the Pennines, the province of seasonal herdsmen moving up from the dales, but also further down-country. There was moor at Ackworth near Pontefract, at Swinton near Rotherham, at Horsforth up-river from Leeds, at Rawcliffe and Hook near Snaith, at Naburn south of York, at Roecliffe near Boroughbridge; and in Lancashire there were extensive moors round Wigan and Manchester as well as at Heaton on the estuary of the Lune.[16]

Marshland and woodland were also ubiquitous. There was marsh along the Mersey and Humber estuaries and the coasts of South Lancashire and Amounderness, and also inland mosses like Chat Moss to the west of Manchester or, in the East Riding, Walling Fen upon which the territories of fifty-eight villages abutted. As for woodland, while the seaward side of Amounderness was "sore destitute", its more

[15] G. Elliott, 'The system of cultivation and evidence of enclosure in the Cumberland open fields in the sixteenth century', *CWAAS*, NS LIX, 1959, pp. 85–104; T. H. B. Graham, 'The common fields of Hayton', *CWAAS*, VIII, 1908, pp. 340–51; *idem*, 'The townfields of Cumberland', *CWAAS*, X, 1910, pp. 118–34; Winchester, *Medieval Cumbria*, ch. 4; PRO SC 11/155–156; PRO C 135/201; Alnwick Castle Mss. X II 23(2).

[16] R. S. Schofield, 'The geographical distribution of wealth in England, 1334–1649', *EcHR*, 2nd ser. XVIII, 1965, pp. 483–510; PRO DL 42/106, f.21; *Feet of Fines for the County of York, 1347–77*, ed. W. P. Baildon, Yorks. Arch. Soc. Rec. Ser., LII, 1915, pp. 71, 84, 180–1; *Inquisitions post mortem Relating to the County of York in the Reigns of Henry IV and Henry V*, ed. W. P. Baildon and J. W. Clay, Yorks. Arch. Soc. Rec. Ser., LIX, 1918, p. 178; *Coucher Book of the Abbey of Kirkstall*, ed. W. T. Lancaster and W. P. Baildon, Thoresby Soc., VIII, 1904, no. 386; *VCH East Riding*, III, p. 79; *Final Concords for the County of Lancaster...1377–1569*, ed. W. Farrer, Lancs. and Cheshire Rec. Soc., L, 1905, *passim*.

eastern parts were "partly woody, partly heathy"; there was a good deal of timber in the districts around Manchester, Sheffield, Barnsley, Escrick, Skipton in Craven, and Beverley; and, while much of Knaresborough Forest was open moorland, it also furnished oaks suitable for the repair of the castle. Further north, when the abbot of Fountains went to christen Sir James Strangeway's son at Harlsey beyond Northallerton in 1453 he paid a boy 2d. *docenti et informanti viam nobis per silvam.* The wild landscape was anything but completely tamed. Some land, too, was liable to flooding, like the drowned acres at Fenwick and Carlton-in-Balne, and some could only with difficulty be made fruitful. Much of Middleton-in-the-Wolds was said to lie in deep valleys which could "at no time be sown or anything got from [them] because of [their] poverty"; at Great Givendale, also in the wolds, a great part of the land was not worth sowing because of its dryness and weakness; and the "poverty" of the land was one reason given for waste oxgangs in 1366 at Carlton and Sandburn in the forest district north of York. In such places the expansion of ploughland in earlier generations appears to have extended onto marginal soils.[17]

In many places, of course, expansion had been checked well before 1349. Yorkshire and Lancashire, for example, had suffered from Scottish raiding, although to a lesser extent than the counties further north, in the early years of the fourteenth century. As late as 1344 Salton, near Pickering, was described as "greatly destroyed and wretchedly cast down by the invasions and burnings of the Scots", and assessments for the ninth in 1341 indicate how widespread damage had been. In Lancashire almost every parish in Lonsdale wapentake was affected, land that had lapsed from cultivation ranging from 19 per cent at Urswick to 73 per cent at Tunstall; and further south half-a-dozen townships in Amounderness, together with Ribchester and Chipping in Blackburnshire, had suffered only a little less severely. There was also a good deal of land out of cultivation in the North Riding and this was specifically attributed to destruction by the Scots at Briggenhall, Danby, and Marske in Swaledale. Even as late as 1363 many Fountains granges were said to be "lost, burned and reduced almost to nothing". Some of these claims may have been made with an eye to tax avoidance, but that does not of necessity deny them all basis in reality.[18]

---

[17] Leland, *Itinerary*, I, p. 51; IV, p. 10; *Yorks. Deeds*, IX, no. 162; *Inquisitions ... Henry IV and Henry V*, ed. Baildon and Clay, pp. 80, 160; *John of Gaunt's Register, 1372–1376*, ed. S. Armitage-Smith, II, Camden 3rd ser. XXI, 1911, no. 1373; *Memorials of the Abbey of Fountains*, III, ed. J. T. Fowler, Surtees Soc., CXXX, 1918, p. 102; *CIPM*, IX, nos. 188, 568; X, nos. 8, 84; XII, no. 8.

[18] *Priory of Hexham*, ed. Raine, II, p. 138; *Memorials of the Abbey of Fountains*, I, ed. J. R. Walbran, Surtees Soc., XLII, 1863, pp. 203–4; *Nonarum Inquisitiones in Curia Scaccarii*, ed. G. Vanderzee, pp. 35–8, 219–43, 436–7.

The returns for the ninth in Yorkshire in 1341, however, also reveal other adverse circumstances. The effects of bad weather can possibly be dismissed as temporary, but the taxors also drew attention to the prevalence of murrain among livestock, to sheep that were dead or putrid or sick, and to land that had lapsed from cultivation because of the "impotence" of tenants, depressed prices, the "debility" or "sterility" of the land, and flooding. Inundation, moreover, continued to present problems in Yorkshire. Rivers overflowed their banks at Adlingfleet and Fockerby in 1369, and in Holderness by that time land was being lost both through flooding along the Humber estuary and coastal erosion in the townships facing the North Sea. Flooding contributed to a reduction of the revenues which the earl of Kent drew from Cottingham in 1353; 240 acres of meadow were inundated on the archbishop's manor at Patrington in 1388; and, while the sea was eating away the coastal townships of Dimlington, Grimston, Withernsea, and Hartburn, the Meaux abbey lands along the estuary were also in full retreat by 1400. Over 500 acres were lost at Tharlesthorpe alone, a loss apparently accepted as irreversible by the abbey, for the buildings of the grange were dismantled.[19]

Long before that time, however, plague had been added to the troubles afflicting the north. Information about its incidence in Lancashire is anything but plentiful. An assertion by the archdeacon of Richmond that 13,180 people died in Amounderness between September 1349 and January 1350 is too exact to carry conviction, although doubtless it correctly conveys an impression of heavy mortality; and there is independent testimony to a high death toll at Everton and Didsbury during these months, and to subsequent outbreaks in the county in 1361, 1379, 1390–1 and 1466. The evidence for Yorkshire seems somewhat better. The number of ecclesiastical benefices vacated by death in plague years has been used as an indicator of the severity of these early outbreaks. In the "first pestilence" they rose to 178 in the twelve months beginning in March 1349, compared with only 16 in the preceding fifteen months; and visitations in 1361–2 and 1368–70, though less dramatically, also pushed up rates of mortality among incumbents. This evidence also suggests that in 1349, while the death rate may have been particularly high in the northern wolds and the Vale of York and somewhat lower in the remoter areas of Craven, Ryedale, and Cleveland, plague affected every part of the county. This last impression is reinforced by many casual indications in manorial records and the severity of this visitation is reflected in the court rolls of the manor of Wakefield and of Knaresborough Forest. At

[19] *CIPM*, x, p. 47; xii, no. 336; *Cal. Inq. Misc.*, v, no. 101; *Chronica Monasterii de Melsa*, ed. E. A. Bond, iii, pp. 241–2, 283–6; C. Platt, *The Monastic Grange in Medieval England*, p. 65.

Wakefield 157 tenants paid heriot or relief on succeeding to holdings in the ten months beginning in September 1349 compared with 11 during the corresponding months of the previous year; and at Knaresborough the court recorded 71 tenant deaths on 29 October 1349 and 36 more three weeks later. In the end nearly half the land in the area changed hands, some of it going to successors other than wives, sons or daughters, suggesting that some whole families may have been wiped out. The 1361–2 and 1369 visitations were seemingly less lethal; but even so the death rate in Knaresborough Forest in 1369 was three or four times higher than normal and outbreaks continued to be reported in remote places, including Healaugh beyond Reeth in Swaledale in 1362.[20]

Nor did peaks of mortality disappear after 1369. That is the implication of evidence furnished by the York probate registers, even though these are sources which largely leave out of the picture those poorer sections of society likely to be most vulnerable to dearth and disease. They suggest that there were at least ten years between 1391 and 1483 when death rates were markedly high, whether as the result of epidemic disease (which may not always have been plague) or, as in 1438, of plague combined with the hunger that followed upon a bad harvest. This periodic heightening of mortality may reasonably be regarded as one influence preventing the recovery of population levels from the blows they suffered during the third quarter of the fourteenth century. Whether it was reinforced, at least down to the mid-fifteenth century, by a parallel decline in fertility as expanding employment opportunities for women led them to postpone marriage, is a more debatable proposition. In the countryside particularly a young man's chances of getting a holding, and therefore a base for raising a family, even in his father's lifetime were far better than they were likely to have been before 1349. Whatever the precise explanation may be, the impression which remains is that, in most places (but not quite all) in the Yorkshire countryside, population levels were substantially lower than before 1349 and sometimes continued progressively to decline at least until some recovery became evident late in the fifteenth century.[21]

The immediate effects of the changing situation are evident enough in the townships of Knaresborough Forest. Most holdings vacated in

[20] A. G. Little, 'The Black Death in Lancashire', EHR, v, 1890, pp. 524–30; VCH Lancs., II, pp. 285–6; R. S. France, 'The history of plague in Lancs.', Hist. Soc. of Lancs. and Cheshire, XC, 1938, pp. 24–8; A. Hamilton Thompson, 'The pestilences of the fourteenth century in the diocese of York', Arch. J., LXXI, 1914, pp. 128–34; B. Jennings, ed., A History of Nidderdale, pp. 86–91, 468–9; Wakefield Court Rolls, 1348–1350, ed. H. M. Jewell, Yorks. Arch. Soc., 1981, passim; CIPM, XI, no. 102; PRO DL 29/465/7604, 30/478/13.

[21] P. J. P. Goldberg, 'Mortality and economic change in the diocese of York, 1390–1514', North. Hist., XXIV, 1988, pp. 38–55.

1349 were taken up again quite quickly, especially in the valley settlements around Knaresborough itself; but even further up Nidderdale only small amounts of land were still unlet in 1384. On the other hand, assarting, which had been active down to 1349, virtually ceased for the rest of the middle ages; and in the moorland townships above Nidderdale and over towards Wharfedale some 15 per cent of the customary land lacked tenants both in 1384 and in 1426. Further, even land that was not abandoned might no longer command its old rent. At Timble in 1378, for instance, the rent payable for five acres which had been in the lord's hand since the great pestilence was reduced by 2s. 6d. to secure a tenant, and that paid for five oxgangs at Aldborough had been long abated *durantibus istis mediocribus annis quousque seculum emendetur*. Here the least rewarding land now attracted no tenants at all and even better land had often to be let on easier terms.[22]

There was nothing unusual about what happened in Knaresborough Forest. A little assarting may have continued in a few places: in the Sheffield region, for example, or around Slaidburn on the Lancashire border; but the gains were minor and often minuscule. Far more common in Yorkshire were notices of land going out of cultivation. Some of these losses, of course, were the involuntary results of flooding or erosion, but even so a contributory influence may have been an unwillingness or inability in hard times to incur the cost of drainage or sea-defence. More commonly, however, where formerly cultivated land lay "waste", the explanation seems to be that there were fewer tenants competing for the land available and, as in Knaresborough Forest, poorer land was the least likely to prove attractive to them. The poverty of the soil at Great and Little Givendale has already been mentioned, so that it is no surprise to find empty holdings in these townships appearing in the records with monotonous regularity.[23]

Even more characteristic was the depressing influence of these circumstances upon rents. The position was put succinctly in relation to an oxgang at Little Barugh, near Pickering: because its late tenant thought it too dear it lay waste, rendering nothing. Faced by reluctance to pay the old rents, especially for poorer land, landlords were driven into concessions, not always successfully, to attract or retain tenants. This compulsion was already being felt in the townships of the manor of Wakefield in the immediate aftermath of the Black Death. With possibly around 300 acres "waste and uncultivated" on Joan of Bar's

[22] Jennings, ed., *History of Nidderdale*, pp. 467–8; PRO DL 29/465/7604, 7607.

[23] T. W. Hall, *Descriptive Catalogue of Sheffield Manorial Records*, I, Sheffield, 1926, pp. 42–3; PRO DL 29/76/1500; *CIPM*, x, no. 84; xi, nos. 427, 515, 547; *Inquisitions... Henry IV and Henry V*, ed. Baildon and Clay, pp. 28, 49, 165, 169.

lands in Warley, Hipperholme, and Crigglestone in September 1350, John del Lathe's threat to abandon completely his holding in Hipperholme unless his rent was reduced was immediately effective; and in the following year, because the reeve could not persuade them to pay more, certain tenants in Saltonstall secured an abatement of their rents by one-third.[24]

Concessions of this sort were probably reversed only with difficulty and, in any case, there are indications that the downward pressure on rents was often progressive and cumulative. At Bowes an increment of 1s. per oxgang had been abandoned before 1399 because of the "impotence" of the tenants; at Forcett rents for bond oxgangs were reduced from 10s. to 8s. by 1394 and subsequently a further 8d. was remitted; at Ripon rents were reduced in the 1390s because holdings could not be let more dearly; at West Gilling rents that had already been reduced by 27 per cent were 15 per cent "decayed" in 1436; at Snape in the 1450s "decay" of rents amounted to some 40 per cent of the total charged. On the Percy estates, too, the period 1416–71 was one of generally falling income from rents: at Tadcaster, for instance, because land was increasingly hard to let, rents for arable and meadow were cut by 20 per cent and 16 per cent respectively, and only began to rise again towards the end of the fifteenth century. This picture of falling rent rolls, however, is one that must not be overdrawn. On the manors of the honour of Pontefract, as elsewhere, there was some land that could no longer be let; and rents paid for demesne land were reduced at Kippax, Elmsall, Altofts and Barwick-in-Elmet, as they were for bond oxgangs at Kippax. On the other hand, the agricultural frontiers of this estate seem to have been substantially preserved and in 1383–4 only three out of sixteen manors showed any significant "decay" of rents. During the fifteenth century, moreover, the impression is one of stabilization, for the charges recorded in the 1425 rental were generally those accounted for in 1484–5. New rents at that time were few and small, but the loss of old rents seems equally uncommon.[25]

What was happening in Lancashire is even less clear-cut. There, too, some land in Blackburnshire, as well as mills at Cliviger and Haslingden, lacked tenants in the 1420s, and at Huyton in 1491 the rent for a pasture had been cut by one-third. On the other hand, some expansion of

---

[24] *Priory of Hexham*, ed. Raine, II, p. 80; *Wakefield Court Rolls, 1348–1350*, ed. Jewell, pp. 260–1; *Wakefield Court Rolls, 1350–1352*, ed. M. Habberjam *et al.*, Yorks. Arch. Soc., 1987, pp. 9, 61.

[25] PRO SC 6/1085/18, DL 42/106, DL 29/507/8226–8, 511/8265; *Memorials of the Church of Ripon*, ed. J. T. Fowler, III, Surtees Soc., LXXXI, 1886, pp. 113, 118; M. Y. Ashcroft, 'Snape in the fifteenth century: account rolls', *North Yorks. RO Jnl*, 5, 1977, pp. 35–8; Bean, *Estates of the Percy Family*, pp. 36–40, 47–8.

cultivation was still taking place: assarting continued at Tottington and Penwortham at least until 1400, land was reclaimed from woodland at Ulnes Walton in 1440, and "new rents" slowly increased the receipts from Colne, Haslingden, and Accrington through much of the fifteenth century. The second half of the fourteenth century also witnessed recovery from some of the worst effects of the earlier Scottish raids, manifested by the rising value of rectories in Lonsdale and Amounderness as grain production increased and sheep farming became more active. John of Gaunt's attempts to negotiate higher rents for his Lancashire vaccaries in the 1370s may also have been a symptom of this recovery, and some recovery of values in west Derbyshire about this same time in part reflected more intensive stock farming. The fifteenth century, on the other hand, appears usually to have been a time of stabilization or retreat, but again there were exceptions: at Mytham in Kirkham parish, for instance, where mosses were reclaimed for cultivation; or at Goosnargh and Whittingham, where the oats acreage was expanded on assarted forest land. Further east, on the Pennine slopes, the immense cattle farms of the great landlords were broken up, and "the moorland was...slowly settled by rent-paying tenants" who improved and often enclosed the land around their homesteads. One result was a rise in the rental values of the Rossendale and Pendle Hill vaccaries in the first half of the fifteenth century which, after a recession in the 1460s, was resumed later in the century. In this part of the county there appears to have been genuine development in the late middle ages, including some increase of the population of a sparsely settled countryside.[26]

Changes, therefore, in the generations after 1349 were not all in one direction. In Yorkshire, particularly, there was evidently some withdrawal from marginal arable, although such land was not necessarily lost to productive use. At Cowton 91 acres of "forland" (assarted land) were "pastured by all the tenants of the vill", and $7\frac{1}{2}$ uncultivated oxgangs at Silsden, near Skipton, still yielded 30s. for herbage. Many Yorkshire villages, however, were reasonably well provided with pasture, with the result that abandoned arable at Azerley, Carlton and Sandburn could be given no value "by reason of the abundance of pasture in those parts"; and in wold villages like Kilham rents for pasture as well as for arable fell sharply. The general impression is that, nonetheless, on the lower grounds in Yorkshire, and most markedly in the wolds, there was some shift from arable to

---

[26] *Court Rolls of the Honour of Clitheroe*, ed. W. Farrer, I, pp. 489, 493–6; II, p. 1; III, p. 2; G. H. Tupling, *The Economic History of Rossendale*, pp. 31–4, 38; PRO DL 29/76/1498, 1500; R. Cunliffe Shaw, *Royal Forest of Lancaster*, pp. 405–8, 471–4, 489–90; *John of Gaunt's Register, 1372–6*, ed. Armitage-Smith, II, no. 1699.

pasture as well as some abatement of rents and a virtual cessation of demesne cultivation. In the Lancashire and Yorkshire Pennines and the Yorkshire moors, where pasture had always predominated, smaller men likewise took over many of the stock farms of landlords. Some of them created little enclosed farms, like the 40-acre close of land, meadow and wood which John Parker occupied at Burnley in 1425, or the 200 acres which Walter Curwen made separate from Quernmore in 1431, or the "messuage called Baxtanclyff with land and closes in severalty" on the Bolton priory estate in 1473. They fitted well enough into a landscape in which large common fields had always been exceptional, where there was enough pasture to make it no hardship if individuals appropriated parcels of it, and where hamlets and isolated farms had been the characteristic products of long-term expanding settlement. This was not only true of the Pennines, where a single township, Northowram (Yorks.), had over forty medieval settlement sites, but also of the north Yorkshire moors. To an increasing extent in the late middle ages the upland zone became a region of large open commons and small enclosed farms. In Lancashire, too, there were also enclosures down-country: of forest assarts at Fulwood, for instance, or as stock farming intensified, in the coastal mosses, the river meadows and even in the mixed farming belt further inland – but, as Leland observed, "always the most part…for pasturage". Some arable, too, seems to have been converted to pasture, like the demesne crofts and fields at Hornby by 1491.[27]

Pasture was plentiful enough in most parts of Lancashire to minimize opposition to piecemeal enclosure and the incentive to depopulating enclosure. The county was an area of light depopulation and therefore was not visited by the 1517 commissioners. The latter came to Yorkshire, however, and noted both enclosures and conversion to pasture. In the North Riding these had occurred in the townships of the Vales of York and Pickering rather than in the moors, and not infrequently the motive seems to have been less an economic one than to create a park for sport. Only in about five villages in the riding do more businesslike considerations appear to have been dominant, most notably in the conversion to pasture and enclosure of 400 acres of arable by the FitzHugh heirs at East Tanfield. Similar instances in the West Riding were fewer still, although the abbot of Kirkstall "prostrated"

[27] BL Add. Ms. 40010, f.30d; PRO E 142/50; *CIPM*, XI, no. 290; XII, no. 8; BL Harl. Roll H5; *Court Rolls of the Honour of Clitheroe*, ed. Farrer, II, p. 6; Cunliffe Shaw, *Royal Forest of Lancaster*, p. 445; *Rental of Bolton Priory*, ed. I. Kershaw, Yorks. Arch. Soc. Rec. Ser. CXXXII, 1970, p. 3; M. L. Faull and S. A. Moorhouse, eds., *West Yorkshire: an Archaeological Survey*, III, pp. 585, 603–6; J. McDonnell, 'Medieval assarting hamlets in Bilsdale', *North. Hist.*, XXII, 1986, pp. 268–79; *AHEW*, IV, p. 81; Leland, *Itinerary*, IV, p. 10; BL Add. Roll 53088.

messuages and ploughs at Morton; but only Henry Pudsay really stands out, having cast down houses, converted 240 acres to pasture and evicted 42 people at Rimington and elsewhere in the unlikely terrain of the Lancashire border. The parishioners of Aldborough, however, may have been more typical when they enclosed 180 acres of arable by agreement, presumably for their mutual use. In the East Riding, too, significant depopulating enclosure was noted only in some three villages, although a "decay" of people, resulting from the accumulation of tenements by individuals or their conversion to pasture without being enclosed, was also reported in a number of places. The explanation may be that tenements were accumulated or converted simply because tenants were hard to find.[28]

The 1517 returns for Yorkshire, however, tell only a part of the story, for especially in the west and south-west enclosure and conversion may well have made as much progress as in Lancashire, and in general meadow and pasture almost certainly gained ground relative to arable. An attempt has been made to chart this progress in Lancashire. In the south-west of that county an earlier "overwhelming preponderance of arable" became much less marked after about 1450. In the period 1450–1508 arable accounted for 56–63 per cent of the productive area (that is, the total area of arable, meadow and pasture, but excluding "waste") in the central region, the Ribble valley and in east and central Fylde, a figure which falls 34–39 per cent in Bowland, Lonsdale, West Fylde and Rossendale, to 26 per cent in south-west Lancashire and to 16 per cent in north Fylde. The inquisitions of Henry VII's reign suggest a broadly similar range of land uses in Yorkshire at the end of the fifteenth century. Arable accounted for 54–66 per cent of the productive area in the Vales of York and Pickering, the Humberhead levels, and in the limestone and sandstone hills, and only for around 40 per cent in the wolds, Holderness, the Pennines, and Craven, and for substantially less than that in the north Yorkshire moors. The fact that moor and waste are excluded from these calculations, moreover, means that in the upland areas of both counties where these pastoral adjuncts were most extensive the importance of arable is considerably overstated by the figures given above.[29]

Equally inescapable is the impression that the populations of many rural settlements were shrinking, even if no very large proportion of

[28] For Lancashire, M. W. Beresford, Lost Villages of England, pp. 41–2, 220, 223, 233; for Yorkshire, I. S. Leadam, 'The inquisitions of 1517', RHS, NS, VII, 1893, pp. 233–53.

[29] F. Walker, Historical Geography of South-West Lancashire before the Industrial Revolution, Chetham Soc., NS, CIII, 1939, pp. 39–40, 54–7; H. B. Rodgers, 'Land use in Tudor Lancashire', Institute of British Geographers, XXI, 1955, p. 97; for Yorkshire, data from CIPM, Henry VII, I and II.

those which would eventually be deserted had totally disappeared by 1500. Desertions in Lancashire have not yet been counted or systematically studied, but some of the lost villages of Yorkshire recall the many catastrophes of the fourteenth century. Some, like Mortham, never recovered from ravaging by the Scots; some were eaten away by flooding or erosion; and a few, although only a few, were so emptied by plague that they died forthwith. This may have been the fate of Flotmanby, Drewton and Gardham in the East Riding and, in the West Riding, of Wheldale, Wothersome and Stotfold (as well as of Bolton by Bradford, subsequently re-established). In general, however, while plague made some places more vulnerable by making them smaller, it only rarely destroyed them outright. Consequently the number of villages which had disappeared before 1400 does not seem to have been large, although some of the tiny hamlets and isolated farms established on the margins of townships may have fared less well. Thereafter the deliberate acts of landlords (of Sir Thomas Fairfax at Caythorpe, of the FitzHugh heirs at East Tanfield, or of the Wilstrops at Wilstrop) precipitated the demise of some settlements; but there are also indications that East Tanfield was a shrinking community long before it was lost, and excavations at Wharram Percy suggest that its depopulation by the Hiltons around 1500 was the end of an extended process of decay. This wold settlement was still a corn-growing open-field village in 1457, but it was already steadily contracting. In a number of instances one house was replacing two on the same site and, still more significantly, in the course of the later middle ages the aisles and chapels of the village church were demolished and its chancel was halved. This tangible evidence of shrinkage, especially on the thin soils of the wolds, is even more typical than testimonies to seigneurial destruction.[30]

No more than a relatively small proportion of the settlements which had existed early in the fourteenth century had been extinguished by 1500, but some had died and others were sufficiently shrunken to make them vulnerable in the future. On the other hand a few new villages were also being born (or at least revived). In 1363 Fountains abbey was allowed to establish villages on the sites of nine of its ruined granges and Jervaulx had apparently already done the same at Newstead, Rookwith, Aikber, Didderston, and Horton in Ribblesdale. Not all flourished, but

---

[30] For a list of desertions in Yorkshire that were known in 1968, Beresford and Hurst, *Deserted Medieval Villages*, pp. 207–12; and see generally M. W. Beresford, 'The lost villages of Yorkshire', *Yorks. Arch. J.*, xxxvii, 1948–51 – xxxviii, 1952–5, and K. J. Allison, *The East Riding of Yorkshire Landscape*, London, 1976, pp. 99–108. For East Tanfield and Wharram Percy, see Beresford and Hurst, *op. cit.*, pp. 132–3 and M. W. Beresford, *Lost Villages of England*, pp. 292–4, 298–9.

land on which Cistercians had planted their granges might well be good enough to attract settlers. To the extent that it did so represents yet another indication of a tendency for population to move from poorer to better land.[31]

There are indications, therefore, of development as well as of difficulties in the Yorkshire and Lancashire countryside. Even so, both counties at the opening of the sixteenth century ranked even lower in assessed taxable wealth than they had in 1334 and the growth of their taxable capacity was well below the average for the country as a whole. It had been lowest of all in Lancashire, suggesting the limited economic potential of such development of stock farming as there had been, and also the slight progress yet made by the woollen industry of Salfordshire and Blackburnshire. The improvement of taxable capacity in the North and East Ridings was little better than in Lancashire and amounted to no more than half the national average. The East Riding, in consequence, fell heavily in the ranking of counties and districts, perhaps mainly because there had been no significant growth of industry to balance a retreat of cultivation, especially in the wolds. In the West Riding, on the other hand, and more particularly in some parts of it, the growth of taxable capacity did approach or even exceed the national average, although this did not improve the ranking of the riding as a whole. This relatively better performance is probably mainly to be explained in industrial rather than agricultural terms, even though industrial development meant an expanding market for foodstuffs and raw materials. The last word, therefore, lies with the craftsman, and especially with the rural craftsman. To the extent that the amount of tax paid per village offers a rough indication of the levels of economic activity, the most prosperous parts of the West Riding in 1334 had been in the south around Doncaster, Sheffield, Tickhill, Selby, and Pontefract, and much the same was true in 1379 save that the Selby district had fallen back and the villages round Ripon had rapidly advanced. At that time, too, the countryside around Doncaster, Tickhill, Sheffield, Pontefract, and Ripon contained nearly two-thirds of the rural clothworkers and metalworkers assessed to the poll tax of that year. This, too, was merely a stage in the development of cloth manufacture in particular which was continuing westward along the valleys of the Aire and Calder, so that by the 1470s Halifax, Bradford, and Almondbury were challenging the centres further east. In the West Riding during the later middle ages, as was subsequently the case in Lancashire, the growth of rural industry offered a compensation for limited potentialities for agricultural development.[32]

[31] C. Platt, *Monastic Grange*, pp. 97–8.
[32] Schofield, 'The geographical distribution of wealth in England', pp. 504, 508–9; H. C.

C. EASTERN ENGLAND

Eastern England, though predominantly an area of fertile, easily cultivated soils, contained areas where arable land was hemmed in by natural pasture and waste. The fenlands, with their fisheries and sheep pastures, stretched far into Lincolnshire, Cambridgeshire, and western Norfolk. Parts of the fenlands were very fertile, but pastoral farming was everywhere prominent there. At Chatteris, in the heart of the Cambridgeshire fens, the fishery of Hunneye was leased, together with a dairy farm of the same name, for £3 6s. 8d. in 1415–16; the pasture, meadows and fishery of Hollode rendered £8 10s. 4d., and a further £7 10s. was received for the hay from 112 acres of meadow called Crowlode. On a manor at Stow Bardolph (Norfolk) leases of marshlands in 1426–7 totalled £9 13s. 8d.; the Newland, comprising 231 acres of land and pasture reclaimed from the fen before 1350, was leased for £7 13s. 9d., and the demesne flock numbered 1,850 sheep.[33] A comparable emphasis on pastures was characteristic of long stretches of coastline. Along the Lincolnshire coast, and farther south among the coastal marshes of the Thames, the Crouch, the Blackwater, and the Colne, demesne pastures greatly exceeded the arable area.[34] Where a marshland sheep farm was remote from the manor to which it belonged, the shepherds lived in the marshes apart from other farmworkers. In Essex such a separate sheep farm was called a *wick*.[35]

A frontier of a different kind, on the landward side, was the region of predominantly poor soils continuing eastwards and south-eastwards from the fens into Norfolk and Suffolk. The Breckland and Norfolk sands were again regions of large sheep flocks, where rabbit warrens replaced the fisheries of the fenlands as a valuable source of income

Darby *et al.*, 'The changing geographical distribution of wealth in England', *J. of Historical Geography*, 5, 1979, pp. 245–62; Tupling, *Economic History of Rossendale*, p. 166; *The Early Yorks. Woollen Trade*, ed. J. Lister, Yorks. Arch. Soc. Rec. Ser., LXIV, 1924, pp. 102–4; W. B. Crump and G. Ghorbal, *History of the Huddersfield Woollen Industry*, Huddersfield, 1935, pp. 25–30. The 1379 poll-tax returns for the West Riding are printed in *Yorks. Arch. J.*, V–VII, 1879–82.

[33] PRO SC 6/765/25r (Chatteris), SC 6/943/13 (Stow Bardolph). For details of Hunneye and Hollode, see SC 6/678/4.

[34] PRO DL 29/242/3888d, 3895d, 3904r (Gedney, Wrangle, Long Sutton), DL 29/243/3912, mm.10r, 11r (*le ffryth iuxta Boston*, Wrangle), DL 43/6/32 (Saltfleetby), SC 6/909/22r, 23, m.1d (Fleet, Frampton); R. H. Britnell, 'Production for the market on a small fourteenth-century estate', *EcHR*, 2nd ser. XIX, 1966; *idem*, 'Agricultural technology and the margin of cultivation in the fourteenth century', *EcHR*, 2nd ser. XXX, 1977; H. E. Hallam, 'The agrarian economy of south Lincolnshire in the mid-fifteenth century', *Nottingham Medieval Studies*, XI, 1967, p. 87.

[35] PRO SC 6/848/13d (Tolleshunt Major); Essex RO, D/DK M86–90 (Bourchier Hall in Tollesbury). For examples of wicks around St Osyth see R. C. Fowler, 'A balance sheet of St Osyth's Abbey', *Essex Arch. Soc.*, NS XIX, 1930, pp. 187–8; P. H. Reaney, *The Place-Names of Essex*, EPNS, XII, Cambridge, 1936, pp. 348–51.

from the wild. At Brandon on the border of Norfolk and Suffolk, 4,020 rabbits sold from the warrens were worth over £40 in 1387. Farther south there were similar heathlands running parallel to the coast between Danbury Common (Essex) and the banks of the Alde about Iken Heath (Suffolk). In some parts heathlands and marshlands lay adjacent, together ensuring a high proportion of pasture, as in the hundreds of Thurstable and Winstree (Essex) and Colneis (Suffolk).[36]

During the later middle ages water encroached on cultivated lands, partly because of changes in the natural environment, partly because of the relaxation of responsibility on the part of landlords and local communities. The level of the sea rose and the cost of maintaining sea walls increased. Sometimes sea defences decayed gradually as at Ingoldmells (Lincs.), but sometimes they collapsed all of a sudden, as in the floods of 1377 in which land was permanently lost on the shore of the Thames at East Ham, West Ham, Barking and Dagenham (Essex), or in those along the Nene which drowned over 10,000 acres in Wisbech, Leverington, Newton, and Tydd St Giles in the Cambridgeshire fenland in 1439.[37] The Norfolk coastline suffered losses chiefly through erosion by the sea rather than through flooding. But not all inundation was on the coast. In eastern Norfolk after the late thirteenth century areas of worked peat were filling with water to form the Broads.[38] The fenlands also suffered losses, and it was indeed here that wildness and wet achieved their most striking victories. A major problem of the fens was peat shrinkage, and this perhaps accounts for the flooding at Chatteris; rent for the pastures of Hollode declined from £26 13s. 4d. in 1404–5 to £5 6s. 8d. in 1454–5, and Crowlode ceased to be valued for its hay after 1452. At Stow Bardolph, the $231\frac{5}{8}$ acres of Newland accounted for in 1426–7 were all that remained of $304\frac{1}{2}$ acres there paying rent "before the great plague", since $69\frac{1}{2}$ acres were now lying in marsh and $3\frac{3}{8}$ were waste.[39]

Other causes brought about a more general withdrawal of land from agriculture, and in some cases the abandonment of former settlements

[36] *Brandon Manor Account Roll, 1386–7*, trans. J. T. Munday (duplicated), Lakenheath, 1971; M. D. Bailey, 'The rabbit and the East Anglian economy', *AHR*, XXXVI, 1988, pp. 1–20; J. Chapman and P. André, *A Map of the County of Essex*, London, 1777, Pls. XIII and XIV; W. R. Fisher, *The Forest of Essex*, London, 1887, p. 275 and map facing.

[37] *Court Rolls of the Manor of Ingoldmells*, trans. W. O. Massingberd, London, 1902, pp. 209, 243, 255–6, 268; *A Terrier of Fleet, Lincolnshire*, ed. N. Neilson, London, 1920, pp. xiv, xlvii–xlviii; H. C. Darby, *The Medieval Fenland*, Cambridge, 1940, pp. 59, 165; *VCH Essex*, v, pp. 215, 238, 285; VI, pp. 17, 75.

[38] R. R. Clarke, 'The Broads and the medieval peat industry', *Norfolk Archaeology*, XXXII, 1961, pp. 209–10; C. Green and J. N. Hutchinson, 'Relative land and sea levels at Great Yarmouth, Norfolk', *Geographical J.*, CXXXI, 1965, pp. 86–90; C. M. Hoare, *The History of an East Anglian Soke*, pp. 164, 173.

[39] PRO SC 6/766/1r, 3r, 4r (Chatteris), SC 6/943/13r (Stow Bardolph).

altogether. In Lincolnshire North Cadeby and Middle Carlton were extinguished by the Black Death in 1349, and perhaps a hundred more villages had disappeared by 1500. Losses were appreciably fewer in Norfolk, where no example of desertion is attributable to the Black Death, and there were not many at any stage of the later middle ages in Cambridgeshire, Suffolk, or Essex. Most deserted villages had been small, as in the case of the adjacent hamlets of Middleton and Barwick (Norfolk), both abandoned during the century following the Black Death. Such desertion was not peculiar to this period. Between 1066 and 1349 changes in manorial structure or economic organization had brought about the disappearance of many small settlements. But from 1349 falling population made the survival of small communities more precarious than ever. Hamlets around greens or on the edge of commons in the claylands of eastern England were particularly vulnerable.[40]

Total desertion was just an extreme case of a more general shrinkage of settlements. Depopulation often reduced villages without finishing them off, and it is not uncommon to find that so-called deserted medieval villages survived the fifteenth century to disappear later. Caldecote (Norfolk) had fewer than ten households in 1428, but the church there was still being maintained in 1489. Pudding Norton (Norfolk) was there in 1557, and the group of deserted villages at West Harling, Middle Harling and Harling Thorpe (Norfolk), on the eastern edge of the Brecklands, was still inhabited in the seventeenth century. Many villages survive to the present day despite severe late-medieval shrinkage. Such are Ludborough and Stallingborough (both Lincs.), where complex earthworks adjacent to the modern village indicate the extent of former settlement. A few villages, like Holt (Norfolk) were deliberately destroyed by landlords to prepare the way for sheep farming, but this occurred chiefly towards the very end of the period and was only a minor feature of the overall picture.[41]

Concentrations of lost villages occur on the Lincolnshire Wolds and the light, sandy soils of western Norfolk. In Essex the small number of lost villages contains a high proportion of heathland settlements from the west and south-west of Colchester. Where village lands were

---

[40] Allison, 'Lost villages', pp. 122–5, 139, 154; G. Becket, 'The Barwicks: one lost village or two?', Norfolk Archaeology, XXXIX, 1984, p. 52; M. W. Beresford, Lost Villages of England, pp. 170–2, 365; G. Platts, Land and People in Medieval Lincolnshire, pp. 165–7; P. Warner, Greens, Commons and Clayland Colonization, Leicester, 1987, p. 39.

[41] Allison, 'Lost villages', pp. 133, 138–40; M. W. Beresford and J. K. St Joseph, Medieval England: an Aerial Survey, pp. 119–20; A. J. Davison, 'West Harling: a village and its disappearance', Norfolk Archaeology, XXXVII, 1980, pp. 295–9; idem, 'The desertion of Caldecote: some further evidence', Norfolk Archaeology, XXXIX, 1984, pp. 53–4; P. Everson, 'Stallingborough – earthworth survey', Lincs. History and Archaeology, XVI, 1981, p. 32; Platts, Land and People, pp. 167, 180–1; C. Taylor, Village and Farmstead, London, 1983, pp. 164–5; VCH Cambs., v, p. 263.

abandoned they were often put down to pasture, and often they were being enclosed by the end of the fifteenth century, as in the former Cambridgeshire villages of Clopton and Shingay. Not all deserted settlements were on exceptionally poor land, though, since the arable of a decayed village might continue to be worked from a neighbouring one, as in instances from the Lincolnshire Wolds. Nor did poor land necessarily drive tenants away. Recent research in the history of the Breckland implies that the extent to which villages there were abandoned in this period has been overstated; seven from the Norfolk Breckland and one from the Suffolk Breckland seem to exhaust the count. The Suffolk Breckland did not fare more adversely than other parts of eastern England in this respect. A region of poor soils might be well adapted to dependence upon other resources. It is not possible, at present, to explain the changing relationship between soils and settlement with any claim to science. A lot depended not on the natural fertility of the soil but upon how it was cultivated, what degree of specialization was possible, and what employment was available outside agriculture.[42]

To some extent land was abandoned for reasons which had been operative before 1349; overcropping of soils without adequate manuring could lead to their deterioration. But a more significant cause of declining arable cultivation was the rising labour cost of working the land and transporting its product, which meant that land which had been ploughed and sown before 1348 could no longer be cultivated at a profit thereafter. Some abandonment of arable resources was well-nigh universal, and even on manors which survived as grain producers land was taken out of cultivation. On the Beaumont manor of Welbourn (Lincs.) in 1427 there were 210 acres of demesne arable, "of which 110 lie in a field called Westfeld and each acre is worth $2\frac{1}{2}$d. a year while the other 100 acres lie waste on the heath in a field called Estfeld, and each acre of these 100 is worth 1d. a year". There are many similar examples in a survey of the Hastings family estates made in 1391. At Saxthorpe (Norfolk) there were 46 acres of wasteland in fields called the Longe Redye and the Holwode. At Lidgate (Suffolk), 16 acres were lying bare as wasteland and a further 51 acres withdrawn from cultivation were enclosed in Badmondisfield Park. In the Colchester region (Essex), despite the growth of urban demand, this same estate shows the retreat of arable at Fordham, where 34 acres in Wolfledefeld had reverted to heath, and at Thorrington, where 163

[42] Allison, 'Lost villages', pp. 131–4, 138; M. D. Bailey, *A Marginal Economy? East Anglian Breckland in the Later Middle Ages*, pp. 9–25, 309–23; M. W. Beresford, *Lost Villages of England*, p. 273; Beresford and Hurst, *Deserted Medieval Villages*, p. 187; Beresford and St Joseph, *Medieval England*, p. 119; *VCH Cambs.*, VIII, pp. 30, 36, 125.

acres had been taken out of cultivation as wasteland pasture. On the Arundel estates similar adjustments had been made by the 1380s; at Langtons in Little Canfield (Essex), for example, there were 94 acres of wasteland used as pasture and valued at 4d. an acre, and at Margaretting (Essex) there were 40 acres lying waste because of debility.[43]

On the heavy Essex soils decline of cereals production was severe. Langenhoe manor, despite an increased amount of land in the lord's hands after 1349, maintained an arable acreage no higher in the 1370s and 1380s than in the second quarter of the century. Reduction of the arable area after the 1380s was accompanied by an increase in the stock of wethers. At Bourchier Hall tenements fell into the lord's hands after the Black Death and so increased the potential size of the demesne, but the arable area of the demesne in the first decade of the fifteenth century was nevertheless 100 acres smaller than it had been in the 1340s. On neither manor were resources used as fully in the early fifteenth century as they had been a century earlier. At Feering the demesne lands of Westminster abbey were considered of good quality in 1289, when they were mostly valued at 6d. an acre, but even here the average sown area fell from $398\frac{1}{2}$ acres in 1332–48 (data for 9 years) to $321\frac{1}{8}$ acres in 1398–1404 (data for 6 years). It is apparent from the decline of receipts at Feering Rectory that the contraction of arable husbandry was not confined to demesne lands. At Writtle the demesne had about 1,300 acres under cultivation in 1328 but only about 565 in 1413 and probably fewer than 400 by 1440. "For more than a century and a quarter, by far the greater part of the demesne arable grew no crops."[44]

Less intensive use of resources after 1350 can help to account for some ambiguities in the classification of land. Pentokkes Close in Mettingham (Suffolk) was described in 1485–6 as containing about 20 acres of arable or pasture.[45] It might be some time before land withdrawn from the growing of crops was acknowledged to have been withdrawn permanently. Classification became difficult, moreover, on soils where cultivation was irregular and rest periods extended. An example of such ambiguities occurs in surveys of certain Norfolk manors of the Hastings family made in 1377 and 1391. The ratio of arable to pasture shows a divergence hardly to be accounted for by real changes in land utilization (Table 2.1). Many acres of poor soil were classed as arable in 1391 but not in 1377; the only manor where the figures are

[43] PRO SC 6/913/4 (Welbourn), DL 43/14/3, ff.12v, 22v, 24r,v, 42r, 43v (Hastings manors), SC 11/33 (Arundel manors).

[44] Essex RO, D/DC 2/11–16, D/DEl M220–9, D/DGe M200, 201 and PRO SC 6/842/24 (Langenhoe); Westminster Abbey Muniments, 25659–25758, Cambridge Univ. Lib., Kk.5.29, f.96r and PRO SC 6/841/6–10 (Feering); Britnell, 'Agricultural technology', pp. 63–5; K. C. Newton, *The Manor of Writtle*, pp. 25–6, 58, 74–8.   [45] BL Stowe 934, f.5v.

Table 2.1. *A comparison of two statements of the acreage of arable and pasture on some Norfolk manors*

	1377		1391	
	Arable	Pasture	Arable	Pasture
Burgh Apton	120	280+	260	?
Gooderstone	230	144	491	?
Foxley	60	40+	$294\frac{3}{4}$	29+
Saxthorpe	180	70	140	51+
Hockham	80	175	209	?
Totals	670	709+	$1,394\frac{3}{4}$	?

Source: PRO E 142/83(5) and DL 43/14/3, ff.4r–6r, 12r–16v.

Table 2.2. *The valuation of acres on some Norfolk manors, 1391*

	1d.	2d.	3d.	4d.	5d.	6d.	7d.	8d.	12d.
Burgh Apton	0	$99\frac{1}{2}$	25	29	60	$34\frac{1}{2}$	5	7	0
Gooderstone	238	69	0	57	0	0	0	8	119
Foxley	0	$165\frac{1}{4}$	$4\frac{1}{2}$	77	0	0	0	48	0
Saxthorpe	0	0	0	0	0	0	0	140	0
Hockham	75	0	31	0	0	103	0	0	0

Source: PRO DL 43/14/3, ff.4r–6r, 12r–16v.

approximately the same is Saxthorpe. Comparison of the acreage of 1377 with valuations of 1391 (Table 2.2) suggests that only land valued at over 4d. an acre was unambiguously arable land, and that Saxthorpe was exceptional for the high and homogeneous quality of its soils.

The switch into sheep farming commonly associated with declining arable farming can nowhere be illustrated as a steady trend. At Writtle, for example, the steep reduction of demesne arable cultivation was not due to an expansion of sheep farming. Though on some manors there were periods when sheep were substituted for cereal crops, there were others when land was abandoned as arable without any corresponding expansion of pasture farming. At Kelvedon (Essex) the sown area of Westminster abbey's demesne fell from 259 acres (1376–86, eleven years) to 205 acres (1391–1402, twelve years), while the average number of fleeces produced fell from 261 to 213.[46] Indeed, permanent

---

[46] Westminster Abbey Muniments, 25829–25880 (Kelvedon); Britnell, 'Production for the market', pp. 386–7.

pasture, like arable land, was commonly in excess supply in the fifteenth century. On the Lincolnshire manors of the Duchy of Lancaster in 1420–1 pastures were not leased for want of a tenant in Long Sutton, Wrangle and *le ffryth iuxta Boston*. At Gooderstone (Norfolk) in 1467–8 decays of rent included £1 "in the distres of the ferme of a pasture with a mershe collyd Helgey, the wyche payd sumtyme 26s. 8d., and nowe yt path [but] 6s. 8d. be yere". This was a recurrent problem for landlords in more pastoral regions, and contributed to severe losses of income.[47] Admittedly some farmers near towns benefited from a rising demand for meat, particularly before 1450. In the early fifteenth century perhaps more sheep were bred for meat than before; the sheep to be slaughtered were usually sold after shearing. In the 1420s the Clere family's manor at Ormesby St Margaret supplied wethers to butchers in Great Yarmouth, Norwich, and elsewhere. Wivenhoe manor in 1425–6 sold 48 wethers, 48 ewes and 80 lambs to Colchester butchers.[48] However, even near towns the raising of livestock for meat did not take up all the resources left idle by shrinking arable husbandry.

As long as land was periodically ploughed it would not grow wild. And fifteenth-century leases sometimes required the eradication of bushes and trees as a condition of tenure on land which had become permanent pasture.[49] So although the area of scrub and woodland increased, this increase was not directly related to reduced intensity of land use. The most permanent additions to woodland were deliberate ones, where parks were enlarged to include former arable lands. At Winfarthing (Norfolk), 15 acres of arable called the Launde were emparked before 1391.[50] In cases such as this, conversion of land to park and wood was an act of investment, even if the land had little alternative use, for enclosures had to be constructed and maintained. On a well-managed estate parks and woods were administered with great care as a valued asset. The timber and underwood of the Hastings manors of Norfolk, Suffolk, and Essex was worth over £9,000 in the winter of 1391–2, with valuations ranging from £2 for an acre of young trees to £6 13s. 4d. for an acre of mature timber. In the 1460s the number of trees felled was a measure of the severity of agricultural depression. Margaret Paston, unable to call in her rents or sell her

---

[47] PRO DL 29/243/3912, mm.6r, 10r, 11r; *The Grey of Ruthin Valor of 1467–8*, ed. R. I. Jack, p. 141; W. O. Massingberd, 'Social and economic history', in *VCH Lincs.*, II, p. 321.

[48] PRO SC 6/939/1, 2, 5, 8A (Ormesby); Essex RO, T/B 122 (Wivenhoe); M. K. McIntosh, *Autonomy and Community: the Royal Manor of Havering, 1200–1500*, pp. 142, 147.

[49] e.g., Essex RO, D/DBw M99, m.5r,d (Witham, Essex).

[50] Essex RO, D/DBw M99, m.16r (Witham); PRO DL 43/14/3, ff.17v, 22v (Winfarthing and Lidgate).

Table 2.3. *Demesne cropping: examples of wheat and oats husbandry* (*percentages*)

Manor	Years (no. of years averaged in brackets)	W	M	R	L	B	D	H	O
Essex									
Boreham	1378–9 (1)	44.7	—	—	6.2	4.0	3.7	—	41.4
Bourchier Hall	1350–7 (4)	36.5	5.9	3.6	4.0	0.3	2.4	—	47.3
Bourchier Hall	1401–6 (3)	44.8	—	—	2.7	6.2	1.9	—	44.4
Claret Hall	1361–4 (3)	42.8	1.1	—	9.6	6.8	5.9	3.4	30.4
Feering	1399–1404 (6)	43.0	—	—	17.9	7.5	0.9	—	30.8
Hatfield Regis	1418–19 (1)	40.1	—	—	14.0	3.9	1.6	1.7	38.7
Hutton	1388–90 (2)	48.7	—	—	10.9	0.6	—	—	39.8
Kelvedon	1391–1402 (12)	40.1	—	0.1	14.4	9.9	—	—	35.4
Langenhoe	1379–1414 (10)	45.8	—	—	3.9	2.8	—	0.8	46.7
Mashbury	1418–19 (1)	25.4	—	—	16.5	11.3	—	—	46.7
Sampford Rectory	1351–60 (8)	51.3	—	—	—	—	—	—	48.7
Tey	1351–2 (1)	53.1	—	—	2.9	—	—	—	44.0
Tolleshunt Major	1397–8 (1)	41.2	4.3	—	—	—	—	—	54.5
Writtle	1412–13 (1)	39.8	—	—	15.1	7.6	5.6	—	31.9
Writtle	1451–5 (4)	19.0	0.5	—	13.5	22.9	3.4	—	40.9
Suffolk									
Hundon	1381–9 (3)	32.8	—	—	12.3	11.7	—	11.8	31.4
Lidgate	1347–8 (1)	46.2	—	2.5	6.1	4.2	—	—	41.0
Woodhall	1351–8 (3)	39.6	1.5	—	1.1	15.2	7.2	3.4	32.1

Note: W = wheat, M = maslin, R = rye, L = legumes, B = barley, D = dredge (oats and barley sown together), H = peasmong and beanmong (oats and peas or beans sown together), O = oats. The dates cited are the earliest and latest in the group; i.e. 1350–7 signifies that the earliest account included is from 1349–50 and the latest for 1356–7. The figure cited for each crop is its average percentage share of the sown area of the demesne.
Sources: PRO SC 6/837/1 (Boreham), SC 6/839/1–4 (Claret Hall), SC 6/841/10 (Feering), SC 6/842/24 (Langenhoe), SC 6/844/8, 30, 31 (Hatfield, Hutton), SC 6/845/18 (Mashbury), SC 6/846/32–9 (Sampford Rectory), SC 6/847/16 (Tey), SC 6/848/13 (Tolleshunt Major), SC 6/1000/1–3 (Hundon), SC 6/1002/16 (Lidgate), SC 6/1008/14–16 (Woodhall); Essex RO, D/DC 14–16, D/DEl M224–228, D/DGe M200, 201 (Langenhoe), D/DK M86, mm.5–8, D/DK M87–90 (Bourchier Hall); Westminster Abbey Muniments, 25739–25758 (Feering), 25857–25880 (Kelvedon); Newton, *Writtle*, pp. 75, 76.

produce, was driven to contemplate felling her woods in 1471, much against her inclination since many other landlords were resorting to the same expedient and prices were low.[51]

Meanwhile, arable husbandry often remained a principal source of cash even where the cultivated area was declining. The proportion of grain which was sold may have been much the same in the fifteenth century as in the early fourteenth, even though total output was smaller. The regions of eastern England were affected very differently in this respect. Commercial prospects remained brightest for estates able to supply London or other towns cheaply because of good communications by water. The most commercially interesting region was the Norfolk coast, both because of its coastal communications and because of its capacity for growing barley. Bromholm priory was selling barley to Cromer in 1415–16. Men from Great Yarmouth, Covehithe, Dunwich, Brightlingsea, and Colchester were buyers of malt at Ormesby St Margaret. Some barley malt went out of the region altogether, to York or to Kent, and the correspondence of William Paston shows that Londoners were customers as well. During the fifteenth century ale was probably more commonly brewed with barley malt in place of oats malt than in the past.[52]

Arable husbandry was responsive to local differences of soil and climate. Though the same crops were to be found everywhere their relative proportions varied greatly. In Essex, southern and eastern Suffolk, and parts of eastern Norfolk the main commercial crop was wheat, and this was cultivated in conjunction with oats as the main spring-sown crop, as at Langenhoe (Essex), where between 1379 and 1414 roughly equal acreages of wheat and oats accounted for 93 per cent of the sown acreage. A similar cropping scheme was practised here in 1440, when 12 quarters of wheat, $24\frac{1}{2}$ quarters of oats and $2\frac{7}{8}$ quarters of barley were sown on unspecified acreages.[53] At Langenhoe the proportion of crops other than wheat and oats was always low, on average under 10 per cent of the sown acreage. Elsewhere the proportion of legumes and barley was often higher, but it was characteristic of this type of husbandry that wheat and oats together accounted for at least two-thirds of the sown acreage and usually more (Table 2.3). Closely related to it is a type of cropping found on sandier

[51] PRO DL 43/14/3 passim; The Paston Letters and Others Letters and Papers of the Fifteenth Century, ed. N. Davis, 2 vols. out of 3, I, nos. 209, 212, 214, pp. 352–3, 359, 362.

[52] PRO SC 6/939/1–12, SC 6/940/1–11, SC 6/941/1–13 (Ormesby); 'The Cellarer's Account for Bromholm Priory, Norfolk, 1415–16', ed. L. J. Redstone, Miscellany (Norfolk Rec. Soc., 17), 1947, pp. 58–61; Paston Letters, ed. Davis, I, no. 71, p. 126; Britnell, Growth and Decline in Colchester, pp. 132, 246–7. For the malting of oats, see PRO SC 6/836/9d, 11d (Bardfield), SC 6/844/36, m.1d (Justicehall), SC 6/849/16d (Wix); Essex RO, D/DC 2/11d (Langenhoe), D/DK M86, mm.1d, 2d (Bourchier Hall).   [53] Essex RO, D/DEl M229d.

Table 2.4. *Demesne cropping: examples of wheat and oats husbandry on sandy soils (percentages)*

Manor	Years	W	M	R	L	B	D	H	O
Essex									
Bradfield	mid-14th c. (1)	25.3	—	23.5	9.9	16.0	3.5	—	21.8
Eastwood	1361–3 (3)	0.8	—	49.1	0.2	—	—	—	49.9
Eastwood	1370–2 (3)	31.0	—	19.0	1.4	—	—	—	48.9
Wivenhoe	1425–6 (1)	—	—	54.8	—	—	—	—	45.2
Wix	1390–4 (3)	26.7	—	11.1	14.9	10.0	3.9	—	33.4
Suffolk									
Acton	1410–15 (4)	31.6	10.1	—	15.0	16.3	5.1	12.0	9.8
Norfolk									
Popenhoe	1390–1 (1)	10.8	37.8	—	—	7.2	1.8	—	42.3
Lincolnshire									
Gedney	1364–5 (1)	33.3	24.3	—	15.0	9.7	2.2	—	15.4

Note: This table has the same form as Table 2.3.
Sources: PRO SC 6/845/24 (Bradfield), SC 6/840/22–5, 31–3 (Eastwood), SC 6/849/19–21 (Wix), SC 6/942/17 (Popenhoe), SC 6/989/12–15 (Acton), DL 29/242/3888 (Gedney); Essex RO, T/B/122 (Wivenhoe).

soils where rye was more prominent in the winter-sown courses. The cultivation of barley and legumes was often prominent on these soils, though oats and oats mixtures remained the predominant spring-sown crop (Table 2.4).

In the more fertile and better populated parts of eastern England north of the river Stour, oats and oats mixtures were of less significance. It is true that on the boulder clay of south Cambridgeshire they grew dredge, a mixture of oats and barley. A similar cropping was practised at Somerton (Lincs.) in the 1370s. But neither dredge nor oats were favoured on better soils. At Thurlby (Lincs.) in 1361–2 no oats was cultivated; barley and peas occupied the place oats would have taken in Essex. At Harrington (Lincs.) no oats was sown in 1387–8 "because no land there is suitable for such seed this year"; wheat, barley and pulses here accounted for 84 per cent of the sown acreage.[54] So few Lincolnshire demesnes were managed directly in the later middle ages that evidence for cropping in the county is too weak to support confident generalizations. For the rest of the region evidence is stronger. The most striking feature of husbandry in East Anglia was the prominence of barley. In High Suffolk it figured more prominently

[54] PRO SC 6/910/11d (Harrington), SC 6/913/12–19 (Somerton), SC 6/914/7d (Thurlby).

Table 2.5. *Demesne cropping: examples of barley husbandry (percentages)*

Manor	Years	W	M	R	L	B	D	O
Cambridgeshire								
Burwell	1398–9 (1)	46.2	—	—	3.2	46.9	—	3.6
Elsworth	1381–4 (3)	33.8	—	—	23.5	—	38.7	4.0
Elsworth	1402–3 (1)	26.6	—	—	40.1	30.3	—	2.9
Fulbourne	1435–6 (1)	29.8	15.1	—	0.6	30.1	24.4	—
Fulbourne	1461–2 (1)	—	10.3	—	—	75.4	—	14.4
Graveley	1391–5 (3)	27.5	—	—	29.4	39.5	—	3.5
Knapwell	1415–16 (1)	18.9	—	—	40.9	—	37.1	3.0
Landbeach	1352–3 (1)	25.1	22.1	—	7.6	31.7		13.5
Oakington	1361–2 (1)	16.5	8.3	—	24.2	—	46.8	4.2
Great Shelford	1363–5 (3)	13.0	17.1	—	—	35.8	30.4	3.7
Great Shelford	1383–4 (1)	19.2	16.2	—	—	60.0	—	4.6
Soham	1354–5 (1)	14.1	16.1	—	10.7	42.3	12.1	4.7
Suffolk								
Brandon	1386–7 (1)	2.7	22.1	—	—	59.1	—	16.1
Exning	1357–9 (2)	17.8	21.2	—	5.8	55.2	—	—
Norfolk								
Bircham	1356–62 (4)	—	—	27.0	3.3	41.4	—	28.3
Brancaster	1367–9 (3)	20.7	—	4.9	4.9	58.5	2.7	8.2
Carrow	1455–6 (1)	14.3	6.5	—	2.4	60.5	—	16.3
Carrow	1484–5 (1)	14.2	13.0	—	—	63.3	—	9.5
Ormesby St Margaret	1424–6 (3)	24.2	—	—	19.6	50.6	—	5.6
Ormesby St Margaret	1450–3 (3)	16.0	—	—	16.5	57.9	—	9.5
Uphall	1372–3 (1)	15.5	—	9.7	7.7	58.0	—	9.2
Lincolnshire								
Somerton	1359–68 (7)	21.3	—	1.7	33.8	—	43.1	—

Note: This table has the same form as Table 2.3.
Sources: PRO SC 6/765/10 (Burwell), SC 6/766/27–9, SC 6/767/2 (Elsworth), SC 6/767/8,9 (Fulbourne), SC 6/767/22, 24, 25 (Graveley), SC 6/769/9 (Knapwell), SC 6/913/12–16, 18, 19 (Somerton), SC 6/930/26–8, 30 (Bircham), SC 6/931/8–10 (Brancaster), SC 6/939/1–3, SC 6/940/9–11 (Ormesby St Margaret), SC 6/944/19 (Uphall), SC 6/996/10. 11 (Exning); *Brandon Account*, trans. Munday (Brandon); 'Three Carrow Account Rolls', ed. L. J. Redstone, *Norfolk Archaeology*, XXIX, 1946, pp. 76–82 (Carrow), F. M. Page, *The Estates of Crowland Abbey*, pp. 274–6 (Oakington); J. R. Ravensdale, *Liable to Floods*, p. 117 (Landbeach); *VCH Cambs.*, II, pp. 60–1 (Great Shelford, Soham).

Table 2.6. *Tithes of grain (in bushels) at some rectories in eastern England*

	Wheat	Maslin	Rye	Peas	Barley	Dredge	Oats
Colne, 1374–5	81	—	—	25	87	—	142
Feering, 1402–3	101¾	—	—	—	—	—	152
Kelvedon, 1390–1	141¼	2	—	42¼	111¼	12¼	126¼
Linton, 1420	160	—	—	32	480	—	24
Hoxne, 1414–15	219	—	32	65	175	—	122
Martham, 1360	329	—	—	96	1072	—	18

Source: PRO SC 6/841/10 (Feering), SC 6/999/19 (Hoxne); Essex RO, D/DPr M13 (Colne); Westminster Abbey Muniments, 25858 (Kelvedon); *VCH Cambs.*, VI, p. 92 (Linton); Campbell, 'Agricultural progress in medieval England', p. 40n.

than in Essex, even on estates such as that of Sibton abbey where wheat and oats were large components of the harvest.[55] In Norfolk, particularly in eastern Norfolk, barley was the dominant cash crop, often occupying over half the sown acreage of demesnes (Table 2.5).

Cropping regions are likely to have been the same for tenant farms as for demesnes. Where there is evidence of tithe receipts the proportions of grain received match the prevailing pattern of cropping on demesne arable. The receipts of Colne, Feering and Kelvedon (Essex) show the preponderance of wheat and oats characteristic of Essex demesnes. At Linton (Cambs.), Hoxne (Suffolk), and Martham (Norfolk) barley was more important (Table 2.6). However, the best evidence of the importance of barley on Norfolk holdings of all sizes is that of barley rents. Sometimes whole demesnes were leased for barley, like that of Suffield manor in 1398–9, or at the manor of Ormesby St Margaret in the 1470s. Even where the demesne was not leased, or was leased for cash, there were commonly barley rents from tenements on lease. Some details from Brancaster in 1366–7 show that forty-two tenants owed 65 quarters 5½ bushels between them for holdings totalling 237½ acres in Depedale and Brancaster. At Uphall in 1372–3 the earl of Pembroke's bailiff received 31 quarters 2½ bushels for about 110 acres leased to different tenants, much of it described as oats land. At Burgh Hall in Holkham in 1376, thirty-seven tenants owed 27 quarters 2 bushels of barley at Michaelmas. At Vaux Hall in Burgh St Margaret in 1423–4 there were rents of 62 quarters 3½ bushels of barley a year from twenty-one tenants holding about 110 acres in Burgh,

[55] *The Sibton Abbey Estates*, ed. Denney, Suffolk Rec. Soc., 2, Ipswich, 1960, p. 32.

Bastwick, Repps, Clippesby and Rollesby, and at Lessingham in 1436–7 barley rents totalled 69½ quarters.[56] The importance of barley crops for all classes of arable farmer is adequately indicated by these examples – indeed, no other crop in East Anglia can be showed to have acquired comparable status as a means of payment. At Terrington and Upwell gild members paid their annual subscriptions in barley.[57] The large quantities of barley entering into trade whetted the entrepreneurial instincts of landlords, who had barley malted in anticipation of bulk sales or sold large consignments of grain to maltsters.[58]

Local differences in cropping can also be related to differences of diet, for though little is known of the bread of different regions there is record of grain paid to farm servants for their subsistence. In many cases wages were partly delivered in the form of millcorn, whose composition is rarely stated precisely, but despite this weakness in the evidence it appears that in wheat and oats regions servants were given a large part of their subsistence in wheat, that in regions of rye cultivation they took more rye or maslin, and that elsewhere much of the allowance was paid in peas or barley (Table 2.7). Often barley rather than maslin or rye constituted the staple diet. The register of Crabhouse nunnery records that in 1438 the nuns ran short of grain, and a relative of the prioress "sente us of his charite an 100 cowmbe malte and an 100 coumbe barly".[59]

Discussion of changes in cropping between 1350 and 1500 may be confined to the one generalization for which there is good evidence – the tendency for the relative importance of barley to increase, except in eastern Norfolk. In some cases the acreage under barley became absolutely larger after 1350 than it had been earlier, as at Writtle between 1413 and 1450. Presumably *per capita* consumption of ale had risen more than *per capita* consumption of bread.[60] Other developments in cropping are unlikely to have been of any significance. In the late thirteenth and earlier fourteenth century the importance of peas had

[56] PRO SC 6/931/5, 8–10 (Brancaster), SC 6/931/27 (Vaux Hall), SC 6/937/16, m.6 (Burgh Hall), SC 6/937/19, m.1 (Lessingham), SC 6/942/1–9 (Ormesby), SC 6/944/11 (Suffield), SC 6/944/19 (Uphall); R. H. Britnell, 'The Pastons and their Norfolk', *AHR*, xxxvi, 1988, p. 134.
[57] C. B. Firth, 'Village gilds of Norfolk in the fifteenth century', *Norfolk Archaeology*, xviii, 1914, p. 195.
[58] *Paston Letters*, ed. Davis, i, nos. 71, 72, 221, 272, pp. 126, 130, 372, 456.
[59] 'The Register of Crabhouse Nunnery', ed. M. Bateson, *Norfolk Archaeology*, xi, 1892, p. 62; W. J. Ashley, *The Bread of our Forefathers*, p. 39.
[60] Bailey, *A Marginal Economy?*, pp. 237, 282–3; Britnell, 'Agricultural technology', p. 65; *idem, Growth and Decline in Colchester*, p. 144; B. M. S. Campbell, 'Field systems in eastern Norfolk during the Middle Ages', Cambridge Univ. Ph.D. thesis, 1975, pp. 106, 109, 265; Newton, *Writtle*, pp. 75, 76. See also Tables 2.3 (Bourchier Hall, Witham) and 2.5 (Elsworth, Fulbourne, Great Shelford, Carrow, Ormesby).

Table 2.7. *Grain payments to farm labourers (percentages)*

	W	M	Millcorn	R	B	L	O
Lincolnshire							
Caythorpe, 1360–1	32.1	—	—	50.2	5.2	12.5	—
Gedney, 1364–5	8.8	91.2	—	—	—	—	—
Harrington, 1387–8	—	—	96.1	3.9	—	—	—
Somerton, 1367–8	50.0	—	—	—	—	50.0	—
Norfolk							
Bircham, 1361–2	—	—	10.4	44.8	44.8	—	—
Brancaster, 1368–9	4.9	—	20.7	1.3	73.2	—	—
Popenhoe, 1390–1	—	100.0	—	—	—	—	—
Stow Bardolph, 1426–7	—	—	—	100.0	—	—	—
Uphall, 1372–3	—	—	—	9.0	91.0	—	—
Cambridgeshire							
Elsworth, 1402–3	50.0	—	—	—	—	50.0	—
Fulbourne, 1435–6	—	100.0	—	—	—	—	—
Fulbourne, 1461–2	27.8	72.2	—	—	—	—	—
Graveley, 1394–5	50.0	—	—	—	—	50.0	—
Knapwell, 1415–16	50.0	—	—	—	—	50.0	—
Suffolk							
Acton, 1355–6	—	85.1	7.5	—	—	7.5	—
Acton, 1420–1	5.0	86.1	—	—	—	9.0	—
Brandon, 1386–7	—	—	—	50.0	50.0	—	—
Exning, 1358–9	—	—	38.8	—	61.2	—	—
Hundon, 1380–1	53.8	—	46.2	—	—	—	—
Lawshall, 1371–2	50.0	—	23.1	—	—	26.9	—
Woodhall, 1357–8	58.4	—	41.6	—	—	—	—
Essex							
Bourchier Hall, 1405–6	80.1	—	—	—	—	3.6	16.3
Claret Hall, 1360–1	50.0	—	50.0	—	—	—	—
Eastwood, 1371–2	4.6	—	—	95.4	—	—	—
Feering, 1403–4	85.5	—	—	—	—	14.5	—
Finchingfield Rectory, 1356–7	79.2	—	—	—	—	20.8	—
Kelvedon, 1392–3	69.0	—	31.0	—	—	—	—
Langenhoe, 1413–14	69.3	—	30.7	—	—	—	—
Messing and Birch, 1350–1	100.0	—	—	—	—	—	—
Tolleshunt Major, 1397–8	71.1	28.9	—	—	—	—	—
Wivenhoe, 1425–6	—	—	—	100.0	—	—	—

Sources: PRO, SC 6/767/2, 8, 9, 25 (Elsworth, Fulbourne, Graveley), SC 6/769/9 (Knapwell), SC 6/839/1, 2 (Claret Hall), SC 6/840/33 (Eastwood), SC 6/842/23 (Finchingfield Rectory), SC 6/848/13 (Tolleshunt Major), SC 6/909/15 (Caythorpe), SC 6/910/11 (Harrington), SC 6/913/19 (Somerton), SC 6/930/30 (Bircham), SC 6/931/10 (Brancaster), SC 6/942/17 (Popenhoe), SC 6/943/13 (Stow Bardolph), SC 6/944/19 (Uphall), SC 6/989/1, 14 (Acton), SC 6/996/11 (Exning), SC 6/1000/1 (Hundon), SC 6/1001/17 (Lawshall), SC 6/1008/16 (Woodhall), DL 29/242/3888 (Gedney); Essex RO, D/DEl M228 (Langenhoe), D/DH X17 (Messing and Birch), D/DK M89 (Bourchier Hall), T/B 122 (Wivenhoe, microfilm); Westminster Abbey Muniments 25758 (Feering), 25862 (Kelvedon); *Brandon Account*, trans. Munday.

increased in many parts of eastern England, most notably in Norfolk but also in parts of Essex, Suffolk, and Cambridgeshire; however, apparently nowhere did this development continue beyond 1350.[61] In some areas the consumption of rye may have declined relative to wheat because of rising dietary standards, but the evidence is too thin to support an argument to this effect.

D. THE EAST MIDLANDS

The East Midlands as here defined comprises a band of five counties, stretching 100 miles from Nottinghamshire's border with the West Riding in the north to Northamptonshire's border with Oxfordshire in the south. It is a land-locked area. Parts of it were isolated, and were in legend the homes of famous outlaws, from Robin Hood in Sherwood Forest to Hereward the Wake in the fenland area around Peterborough. The rector of Lutterworth in Leicestershire from 1374 to 1384 was John Wyclif. The most famous criminal bands of the day inhabited the same area, the Coterel gang and the Folvilles. Yet all these activities were supported by a region whose wealth was greater than the average for the England of the day. The two northernmost of the five counties, Nottinghamshire and Leicestershire, ranked at a middle point in a table derived from the 1334 lay subsidy, with assessed wealth of £12 and £13 a square mile. Of the other three counties, Huntingdonshire and Northamptonshire had a wealth of £17 a square mile, while the not many square miles of Rutland were worth £20 each.[62]

If the south was more wealthy than the north, so the east was more wealthy than the west. In 1334 nine towns and villages in the region had an assessed wealth of more than £225. The county towns of Leicester, Northampton, and Nottingham form one group on this list. In Huntingdonshire only Yaxley figures in the list; in Nottinghamshire, Newark was the most wealthy settlement in the region. In second place lay Peterborough, and the list is completed by a group of villages around Peterborough – Barnack, Castor, and Paston. Barnack was an important centre of the quarrying industry, Castor an ancient Roman settlement, but Paston was only a hamlet at the time of Domesday Book, and its prosperity was based on extensive twelfth- and thirteenth-century colonization. To the north of these villages, Stamford on the Welland played a central part in communications for the East Midland region. It was the rivers that tilted the region towards the east, and

[61] PRO SC 6/838/13d, 14d (Claret Hall), SC 6/1001/9d, 10d (Lawshall); Campbell, 'Agricultural progress in medieval England', pp. 31–3.

[62] R. E. Glasscock, 'England circa 1334', in H. C. Darby, ed., A New Historical Geography of England, pp. 137–43; cf. Schofield, 'The geographical distribution of wealth in England', p. 504.

access to the rivers that determined the prosperity of many of these settlements. Barnack stone was transported great distances via both the Nene and the Welland. Wine was one of many commodities that came in by return: to Nottingham via the Trent, where it might have to be unloaded into smaller craft at Torksey, and to other counties via Boston. In 1422 Roger Petelying of Market Harborough, on the Welland, was retailing wine both in his own town and throughout Leicestershire. Owston abbey in the same county bought fish at Yaxley, and coal at Nottingham. Even the south-western tip of the region was tilted east: Brackley in Northamptonshire was on the Ouse, and received supplies of woad via King's Lynn. And so much of the life of the region was focused on its rivers: at Laneham in Nottinghamshire in 1388 the stock of the manor included two movable gangways (*pontes mobiles*) for the use of passengers on the ferry, which among other things allowed the tenants of the manor access to "their pasture and meadows on the other side of the water of Trent".[63]

The goods to be found on these rivers were the products of a mixed agriculture. The variety of possible land use is a distinctive feature of the midland area in general. It is not by chance that nearly half the aerial photographs that Beresford and St Joseph use to illustrate settlement history come from the East Midlands. A pattern of nucleated villages can be seen, lying 2–4 km apart, over this region as over much of the English lowlands. The Giddings in Huntingdonshire are taken as showing this pattern. Still more characteristic of the midland pattern of land use are the illustrations which show later enclosures overlying the ridge-and-furrow of earlier open-field agriculture, at Leighton Bromswold in Huntingdonshire, and Watford and Onley in Northamptonshire. At Laxton in Nottinghamshire there is still some continuity in open-field farming, though the village plan is now much modified from its medieval aspect. At Braunston in Northamptonshire can be seen the pattern of tofts and crofts, and the back lane which divided the village area from the fields. The photographs show, more clearly than any written text, an area of alternative land use.[64] The working out of these alternatives, and their effect on the landscape, provide the main themes of what follows.

The interaction of arable farming and animal husbandry can be seen in several types of record. A survey of the Northamptonshire manor of

[63] Glasscock, 'England *circa* 1334', pp. 180–2; Eleanora Carus-Wilson, 'The medieval trade of the ports of the Wash', *Med. Arch.*, VI–VII, 1962–3, pp. 182–201, esp. map facing p. 186; E. J. King, 'The town of Peterborough in the early middle ages', *Northants. Past and Present*, 6, no. 4, 1980, pp. 193–5; Margery K. James, *Studies in the Medieval Wine Trade*, Oxford, 1971, pp. 148–9, 156–7, 180–1, 192; Hilton, *Economic Development of some Leicestershire Estates*, pp. 136–8; *Cal. Inq. Misc.*, V, no. 76.

[64] Beresford and St Joseph, *Medieval England*, pp. 13–16, 37–9, 40–2, 61–3, 86–94.

Cottingham, made c. 1400, shows a group of cottars who depended for their livelihood on the keeping of livestock and on rights of pannage in Rockingham Forest. Their sheep were to lie in the lord's sheepfold; by contrast those with larger holdings were expected to have a fold of their own, on their messuages or elsewhere. Almost every set of court rolls that survives from this region will show presented at each court a list of tenants whose animals have damaged growing corn, with the offending beasts numbered and sometimes even named. At Clipston, also on the Northamptonshire uplands, a powerful smell of sheep comes from the court rolls. Richard Wattes had 400 sheep in the wheat field on three occasions, "against the ancient customs of the village"; three other tenants had 300, 200, and 100 sheep respectively. These men also, not surprisingly, had their own sheepfolds, in which their sheep had to be penned in summertime; were they not, the fine for each 100 sheep was 6d., "to the lord and the church equally". By the mid-fifteenth century at Shepshed in Leicestershire on the edge of Charnwood Forest the court did little more than record entries for pannage, and both lord and tenants did their best to protect the waste on which so much of their livelihood depended. The extent of rights of common at Stanton-on-the-Wolds, Nottinghamshire, was debated in 1475, in a case which will be examined further, but the existence of those rights could be taken for granted: "this matter needs no examination, for it is perfectly known both by the tenants and by the inhabitants, for if they had not common for their beasts they might not have lived there".[65]

Because of the constraints of mixed farming, and the need for preserving an accurate record, the region is well provided with sets of by-laws, which provide a major source for the workings of open-field agriculture. An entry from Broughton, Huntingdonshire, in 1405 shows a number of the characteristic concerns of such records:

It was ordered by the lord together with the whole homage that no one should enter a field to harvest or to cart corn during the whole of autumn either in the evening or in the morning whilst it is still dark, under penalty of 40d. And that no one should trample the stubble of another with any animals during the whole of autumn until Michaelmas, under the same penalty; he may do this only on his own lands. And no one should pasture any animals near any corn in the fields, until that corn is removed at least 200 yards away, under the same penalty.

Others of the Ramsey abbey court rolls show the particular concerns of

[65] BL Cott. Nero C VII, ff.95v, 98v; Northants. RO, Brassey Ms. LB 59; BL Add. Ch. 26842–3; Nottingham Univ. Library, Clifton Ms. Cl L 199/6a (reference from Alan Cameron).

a fenland community. The ditches had to be kept clean. The resources of the fens had to be protected. Reeds could be used for thatch or for fencing, turves for fuel. The cutting of turves at Upwood in 1428 was limited according to the size of a man's holding, from the virgater down to a cottager with one acre of land; a cottager without land was not allowed to dig. "This grant was discovered in an old book belonging to the steward." There is no call to be sceptical of that statement. An exact village memory was required for the proper working of open-field agriculture. The agreement at Wymeswold in Leicestershire, made c. 1425 before the three lords and "with the common consent of the whole village", may have been made (it will be suggested later) after reorganization of the fields, for an accurate record. This document also is much concerned with the regulation of cattle. If a man's cattle strayed, "he shall make amends to him that has the harm, and for each foot that is within the corn pay a penny to the church". It is not just the feet of the tenants' beasts that might stray. At Elton, Huntingdonshire, in 1387 Henry Shepherd was accused of allowing the lord's demesne flock in amongst "the community's grain" (bladis communitatis); the same phrase is found, though the malefactors by then were different, in 1405.[66] There is much talk of the community in such records; and no more is this an empty phrase. In the later middle ages it was the community that was under threat. It is from this perspective that the problem of deserted settlements is best considered.

The rivers that brought goods into the heart of the East Midland region may have been the vehicle by which the plague spread in the summer of 1349. On 4 May 1349 the bishop of Lincoln consecrated ground for the burial of plague dead at Great Easton, a village on the river Welland. In certain Duchy of Lancaster manors in the Nene valley around Higham Ferrers 19 out of 51 tenants involved in litigation were reported as having died between courts held on 26 April and 17 May. Figures for plague mortality are not easy to find. The chronicler Henry Knighton, a canon of Leicester abbey, gave figures for three parishes in Leicester of 380, 400, and 700 deaths, which if accurate might represent a mortality of around 30 per cent. The only statistics covering the whole region are those for institutions to benefices, not all vacated by death, and not all deaths caused by the plague. The figures for Nottinghamshire varied between 26 per cent in Bingham deanery and 48 per cent in Newark deanery; in Northamptonshire between 27 per cent in Brackley and Peterborough deaneries, and 54 per cent in Higham Ferrers; in Huntingdonshire between 22 per cent in

[66] Raftis, *Tenure and Mobility*, pp. 112, 120–5; HMC, *Middleton Mss*, 1918, pp. 106–9; BL Add. Ch. 39474, 34818.

Huntingdon itself and 50 per cent in St Neots. In Leicestershire the range was between 28 per cent in Goscote and 44 per cent in Guthlaxton hundreds; in Preston deanery, Rutland, the figure was 35 per cent. There is no clear pattern in these figures, and their interpretation is open to doubt.[67]

In the spring and summer of 1349 men sowed but they did not reap. At Warboys (Hunts.), eight standard holdings and 10 cottages fell into the hands of the lord, the abbot of Ramsey, who sold the corn grown on them for £7 1s. 8d. At Elton there were 23 virgates and 11 cottages vacant at the end of 1349. From each Warboys cottage an acre of grain was harvested, worth 18d. or 2s., while the Elton cottages were rented for 1s. each. In the same year 44 landholders in the village of Kibworth Harcourt (Leics.) died. Tenants were found for the majority of these holdings. Two-fifths of the land thus vacated was taken up by widows or by sons, many of whom were under age; a further two-fifths were taken over by other villagers, either voluntarily or under compulsion; a fifth remained, at Michaelmas 1350, in the lord's hands. If land was taken up, it was chiefly through the amalgamation of holdings; within a generation, the average size of family holdings at Kibworth Harcourt increased from 12 to 24 acres; similarly on the Huntingdonshire manors of Ramsey abbey. Four virgates at Wistow, in the lord's hands in 1351, were taken up in the following year; at Slepe there were eight virgates in hand in 1351, but they had been taken up by 1366, the date of the next account roll. Manorial administrators could preserve much of the rent roll, if not some of the villein incidents or the same forms of tenure. At the end of 1349 the reeve of Elton asked for the remission of tallage, "from various villein tenements in the lord's hand because of the plague" (causa mortalitatis); the auditors noted he had not been charged with the tallage in the first place. On a small lay estate in Pattishall (Northants.), the lady was required to explain why she had not obtained royal licence to lease five virgates of land: "the said tenements", she explained, "were in the hands of my bondmen before the time of the last pestilence, and came into my hands by their death; for the lack of tenants willing to receive them, they remained uncultivated for a long time, and the buildings existing upon them became ruinous".[68] The explanation was accepted; what had happened

[67] J. F. D. Shrewsbury, A History of Bubonic Plague in the British Isles, pp. 100–5; N. Groome, 'The Black Death in the hundred of Higham Ferrers', Northants. Past and Present, 6, no. 6, 1982, pp. 309–11.

[68] BL Add. Ch. 39804; Elton Manorial Records 1279–1351, ed. S. C. Ratcliff, Roxburghe Club, 1946, pp. lxxi–lxxiii, 344; Cecily Howell, Land, Family and Inheritance in Transition: Kibworth Harcourt 1280–1700, pp. 242–3; J. A. Raftis, The Estates of Ramsey Abbey, pp. 256–7; CCR, 1354–1360, p. 605.

here was common form, and the problems created by the first visitation of plague in 1349 were intensified by subsequent outbreaks, both local and more general, of epidemic disease.

If tenant lands might find tenants on the right terms, parcels of demesne, increasingly unprofitable for the lords to cultivate, might be more difficult to dispose of. At Slepe in Huntingdonshire again, 161 demesne acres were farmed in 1347; in 1351 rents could be collected from only 58 of these acres, a figure that had increased to 137 acres in 1366. Some demesne acres went out of cultivation. What was leased was leased in small parcels. A list attached to the 1368–9 account of Warboys (Hunts.), records the "land sown of men of toune". The parcels of demesne, in this bilingual text, were sown in acre and half-acre parcels with *frumentum*, barlic, ote, *dragetum* and pesun. There was also "sale of pastour", the largest entry in which was "for leyns beye strete to the commune 3s.". Such small quantities of demesne arable might go with sizeable holdings of tenant land. In the 1420s William Baron, the bailiff of Castle Donington (Leics.), had six virgates and one bovate of escheated land as well as his own holding of two virgates. In 1421 he leased 10 acres of demesne; in 1426 none at all; and in 1429 he had 24 different acres. The village still worked on a three-course rotation; the demesne land which lay fallow in each year could not be leased out. It is clear from study elsewhere in Leicestershire that the pattern of land use on these large tenements changed as they grew in size. At Kibworth Harcourt men with under 30 acres of land tended to exploit their arable to the full or sublet it. Over this figure the amount of pasture would be increased, with between 50 and 70 per cent put down to grass. On the same manor, it was the pasture attached to untenanted arable that found the most ready market: it could be let for 6s. 8d. per virgate.[69] The bias towards pasture followed not immediately but inexorably from the Black Death.

The area around and to the south of Ramsey abbey was one particularly rich in pasture. At Upwood and Raveley 80 acres of "waste in the marsh was enclosed as meadow" in 1448–9. Both lords and peasants received parcels of this land according to the size of their existing holdings: "for each virgate a width of two perches at each end...for every cottage a width of one perch at each end". This was new wealth, and was confined to these villages. A more open market can be seen further south in the fenland, in Holywell-cum-Needingworth. There in 1370–1, 52 persons leased about 120 acres of meadow, mostly in the fens. Thirteen of these were villagers, six of whom had no holdings of arable land. The remaining thirty-nine were

[69] Raftis, *Estates of Ramsey Abbey*, pp. 256–7; PRO SC 6/874/13; Hilton, *Leicestershire Estates*, pp. 157–62; Howell, *Kibworth Harcourt*, pp. 50, 109.

from neighbouring fenland villages: Wistow, Warboys, Caldecote, Broughton, Slepe, Woodhurst. Men from the neighbouring town of St Ives also took an interest in the Holywell land market. This area of eastern Huntingdonshire appears as a distinctive community, and seemingly one whose wealth was increasing in the later middle ages.[70]

Those settlements deserted in the later middle ages were seldom the main or the primary settlement in their parish. They were for the most part secondary settlements, their origins frequently revealed in their names. Nobottle in Brington (Northants.) was a "new building" old enough to have been a hundred meeting-place; Nobottle in Harrington and Nobold in Clipston are in the same county and have the same derivation. Chilcote in Thornby (Northants.) represents "the young persons' cottages"; it was farmed as a grange of Pipewell abbey, and is now again a group of cottages. Thorpe-in-the-Glebe (Notts.), a well-documented fifteenth-century desertion, was a small parish compared with its neighbours of Willoughby-on-the-Wolds, Wymeswold, and Wysall. It may have been carved out of the pasture areas of neighbouring settlements; in which case its later history shows a reversion to its earlier land use. Some hamlets later deserted may be post-conquest in origin; the name Papley in Warmington (Northants.) may come from the serjeanty holding established there to serve the Peterborough abbey estate. Many of the individuals "deserting" settlements will not have moved out of their parish. Little Newton (Northants.) decayed very rapidly in the late middle ages; there were eighteen families there in 1377, but only four in 1449. But the parish church of Little Newton became the church of the adjacent settlement of Great Newton; and the church of Great Newton decayed.[71] This is an example which emphasizes reorganization rather than discontinuity.

There are a few references to settlements deserted in the second half of the fourteenth century, where desertion is specifically ascribed to the plague. Hale in Apethorpe parish (Northants.) was in 1356 described as a messuage and a carucate of land, worth nothing "because no one dwells nor has dwelt in Hale since the pestilence". Elkington in the same county had thirty persons paying the poll tax of 1377, yet in 1412 the pope was assured that the village was depopulated save for three or four servants of Pipewell abbey, because of plague. Certainly all the arable land of the parish had been converted to pasture by the time of

---

[70] Raftis, *Tenure and Mobility*, pp. 26–30, 213–14; E. B. DeWindt, *Land and People in Holywell-cum-Needingworth*, pp. 60–3, 108–13.

[71] RCHM, England, *County of Northampton*, II, 1979, pp. xlviii, 74, 112–16; III, 1981, pp. 25–6, 49–51; A. Cameron and C. O'Brien, 'The deserted medieval village of Thorpe-in-the-Glebe, Nottinghamshire', *Thoroton Soc.*, 85, 1981, p. 61; E. J. King, 'Estate records of the Hotot family', *A Northamptonshire Miscellany*, Northants. Rec. Soc., XXXII, 1983, p. 47 n. 188.

the dissolution, and 4,000 sheep grazed there in 1547. A more typical set of records will show the final mention of a deserted settlement in the late fifteenth or early sixteenth century. Kingsthorpe in Polebrook (Northants.) was a thirteenth-century acquisition of Thorney abbey. The abbey held a court there in 1386. Ten jurors were listed, of whom four did not attend. Those that remained declared that thirteen *nativi domini* were living outside the lordship. Three of them had gone no further than Polebrook itself. The next recorded court was held in 1483, when the tenant of the manor house was instructed to repair the chamber at the end of the hall. In 1488 there were only two men recorded at Kingsthorpe: one of them held the manor house and what had been the demesne, and the other had engrossed the tenant land. They were instructed to make repairs. There is nothing surprising in the absence of fifteenth-century pottery from the site, rather it confirms the documentary record. The community had gone by 1386.[72]

The absence of fifteenth-century pottery, on sites both shrunken and deserted, is a distinctive feature of the archaeological record. Up to the fourteenth century the finds are plentiful, and some are unusual – at Sywell a Nüremberg token of the fourteenth century, at Dodford a Burgundian coin of the same time. Excavations at Faxton in Lamport (Northants.) revealed an interesting sequence. The three areas surveyed showed dates of desertion ranging from the mid-fourteenth to the mid-fifteenth centuries. The earliest desertion was of the poorest dwellings, while on the site deserted *c.* 1400 there were found coins of Henry III and Edward I, bronze rings, buckles, sheep bells, knives, spurs, and weaving slides. The most recent, post-plague buildings on this site included an oven or kiln for drying corn and peas. Such ovens have been found throughout the East Midland region. They may supply evidence for a deterioration of the climate, as may the crew-yards for wintering cattle, for which published examples are at Thorpe-in-the-Glebe (Notts.), and Perio in Southwick, and Mallows Cotton in Raunds, Northamptonshire.[73]

Archaeological evidence from a few crofts may be thought to supply a spurious exactness to arguments for dating settlement desertion. But it may be taken with other evidence which identifies the early fifteenth century as a crucial period for changes in land use over large sections of the East Midland region. On the claylands in the Nottinghamshire Wolds the changes took place between 1410 and 1440. In 1442 the main

[72] RCHM, England, *County of Northampton*, I, 1975, pp. 8–10; III, pp. 77–80; Northants. RO, Buccleuch Ms. 24/41; A. E. Brown and C. C. Taylor, 'Four deserted settlements in Northamptonshire', *Northants. Past and Present*, 5, no. 3, 1975, pp. 183–8.

[73] RCHM, England, *County of Northampton*, II, p. 81, 87–9, 145; III, pp. 72, 119–23; Cameron and O'Brien, 'Thorpe-in-the-Glebe', pp. 59–60.

estate at Thorpe-in-the-Glebe was leased to a flock-master. A change in land use was reflected in a change in the rent days, from Ladyday and Michaelmas to Midsummer Day and Martinmas, "which fits better with the routine of lambing and wool-clip, and the autumn sales of stock". At Stanton-on-the-Wolds one of the fields went out of cultivation at the same time. In 1475 this was described as 180 acres of land which had been "ley" or pasture land from time out of mind, and there was a complicated dispute as to grazing rights over it. In general terms the villagers could describe the working of open-field agriculture, but in detail their memories were deficient. The confusion over whether a particular piece of land was held in severalty – "it has been several…but whether for all the year or a part thereof would be uncertain" – mirrors a general confusion. It was at just this time also that the customs of Wymeswold were written down. Here, unlike at Stanton, there was a contraction of arable in each of the three fields. Reorganization was followed by a writing down of the customs.[74] The evidence from this part of the midland claylands is particularly good.[75] It was these lands that, as Belloc had it, were "sodden and unkind". They could be worked for arable, but were demanding of manpower. As the manpower moved away, some hamlets and villages ceased to be viable as communities cultivating their own common fields.

Other villages reverted to a form of infield–outfield husbandry. This was true at Stanton-on-the-Wolds. When this happened, the population that the village could support was permanently reduced. In some of the forest villages of Nottinghamshire this tradition of farming had never been abandoned, in part because of the constraints on agrarian change provided by the forest law. A map of Carburton from 1615 shows three small common-fields surrounded by a large outfield of 518 acres, described as "the waste lying in brecks". The brecks were tracts of open forest sheep walks enclosed for arable for a period of between three and nine years. Information from Edwinstowe, though it comes from the sixteenth century, shows that the inner fields were used to provide winter feed for the animals and the crops needed for human consumption. The breck or outfield was used for wheat or mixed grains, which formed the cash crop. The key elements in the village economy were its sheep flock and cattle herd, taken out each day and folded in the tofts and yards at night.[76]

---

[74] *Ibid.*, p. 65; Nottingham Univ. Library, Clifton Ms. Cl L 199/1–6a (quotation from no. 6a).

[75] It has become so through the work of Alan Cameron. The material in this and the following paragraph is derived from Cameron's published and unpublished work, which he has been kind enough to share and discuss with me.

[76] Beresford and St Joseph, *Medieval England*, pp. 45–8; D. V. Fowkes, 'The breck system of Sherwood Forest', *Thoroton Soc.*, 81, 1977, pp. 55–61.

Other parts of the region were from the beginning weighted to grass; enclosures took place early, and often without comment. Such was the area on either side of the Northamptonshire–Leicestershire border. There were some well-recorded enclosures made by religious houses. At Canons Ashby a substantial village, in which eighty-two paid the poll tax of 1377, was enclosed in the late fifteenth and early sixteenth centuries. In the parish of Catesby there were three settlements, all largely deserted, and the site of a Cistercian nunnery. Account rolls from early in the fifteenth century show rent paid "for the pasture of Catesby and Newbold this year, let to divers tenants". In 1491 the priory destroyed fourteen houses, evicted sixty people, and enclosed the land for pasture. The church at Charwelton stands solitary witness to another village in the same area taken over by sheep in the fifteenth century. The Knightleys depopulated Fawsley in the century after 1415 when they bought the estate. There are two deserted settlements in Orlingbury parish, each deserted by the fifteenth century. Substantial flocks found in this area in the early sixteenth century bear witness to a century of gradual enclosure.[77] Alternative land uses might be found. A park was made at Rockingham south of the castle in 1485, "by enclosing a large area of former arable land". In 1474 Lord Hastings had licence to empark and enclose 2,000 acres in each of his two manors of Bagworth and Kirby Muxloe.[78]

The changes in land use in the East Midland region in the late middle ages, though they have left substantial visible remains, were an adaptation which left the five counties close to the median of wealth in the early sixteenth century, just as they had been in the early fourteenth. The midland counties indeed show little fluctuation at any time from Domesday onwards. A few changes can be identified. While the growth in the early middle ages was in the silt-fen, and accounted for the high prosperity of Nassaburgh in the 1334 returns, in the later middle ages there was a significant increase in the values of the peat-fen of eastern Huntingdonshire and adjacent parts of Cambridgeshire.[79] The areas around the county towns of Northampton and Leicester had grown more prosperous also, in each case sustained by an urban community that was beginning to specialize in the leather and allied trades. There were fifty shoemakers in Northampton in 1524. A significant number of craftsmen in each of these places was engaged in

---

[77] W. G. Hoskins, *Essays in Leicestershire History*, Liverpool, 1950, pp. 86–94; RCHM, England, *County of Northampton*, III, pp. 35, 38, 43–5, 88–90; J. M. Steane, *The Northamptonshire Landscape*, London, 1974, pp. 172–4.

[78] RCHM, England, *County of Northampton*, II, pp. 128–9; *VCH Leics.*, II, p. 192.

[79] H. C. Darby, *The Changing Fenland*, Cambridge, 1983, pp. 10–31.

the cloth trade, finishing cloth some of which had been woven in the surrounding countryside.[80] Nottinghamshire, which had been the poorest of the counties in 1334, had slipped further by 1524, with a marked fall in the northern part of the county. The emphasis on cattle farming in the later middle ages is a corrective to the attention which historians have focused upon sheep. The pastoral side of East Midlands farming was its most visible aspect to the travellers of the sixteenth century.

E. THE WEST MIDLANDS

A very varied pattern of the distribution of population in the West Midlands had been established by the early medieval period. The river valleys, especially of the Avon, but also of parts of the Severn and Trent, together with their major tributaries, tended to be old-settled and densely populated. The same is true of the low-lying clay plains in the vales of Berkeley and Gloucester, and in south-east Worcestershire and south-east Warwickshire. More thinly populated and later colonized woodlands occupied much of western Gloucestershire, the northern and western parts of Worcestershire and Warwickshire, and most of Staffordshire and Derbyshire. Limestone hills dominated the southern part of the region, the Cotswolds, and, in the north, the Peak district of northern Staffordshire and Derbyshire. The Cotswolds provided a kinder environment for settlement than the Peak, and were relatively densely peopled. The river valleys, clay plains, and Cotswolds supported large nucleated villages, while hamlets and scattered farmsteads were more characteristic of the woodlands.

The colonizing movement of the twelfth and thirteenth centuries had extended the area of arable at the expense of woods, heaths, and pastures throughout the region. By the early fourteenth century there was an overwhelming predominance of arable in the clay plains and much of the river valleys; in the woodlands, although wood and pasture were mingled with arable, the latter had made great advances. Large areas of the Cotswolds were cultivated, and the plough had penetrated above the 1,000 ft contour in the Peak district.[81]

An indication of land use is given by the transfers recorded in feet of fines, which often give details of the land being conveyed. It should be emphasized that common pastures and unenclosed woodlands would

---

[80] W. G. Hoskins, *Provincial England*, London, 1963, pp. 78–81, 94–7; A. Dyer, 'Northampton in 1524', *Northants. Past and Present*, 6, no. 2, 1978, pp. 73–80.

[81] *AHEW*, II, pp. 224–32.

Table 2.8. *Analysis of land use from the Warwickshire feet of fines,*
1345–55 (in acres)

	Arable	Meadow	Pasture	Wood	Moor, marsh, etc.	Total
Avon valley	2,533	118	12	0	0	2,663
and Feldon	(96%)	(4%)	(0%)			(100%)
Arden	1,790	209	182	328	32	2,541
	(71%)	(8%)	(7%)	(13%)	(1%)	(100%)

Table 2.9. *Analysis of land use from the Warwickshire feet of fines,*
1496–1500 (in acres)

	Arable	Meadow	Pasture	Wood	Moor, marsh, etc.	Total
Avon valley	2,850	475	1,654	48	0	5,027
and Feldon	(57%)	(9%)	(33%)	(1%)		(100%)
Arden	1,193	299	1,319	646	4	3,461
	(34%)	(9%)	(38%)	(19%)	(0%)	(100%)

not be included in these documents, so that the proportion of arable and
meadow is somewhat exaggerated. The lands described in the
Warwickshire fines at the beginning and end of our period have been
analysed in Tables 2.8 and 2.9.[82] In 1345–55 the land use of the south
and east of the county, in the Avon valley and the clay plain of the
Feldon, with their very high proportion of arable and scarcity of
pasture and wood, contrasts with the north and west, the Arden (Table
2.8), while figures in Table 2.9 deriving from the feet of fines of
1496–1500 indicate the changes that affected the county during the
intervening 150 years.

In both parts of the county the proportion of arable had dropped
sharply, and the area described as pasture had increased from less than
a tenth to a third or more of the total. This change was caused partly
by the conversion of arable land to pasture, and partly by the enclosure
of common pastures and wastes, so that these lands were included in the
properties conveyed by fines. The developments tended to reduce the
differences between the Arden and the Feldon, but the northern part of

[82] *Warwickshire Feet of Fines*, III, ed. L. Drucker and F. C. Wellstood, Dugdale Soc., XVIII, 1943,
pp. 1–24, 209–14.

Table 2.10. *Analysis of land use from Gloucestershire inquisitions* post mortem, *1349–54 and 1485–1500 (in acres)*

	Arable	Meadow	Pasture	Wood	Moor, marsh, etc.	Total
1349–54	2,122	214	55	81	80	2,552
	(83 %)	(9 %)	(2 %)	(3 %)	(3 %)	(100 %)
1485–1500	1,390	410	1,042	181	0	3,023
	(46 %)	(14 %)	(34 %)	(6 %)		(100 %)

the county still retained a lower proportion of arable and much more woodland, so that the contrasting landscapes of the county were still notable in modern times.[83]

A similar pattern of change in land use is found in the other counties of the region. In the Staffordshire feet of fines between 1345–55 and 1480–1500 the proportion of recorded arable land fell from 85 to 58 per cent, and pasture rose from 3 to 31 per cent.[84] In Gloucestershire the descriptions of land given in inquisitions *post mortem*, reflecting more strongly than the fines the land use of the demesnes, suggest a comparable trend (Table 2.10).[85]

The lands surveyed in inquisitions *post mortem* for Staffordshire in the same period show a decline in arable from 86 to 52 per cent of the total, while the proportion of pasture and moor rose from 4 to 34 per cent.[86] Finally, a large Worcestershire manor, Bromsgrove and King's Norton, in the woodlands in the north-east of the county, exhibits similar developments in its pleas and conveyances, which, because of the manor's royal demesne status, resemble the form of the feet of fines (Table 2.11).[87]

So a variety of sources from all parts of the region tell a fairly consistent story of a decline in the arable, which at the time of the first plague represented between 70 and 96 per cent of the lands surveyed, but by about 1500 had fallen to between 34 and 58 per cent of the total.

[83] Leland, *Itinerary*, II, p. 47; W. Dugdale, *The Antiquities of Warwickshire*, ed. W. Thomas, London, 1730, I, p. vi.

[84] *Final Concords or Pedes Finium, Staffordshire*, ed. G. Wrottesley, Staffs. Rec. Soc., XI, 1890, pp. 157–68, 241–2, 252–4.

[85] *Inquisitiones Post Mortem for Gloucestershire*, ed. E. A. Fry, Index Library, XL, 1910, pp. 321–56; *CIPM Henry VII*, I–II passim.

[86] *Inquisitions Post Mortem, Staffordshire*, ed. J. C. Wedgwood, Staffs. Rec. Soc., 1913, pp. 129–70; *CIPM, Henry VII*, I–II, passim.

[87] Worcs. RO, ref. b 850 BA 821, parcels 23, 25, 32, 33; *Court Rolls of the Manor of Bromsgrove and King's Norton, 1494–1504*, ed. A. F. C. Baber, Worcs. Hist. Soc., 1963, pp. 63–94.

Table 2.11. *Analysis of land use from the court rolls of Bromsgrove and King's Norton, 1386–96 and 1494–1504 (in acres)*

	Arable	Meadow	Pasture	Wood	Total
1386–96	409	76	12	6	503
	(81 %)	(15 %)	(3 %)	(1 %)	(100 %)
1494–1504	848	278	352	114	1,592
	(53 %)	(18 %)	(22 %)	(7 %)	(100 %)

In reality, allowing for unsurveyed areas of pasture and wood, the amount of land under cultivation in the mid-fourteenth century probably exceeded a half of the overall total, and could be much more – at Marton (War.) in 1376 the arable area can be estimated from tithe-corn receipts to have covered 68 per cent of the parish.[88] By the late fifteenth century, arable in the region as a whole must have retreated to occupy considerably less than half of the land.

Usually the former arable became grassland, but sometimes bushes and trees encroached on old arable and pasture. The areas of productive land lost in this way could be quite large, so that at Duffield (Derbs.) the growth of thorns helped to explain the loss of 77 acres in 1460–1. At Grimley and Newnham (Worcs.) in the 1390s, Budbrooke (War.) in the 1420s, Baddesley Clinton (War.) in the 1440s, and in 1465–6 at Dowdeswell (Glos.), lords employed labour in "stocking" and "eradicating" bushes that had grown over their lands. At Berkeley (Glos.) in 1432, Northfield (Worcs.) in 1447, Stivichall (War.) in 1439, and Baddesley Clinton (War.) in 1465, the eradication of trees and bushes that had taken over fields was made a condition of new tenancies.[89]

Sometimes the extension of trees and grass at the expense of arable was organized through the development of parks. Several new parks were created at this time, notably in Staffordshire, and older parks were extended. At Whitcliff park in Ham (Glos.), Henbury (Glos.), Sedgley and Himley (Staffs.), demesne arable was taken into the parks. At Beaudesert (War.), Beoley (Worcs.), Sedgley (Staffs.), and on the

[88] BL Add. Roll 49748.

[89] I. S. W. Blanchard, 'Economic change in Derbyshire in the late middle ages, 1272–1540', London University Ph.D. thesis, 1967, pp. 92–3; Worcs. Cathedral Library, C586, C657; War. RO, CR 895 8/11, 8/13; C. Dyer, 'A small landowner in the fifteenth century', *Mid. Hist.*, 1, 1972, p. 5; Worcs. RO, ref. 009:1 BA 2636/176 92485; Berkeley Castle Muniments, court roll of Berkeley, 20 November, 11 Henry VI; Birmingham Ref. Library, 518091; Shakespeare's Birthplace Trust RO, DR 10/2444; Ferrers' Ms. 793.

Gloucestershire estates of the Berkeleys the parks spread over former tenant lands.[90] There is evidence also for a widespread expansion of rabbit warrens and fishponds on land previously used for agricultural purposes.[91]

Although the assarting of woodland virtually ceased after 1349, the change in man's relationship with his environment was not so profound as to lead to any drastic increase in the area of dense woodland. Large wooded areas were still confined to such places as the Forest of Dean and Michael Wood in western Gloucestershire; Malvern Wood and Feckenham Forest in Worcestershire; the remnants of the Forest of Arden in north-west Warwickshire; Kinver, Cannock, and Needwood in Staffordshire; and Duffield Frith in Derbyshire. The slackening of the administration of royal forests, notably in Dean, has been taken to reflect a relative plenty of timber, though the forest courts at Feckenham in the 1490s dealt with offences against the *vert* with some vigour. Revenues from sales of timber and branches from the Duchy of Lancaster's extensive woods in Staffordshire and Derbyshire declined in the fifteenth century. This may reflect a deterioration in administrative control, or an attempt at conservation.[92] In much of the region both fuel and building timber were in such short supply that they had to be carried over long distances; for example the monks of Tewkesbury (Glos.) in 1385–6 obtained firewood from Ribbesford (Worcs.), a distance of thirty miles down the Severn. Timber for building a barn at Bishop's Cleeve (Glos.) in 1465–6 came from Hartlebury (Worcs.), again involving a journey of about thirty miles, and for the mill of Brailes (War.) timber was brought twenty-two miles overland from Tanworth-in-Arden (War.) in 1413–14. At the end of our period enclosers in south-east Warwickshire were able to defend the planting of hedgerows on the grounds that they would provide a source of timber in an otherwise treeless landscape.[93]

[90] D. M. Palliser, *The Staffordshire Landscape*, London, 1976, p. 90; Microfilm of Berkeley Castle Mss., Cambridge Univ. Library; Worcs. RO, ref. 009:1 BA 2636/167 92278; Staffs. RO, D 593/0/3/3–4; Birmingham Ref. Library, 168240; BL Egerton Rolls 8661; Staffs. RO, D 593/0/3/4; J. Smyth, *The Lives of the Berkeleys*, II, pp. 12, 14–16.

[91] E.g. expanding rabbit warrens at Minchinhampton (Glos.) in 1380–1, PRO SC 6/856/24; Painswick (Glos.) in 1442, W. St Clair Baddeley, *A Cotteswold Manor*, Gloucester, 1907, pp. 105–17; Caldwall (Worcs.) in 1426–7, Bodleian Lib., Worcs. rolls, no. 3; Beaudesert (Staffs.) in 1443–4, Staffs. RO, D 1734/3/2/1; new ponds at Baddesley Clinton (War.), Dyer, 'A small landowner', p. 11; Walsall (Staffs.), BL Egerton Rolls 8467.

[92] C. E. Hart, *Royal Forest*, Oxford, 1966, pp. 67–75; 'Swanimote Rolls of Feckenham Forest', ed. R. H. Hilton, in *Miscellany*, I, Worcs. Hist. Soc., 1960, pp. 37–52; J. R. Birrell, 'The forest economy of the honour of Tutbury in the fourteenth and fifteenth centuries', *Univ. of Birmingham Hist. J.* VIII, 1962, pp. 117–28.

[93] T. Wakeman, 'On the kitchener's roll of Tewkesbury Abbey', *J. of the Brit. Arch. Assoc.*, XV, 1859, p. 323; Worcs. RO, ref. 009:1 BA 2636/175 92485; Birmingham Ref. Library, 167904; H.

What was the chronology of the decline in cultivation? The beginnings of the process can be seen as early as the 1320s. As might be expected, there is much evidence of a shrinkage in the arable area in the aftermath of the successive plague epidemics of 1348–75. There are frequent references to *frisc*, uncultivated land, in sources of all kinds in the late fourteenth century. Parts of demesnes were said to be uncultivated to explain low valuations in inquisitions, or in manorial accounts when the "sale" of parcels of demesne to tenants was described. Tenant holdings were sometimes reported in the court records to be uncultivated when they came into the lord's hands on the death or departure of a tenant, or new tenants were specifically required to cultivate a holding, or were let off payment of entry-fines because the land was *frisc*. Some tenants were amerced or evicted because they failed to plough their lands. If no tenant was available, uncultivated holdings might be incorporated into the demesne pastures, or rented out for grazing.[94]

Such evidence is difficult to assess in quantitative terms. Usually only a small amount of demesne land was said to be *frisc*, often less than ten acres, and only one or two tenements on a manor were described as uncultivated at any one time. The sown acreage of demesnes was often halved during the fourteenth century, but as much of the land was rented out to tenants it may have continued in use as arable. Occasionally it is possible to show, as at Bibury (Glos.) in the last quarter of the fourteenth century, that about 200 acres of an original 400-acre demesne had fallen out of use as arable. In Derbyshire and Gloucestershire whole carucates of demesne arable were reported as uncultivated between 1369 and 1388.[95]

The first visitation of plague led to an immediate drop in the cultivated area in 1349 or the next few years. For example, there was a striking reduction in receipts from grain tithes in northern Derbyshire; at Roland tithes which had been farmed for £2 6s. 8d. in 1340 brought in only 8s. in 1351. Also holdings throughout the region appear "in the lord's hands" in large numbers in 1349 or the early 1350s. Although some manors recovered slowly from this shock, or never recovered at all in a few cases, vacant holdings were often taken up by new tenants soon after the plague. Recovery at Alrewas (Staffs.)

Thorpe, 'The Lord and the landscape', *Volume jubilaire offert à M. A. Lefèvre*, Louvain, 1964, pp. 106–7.

[94] Estates and manors with frequent references to uncultivated tenant holdings are Gloucester Abbey estate, Glos. RO, D 936a/M2; Ombersley (Worcs.), Worcs. RO, ref. 705:56 BA 3910/39, 40; Burton Abbey estate, Staffs. RO, D 1734/2/1/102, 103.

[95] Dyer, *Lords and Peasants*, p. 123; Blanchard, 'Economic change in Derbyshire', pp. 64–6; *Inquisitiones Post Mortem for Gloucestershire*, ed. E. Stokes, Index Library, XLVII, 1914, p. 92; *Cal. Inq. Misc.*, III, p. 270.

was almost immediate, and at Erdington (War.) vacancies fell from eighteen in 1349 to six in May 1350, and all were apparently filled by the 1360s. New lettings of uncultivated land were made on the Derbyshire manors of the Duchy of Lancaster in the 1360s and 1370s, though this was followed by a new phase of decline in the 1380s.[96] Generalization about the late fourteenth century is rendered difficult by many local variations in the rate of the retreat of arable, and by short-term fluctuations in the cultivated area.

There are few references to a decline in the arable area in the first half of the fifteenth century, but this may reflect the changes in administration, such as the leasing of demesnes, which reduced the interest of seigneurial officials in the state of the land. It could be that this period saw a lull in the decline of cultivation. In the feet of fines for Staffordshire and Warwickshire quoted above, a really decisive increase in the proportion of pasture is not apparent until the 1440s.[97]

From the middle years of the fifteenth century the evidence again becomes more abundant, perhaps partly because of an increasing number of informative village by-laws recorded in court rolls. Sometimes, as in the late fourteenth century, individuals were ordered to cultivate their holdings, as at Stanton (Glos.) in 1453, when John Taylor was presented for failing to sow all of his selions, or at Grimley (Worcs.) in 1479, when Thomas Byrche was enjoined to plough his land. At Cleeve Prior (Worcs.) in 1458, and at Hampton Lucy (War.) on three occasions between 1459 and 1474, all of the tenants were ordered to cultivate their lands, as if the problem were widespread. On a number of manors, such as Honeybourne (Worcs.), Bishop's Tachbrook (War.), and Ashton-under-Hill (Worcs.), arable strips put down to grass, sometimes called leys, were intermingled with cultivated selions in the open fields, causing problems as grazing animals ate the growing corn.[98] A similar problem may lie behind the many by-laws of the period dealing with the prevention of damage to arable crops, but which are not sufficiently explicit to mention leys. The word

[96] Blanchard, 'Economic change in Derbyshire', pp. 64–6; J. R. Birrell, 'Medieval agriculture', *VCH Staffs.*, VI, p. 38; Birmingham Ref. Library, 347853–5, 347864; J. R. Birrell, 'The honour of Tutbury in the fourteenth and fifteenth centuries', Univ. of Birmingham M.A. thesis, 1962, pp. 72–85.

[97] Blanchard, 'Economic change in Derbyshire', pp. 90–1; F. G. Davenport, 'The agricultural changes of the fifteenth century', *Quarterly J. of Economics*, XI, 1897, pp. 205–10; *Warwickshire Feet of Fines*, III, *passim*.

[98] Glos. RO, D678/62; R. K. Field, 'The Worcestershire peasantry in the later middle ages', Univ. of Birmingham M.A. thesis, 1962, pp. 85–7; Worcs. Cathedral Library, E64; Dyer, *Lords and Peasants*, p. 336; Glos. RO, D 678/95; Shakespeare's Birthplace Trust RO, DR10/2607; *VCH Glos.*, VIII, p. 247.

"leys" could suggest either a long-term change from arable to permanent pasture, or a temporary shift in land use in a system of convertible husbandry.

Most of the late fifteenth-century references in court rolls to leys and the non-cultivation of land come from the areas of open-field farming in the "champion" districts of the river valleys, clay plains, and eastern Cotswolds. It was from the same areas that the Enclosure Commissions collected accusations of conversion of arable to pasture in 1517, some of the cases dating back to the years 1485–1500. In Gloucestershire cases were reported on the Cotswolds and in the clay plain in the north of the county. In Warwickshire between 1485 and 1500 a total of 3,166½ acres were said to have been converted to pasture, mainly in the Feldon hundreds of Kineton and Knightlow.[99] The Warwickshire total, though larger than in any other county, represents less than 1 per cent of the area of the whole shire. However, the 1517 commissions caught only the end of a process that had begun much earlier.

The growing number of buildings described in the period as ruinous may be related, at least indirectly, to the decline in cultivation, though decaying buildings may often have been the result of poverty, inefficiency, or the tendency of tenants to take on multiple holdings, allowing the surplus houses and agricultural buildings to disappear. In most series of court rolls there were few presentments of ruinous buildings in the years 1349–70, but presentments tended to increase towards the end of the fourteenth and in the early fifteenth century, and reached a peak in the middle decades of the fifteenth century. Large numbers of presentments continued on some manors after 1480, but often presentments of individuals were reduced, but there were more generalized court orders, suggesting that the problem had not gone away. This is confirmed by the reports of decayed messuages in the reign of Henry VII noted by the Enclosure Commissions in Warwickshire. Again, although presentments of ruinous buildings are found in woodland manors, they are notably less common than in contemporary champion manors.

There is some evidence of a revival of arable farming and the beginning of a new attack on pastures and wastes in the last three decades of the fifteenth century. It was normal throughout the later middle ages for tenants to be presented for accroaching by ploughing an extra furrow or two across a boundary. A larger scale of such activity is suggested at Dunnington (War.) and Sambourne (War.) in the 1480s, when tenants ploughed up common ways, creating whole new selions of arable. There were complaints that wastes and pastures

[99] I. S. Leadam, 'The Inquisitions of 1517', RHS, NS VIII, 1894, pp. 280–97; The Domesday of Inclosures, ed. I. S. Leadam, RHS, 1897, II, pp. 389–453.

were being ploughed up at Salford Priors, Alveston, and Tiddington (War.) in the 1480s. In about 1470 new houses were being built on the waste at Ombersley (Worcs.) and Sedgley (Staffs.). Large numbers of new encroachments on the waste were recorded in the High Peak of Derbyshire in the 1480s and 1490s.[100]

The most extreme consequence of declining cultivation, holdings falling vacant, and buildings becoming ruinous, was the total desertion of villages. In all more than three hundred deserted villages have been identified in the region, mainly distributed over the Avon valley, the clay plain of central Worcestershire, the Warwickshire Feldon, the Cotswolds, and the Tame, Trent, and Dove valleys in Staffordshire and Derbyshire. The highest density of desertions, one of the greatest concentrations of sites in England, is found in south-east Warwickshire, and it has been calculated that 24 per cent of known medieval villages were deserted in Kineton hundred.[101] The distribution of deserted villages tends to coincide with the areas of dense and old settlement, with open-field and predominantly arable economies, though not all such areas, notably the Vale of Evesham in Worcestershire, were affected.

Many of the deserted villages have been identified from archaeological or post-medieval documentary evidence, so that there must be some uncertainty as to the numbers abandoned during our period. However, a unique source for Warwickshire, the list of desertions compiled by John Rous, a local chantry priest and chronicler, shows that sixty villages, or about half of the county's total, had been deserted by about 1486.[102] Can we be more precise about the chronology and causes of desertion?

There is some evidence of desertions in the twelfth and thirteenth centuries. Also villages, mainly upland Cotswold settlements, were losing inhabitants and experiencing a reduction in their cultivated area just before the first plague.[103] The first important phase of total desertion of villages came in the late fourteenth century. Again, Gloucestershire Cotswold villages were most vulnerable. Four such places were said to be uninhabited by the collectors of the 1381 poll tax.

[100] Shakespeare's Birthplace Trust RO, DR18, DR5/2358; Worcs. RO, ref. 705:56 BA 3910/24; Staffs. RO, D593/0/3/3; Blanchard, 'Economic change in Derbyshire', pp. 108–9.

[101] Beresford and Hurst, Deserted Medieval Villages, pp. 34–40, 185, 187–8, 203, 204–6, 207; C. Dyer, 'D.M.V.s in Worcestershire', Medieval Village Research Group Report, XIX, 1971, pp. 5–7; C. J. Bond, 'Deserted villages in Worcestershire', in Worcester and its Region, ed. B. H. Adlam, Worcester, 1974, pp. 36–45; P. V. Bate and D. M. Palliser, 'Suspected lost village sites in Staffordshire', South Staffs. Arch. Soc., XII, 1970–1, pp. 31–6; Beresford, Lost Villages of England, p. 234. [102] J. Rous, Historia Regum Angliae, ed. T. Hearne, Oxford, 1745, pp. 122–7.

[103] AHEW, II, pp. 232–4.

To these can be added Wontley in Bishop's Cleeve (abandoned by 1372), and Upton in Blockley (by 1383). In the Avon valley, Hatton in Hampton Lucy (War.) had lost most of its inhabitants by 1385. For other villages the first stages of desertion can be traced in this period. At Preston (Glos.) in October 1351 twelve holdings were in the lord's hands, and the lord allowed holdings to be engrossed by a non-resident tenant from nearby Kempley. Eleven of the twenty-six holdings in Weston-juxta-Cherington (War.) were vacant in 1355, and the permanence of the loss seems to be indicated by the use of part of the land as demesne pasture as early as 1352–3. By 1392 half of the tenant lands (four yardlands out of eight) lay in the lord's hands at Fulbrook (War.).[104]

The desertions of the late fourteenth century should be seen as an extreme version of a decline in tenant numbers that caused shrinkage in many villages, especially in south-east Warwickshire and the Cotswold area. For example, in 1368 a group of five cotlands, and by 1384 eleven, had been abandoned in Homestall End in Todenham (Glos.); and on three south Warwickshire manors of the bishops of Coventry and Lichfield (Bishop's Tachbrook, Gaydon, and Bishop's Itchington) in 1360 a total of twenty-two messuages and thirteen yardlands lay in the lord's hands. In 1385 there were eleven vacant holdings at Ladbroke (War.).[105]

It would be simplistic to blame the plagues entirely for this downward trend in tenant numbers. The disease is not likely to have directly caused any desertions, as it would not kill everyone in a village. Usually, as we have seen, vacant holdings were taken up soon after 1349. The plague's role was to provide alternative opportunities for the tenants or would-be tenants of land in declining villages, so that the key factor should be seen as migration rather than mortality. The best documented desertion of this period, that of Hatton in Hampton Lucy, can be followed from year to year in the manorial accounts, as villagers died or left in ones and twos between 1371 and 1385. There was no compensatory immigration for the outflow of tenants.[106]

What proportion of villages were abandoned in the late fourteenth century? Much of the evidence depends on the chance survival of

[104] R. H. Hilton and P. A. Rahtz, 'Upton, Gloucestershire, 1959–64', *Bristol and Glos. Arch. Soc.*, LXXXV, 1966, pp. 75–86; Dyer, *Lords and Peasants*, p. 284; C. Dyer, 'Population and agriculture on a Warwickshire manor in the later middle ages', *Univ of Birmingham Hist. J.*, XI, 1968, pp. 116–17; *idem*, 'Deserted medieval villages in the West Midlands', pp. 19–34; Glos. RO, D 936a/M2; Shakespeare's Birthplace Trust RO, DR98/865–6; PRO DL 43 14/3, f.61.

[105] B. F. Harvey, *Westminster Abbey and its Estates*, p. 262; Glos. RO, D 1099/M30/17; Shakespeare's Birthplace Trust RO, DR10/2593; 'The *Status Maneriorum* of John Catesby, 1385 and 1386', ed. J. Birrell in *Miscellany* I, Dugdale Soc. XXXI, 1977, p. 27.

[106] Dyer, 'Population and agriculture', pp. 113–27.

manorial documents, and so no overall picture emerges. Most to-be-deserted villages were able to contribute to the poll taxes of 1377–81, but some small settlements were not taxed separately, and others may still have disappeared in the 1380s and 1390s.[107] Some of the villages whose abandonment is recorded in the early fifteenth century, such as Craycombe (Worcs.) deserted by 1438, or the vills with very small numbers of households in 1428, such as Barcheston, Billesley Trussell, and Hodnell (War.), could have declined before 1400.[108]

Most of our evidence indicates that villages were deserted by a process of slow decline that went on through the fifteenth century. Rentals show that the numbers of tenants at Hill (Worcs.) fell from eleven in 1388 to five in 1447, and at Woollashill in the same county the decline was from about twenty in the fourteenth century to thirteen in 1424, nine in 1442, and two in the mid-sixteenth century. Tenant numbers at Kingston (War.) almost halved between 1393–5 and 1430, and desertion seems to have been complete by 1461, and possibly by 1437, when the manor was leased as a pasture. In 1447 only five tenants remained at Thornton (War.), where there had once been twenty-one. Archaeological evidence from Barton Blount (Derbs.) suggests a gradual abandonment, beginning in the late fourteenth century and continuing into the late fifteenth.[109]

The court rolls relating to Chapel Ascote (War.), Compton Verney (War.), and Woollashill (Worcs.) reflect the decay of the villages, with many land transfers as tenants kept land for a relatively short time, often allowing the buildings to fall into ruin. At Ascote there was a marked discontinuity in tenant families, almost a shifting population. The by-laws and presentments for trespass at both Ascote and Compton suggest that the traditional discipline of open-field husbandry was breaking down; also, boundaries and the separate identity of the old tenements were being forgotten. Such developments can be found in many villages in this period – the villages on the road to desertion experienced them in a very acute form.[110]

A new factor in desertion, depopulation as an act of policy, seems to have first appeared in the middle of the fifteenth century. In the period

[107] Beresford and Hurst, Deserted Medieval Villages, p. 9.

[108] Dyer, Lords and Peasants, pp. 247–8; Feudal Aids, v, p. 187.

[109] Worcs. RO, ref. 009:1 BA 2636/193 92628 1/9; PRO SC 11/819; C. Dyer, 'The deserted medieval village of Woollashill, Worcestershire', Worcs. Arch. Soc., 3rd ser. I, 1965–7, pp. 59–60; R. H. Hilton, 'A study in the pre-history of English enclosure in the fifteenth century', in idem, The English Peasantry in the Later Middle Ages, Oxford, 1975, pp. 165–71; PRO SC 11/819; G. Beresford, The Medieval Clayland Village: Excavations at Goltho and Barton Blount, Soc. for Med. Arch., Monograph 6, 1975, pp. 53–4.

[110] BL Add. Rolls 49395–49400, 49418–49452; Hilton, 'Pre-history of English enclosure', pp. 165–7; Dyer, 'Deserted medieval village of Woollashill', pp. 58–9.

1350–1450, especially after 1400, most lords reacted to the decline of villages on their estates with attempts to prevent decay by lowering rents and entry-fines and by taking measures to keep buildings in good repair. When the officials of John Catesby found that eleven decayed holdings were in the lord's hands on his manor of Ladbroke (War.) in 1385, they calculated the cost of rebuilding the houses. Between 1390 and 1480, particularly in the middle decades of the fifteenth century, lords over the whole region spent substantial sums on tenants' buildings.[111] At Lighthorne (War.) in 1437 nearly a half of the tenements (twenty-four out of fifty-six) were in the lord's hands, and more tenants were threatening to leave, so rents were reduced. In 1411 and 1420 the courts of the earl of Warwick at Brailes (War.) instituted an inquiry into the recent departure of tenants, and ordered serfs to take on the vacant holdings. In one case two serfs who were said to have "incited and instigated" the withdrawal of the tenant of a three-yardland holding (about 90 acres) were themselves required to take on the land. Examples could be multiplied – they show that lords wanted to maintain as large a rent-paying tenant population as possible, and eviction of tenants was a rare last resort when tenants broke the terms of tenure flagrantly.[112] Such policies sometimes failed, however; the lords of Chapel Ascote and Woollashill made efforts to keep buildings sound and reduce rents, but the villages disintegrated nonetheless.

From the middle of the fifteenth century some lords, finding themselves with badly decayed villages on their hands which produced only a feeble rent income, and aware of the high rents commanded by enclosed pastures, or the profits of direct management of such pastures, sought a radical solution to their problems by removing the remaining tenants and converting all of the land to pasture. The earliest recorded example was at Compton Verney (War.), which had been in decline at least as early as the 1390s, and in about 1447 Richard Verney "expelled" the tenants of the rectory.[113] Other examples were reported to the 1517 Enclosure Commissions, but as at Compton Verney the villages were apparently decayed before the acts of enclosure and eviction. At Wormleighton (War.), for example, in 1498 William Cope forced the inhabitants of twelve messuages and three cottages to depart "tearfully", and enclosed 240 acres of arable. Another six

---

[111] 'Status Maneriorum of John Catesby', ed. Birrell, p. 27; R. H. Hilton, 'Rent and capital formation in feudal society', in The English Peasantry, pp. 191–3; Dyer, Lords and Peasants, p. 167.

[112] Shakespeare's Birthplace Trust RO, DR98/685a; Hilton, The English Peasantry, p. 67; Birmingham Ref. Library, 168198, 167901; Dyer, Lords and Peasants, pp. 294–5.

[113] Ministers' Accounts of the Collegiate Church of St Mary, Warwick, 1432–85, ed. D. Styles, Dugdale Soc., XXVI, 1969, p. 77.

messuages were also devastated. Two centuries earlier Wormleighton had forty-five tenants and some 800 acres of arable, so that it seems likely that tenant numbers and tillage had been substantially reduced before 1485. In 1498 Sir Edward Belknap was supposed to have enclosed land and caused the decay of twelve messuages at Burton Dassett (War.). He replied that the decay had taken place over a long period, from the reign of Edward IV, and that there had been "at that time" a slack demand for arable holdings. This explanation fits plausibly with what we know of the economy of other villages in the fifteenth century, and reminds us that the inquiry of 1517 recorded accusations rather than proven cases. In another reply to the commissions, William Willington claimed, again plausibly, that the main decline in tillage at Barcheston occurred before 1489. Reference has already been made to the vacant holdings of Weston-juxta-Cherington (War.) in the 1350s, so that the destruction of seven houses and a cottage and conversion of 350 acres of arable into pasture in the early sixteenth century could mark the final stage of a long process, as a result of which "all was desolated".[114]

The commissioners of 1517 failed to find many examples of large-scale depopulation. In Warwickshire they noted only five cases involving more than ten houses, and in most villages only three or less houses were affected. Were they just catching in their net the tail end of a much more widespread series of deliberate depopulations that had occurred mainly before 1485, and which therefore fell outside the scope of the inquiry? The main support for such an argument has been the list of John Rous, compiled in about 1486. Unfortunately it seems that Rous observed the deeds of some contemporary depopulators, and concluded that all the deserted villages had resulted from similar activities. It can be shown in such cases as Hatton and Kingston that the desertions occurred before Rous's time, and that he had misunderstood the causes. Even the 1517 commissions found many cases of buildings falling into ruin and arable "allowed" to become pasture, a continuation of the long-term trend of decay rather than the consequence of deliberate eviction and forcible enclosure.[115]

A more obscure process in which an element of conscious policy led to desertion could have been the activities of dominant individuals within declining villages engrossing holdings, converting to pasture,

---

[114] *Domesday of Inclosures*, ed. Leadam, II, pp. 403–4, 415–16, 424–5, 652; Thorpe, 'Lord and the landscape', pp. 82–96; N. W. Alcock, 'Enclosure and depopulation in Burton Dassett: a sixteenth-century view', *Warwickshire Hist.*, III, 1977, pp. 180–4; M. W. Beresford, *Lost Villages of England*, pp. 126–7.

[115] I. S. W. Blanchard, 'Population change, enclosure, and the early Tudor economy', *EcHR*, 2nd ser. XXIII, 1970, pp. 427–45.

and making life unbearable for their neighbours. At Upper Ditchford (Glos.), John Dyde had acquired a total of seven yardlands by 1413; arable cultivation declined there so that the annual farm paid for the village's tithe corn fell from £7 6s. 8d. in 1383–4 to £4 6s. 8d. in 1458–9. Grain production ceased entirely by about 1475, when the village fields had become an enclosed pasture. Henry Tracy of Toddington (Glos.) was amerced in 1466 in the court of neighbouring Frampton for enclosing nineteen selions and an acre of arable, and with another man was overburdening the common pasture with an enormous flock of 1,400 sheep.[116] Such activities would be most likely to occur in an already weak village community, where a slack demand for land allowed engrossing and overburdening, and enclosure would meet with little resistance.

Deliberate depopulation seems often then to have given the final blow to already dying villages. Accordingly the underlying causes of desertion should be sought, not in the external agency of the encloser, but in the congenital internal weakness of some villages, which might be discernible in their economy and social structure before decline began. The to-be-deserted villages tended to be smaller and poorer than their neighbours, according to early fourteenth-century tax lists. They often lay near, within a mile of neighbouring villages, so that the desertions had the effect of thinning-out closely packed settlements. The economies of the villages were usually overwhelmingly agricultural. In south Staffordshire many craftsmen were listed among the taxpayers of 1380–1, but there were none at Packington, a village that was probably deserted in our period.[117] Above all, most of the deserted villages are found in open-field districts. The champion village was a highly specialized type of settlement, geared to produce cereals, and it could encounter problems in adjusting to the new balance between arable and pasture that developed in our period. In the woodlands, a shift towards pasture could be easily accomplished as much land was held in severalty and some pasture was already present. In the champion villages initial changes in land use could upset the mechanism of the field system, and become a trauma from which the village might not recover.

The causes of desertion would of course vary from place to place. On the Cotswolds, for example, remote settlements at high altitudes seem to have been particularly vulnerable. It is important to stress, however,

---

[116] Dyer, *Lords and Peasants*, p. 250; Glos. RO, D 678/95.

[117] M. W. Beresford, *Lost Villages of England*, p. 407; C. J. Bond, 'Deserted medieval villages in Warwickshire and Worcestershire', in *Field and Forest: an Historical Geography of Worcestershire and Warwickshire*, ed. P. J. Jarvis and T. R. Slater, Norwich, 1981, pp. 147–71; *The Poll Tax of 2–4 Richard II*, ed. G. Wrottesley, Staffs. Rec. Soc., XVII, 1896, pp. 161–205.

that any abandonment of land in late colonized woodland or hilly districts may have led to the loss of small hamlets and farmsteads, but not to the desertion of many sizeable villages.

What happened to the village fields during and after desertion? There was often a long period of decline when the old arable and new pastoral regimes co-existed. When holdings fell into the lord's hands through lack of tenants, they usually became part of the demesne pastures, and were either used to graze the lord's stock or leased out. The lands were most likely to be used as arable when they were taken piecemeal by the inhabitants of neighbouring villages, as happened at Craycombe in Fladbury and Penton in Alvechurch (Worcs.).[118] When the vacant holdings were engrossed by a few remaining tenants, the resulting units could be very large – accumulations of more than four yardlands are recorded in the fifteenth century at Upper Ditchford (Glos.), Kingston (War.), Roel (Glos.), and Thornton (War.). Such holdings would have been difficult to keep under cultivation, given such problems as the labour shortage, though at Alscot (War.) half of the land in a severely shrunken village was still arable in 1506. Normally the land was converted to pasture.[119]

Enclosure, although it greatly enhanced the value of the new pastures, could follow some time after desertion. For example, the site of Wontley (Glos.), although uninhabited in 1372, was not enclosed until about 1480.[120] Some village sites may not have been fully enclosed during our period, particularly when the old holdings were held separately by many non-resident tenants. If enclosure was carried out, the site of the village and its fields was usually leased as a single unit, or in two or three large blocks. In Warwickshire town-based butcher graziers became the lessees of former village lands at Fulbrook, Heathcote, and Kingston. An enterprising grazier, John Spencer, had by 1497 built up a remarkable network of pastures on the sites of seven deserted or shrunken villages in south-east Warwickshire.[121]

Sheep are inseparably linked in our minds with the late medieval conversion of arable to pasture, but the butcher graziers often kept cattle also. A series of accounts for 1447–58 for the Catesby manor of Radbourn (War.) reveals the variety of ways in which a pasture on a village site could be used. In 1385–6 Radbourn had been a conventional manor, with a demesne containing both arable and pasture, and tenants in the village paying rents of £5 8s. 10½d. By 1443 no villagers

---

[118] Dyer, *Lords and Peasants*, pp. 246–8.

[119] Hilton, 'Pre-history of English enclosure', p. 165; Glos. RO, D 678/95; PRO SC 11/819; VCH Glos., VIII, p. 85.   [120] Dyer, *Lords and Peasants*, p. 245.

[121] *Ministers' Accounts of St Mary, Warwick*, ed. Styles, pp. 18, 91–2, 148; Hilton, 'Pre-history of English enclosure', pp. 169–70; Thorpe, 'Lord and the landscape', pp. 97–9.

remained, and both demesne and tenant lands had been thrown together into a 1,000-acre pasture. The Catesbys, between 1447 and 1458, ran most of this in direct management, keeping a flock of between 1,643 and 1,855 sheep, a herd of up to twenty-nine cows, with as many as forty-five cattle including beasts bought in for fattening, and a horse stud of up to seventeen animals. A large rabbit warren yielded up to 300 couples of conies annually. The wool and some surplus animals were sold, but much of the produce of cheese and meat was consumed in the lord's household. The whole enterprise was very profitable, so that the valuation of the manor increased from £19 0s. 6d. in 1386 to £63 13s. 8d. in 1449.[122]

The desertion of villages contributed much to the general change in patterns of land use in the West Midland region. In the middle of the fourteenth century there was a sharp demarcation between the predominantly arable landscape of the champion districts, and the more balanced combination of arable and pasture in the woodlands. By the late fifteenth century the proportion of pasture had increased in the woodlands, and some Arden demesnes, such as that on the manor of Aston and Haybarn (War.), contained only pasture and meadow.[123] In the champion areas those villages that had survived retained a good deal of arable mingled with selions put down to grass, but interspersed with these settlements were empty parishes and townships with large expanses consisting wholly of pasture. We should not underestimate the radical nature of the changes in land use in the century and a half following 1349 in the region.

F. WALES AND THE MARCHES

The territory covered by the modern national entity of Wales and the shires of Cheshire, Herefordshire, and Shropshire forms an appropriate unit for an examination of changes involving the occupation of land in the later middle ages.[124] The greater part of the whole area, in terms of

---

[122] PRO SC 6/1041/19; 1042/2–7.   [123] BL Egerton Rolls 8598.

[124] I am grateful to Professors Glanville R. J. Jones and J. Beverley Smith who read early drafts of this section and the corresponding sections of chs. 3 and 7; both offered valuable suggestions. The following works are of exceptional value in relation to the subjects covered in this section: A. D. Carr, *Medieval Anglesey*; F. G. Cowley, *The Monastic Order in South Wales, 1066–1349*; R. R. Davies, *Lordship and Society in the March of Wales, 1282–1400*; idem, *Conquest, Coexistence and Change: Wales 1063–1415*; R. A. Griffiths, ed., *Boroughs of Medieval Wales*; B. E. Howells, ed., *Pembrokeshire County History*, III: *Early Modern Pembrokeshire, 1536–1815*; T. Jones Pierce, 'Landlords in Wales: the nobility and the gentry', in *AHEW*, IV; idem, *MWS*; G. R. J. Jones, 'The tribal system in Wales: a reassessment in the light of settlement studies', *Welsh Hist. Rev.*,

physical environment, may be firmly placed in the highland zone whose "cultural character" was typified by continuity. Different and distinctive cultures, however, met in those lands lying alongside Offa's Dyke, the traditional border between England and Wales, and the borderlands, on account of their historical development, may be regarded as an intermediate sector situated between highland and lowland zones. Neither the dyke nor the modern boundary provides effective lines of demarcation for the late medieval period. Moreover, administrative and ecclesiastical boundaries do not correspond to topographical features.[125] Welsh tenurial forms may be observed in the border shires and sizeable Welsh communities had been established in them. Inhabitants from these shires in turn formed a high percentage of the population of alien colonies created in Wales as a result of successive phases of military conquest. Attacks launched in the late eleventh and early twelfth centuries from the Norman strongholds of Chester, Shrewsbury, and Hereford contributed substantially to the formation of the Welsh march, which incorporated a series of lordships established along the border and in south Wales. Following the collapse of the state of Gwynedd in the late thirteenth century, another group of lordships was created in the recently conquered lands of north-east Wales.[126] In several respects localities on both sides of the border were similarly affected by the demographic, social, and economic changes of the later middle ages and numerous settlements situated well to the east of Offa's Dyke experienced devastation during the Glyndŵr rebellion. Despite the dislocation caused at this time, trading links connecting Wales, the marches and the border shires were maintained and these were further strengthened during the remainder of the fifteenth century.[127]

The interaction of physical, political, and economic forces influenced both the pattern of rural settlement in the middle of the fourteenth

i, 1961–2; E. A. Lewis, *The Medieval Boroughs of Snowdonia*; D. Huw Owen, ed., *Settlement and Society in Wales*; T. B. Pugh, ed., *Glamorgan County History*, III, *The Middle Ages*; W. Rees, *South Wales and the March*; D. Sylvester, *The Rural Landscape of the Welsh Borderland*; Glanmor Williams, *The Welsh Church from Conquest to Reformation*; idem, ed., *Glamorgan County History*, IV, *Early Modern Glamorgan*; K. Williams-Jones, ed., *The Merioneth Lay Subsidy Roll, 1292–3*.

[125] C. Fox, *The Personality of Britain*, Cardiff, 1959, p. 42; E. G. Bowen, ed., *Wales, a Physical, Historical and Regional Geography*, London, 1956, pp. 431–513; Sylvester, *Rural Landscape of the Welsh Borderland*, pp. 23, 35; W. Rees, *An Historical Atlas of Wales*, Cardiff, 1951, pp. 30–1, Pls. 32, 33.

[126] *AHEW*, IV, pp. 108–9 for comment on the survival of gavelkind in Herefordshire; R. H. Hilton, *The Decline of Serfdom in Medieval England*, London, 1969, p. 23 refers to the "substratum of Welsh agrarian custom" in Shropshire and Herefordshire; M. Richards, 'The population of the Welsh Border', *Hon. Soc. Cymmr.*, 1971, pp. 86–91; D. Walker, *The Norman Conquerors*, Swansea, 1977, pp. 20–33; R. R. Davies, *Lordship and Society*, pp. 15–33; Rees, *An Historical Atlas*, Pls. 29, 30, 45. [127] Below, pp. 241–2.

century and also the nature of those changes affecting the occupation of land during the later middle ages in Wales and the borderlands. Geological and soil survey data, related to the medieval documentary evidence, emphasizes the significance of altitude, aspect, coastal location, and especially soil quality as crucial influences upon the character and distribution of settlement on the island of Anglesey. The influence of topographical factors upon settlement forms and also agrarian practice may be observed in the Welsh march. Territory located above the 600'-contour line, normally designated the Welshry of the lordship, was characterized by a considerable survival of traditional tenurial customs practised by a largely free population. In the Englishry, the other main subdivision of the lordship and situated in the more accessible coastal and valley areas, lowland villages, with their bond tenants, were adapted to conform to the requirements of a manorial system.[128] Agrarian activity on the manors was based upon the direct cultivation of the demesne by a dependent peasantry, but variations in emphasis were again determined by local conditions.[129]

Most of the demesne lands cultivated in Wales and the borderlands in the mid-fourteenth century were located on the manors of seigneurial lords and the granges of monastic houses.[130] The lordships of the Welsh march at this time were dominated by powerful magnates who included members of the Bohun, Fitzalan, Lancaster, and Mortimer families. The monastic orders controlled vast areas of land and extensive estates were held by the Cistercians despite the injunction prohibiting the acquisition of property situated at some distance from their houses. Widely dispersed granges, located in mid- and south Wales and belonging to the abbey of Strata Florida, were carefully integrated with upland granges utilized for the summer grazing of large flocks of sheep and lowland coastal granges providing winter grazing facilities. On the latter, cereals, especially barley and oats, were cultivated and some granges also served as bases for sea-fishing. The produce of the demesne land maintained on the home grange supplied the domestic requirements of the abbey.[131]

The introduction of the manor into Wales has been attributed to the extension of Norman influence.[132] In some areas, however, which

[128] G. R. J. Jones, 'Rural settlement in Anglesey', in S. R. Eyre and G. R. J. Jones, eds., *Geography as Human Ecology*, pp. 199–230; M. Davies, 'Field systems of South Wales', in A. R. H. Baker and R. A. Butlin, eds., *Studies of Field Systems of the British Isles*, pp. 482–4; Rees, *South Wales and the March*, pp. 28–31.   [129] Below, ch. 3, pp. 247–51.

[130] A reference to customary tenures associated with an episcopal manor may be seen on p. 649.

[131] E. G. Bowen, 'The monastic economy of the Cistercians at Strata Florida', *Ceredigion*, I, 1950–1, pp. 34–7; Cowley, *Monastic Order in South Wales*, pp. 69–83; Glanmor Williams, *The Welsh Church*, pp. 357–9; RCHM, Wales, *An Inventory of the Ancient Monuments in Glamorgan*, III (2), Cardiff, 1982, pp. 245–306.   [132] Rees, *South Wales and the March*, p. 131.

remained under the authority of native Welsh rulers until the late thirteenth century, settlements based upon the *maerdref*, or reeve's township, constituted a focus for a long-established quasi-manorial system whereby bond communities held land by means of *tref gyfrif* tenure. Remnants of this system survived in north-west Wales in the middle of the fourteenth century and nucleated bond hamlets, such as the one in Aberffraw in Anglesey, may be identified.[133] In contrast to the nucleated villages and hamlets associated with the manor and *maerdref*, a "girdle settlement pattern" of dispersed dwellings character-ized *tir gwelyawg* holdings which were usually occupied by groups of free men.[134] In 1352 lineal descendants of the founders of *gwelyau* may be identified as free peasant proprietors on the island of Anglesey. The *rhandir* or shareland comprised open arable fields surrounded by the *tyddynnod* (homesteads) of the free peasants. The establishment of secondary settlements by the co-operative efforts of groups of kinsmen, together with the operation of partible inheritance, occasioned an irregular pattern of holdings in the *rhandir*, with plots belonging to a number of *gwelyau* intermingled in the open fields.[135]

The *gwely* was occupied by members of kindred groupings which were also associated with the *gafael*, a related but yet distinct agrarian and tenurial institution. Evidence derived from the early and mid-fifteenth centuries suggests two differing interpretations of the *gafael*. In the lowlands of Arllechwedd Isaf, in Arfon, the *gafael* comprised a dispersed form of land tenure. Holdings were scattered throughout the township and intermingled with those belonging to other *gafaelion*. The *gafael* was consequently regarded as the product of the partition of an established and older *gwely*. Fragmented *gafaelion* also constituted a significant tenurial feature of upland localities in Merioneth. The evidence relating to these areas in the 1415–20 survey has prompted the suggestion that under certain circumstances the *gafael* represented a specific and compact territorial unit, and a similar claim has also been advanced for *gafaelion* located in the Ogwen valley.[136]

[133] G. R. J. Jones, 'The tribal system in Wales', pp. 119–21; *idem*, 'Rural settlement in Anglesey', pp. 211–13; Jones Pierce, *MWS*, pp. 342–4, 355.

[134] G. R. J. Jones, 'The distribution of medieval settlement in Anglesey', *Anglesey Antiq. Soc.*, 1955, p. 33; *idem*, 'Rural settlement in Anglesey', pp. 207–8, 210–11 for discussion of similar settlement patterns associated with bond *tir gwelyawg* holdings. Jones Pierce, *MWS*, pp. 342–4, suggests that the *gwely* movement originated early in the twelfth century along the English border and then spread westwards into Wales.

[135] Jones Pierce, *MWS*, pp. 253–4, 256–7, 332, 340–2; *idem*, in *AHEW*, IV, pp. 358–60; H. Ellis, ed., *The Record of Caernarvon*, Rec. Comm., 1838, pp. 65–6; G. R. J. Jones, 'The tribal system in Wales', p. 117.

[136] Jones Pierce, *MWS*, pp. 220–4; G. R. J. Jones, 'The distribution of bond settlements in north-west Wales', *Welsh Hist. Rev.*, II, 1964, p. 28; *idem*, 'Field systems of North Wales', in

The sharelands and *gafael* holdings survived as basic elements in the tenurial framework despite being subject to those pressures which accounted for the gradual dissolution of the kindred and manorial systems.[137] The collapse of agrarian and landholding institutions associated with kindred groupings and with the cultivation of the demesne was undoubtedly hastened by the consequences of pestilence and rebellion. Indications of decay may, however, be detected at a much earlier period. Innate physical forces were to a certain degree responsible for the disintegration of a tenurial framework based upon clan holdings. Fragmentation of these holdings resulted from the combined effects of *cyfran*, the Welsh law of partible inheritance, and of the insatiable pressure of an expanding population on limited territorial resources. Excessive morcellation was temporarily prevented by assarting and by encroachments on waste land, but the process of continual expansion was of necessity curtailed by the eventual non-availability of suitable land.[138] External factors also contributed to the dislocation of rural communities and these included the policies adopted by the rulers of Wales both before and especially after the Edwardian conquest of the late thirteenth century. The native rulers of Gwynedd, in their efforts to establish a feudal state during the thirteenth century, had encouraged the introduction of new tenurial forms which weakened the authority of kindred groupings in respect of the occupation and ownership of land. The collapse of this state resulted in an extension of the practice of escheat, already experienced in the march, to the newly conquered lands. Hereditary holdings which were withdrawn from clan ownership passed under the control of the local administration and fluctuations in the extent of escheat were often determined by the proximity of a locality to the appropriate administrative centre.[139] The conquest was also accompanied by a number of social and economic changes. Intensified commutation of customary renders to cash payments, establishment of privileged

---

Baker and Butlin, eds., *Field Systems*, pp. 457–8; C. Thomas, 'Social organization and rural settlement in medieval North Wales', *JMHRS*, VI, 1970, pp. 128–30; J. R. Jones, 'The development of the Penrhyn estate up to 1431', Univ. of Wales M.A. thesis, 1955, p. 174.

[137] Jones Pierce in *AHEW*, IV, p. 365; *idem*, *MWS*, pp. 87–91, 333.

[138] Jones Pierce in *AHEW*, IV, pp. 360–1; G. R. J. Jones, 'Some medieval rural settlements in North Wales', *Institute of British Geographers*, 1953, p. 60.

[139] Jones Pierce, *MWS*, pp. 51, 119–24; D. Huw Owen, 'Tenurial and economic development in North Wales in the twelfth and thirteenth centuries', *Welsh Hist. Rev.*, VI, 1972, pp. 130–5; Rees, *South Wales and the March*, pp. 211–13, 266–7, 270; C. Thomas, 'Patterns and processes of estate expansion in the fifteenth and sixteenth centuries', *JMHRS*, VI, 1972, pp. 334–5; D. Huw Owen, 'The Englishry of Denbigh: an English colony in medieval Wales', *Hon. Soc. Cymmr.*, 1974–5, p. 60.

monopolistic commercial centres, confiscation of hereditary holdings and, in some cases, resettlement of local inhabitants all contributed to the enervation of kindred groupings in the first half of the fourteenth century.[140]

The manors of Wales and the marches were by no means immune from the demographic, financial, and military pressures which disrupted manorial cultivation throughout the whole of western Europe. The direct exploitation of the demesne was thereby progressively abandoned and replaced by the leasing of portions of, or the whole of, the demesne.[141] Evidence derived from many areas illustrates this process, but the chronology of each stage varied from one locality to another. Demesne lands in the lordship of Senghennydd had been leased before 1307 and in the lordship of Chirk by 1324. On the Le Strange estates in Whitchurch, in north Shropshire, a small number of fields had been maintained, from the early fourteenth century, as demesne lands whilst the remainder were leased out annually. In the lordship of Denbigh the manors of Dinorben and Ystrad Owain, which had been developed on the sites of *maerdrefi*, were in a dilapidated condition by 1334 and although still functioning were valued for their rent yields rather than for demesne produce. The other two manors of the lordship, located at Denbigh and at Kilford, had been founded in the late thirteenth century, but by 1334 demesne operations had ceased and both manors had been farmed out.[142]

Economic and political forces, during the remainder of the fourteenth, and throughout the fifteenth century, sustained and accelerated the process leading to a fundamental change in the pattern of land occupation in Wales and the marches. An assessment of the impact of the pestilence presents problems despite the occasional availability of specific evidence. Entries in the financial accounts illustrate the high mortality rate caused by the outbreaks of 1349–50, 1361 and 1369. The actual numbers are provided for the hamlet of Llanllwch, located in the neighbourhood of Carmarthen, and the town of Ruthin. Many holdings in Anglesey and Caernarfonshire were described as vacant in 1351 on account of the poverty or death of the inhabitants. The borough of Caus in Shropshire is considered to have

---

[140] E. A. Lewis, 'The decay of tribalism in North Wales', *Hon. Soc. Cymmr.*, 1902–3, pp. 1–50.

[141] G. Duby, *Rural Economy and Country Life in the Medieval West*, pp. 312–31; below, pp. 650–1 for the effects of leasing upon customary tenure.

[142] J. Beverley Smith, 'The lordship of Senghennydd', in Pugh, ed., *Glamorgan County History*, III, pp. 315–16; Llinos O. W. Smith, 'The lordships of Chirk and Oswestry', London Univ. Ph.D. thesis, 1970, pp. 139–40; A. J. Pollard, 'Estate management in the later middle ages: the Talbots and Whitchurch, 1383–1525', *EcHR*, 2nd ser. xxv, 1972, pp. 556–7; D. Huw Owen, 'The lordship of Denbigh, 1282–1425', Univ. of Wales Ph.D. thesis, 1967, pp. 210–14.

been in a state of decline in the post-plague period and many houses
were unoccupied by 1361. Many victims of the plague were recorded
in the deanery of Middlewich and the high incidence of mortality
caused by earlier outbreaks of the plague, in the sixth and seventh
centuries, in sparsely populated localities prompts one to query the
assumption that extensive woodlands and a low density of population
diminished the impact of the pestilence in Cheshire. The Welsh poets
frequently refer to the plague: *y farwolaeth fawr*; and Ieuan Gethin of
Baglan lamented the deaths of five of his children in elegies which
contained vivid descriptions of the horrifying symptoms of the
plague.[143]

The dramatic and terrifying character of the plague led both
contemporary officials and chroniclers, and also later historians, to
exaggerate its consequences, and the various economic difficulties of
the period have been attributed to outbreaks of the pestilence. Failure
to collect dues, an inevitable result of the flight of bondmen from their
traditional holdings, was often concealed by local officials who excused
themselves by citing the effects of pestilence.[144] There is on the other
hand no doubt that periodic outbreaks of pestilence contributed
substantially to the demographic decline which occurred during the
later middle ages. A correlation of population statistics compiled for the
county of Merioneth in the late thirteenth and mid-sixteenth centuries
reveals that the estimated populations of both the county as a whole and
of individual townships were higher at the earlier date. However, an
awareness of the economic problems experienced in the first half of the
fourteenth century enables one to consider the effects of the plague in
their perspective. A papal bull of 1383, which considered the financial
difficulties of Margam abbey, bore a striking resemblance to a
document prepared in 1336. The bull referred to the effects of
pestilence, but both documents considered excessive hospitality and
livestock diseases as contributory causes for the progressive economic
malaise.[145]

---

[143] W. Rees, 'The Black Death in Wales', *RHS*, 4th ser. III, 1920, pp. 120–3; *VCH Salop*, VIII,
p. 310; Shrewsbury, *History of Bubonic Plague*, pp. 52–3; J. C. Russell, 'The earlier medieval plague
in the British Isles', *Viator (Medieval and Renaissance Studies)*, VII, 1976, p. 76; G. J. Williams,
Traddodiad Llenyddol Morgannwg, Cardiff, 1948, pp. 28–9; Ceri W. Lewis, 'The literary tradition
of Morgannwg down to the middle of the sixteenth century', in Pugh, ed., *Glamorgan County
History*, III, pp. 498–9.

[144] D. L. Evans, 'Some notes on the history of the principality of Wales in the time of the Black
Prince (1343–1376)', *Hon. Soc. Cymmr.*, 1925–6, p. 80.

[145] Williams-Jones, ed., *Merioneth Lay Subsidy Roll*, pp. xliv–xlviii; Glanmor Williams, *The
Welsh Church*, pp. 141, 155; *Cartae et Alia Munimenta quae ad Dominium de Glamorgan pertinent*, ed.
G. T. Clark, Cardiff, 1910, IV, pp. 1199, 1350–1.

The cumulative problems afflicting the economy were further accentuated by the revolt which, led by Owain Glyndŵr, erupted in north-east Wales in 1400 and was sustained for the greater part of the following decade. Considerable and extensive material damage was caused by both the rebels and the opposing royal forces in many areas of Wales and the borderlands. Numerous churches and monasteries were burned, pillaged, and destroyed. Adam of Usk, a contemporary chronicler and possibly a supporter of Glyndŵr, referred to the Welsh leader as "a second Assyrian, the rod of God's anger" and described his activities in the diocese of Llandaff as "deeds of unheard of cruelty with fire and sword". Fierce attacks were launched on the plantation boroughs of north-west Wales, whose privileged status had aroused the hatred of Welshmen denied the opportunity of residence and forced to sell their produce in them. The manorial borough of Pwllheli, which was regarded as an alien institution despite the fact that it was occupied by Welshmen, also suffered from the attention of Glyndŵr's adherents. An account for 1411 described the township as "destroyed and laid waste" and refers to the flight of the tenantry from the commote. Manors located in the Englishries of lordships also represented prime targets for the Welsh forces. Tenements on the manor of Llantrisaint, in the lordship of Usk, were burned and devastated and mills destroyed in the lordship of Gwynllwg had not been repaired by 1434–5.[146]

The border shires also suffered from the hostilities engendered by the rebellion. Burgesses and officials of the city of Chester were fully aware of the threat of devastation and attempts were made to curtail trading activities with Welshmen. Relief from taxes was granted by parliament in 1406 and 1407 to the communities of Shropshire because of "the ravages of Welsh rebels". In 1404 the town of Whitchurch, together with the surrounding countryside, suffered from attacks mounted by Welsh troops. Considerable damage had also been caused in the hundreds of Condover and Ford: the townships of Caus, Marsh, Vennington, Westbury and Tockleton had been relieved from liability for taxation in 1405–6 and houses destroyed at this time by fire on the manor of Minsterley had not been rebuilt by 1445. Numerous churches in Archenfield, a deanery in the diocese of Hereford, were also destroyed at this time.[147] Recovery from the devastation caused during

---

[146] Glanmor Williams, The Welsh Church, pp. 227–9; Chronicon Ade de Usk, ed. E. Maunde Thompson, London, 1904, p. 247; Griffiths, ed., Boroughs of Medieval Wales, pp. 73–101, 165–87; E. A. Lewis, Medieval Boroughs of Snowdonia, pp. 184–5, 191, 203–4; Jones Pierce, MWS, p. 156; PRO SC 6/1175/9, 928/20; Rees, South Wales and the March, p. 278; T. B. Pugh, The Marcher Lordships of South Wales, 1415–1536, pp. 167–9.

[147] J. Gwynfor Jones, 'Government and the Welsh community: the north-east borderland in the fifteenth century', in British Government and Administration: Studies presented to S. B. Chrimes,

the turbulent first decade of the fifteenth century was delayed in many localities. The lingering memory in north Wales of the violence characterizing the rebellion was expressed by Sir John Wynn, who, writing at the close of the Tudor period, commented that "it was Owen Glyndoores policie to bringe all thinges to wast, that the Englishe should find not strength nor restinge place in the Countrey".[148]

The upheaval caused by pestilence and rebellion accounted for the evacuation of a large number of clan holdings, occupied by free and bond inhabitants. Bondmen in particular suffered from the outbreaks of the plague. The nucleated nature of their settlements may well explain the reduction in bond population recorded in evidence relating to *tir gwelyawg* and *tir cyfrif* communities and also from manorial centres.[149] A feature of *tref cyfrif* tenure was that the rents imposed on a township represented a communal obligation and those bondmen who survived the plague were subject to considerable fiscal pressures. The suspension, in some localities of the Principality of North Wales, of the payments of *staurum*, a render traditionally imposed on bondmen, emphasizes the immediate and shattering effect of the plague upon bond communities. The restoration of these payments by 1362 suggests a measure of recovery and, although financial accounts for the remainder of the fourteenth century continued to record vacant holdings, bond townships survived as an integral element of the social structure.[150]

The disturbances associated with the Glyndŵr rebellion, however, provided the bondmen with an opportunity to evade and escape from their fiscal obligations. Entries in fifteenth-century accounts, available from all parts of Wales, illustrate the depopulation and decay of bond settlements. In the north-west the flight of bondmen accounted for the frequent exoneration of *staurum* payments and it was asserted at the beginning of the seventeenth century that "the exaccions were in those dayes soe manyfould that...the boundmen ran awaye and forsooke the kinges land". Bondmen in the marcher lordships of the south-east and north-east borderlands also left their tenements in large numbers.[151]

ed. H. Hearder and H. R. Loyn, Cardiff, 1974, pp. 60–3; *The Shropshire Peace Roll, 1400–1414*, ed. E. G. Kimball, Shrewsbury, 1959, p. 9; Pollard, 'Estate management in the later middle ages', p. 560; *VCH Salop*, VIII, p. 316; PRO E 179/166/37, 48; *The Register of Robert Mascall, Bishop of Hereford, 1404–1416*, ed. J. H. Parry, Hereford, 1916, pp. v–vi.

[148] Sir John Wynn, *The History of the Gwydir Family*, ed. J. Ballinger, p. 53.

[149] Jones Pierce, *MWS*, pp. 39–57; G. R. J. Jones, 'Rural settlement in Anglesey', p. 223.

[150] E. A. Lewis, 'The decay of tribalism in North Wales', p. 44; Jones Pierce, *MWS*, pp. 43–4.

[151] Wynn, *History of the Gwydir Family*, p. 59; Pugh, ed., *Marcher Lordships of South Wales*, pp. 167, 172; Rees, *South Wales and the March*, p. 274; L. O. W. Smith, 'The lordships of Chirk and Oswestry', pp. 229–31.

The process occasionally proved to be profitable for the seigneurial administration and lucrative aspects are illustrated by the records of the lordship of Newport. On the manor of Stow, lands which had been abandoned by bondmen were leased out at increased rents to freemen. Moreover, the reeve of Machen in 1456/7 anticipated the receipt of at least £20 in entry fines if the lord was prepared to let on free tenurial terms vacated bond lands.[152] On the whole, however, the depopulation of bond holdings resulted in a reduction in revenue and this explains the strenuous efforts made by officials in crown and marcher lordships to force bondmen to return to their tenements. In 1417 the marcher lords were required to deliver to royal officials bondmen from the three shires of north-west Wales in order that they might be re-settled "for the king's profit". The adoption of a protectionist policy failed to stem the process of depopulation. The Merioneth section of the Record of Caernarfon, compiled in the period 1415–20, refers to three dozen *gwelyau* or *gafaelion*, predominantly of bond status, which were vacant at this time. Moreover, a petition submitted in 1433 stated that the desolation of extensive areas of crown lands in Wales resulted from the abandonment of bond holdings.[153]

The opportunities presented by the departure of bondmen and the disintegration of bond communities were appreciated by the more ambitious and enterprising freemen. An inquisition *post mortem* of 1390 reveals that Dafydd ap Dafydd ap Madog of Hendwr had held in the commote of Edeirnion a total of 26 *gafaelion*, of which at least 12 were of bond character. A crucial factor in the emergence to prominence of the Wynn family of Gwydir was Maredudd ap Ieuan's decision to move, in the early years of the reign of Henry Tudor, from his hereditary lands in Eifionydd to the commote of Nanconwy so that "he shoulde finde Elbowe roome in that wast countrey amonge the bondmen". The southern townships of Nanconwy which attracted Maredudd's attention had largely comprised, in the mid-fourteenth century, members of bond clan groupings and these had been subjected, in the ensuing period, to the debilitating effects of pestilence, rebellion, and a high incidence of crime perpetrated by the "theives and murtherers" harboured at the nearby "sancturarie" of Yspyty Ifan.[154]

[152] Pugh, ed., *Marcher Lordships of South Wales*, pp. 167, 174.

[153] J. Beverley Smith, 'Crown and community in the principality of North Wales in the reign of Henry Tudor', *Welsh Hist. Rev.*, III, 1966, pp. 152–3; C. Thomas, 'The social and economic geography of rural Merioneth from the dark ages to the Act of Union', in *Merioneth County History*, II, forthcoming. I am grateful to Dr Thomas for allowing me to read a manuscript copy of this chapter prior to its publication.

[154] A. D. Carr, 'An Edeyrnion inquisition, 1390', *JMHRS*, VI, 1969, pp. 1–7; C. A. Gresham, *Eifionydd: a Study in Landownership from the Medieval Period to the Present Day*, pp. 87–9; J.

Encroachments upon bond lands were recorded during the fifteenth century and attempts to reverse the process of depopulation were made by royal officials aware that a diminution in the bond population accounted for a substantial loss of revenue. Prominent freemen resented the restraints placed on them, and the mutual but conflicting interest of royal officials and free communities in the fate of bond settlements forms the background to the negotiations which preceded the grant of a series of charters to the shires and a group of lordships in north Wales in the first decade of the sixteenth century.[155]

The depopulation of bond tenements ensured that on some manors the seigneurial administration was unable to maintain demesne-based agrarian operations. A drastic reduction may be observed in the numbers of customary tenants occupying the manor of Caldicot and in 1362 a fall in revenue was attributed to the fact that "very many of the tenants are dead and their lands are in the lord's hands". Difficulties and also considerable expenditure were encountered in recruiting local labour and in 1366 demesne farming at Caldicot had been terminated.[156] The cultivation of the demesne continued until the next decade on a number of other manors held by the earl of Hereford in the Welsh marches, and the crucial event responsible for a change in agrarian policy in these lands would seem to be the death of Humphrey de Bohun, earl of Hereford, in 1373. The earls of Arundel, on their estates in the lordships of Chirk and Oswestry, did not place great emphasis on the comparatively small arable demesne lands which were at their disposal and interest was largely focused on the rearing of livestock. A connection has been traced between the increased absenteeism of seigneurial lords and the leasing of the demesne on a number of manors in Pembroke.[157] Moreover, the conscious adoption of a new approach to the utilization of manorial centres may be observed at Kilford in the lordship of Denbigh. The total acreage of 886 acres in 1334 consisted of 239 acres of arable, 240 acres of meadow, 248 acres of pasture and 159 acres of rented demesne land, and the messuage

Gwynfor Jones, 'The Wynn family: aspects of its growth and development, c. 1500–1580', NLW Jnl, XXII, 1981–2, pp. 141–4; Wynn, History of the Gwydir family, pp. 50–4.

[155] J. Beverley Smith, 'Crown and community in the principality of North Wales', pp. 145–71; CPR, 1494–1509, pp. 434, 464–5, 471, 523–4, 586–7.

[156] Rees, 'The Black Death in Wales', pp. 124, 128–9; idem, South Wales and the March, pp. 246, 249–52.

[157] Rees, South Wales and the March, pp. 254–5; R. R. Davies, Lordship and Society, p. 114; L. O. W. Smith, 'The lordships of Chirk and Oswestry', pp. 140–55; B. E. Howells, 'Studies in the social and agrarian history of medieval and early modern Pembrokeshire', Univ. of Wales M.A. thesis, 1956, pp. 97, 155; A Calendar of the Public Records relating to Pembrokeshire, ed. Henry Owen, 3 vols., London, 1911–18, I, pp. 74–5; III, pp. 109, 151, 167.

contained two granges, a cowhouse, bakery and dovecote. Reductions in these acreages were recorded in 1362 with the arable comprising 209 acres, meadow-land 57½ acres, and no reference being made to the pasture. The lands withdrawn from the manor had been utilized to form a park which was used as a hunting ground by the Black Prince who held the lordship at this time.[158]

The dislocation caused to numerous manorial centres during the turbulent years of the first decade of the fifteenth century is illustrated by significant developments on the neighbouring manors of Denbigh and Ystrad Owain. Attempts were frequently made to lease the demesne as a unit and the possibility of renewing demesne operations might therefore represent an option for the seigneurial administration at a later stage. The partition of the demesne was therefore frequently undertaken with care and detached portions were usually located at some distance from the manorial centre. The manors of Denbigh and Ystrad Owain had both been leased as units during the second half of the fourteenth century, but by 1410 small plots of land had been carved out of the demesne and offered on leases. In Denbigh, 34 acres, representing 22 per cent of the demesne, had been apportioned into five plots and a much more extensive area in Ystrad Owain, comprising 221½ acres out of the total demesne land of 241½ acres, had been divided into 31 plots and leased to 15 individuals.[159] The involvement of a number of lessees also represented an important change in the pattern of demesne-land occupation. One individual or family was frequently associated with a leased demesne. The manor of Dinorben had been granted to William Curteys, a burgess of Denbigh, in 1342 and Roger de Keswise occupied the demesne lands of Ystrad Owain in 1373 on a 30-year lease. Demesne lands in the Park of Macclesfield were leased in 1386 to John de Macclesfield and members of the Savage family frequently appeared as lessees in the fifteenth century.[160] Similar tendencies were also apparent on the monastic estates. Evidence derived from the late fourteenth century suggests that, whilst demesne lands were still cultivated, the leasing of granges, in portions or as units, was increasingly practised. The entire estate of the abbey of Aberconway was probably leased out by the end of the century. The greater part of the demesne lands of Ince, located in Cheshire, and the property of the

---

[158] D. Huw Owen, 'The lordship of Denbigh', pp. 222–6; PRO SC 6/1182/4–6, 8.

[159] D. Huw Owen, *op cit.*, pp. 217–21; PRO SC 6/1185/12; Rees, *South Wales and the March*, p. 255 for an example of the leasing of an outlying demesne, at Bryndu in 1372, which preceded the farming of the demesne lands and customary works of the main manor of Bronllys, in the lordship of Brecon.

[160] Hatfield House Library, Montague Cartulary; PRO SC 6/1183/9; C. S. Davies, *A History of Macclesfield*, Manchester, 1961, pp. 36–9.

Benedictine abbey of St Werburgh, were farmed in 1439–40 by John Wilkinson.[161] It is significant, however, that a number of tenants also held here plots of arable land which had formerly belonged to the demesne. Multiple tenancies tended to appear with greater frequency in the financial accounts of lay and monastic estates and demesne lands were often described as having been leased *diversis tenentibus*.[162]

The depopulation and devastation of many localities led to a reduction in the extent of cultivated land. Soils of marginal productive quality, which had been brought into cultivation as a consequence of the population explosion of the thirteenth century, were now abandoned and agrarian activity was increasingly concentrated on the richer and more productive lands.[163] This trend again may be observed before the first major outbreak of pestilence. The *Nonarum Inquisitiones* of 1342 reveal a contraction of arable acreage in the early decades of the fourteenth century, and an examination of the returns submitted by parish jurors identified Shropshire as one of four localities where the amount of abandoned land was considerable. Uncultivated land was recorded in more than fifty townships and most of these were located in the uplands to the south-west of the river Severn. The reasons advanced for the vacated holdings included the poverty of tenants, the destruction of crops by unfavourable weather and the prevalence of murrain in sheep. Many villages were in a state of decline during the first half of the fourteenth century and several, including Hampton Wafer in Herefordshire, are believed to have been depopulated at this time.[164]

The encroachments of sea and sand in this period contributed to the depopulation of rural settlements along the southern coast of Wales.[165] The location of a number of declining villages in Shropshire reveals an association with the consolidation of scattered strips of arable land and the enclosure of open fields. A further weakening of the structure of many villages may be observed in the years of pestilence and revolt,

[161] J. S. Donnelly, 'Changes in the grange economy of English and Welsh Cistercian abbeys, 1300–1540', *Traditio*, x, 1954, pp. 445–6; Glanmor Williams, *The Welsh Church*, pp. 173–4; D. H. Williams, *The Welsh Cistercians: Aspects of their Economic History*, Pontypool, 1969, pp. 55–6; Rhys W. Hays, *A History of the Abbey of Aberconway*, Cardiff, 1963, pp. 421–2; Platt, *Monastic Grange*, pp. 210–11.   [162] PRO SC 6/1182/7.10, 1183/3.20.

[163] Duby, *Rural Economy and Country Life*, pp. 308, 310, 342–3; W. G. Hoskins and L. D. Stamp, *The Common Lands of England and Wales*, London, 1963, p. 45.

[164] A. R. H. Baker, 'Evidence in the *Nonarum Inquisitiones* of contracting arable lands in England during the early fourteenth century', *EcHR*, 2nd ser. xix, 1966, pp. 518–32; Vanderzee, ed., *Nonarum Inquisitiones in Curia Scaccarii*, pp. 182–94; T. Rowley, *The Shropshire Landscape*, London, 1972, pp. 109, 112; S. C. Stanford, 'The deserted medieval village of Hampton Wafer, Herefordshire', *WNFC*, xxxix, 1967, p. 88.

[165] Clark, ed., *Cartae et alia Munimenta*, IV, pp. 1358–9; R. R. Davies, 'The lordship of Ogmore', in Pugh, ed., *Glamorgan County History*, III, p. 298.

when the hamlets of Broomcroft and Burfield appear to have been abandoned as a result respectively of the ravages of pestilence and an attack launched by Glyndŵr's forces. Poverty and turbulent conditions were undoubtedly responsible for the decay of market villages such as Clifford, Moccas, and Bridge Sollars in Herefordshire. Moreover, nucleated settlements in the lordship of Laugharne (Dyfed) also succumbed to a combination of pressures accentuated by the consequences of plague and rebellion.[166]

Bond settlements, whose decay during this period has already been noted, were frequently located on favourable soils and thus attracted the attention of acquisitive freemen. Difficulties were occasionally experienced in securing a sufficient number of tenants. A condition of the appointment of Hywel Kemeys as deputy-sheriff of the lordship of Newport in 1444 was that thirty new tenants be found for the locality. In 1474 favourable terms were offered to tenants prepared to occupy and rebuild properties "lying waste and fallen to the ground".[167] The availability of land, however, in the early fifteenth century both stimulated an active and fluid land market and also encouraged the mobility of tenants. The survey of Merioneth undertaken in 1415–20 indicated that several *gafael* holdings were vacant whilst others were of recent origin, and it is possible that this area had witnessed an attempted recolonization of desolate land in the late fourteenth and early fifteenth centuries.[168]

The reclamation of farming land was accompanied by enclosures from and encroachments onto waste and wooded lands. It is true that extensive areas of forest and woodland survived and Sir John Wynn, describing the landscape of north Wales in the fifteenth century, stated that "the countrey of Nanconway was not onelie wooded, but also all Car[narfonshi]r, Merionythshire and denbigh shire seemed to be but one forrest and wood". The gradual clearance of certain forest areas in the border shires may be observed throughout the period. Considerable assarting activity was recorded in several localities in Shropshire in the mid- and late fourteenth century. Tenants of Condover were granted by absentee lords assart licenses which enabled them to clear and enclose parts of Buriswood.[169] The jurisdictional rights attached to forests

---

[166] Rowley, *Shropshire Landscape*, pp. 27–8, 109–10; *VCH Salop*, VIII, pp. 4–5, 93; J. O'Donnell, 'Market centres in Herefordshire, 1200–1400', *WNFC*, XL, 1971, p. 192; *Register of Robert Mascall*, ed. Parry, p. vi; W. S. G. Thomas, 'Lost villages in south-west Carmarthenshire', *Institute of British Geographers*, 47, 1969, pp. 191–200.

[167] Pugh, ed., *Marcher Lordships of South Wales*, pp. 166–7; W. Bell Jones, 'Hawarden Deeds', *Jnl Flints. Hist. Soc.*, 7, 1919–20, p. 33.

[168] C. Thomas, 'Patterns and processes of estate expansion', pp. 129–30.

[169] Wynn, *History of the Gwydir Family*, p. 53; *VCH Salop*, VIII, p. 46 and, for other examples of the clearance of woodland in the county, pp. 28, 29, 183, 184–5.

provided a valuable source of seigneurial revenue, and these rights were often exploited by the rigorous application of forest laws.[170] Encroachments onto waste lands in Wales appear, despite the paucity of documentary evidence, to be well advanced by the close of the fifteenth century. The increased pressure on land may be partly explained by the economic recovery and greater social stability experienced in many localities. A comparison of surveys compiled in 1429 and 1502 for six manors in the lordship of Ogmore shows marked increases both in the number of tenants and in the extent of cultivated land in an area which had experienced extensive dislocation during the Glyndŵr rebellion. Studies of farm names based on *hendre* or *hafod* settlements, associated with traditional practices of transhumance, suggest that the conversion of some *hafodydd*, in origin summer dwellings in the mountain-moorlands, into separate and later independent farms was already well advanced by the sixteenth century.[171] The leasing on a more extensive scale of monastic lands suitable for grazing purposes further confirmed the growing attraction of marginal lands. Trends apparent by the end of the fifteenth century thus anticipate the colonization of large areas of *ffriddoedd* (moorland pasture), which represented a significant landscape feature of the sixteenth century and presage the further and more pronounced upheavals in the occupation and distribution of land in the sixteenth century.[172]

G. THE HOME COUNTIES[173]

In this region there are clear signs that arable cultivation was contracting before 1350. The returns made in 1341 to inquiries into low tax assessment refer in all five counties to land cultivated in 1291 but now

[170] Below, p. 660 for the tension and unrest caused in Cheshire by the adoption of this policy in the middle of the fourteenth century.

[171] Jones Pierce in *AHEW*, IV, p. 379; R. R. Davies, 'The lordship of Ogmore', pp. 300–4; Glanmor Williams, 'The economic life of Glamorgan, 1536–42', in *idem*, ed., *Glamorgan County History*, IV, p. 22; Elwyn Davies, 'Hendre and hafod in Merioneth', *JMHRS*, VII, 1973, pp. 13–27; *idem*, 'Hendre and hafod in Denbighshire', *Denbs. Hist. Soc.*, XXVI, 1977, pp. 49–72.

[172] C. Thomas in *Merioneth County History*, II, forthcoming; *idem*, 'Enclosure and the rural landscape of Merioneth in the sixteenth century', *Institute of British Geographers*, 42, 1967, pp. 153–62; Jones Pierce in *AHEW*, IV, pp. 376–81; Glanmor Williams in *ibid.*, pp. 383–7.

[173] In the sections dealing with the home counties in chapters 2, 3, and 7 I am grateful for permission to make use of the following unpublished dissertations (with the exception that it has proved impossible to trace Miss L. C. Latham): J. Brooks, 'The deserted medieval villages of north Berkshire', Reading Univ. Ph.D., 1982; R. J. Faith, 'The peasant land-market in Berkshire during the later middle ages', Leicester Univ. Ph.D., 1962; P. D. Glennie, 'A commercializing agrarian region: late medieval and early modern Hertfordshire', Cambridge Univ. Ph.D., 1983;

lying untilled: in Berkshire this is mentioned in 16 parishes, in Oxfordshire in 11, in Buckinghamshire in 102, in Bedfordshire in 49, in Hertfordshire in 26. We should be wary of accepting this information at face value; in Hertfordshire no details are given of the amount of land involved in each case, reducing the plea almost to common form, and everywhere we may suspect a tendency to exaggerate the extent of decline. But it cannot be ignored, and it is significant that in all the counties the places involved fall into a recognizable geographical pattern. In Berkshire they are mostly in the west, north of the river Kennet; in Buckinghamshire, the county most affected, they are particularly dense in the south-west, spilling over into Oxfordshire and Berkshire, and along the northern border with Northamptonshire, forming a single belt with similar concentrations in north Bedfordshire and, to a lesser extent, north-east Oxfordshire; in Bedfordshire, apart from those north of the river Ouse, they all lie south of a line drawn through Houghton Conquest, leaving a broad belt of central Bedfordshire apparently free from arable contraction; in Hertfordshire the places affected all lie in the north-east, continuing the marked concentration in south Cambridgeshire.[174] The returns for some places specifically mention a reduction in the number of inhabitants,[175] and it may well be that in other places, too, abandonment of arable was only an aspect of shrinkage of settlement. Detailed work on individual places confirms the reality of the decline. D. Roden found shrinkage of

P. Hyde, 'The Winchester manors at Witney and Adderbury, Oxfordshire, in the later middle ages', Oxford Univ. B.Litt., 1955; P. J. Jefferies, 'A consideration of some aspects of landholding in medieval Berkshire', Reading Univ. Ph.D., 1972; A. C. Jones, 'The customary land market in Bedfordshire in the fifteenth century', Southampton Univ. Ph.D., 1975; L. C. Latham, 'The decay of the manorial system, during the first half of the fifteenth century, with special reference to manorial jurisdiction and the decline of villeinage', London Univ. M.A., 1928; M. H. Long, 'A history of the manors of Mapledurham Gurney and Mapledurham Chazey', Oxford Univ. B.Litt., 1953; D. Roden, 'Studies in Chiltern field systems', London Univ. Ph.D., 1965; D. V. Stern, 'A Hertfordshire manor of Westminster abbey', London Univ. Ph.D., 1978; F. B. Stitt, 'Manors of Great and Little Wymondley in the later middle ages', Oxford Univ. B.Litt., 1951. I am particularly indebted to the work of R. J. Faith and A. C. Jones (much of which is published in P. D. A. Harvey, ed., *The Peasant Land Market*), and to that of D. Roden. My debt to the relevant volumes of the *VCH*, especially to the sections on economic and social history in the topographical volumes of the *VCH Oxon.*, is greater than the many footnote citations might suggest.

[174] *Nonarum Inquisitiones in Curia Scaccarii*, ed. Vanderzee, pp. 1–22, 132–42, 326–40, 431–4; Baker, 'Evidence in the *Nonarum Inquisitiones*', pp. 518–32, where there is particular discussion of the returns from Bedfordshire and Buckinghamshire and also (p. 522) a distribution map for the whole country of the references to untilled arable; cf., for Bedfordshire, A. H. R. Baker, 'Contracting arable lands in 1341', *Beds. Hist. Rec. Soc.*, XLIX, 1970, pp. 7–18, and, for Oxfordshire, C. Dyer in *AHEW*, II, pp. 233–4.

[175] E.g. West Ilsley (Berks.), Meppershall (Beds.), Hambleden (Bucks.): *Nonarum Inquisitiones*, ed. Vanderzee, pp. 8, 17, 334.

settlement in the decades before the Black Death on all four Chiltern parishes that he closely studied: King's Walden, Codicote, Berkhamsted (all in Herts.), and Ibstone (Bucks.). On the plain below the hills, at Cuxham (Oxon.), after many years of a three-course rotation on unvarying areas of the manorial demesne, there was in 1348 an unexplained reduction of the area sown in the spring-corn field, of which nearly one-third must have lain waste. At Iver in south-east Buckinghamshire 38 tenants were presented in the manorial court between 1332 and 1349 for abandoning their holdings or letting them go to waste, and at Padworth (Berks.) on the river Kennet extents of 1251 and 1349 show a great reduction of arable area.[176] Interestingly, not one of these places is among those where lands were reported untilled in 1341.

Certainly from 1349 to the end of the fifteenth century shrinkage of rural settlement is found in all parts of the region, a shrinkage that appears in decreasing numbers of manorial tenants and in the abandonment and decay of dwellings. Thus R. J. Faith, investigating manors scattered throughout west Berkshire, found that on all eight with adequate records the number of tenants fell, on some very considerably. Roden has brought together evidence from all parts of the Chilterns of the abandonment of cottages, larger houses, and mills.[177] There is no lack of examples to show that these same phenomena were widespread throughout the region. Islip (Oxon.) and Sherington (Bucks.) are other instances of villages which have been closely studied and which show a fall in the tenant population.[178] Where a new tenant took over lands and buildings that had formerly supported two or more families he was sometimes given permission to pull down unwanted houses, and there are cases of houses converted to a cowshed and a barn.[179] Far more commonly manorial court rolls

---

[176] Roden, 'Studies', pp. 124, 163, 179–80, 211–12, 266–7, 420–3; D. Roden, 'Changing settlement in the Chiltern Hills', *Folk Life*, VIII, 1970, pp. 64–6; P. D. A. Harvey, *A Medieval Oxfordshire Village: Cuxham, 1240–1400*, p. 165; J. M. Bennett, *Women in the Medieval English Countryside*, New York, 1987, p. 224; Jefferies, 'Consideration of some aspects of landholding', pp. 265–6.

[177] Harvey, ed., *The Peasant Land Market*, pp. 123–4 (Woolstone), 130–1 (Brightwalton), 134–5 (Letcombe Regis), 135–6 (South Moreton), 139 (Sotwell Stonor), 143 (Speenhamland), 150–1 (Englefield), 152–5 (Coleshill); Roden, 'Studies', pp. 124, 179–80, 211–12, 266–7, 302–5, 420–3; Roden, 'Changing settlement', pp. 67–8; D. Roden, 'Field systems in Ibstone', *Records of Bucks.*, XVIII, 1966–70, pp. 52–3.

[178] *VCH Oxon.*, VI, p. 210; A. C. Chibnall, *Sherington; Fiefs and Fields of a Buckinghamshire Village*, pp. 149–50. Case after case of shrinkage is reported in *VCH Oxon.*; some widely scattered examples are at Ardley (VI, pp. 10–11), Headington (V, p. 162), Prescote (X, pp. 206–7), Pyrton (VIII, pp. 141, 171), Waterstock (VII, p. 224); cf. *VCH Bucks.*, II, p. 62 (Fawley, Haversham).

[179] Latham, 'Decay of the manorial system', p. 173 (Brightwalton, Berks., 1439); Roden, 'Studies', p. 124 (King's Walden, Herts., 1359); *The Boarstall Cartulary*, ed. H. E. Salter, Oxford

contain presentments of tenants who had illicitly allowed buildings to fall into decay.[180]

In many places shrinkage of settlement seems to have been initiated by the Black Death of 1349. Its permanent effects, however, did not simply reflect its local severity. In two cases – Tusmore, and Tilgarsley in Eynsham (both in Oxon.) – settlement was apparently abandoned as a direct result of the Black Death.[181] But other villages where all or nearly all the landholders perished had replaced most of their tenants within a few years of 1349. Woodeaton (Oxon.), where it was said that all but two of some 35 tenants had died, had only seven vacant houses in 1366.[182] At Woolstone (Berks.), thirteen half-virgates were still unoccupied at the beginning of 1352; during the year they were all let out but ten of them were divided up to be held by existing tenants under what were intended as temporary leases.[183] In many places the plague produced a small permanent reduction in the number of landholders; this was demonstrably so at Cuxham (Oxon.), where although all vacant lands were occupied by 1355 the total number of tenants was less than before 1349 and two houses remained empty, never to be reoccupied.[184] Cases like these, where the plague left some holdings unoccupied for at least a few years and permanently reduced the number of landholders, seem far more common than those like Chalfont St Peter (Bucks.), where the admission of twelve new tenants in the autumn of 1349 may well have filled all vacancies created by the Black Death.[185] Later outbreaks of plague, if less severe overall, also helped to shrink particular settlements: vacancies from the plague of 1361 were rapidly filled at Great Wymondley (Herts.), but probably led to the abandonment and destruction of cottages at Willington (Beds.), and certainly initiated a long-term reduction in tenants at

---

Hist. Soc., OS LXXXVIII, 1930, no. 337; H. L. Turner, '"The Great Barn", Lewknor: the documentary evidence', Oxoniensia, XXXVII, 1972, pp. 187–91; M. C. J. Morrey and J. T. Smith, '"The Great Barn", Lewknor: the architectural evidence', ibid., XXXVIII, 1973, pp. 339–45.

[180] E.g. Harvey, ed., The Peasant Land Market, pp. 185–6; Long, 'History of the manors of Mapledurham Gurney and Mapledurham Chazey', p. 126.

[181] VCH Oxon., VI, p. 337; K. J. Allison, M. W. Beresford and J. G. Hurst, The Deserted Villages of Oxfordshire, pp. 44, 45; D. Miles and T. Rowley, 'Tusmore deserted village', Oxoniensia, XLI, 1976, pp. 309–15.

[182] In the case of the one half-virgate and two of the six cottage-holdings with empty houses, tenants of other holdings had taken over the appurtenant lands (Eynsham Cartulary, ed. H. E. Salter, Oxford Hist. Soc., OS XLIX, LI, 1907–8, II, pp. 19–24).

[183] Harvey, ed., The Peasant Land Market, p. 124.

[184] Idem, Medieval Oxfordshire Village, pp. 136–7.

[185] E. M. Elvey, 'The abbot of Missenden's estates in Chalfont St Peter', Records of Bucks., XVII, 1961–5, pp. 32–3. By the beginning of the fifteenth century, however, many holdings there were vacant.

Witney (Oxon.), while Codicote (Herts.) is said to have suffered particularly in an outbreak in 1431.[186]

Whether holdings became vacant through death or through the occupants' simply leaving the manor, landlords clearly suffered persistent difficulty in finding new tenants. On some manors this difficulty became particularly severe in the late fourteenth century: at Great Wymondley (Herts.) it was felt from the 1370s on, while at Coleshill (Berks.) losses of this sort between 1394 and 1424 reduced the number of tenants from 44 to 18.[187] But in some vills too there emerged tenants who enlarged their holdings not only by taking over lands of their fellows when they fell vacant but by a more vigorous policy of purchase. The activities of, for instance, John Hyghe and his successors at Marston (Oxon.), or of the Pope family at Sotwell Stonor (Berks.) may well have contributed to the shrinkage of those places in the fifteenth century; the cases reported to the enclosure commissioners of 1517 suggest that population was often reduced as a result of this small-scale engrossment.[188]

Although shrinkage occurred throughout the region, it led to the total desertion of villages and hamlets principally in four well-defined areas. One is north-central Oxfordshire, the broad belt of the Oxford Clay Vale, running north-east from Kelmscott and Burford to the eastern border of the county, and extending southwards into Berkshire only to take in Seacourt in Wytham, Whitley in Cumnor and a few other settlements in parishes bordering the Thames.[189] Another forms a great crescent starting at the eastern border of Bedfordshire near Biggleswade, sweeping south and west up the valley of the Ivel, then turning north towards Cranfield, crossing into Buckinghamshire to include the northern half of Moulsoe hundred, then turning eastward again along the borders of both counties with Northamptonshire.[190]

---

[186] Stitt, 'Manors of Great and Little Wymondley', pp. 139–40; VCH Beds., III, p. 263; Hyde, 'Winchester manors at Witney and Adderbury', p. 175; J. Amundesham, Annales Monasterii S. Albani, ed. H. T. Riley, R.S., 1870–1, I, p. 62. Islip (Oxon.) is another village where the 1361 plague caused temporary dislocation (VCH Oxon., VI, p. 210), and in 1391 Wroxton priory claimed that its lands were almost untilled through the death in plagues of those who should be cultivating them (Cal. of Papal Letters, 1198–1492, HMSO, 1890–1960, V, p. 436).

[187] Stitt, 'Manors of Great and Little Wymondley', pp. 139–40; Harvey, ed., The Peasant Land Market, pp. 153–4.

[188] VCH Oxon., V, p. 216; Harvey, ed., The Peasant Land Market, p. 141; Leadam, ed., The Domesday of Inclosures, II, pp. 502–9, 570–9.

[189] Allison et al., Deserted Villages of Oxfordshire, passim (map at end); VCH Oxon., XI, p. 3; M. W. Beresford and J. G. Hurst, 'Introduction to a first list of deserted medieval village sites in Berkshire', Berks. Arch. J., LX, 1962, pp. 92–7; Brooks, 'Deserted medieval villages of north Berkshire', pp. 235–55 (Barcote, Carswell, Newton), pp. 461–75 (Draycott, Tubney).

[190] A. C. Chibnall, Sherington, p. 153; D. N. Hall and N. Nickerson, 'Sites on the north Bedfordshire and south Northamptonshire border', Beds. Arch. J., III, 1966, pp. 1–6; Beresford and

The third area can be roughly defined as the part of Hertfordshire lying east of Hitchin and north of Welwyn Garden City.[191] The fourth is a small cluster in or beside the eastern half of the Berkshire Downs.[192] There is no simple physical feature common to these four areas and they include a variety of soil types. But they were all areas of intensive arable cultivation, with villages and hamlets closely packed together, and it seems likely that decrease in the demand for land following the Black Death and the general shrinkage of settlements reduced some of these places to a size that made them no longer viable communities; the demands of co-aration, or the simple social and economic amenities of community life, may have imposed a certain minimum size below which a settlement was unlikely to attract new inhabitants. Labour difficulties, too, may have encouraged landlords to abandon such places.[193] Certainly the places that disappeared tended to be smaller and more impoverished than average in the tax assessments of the early fourteenth century. Some of these vulnerable villages and hamlets may have been suddenly abandoned – as Tusmore and Tilgarsley seem to have been – as a direct consequence of plague or other cataclysm. But probably the vast majority simply fell into gradual decay and desertion, a process that has been examined particularly from the archaeological evidence at Seacourt (Berks.) and from documentary sources at Brookend (Oxon.). At Seacourt reductions in tax assessments and in manorial profits point to decline in the first half of the fourteenth century, though it is worth noting that timber buildings in the village were still being replaced by stone ones early in the century. Houses excavated at Seacourt show no sign of occupation after the mid-fourteenth century; the high (50 per cent) relief on tax due in 1351 points to severe loss in the plague, and the village was probably deserted by the end of the century. In 1439 the church was ruinous and there were only two inhabited houses in the parish (both outside the village area).[194] At Brookend there may well have been some decline in the

Hurst, *Deserted Medieval Villages*, p. 183 (mapped in A. C. Jones, 'Customary land market in Bedfordshire', p. 294); D. N. Hall and J. B. Hutchings, 'The distribution of archaeological sites between the Nene and the Ouse valleys', *Beds. Arch. J.*, VII, 1972, pp. 1–16; R. H. Britnell, 'Abingdon: a lost Buckinghamshire hamlet', *Records of Bucks.*, XXII, 1980, pp. 48–51; A. C. Chibnall, *Beyond Sherington*, London, 1979, p. 154.

[191] K. R. Davis, *The Deserted Medieval Villages of Hertfordshire*, Herts. Local History Council, Occ. Paper 4, 1973, *passim* (map on pp. 10–11). These desertions are further discussed by Glennie, 'Commercializing agrarian region', pp. 25–51.

[192] Brooks, 'Deserted medieval villages of north Berkshire', pp. 136–231, 373–93, 578–637 (Compton, Eagle, Lambourn, and Wantage hundreds).

[193] As argued by A. C. Chibnall, *Sherington*, pp. 152–4.

[194] M. Biddle, 'The deserted medieval village of Seacourt, Berkshire', *Oxoniensia*, XXVI/XXVII, 1961–2, pp. 71, 80–4, 118–19; *Cal. of Papal Letters*, IX, pp. 60–1.

decades before the Black Death, which was severe enough at least to cause some economic disruption; the late fourteenth and early fifteenth centuries saw tenants leaving the manor either with formal permission or without, but at first their places were taken by newcomers and it was only from the turn of the century that vacant holdings were taken over by existing tenants, with consequent reduction in the number of landholders. The decay of the uninhabited buildings on these consolidated holdings now made it virtually impossible to attract new tenants and in the 1420s and 1430s Brookend seems to have declined fast; in 1459 a charter, by which Oseney abbey voluntarily relinquished the rectorial tithes to the vicar, mentioned the lack of parishioners and the abandonment of cultivation, and ten years later there were only four tenants there. By then "Brookend had ceased to exist as a hamlet, it was now merely a group of farms".[195]

The general shrinkage of settlement produced local changes in the occupation of the Chilterns, though not in the overall pattern of settlement there. This was not an area simply of nucleated villages; in all parishes there were also isolated farms, and in some the whole population was dispersed in scattered farms and hamlets. Here trends already visible before 1349 accentuated, leading to desertion of some farms and entire hamlets, such as Flexmore in King's Walden (Herts.) and Fastnidge near Wendover (Bucks.).[196] Where population was scattered in this way desertion of sites is far harder to trace than in areas of fully nucleated settlement, and we may suspect a similar pattern of desertion in other parts of the region, in which scattered farms and small hamlets were also important, but which have not been so carefully and thoroughly investigated as the Chilterns. Eastern and southern Berkshire is a particularly likely area.[197]

This general shrinkage, and in some areas desertion, of settlements can be seen in part as a retreat from marginal land. Where there was abandonment of sites, whether of entire villages or of single farmsteads, this must often, perhaps usually, have been because their lands were poor compared with others available in the area. Thus we find that at Seacourt the soil is either poor or apt to be waterlogged and in recent times has supported little arable cultivation; tithes from Chastleton (the parish of Brookend) in the 1340s significantly consisted of rye and

---

[195] T. H. Lloyd, 'Some documentary sidelights on the deserted Oxfordshire village of Brookend', *Oxoniensia*, XXIX/XXX, 1964–5, pp. 120–7; *Cartulary of Oseney Abbey*, ed. H. E. Salter, 6 vols., Oxford Hist. Soc., 1929–36, IV, pp. 330–2. The process of desertion in a less well documented Berkshire (now Oxfordshire) settlement is discussed by J. Brooks, 'Tubney, Oxfordshire: medieval and later settlement', *Oxoniensia*, XLIX, 1984, pp. 121–31.

[196] Roden, 'Studies', pp. 124, 302–5; Roden, 'Changing settlement', p. 68.

[197] Cf. Beresford and Hurst, 'Introduction to a first list of deserted medieval village sites in Berkshire', pp. 94–5.

dredge rather than the richer wheat and pure barley.[198] On the other hand, whereas some abandoned hamlets such as Ilbury in Deddington (Oxon.) were independent economic units with their own field systems, others like Cote in Cottisford (Oxon.) were not, and we ought perhaps to look to social as much as to economic causes for the changes that occurred in the local pattern of settlement, and to see them in part as a simple rationalization that brought a reduced population into communities of workable and acceptable size.[199] As one would expect, we find records of the desertion of churches and the union of parishes, symptoms of depopulation.[200] But there are also cases where new parishes were created, as at Hedgerley (Bucks.) in 1414 and Horley and Hornton (Oxon.) between 1438 and 1448, or where local chapels acquired rights that made them more or less independent of their mother-churches, as at Chesham Bois from 1368, Weston Underwood in 1380, and Boarstall in 1417 (all in Bucks.).[201] Some places flourished throughout the period. Stratton Audley (Oxon.), on the fringe of one of the areas where desertion of settlements occurred, became an independent parish, probably in 1455; in 1412–13 it had more customary tenants than in 1279, and manorial receipts from the early to mid-fifteenth century seem to have maintained a steady level.[202] In some places there are distinct signs of expansion late in the fifteenth century. On the Grey family's manor at Blunham (Beds.), the number of tenants rose from 65 in 1457 to 72 in 1498 and similar slight increases are recorded at Coleshill (Berks.) and Sherington (Bucks.).[203] At King's Walden (Herts.), a Chiltern parish that had suffered the loss of an entire hamlet as well as of individual dwellings both in and away from the main village, new building was going on in the 1490s.[204] Contraction, shrinkage of settlement, was widespread and may have been the norm throughout the period, but it was not universal.

Against this background there appeared, in the mid-fifteenth century, a completely new feature: the deliberate eviction of tenants –

[198] Biddle, 'Deserted medieval village of Seacourt', pp. 76–7; Lloyd, 'Some documentary sidelights', p. 119.

[199] H. M. Colvin, A History of Deddington, London, 1963, pp. 15, 86–7; VCH Oxon., VI, pp. 109, 110; cf. Davis, Deserted Villages of Hertfordshire, pp. 16–17, and B. Holden, 'The deserted medieval village of Thomley, Oxfordshire', Oxoniensia, L, 1986, p. 215.

[200] E.g. VCH Berks., II, p. 20; VCH Oxon., II, p. 18.

[201] VCH Bucks., I, p. 295; VCH Oxon., IX, p. 132. Boarstall has been reckoned a depopulated village, but this did not come about until the seventeenth century, when it played all too prominent a part in the Civil War: S. Porter, 'The Civil War destruction of Boarstall', Records of Bucks., XXVI, 1984, pp. 86–91; Local Maps and Plans from Medieval England, ed. R. A. Skelton and P. D. A. Harvey, Oxford, 1986, pp. 214–15.   [202] VCH Oxon., VI, pp. 328, 330.

[203] Harvey, ed., The Peasant Land Market, pp. 154, 197–9; A. C. Chibnall, Sherington, pp. 149, 154.   [204] Roden, 'Studies', pp. 124, 129–30.

sometimes of entire hamlets – by landlords who wished to convert their holdings to demesne sheep pastures. We have comprehensive evidence for this in the returns made to the commissioners inquiring into enclosures in 1517; but these survive for only three counties of the region – Berkshire, Buckinghamshire, and Oxfordshire – and in any case are not concerned with events before 1485.[205] On the other hand the information at our disposal from other, casual, sources suggests that the geographical range of these evictions is fairly accurately defined by the 1517 returns: they may be seen as a southward extension of the movement in Northamptonshire and Warwickshire, affecting northern and central Buckinghamshire (as far south only as the line of the Chilterns), together with the tongue of north-west Hertfordshire that extends beyond the Chilterns and, more importantly, protruding parts of eastern and northern Oxfordshire. Outside this area evictions of this sort were few and mostly on a small scale; at Milton (Berks.) the manorial staff of eighteen was reduced to two, twelve persons were evicted from two messuages at Chaddleworth (Berks.), fourteen from three messuages at Chesham (Bucks.), all in the 1490s, while Higham Gobion (Beds.) seems to have been completely depopulated between the mid-fifteenth century and 1518.[206] But if the 1517 returns accurately define the area of these evictions they probably fail to reveal the start of the movement in the region. There is doubt over the exact chronology of the process by which Sir Robert Whittingham reduced the village of Pendley, in Aldbury and Tring (Herts.), to uninhabited pastures, but his activities can certainly be dated back to the 1440s; at Attington, a deserted (and now lost) hamlet of Thame (Oxon.), the key figure seems to have been the wool-stapler Geoffrey Dormer, who acquired the manor about 1473 and who was presented for enclosing common pasture elsewhere in the parish in 1481, when his lands there were said to consist of three times as much pasture as arable.[207] Probably the movement was at least well under way in the region before 1485; this would be consistent with what we know of its progress in Northamptonshire and Warwickshire. Even just in the last fifteen years of the fifteenth century there was considerable local disruption within the area affected: the commissioners in Buckinghamshire were told of the total destruction of four hamlets and, apart from

[205] They are printed, with an introduction to each county, in Leadam, ed., *Domesday of Inclosures*, I, pp. 87–214, 319–88; from Bedfordshire there survive the returns to supplementary inquiries in 1518 (*ibid.*, II, pp. 454–76).

[206] *Ibid.*, I, pp. 111–12, 132–3, 208–9; *Visitations in the Diocese of Lincoln, 1517–1531*, ed. A. H. Thompson, Lincoln Rec. Soc., 3 vols., 1940–7, I, pp. 102–3; J. Godber, *History of Bedfordshire, 1066–1888*, p. 139; Harvey, ed., *The Peasant Land Market*, p. 179. A hamlet of Essendon (Herts.) is another possible casualty outside the main region (Davis, *Deserted Villages of Hertfordshire*, p. 15).

[207] *VCH Herts.*, II, pp. 284–5; IV, pp. 214–15; *VCH Oxon.*, VII, pp. 170, 172, 189–90.

these, of the displacement of 120 persons from one village and of 40 from another, besides many smaller-scale evictions.[208] The landlords particularly involved were substantial proprietors, with interests extending beyond a single manor: men such as Thomas Pigott, serjeant-at-law, at Grendon Underwood, Doddershall in Quainton, and Littlecote in Stewkley (all in Bucks.), or Sir Thomas Danvers of Waterstock at Chilworth in Great Milton and Golder in Pyrton (both in Oxon.).[209]

The returns of 1517 and other evidence make it clear that these evictions were combined with the conversion of arable holdings to pasture for grazing sheep. But the deliberate conversion of arable to permanent pasture will have occurred, probably much more commonly, on demesne lands as well. Thus at Garsington (Oxon.) the Louches manor in the mid-fifteenth century included 160 acres of arable and 100 acres of pasture as against 300 acres of arable and unspecified pasture in 1315.[210] Interestingly, D. V. Stern has shown that at Kinsbourne (Herts.), where Westminster abbey expanded the demesne livestock from the 1360s onwards, pastoral husbandry was indeed far more profitable than corn-growing; but this in fact had also been the case at the beginning of the century.[211] How far enlarged holdings led to a similar change to pastoral farming among manorial tenants is impossible to determine, but it seems likely that this often occurred; presentments of such tenants for letting unwanted buildings fall into disrepair can be paralleled by those reporting that lands lay untilled, and even if there is little positive proof there is a great deal of impressionistic evidence for increased sheep farming by tenants.[212] However, Faith has been able to demonstrate the importance of sheep to the villagers of Coleshill (Berks.) from the late fourteenth century onwards, a period that saw (down to 1424) a considerable drop in the tenants' numbers as holdings became concentrated in fewer hands.[213] That pasture could be much valued is shown by the limits imposed on grazing rights: in Oxfordshire 25 sheep per virgate at Shirburn (1493), 30 or 40 per virgate (with other beasts) at Great and Little Milton

---

[208] Tables in Leadam, ed., *Domesday of Inclosures*, II, pp. 570–9.

[209] *Ibid.*, I, pp. 162–5, 342; *VCH Oxon.*, VII, pp. 133–4; VIII, p. 152; Allison et al., *Deserted Villages of Oxfordshire*, pp. 34, 38. Pigott's vigorous attempts to maintain or extend the bounds of Whaddon Chase, of which he was hereditary keeper, are described in detail in *VCH Bucks.*, II, pp. 139–40.   [210] *VCH Oxon.*, V, p. 145.

[211] Stern, 'Hertfordshire manor', pp. 126–7, 207–17, 224–6, 301.

[212] E.g. *VCH Bucks.*, II, p. 61 (Fawley); *VCH Oxon.*, VI, p. 227 (Kirtlington); Harvey, *Medieval Oxfordshire Village*, pp. 117, 138 (Cuxham).

[213] Harvey, ed., *The Peasant Land Market*, pp. 153–4, 171–2; the importance of sheep to particular families is brought out in the detailed accounts of Coleshill tenants in Faith, 'The peasant land-market', pp. 158, 162, 172–4, 185.

(1500), 50 per virgate (with other beasts) at Deddington (1474).[214] It is shown too by the rule at Woodeaton (Oxon.) in 1446 that no tenant was to have any but his own sheep on the manor. And it is interesting that at St Albans (Herts.) rights of common pasture were an important issue both in the Peasants' Revolt of 1381 and in a lesser dispute in 1434.[215]

But if some arable areas were changed to pasture by deliberate conversion, others were changed rather by simple reversion from cultivation to waste. This happened particularly in the early part of the period, when settlement was shrinking as a direct consequence of plague and of landlords' failure to attract new tenants. In the years immediately after the Black Death much arable in landlords' hands was left untilled for want of tenants or a sufficient labour force on the demesne. On Harvies manor in Risley (Beds.), 300 acres of arable were said in 1351 to be of no value because "they are uncultivated and no one wants to occupy them"; at Berkhamsted (Herts.) there were lands in 1360 which were said not to have been sown since the Black Death.[216] In the Chilterns untilled areas seem to have been restored to cultivation within a few years, but elsewhere in the region this state of affairs often continued or got worse.[217] At Rollright (Oxon.) in 1363 two of the four fields were untilled. Of the 800 acres of demesne at Wymondley (Herts.) in 1373, 240 acres were under corn, 120 acres fallow by normal rotation, 100 acres were leased out to tenants, and the remaining 340 acres must have been simply left uncultivated. At Eaton Hastings (Berks.) in 1354–5 there were in demesne 400 acres of arable of which some 150 acres were fallow for pasture (apart from the area fallow by rotation); by 1388 more holdings must have come into the lord's hands, for the demesne arable was now 560 acres, of which 400 acres were fallow for pasture.[218] In such cases a new emphasis on pastoral husbandry, accepting a change in land use from arable to permanent pasture, may have been dictated by circumstances rather than a matter of choice: landlord and tenant alike would simply be putting their land to what use they could with the limited labour available to them. Sometimes they may not even have done this, and the untilled arable will have remained virtually unused; when, in 1441,

---

[214] *VCH Oxon.*, VII, p. 133; VIII, p. 189; Colvin, *History of Deddington*, p. 69.

[215] *VCH Oxon.*, V, p. 314; *VCH Herts.*, IV, pp. 202, 206–7.

[216] *VCH Beds.*, III, p. 158; *Register of Edward the Black Prince*, 4 vols., HMSO, London, 1930–3, IV, p. 353.

[217] Roden, 'Studies', pp. 275–6; Baker and Butlin, eds., *Field Systems*, pp. 327–8. But cf. Roden, 'Demesne farming in the Chiltern Hills', *AHR*, XVII, 1969, pp. 18–19, 20–1.

[218] *Eynsham Cartulary*, ed. Salter, II, pp. 59–60 (this may, of course, have been a consequence of the plague of 1361–2); Stitt, 'Manors of Great and Little Wymondley', p. 85; J. Brooks, 'Eaton Hastings: a deserted medieval village', *Berks. Arch. J.*, LXIV, 1969, pp. 4–5.

a tenant of two virgates in the decaying hamlet of Brookend (Oxon.) gave up his holding and had his chattels impounded for building repairs he had only 12 acres of his 64-acre holding under crop, but his livestock consisted of no more than 16 ewes, 14 lambs, 3 cows, 2 calves, 2 horses and 2 foals.[219] Cases where it is clear that land was untilled through necessity, not choice, recur throughout the period. At Wretchwick in Bicester (Oxon.), in 1433–4, low receipts from manorial rents were explained by the tenants' poverty and by much land being untilled. At Upper Heyford (Oxon.) in 1484 most tenants held part of their holdings in *vaccantlonde* at a lower rent than the rest.[220] These are interesting instances because they come from the fringe of the area where in the second half of the fifteenth century there was deliberate conversion to pasture accompanied by eviction of tenants. They underline how little we still know of the extent or the causes of the change from arable to pasture, and how far these varied between different areas, between different classes of landholder, and between different parts of the period. We can only be certain that over the region as a whole the proportion of permanent pasture to ploughed land was substantially greater in 1500 than it had been in 1350.

That the value attached to pasture varied a good deal is shown by instances both of planting new woods and of converting woodland to pasture. A new wood had been recently planted at Kirtlington (Oxon.) in 1476.[221] At King's Walden (Herts.), woods were reduced to open pasture and at Islip (Oxon.) tenants illicitly used woodland for pasture even though former arable was apparently lying waste.[222] Even the assart of woodland had not entirely died out in the early part of the period; at Charlbury, in the Wychwood area of north-west Oxfordshire, it reached a peak in the 1370s, though it declined in the 1390s, and in Bernwood Forest, in Buckinghamshire, woods were being felled in 1460.[223] Probably, though, the period saw an increasing sense of the importance and value of woodlands throughout the region. Woods played, of course, a particularly important part in the economy of the Chilterns. The south-west and central areas of the hills were thickly wooded, and here the use of the woods tended to be casual; thus at Ibstone (Bucks.), basically a corn-producing manor, the woods were treated as a financial reserve and timber was normally sold only if corn

[219] Lloyd, 'Some documentary sidelights', p. 127.

[220] *VCH Oxon.*, VI, pp. 27, 200 (it need not follow, as suggested there, that because this *vaccantlonde* had been let it had therefore been brought back into cultivation again).

[221] *VCH Oxon.*, VI, p. 220.

[222] Roden, 'Studies', pp. 129–30; D. Roden, 'Woodland and its management in the medieval Chilterns', *Forestry*, XLI, 1968, p. 68; *VCH Oxon.*, VI, pp. 210, 212.

[223] *VCH Oxon.*, X, p. 140; *CPR, 1452–61*, p. 631.

sales were particularly low, if manorial expenses were particularly high, or if trees had been blown down. At the north-east end of the Chilterns woods were fewer and felling tended to be organized on a systematic rotation, as at King's Walden (Herts.) in the fifteenth century. But woodland was exploited in many parts of the region besides the Chilterns. North Mimms (Herts.), for instance, was thickly wooded until the lord of the manor in the mid- or late fifteenth century cut down much of its timber, presumably for immediate profit.[224]

Several areas imparked under royal licence in this period included woodland, perhaps for the timber, which would be endangered by common grazing rights, as well as for the cover it offered to game. Thus, as an example consisting entirely of woodland, Roger de Louthe was given permission in 1360 to impark two woods at Oxhey in Watford (Herts.). Cases of licensed imparking, though few in number, come from all parts of the region: at Chalgrave (Beds.) in 1365, at Olney (Bucks.) in 1374, at Minster Lovell (Oxon.) in 1441, at Yattendon (Berks.) in 1448, and so on.[225] Some half-dozen cases along the east and south border of Hertfordshire from Albury to Rickmansworth and dating from 1360 to 1447 form a cluster that may be significant.[226] In an earlier period licence to impark might mean no more than simple enclosure of an area, enabling a landlord to extinguish common grazing rights over land that he continued to cultivate as arable; such had been the case on the bishop of Lincoln's demesnes at Banbury in 1330.[227] But there is no demonstrable case of this occurring in the present period, and imparking now, with or without royal licence, probably simply extended or added to the already large number of private parks in the region. John Amundesham, the St Albans chronicler, describes the creation of a park by private agreement, also on the south border of Hertfordshire, at Tyttenhanger in Ridge. The abbot of St Albans, after a dispute with Thomas Knollys, lord of North Mimms, about rights of way and rights of rounding up and impounding animals grazing on the heath there, came to an agreement in 1430 which allowed him to enclose 30 acres near his manor house at Tyttenhanger; then, having got the local copyholders

---

[224] Roden, 'Studies', pp. 128, 257–9, 355–7; Roden, 'Field systems in Ibstone', p. 45; Roden, 'Woodland and its managment', pp. 65–6; VCH Herts., II, p. 254.

[225] CChR, 1341–1417, p. 167; Godber, History of Bedfordshire, p. 81; VCH Bucks., IV, p. 432; CPR, 1436–41, p. 376; CChR, 1427–1516, p. 100.

[226] At Oxhey (1360: CChR, 1341–1417, p. 167), Albury and Braughing (1366: ibid., p. 192), Essendon (1406: ibid., p. 430), Rickmansworth and Watford (1426: CPR, 1422–9, p. 351), Stanstead Abbots (1443: CChR, 1427–1516, p. 38; R. T. Andrews, 'The Rye House Castle and manor of Rye', East Herts. Arch. Soc., II, 1902–4, pp. 32–3; VCH Herts., III, pp. 367, 370), Sawbridgeworth and Thorley (1448: CChR, 1427–1516, p. 98).

[227] VCH Oxon., X, p. 50.

to surrender their rights over the adjacent meadows and pastures, the abbot turned the whole area into a park which he stocked with deer. The chronicler breaks into twenty lines of verse to describe the abbot's pleasure in his new park.[228]

H. KENT AND SUSSEX

By the mid-fourteenth century the pressure of population had pushed cultivation into hilly and marginal land in the depths of the High Weald.[229] After the Black Death, however, on some manors assarting virtually ceased. On other manors arable land continued to be claimed from the waste until 1400, although both the pace and scale of assarting was considerably less than it had been a century earlier. As the population fell in the fifteenth century, not only was little new land brought under the plough, but in many places the area under cultivation shrank. Land was converted from arable to pasture or else reverted to scrub and waste. Contraction, however, was not uniform throughout the region. On some of the fertile lands of east Kent the reduction in arable was slight. In contrast on the southern, coastal marshes of Sussex the combined onslaught of French raids and repeated flooding left vast tracts lying waste. Even when population levels began to rise in parts of the area towards the end of the fifteenth century, the coastal marshes of Sussex remained denuded of people and the conversion to pasture was not reversed. In parts of the Kentish Weald, on the other hand, the number of inhabitants increased at the end of the century, as smallholders took advantage of the opportunity for employment in the burgeoning cloth and tanning industries. There thorn bushes were eradicated and some land was brought back into use again.

Despite the severe mortality over much of Kent and Sussex in 1348–9, very little tenant land remained in the hands of a lord for more than a few years. Women, minors, collateral relatives or neighbours were willing to take up holdings at the old rents and services. But arable farming was badly hit by a severe drought in the early 1350s. Yields were halved on some demesne manors and it is exceedingly likely that peasant farmers suffered as much, if not more.[230] Acreage under cultivation was cut back by lack of seed corn as well as by lack of

---

[228] Amundesham, *Annales Monasterii S. Albani*, ed. Riley, I, pp. 254–62; cf. H. Fowler, 'Tyttenhanger', *St Albans Archit. and Arch. Soc.*, 1893–4, p. 36, and *VCH Herts.*, II, p. 387.

[229] For an excellent and detailed description of this process of assarting in east Sussex, see P. F. Brandon, 'Medieval clearances in the East Sussex Weald', *Institute of British Geographers*, XLVIII, 1969, pp. 135–53.

[230] M. Mate, 'Agrarian economy after the Black Death: the manors of Canterbury cathedral priory, 1348–91', *EcHR*, 2nd ser. XXXVII, 1984, pp. 341–54.

workers. Later, in the 1360s and early 1370s harvests in Kent were reduced by outbreaks of mildew and other fungoid diseases. In addition, wages, although held down by the Statute of Labourers, remained above the pre-plague level. Faced with such problems, it is not surprising that so many landholders, both lords and peasants, converted at least some of their land from arable to pasture, especially when animal and wool prices rose markedly. In the period 1365–74, for example, oxen, cows, and even pigs sold for at least 25 per cent and frequently 75 per cent more than in the decade before the Black Death. Wool prices, during most of the seventies, stood at a higher level than at any time since the 1320s. Thus any goods sent to markets produced higher revenues than in the past.

In some places lords built up their sheep flocks and cow herds to utilize the new pasture, but, in other areas, they preferred to rent it out. The monks of Christ Church, Canterbury, for example, on their marsh manor of Barksore in north Kent, cut the acreage under the plough by a third (from 95 to 32 acres), but doubled the size of the sheep flock and cow herd there. At Lydden, in Thanet, on the other hand, the monks kept approximately the same numbers of animals as before the Black Death. The serjeant, however, ploughed no land at all after 1364 and rented out the additional pasture. In 1356 the manor housed 500 "foreign sheep" and pasture revenues averaged £24 a year in the late 1360s and early 1370s. Peasants and local butchers were surely taking advantage of the high meat and wool prices and keeping more animals than before. By the 1420s, as more grass became available with the steady retreat of arable cultivation within the marshes, the demand for the Lydden pasture lessened. Agistment dues averaged just £15 a year. None the less neighbouring townsmen from Deal and Sandwich still needed to fatten their stock on the rich Lydden marshes. Butchers and other townsmen lived in a symbiotic relationship with the monks and their tenants. They would buy young stock from local farmers, then rent the pasture needed to fatten the animals, before selling the meat to their neighbours. A similar situation occurred around the other Cinque Ports and towns such as Battle.[231]

Contraction in acreage under the plough is easiest to document for demesne farms, but with so few accounts surviving it is impossible to plot any clear-cut regional chronology. In north Kent, on the manor of Otford, belonging to the archbishop of Canterbury, the area under cultivation had been cut by the 1350s and remained at this new lower level, with some minor fluctuations, until the manor was farmed out in

---

[231] M. Mate, 'Pastoral farming in south-east England in the fifteenth century', *EcHR*, 2nd ser. XL, 1987, pp. 523–36. See also Searle, *Lordship and Community*, p. 337; A. F. Butcher, 'The origins of Romney freemen, 1483–1523', *EcHR*, 2nd ser. XXVII, 1974, pp. 16–27.

the 1440s.[232] In contrast, on the Battle abbey manor of Alciston, in Sussex, in the 1380s arable farming revived temporarily. Grassland was again brought under the plough and the serjeant sowed 450 to 475 acres a year. The revival, however, was short-lived. By the first decade of the fifteenth century the acreage had been cut by a hundred and it continued to fall, reaching its lowest point, 190 acres, in the mid-1470s.[233] On the other Sussex manors of Battle Abbey the contraction was not so steep, but was still significant. At Lullington 283 acres were sown in 1393–4 and by the time of the last accounts in the 1460s an average of 194 acres were being sown.[234] At Apuldram 209 acres were sown in 1421–2, but by the end of the decade the acreage was halved, before slowly climbing back to an average of 177 acres in the 1440s and 1450s.[235]

On all these manors it was the acreage under oats and legumes that was cut the first and hardest, with the area under wheat and barley remaining relatively stable. Thus at Apuldram, in 1421–2, the serjeant sowed 40 acres of oats and 53 acres of peas and vetch. A few years later he sowed just 16 acres of oats and 20 acres of peas and vetch.[236] Similarly, at Lullington, in 1393–4, oats occupied 23 acres and peas and vetch 35 acres; by 1459–60 just 2 acres of oats and 2 acres of peas and vetch were sown. At Alciston, in the decade 1380–90, 30 per cent of the arable area had been devoted to legumes and oats. By the mid-1470s, however, the sowing of oats and legumes there was negligible – 6 acres of oats, 8 acres of peas and vetch, and 6 acres of beans – compared to 38 acres of oats and 71 acres of peas and vetch sown in 1399. So too at Otford the production of oats declined steadily from 1418 and by 1432 the sowing of legumes had almost ceased. Very little of this unused land was let out to tenants; it appears to have reverted to pasture or waste.

The profits of pasture farming, however, collapsed in the mid-fifteenth century. The winding down of the Hundred Years' War reduced the overseas market. Major outbreaks of sheep disease reduced the size of many flocks over an 11-year period, 1426–37. The bottom fell out of the wool market in the 1440s and 1450s as English trading relations with the Hanse, Burgundy, and France worsened. Not only did wool prices drop, but producers had a hard time finding buyers. On a number of manors wool accumulated unsold.[237] Small tenant farmers

[232] F. R. H. Du Boulay, 'Late continued demesne farming at Otford', Arch. Cant., LXXIII, 1959, pp. 116–24.

[233] P. F. Brandon, 'Arable farming on a scarp-foot parish during the late Middle Ages', Sussex Arch. Colls., C, 1962, pp. 60–72; Judith A. Brent, 'Alciston manor in the later middle ages', Sussex Arch. Colls., CVI, 1968, pp. 89–102.   [234] PRO SC 6/1025/5; 1027/12–15.

[235] PRO SC 6/1017/17.   [236] PRO SC 6/1017/24.

[237] Mate, 'Pastoral farming in south-east England', p. 527.

clearly suffered as much as the great lords. Giles Page at Alciston, for example, held a tenement with two gardens, three crofts and 21 acres in the common fields. In the 1440s and 1450s he was keeping large numbers of sheep – in 1451 he was cited for trespassing with 100 sheep. In 1463, however, Giles "on account of his poverty" relinquished his building called the Sheephouse and most of his land and refused to hold it any longer. The land stayed in the hands of Battle abbey for the next two years and the steward was able to find a taker only by offering special concessions.[238] Page cannot have been alone in his difficulties, for a slump in the demand for pasture that had begun in the 1430s continued and in some places deepened in the 1440s and 1450s. To give but one example: on the Duchy of Lancaster's manor of Willingdon, revenues from the sale of meadow had gone up in the early fifteenth century from £17 to £21 and those from the sale of pasture from £4 to £12. In the 1440s, receipts from the sale of meadow fell below the late fourteenth-century level and receipts from the sale of pasture dropped to £7 7s. 5d.[239]

Behind this collapse lay a marked down-turn in population that reduced both the home market and the demand for land. Plague visited southern England repeatedly in the early fifteenth century.[240] The 1430s, moreover, was a decade of exceptionally bad weather. In 1434 a hard frost gripped the country that lasted until February. Bay trees and tender herbs were killed; a multitude of birds and fowls died from hunger and many old people died from the cold and the scarcity of wood and coal.[241] The following year was just as bad and according to the *Great Chronicle* bread was frozen so hard together that unless men thawed it by the fire they could not eat it, nor cut it with a knife, but hewed at it with an axe or hatchet.[242] Two years later, in 1438, the wheat harvest in many places was just over half the normal amount.[243]

---

[238] PRO E 315/56; East Sussex RO, SAS G18/48. The new renter, William atte Forde, paid a low entry fine of 6s. 8d. and the annual rent was reduced from 24s. 9d. to 15s. 10d. "because of the weakness of the tenement and the land and the scarcity of tenants".

[239] PRO DL 29/441/7098, 442/7106, 442/7114.

[240] Hatcher, 'Mortality in the fifteenth century', pp. 19–38.

[241] *Brut or the Chronicles of England*, ed. Friedrich W. D. Brie, 1908, EETS, OS CXXXII, p. 467; *Great Chronicle of London*, ed. A. H. Thomas and I. D. Thornley, London, 1938, p. 171; *Chronicles of London*, ed. Charles Lethbridge Kingsford (reprinted 1977), p. 137; *English Chronicle of the Reigns of Richard II, Henry IV and Henry V*, ed. John Sylvester Davies, Camden OS LXIV, 1856, p. 55; *The Historical Collection of a Citizen of London in the Fifteenth Century*, ed. J. Gairdner, Camden NS XVII, 1876, p. 178.   [242] *Great Chronicle*, p. 173.

[243] On the Christ Church manor of Barton (Kent), where the wheat yielded, on average, four times the seed, the harvest of 1438 produced just over 6 bushels an acre (1.65 × seed): Cathedral Archives and Library, Canterbury, Caruca Bertona roll 25. On the archiepiscopal manor of Otford the oats yield was normal, but barley yielded 83 per cent and wheat just half of normal: Lambeth Palace Library ED 83. Similarly on the Winchester estates the wheat harvest of 1438 was

Nearly all the chroniclers complained of the great scarcity and the consequent high price of wheat.[244] Prices of rye and barley rose likewise and the poor had to make bread using peas and beans, vetch, and even, in some places, bracken and fern roots. Consequently many people in 1438 may well have died as a result of inadequate food. Furthermore shortages and high prices continued throughout the next year as well, with the price of wheat rising in London in 1439 to 3s. 4d. a bushel (26s. 8d. a quarter). Not surprisingly other prices, including flesh and fish, rose concomitantly and the poor continued to go hungry.

The evidence of rents and services suggests that in mid-century much of the countryside was suffering from an acute shortage of people. In many places land lay unoccupied for lack of a renter. Lords, however, especially in Kent, were very unwilling to give up their rights and make new rentals, permanently reducing their rents. Instead each year they granted the rent collector a respite for rents that could not be collected. Since these concessions were respites, not allowances, they were carried forward as part of the arrears. Thus on the Battle abbey manor of Wye the arrears of 1463–4 amounted to £401 9s. 5½d., but these had been accumulating for twenty years. The amount that was lost each year was roughly £6 5s. – 8 per cent of the total rents.[245] High arrears also accumulated on the archiepiscopal lands. In the late 1420s the arrears at Otford came to £256 19s. 9d. Even though the reeve there was regularly allowed 50s. for loss of rents, this allowance was not sufficient, and, by the 1450s he was petitioning for a further allowance of 42s. "for the loss of different lands and rents lying in the hands of the lord and no way could they be levied". After petitioning in vain for nine years, his claims were heard and in 1460–1 the regular allowance went up to £4 12s. 2d. – just under 31 per cent of the assized rents of £14 17s. 6d.[246] Other archiepiscopal manors had similar problems and even manors very close to London, such as Lambeth, had some difficulty finding tenants for all their properties. So too the reeves on the estates of Canterbury Cathedral priory regularly received an allowance for rents that could not be collected, either for lack of tenants or because no one knew where the property lay.

55.5 per cent of the long-term yield ratio: D. L. Farmer, 'Grain yields on the Winchester manors in the later middle ages', *EcHR*, 2nd ser. xxx, 1977, p. 558.

[244] According to the *Brut* (p. 472) in 1437–8 a bushel of wheat which normally sold for 6d. or 7d. a bushel was selling for 20d. or 2s., and at the end of the year for 26d. (17s. 4d. a quarter). In London, according to the *Great Chronicle* (p. 174), wheat was even selling for 3s. a bushel (24s. a quarter). [245] PRO SC 6/905/20.

[246] Lambeth Palace Library, ED 859, 1240, 1241, 1243. The 50s. regular allocation included a watermill previously worth 7s. and currently totally broken, a smithy or workshop (*fabrica*) in the hands of the lord and occupied by the dogs of the kennel, and at least 13 acres of land lying untilled and being used for pasture.

In parts of Sussex, however, landlords like Syon abbey were prepared to reduce rents in order to attract tenants. On its manor of Ecclesden, for example, the first sign of distress occurred in 1420–1. That year the loss of rents was 22s. 10d., for a virgate which used to rent for 10s. was now 7s. 6d. and other tenements were in the hands of the lord and produced nothing. In the next few years the situation worsened with land remaining for a while in the hands of the lord and then being let out at lower rents. Although the amount of the new rent obviously varied from person to person, in many cases the new tenant paid just two-thirds of the former rent. In 1430–1 the abbess and convent recognized the changed situation and made a new rental that was £3 11s. below the earlier one. Unfortunately this concession did not end the abbey's problems, for that year three more holdings came into the reeve's hands and could not be rented out. When tenants were found for the unoccupied land, they often paid only half the earlier rent. Thus a tenement which had rented for 10s. was re-let for 5s. and a croft which had brought in 12d. was rented for 6d. Once again in 1443–4 another new rental was made in which the assized rents were £6 14s. below the early fifteenth-century level – a drop of 15.36 per cent.[247] The rents never recovered. Although a third, downward readjustment to the rents was made in 1459, the reeve was still allowed 21s. 8d. for loss of rents as late as 1483.[248]

Although not all manors suffered to this extent, in most places some land lay unoccupied, at least for a few years, before eventually being taken up at the same or reduced rents. The new tenants, however, often held other land and were not interested in maintaining the buildings on their new holding. Over and over again court rolls cited tenants for keeping "ruinous" buildings and threatened forfeiture if repairs were not made. Such threats remained for the most part unsubstantiated, for new tenants could not be found. Yet if buildings were abandoned, the holding was not. Hedgerows were often maintained, when former arable reverted to rough but enclosed grazing.[249] None the less in east Sussex, nearly every settlement at the scarp foot of the downs, from Beddingham in the west to Alfriston in the east, showed at least some evidence of shrinkage. On the other hand very few totally deserted medieval villages have been identified in either Kent or Sussex. The majority of these came from the southern coastal regions that were subject to the combined onslaught of French raids, repeated floods and

[247] PRO SC 6/1032/24, 1033/7, 1034/1.   [248] PRO SC 6/1035/16.

[249] This process is well described by C. F. Tebbutt, 'A deserted medieval farm settlement at Faulkners Farm, Hartfield', Sussex Arch. Colls., cxix, 1981, pp. 107–16. The settlement, which consisted of houses and farm buildings, had been established in the late twelfth or early thirteenth century and survived until the mid-fourteenth century.

the persistent pressure of the sea. At least ten sites in Sussex, including Hydneye and Northeye on the Pevensey levels, were destroyed by coastal erosion during the period 1350–1450.[250]

These coastal districts, in the early fourteenth century, had contained some of the most productive cornland in the region.[251] Although sheep keeping was important, much of the land was sown, with oats as the main crop, but substantial acreages of wheat and beans were also grown. Yet a reduction in the acreage occurred even before the Black Death. According to the *Nonarum Inquisitiones* more than 5,600 formerly cultivated acres in Sussex were lying untilled in 1341.[252] In some places the jurors blamed French raiders, who had destroyed property and killed villagers. Elsewhere they attributed the contraction to the sterility of the soils or the poverty of the parishioners. In addition a further 3,500 acres had been flooded by the sea. Such problems continued to affect the coast of both Kent and Sussex in the late fourteenth century. In 1374, for example, some of the sea walls along the Kentish coast collapsed under the force of the tide and on the Christ Church manor of Ebony much of the land was destroyed by salt water. Later, in 1380, "men from the galleys" set fire to the shops of Appledore, destroyed the hay, burned the bridge and the dairy and took five calves and two pipes of cider.[253] Floods also attacked the Sussex coast.[254] Yet, despite these disasters, arable farming continued to form an important component in the economy of the marshland. Indeed, at Appledore the area under cultivation increased with the inning of a new marsh. So too, at Barnhorne in Sussex, in the 1380s and 1390s, beans, oats, and wheat were still being sown on a substantial scale.[255]

Renewed flooding in the first half of the fifteenth century reduced revenues on coastal manors within Kent. Although most of the marshes had been inned, the sewers were not always well maintained and became obstructed with sand, mud, grass, and other filth.[256] The heavy

[250] M. W. Beresford, *Lost Villages of England*, pp. 358–9. See also G. R. Burleigh, 'An introduction to deserted medieval villages in East Sussex', *Sussex Arch. Colls.*, CXI, 1973, pp. 45–83; G. R. Burleigh, 'Further notes on deserted and shrunken medieval villages in Sussex', *Sussex Arch. Colls.*, CXIV, 1976, pp. 61–8.

[251] A. J. F. Dulley, 'The level and port of Pevensey in the Middle Ages', *Sussex Arch. Colls.*, CIV, 1966, pp. 36–7.   [252] Baker, 'Evidence in the *Nonarum Inquisitiones*', p. 523.

[253] Mate, 'Agrarian economy after the Black Death', pp. 349–50.

[254] P. F. Brandon, 'Late medieval weather in Sussex and its agricultural significance', *Institute of British Geographers*, LIV, 1971, p. 5.

[255] P. F. Brandon, 'Agriculture and the effects of floods and weather at Barnhorne in Sussex during the later middle ages', *Sussex Arch. Colls.*, CIX, 1971, p. 82.

[256] Sir William Dugdale, *The History of Imbanking and Draining of Divers Fens and Marshes*, 2nd edn, London, 1872, p. 97; see also L. F. Salzman, 'The Inning of Pevensey Level', *Sussex Arch. Colls.*, LIII, 1910, pp. 32–60.

rains of the late 1420s and 1430s therefore caused extreme flooding. On the Christ Church manor of Ebony, for example, the situation was so bad in 1436–7 that no pasture was available for the animals and the farmer of the lands delivered his stock back to the priory. Not surprisingly the value of the farm dropped from £22 to £13 6s. 8d.[257] Each year the monks of Canterbury Cathedral priory were forced to spend substantial sums on repairs to sea walls, yet their rents and farms continued to fall, as land, flooded by the sea, became less valuable. By 1453–4 the farms of five Christ Church marsh manors – Appledore, Lydden, Agney, Orgarswick, Ebony – totalled just £180 13s. 4d., whereas earlier in 1410–11 they had reached £223. This drop of approximately 18.8 per cent is far higher than the loss in revenues of 5.6 per cent that the priory experienced on its other Kent manors. Since all the manors were leased out, however, it is impossible to determine the extent to which the lessee maintained or changed the old balance between arable and pastoral farming. But at Appledore the "farm" was, in fact, frequently paid in kind, not money. In 1428–9 the farmer supplied 240 wethers, 27 bullocks, 200 geese, 100 quarters of beans, and 100 quarters of oats. Thereafter the farm, when it was paid in kind, was always paid in the form of cheese and stock – some combination of wethers, geese and bullocks.[258] This suggests, although it is by no means conclusive, that arable farming may have become less important at Appledore.

Certainly in Sussex these early fifteenth-century floods not only reduced revenues, but in some places produced an almost total conversion from arable to pasture farming. According to P. F. Brandon, "the final coup de grâce for the Battle Abbey marsh manor of Barnhorne came with the devastating floods of the 1420s, which effectively terminated the old farming economy altogether".[259] Sheep/corn husbandry was gradually replaced by the rearing and fattening of cattle to supply the abbey table. Elsewhere with few demesne accounts available, it is harder to determine what changes, if any, were taking place, but the down-turn in revenues is clear. In the last years of Richard II's reign the demesne lands of Pevensey were leased for £20 a year. On the coming of Henry IV these lands were given to Sir John Pelham, constable of Pevensey Castle, and not accounted for again until 1438–9. By that time the demesne was being leased in fairly small parcels and the total revenues came to £13 2s. 2d. These receipts went steadily down until in 1442–3 just £10 3s. 10d. was received.[260] The main reason for this decline was that much of the land

---

[257] Cathedral Archives and Library, Canterbury, Prior's roll 7.
[258] Lambeth Palace Library, ED 201, 202, 203, 204.
[259] Brandon, 'Agriculture and the effects of floods at Barnhorne', p. 83.
[260] PRO DL 29/441/7098, 442/7117.

Table 2.12. *Number of male inhabitants paying the tithing penny in five Wealden parishes, 1444–87*

	Waldron	Hoathly	Laughton	Chiddingly	Ripe
Fixed fine	60	60	120	120	120
1444	33	26	46	50	68
1487	35	19	27	47	59

was flooded and produced nothing. Land that escaped in 1438–9 was often flooded in the next few years. Thus seventeen acres which had rented for 26s. 8d. in the past, rented for 13s. 4d. in 1438–9 and nothing in 1439–40. Even though some areas dried out and could be rented again, this land, always in imminent danger from the sea, was never the most desirable and parcels remained in the hands of the lord "because no one wished to lease them". For demand was lessened as the population within the marshland fell more sharply than in many other parts of the region.

The clearest evidence for the actual number of male inhabitants in any one area comes from tithing data, recording the payment of a "common fine" or "tithing penny". Originally set at one penny for each male member of the tithing, these payments, in the late fourteenth century, had sometimes been commuted into fixed sums, paid annually by the community as a whole. In the 1440s, in many parts of Sussex, men refused to pay this fine on the grounds that it was too great a burden now that the land had become depopulated. They demanded that from henceforth the fine should be levied at the old rate of one penny a head. Where this request was granted, it is possible to chart year by year the number of adult males over the age of twelve actually paying the tithing penny. Such totals, of course, do not show the total population of an area, for women, clerics, wealthy freemen and migrant workers were excluded along with under-age children. Moreover some men evaded for many years the responsibility of joining the tithing. None the less L. R. Poos, in his detailed study of similar data for Essex, has concluded that it does provide a fairly accurate reflection of the resident tenant population.[261] If that is indeed the case, then it is possible to gauge both the magnitude of the population decline by the mid-fifteenth century and the fluctuations thereafter. Assuming that the fixed common-fine payments approximated to an earlier population level, then in a number of Wealden communities it had fallen by a half or more in the mid-1440s, but remained at that level, with some minor fluctuations, for the next forty

[261] L. R. Poos, 'The rural population of Essex', p. 526.

Table 2.13. *Total number of male inhabitants paying the tithing penny in Aquila honour, Sussex, 1442–1529*

Year	Total number	Year	Total number
Fixed fine	6,700		
1442–3	1,497	1496–7	954
1444–5	1,441	1497–8	1,013
1445–6	1,496	1498–9	1,007
1446–7	1,371	1499–1500	1,006
1449–50	1,451	1500–1	1,063
1450–1	1,364	1502–3	1,069
1453–4	1,389	1504–5	1,089
1454–5	1,237	1505–6	1,053
1455–6	1,088	1510–11	1,033
1456–7	1,078	1516–17	1,085
1459–60	1,079	1517–18	1,055
1460–1	1,160	1520–1	1,215
1461–2	1,214	1521–2	1,136
1462–3	1,151	1522–3	1,001
1485–6	997	1523–4	903
1489–90	1,026	1524–5	937
1491–2	969	1526–7	861
1494–5	961	1527–8	805
1495–6	992	1528–9	750

years (see Table 2.12). In contrast, in the marshlands of east Sussex the population, which had already fallen drastically by the 1440s, continued to fall. By 1485–6 five hundred fewer people paid the tithing penny than in 1442–3 (see Table 2.13). The numbers had not recovered by the end of the century.[262] Part of the reason for the decline could simply be that more people were being exempted or refusing to pay; but that factor alone can hardly account for a drop of 33 per cent. Significant numbers of people must have died or left the neighbourhood for places where opportunities were more favourable.

In the 1460s and again in the 1480s floods devastated many of the southern coastal districts. The sea walls of Appledore were breached in the late 1460s. Some land, such as 100 acres of marsh at Bekard, was

---

[262] See PRO DL 29/442/7117 for the petition to the king requesting relief and the subsequent grant of payment of a penny a person. The loss of revenues was significant. The old assessment had been £26 19s. 8d. and in 1442–3 just £5 17s. 7d. was received. Nine hundreds were involved. The total amount paid by each was usually written in a different coloured ink from the repeated recitation of the royal concession and thus strongly suggests that these figures reflect the actual sums received.

totally submerged, and the former lessee refused to pay the rent of £10 a year after 1465–6.[263] At the same time, on the Christ Church manor of Appledore itself, the rent dropped from £100 to £48 13s. 4d.[264] In 1467–8 the priory spent £39 9s. 3½d. on repairs to sea walls, but this was probably only a small fraction of the total cost of their repair, for, in the obituary of Prior Goldstone I (1449–68) it was claimed that he had spent more than £1,200 defending the lands of the manor of Appledore from the sea.[265] Although the other priory marsh manors were affected to a lesser extent, they did not escape entirely and the tenant at Agney sought an allowance of £5 for grain that had been lost by the inundation of water. Similarly on the Syon abbey manor of Hampton the nuns in 1477–8 paid 72s. 6d. in regard to different tenants because the sea had flooded both the land and the grain stacked in granges. In 1483–4 they allowed £4 18s. 5d. because the irruptions of the sea had damaged different lands so that they rented for less.[266] Three hundred acres of Thomas Sackville's land at Highlant were also drowned.[267] In the area around Pevensey the rents for pasture which had begun to rise in the early 1460s dropped back in 1469–70 as land was flooded by the sea and produced nothing. Thereafter the situation deteriorated still further. In 1485–6, although the actual charged rents came to £11 11s., the reeve was allowed a further £5 1s. for rents that could not be collected.[268]

The slump in pasture revenues at Pevensey lasted until almost the end of the century and even then the recovery was only partial. In 1491–2 the reeve was still being allowed £5 1s. for loss of rents of land that was flooded and a further £1 13s. 4d. for lands the rent of which had been reduced.[269] After the mid-1490s, however, a few rents were restored to their former level. In 1438–9 52 acres in Cokemoresaltes had been leased to John Slegge for 40s. (just over 9d. an acre). The following year the lease was transferred to someone else and the rent increased to 46s. 8d. But then the land was flooded and produced nothing. When it was finally leased again, to Sir Roger Fiennes, he paid just 20s. This pasture then remained in the hands of the Fiennes family, at that low rent, until 1495–6 when a new lessee, Stephen Porter, agreed to pay 45s. Within a few years, by 1497–8, Thomas Fiennes, the new Lord Dacre, had recovered the use of Cokemoresaltes, but he had

---

[263] Lambeth Palace Library, ED 1195. The lessee – the monks of Canterbury Cathedral priory – had rented the land from the archbishop of Canterbury.

[264] Cathedral Archives and Library, Canterbury, Prior's roll 11.

[265] BL Arundel Ms. 68, f.5. He did not build as much as he would have liked because he was prevented both by the calamitous times and the "unaccustomed inundations of water in the maritime manors". [266] PRO SC 6/1035/13, 1035/16.

[267] Salzman, 'Inning of Pevensey level', p. 50. [268] PRO DL 29/443/7137.

[269] PRO DL 29/444/7139.

to pay 40s. a year, double the rent his father was paying a few years before, although no more than the old rent of the early fifteenth century. Similarly when Fiennes, in 1506–7, took over a further portion of pasture – 60 acres in Queensaltes – he paid a higher rent than the former lessee and one that equalled the rent of the late fourteenth century.[270] A number of other parcels, however, never recovered their former prosperity. Three hundred acres called New Land, for example, had been rented by Lewes priory for 50s. 2d. But after this land was flooded in the 1480s the priory naturally refused to pay any rent and for many years the land lay unused. Eventually, in 1505–6, the priory recovered at its "great cost and expense" 92 of the 300 acres and was charged only the low rent of 15s. 2d. (not quite 2d. an acre).[271] It is, of course, quite possible that duchy officials were being unaggressive and failing to charge economic rents. But in the north duchy officials showed no such disinclination. Surely southern officials would have increased more rents, if the condition of the land and the market had allowed it.[272]

These late fifteenth-century floods undoubtedly hastened the process started in the beginning of the century of moving from an arable to a pastoral economy. By the mid-sixteenth century most of the Sussex marshland was in the hands of absentee landlords and was used principally for summer grazing. A comparison of rentals for the manor of Pevensey in the mid-fourteenth and the mid-sixteenth century shows an increase in the average size of tenant holdings and a decrease in the number of dwellings on the manor.[273] The town of Pevensey also declined in size and commercial activity. Barns, stables, and gardens began to occupy the sites of former houses. As less land was brought under the plough, so the chances for employment decreased, and more and more people left the area (see Table 2.13).[274] The situation on the Kentish marshland appears to have been somewhat similar, although arable husbandry retained its importance longer. Clearly land was still being cultivated in the late fifteenth century.

[270] PRO DL 29/442/7114–6, 442/7119, 444/7151. In the depth of the slump, in 1438–9, these 60 acres in Queensaltes had rented for just 26s. 8d. Then the rent slowly climbed until from 1463 to 1506 it was set at 60s. 8d. Thomas Fiennes paid £4.

[271] PRO DL 29/454/7329. Similarly in 1516–17 36 acres in Ilonde that had remained without tenants for many years finally found a taker, but at the very low rent of 3s. 4d., whereas before the floods the same land had leased for 23s. and even earlier at 33s. 4d.

[272] *Duchy of Lancaster's Estates in Derbyshire, 1485–1540*, ed. I. S. W. Blanchard, Derbs. Arch. Soc. Rec. Ser., III, 1967, pp. 2–16.

[273] Dulley, 'Level and port of Pevensey', pp. 38, 43.

[274] For a good discussion of the correlation between population levels and employment possibilities, see C. E. Brent, 'Rural employment and population in Sussex between 1550 and 1640', *Sussex Arch. Colls.*, CXVI, 1978, pp. 41–55.

When, in 1477–8, floods hit the Christ Church manor of Appledore, the farmer there claimed compensation for the damage to 140 acres of pasture and 88 acres sown with wheat, plus 66 acres fallowed ready to sow with barley.[275] So too when the 100 acres in the marsh of Bekard were finally re-leased after the floods, the new lessee promised to plough and sow 80 acres of land there twice within the term. But by the end of the century landlords had become concerned that the land should not be turned over to arable too often. In 1491, for example, when the monks of Canterbury Cathedral priory made an agreement with the lessee of Orgarswick, Thomas Knight, he agreed that all the demesne land would lie waste, not ploughed or sown, for the last five years of the 21-year lease. If he failed to keep the agreement and within that time the land was sown and became of less value, he would pay recompense. A somewhat similar agreement was made between the archbishop and one of his farmers.[276]

Reclamation, however, occurred on a considerable scale in the Romney marshes. Both the archbishop of Canterbury and his cathedral priory were willing to spend substantial sums on repairs to sea walls and the inning of new land. Prior Petham was responsible for inning 600 acres at Kite's fleet or Kitemarsh in Appledore and Fairfield. The total cost of the project is not known but Thomas Chandler, Warden of New College, made a gift of 200 marks to enable the work to be finished and to take in another 200 acres at Agney. This extraordinary expenditure was in addition to the regular but heavy costs of maintaining sea walls and enclosures. In 1472–3 the priory, for example, spent £80 9s. 8d. repairing the sea walls at Appledore, £5 1s. 8d. for repairs at Ebony and £62 for the enclosure of Bekard.[277] Similarly on the archiepiscopal manor of Cheyne Court, the tenant, in 1477–8, spent £43 17s. 5d. (slightly over half the rent) on payments of common scot, the scouring of ditches, the evacuation of water and enclosing the demesne. Although thereafter his expenses did drop, for the rest of the century he still paid between £15 and £19 a year in common scots and other repairs.[278] None the less, despite these and similar expenses on other manors, both the archbishop and the priory probably did recover ultimately the cost of their investment, for, by the early sixteenth century, the rents from their marsh manors had risen by

[275] Cathedral Archives and Library, Canterbury, Misc. accounts 6, f.149. For lack of pasture his animals consumed 26 cartloads of hay. The tenant was also forced to rent 26 acres of pasture at 4d. an acre.

[276] Cathedral Archives and Library, Canterbury, Register S, f.367v. William Brockhill, the tenant for Cheyne Court, promised that in his last term he would not plough or sow any part beyond 20 acres: Lambeth Palace Library, ED 1200 (1484–5).

[277] Cathedral Archives and Library, Canterbury, Register S, f.253; Prior's roll 12.

[278] Lambeth Palace Library, ED 1199, 1200, 1201, 1202.

£55 and £40 respectively. The priory fairly consistently charged 14d.
to 20d. an acre for their land, but the archbishop was either unable or
unwilling to charge that much in the late fifteenth century. In 1484–5
when he leased the first portion of the new marsh, he charged 11d. an
acre, that is, £40 for 829 acres. When a further 300 acres were leased
in 1494, the lessee paid just 8d. an acre. But new leases in the early
sixteenth century, at much higher rates, show that a different archbishop
was able to take advantage of growing demand for good land. In
1516–17, when 100 acres of marsh at Shirley Moor were leased for the
first time, the rent was nearly 29d. an acre – 100 acres for £12.[279]
Although within a few years this rent had dropped to 24d. an acre, it
was still considerably higher than the rents being charged on the
Pevensey marshes. The higher value so frequently placed on Kentish
marshland probably resulted, at least in part, from the closer proximity
of Romney to markets in both London and the continent. The absence
of rich grazing land in other parts of the county also helped to push up
the price.

But while pasture farming was expanding in the marshes, arable
farming remained important in east Kent. Although by the fifteenth
century the Christ Church manors were all leased out, on the east Kent
manors much of the rent was actually paid in grain. Moreover many
of the rectories were kept "in hand" and the grain received went to
supply the house. Thus most years the monks needed to purchase very
little grain on the market. The steady receipt of grain throughout the
fifteenth century at rectories such as Eastry and Monkton (see Tables
2.14 and 2.15) suggests that no further reduction in arable took place
there after 1400 and that tenants were growing substantial amounts of
wheat and barley. Moreover in times of bad harvests, in England or
elsewhere, grain could always be supplied from Kent and parts of
Sussex to make up the deficits. In 1438–9 and again in 1481–2 the
London market was bolstered with wheat and other grains from the
south-east. Similarly in 1474–5, when Castile was suffering from a
severe shortage of grain, Spanish merchants exported over 4,000
quarters of grain from Kentish ports.[280] In good years, however, much
of the barley was turned into malt. Almost every village probably had
several maltsters. At Eastry, for example, in 1487–8, eight different
people took ten quarters of barley from the Christ Church monks and
another man took five quarters.[281] But large-scale production was

[279] Lambeth Palace Library, ED 1207, 1208.
[280] W. R. Childs, *Anglo-Castilian Trade in the Later Middle Ages*, Manchester, 1978, p. 98. In
1474–5 the Christ Church monks sold 315 quarters of barley from their Eastry rectory to John
Archer of Sandwich instead of sending it to the granary of the house.
[281] Cathedral Archives and Library, Canterbury, Beadle's rolls, Eastry.

Table 2.14. *Grain produced at the Christ Church rectory of Monkton, 1455–72 (in quarters)*

	Wheat		Barley		Oats	
	Monkton	Birchington	Monkton	Birchington	Monkton	Birchington
1455–6	37	47	63	80	0	28
1456–7	46	52	75	85	0	15
1460–1	45	53	77	106	0	25
1464–5	44	57	33	34	0	10
1470–1	61	38	97	160	14	31
1471–2	43	59	103	94	7	20
1472–3	57	74	110	130	19	33

Source: Lambeth Palace Library, ED 737, 738, 741, 745, 748, 750. The figures are given to the nearest quarter.

Table 2.15. *Grain produced at the Christ Church rectory of Eastry, 1412–93 (in quarters)*

	Wheat	Barley
1412–13	88	262
1417–18	86	197
1427–8	126	301
1429–30	126	307
1444–5	84	245
1445–6	53	185
1450–1	89	247
1451–2	79	218
1456–7	91	311
1462–3	96	306
1471–2	119	221
1482–3	86	184
1483–4	77	253
1492–3	126	212

Sources: Lambeth Palace Library, ED 396, 401, 404, 417, 417A, 422, 430; also Cathedral Archives and Library, Canterbury, Misc. accounts 4, 6, 8. The figures are given to the nearest quarter.

increasing. In the parliament of 1455 the Commons complained that Kentish brewers were banding together and some men were making as much as 1,800 quarters of malt a year in their own houses.[282] Although this practice was forbidden and no brewer was to make more than 100 quarters of malt, it probably continued. Moreover, not all the malt was used in domestic production. By the early sixteenth century significant quantities were being shipped abroad from Sandwich and smaller amounts from other Kentish ports.[283]

Pasture farming, however, continued its importance within the Weald. There the land by the sixteenth century was divided among a large number of smallholders, a goodly number of medium-sized family farms and just a few larger holdings of 60 to 100 acres.[284] Smallholders kept a few dairy cows, sheep, pigs, and poultry and sowed only a small crop acreage to serve the needs of their family and their animals. This form of husbandry, which was not labour intensive, left men free to engage in other occupations and they frequently worked as ploughmen, shepherds, carpenters, or thatchers for each other and for nearby lords. Some of them also wove and spun linen and woollen cloth. It is not clear, however, whether this pattern of landholding existed a century earlier. Certainly in Sussex, by the mid-fifteenth century, men had gathered into their hands land that in the past had belonged to several different families. Thus, although a few families held very small holdings of two to three acres, the majority of freeholders held 15 or more acres, albeit divided up into a large number of small parcels. In addition a significant number of families held large holdings of 60 to 100 acres, but often made up of bondland. Stock raising was usually their primary occupation. For all families pig keeping was central. A smallholder would usually have just one or two animals, but the larger tenants kept fifteen or more pigs or piglets. In addition most families kept cows and bred cattle for the market. Indeed by the 1490s heriots were most commonly paid in the form of cows or bullocks. Horse breeding was also important, but sheep rearing was never as important in the Weald as it was on the downland. Only the larger tenants kept substantial numbers of sheep and even their flocks rarely went beyond a hundred animals.

Finally, throughout the region the sale of wood products supplemented income from other sources. Although nearly every court roll

---

[282] 1455. *Rot. Parl.*, v, p. 324; *SR*, III, p. 374.

[283] In 1502–3, 1,071 qr of malt were exported from Sandwich, 99 qr from Dover, 120 qr from Faversham, and 70 qr from Queensborough: PRO E 122/129/8.

[284] M. L. Zell, 'A wood pasture agrarian regime: the Kentish Weald in the sixteenth century', *Southern History*, VII, 1985, pp. 69–93. See also C. E. Brent, 'Rural employment and population in Sussex', pp. 40–50.

contained some citations for illegal cutting of trees and firewood, the small fines did not serve as a major deterrent and peasants continued to nibble away at the woods as they had done in the past. Lords also exploited their woodlands, selling timber to their tenants or having it cut and sold as firewood. In 1479–80, for example, Sir John Scott, on his manor of Mote, received £20 17s. 4d. from the sale of billetts of firewood and in 1480–1 he received £12 14s. 10d.[285] Some of this wood was shipped along the coast to London and other English ports, but much of it was shipped across to the continent for fuel.[286] Merchants from the Netherlands, Picardy, and Normandy took timber and firewood back with them and English merchants regularly visited Calais and other ports. In 1470–1 the Calais victualler bought 100,500 billetts of firewood, at Calais, from two Sussex merchants and in 1472–3 he bought 281,175 billetts from both Kent and Sussex merchants.[287] By the end of the century firewood and timber were the major exports from Sussex ports. Although the volume of exports obviously varied from year to year, the total of 1,566,000 billetts exported in 1489–90 was by no means atypical.[288]

By the end of the fifteenth century the economic fortunes of Kent and Sussex had thus become increasingly disparate. Kent was at least four times wealthier than it had been in the early fourteenth century.[289] Wheat, malt, and livestock flowed from the fertile lands of north and east Kent to sustain London households. Kentish wool supplied Essex clothiers with some of their raw material.[290] By the end of the century the local cloth industry was expanding, especially in the area around Cranbrook. In addition a flourishing trade flowed back and forth across the English Channel. Merchants and royal agents, using the resources of the Kentish hinterland, supplied Calais with firewood, grain, cloth, and live animals. Consequently although the land went out of cultivation in Kent as elsewhere, very little reverted to scrub and waste, but rather was used for pasture. The profits of the pastoral economy, however, slumped in mid-century with the disruption of the export trade in wool and cloth and the contraction in the home market, but

[285] East Sussex RO HC 179/8, 179/10.

[286] For the fourteenth-century export figures see R. A. Pelham, 'Timber exports from the Weald during the fourteenth century', Sussex Arch. Colls., LXIX, 1929, pp. 170–82.

[287] PRO E 101/197/12, 197/20.   [288] PRO E 122/35/7.

[289] R. S. Schofield, 'The geographical distribution of wealth in England', pp. 483–510.

[290] Thomas Marsh was authorized to ship from Faversham to Colchester 6,000 fleeces in 1427 and 10,000 in 1429. In 1436 John Cooke of Colchester was licensed to bring 25 sacks of wool from Sandwich. In 1441 licences were granted for the shipment of 11,000 fleeces from Kent, most of them being shipped in barges across the Thames estuary and then carried to Colchester overland: Britnell, Growth and Decline in Colchester, p. 248.

recovery was well under way by 1500. The flood damage in the Romney marshes had been repaired and followed by extensive works of land reclamation. This marshland was obviously teeming with animals by the end of the fifteenth century and becoming increasingly valuable. In contrast the wealth of Sussex appears to have been half that of its neighbour. The Sussex marshes around Pevensey had suffered a marked drop in population, and even though the economy had become primarily a pastoral one, pasture rents were still low. Elsewhere considerable land reverted from arable to rough pasture or waste, rents frequently fell and land changed hands rapidly as men died or left the area and new tenants moved in. Even when demesne lands were kept in hand, the produce was used to supply the seigneurial household. Further from both the London and the continental markets, landholders had less incentive to produce large quantities of grain or stock for sale, especially when prices remained low. Wood products constituted the major exports from Sussex ports, and their value did not compare to the wool and cloth regularly exported from Sandwich.[291] The only forward-looking element was the establishment, in the 1490s, at Newbridge and Parrock, of the first known water-powered blast furnace. Both sites also had powered forges. None the less the Wealden iron industry in the early sixteenth century was no more than "poised on the threshold of greatness".[292] For most of Sussex the fifteenth century had been a time of depression.

I. THE SOUTHERN COUNTIES

A central feature of southern England was the great tract of chalkland stretching from the Isle of Wight and the Hampshire Downs across Salisbury Plain and Cranborne Chase to the Dorset uplands and the central Dorset coast. This was sheep-corn country *par excellence*, with arable "on the hill" (as at Mere in Wiltshire) as well as in the valleys, but also with "great flocks of sheep" which Leland saw. There were 1,300 acres of demesne pasture on the Glastonbury manor of Damerham (Hants.) in 1518, enough for two thousand sheep, and the abbey's tenants also had grazing rights on the heath and Damerham Down.[293]

---

[291] By mid-fifteenth century, wool exports from Chichester and other Sussex ports were either negligible or non-existent. Furthermore, an average of 63 cloths a year were exported compared to the 2,000 cloths that were exported from Sandwich in peak years.

[292] Julian Cornwall, 'Sussex wealth and society in the reign of Henry VII', *Sussex Arch. Colls.*, CXIV, 1976, p. 20; see also C. F. Tebbutt, 'An abandoned medieval industrial site at Parrock Hartfield', *Sussex Arch. Colls.*, CXIII, 1975, p. 150.

[293] *Cal. Inq. Misc.*, IV, no. 156; Leland, *Itinerary*, I, pp. 247–8; R. C. Hoare, *The Modern History of South Wiltshire*, IV(2), pp. 41–2.

This chalkland core was ringed by a variety of other districts. The sandy heathlands of the Hampshire basin and south-east Dorset were judged by Leland to be fitter for cattle than for corn; the Forest of Bere and the New Forest accommodated mixed farming and deer as well as timber; in the wood-pasture lands circling the chalk to north and west dairying had some importance; and beyond them the Vale of Taunton Deane was recognized eventually as the granary of the west. Still further westward Leland found the Quantocks and Exmoor to be barren and moorish ground, with many cattle pastures, but with little or no corn or habitation; northwards lay the coastal marshes along the Bristol Channel and the Somerset wetlands stretching inland to Glastonbury, Athelney, and beyond, where there are many notices of fishing, hunting, and cattle grazing and where some of the best Somerset cheeses were made; and still further north the Mendips and other hills again carried many sheep, but a village like Evercreech, on the margin between Mendip and the clay vale, combined corn growing, dairying and cattle breeding, and sheep farming.[294]

Farmers, of course, had long been at work modifying these natural landscapes. The characteristic settlement pattern of the downlands – a valley centre of habitation, meadows by the river, open-field arable below the down, and wide pastures on the down itself – still gives an impression of elbow room in the early fourteenth century, and the same is true of the very similar settlements in Mendip. In both, however, expanding populations had left their mark in the scatter of isolated farms on the Mendip hilltops, in ploughland "on the hill" already noticed at Mere, and multiplying settlements within the downland parishes. Similar signs of expansion were no less evident elsewhere. Most Somerset parishes contained several hamlets, each commonly having its own fields; in the Vale of Marshwood in west Dorset there were many isolated farms; in the wooded areas of south-eastern Hampshire forest assarts, many of them enclosed, clustered around the original fields; enclosed fields and scattered farms were also characteristic of west Somerset; and, in the wetlands, much of the reclaimed marshes lay in closes even when they were used for pasture. The complex landscape created by expanding settlement is well illustrated at Whiteparish (Wilts.), on the margins of both Salisbury Plain and the New Forest. Already a parish of dispersed habitation in 1086, some seven additional farms or hamlets had been established by the fourteenth century, a new set of open fields had been laid out, and

[294] Leland, Itinerary, I, pp. 168, 275, 284; E. Kerridge, Farmers of Old England, London, 1973, p. 87; Cal. of Mss. of the Dean and Chapter of Wells, HMC 1907–14, I, pp. 288, 324–7, 417, 425–7; Some Manorial Accounts of St Augustine's Abbey, Bristol, ed. A. Sabin, Bristol Rec. Soc., xxii, 1960, pp. 35–8, 190–1; Somerset and Dorset N. & Q., xi, 1908–9, pp. 237–40.

extensive assarts (which were often enclosed) had been carved out of the forest and downs. These complex settlement patterns provided the context for the changes of the late middle ages.[295]

The predominant role of arable farming in the mid-fourteenth century was likewise characteristic of most of the region. Information relating to some 25,000 acres of land in Wiltshire, Dorset, and Somerset in the second half of the fourteenth century suggests that, on average, about 80 per cent of demesne acreages were under the plough. That figure was 77 per cent even in the heathlands; it was still 73 per cent in the Somerset fens (where there were above-average acreages of meadow), and only fell to below 50 per cent on the Somerset moors where there was as much pasture as arable. These figures, of course, are very inadequate measures of land use, since the often extensive areas of common pasture were seldom surveyed. How extensive they were is indicated by the fact that on the Wiltshire downland, for every arable acre, there was grazing for 1.3 sheep.[296] The manure of these large flocks of sheep, on the other hand, also made its positive contribution to arable farming. Half a dozen Winchester manors in the period 1325–48 had over a thousand sheep; but in Hampshire the arable sown averaged 389 acres at Twyford, 473 acres at East Meon, 184 acres at Alresford and 215 acres at Overton; while in Wiltshire the comparable figures were 299 acres at Downton and 280 acres at East Knoyle. To allow for fallow, moreover, in order to establish the primarily arable area these figures need to be increased by half or more likely doubled. Some less promising land than Hampshire and Wiltshire downland was, at least occasionally, under crops. In 1279 there were "men who work their waste land to sow corn" on Exmoor, although their assarts normally reverted to pasture after two or three crops; and Athelney abbey's carucate at Clavelshay, lying at the eastern end of the Quantocks, could only be sown for a single year at ten-yearly intervals because of its debility.[297]

[295] C. D. Drew, 'The manors of the Iwerne valley, Dorset', *Dorset N.H. and Arch. Soc.*, LXIX, 1947, pp. 46–7; R. Athill, ed., *Mendip: a New Study*, Newton Abbot, 1976, pp. 84–9; M. Whitfield, 'The medieval fields of south-east Somerset', *Somerset Arch. and N.H. Soc.*, CXXV, 1981, pp. 17–19; J. H. Bettey, *Wessex from A.D. 1000*, London, 1986, pp. 36–7; *VCH Somerset*, V, pp. 22, 26, 35, 83, 85; *Cal. of Mss. of the Dean and Chapter of Wells*, I, p. 411; C. C. Taylor, 'Whiteparish: a study of the development of a forest-edge parish', *Wilts. Arch. and N.H. Magazine*, LXII, 1967, pp. 83–91.

[296] Material from: *Somerset and Dorset N. & Q.*, IX–XVI, 1904–19; *Pedes Finium ... for the County of Somerset, 1347–99*, ed. E. Green, Somerset Rec. Soc., XVII, 1902; *Abstracts of Feet of Fines relating to Wilts. for the Reign of Edward III*, ed. C. R. Elrington, Wilts. Rec. Soc., XXIX, 1973; *Abstracts of Wilts. i.p.m. ... 1327–77*, ed. E. Stokes, Index Library, XLVIII, 1914; BL Add. Ms. 6165.

[297] J. Z. Titow, *Winchester Yields: a Study in Medieval Agricultural Productivity*, pp. 136–9; E. T. MacDermot, *History of the Forest of Exmoor*, rev. edn, Newton Abbot, 1973, pp. 8, 55; BL Add. Ms. 6165, f.61d.

Expansion was checked from the fourteenth century by a combination of influences. Some were limited in their effects or duration, like French attacks on the south coast which devastated Southampton in 1338, allegedly depopulated Portesham (Dorset) in 1469 and impoverished the Isle of Wight until the 1380s, exercising a permanently depressing effect upon its economy for a further century. The same is true of the "great wind" which did much damage at Somerley (Hants.) in 1366 or the floods which were helping to despatch Wraxall (Somerset) in 1382 towards desertion.[298] Some things may have had longer-term consequences, like the outbreaks of animal diseases some of which seriously reduced wool output, and possibly generally less favourable weather conditions which, especially in the fifteenth century, may have adversely affected both arable and animal productivity.[299]

More important still, however, were basic demographic trends in an area where the fragile balance between land and people had been revealed by the bad harvests of the early fourteenth century. On the Winchester manors at Fareham, Bishop's Waltham and East Meon (Hants.) and at Taunton (Somerset), mortality as reflected in heriot payments rose from an annual average of 73 in the decade before 1315 to one of 126 in the lean years 1315–18. Death rates were still higher with the coming of plague in 1348–9. In that year heriots soared to 1,205 on these same four manors compared with an annual average of 80 in the preceding decade. The impact of plague was also evident elsewhere. In Hampshire, in 1349–50, at Beauworth 25 per cent and at Twyford 22 per cent of the rents due had lapsed *per pestilenciam*; in the diocese of Winchester the death rate among beneficed clergy was around 49 per cent; and at Cheriton in 1351 all the "coterills" were said to be dead. It was the same in other places. In Wiltshire the sale of harvest works produced small returns "for lack of tenants" and heavy mortality was noted at Wanborough, Tidworth, Broughton, West Dean, and East Grimstead; in Dorset (reputed to be the county into which plague first entered the country), Bere Regis and Charminster lay untilled in 1348 because "the present pestilence is so great"; and in Somerset in January 1349 the contagion of pestilence was said to be spreading everywhere. Some 13 per cent of the Nailsbourne rents could not be collected in 1349–50, it looks as though the graveyard at North

---

[298] *CPR, 1350–4*, p. 56; *Somerset and Dorset N. & Q.*, XI, 1908–9, p. 91; *Cal. Inq. Misc.*, IV, nos. 128, 136, 384; S. F. Hockey, *Quarr Abbey and its Lands, 1132–1631*, Leicester, 1970, pp. 136–9; *Cal. Inq. Misc.*, III, no. 605; *CIPM*, xv, no. 501.

[299] M. J. Stephenson, 'The productivity of medieval sheep on the great estates, 1100–1500', Cambridge Univ. Ph.D. thesis, 1986; Lloyd, *Movement of Wool Prices*, p. 20.

Petherton had to be temporarily enlarged, and the court rolls leave no doubt about the catastrophe plague brought to Curry Rivel. No deaths were reported at the manor court in October 1348, but eighteen were notified in December, thirty-five in February 1349 and ten more in March. That this level of mortality was exceptional is clearly implied by the fact that sixteen holdings were unlet in March 1349 and that fifteen of them were still in hand at the end of July.[300]

Nor did plague respect rank, for deaths of Wiltshire tenants in chief in 1348 and 1349 were about four times as numerous as they were on average in the preceding or succeeding decades. There were further periods of enhanced mortality among manorial lords in 1360–1 and 1369, and deaths from epidemic disease in the early 1360s added to the tally of lapsed rents on the Winchester manors, the outbreaks of 1348–9 and 1360–1 still being recalled at Overton (Hants.) in the fifteenth century as the first and second pestilences. Nor do they appear to have been the last. The incidence of epidemic disease in the southern counties has still to be systematically established, but there are indications that it was sufficiently endemic to prevent population levels recovering to anything like the level they had reached before the losses of the third quarter of the fourteenth century.[301]

These indications are necessarily mainly indirect. The heavy mortality of 1348–9 evidently reduced the level of demand for land, but the Winchester records were exploited long ago to demonstrate the remarkable resilience of fourteenth-century village society and its reserves of people. Holdings that were not immediately taken up mostly found new tenants by the mid-1350s, though not always on the old terms; and both failure to re-let holdings and downward revision of rents were still remembered into the fifteenth century. At Downton and Twyford rents for land that had lapsed to the lord *per pestilenciam* were still recorded half a century later; at Burghclere (Hants.) in 1447–8 it was noted that land which had escheated to the lord a century earlier was let for a lower rent than it had once commanded; and at Highclere (Hants.) a virgate and close brought in nothing in 1431 because no one would take them. Overton entries suggest that the "second plague" of 1360–1 had even more serious consequences than the first, and those manors still experiencing difficulties in the 1370s in

---

[300] Postan, *Essays on Medieval Agriculture*, Table 9.1; Shrewsbury, *A History of Bubonic Plague*, pp. 57, 65, 88–90; Levett, *The Black Death*, pp. 165–6, 174, 177; G. G. Coulton, *Medieval Panorama*, Cambridge, 1949, p. 496; WPR 159360; *Abstracts of Wilts i.p.m. ... 1327–77*, ed. Stokes, pp. 199, 204–5, 210; P. J. Leach, 'Excavations at North Petherton, Somerset, 1975', *Somerset Arch. and N.H. Soc.*, CXXI, 1977, pp. 21–2; J. F. Chanter, 'Court rolls of the manor of Curry Rivell in the year of the Black Death', *ibid.*, LVI, 1910, pp. 92–135.

[301] *Abstracts of Wilts. i.p.m. ... 1327–77*, ed. Stokes, *passim*; Levett, *The Black Death*, pp. 135–6; WPR 159449.

letting holdings seem to be those most severely affected by this second major epidemic. Possibly the effort needed to adjust to the results of high mortality in 1348–9 imposed strains upon the resilience of medieval society that made it less capable of sustaining adversities in the future.[302]

The initial resilience displayed by the Winchester manors is not untypical of southern England. Of half a dozen Wiltshire manors where heavy mortality was recorded in 1349, only Cowesfield in Whiteparish was ultimately deserted; the Mortimer lands in the lordship of Bridgwater (Somerset) achieved a new stability of rents, if at a somewhat lower level, within a decade of 1349; and lapsed rents at Wellow in the 1360s and Farleigh Hungerford (both Somerset) in the 1380s were only 6.5 per cent and 3 per cent respectively of the totals due. Early resilience, however, might prove less than permanent. By the mid-fifteenth century the Farleigh Hungerford rent roll may have been reduced by almost a fifth and, even so, 11 per cent of the rents due could not be collected. That figure is comparable to those, ranging from 9 to 16 per cent, for "decayed" rents at Enford in 1403, Aldbourne in 1427 and Collingbourne Ducis (all Wilts.) in 1435.[303] The reason why land could not be let, or had to be let "for a lesser rent than was usual of old", might be that given by the Malmesbury surveyor at Purton (Wilts.) in 1396 (*pro defectu tenencium causa pestilencie*); but lower grain prices from about 1380 and sagging wool prices in much of the fifteenth century also influenced what men were willing to pay for land. These circumstances in combination gave the downward pressure on rents a relentless character. The rent paid by demesne lessees at Manningford Bohune (Wilts.) fell from £20 in 1412 to £12 in the second half of the century and that for Westwood (Wilts.) from £7 in 1365 to £5 a century later; and St Augustine's abbey, Bristol, drew up a new rental for Portbury in c. 1420 to put on record divers reductions of rents conceded at various times in the past, thus giving permanence to what may at first have been regarded as temporary concessions. The sluggish demand for land was still evident at Shapwick (Dorset) in the 1460s and 1470s, when some standard holdings were slow to find new tenants, some found no tenants at all, and some could only be let for as little as half their former rents or even less.[304]

The circumstances making land harder to let, at least on the old terms, also affected landowners as producers. The long-term trend of

---

[302] Levett, *The Black Death*, pp. 82–6, 135–6; WPR 159412, 159414, 159439, 159449.

[303] Holmes, *Estates of the Higher Nobility*, pp. 107–9; PRO SC 6/970/21–3, 971/9, 974/24; BL Harl. Roll X7; PRO DL 29/682/11058, 683/11068.

[304] BL Add. Ms. 6165, f.58; *VCH Wilts.*, x, pp. 209–10, XI, p. 229; *Some Manorial Accounts of St Augustine's Abbey, Bristol*, ed. Sabin, p. 182; PRO DL 30/57/707.

producer prices was for much of the time unfavourable, while labour was both scarcer and dearer and it proved more and more impossible to preserve claims to traditional labour services. Indeed, at Boscombe (Wilts.) in 1362 there were only free tenants because no one there would hold land in bondage. The relaxation of labour services, at least on a temporary basis, had often gone far before 1349: the sale of works at Bishop's Waltham, for instance, yielded just over £36 in 1340–1. This amount was exceptionally large, but there were significant receipts under this head on many other Winchester manors, suggesting that the bishops were entitled to a tally of works greatly in excess of the labour requirements of demesnes on which sown acreages had long been contracting. Before 1349 this surplus could be turned into cash unless, as at Twyford and Bishopstoke (Hants.) in 1340–1, the tenants *operabuntur propter eorum paupertatem.* After the heavy mortality of 1348–9 it still provided a cushion, although vacant holdings reduced its size and, as at Downton in 1350–1, the sale of services produced "so little for lack of tenants". At Meon manor in 1350 and 1360 allowances of works for vacant holdings and to manorial officials, etc., reduced by about a third the total due, and of these the bishop made do with only around 40 per cent, indicating how large the surplus of works theoretically owed had become by the mid-fourteenth century.[305]

In many places services were already much less significant than on the Winchester manors. At Farleigh Hungerford only a little weeding and haymaking was owed in 1352, at Wellow in 1364 only two customary holdings owed works (the rest were in the lord's hand or let at fixed rents), and at Estcourt in Heytesbury (Wilts.) in 1357–8 less than one-fifth of the 1,780 works owed were in fact performed. These tendencies evident in the mid-century continued. At Heytesbury by 1392 all the winter, summer, and autumn works were *in denariis*; and at Aldbourne by 1426 all that were left, with the arable demesne leased out, were some sheep-shearing services and enough haymaking works to provide about a third of the hay the sheep needed in winter. Similarly, at Shapwick and Kingston Lacy (Dorset) in the 1430s, though the customary tenants clipped the sheep, they got paid for doing so, and all other services had gone with the leasing of the arable demesne. At Kingston, however, some works had still been done in the 1390s, although even then the sale of works brought in over £13. The comparable figure in 1433–4 was £15 14s. 7¼d.[306]

This erosion of services was often conceded very reluctantly: thus the bishops of Winchester, even when they used only a proportion of

[305] *Abstracts of Wilts i.p.m. ... 1327–77*, ed. Stokes, p. 315; WPR 159351, 159360, 159371; Levett, *The Black Death*, p. 88.
[306] PRO SC 6/970/14, 974/24, 1052/17, 1053/7; PRO DL 29/682/11046, 11058, 683/11066.

the works due to them, preserved into the second half of the fourteenth century claims to as many traditional villein services as possible. Even on an estate as conservative as this, however, the withering away of labour services continued. At East Meon in the 1440s the sale of works brought in ten times as much as a century earlier; by 1410 all the Overton services were sold except shearing works, harvest boons and a few minor obligations; and at Burghclere the customary tenants had bought out all their works. At Fareham (Hants.), by contrast, while the main burden on the tenants, the *opera manualia*, had been totally commuted by 1441, many other works were still performed, and at Ecchinswell (Hants.) 50–80 per cent of the works owed were actually done. Reluctance to abandon customary claims was evident on other estates. St Swithun's was still calling upon customary labour for the cultivation of its Enford demesne in 1403; the bishop of Salisbury about the same time disposed of about one thousand works a year at Baydon, although by 1438 all the services had gone at Bishopstone (both Wilts.); at East Quantoxhead (Somerset) there were even attempts in 1457 to revive services commuted half a century earlier; and in 1484 works had been only recently commuted on the abbey home farm at Muchelney.[307]

The jettisoning, however reluctantly, of traditional labour dues was not always a direct reflection of a continuing retreat of demesne cultivation. In some places the pre-1349 reduction of demesne acreages was slowed down for a time. The sown acreage on the Winchester demesnes in Wiltshire, Hampshire, and Somerset, which fell on average by 23 per cent between the first and second quarters of the fourteenth century, decreased by only 9 per cent (mainly in the years immediately after the Black Death) between the second and third quarters, and by a similar amount between the 1370s and the end of the century. By 1400, however, the whole of three Hampshire demesnes had been leased, in the three counties all the arable was leased in 13 out of 34 manors by 1409 and in 21 by 1432, and the sown acreage which remained was less than a third of its extent in 1349. By 1449 only one manor in Wiltshire and three in Hampshire had any arable in hand, and the total Winchester arable under cultivation was less than a tenth of what it had been a century earlier. On this estate, none the less, it was only when less favourable prices were added to the problems of rising labour costs that the dispersal of arable demesnes reached something like its term.[308]

[307] Levett, *The Black Death*, pp. 110, 112, 115; WPR 159414, 159437; BL Harl. Roll X7; *VCH Wilts.*, XI, pp. 126–7, XII, pp. 7, 32; *VCH Somerset*, III, p. 43, V, p. 124; PRO SC 6/974/5.

[308] Titow, *Winchester Yields*, pp. 136–9; figures for Winchester acreages provided by Professor David Farmer, to whom I am greatly indebted for data from the Winchester pipe rolls and from

The course followed by demesne livestock husbandry was not quite the same. On the Winchester estates a rapid build-up of sheep flocks began in the late 1340s and continued until the mid-1370s, when there were three times as many sheep on the estate as in 1345. This peak figure was maintained for the rest of the century and only began to fall in the early fifteenth century, when a growing willingness to lease out sheep flocks as well as arable emerged. The initial increase in sheep numbers doubtless reflects a buoyant demand for wool and the high prices downland fleeces commanded, especially in the 1360s and 1370s; while the fact that at this time fleece weights were exceptionally high and that labour costs were lower than for arable cultivation (especially where customary labour could be mobilized for washing and shearing) probably also contributed to the profitability of sheep farming. It became a less attractive proposition when wool prices fell in the late 1370s, during the long periods of depressed prices in the fifteenth century, and at a time when fleece weights too appear to have been falling. By the mid-fifteenth century sheep had gone from the bishop's Somerset manors, where they had never been of great moment; in Wiltshire, where there had been nearly 4,500 demesne sheep in 1370, there were now only 850 at Bishopstone; and only Hampshire retained a dozen or so demesne flocks, with those at Hambledon, Twyford, Crawley, and Overton each still numbering over a thousand head. By that time the estate had only about three-fifths of the sheep it had carried in the 1370s and a third of those that remained were leased out to farmers. On the whole, however, demesne sheep farming proved more resilient than arable cultivation, perhaps because it made less calls upon labour. At a place like Crawley it was doubtless an advantage, too, that even in the mid-fifteenth century the bishop could call upon as many shearing services as had been available in 1389. There the sheep flock was kept in hand after the arable was finally leased in 1448, although by 1487 the sheep had also passed to a farmer.[309]

There were other southern landlords who abandoned sheep farming relatively late, including the Duchy of Lancaster and the Hungerfords on their Wiltshire estates. St Mary's, Winchester, likewise kept its flock at Urchfont until at least 1470 and at All Canning (Wilts.) until 1480; St Swithun's only leased the sheep at Stockton (Wilts.) in c. 1484, nearly a century after giving up the arable; and in the late fourteenth

Glastonbury abbey documents at Longleat House. See also D. L. Farmer, 'Grain yields on Winchester manors in the later middle ages', *EcHR*, 2nd ser. xxx, 1977, pp. 555–66; *idem*, 'Crop yields, prices and wages', pp. 117–55.

[309] Stephenson, 'The productivity of medieval sheep on the great estates', pp. 280–9, 299; Gras, *English Village*, pp. 290–1, 466–8, 478, 486–7.

and early fifteenth centuries the leases of Rowberrow and Abbotsleigh (Somerset) excluded St Augustine's abbey's sheep flocks.[310] In the end, of course, the sheep of these large landowners mostly passed to leaseholders. Some leaseholders, however, were gentlemen and some manorial lords may have continued to run their own sheep farms. Guy Brian's widow had sheep and cattle pastures, and what look like arable furlongs put down to grass, at Haselbury Brian (Dorset) in 1434; a judge holding Heywood, near Trowbridge (Wilts.), left 520 sheep and substantial amounts of wool as legacies; and in Somerset bequests of sheep were made by William Carent of Brimpton (1406), Sir John Wadham (1411), Sir John Stourton of Preston Plucknett (1439) and Henry Burnell, esquire (1490). Evidently some smaller landlords were not pure rentiers.[311]

Other features of the countryside reflected the changed demographic circumstances more directly. At Farleigh Hungerford, for instance, over one hundred acres (about one-third) of the demesne was uncultivated in the 1350s and by the 1380s seems to have been permanently abandoned, at least for corn growing. At Heytesbury in 1392, tenants seem to have been found for similar *terra domini frisca*, but at Abbotsleigh eleven cottage holdings were vacant and decayed in the 1380s, and there were one hundred uncultivated acres at Woodfalls (Wilts.) in 1390 and four hundred acres at Sutton Poyntz (Dorset) in 1434. Some of the thirteenth-century assarts added to the demesne at Downton probably reverted to pasture, at Urchfont in 1460 four cottage holdings and other plots could neither be let nor profitably cultivated, and at Highclere a virgate and a $36\frac{3}{4}$-acre close vacant in 1430 had probably been unlet for many years. There were clearly some long-term losses of land from arable cultivation.[312] Losses, of course, were not always permanent or total. Tenant land falling to the lord was probably most usually re-let, though possibly for a different purpose or on different terms or at a lower rent. Sometimes, on the other hand, lords cropped escheated holdings, as the abbot of Glastonbury did at Monkton Deverill (Wilts.) in 1452; or they might use them as temporary sheep pasture, as the bishop of Winchester did with Robert

[310] Above, p. 142; *VCH Wilts.*, VII, pp. 67, 84, X, p. 26, XI, p. 217; PRO SC 6/971/9; *Wilts. N. & Q.*, IV, 1902–4, pp. 546–51; V, 1905–7, pp. 9–15, 61, 163; *Some Manorial Accounts of St Augustine's Abbey, Bristol*, ed. Sabin, pp. 10–11, 46–53, 193.

[311] *Somerset and Dorset N. & Q.*, XI, 1908–9, pp. 363–4; Hoare, *Modern History of South Wilts.*, II(2), pp. 17–19; *Somerset Medieval Wills, 1383–1500*, ed. F. W. Weaver, Somerset Rec. Soc., XVI, 1901, pp. 22–3, 52–5, 143–6, 290–3.

[312] PRO SC 6/970/14–15, 21–3, 1053/7; *Some Manorial Accounts of St Augustine's Abbey, Bristol*, ed. Sabin, pp. 8–9; *CIPM*, XVI, no. 818; *VCH Wilts.*, XI, p. 35; *Somerset and Dorset N. & Q.*, XI, 1908–9, pp. 365–6; *Wilts N. & Q.*, IV, 1902–4, pp. 547–9; WPR 159449.

Woodcote's tenement at Crawley in 1356–7. Some permanent retreat of the frontiers of cultivation does, however, appear to be undeniable.[313]

At least in some instances, on the other hand, this simply meant that arable was giving way to pasture. The 291 acres of demesne pasture in eleven *culture* at Haselbury Brian in 1434 look very like former ploughland; in Somerset one open field at East Lydford may have become common pasture by 1396, and the rents for demesne land at West Lydford in 1433 were mostly for meadow and pasture; and on Glastonbury's Damerham estate in 1518 only about half the arable at Boulsbury and one-third of it at Toyd were cultivated, the rest being sheep pasture. Sometimes nothing more than a form of convertible husbandry may be implied, but some advance of pasture at the expense of arable was nonetheless involved.[314] Inquests *post mortem* and comparable sources, detailing in all some 38,000 acres of land in the four southern counties, likewise suggest that there was a lesser proportion of arable on the demesnes of the later fifteenth century than there had been in the mid-fourteenth century, or at the very least that there was a greater concern to measure and set a value upon pasture. On average only about half the land surveyed was arable, a figure that was only substantially exceeded in the chalkland and London basin areas of Hampshire, the Cotswold area and some chalkland valleys of Wiltshire, and the central plain of Somerset. Pasture, on the other hand, accounted for more than a quarter of the total area, and pasture and moorland combined for a third, although pastoral resources probably continued to be understated wherever there were large areas of common. Even a coastal village in Exmoor, like Porlock, where only a quarter of tenant land was arable and most of the rest was heath or pasture, had substantial grazing rights not measured in acres: for in aggregate the tenants had common on the moor for over 3,000 sheep, for 189 cattle, and for 13 horses.[315]

At Porlock, too, in the early sixteenth century there appear to have been only 48 acres of open-field land compared with 131 acres on the demesne alone in 1306; and three-quarters of the arable, most of the meadow, and all the pasture save the common moor lay in closes. Enclosure, as well as pasture in the place of arable, seem to have made progress; and while a moorland parish like Porlock is hardly typical of

[313] Data from GAD 9716 provided by David Farmer; Gras, *English Village*, pp. 281, 295–6.

[314] *Somerset and Dorset N. & Q.*, XI, 1908–9, pp. 363–4; *VCH Somerset*, III, p. 121; PRO SC 6/972/1; BL Harl. Ms. 3961, ff.150–2.

[315] Material drawn from *CIPM, Henry VII*, I and II; *Somerset and Dorset N. & Q.*, XI–XVI, 1904–19; BL Add. Ms. 6165; Chadwyck Healey, *History of Part of West Somerset*, pp. 144–5, 202, 409–22.

southern England there are signs of similar tendencies elsewhere. Some of the numerous fifteenth-century closes at Bromham, in the wood-pasture area of Wiltshire, may have been older than the late middle ages; but elsewhere in that county some arable and pasture in Grittleton was said in 1518 to have been newly enclosed, many tenants at Nettleton and Kington had closes of meadow and pasture even though most of their arable was open-field, and at Christian Malford some tenants had a preponderance of enclosed land (including Thomas Stokehamme, with 30 acres of closes compared with $18\frac{1}{2}$ acres in the common fields). The interdependence of sheep and corn husbandry in the chalklands probably made for the preservation of open-field arable, but at Damerham in 1518 much of the land of some holdings was in closes and the demesne on the outlying settlement at Stapleton was almost totally enclosed.[316]

There were similar developments further to the west. While there was still much open field in Dorset, some abandoned arable and intakes from the downs were enclosed for grazing (perhaps like the earl of Northampton's closes at Gussage All Saints and St Michael in 1360). There were also many old enclosures in west Dorset and in the heathlands, and in the late fourteenth century Cirencester abbey was still reclaiming woodland at Pulham in the Vale of Blackmoor and occupying its gains in severalty. There was also much enclosed land, as well as open fields, in many parts of Somerset; on the southern hills at Chaffcombe, Cricket St Thomas and Knowle St Giles; on the hills and coastal areas of the west, where the Luttrell demesne at East Quantoxhead included at least nine large enclosures; on scattered farms, characteristic of the landscape of the Brendons, like those found in Huish Champflower; in the Muchelney marshes where income from the sale of enclosed grazing rose steeply in the fifteenth century; or at Evercreech on the Mendip margins, where closes which lay open were characterized as *ad nocumentum* and the bishop's new enclosure in 1414 was bounded by a quickset hedge.[317]

Despite modifications of the open-field landscape, however, Leland's journeys from Salisbury to Winchester, from Cirencester via Malmesbury to Chippenham, from Queen Camel in Somerset to Sherborne were "al by champayne ground", much of it fruitful in corn. The

---

[316] Chadwyck Healey, *op. cit.*, pp. 245–6, 409–22; *VCH Wilts.*, VII, p. 185; BL Harl. Ms. 3961, ff.6d, 19d–38, 41–61, 68d–9; Hoare, *Modern History of South Wilts.*, IV(2), p. 43.

[317] *Somerset and Dorset N. & Q.*, VIII, 1902–3, pp. 171, 210, X, 1906–7, pp. 233–4; C. C. Taylor, 'Medieval and later fields and field shapes in Dorset', *Dorset N.H. and Arch. Soc.*, XC, 1968, pp. 253–4, 256; *idem, Fields in the English Landscape*, pp. 100, 108–9, 113–17; M. Whitfield, 'Medieval fields of south-east Somerset', pp. 18–19; *VCH Somerset*, III, p. 44; IV, pp. 25, 136, 160; V, pp. 83–5, 124.

open-field frontiers may have retreated somewhat, but in most places the regime itself survived. Where retreat did take place, it was sometimes a manifestation of the shrinkage or desertion of settlements established in earlier periods of expansion. It is not easy to establish the chronology of these processes because, despite the fact that the earliest anti-enclosure statute referred to the Isle of Wight, the southern counties did not figure largely in late medieval and early Tudor debates about enclosure and depopulation. Only Hampshire was visited by the 1517 commissioners, but their findings were trivial and no depopulation was presented even in the Isle of Wight. Deserted or shrunken settlements, however, were numerous in the region, all the more so because (especially in Somerset and Dorset) many fourteenth-century parishes were filled with "tiny hamlets", often sited on poor and difficult soils, which at best were likely to be very modest centres of population.[318] The impression which remains, on the other hand, is one of slow and gradual contraction rather than catastrophe. Some places, and especially minuscule settlements on the remoter agricultural frontiers like the abandoned settlements on Exmoor lying nearer to the common than the modern farms, are likely to have died early; but shrinkage or desertion was commonly a more protracted process which might be far from completion in 1500. An isolated farm like Colber in Sturminster Newton, for instance, may have been quickly abandoned, but the destruction of villages was apt to take a much longer time. Where that did happen in the end, it may perhaps be regarded as the extreme manifestation of the more widespread retreat of arable in areas like the Dorset downland, with reversion to pasture on the high downs and much enclosure of formerly open land in the valleys.[319]

There are similar indications in other places. Allowances against the Dorset lay subsidy in 1511–12, totalling about 16 per cent of the 1334 quota of the county, do suggest that population and settlement had often contracted; but the details do not imply that places ultimately abandoned were yet deserted, even though above average rebates for Bryanston, Whitcombe and Winterbourne Herringston suggest that they were already much shrunken. Small dependent settlements, however, were not assessed separately in the subsidy rolls, which therefore shed no light on the fate of the small isolated farmsteads which are prominent among deserted sites in west Somerset. Some may have died early, although in south-east Somerset the depopulation of hamlets or their shrinkage into farms seem only to have been

[318] Leland, *Itinerary*, I, pp. 130, 151, 269; M. W. Beresford, *Lost Villages of England*, pp. 93, 290, 351–5; Beresford and Hurst, *Deserted Medieval Villages*, pp. 35, 39.

[319] O. Hallam, 'Vegetation and land-use on Exmoor', *Somerset Arch. and N.H. Soc.*, CXXII, 1978, p. 44; C. C. Taylor, *The Making of the English Landscape: Dorset*, pp. 111–19.

completed in the sixteenth century.[320] There was a similar gradual contraction of settlements in Wiltshire. In the west of the county Whittenham was so shrunken by 1428 that it soon amalgamated with Farleigh Hungerford and was absorbed into Somerset; and in the east the retreat of settlement in the formerly colonizing parish of Whiteparish probably reduced the hamlet of Whelpley to an isolated farm sometime in the fifteenth century, by which time customary holdings in the Downton hamlets of Barford and Witherington had in each case been converted into single leasehold farms.[321] There is a similar picture of gradual contraction, especially of the smaller settlements, in the Isle of Wight; while in mainland Hampshire, although the downland settlement at Abbotstone was already shrinking in 1428, not until 1544 can we be sure that its sole inhabitants were John Paulet and his servant. Some arable may have been put down to grass, too, in the lost hamlet of Lomer by the end of the fourteenth century, but its tax rebates did not exceed 10 per cent before 1489 and only in the mid-sixteenth century were its habitations reduced to a few cottages and was its church finally abandoned.[322]

Some settlements contracted and some even disappeared, some arable was turned into pasture, some old field arrangements were modified, some land lapsed altogether from cultivation and a good deal of it was worth less than formerly – all these are features of the countryside of southern England in the late middle ages, but they cannot necessarily be treated as indicators, and still less as measures, of rural decline or depression. Any adequate index of changing prosperity, of course, is simply not available; but for want of a better, the wealth of these counties per thousand acres, as it was assessed for taxation in the early fourteenth and early sixteenth centuries, may provide some pointers to their relative fortunes. These assessments show that, in 1334, Hampshire, Dorset, and Somerset ranked below the average of the English counties and that only Wiltshire was slightly above it. By the early sixteenth century, on the other hand, while Hampshire and Dorset were still ranked rather below the average, Wiltshire and Somerset (at fifth and second respectively) were among the wealthiest.

[320] *Somerset and Dorset N. & Q.*, III, 1892–3, pp. 193–9; M. Aston, ed., 'Somerset archaeology, 1976', *Somerset Arch. and N.H. Soc.*, CXXI, 1977, pp. 117–19; *idem*, 'Deserted settlements in Mudford parish, Yeovil', *ibid.*, pp. 41–5; Whitfield, 'Medieval fields of south-east Somerset', pp. 17–21.

[321] Beresford, *Lost Villages of England*, pp. 389–91; *VCH Wilts.*, VII, p. 70; XI, pp. 54, 76; C. C. Taylor, 'Whiteparish', pp. 92–4; *idem*, 'Three deserted medieval settlements in Whiteparish', *Wilts. Arch. and N.H. Magazine*, LXXIII, 1968, pp. 39–44.

[322] Beresford, *Lost Villages of England*, pp. 93, 103–4, 251, 353–5; I. Sanderson, 'Abbotstone: a deserted medieval village', *Hants. Field Club and Arch. Soc.*, XXXVII, 1971, pp. 57–64; F. Collins and J. Oliver, 'Lomer: a study of a medieval deserted village', *ibid.*, pp. 67–75.

Somerset's wealth, furthermore, had grown especially rapidly since the early fourteenth century, and Wiltshire and Dorset were also in the first eleven counties from that point of view.[323]

Tax data, in other words, suggest that the southern counties had adjusted not unsuccessfully to post-1349 circumstances, perhaps by using some land in ways better suited to its inherent qualities, using it with great flexibility, and sometimes by increasing the numbers of livestock, and especially of sheep, providers of income from wool and meat and also of manure contributing to arable productivity. New wealth, however, was generated by industrial development in villages and small towns as well as by agriculture. There was some expansion of rope-making at Bridport in the fourteenth and late fifteenth centuries, enlarging the market for Dorset and Somerset hemp; the output of the Mendip mines (especially the lead mines) increased during the century after 1433, despite (or perhaps because of) falling prices in the mid-century which reinforced the domination of the industry by "farmer-miners"; but above all cloth-making was coming to dominate the rural industrial scene. The bishops of Winchester had fulling mills in Hampshire at Fareham, Bishop's Waltham, Alresford and Wolvesey; and in Dorset there were also fulling mills at Sherborne, in the adjoining villages, and in the Frome valley north-west of Dorchester, while the Duchy of Lancaster let a site for a second fulling mill at Kingston Lacy in 1390 (the rent for which had risen by 25 per cent by 1430) as well as taking a rent from another man for leave to dig for fuller's earth. Landowners as well as seekers for employment derived benefit from the spread of cloth-making.[324]

Its development was even more marked in Somerset and Wiltshire. Numerous spinners and weavers in east Somerset were presented for taking excess wages in the 1350s, and later Leland found much clothworking at Bath and Wells and Bruton and Frome, many fulling mills on the river Frome, Chew Magna to be a pretty clothing town, and clothing townlets at Pensford and Mells. Further west there was some cloth-making at Nether Stowey and three or four fulling mills at Dunster in 1418 compared with only one in 1259. The aulnage accounts suggest something like a ten-fold increase of the county's cloth output in the second half of the fourteenth century, so that by the 1390s Somerset may have produced around a quarter of the cloth offered for

[323] Schofield, 'The geographical distribution of wealth in England', pp. 483–510.

[324] J. Pahl, 'The rope and net industry of Bridport', Dorset N.H. and Arch. Soc., LXXXII, 1960, pp. 143–5; M. Nathan, Annals of West Coker, Cambridge, 1957, p. 134; I. Blanchard, 'Labour productivity and work psychology in the English mining industry, 1400–1600', EcHR, 2nd ser. XXXI, 1978, pp. 1–24; WPR 159436; Somerset and Dorset N. & Q., XII, 1910–11, p. 311, XIII, 1911–12, pp. 115–16; G. D. Squibb, 'Calendar of medieval Dorset deeds', Dorset N.H. and Arch. Soc., LXV, 1944, p. 94; Leland, Itinerary, I, p. 151; PRO DL 29/682/11046, 11051.

sale in England. The Wiltshire industry, responsible for around one-seventh of the cloth manufactured at that time, is better known. By 1390 there was a specialized clothing area in the south-west of the county which, save for a period of depression in its middle years, continued to grow in the fifteenth century, as did textile working at Castle Combe in the north-west. Later in that century there was also considerable development in the Bradford Avon basin, and it was here that in 1468–9 James Tucker of Trowbridge is found buying pure white wool from the Hungerford manors. This purchase is symptomatic of the interdependence of farming and industry towards the end of the middle ages.[325]

Changes outside agriculture, therefore, cannot be dissociated from the fortunes of the countryside at this time. Industrial development in Somerset has still to be adequately explored, although it was possibly at least as important as that taking place in Wiltshire and the same may be true of development in the Sherborne area of Dorset. The growth of manufacture, of cloth in particular, not only created new employment opportunities: it enlarged the market for foodstuffs as well as wool, helped sometimes to sustain land values, and probably in some cases delayed the leasing of arable demesnes and even more of sheep flocks. The depression of the mid-fifteenth century in the cloth industry persuaded the Duchy of Lancaster to give up its sheep flocks in Wiltshire, but there were other landowners who still kept their sheep in hand; and it is reasonable to suppose that industrial development, and the stimulus that it afforded to agricultural production, help to explain the relative wealth of Wiltshire and Somerset as that was reflected in assessments for the king's taxes in the early sixteenth century, and also the marked growth in their relative wealth in the course of the later middle ages.[326]

[325] B. H. Putnam, *The Enforcement of the Statutes of Labourers during the First Decade after the Black Death, 1349–1359*, App., pp. 205–10; Leland, *Itinerary*, I, pp. 143, 145, 149, 166; V, pp. 98, 103, 105; *VCH Somerset*, V, p. 195; H. C. Maxwell-Lyte, *A History of the Castle, Manor and Barony of Dunster and of the Families of Mohun and Luttrell*, I, pp. 297–9; H. L. Gray, 'The production and exportation of English woollens in the fourteenth century', *EHR*, XXXIX, 1924, pp. 13–35; E. M. Carus-Wilson, 'The woollen industry before 1550', *VCH Wilts.*, IV, pp. 120–35; *idem*, 'Evidences of industrial growth', pp. 190–205.

[326] For Wilts., Hare, 'Demesne lessees', pp. 1–2; *idem*, 'The Wiltshire rising of 1450', pp. 16–19.

J. DEVON AND CORNWALL[327]

It has been said that, for the south-west in the Tudor period, Leland's *Itinerary* makes for "monotonous reading, like a play with only two sets of scenery", tracts of uncultivated land soon giving way to countryside "fertile of corn and grass", in turn followed by more "barren" or "moorish" ground.[328] The patchwork pattern observed by Leland was in many ways a product of changes taking place during the period covered by this volume. For notwithstanding the antiquity of their basic structures, and important later changes, agrarian landscapes in the south-west owe a great deal in their details to the transformations of the later middle ages – to piecemeal enclosure and the emergence of substantial farms (see ch. 7), as well as to changes in the occupation of the land.

Changes in land use were, in general, long and drawn out, as shown by Table 2.16, which is based upon the often rounded figures given in inquisitions *post mortem*. Indeed, at a few places the trend towards pasture had begun before the Black Death, for there are references from the early fourteenth century to arable lying untilled in western Cornwall and on the infertile hill slopes of east Devon, and to tenants too poor to cultivate their holdings. Many of these are classic examples of over-expansion onto marginal lands, although in western Cornwall decline in the local stannary may have contributed to contraction of arable.[329] After these localized beginnings, sharp contraction of arable continued to be restricted to particular localities, for there was no large-scale or sudden acceleration after the Black Death in the rate at which

[327] I am most grateful to those who have answered my queries and provided help: to N. Alcock, A. Barker, B. M. S. Campbell, J. Cloud, A. Goode, P. D. A. Harvey, P. Herring, R. Higham, M. Jones, J. Langdon, R. McKinley, D. Postles, C. Thornton, R. M. Smith, and M. Wickes. I owe special thanks to M. L. Meeres, Lord Talbot of Malahide, and W. A. Roberts for their hospitality; to M. Cherry and M. Kowaleski, co-workers in these fields, for the stimulus of their conversation; to E. Miller for his patience. I could not have carried out this work without constant and cheerful correspondence with O. Padel of the Institute of Cornish Studies: so obscure are the names of some Cornish manors, and the thousands of little places which lie beyond the manor, that research would often have come to a dead end without his expertise backed up, when all else failed, by that of the Rev. W. M. N. Picken. I owe most to the archivists of Devon and Cornwall, particularly P. A. Kennedy, M. Rowe, M. Dickinson, A. M. Erskine, P. L. Hull, C. North, R. Douch, G. Haslam, and all their staffs. Documents in the office of the Duchy of Cornwall were examined with the permission of Sir John Higgs. The Research Board of the University of Leicester contributed something towards costs of research.

[328] Joan Thirsk, in *AHEW*, IV, p. 72.

[329] G. Oliver, *Monasticon Dioecesis Exoniensis*, London, 1846, p. 430 (Cargoll); Hatcher, *Duchy of Cornwall*, pp. 95–7 (Helston-in-Kirrier); PRO C 133/122/12 (Truthall); *The Knights Hospitallers in England*, ed. L. B. Larking, Camden OS LXV, 1857, p. 13 (Bodmiscombe); J. R. Maddicott, *The English Peasantry and the Demands of the Crown 1294–1341*, Oxford, 1975, pp. 14–15 (Ottery St Mary); Dean and Chapter Archives, Exeter, 3672a (Teignmouth).

Table 2.16. *Devon and Cornwall: changes in land use, 1295–1509*

	Total acreage sampled	% arable	% meadow	% pasture	% moor
1295–1325	22,359	66.5	4.6	14.2	14.7
1423–1452	31,929	62.1	3.6	17.7	16.6
1497–1509	67,013	55.4	6.8	12.5	25.3

Sources: 1295–1325: 168 extents in PRO C 133 and 134 (Chancery inquisitions *post mortem*, collated with E 149 and 152 where necessary), C 145 (miscellaneous inquisitions), E 106 (extents of alien priories), SC 11/798 (extent of Monkleigh) and BL Harl. 3660 (extents of the lands of Canonsleigh Abbey). 1423–1452: 156 extents in PRO C 139 (Chancery inquisitions *post mortem*). 1497–1509: profiles of manors and free holdings in *CIPM, Henry VII*, II and III. Readers of the table should bear in mind the following: 1. 'arable' in Devon and Cornwall was convertible land, and variations over time in the proportion actually tilled is a distinct possibility; 2. figures in the first period relate for the most part to demesnes in hand while those in the last relate to leased demesnes and freeholds.

land passed out of cultivation. Confirmation is provided by evidence from demesnes (see below), which shows that until the end of the fourteenth century cultivation continued on large estates, although on a diminished scale. But at the same time demesne managers and husbandmen were reacting to reduced demands for grains by expanding their livestock enterprises, thereby feeding the gradual trend towards pastoral land use. Demesne cultivation was abandoned on most large estates by the 1410s and subsequent decades saw a related slack demand for tenant holdings which aided the building up of multiple tenancies (see below, ch. 7). Under these circumstances, demesnes unwanted by their lords were leased as pasture, some unwanted tenures were abandoned, and parts of newly enlarged tenant holdings fell to pasture or moorland, ultimately leading to the depressed figures for arable land recorded in inquisitions from Henry VII's reign. Alongside these developments shifts may well have taken place in the proportion of the "arable" land which was under grass ley, further increasing the amount of available pasture.

Within two counties which were, in William Marshall's phrase, "strongly marked with natural districts", generalized figures can conceal significant regional differences. In Table 2.17 figures for land use are analysed on the basis of regional divisions outlined by Marshall

Table 2.17. *Devon and Cornwall: changes in land use by region,*
1295–1509

	% arable	% meadow	% pasture	% moor
South Devon				
1295–1325	66.8	4.1	19.3	9.8
1497–1509	62.7	6.8	15.5	15.0
East Devon				
1295–1325	64.6	9.8	10.3	15.3
1497–1509	61.4	6.5	4.4	27.7
Mid- and N. Devon				
1295–1325	71.1	4.4	16.0	8.5
1497–1509	50.9	7.4	11.1	30.6
Devon moorlands				
1295–1325	62.5	5.4	6.3	25.8
1497–1509	56.3	7.5	8.7	27.5
Cornish coastlands				
1295–1325	57.3	2.5	26.7	13.5
1497–1509	54.8	7.0	19.5	18.7
Cornish moorlands				
1295–1325	56.4	4.4	22.9	16.3
1497–1509	16.1	3.1	28.7	52.1

Sources: As for Table 2.16, but excluding extents of those manors which
cannot be precisely located.

and other writers (and shown on Fig. 2.1), the marked contrasts which
it reveals giving some confidence to the assumption that medieval
changes in land use differed regionally according to divisions recognized
at a much later date.[330]

South Devon, the South Hams, at once warns against the dangers of
generalizing at a county level, for Table 2.17 reveals that here only a
modest decline took place in the proportion of the land under arable.
In the short term and in particular places land did go out of cultivation,
as at Bolberry Beauchamp and Harberton in 1361, where two whole
carucates lay "untilled and uncultivated"; or at Abbotskerswell in
1459. Some cases of this kind may have resulted from action by, or fears

[330] W. Marshall, *The Review and Abstract of the County Reports of the Board of Agriculture,
Southern and Peninsular Departments*, York, 1818, p. 549; G. Vancouver, *General View of the
Agriculture of the County of Devon*, London, 1808, frontispiece; Richard Carew, *The Survey of
Cornwall*, ed. Thomas Tonkin, pp. 17–18; R. Fraser, *General View of the County of Cornwall*,
London, 1794, pp. 23–8.

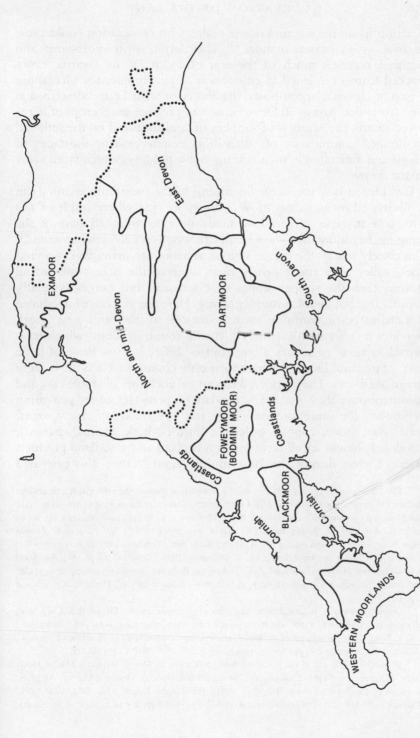

Fig. 2.1 Devon and Cornwall: regional divisions

of action from, the enemies of the realm who on occasion could cause devastation on coastal manors.[331] But despite such short-term and localized reversals much of the soil of south Devon (warm, easily worked loams) remained in cultivation. Opportunities for victualling at two of Devon's largest ports, the ability of what Leland described as the "frutefulest part of all Devonshire" to produce good crops of high-priced grains, the nearness of supplies of sand to spread on the soil – all encouraged continuance of cultivation despite evident shortages of labour and difficulties in maintaining viable holdings which faced some tenant farmers.[332]

East Devon land use at the beginning of the fourteenth century can be illustrated by an extent of Woodbury in 1321 where arable of 100 acres and 20 acres of meadow made up the improved part of the demesne, beyond which was a small oak wood and 200 acres of *vasta*.[333] This closely reflects the region's physical make-up: many well-watered vales, valley sides rising gently over some of the richest soils of all Devon, then the steeper slopes of Greensand hill ranges, virtually uncultivable but useful as rough grazing. Here one is at once introduced to a characteristic common to most regions of the south-west (south Devon is an exception), namely plentiful rough grazings, which have steered its agrarian history along courses different from those of large tracts of midland England where their only counterpart was the meagre forage of fallows. They rendered piecemeal enclosure of arable easy and uncontentious; they yielded a myriad of petty resources providing livelihoods for some and enriching the livelihoods of many – turf, gorse, clay, stone, coppice poles for hurdles, bark, acorns, charcoal, woodcock, hawks are all recorded as wasteland and woodland products in east Devon during the later middle ages;[334] they also provided

---

[331] PRO E 149/19/11; C 139/181. For coastal devastation some of the principal references are: Hatcher, *Duchy of Cornwall*, pp. 144–5 for a manuscript reference to the sacking of Sutton in 1339; *Adae Murimuth Continuato Chronicarum*, ed. E. M. Thompson, Rolls Ser., London, 1889, pp. 89–90 and 109n; *Rot. Parl.*, II, p. 213 and *CPR, 1345–8*, pp. 467–8; *CPR, 1401–5*, p. 298; *Thomae Walsingham, Historia Anglicana*, ed. H. T. Riley, Rolls Ser., London, 1863–4, II, pp. 259–61; *Chronique du religieux de Saint-Denys*, ed. L. Bellaguet, Paris, 1839–52, III, p. 181; *Royal and Historical Letters of Henry the Fourth*, ed. F. C. Hingeston, Rolls Ser., London, 1860, pp. 270–3; *Cal. Papal Letters, 1404–15*, p. 93 and *1455–64*, p. 93; *Register of Edmund Lacy*, ed. Dunstan, II, p. 177 and IV, p. 316.

[332] Leland, *Itinerary*, I, p. 224; below, ch. 3 for crop combinations; Devon RO, Cary Mss., Ashwater court of Oct. 1436 which mentions harvesters migrating *usque lez southammys*; H. S. A. Fox, 'The chronology of enclosure and economic development in medieval Devon', *EcHR*, 2nd ser. XXVIII, 1975, pp. 190–1, 196–7.   [333] PRO C 134/66/21.

[334] Devon RO, CR 522 (Kenn); CR 1288 m.17 (Ottery St Mary); Arundell Mss. at Hook Manor, MA 246, a/c of 1381–2 and court of Nov. 1381 (Clayhidon); Dean and Chapter Archives, Exeter, 5065 (Sidbury); Devon RO, DD 54916 (Holcombe Rogus); BL Add. Roll 64856 (Whimple); Add. Roll 7657 (Rockbeare); Arundell Mss. CR 447, a/c of 1411–12 (Clayhidon);

pasture generously for smallholders.[335] At the height of the early middle ages, arable cultivation, some of it intermittent, was pushed as far as possible onto the hill ranges. During the period covered by this volume, by contrast, there developed in east Devon the most well-rounded pastoral farm economies in all of south-western England.[336] The poorest land reverted to moor (Table 2.17), providing rough grazings on which young stock ran in summer. A little surprising is the relatively slight recorded fall in arable acreage, probably to be explained by the fact that inquisitions here are particularly conservative, still classifying as "arable" rich lands which to all intents and purposes had been given over to grass but which were cropped occasionally. Certainly, early sixteenth-century surveys of properties once belonging to the Bonvilles, concerned more with the *actual* use of each close, reveal some east Devon manors with more pasture than arable. Moreover, they consistently give arable a lower value per acre than pasture, whereas in the thirteenth century the reverse had been the case.[337] Clearly, an inversion of priorities had taken place during the later middle ages.

North and mid-Devon, unlike the east of the county, have few virtually uncultivable soils, but much poor clayey land which, if cultivated, yields but small returns. Relatively lightly exploited at the time of the Norman Conquest, it was this land which, despite its difficulties, was brought into cultivation during the twelfth and thirteenth centuries and then lapsed back very extensively to pasture and rough grazing during the later middle ages.[338] At the prior of Montacute's manor of Monkleigh, the last year of demesne husbandry in 1393–4 saw a sharp rise in sales of pasture from former arable and "untilled land"; thereafter lessees did nothing to reverse the trend, for a demesne rental of 1440–1 is headed *Assessa pasture bertone de Monkelegh*. At Halsford likewise the whole demesne was under pasture in 1408–9, some probably very rough and infested with gorse.[339] Ten

Dean and Chapter Archives, VC 22279 (Sampford Courtenay); PRO SC 6/1118/6 and Devon RO, CR 521 (Aylesbeare).

[335] Devon RO, 123M/TB/349 for a lease of 1 acre together with unstinted common of pasture *in montibus de Northleigh*; PRO E 315/385 for generous stints belonging to cottagers at Churchstanton.

[336] H. S. A. Fox, 'Field systems of East and South Devon. Part I, East Devon', *Devon Assoc.*, CIV, 1972, pp. 91–101, 121–7; below, ch. 3.

[337] PRO E 315/385 and Fox, 'Chronology of enclosure', p. 185 for acreages and valuations. The lapsing of arable to pasture can be clearly seen in accounts of Otterton in 1427–8 and Mohun's Ottery in 1449–50: PRO SC 6/829/14, 829/21. For strictly pastoral holdings see *CIPM, Henry VII*, I, p. 343 and II, p. 319.

[338] Cf. *The Domesday Geography of South-West England*, eds. H. C. Darby and R. Welldon Finn, Cambridge, 1967, p. 242; and Table 2.17 above.

[339] Devon RO, CR 1133 and 1139; Dean and Chapter Archives, 5121. See also an extent of

vacant tenements at Sampford Courtenay were described as *in mora* in
1383–4 and by 1422 their land was being used as common grazing,
while at Hendon in Hartland between 1394 and 1412 eight vacant
holdings deteriorated to become moorland.[340] If multiplied appropriately such examples could account for the increase in the area of
moorland from 8 to 30 per cent which took place in north and mid-
Devon during the later middle ages, more than in any other part of the
county (Table 2.17); moreover, they indicate that, on these particularly
unsuitable soils, the transformation in land use took place more swiftly
than in some other regions. As cultivation declined,[341] the main
specialism in a region remote from large markets became the rearing of
cattle, bred on the best pastures and then allowed to run on land which
had reverted to moor. Later medieval trends in land use gave the region
many of the characteristics which it was to retain after 1500, an empty,
largely pastoral appearance, many patches of moorland, and "vestiges
of... old mounds" testifying to abandoned arable.[342]

Dartmoor is a true highland zone region, having a high inner core
(the "Forest") of about 50,000 acres of rough grazing with a few
islands of reclamation amounting to approximately 1,020 acres on the
eve of the Black Death, and an outer zone of moor-edge manors (to
which the figures in Table 2.17 relate). Within the Forest, a special
appraisal of vacancies in 1350–1 found about 300 acres unoccupied,
although one-third were immediately re-let to formerly landless men;
by the late 1370s only about 75 of the acres reclaimed by 1348 were still
waste (*in chacia*). Moreover, contrary trends were already apparent;
slowly, no doubt almost imperceptibly in the fastnesses, new
reclamations were being made on a small scale, "called landbot by the
custom of the Forest".[343] In the zone of moor-edge manors the early
medieval arable field systems of two hamlets below the rocky slopes of
Hound Tor were abandoned towards the end of the fourteenth
century, as were outfields of about 80 acres and other fields at Venford,
outer boundaries being deliberately broken to give access to com-

the demesne at South Tawton in 1439, which comprised nothing but pasture, turbary, and wood:
PRO C 139/94.

[340] Dean and Chapter Archives, VC 22279 and PRO SC 6/1118/6; Arundell Mss., MA 225
and 227.

[341] For further evidence of declining standards of cultivation in this region (failure to manure
land, cessation of sanding, decline of mill receipts), see Devon RO, W1258M/D/70, court of Oct.
1365 (Werrington); CR 1049a (Manworthy); Cary Mss., Ashwater court of Oct. 1436; Arundell
Mss. MA 225, a/c of 1390–1 (Hartland); Devon RO, W1258M/D/71 (Werrington).

[342] Below, ch. 3; Vancouver, *County of Devon*, p. 290.

[343] Acreage of reclaimed land calculated from figures in two imperfect rentals and an account
of 1350–1: PRO SC 6/828/20, 828/21, SC 11/802. For a sample of accounts detailing subsequent
trends, SC 6/828/21, 829/1, 829/9 (for the custom of "landbot"), 822/3.

moning livestock; all may still be seen under rough grass and bracken today. Yet, when all is said and done, there was no massive abandonment of arable, as Table 2.17 shows. At Venford parts of the field system remained in use during the later middle ages; at Widecombe-in-the-Moor sales of tithe sheaves yielded approximately the same sums in the 1440s as in the 1380s, suggesting that some of the abandoned fields to be seen in the parish today were casualties not of later medieval, but of more recent contraction of cultivation.[344] This resilience may be put down to the fact that Dartmoor was a highly commercialized region during the later middle ages. Thither came "strangers" (*extranei*) with their cattle to exploit limitless rough pastures; the "delinquent men" or surreptitious grazers; *carbonarii*, "digging turves to make charcoal"; *censarii* or landless men and women; migrant tinners; merchants to the stannary towns, from Bristol, Coventry, London; men from Cornwall to dig turf; others seeking more minor moorland products – reeves of the earl of Devon, abbot of Tavistock, and Dean and Chapter for granite millstones, the bishop's reeve to Ashburton for a horse (a tough Dartmoor pony?) to work far away on the demesne at Clyst.[345] Demands for foodstuffs from men in a great diversity of occupations, and from the moor-edge towns, as well as remoteness from other sources of supply, gave a resilience to land use on Dartmoor.

The north and south coastlands of Cornwall are considered together here, as they are in surveys of modern land use.[346] Figures in Table 2.17 reveal that these parts of Cornwall (a county often considered to be largely pastoral)[347] in fact experienced a decline in cultivation smaller than in any other part of the south-west. Relative attractiveness of holdings in the aftermath of the Black Death is indicated by the renewal of tenures made by duchy ministers in 1356: at Trematon, Calstock, and Tintagel there were few reductions, and even some increases, in

[344] G. Beresford, 'Three deserted medieval settlements on Dartmoor', *Med. Arch.*, XXIII, 1979, pp. 150–2; A. Fleming and N. Ralph, 'Medieval settlement and land use on Holne Moor, Dartmoor: the landscape evidence', *Med. Arch.*, XXVI, 1982, pp. 130–2; Dean and Chapter Archives, 5232, 5235, 5237, 5248; E. Gawne, 'Field patterns in Widecombe parish and the Forest of Dartmoor', *Devon. Assoc.*, 102, 1970, pp. 49–69.

[345] For agistment arrangements and *extranei*, PRO C 145/224/3 and *Cal. Inq. Misc.*, v, pp. 120–1; for numbers of animals and the distances travelled, below, p. 319; for *carbonarii*, *censarii*, and delinquents, see the sample of accounts listed in n.343 above and PRO SC 6/Hen.VII/88–92, SC 2/166/45–6; for merchants, *CPR, 1327–30*, pp. 240, 367, 379; for the Cornish, below, p. 740; for exploitation of minor products, BL Add. Roll 64717, Devon RO, W1258M/D/74/6, a/c of 1488–9; Dean and Chapter Archives, 5067; Devon RO, W1258M/G/3.

[346] B. S. Roberson, *Cornwall*, pt. 91 of The Land of Britain, ed. L. D. Stamp, London, 1941, p. 442.

[347] The prejudice has a good pedigree: *The Register of John de Grandisson*, ed. F. C. Hingeston-Randolph, London and Exeter, 1894–9, III, p. 98.

rents and fines, while at Tybesta and Helstone-in-Trigg reductions were small and attributed to temporary insolvency of tenants rather than to any more fundamental "weakness of the land".[348] Later, during the mid-fifteenth-century nadir in demand for land, there are signs of difficulties on individual tenancies on some of the duchy's coastal properties and on the coastal manors of other estates: at Ardevora, exposed to the Fal, a few holdings were described as *vasta* and in 1487 Joan Coryngton's manor of Dorset opposite Fowey was said, perhaps not entirely truthfully, to be valueless "on account of the devastation and desolation of the country".[349] These last examples may possibly have been casualties of French or Breton raids, or more probably refer to the unsuccessful tenures always to be found here and there when low grain prices can lead to under-capitalization in arable farming.[350] In either case they were exceptional, for in general rentals on coastal manors did not decline sharply.[351] There are several reasons why farmers on the coastlands continued to cultivate with some success during the later middle ages. First, these are intrinsically good grainlands, "excellent for all kinds of grain, especially wheat" and yielding "a very good produce of corn", qualities which were recognized in the later middle ages when the region specialized, more than any other, in wheat and barley. Second, the coastlands were close to supplies of sea-sand, resulting in particularly high valuations of arable on creek-sides, 10d. per acre at Markwell in 1428, 8d. at Trelasker in 1447.[352] Thirdly, the men of the nearby stannaries and

[348] Hatcher, *Duchy of Cornwall*, pp. 122–5; PRO E 306/2/1, in which there are few references for reductions on these manors *quia terra morosa* or *propter debilitatem terre*.

[349] Hatcher, *Duchy of Cornwall*, pp. 148–65, and PRO E 306/2/7 for some vacant holdings on the duchy's coastal manors, although few of these became permanent; Arundell Mss. MA 27, 31; *CIPM, Henry VII*, I, p. 94, possibly looking back to the raid on Fowey described by Leland and Carew (for which see n.350 below).

[350] For coastal devastation some of the principal references are *Rot. Parl.*, III, p. 42; *Cal. Inq. Misc. 1377–88*, p. 77; *Thomae Walsingham*, ed. Riley, I, pp. 374–5; M. Oppenheim, 'Maritime history', in *VCH Cornwall*, I, pp. 481–2; *Register of Edmund Lacy*, ed. Dunstan IV, p. 262; Leland, *Itinerary*, I, p. 204 and Carew, *Survey of Cornwall*, ed. F. E. Halliday, p. 209.

[351] On the bishopric's manor of Tregaire a valor of 1484–5 gives the rental (minus defects of rent) at only a little lower than that in a similar document of 1308, while, despite some uncollected rents, cash received from tenants remained remarkably stable in a sample of accounts from 1396 to 1496: Devon RO, W1258M/E/24 and Oliver, *Monasticon Dioecesis Exoniensis*, p. 430; BL Add. Roll 64934; Devon RO, CR 470, 473, 475, 481. At the Arundells' manor of Lanhadron there was a slight increase in rents over the course of the fifteenth century: Arundell Mss., MA 33, 41, 70 and Devon RO, CR 1407. Hatcher, *Duchy of Cornwall*, pp. 262–6 for Calstock, Liskeard, Helstone-in-Trigg, and Tybesta, on all of which rents held up far better than on manors with much moorland, e.g. Tewington, Moresk, and Helston-in-Kirrier.

[352] Carew, *Survey of Cornwall*, ed. Tonkin, pp. 17–18; Fraser, *County of Cornwall*, p. 26; see ch. 3 below for medieval crop combinations; PRO C 139/35, 139/126 and ch. 3 below for sandways.

numerous ports, including Plymouth, provided ready markets for foodstuffs. Only the remotest of coastal farms were more than a few miles away from these sources of demand which, on occasion, could even encourage imports of grain by aliens.[353]

By contrast, dramatic changes in land use took place on the Cornish moorlands – "Bodmin" Moor (properly Foweymoor), Blackmoor, and the moory landscapes northwards and westwards of Truro, on all of which there had been early medieval reclamations associated in part with expanding tin production. At Corndon on Bodmin Moor a reclamation described as "a certain parcel" in 1337 later became four parcels and a messuage, indicating its precarious establishment as a holding, but it decayed during the later fourteenth century and then disappears from the record, reclaimed back by moor, during the fifteenth. At Enniscaven, environed by the wastes of Blackmoor, and on Carminowe manor in the far west we read of holdings "remaining waste" from which "it is not possible to levy herbage payments" – presumably because surrounding common moors gave graziers all that they needed. Almost all tenants in the uplands of Helston-in-Kirrier were excused fines in 1356 and the reasons given – "because the land is inclined to moor" (*morosa*), "because of the weakness of the land" – allow us almost to witness a return to waste which was rapid and permanent (at least during the time-span covered here) on this classic example of a manor which underwent "over-expansion" during the early middle ages. The trend is eloquently reflected in the farm of the mills at Helston which fell from over £9 to 28s. between 1347 and 1465.[354] It is interesting to note that there are many other references to mills which were "ruinous" or "all waste and fallen" around each of the Cornish moorlands.[355] In the thirteenth century the population of the county had been great enough to encourage reclamation and cultivation of relatively poor soils on the moorland fringes, but with demand reduced after the Black Death, the more fertile and productive nearby coastlands became the main producers of grains, and cultivation

[353] Hatcher, *Duchy of Cornwall*, p. 147.

[354] P. L. Hull, ed., *The Caption of Seisin of the Duchy of Cornwall (1337)*, Devon and Cornwall Rec. Soc., NS 17, 1971, p. 16, PRO E 306/2/1, 2/16, Duchy of Cornwall Archives, 475; Arundell Mss. MA 61; PRO E 306/2/1 and Hatcher, *Duchy of Cornwall*, p. 177. At Helston the letting of some moorland holdings was regarded as hopeless, and the baliff converted them into a "chace", yielding profits only from agistment, sales of gorse and heath, turbary, and toll of tin: PRO SC 6/817/3.

[355] Arundell Mss. MA 29 (Bodardle); MA 5 (Cardinham); PRO SC 6/1138/2 and Devon RO, W1258M/E/24 (Cargoll); Arundell Mss. R&S 8, 14 (Carminowe); PRO SC 6/823/28 (Hamatethy); Arundell Mss. MA 34 (Lambroun); PRO C 139/103 and SC 6/823/38 (Merthen); PRO SC 6/823/38 (Treloweth).

on the moorlands suffered accordingly. J. Hatcher has repeatedly, and rightly, stressed the local effects of buoyancy of demand for farm products in later medieval Cornwall, and this concentration of grain production where it was most profitable is a further illustration.[356] Lapsed arable on the moorlands was not, of course, totally valueless. The most productive residual use was permanent pasture, the acreage of which rose significantly around the moorland borders (Table 2.17) during the later middle ages as livestock-rearing enterprises there became increasingly important. Uninhabited holdings at Trenuth and Tregoodwell on the flanks of Bodmin Moor were occupied in the late fifteenth century by tenants with principal holdings on soils more fit for cultivation and almost certainly became what a later age was to call "feeding farms", their land "all pasture ground, the inner hedges down".[357] Second, abandoned arable could revert to intercommoned rough grazing. Finally, the agricultural value of the land could be totally devastated by tinners. In 1361 John de Treeures complained that, because of the presence of tinners on his manor, "nothing will remain of all that good land except great stones and gravel", and if the figure of 300 acres per year destroyed by Devon tinners has any validity, the rate of destruction in the Cornish stannaries must have been even greater.[358] More than this, peat charcoal was the standard fuel throughout the generally treeless stannaries, sale of turves bringing in 29s. to Sir John de Dynham at Cardinham in 1435–6 and 17s. to the Lambrouns at Lambroun in 1398–9. A deft calculation might allow estimates to be made of the acreage so devastated, as has been done for the turbaries of the Norfolk Broads; it was certainly enough for Cornish tinners to complain to Edward IV, with some exaggeration, that "the lands…in their own county have been so devastated of turf…that they cannot get enough to melt their tin".[359]

[356] Hatcher, *Duchy of Cornwall*, pp. 29–32, 258. For examples of documentary evidence of early medieval reclamations on the Cornish moorlands, PRO C 145/87/1 (Tremoddrett); SC 6/811/5 (Helston-in-Kirrier); *The Cartulary of Launceston Priory*, ed. P. L. Hull, Devon and Cornwall Rec. Soc., 30, 1987, pp. 36–7; Hull, ed., *Caption of Seisin* for reclamations called *landioks*, as at Calstock and Stoke Climsland, pp. 99–101, 109–15. It is likely that the produce of these reclamations was sold to tinners, which may have been the purpose of the stalls set up from time to time on the moory and metalliferous manor of Tywarnhayle, present in 1337 but, significantly, not thereafter: *ibid.*, p. 83.

[357] PRO E 306/2/16. There are later portrayals of such decayed feeding farms in maps of Stuffle and Medland in the Lanhydrock Atlas, Lanhydrock House.

[358] *Register of the Black Prince*, II, p. 178; *Rot. Parl.*, I, p. 312. For other evidence of devastation by tinners in the south-west, *ibid.*, pp. 190, 297–8 and II, p. 190; *CCR, 1385–9*, p. 510 and *1392–6*, pp. 159–60.

[359] D. Woolner, 'Peat charcoal', *Devon and Cornwall N & Q*, xxx, 1965–7, pp. 118–20, and N. Quinnell, 'A note on the turf platforms of Cornwall', *Cornish Arch.*, 23, 1984, pp. 10–11; Arundell Mss. MA 2 and 33; *CPR, 1461–7*, p. 482. Manorial documents often value turbaries

Local histories sketched in the preceding paragraphs show that later medieval farmers in the south-west participated in an important *divergence* in land use between one region and another. In his work on peasant livestock in Wiltshire, M. M. Postan observed that thirteenth-century population pressure and the need to produce grains for subsistence led to a convergence in regional characteristics, so that any expected regional differentiation turns out "to be something of a phantom".[360] It was the same in the south-west, where similar demands reduced regional differences in land use during the early middle ages, encouraging cultivation even of the poor clays of mid-Devon and the boulder-strewn slopes of Carnmenellis in western Cornwall. Removal of those pressures during the later middle ages strengthened regional contrasts as farmers adjusted land use according to the best capabilities of the land and the survival or otherwise of local markets. For example, in Cornwall the moorland borders became predominantly pastoral while arable cultivation came to be concentrated on the coastlands; in Devon, there was a very marked divergence between the south, where natural fertility and proximity to markets encouraged continued cultivation, and mid-Devon where poor soils and remoteness from markets combined to encourage a swift movement towards extensively used pastures. It was not always that slight early medieval emphases were strengthened during this process of divergence (although this could be the case), for mid-Devon had a heavy but unsuitable arable bias in the thirteenth century yet had become predominantly pastoral by the beginning of the fifteenth. Nor was it always that the regions of most recent reclamation were those which most surely returned to pasture and moor, for local demand could, under certain circumstances, bolster the farm economies of such areas. The resilient holdings of the Dartmoor borders, some of them in the mid-fourteenth century relatively recently reclaimed, illustrate this last point very well for most were adjacent to tin workings and, moreover, the workings were in many cases distant, over rugged terrain, from other sources of foodstuffs. On the Cornish moorlands, by contrast, demands from stannary workers did not have the same effect, most tin workings being only a few miles away from the coastlands, which were better suited for grain production.

Expansion of pastoral land use in many regions was accompanied by, and in part a result of, a very marked expansion in the size of holdings, as chapter 7 shows. When we come to ask how these changes affected

along with toll tin: PRO C 139/35, 93, 107; *Cal. Inq. Misc.*, VI, p. 127; Arundell Mss. MA 32, 56, 70.

[360] M. M. Postan, 'Village livestock in the thirteenth century', *EcHR*, 2nd ser. XV, 1962–3, p. 247.

settlements we at once recall the deserted villages of the English midlands, which were casualties alike of pastoral farming and of a good deal of long-term social change involving amalgamation of tenures.[361] Yet no true deserted village sites have been identified in the south-west. Speculations that this points to little change in land use during the later middle ages are clearly inappropriate in the light of what has been said above.[362] It is simply due to the fact that the nucleated village was never a common settlement form in Devon and Cornwall. Indeed, Charles Henderson's unrivalled knowledge of the early topography of Cornwall led him to observe that there were no true medieval villages in the county, an observation fully confirmed by a detailed analysis of thirteen manors on the estates of the Duchy of Cornwall, the Arundells and the bishops of Exeter. Unfree tenants on these manors lived among a total of 223 settlements, many of them hamlets typically containing between two and six messuages, the rest of them isolated farms.[363] In Devon a small number of true nucleated villages, mostly hundredal centres and market villages with a strong chance of survival, accompanied the predominantly dispersed settlement pattern: Sidbury, for example, with its many houses and cottages in 1394–5, its *shoppe* and market place. Elsewhere, as in Cornwall, isolated farmsteads and small hamlets were the rule.[364] Amalgamation and decay of holdings can have profound effects on settlement structures of this type, for reduction in occupied farmsteads, let us say by half, will not destroy a nucleated village but can substantially modify a pattern of scattered farms. The best approach to the subject is through detailed studies of manors with series of topographically arranged rentals naming individual farmstead and hamlet sites (Table 2.18).

Of the three Devonshire manors analysed in the table, contraction of settlement was most severe on Hartland manor in the remote countryside of north Devon; here almost all hamlets dwindled in size during the fourteenth and fifteenth centuries (Table 2.18, middle lines). Contraction took place as a result of several processes. First was total abandonment of land, best illustrated by the history of the hamlet of

---

[361] Dyer, 'Deserted medieval villages in the West Midlands', pp. 20–5, 29–34.

[362] J. Hall and A. Hamlin, 'Deserted medieval settlements in Devon', *Devon Historian*, 13, 1976, p. 2.

[363] C. Henderson, *Essays in Cornish History*, Oxford, 1935, p. 19; see Table 2.18 for sources for Helston-in-Kirrier, Helstone-in-Trigg, and Tybesta; Arundell Mss. R&S 14 for the manors of Carminowe, Tregarne, Trembleathe, Treloy, Lanherne, Connerton, Lanhadron, Bodwannick; Devon RO, W1258M/E/24 conventionary fines, and 382/ER/2 for Cargoll and Tregaire.

[364] Dean and Chapter Archives, 2945 for Sidbury and, for another example, Fox, 'Field systems: East Devon', pp. 112–33. For contemporary descriptions of dispersed settlement see PRO C 136/25/2 which mentions rights *in minutis hameletis* within Hackpen manor, and Eton College Mss. 1/140 which mentions collection of rents *in diversis locis in parochia de Modbir*.

Table 2.18. *Settlement contraction in six south-western manors*

		Hartland	Ashwater	Helston-in-Kirrier	Stokenham	Tybesta	Helstone-in-Trigg
All occupied settlement sites	pre-1348	43	25	45	24	20	21
	late 14th cent. or early 15th	40	22	40	24	21	18
	late 15th cent. or 16th	33	21	31	24	19	18
Settlement sites declining in size	14th cent.	24	9	17	14	7	10
	15th cent.	23	2	20	16	10	12
Sites occupied by single farms	pre-1348	8	14	21	2	7	4
	late 14th cent. or early 15th	14	14	26	4	8	3
	late 15th cent. or 16th	20	15	28	8	12	4

Sources: Hartland: Arundell Mss., R&S 5 collated with PRO C 133/102/2 (for 1301); R&S 5 (for *c.* 1365); Devon RO, Survey of Lord Dynham's lands (for 1566). Settlements in parts of the manor lying outside the parish, and in areas for which the rental of *c.* 1365 is missing, have not been reconstructed. Ashwater: Devon RO, Cary Mss., rentals of 1346 and 1397 and survey of 1523. Settlements lost to, or gained by, the manor in 1425 have not been reconstructed. Stokenham: PRO SC 11/765 (for *c.* 1347); Huntington Library, San Marino, HAM box 64, rental of "1577" (for *c.* 1360); PRO SC 11/168 (for 1548–9). Identification of settlement sites from DRO, Hartland tithe map and 1201A/PW/3 (for Hartland); A. Barker, 'Pre-Conquest and medieval settlement on the Culm Measures of Devon', Leicester Univ. M.A. thesis, 1985, pp. 44–9 (for Ashwater); Huntington Library, HAM box 64, rental of 1580–1 (for Stokenham). Helston-in-Kirrier, Tybesta, and Helstone-in-Trigg: *The Caption of Seisin of the Duchy of Cornwall* (1377), ed. P. L. Hull; Duchy of Cornwall Archives, 475, 480; PRO E 306/2/2, 5, 7, 14, 16. Settlements containing only free tenements have not been reconstructed, because the sources do not regularly enumerate free tenures. Identification of settlement sites from Cornwall RO, maps drawn for the Assessionable Manors Award Act, 1848; J. E. B. Gover, 'The place-names of Cornwall' (Ms. at Royal Institution of Cornwall); *The Parliamentary Survey of the Duchy of Cornwall*, ed. N. J. G. Pounds, Devon and Cornwall Rec. Soc., NS 25, 27, 1982–4.

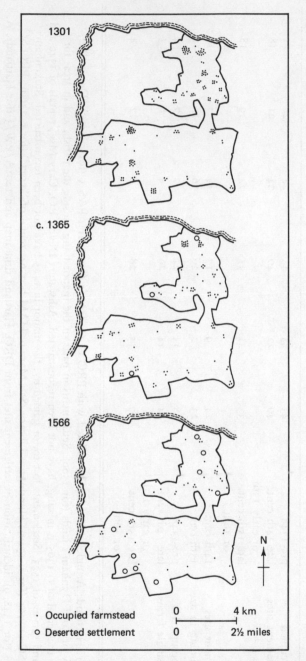

Fig. 2.2 Settlement and contraction on Hartland manor (for the area mapped and for sources see Table 2.18)

Hendon which was occupied by eight smallholders in the early fourteenth century, already in decay with two holdings vacant "through want of tenants" in 1365, and completely abandoned by the early fifteenth century when all holdings appear in reeves' accounts as agisted waste; until recently parishioners amused themselves with the ditty "Yennon [Hendon] was a market town / When Lunnon was a vuzzy down." A second process leading to desertion was attachment of the land of one settlement to a holding in another; sometimes the two were at some distance, probably indicating that the attached holdings were converted to pastoral appendages of the main farm. Working alongside these two processes was a third, internal engrossing, which did not result in total desertion of sites but in an equally important later medieval development throughout the south-west, namely the dwindling of a hamlet in size until it became a single isolated farmstead (Table 2.18, bottom lines). Whereas the small hamlet inhabited by often interrelated smallholders had been the characteristic type of settlement at Hartland in the early fourteenth century, the deserted site and the isolated farmstead were dominant by the sixteenth century (Fig. 2.2).[365]

At Ashwater, 18 miles to the south of Hartland, four sites became deserted through attachment of their land to neighbouring settlements, and almost all hamlets dwindled in size.[366] Much contraction of settlement is to be expected in a region where cultivation declined sharply after 1348, to be replaced by livestock rearing of an extensive type. North and mid-Devon had begun to assume that empty air, with large, widely spaced farms, which they still wear today.[367]

On the high moorlands of Devon and Cornwall, settlement contraction was closely related to the degree to which land reverted to pasture and waste. Dartmoor is the prime example of a moorland region where demands for foodstuffs from those in industrial occupations helped to preserve patterns both of land use and of

[365] Principal sources are rentals and surveys listed in note to Table 2.18; Arundell Mss. MA 225–41, CR 427–38; PRO C 139/40, 170; Bodleian Library, Top. Devon. b.1; R. P. Chope, *The Book of Hartland*, Torquay, 1940, p. 8. Further details in H. S. A. Fox, 'Contraction: desertion and dwindling of dispersed settlement in a Devon parish', *Ann. Rept. Medieval Village Research Group*, 31, 1983, pp. 40–2.

[366] Rentals listed in note to Table 2.18 and Devon RO, Cary Mss., Ashwater court rolls.

[367] Below, ch. 7, n.331 for decline of population in mid-Devon. For two excavated deserted sites in this region see E. M. Jope and R. I. Threlfall, 'Excavation of a medieval settlement at Beere, North Tawton, Devon', *Med. Arch.*, II, 1958, pp. 112–40 and R. Bridgewater and T. Miles, 'A trial excavation at Kigbeare, Okehampton Hamlets', *Devon. Arch. Soc.*, 36, 1978, pp. 241–4. Other sites may be identified through locative personal names recorded before 1350, but later only borne by woods or moors: J. E. B. Gover, A. Mawer and F. M. Stenton, *The Place-Names of Devon*, EPNS, 1931–2, pp. 78–9, 115.

settlement for, although deserted sites are indeed very numerous there, it is wrong to jump to the conclusion that most were marginal settlements abandoned when pressure of population became less acute, and climate perhaps more severe, in the later middle ages. To be sure, excavation has demonstrated desertion towards the end of the fourteenth century at a number of hamlets and single farms,[368] but many other now visible deserted sites were casualties of post-medieval changes in the exploitation of the region.[369] The history of Dartmoor's "ancient tenements" – holdings within the core of the moor – confirms this interpretation: at the very most perhaps nine sites were abandoned during the later middle ages, but about twenty remained inhabited. At short distances from tin workings, their tenants may have been part-time miners or engaged in the lucrative supply of foodstuffs to miners; they certainly enjoyed the right to pasture an unlimited number of animals on the moor, a right which became all the more profitable in the later middle ages.[370] In other high moorland regions, by contrast, settlement contraction was more severe. On the Cornish moorlands tin production did not bolster agriculture and settlement in the same way as on Dartmoor, for the Cornish stannaries were everywhere very close to more easily worked lands around the coasts. Retreat of cultivation and of settlement could therefore be pronounced, as shown by the figures for Helston-in-Kirrier (Table 2.18), where as many as fourteen moorland sites became deserted during the later middle ages, although some of them were later reoccupied. By the fifteenth century, despite continued activity in the manor's tin works, the moorland farming landscape of Helston-in-Kirrier presented a wrecked appearance of single farmsteads (the results of internal engrossing in former hamlets until one tenant held "the whole vill") and deserted tofts and messuages resulting from total abandonment of farmhouses and farmland.[371] On Bodmin Moor a settlement at Corndon, probably newly reclaimed in the first half of the fourteenth century, was abandoned by 1371, the internal hedges of the farm

---

[368] G. Beresford, 'Three deserted settlements', pp. 98–158. A date of desertion after 1397 could perhaps be suggested for Hound Tor, because the tithing was represented in the sheriff's tourn in that year; difficulties with arable farming at Dinna Clerks are suggested by the fact that tithe collectors found "nothing cultivated" within its manor in the 1380s: Devon RO, W1258M/X/1; Dean and Chapter Archives, 5232, 5234.

[369] C. D. Linehan, 'Deserted sites and rabbit-warrens on Dartmoor, Devon', *Med. Arch.*, x, 1966, pp. 124–5, 135, 139 and Table II; H. French and C. D. Linehan, 'Abandoned medieval sites in Widecombe-in-the-Moor', *Devon. Assoc.*, xcv, 1963, pp. 169–71.

[370] Rentals as in n.343 above; PRO SC 6/828/28; Dartmoor Preservation Association, *A Short History of the Rights of Common upon the Forest of Dartmoor and the Commons of Devon*, Plymouth, 1890, pp. 89–90. Figures for the ancient tenements are inevitably very rough and ready because of the difficulty of matching place-names with places.

[371] Sources as for Table 2.18 and, for their deployment, M. W. Beresford, 'Dispersed and grouped settlement in medieval Cornwall', *AHR*, xII, 1964, pp. 13–27. See also n.354 above.

decayed and its herbage rented by a syndicate of tenants from elsewhere; at Goosehill by the third quarter of the fourteenth century all the land was in the hands of a single tenant with a more fertile farm three miles away, and later the hamlet became simply "pasture called Gosehill...in waste", its messuages forgotten, its land reclaimed by the moor. Such developments went hand in hand with a marked increase in the proportion of the land under waste and pasture on Bodmin Moor and are confirmed by archaeological evidence for abandoned and shrunken hamlets.[372]

It is to be expected that settlements in the arable South Hams of Devonshire and on the Cornish coastlands, because of their distinctive role as grain producers, were affected in a different way from those in regions which became predominantly pastoral. The South Hams is represented in Table 2.18 by Stokenham, where three rentals of c. 1347, c. 1360, and 1548 indicate a long-drawn-out decline in the size of the manor's many hamlets through internal engrossing until some became single farms, but show relatively little attachment of all the land of one hamlet to tenures in another distant settlement, and no total desertion of sites. Both characteristics may be explained by a continuing emphasis on arable, which made it difficult (especially under conditions of labour scarcity) for many husbandmen to expand holdings above a certain threshold, to build up those huge multiple tenancies which were to be found where pastoral farming of an extensive type prevailed, and to cultivate land at a distance. Changes of the same order and type took place in settlement on the two nearby South Hams manors of Stoke Fleming and Blackawton where, despite short-term vacancies, few sites became totally deserted.[373] Few settlements on the Cornish coastlands, represented in the table by Helstone-in-Trigg and Tybesta, were totally deserted, and for the same reasons, although many hamlets declined in size to become pairs of farms or single farms. Some examples can nevertheless be found on the coastland of sites deserted during the later middle ages, such as "Cornkee" in Tregaire manor, where the land was

[372] Sources for Corndon and Goosehill as in n.354 above; D. Dudley, 'The medieval village at Garrow Tor, Bodmin Moor, Cornwall', Med. Arch., VI–VII, 1962–3, pp. 272–94; P. C. Herring, 'An exercise in landscape history: pre-Norman and medieval Brown Willy and Bodmin Moor, Cornwall', University of Sheffield M.Phil. thesis, 1986, II, p. 115; P. M. Christie and P. Rose, 'Davidstow Moor, Cornwall: the medieval and later sites', Cornish Archaeology, 26, 1987, pp. 178–82; S. Baring-Gould, 'An ancient settlement on Trewortha Marsh', Roy. Inst. Cornwall, II, 1892–3, pp. 57–70. Exmoor was another moorland region, distant from markets, where there was a good deal of contraction of arable and desertion of settlement: PRO C 135/164/11 (North Molton), SC 6/828/21–3 (Badgworthy and other settlements); Med. Arch., VI–VII, 1962–3, p. 343; M. Aston, 'Deserted farmsteads on Exmoor and the lay subsidy of 1327 in West Somerset', Somerset Arch. and N.H. Soc., CXXVII, 1983, pp. 71–104.

[373] Rentals for Stokenham as in note to Table 2.18; Devon RO, 902M/M/21 and Cary Mss, Stoke Fleming rental of c. 1522 for the single deserted site, at "Yartecomb", in Stoke Fleming; Trinity College Dublin Mss., E.5.15, f.131 and Devon RO, W1258M/G/1/38 for Blackawton.

described as "waste" in 1425–6 and was still "one parcel of moor" in 1538–9. But for the most part references to "tofts" here, increasingly frequent from the reign of Henry VI, reflect shrinkage but not total abandonment of settlement.[374]

In Devon and Cornwall, as in other areas marked by dispersed farmsteads,[375] patient documentary work can therefore uncover deserted settlements which are in some ways equivalents of the more visually dramatic deserted villages in the midlands. But the comparison should not be taken too far, for contraction of settlement in the south-west proceeded with less dislocation to rural society than occurred in districts where villages rather than dispersed farms were the character-istic settlement forms. Field systems could easily be adapted to reduced numbers of tenants; the limited lands of a hamlet of, say, four smallholders could, under the prevailing system of convertible husbandry, pass to a single occupier without the severe difficulties of running a field system for long in low gear or in transition (with too few or too many livestock), which faced some larger communities in decline elsewhere in England.[376] Nevertheless, we should not think of the transition to fewer and smaller settlements as an entirely easy one. During the period of great epidemics after 1348 there were attempts to preserve the established structure of holdings and settlements. On one manor a new custom was introduced on behalf of "the whole homage": that surviving tenants of a hamlet with vacant tenures should occupy the vacancies. On other manors the whole vill, or the tithing, or neighbours held themselves responsible for the maintenance of vacancies, and we find empty holdings being held *in communi* by survivors.[377] Such practices perhaps suggest a conservative desire among tenant farmers to maintain traditional farming systems, but this was an attitude which was perforce eroded as population levels failed to make any recovery.

Landlords, too, attempted to minimize dilapidations and certainly played no destructive part in the contraction of settlement. Cases can

---

[374] Devon RO, CR 473, 481 and 382/ER/2, BL Add. Roll 64536, PRO E 306/2/6; for examples of tofts, PRO C 138/50, 139/31, 103, 110. Other deserted sites away from the moorlands are listed in the checklists in *Cornish Archaeology*, e.g. vol. 7 (1968) for Creed and vol. 14 (1975) for Morwenstow, although some of these may be post-medieval desertions. For an excavated example see G. Beresford, 'Tresmorn, St Gennys', *Cornish Archaeology*, 10, 1971, pp. 55–73.

[375] *VCH. Salop*, VIII, pp. 4–5; Faull and Moorhouse, eds., *West Yorkshire: an Archaeological Survey to AD 1500*, II, pp. 294–579; Aston, 'Deserted farmsteads on Exmoor'.

[376] Dyer, 'Deserted medieval villages', p. 32.

[377] Huntington Library, San Marino, HAM box 64, Stokenham rental of "1577" and PRO SC 6/1118/6 (Sampford Courtenay); BL Add. Ms. 28838, ff.129v, 135; Devon RO, W1258M/D/84/22 and D/84/44, f.27v; Dean and Chapter Archives, 2937; Arundell Mss. R&S 5, 8 (Trembleathe), MA 41 (Trink), 56 (Tregarne), 61 (Lanherne).

be found in the late fourteenth century of lords who reaped the crops from vacated holdings or used them for grazing, but this was hardly eviction.[378] It was a fear, in the words of the reeve of Rillaton, that "remaining tenants would relinquish their holdings through poverty", which encouraged a meeting of the council of the Black Prince to remit payments from many tenants in the years immediately following 1348. Thereafter, as Hatcher has shown, duchy tenants were governed with considerable benevolence, the Black Prince himself "marvelling" that his council was prepared to listen sympathetically to "poor folk…importuning him and his council so much, bringing their suit to him from such distant parts and on such petty matters".[379] Payments made by landlords, who were increasingly rentiers, for repair of tenants' buildings were, after reductions in rent and fines, their most substantial contribution to their efforts to retain tenants and are especially relevant in the context of settlement contraction. In certain circumstances landlords did sanction decays, as when John Foterell of Stoke Fleming was allowed to maintain only a hall, bakehouse, and barn on four engrossed holdings, no doubt because the upkeep of several vacant houses was too great a charge on a single holding.[380] But a *principal* messuage which was habitable, and a well-hedged holding, were essential for successful re-letting, and it was for this reason that lords are to be found carrying out repairs of all kinds, a course preferable in most cases to eviction on account of dilapidations. A vacant dwelling might be shored up until eventually, if no takers were found, it was reported as "totally prostrate" or decayed *ad terram*, but most seigneurial repairs were done on occupied holdings. Repairs could be very elaborate, as when the Dean and Chapter of Exeter completely renewed Richard Wyse's house at Sidbury in 1460–1: stone foundations, "le quabbewalle" (cob wall), timber prepared by a master carpenter, door and window frames, thatch, and other materials cost a total of £7 3s. A valor of the bishop of Exeter in 1484–5 set repairs to tenants' houses against total income on some of his Cornish manors, yet this was not simply episcopal charity, for similar assistance was given on estates of all sizes, as might be expected of expenditure designed to prevent deterioration of income from rents.[381] Repairs by landlords, as

---

[378] Devon RO, DD 54888; Somerset RO, DDCN box 3 no. 14, a/c of 1394–5; Arundell Mss. MA 56 (Lanherne and Carminowe) and CR 446, a/c of 1366–7.

[379] Duchy of Cornwall Archives, 4 (Rillaton); Hatcher, *Duchy of Cornwall*, pp. 104–21, 127–8; *Register of the Black Prince*, II, p. 22.   [380] Devon RO, 902M/M/22.

[381] Huntington Library, San Marino, HAM box 74, a/c of "Salisburysland" (Yealmpton) and BL Add. Roll 13776; for repairs to *vacant* tenements BL Add. Roll 64513 (Roskymer) and PRO SC 6/823/34; Dean and Chapter Archives, 5055 for Sidbury; Devon RO, W1258M/E/24 and, for examples of other repairs on the episcopal estate, BL Add. Rolls 64392, 64546, Devon RO, CR 470, W1258M/E/24, a/c of 1399–1400, N. W. Alcock, 'The medieval cottages of Bishops Clyst, Devon', *Med. Arch.*, 9, 1965, pp. 146–53; for a sample of other estates, PRO SC 6/822/16,

well as the comparative ease of the transition from smallholdings to larger farms, helped to create viable rather than enfeebled tenures, secure from and giving little encouragement to the depopulator, so that when Wolsey's commission set out to investigate houses deliberately cast down since 1488 it did not see any need to visit the counties of Devon and Cornwall.[382]

The renovation of tenants' houses with the use of seigneurial incomes provides an interesting example of redistribution of wealth during the later middle ages, for many manor houses themselves were becoming ruinous during this period as lords ceased to occupy some manors and concentrated increasingly expensive repairs on principal residences. On the Courtenay estate the manor house at Topsham was in ruins by the 1440s and at Musbury only the toft remained; repairs and new buildings were clearly being concentrated at Tiverton with its "many buildings and gardens". There the family was to build or repair a deer-house in the park, a salthouse, a woodhouse, a storehouse, stables, gun-carriages, and the doors of two towers – these last preparations, in 1455, being no doubt occasioned by the simmering violence, in that violent year, between Thomas Courtenay and William Bonville. Likewise, on the Pomeroy estate, the manor house at Stockleigh was allowed to decay and building was concentrated at Berry Pomeroy, both on fortifications and more peaceful improvements, including the new arbour assigned in dower to Elizabeth Pomeroy in 1496.[383] Where all that remained in place of a manor house was a steward's chamber, as at Tregaire and Sherford, Yealmpton and Stokenham, there could be no better expression of the development of a system of management under which lordship was physically expressed only by occasional visits of an official to hold manorial courts.[384]

This reduced commitment to seigneurial building was associated with a decline in direct demesne management on large estates and with

6/823/38 (Winnianton), Arundell Mss. MA 34 (Lanherne, Trembleathe), Duchy of Cornwall Archives, 475 (reductions in fines at Helston-in-Kirrier and elsewhere as subsidies for repair).

[382] M. W. Beresford, *Lost Villages of England*, p. 218.

[383] PRO C 139/104; BL Add. Rolls 64714, 64717; Devon RO, CR 292, 503; and M. Cherry, 'The struggle for power in mid-fifteenth-century Devonshire', in R. A. Griffiths, ed., *Patronage, the Crown, and the Provinces in Later Medieval England*, Gloucester, 1981, pp. 134–8; PRO C 139/122 for the *vacuus situs* at Stockleigh; D. Seymour and J. Hazzard, *Berry Pomeroy Castle*, Torquay, 1982, pp. 17–22; J. R. Kenyon, 'Early artillery fortifications in England and Wales: a preliminary survey and reappraisal', *Arch. J.*, CXXXVIII, 1981, p. 227; *CIPM, Henry VII*, I, pp. 516–17.

[384] BL. Add. Roll 64534 and Devon RO, CR 471; BL Add. Roll 13091; Huntington Library, San Marino, HAM box 74, a/c of "Salisburysland" for Stokenham and Yealmpton. Unused and decaying manorial buildings were often let to a number of tenants, as at Slapton, Filleigh, and Newton St Cyres: Bury St Edmunds and W. Suffolk RO, 449/1/E3/15.101/2.2; Devon RO, 1262M/M/100; BL Harl. Ms. 4766, f. 7.

a related tendency for lords to become less residentially mobile. Direct management of demesnes continued into the last quarter of the fourteenth century, even on the south-western manorial outliers of estates with centres elsewhere.[385] It was usually, however, management which reduced expenditure on arable farming (except on "home farm" demesnes) and which concentrated more upon livestock, especially dairying and cattle breeding.[386] On large and medium-sized estates the end came in the last decades of the fourteenth century and the first two decades of the fifteenth. When, in 1377, Edward Courtenay succeeded to the earldom of Devon, most of his demesnes were under cultivation, yet by 1422, three years after his death, all were leased.[387] On the estates of the Dynhams, of Plympton priory, and of the Dean and Chapter of Exeter the end also came during these decades.[388] On most large estates a meadow for the lord's horses, or an orchard and cider press, might be kept in hand after the first quarter of the fifteenth century, but the age of large-scale direct occupation was over.[389] When, in the late summer of 1538, the abbot of Tavistock's bailiff at the home farm of Hurdwick set his villeins about their customary tasks of reaping at the very time that preparations were being made elsewhere for the abbey's deed of surrender, this was by now conservative practice for most estates of the same size, archaic and long forgotten.[390]

[385] For examples of the latter see *Cal. Inq. Misc.*, VII, p. 71 (John, Earl of Salisbury at Stokenham) and Devon RO, CR 1131–3 (prior of Montacute at Monkleigh).

[386] *The Register of Walter de Stapeldon*, ed. F. C. Hingeston-Randolph, London and Exeter, 1892, pp. 570–5; *Trevelyan Papers*, ed. J. P. Collier, Camden Soc. OS LXVII, 1857, pp. 5–17 and Devon RO, Diocesan records 1057 for the bishopric estate as a whole; Devon RO, W1258M/G/3 (Bishop's Clyst), DD 54888–54921 (Holcombe Rogus), Arundell Mss. CR 446 and MA 246 (Clayhidon), Somerset RO, DDWO 46/1 (Whalesborough) for examples of the trend on individual manors. See also Table 3.22.

[387] PRO C 135/260/3, BL Add. Roll 64318, Devon RO, CR 513, 531, 584, and Dean and Chapter Archives, VC 22279, for direct management on some of the earl's Somerset and Devonshire manors, and of his wife's Cornish inheritance, into the 1380s and 1390s; PRO SC 6/118/6 for leasing.

[388] We know only of termination of direct management at the principal Dynham manors of Clayhidon (by 1411–12) and Kingskerswell (by 1452–3): Arundell Mss. CR 447, a/c of 1411–12, and MA 251. In the first decade of the fifteenth century the family may still have been engaged in fattening cattle at Nutwell, for which see below, ch. 3, n. 347. For the Dean and Chapter estate we have only "outside" dates, which may post-date termination by several years, for Clyst Honiton (by 1425), Culmstock (by 1404), Dawlish (by 1419), Halsford (by 1408), Salcombe Regis (by 1444), and Sidbury (by 1425): Dean and Chapter Archives, 5117, 5109, 5031, 5121, 5137, 5054. Prior of Plympton: BL Harl. Ms. 4766, ff. 7, 10v, 14v, 18v, 20.

[389] BL Add. Roll 64714 for an example of meadows in hand (for the earl of Devon's huge number of horses) and below, ch. 3, for orchards.

[390] Devon RO, W1258M/D/52/2, a/c of 1537–8. This is an example of late continued cultivation at a "home farm", as at Otford: Du Boulay, 'Demesne farming at Otford', p. 116.

From these generalizations we must to a degree exempt the houses and demesnes of minor knightly families, esquires and gentlemen, all of whom were very numerous in both counties.[391] Their demesnes, by virtue of their origins as sub-infeudations in manorial backwoods, tended to be small and home farming for the household had always been important; direct management on such properties was little affected by sluggish market prices. Thus the mid-fifteenth-century *compoti* of Ralph Reskymer esquire, while exhibiting nothing of the complicated system of grange and livestock accounting which an earlier age had demanded of its reeves, contain oblique references to continued cultivation and employment of a shepherd.[392] In the records of the Blewetts, esquires of Holcombe Rogus, we can observe the decline of formal accounting for stock and crops in the 1430s, although some demesne cultivation was still carried on at a reduced scale. The Blewetts probably continued husbandry in a small way on their home farm of Holcombe into the sixteenth century when they rebuilt the great front of Holcombe Court; just as the Fortescues combined involvement in husbandry at Weare Giffard with the rebuilding in the late fifteenth century of the gatehouse and hall which still survive; or like the Malherbes of Payhembury, details of whose farm stock and improved house survive in an inventory made after the death of William Malherbe in 1498.[393] This continued occupation of demesnes on small estates in the south-west confirms the suspicion of other historians that small landowners were often able to maintain their lifestyles with comparatively little dislocation during the later middle ages.[394]

---

[391] See C. J. Tyldesley, 'The Crown and the local communities in Devon and Cornwall from 1377 to 1422', University of Exeter Ph.D. thesis, 1978, p. 22, for lack of any great landed estates in Cornwall; W. G. Hoskins, 'The estates of the Caroline gentry', in Hoskins and Finberg, *Devonshire Studies*, p. 334, for an estimate of about 400 Devon gentry in 1600, a figure confirmed by BL Harl. Ms. 5827, ff. 96–138v, Hooker's list of gentry residences in the county.

[392] PRO SC 6/823/37–8. For similar involvement in husbandry, despite lack of formal accounting, on the estates of Wm Lambroun knight and on the Bottreaux estate, see Arundell Mss. MA 33; Devon RO, CR 1407; Somerset RO, DDWO 46/1, a/c of 1414–15 and 47/3, a/c of 1438–9.

[393] Devon RO, DD 54925; 1262M/M/106–8, 98, a/c of 1480–1, 101 (heriots and strays sent *ad instaurum apud Were*); BL Add. Ms. 28838, f.65v for the inventory, f.151v for what was probably the Malherbe house, and f.119 for instructions on building. For another example of pride in building on a gentry estate, see *The Hylle Cartulary*, ed. R. W. Dunning, Somerset Rec. Soc., LXVIII, 1968, p. 245.

[394] M. M. Postan, in *CEcH*, I, 2nd edn, p. 596; C. Carpenter, 'The fifteenth-century English gentry and their estates', in M. Jones, ed., *Gentry and Lesser Nobility in Late Medieval Europe*, pp. 47–51.

CHAPTER 3

FARMING PRACTICE AND TECHNIQUES

A. THE NORTHERN BORDERS

The study of the fine series of Percy estate maps has made it clear that in the sixteenth century much of eastern Northumberland was open-field country, and some of the earlier generalizations about the field systems of that county are now, rightly, discounted. At the same time, much evidence for the open-field character of many parts of Cumberland in the sixteenth century has come to light. For the later medieval period, however, evidence for the field systems of the northern counties is sparse by comparison, and there is an obvious temptation to use sixteenth-century evidence to illuminate the much darker period which preceded it. There are, however, grounds for believing that some of the open fields of sixteenth-century Cumberland were of fairly recent origin, and instances from Northumberland of the rearrangement of fields in the sixteenth century suggest that maps dating from the end of the century may not be a reliable guide to fourteenth- and fifteenth-century conditions. It is as well, therefore, to limit the discussion as far as possible to the evidence from the late medieval sources.[1]

In east Durham and east Northumberland, the overwhelming bulk of arable land was in open fields, laid out in strips. The terrier of Hawkwell (c. 1370) presents a vivid and detailed picture of ploughed strips or selions dispersed through the three open fields of Killingworth in south-east Northumberland, and a lease of 1392 gives a similar picture of the land on Durham priory's vill of Nun Stainton. At Killingworth the open fields were divided into a number of parcels called flats, and within each flat were strips or selions which varied in size from one rood to five acres. A similar system prevailed at Nun Stainton, and these two vills may serve as examples of the field system

[1] R. A. Butlin, 'Northumberland field systems', *AHR.* xii, 1964, pp. 99–120; Butlin, 'Field systems of Northumberland and Durham', in Baker and Butlin, eds., *Field Systems*, pp. 93–144, esp. pp. 140–2; G. Elliott, 'Field systems of north-west England', *ibid.*, pp. 41–6; *idem*, 'System of cultivation and evidence of enclosure', pp. 86–90, 100; *NCH*, xiv, pp. 212–13.

of the arable vills of the coastal plain. Open fields, however, were not confined to the arable east. They were widespread in the inland valleys of Northumberland, especially in Tynedale, and in much of Cumberland. By the sixteenth century at least 220 out of 288 townships in the county had open fields, some of which had been created within the previous century, and the system existed everywhere except in the dome of the Lake District and the border districts of north-east Cumberland.[2]

Open-field farming thus prevailed over most of the lower-lying parts of the region; but this generalization conceals much variety in farming techniques and in field patterns. In lowland Cumberland and north Westmorland the usual pattern seems to have been for each vill to have one "town field" which was kept permanently under cultivation and heavily manured, though in some of the lowland parts of Cumberland in the fifteenth century an "infield" and "outfield" system began to develop. In the south and east of Durham, however, and on the better lands of the Northumberland coastal plain, the predominant pattern was one of three or more open fields. At Killingworth, Nun Stainton, and Sacristonheugh in the fourteenth and fifteenth centuries there were three open fields, and in the sixteenth century townships with three or more open fields were numerous in east Northumberland. In both the single-field townships of Cumberland and the multiple-field vills of east Northumberland, there was abundant surrounding waste land that provided ample pasturing for animals and a reserve of arable land that might be broken up and taken in as necessary. Indeed in Cumberland this is probably how the "infield" and "outfield" system took shape in the fifteenth century. In Northumberland in the vill of East Matfen in the fifteenth century provision was made for land taken in from the waste in this way to be allocated by lot, and sixteenth-century evidence from other Northumberland vills suggests that allocation of newly cultivated waste by lot was a widespread practice. The evidence for the periodic reallocation by lot of strips in the established open fields is much sparser, though, as R. A. Dodgshon has shown, a concern for equality in the distribution of land when open fields were reallocated was an important characteristic of some Northumberland communities in the sixteenth century. The availability of abundant waste land, however, not only ensured the survival of the idea of division by lot, but also gave an unusually fluid and diverse character to the field systems of Northumberland and Cumberland.[3]

[2] Newcastle-upon-Tyne City Library, Ms. K46T: *Feodarium Prioratus Dunelmensis*, ed. W. Greenwell, Surtees Soc., LVIII, 1872, pp. 164–7; Elliott, 'System of cultivation and evidence of enclosure', p. 89; Winchester, *Medieval Cumbria*, pp. 68–77.

[3] Newcastle-upon-Tyne City Library, Ms. K46T; S. L. Greenslade, 'Sacristonheugh', *Archit.*

In the open-field townships of the east, communally agreed crop rotations with one-year fallows appear to have been the rule. At Sacristonheugh in the fifteenth century, for instance, there were three open fields, one sown with wheat, one with oats, and one fallow. But the communal routine was enforced only with some difficulty after the Black Death: in 1352 the steward of Durham priory's manor of Sedgefield had to force the villeins to adhere to the traditional routine of allowing one-third of the land to lie fallow each year, but the tenants continued to sow the fallow field. In 1373 the steward of the manor of East Merrington in Durham ordered each tenant to have his lands under crops when everyone else did, and let them lie fallow at the same time as the others; and at Allerwash in Northumberland in 1369 Thomas Lucy insisted that the lessees of his demesne lands there should allow the land to lie fallow every third year. In Cumberland, the town fields were generally cultivated continuously, though in Holm Cultram parish there was a large open field taken in from the waste, probably at the beginning of the sixteenth century. It was divided into four "rivings"; each riving was cultivated for three years and was then to "lie as pasture and common for nine years".[4]

The type of crop grown varied greatly from one part of the region to another, and the traditional belief that the northern counties depended mainly on oats requires serious modification. As in all other aspects of farming in the region, there was a close relationship between type of crop and climate and topography. In Cumberland and Westmorland, there is little doubt that oats was the predominant crop, for the prevailing climate made it difficult to grow wheat or barley successfully, except perhaps in the Eden valley. The great religious houses of the west, such as Cartmel, Furness, and Holm Cultram, and the town of Kendal, depended for their supplies of wheat on imports from Ireland, and this may have been one motive for the acquisition earlier in the middle ages by Furness and Holm Cultram of land in eastern Ireland. In the upper reaches of the Tyne valley oats was probably the most important crop, for in the Allerwash lease of 1369 Thomas Lucy had to insist that the lessees sowed at least 2 acres of barley each year, the implication perhaps being that oats was a much easier crop to raise. In west Durham, oats and barley predominated

and Arch. Soc. of Durham and Northumberland, x(3), 1950, p. 257; Elliott, 'System of cultivation and evidence of enclosure', p. 92; Butlin, 'Field systems of Northumberland and Durham', pp. 107–8; Winchester, Medieval Cumbria, pp. 74–5; Priory of Hexham, ed. Raine, II, pp. 5–9, 50; NCH, IX, pp. 324–5; R. A. Dodgshon, 'The landholding foundations of the open-field system', PP, no. 67, 1975, pp. 3–29, esp. pp. 19–20.

[4] Greenslade, 'Sacristonheugh', p. 257; PRO Dur., 3/12 f.68d; Halmota Prioratus Dunelmensis, ed. Longstaff and Booth, p. 122; Lucy Cartulary, National Register of Archives calendar of the original in Carlisle RO (Cockermouth Castle Mss.), No. 197; Elliott, 'System of cultivation and evidence of enclosure', pp. 96–8.

over wheat: in 1349–50 the bailiff of Auckland received a total of 31 quarters and 1 bushel of wheat from the tenants of Heighington, Auckland, and nine other vills, together with 60 quarters, 1 bushel of oats and 233 quarters, 4 bushels of malt; and at Killerby each six bovates of land was burdened with a render of 1 quarter of wheat, 2 quarters of oats and 10 quarters of malt. On Durham priory's manor of Elvethall, close to Durham city, barley was the predominant crop in the fifteenth century; oats was only slightly less important, but wheat accounted for barely one-fifth of the total yield of grain. At Temple Thornton in the Wansbeck valley in Northumberland oats was the predominant crop in the early fourteenth century, although wheat, barley, rye, and maslin were also grown, and on the poor soil of Tynemouthshire the 1539 survey suggests that oats and barley were the most important crops.[5]

In some parts of Durham, on the other hand, much more wheat was grown than has sometimes been supposed. At Sacristonheugh in the fifteenth century, for example, the normal routine was 10 acres of wheat, 12 acres of oats, and 10 acres fallow. In south-east Durham in particular tenants regularly grew wheat alongside barley, with little evidence that oats was a significant crop. Tenants sold wheat to the priory, and produced enough for themselves for us to be reasonably confident that wheaten bread formed part of their diet. At Bellasis in 1373, 56 acres of wheat were sown, 7 acres of barley, 48 acres of peas, and 20 acres of rye and maslin; at Fulwell in 1446, $28\frac{1}{2}$ acres were sown with wheat, 11 with blandcorn, 14 with beans, and $13\frac{1}{2}$ with oats, while at Hesleden in 1380 a bondage holding was sown with 5 acres of wheat, $3\frac{1}{2}$ acres of barley, and 4 acres of peas and oats. At Cowpen Bewley wheat was predominant, while at Ketton and Westoe wheat provided just under one-half of the total yield of grain in the 1370s, with oats and barley together being roughly equivalent to the wheat in yield. It is unfortunate that virtually no evidence survives for the variety of crops grown on the north Northumberland coastal plain between Wark-worth and Berwick and in Glendale Ward. Open-field farming prevailed over most of this area, and in all probability wheat formed one element in the rotation of crops. At the end of the thirteenth century wheat was the most important crop at Bamburgh, and in 1333

---

[5] W. Farrer, *Records Relating to the Barony of Kendal*, I, CWAAS, Rec. Ser. IV, 1923, p. 28; *Register and Records of Holm Cultram*, ed. F. Grainger and W. G. Collingwood, CWAAS, Rec. Ser. VII, 1929, pp. 21, 95, 97, 138; *Cal. Close and Patent Rolls of Ireland*, ed. E. Tresham, Dublin, 1828, p. 224; *Coucher Book of Furness Abbey*, II, ed. J. Brownbill, pt 3, Chetham Soc., NS LXXVIII, 1919, pp. 716–19; *Lucy Cartulary*, no. 197; *Bishop Hatfield's Survey*, ed. Greenwell, pp. 23–4, 207; R. A. Lomas, 'A northern farm at the end of the middle ages: Elvethall manor, Durham, 1443/4 – 1513/14', *North. Hist.*, XVIII, 1982, pp. 26–53; J. C. Hodgson, 'Temple Thornton farm accounts', *AA*, 2nd ser. XVII, 1895, pp. 40–52; *NCH*, VIII, p. 229.

an inquiry into damage done by royal troops at Belford showed that wheat, barley, oats, and peas were sown: a slightly greater acreage of oats than of wheat was sown, but barley was much less important.[6]

The yield of crops was very respectable by medieval standards. At Ketton, Fulwell, and Cowpen Bewley in the 1370s the yield of both wheat and barley was above the average recorded for Ramsey in Huntingdonshire in the fourteenth century, and noticeably higher, in the case of wheat, than Lord Beveridge's average for the whole of the thirteenth and fourteenth centuries. T. Lomas has demonstrated similar good returns for barley on the manor of Elvethall. On the Durham manor of Ketton, wheat yielded a return on seed of 1:4.31 in 1371–7 and barley a return of 1:4.69 in 1373–7, while at Cowpen Bewley in 1371–3 the return was 1:4.25 for wheat and 1:5.73 for barley. In south-east Durham, wheat was not only grown extensively; it was also grown at least as successfully as in some other parts of the country, and this alone should dispose of some of the more extravagant generalizations about the poverty of the northern rural economy in the later middle ages. In other parts of the region wheat growing was almost as successful: at Elvethall near Durham city a four-fold return was usual, and at Temple Thornton in Northumberland wheat yielded a return of 1:3.5, though the yield of oats was 1:7. Evidence for crop yields in Cumberland and Westmorland in the fourteenth and fifteenth centuries is wholly lacking.[7]

Away from the east-coast plain and certain inland valleys, stock rearing was more important than arable farming throughout the later middle ages, although most pastoral communities had some arable land. In general, the pattern was one of dispersed settlement, small enclosed fields, and large areas of unenclosed common grazing land. In parts of Cumberland, enclosure of small portions of the waste seems to have gathered pace from the mid-fifteenth century onwards. The system of farming was more individualistic in these pastoral vills than in the arable vills of the east. At Thirlwall in west Northumberland, the tenants of the priory of Hexham held their small enclosed fields and their meadow lands in severalty, as did the tenants of Furness abbey in Borrowdale in Cumberland. Nonetheless, certain communal features

[6] T. Lomas, 'South-east Durham', in Harvey, ed., The Peasant Land Market, pp. 318–21; Greenslade, 'Sacristonheugh', p. 257; Halmota Prioratus Dunelmensis, ed. Longstaff and Booth, pp. 120–1, 165; Scriptores Tres, ed. Raine, p. ccxciii; N. Morimoto, 'On the arable farming of Durham Cathedral priory in the fourteenth century', Nagoya Gakuin University Review, XI, 1975, p. 271; NCH, I, pp. 119, 384–5.

[7] Morimoto, 'Arable farming of Durham Cathedral priory', p. 274; Dobson, Durham Priory, p. 281; R. A. Lomas, 'A northern farm at the end of the middle ages', pp. 33–4; Hodgson, 'Temple Thornton farm accounts', pp. 45–51.

survived. Grazing rights on the unenclosed land were held in common, and in certain places there were common fields: at Wasdale Head in the sixteenth century, for instance, there was an open field of 345 acres, presumably given over to oats, surrounded by 6,000 acres of common grazing. In these districts, stock rearing was clearly the mainstay of the agrarian economy. At Thirlwall there is no mention of any arable land, and in Borrowdale those tenants whose holdings are described in detail have more meadow than arable land. The absence of open fields in the townships of north-east Cumberland, together with the importance of summer grazing rights there, suggests that there too stock raising was the most important activity.[8]

In west Durham there were many more cornage vills than in the east of the county, and this presumably reflects the mainly pastoral nature of farming there. At Wolsingham in Weardale the cottagers' services were mainly connected with haymaking, and at Lanchester the bond tenants' obligations were to make hay and take the pigs to pannage. The great religious houses of the region carried on stock farming on a large and highly organized scale. The priors of Durham had a large cattle farm at Muggleswick on the west Durham moors, and an extensive sheep ranch at Le Holme on the flats of the Tees estuary. At Le Holme the prior had 1,208 breeding ewes in 1341, a figure that had risen to 1,439 in 1416–17. At Stanhope Park in Weardale, according to J. L. Drury, there was grazing for 944 cattle, 472 sheep and 30 horses in 1438, and here the grazing of livestock was developed at the expense even of deer in the fifteenth century. Furness abbey had surprisingly little stock in its immediate vicinity, since the woodlands of High Furness had to be conserved to provide charcoal for the ironworking which was so important a source of wealth to the abbey; but the monks acquired extensive grazing rights for their sheep and cattle in Borrowdale in Cumberland. Holm Cultram developed the Solway shore for raising sheep and cattle, while in Northumberland the monks of Newminster acquired pasture for sheep and cattle on Kidland in upper Coquetdale.[9]

In some of these upland districts transhumance was practised. The monks of Newminster had summer grazing grounds on Kidlandlee,

[8] Winchester, *Medieval Cumbria*, pp. 52–4; Elliott, 'System of cultivation and evidence of enclosure', pp. 89–90; Alnwick Castle Mss. x ii 3(ii); *Priory of Hexham*, ed. Raine, ii, pp. 17–18; *Coucher Book of Furness Abbey*, ii, ed. Brownbill, pt 3, p. 643.

[9] *Bishop Hatfield's Survey*, ed. Greenwell, esp. pp. 61, 109–10; *Feodarium Prioratus Dunelmensis*, ed. Greenwell, pp. 207–8; *Extracts from the Account Rolls of Durham Abbey*, ed. J. T. Fowler, ii, Surtees Soc. c, 1899, pp. 311–17; J. L. Drury, 'Early settlement in Stanhope park, Weardale, c. 1406–79', *AA*, 5th ser. iv, 1976, p. 141; *Coucher Book of Furness Abbey*, ed. Brownbill, ii, pt 2, pp. 568–80; *Register and Records of Holm Cultram*, eds. Grainger and Collingwood, pp. 1–2, 96, 126–7; *NCH*, xv, p. 449.

and remains of their shielings survive. In north-east Cumberland the lords of Burgh-by-Sands and of Gilsland had summer pasturing for their cattle on the Bewcastle Fells and on Askerton North Moor, and in Tynedale and Redesdale transhumance was a regular feature of stock management. In these two valleys, however, the lower-lying land is more productive than the mosses at similar altitude in north-east Cumberland, and by about 1300 permanent grazing had become established at 400 feet in the valley of the Chirdon Burn and at 500 feet in the valley of the Wark Burn, but the higher land at the heads of these valleys was used for summer pasturing in the fifteenth century. There is no medieval evidence for the organization of summer pasturing or the division of the shieling grounds. The earliest account of the system is contained in the 1604 *Survey of the Border Lands*. The men of Redesdale, according to this survey, "sheylde together by Surnames; not keepinge Cattle accordinge to the proporcion of the rent, but eatinge all in Common without stinte or number", but the men of Tynedale shielded "by agrement among themselves accordinge as the season falleth out".[10]

The stock farmers of Cumberland and Northumberland had to face one hazard which their southern counterparts were spared: attack from the Scots. Protection from Scottish raids is thus an important aspect of stock management in the region. Sixteenth-century surveys of the border lands suggest that sheep and cattle stealing was commonplace; evidence from the fourteenth and fifteenth centuries is less substantial. In the early fourteenth century Scottish raiders concentrated mainly on the lowland arable vills and on the destruction of standing corn rather than the carrying off of livestock. J. Scammell has shown that in 1320 the monks of Durham priory drove their cattle on to the moor of Spennymoor, only six miles from Durham, rightly thinking that they would be safe there. In the later fourteenth and fifteenth centuries livestock were seized on raids into Northumberland and Cumberland; but sixteenth-century commentators recalled that the uplands of Northumberland had not always been as disorderly as they then were. Men in Kidland reported that the district had been inhabited "when Teviotdale was English" (probably meaning the mid-fourteenth century), and that Redesdale had at that time been kept in such order that the inhabitants there did not spoil and steal their neighbours' cattle as they did now.[11]

[10] *NCH*, xv, pp. 277–8, 449; H. G. Ramm, R. W. McDowell and E. Mercer, *Shielings and Bastles*, RCHM, England, London, 1970, pp. 5–6; *Survey of the Debateable and Border Lands AD 1604*, ed. R. P. Sanderson, Alnwick, 1891, pp. 52, 104.

[11] J. Scammell, 'Robert I and the north of England', *EHR*, LXXIII, 1958, p. 391; J. Hodgson, *History of Northumberland*, III (2), Newcastle-upon-Tyne, 1828, pp. 222–3.

It may be, therefore, that there was a substantial increase in sheep and cattle raiding in the early sixteenth century, both across the border and within the disorderly districts of Bewcastle, Tynedale, and Redesdale. It was at this time that the farmers of the border district were forced to abandon pasturing altogether on the Bewcastle Fells and on Kidlandlee, and it is from this period that most of the fortified farms or bastles with barmkins for stock protection date. Such buildings were designed to shelter stock as well as humans, and although it was obviously impossible to provide protection for all the thousands of sheep and cattle that grazed at will on the upland pastures, some stock at least could find shelter within the barmkins or on the ground floors of fortified dwellings.[12]

The architectural and archaeological evidence suggests that the proliferation of fortified dwellings of this kind was a sixteenth-century phenomenon. Such buildings, uncompromisingly stark and simple, are extremely difficult to date, but the written evidence from the same period for regular and substantial cattle raiding makes a sixteenth-century date for such buildings probable, and implies that this aspect of stock management only became of major importance at the end of the period. Until then, the stock farmers of the region, like their arable counterparts, had perhaps come to terms with the intermittent nuisance of Scottish raids, and it is hard to find any evidence that the pastoral economy of the region away from the immediate border area was seriously disrupted by Scottish raids until the sixteenth century. Just as conclusions about the late medieval arable economy of the region should not be drawn merely from sixteenth-century evidence, so it should not be assumed that the pastoral, raiding society of the border ballads was fully formed in the fourteenth and fifteenth centuries.

B. YORKSHIRE AND LANCASHIRE

In Yorkshire and Lancashire, as elsewhere, evidence regarding farming practice becomes scarcer in the late middle ages as the larger landowners, the main keepers and preservers of records, abandoned direct cultivation. It does seem clear, however, that in both counties the importance of pastoral farming was considerable and was probably increasing. It has already been noted that, at the end of the middle ages, ploughland in Lancashire occupied at best only about two-thirds, and in some districts a third or less, of the total "productive area" (a total which leaves out of account the often very extensive common pastures). Meadow and pasture, in other words, were frequently

---

[12] Ramm *et al.*, *Shielings and Bastles*, pp. 65–6.

important constituents of holdings. The monks of Merevale, for instance, as well as 200 acres of arable, had 200 acres of meadow and 1,000 acres of pasture at Altcar in 1377; and, at the other end of the social scale, 28 tenants at Brandwood in 1539, with 108½ acres of arable between them, shared 65 acres of meadow and 116 acres of pasture in addition to possessing unspecified rights of common.[13]

Arable in lowland Yorkshire often occupied a higher proportion of the productive area than in Lancashire, although Leland found much low pasture and moor between Northallerton and the Tees and also forest land to the north of York lying as a "great plaine commune". There were also extensive meadows and pastures in Holderness and Humberhead: the archbishop had much hay-meadow at Cawood and 400 acres of meadow and pasture at Patrington, even after some of his manor there had been flooded; and there were over 1,600 acres of meadow and pasture on eight Meaux granges c. 1400. In the wolds, north Yorkshire moors and the Pennines, in addition to arable, there was meadow and improved pasture in the valleys and dales, and the higher lands were mainly sheep or cattle country. At Bishop Wilton in the wolds the archbishop of York had pasture for 3,800 sheep, worth twice as much in 1388 as his arable and meadow put together, and the 1341 tax returns clearly demonstrate the importance of sheep farming for the townships of Teesdale, Swaledale, Wensleydale, and the north Yorkshire moors. In Wharfedale, while there was a fair amount of arable at Skipton and even uphill at Skibeden, there were cattle farms on the higher land of Barden and Rombald's moors; and further north, between the Swale and the Tees, there was little else in the New Forest and Arkengarthdale but vaccaries. The remoter the location the more predominant pasture was likely to be. At Hawkswick in Littondale in 1437 there was a dispute about a messuage, half an arable oxgang, and 1,000 acres of moor and pasture. This is the further extreme from the overwhelmingly arable character of farming in the Yorkshire plain.[14]

Even at Hawkswick, however, there was some arable, just as there was some arable attached to the "dairyhouse" at Bouthwaite in Fountains Earth. How arable land was disposed, therefore, is a reasonable point of departure for any review of farming practice. In this respect much of lowland Yorkshire was an extension of

[13] Above, p. 50; R. Cunliffe Shaw, *The Royal Forest of Lancaster*, p. 469; *Coucher Book of Whalley Abbey*, ed. W. A. Hulton, IV, Chetham Soc., os XX, 1849, pp. 1128–34.

[14] Leland, *Itinerary*, I, p. 68; IV, p. 12; PRO SC 6/1088/18, 1144/7; PRO E 142/50; *Cal. Inq. Misc.*, V, nos. 100–2; BL Egerton Ms. 1141, ff.169–74; *Nonarum Inquisitiones*, ed. Vanderzee, pp. 231–43; B. Waites, *Moorland and Vale-land Farming in North-East Yorks.*, Borthwick Papers, 32, York, 1967, pp. 27–8; *Yorks. Deeds*, V, no. 235.

the great midland plain and shared the same open-field landscape. There are many indications of a three-field layout: at Kippax, Barwick-in-Elmet, and Naburn, for instance, or at Lotherton where land was distributed in intermixed parcels grouped in furlongs or riggs in three named fields. Traces of a basically three-field regime are found in a number of Humberhead townships, but also as far north as Holme in Ainderby Quernhow and possibly Bedale, as well as at Marske and (associated with a small fourth field) at Skelton between the moors and the sea. In Holderness there were three fields at Burstwick, but only two at Great Cowden and Brandesburton, and two fields were later the norm in this district. In the wolds there also seem to have been two-field systems at Raisthorpe and Kilnwick Percy, but in some places additional land was temporarily taken in from the wold and cropped for a time before being allowed to return to grass. In these cases an infield–outfield regime supplemented an open-field system.[15]

Even in lowland Yorkshire, however, segregation of the arable in two or three large fields was far from universal. At Ackworth, Altofts, and Elmsall, for instance, it was disposed in various "flats" and crofts, or lay in a single field with many subdivisions; and a very similar disposition of arable parcels is found at Little Humber in Holderness. In some townships, too, only a part of the arable lay in open fields: thus at Barwick-in-Elmet the new demesne was divided more or less equally between three fields, but the old demesne consisted of a variety of plots of varying size up to 50 acres. In the southern part of the Vale of York blocks of "foreland" of relatively recent reclamation, some of them subdivided into furlongs and selions, frequently lay outside the limits of the open fields; and a similar arrangement may be implied by the description of the Hexham demesne at Salton in the Vale of Pickering. Of this land 72 acres *jacent discontinue per diversas partes inter terras tenentium*, but a similar acreage lay in severalty in four "flats".[16]

The irregular patterns in the disposition of arable found in association with open fields in the plain of York become the rule in the south-west,

[15] See generally M. W. Beresford, 'Glebe terriers and open field, Yorks.', *Yorks. Arch. J.*, XXXVII, 1950, pp. 325–50, and Baker and Butlin, eds., *Field Systems*, pp. 167–72; also *Fountains Abbey Lease Book*, ed. D. J. H. Michelmore, Yorks. Arch. Soc. Rec. Ser. CXL, 1981, no. 205; PRO DL 42/106, f.26, C 135/144/8, SC 6/1083/1; *Yorks. Deeds*, I, no. 279; IV, no. 405; VI, nos. 340–3; IX, nos. 248, 344, 419–22; X, nos. 45–6; *Miscellanea*, IX, Thoresby Soc., XXVIII, 1928, pp. 238–9; BL Add. Ms. 40010, f.21d; *Inquisitions…Henry IV and Henry V*, ed. Baildon and Clay, pp. 69–74; A. Harris, *Open Fields of East Yorkshire*, East Yorks. Local Hist. Ser., 1959.

[16] PRO DL 42/106, ff.18, 23d, 38; PRO SC 6/1082/7–8; *Yorks. Deeds*, V, nos. 63, 172, 177; VI, nos. 218, 226; VIII, no. 153; IX, nos. 113, 118, 225, 229, 349; *Priory of Hexham*, ed. Raine, II, p. 72.

the Pennines and the moors, where ploughland was apt to be dispersed in a disorderly multiplicity of "fields", furlongs, and closes. Land at Cudworth, for example, lay in Thorwellflat, at the Cloghes, in the north field, the south field, the old field, in Rawlande and in Smallbryg field; at Great Houghton some arable lay in a 5-acre close in Odstorth field, and meadow and arable were intermixed in the fields; and pasture was intermixed with arable in the fields of Carlton-by-Snaith. Multiple irregular fields are also found at Tickhill, at a group of townships around Wakefield, at Fixby near Halifax, and at Glusburn near Skipton; while in the dales of the north Yorkshire moors arable, meadow and pasture was often scattered in parcels within the woodland.[17] Lancashire closely resembles west Yorkshire in the way in which land was disposed. The lands of Whalley abbey at Garston were intermixed with those of other men in 28 different "fields", including a high field, an old field, and a long furlong; there were also numerous fields at Kirkdale and Speke which included various crofts; and at Speke these parcels were sometimes described in aggregate as the township's field. The arable layout at Farrington near Preston and Bolron near Lancaster appears very similar; and at Lytham the arable was not continuous, but divided by intervening marsh. The permanent arable in some places was temporarily augmented by ploughing up intakes from the waste, although the lord's licence for such an improvement was needed at Cockerham and doubtless elsewhere. There are traces of a similar practice in west Yorkshire, for at Holme, near Wakefield, a Horbury man fined in 1349 to be allowed to return 6 acres to the waste and to take in a similar amount of land in their place.[18]

Arable holdings were frequently as fragmented in Lancashire and upland Yorkshire as in the open-field lowlands. At Newhall in southern Yorkshire, for instance, $2\frac{1}{4}$ acres were dispersed in at least six selions in four locations in the west field. In these areas of irregular fields, where arable and for that matter meadow and improved pasture were often the fruits of relatively recent reclamation, enclosure had already made significant progress by the mid-fourteenth century and was continued

[17] *Abstracts of the Chartularies of the Priory of Monk Bretton*, ed. J. W. Walker, Yorks. Arch. Soc. Rec. Ser. LXVI, 1924, nos. 61, 75–6, 81, 243; *CIPM*, XII, no. 232; *Yorks. Deeds*, I, no. 350; III, no. 108; IV, nos. 418–24; VI, no. 46; X, nos. 448–56; *Pudsay Deeds*, ed. R. P. Littledale, Yorks. Arch. Soc. Rec. Ser., LVI, 1916, no. 210; Waites, *Moorland and Vale-land Farming*, pp. 6–9.

[18] *Cal. of Norris Deeds*, ed. J. H. Lumby, Lancs. and Cheshire Rec. Soc., LXXXVIII, 1936, nos. 22, 75, 222, 1102; BL Add. Ms. 36924, ff.127–7d; F. J. Singleton, 'The influence of geographical factors on the development of the common fields of Lancs.', *Hist. Soc. of Lancs. and Cheshire*, CXV, 1963, pp. 38–9; R. Cunliffe Shaw, 'The townfields of Lancashire', *ibid.*, CXIV, 1962, p. 25; 'Two custumals of the manor of Cockerham', ed. R. S. France, *Lancs. and Cheshire Antiq. Soc.*, LXIV, 1954, p. 48; *Wakefield Court Rolls, 1348–1350,* ed. Jewell, p. 143.

during the ensuing century and a half. Some enclosures were also appearing within common fields, although for that to be possible consolidation of the scattered parcels of which holdings were normally composed was a necessary preliminary. At Stainall (Lancs.) in 1518 lords and tenants jointly determined to "deyle theyr land and to lay it in dalez together", but the same end was sometimes achieved by the slower process of individual exchanges. Self-contained enclosed farms were appearing, especially on the moors and in the dales, together with a landscape of enclosures more generally in Lancashire and south-west Yorkshire and expanding pockets of closes even in open-field territory. Leland found much "champion" country in Yorkshire; but he also noticed a partly enclosed countryside around Pontefract, Wakefield, Tickhill, and Doncaster, as well as in Howdenshire, in the forest vills north of York, and in the Ure valley around Middleham. Enclosure permitted a more flexible use of land, which might well be a pastoral use. This appears to have been the case at Middleham and at Kettlethorpe near Wakefield, where beasts straying into a close ate up grass to the not inconsiderable value of 20s. At Ulnes Walton (Lancs.), too, enclosed assarts were grazed and "not further approved". Changes in these directions, of course, must not be exaggerated. In 1500 many holdings in Lancashire still lay intermixed in town fields and even at the end of the seventeenth century there were still open fields in some two-thirds of the townships of the central Yorkshire plain, the wolds and Holderness. The transformation of the older framework of farming, all the same, was well under way by the close of the middle ages.[19]

Details of how fields were cultivated are scarcer than might be desired, but in Lancashire oats probably continued to be the principal cereal crop. Much of the arable, therefore, was spring sown and could be manured by grazing stock for half the year. It may, therefore, have been possible to crop it continuously, although some ploughland was probably rested periodically as self-sown leys or meadow. Oats was not the sole crop, however, for the Cockerham customs imply a three-course rotation, wheat was certainly grown at Standen in the Ribble valley, and Nicholas Haryngton had stocks of wheat, rye, and barley (as well as oats) at Farleton in Lonsdale. Small amounts of winter grains may have been grown in crofts or closes, but where they were sown in town fields there must have been some approximation to the

[19] Faull and Moorhouse, eds., *West Yorkshire*, III, pp. 656–63; Cunliffe Shaw, 'The townfields of Lancashire', p. 28; *Abstracts of the Cartularies...of Monk Bretton*, ed. Walker, no. 347; Jennings, ed., *History of Nidderdale*, p. 91; Leland, *Itinerary*, I, pp. 35–59, 80; PRO DL 29/76/1500; *Wakefield Court Rolls, 1350–1352*, ed. Habberjam *et al.*, pp. 40, 48–9; M. W. Beresford, 'Glebe terriers and open field', pp. 348–9.

rotational schemes familiar elsewhere. Oats was also the principal crop in upland Yorkshire as is indicated by the tithe corn that came from Ingleby Greenhow and Ayton-in-Cleveland or from Gargrave and Stainton-in-Craven, and also by the corn stocks at Whitby's granges on the coastal plateau of north Yorkshire and at Sawley's granges in Ribblesdale. On the other hand, even in Craven or Ribblesdale or the north Yorkshire coastlands some wheat and perhaps a little barley were sown as well as wheat; and references to crops in the mid-fourteenth-century court rolls of Wakefield manor, while suggesting the clear primacy of the oat crop and the very modest amounts of land under wheat, barley, and pulses, do appear to indicate that there was a significant amount of land under rye. On the lower land in Yorkshire, on the other hand, there was probably something more like a balance between winter and spring crops.[20]

Even on these lower lands, however, there was much diversity of cropping. Wheat seems to have been the main winter-sown crop, but rye had a certain importance at Rotherham in the south, at Marton-le-Moor and Whixley near Knaresborough, on the archbishop's manor at Cawood on the Ouse, and at Seamer and Hackness on the northern flank of the Vale of Pickering. Among spring crops, barley provided a third of the harvest at Whitgift and Reedness, followed by drage, then beans and peas, and finally oats; at Flamborough peas led, followed by barley, with oats and drage of small account; in Holderness, at Burstwick, beans occupied 43 per cent of the land sown (more than the acreage under wheat), while at Little Humber the demesne was mainly under wheat and pulses and no barley was grown at all. Barley comes into its own, however, in the wolds and on the margins of the Vale of Pickering. It seems to have been the principal crop at Seamer and Burton Fleming, and only the wheat acreage matched that under barley at Sewerby in 1377 or on Thomas de Westhorpe's lands at Brompton and elsewhere in 1366.[21]

In much of Yorkshire, then, the arable was sown with winter and spring grains in fields that were to varying degrees open. To preserve fertility part of this arable was fallowed each year: presumably a half

---

[20] 'Two customals of the manor of Cockerham', ed. France, p. 47; *Coucher Book of Whalley Abbey*, ed. Hulton, IV, pp. 1158–61; *Cal. of Norris Deeds*, ed. Lumby, no. 1001; *Cartularium Abbathiae de Whitby*, ed. J. C. Atkinson, Surtees Soc., LXIX, 1879, and LXXII, 1881, I, pp. 318–20, and II, pp. 568–9, 577–8, 584; T. D. Whitaker, *History and Antiquities of the Deanery of Craven*, Leeds, 1878, pp. 63–5.

[21] *Miscellanea*, VI, ed. C. E. Whiting, Yorks. Arch. Soc. Rec. Ser., CXVIII, 1953, pp. 47–9; BL Add. Rolls 75467–71; PRO SC 6/1082/7–8, 1083/1; B. Waites, 'A Yorkshire farmer in the memoranda rolls', *Yorks. Arch. J.*, XLI, 1966, pp. 447–8; *idem*, 'Aspects of thirteenth and fourteenth century arable farming on the Yorkshire Wolds', *ibid.*, XLII, 1968, pp. 138–9; *Cartularium Abbathiae de Whitby*, ed. Atkinson, II, pp. 566, 575, 583; *Yorks. Deeds*, VI, no. 422.

in places where there were two open fields, but perhaps more usually one-third, irrespective of whether a regular field system had developed or not. At Burstwick in 1350–1, for instance, the east and west fields were under crops while the middle field was fallowed; but at Little Humber eight "lands" and crofts of varying sizes were grouped into three shifts of roughly equal acreages which, in successive years, were under (1) wheat, (2) beans or peas or oats, and (3) fallow. When one of the sown fields was much larger than the others, as at Burstwick, it had to accommodate both winter- and spring-sown crops; and the same may have been the case when, as at Bishop Burton or Otley, the acreage under either winter or spring grains was disproportionately large.[22]

Further information about arable routine is scanty, but one Yorkshire lease implies that the norm of good husbandry was that corn land ought to be manured, ploughed twice, and weeded. Manuring was chiefly a matter of running stock on the arable, and for this reason the fallow at Little Humber was put in the charge of the stockman and at Burstwick was grazed by the king's sheep. Fountains abbey, however, also bought marl for its fields and a Marton lessee was required to cart soil onto the land in order to improve it. Sowing rates varied from grain to grain and from place to place: for what they are worth, in Holderness and on the archbishop's manors in the 1350s, the rates per acre were $2\frac{1}{4}$–$3\frac{1}{4}$ bushels for wheat, $2\frac{1}{2}$–3 bushels for rye and pulses, 4 bushels for barley and 4–5 bushels for oats. Runs of accounts which would provide soundly based yield ratios are unfortunately not available and evidence about the arable farmer's equipment is scarcely better. At Flamborough, since there were no oxen, horses must have been used as plough beasts, as they certainly were both by lord and tenants at Wetwang (sometimes, apparently, in teams of four). Oxen, however, seem to have been the more usual draught animals in Yorkshire, especially for ploughing; and on the Meaux granges and at Burstwick, Bishop Wilton, Bishop Burton, Sherburn-in-Elmet, and Cawood they were numerous enough to suggest eight-ox demesne teams. Oxen also appear to have been the normal plough beasts in Lancashire and even some quite small estates were quite well provided with them. There were 20 at Standen in 1376, Nicholas Haryngton had 16 at Farleton in 1429, and Henry Norris in 1524 had 20 at Speke (together with five work horses) for only 69 acres of standing corn.[23]

The prominence of oxen reflects the fact that much of Yorkshire and

[22] PRO SC 6/1082/7–8, 1083/1, 1144/7.

[23] *Yorks. Deeds*, VI, no. 422; IX, no. 308; *Memorials of Fountains*, III, ed. J. T. Fowler, Surtees Soc., CXXX, 1918, pp. 14–15, 182; BL Add. Rolls 75467–71; BL Cott. Vitellius C VI, ff.239–41; PRO SC 6/1083/1, 1144/7, 1144/10; *Cal. of Norris Deeds*, ed. Lumby, nos. 101, 1001.

Lancashire was cattle country. In the 1390s, for instance, Meaux was leasing out one vaccary for 30 cows and itself kept in hand 132 cows (most of them in three specialist dairying granges). The duke of Gloucester, too, had 81 cattle at Burstwick and 50 at Cleeton in Holderness in 1396, Selby abbey had 105 cows in the Humberhead lowlands in 1368 and, at about the same time, Thomas de Westhorpe had 152 cows, 55 yearling oxen, and 46 calves on the margins of the Vale of Pickering. In these places cattle were part of a mixed farming economy, but in some parts of upland Yorkshire they had a predominant role. There were at least fifteen vaccaries between Bowes and Reeth and 1,560 cattle at Castle Bolton in 1395; Robert Clifford had vaccaries on the moors above Skipton, and Bolton priory vaccaries on Appletreewick moors; and it looks as though Fountains in the late middle ages may have deliberately concentrated on cattle farming at the expense (although not to the exclusion) of sheep.[24] In Lancashire demesne cattle farming still continued on the Bowland vaccaries in 1422, although these too would soon be leased as the Blackburnshire vaccaries had been earlier. Cattle farming remained, however, the basic occupation of the lessees and other tenants of much of the Lancashire uplands and was far from unimportant in many townships on Merseyside or in the valleys of Ribble and Lune. In Lonsdale Nicholas Haryngton's cattle at Farleton were valued at £24 15s. (out of the total value of £32 12s. 8d. set on his goods), without bringing into the account a debt owed to him of £8 2s. 6d. for eighteen cows he had sold on credit. In areas like the moorland edges of the Pennines, moreover, cattle farming probably continued to demand some agricultural progress if only to improve land for "hay-getting", the vital importance of which was recognized in the lease of the Fountains dairyhouse at Bouthwaite in Nidderdale in 1512. Like sheep, too, cattle were sometimes driven out to higher land for summer pasturage, helping to push uphill the available "productive land".[25]

In very many places, however, sheep greatly outnumbered cattle and sheep farming was much more widely distributed than cattle farming on any scale. There were sheep as well as cattle on Merseyside, on

[24] BL Cott. Vitellius C VI, ff.235–5d; BL Egerton Ms. 1141, f.183d; Cal. Inq. Misc., VI, no. 348; G. S. Haslop, 'The abbot of Selby's financial statement, 1348', Yorks. Arch. J., XLIV, 1972, pp. 166–8; Waites, 'A Yorkshire farmer in the memoranda rolls', p. 448; PRO SC 6/1085/18; Yorks. Deeds, II, no. 118; Rental of Bolton Priory, ed. I. Kershaw, Yorks. Arch. Soc. Rec. Ser., CXXXII, 1970, p. 10; R. A. Donkin, 'Cattle on the estates of medieval Cistercian monasteries in England and Wales', EcHR, 2nd ser. XV, 1962, pp. 35, 40; J. McDonnell, 'The role of transhumance in northern England', North. Hist., XXIV, 1988, p. 11.

[25] PRO DL 29/76/1498; Cal. of Norris Deeds, ed. Lumby, no. 1001; J. Langdon, Horses, Oxen and Technological Innovation, pp. 88, 98; Fountains Abbey Lease Book, ed. Michelmore, no. 205; Faull and Moorhouse, eds., West Yorkshire, III, p. 761.

occasion sheep overcharged commons in Blackburnshire, and sheep numbers may have been increasing in coastal Lancashire during the late middle ages. In the Yorkshire Pennines, too, there were large flocks at Gargrave in Craven, Appletreewick in Wharfedale, and Castle Bolton in Wensleydale; Easby abbey had sheep in Swaledale in 1388; and there were at least 3,000 sheep belonging to Fountains even in 1495. Similarly, in the north Yorkshire moors, the Whitby abbey flock numbered over 3,200 in 1393, Thomas de Westhorpe had 2,700 sheep at Brompton and Ebberston in 1366, and the Percies had a flock of 1,400 sheep at Seamer as late as 1405. The management of these large upland flocks often involved a degree of transhumance. To the end of the middle ages the Fountains sheep were summered on the Craven moors beyond Malham and brought down to the lower parts of Nidderdale in winter – to Bewerley and Dacre, to Bollershaw and Braisty Woods, or even to Warsill and Haddockstones. Further north, too, dale settlements at Danby and Hackness used the high moors for summer grazing, as did the Stokesley flocks in a detached part of the parish on Westerdale moor. Yorkshire sheep farming, however, was by no means confined to the highlands nor was it the sole province of landlords. The sheep and barley husbandry of the wolds was already well developed; and, if the archbishop's sheep pasture was the dominant feature of Bishop Wilton, the demesne flock at Flamborough in 1355 numbered only about 360 compared with at least 1,120 sheep belonging to the tenantry. Holderness, too, had its sheep flocks. Meaux abbey had 3,000 sheep on its granges in 1396, of which less than one-third were at Wharram-le-Street in the wolds; and in the following year there were more than 3,500 sheep and lambs at Keyingham. Here again, however, there were small flocks as well as large. The mainly arable manor at Sewerby had a stock of 70 sheep and lambs and at Sutton-in-Holderness Isabella de Preston, with only half an arable oxgang, had pasture for 300 sheep.[26]

Much less is known about other types of livestock. Villagers had pigs grazing on the common fields at Ashton-under-Lyne (Lancs.) and in the woods at Wensley (Yorks.). Evidently many of them had hens, and geese and sometimes ducks are mentioned in Holderness and Humberhead. Some larger properties, too, might have a few breeding mares, but for most holdings sheep and cattle were the stock that

---

[26] Cunliffe Shaw, *Royal Forest of Lancaster*, pp. 406–8, 469; *Court Rolls of the Honour of Clitheroe*, ed. Farrer, I, pp. 5, 24, 218; Whitaker, *History of Craven*, p. 64; *Cartularium Abbathiae de Whitby*, ed. Atkinson, I, p. 318; II, p. 575; Waites, 'A Yorkshire farmer in the memoranda rolls', p. 448; *idem, Moorland and Vale-land Farming*, pp. 27–8; *Fountains Abbey Lease Book*, ed. Michelmore, pp. lviii–ix; McDonnell, 'The role of transhumance in northern England', pp. 11–15; BL Add. Rolls 75467–71; *Cal. Inq. Misc.*, V, no. 100; VI, no. 348; BL Cott. Vitellius C. VI, ff.235–5d; *CIPM*, IX, no. 384.

mattered. The returns were manifold. Flamborough sheep provided Bridlington priory with a little mutton, everywhere pigs furnished some pork or bacon, and old cows were fattened off on the Fountains estate and doubtless some of them ended up in the refectory. So far as sheep were concerned, however, the sale of ewes and wethers was a more important consideration than meat for the table, and the sale of wool was most important of all. Dairy cattle provided butter and cheese, and liveries of these foodstuffs to Meaux and Fountains were an important element in the payments made by the keepers or lessees of their vaccaries. Keepers and lessees, in addition to dairy produce and old cows, normally also had to deliver so many stirks or calves each year, a source of replacement cows, of oxen for use on the estate or for sale, and of store cattle for the market. Even the hides of cattle killed for the larder or dying of disease were not neglected: to exploit them Meaux abbey had a tannery at North Grange and Fountains a "barkhouse" which was still operative in 1532.[27]

Animal feed was principally provided by grazing, although hay (and sometimes straw) might be fed to oxen and horses, and hay might be fed, especially in winter, to sheep and also to cows and young stock on upland cattle farms. It was for this reason that the lessee of the Fountains "dairyhouse" at Lofthouse in Nidderdale was required "to do all manner of labours...appertaining to the sustenance and nourishing of the cows and of all other cattle...as in mowing and getting of hay and foddering of them". Peas and oats, too, were sometimes fed to horses and oxen, peas and beans were used for fattening pigs, and occasionally cows' milk was provided for lambs. Supplementary feeding, however, was commonly insignificant in amount, and livestock depended above all upon the nutrient of grass, possibly augmented by "browsing" on cut holly or other underwood. Most other indications of how livestock were managed relate to sheep. Tar and grease were bought to dress sheep affected by scab and other ills; and some monastic establishments continued to prepare wool carefully for marketing, as the classification of Fountains wool into a variety of grades clearly indicates. This is not to say that Yorkshire wool, by and large, was of the highest quality. The minimum price fixed for most of the county's wool in 1454 was about 20 per cent below the national mean price for the year and only wolds wool was somewhat above that mean. There is other support for these government estimates. Craven wool in 1381, Holderness wool in 1397, and the Fountains clips in 1457–9 all sold for below national mean prices, although once again some wolds wool sold above them. More

---

[27] *Three Lancashire Documents of the Fourteenth and Fifteenth Centuries*, ed. J. Harland, Chetham Soc., OS LXXIV, 1868, pp. 111–12; BL Add. Ms. 40010, f.35; BL Egerton Ms. 1141, f.183d; Cunliffe Shaw, *Royal Forest of Lancaster*, pp. 375–7; Platt, *Monastic Grange*, pp. 224–5; *Fountains Abbey Lease Book*, ed. Michelmore, no. 232.

surprisingly a good deal of the wool for which payment was owing in the Wakefield area in 1348–52 was priced at 4s. a stone, well above the national mean at that time, but these may be the prices small craftsmen had to pay for their raw material (as distinct from wholesale producer prices paid to farmers), and they may even conceal an element of interest. If wool prices were relatively low, however, there are some indications of relatively high fleece weights, with an average of 1.7 lb at Keyingham in 1397 and of around 2 lb at Flamborough in the 1350s. The evidence is insufficiently continuous to be conclusive, but the productivity of Yorkshire sheep may have helped to compensate for the prices their wool commanded. If this was so, it gives support to indications of relatively heavy Yorkshire fleeces from Holderness and elsewhere in the late thirteenth and early fourteenth centuries.[28]

Comparable information about Lancashire wool is virtually non-existent, but such evidence as there is suggests that in both Yorkshire and Lancashire the productivity of breeding stock was often very modest. Cows did relatively well at Flamborough in 1348–57 and at Burstwick in 1350–1, for 80 per cent or more of them produced calves; but around 1500 the monks of Fountains only required their lessees to deliver 13 calves from 20 cows, and in 1422–3 more than half the 177 cows in the Bowland vaccaries were sterile. At Flamborough, with a lambing rate of around 70 per cent, ewes did rather less well than cows, while there and at Whitgift sows each produced two litters a year totalling 10–20 young pigs. These figures, of course, need also to be read in the context of considerable mortality amongst stock and especially of young stock; at Flamborough, for example, 8–10 per cent of the sheep, 16 per cent of lambs and calves, and up to 25 per cent of young pigs were lost annually in the 1350s. As for milk yields from cows, the rents of the Fountains dairy farms suggest an expectation of only 40 gallons per cow (yielding 16 lb of cheese and 8 lb of butter) each summer milking season. Even if that figure is doubled to allow for a share of the milk being retained by the keeper or lessee and for some initial suckling by calves, it still looks as though Nidderdale milk yields were low when compared with those expected by the authors of thirteenth-century treatises on husbandry.[29]

---

[28] *Fountains Abbey Lease Book*, ed. Michelmore, p. lxiii and no. 277; *Memorials of Fountains*, III, ed. Fowler, pp. 37, 78–9; *Rot. Parl.*, v, p. 275; Lloyd, *Movement of Wool Prices*, Table 1; BL Add. Rolls 75467–71; Whitaker, *History of Craven*, p. 64; *Cal. Inq. Misc.*, VI, no. 348; *Wakefield Court Rolls, 1348–1350*, ed. Jewell, pp. 130, 188, 250; *Wakefield Court Rolls, 1350–1352,* ed. Habberjam et al., pp. 1, 18; M. J. Stephenson, 'Wool yields in the medieval economy', *EcHR*, 2nd ser. XLI, 1988, pp. 372–3; J. P. Bischoff, 'Fleece weights and sheep breeds in late thirteenth and early fourteenth century England', *Agric. Hist.*, LVII, 1983, p. 156.

[29] BL Add. Rolls 75467–71; PRO DL 29/76/1498, SC 6/1083/1; *Miscellanea*, VI, Yorks. Arch. Soc. Rec. Ser., p. 51; *Fountains Abbey Lease Book*, ed. Michelmore, pp. liv–lvi.

Despite limits to its productivity, the relative importance of animal husbandry in Yorkshire and Lancashire during the late middle ages must not be minimized. The chance survival of information about two individuals, already mentioned more than once, makes that clear. Thomas de Westhorpe in 1366 had been farming on a considerable scale on the margins of the Vale of Pickering, where he had $238\frac{1}{2}$ acres sown with grain and the value of his growing crops, together with that of his working oxen and horses, totalled £108; but his cows, cattle, sheep, and pigs were worth nearly three times as much. Later, in 1524, Henry Norris had 69 acres under corn and 27 working animals at Speke in Lancashire, but he also had 74 cows, cattle, and calves, 68 sheep and lambs, and 28 pigs. The balance between plough and pasture was doubtless very different in the lowlands of the Vale of York, but neither Thomas nor Henry were inhabitants of the remoter dales. They were mixed farmers for whom livestock husbandry provided no small part of their living. Nor was stock farming important merely for its contribution to the resources of individuals. The manure of cattle and sheep helped to maintain the fertility of arable fields and, even in a period of agrarian contraction, the needs of livestock continued to require some degree of agricultural improvement. Some meadow was ploughed up from time to time to regenerate the grass and some pasture was turned into meadow in order to provide the vitally necessary winter hay. Meadow and pasture, too, were often carefully managed. The enclosed pastures around Wakefield enabled cattle men to exercise a certain amount of grazing management; burning off the old grass in early spring on the marsh meadows of the Vale of Pickering encouraged lush, new growth; and even on the moors the old heather was burned off from time to time to produce a new growth on which sheep could feed.[30]

Some land that was not principally agricultural was also subjected to a degree of management. This applied most especially to woodland. Trees, as sources of fuel, building timber, and industrial raw materials, were too valuable and in some places too scarce to be left to random exploitation. The rights of tenants to take wood for their own uses were strictly controlled and, at Pudsey and elsewhere, the activities of charcoal burners were subject to specific agreements. Narrow strips of trees were often carefully preserved along the boundaries both of enclosed and of open fields and many woods were periodically cropped

[30] Waites, 'A Yorkshire farmer in the memoranda rolls', pp. 447–8; *Cal. of Norris Deeds*, ed. Lumby, no. 101; Faull and Moorhouse, eds., *West Yorkshire*, III, pp. 660–3, 670–1; B. Waites, 'Pastoral farming on the Duchy of Lancaster's Pickering estate in the fourteenth and fifteenth centuries', *Yorks. Arch. J.*, XLIX, 1977, p. 85.

by coppicing. This method of exploitation was already being followed in the manor of Wakefield early in the fourteenth century and, at the end of the middle ages, it is much in evidence on the Fountains estate. The abbey's leases not only normally reserve timber for its own use, but lay down detailed prescriptions for the regeneration of coppices after they had been cut. The rule seems to have been to keep them fenced thereafter for a period of seven years, during which time no livestock would be allowed to enter and feed on the new growth. Many woods were part of a surviving natural landscape, but like the rest of the land they were, to varying degrees, a managed element in the agricultural scene.[31]

C. EASTERN ENGLAND

Eastern England in the middle ages cannot be treated as a single region as far as agricultural methods were concerned. So much is apparent even from the field systems there.[32] In Lincolnshire and western Cambridgeshire holdings were distributed between a few large fields subject to common pasture rights when not under crops. Almost everywhere else this type of organization was absent and the layout of fields suggested nothing in particular about cropping and pasturing practices.

Where a regular rotation of crops was practised the same lands would tend to be sown together each year whether or not they were in the same field. At Ovesham Hall in Matching (Essex) in 1391 there were 240 acres of demesne land free of commoning of which two-thirds were sown each year. On such a manor lands were grouped into three shifts. Accountants and surveyors might refer to the "wheat shift" (*seisona frumenti*), meaning lands sown with wheat in a particular year, or they might use a phrase like the "Westfeld shift" (*seisona de Westfeld*) to define the lands cropped alike each year. This terminology was frequently employed on the demesnes of Essex, Suffolk, and Cambridgeshire. Though on some manors, like Claret Hall (Essex) or Eastwood (Essex), regular rotations and compact courses created a kind of field system for the demesne (Table 3.1), the relationship between fields and shifts was normally complicated. First, it cannot be assumed that lands constituting a shift lay together. At Writtle (Essex) this was clearly not so; lands in one shift were separated by lands in others. Secondly, a field might be divided between two or more shifts. Even small fields were often so divided, as at Bircham (Norfolk), where in

---

[31] Faull and Moorhouse, eds., *West Yorkshire*, III, pp. 685, 688–9; *Fountains Abbey Lease Book*, ed. Michelmore, pp. lxii–iii and nos. 202, 279.

[32] H. L. Gray, *English Field Systems*, chs. 1, 8, 9; Baker and Butlin, eds., *Field Systems*, chs. 6, 7, 8.

Table 3.1. *The rotation of crops at Eastwood (Essex), 1366–74 (acres:*
winter-sown acreages in italics)

	Brounisfeld	Westfeld	Southfeld	Grymesfeld
1365–6	*119*	*31*	140	—
1366–7	119	31	—	*133*
1367–8	—	—	*140*	133
1368–9	*119*	*32*	140	—
1369–70	119	32	—	*133*
1370–1	—	—	*140*	133
1371–2	*119*	*32*	140	—
1372–3	119	32	—	*133*
1373–4	—	—	*143*	133

Source: PRO SC 6/840/27–35.

the years 1356–8 Ethelhowe was divided into two pieces containing 7
and $7\frac{3}{8}$ acres respectively. Thirdly, the permanence of the shift as a
cropping unit depended upon the regularity with which a rotation was
repeated; under a flexible system no permanently defined units
emerged and there was no fixed relationship between fields and shifts.
Naturally this was the case with outfields, which were only cropped
occasionally. It was also true where lands were fallowed at irregular
intervals or where there was a broad choice of cropping sequences, as
in much of East Anglia. This explains why commoning arrangements
in Norfolk and Suffolk often led to a disposition of folds more flexible
than that permitted by the common-field system.[33]

Fourteenth-century cropping patterns in Essex present few difficulties. Arable was usually fallowed one year in three in preparation for
a winter-sown crop, to be followed the next year by a spring-sown
crop. The sequence was generally (1) fallow, (2) wheat, rye, or maslin
(wheat and rye mixed together), (3) oats, barley, dredge (oats and
barley mixed together), peas or beans. The three shifts sometimes

[33] PRO SC 11/33 (Matching); PRO SC 6/838/4–30, SC 6/839/1–4 (Claret Hall), SC
6/930/27d, 28d (Bircham); for Eastwood, see Table 3.1; Bailey, *A Marginal Economy?*, pp. 57–65;
B. M. S. Campbell, 'Field Systems in Eastern Norfolk during the Middle Ages', Cambridge
Univ. Ph.D. thesis, 1975, pp. 323–4; idem, 'The complexity of manorial structure in medieval
Norfolk: a case study', *Norfolk Archaeology*, XXXIX, 1986, pp. 249–50; idem, 'The regional
uniqueness of English field systems? Some evidence from eastern Norfolk', *AHR*, XXIX, 1981, p.
17; D. Cromarty, *The Fields of Saffron Walden in 1400*, Chelmsford, 1966, pp. 8–13 and maps 1–5;
M. R. Postgate, 'The field systems of Breckland', *AHR*, X, 1962, pp. 82, 88–92; Newton, *Writtle*,
pp. 23–7 and map IV.

MILLS COLLEGE
LIBRARY

Table 3.2. *The rotation of crops at Langenhoe (Essex), 1379–84 (acres:
winter-sown acreages in italics)*

	1378–9	1380–1	1381–2	1383–4
in Bawysdoune	20	*14*	14	*14*
in the field towards the rectory	15	*21 + 1½*	23	*23*
in the Kechenefeld	24¾	*21 + 4*	25	*25*
in Cherchefeld (i)	—	23	—	32
at the lower end of the same field	—	3	—	3
in Baufeld	—	25	—	25
in a piece abutting on to Scruttiswall	(*33*)[a]	—	—	—
in two pieces below Katelenegraue	(*10*)[a]	—	—	*10*[b]
in Oxelace	*20 + ¾*	—	20	—
in Cherchefeld (ii)	—	—	*40*	—
in three Bawyscrofts	—	*14*	14	—

[a] 43 acres sown "in a certain piece of land abutting on to Scruttiswall and
in two pieces below Katelenegraue"
[b] 10 acres sown "in two pieces below Katelenegraue"
Source: Essex RO, D/DC 2/14d, D/DGe M200d, D/DEl M225d, 226d.

corresponded to field divisions as at Eastwood between 1366 and 1374
(Table 3.1), but demesnes were more commonly made up of numerous,
irregular fields. Eastwood was also unusual for the constancy of the
sown acreage in each field; it was more normal to allow additional
periods of rest. The example of Langenhoe (Table 3.2) illustrates such
irregular fields and the practice of allowing parcels to go temporarily
out of cultivation (Churchefeld in 1378–9), as well as the use of
outfields for growing oats (the three Baucrofts in 1380–1 and 1381–2).
Looser rotations were encouraged by the reduction of cereal
cultivation during the fourteenth century. At Bourchier Hall in
Tollesbury no regular shifts were recognizable by 1404.[34] At Langenhoe
rotations became less regular as the arable acreage was reduced in the
1390s; under a strict sequence the same lands would have been sown
with the same crops in 1395–6, 1404–5 and 1413–14 (Table 3.3).

The Essex pattern recurred on the loams of Suffolk, but here it was
also common to sow barley as a cash crop after a fallow year, followed
by peas or oats. This practice was introduced on the Clare manors of
Woodhall (Table 3.4) and Hundon in the mid-fourteenth century. On
both manors the rotations became (1) fallow, (2) wheat or barley, (3)

[34] Britnell, 'Agricultural technology', *EcHR*, 2nd ser. XXX, 1977, pp. 59, 64–5; *idem*,
'Finchingfield Park under the plough, 1341–42', *Essex Arch. and Hist.*, IX, 1977, p. 107; *idem*,
Growth and Decline in Colchester, p. 145.

Table 3.3. *The rotation of crops at Langenhoe (Essex), 1396–1414*
(acres: winter-sown acreages in italics)

	1395–6	1396–7	1404–5	1413–14
in Twentiacres	*18+4*	—	—	—
in Alaynesshot	*19*	—	—	—
in 12 acres	*12*	12	—	—
in Threacres	*3*	3	—	—
in Catelyne	—	29^a	$33\frac{1}{2}^b$	$34\frac{1}{2}+8^c$
in Catelynedoune	6^d	—	6^e	$5\frac{1}{2}^f$
to the west of Scruttis and elsewhere	—	—	12	—
in Gyffreyspetshot	—	—	$6\frac{1}{4}+2\frac{3}{4}$	—
in Estcroft	6	$5\frac{1}{2}$	6^g	—
in Estlond	7	—	—	—
in 40 acres	19	—	—	—
in Benfeld	15	—	—	—
in Westfeld, including Bawesdoune	—	—	$32\frac{1}{2}$	$4+?^h$
in a piece beside Westfeld	—	—	—	$?^h$
at Rysyng	—	—	$16\frac{3}{4}$	—
in the Northfeld	—	49	—	—

[a] in the land broken up opposite Catelenesgroue
[b] on the south side of the house called Catlynehomez
[c] in Catelyne next to the Esthous on the southern side
[d] in the Doune
[e] in a croft called Catelynedoune
[f] in the Catelynedoune next to the marsh
[g] in another croft
[h] $44\frac{1}{2}$ acres of oats were sown in Westfield and in a piece on the east side of it
Source: Essex RO, D/DC 2/15d, 16d, D/DEl M228d, D/DGe M201d.

oats, dredge, or peas. A similar rotation occurs at Acton (Suffolk) in 1356, at Long Melford (Suffolk) in 1372 and at Lawshall (Suffolk) in 1374 and 1377. By a further modification of Essex practice the Bures family at Acton took two successive barley crops, as in both 1410 and 1411; in both years 24 acres were sown with barley in Millefeld and $1\frac{1}{2}$ acres in Hygynsfeld. The three-shift system here may be expressed as (1) fallow, (2) wheat, maslin, or barley, (3) oats, barley, dredge, peas, or bullimong (oats and peas mixed together).[35] Suffolk farmers

[35] PRO SC 6/989/1–20 (Acton), SC 6/999/23d, 26d, 27d, SC 6/1000/1d, 2d, 3d (Hundon), SC 6/1002/1d, 2d (Lawshall); BL Add. Ms. 14849, f.108r (Melford).

Table 3.4. *Barley sowing at Woodhall (Suffolk), 1346–58 (acres)*

	sown in the wheat shift	sown in the oats shift
1345–6	—	$13\frac{1}{2}$
1347–8	3	$16\frac{1}{2}$
1350–1	$7\frac{3}{4}$	$16\frac{1}{2}$
1356–7	8	12
1357–8	$18\frac{3}{4}$	—

Source: PRO SC 6/1008/12–16.

probably used extended versions of the Essex rotation with six or nine courses in order to include an occasional wheat or maslin crop on all parts of the cultivated area. Variants of the Essex system were also to be found in the chalk regions of Cambridgeshire. At Burwell in 1399 there was wheat in one field and spring-sown crops, including barley, in another. At Fulbourn in 1436 the winter-sown crops were all "in the shift of the fields of Corsefeld and Colvylescrofte" and all the spring-sown crops, except for 2 acres were "in the shift of the fields of Wodebrugg and Yee". Here too, in 1462, the barley acreage was increased by taking two barley crops in succession, to judge from the large proportion of barley in the cropping of the demesne and its occurrence in the same shift as the wheat.[36]

On the boulder clays of southern Cambridgeshire the cropping patterns bore little relationship to others in eastern England. The land was fallowed every fourth year, and during the three years when the land was cropped two cereal harvests were separated by a course of legumes. This created a four-shift rotation of (1) fallow, (2) barley or dredge, (3) peas, (4) wheat. The wheat would benefit from the combined nitrogen produced by the roots of the pea plants. M. R. Postgate accounts for the existence of four-field Cambridgeshire villages by reference to such rotations. Details of this husbandry are outlined on demesnes of Ramsey abbey at Elsworth, 1381–4 (Table 3.5), Graveley, 1391–5, and probably at Knapwell in the 1360s and 1370s.[37] Inevitably there were differences from manor to manor. At Elsworth the shifts were cropped regularly but generous extra fallowing was allowed in the peas shift. At Graveley, besides this, wheat might be

[36] PRO SC 6/765/10d (Burwell), SC 6/767/8d, 9d (Fulbourn).

[37] PRO SC 6/767/22d, 24d, 25d (Graveley), SC 6/769/2–6 (Knapwell); Baker and Butlin, eds., *Field Systems*, p. 297.

substituted for barley or dredge in part of the shift succeeding the fallow. This might be formalized as (1) fallow, (2) barley, dredge or wheat, (3) peas or fallow, (4) wheat.

In Norfolk husbandry peas and beans were less important but the schemes used here were again different from those of Essex and most of Suffolk. The length of rotations was frequently indeterminate, either because periods of rest were of irregular length or because cropping sequences varied. At Bircham in the Good Sands the rotation in the 1340s and 1350s was (1) rest for one year or more, (2) barley, (3) rye, (4) oats. Here the irregularity of resting was the chief variable (Table 3.6). A more intensive cultivation occurred on the light loams. Fallowings were less frequent than elsewhere in eastern England and a large proportion of barley was achieved by taking successive barley crops from the same soil. A rotation often used at Brancaster in the 1360s seems to have been (1) fallow or peas, (2) wheat, (3) barley, (4) barley. A similar scheme can be illustrated from the Broadlands manor of Ormesby St Margaret (Table 3.7); intensive manuring by the cart and by the fold regularly permitted more than three successive crops.[38] Table 3.7 implies that land was sometimes under crops for eight or more successive years; the five parcels whose cropping is illustrated cannot all have been fallow in 1426–7, the year for which evidence is wanting. This was the most intensive arable farming in eastern England. It depended upon good, light barley soil, abundant manure and easy communications with urban markets.

Pasture rights on the arable in eastern England varied as much as cropping patterns, but some broad divisions are distinguishable. In Lincolnshire, except in parts of the southern fenlands, villagers usually had rights over open fields. Most of the country was subject to a two-field regime where half the cultivated area was fallowed, as at Grimsby. Common grazing had probably become widespread and systematic by the mid-fourteenth century.[39] In Essex, by contrast, communal organization of pasturing on the fallows was weakly developed. Examples of arable lands lying in common when not under crops occur in even the most enclosed regions, but such arrangements did not bring about the grouping into blocks of all the lands in the same shift. Nor, probably, did they affect as much of the village community as the common fields on the midland pattern did. In many villages,

---

[38] PRO SC 6/931/8–10 (Brancaster); B. M. S. Campbell, 'Agricultural progress in medieval England'; idem, 'Arable productivity in medieval England: some evidence from Norfolk', J. of Economic Hist., XLIII, 1983, pp. 390–3; idem, 'The regional uniqueness of English field systems?', pp. 21–2.

[39] Gray, English Field Systems, pp. 474–5; J. Thirsk, 'Field systems of the east Midlands', in Baker and Butlin, eds., Field Systems, pp. 279–80.

Table 3.5. *The rotation of crops at Elsworth (Cambs.), 1381–4*

	1380–1		1381–2		1382–3		1383–4	
	shift	ac.	shift	ac.	shift	ac.	shift	ac.
Wheat	A^a	78	B	10	[C]	?	D	69
Peas and beans	B^b	60	C	60	[D]	?	A	55½
Dredge	C^c	95	D^d	92	[A]	?	B	102½
Oats	—	10	—	10	[?]	?	—	10
Fallow	[D]	?	[A]	?	[B]	?	[C]	?

^{a} sown on Westdole, Laydole, Oldorchierdole, Middelbullocdole, Ouerbullocdole, Suinesgore, Schortbenlond and nine other parcels
^{b} sown on Over Madehil, at Bournende, at Knapwelleweie, Blacmerheuedyn and six other parcels
^{c} sown on Inlondole, Grenedole, Fordole and twelve other parcels
^{d} sown on Hungrydole, Standartdole, Woldhil, Woldweye, Grendich, Wardeboyscroft, Portersdole, Hebbesweye, Portersweye, Schortamberlond, Longamberlond, two pieces on Kyngestonhil, Buryete, Brodedole
Source: PRO SC 6/766/27d, 28d, 29d

meanwhile, there were no common rights on cultivated land; men pastured their animals on common woodlands and wastes or on their own holdings.[40]

In Norfolk and parts of Suffolk the folding of sheep was subject to an exceptional degree of control by manorial lords. After a period of varying length after the harvest when feeding off the stubble was fairly unrestricted (the period of shack), grazing became subject to tighter control. Sheep grazed the common pastures by day and were penned in with hurdles on particular pieces of arable land at night. It was in the interests of landlords to have their tenants' lands adequately manured, but so long as the demesnes remained intact they used their powers of regulation for the benefit of demesne lands in particular. Two main variations of practice may be distinguished. In eastern Norfolk the extreme fragmentation of peasant holdings, the complexity of rotations and the slighter importance of sheep for the manorial economy meant that folds were confined to demesne lands for part of the year and tenants manured their lands in severalty at other times. On the manor of Ormesby St Margaret, where the sown and fallow areas together averaged 216¾ acres between 1440 and 1455 (average of ten years), the

[40] R. H. Britnell, 'Agriculture in a region of ancient enclosure, 1185–1500', *Nottingham Medieval Studies*, XXVII, 1983, pp. 53–5.

Table 3.6. *The rotation of crops on parcels of demesne at Bircham (Norfolk), 1342–53 (acres)*

	Houtonwong		Shephouscroft	Popenhodele		Boterowe	
1341–2	5¼ barley	—	3½ barley	—	—	6½ rye	—
1342–3	5¼ rye	—	3½ rye	5¾ barley	—	6½ oats	—
1343–4	5¼ oats	—	3½ oats	5 rye	5½ barley	—	—
1344–5	—	6½ barley	—	4½ oats	5½ rye	—	—
1345–6	? (barley)	? (rye)	? (barley)	?	? (oats)	?	?
1346–7	4½ rye	6½ oats	2¼ rye	—	—	6½ barley	—
1347–8	4¾ oats	—	2¼ oats	—	—	6½ rye	6½ barley
1348–9	—	5¼ barley	—	—	—	6½ oats	6½ rye
1349–50	?	? (rye)	? (barley)	?	?	?	? (oats)
1350–1	—	6 oats[a]	3½ rye	—	6 barley	—	—
1351–2	—	—	3½ oats	—	5 rye	—	—
1352–3	—	—	—	5¾ barley	5 oats	—	—

[a] "in le Wong"

Note: the continuity between the parts of Hotonwong, Popenhodele and Boterowe is hypothetical

Source: PRO SC 6/930/17–25.

Table 3.7. *The rotation of crops on parcels of demesne at Ormesby St Margaret (Norfolk), 1424–31 (acres)*

	Nether-rannowe	Lullewelle	le Ston	Over-skynewelle	Nether-skynewelle
1423–4	7 wheat	12 wheat	5 grey peas	6 barley	8 barley
1424–5	7 barley	12 barley	5 wheat	6 grey peas	8 oats
1425–6	7 barley	12 barley	5¾ barley	6 wheat	8 grey peas
1426–7	(oats, peas, or fallow)	(oats, peas, or fallow)	(barley)	(barley)	(wheat)
1427–8	7 wheat	12 wheat	(oats)	6 barley	8 barley
1428–9	7 barley	(12) barley	5 grey peas	(oats)	8 barley
1429–30	7 barley	12 barley	5 wheat	6 wheat	8 grey peas
1430–1	7 fallow	12 oats	5 barley	6 barley	8 wheat

Note: In neither 1427–8 nor 1428–9 was the oats sowing described in detail. But neither le Ston in the former year nor Overskynewelle in the latter are listed among the fallowed lands, so it is more likely that they were sown with oats than that they were left unsown.
Source: PRO SC 6/939/1–8A.

acreage manured with the fold averaged 35½ acres (average of eight years), implying that a sixth of the cultivated area could be manured in this way every year. This proportion was about normal for the region. At Ormesby St Margaret the fold was chiefly used between consecutive crops in preparation for wheat or barley. Meanwhile in western Norfolk and the Breckland, adjacent pastures and arable lands were grouped into separate foldcourses each one of which was reserved for a particular flock. Sometimes the whole area of a village was partitioned in this way. There was often more than one manor in a village, each with its own foldcourses, and in the Breckland some tenants had their own folds. Since ewes and lambs were usually folded separately from wethers, the pasturing arrangements in some villages were very complex. B. M. S. Campbell uses the term "liberty of the fold" for the practice of eastern Norfolk to distinguish it from the "foldcourse system" of western Norfolk and the Breckland.[41] Landlords entitled to

[41] PRO SC 6/940/3–11, SC 6/941/1 (Ormesby); Bailey, *A Marginal Economy?*, pp. 65–85; Campbell, 'Agricultural progress in medieval England', p. 35; *idem.*, 'The complexity of manorial structures', pp. 248–50; *idem*, 'The regional uniqueness of English field systems?', pp. 16–28; Gray, *English Field Systems*, p. 349; M. R. Postgate, 'Field systems of East Anglia', in Baker and Butlin, eds., *Field Systems*, pp. 315, 317. For an example of foldcourses in north-west Essex, see Cromarty, *Fields of Saffron Walden*, pp. 14–17 and map 3.

Table 3.8. *Preparation for the cropping of 1452–3 at Ormesby St Margaret (Norfolk)*

Crop	Acres	Preceding crop	Number of summer ploughings
Wheat	12	mixed peas	—
	9	fallow	4
	8	fallow	3
Grey peas	12	?	—
Mixed peas	18	barley	—
Barley	18	wheat	—
	11	grey peas	—
	2	mixed peas	—
	$57\frac{1}{4}$	barley	—
	$18\frac{3}{4}$	?	—
Oats	$20\frac{1}{4}$	barley	—

Source: PRO SC 6/940/10d, 11d.

raise folds could make over their rights to others and frequently did so. At Stow Bardolph (Norfolk) in 1426–7 a manorial shepherd's lands were composted by the fold. At Bircham rights of foldage were leased to others even while direct demesne management continued; in 1355–6 a shilling was received "for the liberty of a fold of the lady's leased to Sir John Nichole". After the abandonment of direct demesne management folds might be leased with the demesne lands or separately.[42]

Besides an appropriate rotation and an adequate supply of manure, good crop husbandry required that the seedbed should be properly broken up and cleaned by the plough. Walter of Henley thought that each year sown lands should be ploughed once and fallow lands twice. This was the practice on some Suffolk manors of the abbot and convent of Bury St Edmunds in the mid-fourteenth century. In one instance most of the fallow course had to be ploughed three times.[43] An even greater commitment to ploughing was common in Norfolk. At Ormesby St Margaret in the fifteenth century the fallows were prepared with up to six ploughings whether or not they were dunged at the same time; this was possible because so little land was drawn

[42] PRO SC 6/930/26r (Bircham), SC 6/943/6r (Runcton, Norfolk), SC 6/943/13r, d (Stow Bardolph), SC 6/944/12r (Swaffham, Norfolk); Davenport, *Economic Development of a Norfolk Manor*, App. IX, p. 1; J. R. Ravensdale, *Liable to Floods*, pp. 79–80.

[43] BL Add. Ms. 14849, ff.91v–92v, 102v–103r, 108r; *Walter of Henley and other Treatises on Estate Management and Accounting*, ed. D. Oschinsky, pp. 314–15.

Table 3.9. *Ploughing at Eastwood (Essex), 1366–74 (acres)*

	at winter ploughing	at Lent ploughing	at fallow ploughing
1365–6	150	140	50[a]
1366–7	133	150	40[a]
1367–8	140	133	50[a]
1368–9	151	140	55[b]
1369–70	133	151	60[b]
1370–1	140	133	58[b]
1371–2	151	140	52[c]
1372–3	133	151	48[c]
1373–4	143	133	52[a]

[a] April and May; [b] March, April and May; [c] March and April
Source: As Table 3.1, with which this needs to be compared.

from fallow in any one year (Table 3.8). Such thoroughness was not characteristic of the Essex tradition. At Eastwood in the 1360s summer ploughings never exceeded half the fallow area (Table 3.9).

The plough itself was subject to variation both from region to region and from season to season. Wheeled ploughs were to be found on the light soils of Norfolk but not on the clays of Essex or Suffolk.[44] Even on the same manor larger ploughs than usual were sometimes used in early summer when hard fallow lands were first broken up.[45] Ploughs were among the least durable items of equipment and rarely lasted more than a season before being taken apart. A tenant's plough may have lasted longer, since it might not have to plough so many acres in a year as a demesne plough, but it can hardly have performed more duty. The heavily bound ploughs of the royal demesne at Eastwood between 1367 and 1372 worked 56 acres on average before having to be reconstructed.[46] Many demesnes contracted annually with a smith for the upkeep of the ironwork of their ploughs. By this arrangement the iron required would usually be supplied by the smith. Some impression of the quantities of metal used may be taken from the Eastwood accounts. Each plough there required annually a sheaf of steel and over sixteen pounds of iron in addition to the iron in the plough-foot, the drail, the straddleclout, ties for the beam and the spitclout. The

[44] PRO SC 6/939/1r, 6r, 8Ar, etc. (Ormesby), SC 6/944/19r (Uphall in Ashill, Norfolk); Davenport, *Economic Development of a Norfolk Manor*, App. VIII, p. xxxiii; Langdon, *Horses, Oxen and Technological Innovation*, pp. 132–41.

[45] BL Add. Ms. 14849, ff.91v–92v (Clopton, Suffolk); PRO SC 6/840/29r (Eastwood), SC 6/1000/3r (Hundon).   [46] PRO SC 6/840/29–33.

main metal parts were the ploughshare and coulter, and the coulter of a new Suffolk plough might alone weigh ten pounds.[47] The principal wooden parts were the main beam, sharebeam, and handles, together in Norfolk with the wheels; they were often of ash.[48] Differences between manors were not so great as to preclude a market for plough parts. Throughout the later middle ages it was common for bailiffs to buy wooden ploughs ready-made and to buy ready-made iron parts for them. The mid-fifteenth-century officials at Ormesby St Margaret acquired ploughs at various times from ploughwrights at Upton, Hemsby, and Yarmouth; the ploughs were bought without wheels, which could be obtained from wheelwrights as required. Even when ploughshare and coulter were made to order a bailiff would often buy smaller parts from ready stock. At Eastwood in 1364 the cost of a new plough included 1s. 4d. for purchased metal parts as against 1s. 9d. for unworked iron and steel.[49]

The size of ploughteams varied with the heaviness of the soil, and the major differences between one region and another persisted throughout the period. Outside Norfolk mixed teams of horses and oxen were employed everywhere. At Harrington (Lincs.) on the edge of the wolds the team comprised two mares and four oxen. In Essex and Suffolk bigger teams of four horses and four oxen, or six horses and two oxen, were common, while on London clay and the heavier loams were to be found teams as large as six horses and three oxen, or six horses and four oxen.[50] The higher costs of ploughing in these districts must have contributed to the frequently severe reduction of arable acreage there in the late middle ages. Oxen might be shod only on their front feet[51] or not at all, whereas horses were shod on all four feet. In Norfolk light wheeled ploughs were drawn by small teams, usually of horses. In the Breckland a four-horse plough occurs at Uphall in Ashill (Norfolk) in 1372–3 and a two-horse plough at Brandon (Suffolk) in 1386–7. At Bircham the ploughteam had two or three horses during the 1360s. In

---

[47] PRO SC 6/840/25r (Eastwood), SC 6/1008/16r (Woodhall, Suffolk). A lighter Norfolk coulter weighing 8¾ lb occurs in *Paston Letters*, ed. Davis, I, no. 11, p. 20.

[48] e.g. 'For an ash bought from Roger Dextere from which to cut plough timbers, 16d.', PRO SC 6/989/14r (Acton).

[49] PRO SC 6/840/26r (Eastwood), SC 6/939/1r, 4r, SC 6/940/5r (Ormesby); F. M. Page, *The Estates of Crowland Abbey*, p. 272.

[50] BL Add. Ms. 14849, ff.32v, 108r (Melford and Redgrave, Suffolk); PRO SC 6/836/10d (Bardfield, Essex), SC 6/839/1r, 2r, 3, m.2r, 4r (Claret Hall), SC 6/841/9d, 10r (Feering), SC 6/846/31, m.2r, 32, mm.4r, 5r, 33r, 34r (Sampford, Essex), SC 6/848/13r (Tolleshunt Major, Essex), SC 6/849/3, m.1r (Walkfare, Essex), SC 6/910/11r (Harrington, Lincs.), SC 6/1002/16r (Lidgate, Suffolk); Essex RO, D/DGe M20or (Langenhoe), D/DK M86, mm.6r, 7r (Bourchier Hall); Langdon, *Horses, Oxen and Technological Innovation*, pp. 109, 112, 215–18.

[51] PRO SC 6/989/13r, 17r (Acton), SC 6/1001/10r (Lawshall).

eastern Norfolk ploughs at Ormesby St Margaret probably had only two horses in the 1420s and 1430s, and ploughs of this sort were used on the Paston manors at Drayton in 1465. Such light ploughs saved labour as well as horsepower since they could be managed by a single ploughman; in much of Norfolk it was already true in the fourteenth century that "two horses with one boy doe plow or care".[52]

By the nature of the evidence it is easier to describe regional differences in arable farming than to assess their implications for productivity. Table 3.10 demonstrates that yields of wheat were low in varying degrees, but does not show any definite pattern of local variation. Regional differences in arable productivity were in fact more clear-cut than these figures suggest. Seed was sown more thickly on some soils than on others; even within eastern Norfolk sowing rates varied between two and four bushels to an acre. The average productivity of an acre of land was also affected by the proportion of the arable which was cropped each year and by the pattern of cropping, since barley and legumes were higher yielding than other crops. Northeastern Norfolk, with its high sowing ratios and intensive farming practices, was distinctly more productive than other parts of eastern England.[53]

The custody of plough beasts and dairy cattle in the later middle ages did not develop any important new principles. Specialized veterinary skills were confined to horses, for whom manorial officers sometimes called upon the services of a marshal or farrier.[54] Other livestock were treated by the regular herdsmen. Levels of productivity are only roughly known. In the case of plough beasts there were considerable regional variations according to different qualities of soil. At Eastwood ploughing rates work out at $20\frac{3}{4}$ acres a year for each plough beast between 1362 and 1374, whereas at Ormesby St Margaret the average rate between 1424 and 1431 was about $43\frac{1}{4}$ acres.[55] Both teams contained horses only, so the difference is attributable chiefly to the difference between working Essex clays and light Norfolk loams.

Dairy management is imperfectly recorded because manorial dairies were usually leased out, even on demesnes which were directly managed. The tenant paid rent according to the number of cows in milk. Average milk yields were depressed by high sterility ratios

[52] PRO SC 6/930/29d, 30d (Bircham), SC 6/939/1r, d, 2r, d, etc. (Ormesby), SC 6/944/19r (Uphall); *Brandon Manor Account Roll, 1386–7*, trans. J. T. Munday, Lakenheath, 1971; 'Old poem on Norfolk', ed. J. P. Boileau, *Norfolk Archaeology*, v, 1859, p. 162; *Paston Letters*, ed. Davis, i, no. 180, pp. 295–6; Campbell, 'Agricultural progress in medieval England', pp. 36–7; Langdon, *Horses, Oxen and Technological Innovation*, pp. 101, 103, 215.

[53] Campbell, 'Arable productivity', pp. 387–94.

[54] PRO SC 6/840/30r (Eastwood), SC 6/999/20r (Hundon); *Paston Letters*, ed. Davis, i, no. 175, p. 288.   [55] PRO SC 6/840/23–35 (Eastwood), SC 6/939/1–8A (Ormesby).

Table 3.10. *Wheat yields per seed sown on some manors in eastern England*

	Number of years averaged	average	minimum	maximum
Claret Hall, Essex (1350–63)	7	3.4	1.7	6.4
Eastwood, Essex (1363–73)	10	3.7	3.1	4.5
Feering, Essex (1399–1403)	5	2.9	2.2	4.1
Kelvedon, Essex (1377–1401)	20	3.2	1.6	4.7
Langenhoe, Essex (1381, 1396)	2	3.7	3.4	3.9
Fornham All Saints, Suffolk (1400–20)	11	2.9	2.1	3.6
Risby, Suffolk (1352–77)	4	3.9	2.0	6.3
Martham, Norfolk (1400–24)	11	3.9	2.5	6.0
Ormesby, Norfolk (1423–52)	18	4.8	2.7	6.8

Sources: PRO SC 6/838/24–30, SC 6/839/1–4 (Claret Hall), SC 6/840/25–35 (Eastwood), SC 6/841/10 (Feering), SC 6/939/1–13, SC 6/940/1–11 (Ormesby); Westminster Abbey Muniments, 25739–25758 (Feering), 25829–25880 (Kelvedon); Essex RO, D/DC 2/15, 16, D/DEl M224, D/DGe M200 (Langenhoe); Bailey, *A Marginal Economy?*, pp. 102–3 (Fornham, Risby); Campbell, 'Agricultural progress in medieval England', p. 38, with additional information from Dr Campbell (Martham).

and cattle diseases. Some calculations from Sibton abbey estates in Suffolk shortly after 1500 show an average annual production of 0.6 weys of cheese and 3.1 gallons of butter per cow, besides small quantities of milk and cream reserved for use at Sibton. These ratios were no higher than those envisaged by Walter of Henley in the thirteenth century.[56]

The management of sheep flocks depended upon the size of an estate, the distance between its parts and the distribution of pasture lands between them. On small estates and isolated manors of large estates lacking extensive pastures the flocks contained sheep of all categories. At Somerton (Lincs.) in the 1360s the flock had this composite character and no transfers took place between Somerton and other manors. Large wool producers usually aimed at more specialized shepherding than this. On manors with extensive grazing they divided different

[56] PRO SC 6/844/23–8 (Hutton, Essex), SC 6/846/32–5 (Sampford); *The Sibton Abbey Estates*, ed. Denney, p. 38.

categories of sheep between separate folds each with its own shepherd. On the duke of Exeter's manor of Stow Bardolph in 1426–7 there were shepherds of ewes, wethers, ewe-hogs, and wether-hogs, and an assistant was employed at lambing. There was another shepherd of ewes at Wormegay attached to this manor. At Bourchier Hall in 1404–6 there were shepherds of wethers, ewes, and lambs. Alternatively, where grazing was more limited but where an estate had a number of manors, each manor might constitute a specialized fold. The Suffolk manors of the Clare estates exhibited such inter-manorial specialization in the 1350s. At Hundon, for example, there were no ewes. Lambs were born on the lower pastures in Clare and then sent to Hundon in time for their first winter. The following summer, after shearing, the young females were sent back to Clare to rejuvenate the breeding stock while the wethers were kept at Hundon to produce wool. A similar pattern of sheep farming was practised on the Paston family estates in Norfolk in the third quarter of the fifteenth century; the wethers were kept at Sparham, the ewes at Hellesdon, the young sheep at Drayton. Such specialization between manors often involved sheep in long journeys. In 1360–1 Writtle manor in central Essex received 80 year-old lambs from Walden, over twenty miles to the north-west, and sent 110 year-old lambs to Foulness Island, over twenty miles to the south-east.[57]

Death rates of medieval sheep were affected by endemic diseases, usually loosely described as murrain, which caused periodic epidemics. On Sibton abbey estates heavy losses recurred in 1363, 1365 and 1372, about a third of the flock being lost on each occasion. Murrains were often local in their incidence, so that sheep could be replaced from another manor or bought from outside the estate. Even so, they were costly, especially if a flock was struck before lambing. The rate of reproduction was a serious matter for large sheep owners. It was chiefly to meet the requirements of breeding that they separated ewes and their lambs from other sheep; in this way they could ensure that in the breeding grounds the pasture, the shepherding, and the composition of the flock were all favourable for lambing. Ewes were served by more rams in the middle ages than in the sixteenth and seventeenth centuries. A ratio of one ram to thirty or forty ewes was normal, and higher rates were adopted on well-administered estates. At Eastwood between 1361 and 1374 there was a ram to every twenty ewes; here lambing rates averaged about one lamb for every ewe on the manor the Michaelmas before lambing. At Wix (Essex) in the 1380s there was a

---

[57] PRO SC 6/913/12–19 (Somerton), SC 6/943/13r, d (Stow Bardolph), SC 6/999/27d, SC 6/1000/1d (Hundon); Essex RO, D/DK M89d (Bourchier Hall); *Paston Letters*, ed. Davis, II, no. 731, p. 359; Newton, *Writtle*, pp. 64–5, 118–20.

ram to every eighteen ewes. The lambing rate was more likely than the mortality rate to be significantly affected by good estate management and expert shepherding. However, a lambing rate of one lamb to each ewe was as high as shepherds could hope for, and much lower rates are recorded.[58]

The main object of sheep rearing was to produce wool. The wools of eastern England were not, on the whole, of the first quality. The best came from Lincolnshire, whose Lindsey wools had an established reputation at home and abroad, though they were cheaper than the best wools of the Cotswolds and the Welsh marches. Wool from Essex and Suffolk was among the poorest in England, and it was often fouled with tar and grease to soften it. The fleeces whose weights can be assessed varied sufficiently widely to suggest that different types of sheep were kept on different estates. At Claret Hall the average weight of a fleece was 2.3 lb in four years between 1350 and 1358. At nearby Acton (Suffolk) the average weight was 1.3 lb in four years between 1415 and 1423. The latter weight was more nearly representative of the region than the former. Fleeces weighed 1.2 lb at Mildenhall (Suffolk) in 1418 and 1420, 1.4 lb on the Sibton abbey estates in 1366, 1.4 lb at Ormesby St Margaret in 1425 and 1.6 lb at Eastwood between 1363 and 1374. The Townshend flocks in Norfolk in 1481–2 averaged 1.3 lb a fleece, though there was a difference between ewes' fleeces which were below this average and wethers' which were above it.[59]

Even this brief sketch can illustrate how, in every particular capable of being studied, agricultural practice varied with different circumstances of soil, climate, and estate organization. It is striking how uniformly low productivity levels were by the standards of later centuries and, at the same time, how difficult it is to be sure of any advance on the standards of earlier ones. Because of the reduction in labour inputs, grain yields on Norfolk demesnes were in fact lower after 1350 than they had been before.[60] The variety of medieval techniques represents not a pattern of contrasts between new knowledge

[58] PRO SC 6/840/22–35 (Eastwood), SC 6/849/16, 17 (Wix); Essex RO, D/DC 2/13–16, D/DEl M224–6, D/DGe M200 (Langenhoe), D/DK M88d, 89d (Bourchier Hall); *Brandon Account*, trans. Munday; *The Sibton Abbey Estates*, ed. Denney, p. 25; K. J. Allison, 'Flock management in the sixteenth and seventeenth centuries', *EcHR*, 2nd ser. xi, 1958, p. 104; Davenport, *Economic Development of a Norfolk Manor*, App. ix, p. lxvii.

[59] PRO SC 6/838/24–30 (Claret Hall), SC 6/840/22–35 (Eastwood), SC 6/989/15–18, 20 (Acton), SC 6/931/1r, 2r, SC 6/939/2r (Ormesby); *Brandon Account,* trans. Munday; *Sibton Abbey Estates*, ed. Denney, pp. 25, 29; Allison, 'Flock management', p. 105; Bailey, *A Marginal Economy?*, p. 127; Davenport, *Economic Development of a Norfolk Manor*, App. ix, p. lvii; R. Trow-Smith, *A History of British Livestock Husbandry to 1700*, pp. 162–3.

[60] Campbell, 'Agricultural progress in medieval England', p. 39; *idem*, 'Arable productivity', p. 384.

and old, but rather a set of local adaptations to different environments.[61] It is nevertheless instructive to see the matrix from which later developments could arise. Regional diversification of agrarian methods did not have to wait for agrarian capitalism but was born of variations in experience over many centuries. Medieval farmers had already established the regional variations in husbandry which were developed by their more experimental successors. Intensive rotations in eastern Norfolk presaged the intensive Norfolk husbandry of the seventeenth and eighteenth centuries, just as intermittent cropping on some claylands was a precursor of later patterns of convertible husbandry. Much of the local knowledge which was commonplace in the fifteenth century was a necessary foundation for later advances.

D. THE EAST MIDLANDS

In 1959 one of the duties of the Ministry of Agriculture was to regulate the use of the open fields in the village of Laxton. In particular it was concerned with regulating the access of animals to the three fields, to two of the fields between the harvesting of one crop and the sowing of the next and to the third field which lay fallow. The fields were named according to the crops which they grew: there was the Wheat Field, the Bean and Clover Field, and the Fallow Field. The regulations were enforced by a jury of the tenants. Each field was the special responsibility of a foreman. One of the tenants was bailiff and pinder (responsible for the impounding of stray animals in the pinfold). He was responsible to the steward, who was responsible to the lord, in this case the Minister. Laxton is still farmed in this way. The regulations are made, and they are enforced, by the community of the village. Only a note at the end of the 1959 regulations destroys the illusion that this might be late medieval England. "The Commission appeal to the Minister's tenants, in their common interests, to help him and the foreman of the juries to carry out these rules." The plaintive note of appeal gives the game away: this is a method of farming that has been passed by.[62]

No such plaintive tone, but rather an anxious solicitude, informs the agreement made by the men of Harlestone in 1410. A century earlier, in the time of Henry de Bray, there had been two fields in Harlestone, the North Field and the South Field; by the early fifteenth century a third field, the East Field, had been added. But in each third year the yields were inadequate, and so the boundaries of the fields were redrawn. The fields are described, as at Laxton, in terms of the grains

[61] Britnell, 'Agricultural technology', p. 55; Campbell, 'Arable productivity', pp. 397–8.

[62] J. D. Chambers, *Laxton: The Last Open-Field Village*, London, 1964; C. S. and C. S. Orwin, *The Open Fields*.

to be sown in them: "in each year one field shall be sown with wheat and barley, and another field with beans and peas, and the third field shall lie fallow". The document is an agreement between six different lords and "the lawful men of the whole village of Harlestone". They elected a jury of nine, a body which survived at least until the early sixteenth century. Much of the work it had to do concerned the management of stock; the regulations match, though they are more detailed than, those of the modern community at Laxton. The proper working of enclosure was a vital part of communal agriculture. "All the meadow and pasture within the three fields shall be enclosed when those fields are being sown"; they shall lie as common "when the needs of those fields and of the village shall render customary". Each of the lords was to make a proper enclosure around his own demesnes, and maintain it with care. They were to release animals that strayed into their enclosures, unless these were "rude and incorrigible cattle", in which case they could be impounded. On the first and second offence the beasts were then to be released without penalty, on a third occasion only after satisfaction had been given. As is clear from both the documents cited, this is an area of mixed husbandry, in which livestock plays a prominent part.[63]

A similar agreement survives from Wymeswold in Leicestershire c. 1425, made before the three lords and "with the common consent of the whole village". This represents the collection of a series of by-laws, primarily though not exclusively concerned with regulating the movement of cattle. This document also thinks in terms of three fields, "the qwyte corn feld", "the pesse corn feld", and the fallow. A man had to keep animals off his neighbour's grassland and his growing corn, otherwise "he shall make amends to him that has the harm, and for each foot that is within the corn pay a penny to the church". The terms under which the poor might glean both in the wheat and the peas field were regulated. "No man should glean for any manner of corn that is able to work for his meat and twopence a day to help to save his neighbour's corn." The sense of community comes over very clearly here. Elsewhere in the region there are by-laws from Ramsey abbey manors in Huntingdonshire, custumals from Kingsthorpe and Brigstock in Northamptonshire, and individual regulations in most sets of court rolls. Each village has its own particular preoccupations, "according to the needs of the fields and of the village", but the similarities are great, for the common constraints on men were those of original sin and of the agricultural calendar.[64]

[63] Joan Wake, 'Communitas Villae', *EHR*, XXXVII, 1922, pp. 406–13.
[64] HMC, *Middleton Mss.*, London, 1918, pp. 106–9; Raftis, *Tenure and Mobility*, pp. 111–27; J. H. Glover, *Kingsthorpiana*, London, 1883, pp. 38–45; Northants. RO, X371 (trans. *ibid.* Misc. Ledger 141, pp. 93–106); W. O. Ault, *Open Field Farming in Medieval England*.

The by-laws are valuable in showing not just what had to be regulated but what could be taken for granted. It was taken for granted that agricultural production was organized through the sowing of a narrow range of crops on a small number of large, open fields. The narrowness of the range and the numbers of fields were often modified, but these modifications were not such that men's terminology needed to be altered at the time. In Leicestershire, Rutland, and Huntingdon-shire four-fifths of the villages had three fields. Three fields predominated also in northern Northamptonshire. To the north and the south of the band of territory thus formed there was more variety. In southern Northamptonshire, at Alice Perrers's two manors of Culworth and Radstone and at Kingsthorpe, which the men of the village leased from the crown, there were two fields. The Nottingham-shire inquisitions suggest that in the north of the region three fields were most common, as still at Laxton, but that many villages had two fields.[65]

The neat open-field arrangement might suggest that a narrow range of crops was sown, and that under a three-course rotation fallow would be followed by a winter-sown crop, such as wheat or rye, and this would in turn be followed by a spring-sown crop such as barley or peas. In fact cropping was more complicated than this picture would suggest. No account consulted shows only two crops sown on a manorial demesne: there could be as many as six different grains. It will be shown that peasant land use was just as varied. Before discussing cropping then, it is necessary to examine how the holdings of the lords and the peasants lay within the fields. In particular it is necessary to stress the importance of the furlong, as a unit of cultivation and as a unit of consolidation also. A survey made c. 1500 of the land of Giles Colyer in Orton Saucey (Leics.) provides a point of departure. He had 43 acres $5\frac{1}{2}$ roods of land, lying as follows: in the East Field 13 acres, in the South Field 18 acres 2 roods, and in the West Field 12 acres $3\frac{1}{2}$ roods. In all 55 parcels of land are listed. An acre is both the largest and the most common unit described: other parcels are of $\frac{1}{2}$ acres, 3, 2, 1 and $\frac{1}{2}$ roods. One point where the Orton survey may not show an entirely typical picture is in the size of the individual plots of land. The demesnes of Leicester abbey at Barkby (Leics.) amounted to about 148 acres and lay in 231 different parcels, nearly a half of which were less than half an acre in size. This was a manorial demesne, though one formed at a comparatively late date. The peasant strips would be no larger: an early

[65] Baker and Butlin, eds., *Field Systems*, pp. 256–7; Gray, *English Field Systems; Cal. Inq. Misc.*, IV, no. 13; Kingsthorpe parish records, memoranda rolls 1377 (consulted at Northants. RO by courtesy of P. I. King and the rector of Kingsthorpe); *Inquisitions post Mortem relating to Nottinghamshire, 1350–1485*, Thoroton Soc., XII (1), XII (2), XVII, 1948, 1951, 1956.

fifteenth-century deed from Bottesford mentioned 14 parcels of land, 10 of which were single strips of probably not more than one-third of an acre. These strips of land corresponded to the ridges within the pattern of ridge and furrow. Measurement of the ridges at Kibworth Harcourt showed the ridge to equate roughly with a rood of land, and to measure just over a quarter of an acre.[66]

At times a manorial demesne followed this pattern, of a large number of small parcels of land scattered over the open fields, just as the peasant holdings lay. At Kirby Bellars (Leics.) the demesne was scattered over 113 furlongs in the three fields; the demesne of Owston abbey in King's Norton was spread over 71 furlongs. Elsewhere, however, the demesne lay largely apart and enclosed; this is suggested for Laxton, for Eaton (Leics.) in 1396, and is implied by the Harlestone agreement already quoted. And possibly it was still more common for the demesnes to be distributed around the fields, but in larger parcels than the peasant holdings. Peterborough abbey had a large manor in Peterborough itself. When it was surveyed in 1393 there were five fields, in which a demesne of 547 acres lay in 39 separate parcels of land. Sometimes the unit is called a *cultura* or furlong, but more often it is a *pecia* or plot of land. The other Peterborough demesnes, and that of the archbishop of York's great manor of Southwell, show a similar pattern. In 1388 the jurors described the latter as having a demesne of 542 acres of arable, which were described as lying in eighteen parcels only. The largest parcel was 142 acres in *Mikelthwayth*; this was surely a field, not a furlong.[67]

It was the furlong not the field which was the unit of cropping. It was normal practice by the mid-fourteenth century for accounts to specify on which furlongs or in which areas and fields the different crops were sown. A few surviving accounts from Peterborough in the later fourteenth century show the six different crops each confined to a particular region of the demesne. Here there were five fields, and such a neat arrangement cannot have been difficult to organize. A similar neatness, on a much smaller scale, is found on the rectorial demesne on the Westminster abbey manor of Oakham. Here in the mid-fourteenth century the abbey grew wheat, barley, and legumes in three fields described in the accounts as the north, south, and west fields. In 1350–1 24 acres of wheat and 18 acres of barley were in the south field, and 32 acres of legumes in the north field. In the following year wheat

---

[66] R. H. Hilton, 'Medieval agrarian history', *VCH Leics.*, II, pp. 157–61; Huntington Library, San Marino, Hastings Mss., Leics. Manorial papers, outsize box 65; Howell, *Kibworth Harcourt*, pp. 90–1.

[67] Hilton in *VCH Leics.*, II, pp. 157–9; Chambers, *Laxton*, pp. 12, 19; Wake, 'Communitas Villae', p. 410; BL Cott. Nero C VII, ff.145r–147v; *Cal. Inq. Misc.*, v, no. 65.

and barley were sown in the west field, and barley and legumes in the south field. At Kirby Bellars in 1395 the small amount of wheat was sown in both the fields cropped that year; in 1399 and 1406 one field was devoted to peas, while barley, oats, and wheat were grown on the other field. It is interesting to compare this pattern of cropping with the normal terminology of the by-laws; if the wheat field was in some sense a fiction, the pea field was not.[68]

The question of which crops were sown will now be considered more systematically, taking first the crops sown on the demesnes of the lords, and then the crops grown by villeins. Manors directly farmed for which grange accounts survive are rarities in the later middle ages, and they become steadily more rare. Most of the evidence relates to the first half of the period, before 1425. For Northamptonshire it is possible to find a good mixture of lay and ecclesiastical estates. The manors in Table 3.11 are Peterborough, Longthorpe by Peterborough, Biggin Grange in Oundle, and a group of five manors centred on Brampton Ash. For the Peterborough abbey manors, a figure from the early fourteenth century has been added for the purpose of comparison. At Longthorpe there are two contemporary accounts from the same village, one from the abbey demesne and the other from the farm of justice William Thorpe, whose manor house is now one of the best-known monuments of the region. It can be seen from Table 3.11 that the amount of oats sown decreased during the fourteenth century to around 10 per cent of the total acreage, though the figures for drage must be added to this. The amount of wheat had decreased also, and winter-sown grain represented between 24 and 30 per cent of the later fourteenth-century sample. The increase was in the sowing of barley and of vetches.[69]

Figures for grain receipts at Leicester abbey allow the farming of a different region to be examined. The figures for the years 1393, 1399, 1401, and 1470 suggest there was little variation over the period. Of total receipts of grain, 13.3 per cent were wheat, 5.2 per cent rye, 43.2 per cent barley, 30.8 per cent peas and 7.5 per cent oats. These figures include peasant tithe corn as well as renders from the abbey demesne. If we move to the Ramsey abbey estate, we find that cropping has become more narrowly focused than elsewhere in the region. The abbey continued to sow a large acreage of wheat in the years just before the demesnes were leased out. At Upwood it was 21 per cent of the total crop, but elsewhere the proportion varied between 26 and 33 per

[68] Northants. RO, PDC a/c rolls, box 1, nos. 5, 6, 10, 18; Westminster Abbey Muniments, 20267, 20270; Hilton in *VCH Leics.*, ii, p. 161.

[69] Northants. RO, Fitzwilliam/Milton Mss., nos. 233, 267, 2389; *ibid.*, PDC a/c rolls, box 1, nos. 4, 4b, 5, 6, 10, 18; *Cal. Inq. Misc.*, v, nos. 30–4.

Table 3.11. *Crops sown on Northamptonshire manors*

Manor/year	Percentage sown with each crop						Total acreage sown
	Wheat	Rye	Vetches	Barley	Drage	Oats	
Peterborough 1307–8	26.3	6.8	6.9	23.7	8.4	27.9	541
Peterborough 1373–4	14.2	9.6	10.7	26.8	27.0	11.7	563
Peterborough 1412–13	11.6	—	18.4	60.7	—	9.3	355
Biggin Grange 1309–10	40.8	—	8.7	10.2	6.1	34.2	440
Biggin Grange 1373–4	28.0	—	34.2	26.3	—	11.5	286
Longthorpe 1309–10	38.7	9.1	7.0	12.2	10.3	22.7	246
Longthorpe 1371–2	14.5	10.6	17.5	31.0	15.5	10.9	258
Longthorpe lay estate, 1371–2	29.9	—	22.2	29.6	—	18.3	164
Brampton Ash lay estate, 1388	11.5	3.2	34.8	42.9	—	7.6	557

cent. The specialization in barley and vetches follows a pattern that has been seen elsewhere. The amount of barley sown was greatest at Houghton where it was 43 per cent, but elsewhere it varied between 32 and 38 per cent. The amount of vetches sown varied over a greater range, from 24 to 40 per cent. Oats had all but disappeared. Table 3.12 gives the percentages sown with the different crops. On each of these manors about 200 acres were sown each year, with the exception of Upwood, where the figure was about 170 acres a year.[70]

A broader geographical range is provided by the inquisitions, but their information is more limited, for the juries normally answered only for crops in the granary and not seed in the ground. But they show that certain areas of Northamptonshire continued to grow significant amounts of oats in the late fourteenth century, for there were oats at Long Buckby and Potterspury in 1397. They also extend the range of the ryelands, for rye was found at Laneham and Gresthorp in

[70] Hilton, *Leicestershire Estates*, pp. 62–4; Raftis, *Estates of Ramsey Abbey*, pp. 188–90.

Table 3.12. *Crops sown on Huntingdonshire manors*

| | | No. of | Percentage of acreage sown | | | |
Manor	Range of years	years	Wheat	Barley	Vetches	Oats
Broughton	1380–92	3	32.9	35.3	28.5	3.3
Houghton	1379–99	9	33.5	42.8	23.7	0.3
Slepe	1387–1417	3	30.5	35.5	30.8	3.2
Upwood	1385–1420	7	21.1	38.2	40.1	0.6
Wistow	1379–1403	6	26.1	32.4	37.7	3.8
Warboys	1379–1413	4	31.5	33.6	33.9	1.0

Nottinghamshire in 1388, and at Culworth in 1377, where "goods of the said Alice Perrers were found as follows: 40 quarters of rye, 10 quarters of wheat and 16 quarters of drage". There were barley and peas in every granary in the sample save this one, and wheat everywhere save at Laneham. The peas were sometimes threshed, but sometimes remained in stacks. At South Wheatley (Notts.) there were several stacks of peas; one of the current year estimated to contain 40 quarters, one of the previous year estimated at 20 quarters and one that was "old" and estimated at 60 quarters. It is clear from these entries, as it is from the account rolls, that much of the pea crop was intended as fodder for the animals. In these inquisitions the proportion of peas found seems low; it may be that in some cases juries only estimated the threshed corn, and ignored corn in stacks.[71]

The account rolls give information on sowing rates and on yields. The information on sowing rates is presented in Table 3.13 and does not call for further comment.[72] On yields the accounts show both the concern of the auditors and the unresponsiveness of the soil. Granted the scattered nature of the accounts, the figures for yields would be flattered by tabulation. The best series is that of Ramsey abbey. In Huntingdonshire, excluding Warboys, the yields per seed were 4.5 for wheat, 4.1 for barley, 2.0 for legumes and 1.6 for oats. At Warboys the yields were 5.9 for wheat, 7.8 for barley, 2.6 for legumes and 1.0 for oats. The Warboys figures may have been near to the maximum which was possible in this region over an extended period. Only at Oakham

[71] *Cal. Inq. Misc.*, IV, no. 13; V, nos. 91, 96, 201; VI, no. 301.

[72] Raftis, *Estates of Ramsey Abbey*, p. 185; Northants. RO, PDC a/c rolls, box 1; Gwendoline Brett, 'The economic development of some lay estates in north Nottinghamshire in the fourteenth century', Univ. of Sheffield M.A. thesis, 1971, p. 93; Westminster Abbey Muniments, 20267, 20270.

Table 3.13. *The East Midlands: sowing rates*

	Wheat	Rye	Barley	Drage	Peas	Oats
Huntingdonshire	$2\frac{1}{2}/3$	—	4/5/6	—	$2\frac{1}{2}/3/3\frac{1}{2}$	4/5
Northamptonshire	$2\frac{1}{2}/3$	$2/2\frac{1}{2}/3$	4	4/5	$2\frac{1}{2}/3$	3/4/5
Nottinghamshire	2/3	—	5/6	—	3	6/9
Rutland	2	—	$4/4\frac{1}{2}$	4	$2\frac{1}{2}$	4

Note: All figures represent bushels per acre.

were comparable yields noted by auditors. In 1350–1 they surcharged the reeve to bring the wheat yield up to four times the seed, the combined legumes and oats yields to three and a half times, and the oat yield to three times. Elsewhere very low yields were noted without comment. Both at Maidwell in 1351–2 and at Peterborough in 1389–90 the reeves declared yields for all crops of around two times seed, and the figures were accepted without comment. Here the reader may feel that he is not being told of agrarian conditions but is seeing a manorial administration that has thrown in the towel. Auditors who did try would often ask for details of which furlongs had been sown. Thus at Peterborough in 1373–4 the barley yield was a little over four and a half times the seed, "but this was better than in the same ground last time for the same seed"; there is a similar entry for vetches.[73]

It is necessary to consider now whether the picture that has been given of crops sown on demesnes adequately reflects peasant farming practice. It is evident that barley and peas became on most demesnes the two dominant crops of the later middle ages. They dominate also on the peasant land, but not to the exclusion of all else. Statistics for tithe corn are the best source for the crops sown by the peasantry. Table 3.14 gives the figures for Barkby, Leicestershire. Hilton commented: "it would seem that in the early years the tithe-payers tended to grow more wheat than was grown on the demesne and less peas". On four of the five manors the amount of winter-sown grain harvested averaged 22 per cent, an average comparable with the figures that have been found for the demesnes.

It is comparable also with the figures for the tithe grain collected at Oakham (Rutland) in the mid-fourteenth century. In five accounts between 1337–8 and 1353–4 the average of winter-sown grain was just under 24 per cent. In the last two accounts of this series, between 1352 and 1354, the corn harvested was in the ratio 22.5 per cent wheat, 2.9

---

[73] Raftis, *Estates of Ramsey Abbey*, pp. 173–8; Westminster Abbey Muniments, 20267; Northants. RO, Finch Hatton Ms. no. 481; *ibid.*, PDC a/c rolls, box 1, no. 10.

Table 3.14. *Peasant and demesne cropping compared at Barkby (Leics.)*

Year	Source of grain	Percentage receipts of each crop				
		Wheat	Rye	Barley	Oats	Peas
1393	Tithe	16.9	4.5	65.6	—	13
1393	Demesne	3.1	4.2	42.2	1.5	48.4
1401	Tithe	12.2	8.5	60	5.8	13.5
1401	Demesne	10.9	7.6	44.5	1.8	36
1470	Tithe	13	14	18	15	48
1470	Demesne	14	6	50	4	30

per cent rye, 46.9 per cent barley and 27.7 per cent *pulmentum*. The last of these, *pulmentum* or bulimong, is a mixed crop, described in the Maidwell accounts as a mixture of vetches and "the lighter grain of oats". Oakham was set in a fertile arable region, a measure of which was the 775 quarters of corn and vetches collected at Oakham and Langham in 1339 as tithe alone. Other sources for peasant cropping, though they must be more impressionistic, extend the geographical range a little. Crops are sometimes specified in peasant litigation for debt. At Loughborough in north-west Leicestershire, on poorer land, rye is the crop most frequently mentioned; and there are wheat, oats, barley, and peas. The Ramsey abbey *Liber Gersumarum* shows that barley and peas, and some wheat, comprised the seed delivered to a new tenant. In October 1412 at King's Ripton and again in December 1423 at Abbot's Ripton tenants taking over substantial holdings were given 4 bushels of wheat, and 3 quarters each of peas and of barley. At Wistow early in 1425 John White and his wife received 6 acres of demesne land: 3 roods were sown with wheat, 2 acres with barley and one acre with peas, giving a sown acreage of just under 4 acres of land. The mixed grains have not been noted on peasant land; if bullimong was collected at Oakham it was because peas and oats were sown together on the same ground.[74]

Entries on court rolls provide incidentally the only information on the rotation of crops on peasant holdings. The two entries which follow are from Peterborough in 1391:

[74] Hilton, *Leicestershire Estates*, p. 66; Westminster Abbey Muniments, 20253–4, 20260, 20271, 20359; Huntington Library, Hastings Mss., Leics. Manorial Papers, box 11; E. B. DeWindt, ed., *The Liber Gersumarum of Ramsey Abbey*, nos. 1141, 2056, 2180. Peas and oats are often found together on the same land: at Longthorpe in 1372 they were grown in *Pabenho* and *Pabenhopittes*, and at Peterborough in 1390 they were grown in *Estfeld* and *inter Estfeld et Garton* (Northants. RO, PDC a/c rolls, box 1, nos. 4, 10).

Henry Dravat destroyed the crop of a headland of John Gere, sown with various grains over the past three years, causing the loss of 1 peck of wheat valued at 2½d. and 1 peck of peas valued at 1d.

And then

John Gere destroyed with his sheep the wheat growing on 2 acres of land belonging to Henry Dravat, to the damage of 1 bushel of wheat valued at 5d.

John Gere's sheep, as they munched contentedly away, cannot have known that they were the instruments of revenge, but by the time they were driven off they had with some exactness secured restitution for their master. There was more than one way to secure such restitution, and more than one kind of animal that could be pressed into service. At Shepshed (Leics.) at the Easter court of 1393 it was the misdeeds of the geese of Robert Froreman that were described. For the past several years they had damaged the crops sown by Geoffrey Nicholson on three selions of land. Four years before it had been sown with barley, three years before with peas, and the previous year with barley again. Damages were assessed at 6s. 8d. But Geoffrey had not waited to be awarded damages; he had, his adversaries complained, entered their house and taken divers goods and chattels. In one case here we are given and in another we can surmise the crop rotation: at Shepshed fallow/barley/vetches, and at Peterborough fallow/wheat/vetches. At Oakham, between these two places, the rotation was fallow, then wheat or barley, then vetches. On the Huntingdonshire demesnes of Ramsey abbey there was a more complicated four-course rotation: first fallow, second barley (or wheat), third vetches, fourth wheat (or barley).[75]

The farms both of peasants and of lords carried a wide range of livestock.[76] The working beasts of the medieval farm were horses and oxen. The oxen were specialist and were the traditional plough beasts. The horse was more versatile, being used for carting and harrowing, as well as ploughing. Its versatility made it more popular than oxen amongst the peasantry, and led to an increase in its use in demesne agriculture during the later middle ages. Over the region as a whole 35 per cent of the "great beasts" were horses. The lowest proportion of horses to oxen was in Nottinghamshire where it was 20 per cent, the highest was in Rutland with 52 per cent. In every county the figures were higher than in the pre-Black Death period; in Leicestershire they

[75] Northants. RO, PDC court rolls, box 1, no. 9; BL Add. Ch. 26842; Westminster Abbey Muniments, 20267–8, 20270; Raftis, *Estates of Ramsey Abbey*, pp. 186–7.

[76] The remainder of this section is much indebted to the work of two scholars: John Langdon, *Horses, Oxen, and Technological Innovation*, and Martin Stephenson, 'The productivity of medieval sheep on the great estates', Cambridge Univ. Ph.D. thesis, 1986.

had risen from 20 to 35 per cent. These figures suggest the use of mixed ploughteams, of two horses and six oxen, though on larger demesnes it would be possible to use both ox and horse ploughs – in 1351 the reeve of Elton had four ox ploughs and one horse plough in his manorial inventory. The working animals had first claim on the winter feed. The cart horses were heavy consumers of oats, consuming around 6 quarters per animal in this region; the plough horses and the oxen relied more on hay and straw. The care with which they were treated was reflected in a low rate of loss in an average working-life that has been calculated as seven years for cart horses and five years for plough horses and oxen. On the Ramsey estate losses were between 5 and 8 per cent a year, and often were due to accidents in the marshes. The mortality of cows on the same estate was 4–5 per cent a year. Even in the fenlands the number of cattle was not large, and there is no sign of commercial dairy farming. Cows would yield on average 150–225 gallons of milk a year. Figures for milk-yield are not often found, however: auditors judged the efficiency of the dairy by its production of butter and most importantly cheese. During the cheese-making season, which began towards the end of April and lasted until Michaelmas, one cheese was made each day on each of the Ramsey manors.[77]

The numbers of each of these working animals fluctuated little on manors for which accounts survive. In demesne flocks of sheep there are much greater fluctuations in numbers to be observed, the result of heavier mortality of stock and changes in estate policy. After the Black Death, pastoral farming showed a better rate of return than arable farming. The wool of the East Midland region was of a good average quality. In 1454 the prices suggested of between £4 and £5 a sack were all above the national mean price for that year. In this and in other price series Northamptonshire wool was at the bottom of the local range, and Nottingham, particularly Newark, wool was at the top. Only a few fleece weights are recorded, and those from early in the period. In 1358 the Owston abbey sheep at Norton seem to have produced fleeces weighing 2.1 lb each. A total of 4,306 fleeces sent to Ramsey abbey from its manors in 1361 weighed an average 1.5 lb a fleece. The same document shows the extent to which the Ramsey abbey flocks had been built up after the Black Death. Abbots Ripton, Warboys and Broughton had each flocks of around 1,000 sheep in the early 1360s. There followed an epidemic, which may or may not have been a national epidemic, but which decimated flocks in Huntingdonshire.

[77] J. Langdon, 'The economics of horses and oxen in medieval England', *AHR*, xxx, 1982, pp. 31–40; *Elton Manorial Records*, ed. Ratcliff, pp. liii–lv, 123; Raftis, *Estates of Ramsey Abbey*, pp. 129–40.

Thus at Warboys in 1362 the mortality was 3.7 per cent, but in the following year 182 of the 318 wethers died before the time of shearing. At Holywell the whole flock of ewes was lost in 1364. Over the fourteenth century as a whole mortality ranged between 5 and 6 per cent at Upwood and Broughton and 17.6 per cent at Wistow. For ewes the range was between 6.7 per cent at Elton and 39.3 per cent at Holywell. These great fluctuations depend solely on whether accounts survive for the years of heavy mortality. For lambs the range of mortality was between 10.6 per cent at Warboys and 27.5 per cent at Weston, with several manors just a little below the latter figure. The lambing rate on the same estate was between 64 and 90 per cent, with the ten Huntingdonshire manors stretched out evenly over this range. The fullest set of accounts is from Warboys, and there the lambing rate was 83 per cent. These figures continue no further than the early fifteenth century.[78] The continued importance of sheep farming thereafter is not in doubt, but the evidence must be looked for elsewhere (see Chapter 2, D).

In most midland villages the total peasant flocks would have surpassed the demesne flocks, even when the latter were at their greatest extent. Ramsey abbey took a tallage at Michaelmas at the rate of $\frac{1}{2}$d. for a horse, $\frac{1}{2}$d. for a beast, 1d. for 8 pigs, and 1d. for 8 sheep. It has been calculated that the amounts paid at Wistow in the late fourteenth century are commensurate with a virgater having 1–2 horses, 4 beasts, 16 pigs, and 40 sheep.[79] It is clear from court records that these figures are of the right order of magnitude. Stints of 30 or 40 sheep per virgate were common in this region, and they might go higher; the men of Clipston thought in hundreds. It may be, however, that the figures for the great beasts should be adjusted to reflect the peasantry's preference for horses over oxen. At Wistow in 1429 a virgate was transferred along with "a plough with equipment for three horses". Here we have a small, all-horse, ploughteam; though elsewhere, particularly in Nottinghamshire and Leicestershire, mixed teams continued to operate on peasant holdings. Overall, the peasantry probably had as many horses as cattle. The average holding of pigs would probably be smaller than sixteen, for whilst there was a "plenitude of pasture" in Charnwood Forest a list of payments for pannage shows thirty-one different tenants paying for 155 pigs in

[78] *Ibid.*, pp. 144–52; Stephenson, 'The productivity of medieval sheep', *passim*; Lloyd, *Movement of Wool Prices*, EcHR, supplement no. 6, 1973, pp. 10–11, 70–1; Hilton, *Leicestershire Estates*, p. 133.

[79] Mary P. Hogan, 'Wistow: a social and economic reconstitution in the fourteenth century', Univ. of Toronto Ph.D. thesis, 1971, pp. 170–2; this modifies the figures in Raftis, *Tenure and Mobility*, pp. 23–5.

1454–5. At the bottom level in terms of subsistence were the fowl. Hens can be seen scratching around in the peasant yards; they were paid as rent by the cottagers, and widows in the Ramsey *Liber Gersumarum* reserved the right to keep them when making maintenance agreements. There was a little more flesh on the goose. Two went "in hochepot" at Maidwell in 1384–5. Eight escaped at Elton in 1350–1 and swam off down the Nene: "perierunt" said the reeve, "alienated" said the auditors, suspecting that flooding was not invariably fatal even for the most domesticated goose.[80]

E. THE WEST MIDLANDS

The agricultural economy of the West Midland region retained its basis in arable cultivation in spite of the expansion of pasture. This is readily apparent from the accounts of manors with arable demesnes directly managed by landlords, which are plentiful in the late fourteenth century, and occur sporadically in the first half of the fifteenth century. Once the demesnes had been leased, more fragmentary evidence suggests that demesne farmers continued to keep some land under the plough. The peasants, in whose hands lay the bulk of the region's arable, produced as much as possible of their own needs of cereals and legumes, and provided a high proportion of the crops on the market.

The essential local variations in the field systems of the region were established well before 1349. In the champion south-east – the Gloucestershire Cotswolds, south-east Worcestershire, and the Warwickshire Feldon – two-field systems prevailed, in which the arable was divided into two halves, and each holding was evenly divided between them.[81] The number of field divisions in each system tends to multiply as we move to the north and west. Three-field systems are known in some quantity from post-medieval times in north-east Warwickshire, the Trent valley in Staffordshire, and parts of lowland Derbyshire, but in only a few cases can a regular division of

---

[80] Hilton in *VCH Leics.*, II, pp. 164–5; Northants. RO, Brassey Ms LB 59; Raftis, *Tenure and Mobility*, p. 73; BL Add. Ch. 26843; DeWindt, ed., *Liber Gersumarum*, nos. 4121, 4127, and *passim*; Northants. RO, F.H. 482; *Elton Manorial Records*, ed. Ratcliff, pp. 382–3.

[81] *AHEW*, II, pp. 369–73; Baker and Butlin, eds., *Field Systems*, pp. 221–5. References to two-field systems within our period are North Cerney (Glos.), Glos. RO, D 621 M7; Sherborne (Glos.), R. H. Hilton, 'Winchcombe Abbey and the manor of Sherborne', in *Gloucestershire Studies*, ed. H. P. R. Finberg, Leicester, 1957, p. 101; Temple Guiting (Glos.), Corpus Christi College, Oxford, Ms. F2/21, f.401; Burton Dassett (War.), Shakespeare's Birthplace Trust RO, DR98/188; Farnborough (War.), Shakespeare's Birthplace Trust RO, Archer Coll. no. 2116; Grandborough (War.), Staffs. RO, D641/1/4v/2; Ladbroke (War.), PRO SC 12/16/27; Weston-juxta-Cherington (War.), Shakespeare's Birthplace Trust RO, DR98/866.

land into three fields be traced back to before 1500. Instead in the north and west of the region complex field systems predominated, with arable land divided into five or more fields, often of unequal size. In such areas the term "field" was not in universal use, the arable areas often being called "crofts", "furlongs" and a variety of other names. In many woodland settlements, for example in the Warwickshire Arden, a core of open field was surrounded by small enclosed plots, the products of early medieval assarting. The proportion of enclosed land varied a good deal, though there was hardly ever a total exclusion of open field. Shifting cultivation, even infield–outfield systems, may have existed in the Peak District of Derbyshire.[82]

The irregularity of the layout of fields in much of the region, and the prevalence of old enclosures, did not preclude a good deal of control by the village community over rotations and common grazing, so that even in systems with much land held in severalty the cultivators were expected to follow a three-course rotation.[83] In theory, then, we might expect to find as the main crop rotations two-course (in the two-field villages of the south-east), and three-course (in the north and west). The reality diverges from these norms; these were not necessarily post-1349 developments, but there can be no doubt that field systems and rotations were being adapted during our period to new circumstances.

The regular two-field systems, attached to close-knit village communities and governed by ancient customs and regulations, might be thought to have been the least adaptable to change, yet even before 1349 they had adopted a system of "inhoking", or cropping of part of the fallow. The area taken in for more intensive cultivation was called the "hiche" or "hechyng"; its use was defined clearly at Grandborough (War.) in the 1490s as "every year's land", in contrast with the land subject to a two-course rotation, "every other year's land". The extent of inhoking can be appreciated from the area of south-east

[82] Baker and Butlin, eds., Field Systems, pp. 205–21, 225–30; Hilton, English Peasantry, pp. 134–8; V. H. T. Skipp, 'The evolution of settlement and open-field topography in north Arden down to 1300', in The Origins of Open-field Agriculture, ed. T. Rowley, London, 1981, pp. 162–83; VCH Staffs., VI, pp. 12–17; J. C. Jackson, 'Open-field cultivation in Derbyshire', Derbs. Arch. J., LXXXII, 1962, pp. 54–72; R. H. Hilton, 'Old enclosure in the west Midlands', Annales de l'Est, 1959, pp. 272–83.

[83] E.g. Bromsberrow (Glos.), Gloucester Public Library, R59.4; Haresfield (Glos.), VCH Glos., x, p. 194; Lydney (Glos.), Glos. RO, D 421/M19; Coughton (War.), Shakespeare's Birthplace Trust RO, DR5/2191; Keresley (War.), VCH War., VIII, p. 80; Sutton Coldfield (War.), Nottingham Univ. Library, MiM 134/5; Broadwas, Hagley, Stoke Prior (Worcs.), Field, 'Worcestershire peasantry', p. 280; Hanbury, Hartlebury (Worcs.), Dyer, Lords and Peasants, p. 322; Farewell (Staffs.), Staffs. RO, D1734/2/1/379 (I am grateful to Miss J. R. Birrell for allowing me to use her transcripts of this and other Staffordshire documents. Subsequent references based on these will be followed by the initials J. R. B.).

Worcestershire between Bredon Hill and the Avon. The lords of Elmley Castle (for most of the period the Beauchamp earls of Warwick) were able to demand payments from eight nearby two-field villages if part of the fallow was inhoked. Every village is not recorded as inhoking each year, and normally the area specified, between 2 and 36 acres, represented only a small proportion of the fallow. However, the process sometimes involved whole furlongs and fields, and by the 1440s it is clear that the village of Ashton-under-Hill had taken "hechyng" so far that much of its land could be regarded as being run on a three-course rotation, and the village of Netherton had evidently changed to a four-course rotation. Similar evidence from another Beauchamp manor in central Worcestershire, Wadborough, shows that the villagers of Churchill and Broughton Hackett were sowing on the fallow every year in the early fifteenth century. Elsewhere there were cases of individuals in two-field villages, such as Hampton Lucy (War.) in 1476, cultivating fallow land to the annoyance of their fellow villagers.[84]

For a two-field village moving towards greater intensity of cultivation the ultimate development would be to divide each field and create a four-field system. At Adlestrop (Glos.) such a change was ordered in the manor court in 1498, and four fields had come into existence at Church Honeybourne (Worcs.) by 1469. The poverty of documentation may conceal a more widespread reordering of the two-field systems of the region. Certainly by the mid-sixteenth century four-field arrangements were common in the former two-field villages of south-east Worcestershire.[85]

More frequent croppings than either the two- or three-course rotations allowed are also found in the west and north of the region. For example, on the demesne of Cam (Glos.) the irregular fields were organized into cropping units called "seasons", and three of these were planted in 1354–5, giving a total of 162 acres under crops, while an area of $53\frac{3}{4}$ acres lay fallow, approximating to a four-course rotation. Similar practices are suggested by references at Middleton (War.) in the 1390s to peasants departing from the customary three-course regime by cropping closes in the third, supposedly fallow, year.[86]

[84] Staffs. RO, D641/1/4v/2; Worcs. RO, ref. 899:95 BA 989/1/2 – 989/2/30; Birmingham Reference Library, Keen Coll. 245; C. Dyer, *Warwickshire Farming, 1349–c. 1520*, Dugdale Soc. Occasional Paper 27, p. 28.

[85] C. Elrington, 'Open fields and inclosure in the Cotswolds', *Proceedings of the Cotteswold Naturalists' Field Club*, xxxiv, 1962–3, pp. 37–44; Worcs. RO, ref. 008:7 BA 3590 vol. I, pp. 27–8; J. Yelling, 'The combination and rotation of crops in east Worcestershire, 1540–1660', *AHR*, xvii, 1969, pp. 30–3.

[86] Berkeley Mss., microfilm in Cambridge Univ. Library; Nottingham Univ. Library, MiM 131/32.

Many of the cropping practices suggest the use of irregular and unconventional systems of husbandry. The managers of the demesnes, while allowing parts of the arable to go down to grass, were ploughing up pastures, meadows, and even sections of parks. Furlongs and parcels within demesnes were being cropped for three, four, and five years in succession. Peasants also ploughed former grassland, put down arable strips to "leys", planted in the fallow field, grew spring crops in areas reserved for wheat and rye, or failed to cultivate "at the correct time". In some cases we are told that they were departing from the old system, without our knowing the specific changes being made. We must conclude that land was being used with much flexibility, in which it is difficult to see any general pattern, except perhaps a growing frequency of cropping on the remaining arable, as an increasing amount of land was being temporarily or permanently converted to pasture.[87]

More freedom in the use of land was facilitated by the extension of enclosures. "Enclosure" describes a variety of changes. One type, prevalent in woodland areas, involved the extension of individual rights over existing closes by excluding common grazing "in the open time", in the case of arable on the stubble and fallow. Court rolls contain many complaints of the denial of common pasture in old enclosures. In Gloucestershire they occur in large numbers at Thornbury in the 1430s and at Stonehouse in the 1490s. Worcestershire examples appeared at Chaddesley Corbett in 1375, and were particularly numerous in the Severn valley and the woodlands in the north of the county between 1440 and 1480. In Derbyshire and Staffordshire cases were common in the first two decades in the fifteenth century.[88] Such enclosures were often for the "improvement" of pasture (to quote an example at Almondsbury (Glos.) in 1492), and lords might find it difficult to attract tenants to pastures and meadows in woodland

---

[87] Dyer, 'A small landowner', p. 6; Worcs. Cathedral Library, C 657, C659 (cultivation of pastures and meadows at Baddesley Clinton, War., and Newnham, Worcs.); Staffs. RO, D641/2/133 (cultivation in Eastwood Park, Thornbury, Glos.); Dyer, Lords and Peasants, pp. 125–7 (successive cultivation); Dyer, Warwickshire Farming, p. 29 (ploughing of grassland); see above, pp. 83–4, for leys; Birmingham Reference Library, 422743; Shakespeare's Birthplace Trust RO, DR5/2748 (for cultivation of fallow at Elmley Lovett and Chaddesley Corbett, Worcs.); Worcs. RO, ref. 899:95 BA 989/1/9 (barley and pulse sown instead of wheat at Elmley Castle, Worcs.); Field, 'Worcestershire peasantry', pp. 85–7 (failure to sow at the correct time at Himbleton (Worcs.), and departure from the 'old cultivation' at Hanbury (Worcs.)).

[88] Staffs. RO, D641/1/4c/7 (Thornbury); C. Swynnerton, 'Some early court rolls of the manors of Stonehouse, King's Stanley, Woodchester and Achards', Bristol and Glos. Arch. Soc., XLV, 1923, pp. 228–9; Shakespeare's Birthplace Trust RO, DR5/2737 (Chaddesley Corbett); Birmingham Reference Library, 422744–53 (Elmley Lovett); Worcs. RO, ref. 705:56 BA 3910/22, 24 (Ombersley); Dyer, Lords and Peasants, pp. 331–3 (other Worcestershire manors); Blanchard, 'Economic change in Derbyshire', p. 88; Staffs. RO, D1734/2/1/427, 428 (J.R.B.); D1734/2/1/176 (J.R.B.) (Haywood, Cannock and Rugeley).

districts if they were not enclosed – for example at Caldwall (Worcs.), where a pasture lay waste in 1426–7 for this reason. Some lords were willing to license enclosures, in some numbers at Halesowen (Worcs.) in 1350–1450, and in Derbyshire after 1440.[89]

Another type of enclosure was the fencing of portions of the waste or common pasture, a long-term process which landlords conducted on a large scale before as well as after 1349. They included Richard de Lichfield, who acquired exclusive rights to 70 acres of Bloreheath (Staffs.) in 1355, and John Ombersley, abbot of Evesham, who created a 300-acre park at Ombersley (Worcs.) in the 1370s. Smaller-scale encroachment on the waste by humbler men is found in such places as Atherstone and Berkswell in the Warwickshire Arden, and on Cannock Chase (Staffs.) in the fifteenth century.[90]

The most radical type of enclosure involved the consolidation of parcels within open fields and the erection of fences around the resulting plots. Landlords were well placed to accomplish this because their demesnes often lay in compact furlongs. Winchcomb abbey negotiated agreements with neighbouring landowners to enable it to enclose three furlongs near Winchcomb in the mid-fourteenth century, and in 1457 made an exchange in order to enclose $63\frac{3}{4}$ acres in the North Field of Stowell (Glos.). Demesne farmers carried out similar enclosure policies, for example in the 1440s at Stratford-on-Avon (War.), Whitstones (Worcs.), and Wick Episcopi (Worcs.).[91] Peasants also exchanged and enclosed, on a smaller scale, and probably with more difficulty. For example, Robert Culs of Norton (Glos.) in 1439 exchanged three butts of land with neighbours in order to extend his existing close into the adjoining open fields, and William Paxford in 1488 was said to have set up a hedge in the fields of Tysoe (War.) which caused another tenant to lose three selions of arable. There are many individual examples of this type in the region, and they may have done no more than to nibble at the edges of open fields; but the possible scale of combined peasant enclosure is indicated at Sambourn (War.), a woodland village with extensive open fields, of which about 240 acres were enclosed by agreement among sixteen tenants just before 1478.

[89] Some Manorial Accounts of St Augustine's Abbey, Bristol, ed. A. Sabin, p. 84 (Almondsbury); Bodleian Library, Worcs. rolls, no. 3 (Caldwall); Field, 'Worcestershire peasantry', pp. 81–4; Blanchard, 'Economic change in Derbyshire', pp. 92–3.

[90] Inquisitions Post Mortem, Staffordshire, ed. J. C. Wedgwood, Staffs, Rec. Soc., 1913, pp. 160–1; Chronicon Abbatiae de Evesham, ed. W. D. Macray, Rolls Ser., 1863, pp. 300–1, and CPR, 1374–7, p. 296; Staffs. RO, D641/1/2/270; Ministers' Accounts of the Warwickshire Estates of the Duke of Clarence, 1479–80, ed. R. H. Hilton, Dugdale Soc., XXI, 1952, p. 60; Staffs. RO, D(W)1734/2/1/178 (J.R.B.).

[91] Landboc sive Registrum Monasterii Beatae Mariae Virginis et Sancti Kenelmi, ed. D. Royce, II, pp. 145–6, 550–2; Dyer, Lords and Peasants, pp. 214, 333.

Complete field systems, too, were enclosed when villages were deserted, a process to which lords, demesne farmers and the pre-abandonment peasant tenants may all have contributed. By 1500, however, enclosed field systems had been extended over whole townships, not just in the deserted villages, but also in some woodland settlements like Bordesley (War.), where there was a considerable legacy of enclosure from the period of colonization. At the same time, much open field remained untouched by the enclosure movement.[92]

The choice of crops grown on demesnes depended both on the local soils and climate, and on the needs of the lords. In the far west of Gloucestershire, in the vicinity of Bristol, wheat and oats took up most of the planted area, three-quarters or even more of the acreage; there was a similar preponderance of these crops in the extreme north-west of Worcestershire. In the Vale of Berkeley (Glos.), wheat and oats were major crops too, but legumes, especially beans, were also grown in quantity. One demesne (Ham, in 1375–6) produced wheat and beans only. In contrast Cotswold demesnes concentrated on barley and/or dredge, which often occupied a half or more of the sown area, together with wheat and oats, but only a small proportion of legumes (peas or pulse). The area under oats in the Cotswolds could be as high as 40 per cent, especially in the region around Stroud. On the clay lands of the Vale of Gloucester, the northern slopes of the Cotswolds, and the Warwickshire Feldon the normal combination was of wheat, barley and/or dredge, and peas, often in roughly equal proportions, with a tenth or less of the area given over to oats. On some Feldon manors no oats were grown at all, except as a mixture with barley in dredge. On the lighter soils of the Avon valley in Worcestershire and Warwickshire the same crops predominated, except that the winter corn usually included rye, which sometimes exceeded the area under wheat. Rye was also cultivated in quantity in the Severn valley in Worcestershire, together with dredge and oats; legumes there were of little importance. West of the Severn in south-west Worcestershire the main crops were wheat and pulse, with barley, dredge, and oats. In the woodlands of north Warwickshire and north Worcestershire oats tended to cover a large area, up to a half of some demesnes, but there were pockets of better soils, in the valleys of the Salwarpe or the Thame, for example, where wheat was extensively grown.[93]

[92] Glos. RO, D621 M1 (Norton); Dyer, *Warwickshire Farming*, pp. 26–7 (Tysoe and Sambourn); *The Records of King Edward's School, Birmingham*, ed. W. F. Carter, Dugdale Soc., IV, 1924, pp. 28–50.

[93] Information about crops, and other aspects of demesne agriculture to follow, comes from these sources (mainly accounts, or secondary sources based on accounts): *Gloucestershire*:

The restricted amount of evidence makes generalization about demesne crops in Staffordshire and Derbyshire more difficult. In south and central Staffordshire a good deal of wheat and rye were grown, and barley, legumes, and oats. Further north, at Chesterton (Staffs.) and Haddon (Derbs.), oats took up as much as two-thirds of the area under crops. In the northern uplands it is likely that a monoculture of oats, known from the early fourteenth century, continued.[94]

The crops grown on peasant holdings are known from their occasional seizure by lords after the departure or death of a tenant, from records of trespass and theft, or can be inferred from tithe receipts. When comparison can be made between demesne and peasant crops differences are often found, reflecting divergences in the needs of the cultivators. In the Severn and Avon valleys in Worcestershire, at

Alkington, Cam, Ham, Berkeley Mss., microfilm in Cambridge Univ. Library and Berkeley Castle muniment room; Awre and Blakeney, Glos. RO, D421 M4; Ashelworth, Horfield, *Manorial Accounts of St Augustine's Abbey*, ed. Sabin, pp. 54–60, 120–32; Bibury, Blockley, Bishop's Cleeve, Henbury-in-Salt-Marsh, Stoke Bishop, Worcs. RO, ref. 009:1 BA 2636/157, 159, 160, 161, 162, 165, 166, 167, 170, 171, 192, 193 (and see also Dyer, *Lords and Peasants*, pp. 119–52); Bourton-on-the-Hill, Hardwicke, Westminster Abbey Mss. 8282, 8290, 8299, 8438A, 8444; Cowley, PRO SC 6/853/14; Hawkesbury, PRO SC 6/854/15; Horsley, PRO SC 6/855/6; Minchinhampton, PRO SC 6/856/24; Sherborne, Hilton, 'Winchcombe Abbey and the manor of Sherborne', pp. 107–8; Thornbury, Staffs. RO, D641/1/2/133, 134, 136, 138A, 140, 141, 144, 150; Todenham, Glos. RO, D 1099 M30/10, 12, 14, 17, 18, 22. *Warwickshire*: Alderminster, PRO SC 6/1063/23; Baddesley Clinton, Shakespeare's Birthplace Trust RO, DR3/799–805 (see also Dyer, 'A small landowner', pp. 5–8); Bidford, PRO SC 6/1038/3, 4, 5; Blackwell, Worcs. Cathedral Library, C 538; Brandon, PRO SC 6/1038/9; Budbrooke, War. RO, CR 95 8/2, 8/10–22; Chesterton, Shakespeare's Birthplace Trust RO, DR98/393b; Hampton Lucy, Worcs. RO, ref 009:1 BA 2636/163, 164; Long Itchington, PRO SC 6/1039/14; Knowle, Westminster Abbey Mss., 27705; Ladbroke, PRO SC 6/1041/13; Ladbroke, Radbourn, Shuckburgh, '*Status Maneriorum* of John Catesby, 1385 and 1386', ed. J. R. Birrell, in *Miscellany* I, Dugdale Soc., XXXI, 1977, pp. 23–6; Lea Marston, Nottingham Univ. Library, MiM 165; Lighthorne, Shakespeare's Birthplace Trust RO, DR98/672a–672d, 674; Oversley, Shakespeare's Birthplace Trust RO, DR5/2254–5; Quinton, Magdalen College, Oxford, SH III BU2; Snitterfield, BL Egerton Roll 8624; Sutton-under-Brailes, Glos. RO, 1099/M31/46, 50; Weston-juxta-Cherington, Shakespeare's Birthplace Trust RO, DR98/865; Willoughby, Magdalen College, Oxford, Will. B 169 (1). *Worcestershire*: Bredon, Worcs. RO, ref. 009:1 BA 2636/157, 158 (see also Dyer, *Lords and Peasants*, pp. 119–52); Caldwall, Bodleian Library, Worcs. rolls, nos. 2, 3; Cropthorne, Grimley, Hallow, Harvington, Henwick, Lippard, More, Newnham, Overbury, Sedgeberrow, Worcs. Cathedral Library, C 565d, C 586, C 596, C 600, C 610, C 633, C 678, C 649, C 650A, C 657, C 659, C 662, C 667, C 705, C 709, C 719, C 721, C 759A, C 760, C 766, C 764, C 762; Elmley Castle, Worcs. RO, ref. 899:95 BA 989/4/70; Hewell Grange, PRO SC 6/1668/11; Longdon, Morton (i.e. Castlemorton), Westminster Abbey Mss. 21023, 21055; Peachley, *Early Compotus Rolls of the Priory of Worcester*, ed. J. M. Wilson and C. Gordon, Worcs. Hist. Soc., 1908, pp. 54–70; Westwood (with *Clethale* and Crutch), Worcs. RO, ref. 705:349 BA 3835/10 (xii).

[94] *Staffordshire*: Chesterton, J. C. Wedgwood, 'Court rolls of the manor of Tunstall', *North Staffs. Field Club*, LIX, 1925, pp. 73–8; Elford, Bodleian Library, Ms. DD Weld C9/1; Farewell, Staffs. RO, D1734/3/3/34 (J.R.B.); Perton, *VCH Staffs.*, VI, p. 45; Stafford, PRO SC 6/988/12 (J.R.B.). *Derbyshire*: Haddon, Blanchard, *op. cit.*, p. 28.

Hallow, Grimley, and Cropthorne, where both rye and wheat were grown as winter corn, the peasants, in contrast with the demesne managers, showed a marked leaning towards wheat rather than rye. Perhaps the peasants were anxious to gain as much as possible from the sale of the higher-priced wheat, or they may have preferred wheat bread for their own tables. The prejudice cannot have been a general one, as peasants elsewhere, at Chaddesley Corbett (Worcs.), and Cannock and Rugeley (Staffs.), for example, grew a good deal of rye. A more general tendency was for peasants to grow large quantities of barley and dredge – this is apparent at Cropthorne, where dredge made up a half of the tithe crops, but only a third of demesne production. The contrast is greater in the Vale of Berkeley where the peasants in the 1490s grew a combination of wheat, barley, and legumes, with very little oats, while the late fourteenth-century demesnes had concentrated on wheat, legumes, and oats, and had scarcely cultivated barley at all. However, this may reflect changes over time as well as the different priorities of large and small cultivators. When the evidence is exactly contemporary, as at Long Itchington (War.) in 1367–8, it is possible to show that peasants grew twice as much dredge as did the demesne (70 per cent compared with 36 per cent), and a similar difference (38 per cent of the tithe corn, 11 per cent of the demesne) is apparent in the barley grown at Lea Marston (War.) in 1394–5.[95]

A relatively low proportion of legumes among peasant crops in the late fourteenth century is apparent at Long Itchington, Lea Marston, and also Bourton-on-the-Hill (Glos.). This is surprising, as peas were eaten by peasants, and in particular formed a welcome item in the diet as green vegetables in the early summer, available under custom as declared at Weston Subedge (Glos.) to the poor of the village as well as the cultivators. Peas were certainly grown in some villages in quantity in the 1370s, representing between a fifth and a quarter of the crop at Burton Hastings, Marton, and Wibtoft, in north-east Warwickshire, and some very high proportions of legumes – 40 per cent or more – are recorded in the fifteenth century, notably in the Vale of Berkeley. Perhaps by this date the peasants, like the demesne managers earlier, were feeding legumes to animals.[96]

On both demesnes and tenant land over the whole region, except in

[95] Tithes of Hallow, Grimley, Cropthorne: Field, 'Worcestershire peasantry', pp. 283–93; Chaddesley, Cannock and Rugeley: Shakespeare's Birthplace Trust RO, DR5/2737–2754; Staffs. RO, D1734/2/1/176–179 (J.R.B.); Some Manorial Accounts of St Augustine's Abbey, ed. Sabin, pp. 106–9; PRO SC 6/1039/14; Nottingham Univ. Library, MiM 165.

[96] For Long Itchington, Lea Marston, and the Berkeley tithes, Some Manorial Accounts of St Augustine's Abbey, ed. Sabin, pp. 106–9; PRO SC 6/1039/14; Nottingham Univ. Library, MiM 165. For peas at Weston Subedge, Dorset RO, D10/M229/1–5; for Burton Hastings etc., BL Add. Roll 49, 748.

the districts concentrating on the cultivation of wheat and oats, the winter-sown grains, wheat and rye, usually occupied less than half of the cultivated area, leaving room for the more versatile spring-sown crops, which were potential sources of drink, pottage, and animal-feed as well as bread.

Over the period the choice of crops changed on some demesnes, though it is difficult to see strong common patterns. In the late fourteenth century on at least five demesnes the area under legumes expanded; however in one case, Bibury (Glos.), attempts to grow peas were abandoned after a disastrous harvest in 1393. On two manors with records in the fifteenth century, Bidford-on-Avon (War.) and Sherborne (Glos.), the legume acreage dwindled.

The yields of demesne crops were generally poor, even by medieval standards. From a sample of 332 yield ratios, calculated by dividing the total harvested by the amount sown, 277 fall between two and five, the median figure being between three and four. Ratios in excess of six were very rare indeed. The normal sowing rates in the region were two bushels per acre for wheat and rye, and three or four bushels for spring-sown crops. This meant that yields per acre, which often lay in the region of eight bushels for wheat, could rise to twelve or even as much as fifteen bushels for barley, the highest yielding of the spring crops. Many of our yield figures come from the years 1350–75, notorious for their bad weather, but even allowing for this distortion no marked improvement to yields is apparent in the period of direct management. Demesnes may have become more productive under the management of their lessees, but the overall stagnation or decline of leasehold rents for arable demesnes in the fifteenth century gives no cause for optimistic speculations.

The information on the yields obtained from peasant land is meagre. Walter Shayl's holding at Hatton-on-Avon (War.), which yielded about ten bushels per acre in 1377, and tenements left in the lord's hands at Bourton-on-the-Hill (Glos.) after the plague in 1349–50, which seem to have produced less than eight bushels per acre, both show performances inferior to those of the demesnes. The grain produced from the holding of John Kent of Stivichall (War.) in 1481 can be variously estimated at between nine and twenty bushels per acre, with a probability in favour of a figure above eleven bushels, but the calculation is uncertain, and would be a slender basis for a theory of long-term increases in peasant yields.[97]

Low yields are difficult to explain in terms of the changes in agricultural methods. The normal explanations of poor medieval

[97] Hilton, *English Peasantry*, pp. 201–2; Westminster Abbey Ms. 8282; Dyer, *Warwickshire Farming*, pp. 29–30, 41.

agricultural productivity, notably the excessive cultivation of marginal
lands and the shortage of manure, can scarcely be invoked in a period
of shrinking arable acreages and developing pastoral agriculture. Any
long-term consequences of soil exhaustion should have been counter-
acted by the flexible land use implied by such practices as the creation
of leys. The real value of capital investment in agriculture does not
seem to have declined. The managers of the demesnes carried out the
usual procedures to improve the fertility of the soil – manure was
spread regularly (though the quantities are not known); sheep were
folded on the arable; fallows were ploughed and re-ploughed in
preparation for sowing; weeding was a regular practice; and legumes
were grown on nine out of every ten demesnes, usually occupying
between a tenth and a third of the cropped areas, and assisting in the
improvement of the fertility of the soil for the succeeding crops. None
of these were innovations, however. Nor did techniques of cultivation
change. The occasional use of mixed teams of horses and oxen for
ploughing, and the adoption of a wholly horse team, working
alongside an ox-team at Bourton-on-the-Hill (Glos.) in the 1360s, can
both be paralleled in the region in the thirteenth century. Throughout
the later middle ages most demesne ploughs were hauled by teams of
six to ten – normally eight – oxen.

The effectiveness of demesne cultivation may have been adversely
affected by social and demographic changes. Landlords found increasing
difficulties in disciplining slack reeves and inefficient or dishonest
famuli.[98] Labour shortages probably led to a lack of thoroughness, even
neglect, of such work as fallow ploughing, weeding, and manuring.
The quality of arable husbandry varied from manor to manor. On the
Beauchamp manor of Lighthorne (War.) in the 1390s a small band of
famuli were hard pressed to do all of the necessary work. No extra
labour was hired for weeding, so thistles may have grown unchecked.
The reeve complained that the lord's rabbits were causing extensive
damage to the crops. Yields were correspondingly low. Yet on the
Berkeley estate in Gloucestershire in the late fourteenth century money
was spent on weeding all of the cereal crops, and bean seeds were
dibbled. On the Bordesley abbey grange at Bidford-on-Avon (War.),
care was taken to ensure that sheep were folded on the arable, and in
1448–9 half of the seed-corn was either purchased or brought in from
outside, in contrast with the prevalent use elsewhere of seed from the
previous year's crop. Perhaps because of such measures barley yielded
almost eight times in 1448, one of the highest ratios on record in the
region.

[98] Manorial courts heard presentments about the misdoings of reeves and *famuli*, see Dyer,
Warwickshire Farming, p. 15.

How did standards of peasant husbandry compare with that of the demesnes? Holdings of a half-yardland and above were provided with the standard types of equipment – a plough, harrow, and a cart or wain, though the vehicles were sometimes "bare", that is, lacking in iron fittings. Tenants with less than a half-yardland did not usually own heavy implements, so they either borrowed (or hired) them, or made do with hand tools, for most owned a spade or mattock.[99] Many peasants possessed less than four draught animals, so they either ploughed with a light team, or pooled beasts to make up teams of eight, a practice that has to be assumed in the absence of specific evidence. Perhaps peasants used horses for ploughing more often than did the demesne managers; horses often accounted for as much as a third or even a half of peasant draught animals, and litigation at Keele (Staffs.) in 1374 records a peasant ploughing with an illicitly borrowed horse. However, peasant horses seem often to have been of such poor quality that it is doubtful if their use gave the cultivator any gain in efficiency.[100]

Peasants certainly appreciated the value of manure, which was bought, sold, borrowed, and stolen, leading to disputes between villagers before manorial courts. A normal thoroughness in manuring is suggested by a complaint at Thornbury (Glos.) in 1438 by a tenant that his sub-tenant had failed to manure his land every year. As peasant flocks and herds increased, manure presumably became more plentiful. In addition, unlike the demesne managers, peasants used marl a good deal, judging from the number of marlpits that they are recorded as owning or using.[101]

Cereals and legumes occupied the bulk of the cultivated land, but the existence of other crops should not be ignored. Seigneurial gardens produced leeks, onions, apples, and might be planted with vines or even hemp. Flax was widely grown by peasants, and there is some evidence that production increased as former pastures were ploughed up for the crop. Peasant gardens were used to grow apples, nuts, garlic, and peas and beans, though references to grass in the gardens of both lords and

[99] R. K. Field, 'Worcestershire peasant buildings, household goods, and farming equipment in the later middle ages', *Med. Arch.*, IX, 1965, pp. 121–5, 137–45; for loans see Hilton, *English Peasantry*, p. 49.

[100] Keele Univ. Library, Sneyd Mss., S 144/7 (J.R.B.); J. Langdon, *Horses, Oxen and Technological Innovation*, pp. 205–53.

[101] Staffs. RO, D641/1/4c/7. On transactions involving manure, see *VCH Staffs.*, VI, p. 32; Dyer, *Warwickshire Farming*, p. 29; for marl-pits, Rugeley (Staffs.), 1461–2, Staffs. RO, D1734/3/2/2 (J.R.B.); Coleshill (War.), 1414, Birmingham Reference Library, Wingfield Digby Mss. A468; Baddesley Clinton (War.), 1356, Shakespeare's Birthplace Trust RO, Archer Coll. no. 2014. John Smyth of Nibley thought that marl-pits had been abandoned in the Vale of Berkeley in the mid-fifteenth century; see *Lives of the Berkeleys*, II, p. 40.

peasants suggest that even these small plots were not immune from the advance of pasture. The urban and suburban gardens of Warwick in the fifteenth century were the source of considerable quantities of onions, garlic, flax, hemp, apples, pears, and saffron.[102]

An expansion in the animal population must have accompanied the shift from arable to pasture. In the late fourteenth century, before the wholesale leasing of demesnes, the stock keeping of landlords was relatively unspecialized. Horses and oxen were kept everywhere as draught animals. Most manors had some cows, with the largest herds of between twenty and fifty animals on the pastures of the Severn estuary, in the Avon and Severn valleys, and in the woodlands of south Staffordshire and Derbyshire. Large herds of pigs, often in excess of fifty head, were kept on manors throughout the region, and were sometimes driven in transhumant herds to woodland in the autumn. Sheep flocks of two to five hundred were commonplace, not just on the Cotswolds, though they were less numerous in the woodlands in the north of the region. The separate administration of sheep under a sheep-reeve or master-shepherd on the larger estates, and the central marketing of the wool-clip, allow us to calculate the total number of sheep owned by some landlords. These were usually rather below the peak of the period around 1300, but could still be substantial – from 4,326 to 4,619 were kept on the Duchy of Lancaster's pastures in the Derbyshire High Peak in the 1350s and 1360s; the bishop of Worcester owned 4,638 in 1389; and the flocks of Worcester Cathedral priory (in 1351–2) and Thomas Beauchamp, earl of Warwick (in 1397), can both be estimated to have exceeded four thousand animals.[103]

When landlords leased out their arable demesnes, they often kept some pastures in hand and continued with stock keeping. This could be unspecialized in character, indicated by the horses, cattle, pigs, sheep, and goats kept by the successive bishops of Coventry and Lichfield at Haywood and Beaudesert (Staffs.) in the fifteenth century. Often the

---

[102] Seigneurial gardens: Caldwall (Worcs.), Bodleian Library, Worcs. rolls, no. 2; Thornbury (Glos.), Staffs. RO, D641/1/2/133; Bromsgrove (Worcs.), Worcs. Cathedral Library, C 554; Bishop's Cleeve (Glos.), Corpus Christi College, Oxford, B/14/2/3/1. On flax see Dyer, *Lords and Peasants*, p. 321. For peasant gardens: Lydney (Glos.), Glos. RO, D421/M19; Hartlebury (Worcs.), ref. 009:1 BA 2636/11, no. 43700, f.64; Bromsberrow (Glos.), Gloucester Public Library, R59.2; Erdington (War.), Birmingham Reference Library, 347856, 347863; Haywood (Staffs), Staffs. RO, D1734/2/1/427 (J.R.B.). Urban gardens: *Ministers' Accounts of the Collegiate Church of St Mary, Warwick, 1432–85*, ed. D. Styles, Dugdale Soc., xxvi, 1969, pp. 81–2, 125–8, 159.

[103] Blanchard, 'Economic change in Derbyshire', p. 179; Dyer, *Lords and Peasants*, pp. 134–7; *Early Compotus Rolls of the Priory of Worcester*, ed. Wilson and Gordon, p. 47; BL Egerton Roll 8769.

remaining pastures were used for specific types of animal husbandry. For example, on many estates a horse-stud was maintained, characteristically as one of the uses of a park, at Henbury (Glos.), Beoley (Worcs.), Budbrooke (War.), and Tutbury (Staffs.). Specialist dairying and cattle-breeding establishments were a feature of the northern part of the region, like the vaccary of a hundred animals managed by the Duchy of Lancaster in the High Peak in the early fifteenth century, or the Vernons' cattle operation at Haddon (Derbs.), which in 1429 had 59 cows and 100 other beasts. At Baddesley Clinton (War.) in the mid-fifteenth century, and at Walsall (Staffs.) at the end of the fourteenth, store cattle, often from Wales, were fattened for the market. Similar activities in Wedgnock Park near Warwick were combined with dairying in the 1420s and 1430s.[104]

Further south landlords of all kinds continued with sheep farming in the first half of the fifteenth century. Many gave up this last direct involvement in agriculture by about 1460, but Coventry priory, Winchcomb abbey, and Worcester Cathedral priory still kept sheep as late as the 1480s and 1490s. The scale of these fifteenth-century sheep-farming operations marked a further stage in the decline of the previous century. The bishopric of Worcester owned between two and three thousand sheep in 1412–50; the Pershore abbey sheep-reeve was responsible for 1,847 animals in 1416; Winchcomb abbey's flock fluctuated between 1,900 in 1468 and 2,900 in 1485; and there were 1,418 sheep on the Worcester Cathedral priory estate in 1446.[105] An exception to the tendency towards decline in the flocks of landlords is provided by some lesser and middling lay landowners, notably the Warwickshire Catesbys with as many as 2,742 sheep in 1476, the Vernons of Derbyshire who owned 1,071 sheep in 1424, and the Gloucestershire Giffards whose leasehold of Combe pasture near Chipping Campden enabled them to keep a flock of 2,156 in 1445.[106]

With the pastures coming into the hands of lessees, we normally lose sight of large-scale stock keeping. Clues as to the size of their operations

---

[104] VCH Staffs., VI, p. 42; Worcs. RO, ref 009:1 BA 2636/166; BL Egerton Roll 8661; Ministers' Accounts of the Warwickshire Estates of the Duke of Clarence, ed. Hilton, p. 29; J. R. Birrell, 'The honour of Tutbury in the fourteenth and fifteenth centuries', Univ. of Birmingham M.A. thesis, 1962, p. 170; Blanchard, 'Economic change in Derbyshire', pp. 171, 187–9; Dyer, 'A small landowner', pp. 6–8; VCH Staffs., XVII, p. 183; War. RO, Warwick Castle Mss. 488.

[105] D. Greenblatt, 'The suburban manors of Coventry, 1279–1411', Univ. of Cornell Ph.D. thesis, 1967, p. 47; Hilton, 'Winchcombe Abbey and the manor of Sherborne', pp. 111–12; Dyer, Lords and Peasants, pp. 150–1; PRO SC 6/1071/24; Worcs. Cathedral Library, C3; Compotus Rolls of the Priory of Worcester, ed. S. G. Hamilton, Worcs. Hist. Soc., 1910, pp. 79–80. See also comments in Lloyd, Movement of Wool Prices, p. 26.

[106] PRO SC 6/1043/10; Blanchard, 'Economic change in Derbyshire', pp. 180–1, 185–7: Dorset RO, D10/M231.

are provided by occasional stock and land leases, like that granting 2,500 sheep with the pasture of Blockley (Glos.) in 1454, or the 400 animals leased to a "tucker" at Bisley (Glos.) in 1455. Pasture for 800 sheep was leased with a substantial arable holding at Temple Guiting (Glos.) in 1484. The butcher-graziers of Warwickshire who took on large pastures probably kept substantial herds of cattle; the size of the flocks and herds owned by the chief grazier of the county, John Spencer, must have run into many thousands, judging from the vast acreage at his disposal.[107]

On the large estates, under their master-shepherds, sheep received special treatment. Transhumance allowed the most efficient use of both upland and valley pastures in the late fourteenth century, but with the leasing out of demesnes the practice went into decline, and was to some extent superseded by some estates keeping the older wethers only on the hills, and replacing them by purchase rather than breeding new animals from within the flock.[108] Sheep usually needed to be fed with hay and peas in the winter, and their lambs were given cows' milk, oats, and bran. Fodder, and some shelter, was provided for sheep flocks in sheep-cotes which were built solidly and to a considerable size. There was much concern with the prevention and cure of disease, and tar, grease, and other substances were bought regularly for use by shepherds, yet epidemics caused high levels of mortality, notably the severe pox outbreak of 1349–50, and sporadically throughout the period. In 1428–9, for example, murrain killed the whole flock of 70 wethers at Budbrooke (War.). In spite of these set-backs sheep farming in the region may be judged to have achieved a high level of productivity; Cotswold fleeces were relatively heavy, often reaching 1.6 lb or above, and were also highly priced. Urban butchers also valued the old wethers at the end of their wool-producing days. Ewes were milked on some manors, for example at Haddon (Derbs.) and Thornbury (Glos.).

The normal method of management for cows was to lease out the "lactage" of each animal at an annual rent of about 5s. When the dairy was directly managed, as at Hallow and Grimley (Worcs.) in the late fourteenth century, it is possible to calculate the annual yield of butter and cheese per animal at between 72 and 98 lb, the larger figure being high by medieval standards.[109] The demand for beef made the fattening

[107] Dyer, *Lords and Peasants*, p. 151; Corpus Christi College, Oxford, F2/22, f.345; F2/21 ff.263, 269; H. Thorpe, 'Lord and the landscape', pp. 97–9.

[108] e.g. PRO SC 6/858/26, which shows the management of Evesham abbey's flock of wethers at Slaughter (Glos.) in 1390/1.

[109] Worcs. Cathedral Library, C 586, C 598; cf. the yields suggested in *Walter of Henley*, ed. Oschinsky, p. 376.

of cattle a profitable activity; pigs were also fattened on late fourteenth-century manors by feeding with peas, but usually for household consumption rather than for sale. The hides of cattle formed an important by-product of stock keeping, and Tewkesbury abbey's tannery, which sold 373 hides in 1380, is a remarkable example of seigneurial involvement in the processing of animal products.[110]

The changes in the ecology of the late medieval countryside allowed lords to take some new directions in animal keeping. Goats had been discouraged in the thirteenth century because of the damage that they caused; as the pressure on resources relaxed in the fourteenth century large herds of goats were kept by the Berkeleys in the west Gloucestershire woodlands, and are also recorded at Minchinhampton (Glos.) and in south Staffordshire. An increasing deer population is implied by the expansion of parks, and as a growing number of lesser lords created parks, the keeping of deer became more widely disseminated through landed society. More rabbit warrens were set up, and these animals, as well as occupying sections of pastures, were occasionally fed with grain.[111]

While most lords reduced their numbers of animals with the decline in direct management, the initiative in stock keeping passed to the demesne farmers and peasants. Since the total amount of land in the hands of the peasantry greatly exceeded that in the hands either of lords or of the farmers, their cumulative holdings of stock could be very large. For example, tithe receipts at Bishop's Cleeve (Glos.) in the 1390s suggest that in one Cotswold-edge parish there were about 4,000 sheep. Trespass cases reveal at Northleach (Glos.) in 1412 that five tenants owned a total of 1,160 sheep, and ten tenants of Teddington (Glos.) had 759 sheep between them in 1427.[112]

Examination of the size of flocks and herds mentioned in court rolls in presentments of overburdening or trespass suggest a considerable increase in the numbers of animals owned by individual tenants in the fourteenth and fifteenth centuries. The normal maximum recorded before 1349 was a hundred sheep or a dozen cattle. In the court rolls of the Worcester Cathedral priory estate peasant flocks exceeding a hundred appear after 1358. Flocks of two or three hundred are recorded throughout Gloucestershire – at such places as Bisley, Hazleton, Norton and Weston Subedge, Moreton-in-Marsh, Northleach, Snowshill, and Swell – mainly in the fifteenth century. In Warwickshire and

[110] T. Wakeman, 'On the kitchener's roll of Tewkesbury Abbey', *J. of the British Arch. Assoc.*, xv, 1859, pp. 321–6.

[111] Smyth, *Lives of the Berkeleys*, I, p. 302; PRO SC 6/856/24; *VCH Staffs.*, vi, p. 42; Blanchard, 'Economic change in Derbyshire', p. 182; Staffs. RO, D593/o/3/3 (J.R.B.).

[112] Dyer, *Lords and Peasants*, p. 329; Glos. RO, D936a/M5; Worcs. Cathedral Library, E53.

Worcestershire such large flocks are less frequently noticed, but are known from Chaddesley Corbett, Cropthorne, and Long Marston. They are also found in south-east Staffordshire, in the Trent valley, in the vicinity of Lichfield, and in Needwood.[113]

In the woodlands some peasants kept sheep, but they tended to be outnumbered by cattle and pigs. Individuals owning twenty or more cattle are known from Baddesley Clinton (War.), Bromsgrove (Worcs.), Erdington (War.), Middleton (War.), Northfield (Worcs.), Shottle Park (Derbs.), Tanworth-in-Arden (War.), and Wroxall (War.). There are also many examples from Staffordshire of herds of up to forty beasts.[114] Pig keeping is less thoroughly recorded, but herds of eighteen or more were kept by individuals at such places as Baddesley Clinton (War.) and Kempsey (Worcs.). Among the pig owners of Bisley (Glos.) in 1431, one had forty animals, another had seventeen, three owned ten pigs each, and two owned eight.[115] All of these herds and flocks mentioned so far were so large as to indicate production for the market among peasants on a considerable scale. But the largest holdings of animals were most likely to be mentioned in court records, and they tell us about the pastoral specialization among the wealthy minority, not the overall distribution of stock among the peasantry.

Occasional evidence of confiscation of animals by landlords, together with trespass cases, and the stints limiting the number of animals allowed on the commons, suggest that peasants with holdings of a yardland might have no more than six cattle and forty to eighty sheep. At the bottom of village society were the cottagers who might be limited by stints to owning a single animal. The collection of the lord's heriot when tenants died provides some guide to the extent of animal ownership among a wide range of tenants, including many old people. Within our period we find that as few as 9 per cent or as many as 16 per cent were said to lack any animal at all at the time of their deaths.[116]

[113] E. K. Vose, typescript on the estates of Worcs. Cathedral priory, School of History, Univ. of Birmingham; PRO SC 2/175/7; Glos. RO D678/62, 94; Dorset RO, D10/M229/1–5; D10/M233; *Eynsham Cartulary*, ed. H. E. Salter, Oxford Hist. Soc., LI, 1908, II, p. xxx; Glos. RO, D936a/M5; Gloucester Public Library, RF296.3 (1–5); Shakespeare's Birthplace Trust RO, DR5/2737; Hilton, *English Peasantry*, p. 44; Glos. RO, D678/62; *VCH Staffs.*, VI, pp. 45–6.

[114] Dyer, 'A small landowner', p. 12; Worcs. RO, ref. b.850 BA 821/32; Birmingham Reference Library, 347853, 518078; Nottingham Univ. Library, MiM 131/34; Birrell, 'The honour of Tutbury', pp. 175–6; Bodleian Library, Ms. Top. Warwick, C1, f.68; PRO SC 2/207/94; *VCH Staffs.*, VI, p. 46.

[115] Shakespeare's Birthplace Trust RO, DR3/791; Worcs. RO, ref. 705:4 BA 54; PRO SC 2/175/10.

[116] The lower percentage is found on the Winchcomb abbey estate in 1361–2, Glos. RO, D678/99, the higher at Ombersley in the late fourteenth and early fifteenth centuries, Worcs. RO, ref. 705:56 BA 3910. On the bishopric of Worcester manors the fifteenth-century figure was 12 per cent: see Dyer, *Lords and Peasants*, p. 323.

These figures show that at least a minority were not involved in pastoral farming, though the presence of some retired people among those liable to pay heriots would mean that the number of active cultivators among the animal-less was a very small minority. Even retired people might continue to own surprisingly large numbers of stock, like the couple at Temple Guiting (Glos.) in 1453 who expected to keep a horse, two cows, and twenty-six sheep.[117]

The chief problem for the peasant pastoralist was finding sufficient foodstuffs. Clearly the expansion in animals outstripped the grazing resources, especially by the middle of the fifteenth century, when complaints of over-burdening commons became especially numerous. By-laws multiplied in the fifteenth century, designed to keep animals out of growing crops, to prevent them being turned on to stubbles before the completion of the harvest, to stop villagers taking strangers' animals (often butchers' and drovers' stock) for pasture on the commons, to limit the damage caused by pigs by insisting that they be ringed or yoked, and to force everyone to put their stock under the care of the common herdsman. These rules and regulations were often broken, judging from the presentments of offenders, and the frequent repetition and modification of the by-laws. The fixing of stints, especially numerous after 1440, is a useful indication of the pressure on the common pastures that led to closer definitions of the rights of individuals.[118]

F. WALES AND THE MARCHES

Climatic, soil, and topographical factors have accounted for the suitability of pastoral agrarian activities in many areas of Wales and the borderlands.[119] Extensive pasturelands were particularly associated with upland and forested regions such as the forests of Delamere and Macclesfield in Cheshire and the Great Forest of Brecknock, whilst the coastal marshes of Gwent were utilized for pastoral purposes by the monastic authorities of Tintern abbey.[120] The documentary and

[117] Corpus Christi College, Oxford, Ms. F2/21 f.401.

[118] On over-burdening see Blanchard, 'Economic change in Derbyshire', pp. 205–23; on stints, Field, 'Worcestershire peasantry', pp. 97–101, 295–8; Hilton, English Peasantry, pp. 203–4; Dyer, Lords and Peasants, pp. 325–8, 331.

[119] In addition to the works cited above in Ch. 2, n.124, the major sources for what follows here include: M. Davies, 'Field systems of South Wales' and G. R. J. Jones, 'Field systems of North Wales', in Baker and Butlin, eds., Field Systems; F. G. Payne, 'The Welsh plough-team to 1600', in J. Geraint Jenkins, ed., Studies in Folk Life.

[120] H. J. Hewitt, Medieval Cheshire, Chetham Soc., NS LXXXVIII, pp. 48–51; M. B. Husain, 'Delamere Forest in late-medieval times', Hist. Soc. of Lancs and Cheshire, CII, 1952, pp. 23–9; W. Rees, The Great Forest of Brecknock, Brecon, 1966, pp. 3–11; D. H. Williams, The Welsh Cistercians, p. 64.

literary evidence of the later middle ages emphasizes the significance of arable farming in those localities where conditions were conducive, and even under adverse conditions dietary considerations in communities which were largely self-sufficient explain the occasionally limited extent of crop cultivation. Despite the absence of detailed information on levels of grain yields and on animal husbandry, the extant sources clearly indicate that mixed farming, with a variable arable/pastoral content, was widely practised. The close relationship between the two agrarian processes is illustrated by the premium placed on meadowlands by both the arable and pastoral farmer. The hay and grazing facilities of meadows contributed to the cattle-rearing enterprises at Maccles-field, and the relative importance of meadows in lowland manors is suggested by their scarcity and also by valuations which often exceed those of arable lands. A significant differentiation between arable and meadowland was made at the manor of Dinorben in the lordship of Denbigh: 201 local acres of arable land were valued at either 1s. 3d. or 1s. per acre, whilst demesne meadowlands amounting to 23 local acres were worth 60s. 8d. The hay provided for the winter fodder of animals was highly regarded by both lord and peasant farmer. In the lordship of Oswestry, meadows were retained in the lord's hands even after the arable land had been leased out to tenants. In the neighbouring lordship of Chirk, where only a limited amount of meadowland was held by the lord, he was occasionally obliged to purchase hay from his tenants.[121]

The inter-dependence of arable and pastoral farming practices is underlined by the crucial role of livestock in ploughteams and in soil fertilization. Local factors influencing the predominance of an arable or pastoral economy determined the employment of cattle in specific agrarian activities and explain regional emphases on the provision of ploughteams or the requirements of milk or beef production. Specialization within pastoral regions may also be observed. In some areas of north Wales the rearing of cattle, rather than that of sheep, was of prime importance and the limited extent of sheep farming in these localities was caused by the unsuitability of the terrain, the prevalence of disease, and marketing difficulties.[122] In Cheshire northern areas tended to concentrate on cattle rearing and fattening whilst in southern and western localities the heavier soil proved to be more suitable for

[121] C. Elliot, 'Field systems of northwest England', in Baker and Butlin, eds., *Field Systems*, pp. 62–3; M. Davies, 'Field systems of South Wales' in *ibid.*, p. 528; P. Vinogradoff and F. Morgan, eds., *Survey of the Honour of Denbigh, 1334*, B. Acad. Records of Social and Economic History, I, pp. 230–1; L. O. W. Smith, 'The lordships of Chirk and Oswestry', pp. 287–8; W. J. Slack, *The Lordship of Oswestry, 1393–1607*, p. 159.

[122] C. Thomas, 'Thirteenth-century farm economies in North Wales', *AHR*, XVI, 1968, pp. 3–11; *Merioneth Lay Subsidy Roll*, ed. Williams-Jones, pp. cxiv–cxvi.

dairy farming. Sheep farming represented a relatively insignificant role in the local economy and in this respect Cheshire may be contrasted to the other border shires of Hereford and Shropshire, both of which made a significant contribution to the medieval wool trade. Moreover, the importance of cattle rearing in fifteenth-century Shropshire is illustrated by the substantial number of recorded offences involving the custody of livestock in the period 1400–14, whilst towards the end of the century there was an increased emphasis on beef production.[123]

Some localities were particularly renowned for the quality of their cattle and sheep. Herds of cattle were driven to Cheshire from north Wales and of these the Flintshire and Vale of Clwyd quotas were highly regarded. Information is occasionally provided on the value of livestock but insufficient evidence is available to denote significant trends in valuations during the entire period. A cellarer's roll compiled for Tintern abbey in 1411–12 records the sale of calves at 1s. 8d. each and of cows at 10s. apiece. Assessments of stolen cattle in Shropshire at approximately the same time reveal marked similarities: cows were priced at between 6s. and 10s. and oxen between 10s. and 13s. 4d.[124] Variations in the standards of wool produced in Wales and the borderlands reflect the local predominance of distinctive breeds of sheep. The wool produced in south-east Wales, Herefordshire, and Shropshire was of an exceptionally good quality and the flocks of Abbey Dore, Margam, and Tintern gained a reputation for their high-grade wool. The two border shires appeared prominently in wool price-lists compiled on a county basis during the fourteenth and fifteenth centuries, and Herefordshire headed the lists for 1337 and 1454. In these areas light-weight fine and short-woolled sheep, forerunners of the Ryeland breed, may be identified. A valuable breed is believed to have been reared in the vicinity of Leominster and the sheep flocks of Clun Forest, Kerry Hill and Wenlock Edge were also associated with the production of good-quality clothing wool.[125] On

---

[123] Hewitt, *Medieval Cheshire*, pp. 44, 48–56; J. T. Driver, *Cheshire in the Later Middle Ages, 1399–1540*, Chester, 1971, pp. 92–4; E. Power, *The Wool Trade in English Medieval History*, pp. 21, 23; *The Shropshire Peace Roll*, ed. Kimball, p. 46; D. G. Hey, *An English Rural Community: Myddle under the Tudors and Stuarts*, Leicester, 1974, p. 57.

[124] Hewitt, *Medieval Cheshire*, p. 55; D. H. Williams, *The Welsh Cistercians*, p. 73; NLW, Badminton Deeds and Documents 1575; *The Shropshire Peace Roll*, ed. Kimball, p. 48.

[125] R. A. Pelham, in *An Historical Geography of England before A.D. 1800*, ed. H. C. Darby, Cambridge, 1936, p. 244; Power, *The Wool Trade*, p. 23; D. H. Williams, *The Welsh Cistercians*, p. 68; Trow-Smith, *A History of British Livestock Husbandry*, pp. 162–4; M. L. Ryder, 'The history of sheep breeds in Britain', *AHR*, XII, 1964, pp. 10–11; E. Kerridge, 'Wool growing and wool textiles in medieval and early modern times', in J. Geraint Jenkins, ed., *The Wool Textile Industry in Great Britain*, London, 1972, p. 24.

the other hand, disparaging comments were made on the standard of wool exported from Carmarthen and in 1341 Welsh wool was described as "being coarse and of little value". The hardy mountain breeds of sheep found in numerous localities in Wales yielded short hairy wool which proved to be particularly suitable for the production of cottons and flannels.[126]

The cattle of late medieval Wales comprised a variety of breeds and of colours and detailed and vivid descriptions are provided in the poetry of the period. Qualities which were particularly admired by the poets included healthy appearance, size, and strength, whilst breeding capacity rather than working ability constituted the prime function of a bull.[127] A distinctive feature of draught oxen was the excessive length of horns, described by Ieuan Deulwyn as "pibay gyrn ar bibay gwin" (horn pipes on pipes of wine). Despite the suggestion in this particular instance of a red colouring most oxen, from the bardic evidence, were of a black colour. Tudur Aled thus saw them as "Cameliaid, wisg cwmwl du" (camels within black clouds), and pictured a bull's "flew clyd o flac y lir" (snug coat of black of Lyre). His contemporary, Tudur Penllyn, referred to a bull "trom dar yn ei dabar dŷ" (massive as an oak in his black tabard) and wearing "blew dŷ ffris fel dwbled ffwl" (a black frieze coat like a fine doublet). Black cattle, forerunners of the renowned Welsh blacks of later centuries, represented one of the most prevalent breeds in fourteenth- and fifteenth-century Wales. Bulls of a red colour also appeared prominently in poetic compositions and a bull from Glamorgan was stated to have "blew yscarlad a roddai lifrai i'r wlad" (scarlet hair enough to provide livery for his land). Red cattle with white faces were commonly found in south-east Wales and a relationship may be traced between this type of cattle and the modern Hereford breed. Brindled cattle were also in evidence at this time and constituted another commonly found breed in late medieval Wales.[128]

The importance of cattle rearing in the economic life of Wales and the border shires is underlined by the evidence of a flourishing livestock trade and also in the widespread distribution of vaccaries or cattle farms. Trading links involving north Wales and Cheshire in the mid-fourteenth century clearly reflected the Black Prince's dual role as prince of Wales and earl of Chester, and livestock were driven from

---

[126] *CPR, 1340–3*, p. 272; Kerridge, 'Wool growing and wool textiles', p. 24.

[127] Payne, 'The Welsh plough-team to 1600', pp. 237–8, 250.

[128] *Gwaith Ieuan Deulwyn*, ed. Ifor Williams, Brecon, 1909, p. 46; *Gwaith Tudur Aled*, ed. Ifor Williams, Cardiff, 1926, II, pp. 437, 441; *Gwyneddon Ms. 3*, ed. Ifor Williams, Cardiff, 1931, pp. 146, 159; Payne, 'The Welsh plough-team to 1600', pp. 247–50; C. A. J. Skeel, 'The cattle trade between Wales and England from the fifteenth to the nineteenth centuries', *RHS*, 4th ser. IX, 1926, p. 136.

north Wales to stock cattle farms in Cheshire. Cattle were brought into the western hundreds of Cheshire even after the imposition of prohibitions during the Glyndŵr rebellion and in 1406 Gruffudd ap Maredudd Bottyn succeeded in breaching an apparently ineffective policy of trade sanctions. The livestock trade between Wales and the border shires was also threatened by the prevalence of cattle stealing, and Shropshire in particular suffered from predatory cattle thieves.[129] Despite these difficulties the transportation of cattle to the border shires was maintained throughout the later middle ages. Cattle were also despatched even further afield. Lordships in Wales often formed component parts of extensive estates and livestock were sent from Welsh lands both to re-stock manors in England and to provide food for seigneurial households. In 1349 twenty drovers were employed to drive 400 head of cattle from Brecon to Essex and in the following year cattle from the same lordship were delivered to Huntingdonshire and Wiltshire. The household accounts of the Howard family of Suffolk in 1463 included payments of £18. 7s. for the purchase of 33 oxen at Wrexham and of 10s. for transporting them to East Anglia. Welsh cattle also supplied food for the armies in France and in 1413 93 cattle were ordered to be killed and salted in London in order that the meat be sent to Calais.[130]

The establishment of vaccaries in parts of north-west Wales in the thirteenth century formed part of the commissariat policies of the rulers of Gwynedd and represented an integral feature of their strategy of military defence. Vaccaries were frequently associated with the pasture lands of forested areas and the financial accounts of the mid- and late fourteenth century throw light on the organization of cattle farms located in the forests of Macclesfield and of Brecknock. Responsibility for the breeding and fattening of cattle at the farm located in the Park of Macclesfield was given to a stock keeper. He also sold some of the cattle at a local fair and supervised the movement of cattle to the farm from other localities. Vaccaries established in Fforest Fawr and Fforest Fach in the lordship of Brecon, and supervised by stock keepers, provided for the requirements of both the castle and manors of the lordship, and also of other estates held by the lord. The minister's account compiled for Caernarfonshire in 1350–1 records the employment of Ririd ap Cad' as *magister vaccariarum* at the manor of

[129] Hewitt, *Medieval Cheshire*, pp. 54–6, 84; *Cal. Recognisance Rolls of the Palatinate of Chester*, in *36th Annual Report of the Deputy Keeper of the Public Records*, 1875, App. II, pp. 333, 340, 534, 224; *The Shropshire Peace Roll*, ed. Kimball, pp. 46, 104.

[130] R. R. Davies, *Lordship and Society*, p. 116; PRO DL 29/671/10810; SC 6/1156/18, 1157/2; Skeel, 'The cattle trade between Wales and England', pp. 137–8; T. H. Turner, ed., *Manners and Household Expenses of England*, Roxburgh Club, 1841, p. 184; J. H. Wylie, *The Reign of Henry the Fifth*, I, Cambridge, 1914, p. 39.

Pwllheli. Moreover, the significance of cattle breeding in the economy of western Shropshire is denoted by the activities centred on the demesne pastures of the manor of Pontesbury. The danger of flooding in the low-lying lands of the Rea valley partly explains the emphasis in this area on cattle breeding rather than on sheep rearing.[131]

In this area of Shropshire, as in several other cattle-rearing centres, the breeding of horses proved to be a profitable pursuit. In the Park of Macclesfield an official was responsible for that section of the forest set aside for horse breeding, and a separate account was compiled for those expenses incurred in providing for a highly prized stallion. Horse studs were also maintained in the Forest of Brecknock and on the estates of Margam, Neath, and Strata Florida.[132] Conditions in the forest areas also favoured the rearing of pigs. In Cheshire an abundant local supply of salt for preserving the meat partly accounted for the production of considerable quantities of pork and bacon. Extensive woodlands were utilized by peasants for pasturing their pigs in the autumn months and although the pig was primarily regarded as a peasant animal large herds of swine were maintained on some manors.[133]

The rearing of sheep constituted a significant feature in the economies of many localities of Wales and the borderlands, despite the prevalence of adverse conditions in certain areas. This was reflected in south-west Wales, where the increasing importance of wool production was denoted by the designation of Carmarthen in 1353 as the sole staple town of Wales. Sheep-farming enterprises in the second half of the fourteenth century were particularly associated with the estates of several Cistercian abbeys and marcher lords. The statistics contained in the *Taxatio Ecclesiastica* of 1291 and the poll-tax return of 1379 should be handled with caution but even so they clearly illustrated the maintenance of large sheep flocks on the estates of Margam, Neath, and Tintern. On the lands of Strata Florida in mid- and west Wales, sheep-rearing activities were based on an integrated system of dispersed granges with the uplands used for summer grazing and the sheep driven to the lowlands for the winter months.[134] An increasing awareness in

[131] G. R. J. Jones, 'The defences of Gwynedd in the thirteenth century', *Caerns. Hist. Soc.*, xxx, 1969, pp. 38–9; Hewitt, *Medieval Cheshire*, pp. 52–6; Rees, *Great Forest of Brecknock*, p. 10; R. R. Davies, *Lordship and Society*, p. 116; PRO DL 29/671/10810; T. Jones Pierce, 'Lleyn ministers' accounts, 1350–51', *Bull. BCS*, VI, 1932, p. 265; *VCH Salop*, VIII, pp. 277–8.

[132] Hewitt, *Medieval Cheshire*, pp. 56–8; PRO SC 6/802/13; *Accounts of the Chamberlains and other Officers of the County of Chester, 1301–1360*, ed. R. Stewart-Brown, Lancs. and Cheshire Rec. Soc., LIX, 1910, pp. 6, 11, 26, 44; Rees, *Great Forest of Brecknock*, p. 10; D. H. Williams, *The Welsh Cistercians*, p. 64. [133] Hewitt, *Medieval Cheshire*, pp. 58–9.

[134] J. E. Lloyd, ed., *A History of Carmarthenshire*, II, Cardiff, 1939, p. 315; Cowley, *Monastic Order in South Wales*, pp. 86–9; Glanmor Williams, *The Welsh Church*, p. 174; E. G. Bowen, 'The monastic economy of the Cistercians at Strata Florida', *Ceredigion*, I, 1950–1, pp. 34–7.

the Welsh marches of the lucrative potential of sheep farming reflected influences radiating from the important wool-producing counties of Shropshire and Herefordshire. The lordships of Oswestry and Clun constituted two of the main sheep-rearing centres within the whole complex of the Arundel estate. The Bohun lands in the marches were also utilized for an extensive sheep-farming enterprise and approximately 3,000 sheep were maintained by the earl of Hereford in the lordship of Brecon in 1372. Permanent sheepfolds had been built at Bronllys, the main sheep farm, and at Bryndu, and slate-roofed sheds sheltered the sheep during the winter and lambing periods. In the period 1367–72 over 18,000 fleeces were produced on the Bohun manors and in 1371 a substantial number were despatched from Brecon and prepared for sale in London.[135]

The involvement of these lordships in the wool trade was based upon the application of a seigneurial policy and, subject to the financial pressures of the period, was terminated before the end of the fourteenth century. In other respects conditions during the late fourteenth and the fifteenth centuries favoured the rearing of both cattle and sheep. Declining soil fertility and a deteriorating climate, combined with the depopulation and devastation experienced in many localities as a result of pestilence and rebellion, contributed to the conversion of arable land to pasture. For the greater part of the period the scarcity of tenants, rather than the price of wool, proved to be the main incentive for an expansion in sheep-farming activities.[136] It is true that the Customs' Accounts of the fifteenth century confirm a reduction in the amount of wool exported from Welsh ports, but they also reveal an increased emphasis on cloth production. The expanding English cloth industry of the fifteenth century was not primarily dependent upon local supplies of high-quality wool. Thus Herefordshire and Shropshire, which produced the highest graded wool in 1454, were not included in the premier group of textile-industrial regions in England. The two border shires did, however, contain some cloth-making centres and also provided wool for processing in the west country, which represented one of the three predominant regional centres of the cloth industry.[137]

The distribution of fulling mills, or *pandai*, usually located on the

---

[135] L. O. W. Smith, 'The lordships of Chirk and Oswestry', pp. 144–8; Rees, *South Wales and the March*, pp. 256–7; PRO SC 6/1156/13, 15, 18.

[136] Duby, *Rural Economy and Country Life*, pp. 350–1; G. R. J. Jones, 'Field systems of North Wales', p. 451; E. A. Lewis, 'The decay of tribalism in North Wales', *Hon. Soc. Cymmr.*, 1902–3, p. 47; Lloyd, *Movement of Wool Prices*, pp. 28–30.

[137] E. A. Lewis, 'The development of industry and commerce in Wales during the middle ages', *RHS*, NS XVII, 1903, pp. 151–61; A. R. H. Baker in Darby, ed., *A New Historical Geography of England*, pp. 222–5; E. M. Carus-Wilson, 'The woollen industry', *CEcH*, II, 2nd edn, pp. 672–3, 678–83.

upper reaches of fast-flowing streams, denotes the existence of cloth-producing centres in many localities in Wales, and concentrations of these mills may be observed in the south-west and in the northern and southern borderlands. A flourishing cloth industry was located in the lordship of Ruthin: at least five fulling mills were operated in the 1460s and the ordinances of a gild of weavers and fullers, enrolled in 1447, denote active seigneurial support for the enterprise. The construction of fulling mills towards the end of the fifteenth century on the estates of Basingwerk and Margam abbeys reflects an intensification of the process whereby wool production was geared to the requirements of a textile industry.[138]

Cloth produced in Wales was also sold locally, taken to markets in border towns, notably Oswestry, Shrewsbury, Ludlow, and Hereford, or sent to the annual St Bartholomew Fair in London. Substantial quantities of friezes were also exported to overseas markets either directly from Welsh ports such as Beaumaris, Carmarthen, and Rhuddlan or from Bristol, which as a major manufacturing centre and port contributed significantly to the Welsh export trade. The primary commodities of wool, hides, and cloth were transported by land and sea to Bristol for the use of the numerous and various craftsmen of the city. The importance of Bristol's trading relationships with Wales, the marches and the border shires is illustrated by the contingent of Welsh merchants resident in the city, the abbot of Tintern's membership of the Staple in Bristol, and the indications of heavy traffic in this period on the Bristol–Chester road.[139]

Commercial activity involving the movement of cattle and sheep, and of meat, hides, wool and cloth, emphasize the extent and significance of pastoral agrarian pursuits in late medieval Wales. Studies of arrangements associated with the practice of arable farming in Wales and the borderlands have identified a "Celtic System" which, practised in Wales and in some parts of the border shires including Cheshire, was characterized by small open arable fields surrounded by extensive areas of pastureland. The fields might contain the inter-mingled strips of tenants but other integral features of the "midland" two- and three-field open arable systems, involving the division of the

[138] Lewis, 'Development of industry and commerce in Wales', pp. 156–8; R. I. Jack, 'The cloth industry in medieval Wales', Welsh Hist. Rev., x, 1979–80, pp. 10–25; idem, 'The cloth industry of medieval Ruthin', Denbs. Hist. Soc., XII, 1963, pp. 10–25; D. H. Williams, The Welsh Cistercians, p. 68; W. de Gray Birch, History of Margam Abbey, London, 1897, p. 349.

[139] Lewis, 'Development of industry and commerce in Wales', pp. 159–61; T. H. Lloyd, The English Wool Trade in the Middle Ages, pp. 54–5, 132; E. M. Carus-Wilson in E. Power and M. M. Postan, eds., Studies in English Trade in the Fifteenth Century, London, 1933, pp. 185–8, 234; D. T. Williams in Darby, ed., An Historical Geography of England, pp. 284–91.

ploughland into fields of roughly equal size, and the systematic rotation of crops, were absent. The distinction recently drawn between open and common field systems is particularly applicable to those localities subjected to the "Celtic System". Considerable evidence is available to indicate the widespread distribution of open fields but for a variety of reasons the specified requirements of a fully developed common-field system were not always fulfilled.[140]

Contemporary and later sources throw light on the various field systems adopted. Medieval deeds and manorial records contain frequent references to open fields incorporating arable strips. Difficulties of interpretation are occasionally presented by the terminology employed: documents in estate collections relating to lands in north-east Wales and the border shires describe the open field as a *campus*, "field", or *maes* and the arable strip as a "butt", *cefn*, or selion. The term *cae* normally represented an enclosed field and the prevalence of field arrangements associated with both the *cae* and *maes* in Maelor Saesneg, in the northern borderlands, illustrates the complexity of field patterns in many localities in the late fifteenth century.[141]

The writings of sixteenth-century commentators confirm the prevalence of an open-field landscape. Rice Merrick in 1578 referred to the Vale of Glamorgan as "a champion and open country, without great store of Inclosures" and George Owen attributed the survival of open fields with intermingled holdings in north Pembrokeshire to the Welsh inheritance law of gavelkind. Post-medieval documents contain references to unfenced arable quillets and strip fields which represent remnants of a medieval field system embracing communal forms of cultivation and intermingled holdings. Information contained in tithe maps compiled for west Cheshire suggests that in several townships over three-quarters of the total area incorporated open fields. Fossilized traces of arable fields divided into strips may also be discerned in manorial and tithe surveys relating to all the shires of south Wales and in some instances arable strips separated by balks have survived to the present day.[142]

[140] Gray, *English Field Systems*, pp. 171–90, 195–205, 249–58; Orwin, *The Open Fields*, 3rd edn, pp. ix–xi, 65–6; J. Thirsk, 'The common fields', *PP*, no. 29, 1964, pp. 3–4.

[141] G. R. J. Jones, 'Field systems of North Wales', pp. 471–6; Vinogradoff and Morgan, eds., *Survey of the Honour of Denbigh*, pp. 4, 52, 231; NLW, Pitchford Hall Deeds and Documents 161, 167, 185; NLW, Plymouth Deeds and Documents 15, 39; UCNW, Mostyn Coll. 1533, 1631; NLW, Bettisfield Manuscripts and Documents 424, 354.

[142] Rice Merrick, *Morganiae Archaiographia: a Book of the Antiquities of Glamorganshire*, ed. Brian Ll. James, Barry, 1983, p. 14; George Owen, *The Description of Penbrokeshire*, ed. H. Owen, Hon. Soc. Cymmr. Rec. Ser., I, 1902, p. 61; V. Chapman, 'Open fields in west Cheshire', *Hist. Soc. of Lancs. and Cheshire*, CIV, 1952, pp. 53–4; M. Davies, 'Field systems of South Wales', pp. 480–529;

In south Wales and parts of the borderlands the main determinant responsible for open-field cultivation was the suitability of soil, and topographical conditions for both arable farming and also for Anglo-Norman settlement. Communal forms of agrarian and tenurial procedures in the pre-conquest period were assimilated on the manors established in the coastal lowlands and the broad river valleys. Regional peculiarities and variations in the field systems resulted from the influence of earlier practices, the impact of different arrangements in neighbouring upland areas geared to a pastoral economy, and the physical definitions of local landscape features.[143]

Some of the closest approximations in the borderlands to the "midlands" three-field system were to be found in Shropshire and in Herefordshire. Communal arrangements may be observed in various parts of Shropshire and an examination of the relationship between field systems and settlement sites in western localities reveals the widespread utilization of the three-field system. On the eastern manors of the lordship of Oswestry the fields were of a relatively large size, and two or three open fields were often identified with one township. Field names often provide information relating to their origins and those denoting clearances from woodland areas indicate that in some cases the assarted land was brought into an open-field system; in others it retained a separate existence and was enclosed at an early stage in fields of an irregular shape. The enclosure of the open arable fields of Shropshire was largely effected from the sixteenth century onwards, and some fifteenth-century examples of enclosure were associated with abandoned and decayed settlements.[144] In Herefordshire, 12 acres of arable land on the manor of Stretton in 1410 were cultivated as common land in alternate years. A carefully regulated three-course rotation involving wheat, oats and peas, and fallow had been operated at Bunshill in the upper Wye valley in the period 1326–44, whilst three open fields of 22, 30 and $23\frac{1}{2}$ acres may be observed at Weobley in 1403. Irregularities frequently characterized field arrangements and rotational systems. Crops were occasionally sown in one field only and smaller fields were occasionally added to existing three-field systems. Modifications to accepted field arrangements undoubtedly resulted from the assarting of woodland areas and the acquisition of arable strips by

RCHM, Wales, *An Inventory of the Ancient Monuments in Glamorgan*, III(2), Cardiff, 1982, pp. 307–12.

[143] Rees, *South Wales and the March*, pp. 25–9; M. Davies, 'Field systems of South Wales', pp. 480–5.

[144] L. O. W. Smith, 'The lordships of Chirk and Oswestry', pp. 278–9; T. Rowley, *The Shropshire Landscape*, London, 1972, pp. 137–42; *VCH Salop*, VIII, pp. 185–6, 248–50, 300.

enterprising and prosperous tenants anxious to form compact holdings of land.[145]

Open-field patterns in Cheshire were also influenced by the reclamation of land and the redistribution of arable quillets. Numerous references to assarts and riddings denote an extension of open-field cultivation and the purchase and exchange of parcels of land illustrate efforts to consolidate strip holdings. Despite suggestions to the contrary, open fields constituted a feature of the landscape of medieval Cheshire. At least 250 examples of open arable lands have been identified and a distinctive designation, the town field, was frequently given to the arable lands cultivated in open strips. The arrangement of open lands involved the adoption of a variety of systems. The primitive agrarian organization of an infield and outfield seems to have been practised and in view of the absence of references to an outfield it has been suggested that the "ridding", which appears frequently in the documentary evidence, may well have fulfilled this function. Several multi-field manors on which co-aration was practised were located on the estates of Vale Royal abbey. Insufficient and occasionally contradictory information relating to three-field townships suggests that the application of a carefully regulated three-field system was extremely restricted in Cheshire.[146]

In south Wales also only a limited number of references illustrate the adoption of a three-field system. Two parts of three carucates at Carew in south Pembrokeshire were sown in 1369, whilst a third lay fallow. An inquisition *post mortem* compiled in 1376 reveals that at nearby Llangwm two-thirds of two carucates, valued at 13s. 4d., had been sown whilst a third part was described as "lying waste and in common". Ministers' accounts compiled for the manor of Llantrisaint in the lower Usk valley in the years 1323–6 illustrate the arrangement of fields into three groups with the predominant crops being oats and wheat. Climatic and soil conditions accounted for the widespread cultivation of oats, which both provided a staple diet in medieval Wales and also constituted a source of winter fodder for animals. Corn production was generally restricted to the fertile coastal lowlands and river valleys and featured in the agrarian enterprises of manorial centres and monastic granges. Occasionally some portions of the demesne

---

[145] A. J. Roderick, 'Open-field agriculture in Herefordshire in the later middle ages', *WNFC*, XXXIII, 1949, pp. 55–67; Sylvester, *Rural Landscape of the Welsh Borderland*, p. 368; BL Harl. Ms. 7366, p. 14.

[146] D. Sylvester, 'The open fields of Cheshire', *Hist. Soc. of Lancs. and Cheshire*, CVIII, 1956, pp. 1–2, 20–7; *idem*, 'Rural settlement in Cheshire', *ibid.*, CI, 1949, pp. 32–4; Chapman, 'Open fields in west Cheshire', pp. 53–4, 58.

proved to be unsuitable for the cultivation of wheat, and this explains irregularities in the systematic application of a three-course rotation. At Llantrisaint an unequal balance may also be observed in the apportionment of the grouped fields. The fields on which wheat and oats were cultivated comprised between 50 and 60 acres, whilst fields reserved for the less important crops of barley, peas and beans amounted to under 10 acres.[147] The absence of a two- or three-field system in localities in the north of the former shire of Pembroke is suggested by George Owen's observation that winter corn was not sown. Spring crops were sown in a section of the open fields but the remainder was allowed to lie fallow and the fields during the winter months were utilized for the unrestricted grazing of livestock. An infield–outfield arrangement was also practised in both north and south Pembrokeshire. Regular cultivation of the infield or "arable land" was in contrast to the occasional cropping but more frequent grazing of the outfield or "arable and pasture-land". Temporary forms of cultivation were practised in other upland areas of Wales and lands described as *terra montana* or *tir y mynydd* frequently corresponded to the "outfield".[148] The observations of George Owen also indicated that the cultivation of arable lands in some localities was accompanied by the use of marl as a fertilizer. He distinguished between stone marl and clay marl, and earlier evidence suggested that marling had been practised as early as the thirteenth century on the lands of the episcopal manor of Lamphey. The yield of arable lands was also stimulated in Cheshire, where the sowing of wheat was often preceded by the process of marling. John Leland, during his visit to the county in the sixteenth century, commented upon the beneficial consequences of the application of marl upon corn production.[149]

Agrarian arrangements involving the cultivation of open fields were also associated with the two main settlement forms which have been identified in those areas of Wales where native rule was maintained down to the end of the thirteenth century. In localities subject to *tir gwelyawg* tenure the homestead (*tyddyn*), set in its own enclosure, was

---

[147] Rees, *South Wales and the March*, pp. 140, 190–3; PRO C 135/169/4; SC 6/923/29–30, 924/1–3; B. E. Howells, 'Open fields and farmsteads in Pembrokeshire', *The Pembrokeshire Historian*, 3, 1971, p. 11; *A Calendar of the Public Records relating to Pembrokeshire*, ed. H. Owen, I, London, 1911–18, p. 122.

[148] B. E. Howells, 'Pembrokeshire farming *circa* 1580–1620', *NLW Jnl*, IX, 1955–6, pp. 324–6; G. Owen, *The Description of Penbrokeshire*, ed. H. Owen, I, p. 61; G. R. J. Jones, 'Field systems of North Wales', pp. 422–4, 470–1.

[149] Howells, 'Pembrokeshire farming', p. 247; B. G. Charles, *George Owen of Henllys, a Welsh Elizabethan*, Aberystwyth, 1973, pp. 148–51; G. Owen, *Description of Penbrokeshire*, I, pp. 71–5; Leland, *Itinerary*, V, p. 6.

occupied by a clansman who held small arable plots arranged in open fields. The plots comprised arable strips or quillets which were dispersed among one or several share-lands (*rhandiroedd*). The *rhandir* formed part of a single *gwely*, or in more complex circumstances was related to the holdings of several *gwelyau*. The reconstruction of the mid-fifteenth-century *rhandir* of Llwydfaen in the Conway valley reveals that it contained numerous homesteads and arable plots which, of a dispersed character, belonged to clan groupings and in this instance were designated *gafaelion*. The fragmentation of individual holdings resulted from the consequences of *cyfran* or partible inheritance, and the average arable holding in the fourteenth century comprised plots scattered over a number of open-field *rhandiroedd*.[150] Attempts were made by the members of kindred groupings to circumvent the disruptive effects of dispersion and fragmentation. Co-operative measures adopted included co-tillage, and legal texts specify the contributions required of a 12-man ploughing team. The detailed stipulation of communal arrangements suggests that common-field cultivation was practised and compensatory provisions for the damage caused by grazing animals indicate the location of arable lands in open fields. This impression is strengthened by references in the legal texts to the *talar* (headland) used for turning the plough and turf balks which, measuring eighteen inches wide, separated the ploughing strips. Attempts made to retain individual shares of arable were motivated by the desire to prevent excessive morcellation caused by the strict application of *cyfran*. Physical limitations inherent in the *gwely* system ultimately occasioned fragmentation, and the more enterprising peasant proprietors seized the opportunity to acquire additional arable quillets. Scattered properties were consolidated into compact holdings and the fields of the consolidated farms were enclosed by hedges which replaced the turf balks.[151]

Open fields also constituted a basic feature of those settlements

[150] G. R. J. Jones, 'Medieval open fields and associated settlement patterns in north-west Wales', in *Géographie et Histoire Agraires*, Annales de l'Est, Mémoire 21, Nancy, 1959, pp. 313–28; Jones Pierce, *MWS*, pp. 332–6; *idem*, 'The gafael in Bangor Ms. 1939', in *MWS*, pp. 195–227; C. A. Gresham, 'The Bolde rental (Bangor Ms. 1939)', *Caerns. Hist. Soc.*, XXVI, 1965, pp. 31–49; G. R. J. Jones, 'Field systems of North Wales', pp. 446–8. For further discussion on *gwely*, *gafael*, and *rhandir*, see pp. 95–7 and 649–50.

[151] G. R. J. Jones, 'Field systems of North Wales', pp. 436–9, 448–9; *Llyfr Iorwerth*, ed. A. R. Wiliam, Cardiff, 1960, pp. 96–9; *Llyfr Colan*, ed. D. Jenkins, Cardiff, 1963, pp. 10–12, 68–73; Vinogradoff and Morgan, eds., *Survey of the Honour of Denbigh*, pp. 17–8, 40–3; above, pp. 96–102 and below, pp. 650–60. G. R. J. Jones, 'The Llanynys quillets: a measure of landscape transformation in North Wales', *Denbs. Hist. Soc.*, XIII, 1964, pp. 133–58, and *idem*, 'Field systems of North Wales', pp. 471–6, for discussion on the survival of sharelands at Trefechan, near Llanynys in the Vale of Clwyd. The turf balks separating the quillets were eventually ploughed out in 1970 and 1971.

centred on the *maerdref* and characterized by *tref gyfrif* tenure. Frequently amounting to several hundred acres, the fields were cultivated by bondmen who, liable for a variety of renders and labour services on the demesne (*tir bwrdd*), held small arable quillets which were dispersed in the open fields. The rights exercised over the arable lands were shared equally among all the male members of the hamlet or village community and the regular redistribution of arable land therefore accompanied local demographic changes. Grazing rights were also exercised on the surrounding waste lands and, following the harvesting of the arable quillets, these plots in the open fields reverted to common land and were utilized as pasture.[152] Some *maerdrefi* in the period which followed the Edwardian conquest were adapted to form manors and a deliberate effort was made to promote demesne farming. Arable demesne land on the manor of Dinorben Fawr, in the lordship of Denbigh, amounting to 201 local acres, had been systematically organized by 1334 into three seasons which included lands held *in culturis* and *in forlongis*. Dispersed meadow and pasture lands were also associated with the demesne, whilst the *maerdref* hamlet was occupied by bondmen. Their customary services had been commuted into cash renders and agrarian activities at Dinorben by this time were dependent upon hired labour. The manor, however, was evidently in a state of decline and demesne farming, although still practised in 1334, was soon terminated and the leasing of the manor proved to be a more lucrative proposition for the seigneurial authorities. Similar trends may also be observed in Anglesey on the manor of Aberffraw, which superseded a *maerdref* located near to the main residence of the native rulers of Gwynedd. Arable demesne lands whose produce maintained the royal court were laid out in open fields and were interspersed with the lands of free and bond tenants. Despite the farming and leasing of parts of the demesne in the later middle ages, the survival of open-field tenurial arrangements is indicated by sixteenth-century surveys which record both the intermingling of crown demesne, tenant, and glebe lands in the "feldeland" and also the use of turf balks as boundaries for the arable plots.[153]

The nature and scope of ploughing arrangements are illuminated by an examination of the narrative and literary sources of the period. Legal

---

[152] G. R. J. Jones, 'Medieval open fields and associated settlement patterns', pp. 320–3.

[153] D. Huw Owen, 'The lordship of Denbigh, 1282–1425', Univ. of Wales Ph.D. thesis, 1967, pp. 210–11, 214–16; Vinogradoff and Morgan, eds., *Survey of the Honour of Denbigh*, pp. 230–2; Hatfield House Library, Montague Cartulary, f.48; PRO SC 6/1183/20, 1184/22, 1185/4; G. R. J. Jones, 'Field systems of North Wales', pp. 461–9; *idem*, 'Rural settlement in Anglesey', pp. 211–14.

texts which enshrined Hywel Dda's codification of the tenth century were compiled from the twelfth century onwards and reflected contemporary agrarian practices. The working day for ploughing purposes extended from early morning until noon. Oxen were specified as the only plough animals and the unsuitability of horses in ploughteams was emphasized. Financial penalties and valuations enumerated in the laws denote the *desiderata* of the plough ox; these included age (six years being regarded as the age of maturity), strength, and the ability to plough both in the furrow and on the land. Regulations relating to the practice of co-tillage suggest an ideal arrangement involving the cultivation of twelve "acres" with one acre each belonging to the ploughman, the ox-driver, the owners of the plough-frame and plough-irons, and the owners of the eight oxen which formed the ploughteam. The duties of the various parties involved were also specified: the ploughman was required to possess a mechanical knowledge of his plough and the ox-driver, who was expected to provide the yoking equipment, was responsible for the direction and speed of the ploughing: the latter, in fact, was undertaken by "calling" or singing to the ploughteam. Two main forms of ploughteam arrangement are recorded: the long yoke with the oxen lying abreast of one another and the long team, whereby the oxen were grouped in pairs with one pair following the other.[154]

Valuable information relating to agricultural techniques is also contained in contemporary poetry and in this respect an examination of the *cywyddau*, the distinctive metrical verse form of the period, has proved to be particularly rewarding. *Cywyddau* composed by Ieuan Deulwyn towards the end of the fifteenth century refer to a late-surviving example of the long yoke, involving eight oxen arranged four abreast of each other and also to the formation of a long team which represented a more popular arrangement by this time.[155] A detailed description of the fourteenth-century plough is contained in Iolo Goch's *cywydd* in praise of the ploughman and the plough, and the vivid use of figurative language conveys the poet's intense admiration for his subject. The component parts of the mould-board and ploughshare are suggested by the couplet:

E' fynn ei gyllell a'i fwyd
A'i fwrdd dan fôn ei forddwyd.

It likes its knife and table
And its food under its thigh.

[154] Payne, 'The Welsh plough-team to 1600', pp. 236–42; *Ancient Laws and Institutes of Wales*, ed. Aneurin Owen, London, 1841, I, pp. 274, 314, 316, 318, 320, 322.

[155] Payne, 'The Welsh plough-team to 1600', pp. 243–4; *Gwaith Ieuan Deulwyn*, ed. I. Williams, pp. 42, 44.

Comparisons drawn between the plough, and a "crud" (cradle), and a "cawell" (creel) suggest a rectangular shape, and the plough is also pictured as

> y creir glŵys...
> Crehyr a'i hegyr hoywgŵys.
>
> A precious thing...
> Crane opening fine furrows.[156]

In the fifteenth century Lewis Glyn Cothi described a rectangular wheeled plough with two oxen and one chain to each yoke and the manuscript of a legal text compiled in Ceredigion contains an illustration of a plough.[157]

The content, language, and imagery of poetry composed at this time constitute an informative source for an understanding of practices adopted during the process of crop cultivation.[158] Information is occasionally provided which also indicates the contemporary importance of animal husbandry. Guto'r Glyn and Tudur Penllyn were employed in the fifteenth century as sheep-drovers and they sold wool in English fairs. In one poem Guto presented a detailed description of a remarkable expedition to Coventry, Lichfield, and Stafford and the hazardous nature of his work is conveyed by the final observation:

> Pe ceid am ddafad ddeufwy
> O dda'n y Mars, ni ddown mwy.
>
> If I obtained twice as much for my sheep
> I would not go again.

His clerical patron, Sion Mechain, "person ni chel pwrs na chost" (a parson who never hid his purse), seems to have been a prosperous sheep breeder in Deuddwr, an area lying to the south of Oswestry.[159] Various kinds of agrarian activity are both selected by the poets as their main

---

[156] F. G. Payne, *Yr Aradr Gymreig*, Cardiff, 1954, pp. 73–7; *Cywyddau Iolo Goch ac eraill*, eds. H. Lewis, T. Roberts and Ifor Williams, Cardiff, 1972, p. 80; J. P. Clancy, *Medieval Welsh Lyrics*, London, 1965, p. 139.

[157] Payne, *Yr Aradr Gymreig*, pp. 59–60, 78–86; *The Laws of Howel Dda*, ed. T. Lewis, London, 1912, frontispiece; NLW, Llanstephen Ms. 116.

[158] F. G. Payne, 'Cwysau o Foliant Cyson', *Y Llenor*, XXVI, 1947, pp. 3–24; *idem*, 'The Welsh plough-team to 1600', pp. 242–7.

[159] Skeel, 'The cattle trade between Wales and England', pp. 157–8; *Gwaith Guto'r Glyn*, eds. Ifor Williams and J. L. Williams, Cardiff, 1939, pp. 84–6, 273; T. Roberts, 'Tudur Penllyn', *Y Llenor*, XXI, 1942, p. 145; *Gwaith Tudur Penllyn ac Ieuan ap Tudur Penllyn*, ed. T. Roberts, Cardiff, 1958, pp. 40–1; Glanmor Williams, *The Welsh Church*, p. 263.

themes and are extensively used as allegorical material to illustrate their view of more general subjects. Moreover the large number of references, together with the detailed knowledge displayed, further confirms the significance of both arable and pastoral forms of agriculture in the economic and social framework of Wales and the marches in the later middle ages.

G. THE HOME COUNTIES

In its arable field systems the region falls into three broad divisions. The first, and by far the largest, consists of west Berkshire, the parts of Oxfordshire, Buckinghamshire, and Bedfordshire north of the Chiltern Hills, and the northernmost part of Hertfordshire, from Hitchin eastwards. The second consists of the Chilterns themselves, and the third the areas to the south: east Berkshire, the southern tip of Buckinghamshire, and most of Hertfordshire.

In the first of these divisions open common fields predominated; these were the fundamental cropping units that formed the basis for a two- or three-course rotation. At the eastern end of this division – the relevant parts of Buckinghamshire, Bedfordshire, and Hertfordshire – two- and three-field systems were intermingled, forming no recognizable geographical pattern. However, in west Berkshire, and in Oxfordshire west of the Cherwell and north-east from the Heyfords, it was nearly always a two-field system (sometimes with four fields instead of two), with a few three-field villages around the upper Thames; and in the part of Oxfordshire between Oxford and the Chilterns there were mostly three-field systems.[160] In the part of Oxfordshire between these two areas, north-east from Oxford, change from two- to three-course rotation is recorded in a number of places, as also in the neighbouring area of north-west and northern Buckinghamshire.[161] This change can seldom be precisely dated; in some places it may have been made before 1350, but it probably mostly occurred during the present period or later. Thus at Hethe (Oxon.)

[160] The evidence for the distribution of two- and three-field systems is drawn principally from the relevant topographical volumes of *VCH*, from Gray, *English Field Systems*, and from the indications of two- or three-course cropping provided by the inquisition *post mortem* valuations for Bedfordshire, Buckinghamshire, and Hertfordshire that are tabulated by J. A. Raftis, *Assart Data and Land Values*, Toronto, 1974, pp. 27–37. H. S. A. Fox, 'The alleged transformation from two-field to three-field systems in medieval England', *EcHR*, 2nd ser. XXXIX, 1986, p. 542, in a discussion of great interest, comments on the distribution of the two systems in Oxfordshire.

[161] Thus *VCH Oxon.*, V, p. 67 (Beckley); VI, pp. 62 (Bletchingdon), 163 (Hampton Poyle); XI, pp. 11–12 (North Aston: an outlier of this area); B. Holden, 'The deserted medieval village of Thomley, Oxfordshire', *Oxoniensia*, L, 1985, pp. 223–5; Fox, 'The alleged transformation', pp. 538–41, 543.

there were only two fields in 1349 but three by the early seventeenth century; at Woodeaton (Oxon.) in 1366 there were basically two fields, but some furlongs were cropped on a three-course rotation.[162]

Where change occurred within the open-field division of the region it seems hardly ever in the present period to have taken the form of a straightforward conversion of a village's field system, though there is at least one possible case – at Cropredy in north Oxfordshire – of the change from a three- to a two-field system that might seem a sensible response to contracting arable cultivation.[163] In many places open-field cultivation on the two- or three-field system continued long after 1500.[164] Elsewhere modifications were introduced, which can be exemplified by what happened at Boarstall (Bucks.). In the early fourteenth century the arable there had been divided between four open fields; between 1350 and the 1440s two of these fields were amalgamated, and as individual strips and furlongs at Boarstall are commonly identified without naming the field in which they lay, it seems likely that what we have here was not a change in crop rotation, but rather fields that were not cropping units at all.[165] In some other places we find that in the course of the period lands come to be referred to, or even listed at length, by the names of furlongs alone, not fields, arguably pointing to a decline in the importance of the fields as the basis of crop rotation; examples of this include Kempston (Beds.), Pyrton (Oxon.), and Stewkley (Bucks.), and it may be significant that none come from the two-field areas of Berkshire and Oxfordshire.[166] From a group of places in north-east Oxfordshire we can draw other very clear evidence of the way regular field systems were modified and this was probably typical of many other districts as well: at Bicester in 1399 some furlongs of the three-field system at Market End could be sown in a particular year "if it was so agreed", at Stratton Audley a survey of 1412–13 shows that a former two- or three-field system had given

[162] VCH Oxon., VI, p. 177; Eynsham Cartulary, 2 vols., ed. H. E. Salter, Oxford Hist. Soc., OS XLIX, LI, 1907–8, II, pp. 15–17.

[163] VCH Oxon., X, pp. 164–5; interestingly, the change (if the evidence is rightly interpreted) occurred early, between 1332 and 1349.

[164] As can be demonstrated by seventeenth- to nineteenth-century maps: Sixteen Old Maps of Properties in Oxfordshire, ed. J. L. G. Mowat, Oxford, 1888; Buckinghamshire Estate Maps, Bucks. Rec. Soc., 1964; F. G. Emmison, Some Types of Common-field Parish, London, 1965, which draws its evidence from Bedfordshire.

[165] The evidence, taken from the mid-fifteenth-century cartulary of the Rede family (Bucks. RO, archives of Sir John Aubrey-Fletcher, Bart.), is set out in Local Maps and Plans from Medieval England, ed. R. A. Skelton and P. D. A. Harvey, Oxford, 1986, pp. 215–16. The published calendar of the cartulary (The Boarstall Cartulary, ed. H. E. Salter, Oxford Hist. Soc., OS LXXXVIII, 1930) unfortunately omits field names and is thus inadequate in this connection.

[166] VCH Beds., III, p. 301; VCH Oxon., VIII, p. 160; [G. Eland], 'Terrier of land at Littlecote – 1514', Records of Bucks., XIII, 1934–40, pp. 353–4.

way to an arrangement which divided the tenants' lands between at least five fields, and at Marston a new fourth arable field was formed in Henry VII's reign from newly drained land beside a stream.[167] Returning to Boarstall we find that by the late seventeenth century the three fields of the 1440s had shrunk to mere relics, most of the land having been carved away in closes.[168] This erosion of open-field arable by the formation of closes seems to have occurred quite often; at Boarstall the process may or may not have begun before the sixteenth century, but in some places it was demonstrably well advanced by then.[169] Occasionally we get a glimpse of the process of enclosure. In 1367 the accounts of the Grey family's estates in Bedfordshire mention the costs of enclosure at Blunham, Brogborough, and Harrold; new closes were created at Coleshill (Berks.) between 1394 and 1424; in 1448 it was agreed that each tenant of Woodeaton (Oxon.) should have a close which he was to hedge at his own expense and for which he was to pay a fee to the church and to Eynsham abbey as lord of the manor; in 1476 and subsequently, a tenant at Kempston (Beds.) was presented for not allowing common on his close, presumably newly created; New Close at Henton in Chinnor (Oxon.) first appears in 1481. This piecemeal enclosure, which seems to have occurred throughout the open-field division of the region, did not necessarily mark a change to permanent pasture; thus at Kirtlington (Oxon.) a 1476 rental mentions not only six closes of pasture (totalling 39 acres) but also eight closes of arable (60 acres).[170] In this it differed from the enclosure movement which affected Buckinghamshire and neighbouring parts of Hertfordshire and Oxfordshire in the second half of the fifteenth century and which involved not only the enclosure of both demesnes and former tenants' lands but also their conversion to pasture for sheep farming.[171]

The field systems of the Chilterns were markedly different from the open-field division of the region, and seem to have been less subject to change in this period. Open common fields there certainly were throughout the Chilterns, though they were more prominent in the parishes of the north-east, where they might contain up to half the agricultural land, than in the south-west, where in some places, such as

[167] VCH Oxon., v, p. 216; vi, pp. 26 (citing W. Kennett, Parochial Antiquities, ed. B. Bandinel, 1818, ii, pp. 186–7), 329.

[168] As shown on a map of 1697 (Bucks. RO, D/AF/266); a deed of 1632 refers to one of the three fields as a close (Bucks. RO, D/AF/3/19).

[169] E.g. VCH Oxon., v, pp. 38–9 (Marsh Baldon and Toot Baldon); vii, p. 188 (Attington in Thame).

[170] Godber, History of Bedfordshire, pp. 137, 143; Harvey, ed., The Peasant Land Market, p. 154; L. Clare Latham, 'The decay of the manorial system, during the first half of the fifteenth century', London Univ. M.A. thesis, 1928, p. 169; VCH Oxon., v, p. 314; vi, p. 225; viii, p. 68.

[171] See above, ch. 2,D.

Ibstone (Bucks.), they were entirely lacking. But the number of common fields in a single parish varied greatly, and they tended to be numerous and small; at Codicote (Herts.) there were as many as twenty, at Berkhamsted (Herts.) even thirty or forty. In some places the common fields were divided into groups attached to particular hamlets but although a three-course rotation had become the norm throughout the hills by the mid-fourteenth century the cropping unit would be not one but several of these multiple fields which might lie in different parts of the township. Individual holdings were often concentrated in a small number of fields in the neighbourhood of the particular homestead, even though this might mean very uneven division between cropping units. This was practicable because everywhere much arable was held in closes which could be used to make up for uneven cropping in the common fields; probably nearly all holdings included some enclosed land and many, particularly manorial demesnes, were entirely enclosed. In the mid-fourteenth century there was a general distinction between closes on demesnes and those held by tenants: the former were very much larger, of 50 acres or more, whereas from 5 to 10 acres would be a normal size for a tenant's close. There remained substantial areas of woodland in the Chilterns, often interspersed with the arable, as well as much unenclosed waste in the form of heaths, where the soil was too poor for agriculture.[172]

Changes that occurred in the Chilterns in the late middle ages did not alter this general pattern. There was a little enclosure of common fields, mostly by manorial lords, but this was not for conversion to pasture. At Codicote (Herts.) in the late fifteenth century, presentments of tenants who had enclosed strips or blocks in the common fields foreshadowed a more general move towards enclosure in the sixteenth century. Consolidation of holdings through purchase and exchange probably paved the way to this enclosure both on demesnes and on tenants' lands; it certainly led to increasing irregularity in the size of common-field strip-holdings in the course of the later middle ages. Some local changes that occurred belonged simply to the existing pattern of agrarian organization in the Chilterns. Thus the subdivision of some common fields, as at Great and Little Missenden (Bucks.) and, probably, Berkhamsted (Herts.), reflects a certain fluidity and flexibility in field divisions. At Berkhamsted there was probably also subdivision of tenants' closes in this period, and this too accords with an established

[172] This paragraph is based on D. Roden, 'Studies in Chiltern field systems', London Univ. Ph.D. thesis, 1965, especially pp. 39–42, 189–90, 226–7, 248, 312–19, 323–5, 355–63; its conclusions for the medieval period are summarized in Baker and Butlin, eds., *Field Systems*, pp. 325–38. Some points are also drawn from D. Roden, 'Demesne farming in the Chiltern Hills', *AHR*, XVII, 1969, pp. 15, 18.

tendency to fragment and recombine lands without destroying the identity of the individual close. On the other hand the division of the large demesne closes into smaller units was a new and widespread development in this period; the details of the process are not known, though it may be connected with increasingly intricate cropping arrangements which sometimes led to spring and winter corn being sown side by side in the same demesne closes. Permanent contraction of arable cultivation was not a problem in the Chilterns, but what happened at Ibstone (Bucks.) in the 1350s is of interest: the amount of demesne land sown each year was reduced by about two-thirds, but instead of converting a proportionate part of the arable to permanent pasture the sown areas were apparently shifted from year to year within fields that mostly lay fallow, so as to follow a sort of outfield cultivation.[173] Arrangements not unlike this, involving a form of convertible husbandry with grass leys, may well have been common throughout the region, particularly in the parts away from the Chilterns where contraction of arable continued for the whole period.[174]

In the third division of the region, the lands south-east of the Chilterns, the field organization was very similar to that in the hills.[175] Thus there were common fields in all areas – they occur, for instance, at Ware (Herts.), Eton (Bucks.), and Sonning (Berks.) – and these were not the complete cropping units of the midlands, but the multiple fields of the Chilterns, with individual holdings concentrated in a particular area, not necessarily evenly distributed between the different courses.[176] Everywhere substantial amounts of land were held in closes, though the proportion varied a good deal. Thus at Cheshunt (Herts.) most of the arable seems to have lain in common fields; nearby, at Essendon (Herts.) the manor of Hornbeamgate consisted in 1468 almost entirely of individually owned fields and crofts, possibly in consequence of consolidation and enclosure; while at Stratfield Mortimer (Berks.) all tenants' lands apparently lay enclosed adjacent to the particular homestead.[177] Evidence of change during the present period is lacking,

[173] Roden, 'Studies', pp. 132–3, 136, 141–5, 147–8, 171–5, 222–4, 226, 227, 251–2, 312–15, 326–30, 342–6; Baker and Butlin, eds., Field Systems, pp. 328, 333, 336; D. Roden, 'Field systems in Ibstone', Records of Bucks., XVIII, 1966–70, pp. 50, 51.

[174] Cf. the existence of scattered strips under grass in the common fields at King's Walden (Herts.) in 1472–3 (Roden, 'Studies', p. 136).

[175] General descriptions of field systems in this area are given by Gray, English Field Systems, pp. 369–81, 384–6, and by D. Roden in Baker and Butlin, eds., Field Systems, pp. 338–45.

[176] Gray, English Field Systems, pp. 375, 385–6, 553–4; VCH Bucks., III, p. 274 (refers to "le Suthfelde").

[177] Gray, English Field Systems, pp. 376, 550 (the picture Gray gives from the Cheshunt survey of 1621–2 can be carried back to the middle ages by earlier surveys, of 1562 (Ms. in Cheshunt

but references to crofts lying in particular fields at Eton (Bucks.) in 1440 and at White Waltham (Berks.) in 1467 may point to recent enclosure, and certainly in the Lea valley there seems to have been some conversion of common fields to individually held closes in the fifteenth and early sixteenth centuries.[178] There are signs that a three-course rotation was normal in the relevant areas of Hertfordshire, a two-course one in Berkshire and Buckinghamshire.[179]

Looking at the distribution of crops throughout the region it is clear that wheat was everywhere the predominant winter-corn crop.[180] There are references to rye or maslin in Berkshire, Oxfordshire, and Buckinghamshire, but they are widespread only in the 1350s. It may be that it was generally grown as a peasant crop, and is recorded during those years because so many tenants' holdings were in their lords' hands; it is certainly for this reason that it appears on the manorial accounts of Cuxham (Oxon.) in this decade.[181] But on the demesne lands of West Wycombe (Bucks.) we find that maslin, which in the previous eight years had accounted for some two-thirds of the area sown with winter corn, suddenly in 1353–4 stopped being grown; it may well be that here and elsewhere reduced demand led to the cultivation of other crops instead on manors which had normally grown at least a proportion of rye.[182] After the 1350s references to rye and maslin all come from a single area, central and north-east Oxfordshire and north Buckinghamshire. In every case wheat was also grown, and was usually the more important crop; this was not the case, however, at Broughton (Oxon.), where it may be significant that the record is of corn grown by tenants, nor at the nearby Adderbury.[183]

Public Library) and c. 1500 (P. E. Rooke, 'Medieval Cheshunt: a rental of all the lands belonging to Henry Coote in the parish of Cheshunt about 1500', East Herts. Arch. Soc., XIII, 1950–4, pp. 172–203); K. R. Davis, 'An account of the excavations at Coldharbour Moat, in Friday Field, Essendon, Herts.', ibid., XI, 1940–4, pp. 22–5; note by F. Turner in Berks., Bucks. and Oxon. Arch. J., XXXV, 1931, p. 89.

[178] VCH Bucks., III, p. 274; VCH Berks., III, p. 175; P. D. Glennie, 'A commercializing agrarian region: late medieval and early modern Hertfordshire', Cambridge Univ. Ph.D. thesis, 1983, pp. 294–5.

[179] Levett, Studies in Manorial History, pp. 183–4 (Tyttenhanger in Ridge; Cashio); Gray, English Field Systems, p. 453 (Cookham); Raftis, Assart Data, p. 33 (Oak End in Hedgerley).

[180] This paragraph is based primarily on the tables of corn prices in J. E. T. Rogers, A History of Agriculture and Prices in England, 1259–1793, II, pp. 126–70, 176–7, 590–3; III, pp. 4–80, 687–8.

[181] Harvey, Medieval Oxfordshire Village, p. 130.

[182] Roden, 'Studies', pp. 444–6. Cottisford (Oxon.), where in 1391 wheat and maslin had replaced the rye formerly grown (VCH Oxon., VI, p. 110), might be another example of the same trend. The corn prices from the region, as recorded in Rogers, Agriculture and Prices, are not inconsistent with this explanation.

[183] Rogers, Agriculture and Prices: Whaddon (Bucks.) 1362–3, Steeple Claydon (Bucks.) 1364–5, Somerton (Oxon.) 1365–8, Tingewick (Bucks.) 1380–1, Tackley (Oxon.) 1400–1,

Turning to spring corn, barley was grown everywhere, either alone or – as on estates at Steeple Aston (Oxon.) and Penn (Bucks.) – only combined with oats as dredge. In late fifteenth-century Bedfordshire it seems to have been the most common of all corn crops, and it is interesting that when maslin stopped being grown on the demesne at West Wycombe its place was taken by increased sowings of barley as well as of wheat.[184] Pure oats were found nearly as widely. On some manorial demesnes in north-east Berkshire, central and north-east Oxfordshire, and northern Buckinghamshire we find oats being sown only with barley as dredge or not at all.[185] However, at Water Eaton (Bucks.) in 1394–5 we find tenants' renders of oats accounted for although none were sown on the demesne, and it may be that in this area they were cultivated largely as a peasant crop.[186] Leguminous crops – peas, beans (sometimes sown together as pulse), and vetch – appear on most manors; the proportion of demesne arable devoted to them varied a lot from one manor to another and on some this proportion was increasing, but the general increase found in the first half of the fourteenth century does not seem to have continued into this period.[187] On any one manor there was usually little change from one rotation to the next in what was grown and where, as can be illustrated by furlong names at South Newington (Oxon.), a two-field vill: Peas Breach, Bean Land, Barley Hill, Oat Hill.[188] Only in one part of the region was there a specialized local crop; this was in the extreme east of Hertfordshire, where saffron was grown in a district that extended into the neighbouring parts of Essex. However, at Sawbridgeworth, where it had been grown in large quantities in the fifteenth century, its cultivation was in decline by the early sixteenth.[189] Among non-field

Bicester (Oxon.) 1451–2; *VCH Oxon.*, VII, p. 13 (Chislehampton 1422); VIII, p. 159 (Pyrton 1387–8: *mixtum*); IX, p. 93 (Broughton); F. W. Ragg, 'Fragment of folio M.S. of archdeaconry courts of Buckinghamshire, 1491–1495', *Records of Bucks.*, XI, 1920–6, pp. 328–9 (Addington 1494); P. Hyde, 'The Winchester manors at Witney and Adderbury, Oxfordshire, in the later middle ages', Oxford Univ. B. Litt. thesis, 1955, pp. 319, 362–7.

[184] *VCH Oxon.*, XI, p. 35; Roden, 'Studies', pp. 444–6; Harvey, ed., *The Peasant Land Market*, p. 181.

[185] Brightwell and Harwell 1350–1453 (Farmer, 'Grain yields on the Winchester manors', p. 559n); Culham and Drayton 1355–6 (*Accounts of the Obedientiars of Abingdon Abbey*, ed. R. E. G. Kirk, Camden Soc., 2nd ser. LI, 1892, pp. 10–11); Stratton Audley 1409–10 (*VCH Oxon.*, VI, p. 328); Chislehampton 1422 (*ibid.*, VII, p. 13); cf. the debts in wheat, rye, and barley due at Addington in 1494 (Ragg, 'Fragment of folio M.S.', pp. 328–9) and the general decline in oats-growing in the Chilterns in the fourteenth century (Roden, 'Studies', pp. 279–80).

[186] E. Hollis, 'Farm accounts – late 14th century', *Records of Bucks.*, XII, 1927–33, pp. 182–6.

[187] Farmer, 'Grain yields on the Winchester manors', p. 564; D. Farmer, 'Grain yields on Westminster abbey manors, 1271–1410', *Canadian J. of History*, XVIII, 1983, pp. 340–1; C. Dyer in *AHEW*, II, p. 379.   [188] *VCH Oxon.*, XI, pp. 150, 151.

[189] *VCH Herts.*, III, p. 346; *East Herts. Arch. Soc.*, XII, 1945–9, p. 155; *VCH Essex*, II, p. 360.

crops it is interesting that vineyards are recorded not only at Abingdon abbey in the late fourteenth and early fifteenth centuries and at Windsor Castle in 1472 but also on humbler manorial establishments at Astwick (Beds.) in 1479 and, possibly, Great Wymondley (Herts.) in the late fourteenth century.[190]

It is possible to calculate yield ratios for arable crops on a number of manors (on most of which the gross yield would probably have been one-ninth larger, since tithe would have been taken from the corn in the field). Usually, however, the relevant information is available for relatively short periods of time: only the records of Westminster abbey and the bishops of Winchester are sufficiently continuous to give some confidence that the grain yields they document are not distorted by temporary circumstances, and at the same time to reveal any secular trends.[191] The mean yield ratios on the manors of these two estates have a wide range: for wheat from 2.21 (Islip, 1349–80) to 5.59 (Brightwell, 1381–1410), and with the Winchester manors in Berkshire generally doing well; for barley from 2.62 (Islip, 1349–80) to 6.97 (Kinsbourne, 1381–1410); and for oats from 1.96 (Islip, 1349–80) to 4.07 (Wargrave, 1411–53), although since this last figure is based on comparatively few entries the ratio of 3.71 at Adderbury in 1381–1410 may provide a better upper limit. Where the information is available, wheat and barley yields in 1411–53 were lower than they had been in 1381–1410. On the other hand, on rather more than half the Westminster and Winchester manors in the region, and especially in Berkshire and Hertfordshire, wheat yields were higher in 1381–1410 than they had been in the quarter century before the Black Death, as were barley yields at West Wycombe, Kinsbourne and Stevenage; and in some cases this continued an improvement of yields already evident in the

[190] *Accounts of the Obedientiars*, ed. Kirk, pp. 17, 52, 53, 55, 75; C. J. Bond, 'The reconstruction of the medieval landscape; the estates of Abingdon Abbey', *Landscape History*, I, 1979, p. 63; F. Madden, 'Narratives of the arrival of Louis de Bruges, Seigneur de la Gruthuyse, in England', *Archaeologia*, XXVI, 1836, p. 278; *VCH Beds.*, II, p. 203; F. B. Stitt, 'Manors of Great and Little Wymondley in the later middle ages', Oxford Univ. B.Litt. thesis, 1951, p. 32.

[191] Adderbury, Brightwell, Harwell, Ivinghoe, Moreton, Wargrave, West Wycombe, Witney: Farmer, 'Grain yields on the Winchester manors', p. 559. Aldenham, Islip, Kinsbourne, Stevenage, Turweston, Wheathampstead: *idem*, 'Grain yields on Westminster abbey manors', pp. 335–6 (figures year by year for Kinsbourne are in D. V. Stern, 'A Hertfordshire manor of Westminster abbey', London Univ. Ph.D. thesis, 1978, pp. 329–44). Cuxham: Harvey, *Medieval Oxfordshire Village*, p. 58 (deducting the allowance for tithe; figures year by year are in *Manorial Records of Cuxham, Oxfordshire, circa 1200–1359*, ed. P. D. A. Harvey, Oxon. Rec. Soc., L, and HMC, 1976, pp. 739–49). Great Wymondley (auditors' figures): Stitt, 'Manors of Great and Little Wymondley', p. 161. Higham Gobion: Godber, *History of Bedfordshire*, p. 94. Ibstone: Roden, 'Field systems in Ibstone', p. 49. Kintbury (auditors' figures): BL Add. Roll 49256. Knebworth: Roden, 'Demesne farming in the Chiltern Hills', p. 13.

period 1349–80. The explanation of these trends is seldom self-evident, although on the Westminster manors of Aldenham, Kinsbourne and Wheathampstead better than average yields appear to have been secured by sowing barley on the just fallowed winter-corn field.

Yields of oats on these estates, meanwhile, were higher on half the manors for which evidence is available in 1349–80 than they had been in the pre-Black Death generation, and were higher on all manors in 1381–1410 than they had been in 1349–80. This improvement, moreover, continued at Wargrave, Ivinghoe, and West Wycombe (the only manors from which information survives) in the period 1411–53.[192] In comparing one part of the region with another yield ratios for much shorter periods of time from manors on other estates are often reasonably compatible with those derived from the Westminster and Winchester estates. There are significantly high figures from places lying just below the Chiltern scarp, from Higham Gobion (Beds.), with wheat yields of 3.4 in the 1380s, to the even better results at Harwell with a yield ratio of 5.35 in the period 1349–80 – figures which tally with those for an earlier period, indicating that this was a particularly fertile area.[193] The short series of barley yields at Great Wymondley (Herts.) for 1352–6 and 1366–73, running as high as a six-fold return, likewise mirror the good barley yields Westminster abbey got on its Hertfordshire manors. At Cuxham (Oxon.) in the 1350s wheat yields, too, were not out of line with those in neighbouring places, but at 1.9 the yield ratio for oats was perhaps somewhat low; and the yield ratios achieved at Ibstone (Bucks.) in 1346–58 appear rather lower than those obtained over a longer period, except possibly for oats, on the Westminster and Winchester manors in the county. It must be remembered, however, that the figures for Cuxham and Ibstone derive from relatively short periods, which include the difficult years of the Black Death and its aftermath.

Some decrease in recorded yields may merely reflect a decline in manorial officers' honesty or in their lords' supervision. In 1367 Westminster abbey found that the acres of standing corn allotted to the manorial servants at Kinsbourne were twice as productive as the rest of the demesne. It has, however, been suggested that, at Kinsbourne and elsewhere, there is a direct correlation between medieval crop yields and the number of animals maintained on a manor, the land being

---

[192] Farmer, 'Grain yields on the Winchester manors', pp. 559–60; *idem*, 'Grain yields on Westminster abbey manors', pp. 334–6, 344.

[193] Titow, *Winchester Yields*, pp. 129–31; a notable exception was Moreton, where yields had always been low; cf. the contrast in yields throughout the period from the 1290s to the 1350s between Ibstone (in the Chilterns) and Cuxham (below the scarp): Roden, 'Field systems in Ibstone', p. 49; Harvey, *Medieval Oxfordshire Village*, p. 58.

chronically under-fertilized. The yields from the Westminster and Winchester manors do not support this view in this region, as on each demesne there seems nearly always to have been proportionately more livestock per acre sown than in 1325–49.[194] However, it is clear that animal manure was generally used and highly valued. Direct dunging from the sheepfold may have been the principal source. At Coleshill (Berks.) in 1383 it was ruled that a villein leasing out the pasture rights of a virgate to someone else should require a half-acre of arable to be well manured; at Cottisford (Oxon.), when the manor was being leased in 1391, there were 20 acres of fallow on the demesne, of which 12 acres were being ploughed for the third time and manured with the fold; fifteenth-century leases of Adderbury (Oxon.) rectory by New College, Oxford, required the lessee to put all dung on the demesne arable.[195] Other leases confirm that it was regular practice to manure either all the fallow or part of it (perhaps by rotation). At Berkhamsted (Herts.) in 1347 lands leased out included 89 acres of fallow ploughed three times, of which 18 acres had been manured from the sheepfold; at Bloxham (Oxon.) in 1431–2 the lessee was required at the end of the term to hand back the demesne in the West Field well fallowed by being ploughed three times and manured, while the requirement in the next lease, in 1435–6, was for the return of 20 acres well fallowed, 7 acres ploughed three times, and 29 acres manured.[196] Farmyard and other manure was also used; at Berkhamsted in 1347 and 1353 the castle and stables, as well as fallen leaves and droppings from the deer park, were mentioned as sources of supply. There is a reference to a pit being dug to take manure at Churchill (Oxon.) shortly before 1362.[197] Marling is hardly ever mentioned in this period, and this may have been too expensive a method of fertilizing at a time of high labour costs and low profit margins; at Kinsbourne (Herts.) there was some marling in the late fourteenth century, but the reaping works "called *marlure*" suggest that regular, more extensive, marling services had been replaced by extra works at harvest.[198]

[194] Stern, 'Hertfordshire manor', pp. 302–5; Titow, *Winchester Yields*, pp. 30–1; Farmer, 'Grain yields on Westminster abbey manors', pp. 341–2; *idem*, 'Grain yields on the Winchester manors', pp. 563–4.

[195] Harvey, ed., *The Peasant Land Market*, p. 172; *VCH Oxon.*, VI, p. 109; Hyde, 'Winchester manors at Witney and Adderbury', pp. 209–10.

[196] *Register of Edward the Black Prince*, 4 vols., HMSO, London, 1930–3, I, pp. 148–9; *VCH Oxon.*, IX, p. 66.

[197] *Register of Edward the Black Prince*, I, pp. 148–9; IV, p. 82; F. N. Macnamara, 'King John's palace at Little Langley, Oxfordshire', *Berks., Bucks. and Oxon. Arch. J.*, V, 1899–1900, pp. 44–5.

[198] Stern, 'Hertfordshire manor', pp. 135, 263–4. There are more references to marling in the region before the mid-fourteenth century (e.g. Roden, 'Demesne farming in the Chiltern Hills', p. 16).

The increased proportions of livestock on the demesnes of Westminster abbey and the bishop of Winchester typified a new emphasis on pastoral farming in the region, corresponding to the contraction of arable cultivation. Probably the only areas not affected were the Chiltern Hills, where there was little permanent change in the arable area, and perhaps the Berkshire Downs, already well supplied with flocks.[199] In a few places we can see this occurring as a deliberate new policy on a particular manorial demesne – as at Witney (Oxon.) in the 1350s, Coleshill (Berks.) in 1421, Islip (Oxon.) in 1340, and, perhaps, Wymondley (Herts.) in the 1330s or 1340s.[200] It is interesting that these last two cases occurred before 1350, recalling the evidence for a decline in arable before the start of our period. This swing to pastoral farming was based above all on sheep; although increases in flocks can be formally demonstrated only on relatively few manorial demesnes, there is much widespread evidence for sheep owning on every scale, from a few head to flocks of one or two thousand.[201] At the same time such towns as Banbury or Bedford developed as wool-collecting centres.[202] On estates that ran their manors by demesne farming, sale of wool was often organized centrally, not by the reeve or bailiff on the spot.[203] A corollary was that when demesnes were leased out sheep and their pastures might be excluded from the lease, continuing to be exploited directly by their estate owners; this was, for instance, the case at Coleshill and Woolstone (both Berks.).[204] However, lords who leased out their manors organized their flocks in various ways. The bishop of Winchester first leased out his demesne at Adderbury (Oxon.) in 1405 on a stock-and-land lease that included the manor's sheep, but in 1436 arranged that the lessee should look after a flock

---

[199] The statement in *VCH Berks.*, II, p. 170, that there was little sheep farming in the Vale of the White Horse is probably untrue of the later middle ages: cf. the growth of sheep farming at Coleshill (see above, ch. 2, G).

[200] Hyde, 'Winchester manors at Witney and Adderbury', pp. 173–4; Harvey, ed., *The Peasant Land Market*, p. 171; *VCH Oxon.*, VI, p. 213; Stitt, 'Manors of Great and Little Wymondley', pp. 77–8.

[201] E.g. Harvey, ed., *Peasant Land Market*, pp. 171–2 (Coleshill, Berks.), 180–1 (Bedfordshire); Ragg, 'Fragment of folio M.S.', pp. 63, 71 (Buckinghamshire); *VCH Herts.*, III, p. 174 (Weston); *VCH Oxon.*, VII, p. 133 (Great Milton). However, direct comparison with earlier periods can seldom be made, and we should not underestimate the number of sheep owners in the early fourteenth century; in 1297 at least one-third (probably rather more) of the peasants assessed for subsidy in Barford, Biggleswade, and Flitt hundreds (Beds.) owned sheep (*The Taxation of 1297*, ed. A. T. Gaydon, Beds. Hist. Rec. Soc., XXXIX, 1959, pp. xxx–xxxi).

[202] Godber, *History of Bedfordshire*, p. 118; *VCH Oxon.*, x, p. 62.

[203] E.g. at Wymondley (Herts.): Stitt, 'Manors of Great and Little Wymondley', p. 102.

[204] Latham, 'Decay of the manorial system', pp. 160–2; at Woolstone in 1440, however, sheep were included in the stock leased (Harvey, ed., *The Peasant Land Market*, p. 167).

belonging to the bishop, then in 1444 included 300 sheep in the lease again. At Witney (Oxon.), another manor of the bishop, leases of the demesne between 1398 and 1449 sometimes included some or all of the bishop's sheep there, sometimes not. Another example from northern Oxfordshire of a manorial lease that included sheep is at Cottisford in 1391, while at Upper Heyford in 1410 the manorial lord neither maintained nor leased out a demesne flock, so that sheep farming was entirely at the farmer's discretion. At Codicote (Herts.), St Albans abbey seems to have leased the sheep out separately from the rest of the manor. An account for Oseney abbey's centrally organized flocks in 1476–7 shows them divided between nine manors; breeding stock was kept on four or five of them and the others were for wool production only.[205]

Throughout the period some manorial tenants seem to have specialized in sheep farming, such as John and Thomas Marshal who were acquiring properties in Cuxham and Watlington (both Oxon.) in the 1350s, or the Pulker family of Cowley (Oxon.) in the fifteenth century; we even find sheep being hired, as at Blunham (Beds.) in 1432, where both parties were villagers, or at Spelsbury (Oxon.) in the early sixteenth century, where the churchwardens seem to have bought sheep as an investment simply in order to hire them out.[206] But probably most tenant sheep owners kept their small or substantial flocks simply as one element in a balanced mixed farm, such as the villein of King's Walden (Herts.), whose property in 1413 included 45 sheep, but also 4 plough horses, 8 cattle, 7 pigs, and, in his barn, stocks of wheat, barley, oats, and peas. The three pairs of shears found at Seacourt (Berks.) are a tangible relic of the small-scale sheep farming that was probably common in every part of the region. Almost certainly the object was normally the sale of wool, but at Great Gaddesden and Knebworth (both Herts.) in the late fourteenth century we find wethers being bought for fattening; here the London market for meat may have been important.[207] One interesting aspect of sheep farming was the provision of sheephouses; this was probably a practice of the west of England, and most of the cases recorded were in the west of

[205] *VCH Oxon.*, VI, pp. 110, 119; IX, p. 26; Hyde, 'Winchester manors at Witney and Adderbury', pp. 184–7; J. Amundesham, *Annales Monasterii S. Albani*, ed. H. T. Riley, Rolls Ser., 1870–1, II, p. 275; D. Postles, 'The Oseney abbey flock', *Oxoniensia*, XLIX, 1984, pp. 142–4, 146–52.

[206] Harvey, *Medieval Oxfordshire Village*, p. 138; *VCH Oxon.*, V, p. 86; A. C. Jones, 'The customary land market in Bedfordshire in the fifteenth century', Southampton Univ. Ph.D. thesis, 1975, p. 36n; J. Oldfield, 'A churchwarden's account book', *Berks., Bucks. and Oxon. Arch. J.*, XVI, 1910–11, pp. 10–11.

[207] Roden, 'Studies', pp. 118, 281; M. Biddle, 'The deserted medieval village of Seacourt, Berkshire', *Oxoniensia*, XXVI/XXVII, 1961–2, pp. 172–3.

Berkshire and Oxfordshire, but we find them being built also at Aston Abbots in central Buckinghamshire at the turn of the fourteenth century.[208]

Whereas the flocks and grazing grounds were often the last part of a manor to be put to farm by its lord, the opposite was true of the cows and poultry: by the mid-fourteenth century these were often being leased out even though the demesne as a whole was run by a reeve or bailiff. We find this, for instance, at Cuxham (Oxon.) from 1353–4 and at Water Eaton (Bucks.) in 1394–5.[209] In most of these cases the cows were simply a normal part of the demesne stock, but there were also landlords who built up specialized small dairy farms, as at Hitchin (Herts.) where in 1376 there were only two sheep on the demesne but twenty-nine cows. These dairy herds might be leased out as going concerns. This occurred at Wretchwick in Bicester (Oxon.) in the 1430s and at Essendon or Hatfield (Herts.) in 1475. The dairy herd at Rye House in Stanstead Abbots (Herts.) may be typical of others attached to large mansions which were otherwise not directly involved in farming; William Worcestre tells us that there were thirty cows there in 1454.[210] Cattle were also, of course, used for ploughing; on the Chilterns some ploughing was done by teams of horses, but on manorial demesnes elsewhere in the region mixed teams or (except in Hertfordshire) teams of oxen alone were used. Hertfordshire differed

[208] Brookend in Chastleton (T. H. Lloyd, 'Some documentary sidelights on the deserted Oxfordshire village of Brookend', *Oxoniensia*, xxix/xxx, 1964–5, p. 127); Milton-under-Wychwood (Macnamara, 'King John's palace', pp. 44–5); Shellingford (*Accounts of the Obedientiars*, ed. Kirk, p. 146); Coleshill (R. J. Faith, 'The peasant land-market in Berkshire during the later middle ages', Leicester Univ. Ph.D. thesis, 1962, p. 158 (*aula bidentium*); cf. pp. 44–7 for sheephouses just across the Wiltshire border at Eastrop in Highworth); Newton in Buckland (J. Brooks, 'The deserted medieval villages of north Berkshire', Reading Univ. Ph.D. thesis, 1982, pp. 250–1); Thomley (Holden, 'Deserted medieval village of Thomley', pp. 222–3). It was reported in 1517 that enclosers at Ardington and at Betterton in Lockinge had converted dwellings into sheephouses (Leadam, ed., *The Domesday of Inclosures*, I, pp. 115, 116). The sheephouses at Aston Abbots were put up under John de la Moote, abbot of St Albans in 1396–1401, whose mania for building was such that he might well have ordered houses for sheep in an area where no one else would think of building them (T. Walsingham, *Gesta Abbatum Monasterii Sancti Albani*, ed. H. T. Riley, RS, 1867–9, III, p. 444). This distribution of sheephouses in the region strongly supports D. Oschinsky's suggestion that the references to sheephouses in Walter of Henley's 'Husbandry' point to a western origin for the treatise or its author (*Walter of Henley*, ed. Oschinsky, pp. 183–4).

[209] Harvey, *Medieval Oxfordshire Village*, p. 74; Hollis, 'Farm accounts', p. 169. Ibstone (Bucks.) in 1351–2 and Wymondley (Herts.) throughout the fourteenth century provide further examples (Roden, 'Field systems in Ibstone', p. 56; Stitt, 'Manors of Great and Little Wymondley', pp. 57, 101).

[210] R. L. Hine, *The History of Hitchin*, London, 1927–9, I, p. 38; *VCH Oxon.*, VI, p. 28; C. E. Johnston, 'A collector's account of 1475 for Bedwell, Little Berkhamstead and Lowthes', *East Herts. Arch. Soc.*, IV, 1908–11, pp. 190–7; *William Worcestre, Itineraries*, ed. J. H. Harvey, pp. 47–8.

from the rest of the region in that (as in Essex) some two-thirds of demesne draught animals were horses in 1350–1420; in the other four counties the proportion was about one-third, having risen in Berkshire and Oxfordshire from about one-quarter in 1250–1320.[211] Among tenants' draught animals the proportion of horses was probably a good deal higher than on manorial demesnes, but there is likely to have been much local variation and throughout the period there is no difficulty in finding manorial tenants who owned oxen; thus oxen were among the animals making up a virgate's customary stint for pasture at Great and Little Milton (Oxon.) in 1500.[212] J. Langdon's recent analysis of plough types in 1350–1420 shows that in this region wheeled ploughs barely extended north of the Chilterns, foot ploughs were mostly used in north Buckinghamshire, north Oxfordshire, and along the middle Thames, and swing ploughs mostly appeared north of the Chilterns, no example being found in Berkshire. Among cart types, the heavy, often ox-hauled, vehicles called *carri* or *plaustra* in the records do not appear in the region – only the common light farm carts called *carecte*.[213] Pigs, found everywhere in the region, were possibly of particular importance where woodland was available for pannage.[214] Of other livestock it is of interest that on the manor of the Argentein family at Wymondley (Herts.) a heronry was started in the 1350s, a swannery in the 1360s.[215]

Despite the apparent new emphasis on sheep farming, the region was primarily a corn-producing area throughout the period. This is borne out by the number of large and substantial barns that were built; some still stand. They figure prominently in the astonishing list of building works undertaken by John de la Moote in his five years as abbot of St Albans (1396–1401): he was responsible for about a dozen new ones on the abbey estates, several of them being described as *optima* or even *incomparabilis*. They probably included two still standing at Kingsbury in St Albans and at Croxley that are almost identical in plan and construction, though different in size.[216] A further eight barns were

[211] Langdon, *Horses, Oxen and Technological Innovation*, pp. 88, 96–7, 100, 102–4 (cf. pp. 164–8, where the adoption of all-horse farming at West Wycombe in the early fourteenth century is examined in detail), 108–11; Roden, 'Studies', pp. 118, 119, 220–1, 282, 330; Roden, 'Field systems in Ibstone', p. 48.

[212] Langdon, *Horses, Oxen and Technological Innovation*, pp. 197–8, 211; *VCH Oxon.*, VII, p. 133.   [213] Langdon, *op. cit.*, pp. 128–41, 142–53.

[214] E.g. *VCH Oxon.*, V, p. 119; Roden, 'Studies', p. 282.

[215] Stitt, 'Manors of Great and Little Wymondley', pp. 101–2.

[216] Walsingham, *Gesta Abbatum Monasterii Sancti Albani*, III, pp. 441–7; S. A. Castle, 'The medieval aisled barns at Kingsbury manor farm, St Albans, and Croxley Hall Farm', *Herts. Archaeology*, III, 1973, pp. 134–8 (barns at Kingsbury and Croxley are among those listed by Walsingham). Other barns still (or until recently) standing on the St Albans abbey estates are described by: O. J. Weaver, 'A medieval aisled barn at St Julian's Farm, St Albans', *Herts. Archaeology*, II, 1970, pp. 110–12; S. A. Castle, 'The aisled barn at Parsonage Farm, Abbots

built by a later abbot, John Whethamstede (1420–40 and 1452–65).[217] Barns elsewhere include one built by Winchcomb abbey at Church Enstone (Oxon.), dated 1382 in a surviving inscription, and those built in the fifteenth century by Cholsey and Abingdon abbeys close to the monasteries themselves at Cholsey and Shippon (both Berks.). Two barns put up at Little Langley in Shipton-under-Wychwood (Oxon.) in 1352 are described as timber-built. At Seacourt (Berks.) it seems that the threshed grain was stored in granaries raised above the ground on wood or staddle-stones.[218]

H. KENT AND SUSSEX

P. F. Brandon, in his study of the husbandry of Battle abbey and other Sussex estates in the late fourteenth century, stressed both its innovative quality and its efficiency.[219] Distinguished by the use of legumes as a partial alternative to fallow and the thick sowing of crops, these estates produced high yields per acre. Similar methods were followed on many Kent estates, especially those belonging to the archbishop of Canterbury and his cathedral priory of Christ Church. In addition great lords, in both areas, practised convertible husbandry – taking the plough round the pasture – thus tapping the stored fertility of land that had lain under grass for several years. But, as Brandon himself realized, such husbandry was expensive. "High cultivation costs were profitable only in districts where the demand for grain was high."[220] By the mid-fifteenth century, as the population continued to fall, demand dropped, and, with its fall, grain prices slumped. In many places the area under cultivation contracted. Under the new circumstances, some lords modified or abandoned earlier practices.

The exceedingly high seeding rates were cut back almost everywhere. On some of the archiepiscopal estates, the reduction occurred in the immediate post-plague year, 1349–50, and elsewhere the density of sowing decreased some time in the late fourteenth or early fifteenth centuries.[221] On some Battle abbey estates the reduction of seeding densities accompanied the introduction of new measures, which makes

Langley', *ibid.*, III, 1973, pp. 131–4; A. V. B. Gibson, 'The medieval aisled barn at Parkbury Farm, Radlett: thirteenth century rafters re-used', with O. J. Weaver, 'A note on the history of Parkbury', *ibid.*, IV, 1974–6, pp. 158–64.

[217] Amundesham, *Annales Monasterii S. Albani*, II, pp. 199–200, 262–3, 273.

[218] R. B. Wood-Jones, 'The rectorial barn at Church Enstone', *Oxoniensia*, XXI, 1956, pp. 43–7; W. Horn, 'The great tithe barn of Cholsey, Berkshire', *J. of the Soc. of Archit. Historians*, XXII, 1963, pp. 13–23; Bond, 'Reconstruction of the medieval landscape', pp. 65, 66; Macnamara, 'King John's palace', pp. 44–5; Biddle, 'Deserted medieval village of Seacourt', p. 108.

[219] Brandon, 'Cereal yields', pp. 403–20.   [220] *ibid.*, p. 410.

[221] F. R. H. Du Boulay, *The Lordship of Canterbury*, p. 211.

it difficult to determine the extent of the change. But at Apuldram the changes in seeding rates appear to be independent of any changes in measures and the reduction is clear. Wheat, which had been sown at three bushels an acre, was sown at two bushels an acre after 1427, and barley was sown at four bushels instead of six.[222] Although the Christ Church monks, on their home farm of Barton in the early fifteenth century, were still sowing at the traditional high rates of four bushels an acre for wheat and six bushels an acre for barley and oats, by the 1440s seeding rates had become variable. Wheat fluctuated between three and four bushels an acre, barley between four and five bushels an acre and oats between five and six bushels an acre.[223] Lay lords, like the Pelhams, were also willing to vary rates, sowing wheat sometimes at two bushels and sometimes at three bushels, and oats sometimes at four bushels and sometimes at five bushels.[224] The reasons for these changes are hidden and one can only hazard a guess. But high ratios of seed produced high yields per acre. Even though a large quantity of grain was required for seed, there was still plenty left over for sale and other purposes. By the mid-fifteenth century, however, grain prices had fallen, so any surplus that was sold produced low revenues. Thus the incentive to produce extra for the market was lessened. Lords may have decided that lower seeding rates could still produce sufficient grain for household needs and modest sales. None the less, despite the widespread reductions, grain continued to be sown throughout most of Kent and Sussex at higher rates than elsewhere. There wheat was frequently sown at three bushels an acre, barley at four bushels an acre, and oats at four or five bushels an acre, whereas in much of the country seeding rates of one and a half to two bushels for wheat, and two and a half to three bushels for oats and barley were quite common. The seeding rates adopted in Kent and Sussex were now more in line with those of other regions, but the differences had merely been lessened, and not eliminated.

The extensive use of legumes – a characteristic of arable husbandry in Kent and Sussex from the mid-thirteenth century – was also cut back in some parts of Sussex during the course of the fifteenth century. On the Battle abbey estates in the late fourteenth century, between one-third and one-half of the total arable acreage was under a continuous sequence of crops. This intensive cultivation was made possible by diligent deep ploughing with turn-wrest ploughs, by folding the sheep nightly on the arable, and by sowing legumes on land that would

[222] Brandon, 'Cereal yields', pp. 411–12.

[223] Cathedral Archives and Library, Canterbury, *Caruca Bertona* rolls.

[224] Oats, for example, were sown at 4 bushels an acre in 1421–2 and 1446–7, and at 5 bushels an acre in 1409–10 and 1437–8. BL Add. Rolls 32145, 32154, 32196, 32239.

otherwise have lain fallow.[225] The Battle monks, however, were probably not aware of the fertilizing properties of these legumes.[226] Peas and vetch were used primarily for forage – for fattening pigs, for feeding horses, and occasionally cows and ewes as well. But in the course of the fifteenth century both the area under cultivation and the size of the sheep flocks and cow herds were cut back, thus producing more pasture for fewer beasts. Thus it is exceedingly likely, but by no means certain, that the monks decided to sow fewer legumes because they had less need for supplementary forage. At Lullington the reduction occurred gradually. In the late fourteenth century an average of 40 acres of legumes was sown. This was cut back to 25 acres in the early fifteenth century and to 10 acres in the 1430s (a decade of bad weather and rampant sheep disease). In the 1440s as sheep flocks were temporarily rebuilt, the legume acreage went back to an average of 18 acres, but it dropped back in the 1450s to 10 acres and in the last three accounts of the 1460s just 5, 2, and 4 acres were sown. At Alciston the fluctuations were somewhat similar, but not identical, as the bailiff responded to different local conditions. In the late fourteenth century an average of 75 acres of legumes was sown (18.7 per cent of the total acreage). This was cut in half in the early fifteenth century, before rising in the 1440s to an average of 43 acres (16 per cent of the total acreage). In the late 1460s, as the total acreage contracted producing more pasture, so the legume acreage began to drop sharply, reaching its lowest point in the mid-1470s, when just 12 acres were sown (6.8 per cent of the area under cultivation). Then, as more land was brought under the plough in the 1480s and 1490s the area under legumes increased again, and in the last accounts an average of 30 acres was sown (11.49 per cent of the total acreage).

With so few demesne accounts available, it is hard to say to what extent the Battle abbey experience was typical or atypical, but on the lay manor of Chalvington, owned by the Sackvilles, a similar reduction in the area under legumes did take place.[227] In the late fourteenth century roughly one-quarter of the total acreage was sown with beans. These formed part of the grain livery of the *famuli* on the manor and any not needed for that were used to fatten pigs or sold. In the late 1420s the acreage under cultivation was halved. The ploughmen were hired by the day and paid a money wage and the one *famulus* of husbandry who was hired by the year received all his grain livery in oats. With less need for beans, fewer were sown, with percentages fluctuating between 10 and 18.5 per cent. But in the last surviving

[225] Brandon, 'Cereal yields', p. 406.

[226] For a discussion of this point, see M. Mate, 'Medieval agrarian practices: the determining factors', *AHR*, XXXIII, 1985, pp. 22–31.   [227] East Sussex RO, SAS CH251–85.

account, in 1444–5, the bailiff sowed 60 acres of oats and 2 acres of peas, with no beans at all. In future years the acreage under legumes may have increased, but, if the experience of the Battle manors was in any way typical, then the level of the late fourteenth century was probably not regained.

In Kent, as in Sussex, legumes constituted a significant part of the total area under the plough in the late fourteenth and early fifteenth century. The percentage obviously varied from place to place, but ranged from 21 per cent of the total acreage on the Battle abbey manor of Wye, through 24 and 25 per cent on the lay manors of Lymingsbourne and Bekesbourne, to 29 per cent on the Christ Church marsh manor of Elvington, and 34 per cent on its east Kent manor of Monkton.[228] Unfortunately all these accounts are isolated ones, so it is very difficult to determine what changes, if any, took place over the century as a whole. But for the Christ Church home farm of Barton there is a fairly continuous series of accounts and there the percentage does not change. Each year, from the earliest accounts through to the 1460s, between 20 and 25 per cent of the total acreage was sown with vetch, peas, or beans. In the case of the peas and beans, these crops went to feed the plough horses and cart horses and in some years nothing was kept for seed. The serjeant bought the necessary seed from outside. Horses, unlike oxen, are grain rather than grass consumers. Thus any manor which housed a significant number of horses would not be able to sustain them with any increased pasture that became available, but would still need to grow oats or legumes for forage. Thus on those manors, like Barton, where the prime reason behind the sowing of legumes was the need to provide horse fodder, it probably continued throughout the century.

By the mid-thirteenth century, manors in Kent were relying on horse power to a far greater extent than those in Sussex. John Langdon, in his sample of demesne manors, found that in Kent, for the whole period 1250–1420, there were approximately as many work horses as oxen. In contrast, in Sussex, in the period 1250–1320, the percentage of work horses to oxen was just 11.3 per cent and it increased only slightly, to 18.4 per cent, in the period 1350–1420.[229] But these figures hide considerable variation even within a county. Some Kent estates, by the fifteenth century, relied totally on horse power. In 1434–5 the manor of Lymingsbourne, belonging to John Doget, contained no oxen, but thirteen horses.[230] When Christ Church manors were in hand, in the

---

[228] For Lymingsbourne and Bekesbourne see BL Harl. Rolls Z3 and S11. The Christ Church material can be found in the beadle's rolls.

[229] Langdon, *Horses, Oxen and Technological Innovation*, p. 88 (Table 11).

[230] BL Harl. Roll Z3.

early fifteenth century, they usually contained four cart horses and six to twelve plough horses, depending on the number of ploughs. On their home farm of Barton, however, they frequently had as many as eight cart horses and sometimes two pack-horses, in addition to the six to eight horses used to pull their three ploughs. These were all prime animals, for when the horses became too old or sick for useful work they were sold and replaced with new stock. Moreover, the Christ Church monks were willing to pay high prices – an average in mid-century of 26s. for a cart horse and 18s. for a plough horse. Such animals were obviously very sturdy and seem to have been combined in two-horse ploughteams.[231]

In contrast, in Sussex, oxen were still used throughout the fifteenth century not only for ploughing but, in many places, for hauling as well. The one agricultural operation that was clearly performed by horses was harrowing. Oats were frequently fed to horses while they were harrowing and at Chalvington, when the lord hired tenants with their equipment to work for him, he always hired a harrower "with a horse", although in one instance he hired someone with two mares.[232] Ploughing, on the other hand, seems to have been done primarily with oxen, in large teams. Since oxen, however, frequently ended up on the lord's table, the presence of a large number of oxen on any one manor is not necessarily a guarantee of their use for ploughing. They could be there to be fattened before slaughter. Thus, on the Battle abbey manor of Alciston the number of oxen left over each year could fluctuate markedly from year to year, for example, from thirty-six to fifty-four beasts. In addition, in the early fifteenth century, the bailiff regularly kept nine horses on the manor, so it is possible that the five ploughs were drawn by mixed teams of horses and oxen. Elsewhere, on the other Battle abbey manors, a ten-oxen ploughteam seems to have been quite common, although, as at Alciston, manors frequently housed more oxen and horses than were immediately needed for ploughing. Apuldram, for example, in the 1440s, was handed over to a tenant with one plough, five horses, and sixteen oxen. Lay estates followed similar practices. The clearest evidence comes from the Pelham manor of Laughton, where, in 1409–10, the free tenants carried out thirty-five works of ploughing, using seven ploughs, "each plough with ten oxen".[233] At Chalvington, in 1293–4, with one plough, there were ten

---

[231] The number of plough horses remaining at the end of the year obviously varied, sometimes 6, sometimes 7, and sometimes 8. Unless one of the more expensive cart horses was occasionally used for ploughing, it is hard to see how the three ploughs could have been in operation simultaneously using more than two horses. In the mid-fifteenth century the national price level for a plough horse was 10s. 8d.: Farmer, 'Crop yields, prices and wages', p. 144.

[232] East Sussex RO, SAS CH280.   [233] BL Add. Roll 32145.

oxen and one mare. By the mid-fourteenth century the manor was keeping three to four mares, partly for breeding but also for work, for in 1346–7 all the mares aborted with the heavy labour of marling. At the end of the fourteenth century, when two ploughs were in operation, the manor had 21 oxen, but, as the acreage contracted in the fifteenth century, the second plough was abandoned and the complement of oxen dropped to 12–14 beasts. By the 1440s, however, the ploughing was all being done by hired labourers, who provided their own ploughs and beasts. Thus in the last account there were just two oxen on the manor, presumably used for hauling, for at the time of the harvest some of the grain was carried in the *plaustrum* (wain) of the lord.[234]

The continued use of oxen for hauling in Sussex was a considerable anomaly. By the end of the fifteenth century, 65–70 per cent of demesne hauling, across the country, was being performed by horses yet in Sussex very few demesnes had made the switch. Moreover, as far as can be ascertained, oxen continued to be used throughout the fifteenth century, with lords buying new *plaustra* when old ones broke. An ox, however, was able to make up for its slow speed by its ability to carry a heavier load. Thus, it is not surprising that when the nuns of Syon abbey needed additional resources in the mid-fifteenth century, to carry a large amount of timber from their manor of Worminghurst to their house at Kingston, they spent £17 15s. 5d. on the purchase of both oxen and *plaustra*.[235] At a time when pasture was plentiful it made sound economic sense for both peasants and lords to use oxen for most hauling tasks. None the less horses were being used to carry light loads over long distances. When in the 1440s the Sackvilles hired tenants to carry for them, they used ox-drawn wains for carrying grain from the fields to the barn and from one manor to another, but for the carriage of salt, herrings, and salt-fish from the coast at Seaford to the manor of Chalvington, they hired a man with a cart (*biga*) and a mare.[236] The horse, with its greater speed, could do the journey in less time.

With less land under cultivation, cropping patterns on the Battle abbey Sussex manors became extremely flexible. At Alciston, in the late fourteenth century, the main part of the demesne land lay in severalty in unenclosed blocks of land contiguous with the common fields and was cultivated fairly continuously. In addition there was a group of intermittently cultivated fields that were generally under

---

[234] John Langdon has argued convincingly that *plaustra* were heavy, two-wheeled vehicles, larger and wider than carts, and pulled by oxen: *Horses, Oxen and Technological Innovation*, pp. 151–6.   [235] *Ibid.*, pp. 115, 147, fig. 39; PRO SC 6/1037/5.
[236] East Sussex RO, SAS CH280.

Table 3.15. *Rotation of crops at Barton (Kent), 1444–8 (in acres)*

	1444–5	1445–6	1446–7	1447–8
Bartonfield	15½ peas	5 oats, 39 wheat	73 barley	10 beans, 19 barley
Bishopfield	38 barley	4½ beans, 17½ vetch, 15 peas	36 wheat	26 barley
Chelefield	42 wheat	42 barley	10 vetch, 23 peas	42 wheat
Paverigge	24 barley	28 barley, 8 wheat	32 barley	28 barley
Bagbury	5 barley	5 barley	fallow	5 barley
Hecchescroft	14 wheat	13 barley	3½ oats, 7 beans, 1½ barley	13 wheat
Les Vines	4 oats, 13 peas, 3 rods beans	14 oats	11 barley, 8 wheat	18 oats
Gravelpit	fallow	4 oats	3 peas	fallow
Torolcroft	fallow	8 peas, 6 beans	2 beans, 6 wheat	6 beans, 5 oats, 8 barley, 5 wheat

pasture but were tilled occasionally and sown with oats and legumes.[237] This system is analogous to the infield–outfield system existing on the Kent manor of Westerham.[238] In the fifteenth century some of the fields that had been cropped so intensely earlier reverted to out-field status and were sown just occasionally. Other fields dropped out of cultivation altogether. Even the infields were cropped less intensely and frequently remained fallow or with just a small sowing of legumes for two or even three years before being sown again. As the century progressed, the length of time between sowings increased. One field, in the early fifteenth century, followed the rotation: wheat / barley/ fallow-legumes / fallow-legumes / wheat / fallow-legumes / wheat / barley / fallow / fallow-legumes / barley / fallow-legumes / fallow / fallow / fallow-legumes / wheat. The crops that were sown were scattered. Thus, in 1409–10, 122 acres of barley were sown in nine different fields. Furthermore, as tenant land came into the hands of the lord for lack of takers, it was utilized for demesne crops. In 1413–14,

[237] P. F. Brandon, 'Arable farming in a Sussex scarp foot parish during the late Middle Ages', *Sussex Arch. Colls.*, C, 1962, pp. 60–72. See also Brandon, 'Cereal yields', pp. 406–7, and Baker and Butlin, eds., *Field Systems*, pp. 425–9.

[238] T. A. M. Bishop, 'The rotation of crops at Westerham, 1297–1350', *EcHR*, IX, 1938–9, pp. 38–44.

for example, some of the demesne barley was sown "in the wist of John Colyn".[239] Clearly by the fifteenth century land at Alciston was being rested for far longer periods than had been the case in the late fourteenth century. In contrast, on the Battle abbey manor of Apuldram, the reverse situation occurred. There, as the area under cultivation contracted, the wheat, barley, and legumes were sown in just one field, the Homefield, which was cropped continuously. In 1428–9, for example, the Homefield was sown with 24 acres of peas and vetch, 48 acres of barley, and 52 acres of wheat.[240] The field was probably large enough that some land lay fallow each year, and it is quite likely that the bailiff practised a rotation within the field, sowing wheat on the patch that had been sown with legumes the year before. None the less the land was clearly under fairly continuous use. Oats, on the other hand, were usually sown on outlying patches that most of the time were under pasture. In 1421–2, for example, 20 acres of oats were sown in Boriscroft and 20 acres in Mellefield. In 1422–3 the pasture of Boriscroft was leased for 4s. and in 1423–4 the pasture of Mellefield was leased for 6s.[241]

Similar flexibility was used in the fifteenth century in the cropping arrangements on the Christ Church manor of Barton (see Tables 3.15 and 3.16). Some fields, such as Bishopfield and Chelefield, followed a standard three-course rotation – wheat/barley/legumes – with the legumes replacing the fallow, and they appear to have been continually cultivated throughout the century. Other fields, such as Bagbury, were cultivated equally intensely, but were sown primarily with barley, with just an occasional year of fallow or legumes. Moreover Bagbury was not cultivated at all before 1434–5 and was probably pasture until then. Similarly Paverigge had been sold as pasture for 2s. 6d. in 1431–2 but in the 1440s was sown every year with barley. By the early 1450s, however, the field was being used less intensely and lay fallow, with just a small inhoking of legumes for several years in succession. Other patches such as Les Vines were also continually cultivated, but primarily with legumes and oats. As the century progressed, fields like Bagbury, Paverigge and Les Vines probably reverted to pasture and were cropped just intermittently. For there seems to have been a definite pattern of bringing land into cultivation for a few years and then allowing it to rest and recover its fertility. Bartonfield, for example, had been cultivated intensely in the early part of the fifteenth century. In the period 1406–39 (with nine scattered accounts) the average area under the plough was 66½ acres. In mid-century it was still

---

[239] East Sussex RO, SAS G44/67, G44/70.   [240] PRO SC 6/1017/25.
[241] PRO SC 6/1017/17, 1017/18, 1017/20.

Table 3.16. *Rotation of crops at Barton (Kent), 1451–4 (in acres)*

	1451–2	1452–3	1453–4
Bartonfield	18 barley	36 barley	fallow
Bishopfield	36 barley	36 wheat	36 barley
Chelefield	fallow	14 vetch, 11 barley	42 wheat
Paverigge	3 vetch	14 peas	8 vetch, 32 barley
Bagbury	5 barley	5 barley	9 vetch
Hecchescroft	fallow	$5\frac{1}{2}$ peas, 8 beans, $\frac{1}{2}$ barley	$13\frac{1}{2}$ wheat
Les Vines	11 peas	12 oats	12 oats
Gravelpit	5 barley	fallow	fallow
Torolcroft	42 oats, 8 beans, 8 barley	8 wheat	fallow

Source: Cathedral Archives and Library, Canterbury, *Caruca Bertona* rolls.

occasionally all ploughed (73 acres of barley were sown in 1446–7 and 78 acres of wheat in 1463–4), but most years it was just partially used or left fallow. In addition to these infields, which were cultivated even if only partially on a fairly regular basis, the manor contained a large number of outfields. In 1452–3 the serjeant sowed oats, peas, and barley on seven small patches, not one of which had been cultivated in the 1440s.

Although the evidence is very sparse, some form of convertible husbandry with frequent recuperative breaks appears to have been fairly common throughout the region. At Ticehurst, in the Weald, a contract from the late fifteenth century prohibited the ploughing of meadows in the last two years of a seven-year lease. Similarly at Barnhorne, in the coastal marshes, the plough clearly moved around the farm. A field was sown for a few years until it was exhausted and then it reverted to grass, while new pasture was turned over. But there, as in so many other places, the infields, which received the bulk of the manure, were cropped fairly continuously. Some of the outfields, however, remained primarily pasture and were just turned every ten or so years. Other patches, as at Barton, were cropped for three to five years in succession and then left to recuperate for a similar period.[242]

[242] Brandon, 'Agriculture and the effects of floods at Barnhorne', pp. 74–6.

The land was kept in good heart by manuring and folding the sheep on the fields at night. Even when manors were leased out, the leases sometimes stipulated that all manure and straw waste from demesne barns was to be used for composting the demesne lands and that sheep pasturing on the demesne pasture of the manor should be folded on the demesne lands there.[243] Marling clearly continued on tenant land, but became less common on demesne land, as fields were cultivated less intensely. On the Battle abbey manor of Lullington, on at least one occasion, sand was carried from the sea, presumably to mix with the soil.[244] The Christ Church monks at Barton were also prepared to pay more to buy seed from outside the manor. In 1467–8 they bought 2 qr 4 lb of wheat at Sandwich "for seed" and 13 qr of wheat at Calais "for seed".[245] In addition the Christ Church monks spent £8 to £10 a year maintaining the Barton ploughs and carts. This is three to four times what was spent on the maintenance of Battle abbey equipment, and suggests that the Christ Church vehicles may have been superior in construction. The money, however, appears to have been well spent, for by the 1440s these demesne ploughs and carts were being leased to tenants and the revenues (roughly £10 a year) equalled or exceeded the cost of maintenance.

The high grain yields at Barton show the success of these methods. In the early fifteenth century, however, the priory paid both the threshers and reapers in grain – the latter receiving a share of every tenth sheaf harvested. Thus, although the money paid for harvesting was low – 20s. to 30s. a year for food – the siphoning of grain to harvest workers meant that the net yields received by the monks were not outstanding (roughly 3 × seed for wheat, $2\frac{1}{2}$ × seed for barley and $1\frac{1}{2}$ × seed for oats). It is not until the mid-1440s, when reaping was paid for in money and the wages of the threshers were included in the grain receipts, that it is possible to determine more precisely the productivity of the soil. Unfortunately at the same time seeding rates became variable, so that unless one has consecutive accounts it is impossible to calculate the exact yield per seed, but the range was five to six times the seed. The yields per acre (see Table 3.17) equalled those received on the most productive estates in eastern Norfolk.[246]

The highest yield was that for oats in 1445–6, when, as the serjeant noted, he received 4 qr 4 b. an acre. The year before he had sown 23

---

[243] Lambeth Palace Library, CM XX (lease of Westwell).

[244] PRO SC 6/1027/3.

[245] The wheat bought at Calais cost 7s. 2d. a quarter, whereas their own wheat was selling for 6s. 8d. a quarter: Cathedral Archives and Library, Canterbury, *Caruca Bertona* roll 33.

[246] Campbell, 'The regional uniqueness of English field systems?', p. 21; *idem*, 'Agricultural progress in medieval England', p. 31.

Table 3.17. *Grain yields per acre on the Christ Church manor of Barton (Kent), 1444–72 (in bushels)*

Year	Wheat	Barley	Oats
1444–5	15.33	25.51	14.90
1445–6	11.25	26.49	36.63
1446–7	17.54	22.77	28.28
1447–8	14.62	17.12	18.00
1451–2	13.60	28.86	18.35
1452–3	21.63	21.31	20.03
1453–4	15.81	29.44	18.32
1463–4	11.89	19.18	15.61
1470–1	14.51	23.50	25.00
1471–2	12.57	19.55	26.93

acres of oats at five bushels an acre in four different patches – 8 acres of land next to the aqueduct, 8 acres next to the gate, 3 acres in Middlecroft, and 4 acres in Les Vines. The first three patches were not in general cultivation and had probably lain fallow or been used as pasture for some time. Thus one reason for these high yields could be that the oats were grown on virgin soil, or at least land that had been rested for long periods. But the weather could also have been kind that year, for when the Barton serjeant sold 71 qr of these oats he received just 19d. a quarter. This suggests that plenty of oats were available in the neighbourhood and that other farmers must also have had good yields.

The importance of weather in determining yields is also suggested by an analysis of grain yields on the Battle abbey manor of Alciston in the fifteenth century (see Table 3.18). Weather patterns that were disastrous for one grain frequently allowed another grain to flourish. Thus the 1420s produced low barley yields but exceedingly high oats yields. Similarly the low barley and oats yields of the 1460s were counterbalanced by some of the best wheat yields of the century. Moreover, the minimum and maximum figures indicate just how flattening the averages can be. Barley yields fluctuated from under twice the seed to over five times, and oats yields from under twice to over nine times the seed. It is, however, hard to agree with the assessment of P. F. Brandon that "at Alciston the yields of wheat and barley were in marked and persistent regression for most of the fifteenth century".[247] Barley, according to Brandon's calculation, had

[247] Brandon, 'Cereal yields', p. 413.

Table 3.18. Net yields of barley, oats, and wheat per seed at Alciston (Sussex), 1399–1492[a]

	Barley			Oats			Wheat		
	Average	Minimum	Maximum	Average	Minimum	Maximum	Average	Minimum	Maximum
1399–1421	3.35	2.24	5.14	4.91	3.72	7.82	4.37	3.60	4.74
1422–1432	2.90	1.89	3.88	6.03	3.80	9.16	3.61	2.75	4.67
1433–1441	3.28	2.43	4.91	3.95	2.00	7.02	3.44	3.16	3.71
1442–1460	3.23	2.56	3.76	4.11	2.00	7.50	4.89	3.32	6.39
1461–1476	2.96	1.82	4.38	2.87	1.90	3.88	3.18	2.35	3.67
1477–1479	3.06	1.75	5.04	4.52	3.50	5.41			
1480–1492	2.57	2.07	3.06	3.06	2.40	3.70	4.32	3.06	5.68

Source: East Sussex RO, SAS G44/54–132.
[a] After deducting one-tenth for wages.

Table 3.19. *Grain yields at Apuldram (Sussex), 1420–59*

	Wheat per acre	Wheat per seed	Barley per acre	Barley per seed	Oats per acre	Oats per seed
1420s	6.77	2.25	11.72	2.93	8.38	2.09
1430s	10.53	5.26	15.68	3.92	14.67	3.66
1440s	9.04	4.52	13.58	3.39	19.26	4.81
1450s	10.06	5.33	13.50	3.37	16.80	4.20

yielded 2.77 × seed in the period 1356–73 and exceeded that ratio in most years of the following century. Wheat produced just as well in the 1460s as it had done in the late fourteenth century. If the poor harvest of 1461–2 is excluded from the calculation, the average wheat yield in the 1460s was 5.15 × seed (with six accounts) compared to a yield ratio of 5.11 in the period 1376–93. Oats, on the other hand, did not show "the marked improvement...throughout the fifteenth century" that Brandon postulated, but fluctuated rather wildly from year to year.

Figures for yields per acre, however, reflected the size of the bushel in use, which might and often did change over time. At Alciston, in the early fifteenth century, the yields per acre were comparable to those received at Barton – 13.01 bushels for wheat, 20.9 bushels for barley and 23.21 bushels for oats. But the return to larger local measures, based on a heaped bushel, naturally reduced the number of bushels received, although not necessarily the amount of grain. At Apuldram, although the seeding rate changed, the size of the bushel did not and it appears to have been the same as the one used at Barton. The 1420s, however, were years of flooding and Apuldram, a low-lying coastal manor, was particularly affected. The wheat harvest of 1425 was exceedingly poor and yielded just 2.02 bushels an acre (0.67 × seed).[248] The average yields for this decade, therefore, are far below those of the rest of the century (see Table 3.19). Thereafter the yields per seed improved and in many years exceeded those received at Alciston, although, except for wheat, they did not reach the five to six times so frequently received at Barton. By the 1430s, however, wheat at Apuldram was being sown at two bushels an acre, so that even with a yield of five times the seed the yield per acre was fairly low – just over ten bushels an acre, whereas at Barton, with similar yields per seed but a higher seeding rate, the yields per acre averaged nearly fifteen bushels an acre.

[248] The serjeant responded to the bad 1425 harvest by cutting back the acreage under the plough, presumably because there was not enough grain for seed.

Animal husbandry, at least on the Battle abbey estates, does not appear to have been equally productive. At Alciston a significant number of the ewes each year were sterile. On two occasions nearly a third of the animals did not conceive (167 ewes out of 503) and on an average (with fifteen accounts) 14 per cent of the ewes remained sterile per year. The death rate for lambs was also higher than on some other estates.[249] In one year (1480–1) 98 per cent of the newborn lambs died (160 out of 163), and in four other years 49–50 per cent died. These figures, however, should be weighed against the five years in which the death rate was under 10 per cent. If all the bad years are included, the average death rate for the lambs at Alciston, in the fifteenth century, was nearly 22 per cent (with 30 accounts). If the years when the death rate was around 50 per cent or higher are excluded, on the grounds that these represent atypical years when disease was rife, then the average death rate drops to 17.84 per cent. The situation on the marsh manor of Apuldram was slightly worse. There too all the lambs died one year (1428–9) and on another occasion 93.1 per cent died (54 out of 58) and in a third year 75.5 per cent died. If these three accounts are excluded, the average death rate for the lambs was 18.66 per cent, but if they are included the average rises to 30.88 (18 accounts). The death rate, moreover, would probably have been higher if the "weak lambs" had not been regularly sold in the neighbourhood for the low price of 4d. each.

These flocks were being kept partly for their wool, but they also produced useful manure for the fields, the ewes were milked, and the culls of the herd were sent regularly to the abbey table. The wool, however, was not of the highest quality and each fleece, even from mature animals, weighed just over 1 lb. In the beginning of the fifteenth century, abbey officials were being paid 4d. or 4½d. a fleece, and with 1,500–2,000 ewes and wethers kept either at Alciston itself or nearby Lullington, the revenues from the sale of wool fluctuated between £30 and £40 a year. As wool prices began to fall in the 1420s, so obviously did revenues. In 1457–8, for example, 1,374 fleeces were sold for £10 18s. 4d. (just under 2d. each). But the animals still provided valuable manure and the high ratio of livestock to the area under cultivation must surely have contributed to the general productivity of the land.[250] In addition some of the ewes were milked, providing cheese for the abbey household. Furthermore each year a significant number of animals – between 100 and 300 – were sent to the

---

[249] For some comparative data, see Mate, 'Medieval agrarian practices', pp. 24–5.

[250] David Farmer, in his study of grain yields on the Winchester estates, concluded that "the manors where cereal productivity improved most tended to be those with the highest ratio of livestock to demesne arable", 'Grain yields on the Winchester manors', p. 566.

cellarer to provide meat for the monks and their guests. The serjeant, however, sold very little mature stock in the local markets, although some years he did sell new-born lambs.

The Christ Church monks, on their home farm of Barton, were more market oriented. Even though they kept quite a small flock of ewes, they usually sold some of the lambs to butchers and other men in the locality; and for a few years in the 1440s, when lambs were selling for 10d. each, they sold all the issue. In addition they bought yearling lambs from the Isle of Harty and elsewhere at 12–16d. each. These they then fattened and sold in subsequent years for 22–26d. before clipping and 18d. after clipping. Since their fleeces were selling for 2.4d. each (20s. a 100), they were making a good profit on the animals they sold before clipping. By the 1460s the profit margin had been reduced, for yearling lambs were bought at 17d. and 18d. and the wethers sold in gross for just over 21d. None the less significant numbers of animals were sold each year – 202 in 1463–4 and 303 in 1467–8. In addition, as earlier, many of the new-born lambs were sold, but the price had increased to 12d. each. The serjeant also sold roughly half the pigs and piglets each year. With eight to eleven sows on the manor and three to four boars, a large number of piglets were born (minimum 50, maximum 181, average 87). Some of these animals were sold, some were sent to the households of the prior and the bartoner, and some were kept until they became more mature animals. Then they, in their turn, were either sold to butchers and others or used for meat in the various priory households. The revenues from these sales – with pigs selling for 2s. 6d. and 3s. each – undoubtedly contributed to the priory's financial well-being.

Cattle rearing was also undertaken for a variety of purposes. The milk from cows was made into cheese and butter and then used to feed the household or sold. Cows were also eaten when they became old; but breeding was their main function. A steady supply of oxen, particularly in Sussex, was needed for hauling and ploughing as well as for food. By the mid-fifteenth century people were eating large quantities of beef and utilized animals at every stage of life from young calves to fully mature beasts. On the Battle abbey manor of Alciston, for example, each year at least half, and in some years over half of the new-born calves were sent to the cellarer. Elsewhere oxen were fattened for the table. On the manor of Heighton, in 1547–8, there were 66 oxen, of which 40 were needed for husbandry and 26 were to be fattened. That year 15 new oxen joined the herd from the stock of the manor and 61 animals were bought, bringing the total herd to 142 animals. But during the course of the year, 48 oxen were either killed for the expenses of the household or delivered to a local butcher. Of the

94 animals left, the serjeant noted that 46 were needed for husbandry and 48 were to be fattened.[251] On some manors cattle were reared solely for food. When Sir John Scott took his Sussex manor of Mote in hand in the 1470s, very little land was ploughed – 16 to 21 acres. Cattle were kept to supply his household in Calais and 28 to 30 oxen were sent abroad each year. The serjeant, however, did not rear all these animals on the manor, but kept just a small herd of eleven cows. He preferred to buy third- or fourth-year bullocks and then fatten them up for a year or two. Animals not needed for the household were then sold to local butchers and others.[252] Tenants with smaller households to feed were probably more market oriented and reared both young animals to be fattened elsewhere, and other animals to be sold to butchers. Certainly every court roll by the late fifteenth century accuses men of trespassing with young bullocks (*boviculis*) as well as with oxen and with third- or fourth-year bullocks (*bovettis*).

How profitable was farming at this time? Was Brandon correct when he stated that high cultivation costs were justified only when the demand for grain was high? When demesnes were kept in hand, much of the produce – both grain and stock – went to supply the household. Even though these goods were usually valued by the auditor, it is not certain that the genuine market price was given. Thus any calculation of profitability can only be estimates at best. On the Christ Church manor of Barton, the serjeant, even in the doldrums of the mid-fifteenth century, continued the expensive practices of a century earlier. He sowed at a fairly high rate of seed, he relied totally on horse power, buying high-quality animals, and he planted roughly a quarter of his sown acreage with legumes, which were then consumed by animals in the fields. Moreover, by the 1440s the cost of bringing in the harvest had become a major drain on resources. The *famuli* harvested only a small amount and for the remainder the serjeant paid the reapers 16d. an acre. Thus the total cost of the harvest was c. £15 a year. Another £8 a year went on wages and clothing for the *famuli* responsible for the ploughing and the other agricultural tasks. On the other hand, the cost of maintaining the ploughs and carts was mitigated by the practice of leasing them out. None the less in years when grain prices were low, the difference between the value of the grain received (both sent to the house and sold) and the cost of producing it was either very low or on the debit side, especially if one takes into account the purchase price of the horses and the value of the forage they consumed. But these expensive practices did produce high yields per acre and in years when prices were moderate it was possible to make a reasonable profit. In

[251] East Sussex RO, SAS G1/48.   [252] East Sussex RO, SAS HC179/3–8.

1445–6, for example, wheat was valued at 5s. a quarter and barley at 3s. and 3s. 4d. a quarter. The barley yielded 26½ bushels an acre. The Barton serjeant was able to send 124 quarters to the monastic granary, pay the grain livery of the *famuli* and the wages of the threshers and still have 47 quarters available for sale after the seed for the following year had been subtracted. The difference between the estimated value of all the grain and the cost of producing it was around £20. In addition the serjeant could rely on substantial revenues from the pastoral side of the manor. Even though he received just £3 5s. from the sale of wool from the wethers, he received £11 11s. from the farm of 33 cows at 7s. a year, and £6 profit from the sale of sheep and pigs. His pastoral expenses, on the other hand, were fairly low, for he employed just one shepherd and one pigman (paid respectively 20s. and 15s. 8d. a year).[253] Even so the margin of profit in the mid-fifteenth century was undoubtedly lower than it had been in the late fourteenth century, when prices were higher and costs lower.[254] This factor probably lies behind much of the arable and pastoral contraction that took place. Yet it is important to remember that so long as yields were good, in most years it was possible to make a modest profit. Moreover, lords frequently reduced costs by using part-time and female labour.[255] Demesne farmers presumably did likewise. They did not have to do all the work themselves or with family members to break even.

In some respects farmers in Kent and Sussex followed similar practices in the late middle ages. They cut back slightly on their rate of seeding, but continued to sow at higher rates than in many other parts of the country. They practised some form of convertible husbandry and periodically turned over the pasture, sowing the land with oats and legumes. On the infields nearest to the house they used extremely flexible cropping patterns that included, but were not limited to, a three-course rotation (wheat/barley/fallow). But in other areas they adopted different techniques and these differences became accentuated in the course of the fifteenth century. Kent farmers relied more and more on horse power for all agricultural work, whereas Sussex farmers preferred to use oxen for ploughing and even for most hauling tasks.

[253] Cathedral Archives and Library, Canterbury, *Caruca Bertona* roll 38.

[254] On the Battle abbey manor of Alciston, at the turn of the century, the sheep produced revenues of £80 or more and the value of the grain produced was over £96. By the mid-1440s the lower prices and the cutback in the size of the sheep flocks and the area under the plough produced revenues that were approximately one-third of their former level.

[255] The Sackvilles, on their manor of Chalvington, often employed husband and wife teams to reap the grain and mow the meadow. Women, when employed alone, were usually paid less than men. Thus the Chalvington serjeant, in the 1432 harvest, hired six men for one day, each at 4d. a day, and seven women for one day, each at 3d. a day: East Sussex RO, SAS CH273, 279, 280. The Battle abbey officials at Alciston and Wye relied increasingly on part-time labour.

The planting of legumes was cut back on many Sussex estates, but appears to have continued with little reduction in much of Kent. Even so, estates in both Kent and Sussex continued to enjoy good yields, both per seed and per acre, for the lack of nutrients from legumes was offset by leaving the land fallow for longer periods and folding more stock on it. Except for a few years, when prices were exceedingly low, farming appears to have been a profitable enterprise.

I. THE SOUTHERN COUNTIES

How land was used, in southern England as elsewhere, depended in the first place upon the land itself. Much downland found an obvious use as "hill pasture for sheep", although there were also sheep in many other places and they even outnumbered cattle and horses on Porlock common in Exmoor. There were some fair-sized pig farms where woodland pannage was available, as on the St Swithun's manor at Wootton (Hants.); and the meadows of the vale country, the Somerset marshes and some downland valleys made some concentration upon cattle farming possible. Almost everywhere, however, arable and livestock farming were combined, with natural conditions influencing only the character of the mixture. Thus, on Glastonbury's Dorset estate on the eve of the Black Death, Sturminster Newton in the Stour valley lowlands had about 70 per cent of its land as arable, 16 per cent was pasture and it was reasonably well provided with hay meadows. The downland manors of Buckland and Plush further south, by contrast, had only 16–18 per cent of their acreage as arable and they had little meadow, but they were lavishly endowed with pasture. The 1,900 acres of abbey land at Buckland and Plush, therefore, produced less corn than the 500-acre manor at Sturminster Newton; Sturminster grew enough hay to support a herd of dairy cows and its sheep, but the Buckland sheep flock was much larger and its dairy output was made from ewe's milk.[256]

The subsistence needs of both landlords and tenants also encouraged mixed farming. The Glastonbury abbey granger still received large consignments of grain from the house's Dorset and Somerset estates in the 1360s; the St Augustine's lessee at Pawlett (Somerset) in the 1440s paid his rent in grain, oatmeal, mustard seed, eggs, and large quantities of cheese; and liveries to the household of the lady of Porlock in 1419–20 included wheat, a couple of riding horses, 15 oxen, sheep, poultry, young pigs, even 7 stones of wool for making cloth. If lords and ladies made demands of this sort on their lands we may be sure that

[256] I. Keil, 'Farming on the Dorset estates of Glastonbury abbey in the early fourteenth century', *Dorset N.H. and Arch. Soc.*, LXXXVII, 1965, pp. 234–47.

ordinary villagers did so too, although individually on a much more modest scale. At the same time mixed farming was also favoured by the fact that livestock and arable were interdependent. Arable fields as well as meadows supplied winter food for livestock and, still more indispensably, livestock provided the manure which fertilized the arable. Especially on the thin downland soils, sheep were as vital for sustaining harvest yields as for producing the wool which nourished the export trade and the developing cloth industry at home.[257]

Arable production remained the dominant branch of farming in much of southern England, very often conducted within the traditional open-field context. A two-field system (or at least two-course rotation) was very common, especially in the downlands, but it was intermingled with a three-field system (or at least three-course husbandry) where the land would stand it. At Burghclere (Hants.) in 1381–2 there was what looks like a straightforward three-field system: 96 acres in Church Field were sown with winter grains, $94\frac{1}{2}$ acres in *La Cley* were under spring grains, and presumably a similar acreage was fallowed. The much larger sown acreage at Enford (Wilts.) in 1403 needed more numerous fields: South Field and *Oldedyche* Field for wheat, Middle Field for barley, *Suthewodecombe* for oats and *Cheselhulle* for peas and vetches; while at Chilton Cantelo (Somerset) in 1392 there were few signs of an organized field system, various furlongs and crofts (including some lying in the park) being combined for the purposes of cultivation.[258] Some lords and demesne lessees also held some open-field land in large consolidated plots, like the 80-acre parcel of demesne on the Glastonbury manor of Idmiston (Wilts.) in 1518. Holdings of this kind might offer encouragement to attempts to exclude all other users from them, although such attempts faced formidable obstacles in the rights of commoners to graze them when they were not under crops. How powerful those rights were is indicated by the very common assumption that no value could be placed upon demesne arable in the fallow year, since then it lapsed into common pasture. Where lords did have large blocks of land, however, they might be able to use them with a certain flexibility. The bishops of Winchester possibly adopted something like a four-course rotation on the $75\frac{1}{2}$ acres of Combe-furlong at Crawley; and there are indications of a wheat/two spring crops/fallow cycle, and even of a wheat/barley/wheat/fallow sequence, on some furlongs of the Glastonbury manors at Longbridge and Monkton Deverill. Holdings consisting of numerous small parcels

---

[257] I. Keil, 'Account of the granger of Glastonbury abbey, 1361–2', *Somerset and Dorset N. & Q.*, XXVIII, 1968, pp. 86–90; *Some Manorial Accounts of St Augustine's Abbey*, ed. Sabin, pp. 35–8; Chadwyck Healey, *West Somerset*, pp. 426–7.

[258] WPR 159388; BL Harl. Roll X7; PRO DL 43/14/3, ff.73–3d.

intermixed with the land of others, on the other hand, must have imposed stronger constraints to follow the common rotational patterns.[259]

The principal crops in most of the region were likely to be wheat, barley, and oats, although a place like Nettlecombe (Somerset) in the Brendon Hills might grow mostly oats and rye. The Winchester manors in Wiltshire and Hampshire are more typical. Over the period 1345–1433, on average, about 40 per cent of the demesne acreage sown was under wheat, 20 per cent rising over the period to 24 per cent under barley, and 35 per cent falling to about 25 per cent under oats. Other crops, of which legumes with 7–8 per cent of the sown acreage were the most important, show no very significant trend save that mancorn (mixed wheat and rye), once popular especially in northern Hampshire, continued its long-term decline. Wide differences between individual manors, of course, are concealed by these averages, and on other estates, too, there were variations on what was still something of a common theme. There was a proportion of land under wheat rather lower than the Winchester average at Enford in 1403, at Wootton St Lawrence (Hants.), and at Porlock in 1422–5 (but not in 1425–6); but at Heytesbury, Wellow, Farleigh Hungerford and Muchelney this proportion on occasion was as high as 60 per cent. Except at Heytesbury, on the other hand, a smaller acreage of barley was sown than on the average Winchester manor, and no legumes were grown at Wellow and Farleigh Hungerford. The Luttrell manor at East Quantoxhead was perhaps most idiosyncratic: there, in the early fifteenth century, some 72 per cent of a demesne consisting mainly of substantial closes was under wheat. In a few places (including Heytesbury, Longbridge Deverill, and Cheriton) drage, mixed oats and barley, had a certain importance: its advantage was its suitability for either human or animal consumption according to need.[260]

Harvest results depended upon many things, including weather, standards of husbandry, soil qualities, and seeding rates. On the Winchester manors, which alone have long runs of accounts, mean yield ratios per seed during the century after 1349 were 3.66–3.88 for wheat, 3.53–4.14 for barley and 2.43–3.03 for oats. Some manors for some part of this century performed significantly better than during the

[259] BL Harl. Ms. 3961, f.138; Gras, *English Village*, pp. 34–6, 274–5, 282–3; data from GAD 9732, 9744–51, 10624, 10716 communicated by David Farmer.

[260] Winchester acreages under crops communicated by Farmer. For other places, *The Manor of Manydown*, ed. G. W. Kitchin, Hants. Rec. Soc., 1895, pp. 159–60; Chadwyck Healey, *West Somerset*, pp. 425–43; *VCH Somerset*, III, p. 43, V, p. 124; PRO SC 6/970/13–15, 21–3, 974/24–5, 1052/17, 1053/7; BL Harl. Roll, X7. On drage, I. Keil, 'Impropriator and benefice in the middle ages', *Wilts. Arch. and N.H. Magazine*, LVIII, 1961–3, p. 359.

quarter-century before 1349. Cheriton wheat yields, for example, were higher in the period 1349–80 and those at Twyford, Sutton, and Downton in the period 1381–1410, when three-quarters of the manors growing barley and all but two of the manors growing oats achieved better yields than before the Black Death. If barley yields fell back somewhat after 1410, moreover, the improved yields of oats were maintained. Only on the bishop's Somerset manors, producing high yields earlier in the fourteenth century, was there a downward trend or at best stability after 1349. Averages, of course, conceal wide variations between manors and from year to year, making it dangerous to compare the Winchester results with more sporadic data from other estates; but some places give the impression of doing well in the late fourteenth century. In the 1380s wheat yields of around seven-fold and barley yields of 5.3–6.3-fold were achieved at Farleigh Hungerford.[261]

Harvest returns, however, also depended upon sowing rates which varied from place to place (though some variations may reflect different customary measures of area and volume). Rates of sowing on the Winchester manors before 1349, which do not seem to have changed greatly in the ensuing century, were 2–2$\frac{1}{2}$ bushels per acre for wheat except in Somerset where they were 1$\frac{1}{2}$ bushels; for barley 3$\frac{1}{2}$–4 bushels, but only 3 bushels at Taunton and as high as 5–5$\frac{1}{2}$ bushels at Fareham; and commonly 4 bushels for oats, but up to 5 bushels at Crawley and a few other manors and often below 4 bushels at Taunton.[262] Given these varying yield ratios and sowing rates, productivity per acre must likewise have varied considerably. Extrapolation from the yields per acre on some Winchester manors in the period 1325–49, as these have been calculated by J. Z. Titow, and in the light of the subsequent trend of yield ratios, suggests average yields per acre on these manors in the period 1381–1410 of 6–11 bushels for wheat, 14–24 bushels for barley and 9–19 bushels for oats. Some figures occasionally available from other estates are perhaps not wildly out of line with these estimates: wheat yields of 8–9 bushels an acre at Farleigh Hungerford; barley yields of 17 bushels at Wellow, 13–15$\frac{1}{2}$ bushels at Farleigh Hungerford and 14 bushels in 1424 at Porlock; and oats yields of 7–9 bushels at Farleigh, 10 bushels at Porlock and 12$\frac{1}{2}$ bushels at Wellow.[263] Even if such estimates are accorded a degree of validity, however, they remain an inadequate measure of the productivity of medieval arable farming. The intensity with which land was cropped varied between and even

---

[261] Farmer, 'Grain yields on the Winchester manors', pp. 555–66; PRO SC 6/970/22–3.

[262] Titow, *Winchester Yields*, pp. 40–2; Gras, *English Village*, pp. 274–5, 281, 300–1, 309–10.

[263] The Winchester manors are Fareham, Cheriton, Twyford, Crawley and East Meon (Hants.), Downton (Wilts.), Rimpton and Taunton (Somerset), for which 1325–49 yields are in Titow, *Winchester Yields*, pp. 121–35. Sources for the other places mentioned are listed in n.260 above.

within manors. A manor following a two-course rotation, like many downland manors, even with good yield ratios and yields per acre, might ultimately produce only marginally more than places like Rimpton and Taunton where two-thirds of the arable were cropped each year.[264] The most important conclusion to be drawn from the Winchester records, therefore, is that wheat yields may have improved in some places, but by no means everywhere, in the second half of the fourteenth century; that in most places (but not quite all) the yields of barley and oats improved; and that in the case of oats this improvement was continued into the fifteenth century.

To explain these productivity trends is another matter. In part they may reflect the long-term tendency of landlords to shed demesne land, presumably including some that was least productive; but the rate at which they were withdrawing from direct cultivation slowed down for a time in the second half of the fourteenth century. Nor can any improvement in yields be linked with any certainty to expanded cultivation of legumes, although at Rimpton vetches were sometimes sown on the fallow "to fertilize the land". In fact, however, there is no very evident increase in legume cultivation in most places. At Downton, where it did increase, the yields of barley and oats improved but wheat yields fell somewhat; at East Meon where wheat yields and at Hambledon where barley yields were high, the legume acreage was small; and there were also good cereal yields at Wellow and Farleigh Hungerford even when no legumes were grown. They might be sown because, as at Downton and Porlock, there was evidently a local market for them, or because, as at Rimpton, they were a traditional component of the liveries to manorial employees; still more frequently they were fodder for livestock – for horses and oxen at Brockhampton (Hants.) when hay was short, for *porci campestres*, and above all for sheep. They were grown at Crawley either for seed or for the sheep; they nourished ewes at lambing time at East Knoyle and Burghclere or weakly wethers and hoggasters at Fareham and North Waltham; and they were bought in to feed the flocks at Collingbourne Ducis and Everleigh. Any effect of growing legumes upon the yields of other crops, at least in intention, was probably coincidental: as has been pointed out, they were often sown in the year before land was fallowed, so that the principal beneficiaries were the fallow weeds.[265]

Weather and sheep flocks may have been more important influences upon cereal productivity. The high proportion of "harvest successes"

[264] *Medieval Customs of the Manors of Taunton and Bradford on Tone*, ed. T. J. Hunt, Somerset Rec. Soc., LXVI, 1962, pp. xxix, 92–4.

[265] WPR 159371, 159388; PRO DL 29/683/11068; Gras, *English Village*, pp. 300, 309–10; Farmer, 'Crop yields, prices and wages', pp. 132–3; *idem*, 'Grain yields on Westminster Abbey manors', *Canadian J. of History*, XVIII, 1983, pp. 346–7.

in the years 1381–1410 may in part reflect the fact that the weather in these years was kind to arable farmers.[266] Increased livestock, and especially sheep, numbers may have been even more influential, in that the intensity of cultivation and the productivity of the land was governed in part by the availability of manure. Thus in Somerset, yields at Farleigh Hungerford, at least of wheat and barley, look rather better than those at Taunton and Rimpton: one reason may have been Farleigh's relatively larger sheep flock.[267] Realization of the importance of manure for good harvests is evident. Carting horse and cattle manure onto the fields occupied many of the surviving labour services at Crawley even in 1448–9; the stables at Taunton Castle provided manure for Holway fields; but on the chalklands especially, sheep were the principal providers. The routine for folding the sheep flock on the arable each night was laid down in great detail at Bincombe (Dorset), and the task of moving the lord's sheepfold round his land was a common servile obligation. Tenants, at Urchfont for instance, might be compelled to fold their sheep on the lord's arable, although at least initially large demesne flocks may have been a more important source of manure, a fact which tenants too might appreciate. At Longbridge Deverill in 1450–1 the demesne flock manured most of the abbey's arable still cultivated, but ten years later it also fertilized 16 acres of *terra villanorum*; at Monkton Deverill, as arable cultivation was run down in the mid-fifteenth century, tenants paid 1s. per acre to have the manure of the lord's sheep; and rather earlier tenants at Aldbourne paid 2d. per night to have the lord's fold on their land. A similar appreciation of sheep as providers of manure is indicated by the Charlton (Wilts.) by-law allowing sheep to be pastured on the sown wheat field, providing that there was a shepherd over them and that they were gone by 17 October when the corn was sprouting.[268]

The routines of arable husbandry appear only incidentally. Oxen were still the principal plough beasts, although the bishop of Wells had only horses on his Muchelney demesne in 1440 and the horses at Kingston Lacy in 1430, although there were also oxen there, were said to be *pro carecta et caruca*. The primacy of oxen as draught animals, however, is perhaps underlined by John Stourton's will providing for his body to be taken for burial from Preston Plucknett to Stavordale priory "in my best wagon...drawn by my ten best oxen". It looks as though, for ploughing, eight-ox teams may not have been uncommon

---

[266] 'Harvest successes' are defined by Farmer, 'Grain yields on the Winchester manors', pp. 557–8.   [267] *Ibid.*, pp. 563–4.

[268] Gras, *English Village*, pp. 485–7; WPR 159414; *Somerset and Dorset N. & Q.*, x, 1906–7, p. 45; *Wilts. N. & Q.*, v, 1905–7, p. 104; data from GAD 9702, 9837, 9880, 9883, 9945 communicated by David Farmer; W. O. Ault, 'Open-field husbandry and the village community', *American Philosophical Soc.*, NS LV(7), 1965, p. 25.

on demesnes, although there were possibly some mixed teams by the fifteenth century. The two main ploughing seasons preceded the winter and spring sowing, but the fallow was also ploughed in summer as a cleaning operation: indeed, at Longbridge Deverill in 1372 most of the fallow was ploughed twice and some of it three times, and in 1353 a third plough was put into service at Farleigh Hungerford to double-plough the fallow. The seed used usually came from the previous year's harvest, but from time to time a little was bought and that this was carefully selected is suggested by the fact that the reeve of Porlock paid 2d. or 3d. a bushel more for seed wheat than he got for the wheat he sold. The expenditure of nearly £20 on new seed at Crawley in 1356–7, on the other hand, was exceptional, probably representing a decision to change the seed more or less completely after a disastrous harvest in 1356. The change of about half the seed at Heytesbury in 1357–8 may have had a similar explanation.[269]

Much work remained to be done, of course, between seed-time and harvest. The growing crops needed weeding, especially if (as at Holway in 1412 and Ecchinswell in 1442) thistles were exceptionally prolific, a task for which customary labour was still being used at Ecchinswell. If services were not available, wage-labour was hired for this essential task. Weeding was a matter of handwork as was the harvest itself and stacking and threshing the corn which came from it. That fact explains the modest *utensilia* needed even on arable demesnes. At Crawley in 1449 they consisted of three ploughs, two harrows with iron and three with wooden teeth, a cart, harness, dairy equipment and so forth, valued at just over £3; and the "dead stock" delivered to the demesne lessee of Fifehead Magdalen (Dorset) in the late fifteenth century included a plough, two iron chains, two yokes for oxen, two horse harrows with iron teeth, a corn cart and a rope for securing loads, a dung hook, an iron fork, a bushel measure, a seed basket, a two-gallon jar, a pitcher, a pair of tripods, ox rings, cheese tubs and vats, and tables, trestles, and dishes. Such equipment often represented a much smaller investment than the draught animals which pulled the ploughs and carts. The 17 oxen and 7 horses in the hands of the Crawley lessee in 1449 were valued at nearly £13, four times what the *utensilia* were worth.[270]

The grain crop was seldom the sole return from land and in many places income derived from pastoral farming was very considerable. The gross income from animal husbandry at Crawley (the wool

[269] Langdon, *Horses, Oxen and Technological Innovation*, pp. 88–9; *VCH Somerset*, III, p. 45; PRO DL 29/682/11051; *Somerset Medieval Wills*, ed. Weaver, pp. 143–6; GAD 9905; PRO SC 6/970/14, 1052/18; Gras, *English Village*, pp. 280–1.

[270] WPR 159414, 159437; PRO SC 6/970/21, 974/24; Gras, *English Village*, pp. 281, 484–5; *Some Manorial Accounts of St Augustine's Abbey*, ed. Sabin, p. 73.

despatched for sale centrally being valued at the prevailing price in the locality in the years in question) was about £27 in 1355–6, £39 in 1409–10, £33 in 1410–11 and £19 in 1448–9, compared with gross income from grain sales in these same years of £37, £34, £37, and £24. To achieve these latter results, moreover, was likely to require heavier outlays. Sheep and cattle were the most important livestock and in most of the region sheep greatly outnumbered cattle. They were part of the stock on every sort of holding: on the lands of manorial tenants, of great noblemen, of bishops and religious houses, of New College, Oxford, when it got the former Hungerford manor at Stert (Wilts.); and of a gentleman like Sir Thomas West, whose 650 sheep at Bridmere and Swallowcliffe (Wilts.) in 1380 were valued at about £43 compared with other livestock worth £10, implements and draught animals worth £28, and arable crops also worth £28. For the management of these flocks, however, it is necessary once again to rely principally upon the records of some of the larger estates, some of which had very large numbers of sheep. The mean size of the Winchester flocks in Hampshire and Wiltshire in the later fourteenth century was around 22,000 sheep, with nearly 1,400 at Overton, over 1,500 at Downton, nearly 1,800 at East Knoyle, nearly 2,000 at East Meon and over 2,000 at Twyford. St Swithun's, too, had over 20,000 sheep on its manors at the end of the fourteenth century; the abbess of Romsey had over 2,000 at Edington (Wilts.) in 1414; and at Michaelmas 1391 there were 1,785 lambs and wethers on the Hungerford manor at Heytesbury. Even in Somerset the bishop of Wells had 857 sheep and lambs at Evercreech in 1383 and the Luttrells had up to 644 sheep to clip at East Quantoxhead in the early fifteenth century.[271]

On these large estates many manors supported a specialized flock and, even when this was not so, sheep farming was centrally managed on an intermanorial basis.[272] On the Winchester estate, for instance, there seem to have been several "clusters of manors" centred on a manor or manors with a large ewe flock: thus the Ecchinswell wether flock was kept up to strength with lambs from Burghclere or bought in the market, some of which were sent on as hoggasters to Burghclere, Highclere and Ashmansworth. Even Crawley, which carried both ewe and wether flocks, sent culled ewes and rams to Bishopstoke and

[271] VCH Wilts., VIII, pp. 243–4; X, p. 156; Wilts. Extents for Debt, Edward I – Elizabeth I, ed. A. Conyers, Wilts. Rec. Soc., XXVIII, 1973, no. 22; Stephenson, 'The productivity of medieval sheep on the great estates', pp. 278–82; Hare, 'Demesne lessees', pp. 1–2; PRO SC 6/1053/6; Somerset and Dorset N. & Q., XI, 1908–9, pp. 237–40; VCH Somerset, V, p. 124.

[272] R. Trow-Smith, History of British Livestock Husbandry, pp. 111, 144–5, draws heavily upon the pioneering work of R. C. Payne, 'Agrarian conditions on the Wilts. estates of the Duchy of Lancaster, the lords of Hungerford and the bishopric of Winchester in the 13th, 14th and 15th centuries', London Univ. Ph.D. thesis, 1939.

surplus hoggasters to Bishop's Waltham. There were even more complex arrangements on the Hungerford estates. The ewe and wether flocks at Farleigh Hungerford were given up in the early 1350s, the manor becoming a place for fattening culled stock from Heytesbury and Colerne (Wilts.); but by the 1380s it had a ewe flock once more, reinforced by drafts from Heytesbury, Teffont (Wilts.), Holt (Somerset), and Down Ampney (Glos.). Heytesbury, in turn, was a "nursery of lambs" for Farleigh, Wellow, Holt, and Teffont, and supplied these manors with hoggasters in due course. Wool was also centrally marketed. There were similar arrangements on the southern English estate of the Duchy of Lancaster, where ewe flocks at Collingbourne Ducis and Lambourne (Berks.) helped to support the large wether flocks at Aldbourne, Everleigh and Berwick St James, and on the St Swithun's estate in Hampshire and Wiltshire. In Somerset, too, the wether flock of the bishop of Wells at Evercreech was reinforced by drafts of lambs and wethers from Wells and Cranmore and of wethers from the bishop's other Mendip manors at Wookey, Westbury, Cheddar, and Compton Bishop.[273]

Underlying these forms of organization was an intention that, at least within groups of manors, sheep flocks would be self-sustaining. This was achieved by a bewildering movement of sheep between manors on the Hungerford estate, while at Crawley in the three decades after 1350 the ewe and wether flocks were usually kept up to strength from the manor's own hoggasters recruited from the manor's own lambs. Significant numbers of lambs were bought only after heavy mortality among lambs on the manor like that which occurred in 1372–3, 1377–9 and 1387–9. From that point on, however, purchases of lambs became much more regular, probably because the manor's ewe flock was declining from its peak numbers. The wether flock of the nuns of St Mary's, Winchester, was likewise being kept up to strength in the 1460s by purchases of adult stock, hoggasters and lambs, often at relatively high prices.[274]

The underlying intention that sheep flocks should at least reproduce themselves gives a special importance to lambing rates and lamb mortality. The number of lambs born per hundred ewes on four Winchester manors (Downton, East Knoyle, Twyford, and East Meon) ranged from a mean of 80 at East Meon in the period 1411–54 to one

[273] Stephenson, op. cit., pp. 59–61; WPR 159414; Gras, English Village, pp. 275, 283–4, 310–11; PRO SC 6/970/13–15, 21–3, 974/24–5, 1052/17, 1053/6–7; VCH Wilts., IV, pp. 19–20; X, p. 156; XI, p. 194; XII, p. 132; PRO DL 29/682/11058, 683/11068; Lloyd, Movement of Wool Prices, p. 25; BL Add. Ch., 24395–7; Somerset and Dorset N. & Q., XI, 1908–9, pp. 239–40.

[274] Gras, English Village, pp. 372–425; Wilts., N. & Q., V, 1905–6, pp. 10–16; BL Add. Roll 66603.

of 92 at Twyford in the period 1381–1410. Of these lambs 22–4 per cent died before weaning in the period 1349–80, 17–25 per cent in the period 1381–1410, and 17–30 per cent in the period 1411–54. Such general figures may be put more concretely. Another Winchester manor, Crawley, normally had a fairly good lambing rate of 85–90 per cent, and began the year 1409–10 (a reasonably good year) with 385 ewes. Of these 4 died before lambing and 30 were sterile or aborted, so that only 351 lambs were produced. Of the lambs born, 41 died before weaning and others had to be given as tithe or customary gifts so that the initial 385 ewes provided the bishop with only 279 lambs by weaning time, and a few more were lost before the following Michaelmas.[275]

Sporadic information from elsewhere is not inconsistent with that from the Winchester estate. At Wellow there was an 88–9 per cent lambing rate in the 1360s; and at Farleigh Hungerford, although the rate was as low as 78 per cent in 1385–6, it rose to 88–90 per cent in the following years, only offset in 1387–8 by the loss of 15 per cent of the lambs before weaning. At Kingston Lacy in 1390–1 a lambing rate of 87 per cent was said to be as low as that because only 40 per cent of the gimmers added to the ewe flock produced lambs. Everywhere, of course, there were exceptionally bad years. At Crawley in 1372–3, 60 per cent of the lambs died and in 1373–4 39 per cent of them in a year when the lambing rate was only 59 per cent. At Enford, too, 41 per cent of lambs were lost in 1403 and at Collingbourne Ducis in 1435 a ewe flock numbering 444 at the start of the year produced only 85 surviving lambs, because many of the ewes died of disease; and the lambs of 240 more "were still-born and are called slynkittes". Disasters, on the other hand, did not come every year, so that at Crawley the bishop of Winchester could expect to have on average during the century after 1349 two surviving lambs for every three ewes on the manor at the start of each year. Disastrous years, moreover, did not only affect ewes and lambs. At Kingston Lacy the mortality rate of wethers had been only 3 per cent in 1391 and in 1430–2, but it rose to at least 33 per cent in 1434. King's Somborne (Hants.) suffered even more severely in 1434–5 when 12 per cent of the wethers and 35 per cent of the hoggasters died during the winter, and 12 per cent of the ewes also died (mostly after lambing) together with two-thirds of the lambs. The sheep breeder's returns were perhaps always relatively modest, but from time to time both returns and his basic stock were severely reduced by disease.[276]

---

[275] Stephenson, 'The productivity of medieval sheep on the great estates', pp. 310–13; Gras, *English Village*, pp. 301–2.

[276] PRO SC 6/970/21–3, 974/24–5; BL Harl. Roll X7; PRO DL 29/682/11046, 11051, 683/11064, 11066–7.

His returns, of course, were not only represented by lambs to reinforce his own flocks. There was also a market for lambs culled because of their quality or because they were in excess of the needs of the estate producing them, like the 89 lambs *de refusis* sold at Wellow in 1365–6. There was also a market for hoggasters, wethers, ewes, and rams culled because they were surplus to requirements or below standard, or because they had outlived their useful lives. At Urchfont 143 wethers were sold in 1463–4 as "kebbs" (inferior stock) and 68 others were put into a special flock with 74 wethers weeded out in the previous year to be fattened for sale. The proportion of stock culled each year varied considerably, but at Crawley the annual average was around 14 per cent both of ewes and wethers. With losses from disease averaging about 7 per cent, here as elsewhere on the Winchester estate both ewes and wethers seem to have needed replacement after about five years. That figure also looks to be about right for ewes at Kingston Lacy and wethers at Shapwick on the Duchy of Lancaster estate, but wethers at Kingston Lacy may sometimes have been kept a little longer.[277]

The market for sheep supplied farmers without sufficient replacement stock of their own (the Luttrells of East Quantoxhead even bought wethers from Wales); but rejected "kebbs", like the Aldbourne sheep sold to a London butcher in 1426–7 or those the Hungerfords sold to local butchers about the same time, were more likely to go into the fat-stock market, although some might provision the lord's or lady's larder. Stock sales, therefore, provided revenues both in cash and kind, representing at Crawley in the two decades 1354–64 and 1409–19 a quarter to one-third of the manor's gross returns from sheep farming.[278] Sheep also produced a few other minor sources of income: from the sale of the fells or skins of dead stock, or of butter and cheese made from sheep's milk, and from lactage payments from those who rented the milking ewes between weaning time in early May and the beginning of August. The practice of milking ewes, however, seems to have been declining. On the Hungerford estate there was some income from lactage payments at Farleigh and Wellow in the mid-fourteenth century, but none at Farleigh in the 1380s, the milk from the ewes being said to be reserved for the lambs in 1388. Ewes were still milked at Wootton St Lawrence in the 1390s, at Enford in 1403, and on some Winchester manors until the second decade of the fifteenth century; but at this point lactage payments disappear from the Winchester

[277] PRO SC 6/974/25; BL Add. Roll 66603; Stephenson, *op. cit.*, pp. 49, 300–7; PRO DL 29/682/ 11046, 11049, 11051, 683/11064.

[278] *VCH Somerset*, v, p. 124; PRO DL 29/682/11058; Stephenson, *op. cit.*, pp. 46–8; Chadwyck Healey, *West Somerset*, p. 426; Gras, *English Village*, p. 280.

records, nor are they mentioned in the fifteenth-century accounts of Monkton and Longbridge Deverill (where they had been a regular source of income in the 1370s). Where a reason is given, it is usually the weakness of the ewes, milking being apparently increasingly regarded as incompatible with their breeding role. At Crawley, indeed, the cessation of milking was followed by two decades in the 1420s and 1430s of better lambing rates and lower death rates of both lambs and ewes, although both rates deteriorated in the 1440s. Medieval sheep farmers could learn from observation without necessarily guaranteeing results that were successful in the long term.[279]

For most sheep farmers, however, wool was the most important revenue-producing product: at Crawley, for example, providing nearly two-thirds of the gross returns from sheep farming. In this respect growers were at the mercy of many circumstances they could control imperfectly or not at all: hard winters, dry summers, visitations of disease that were exceptionally severe in the 1370s and the 1440s, and fluctuations in the national and international demand for English wool. Sagging wool prices in the mid-fifteenth century, a result of the simultaneous contraction of overseas and domestic demand, helped to persuade some large producers (including the Duchy of Lancaster in Wiltshire) to give up their sheep flocks, because wool was hard to sell even at falling prices, production costs were relatively high, and profits were relatively low.[280]

A further consideration may have been that changes had taken place in the productivity of sheep as wool producers. From the second decade of the fourteenth century Crawley fleeces were markedly heavier than they had previously been, and they averaged 1.76 lb in the 1350s and 1.63 lb in the 1360s. Still averaging 1.79 lb in 1372, they then dropped to 1.16 lb in 1373 and remained at well below their mid-century level, averaging under 1.10 lb in the 1380s and 1390s, about 1.20 lb in the 1420s, and 1.15 lb or less in the 1430s and 1440s. Crawley's experience was not exceptional among Winchester manors. In the period 1381–1410 average fleece weights at Downton and Twyford were 17 per cent lower, and at East Knoyle 12 per cent lower, than in the period 1349–80; the average at East Meon was 18 per cent lower than before 1349; and on all these manors the lower weights persisted after 1410. Lower yields of wool may have contributed to the decision on some estates to abandon demesne flocks or to concentrate on flocks of wethers, with heavier fleeces than ewes, necessitating the buying in of replacement stock with a consequent increase of production costs. How

---

[279] PRO SC 6/970/13, 21–3, 974/25–6; *Manor of Manydown*, ed. Kitchin, p. 169; BL Harl. Roll X7; WPR 159414, 159423; information on the Deverills from D. Farmer.
[280] Lloyd, *Movement of Wool Prices*, pp. 20–6.

general the fall of fleece weights was, and how it is to be explained, is less certain. The Wiltshire lands of the Duchy of Lancaster in the 1430s produced fleeces more or less comparable to those from the Winchester manors at that date. Heytesbury fleeces in the 1390s (1.66–1.91 lb), Stockton fleeces in 1399–1403 (1.55–1.86 lb) and Enford fleeces in 1403 (1.60 lb), on the other hand, were significantly heavier; but Somerset fleeces from Abbotsleigh averaged only 1 lb or less in the 1380s, from Evercreech just over 1 lb in 1383, and from Porlock only 0.66 lb. Some other Duchy of Lancaster manors in the 1390s and 1430s performed somewhere between these extremes, although rather better than Crawley, with fleece weights of 1.4 lb at Longstock in Hampshire and of 1.3–1.6 lb at Shapwick and Kingston Lacy in Dorset.[281]

How cost-effective sheep farming was is not easily determined. The Duchy of Lancaster in 1434–5 got well above the national mean price for its Wiltshire wool, but also rather less than the average price that year for downland wool; but Hungerford wool from Wellow and Farleigh Hungerford in the 1360s sold at above both national and Somerset means. Possibly the implication is that centralized management might, but did not necessarily, enhance returns. It might, of course, also enhance costs, and medieval landlords have been accused of "pampering their sheep". Certainly the Hungerfords, the bishops of Winchester, the Duchy of Lancaster and many others bought gallons of tar and grease to treat the ills of their sheep; they hired extra help at lambing time and often to wash and clip the sheep; they rented extra pasture for them when summers were dry; they fed them hay, vetches, and oats, sometimes bought for the purpose, during winter and lambing; they paid out large sums for haymaking which often had the winter needs of sheep in mind. Obviously these outgoings raised the production costs of wool, the sheep farmer's principal cash crop; and, on large estates, when added to the cost of a large administrative staff, they may have narrowed profitability almost to vanishing point, especially in the middle decades of the fifteenth century when they were faced in combination with contracting markets, falling prices, and low productivity. This is not necessarily to say, however, that landlords were "inefficient producers". Some of them seem to have been relatively efficient in the circumstances of their times in making the best use they could of their stock and their land.[282]

[281] M. J. Stephenson, 'Wool yields in the medieval economy', pp. 368–91; Gras, *English Village*, pp. 372–425; Lloyd, *op. cit.*, p. 25; PRO SC 6/1053/6–7, DL 29/682/11049, 11051, 683/11062, 11066–7; BL Add. Ch. 24395–8, Harl. Roll X7; *Some Manorial Accounts of St Augustine's Abbey*, ed. Sabin, p. 8; Chadwyck Healey, *West Somerset*, p. 427.

[282] Lloyd, *op. cit.*, p. 28; PRO DL 29/683/11068, SC 6/974/24–5; Gras, *English Village*, pp. 272–5.

On some manors, including Crawley, sheep were the only livestock apart from draught animals; but on at least thirteen of the Winchester manors in Hampshire and Wiltshire there were dairy herds, usually of about twenty cows, but double that number at Bitterne (Hants.). Some cheese and butter was made from their milk, together with ewes' milk, until the 1360s, after which time the milk was leased out for lactage payments which in 1371 ranged from 3s. to 4s. 6d. per cow. Dairy produce, however, was seldom the main purpose for which cows were kept. The twenty cows or so that Glastonbury kept at Sturminster Newton in the early fourteenth century were intended to produce calves that would provide replacement cows and oxen for the manor, some stores for sale or transfer to other manors, and some meat for the abbey. The bull and twelve cows at Farleigh Hungerford in the mid-century had a similar purpose: they enabled the reeve to replace one or two cows and one or two oxen each year from young stock on the manor. All the calves beyond the six deemed necessary to ensure that these replacements would be available were sold. At Crondal (Hants.), where there were twice as many plough beasts as at Farleigh, there was a herd of twenty-four cows in 1390. There, too, "kebb" cows and oxen were weeded out and sold; they were replaced from the steers and heifers, any of the latter not needed for this purpose being sold; and of the calves born each year, sixteen were selected by the reeve as the fittest to be reared to reinforce the lord's cows and oxen in the future.[283]

In all this the commercial element was secondary, although undoubtedly there was a market for cattle. Crawley, because it had no cows, had to buy in its oxen; and Farleigh Hungerford, after replacing ageing plough beasts with drafts from Heytesbury in 1386–7, sold most of these recruits the next year and bought others in their place. Here there seems to have been more faith in the market than in intermanorial provision, and intermanorial arrangements involving cattle in fact seem to have been less common than in sheep farming. At Evercreech, however, calves were brought in from the other manors of the bishop of Wells and young beasts were sent off to be grazed at Cheddar. There were also some places where cattle farming was something more than an adjunct of arable cultivation. At Bitterne, by the Itchen estuary, the bishops of Winchester about 1380 abandoned arable and sheep farming altogether and enlarged the dairy herd from twenty-four to about fifty cows, the income from which derived almost equally from the sale of calves and culls on the one hand, and from lactage payments on the other. Bitterne, of course, lay in a part of Hampshire Leland deemed

[283] WPR 159380; information relating to Glastonbury manors from David Farmer; Keil, 'Farming on the estates of Glastonbury abbey', pp. 240, 246; PRO SC 6/970/13–15; *Records and Documents relating to the Manor of Crondal*, ed. F. J. Baignent, Hants. Rec. Soc., 1891, pp. 497–9.

fitter for cattle than corn, as did the Dorset heathland between Weymouth and Lulworth, where a father's wedding gift to his daughter in 1430 was common for seventy cattle. Cattle farming on some scale is also found on the coastal pastures of north Somerset, where a Pawlett lessee in 1440 owed 200 stones of cheese for rent, in the inland marshland where so large a proportion of manorial acreages was meadow, on the Quantocks and on Exmoor, and in the Vale of Blackmoor where Fifehead Magdalen was handed over to a lessee with a herd of twenty cows and thirty loads of hay for their nourishment.[284]

In general cattle farming seems to have been conducted with reasonable efficiency even though its objectives were often rather limited. Calving rates were reasonably good, though inevitably there were bad years: at East Meon in 1440–1, for instance, 3 out of 29 cows died before calving and 5 more were sterile or aborted. On the other hand, at Farleigh Hungerford in the 1350s, 12 cows produced 35 calves in three years, even a couple of them culled as "kebbs" having calves taken from them before they were sold; on the Winchester estate 95 per cent of the cows on half a dozen manors produced calves in the years 1361, 1382, and 1412; and at Kingston Lacy in 1391, 22 cows had 19 calves despite the fact that some of the cows may have been on the old side. The calves to be retained were carefully selected and carefully scrutinized over the next two years, any "useless" stock being discarded, until in their third year the survivors reinforced the ranks of the cows or oxen. On the Winchester estate it looks as though oxen had a 3–5 year working life and cows, too, may have been kept for five years or so before being culled. Losses from disease seem normally not to have been particularly heavy, and some care was taken for the sustenance especially of the working and breeding stock. Special pastures were reserved for the oxen and horses at Idmiston and Gomeldon; 80 acres of hay, much of it for cattle, was made at Evercreech; and when hay was in short supply oats in the sheaf were fed to oxen, especially in the main ploughing seasons, and at Brockhampton even rye and vetches were used for that purpose.[285]

How productive cows were as dairy animals is harder to determine, since so often their milk was rented out. At the end of the fourteenth century, however, there was still dairying on the St Swithun's manors

[284] Gras, *English Village*, pp. 298, 307; PRO SC 6/970/22–3; *Somerset and Dorset N. & Q.*, XI, 1908–9, pp. 238–9; XVI, 1918–19, p. 273; WPR 159388; Leland, *Itinerary*, I, pp. 161, 168, 253, 275; *Some Manorial Accounts of St Augustine's Abbey*, ed. Sabin, pp. 35–8, 70–2, 190–1; M. Williams, *The Draining of the Somerset Levels*, Cambridge, 1970, p. 79.

[285] WPR 159371, 159388, 159414, 159436; *Somerset and Dorset N. & Q.*, XI, 1908–9, pp. 238–9; PRO SC 6/970/13–15, DL 29/682/11046; BL Harl. Ms. 3961, ff.138d–9.

at Wootton St Lawrence and Enford, although unfortunately the milk of both cows and ewes was used in unrecorded quantities. If the Winchester assumption that a cow gave as much milk as twenty-four sheep is applicable in these places, on the other hand, at Wootton during the summer milking season in 1398 each cow produced about 10 lb of butter and 71 lb of cheese, and at Enford in 1403 did just a little better than that. If indeed they did so, these figures are rather better than those the canons of Bolton achieved at the beginning of the century on their Yorkshire vaccaries; and the rich pastures of northern Somerset may possibly have shown figures that were better still.[286]

Other livestock were apt to have a lesser role than cattle and sheep. Many places had a few breeding mares as well as working horses: their foals provided the work horses of the future, although they might be rejected and sold if, like one of the three born at Farleigh Hungerford in 1354, they were thought too small.[287] Pigs were more numerous and ubiquitous. The St Swithun's manors provided the priory with 499 pigs in 1398, and at Michaelmas that year there were 80 pigs and 38 young pigs at Wootton St Lawrence alone. The Hungerfords, too, kept two or three sows at Heytesbury, the bishops of Winchester two at Poundisford (Somerset), the bishops of Wells two at Evercreech, and the Duchy of Lancaster three at Kingston Lacy, all of which justified the expectations of the agricultural treatises by producing, with suspicious unanimity, two litters each every year totalling neither more nor fewer than 15 young pigs. There were some losses from disease of both older and younger stock (and at Heytesbury in 1391–2 the lord's dogs killed a whole litter); but at Rimpton and Poundisford most of the pig stock survived in most years to be sold off as year-old hogs or as mature pigs a year later, while the pigs bred at Evercreech supplied a replacement sow in 1382, hogs and young pigs for the bishop's larder, hogs for despatch to Wookey (perhaps for fattening), and young pigs to be sent to market.[288]

Pigs seem commonly to have been left to root for much of their sustenance and fared particularly well when acorns and beech mast were plentifully available; but even *porci campestres* got some peas in winter at Fareham, at Enford suckling sows and pigs being fattened for the larder got some barley, and beans were also fed to the pigs at Sandford Orcas (Dorset) in 1398–9. There the reason may have been that the winter that year was hard, for barley was also fed to the

---

[286] *Manor of Manydown*, ed. Kitchin, p. 162; BL Harl. Roll X7; I. Kershaw, *Bolton Priory*, pp. 101–2.   [287] PRO SC 6/970/15.

[288] *Manor of Manydown*, ed. Kitchin, pp. 162, 169; PRO SC 6/1052/17–18, 1053/6–7; WPR 159371, 159388, 159414; *Walter of Henley*, ed. Oschinsky, p. 472; *Somerset and Dorset N. & Q.*, XI, 1908–9, p. 240; PRO DL 29/682/11046.

poultry, which seems more commonly to have been left to pick up what it could around the farmyard. Poultry management, however, was possibly rather better at Heytesbury. In 1391–2 the swannery there provided birds for the household at Christmas and in harvest, and 8 geese, 30 capons, 61 cocks and hens, and 121 pigeons were despatched to the lord's larder. Chicks were hatched to keep up the poultry stock, and also to maintain the flock of peacocks and peahens, the sale of whose feathers made a modest contribution to manorial revenues. Hungerford farming was manifestly versatile.[289]

There were other forms of diversification. There was a vineyard at Dunster until the Luttrells abandoned it in the fifteenth century and another on a modest estate at West Grafton (Wilts.). Apple orchards, some devastated in the great gale in c. 1360, produced a certain amount of fruit for sale in various places; dovecotes provided some pigeons for sale and tithe birds for the parish church; and the sale of salmon at Bitterne in 1371 brought in nearly £20.[290] Many landlords also managed their rabbits profitably. It has been said that the references to rabbits on the Isle of Wight are so frequent as to suggest that the island was one large warren; 1,000 rabbits were sold to a London poulterer from Overton (Hants.) in 1382; *grasses and covenables* rabbits were sent from Aldbourne to John of Gaunt's household in 1371–2, provided a present for the Lady Mohun in 1375, and in 1380 were to be delivered to the duke's household at the rate of six dozen a week in the season. The Aldbourne warren was leased for £40 a year in 1426 and for £42 in 1432; but these rents may have been excessive, for it was in hand again in 1434 when 762 pairs of rabbits were taken from it, mostly for the king's household, worth about £16, only £4 less than the value of the Aldbourne wool clip that year.[291]

Another product was put under contribution at Collingbourne Ducis. Because the pallisade of Everleigh park was ruinous, John of Gaunt in 1374 ordered that sufficient wood to repair it, and sufficient saleable timber to cover the cost of repairs, should be cut in Collingbourne "foreign wood". Much woodland, in fact, was exploited very systematically by cropping it regularly for underwood, apparently including the hundred acres at Collingbourne according to

---

[289] WPR 159371; BL Harl. Roll X7; *Somerset and Dorset N. & Q.*, III, 1892–3, p. 315; PRO SC 6/1053/6–7.

[290] Maxwell-Lyte, *History of Dunster*, I, p. 325; *Wilts. Extents for Debt, Edward I – Elizabeth I*, ed. Conyers, no. 11; *VCH Somerset*, IV, p. 45; PRO SC 6/970/13–14, 974/25; WPR 159380.

[291] S. F. Hockey, *Quarr Abbey and its Lands, 1132–1631*, Leicester, 1970, p. 197; WPR 159388; *John of Gaunt's Register, 1372–6*, ed. S. Armitage-Smith, Camden 3rd ser. XX–XXI, 1911, I, no. 265; II, nos. 876, 889, 1126, 1694; *John of Gaunt's Register, 1379–83*, ed. E. Lodge and R. Somerville, Camden 3rd ser. LVI, 1937, I, no. 441; PRO DL 29/682/11058, 683/11068, 710/11433.

a valuation of 1361. Woods in the south may have been cropped rather less frequently than those in eastern England, for a 16–18-year cycle seems to be assumed in 1518 at Kington St Michael and Christian Malford in Wiltshire, always provided that the woods were well supervised. Much of the timber cut was used for fuel and fencing, but sales of timber in some years brought in over £10 at Merdon (Hants.), where 25 acres were cropped in 1350–1, and at Fareham, and nearly £18 at Aldbourne in 1426–7. There were also substantial sales of charcoal at Bishop's Sutton (Hants.), where there were also regular sales of beech saplings. Other manors, however, had only large timber, like that in the Cerne abbey wood at Symondsbury (Dorset). Tall timber, of course, could only be cut at longer intervals than underwood but, as in the case of the 160 ash trees sold from Highclere in 1431, it was the source at least of an irregular income.[292]

Once again the mixed-farming character, at least of the larger agricultural enterprises, in most of southern England is apparent. They made what use they could of all the resources which nature provided, not only ploughland and pasture, but also of woodland and even water. At the same time many of the branches of farming supported each other. There were, of course, crops that were principally cash crops, like the wool from the great sheep flocks and some of the cereals, yet some Porlock wool went to the lady's household, and the Crawley grange accounts show the many uses of grain crops. The harvest usually provided most of the seed for the next year's sowing, perhaps a quarter or so of what had been harvested; full-time workers received as liveries a quarter of the barley crop as well as small amounts of oats; oxen and horses ate up a quarter of the oat harvest, and sheep sometimes consumed all the vetches left after seed had been taken out. Only what remained was available for sale, and on many estates sales were at least partly book-keeping entries for grain delivered to the household of lord or lady. Livestock and rabbits, fish and poultry, butter and cheeses flowed alternately into household and market, and the milk given by the one cow left at Farleigh Hungerford in 1387 was reserved for the lord's consumption. Conversely the harvest, perhaps particularly on the thin downland soils, needed the manure provided by the sheep flocks, just as the sheep in turn might need to supplement their grazing with a few sheaves of vetches or a little hay. The great estates sometimes grouped their properties so that these interlocking needs might be

[292] *John of Gaunt's Register, 1372–6,* ed. Armitage-Smith, II, no. 1433; *Abstracts of Wiltshire Inquisitions Post Mortem...1327–1377,* ed. E. Stokes, p. 288; BL Harl. Ms. 3961, ff.41, 65; O. Rackham, *Trees and Woodland in the British Landscape,* p. 90: WPR 159351, 159360, 159380, 159400, 159407, 159414, 159436, 159449; PRO DL 29/682/11058; *Somerset and Dorset N. & Q.,* X, 1906–7, p. 332.

satisfied on an intermanorial basis, but this extension merely went to further the mutually sustaining objectives of many of the mixed farming operations.

J. DEVON AND CORNWALL

An overall view of arable farming, of diminished but persistent importance in later medieval Devon and Cornwall, reveals certain special features in crop preferences which mark the two counties out as a distinctive agricultural province. First, there was a notable emphasis among farmers and consumers in most parts of the south-west on the coarser grains of rye and oats, an emphasis which is clear from details of multure, of peasant chattels, and of purveyance as well as from demesne accounts.[293] On some manors sowing of "small oats" (*avena minuta*, the "naked oats" of later writers) persisted throughout the later middle ages.[294] This was not a backward husbandry constrained simply by soils and by climatic conditions, for in later centuries barley and wheat became as important in Devon and Cornwall as rye and oats were in the later middle ages.[295] Lying behind the persistence of oats and rye was preference for the two crops in bread and beer, old and well established already by the fourteenth century, very slow to change except in specific localities, and certainly not affected generally by the trend towards the phasing out of rye which took place in some other parts of England during the middle ages.[296] Rye was the most usual dole in liveries paid to manorial *famuli* in the south-west and also features frequently in miscellaneous payments sanctioned from

[293] For multure, see n.298 below; Devon RO, DD54888, Arundell Mss. at Hook Manor, MA 246, court of Michaelmas 1381, and *Register of the Black Prince*, II, pp. 33, 65; PRO E 101/554/1, 555/12, 32B, 33; *CPR, 1321–4*, p. 93; *CCR, 1330–3*, p. 16; *Cal. Inq. Misc.*, II, p. 269.

[294] *Avena minuta*, the "naked oat" of Ray, the *avena nuda* of Gerard and the *pylas* of the Cornish language, survived in Cornwall into the eighteenth and nineteenth centuries: J. Ray, *Historia Plantarum*, London, 1686–8, II, p. 1254; J. Gerard, *The Herball*, London, 1633 edn, p. 74; W. Borlase, *The Natural History of Cornwall*, Oxford, 1758, pp. 59, 87; N. J. G. Pounds, 'Pillas, an extinct grain', *Devon and Cornwall N. & Q.*, XXI, 1942–6, pp. 199–200; *Oxford English Dictionary*, s.v. pillas. It was also grown in Somerset, south Wales and East Anglia: Hants. RO, Ecclesiastical Commissioners, 2/159308 (Nailsbourne); C. E. H. Chadwyck Healey, *West Somerset*, pp. 423, 440, 443; Rees, *South Wales and the March*, p. 188; Gerard, *op. cit.*, p. 74. H. P. R. Finberg, (*Tavistock Abbey*, p. 96) was wrong in hazarding the guess that the large oat (*avena grossa*) replaced *avena minuta* in the south-west during the later middle ages. *Grossa* is found well before 1350: Devon RO, 1262M/M/84; K. Ugawa, 'The economic development of some Devon manors in the thirteenth century', *Devon. Assoc.*, XCIV, 1962, pp. 635–6. For late-continued use of *minuta*, see Devon RO, W1258M/G/3, D/52/2 (Hurdwick), and D/52/2, a/c of 1496–7 (Leigh).

[295] G. V. Harrison, 'The South-West', in *AHEW*, V, p. 367; R. Carew, *The Survey of Cornwall*, ed. F. E. Halliday, p. 102; *idem, Survey of Cornwall*, ed. Tonkin, pp. 17–18; R. G. F. Stanes, 'A georgicall account of Devonshire and Cornwalle', *Devon. Assoc.*, XCVI, 1964, p. 289.

[296] M. M. Postan, in *CEcH*, I, p. 583.

seigneurial granaries – to threshers at Hamatethy, to tenants at Holcombe Rogus as a special gift, and to poor widows at Hele. "Grey" rye loaves were given to the poor by the almoner of Tavistock abbey. The rye loaf of the country was also distributed at boon-works and at harvest revels, as at Hurdwick, where the proportion of rye used "for autumn" actually increased at the expense of wheat during the fifteenth century. These references relate, of course, to the diet of labourers, yet monks at Tavistock themselves consumed rye bread and wheaten bread in equal quantities and the household's baker at Holcombe Rogus used rye, although whether for the lord's table or for servants is uncertain.[297] Some oats went towards an oatmeal pottage, which we can see in the small amounts of gruel often given to labourers "by custom", but the majority was used as the common drink grain of the country.[298] Ale made from oats was still popular locally in the sixteenth century, when it received a universally bad press from outsiders: Cornish ale was "lyke wash as pygges had wrestled dryn", while an especially local variety in mid-Devon induced vomiting in strangers, "notwithstandinge the people of that countrie...doe endure the same very well".[299]

A second distinctive feature of crop preferences was the small part played by legumes at a time when significant increases have been noted in other parts of England. On demesnes legumes were grown on minute acreages, not as part of established rotations but often separately "in the lord's garden". The only statistical indications for tenants' holdings come from tithe accounts of Buckerell, Holcombe Rogus, and Hartland, where legumes comprised about 4, 5, and 1 per cent respectively of all tithes by volume.[300] Nowhere in Devon and

---

[297] PRO SC 6/823/28, Devon RO, DD54925, a/c of 1433–4, Somerset RO, DDCN box 3 no. 14, a/c of 1368–9; Devon RO, W1258M/D/42/9, a/c of 1395–6; Devon RO, W1258M/D/52/2 for Hurdwick and, for another example, BL Add. Roll 7656; Finberg, *Tavistock Abbey*, p. 98 and Devon RO, DD 54890, 54907.

[298] For examples of oatmeal pottage, see PRO SC 6/830/29, BL Add. Roll 13091, Devon RO, W1258M/D/38/15, Milton a/c of 1397–8, West Devon RO, 70/92–6, Arundell Mss. CR 246. The best evidence for the dominance of oats in tenants' brewing comes from multure accounts in which coarse malt of oats was almost everywhere brought to mills in larger quantities than best malt: PRO SC 6/828/10–11, 1118/6 (Sampford Courtenay, Aylesbeare, "Exilond"); Devon RO, CR 1434, W1258M/D/74/6 and DD 54888, 890, 892, 901, 902, 915–18, 921, 923; Dean and Chapter Archives, Exeter, 5030; Arundell Mss. CR 446. Even rye was occasionally used to make ale: Somerset RO, DDCN box 3 no. 14, a/c of 1372–3.

[299] A. Borde, *The First Boke of the Introduction of Knowledge*, ed. F. J. Furnivall, EETS extra ser. x, London, 1870, p. 122; W. J. Blake, 'Hooker's Synopsis Chorographical of Devonshire', *Devon. Assoc.*, XLVII, 1915, p. 345. See also Carew, *Survey of Cornwall*, ed. Halliday, p. 103.

[300] Hilton, *Leicestershire Estates*, pp. 65–6, 135; D. Roden, 'Demesne farming in the Chiltern Hills', *AHR*, XVII, 1969, p. 14; Devon RO, DD 54888, 892, 902 and W1258M/G/3, a/c of 1403–4; Dean and Chapter Archives, 5116, a/c of 1368–9, Devon RO, DD 54892, Arundell Mss.

Table 3.20. *Devon and Cornwall: demesne cropping (percentages)*

(a) Crop acreages

	wheat	barley	oats	rye	legumes
South Devon	35.7	12.0	49.1	2.1	1.0
East Devon	24.0	1.7	61.8	11.3	1.2
Mid- and N. Devon	20.8	—	42.4	36.8	—
Cornish coastlands	47.0	4.5	48.2	0.3	—

(b) Crop combinations
(Figures are percentages, for each region, of all calculations for that region)

	Crops in rank order								
	WO	WOB	OBW	OWB	OW	OWR	ORW	OR	ORB[a]
South Devon	—	9	—	64	18	9	—	—	—
East Devon	—	—	1	7	34	24	15	16	3
Mid- and N. Devon	21	—	—	—	3	15	51	10	—
Cornish coastlands	15	15	—	40	30	—	—	—	—

[a] B = barley, O = oats, R = rye, W = wheat.
Notes on the crop combinations: 1. For each place any fourth-ranking crop or crop occupying less than 5% of the total cropped acreage has not been taken into account. 2. Three calculations which reveal that oats only were sown have also been excluded. 3. For the regions see Fig. 2.1.
Sources: (figures in brackets give numbers of calculations for each place): *South Devon*: Denbury, 1392–3 (1): Devon RO, W1258M/G/3. Goodrington, 1414–15 (1): BL Add. Roll 13770. Maristow, 1379–98 (5): West Devon RO, 70/92, 3, 5, 6. Morwell 1496–7 (1): Devon RO, W1258M/D/52/2 (composite account). North Huish, 1365–6 (1): Devon RO, 158M/M/11. Sherford, 1391–2 (1): BL Add. Roll 13091. Yealmpton, 1395–6 (1): PRO SC 6/830/29. *East Devon*: Bishop's Clyst, 1373–1419 (16): Devon RO, W1258M/G/3. Buckerell, 1365–9 (4): Dean and Chapter Archives, 5116. Canonsleigh, 1377–8 (1): BL Add. Roll 7656. Clayhidon, 1359–90 (13): Arundell Mss. CR 446 and MA 246. Dawlish, 1388–9 (1): Dean and Chapter Archives, 5030. Fluxton, 1373–1411 (6): Devon RO, W1258M/G/3. Hele in Bradninch 1354–95 (12): Somerset RO, DDCN box 3 no. 14. Holcombe Rogus, 1369–1434 (15): Devon RO, DD 54888, 90, 92; 54901, 2, 7, 15–19, 21, 23–5. Langacre in Broad Clyst, 1384–5 (1): PRO SC 6/828/9. Langford in Cullompton, 1356–7 (1): Corpus Christi College, Oxford, Ms. Kn 3/1. Pinhoe, 1395–6? (1): PRO SC 6/829/22. Rockbeare, 1377–8 (1): BL Add. Roll 7657. Yarcombe, 1368–73 (5): Devon RO, CR 1434. *North and mid-Devon*: Bishop's Nympton, 1378–9 (1): Devon RO, W1258M/G/6/10. Burrington, 1357–8 (1): Devon RO, W1258M/G/1/42. Hockford, 1377–8 (1): BL Add. Roll 7658. Hurdwick in Tavistock, 1398–1498 (30): Devon RO, W1258M/D/52/2. Leigh in Milton Abbot, 1397–c. 1500 (3): Devon RO, W1258M/D/38/15, D/52/2 (composite account), D/71/9. Ottery in Lamerton, 1380–96 (2): Devon RO, W1258M/D/42/9. Sampford Courtenay, 1383–4 (1): Dean and Chapter Archives, VC 22279. Week in Milton Abbot, 1381–2 (1): Devon RO, W1258M/D/38/15. Werrington, 1399–1499 (20): Devon RO, W1258M/D/71. *Cornish coastlands*: Burniere, 1399–1403 (3): BL Add. Rolls 64391–2 and Devon RO, CR 435. Cargoll, 1399–1412 (13): Devon RO, W1258M/E/24. Lanherne, 1386–7 (1): Arundell Mss. MA 16. Penheale, 1400–1 (1): PRO SC 6/823/41. Whalesborough, 1373–1404 (3): Somerset RO, DDWO 46/1.

Cornwall, it seems, could be found great acreages under legumes, such as those seen by Leland in Somerset.[301] In the far south-west they were not able to oust rye and oats, so strongly entrenched as "coarse" ingredients in diet, while farmers had their own old-established means

MA 412. Small quantities of legumes are to be found among peasant chattels: Devon RO, DD 54888, Arundell Mss. MA 246, court of Michaelmas 1381.

[301] Leland, *Itinerary*, I, p. 168, an observation confirmed by manorial accounts, e.g. Longleat House Mss. 10655, 11216 (Zoy and Brent).

of maintaining soil quality, and early springing grass, a product of mild winters, meant that they were not necessary as livestock feed.

Underlying these general features was a well-developed regional mosaic of crop combinations which makes one wary of generalizing about arable farming in any county or province of medieval England. In Table 3.20 we analyse regionally crop combinations in all known later medieval demesne grange accounts from Devon and Cornwall. The regions in which the peculiarities of the province at large were most strongly expressed were north and mid-Devon, the high moorlands, and east Devon. North and mid-Devon was oats and rye country *par excellence*. On many demesnes, for example at Sampford Courtenay, Nympton, Leigh, and Hayne, no wheat, or only a very little, was sown; at Monkleigh the demesne was described as *terra siliginosa et avenosa*.[302] That demesne cropping reflects the local practice of the country is shown by evidence for grains grown on tenant holdings in north and mid-Devon. Rye completely dominated multure at Nympton and the mill at Sampford Courtenay ground mostly rye, some oats, and some of an unspecified crop; at Hockford the miller's rent was rye in kind while oats predominated in tithe payments from the parish of Hartland.[303] There could be no better confirmation of the value of demesne cropping patterns to characterize the main outlines of regional farming. Rye and oats had probably become entrenched in local diet as the many marginal lands of north and mid-Devon were broken in during the early middle ages, and remained popular despite retreat of cultivation later. The borders of the high moorlands of Devon and Cornwall have no manors with surviving grange accounts but there are indications – from tithe payments by tenants at Hamatethy and Altarnun adjoining Bodmin Moor, from a demesne inventory for Lustleigh on the edge of Dartmoor and from multure payments at nearby South Teign – that oats and rye also dominated arable farming around these granitic uplands.[304]

The crop combinations of two regions, south Devon and the Cornish coastlands, covering a small proportion of the peninsula, stand out as distinct. In south Devon oats still usually ranked as the dominant crop on demesnes, but rye was found scarcely at all and barley, seldom grown elsewhere in the county, often ranked third. These emphases were present, too, in local diet: of crops mentioned before the court of

---

[302] See notes to Table 3.20 and, for Hayne, *Cal. Inq. Misc.*, v, p. 1; Devon RO, CR 1133. At Sampford Courtenay and Nympton the tolerant *avena minuta* was the only type of oats sown in large quantities. The dominance of oats and rye in the figures for north and mid-Devon in Table 3.20 would be even greater if one aberrant demesne were excluded.

[303] See notes to Table 3.20 and, for Hartland, Arundell Mss. MA 412.

[304] PRO SC 6/823/28; Dean and Chapter Archives, 5252; Devon RO, 410Z/F/1; PRO SC 2/168/29, courts of 12 Henry IV.

Stoke Fleming, in presentments for minor offences of trespass and theft, wheat dominates, but barley is also referred to.[305] The best evidence for cropping on tenants' holdings in south Devon comes from Plymstock; here abbots of Tavistock used the manor as a major source of grain for their bakery, via a food rent of antique appearance paid in wheat. When the tenants of Plymstock had thus paid their rents in kind, and stored some grain for sale, they took the rest to the mill from which multure payments reveal that oats formed the most important crop, quite closely followed by wheat, with barley third. Almost all of the oats went to make malt, indicating that ale from oats remained the traditional drink; wheat and barley were presumably used for bread; oatmeal disappears completely from these records in the early fifteenth century.[306] It is interesting to note that rye also disappears from view in Stoke Fleming court rolls after the end of the fourteenth century. Are we seeing the end of a replacement of oats and rye by wheat and barley in the solid diet of the inhabitants of south Devon? If so, we can only speculate upon the reasons: realization, perhaps, that soil conditions and very easy access to sea-sand allowed these relatively demanding crops to be grown with profit, and perhaps an influence from markets for these grains in ports along the coastline.

Figures from the coastlands of Cornwall, with their emphasis on wheat and barley as well as oats, might seem surprising in light of common suppositions about the unproductive and largely pastoral nature of Cornish medieval agriculture, but will not be unexpected after what has been said in Chapter 2 about the concentration of arable production taking place in favoured coastal areas after the mid-fourteenth century; these areas so impressed Leland that he dubbed the county "fertile Cornwall" in his poem celebrating the birth of a future duke in 1537. Figures for Cornwall in Table 3.20 are drawn largely from the episcopal demesne of Burniere, at the water's edge on the sandy estuary of the Camel, with easily worked soils developed from Devonian slates; the Arundells' at Lanherne, nearby in the sheltered Vale of Mawgan; Cargoll, also episcopal and with similar soils and close to the sea; and the Bottreaux demesne at Whalesborough a mile or so from renowned supplies of sand at Widemouth Bay. We can say that they are typical of demesnes on the coastlands at large, for grains reserved for sowing on the small coastal properties of alien priories seized by the crown in 1324 included little rye and much wheat and barley, while the lands of Sir Robert Tresilian, forfeited after his impeachment in 1388 by the Merciless Parliament, included wheat-growing demesnes. We read too of land which bore "wheat, barley, oats, hay and peas...as good and fair as any soil in Cornewaille". It is

---

[305] Devon RO, 902M/M/2–31 and 55/13/2.   [306] Devon RO, W1258M/D/74/6.

Table 3.21. *Comparative demesne grain yields (yield per seed sown)*

	Devon and Cornwall	Winchester estate, 1349–1453	Norfolk, 1350–1500	England at large, 14th and 15th cent.
Oats	3.2	2.8	2.7	2.7
Rye	6.1	—	3.5	4.5
Wheat	4.8	3.7	4.2	4.6
Barley	3.8	3.8	3.2	4.6

Note: Figures for Devon and Cornwall, and for the Winchester estate, are for productivity minus tithe.
Sources: Devon and Cornwall: accounts, from among those listed in Table 3.20, which are consecutive or from which a calculation is possible from the *oneratio* or the *responsio. Winchester estate*: D. H. Farmer, 'Grain yields on the Winchester manors in the Later Middle Ages', p. 560. *Norfolk*: B. M. S. Campbell, 'Arable productivity in medieval England: some evidence from Norfolk', p. 384. *England at large*: B. H. Slicher van Bath, *Yield Ratios, 810–1820, A. A. G. Bijdragen,* 10, 1963.

the same on tenant holdings: at Roseworthy crops seized illegally in 1352 comprised 45 acres of wheat and barley as well as 30 acres of oats, while tenants at Callington took more wheat to the mill than any other crop. Multure accounts for the mills at St Columb in 1451–2 and later show that by then wheaten bread predominated in the diet and barley had partially replaced oats in brewing, indicating a divergence in these favoured coastlands, as in south Devon, from the coarser fare which prevailed throughout much of the south-west.[307]

Evidence on crop yields comes of necessity only from demesnes. Ratios of yield per seed sown were good by the standards of other parts of the country; means from all demesnes with suitable data show that crops which were of most importance to farmers in the south-west gave significantly higher yields than those in samples from elsewhere in England (Table 3.21). There were of course differences from estate to estate, and manor to manor. On Tavistock abbey's demesnes, where yields of most crops tended to be higher even than the provincial mean, the steward's "expectation" was for wheat to yield eight times, rye twelve times and oats four times, figures rarely reached but often approached quite closely. The prior of Plympton's south Devon

[307] *Itinerary of John Leland,* ed. T. Hearne, London, 3rd edn, 1768–9, IX, p. xxi; sources for demesnes as in Table 3.20; PRO E 106/6/11; *Cal. Inq. Misc.,* v, pp. 61, 83, 84; *Register of the Black Prince,* II, p. 178; *ibid.,* pp. 32–3; PRO SC 6/822/8; Arundell Mss. MA 47, 56, 57. For barley beer at Whalesborough, see Somerset RO, DDWO 46/1, a/c of 1403–4.

property of Maristow was another high-yielding demesne, where the usual expectation for wheat was a five- or six-fold yield, even eight-fold when "the year was good". A correlate for high yield ratios might turn out to be closeness of a demesne to the principal residence of an estate, bringing with it ease of supervision and a close personal interest by lords and their stewards in home farming, as at the Franceis demesne of Hele, at Bishop's Clyst, the nearest episcopal retreat to Exeter, or at Hurdwick by Tavistock.[308] One could extend the argument to suggest achievement of high yields by the most successful of tenants.

Rotations must be considered first in any explanation of the generally high yield ratios of Devon and Cornwall, for in rotational practices as in crop combinations the two counties stand out as a distinctive agricultural province. Estimates of the proportion of arable which was cropped are not easy to make, because of the very irregularity of rotations, but at Hurdwick, Rockbeare, and Burniere the average figure was only 26 per cent, at Clyst 45 per cent, and 51 per cent on the Devonshire estate of the Courtenays in 1377.[309] These are low figures compared with a theoretical 66 per cent cropped under a three-field system, or the mean of 85 per cent under the very intensive rotation systems practised in eastern Norfolk.[310] Uncropped acres were normally rested under grass, in a convertible system, rather than with a bare fallow. At Cargoll in the first decade of the fifteenth century a close called "Parknewith" was used as pasture for the lord's animals for several consecutive years, was sown for the next four and then returned again to grass. Where a series of accounts is less precise, a sure sign that fields were normally returned to grass after being cropped is the infrequency of occurrence of most field names; sporadically occurring field names in a set of accounts indicate a lengthy period of ley between crops, as we should expect in an era when grassland expanded at the expense of cropped land.[311] In addition, references to beat-burning (*baticium*) – the firing of turf pared from the surface when a field was returned to crops – leave no doubt of a system of convertible husbandry. At Cargoll we read of a labourer "rooting out gorse before the plough" in a field which had been so long unploughed that it had become infested with the plant; at Burrington of "hoeing out gorse in

---

[308] Finberg, *Tavistock Abbey*, pp. 110–15 and accounts for Burrington, Denbury, Leigh, and Milton Abbot as in Table 3.20. Sources for other places as in Table 3.20. The Devon home of the Franceis family was sometimes at Chevithorne, a few miles from Hele.

[309] Devon RO, W1258M/D/52/2 and Finberg, *Tavistock Abbey*, p. 106; BL Add. Roll 7657 and Harl. Ms. 3660, f.143; BL Add. Rolls 64391–2, Devon RO, CR 435 and 382/ER/2; Devon RO, W1258M/G/3 and Alcock, 'An East Devon manor', 1, p. 167; PRO C 135/260/3.

[310] Campbell, 'Arable productivity', p. 393.

[311] Devon RO, W1258M/E/24; DD 54890 and subsequent accounts; Arundell Mss. MA 246 and CR 446.

order to burn it"; at Sampford Courtenay of the burning of pasture and "scattering" of the ashes; at Whalesborough of "removing thorns before ploughing".[312] That tenants were thoroughly familiar with the method is clear from the evidence of labour services, from leases, and from a statement in 1487 that beat-burning was the common custom of the whole countryside – *usus et modus patrie*.[313] Convertible husbandry was highly suited to the relaxed conditions of the later middle ages, for it was ideal for the fruitful integration of livestock and arable enterprises, while leys could easily be lengthened to take into account reduced demands for grain. But the system was not a later medieval innovation, as it has sometimes been portrayed:[314] accounts and leases, as well as evidence of labour services incorporating beat-burning, show it in use well before 1350.[315] That even thirteenth-century pressures to increase cropland could not eradicate the practice suggests that it was deeply rooted in the routines and calendars of husbandmen in the south-west. Thence it may well have been imitated elsewhere in the later middle ages, just as in the seventeenth century beat-burning was being praised and advocated abroad under the name of "Denshiring" ("Devonshiring").[316]

Convertible husbandry probably goes far in accounting for high yield ratios in the south-west, but other aspects of crop and soil management contributed too. In some regions rotations which included only the relatively undemanding crops of rye and oats *and* a long ley were far from punishing to the land. In such rotations rye was normally the crop which followed conversion of a field from pasture, accounting

[312] Devon RO, W1258M/E/24, a/c of 1411–12, W1258M/G/1/42, Dean and Chapter Archives, VC 22279, Somerset RO, DDWO 46/1, a/c of 1399–1400. See also Devon RO, W1258M/G/3, a/c of 1396–7, where there is a reference to "cutting gorse and thorns before the plough", W1258M/D/42/9, a/c of 1395–6, for a reference to the mattock used in paring the turf.

[313] PRO SC 6/822/15, 826/15, BL Add. Roll 64349, Devon RO, CR 496, W1258M/G/1/42, a/c of 1357–8, Arundell Mss. MA 277 for *baticium* as a labour service at Bovey Tracey, Halton, Botelet, Plympton, Burrington, and South Pool; Devon RO, W1258M/D/53/25, 124. That beat-burning time, like harvest, was an important point in the farming calendar is suggested by the practice at Hurdwick of slaughtering a ewe in celebration: Devon RO, W1258M/D/52/2, a/c of 1411–12.

[314] J. L. Bolton, *The Medieval English Economy 1150–1500*, London, 1980, p. 244.

[315] For early medieval references to beat-burning on improved land (which implies convertible husbandry), see PRO C 133/126/4 and 134/8/14; Devon RO, W1258M/D/38/5, D/43/1, 1262M/M/81; PRO SC 6/1138/1; Ugawa, 'Some Devon manors', p. 635.

[316] For convertible husbandry in other parts of England during the later middle ages, see Searle, *Lordship and Community*, p. 275, and Dyer, *Warwickshire Farming*, pp. 14, 29. Elsewhere, beat-burning did owe something to Devonshire practice: *Survey of the Lands of William, first Earl of Pembroke*, ed. C. R. Stratton, 1909, I, p. lxii, and II, p. 543. Later, the south-western example was certainly imitated: J. Norden, *The Surveior's Dialogue*, London, 1607, pp. 227–8; T. Risdon, *The Chorographical Description or Survey of the County of Devon*, London, 1811, p. 11; J. E. B. Gover, A. Mawer and F. M. Stenton, *The Place-Names of Surrey*, EPNS, 1934, p. 368.

for very high rye yields on some demesnes.[317] Between each crop the
land benefited from the dung of livestock and also from the more
unusual practice of spreading sea-sand on the land. Where sand
contained pulverized calcareous shells, sanding amounted to liming.
Where it did not, sand lightened soils, making it easier to keep them
free of weeds, so that smothering by sowing at excessive rates was not
necessary.[318] In either case sanding was to the advantage of yields. In
east Devon alone, later called the "marl countrie" of the south-west,
we read of marling,[319] but elsewhere only of sand. From the mouth of
the Taw and Torridge sand was loaded onto barges to be taken
upstream to Tawstock and Monkleigh, thence by pack-horse into mid-
Devon. The Tamar, penetrating deeply inland, was another major
artery on which plied barges to Maristow, Morwellham, and, on the
Cornish side, to Halton. From the Erme radiated a number of sand-
ways on which lords took toll from passing pack-horses, an expected
300 each year at Ermington alone. Cornish sand-ways led inland from
beaches at, for example, Widemouth, Porthtowan, and Winnianton
Towans. The practice gave employment to the sanders mentioned in
demesne accounts, to John Scotte of Monkleigh who in the 1440s
combined barge building and sand carrying, and to pack-horse men
whom we glimpse at Halton in the 1410s renting pasture for their
horses. We hear of sanding as the "custom of the manor" on tenant
holdings, of two Monkleigh tenants who obtained a reduction of rent
in 1456 because of the expense of sanding their holdings, and of the men
of Helston-in-Kirrier who complained to the Black Prince in 1357 that
their lands lay untilled because of interference with carriage of sand.[320]

[317] Devon RO, W1258M/D/38/15, a/c of 1381–2 and 1397–8, G/6/10, Dean and Chapter
Archives, VC 22279 for examples of rye sown on "beat land".

[318] Stanes, 'A georgicall account', pp. 301–2. Sowing rates in the south-west during the later
middle ages were roughly similar to those recommended in the thirteenth century by the
Husbandry, although, significantly, they were lower on recently burnt land: W1258M/D/38/15,
Week a/c of 1381–2, G/6/10, Dean and Chapter Archives, VC 22279.

[319] Stanes, *op. cit.*, pp. 282–7 for the "marl countrie" and, for late medieval references: BL
Add. Rolls 7657 (Rockbeare), 7656 (Canonsleigh), Arundell Mss. CR 446, a/c of 1360–1
(Clayhidon). The first reference indicates marling by tenants.

[320] PRO C 136/69/1, Devon RO, CR 1131–3, and Nottingham Univ. Library, Middleton Ms.
M 149/3 for traffic on the Taw and Torridge; West Devon RO, 70/92, 93, 95, Devon RO,
W1258M/D/71/9, PRO SC 6/822/15–20, and Hatcher, *Duchy of Cornwall*, p. 13 n.4 for the
Tamar route; *Cal. Inq. Misc.*, I, p. 521, PRO SC 6/827/34, Devon RO, 158M/M/11 for the
Erme; Devon RO, W1258M/D/71, Arundell Ms. R&S 8 (Connerton), Duchy of Cornwall
Archives, 3 (Tywarnhaile), and *Register of the Black Prince*, II, pp. 130–1, 179–80 for the Cornish
coastlands; PRO SC 6/830/29 for an example of a *zabulatarius*; Devon RO, CR 1097, court of
June 1452, and PRO SC 6/822/17; PRO SC 2/158/12, court of Oct. 1470; Devon RO, CR 1144;
Register of the Black Prince, II, pp. 130–1. Pleas of debt also indicate sanding on tenant holdings:
Devon RO, W1258M/D/70, court of Sept. 1366, CR 1096, court of Jan. 1448, Cary Mss.,
Ashwater court roll of June 1409.

Such references testify to the belief among farmers that sanding, another distinctive provincial practice, was beneficial to cultivation.

Consideration of yields must also take into account the nature of field systems. By the late fourteenth century (from which most of our yield calculations come) the majority of demesnes were divided into securely hedged, severally held closes. Field systems of this type were likely to abet high yields for they prevented deterioration of grain, allowed the best use of labour in an age when optimal use of work was essential for successful farming, and they rendered easy the concentration of animals on cropland. Enclosure and consolidation of demesnes[321] had begun in the thirteenth century, but the final stages belong to the period covered by this volume, as in 1394 when Walter de Bury, finding the intermixture of his land at Brownstone to his "grave damage", arranged a comprehensive exchange.[322] By the fifteenth century rentals and other documents begin to provide the first really detailed pictures of these enclosed demesnes. At Payhembury a jury of parishioners viewed the inheritance of William Malherbe – gardens next to the manor house, "two little closes" of an acre each, meadowland, then the main convertible land of the demesne in a compact block of five closes of 18, 20, 10, 14, and 8 acres. At Trelawne the demesne, on lease to the bailiff, comprised ten closes, ideal for a ten-course rotation of, say, three years under crops and seven under ley.[323] Upkeep of enclosures involved not inconsiderable expenses: at Hamatethy a special "keeper of hedges" was employed around the demesne in the early fifteenth century, while renovation of thousands of perches of hedge with quicksets (*cum plantis vivis*) was recorded as one of the good deeds of Abbot Mey of Tavistock. Against such expenses could be set income from "loppings", "clippings", and "parings" when hedges were trimmed.[324]

A final determinant of yields to be considered here is the part played

[321] For enclosure on tenant holdings see below, Ch. 7.

[322] Devon RO, Z1/10/26. For other Devon examples and for the early medieval origins of the movement, see Fox, 'Chronology of enclosure', pp. 186–7. For a Cornish example, at Trevollard, Cornwall RO, DDR 2068–9.

[323] BL Add. Ms. 28838, f.126; PRO E 315/385. Examples of accounts and rentals giving details of demesne closes are PRO SC 6/827/40 (Haccombe), Devon RO, 48/13/4/1/12 (Cockington), 1262M/M/98, a/c of 1475–6 (Filleigh), Cary Mss., rental of 1464–5 (Ashwater), Royal Institution of Cornwall, HB/20/12 (Parkham), Arundell Mss., MA 41 (Carminowe and Lanherne), Huntington Library, San Marino, HAM box 74, a/c of "Salisburysland" (Yealmpton), BL Add. Roll 64348 (Botelet), PRO SC 6/822/15 (Halton), the last two references being to the *parci* of the demesne, a Latinized version of the Cornish word for an enclosed field, *park*.

[324] PRO SC 6/823/28; BL Egerton Ms. 3671, ff.13v, 24 for the sycophantic account of Mey, and Devon RO, W1258M/D/38/15, Leigh a/c of 1397–8, for but one example of details of hedge making on the Tavistock estate; Devon RO, W1258M/D/71/5, a/c of 1453–4, G/3, a/c of 1410–11, West Devon RO, 70/92.

by livestock. Animal numbers may be expressed in terms of the "animal ratio" devised by J. Z. Titow, which gives a measure of livestock in relation to the acreage of land under crops; ratios from all demesnes for which the relevant information survives are summarized in Table 3.22. The figures raise two points. First, they are relatively high when compared with the only other easily available series, from the Winchester estate in southern England.[325] This is to be expected, for many Winchester manors had field systems of an "open" kind, which tended to restrict animal numbers through insistence on stinted bare fallows, whereas in the south-west abundance of enclosed ley pastures and wastes had the opposite effect. Second, the table shows clear evidence of an increase in the number of animals per acre of cropland, a result of declining arable acreage discussed in Chapter 2, coupled with increases in demesne flocks and herds.[326] The only documents which allow a precise calculation of an animal ratio on tenant holdings come from manors of the Duchy of Cornwall. John Randolf of Liskeard, who died in 1409, left 14 cattle and 60 sheep and farmed a holding of 40 acres. If we assume that 10 acres of the holding were cropped, almost certainly an overestimate on the basis of our knowledge of rotations and of the value of John's grain, this gives an animal ratio of 290, in all probability a conservative figure. A similar calculation for another, smaller holding on the estate, with 19 cattle and 40 sheep, reveals an even higher animal ratio.[327] It seems that the most successful of tenant farmers maintained animals in large enough numbers to be of great benefit to arable farming.

Of course, animals only have an effect on yields if they are managed in such a way that their manure can be channelled towards cropland. As for oxen and cows, there is no indication in the sources that the milder winters of the south-west discouraged over-wintering in byres, for a *boveria* and other animal houses were standard in demesne building complexes, even in the western parts of Cornwall;[328] from these buildings dung was carted onto the fields. That tenants were expected to manage their holdings in the same way is clear from the

[325] A mean animal ratio of 169 on one group of manors, 159 on another: Farmer, 'Grain yields on the Winchester manors', pp. 563–4.

[326] It must be noted that the high figures for the fifteenth century owe much to inclusion of manors in the cattle-rearing region of mid-Devon.

[327] Based on figures in Hatcher, *Duchy of Cornwall*, p. 255. The second tenant was Richard de Fentenwausaut, whose holding, according to the duchy's assession rolls, was probably of 20 acres. Cases relating to trespass can reveal substantial flocks and herds belonging to tenants: *ibid.*, pp. 171 n.2, 254; Dean and Chapter Archives, 4936; Devon RO, 902M/M/17.

[328] PRO SC 6/823/33 and Arundell Mss., MA 34 for sheep houses at Winnianton and Prospidnick; Devon RO, W1258M/E/24, a/c of 1411–12 for a house for cows and calves at Cargoll; Arundell Mss., MA 28 for an ox-house at Lambroun.

Table 3.22. *Devon and Cornwall: (demesne averages) animal ratios*

1350–75:	151
1375–1400:	180
1400–25:	164
1425–75:	222
1475–1500:	319

Calculations: According to the method devised by J. Z. Titow, *Winchester yields: a study in medieval agricultural productivity,* p. 136.
Sources: Accounts, from among those listed in Table 3.20, in which the relevant information is complete (excluding those from estates where flocks may have been accounted for separately).

presentment of Richard Webber of Manworthy for cultivating "without dung to the destruction of his land", and from other references to manuring on tenant holdings.[329] In summer cows and oxen were brought out from byres onto the enclosed farmland and rougher pastures beyond the enclosures were used by animals less often needed around the farmyard. At Cargoll in 1407–8 the bailiff explained that some animals "should common on the waste land", while bullocks and wethers were sometimes sent from Clyst to a property with access to extensive wastes, and horses from Hurdwick to the rough grazings of Dartmoor; "feeding farms" served the same purpose.[330] Where wastes were at a distance the practice prevented the over-burdening of the better grasslands; where they were close, animals might be pastured on them during the day, traditionally "from sunrise to sunset" for Dartmoor-border farmers, and then brought onto the cropland, thereby replenishing it with nutrients derived from elsewhere. Occasional references to folds show that animals might be concentrated on small areas of arable: at Clyst folding was practised immediately after beat-burning while a lessee of the Dean and Chapter at Branscombe folded a quarter of his land in 1463.[331] All of these systems of livestock management were very different from the more extensive practices traditional under midland field systems, and doubtless played a part in sustaining yields.

[329] Above ch. 2, n.341 for Manworthy and other similar references; Devon RO, CR 72, CR 19, court after Trinity 1380, Dean and Chapter Archives, 2937, PRO E 306/2/2 (Tybesta).

[330] Devon RO, W1258M/E/24 and, for a similar reference to sheep in summer on the wastes of Winnianton, PRO SC 6/823/33; Devon RO, W1258M/G/3 and D/52/3, a/c of 1479–80; above, ch. 2, for "feeding farms".

[331] *Cal. Inq. Misc.,* IV, p. 94 and V, pp. 120–1; W. S. Cooter, 'Ecological dimensions of medieval agrarian systems', *Agric. Hist.,* 52, 1978, pp. 468–9; Devon RO, W1258M/G/3, a/c of 1398–9; Dean and Chapter Archives, 6017/2.

The importance of the later middle ages in the long-term evolution of south-western arable farming lies in the more relaxed systems of land use which characterized the period; in most regions there was less cropland than in the early fourteenth century and leys in convertible rotations became longer. The acreage which a farmer devoted to crops in any one year was relatively small. This meant, on the one hand, that despite respectable yield ratios per seed sown the total productivity of arable husbandry was lower per acre of farmland in comparison with that of farming systems in which much more of the land was sown annually; the absence of high sowing rates and, in some regions, of high yielding crop types, further contributed to low productivity. On the other hand, small cropped acreages meant that, in the realm of soil preparation, the traditional labour-intensive techniques of the province could be maintained despite high labour costs. The period was not one of startling innovation in arable farming: the husbandmen of Devon and Cornwall did not adopt leguminous crops on even a moderate scale, while beat-burning and sanding were already practised in the thirteenth century. Many farmers persisted in sowing the lower priced crops of rye and oats, even of small oats, but in coastal regions these were phased out during the later middle ages. This regional adaptation in crop combinations was one important development of the period. Another, perhaps the most significant improvement, was a structural one, the enclosure of arable land. When, in the sixteenth and seventeenth centuries, the old dominance of oats and rye was finally eroded, leys were shortened and clover added to convertible rotations, these trends – married to intensive techniques of cultivation which survived the labour scarcity of the later middle ages, and taking place on land which had benefited from enclosure and recuperation – could produce arable farming of very high standards indeed.[332]

Livestock husbandry also differed in its scale and prime objects from region to region within the south-west. Demesne accounts reveal those regions in which farmers had an especial interest in sheep and those which, in the management of cattle, specialized not in rearing but in dairying, this emphasis being reflected in herds with relatively few calves or other young bovines (Table 3.23). The two prime dairying regions were south Devon and the Cornish coastlands, both with quick markets near to hand;[333] in both the proportion of meadowland increased, in some cases through rudimentary "floating" schemes,

---

[332] For barley and clover, Carew, *Survey of Cornwall*, ed. Halliday, p. 102, and Harrison in *AHEW*, v, pp. 365, 367.

[333] Cheese was prominent in miners' diet according to Beare's account of the stannaries, written in the sixteenth century: BL Harl. Ms. 6380.

Table 3.23. *Devon and Cornwall: average numbers of demesne livestock*

	Cows	Young bovines	Sheep
East Devon	17	24	314
South Devon	10	14	190
Mid- and N. Devon	22	36	202
Cornish coastlands	17	14	254

Notes: Figures for sheep exclude lambs and exclude manors from estates where flocks may have been accounted for centrally. For the regions, see Fig. 2.1.

Sources: Accounts, from among those listed in Table 3.20, in which the relevant information is complete and also the following additional accounts and inventories of livestock (figures in brackets give numbers of additional calculations for each place). *South Devon*: Aveton Gifford, 1393 (1) and Flete Damarle, 1393 (1): Devon RO, 410Z/F/1. Morwell, 1501 (1): Devon RO, W1258M/D/71. Plympton, 1383 (1): BL Add. Roll 64318. Stokenham, 1400 (1): *Cal. Inq. Misc.*, VII, p. 71. *East Devon*: Bishop's Clyst, 1373–94 (2): *The Trevelyan Papers*, ed. J. P. Collier, Camden OS LXVII, 1857, pp. 5–17 and Devon RO, Diocesan records 1057. Chudleigh, 1373–94 (2): as Bishop's Clyst. Crediton, 1373–94 (2): as Bishop's Clyst. Peterhayes, 1394 (1): as Bishop's Clyst. Salcombe Regis, 1353 (1): Dean and Chapter Archives, 2856. *North and mid-Devon*: Bishop's Nympton, 1373 (1): as Bishop's Clyst. Bishop's Tawton, 1373–94 (2): as Bishop's Clyst. Brendon, 1422–9 (7): PRO SC 6/826/21–3. Holloway in Northlew and Highampton, 1388 (1): *Cal. Inq. Misc.*, V, pp. 44–5. Leigh in Milton Abbot, 1501 (1): Devon RO, W1258M/D/71. Sampford Courtenay, 1383 (1): BL Add. Roll 64318. Werrington, 1501 (1): Devon RO, W1258M/D/71. *Cornish coastlands*: Burniere, 1373–94 (2): as Bishop's Clyst. Cargoll, 1373–94 (2): as Bishop's Clyst. Carminowe, 1434 (1): Arundell Mss. MA 34. Lawhitton, 1373 (1): as Bishop's Clyst. Nansladron, 1401 (2): Arundell Mss. MA 33. Pawton, 1373–94 (2): as Bishop's Clyst. Portlooe, 1394 (1): Devon RO, CR 584. St Germans, 1373–94 (2): as Bishop's Clyst. Sheviock, 1383–c. 1390 (2): BL Add. Roll 64318 and Devon RO, CR 513. Tregaire, 1373 (1): as Bishop's Clyst. Tremadart, 1388 (1): *Cal. Inq. Misc.*, V, pp. 61–2. Tresillian, 1388 (1): *ibid.*, p. 83. Whalesborough, 1411–15 (4): Somerset RO, DDWO 46/1.

during the later middle ages.[334] On some demesnes here, at Lambroun, Cargoll, Pawton, Carminowe, Sheviock, Goodrington and Morwell, many calves, born in spring, were sold off early in the year and an account from Penheale specifies the expenses of weaning (*separatio*)

[334] Devon RO, W1258M/E/24, a/c of 1411–12 for a reference to cleaning out the *rivuli* of a meadow at Cargoll; also Devon RO, CR 718. John Norden noted rudimentary water meadows in Devon: *The Surveyor's Dialogue*, London, 1618 edn, p. 205.

which ensured that as much as possible of their mothers' milk was reserved for the dairy.[335] The productivity of dairies in both regions was markedly higher than elsewhere in the south-west.

North and mid-Devon and the borders of the high moorlands of both counties specialized, by contrast, in cattle rearing, as in later times.[336] Rearing is revealed in demesne accounts by small sales of calves and large numbers of young stock classified carefully by age and sex; typical are fifteenth-century accounts of the abbey of Tavistock's aptly named demesne of Hurdwick where an average of only four calves was sold annually, but where the large herd yielded a yearly average of fourteen mature cows, oxen, and three-year-olds, most of them for sale but some for the larder, as in 1449–50 when an ox (*vocatur Babe*) was sent to the cellarer. Such patterns of management, in which few calves, yearlings, or two-year-olds were sold, could result in herds of impressive size, the bishop's of 97 at Nympton in 1378–9, for example, or the herd of 98 kept by John Blake, a very minor landlord, at Hayne in the same parish.[337] Moving downwards in the scale of farm sizes, tenant farmers at Hartland in the 1440s and 1450s sold large numbers of oxen and three-year-olds, while a bullock-herd employed by the bishop on his home farm near Exeter was brought thither from Tawton in north Devon – suggesting a special esteem for the products of and expertise in rearing here, noticed even by Leland when he commented that Hartland was "very good for broode of catelle". The best enclosed pastures, in a region where cultivation declined sharply during the later middle ages, were probably reserved for breeding stock while young animals ran on the region's many moors, in some cases becoming virtually "wild".[338] Farms on the borders of the high moorlands also engaged in cattle rearing. At Brendon on Exmoor, Elizabeth Harington kept a vaccary (with no cultivation) in the 1420s, amounting to over a hundred animals, while complex tithing arrangements were agreed to apportion the tenths of cattle being moved from parish to parish as they were reared on the southern flanks of the moor. Around Bodmin Moor, rearing is evidenced by 390 head

---

[335] Arundell Mss. MA 28; Devon RO, W1258M/E/24; Devon RO, Diocesan Records, 1057; Arundell Mss., MA 34; BL Add. Rolls 64318, 13770; Devon RO, W1258M/D/71/7; PRO SC 6/823/41.

[336] C. Vancouver, *General View of the Agriculture of the County of Devon*, London, 1808, pp. 325, 329.

[337] Sample from Devon RO, W1258M/D/52/2; G/6/8; *Cal. Inq. Misc.*, v, p. 1. For other herds of this type see Devon RO, W1258M/G/1/42 (Burrington), D/42/9 (Ottery).

[338] Arundell Mss., MA 236, a/c of 1448–9; Devon RO, W1258M/G/3, a/c of 1378–9; Leland, *Itinerary*, I, p. 172; above, ch. 2, for decline of cultivation; *Cal. Inq. Misc.*, v, p. 45. Cattle were red in this region, as in later times: Devon RO, W1258M/D/70, court of 1366 and PRO SC 2/167/34.

of tenants' cattle on Hamatethy moors in 1451–2 and a herd of 500 illegally pastured there in 1358. Related to this specialism was the occupation of vacant tenements as "feeding farms", disputes over tithe calves in 1426 and over summer grazing in 1476, and the construction of tanning mills in the fifteenth century – these last developments probably reflecting a growing commercialization of rearing enterprises which produced those "numberless flocks and herds" of which John Leland sang in verse.[339]

Of all regions, east Devon, with urban markets for meat and dairy produce close to hand, was the most rounded pastoral district. At Bishop's Clyst dairy products brought in the steadiest income from the herd, but there were also profits from sales of calves and mature beasts; figures for bovines in the accounts reveal a pattern intermediate between that of a strictly dairy herd and that of a rearing herd. Income from sheep came from wool and from sales of animals *de extra*, surplus to the desired flock size – lambs before shearing (thus reserving some of the milk of ewes for the dairy), ewes, and wethers. Cows and ewes were kept always around the barton with its large meadows along the winding Clyst, but other stock were sometimes sent in summer, with their own bullock-herd and wether-herd, to a linked property with access to one of the region's rough hill grazings.[340] The alternating hill and vale countryside of east Devon was ideal for both intensive and extensive livestock management, lush low-lying vale pastures taking care of breeding stock while immature beasts ran on the moors of the hill ranges; demesnes could therefore concentrate on both dairying and rearing.[341] Many tenant holdings also had a share of both types of land use, William Haydon's at Southleigh, for example, comprising 5 acres of meadow, 16 of arable, 16 of pasture, and 32 of several moorland in addition to rights for 110 sheep and 5 bullocks on the common moor. The number of cattle kept by tenants is difficult to ascertain, but a Culmstock tenant trespassed with 30 beasts in 1392 and in the 1520s stints of larger holdings with access to Woodbury Down were of 8 or 12 (or in one case 20) beasts which, if demesne practice was followed,

---

[339] PRO SC 6/826/21–3; Stafford County RO, D593/A/1/14/4; PRO SC 6/823/13; *Register of the Black Prince*, II, pp. 142–3; above ch. 2, for "feeding farms"; *Register of Edmund Lacy*, ed. Dunstan, I, pp. 155–7; J. Maclean, 'An ancient Cornish deed in English', *Roy. Inst. Cornwall*, IX, 1886, pp. 33–6; Arundell Mss. MA 5 for a "newly constructed" tanning mill at Cardinham and PRO SC 11/968 for a tanning mill near Launceston; *Itinerary of John Leland*, ed. Hearne, IX, p. xxii.

[340] Devon RO, W1258M/G/3. See also Alcock, 'An East Devon manor', I, pp. 158–67. The linked property was at Fluxton in Ottery St Mary, where the bishop's free tenure gave him access to plentiful rough grazing: BL Add. Ms. 28838, f.78. Other accounts revealing patterns similar in many respects are those of Yarcombe, Clayhidon, and Langacre, for which see sources in Table 3.20.   [341] Vancouver, *County of Devon*, p. 351.

comprised only part of each tenant's herd. On occasion lords sold some of the lactage from demesne cows to tenants and on some manors a cow was usually deemed the best beast, both practices probably a reflection of dairy farming among tenants. Stints for sheep on the region's hill pastures in the 1520s generally ranged from thirty to sixty "in the summer time" (minimal figures, for some sheep were kept on the enclosed pastures below) and indeed the poll tax on sheep of 1549 shows that the largest tenant flocks in the region might number about 150 animals.[342]

Regional specialization in types of pastoral husbandry was bound to lead to inter-regional movements of livestock, best seen, though then only rather dimly, for cattle. Movements took place towards the summer grazings of the high moors, to Exmoor where the practice among moorland border farmers of taking in stock ("stranger beasts") from elsewhere is recorded in the fourteenth and fifteenth centuries,[343] and to Dartmoor. Over eight thousand cattle were pastured there by "strangers" (outsiders) in the summer of 1477, a figure well above those for the late fourteenth century, and this total does not include the animals of men from privileged vills immediately adjoining the moor who paid a collective fine for agistment. Some "strangers" were men with less than ten beasts, others in care of herds numbering several hundred, in all probability the property of more than one farmer; sources of manorial provenance show that Dartmoor attracted graziers from ten or even twenty miles away.[344] Just as interesting as these seasonal movements were permanent transfers of cattle from region to region. From coastal manors which specialized in dairying, young calves were sent to rearing manors inland.[345] And there are hints, too, that farmers in regions specializing in rearing were already sending beasts for a final fattening closer to their point of sale, just as they did in later periods.[346] The best evidence comes from Hartland in north

[342] PRO E 315/385; Dean and Chapter Archives, 4936; PRO E 315/385; Devon RO, DD 54890, 54901, 54902, 54915–19, CR 1431–2, Somerset RO, DDCN box 3 no. 14, Dean and Chapter Archives, 4798–4835 for lactage and heriots; PRO E 315/385 for stints at Churchstanton and Woodbury; E 179/99/315.

[343] PRO SC 6/826/23; Stafford County RO, D593/A/1/14/4.

[344] PRO SC 6/822/3; SC 6/Hen.VII/88–92 and SC 2/166/45–6 for names of graziers; PRO SC 6/823/24, Devon RO, W1258M/D/52/2, a/c of 1479–80, CR 1132, and Cal. Inq. Misc., v, p. 45 for seasonal movements to Dartmoor, the last reference mentioning beasts recovered there "at great labour and expense". For agistment arrangements see Cal. Inq. Misc., v, pp. 120–1 and E. G. Fogwill, 'Pastoralism on Dartmoor', Devon Assoc., LXXXVI, 1954, pp. 89–114. "Drover" as an occupation is recorded at Ermington, just south of Dartmoor: The Stonor Letters and Papers, 1290–1483, ed. C. L. Kingsford, I, Camden 3rd ser. XXIX, 1919, p. 66.

[345] See n.335 for sales of calves; Devon RO, 158M/M/11 for transfers of calves from coastal Aveton Gifford and Flete to inland North Huish.

[346] Vancouver, County of Devon, pp. 325, 329.

Devon rearing country, whose tenants in 1448–9 sold to Sir John Dynham twenty-five oxen and three-year-olds, driving them 70 miles or so across difficult country to his seat at Nutwell in east Devon. The distance involved, and the fact that Nutwell was close to more convenient supplies of meat for the kitchen, makes it unlikely that the whole herd was destined immediately for the table; the animals were no doubt being sent for fattening from the relatively rough grazings of north Devon to the lusher pastures of the Exe valley. The ultimate destinations of such movements were no doubt the meat and hide markets of Exeter and its prosperous satellite towns.[347]

The productivity of flocks and herds in the south-west was not, in general, remarkable and, as with arable husbandry, we can perhaps conclude that the place of the later middle ages in the evolution of pastoral farming within the two counties lies with relaxed pressure on the land, which allowed the development of *systems* of stock management – both regional systems and systems within individual holdings – rather than with any great strides in yields, which were to come later. Fleece weights were low, to judge from the few figures available; the scarcity of data is a result of the practice of selling the clip of demesne flocks *in grosso*, in some cases even before shearing.[348] On the bishop of Exeter's manor of Clyst where, contrary to the usual practice, fleeces were weighed before sale, the mean weight in nine accounts was 1.1 lb; five early fourteenth-century accounts from Uplyme give a mean of 0.9 lb; a single account from Leigh gives 1.1 lb.[349] These are paltry figures. It is unlikely that the quality of pastures can have been responsible, for although some sheep were grazed for part of the year on relatively thin moorland herbage, as the remarks above on east Devon show, this did not apply to whole flocks or for the whole of the year, and the lushness of the early and "new springnynge grasse" of the south-west, as well as the presence of permanent pasture and long ley in well-enclosed severalties, can only have been beneficial to fleeces.[350] It therefore seems plausible to suggest

[347] Arundell Mss. MA 236, a/c of 1448–9 and, for a possible similar movement of livestock from Hockford to Canonsleigh, BL Add. Roll 7658; information on meat and hide markets from M. Kowaleski. Medieval Exeter citizens ate cuts from mature, but not antiquated, cattle according to bovine dental remains: M. Maltby, *The Animal Bones from Exeter, 1971–1975,* Sheffield, 1979, pp. 31–2.

[348] For example, PRO SC 6/830/29; Devon RO, W1258M/G/1/42, a/c of 1357–8; Finberg, *Tavistock Abbey,* p. 146.

[349] Devon RO, W1258M/G/3; Longleat House Mss. 11216, 10656, 11271, 11272, 10655; Devon RO, W1258M/D/38/15.

[350] W. J. Blake, 'Hooker's Synopsis Chorographical of Devonshire', *Devon Assoc.,* XL, 1915, p. 344. Nor can these low fleece weights be attributed to lack of wethers (with heavier fleeces), for all of the flocks analysed here contained some animals of this type.

a genetic explanation and to conclude that the short-woolled, coarse-woolled breed which distinguished the south-west in the sixteenth century, and which provided the wool for the coarse cloth industry of the province, can be traced back to the later middle ages.[351] Certainly, the poor nature of fleeces from Devon and Cornwall was noted by contemporaries: by the sheriff of Devon in 1322 when he stated that the quality of his county's fleeces was too poor to attract major merchants; by those who drew up the ordinance of 1343 fixing minimum rates to be paid for wool, with the two counties at the foot of the list; by the cloth makers of the countryside south and west of Dartmoor who in a petition to parliament spoke of their wool supplies as gross and stubborn.[352]

The productivity of south-western dairies was likewise far from exceptional. Calculations of productivity per cow are, as usual, complicated by the practice of adding the milk of ewes to that from cows; at Burniere in 1401–2 and at Yealmpton in 1395–6 reeves explained poor performance of the dairy by reference to murrain among sheep. If the milk of seven ewes is taken to equal that of one cow, as sometimes claimed, and if their contribution is deducted, yields per cow were very low indeed: 24 lb of summer cheese, butter, and some cream at Clyst, 21 lb at Hurdwick. The "expectation" imposed upon the reeve of Hurdwick in 1426–7 was likewise low, 28 lb of summer cheese per cow and butter in proportion, compared to a figure of about 100 lb mentioned in the *Husbandry*.[353] We cannot explain this low performance through any lack of nourishment among herds and flocks, for although it was not normal practice in the south-west to feed livestock (except horses and pigs) with oats or legumes, the plentiful supply of lush grasses must have amply compensated.[354] Rather, it can

[351] P. J. Bowden, *The Wool Trade in Tudor and Stuart England*, London, 1962, pp. 27–8, 49. For suggested genetic differences among England's medieval sheep, and for contrary views, see J. P. Bischoff, "'I cannot do't without counters'": fleece weights and sheep breeds in late thirteenth- and early fourteenth-century England', *Agric. Hist.*, LVII, 1983, pp. 143–60.

[352] J. C. Davies, 'An assembly of wool merchants in 1322', *EHR*, XXXI, 1916, p. 600; T. Rymer, *Foedera*, edn of 1816–69, II, pp. 1225–6; *Rot. Parl.*, V, p. 621. See also *Studies in English Trade in the Fifteenth Century*, eds. E. Power and M. M. Postan, London, 1933, p. 50 n.56.

[353] BL Add. Roll 64391; PRO SC 6/830/29; Trow-Smith, *History of British Livestock Husbandry*, p. 120; Devon RO, W1258M/G/3 and sample of accounts from W1258M/D/52/2; *Walter of Henley*, ed. Oschinsky, p. 431. The earliest reference to cream at Clyst is in 1413–14, when it was sent from the dairy to the bishop's household. For cream, see also Somerset RO, DDCN box 3 no. 14, Hele a/c of 1394–5 (purchase of cream for the Franceis family), Devon RO, W1258M/Add.1/5 (by Tavistock abbey cellarer). See Finberg, *Tavistock Abbey*, p. 138 for a hypothetical account of cream.

[354] There are occasional references to the feeding of cattle with oats under special circumstances, e.g. of illness or before fattening for the lord's larder: Devon RO, W1258M/D/52/2, Leigh a/c of 1496–7, D/38/15.

be suggested that, in general, care and expertise in herd management were directed towards rearing rather than dairying, a suggestion which is certainly borne out by very low mortality rates among calves.[355] Only in those regions, covering a minority of the face of the peninsula, where dairying was the prime object of cattle husbandry, were yields per cow somewhat above the generally low level.[356]

No discussion of farming technique in south-western England could end without mention of cider. Although there are isolated references to the drink from most parts of the province during the later middle ages, nine out of ten come from south Devon and east Devon, which were still the main areas of commercial production in the eighteenth century.[357] Tenants grew apple trees in their hedges – raising the interesting speculation that, in England at large, there is a connection between fruit growing and early enclosure – and in small orchards such as those leased in the fifteenth century to a tenant at Aylesbeare "to improve his tenure". That their apples were destined for cider is clear from evidence relating to the "manorialization" of pressing: the fruit was taken to the lord's pound, and a small tax or payment in kind (equivalent to multure) exacted. The fine which a Stoke Fleming tenant paid in "wine" (almost certainly cider) and the custom at Culmstock whereby the lord reserved one tree's apples as a gift to tenants are further examples of the place of cider in relations between lord and tenant.[358] Who drank the cider from these orchards? The question is raised because cider was rarely used instead of ale in gifts or in payments to labourers; it seems not yet to have assumed its later place as a common item in diet. Victualling in the ports of the south Devon coast may have been one possible outlet and another may well have been the seigneurial household. Lords certainly prized their orchards, keeping them in hand long after the rest of the demesne had been leased. At Kingskerswell in south Devon the Dynhams were still using and repairing their pound in 1451–2. At Cockington in the same region

---

[355] 18 per cent at Clyst and 12 per cent at Hurdwick (sources as in n.353), figures which compare very favourably with the best of those reported from other parts of England: Trow-Smith, *History of British Livestock Husbandry*, pp. 108, 117, 124–5, 128–9; Kershaw, *Bolton Priory*, p. 100.

[356] 53 lb at Bolberry Beauchamp, 37 lb in good years at Cargoll, and over 60 lb at Lanherne: Central Library, Bradford, Swinton coll., Bolberry accounts; Devon RO, W1258M/E/24; Arundell Mss. MA 16.

[357] Harrison in *AHEW*, v, pp. 382–3. Climate, contacts with Brittany and Normandy, and the demands of victualling in the many ports of these regions could perhaps account for the distribution. For use of cider in victualling see *VCH Kent*, III, p. 426, *VCH Hants.*, v, p. 475.

[358] For Aylesbeare, Devon RO, CR 521 and, for other references to apple trees in tenants' hedges, Dean and Chapter Archives, 4801, 4939; for toll on cider at Plymstock, South Pool, Whimple, and Shute, see Devon RO, W1258M/D/74/6, Arundell Mss. MA 277, BL Add. Rolls 13176, 64856; Devon RO, 902M/M/2; Dean and Chapter Archives, 4934.

the Carys re-planted their orchard when all other branches of demesne husbandry had withered away, repaired their pound and paid men and women labourers to gather and press the apples: watching "the last ouzings, hours by hours".[359]

[359] Arundell Mss. MA 251; Devon RO, 48/13/4/1/2. For purchase of cider for seigneurial households, see Devon RO, CR 535, W1258M/G/1/42, a/c of 1357-8, D/74/6, a/c of 1474-5.

CHAPTER 4

MARKETING THE PRODUCE OF THE
COUNTRYSIDE, 1200–1500[1]

A. INTRODUCTION

"He who offers the higher price shall have it", wrote the author of the *Seneschaucy* with splendid simplicity. "Manorial produce which could be sold should not be taken away by anybody but all is to be shown and bargained for in public at fairs and markets."[2] This advice was already out of date by the time it was written, in the third quarter of the thirteenth century: wholesalers had been buying wool directly from manors or estates for at least a century, grain for over fifty years, and cheese for a decade or more; and the controllers of fairs and markets had begun to curb the vendor's search for "the higher price". The primary sources for the study of medieval marketing start with the manorial accounts, particularly those enrolled in the pipe rolls of the bishopric of Winchester from 1208–9 onwards, and in the more informative individual *compoti* of manors such as the Merton College properties at Cuxham and Holywell (Oxon.) and Elham (Kent). The Monkton Deverill and Longbridge Deverill (Wilts.) accounts have excellent records of the markets and fairs where those distant Glastonbury abbey manors traded in the fourteenth century, and accounts of the remoter Westminster abbey manors, like Birdbrook in north Essex, show something of post-Black Death marketing in places which did not usually send provisions to the abbey community.[3] The accounts of the Peterborough abbey obedientiaries, especially those of the abbot's receiver, are among the best sources for trading links in the fifteenth century.[4] Most manorial *compoti* are much less helpful, however: they rarely name the purchasers of produce or the suppliers

---

[1] The research for this chapter, and the writing of it, had to be completed in haste and without adequate library resources. Most of my conclusions are therefore cautious and tentative, and what follows is not a definitive study.　　　[2] *Walter of Henley*, ed. Oschinsky, p. 271.

[3] I am grateful to St Thomas More College, University of Saskatchewan, for buying for my use the microfilms of the Glastonbury abbey manorial accounts, and to J. R. L. Highfield and Merton College for allowing me to purchase duplicates of the college's microfilms of its manorial documents.

[4] *Account Rolls of the Obedientiaries of Peterborough*, ed. J. Greatrex, Northants. Rec. Soc., XXXIII, 1984.

of stock, or say where the transactions took place. The student of marketing may do a great deal of reading for very little reward. The other manorial documents offer less. Court rolls sometimes name the buyers of underwood, or of grazing in pasture, or of pannage in woodland, and fairly often cite those who brewed or baked *contra assisam* in their communities, and who were therefore likely to be buyers of grain; occasionally a careful analysis may uncover, as at Writtle (Essex), a complex network of commercial and credit arrangements among the villagers themselves.[5] Custumals and extents may list the towns to which peasants might have to carry grain or drive animals for sale but, unless there survive for the same manor *compoti* which detail the "works" performed, or "sold" back to the peasant, one cannot tell whether the *averagia* described were exacted or not.

Most of the crown's grants or confirmations of markets and fairs appear in the charter rolls, or, less commonly, the close rolls or patent rolls. A few other places of trade are mentioned in the hundred rolls, the inquisitions *post mortem*, the exchequer pipe rolls, and the liberate rolls. While the king expected that every market or fair should have its charter, and every charter ensure that its market or fair took place as granted, this did not happen. Some of the markets granted were never held; on the other hand, the accounts record trading at markets and fairs which seem never to have received official warrant. In the absence of topographical surveys such as delighted a later England, one cannot know in how many villages in 1300 or 1400 there was a weekly market to quicken the pulse, or whether there was a fair to celebrate riotously the patronal festival of a local church.[6] The records of boroughs show something of the consumers' concern for hygiene, honest measures, and fair dealing, as well as the town's opportunities for making money out of visiting traders and the arrangements for preserving the burgesses' advantages in their communities. Urban charters and by-laws may state special conditions of trade or unusual practices, lists of tolls and pontage and murage dues may suggest what goods were expected to come to the town, and records of pie-powder and other borough courts – especially the pleas of debt – may demonstrate the ties between the groups of processors, tradesmen, and merchants both resident and visiting. While the London documents are invaluable, this material is at times richer for Exeter than for any other English town.[7] Records of

---

[5] E. Clark, 'Debt litigation in a late medieval English vill', in J. A. Raftis, ed., *Pathways to Medieval Peasants*, Toronto, 1981, pp. 247–79.

[6] For this reason, and because of the space even an incomplete record would occupy, I have not included lists of markets and fairs, or maps of their distribution throughout England and Wales.

[7] *Calendar of Letter-Books...of the City of London*, ed. R. R. Sharpe, London, 1899–1912; *Calendar of Early Mayors' Court Rolls...A.D. 1298–1307*, ed. A. H. Thomas; *Calendar of Plea and*

debts and contracts were often enrolled among the documents of central government; these show, as the manorial accounts usually do not, the names of the contracting parties, and they sometimes provide evidence for regions from which no *compoti* have survived. The close rolls for December 1291, for instance, note that the abbot of Fountains owed William de Hamelton 140 qr of wheat and 190 qr of oats as well as money, to a total value of £209 6s. 8d.[8] Valuations of debtors' possessions show not only commercial connections but also how easy it was for those of little substance to obtain large loans. Fourteenth- and fifteenth-century close rolls also record export licences, such as that of 1391 allowing a London merchant to export a thousand *tuns* of wheat to Pisa and Genoa.[9]

Royal proclamations, statutes both parliamentary and informal, and even Magna Carta, usually exemplify the aims of those in power, rather than the practical realities of the market place. Records of the justices' attempts to enforce the Statute of Labourers, and local efforts to prohibit forestalling and regrating, show how wide might be the gap between principle and practice. Legislation is therefore an inadequate guide to what happened in the markets. On the other hand, after long academic exile for unreliability, the customs accounts are returning to favour as evidence of overseas trade.[10] Narrative sources are few. There is Fitz Stephen's excited account of London's public cook-shop and Smithfield's market for horses, swine with long flanks, cows with full udders, and implements of husbandry; there is the indignation of monastic chroniclers like Jocelin of Brakelond at Bury and Matthew Paris at St Albans, fuming angrily at any threat to their abbeys' trading privileges and recording incidentally how Londoners used to pass through Bury St Edmunds with cart-loads of herrings they had bought at Yarmouth; and there is a certain tiresome moralizing from theologians opposed to Sunday trading and to most forms of retailing – despite the prominence of other churchmen in both activities.[11]

In all, the primary sources for medieval marketing are patchy and inconsistent. One weakness is the dearth of correspondence, except for the Cely papers and the Paston letters in the later fifteenth century (and the Paston letters are only of marginal interest); another is the difficulty

Memoranda Rolls...A.D. 1323–1482, ed. A. H. Thomas and P. E. Jones; M. Kowaleski, 'Local markets and merchants in late fourteenth-century Exeter', Toronto Univ. Ph.D. thesis, 1982.

[8] *CCR, 1288–1296*, p. 246.

[9] Extents on Debts, PRO C 131; *CCR, 1389–1392*, p. 322.

[10] S. H. Rigby, 'The customs administration of Boston in the reign of Richard II', *Bull. IHR*, LVIII, 1985, pp. 12–24.

[11] *English Historical Documents*, II, *1042–1189*, ed. D. C. Douglas and G. W. Greenaway, London, 1968, pp. 958–9; *The Chronicle of Jocelin of Brakelond*, ed. H. E. Butler, London, 1949, p. 76.

of revealing peasant transactions, except where the villagers sold to their lords or bought from them; another is the lack of material from Wales, and (except for Durham) from England north of the Trent; another is the disappearance of full *compoti* when the manors went out to farm, with the consequence that almost all the evidence to be examined in these pages is from the two centuries prior to 1400. The great strength of the primary sources, even so, rests on the manorial accounts. Despite the vagueness of most entries, the *compoti* may bring one closer to the men and women of the countryside than the other sources do for later centuries. It is on the evidence from these sources, and not on the records of towns or cities like London and Winchester, that this chapter is largely based.

Of the secondary sources on medieval marketing, the most comprehensive are Ephraim Lipson's account in the first volume of his monumental *Economic History*, and L. F. Salzman's genial study of many aspects of English trade. The history of wool marketing inspired a much-loved essay from Eileen Power, and T. H. Lloyd's later and more detailed study. N. S. B. Gras's work on the grain trade was a pioneer in its day, but some parts need revision. The marketing of livestock, hides, dairy produce, and timber deserves fuller attention than it has received hitherto, though Oliver Rackham's studies of English woodland economy have opened this important area to historians lacking his botanical knowledge. On other aspects of marketing, one must pay tribute to Michael Postan's examination of credit in medieval trade, to the many excellent urban histories (most notably of Winchester), and to Sylvia Thrupp's studies of London gilds; how one regrets that the second world war distracted her from writing the economic history of the capital![12]

B. MARKETS, FAIRS, AND TRANSPORT[13]

By the end of the twelfth century, bailiffs and reeves and the estate officials who supervised them already had many ways to market the produce that was surplus both to the demands of the lord's household

[12] E. Lipson, *The Economic History of England*, 10th edn, London, 1949; L. F. Salzman, *English Trade in the Middle Ages*, Oxford, 1931; E. Power, *The Wool Trade in English Medieval History*; Lloyd, *The English Wool Trade*; N. S. B. Gras, *The Evolution of the English Corn Market*; O. Rackham, *Ancient Woodland*; M. M. Postan, *Medieval Trade and Finance*, Cambridge, 1973, pp. 1–91; D. J. Keene, *Survey of Medieval Winchester*; S. L. Thrupp, *The Merchant Class of Medieval London*, Ann Arbor, 1948, p. 93, n.169.

[13] The fourth volume in this series, with Alan Everitt's celebrated study of marketing in the sixteenth and seventeenth centuries, led many scholars to examine the location and distribution of markets. R. H. Britnell has been pre-eminent among them, and I am much in his debt for advice and for advance copies of works he was preparing for publication. M. Kowaleski, whose study of the Exeter court records has unravelled the pattern of marketing in a small city, has been

or the monastic community and also to the manors' own needs for stock and seed-corn. Stimulated by a price rise, and at the same time seeking more money for the luxuries appropriate to their status, landlords increased production to channel it into these profitable routes. So did their tenants, who likewise needed cash to pay their rents, entry fines, and taxes, and to buy salt, fish, cloth, farming tools, and other essentials. An expanding population furnished the purchasers: those who lived on small burgage tenements in village or town, the landless many in the countryside who worked for money wages and had to buy their food, the settlers on marginal land unable to produce breadcorn, the ambitious entrepreneurs who linked the English wool growers and cheese-makers to the commerce of continental Europe. One of these routes was through direct sales to the lord's tenants and other local villagers, or to travelling wholesalers like wool merchants and cornmongers; frequently, the entire wool clip of an estate would be sold to a single purchaser, often without inspection. A second route was to take the surplus produce to one of the great annual fairs, such as St Botolph's fair at Boston, or to its regional or local imitation in town or village. A third outlet was to despatch it to a regular market in a nearby village or an urban centre like Winchester or Norwich, wherever there were consumers who could not produce the victuals they required, or traders who would buy it for re-sale in a more distant city such as London or Bristol or perhaps for export. The first method often brought the most money to the lord, sometimes, as with the Cistercian wool contracts, even before the goods were delivered.[14] The second brought the most excitement to the community the fair touched. And it was the third, the regular market, which proved the most enduring.

Medieval England was, of course, predominantly rural. In the 1370s there were probably fewer than forty towns with populations of two thousand or more.[15] Even London, far ahead of its nearest rival, can hardly have held more than 3 per cent of the country's population at the end of the fourteenth century, and barely 2 per cent before the

generous with her help. Edward Miller on many necessary occasions has supplied information, guidance, and encouragement.

Like the manorial accounts themselves, this chapter arranges most of its information by categories of produce: grain, livestock, animal products such as wool and cheese, and timber and firewood. The vagueness of the material and the difficulty of defining, for example, what a town was, dictated this plan; it differs, therefore, from the patterns followed in the succeeding volumes of the *Agrarian History*. Of the secondary material consulted in preparing this chapter, roughly half has been published since I completed my other contribution to this volume. Fortunately, the enthusiasm of younger scholars shows no signs of abating, and their studies will doubtless add much more to our knowledge of medieval marketing.

[14] Lloyd, *The English Wool Trade*, p. 289.

[15] R. H. Hilton, 'Lords, burgesses and hucksters', *PP*, no. 97, 1982, p. 4.

Black Death. A sizeable town like Colchester, with about three thousand inhabitants, seldom had to bring in food more than about eight miles by road.[16] Exeter, with a similar population, also relied mainly on suppliers living in or near the city: about two-thirds of the non-Exeter residents appearing before its courts as debtors and creditors lived within five miles of the city.[17] Most of the places from which the larger city of Winchester obtained grain and livestock were no more than seven miles away, though its charcoal and fish came from further afield; most of the villages from which men came regularly to trade in Gloucester were also within seven miles.[18] The majority of agrarian producers, however, lived at greater distances than these from towns of comparable size. It was in the villages and the small towns that lords and peasants found most of the customers for their surplus corn and cheese, livestock and poultry. Markets in the larger towns left the better records, but the local markets and the communities around them were the more important outlets for the produce of the countryside – the grain, malt, livestock, bread and ale, and the cheap cloths and leather goods made in the district, which were, with fish, the most important commodities traded in places like Halesowen, Pershore, Thornbury, and Cheltenham in the fourteenth and fifteenth centuries.[19]

In the thirteenth and early fourteenth centuries, markets multiplied in all parts of England and Wales, manifesting the optimism of an age of expansion, continuing even after the economy had started to contract. In the counties which formed 55 per cent of England's surface, there were 329 early markets, of which "probably most were founded before the thirteenth century". By 1350, in those same counties, 1,002 places had markets, or had been licensed at some time to hold them.[20] If these counties form a representative sample, one may estimate that England in 1200 had the better part of 600 markets, and that by the Black Death markets had been held (though often only briefly) in over 1,800 places. Their distribution, however, was uneven: in relation to their areas, Suffolk had nine times as many sites as Durham, and Norfolk, Hertfordshire, and Essex were more generously supplied than, for example, the North and West Ridings of Yorkshire. Areas of nucleated settlements, like the Thames valley, had their markets concentrated in a limited number of towns, such as Abingdon, Wallingford, and Henley; regions of scattered farms and villages, such

---

[16] R. H. Britnell, *Growth and Decline in Colchester*, p. 44.

[17] Kowaleski, 'Local markets and merchants', p. 329.

[18] Keene, *Medieval Winchester*, I, p. 270; *VCH Glos.*, IV, p. 47.

[19] R. H. Hilton, 'Medieval market towns', *PP*, no. 109, 1985, p. 8.

[20] R. H. Britnell, 'The proliferation of markets in England, 1200–1349', *EcHR*, 2nd ser. XXXIV, 1981, pp. 209–10.

as the arable parts of Devon sandwiched between moorland and sea, probably had more markets than their population justified.[21] Table 4.1 demonstrates some of these anomalies. Yet even in counties like Derbyshire, as well as in better endowed ones such as Buckinghamshire and Staffordshire, most producers had a choice of several markets within easy reach, about two hours' travelling time.[22]

Even by 1200 there were markets in settlements varying in size and importance from cities like London and Winchester and decaying Domesday boroughs such as Lydford (Devon) to hundredal manors like Frome and Crewkerne (Somerset) and recent creations such as Newborough (Staffs.), and Essex villages like Witham, St Osyth, and Hadstock.[23] Some emerged spontaneously, perhaps out of the gathering of villagers at the local church; others were the deliberate creations of abbey or noble, protected from the start by royal charters, such as those which by 1154 had authorized markets in places as scattered as Norton (Durham), Yaxley (Hunts.), and Thatcham (Berks.).[24] At least until the reign of John, the owners of markets fiercely resisted competition. Oxford and Wallingford, for example, opposed Henry I's grant to Abingdon abbey, and wrung from his grandson the concession that no one but the abbot should bring goods by water – a rule which probably prevented Abingdon developing a grain trade comparable to its famous market for livestock.[25] Abbot Samson of Bury St Edmunds sent the abbey bailiffs and six hundred armed men to destroy the rival market which the monks of Ely had paid the king to have at Lakenheath, fifteen miles from Bury.[26] It may have been this experience which made the crown more cautious: John subsequently chartered markets on the condition that they should not be harmful to others already in the vicinity. As late as 1224, though, in a Lancashire almost empty of markets, one at North Meols was suppressed as injurious to its neighbours even though the nearest, Preston, was thirteen miles away.[27] By that time, the pace of foundations elsewhere was

[21] Hoskins and Finberg, *Devonshire Studies*, map facing p. 225.

[22] B. E. Coates, 'The origin and distribution of markets and fairs in medieval Derbyshire', *Derbs. Arch. and N.H. Soc. J.*, no. 85, 1965, p. 106; M. Reed, 'Markets and fairs in medieval Buckinghamshire', *Records of Bucks.*, xx, 1975–8, p. 569; D. M. Palliser and A. C. Pinnock, 'The markets of medieval Staffordshire', *North Staffs. J. of Field Studies*, no. 11, 1971, p. 56.

[23] R. H. Britnell, 'English markets and royal administration before 1200', *EcHR*, 2nd ser. xxxi, 1978, pp. 183–9; *idem*, 'Essex markets before 1350', *Essex Arch. and Hist.*, 13, 1981, pp. 15–16.

[24] *Regesta Regum Anglo-Normannorum, 1066–1154*, ed. H. W. C. Davis *et al.*, Oxford, 1913–68, I, no. 477; II, no. 1576; III, no. 710.   [25] *VCH Berks.*, IV, pp. 438–9.

[26] *Jocelin of Brakelond*, ed. Butler, pp. 132–4. In this chapter all distances are measured "as the crow flies".

[27] R. H. Britnell, 'King John's early grants of markets and fairs', *EHR*, xciv, 1979, pp. 93–6; G. H. Tupling, 'Markets and fairs in medieval Lancashire', in *Historical Essays in Honour of James Tait*, ed. J. G. Edwards *et al.*, Manchester, 1933, p. 345.

Table 4.1. *The distribution of markets in medieval England*

County	Area (square miles)[a]	Early markets[b]	Markets added 1200–1349	Total sites by 1349[c]	Market sites per 100 sq. miles, 1349
Bedfordshire	473.0	10	12	22	4.65
Berkshire	724.7	13	14	27	3.73
Buckinghamshire	749.1	10	24	34	4.54
Derbyshire	1,005.6	6	23	29	2.88
Devon	2,611.9	32	62	94	3.60
Durham	1,014.8	8	3	11	1.08
Essex	1,528.2	24	54	78	5.10
Gloucestershire	1,257.7	16	40	56	4.45
Hampshire	1,503.4	23	23	46	3.06
Hertfordshire	632.1	16	19	35	5.54
Huntingdonshire	365.6	5	13	18	4.92
Lancashire	1,877.9	16	24	40	2.13
Norfolk	2,053.6	39	82	121	5.89
Nottinghamshire	843.8	6	22	28	3.32
Rutland	152.0	2	2	4	2.63
Staffordshire	1,153.5	10	33	43	3.73
Suffolk	870.9	29	58	87	9.99
Surrey	721.6	12	13	25	3.46
Warwickshire	982.9	8	30	38	3.87
Worcestershire	699.9	7	14	21	3.00
Yorkshire, E.R.	1,172.5	12	31	43	3.67
Yorkshire, N.R.	2,127.8	12	34	46	2.16
Yorkshire, W.R.	2,790.3	13	43	56	2.01
All 21 counties	27,312.8	329	673	1,002	3.67

[a] 1970 county boundaries.
[b] Probably most were founded before 1200.
[c] This total includes some sites where markets had already been discontinued before 1349.
Source: Based on R. H. Britnell, 'The proliferation of markets in England, 1200–1349', EcHR, 2nd ser. XXXIV, 1981, p. 210, and reproduced with the kind permission of the author and the EcHR.

accelerating sharply, especially in the West Midlands: four counties there, with at most only 41 markets which might be older than 1200, gained 47 more by 1250 and another 45 by 1300. In the West Midlands, in East Anglia, and in the north, more new markets began in 1250–74 than in any other quarter-century of the middle ages.[28]

[28] Britnell, 'The proliferation of markets', p. 210.

Before 1066, Wales seems to have been a land with very little commercial exchange, few towns or merchants, and no markets. The castles of the Normans who occupied the south in the twelfth century may have stimulated local trade and marketing in the provisions needed by builders and soldiers, and Henry III granted or confirmed markets at Montgomery, Carmarthen, Cardigan, Deganwy, New-moat, and Kidwelly. In 1283 Edward I ordered merchants from several places to take "victuals of any sort" to the Merioneth coast, and these instructions perhaps indicate the towns and market centres where he believed supplies would be available: Bristol and Aust (Glos.); Swansea and Cardiff; Pembroke, Haverfordwest, and Cilgerran (Pembs.); Laugharne, St Clears, Llanstephan, and Kidwelly (Carms.); Monmouth, Abergavenny, Chepstow, Usk, and Kemeys (Mon.); Brecon and Blaen-Llyfni (Brecons.). Most of these had castles, and most were near the south coast. Earlier, in a 1279 dispute between Welshpool and Montgomery, Griffin son of Wenumwen had argued that, according to Welsh law, markets need be only four miles apart, and that "there are more markets in Wales where one is distant from another only three miles; and more which are distant from another only two miles". Griffin lost his case, but by the end of his reign Edward I had chartered some fifty markets; on a single day in 1290 he granted three markets and eleven fairs to the bishop of St David's.[29]

These developments benefited almost everyone. For the lord, a market provided direct income, as well as an occasional outlet for the produce of his demesne and source of what he needed. He collected tolls on goods sold, rents for stalls and "selds", levies such as picage (when pegs or poles were driven through the road surface to anchor the booths more securely), the profits of the pie-powder court and, ultimately, of the assize of bread and ale. If he planned to create a borough, a market was almost essential, for rural craftsmen and artisans living on burgage tenements had to buy most of their food. Without a market, investments such as the bishop of Worcester's creation of Stratford-upon-Avon would have failed, instead of yielding a rich crop of burgage rents at a shilling a year for a quarter-acre – fifteen times the value of farm land there.[30] The profits to be expected from borough and market led the bishop of Winchester to carve the boroughs of Hindon out of his manor of East Knoyle (Wilts.) and New Alresford (Hants.) out of Old. The bishop of Salisbury moved both the cathedral

---

[29] W. Davies, *Wales in the Early Middle Ages*, Leicester, 1982, p. 57; *Calendar of Chancery Rolls, 1277–1326*, p. 279; *CChR*, II, p. 343; *Select Cases concerning the Law Merchant*, III, ed. H. Hall, Selden Soc., XLIX, 1932, pp. 141–2.

[30] E. M. Carus-Wilson, 'The first half-century of the borough of Stratford-upon-Avon', *EcHR*, 2nd ser. XVIII, 1965, pp. 50–1.

and the town of Old Sarum down to a corner of his manor two miles
away. The bishop of Lincoln built New Thame on a fragment of his
Oxfordshire manor. In Hertfordshire, the Templars founded Baldock
on the edge of their manor of Weston. The king created New
Winchelsea on part of the manor of Iham in Icklesham, and laid it out
with as neat a chequer-board pattern as the site allowed. On a much
smaller scale, the lord of Berry Pomeroy set aside a few acres to found
Bridgetown, across the Dart from Totnes; and in another part of
Devon Robert de Tony, lord of South Tawton, marked out what was
to become the moorland borough of South Zeal.[31] For those larger
settlements which succeeded as boroughs, and secured some degree of
self-government, a prosperous market was even more essential than for
the lords: to safeguard the residents from dearth, to provide
employment and profit for the many in the victualling trades, and to
help pay the town's "farm" to its lord and finance works such as
repairing the walls. These aims, though, might be hard to reconcile:
excessive tolls, or an aggressive pie-powder court, would deter traders.
Too much competition from outsiders could injure the freemen in the
town oligarchies, particularly in the food trades, for it was only in the
weekly markets and annual fairs that outsiders could compete on fairly
equal terms with the residents. The concluding section of this chapter
will examine some of the conflicts.

The king, a unique lord, could also use markets for political
purposes. Edward I planned his Welsh boroughs to complement the
great castles of the conquest, and peopled them with English burgesses
as an essential part of his settlement of north Wales. Although a very
high proportion survived as market centres into the sixteenth century,
their earlier years were troubled. Edward I had to listen to the
complaints of the burgesses of Rhuddlan that there were so many
Welsh lodged outside the town that "they disturb the profit and
market of the English, and give voice to much treason among them".
His successor received the complaints of Conway, that the burgesses
could not repair the walls because the only merchants who came there
were from the towns of Dublin, Drogheda, Chester, Shrewsbury,
Rhuddlan, Denbigh, Caernarfon, and Beaumaris, all of them exempt
from tolls and murage dues in Conway. And in 1330 the burgesses of
Beaumaris protested because the Welsh were trading among themselves
and evading the town's market.[32]

It was primarily the villagers and people in small towns that the
markets served. They helped the virgaters and half-virgaters to sell
their surplus grain, their old livestock, their hens and eggs, perhaps

[31] M. Beresford, *New Towns of the Middle Ages*, London, 1967, *passim*.
[32] *Cal. Ancient Petitions Relating to Wales*, ed. W. Rees, Cardiff, 1975, pp. 311, 461, 469.

their cheese and wool, and to buy from the world outside essentials like salt and fish. The smallholder and landless labourer could buy in them the food they could not themselves produce, and perhaps arrange for casual employment at hay-making or harvest. The village craftsmen might find there iron for the smithy, timber and boards for the carpenter, straw or reeds for the thatcher, yarn for the weaver. For the villagers' families, too, markets offered social contact with neighbours, and also chances for family members, particularly unmarried women, to make precarious livings as stallholders or hucksters. In Halesowen (Worcs.), and probably smaller places as well, most of the early immigrants apparently depended on the retail trade for their living.[33] Typically, most of the immigrants who colonized the new market villages and towns came from nearby: within five miles at Halesowen, five or six at Thornbury (Glos.), six at Stratford-upon-Avon.[34] Despite the attractions of borough life, one may guess that many of them kept in contact with their places of origin, some to buy privately for their own consumption, others to re-sell to their friends in the new settlement, in the market formally, or informally at the cottage door. This happened on a grand scale even in London, where the fourteenth-century "bladers" maintained family and commercial ties with the East Anglian towns from which so many had come.[35]

Paradoxically, one attempt at Church reform may have promoted this class of petty retailers so much criticized (not least by the churches) in later years. When, in the twelfth century, almost all markets took place on Sundays, the peasant could buy and sell for himself, with little need for professional small traders except those bringing salt and fish. Moreover, when all markets met on the same day the interchange of perishable commodities between adjacent markets was difficult. But in John's reign Abbot Eustache de Flay led a campaign against Sunday shopping, and all the markets granted or confirmed by Henry III scrupulously avoided that day. After the 1230 *Decretales*, Gregory IX prompted Robert Grosseteste to start a further successful attack on Sunday and feast-day markets. Some lords changed their markets to week-days by charter; others, like the abbot of Winchcomb, found the justices sympathetic when they moved the market to a week-day without specific royal approval.[36] So the market of Bardney (Lincs.)

[33] Hilton, 'Lords, burgesses and hucksters', pp. 7–8; R. H. Hilton, 'Women traders in medieval England', *Women's Studies*, 11, 1984, p. 149. I use "huckster" to mean those selling door-to-door, rather than (as Hilton suggests) all retailers selling what others had produced.

[34] Hilton, 'Lords, burgesses and hucksters', pp. 10, 13; Carus-Wilson, 'The first half-century of Stratford', p. 53.

[35] G. A. Williams, *Medieval London: from Commune to Capital*, pp. 162–4.

[36] J. L. Cate, 'The church and market reform in England during the reign of Henry III', in *Medieval and Historiographical Essays in honor of J. W. Thompson*, ed. J. L. Cate and E. N. Anderson, Chicago, 1938, pp. 27, 34, 37, 40, 41, 48.

changed from Sunday to Thursday in 1232; that of Brenchley (Kent) to Wednesday in 1230 and then to Saturday in 1233, as its owner sought the day which would attract most visitors.[37] By the middle of the century, the days on which neighbouring markets were held, as well as their proximity, determined whether a market newly instituted would be judged harmful and its grant therefore invalid. In Bracton's words,

A market may be called neighbouring, and a wrongful nuisance because it is harmful whenever it is held within six leagues [miles] and a half and a third of a half...If it is beyond this limit though harmful it will not be wrongful, because it is remote and not neighbouring. A market may also be neighbouring and within the aforesaid limits and yet not wrongful, because not harmful but rather beneficial, as where the one newly established is held on the second or third day or longer after the date of the other market; if before the second or third day it will be wrongful because harmful.[38]

A market, therefore, would be likely to benefit if traders came to it to buy goods to re-sell in other markets nearby. Ultimately, a market's success depended largely on whether it came to function as a regional entrepôt for distributing the produce and requirements of the countryside. In some districts there were apparently cycles of markets which traders could attend on successive days of the week, exchanging the specialities of one village for those of another.[39] Some towns clearly had their markets integrated with those of the immediate hinterland. Exeter held markets on Mondays, Wednesdays, and Saturdays, while the six nearest market villages held theirs on Tuesdays or Thursdays; one would have to cross the Exe and climb Haldon Hill to find at Chudleigh, nine miles away, the closest market held on one of Exeter's market days. Oxford's Wednesday and Saturday markets had no rivals nearer than Bampton and Watlington, each about twelve miles distant.[40] Such arrangements obviously facilitated the interchange of the produce of town and country. While most of the trade at village markets remained local, there was often superimposed upon it a pattern which stretched further afield. For example, Sherston (Wilts.) and Hawkesbury (Glos.), less than five miles apart, competed for the *mercatores bladi* supplying grain to Bristol, eighteen or twenty miles away.[41] As we shall see, those markets with a reputation for livestock lured dealers and drovers much longer distances to supply the meat trades of London and York.

[37] *CChR*, I, pp. 123, 147, 182.

[38] *Bracton on the Laws and Customs of England*, ed. S. E. Thorne, Cambridge, Mass., 1977, III, pp. 198–9.

[39] T. Unwin, 'Rural marketing in medieval Nottinghamshire', *J. of Hist. Geography*, 7, 1981, pp. 241–2; Reed, 'Markets and fairs in medieval Buckinghamshire', p. 572.

[40] M. Kowaleski, 'Local markets and merchants', p. 271; D. Postles, 'Markets for rural produce in Oxfordshire, 1086–1350', *Mid. Hist.*, XII, 1987, pp. 15–16.

[41] *Roll of the Shropshire Eyre of 1256*, ed. A. Harding, Selden Soc., XCVI, 1980, pp. 161–2.

Gregory IX's *Decretales* had attacked not only Sunday trading but also the common practice of holding markets in churches and churchyards. While archdeacon of Northampton in 1235, Robert Grosseteste persuaded the town to get royal leave to move both market and fair out of All Saints' church and churchyard to a site further north. But it was 1334 before the bishop of Bath and Wells petitioned for the Wells fairs to be moved out of the cathedral and its cemetery ("whereby much mischief, unseemly to holy church, has happened and happens to the said church and cemetery"), and as late as 1349 the main market in Winchester was still held in the cathedral churchyard.[42] In other towns and villages the street was the market place. At Oxford, the bread stalls were at Carfax, and the cornmarket by the North Gate; the poultry and butchery stalls were on the south side of High Street, with the sellers of pigs, straw, and timber outside All Saints' and St Mary's. South of Carfax were the fishmongers and the firewood sellers. To the west were cook-shops and more fishmongers. As well as the cornmarket, Northgate street had yet more fishmongers, and sellers of faggots, hay, and hides. The future Broad Street was already known by the thirteenth century as Horsemonger Street.[43] All these streets were fairly wide, spacious enough for market stalls. In many villages and towns today the sudden widening of a road often reveals the old market place, even though corners of the site may have become congested where stall sites became building plots for permanent shops, as at Brackley, Baldock, Wallingford, and Chipping Campden.[44] The Oxford cornmarket remained unroofed until the sixteenth century, but the founders of some other markets made better provision from the start. When the bishop of Winchester obtained in 1318 a market for his manor of Ivinghoe (Bucks.), his first act was to spend 28s. 2d. on building a lath-and-plaster "seld" 54 feet long and 10 feet wide, in effect a small market hall.[45]

Ivinghoe succeeded as a market village, attracting there within a generation settlers with names such as Carpenter, Sawyer, Cooper, Smith, Threadman, Capper, and Chapman, all of whom paid the bishop for permission to live "within the liberty".[46] Perhaps its location, on the frontier between good arable to the north and the woodlands on the Chiltern escarpment to the south, helped it to survive as a place to exchange the produce of two economic zones. Very few

---

[42] *VCH Northants.*, III, p. 23; *CChR*, IV, p. 309; Keene, *Medieval Winchester*, pp. 253, 265.

[43] O. Ogle, 'The Oxford market', in *Collectanea*, Oxford Hist. Soc., XVI, 1890, map facing p. 13; *VCH Oxon.*, IV, p. 26.

[44] Beresford and St Joseph, *Medieval England*, pp. 187–8, 195–7, 228–31.

[45] WPR 159333.   [46] WPR 159348.

Table 4.2. *Markets founded before 1349 which survived to the sixteenth century*[a]

	Founded early[b]	Founded 1200–49	Founded 1250–99	Founded 1300–49
South (Berks., Hants., Surrey)	34 (71)	4 (22)	1 (7)	1 (8)
East Midlands (Beds., Bucks., Herts., Hunts., Rutland)	28 (65)	11 (48)	5 (19)	3 (14)
West Midlands (Glos., Staffs., War., Worcs.)	32 (78)	22 (47)	13 (29)	3 (12)
East Anglia (Essex, Norfolk, Suffolk)	50 (54)	18 (30)	14 (15)	2 (5)
Northern (Derbs., Durham, Lancs., Yorks. W.R., E.R., and N.R.)	53 (73)	17 (44)	18 (20)	2 (4)
South-west (Devon)	22 (69)	8 (42)	8 (25)	2 (18)

[a] The test of survival is whether the market was listed by Alan Everitt in *AHEW* IV, pp. 468–75. Figures in brackets show the percentages of those founded in each period which survived.
[b] Probably most were founded before 1200.
Source: Reproduced from Britnell, 'The proliferation of markets', p. 219, by kind permission of the author and the *EcHR*.

other markets planted in England so late were able to take root. Of the 165 founded in 1300–49 in twenty-one English counties, only 13 were still alive in the sixteenth century. The 1,002 market sites known in those counties before 1350 contracted to 426 by Tudor times.[47] As Table 4.2 shows, the later the foundation, the less the chance of survival.

Why did so many fail, and why were newcomers the most vulnerable? The earliest markets probably had the best sites, where roads crossed rivers by bridge or ford, or where the markets served existing settlements of artisans and craftsmen. It was hard for interlopers to disturb established patterns of trade, especially in long-settled counties like Berkshire, Hampshire, and Surrey. The carrying services the lord might require of his customary tenants were often to specified places, so that manorial tradition directed demesne produce to the oldest markets even if there were new rivals closer to hand. But the village markets, those with the highest casualty rates in the later middle ages, served primarily the peasants and rural craftsmen, and were

[47] *AHEW*, IV, pp. 468–75.

chiefly sensitive to changes in the circumstances of those classes. The early thirteenth century had been a time of general economic development, when additional markets were a logical complement of expanding population, high prices and more money circulating, and the vigorous exploitation of marginal land. By the third quarter of the century, in many regions, that expansion had halted. New markets founded in England after 1275 were more modest in scale.[48] Well before the Black Death, revenues from markets were tumbling. The tolls at Witney (Oxon.) fell from 89s. 2d. in 1220–1 to 30s. 2½d. in 1262–3 and to 12s. 9d. in 1301–2, and were then farmed for an annual 18s. from 1308–9 to 1447–8, when the bishop of Winchester remitted the payments entirely for ten years.[49] At Alresford, the most successful of the bishop's new towns, tolls and stall rents yielded 56s. in 1227–8, 26s. 2d. in 1306–7, 6s. 8¾d. in 1342–3, and only 4s. 8½d. in 1382–3.[50] At Taunton, in an area where customary tenants still paid enormous entry fines until the Black Death, the combined yield from the tolls of the market and St Botolph's fair shrank from £7 18s. 8d. in 1284–5 to £3 12s. in 1300–1, and then fluctuated in the 1340s between 20s. and 30s. a year.[51] Then they too were farmed. Sometimes there was a special reason for the drop: Edward I's campaigns against Scotland in the 1290s, for example, had a disastrous effect on commerce. York's revenues fell from £124 in 1292–3 to £74 in 1294–5 through the collapse of trade; the earldom of Cornwall properties in Knaresborough and Boroughbridge lost income in 1296–7 *propter guerram Scocie et pro simplici precio bladi et pro defectu markandise lane et [bosce]*; and the merchants stayed away from Witney through fear of prises made by the king's officers at Woodstock.[52]

The main reasons for the early decline, though, were that by the late thirteenth century agricultural production was falling off, and the countrymen were finding other ways of selling their produce, ways which evaded the tolls collected in the market. The increased use of horse-drawn carts made it easier to carry goods to or from the more important markets, where produce might fetch higher prices and where there would be a wider choice for buying what lord or peasant needed. In the West Midlands, and in Lincolnshire, at least half of the village markets disappeared by the sixteenth century, whereas almost all the small urban markets survived. Some of the smallest sites had never used their charters at all: Sandiacre in Derbyshire had been

[48] Britnell, 'The proliferation of markets', p. 220.

[49] WPR 159277, 159294, 159448, 159408.

[50] WPR 159304, 159322, 159353, 159389.   [51] WPR 159306; 159319.

[52] *VCH Yorks., City of York*, p. 35; *Ministers' Accounts of the Earldom of Cornwall, 1296–1297*, ed. L. M. Midgley, II, p. 195; WPR 159315, 159319, 159448.

granted both market and fair in 1252, but had not held either by 1330.[53] During the fourteenth century repeated attacks of plague perhaps halved the number of mouths in the country; the survivors, with more land *per capita*, had less need to buy grain from others, and the cattle they raised were more likely to be sold directly to drovers. Village markets had played an invaluable role in the thirteenth century in channelling agrarian produce to those who needed it, but by the fifteenth century few markets survived unless they served a substantial number of town dwellers as well.

The proliferation of fairs in the thirteenth century matched that of markets. Both offered the proprietor similar chances of profit from tolls, rents, and pie-powder courts, as well as convenience to lord, townsman, and villager, for at fairs trading was open to all, burgesses or outsiders, though fair tolls were usually higher than market tolls. The crown's enthusiasm for fairs, at least in the thirteenth century, exceeded that for markets, as large parts of the royal purchases of cloths, wines, and furs were made at fairs, and the kings were careful to protect the merchants who brought them.[54] In the century between 1227 and 1326, the charter rolls alone record grants of nearly 1,500 fairs, almost all of them jointly with the licence for the weekly markets. A small proportion of the charters repeat earlier grants, or approve alterations in a fair's date or duration, while others record the award of two or occasionally more fairs at the same place; in total, though, the charters show that villagers in all parts of England and many parts of Wales, by 1300, had easy access to several fairs every year.[55] Most grants were for fairs lasting three days, commonly the vigil, feast, and morrow of the village church's patron saint, or of a major holy day. Longer fairs took place in the larger towns, or in isolated areas where a single fair had to serve a wider area, as in north Wales: in 1252, for example, Henry III authorized a ten-day fair in the town of Huntingdon, and a nine-day fair at Deganwy (Caerns.).[56]

Most fairs were in the summer and early autumn. Those in the early summer offered the chance to buy young stock, or to dispose of sheep after shearing; those in September supplied cattle to drovers and graziers for fattening before slaughter; those in November a last

---

[53] Hilton, 'Medieval market towns', p. 10; Coates, 'Markets and fairs in medieval Derbyshire', p. 101.

[54] E. Wedemeyer Moore, *The Fairs of Medieval England*. I am grateful to Dr Moore for sending me a copy of the page proofs prior to publication; in a few cases my interpretation of her data differs from her own.

[55] *CChR*, I–III. These calculations exclude earlier grants, those recorded elsewhere, and prescriptive fairs not confirmed by charter.   [56] *CChR*, I, pp. 378, 379.

opportunity to sell the culls which were not to be kept over the winter. When Easter fell on or before the median date of 5 April, two-thirds of the fairs were wholly or mainly within the months of June, July, August, and September; a later Easter would move into that period the large number of fairs at Whitsun and perhaps those at Trinity as well. In contrast, the five months from December to April saw barely 6 per cent of the total, many of these being in large towns. The men of Salisbury had an eight-day fair starting on the vigil of St Remigius (12 January), and one of Westminster's fairs was also held in January; Leicester had a fifteen-day fair starting on the morrow of Candlemas, and, when Easter was early, Peterborough's fair too would fall in February. But most fairs, urban and rural, came in the summer months, followed by a quiet October and a busy November with fairs at All Saints' and Martinmas. Figure 4.1 illustrates this distribution, and shows that, for obvious reasons of weather, the northern counties avoided the winter months and had a high concentration of October and November fairs, as befitted the pastoral bias of their economy. The crowding into the summer months brought competition between fairs held at the same time: the feast of St Lawrence, for example, in August while harvesting might still be in progress, saw fairs in Devon at Crediton, Newton Abbot, Ashburton, and Sheepwash.

Otherwise, the link between fair and patronal festival was mutually beneficial, swelling attendance at the church for the spiritual benefit therein, and increasing the more worldly profit outside. Parliament, though, in 1448–9 entered a late protest against:

The abominable Injuries and offences done to Almighty God ... because of Fairs and Markets upon ... high and principal Feasts...: in which principal and festival Days, for great earthly Covetise, the people is wilfully more vexed, and in bodily labour defouled than in other ferial Days, as in pycchyng and making their Booths and Stalls, bearing and carrying, lifting and placing their Wares outward and homeward, as though they did nothing remember the horrible Defiling of their Souls in buying and selling, with many deceitful Lyes, and false Perjury, with Drunkenness and Strifes...[57]

But, as with markets, many churches gained from the stall-rents and tolls they levied at fairs. The church's own land often provided the fair site; in 1246 the pious Henry III's charter to Marlborough (Wilts.) allowed a fair on the feast of St Peter and St Paul "about the church within and without the graveyard", and Westminster abbey's fairs at first took place within the abbey's walls. In a few cases special sites were reserved for fairs – on St Giles's Hill east of Winchester, on the banks of the Ouse by St Ives (Hunts.), in the space on the Boston waterfront,

[57] *Statutes of the Realm*, II, pp. 351–2; *Rot. Parl.* V, p. 152.

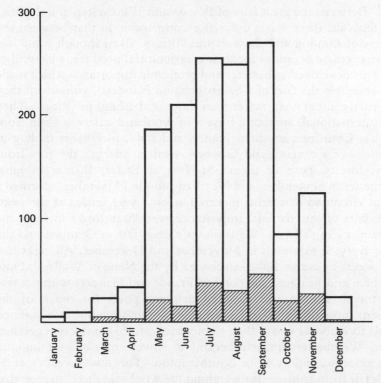

Fig. 4.1 Temporal distribution of fairs chartered in England and Wales, 1227–1326. This diagram takes 5 April as the date of Easter; both Whitsun and Trinity fall in May. The shaded areas show the distribution of fairs in the northern counties: Lancs., Westmor., Cumb., Yorks., Durham and Northumb. The only source used is the *Calendar of Charter Rolls*.

and, eventually, outside Westminster abbey's precincts – and the fair owners built, or allowed others to erect, permanent stalls and shops, from whose open windows the goods were sold. More commonly, the fair spilled over from the usual market place into the streets around, and sometimes beyond the walls, despite the greater difficulty of collecting tolls.

In size and prosperity fairs ranged from the great international fairs like St Botolph's at Boston, with receipts of £289 in 1280, and St Giles's at Winchester, yielding £163 in 1239, to regional fairs like Embsay (Yorks.), worth £11 16s. 3d. in 1297–8, and down to modest events worth a few shillings or less; in 1296–7 that at Henley-on-Thames (already a prosperous inland port) produced only 3s. 10½d. Others were even less promising; the proprietors of a fair licensed in 1251 at Rockland (Sussex) admitted in 1325 that it had never been

held.[58] Between the great fairs of Boston and Winchester, and the brief
local festivals, there was a difference comparable to that between the
markets of London and those of the villages. Even though some had
started as yearly occasions for selling agricultural produce, a handful of
great fairs developed a character and economic importance which made
them resemble the fairs of Champagne and Flanders (with which they
were partly integrated), rather than those of the English villages. They
were international, attracting buyers of wool and sellers of cloth from
the Low Countries, southern France, and Italy, merchants trading in
the wines of Germany and Gascony, dealers offering the furs from
distant forests. Four of them – St. Ives at Easter, Boston in June,
Winchester in September, and Northampton in November – formed a
regular circuit so that debts incurred at one were settled at the next.
Other fairs of international importance were Stamford's in Lent, the
July fair at King's Lynn, Westminster's main fair in October, and the
fair at Bury St Edmunds in November and December. All eight had
good access by water, linked to the sea by the Nene or Welland, Ouse
or Itchen, and bringing the ports of France and Flanders within a few
days travel. Boston was also the delivery point for much of the
northern monasteries' wool, taken there at fair-time not to be offered
for sale to whoever was willing to buy but to fulfil contracts negotiated
earlier. Winchester similarly became a convenient place for bulking
wool prior to export from Southampton. The low revenues at St
Giles's fair from tronage (for weighing the wool sold there) suggest that
most of the bargains and settlements were made outside the fair.[59] The
concourse of domestic and alien traders at the fairs obviously facilitated
commercial contacts which could lead to private marketing un-
hampered by the formalities and tolls of the fair.

It is not easy to assess what part these international fairs played in
marketing agricultural produce. For their towns, and their immediate
neighbourhoods, they served as local fairs more than as sources of
expensive exotica. The records of St Ives fair between 1270 and 1324
contain the names of 201 people from places less than ten miles away,
and 311 from more distant places, mainly the townsmen of Boston,
Bury St Edmunds, Cambridge, Ely, King's Lynn, Leicester, Lincoln,
London, Northampton, and Stamford, as well as aliens from Flanders,
France, and even Italy.[60] Most of the fairs came too early in the year to
trade in grain from the current harvest; all but one were in eastern
England, north of the Thames, and so left most of the country
unserved. At St Ives fair in 1278, the only grain offered seems to have

[58] Moore, *Fairs*, p. 16; Keene, *Medieval Winchester*, II, p. 1124; Kershaw, *Bolton Priory*, p. 29; *Accounts of the Earldom of Cornwall*, ed. Midgley, pp. 91, 218; *CChR*, III, p. 479.

[59] Keene, *Medieval Winchester*, II, pp. 1124–5.   [60] Moore, *Fairs*, pp. 77–87.

been oats, sold from seven boats moored in the Ouse, but (as Dr Johnson was later to remark) in England this was food for horses, not men, and was probably sold for the mounts of visiting merchants.[61] While Henry III occasionally bought horses at Winchester fair, the later Winchester pipe rolls show that the toll income from livestock sales was normally much less than that from selling grazing for the visitors' horses (except in 1321, when more beasts may have been driven to the fair for sale to manors needing to replace those lost in the recent murrains).[62] Even so, regulations tried to compel residents to buy their needs at the fairs: the market and shops of Winchester closed during the St Giles's fair, and the king ordered London's shops to shut during Westminster's.[63] And, as prime links in the chain which brought continental luxuries and some necessities to England, supplying traders with goods they took to lesser fairs or distributed to village markets; as places for assembling wool for export; and as occasions for settling debts and arranging contracts, the international fairs had some importance in attracting to market the produce of the countryside.

The regional and local fairs were of more obvious and more lasting use in agrarian marketing. Many regional fairs were famous for livestock, luring London buyers to Abingdon or Woodstock and enticing Merton College bailiffs to the fairs of Winchcomb and Chipping Campden. Bolton fair, where the stockman was allowed 8s. 6d. for expenses, seems to have been the main outlet for the 385 head of cattle sold from Henry de Lacy's Blackburnshire vaccaries in 1304–5, and the same lord's fair at Halton (Cheshire), which collected that year £17 0s. 10d. in tolls alone, were obviously very important in the north-west. Across the Pennines, Durham Cathedral priory in the fourteenth century regularly bought large numbers of oxen, and occasionally horses, twenty miles away at Corbridge fair. At the very end of our period, Peterborough abbey's officials went as far as Coventry fair, sixty miles distant, to buy oxen: fourteen in 1504–5, twenty-three the next year.[64]

As well as livestock, the regional fairs were important sources of farm equipment: carts and wheels, harness, horseshoes, nails, sawn timber, the tar and fearsome chemicals needed to treat sheep-scab, perhaps the canvas for grain sacks, wool sarplars, or windmill sails. Stourbridge fair, on the outskirts of Cambridge, and the greatest fair of

[61] *Ibid.*, p. 147. [62] WPR 159334.

[63] *VCH Hants.*, v, pp. 37–8; A. G. Rosser, 'Medieval Westminster: the vill and the urban community', London Univ. Ph.D. thesis, 1984, p. 48.

[64] PRO DL/29/1/2; N. Morimoto, *Monastic Economy and Medieval Markets*, Kyoto, 1983, pp. 276–310; *Account Rolls of the Obedientiaries of Peterborough*, ed. J. Greatrex, Northants. Rec. Soc., XXXIII, 1984, pp. 181, 195.

late medieval England, provided salt for Gamlingay (Cambs.) in 1316 and Claret (Essex) in 1340, "terpic" for Chevington (Suffolk) in 1396, hurdles and more tar for Wisbech Barton (Cambs.) in 1412–13.[65] Cheddington (Bucks.) bought canvas at Oxford fair in 1358 and 1370. Hinderclay (Suffolk) bought steel at Bury St Edmunds on several occasions in the thirteenth century, and a cart-load of firewood at Thetford fair in 1368.[66] Wisbech Barton bought oak and ash timbers at Barnwell fair in 1415. Cuxham purchased plough-shares and wheels at nearby Crowmarsh fair in 1289; in 1298 it obtained iron at the fairs of Crowmarsh and Reading. Holywell got cartwheels and axles at Godstow fair in 1309, and wheels at Woodstock fair in 1362. Gamlingay bought horseshoes and nails at St Neots fair in 1316, and wheels at Bedford fair in 1334. Other Merton College manors bought horseshoes at fairs at Aylesbury (Bucks.) and Wye (Kent).[67] Sibton abbey bought horseshoes at Framlingham fair (Suffolk) in 1364–5. Exeter Cathedral regularly bought horseshoes at Lopen fair (Somerset), thirty-seven miles away, as well as nails and other ironmongery, before turning to local sources at Topsham, Dartmouth, and Ottermouth; the cathedral builders had even sent to Boston fair for lead in 1302, 1304, and 1311, before it became available at Teignmouth and the other ports of south Devon.[68]

In contrast, the regional and even the village fairs apparently played little part in marketing grain. Many were too early for the current crop; others came too soon after the harvest to offer anything but seed-wheat hurriedly threshed for the autumn sowing. The bulk and weight of grain made it costly to take to a fair where there was no assured buyer. Peterborough abbey bought 4 qr of wheat *de novo grano* at Stourbridge fair in 1330 (out of total purchases exceeding 260 qr), and Wisbech Barton bought 10 qr of wheat there in 1342 as seed for the coming year. Gamlingay sold small quantities of rye there in 1343 and 1345, perhaps taken as loads for the outward journeys of carts sent to Stourbridge to fetch the manor's purchases.[69] It is of course possible that villagers made more use of fairs for selling grain than the lords did (though the cost of transport would restrict them at least as much), and

---

[65] MCR 5372; PRO SC 6/838/15; Suffolk RO, E3/15.3/2.20(a); Cambridge Univ. Library, D8/3/21.

[66] MCR 5586, 5597; Regenstein Library, Chicago, Bacon Mss. 406, 409, 419, 483.

[67] Cambridge Univ. Library, D8/3/23; MCR 5808, 5818, 4486, 4518, 5372, 5387, 5533, 5268.

[68] BL Add. Ms. 34560; *The Accounts of the Fabric of Exeter Cathedral, 1279–1353*, ed. A. M. Erskine, Devon and Cornwall Rec. Soc., NS 24, 26, 1981–3, pp. 19, 22, 33, 35, 46, 58, 61, 68, 77, 106, 117, 150, 220, 268.

[69] *Account Rolls of Peterborough*, ed. Greatrex, p. 119; Cambridge Univ. Library, D8/1/15; MCR 5396, 5398. These are the only certain examples I have found of manors dealing in grain at any fair.

that some of the grain sold by lords in markets or at the granary door was then re-sold by the purchasers at fairs; certainly, fairs would have provided illicit opportunities for bailiffs to exhibit samples and arrange contracts which allowed buyers to fetch grain from manors without paying fair tolls. But probably fairs played only a minor part in marketing grain.

This may be true also of dairy products. Demesnes did not normally send their cheese and butter to fairs, or buy from them, though a late account of Barnhorne (Sussex) for 1487–8 records 18d. spent on carrying cheese to the fairs of Maresfield and Shoreham.[70] The dairymen who leased the cows and ewes in later years may well have sold the cheeses at fairs, but such dealings do not appear in manorial accounts. On the other hand, hides both undressed and tanned might be sold at fairs. The Glastonbury abbey manor of Damerham in 1258 received 8d. for a heifer's hide sent to Winchester fair, and in 1275 the abbey tanner himself took tanned hides to the fairs of Sherborne, Tintinhull, and Ilchester.[71] Fairs served another purpose when some lords ordered tenants to deliver their rents at specified fairs, perhaps out of the proceeds of stock sales: the large number of fairs at midsummer and Michaelmas fell conveniently at two of the usual times for payment, and helped tenants to pay rents out of what they received for stock sales. The midsummer fair at Corbridge functioned in this way, and Stourbridge fair served for collecting rents from Peterborough abbey's tenants.[72]

Despite such services to the trades in wool, animals, and leather, and to the rent collectors, fairs seem to have been occasions when lords made their purchases, rather than their sales. The markets in town and village provided regular opportunities to buy and sell the staple items of diet, the fairs the chance to buy luxuries and livestock. Agrarian producers made money at markets, and spent it at fairs. For this and other reasons, the history of fairs in the later middle ages differs somewhat from that of markets. All the international fairs, whose prosperity had rested on the wool and cloth trades, were in decline well before the Black Death. Winchester's revenues dropped from about £160 in 1250 to £66 in 1300 and £31 in 1347; between 1400 and 1451 they averaged less than £12, and came mainly from fines in the Pavilion Court.[73] Westminster abbey's October fair had made profits of about £120 a year in the 1330s, but after 1372 the tolls never realized more than a few shillings, and the fair probably ceased altogether about

[70] Huntingdon Library, Mss. BA 422. This is also the only reference of its kind I have found.
[71] GAD 10762, 11244.
[72] NCH, x, pp. 34–5; Account Rolls of Peterborough, ed. Greatrex, pp. 14n, 183.
[73] Keene, Medieval Winchester, II, pp. 1124–5. See also Table 4.3.

Table 4.3. Some revenues of St Giles's fair, Winchester

	Net income[a] £ s. d.	Rent income[b] £ s. d.	Gate and fair tolls[c] £ s. d.	Stock[d] £ s. d.	Pavilion Court[e] £ s. d.
1292	63 7 9½	36 19 10	11 7 0	5 12 2	4 17 7
1302	48 11 11½	33 9 0½	4 18 9	4 16 10	2 1 4
1310	48 6 11½	27 19 7½	6 15 1½	5 13 7	3 5 6
1321	47 18 3¾	25 6 11½	8 19 1½	6 16 8	2 17 4
1331	37 2 8¼	24 5 3	5 10 11	4 2 10	2 3 9
1341	22 15 5½	18 7 8½	2 16 3	3 8 8	1 11 3
1352	26 11 0	16 12 5	3 9 0¼	3 0 0	5 8 2
1362	5 13 11½	8 1 5	1 17 9	3 7 4	6 8 2
1371	16 18 10½	8 10 0½	1 14 1	2 0 7	7 0 10
1377	13 12 1½	7 9 6½	1 0 0	1 17 7	5 1 7
1387	12 3 5	5 6 4½	1 4 4	1 8 0	5 5 2
1394	9 3 7½	1 2 11	—	1 0 4	4 15 6
1403	8 10 7½	2 18 11	—	16 4	5 10 6
1412	9 7 5	1 7 10½	—	6	10 2 11
1422	2 5 3	8 8	—	5 2	7 12 3
1430	10 13 1	7 4	—	12 3	12 8 10
1441	14 17 8	7 4	—	13 2	16 1 2
1450	11 11 1	7 4	—	9 5	13 5 8

[a] Net after deducting fair expenses and the cost of the bishop's household during the fair. For revenues without these deductions, see D. J. Keene, *Survey of Medieval Winchester*, II, pp. 1124–6.
[b] Includes payments for terrage, locage, and seldage.
[c] Gate receipts and fair entry payments.
[d] Boage, and payments for animals agisted during the fair.
[e] Figures for 1412 and 1441 (and for several other years not included in this table) include £2 from the men of Southampton for permission to sell at the fair. It is possible that other court revenues may also have been in lieu of tolls.

1487.[74] For those fairs which had prospered from selling furs, fine cloths, wines, and spices to those who paid for them out of the profits of wool exports, the manufacturing changes and increased government interference in the fourteenth century by taxation and regulation were chill economic winds bringing disaster.[75]

Those local and regional fairs, though, which had gained acceptance in earlier years, continued to fill an economic and social role for the countrymen of the fifteenth century. Such were, in one corner of

[74] Rosser, 'Medieval Westminster', p. 64.   [75] Moore, *Fairs*, pp. 216–22.

England, the fairs at Priddy, Binegar, Hindon, Castle Cary, Somerton, Warminster, and Heytesbury, where the bishopric of Winchester and Glastonbury abbey manors in Wiltshire bought and sold livestock both before and after the Black Death. It was still possible, in the fourteenth and fifteenth centuries, for Stourbridge to develop as the most important agricultural fair of the middle ages and beyond. There are only a few of the smaller fairs whose revenues can be calculated over a long period, but the bishop of Winchester's fairs at Staplegrove (Somerset) and at Otterford (Somerset) kept up their incomes fairly well – in contrast to the bishop's fair at Winchester and the market revenues of the new boroughs he had created. Staplegrove's Mill Lane fair in July brought in between 20s. and 30s. in most years between 1312 and 1453; Otterford's St Leonard's fair between 2s. and 3s. until it was leased to John Rooke, farmer of Otterford, for 2s. 6d. a year about 1440. While the bishop of Worcester's fair at Blockley (Glos.) dropped in value by about half between 1300 and the later fifteenth century, the drop was much less than that of the market tolls of Cheltenham.[76] Fifteenth-century England still had rural craftsmen and weavers with money to spare, and the will to walk five or ten miles to a fair promised some break in the routine of rural life, and some chance for village wives to buy the wares of travelling pedlars who did not come to the local market. And it would be wrong to ignore the non-marketing functions of the fairs, great, middling, and small: the entertainments by jugglers and girls of doubtful virtue, the chance to exchange the gossip from a wider area – news of the plague, or the French war, or rumours of taxation and unrest. To the ploughboys and cloth workers, carpenters and ale-wives, the fair brought a touch of the exotic and a hint of the world over the horizon. These excitements may have helped the lesser fairs to survive as social events even when the growth in private trading had reduced their importance in marketing agrarian produce.

By the early thirteenth century, the English and Welsh centres of agrarian production supplied their markets through adequate roads and drove-ways, along convenient rivers, and by shipping routes around the coasts and across the Channel and North Sea. Much of the transport came from *averagia*, or carrying services required of customary tenants on foot, or with pack-horse, cart, or boat. The full-time *famuli* of the demesne shared in the task. An important and increasing part fell to the men and lads whom the manors hired with their carts or barges, and also to the drovers who took livestock to the centres of distribution and

[76] WPR 159436; Dyer, *Lords and Peasants*, p. 340.

consumption. Distance proved no obstacle to moving millstones and timber, and even less so to the carriage of grain, when the means of transport were efficiently integrated.

The estates of the abbey and bishopric of Ely, according to the mid-thirteenth-century Coucher Book, claimed *averagia* which linked their manors to some thirty towns and villages, apart from other Ely manors: from Boston in the north to Peterborough, King's Lynn, Bury St Edmunds, Hertford, and even London.[77] The cottar of Colne and Bluntisham (Hunts.), for example, did his carrying service on foot with a load on his back, *super dorsum suum*, to Ramsey, St Ives, Sawtry, Huntingdon, or Cambridge. The Little Downham (Cambs.) villein had to accompany the bailiff to buy livestock at Bury St Edmunds, Wisbech, or St Ives; his fellow at Feltwell (Norfolk) had to go to Thetford with horse and cart or saddle bag to buy or sell the lord's grain, while the Hardwick (Cambs.) villein had to go to Cambridge or to other Ely manors *ad bladum vendendum vel cariandum ad opus episcopi*. One of the most remote Ramsey abbey manors was comparably endowed: Lawshall (Suffolk), had *averagia* to Burwell, Reach, Colchester, Ipswich, and Bury St Edmunds.[78] The Glastonbury abbey manors of Longbridge Deverill and Monkton Deverill sweetened the task with small payments to the customary tenants who carried wheat to market – ½d. per quarter for journeys of seven leagues or under, 1d. per quarter for the longer hauls to Glastonbury, Salisbury, Shaftesbury, Sherborne, and Wells, *de consuetudine quia ultra vij leucas*.[79] In the same county, a Bishopstone (Wilts.) tenant of the bishop of Winchester had to carry the lord's grain for sale to the four nearest markets, two quarters each trip, and received only ½d. recompense. John Spareke, one of the bishop's virgaters at Rimpton (Somerset), had to carry grain *ad marchetum* at Ilchester, Sherborne, Yeovil, or Castle Cary. At East Meon (Hants.) six men found a cart to carry the bishop's wool for sale anywhere within the country, while a Hambledon (Hants.) tenant had the task of driving the bishop's livestock *de foris ad fora vel ad lardar'*. If the bishop wished to buy or sell grain in the markets of Alton or Winchester, the Ropley half-virgaters each had to carry one quarter of wheat, or more of oats.[80] These quantities imply the use of carts; no led pack-horse could carry a quarter of wheat weighing over 500 lb.

Many of these *averagia* were commuted, especially in later years, but

---

[77] Cambridge Univ. Library, EDR G/3/27. I am indebted to Edward Miller for these details, and for those on p. 351 below.

[78] *Cartularium Monasterii de Rameseia*, ed. W. H. Hart and P. A. Lyons, 1893, III, p. 282.

[79] GAD 10689; see D. L. Farmer, 'Two Wiltshire manors and their markets', *AHR*, 37, 1989, pp. 1–11.

[80] BL, Egerton Ms. 2418; *The Medieval Customs of the Manors of Taunton and Bradford on Tone*, ed. T. J. Hunt, Somerset Rec. Soc., LXVI, 1962, p. 27.

the Winchester pipe roll for 1381–2 shows many still performed, sometimes specifically for carrying to market: Highclere (Hants.) used eight to carry cheese and four to carry barley *ad diuersa fora ad vendendum*, while Burghclere (Hants.) used thirty-four services to carry 33 qr of wheat and 18 qr 4 b. of other grain to various markets for sale.[81] Cuxham's customary tenants had the duty of carrying grain to Wallingford or Henley even before the manor passed to Merton College, and it was their labour which carried most of the Cuxham wheat over the Chiltern ridge to Henley before the Black Death, and at least briefly after it.[82] These examples suffice to illustrate the value of *averagia* in moving demesne produce overland to markets, or in fetching back what the manor needed. But not all, and perhaps not most, of the carrying services were used in this way: where works accounts survive in the manorial rolls, usually in the mid- or late-fourteenth century, most of the *averagia* seem expended on inter-manorial transfers, on transport to the lord's residences, or were simply "sold" back to the tenant. Even an inter-manorial transfer, though, may have been the first stage of a journey to market, as with the grain which other Ely manors sent to Fen Ditton to begin a journey by river to King's Lynn and then by sea to London or Newcastle or abroad. Similarly, the Winchester estates used inter-manorial movements to assemble their wool clip at Southwark, or Wolvesey Castle, or Downton, prior to sale to purchasers.

By 1210–11, about half the Winchester manors already had *famuli* designated as carters: Bishop's Waltham (Hants.) had three, Downton (Wilts.) and North Waltham (Hants.) two each.[83] During the thirteenth century, horse-drawn carts largely supplanted oxcarts on the demesnes and also among the peasants, for the former travelled at twice the speed, and a single horse (though not as strong as an ox) could still pull as much grain as a producer would normally wish to offer at one time, up to four quarters in flat country. Improved techniques of harnessing horses allowed them to be used in tandem to drag heavier loads; the Luttrell Psalter of *c.* 1340 shows a three-horse cart with iron-shod wheels.[84]

Those manors with inadequate *averagia* had to use their demesne carts, or hire peasant haulage contractors, to market their produce. Thus Combe (Hants.) could require its virgaters to carry cheese to Southampton for shipment to the mother-house at Bec, or to go *ad villas mercandas* to fetch food if the abbot visited the manor; but when

[81] WPR 159388. [82] *Manorial Records of Cuxham*, ed. Harvey, pp. 607, 657.

[83] *The Pipe Roll of the Bishopric of Winchester 1210–1211*, ed. N. R. Holt, *passim*.

[84] J. Langdon, 'Horse-hauling: a revolution in vehicle transport in twelfth- and thirteenth-century England?', *PP*, no. 103, 1984, pp. 54, 58, 63–6.

the reeve travelled to the markets at Andover and Newbury to sell grain, as he did seventeen times in the summer of 1307, he used no carrying services. This the works account confirms. As there were no payments for hiring transport, the task must have fallen to the resident carter and his three cart horses.[85] Details of *famuli* cartage work are rather scarce in the accounts, appearing incidentally, as when the Wellingborough (Northants.) carters, taking grain the twenty-three miles to Yaxley in 1322, were allowed 4d. to buy horsebread, or when the Cuxham *famuli* hurried 21 qr 4 b. of wheat to Henley in September 1357.[86] At Kelvedon (Essex), in 1383–4 and 1384–5, the manor carts joined with hired carts in taking wheat to Colchester. Brightwell (Berks.) in 1387–8 allowed the reeve 14s. 8d. for the expenses of men and horses taking wheat and malt to Henley on various occasions, driving oxen and pigs to London, and carrying cocks and hens to Oxford for the lord's hospice there; as the works account records that the *averagia* were cancelled "because they were not needed this year", the work was clearly done by the *famuli*, not the customary tenants.[87] The Black Death increased the use of demesne transport; in 1343–4 Hinderclay had used all its 120 horse *averagia* to move grain, and also 10 of its 36 carrying services on foot, but ten years later all the customary tenements were in the lord's hands, and the bailiff – one assumes – had to rely on the *famuli* and the four demesne cart horses. Other *famuli* took obvious roles in marketing livestock: in 1411–12 the Monkton Deverill reeve took the shepherd with him to sell sheep at the St Luke's fair at Hindon, incurring expenses of 18d., and in 1420–1 two shepherds and a carter, as well as the bailiff and reeve, went to Hindon fair for the same purpose.[88] In the summer of 1355 Woolford (Worcs.) sent its *tentor* to Winchcomb fair, hiring another man to look after the plough in his absence. The bailiff of Elham, who attended Winchcomb fair regularly, shared in leading the horses back to Kent for sale to the villagers. For one important traffic it was necessary for the producers to provide transport: Cistercian wool crossed England free of toll only while it remained in monastic hands, and the houses therefore used their lay-brothers to cart it to York or Boston or London.[89]

Hired transport, of one sort or another, also played a large part in marketing produce. In 1171, Henry II had hired carts to take wheat

---

[85] *Select Documents of the English Lands of the Abbey of Bec*, ed. M. Chibnall, Camden 3rd ser. LXXIII, 1951, pp. 149, 157–8.

[86] *Wellingborough Manorial Accounts, A.D. 1258–1329*, ed. F. M. Page, Northants. Rec. Soc., VIII, 1936, p. 129; *Manorial Records of Cuxham*, ed. Harvey, pp. 573, 578.

[87] WAM 25845, 25847; WPR 159394.

[88] Regenstein Library, Chicago, Bacon Mss. 466, 472; GAD 9694, 9880.

[89] MCR 4411, 5275; R. A. Donkin, *The Cistercians: Studies in the Geography of Medieval England and Wales*, Toronto, 1978, pp. 139–42.

from Oxford to Bristol for his Irish campaign, the journey across the Cotswolds adding about 35 per cent to the cost of the grain.[90] More than half the accounts in the 1210–11 Winchester pipe roll seem to include payments for hired carriage by cart or, possibly, pack-horse: of wool from many manors to London, of cider from Bishopstoke (Hants.) to Bishop's Waltham and Marwell (Hants.), of timber from West Wycombe (Bucks.) to Marlow. East Meon church (Hants.) that year spent 45s. 10d. in carrying grain to Winchester, Bishop's Waltham, Fareham, Marwell, Lovington, and Stanstead.[91] In 1298 the king bought 1,177 qr 3 b. of wheat, peas, and oats in Yorkshire for £151 15s. 10d., and spent £15 9s. on transporting it by land to the ports of Whitby and Scarborough and on renting granaries there. By the time the supplies reached the army at Berwick, the costs of carriage, storage, loading, and supervision added about 40 per cent to its original purchase price.[92] The reeve of Kelvedon claimed 21s. 8d. for the cost of hiring carts to take 47 qr 2 b. of wheat ten miles to Colchester in 1383–4, at 5½d. a quarter, though the auditors allowed him only 18s. in all. In 1395–6, though, the reeve of the adjacent Westminster manor of Feering (Essex) was allowed to pay 6d. per quarter for wheat taken a slightly shorter distance to Colchester, by seven carts which together carried 28 qr 1 b., averaging 2,025 lb or about 18 cwt per load. A Turweston (Bucks.) carter in 1338–9 had carried 53 qr of dredge malt sixty miles to London for sale, in nine journeys, probably with slightly heavier loads.[93]

The most impressive evidence in manorial accounts of long-distance road transport may be that for carting millstones. In 1339–40 West Wycombe bought a millstone at Tewkesbury, paying only 25s. 10d. for the stone (presumably a small Welsh one), drilling and preparing it, and carrying it back sixty hilly miles to the Chilterns. Claret bought a new millstone at Ipswich in 1318–19 for 39s. 6d.; the cart to carry it twenty-four miles cost 7s.[94] Holywell in other years bought millstones in London or at Brackley, but in 1335–6 it purchased two in Southampton, for 73s. 9d. and 47s. 3d.; leaving the miller in Southampton to drill the stones, the serviens returned to Oxford, collected four men and two carts, and fetched the stones back from Southampton at a cost of 4s. 7d. for the men's expenses, 3s. 9½d. on horsebread, 10½d. on hay, 7d. on shoeing, and 13d. in tolls, in addition to the costs of loading and packing the stones in the carts. These were,

[90] D. L. Farmer, 'Some price fluctuations in Angevin England', EcHR, 2nd ser. IX, 1956, p. 35.

[91] Pipe Roll of Winchester, ed. Holt, pp. 28, 80, 127.

[92] Scotland in 1298: Documents Relating to the Campaign of Edward I in that Year, ed. H. Gough, London, 1888, pp. 273–4.

[93] WAM 25845, 25732. This calculation takes 63 lb as the weight of a bushel of wheat. A bushel of dredge malt would weigh less.   [94] WPR 159355; PRO SC 6/838/4.

however, demesne carts accompanied by *famuli*; during their absence the manor incurred extra costs of 8s. 10d. for help in gathering hay. In an earlier year, three millstones bought in London had been hauled by road from Henley with three carts, five men, and thirteen horses; the round trip between Holywell and Henley, 21 miles "as the crow flies" from Oxford, needed only three days. Birdbrook fetched its millstones by road from Ipswich (27 miles away), Cambridge (20 miles) and, in later years, from Colchester (20 miles). The bishop of Winchester's manors in Somerset bought Welsh millstones at Bridgwater or Taunton, and French millstones usually at Wareham on the Dorset coast, 46 miles distant; transporting two stones bought at Wareham in 1301–2 for £4 0s. 5d. cost 30s.[95] Movements of heavy timber across the country also illustrate how carts and roads could carry heavy burdens long distances. By the mid-fifteenth century, professional hauliers were travelling routinely between the midlands, London, Oxford, Bristol, Salisbury, and Southampton; over 1,600 carts a year passed through Southampton's gates, mainly carrying the needs of the cloth industry, but sometimes with wheat, malt, hogs, or other produce. Of the several millstones carted from Southampton in 1478, one was bound for Abingdon. Hardly any of Southampton's trade went by pack-horse.[96]

It was by cart, too, that the Celys and other merchants moved their wool from the Cotswolds to London in the late fifteenth century, at an average cost of 18s. 9d. a load, about 2 per cent of the selling price.[97] The normal waggon load was six sacks, weighing about one ton; a strong team might haul 30 cwt. By that time the pack-horse seems to have become limited to taking small loads of grain or wool to centres where it could be bulked for onward travel by cart or boat, or to hill regions such as the Lake District, where roads were inadequate and bridges too narrow for carts. Even the sacks bought by manors – usually of five-bushel capacity – would have been too heavy when filled with wheat to be moved by pack-horse. Although London had easy access to river and sea, cart traffic provided London Bridge with more toll income than ships did, despite the high charges imposed on the latter for lifting the drawbridge at Southwark; and one may concur with the old judgement that, in the fourteenth-century, the burden of transport was borne by the cart, rather than the pack-horse or barge.[98]

[95] MCR 4496, 4491; WAM 25415, 25441, 25471; WPR 159448.

[96] Rackham, *Ancient Woodland*, p. 152; *The Brokage Book of Southampton, 1439–40*, ed. B. D. M. Bunyard, Southampton Rec. Soc., 1941; *Brokage Book, 1443–44*, ed. O. Coleman, Southampton Rec. Ser., IV, 1960–1, pp. xx, 54; *Brokage Books 1477–8 and 1527–8*, ed. K. F. Stevens and T. E. Olding, Southampton Rec. Ser. XXVIII, 1985, p. 80.

[97] A. Hanham, *The Celys and Their World*, Cambridge, 1985, p. 119.

[98] G. H. Martin, 'Road travel in the middle ages', *J. of Transport Hist.*, NS III, 1976, p. 161; J. F. Willard, 'The use of carts in the fourteenth century', *History*, XVII, 1932, p. 250.

The roads, and the clearings alongside, also carried a great traffic in livestock. Much of it was inter-manorial – such as the assortment of 33 head of cattle and 1,517 sheep which John the barber, valet of Edward II, conducted in 1323 from royal manors in Lincolnshire to others in Yorkshire – but a lot was on the hoof to market, feeding on the wide grassy verges as the *famuli* or villagers drove the animals on.[99] Fodder costs were minimal, except for horses, and it was rare to hire shelter for livestock, though when two men drove a boar and twenty pigs from Islip (Oxon.) to Eybury in November 1346 they rented a *domus* at Stokenchurch for the animals, at a cost of 4d.[100] At least by the mid-thirteenth century there was a regular trade in cattle from Wales; Welshmen brought their beasts to Ross-on-Wye on Thursdays, spent Friday nights at Newent, seven miles further on, and continued the eight miles to Gloucester in time for the Saturday market; they took the unsold beasts to the Sunday market at Newnham, ten miles away, and were back again at Newent on Tuesday and at Gloucester for its Wednesday market, before returning to their homes with purchases of, perhaps, salt and cloth.[101] The medieval cattle trade will be studied more fully in later pages, and here one needs only to observe that moving livestock to market was cheap and easy, albeit slow, whether entrusted to manorial servants or hired helpers, or in the hands of drover-entrepreneurs who owned the beasts they planned to sell.

For heavy or bulky loads, though, the waterways were more economical than the roads. Millstones again provide some of the best examples. In 1304–5, Witney bought a new millstone in London for 40s. 3d.; loading it from wharf to ship cost $13\frac{1}{2}$d., but sailing it upstream to Henley only 2s. Thereafter it cost 9d. to transfer it to a cart, 4d. in toll at Wallingford, and 18d. for the expense of two *famuli* taking it to Witney with four horses. The 1330–1 Cuxham account records buying five millstones in London for £15 16s. 8d. and paying 11s. 2d. for the journey up the Thames to Henley; even though incidental costs added another 7s. $3\frac{1}{2}$d., the carriage charges thus amounted to less than 6 per cent of the purchase price.[102] Most English waterways flowed in the direction of trade, and by the early thirteenth century much of the produce of the countryside went to market by water. In 1210–11 Brightwell, Harwell, Wargrave, and West Wycombe hired boats to carry 1,130 qr of grain to London, at 3d. or $2\frac{1}{2}$d. per quarter of wheat; even the higher price, paid by Brightwell and Harwell, represented only some 6 per cent of what the wheat fetched when sold at

[99] F. M. Stenton, 'The road system of medieval England', *EcHR*, VII, 1936, pp. 18–19.
[100] WAM 14794.
[101] H. P. R. Finberg, 'An early reference to the Welsh cattle trade', *AHR*, II, 1954, pp. 12–13.
[102] WPR 159408; MCR 5853.

Southwark.[103] In later years, though, the bishop of Winchester's Thames valley manors usually sent their grain to rented granaries at Henley, and the bishop soon ceased to sell wheat at Southwark, so the accounts fall silent on grain shipping costs (though a great deal of timber and firewood was still sent by the river directly from Wargrave to Southwark). The customary services the bishop claimed from his tenants also reflect the river's importance. The Harwell (Berks.) virgaters had the duty of carrying grain the seven miles to Wallingford, loading it in the ship hired by the lord, and, jointly, of supplying someone to accompany the ship until it reached London. The virgaters of Wargrave (Berks.) and its sub-manors had to load grain in the bishop's boat moored by the bank.[104] The bishop of Ely had a remarkable network of watery *averagia* to link his manors to collecting points like Fen Ditton on the Cam, or to King's Lynn itself. The Linden End (Cambs.) villeins, for example, had carrying services by water to Reach, Lakenheath, and King's Lynn, and (except for the cottars) combined to take two boatloads of grain to King's Lynn, the boats and steersmen being provided by the bishop. The customary tenants at March (Cambs.) had to take a boatload of cheese each year from Marchford to King's Lynn. From Ely itself, villeins had carrying services by water to Peterborough, Yaxley, and Wisbech, as well as to King's Lynn and Fen Ditton. These were services to which the lord was entitled, and were not necessarily imposed. But the Wisbech Barton accounts confirm that the bishop's officials used the waterways, for example, in 1322, to carry 30 qr of oats from Wisbech to Fen Ditton at 2d. per quarter, and to carry 8 qr of wheat and 12 qr of oats on the same route at 3d. per quarter.[105] Carrying wheat by water from Burwell (Cambs.) to Peterborough in 1404–5 cost 2½d. or 3d. per quarter for a distance of thirty-two miles, much less than the 6d. per quarter Feering had paid a few years before to cart wheat nine miles to Colchester; and shipping oats eighteen miles from Wisbech cost Peterborough only 1½d. per quarter.[106] These rates were for straightforward commercial transactions, uncomplicated by customary or *famuli* labour, and perhaps imply some recognition of standard freight charges by volume, both for carts and for barges.

In the west country, the Severn carried wheat collected at Worcester down to Bristol, and moved the grain of Hardwicke (Glos.) from Deerhurst to Gloucester. The Avon carried Bredon's grain to Tewkesbury.[107] Even livestock sometimes took to the waters;

[103] *Pipe Roll of Winchester*, ed. Holt, pp. 57, 61, 80.   [104] BL, Egerton Ms. 2418.

[105] Cambridge Univ. Library, EDR G/3/27; D8/1/5.

[106] *Account Rolls of Peterborough*, ed. Greatrex, pp. 118–19; above, p. 351.

[107] *Rot. Parl.*, IV, pp. 332, 351, 379; WAM 8433, 8434; Worcs. RO, BA 2636/009: 1/158/92020.

Crowland abbey in 1364–5 paid 5s. to ship twenty-one pigs from Cambridge to Crowland thirty-five miles away, and it also used the streams and ditches to move its sheep around the "parts of Holland".[108] Some Cistercian monasteries probably used waterways to move their wool to delivery points – Fountains abbey, for example, was exempt from tolls on the rivers Ouse, Swale, and Ure – but land transport for their precious traffic was more usual. William de la Pole used a combination of methods to get his wool to Hull in 1337: his purchases in Nottinghamshire went by cart and pack-horse to Blyth, by cart from Blyth to Bawtry, and thence by boat. The fleeces he bought in Lindsey were carted to Lincoln, or taken there by pack-horse for putting into sacks; then they went by cart to Barton-on-Humber to be ferried across to Hull. His wool from north Yorkshire reached York by pack-horse or cart, and then went on to Hull by boat. Durham Cathedral priory also used a combination of methods to bring its purchases back from Boston fair: in 1303 they travelled by boat from Boston to Lincoln, by cart from Lincoln to Torksey, by boat on the Trent and Ouse between Torksey and Aldwark, and finally by cart again from Aldwark to Durham.[109]

The estuarine and coastal shipping routes, and those across the Channel and North Sea, and to Ireland, completed the network of transportation facilities, and demonstrate how customary, demesne, and contractual carriage could be integrated. When the Kelvedon demesne carts had taken 16 qr of wheat to Colchester in 1383–4, and those the manor hired a further 47 qr 2 b., the total went by water to Westminster for 26s. 4¼d. at 5d. per quarter; the same rate was paid for a similar consignment for next year. Feering paid 54s. 7d. in 1382–3 to send 131 qr to Westminster by water, again at 5d. per quarter, but paid an extra 16d. to have London Bridge raised on two occasions. By 1395–6, Feering had to pay 6d. per quarter to ship wheat from Colchester to London, and the rate was the same two years later;[110] 6d. per quarter, it will be remembered, was what Feering had to pay to cart the wheat to Colchester. The total transport cost of 1s. per quarter was a substantial levy when, as in 1395–6, wheat sold in London for less than 4s. per quarter; the implications of these rates will be considered in the next part of this chapter. But most information on shipping routes and coastal and overseas trade comes from customs records, export licences, or the complaints of merchants against pirates, rather

---

[108] Cambridge Univ. Library, QC6/3; F. M. Page, 'Bidentes Hoylandie', *Econ. Hist.*, I, 1929, p. 605.

[109] Donkin, *Cistercians*, p. 142; E. B. Fryde, *The Wool Accounts of William de la Pole*, pp. 16–17; *Extracts from the Account Rolls of the Abbey of Durham*, ed. J. T. Fowler, Surtees Soc., C, 1899, II, p. 504. [110] WAM 25845, 25847, 25712, 25732, 25735.

than from the manorial accounts. Here this chapter must rest on the work of others, to show how the grain which had been carried, carted, or ferried to King's Lynn or Yarmouth then passed to merchants like Thomas and William de Melcheburn or their contemporary John de Wesenham for shipment around the coast to London or Newcastle, or across the seas to Norway, Holland, Flanders, Zealand, or Gascony; how the licence given to Robert Sturmy of Bristol in 1457 to ship to Italy 400 qr of wheat in the *Katherine* and her two accompanying carvels took him to his death at the hands of the Genoese; how, for example, Edmund Grey in 1487 obtained a licence to export over a hundred oxen; and how a town like Exeter relied on the coastal trade for supplies of wheat from East Anglia and coal from Newcastle.[111]

In the fourteenth and fifteenth centuries, the patterns of maritime transport shifted, and the techniques improved. The ports of the south became more busy, those of the east less so. By 1400, cost-efficient large hulks had reduced freight charges for bulky goods like grain and salt, and the Genoese galleys, which had first come to Southampton in 1278, had so increased their capacity that transport added only 15 per cent to the cost of Flemish cloth in Italy. Then, during the fifteenth-century, the full-rigged ships of the north and carracks of the Mediterranean outclassed both hulk and galley.[112] But by that time little of the unprocessed produce of the English countryside found its way overseas.

A few questions remain, to cast a little doubt on the arrangements for carrying and marketing the produce of the countryside. How safe was travel by road, even after the 1285 Statute of Winchester had ordered underwood to be cut back two hundred feet from each side of the roadway where "a man may lurk to do hurt", and did the bishop of Winchester really need a private army to guard the pass at Alton to protect Londoners travelling to St Giles's fair?[113] The manorial accounts, at least, record that demesne grain, livestock, and carts were in greater danger from the king's agents than from other thieves; royal prises, and the blackmail threatening them, were much more common and costly than the occasional loss to robbers. In 1333–4 the Durham bursar paid a total of £7 15s. 7d. in gifts to the officials of the king and queen *pro bladis et fenis salvandis*. Yet Alton, like Royston and Grantham on the main road north, had an evil reputation.[114]

---

[111] Gras, *Corn Market*, pp. 172–3; E. M. Carus-Wilson, *The Overseas Trade of Bristol in the later Middle Ages*, Bristol Rec. Soc., VII, 1937, pp. 115–18; *The Grey of Ruthin Valor*, ed. Jack, p. 50; Kowaleski, 'Local markets and merchants', p. 293.

[112] Carus-Wilson and Coleman, *England's Export Trade*; R. W. Unger, *The Ship in the Medieval Economy*, London, 1980, pp. 166–71, 176, 216–27.

[113] *SR*, I, p. 97; *VCH Hants*., v, p. 39.

[114] *Account Rolls of Durham*, ed. Fowler, II, p. 524; *English Historical Documents, 1189–1327*, ed. H. Rothwell, London, 1975, p. 882.

Were tolls a serious restraint on trade? Manorial accounts almost never mention them, except occasionally when they were levied on sales in markets, and it is hard to believe that they were always concealed among the miscellaneous expenses of a journey. Occasionally small payments appear for river-crossings. The Cuxham reeve had to pay when crossing the Thames at Nuneham with stock taken to Abingdon or purchased there: 2d. *in passagio aque* for thirty wethers in 1317–18, for example. Adderbury (Oxon.) paid 6d. for ferrying 150 wethers across the Thames at Bablock Hythe in 1345–6, and Holywell paid 2d. there in 1360–1 for two oxen it had bought at Stanlake.[115] While these payments were trivial, over a year they might accumulate usefully; the earldom of Cornwall collected £7 8s. 8d. in 1296–7 at the two crossings of the Tamar by Saltash.[116] Northampton was so determined to collect its legal tolls on goods in transit that it stationed the collectors at distant places to prevent evasion – at Slipton on the Kettering road, Billing Bridge on the way to Wellingborough, and Syresham Cross fifteen miles away towards Brackley – and it abandoned these tolls only in 1836, as the London to Birmingham railway (which would undoubtedly have made collection difficult) was under construction.[117] Bailiffs and peasants certainly knew which routes were cheapest to travel; when a toll-free bridge over the Thames at Abingdon opened in 1416, it brought much of the trade to Gloucester and the west of England through the town, thus avoiding the tolls at Wallingford or the crossing at Nuneham.[118] Tolls, perhaps, redirected trade rather than impeded it.

Nor was the weather a serious problem for road travel. February and March were the busiest months of the year for the Southampton cart traffic, with over two hundred carts passing through the gates in those months of 1440, and only fifty or so in May and June.[119] The wide swathes cleared on either side of the road, in accordance with the Statute of Winchester, gave riders and carts the chance to avoid boggy patches in wet weather, and the large-diameter cart wheels saved *carectae* from sticking in holes which would trap modern vehicles. Many hundreds of bridges carried roads over the swollen rivers in the wetter months, and even the fellows of Merton College were willing to visit their northern properties at almost any time of year.[120]

River traffic, sometimes subject to tolls and possibly affected by too much water or too little, faced a special problem in weirs and fish traps.

---

[115] *Manorial Records of Cuxham*, ed. Harvey, p. 319; WPR 159355; MCR 4517.

[116] *Accounts of the Earldom of Cornwall*, ed. Midgley, p. 237.

[117] *VCH Northants.*, III, pp. 25–6.   [118] *VCH Berks.*, III, p. 535; IV, pp. 435–7.

[119] *Brokage Book, 1439–40*, ed. Bunyard, p. xxi.

[120] *The History of the University of Oxford*, I, ed. J. I. Catto, Oxford, 1984, pp. 336–41.

Magna Carta, perhaps in deference to Londoners, had ordered fish weirs to be removed from the Thames and Medway, and "throughout all England", but in 1347 the Commons were petitioning for the four great rivers of England – the Thames, Severn, Ouse, and Trent – to be cleared of such obstacles.[121] In the meantime, though, the earl of Devon had blocked the Exe by 1245 with the first of a series of salmon weirs, compelling trade between Exeter and the sea to pass through the earl's town of Topsham.[122] In 1315 the people of Gloucestershire and Herefordshire complained that "the river Wye is the King's highway where ships... were wont, from time without mind, to pass from Bristol up to Monmouth with all manner victuals and merchandise without disturbance, until Earl Gilbert of Gloucester raised a weir in his land of Trellech across the said river so that no ship, barge, or boat, can pass there..."[123] Whatever the difficulties these nuisances caused, the rivers of eastern England, and the Thames from Henley downstream, remained open to traffic in the later middle ages.

The coastal trade not merely survived but prospered in the same period. Of Exeter's import business in the late fourteenth and early fifteenth centuries, a healthy proportion came through the coastal trade with the ports of Devon, Cornwall, and Dorset, relatively unaffected by wars and pirates or the hazards of navigation, even though several of the south-coast ports were burnt by French and Breton raiders during the Hundred Years War.[124] On the broader waters, Bristol merchants sailed in those years with grain, wool, or hides to Gascony, Portugal, Italy, and Norway, with few violent interruptions. One may reasonably conclude that English communications at home and abroad were fully adequate for marketing the produce of the countryside.

C. MARKETING GRAIN

Growing grain was the principal purpose of medieval agriculture. In midland England, East Anglia, and the south, most villein labour services were for growing and harvesting the grain – wheat and rye for bread, barley and dredge for malt and ale, oats for the riding horses of the lord or for the working cart and plough horses of the manor – and for carrying it to the barn for threshing and then taking it to its final destination in monastery, castle, or market. The patterns of distribution established in the early years of high demesne farming proved very persistent, overlapping with survivals of even older practices.

[121] Magna Carta, c. 33; *Rot. Parl.*, II, p. 169.
[122] A. M. Jackson, 'Medieval Exeter, the Exe, and the earldom of Devon', *Devonshire Assoc.*, CIV, 1972, pp. 59–71.   [123] *Cal. Ancient Petitions Relating to Wales*, ed. Rees, p. 67.
[124] Kowaleski, 'Local markets and merchants', p. 291.

Of these, the most widespread was the food-farm, whereby the provisions, which had once been consumed on the spot by the visiting lord and his household, were now taken to one or other of his residences in quantities calculated to last the lord or the monastic community for a given period. Thus the thirteenth-century list of the "farms" the canons of St Paul's Cathedral expected from their manors shows that the Essex manors of Sandon, Beauchamp, and Chingford had to deliver food for ten, six, and two weeks respectively each year, not at one time but spaced at intervals so that the supplies could be taken to London by the customary tenants. The thirteen manors contributing to the food-farm sent each year about 1,575 qr of grain to St Paul's. On some Ramsey abbey manors the food-farms seem even to have increased about 1200, and they ended only after the Black Death.[125]

This practice, of supplying the lord with grain from his own land, continued when the manors were cultivated directly, with the arable "in hand". It persisted even in the fifteenth century on some manors leased out to *firmarii* for cash rents: Westminster abbey's treasurer, for example, bought large quantities from the lessees of those manors which had previously delivered grain and malt directly to the abbey bakehouse and brewery. Peterborough abbey also bought some of its grain from the farmers of its manors.[126] For the lord, clerical or secular, an assured supply of produce from his own estates protected the convent or household from the risk of shortages. By the end of the thirteenth century, the auditors usually gave the bailiff a cash or credit allowance at fair market value for the grain and other victuals sent *ad hospicium domini*, and sometimes also for those consumed by the *famuli* on the manor. These were not regular sales, of course, and the bailiff or reeve had no choice in the matter. Many accounts, though, do not make it clear when a sale was of this fictitious sort, and, as a result, one may easily exaggerate the amount of grain a manor sold to outsiders. Other consignments of grain despatched from a granary were inter-manorial exchanges, arranged either because of a shortfall in one manor's harvest or because, as Walter of Henley advised, "more increase shal you have of the seeds that grew upon an other mans lande then by that which groweth upon your owne lands".[127] Transfers between properties of the same lord — a practice very common on the manors of Bury St Edmunds abbey — were not sales, even if, for

[125] *The Domesday of St Paul's*, ed. W. H. Hale, Camden Soc., LXIX, 1858, pp. 154–64; Gras, *Corn Market*, p. 5; Raftis, *Estates of Ramsey Abbey*, pp. 91, 137.

[126] WAM 19896; *Account Rolls of Peterborough*, ed. Greatrex, p. 179, 193.

[127] *Walter of Henley*, ed. Oschinsky, p. 325.

accounting purposes, a monetary value was assigned to them. It was only the surplus, after these prior needs had been met, that went to market.

Other practices reduced still further the fraction of the harvest which the bailiff or reeve had to sell in some way or other. On the bishop of Winchester's manors near Taunton, the customary tenants had to purchase quantities of wheat and oats each year from the demesne granaries; often these were the only sales those manors made. The villeins had to pay high prices, usually 2d. a quarter more than the highest other prices in that area; the additional payment may be a surcharge levied in lieu of the carrying service which would have been demanded if the bishop had sent the grain to market. The Winchester pipe rolls have other evidence of compulsory purchase by the villagers at some earlier date, though now commuted: Downton collected 20s. *de hominibus ville pro relaxatione emptionis medie*, Witney 20s. *de hominibus de Uppelanda pro tasso refutato*, and Adderbury 20s. *pro tasso recusato*.[128] The Taunton manors, Witney, and Adderbury were all a long way from Winchester; perhaps these payments are reminders of an earlier time when the lord had guaranteed himself a market among his own tenants for grain which it would have cost too much to take to his palaces. The standard fee of 20s. suggests that it was a central official, such as the bishop's steward, who had authorized the remission. Again, this does not deserve to be called marketing.

Of those sales which were genuine market transactions, some are labelled *in foro*, *in patria*, or *per mutuum* (occasionally, *de mutuo*). The *per mutuum* sales appear mainly in the Winchester pipe rolls, and there is usually nothing to explain their meaning. Lord Beveridge suggested that the term "might indicate either a credit transaction or an exchange", but the bailiffs inserted nothing in the accounts – in the cash deliveries, the grain purchases, or the granary accounts – to show that it was either of these. In medieval commerce such sales were often devices to charge interest on loans but the prices received for *per mutuum* grain sales seem no higher than for other dealings. The manors do not seem to have incurred any expense in transporting *per mutuum* grain to a market. Sometimes the accounts note that the sales were to the lord's tenants. The Brightwell grange account for 1372–3 goes further, stating that, of the total of 76 qr 4½ b. of wheat sold, 39 qr were sold *custumariis tenentibus domini per mutuum*, at 8s. per quarter, the same price as that allowed for wheat "sold" to the lord's hospice.[129] As the quantities sold *per mutuum* varied from nothing at all to the whole of

---

[128] W. H. Beveridge, 'Wheat measures in the Winchester rolls', *Econ. Hist.*, 1930, pp. 41–3; *Medieval Customs of Taunton*, ed. Hunt, pp. xxxi, 32; *Pipe Roll of Winchester 1210–11*, ed. Holt, pp. 33, 64, 69.   [129] Beveridge, 'Wheat measures', p. 41; WPR 159383.

what the manor had beyond its internal needs, the bailiffs cannot have been compelling the tenants to buy. Most likely, these were voluntary transactions between the manor and the villagers. The term *per mutuum* does not appear in the Winchester records until the 1320s – and by then the Winchester estates were already suffering falling yields and were abandoning much of their arable – and it seems probable that such sales to willing purchasers among the tenantry went back at least to the times of heavier harvests in the previous century.[130] So, while one cannot be certain, the *per mutuum* sales are most likely to have been local.

Even so, by the later fourteenth century the sales identified as *per mutuum* could be very large. East Meon in 1360–1 sold in that way 150 qr 4 b. of the 187 qr 5 b. the bailiff counted as sold, with 24 qr 1 b. *in foro* and 13 qr allowed for the fictional sale to the lord's hospice.[131] In the same year Merdon (Hants.) sold 116 qr *per mutuum* out of a total of 118 qr, and Twyford (Hants.) all but 1 qr of the 55 qr 7 b. it sold. Marwell, Hambledon, East Meon church, and Crawley (Hants.) made all their sales *per mutuum*, though Crawley had at least one customer outside the village, as it sold 4 qr *per mutuum* to the prior of St Denis. Only Winchester's more northerly manors like Ivinghoe and Harwell, and Bentley (Hants.), recorded more sold *ad hospicium domini* than *per mutuum*. Table 4.4 shows how extensive were the sales *per mutuum* in 1372–3 and in 1387–8, on manors whose accounts state the nature of all their wheat sales (see p. 362). In the earlier year, with prices high after a poor crop, the bailiffs of the listed manors sold 399 qr 3½ b. *per mutuum* and only 141 qr 6 b. in the market. In the later year, with low prices following a good harvest, those manors sold 545 qr 5½ b. *per mutuum*, 400 qr 3½ b. *in foro*, and supplied only 107 qr 4 b. *ad hospicium domini*.[132] Perhaps the bailiffs gave the tenants the first chance to buy the demesne grain before sending the rest to market. When the compulsory sales to the Taunton customary tenants are added, it looks as though in the fourteenth century, and probably in the thirteenth as well, bailiffs and reeves were selling most of the demesne crop to very local purchasers. The figures cited above are for an England already ravaged by three outbreaks of plague, with peasant holdings increased in size and, at least in 1387–8, likely to be sharing somewhat in the good harvests achieved on the demesne.

The other terms, *in patria* and *in foro*, also imply local sales for the most part. The Battle abbey manors frequently used the former term for sales of grain and purchases of livestock, and there seems no reason to doubt that these transactions took place within a few miles of the

[130] Titow, *Winchester Yields, passim.*   [131] WPR 159371.
[132] WPR 159394.

Table 4.4. *Wheat sales by the bishopric of Winchester manors in the late fourteenth century*

	1372/3 (WPR 159383)				1387/8 (WPR 159394)			
	H.D.	V.C.	P.M.	foro	H.D.	V.C.	P.M.	foro
Holway	39 qr 2 b.	27 qr			39 qr 2 b.	24 qr 1 b.	20 qr	
Poundisford	24 qr 5½ b.							
Bishop's Hull	27 qr 4 b.	20 qr	5 qr 2 b.		27 qr 4 b.	30 qr 3 b.	11 qr 7½ b.	
Staplegrove					28 qr	13 qr	6 qr 4 b.	
Nailsborne	20 qr 6½ b.				20 qr 0½ b.			
Downton							21 qr	50 qr
East Knoyle							30 qr	27 qr 2½ b.
Bishopstone							29 qr	49 qr 2 b.
Bishop's Fonthill							34 qr 4½ b.	
Upton Knoyle							15 qr	13 qr 4 b.
Brightwell	12 qr 7 b.		39 qr	24 qr 5½ b.				
Harwell	12 qr 4 b.		73 qr 5½ b.	31 qr			40 qr 2 b[a]	
Waltham St Lawrence	13 qr		32 qr 1 b.					
Highclere							7 qr 7 b.	10 qr 3 b.
Burghclere					40 qr		36 qr	38 qr 3 b.
Ecchinswell					25 qr		30 qr	6 qr 6 b.
Overton	14 qr 1 b.		5 qr 5½ b.	5 qr			21 qr	
North Waltham	3 qr		16 qr 3 b.					
Farnham	18 qr 1 b.		34 qr 1 b.		2 qr			19 qr 5 b.
Twyford							40 qr	28 qr 2 b.
Bishopstoke	1 qr		12 qr					
Crawley	28 qr 7 b.		4 qr				25 qr	18 qr 1½ b.
Merdon	6 qr		73 qr 4 b.	19 qr 5 b.			51 qr 4½ b.	41 qr
Bishops Sutton							48 qr	10 qr 5 b.
Alresford							37 qr 7½ b.	
Wield			27 qr 1 b.				31 qr 1 b.	
Cheriton	2 qr		83 qr 5 b.	14 qr 4 b.				
Wolvesey					4 qr 4 b.			28 qr 4 b.

H.D.: fictional "sales" *ad hospicium domini*.
V.C.: compulsory sales to lord's customary tenants.
P.M.: sales *per mutuum*.
foro: sales in the market.
[a] This is described as "sold in the market and to the customary tenants". In the calculation on p. 361 this total is divided equally between *per mutuum* and *in foro* sales.
Note that figures are given for manors only when all the grain sold is described under one or more of the above headings.

manor. But how distant might an *in foro* sale be? Does such an entry in a Brightwell account mean the market in Wallingford, two miles away, or might it be in Newbury or Winchester (both of which were accessible through the *averagia* the manor could demand)? When Islip paid a penny a quarter to carry 128 qr of grain *ad forum ad vendendum* in 1367–8, was it to Oxford market, or to Islip's own market, chartered in 1245 and still important enough for Wargrave to buy a millstone there in 1387–8? A West Wycombe entry for 1370–1 adds to the uncertainty, for 79 qr 5 b. of malt described as sold *in foro* are also described as sold *apud London*.[133] Only in a few cases are there lists of expenses or details in the works accounts which allow one to investigate with some accuracy the patterns of distribution. For nearly forty years the bailiffs of Longbridge Deverill and Monkton Deverill, two Wiltshire manors of Glastonbury abbey, recorded fairly consistently the markets to which they sent the grain, because the customary tenants received a small payment, scaled according to distance, for taking it there. These manors were remote enough from Glastonbury not to be a regular part of the abbey's own supply system, far enough from Salisbury not to be dominated by its market, and on no navigable river whose flow might have drawn the produce to a market downstream. On the other hand, the area was well served by ancient roads and tracks. Most frequently the grain went to Frome, by then a prospering cloth town some seven miles away over the Somerset border, with markets twice a week, or to Trudoxhill, a Somerset hamlet about eight miles away and, apparently, without any charter for a market. Next in frequency came Nunney, nine miles away, and Hindon, five miles distant, where the bishop of Winchester had created a borough by his manor at East Knoyle. There were a number of long hauls to Glastonbury, and a few journeys to Mere, Maiden Bradley, Salisbury, Shaftesbury, and Sherborne. The average journey was about nine miles. But only one-third of the grain those manors sold was carried away to market, and it was only in those years when the price of wheat rose above 6s. per quarter that most of the grain transported went to the more distant markets, those beyond seven leagues. The destinations range from county towns to the smallest of settlements, but the accounts call them all markets. Figure 4.2 illustrates their distribution. Some other evidence from the same area shows how varied the local pattern might be: a list of grain stocks in the hundred of Downton in 1357 records only five sellers in East Knoyle and Hindon, with 135 qr between them, whereas in Bishop's Fonthill thirteen men held 79 qr for sale, six of them with no more than four bushels each.[134]

One searches in vain for any comparable information in the accounts of Winchester or Battle abbey or Canterbury Cathedral priory. But sometimes the bailiffs on the Westminster abbey and Merton College estates become loquacious, and name the buyers or say where they lived. In 1381–2 the Birdbrook bailiff (and the events earlier in 1381 in Essex may have given a special reason for recording the details) listed among the buyers people from Halstead, Stambourne, Foxearth, Clare, Horseheath, Bumpstead, and Bardfield, and the next year there were

---

[133] WAM 14804; WPR 159380.
[134] *Select Cases concerning the Law Merchant*, III, ed. Hall, p. 182.

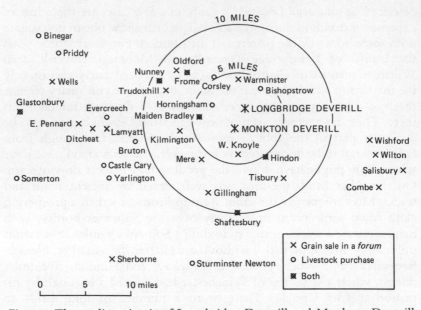

Fig. 4.2 The trading circuit of Longbridge Deverill and Monkton Deverill, Wilts.

men from Haverhill and Belchamp as well. These lay an average of five miles from Birdbrook, as Figure 4.3 shows. But this is a misleading calculation, because the bailiff made most sales to people who did not need to be identified by their places of origin, probably because they were Birdbrook villagers well known to the bailiff. Here, on the densely populated borders of Essex and Suffolk, grain need not travel as far as in the empty corner of Salisbury Plain served by Longbridge Deverill and Monkton Deverill. On the other hand, even in East Anglia, a major market centre such as Bury St Edmunds might draw trade from further afield: the Earl Marshal's manor of Kennet (Cambs.) in the early 1270s sent both wheat and barley (the latter in large quantities) the ten miles to Bury, as well as selling small amounts to local villagers. In those years Kennet also bought oats and seed in Bury.[135]

A final example, from a manor on the edge of a sizeable market, shows another pattern of sales. As in most years, probably all Holywell's grain sales in 1365–6 were made to the people of Oxford or to those of the manor itself. The contrast here is between those who bought a lot, and those who bought very little. In seven separate

[135] WAM 25477, 25478; PRO SC 6/768/5, 6.

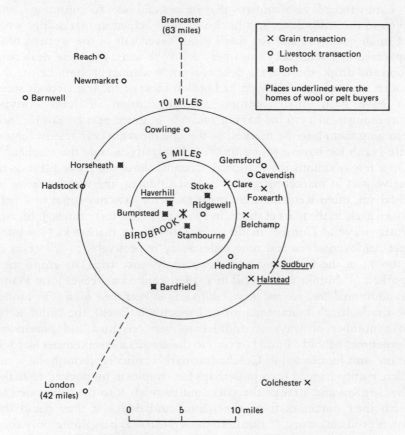

Fig. 4.3 The trading circuit of Birdbrook, Essex

transactions, Margery Crook paid a total of £21 1s. 1d. for 15 qr 4 b. of wheat, 74 qr of barley, 20 qr of dredge, and a quantity of straw. Agnes Clerk, in five deals, spent £4 18s. 3d. on 6 qr of wheat, 12 qr of barley, and 9 qr 6 b. of dredge. John Desier bought 10 qr of barley and 2 qr of tithe wheat. The other men bought only once from the manor, and in small quantities, such as the 1 qr of barley bought by Leonard the Bedell, or the single bushels of tithe wheat bought by William the Thresher and his companion Stephen. These details suggest that the Holywell bailiff was selling partly to dealers who would supply Oxford's bakers and cook-shops, and partly to small customers who could carry their purchases home, if need be in bags thrown over their shoulders.[136]

[136] MCR 4520.

Court records also confirm that most grain sales to consumers, and even to the stallholders and hucksters who helped in marketing, were of small quantities and for small sums. Over half of the women who appeared in Exeter debt cases between 1378 and 1388 were dealers in food and drink; the average debt of a single woman brought before the courts was only 4s. 6d. Even in London most of the transactions seem to have been small: witness the prosecution of John Amyas, cornmonger, in 1376 for having sold 6 b. of green peas by sample, not bringing them into the market, or the case the same year against Simon atte Nassh for having sold 2 qr of malt secretly outside the market.[137] On a few occasions the manorial accounts show the reeve playing an active part in marketing grain. Robert Oldman, the veteran reeve of Cuxham, often went the nine miles to Henley twenty times in a year to sell grain in the market there; in 1301–2 he went forty times. John atte Putte, reeve of Combe, made seventeen trips to market in Newbury and Andover, seven and nine miles away respectively, to sell grain in 1306–7; in the following year he made twenty trips, to unspecified markets.[138] Monkton Deverill in 1338–9 granted its reeve, John Petur, an additional 20s. *pro sua magna diligencia in venditione bladi.* On Lionel de Bradenham's solitary manor of Langenhoe (Essex), the bailiff acted in a number of ways as middleman between lord and purchaser. Sometimes he sold a bushel or two to the *famuli,* and sometimes he took grain with him to sell in Colchester market; usually, though, he went there empty-handed (except perhaps for samples in his pocket) to make the bargains and arrange the sales, and then left it to the townsmen to fetch their purchases from the manor and dodge if they could the town's toll collectors.[139] But here the *serviens* was bargaining only four miles from his manor, and his tactics would have been impossible in a town, say, twenty miles away, where he would not be known, and to which the townsfolk could not easily carry back from the manor what they had bought. These examples are so rare, though, that one may question how far lords left it to their reeves and bailiffs to arrange the marketing of the main cash crop.

Certainly many of the sales were negotiated by the estates' more senior officials. The Glastonbury abbey chamberlain, who usually arranged the wool sales, sometimes sold grain as well: a total of 32 qr of wheat and 20 qr of barley in 1332–3, for example, at Longbridge Deverill, and 20 qr of wheat at Monkton Deverill the same year; some

---

[137] Kowaleski, 'Local markets and merchants', pp. 200, 202; *Cal. Plea and Memo. Rolls 1364–1381,* ed. Thomas, pp. 227, 228.

[138] MCR 5819; *Documents of the English Lands of Bec,* ed. Chibnall, pp. 149, 162.

[139] GAD 9689; R. H. Britnell, 'Production for the market', p. 382.

of the other sales there were described as *per literas domini*.[140] Those manors which were grouped in regional bailiwicks on the larger estates (such as those of Westminster abbey and the bishop of Winchester) often made their grain sales on the authority of the area bailiff, not that of the manorial reeve: thus the Feering account for 1368–9 records the sale of 36 qr of wheat for £12 *per Warantum balliui*, and no more because the wheat was "vetchy". Islip in 1347–8 sold some of its wheat at a modest price because it was poor and unsuitable for seed *per literam domini et per visum domini Ade Capellani*, the bailiff. At Pershore (Worcs.), another Westminster manor, the bailiff Richard Lacock arranged all the grain sales in 1343–4, as well as most of the large transactions except the purchase of cattle, which was left to Thomas Sexy who came to the manor on several occasions to supervise the livestock.[141] On the Winchester manors, the central management of marketing grain is evident from the early thirteenth century, first in the practice of sending supplies from manors near the Thames down-river to the bishop's property at Southwark, where much of it was sold, and then in the bargains made whereby all the crop of a manor was sold *in grosso* to a single unnamed purchaser: as early as 1220–1 Brightwell, Harwell, and Wargrave sold all their grain in gross, not even keeping back the seed-corn for next year. Transactions of this magnitude – Wargrave alone received £84 13s. 4d. for its harvest that year – are not likely to have been arranged by anyone of less authority than the bishop's steward.[142]

At this stage it is necessary to consider how London was supplied with grain. We have seen how the largest ecclesiastical corporations obtained their needs – St Paul's from the food-farms carried from its manors in the surrounding counties, Westminster abbey from the demesne crops of its Essex and Hertfordshire lands, brought by the manor carts or, occasionally, shipped around the coast from Colchester – and how (like other bishops) the bishop of Winchester sent grain to his London residence; and how at least one great church estate in East Anglia had a network of carrying services it could use to move grain by land and water to Fen Ditton, Wisbech, and King's Lynn for shipment to London. But it is easy to exaggerate London's importance as a centre of consumption, particularly prior to the Black Death, and it may be that, in trying to show how London was fed, N. S. B. Gras presented a slightly distorted picture of the medieval grain trade. In *The Evolution of the English Corn Market*, the first study to make much use of the

---

[140] GAD 8083, 9730. [141] WAM 25691, 14795, 22121.
[142] WPR 159277.

Winchester pipe rolls, Gras asserted that the bishop's Thames valley manors regularly sent wheat to Southwark for sale to the Londoners. For perhaps a decade, this indeed happened: Southwark in 1210–11 received over £167 by selling 785 qr of wheat and 166 qr of other grains sent to it from Harwell, Brightwell, Wargrave, and West Wycombe.[143] The circumstances, though, were exceptional. Southwark then was still the administrative centre of the bishop's estates and, as a confidant of King John, Bishop Peter des Roches was deeply involved in the business of his secular master. Perhaps the steward was keeping Southwark well-provisioned in those years in case the bishop's large household needed bread or fodder, and the Southwark *serviens* was merely selling off the surplus before it deteriorated. By 1220, if not before, the practice had ceased entirely. While many of the subsequent pipe rolls have no account for Southwark at all, none of those which survive mentions any such sales again. To judge from the prices received by Southwark for the sales in the 1210s, there was no economic reason for the steward to have grain sent from the middle Thames valley to be marketed there: the prices obtained for their wheat at Southwark seem, if anything, rather lower than the supplying manors received from the grain they sold locally. Table 4.5 shows that the prices at which wheat was sold in the Thames valley were, at least until the Black Death, usually as high as those paid to manors at London's gates.

Gras's statistics of the production and sale of grain on the Winchester manors in 1208–9, 1299–1300, and 1396–7 are also not quite what they seem, for he included among the sales the grain transferred *ad hospicium domini*, certainly in 1396–7 and probably in 1299–1300 as well.[144] As he did not see the special nature of the *per mutuum* sales, which this chapter argues were mainly local, he again probably exaggerated the degree to which the bishop's manors were supplying distant markets. N. S. B. Gras, writing more than a decade before Lord Beveridge and his colleagues began examining the *minutiae* of the Winchester account, and before Beveridge drew attention to the use of measures of varying capacity in different areas, can hardly be blamed for these omissions, but they are reasons for treating cautiously his scheme for a general pattern of marketing based on regional price differences. Similarly, the very early commutation of carrying services to London – Ivinghoe's, for example, were usually "sold" back to the tenants from the 1220s – weakens Gras's attempt to cite them to show a regular flow of grain to the capital.[145] In the later fourteenth century, when works accounts

---

[143] Gras, *Corn Market*, p. 21: *Pipe Roll of Winchester*, ed. Holt, 153, 156.
[144] Gras, *Corn Market*, pp. 261–70.   [145] Gras, *Corn Market*, pp. 20–1.

Table 4.5 *Wheat sale prices, per quarter, on some upper Thames and London area manors*

	Brightwell	Harwell	Wargrave	W. Wycombe	Cuxham	Southwark	Knights-bridge	Eybury
1210–11		3s. 10d.		4s. 2d.		3s. 10$\frac{1}{2}$d.		
1211–12	2s. 11$\frac{1}{2}$d.	2s. 8d.	2s. 7d.	2s. 7d.		2s. 7d.		
1213–14	2s. 8d.	2s. 0$\frac{1}{2}$d.	2s. 4d.	2s. 9d.		2s. 6d.		
1295–6	8s. 0d.	8s. 0d.	11s. 1$\frac{1}{4}$d.	7s. 11$\frac{1}{4}$d.			7s. 10d.	7s. 0$\frac{1}{2}$d.
1296–7	5s. 3$\frac{1}{2}$d.	5s. 4d.	7s. 0d.	4s. 8d.	5s. 2$\frac{1}{4}$d.		5s. 4d.	4s. 1$\frac{3}{4}$d.
1300–1	5s. 11$\frac{3}{4}$d.	5s. 10$\frac{3}{4}$d.	6s. 0d.	5s. 0d.	5s. 1$\frac{1}{4}$d.		5s. 0d.	5s. 5$\frac{1}{2}$d.
1302–3	4s. 11$\frac{3}{4}$d.	5s. 2d.	5s. 0d.	5s. 0d.	4s. 10$\frac{1}{2}$d.		5s. 10$\frac{1}{2}$d.	
1345–6	4s. 0d.	4s. 4$\frac{1}{2}$d.	4s. 0$\frac{1}{4}$d.	4s. 0d.				4s. 4d.
1346–7	9s. 1$\frac{1}{4}$d.	9s. 6$\frac{1}{2}$d.	8s. 4d.	6s. 0d.	6s. 2$\frac{1}{2}$d.			7s. 4d.
1354–5	6s. 2d.		5s. 1d.	6s. 8d.	6s. 2$\frac{1}{2}$d.		7s. 0d.	
1355–6	7s. 0d.	6s. 7$\frac{1}{2}$d.	6s. 0$\frac{1}{2}$d.	6s. 9$\frac{3}{4}$d.			8s. 0d.	
1356–7	6s. 7$\frac{1}{4}$d.	6s. 5d.	6s. 1$\frac{3}{4}$d.	6s. 0$\frac{1}{4}$d.	5s. 4$\frac{3}{4}$d.		8s. 0d.	8s. 0d.
1386–7	4s. 0d.	4s. 0d.	5s. 4d.	3s. 4d.				4s. 11d.
1388–9	3s. 10$\frac{1}{4}$d.	3s. 6$\frac{3}{4}$d.	3s. 7$\frac{1}{4}$d.	2s. 10$\frac{1}{4}$d.				3s. 10$\frac{1}{2}$d.
1390–1	9s. 6d.	10s. 3d.	9s. 9$\frac{1}{2}$d.	8s. 6d.				9s. 8$\frac{1}{2}$d.

in the pipe rolls state how the *averagia* were used (if they were not commuted), most of the carrying services went in taking grain or other victuals *ad hospicium domini* – to Southwark, Esher, Highclere, Farnham, or Wolvesey, wherever the bishop kept a residence.

If the bishop's steward did not send grain to market in London, who did? It was probably the cornmonger. As early as 1148 there was one living outside Winchester's west gate; another appears in the Exchequer pipe roll for 1204; another as a tenant at Farnham (Surrey) in 1210–11; another is mentioned in 1222 as the former tenant of a half-virgate at Sandon (ironically, the St Paul's manor with the heaviest food-farm.)[146] These, doubtless, were small-scale dealers, perhaps working mainly as retailers. But one may infer the presence of others, traders on a much larger scale, wealthy enough to buy *in grosso* the crop of a manor or the great tithes of a church. Only wealthy purchasers, or perhaps people to whom the bishop owed a lot of money, could have bought up all the harvests of Winchester's Thames valley manors in 1220–1. A likely customer would be a merchant with ships which had brought cargoes up river to Henley or perhaps Wallingford, searching for freight for the return journey. One group of merchants looks the most probable: the vintners of London. They had the boats, the capital, the trading connections with the castles and estates of the Thames valley on the one hand, and on the other hand potential customers in London, north-east England, and even Gascony and Germany. For most of the thirteenth century this is speculation, as the accounts do not name the buyers. By the end of that century, though, material from other sources leaves no doubt that merchants working as vintners, fishmongers, and cornmongers or "bladers" had control of an extensive trade in grain, stretching from entrepôts like Henley and King's Lynn and Yarmouth to the quays of London, the corn dealerships, the mills, and even the bakeries and breweries of the city. It was a remarkable early example of the horizontal and vertical integration of an industry. The most prominent of the grain dealers, such as Roger le Palmer (who owned lands in Berkshire, granaries in Henley, and bakehouses in London) and Hamo Chigwell (who was a wine importer, fishmonger, and alderman, as well as grain merchant) were men of great wealth and political power. Palmer, for example, contrived to have the haulage dues abolished at Queenhithe market, undertook much of the victualling of Edward II's Scots campaigns, and shared in the custody of the Templars' lands after the Knights were suppressed. Together, the fishmongers and bladers apparently owned about two-thirds of the ships mentioned in the London court records between 1300 and

---

[146] *Winchester in the Early Middle Ages*, ed. M. Biddle, Oxford, 1976, p. 85; *Pipe Roll of Winchester*, ed. Holt, p. 39; *Domesday of St Paul's*, ed. Hale, p. 15.

1340.[147] Many of the London bladers also had agents and granaries at King's Lynn, trading in the grain sent downstream from Fen Ditton and Peterborough, Crowland, and Huntingdon. Other merchants themselves stayed in King's Lynn, making it the centre of their trading empires, as John de Wesenham and the de Melcheburne brothers did in the second quarter of the fourteenth century.[148]

The wholesale blader, then, was active in the thirteenth century, negotiating with the lord or his steward to buy in gross the harvest of a demesne, and also buying up the grain brought to market in certain known centres. The blader's activities demanded collection points with storage facilities; transport by road or river to the delivery point; granaries or warehouses there to store it for future distribution; and either direct access to a market on advantageous terms (that is, as a burgess entitled to trade freely), or at least a network of local corn dealers or stallholders who would deliver the grain to the market place. In the Thames valley, Henley had developed early as the main distribution centre for cargoes brought upstream and the main collecting centre for grain to be sent to London and perhaps beyond. In 1279 the tenants of Cuxham swore that they were not obliged to carry the lord's grain except to Henley, Wallingford, and the adjacent manor of Ibstone, *nec ulterius nec alibi*. This suggests that the duty was of ancient origin, now embedded in manorial custom (for carriage to Oxford would normally have been easier than hauling grain over the Chiltern escarpment), and that the Henley market was by then long established. Ibstone (Bucks.) also sent grain there, hiring granaries in 1293–4 and 1294–5 to store it. One year Holywell spent 5s. 11½d. on carrying grain from Oxford to Henley.[149] Brightwell and Harwell regularly rented granaries there after the Black Death, to store grain awaiting shipment *ad hospicium domini* at Southwark or at Esher (which William of Wykeham seems to have preferred after the rebels of 1381 had killed his archbishop only a river's width away from Southwark). Marlow was another centre for grain shipments, the river port normally used by West Wycombe, for example. One Marlow cornmonger owned in London various properties (which Gras believed probably included granaries) and leased them for thirty years to another cornmonger.[150] Henley's merchant gild, in existence by 1269, had forty-six members by 1296, each of whom paid the earldom of Cornwall five pence a year, yielding in all more than the market tolls did. By the later fifteenth century the borough had to regulate the fees charged by the grain porters – five pence for measuring and carrying

---

[147] Williams, *Medieval London*, pp. 161–4.   [148] Gras, *Corn Market*, pp. 172–3.

[149] *Records of Cuxham*, ed. Harvey, p. 607; MCR 5062, 5063, 4474.

[150] Gras, *Corn Market*, p. 165.

from granary to wharf twenty quarters of wheat, malt, peas, mixtil, or oats, and six pence for twenty quarters of other grains (presumably barley, unpleasant to handle). In the sixteenth century Henley was still the most important single source of London's grain.[151]

So the route by which London obtained much of its grain from the middle Thames valley began early and lasted late. One may imagine Robert Oldman, the reeve of Cuxham, measuring the grain into sacks to be carried by the horses or carts of the customary tenants; the carts climbing the Chilterns by what the accounts call Broadhill, and dropping to the valley below as they moved to the Henley market place, where the reeve made his bargains with the bladers' agents. Then the wheat would be emptied into the merchants' granaries (for the manor needed to take back for re-use sacks which had cost five or six pence each); when enough for a shipment had been assembled, it would be measured under supervision, put into the bladers' own sacks, and carried by the porters to the barges for transport down-river. At London, the sacks would be unloaded, carried to the bladers' granaries or storehouses, and kept for release when the price was right. Some of the grain was probably sold directly to consumers, particularly those buying in bulk; most of the remainder went to retailers in the markets at Billingsgate, Queenhithe, Newgate, and Gracechurch. Sometimes the London bladers could profit from a sudden demand brought on by war: in 1322–3, when Edward II spent £2,700 on grain for his war against the Scots, nine Londoners provided most of it; two of them, Robert de Ely and Walter Neel, together supplied the crown with grain worth over £1,100. London merchants were also well placed to export grain if they could obtain the necessary licences: in six months in 1450, London exported nearly 1,800 qr, though its export trade in the fifteenth century was generally overshadowed by the grain exports from King's Lynn, Yarmouth, and Bridgwater.[152]

While the trade down the Thames to London continued, the great cornmongers apparently lost much of their control over it after the Black Death. It is not clear why. Some of the bladers may have suffered through their involvement with wool and cloth marketing in the difficult years of the Hundred Years War; perhaps it became harder for them to buy in bulk as estates leased out their demesnes; perhaps the *firmarii* who rented the manors were more likely to take the grain themselves to the major markets. But the circumstances of the later fourteenth century, with London almost certainly sheltering a larger proportion of England's population than in the preceding centuries,

[151] *Accounts of the Earldom of Cornwall*, ed. Midgley, I, p. 91; *Henley Borough Records, 1395–1543*, ed. P. M. Briers, Oxon. Rec. Soc., XLI, 1960, pp. 74–5; Gras, *Corn Market*, pp. 300–2.

[152] Gras, *Corn Market*, pp. 283–4, 288–91, 294–5.

Table 4.6. *Prices of wheat sold by manors in the Lower Thames area and in some other areas which supplied London*

	1326/7–1347/8		1355/6–1379/80	
	Mean price per qr (shillings)	% of Lower Thames price	Mean price per qr (shillings)	% of Lower Thames price
Lower Thames	5.02	—	8.30	—
Upper Thames	4.99	99	7.09	85
Chilterns	4.72	94	6.78	82
Kent	5.26	105	7.16	86
Essex	4.97	99	6.46	78
Norfolk and Suffolk	4.99	99	6.65	80

Percentage price increase by area between 1326/7–1347/8 and 1355/6–1379/80

Lower Thames	+65	Kent	+36
Upper Thames	+42	Essex	+30
Chilterns	+44	Norfolk and Suffolk	+33

should have made it easier for the bladers to establish a monopoly. The city did not regulate them strictly, and, as we have seen, some of them had built up processing empires stretching from the manorial granges to the bakers' shops, with opportunities for multiplying profits at every stage. As Table 4.6 shows, the prices at which manors in the London and lower Thames area sold wheat in the third quarter of the fourteenth century were much higher than in the second quarter, whereas prices in those areas which supplied London with grain rose less – by about one-third, rather than by two-thirds. Yet, by some process, the great bladers like Palmer and Chigwell and de Ely lost control of London's markets. Their places seem to have been taken by humbler wholesalers, ancestors of the broggers or badgers so much blamed for rising prices in Tudor England. How London got its grain supply in the fifteenth century remains obscure. Alderman Simon Eyre's construction of a public granary at Leadenhall, enlarged in 1445 when the parish of St Dunstan's-in-the-East made over a tenement in Gracechurch Street, suggests that the supply merchanism may have been at times inadequate.[153]

Though the evidence is even more slender, several of the midland towns appear to have had grain wholesalers by the end of the thirteenth

[153] *Cal. London Letter-Book K*, ed. Sharpe, pp. li, lii.

century. The victualling arrangements for Edward I's Welsh campaigns name some of them. In 1282, as one would expect, the king ordered the sheriffs of coastal counties like Essex, Kent, and Hampshire to help to collect supplies of wheat and oats for the offensive, but he also issued safe-conducts to several merchants to take grain to the army in Wales. These included William Wilcher of Lichfield, Humphrey le Sauser of Burton-on-Trent, John de la Corner of Derby, John Scurry of Grimsby, Robert le Barbour of Stafford, and Gilbert le Mareschal and Henry Bras, both of Preston, as well as two Irish merchants.[154] Edward also gave safe-conducts to merchants from Shrewsbury, Leicester, Southampton, Bristol, and the Channel Islands to take unspecified victuals to Wales.

In the north, several wool merchants became grain wholesalers, almost by accident. The monks of Durham Cathedral priory, having fallen in debt to the Beverley merchant Thomas of Holme by failing to deliver the wool for which he had paid them in 1328, had to make over to him all the tithes of Eastrington. John of Kelloe, merchant of Darlington, farmed the tithes of Sheraton, Hutton Henry, Ludworth, and Newton Bewley for nearly twenty years after the convent had first fallen into debt to him. Robert de Castro of Newcastle supplied the Durham monks with wine in 1334–5 and malt the next year, and by 1340–1 he was farming the great tithes of seven of the priory's manors.[155] Before long, whether because such merchants slipped from prominence in the north as well as in the south, or because the local markets proved sufficient, or because his credit was exhausted, the Durham bursar was buying most of the monks' needs on the cash market from the local villagers, rather than from powerful wholesalers.[156] This entailed no hardship: the purchases made by the cellaress of Wilton abbey in the local market in 1299 show the wide choice available in a decaying borough, and Shrewsbury's monks in a later century also seem to have relied mainly on local supplies.[157] In expanding Coventry, however, the wholesale brogger was more necessary, and a proclamation by Mayor John Leeder in 1421 warned "badgers" not to hide corn in their houses or elsewhere but to take it to the "Chepyng" or market and sell it there. Some of those who supplied Peterborough abbey in the fifteenth century are also likely to have been wholesalers: Thomas Peer, who supplied over 160 qr of wheat in 1404–5, Nicholas Othehill, who sold the abbey 300 qr in

[154] Cal. Chancery Rolls 1277–1326, pp. 217, 222, 228, 230, 236, 239, 246.

[155] C. M. Fraser, 'The pattern of trade in the north-east of England, 1265–1350', North. Hist., IV, 1969, pp. 50–1, 53.　　　　[156] R. B. Dobson, Durham Priory, p. 263.

[157] 'Fragment of an account of the cellaress of Wilton Abbey, 1299', ed. E. Crittall, in Collectanea, Wilts. Arch. and N.H. Soc., XII, 1956, pp. 142–56; VCH Salop, II, pp. 32–3.

1433–4, and perhaps William Baker, through whom the abbot's receiver bought 300 qr in 1504–5. On the other hand, the abbey also bought substantial quantities of wheat and malt in the market, or from its *firmarii*, and sometimes small quantities from people with only four or five quarters (perhaps a cart-load) to sell.[158] In late medieval Winchester, those with grain to sell stored it in houses in the city and employed agents to sell it for them. Bakers often acted as the agents. As in the fourteenth century bakers had been among the tenants of the city's larger water-mills; this suggests that, in Winchester as in London, the final stages of distributing grain to the consumer were to some degree integrated. By 1430, though, there were only two or three bakers remaining, distributing their bread through a network of women selling loaves from baskets in Winchester's streets.[159]

One would like to know how tithe farmers disposed of the grain they had acquired, and what their relationship was to the wholesalers or broggers. Oakham (Rutland), one of Westminster abbey's most distant manors, had sent its tithe grain to Stamford by the cart-load before the Black Death – twenty-five loads in 1337–8 – but thereafter farmed the tithes. One of the tithe farmers in 1400–1 was Roger Flore, the steward, still collecting a modest fee of 13s. 4d. for his office and getting cloth worth 14s. 2½d. for his robe, but able to pay the abbey £33 for the tithes of Oakham and Egleton, and the rectory demesne, and to join with a partner in farming the Langham tithes as well for an extra £28; did Stamford remain an adequate outlet, or did Flore perhaps take the grain to the market in Leicester, only a few miles further? Possibly he did neither, preferring to entice buyers to come to his barns by offering discounts. The common practice of giving the grain buyer an extra fraction *in avantagio mercatoris*, usually one free quarter with every twenty paid for, had probably started when manors were bargaining with major grain merchants in the thirteenth century, for bulk purchases saved manors the supervisory and transport costs of marketing in small quantities; then it became more widespread, as reeves allowed the extra grain even to small purchasers if they would fetch it themselves.[160] The higher transport costs by 1400, if no *averagia* were available, made this an attractive alternative.

After the Black Death, transport costs to London were a lot higher, and may have narrowed the area which supplied the capital. This may have been one of the reasons why the city took measures it had avoided

[158] *The Coventry Leet Book*, ed. M. D. Harris, EETS, CXXXIV, London, 1907, I, p. 26; *Account Rolls of Peterborough*, ed. Greatrex, pp. 118–19, 165, 179.

[159] Keene, *Medieval Winchester*, I, pp. 252, 254–5.

[160] WAM 20253, 20315; R. H. Britnell, '*Avantagium Mercatoris*: a custom in medieval English trade', *Nottingham Medieval Studies*, XXIV, 1980, pp. 37–50.

in earlier times of high prices – rye imports from the Baltic and a public granary to store against dearth. If carters and bargemen charged whatever the market would bear, the result would enhance prices in London, or depress them in the supplying districts. As prices were firmer in those places which had access to a large market than in those which were more remote, initially at least it was the consumer who bore the burden. In the 1350s and 1360s, in the years when the two Westminster abbey manors both sold wheat, Feering in south Essex obtained 1s. 2d. per quarter more on average than Birdbrook in north Essex did, too far removed to be able to supply London economically.[161] Not that carriage from Feering was cheap: by the 1390s, it was noted earlier, the cost of sending grain by contract haulage to the abbey from Westminster's south Essex manors totalled 12d. a quarter: 6d. for cart transport to Colchester, and 6d. more for shipment to London.[162] Ivinghoe, which sent large quantities of malt to the bishop's residence at Southwark, revived the *averagia* it had usually commuted since the early thirteenth century, and supplemented them with hired transport; for the latter, it too had to pay 12d. a quarter in the 1390s, though the Winchester pipe rolls do not make it clear whether this was for carriage by road or by river.[163] Henbury and Stoke, two of the bishop of Worcester's manors which produced for the large Bristol market, commanded 21 per cent more for their wheat in the later fourteenth century than the bishop's more rural manors like Bredon and Bibury; again, the higher cost of transport may have put a premium on the price of grain in places from which it could readily be taken to market.[164]

For the grain sent to market, a few more formalities remained, some of which cut a little into the dealer's profits. The officials of the borough or seigneurial market decreed the time and place of sale, checked the quantities against their standard measures (defective though those might be, even in London), and took a scoopful of grain out of each sack as market toll. In some towns the freemen and their families claimed the right to buy first; commonly, the loathed but indispensable retailers who bought to sell again would be forbidden to do so until more honest townsmen had secured their needs. Then the assize of bread determined the weight of the standard loaf, according to the current market price of grain, in the process summarized admirably by

[161] My calculations from WAM 25447–25465 and 25668–25693.

[162] Above, p. 354. This carriage made little economic sense, for the price at which Eybury (adjacent to Westminster) sold wheat in 1395–6 was about 2s. per qr *less* than the 6s. per qr which Feering received from its customers in Essex.

[163] WPR 159398, 159399, 159403A, 159403B, 159406.

[164] Dyer, *Lords and Peasants*, p. 132.

Lord Beveridge.[165] The assize of ale required that anyone intending to sell part of a brew must display a post by the house door, wait until the officials had tested the ale for quality, and then sell it outside the house (on a level doorstep) in approved measures of one gallon or half a gallon, at the approved prices.[166] The earliest manorial court records rarely mention such matters: the 1210–11 Winchester pipe roll cites, among the records of the courts on nearly forty manors, two Fareham (Hants.) men fined *pro falso pane*, two at Bishop's Waltham *pro mala cervisia* and one *pro parva cervisia*, one at Winchester *pro cervisia facta contra assisam*, and possibly one at Harwell described simply as *pro cervisia*.[167] By the end of the thirteenth century, though, these offences were more frequent than any others. Norwich fined 290 brewers in 1288–9, and 250 in 1312–13. With a population of about three thousand, Exeter between 1378 and 1388 imposed fines for 4,579 brewing offences – for selling ale at 2d. per gallon rather than the prescribed 1½d., or the use of unapproved measures, or other infractions.[168] That the sins might be legion, moralists like the author of *Piers Plowman* had no doubt; witness Rose the Regrater, who had inferior ale "For laboreres and for louh folke", but sold her best in the parlour and snug by unlicensed measures at "A galon for a grote".[169] But in the end, with the ritual harassments of retailers, brewers, and bakers completed, the villagers and townsmen alike were left to enjoy what remained of the medieval grain harvests.

D. MARKETING LIVESTOCK

On balance, manors sold grain but bought livestock. Bailiffs and reeves, and those over them, were therefore purchasers more often than vendors of livestock at markets, and especially at fairs. Most manors in the arable parts of England lacked enough pasture to raise their own replacement plough beasts, and the earliest accounts show them buying oxen and plough horses from outside. In 1210–11 twenty-six out of the thirty-four Winchester manors had to buy oxen, to a total of 218, for some £70. Even with the shrunken demesne ploughlands of later years, investment in plough animals continued to be a major expense: in 1366–7, for example, the Winchester manors bought 96 oxen for about £89, and in 1387–8 63 more for some £43. On the other hand, the bishop's estates in the early thirteenth century had been self-sufficient in

---

[165] W. H. Beveridge, 'A statistical crime of the seventeenth century', *J. of Business and Economic Hist.*, I, 1928–9, pp. 503–5.   [166] Hilton, 'Lords, burgesses and hucksters', p. 14.

[167] *Pipe Roll of Winchester*, ed. Holt, pp. 60, 108, 114, 161.

[168] Hilton, 'Lords, burgesses and hucksters', p. 8; Kowaleski, 'Local markets and merchants', pp. 204, 238.

[169] William Langland, *Piers Plowman*, ed. D. Pearsall, Berkeley, 1978, p. 119. I have translated very freely line 228 – "Ac þe beste ale lay in my bour and in my bedchaunbre."

sheep, with only four manors buying any in 1210–11, to a modest total of 138 ewes and wethers and 88 lambs. Later, with the spread of diseases like scab – which in 1210–11 was recorded among the flocks only at Alresford, Brightwell, and Hambledon – the Winchester manors spent more replacing their sheep than their plough beasts: nearly three times as much in 1387–8, when they paid in all £123 for 774 adult sheep alone. Inter-manorial transfers were obviously not enough; nor, frequently, were the locally reared animals offered at the nearest markets and fairs. The patterns of trade for supplying manors with their livestock, and for selling slaughter cattle and other animals, consequently differed from the patterns of trading in grain.[170]

The large sums of money involved, and the risk of fraud, led some estates to supervise closely what animals their bailiffs or reeves bought and sold; thus Bishop's Waltham in 1210–11 bought three horses *per preceptum Episcopi*. In later years the bishops used officials such as Henry Baret, bailiff of Crawley and described as *Instaurer*, to make purchases on behalf of other manors.[171] Monastic estates despatched their obedientiaries to oversee their reeves, sometimes using the View of Account as an early opportunity to decide which animals should be replaced, and institutions like Merton College sent their fellows and sometimes the warden to aid the purchasing process. Despite the inconvenience to conventual and collegiate life, the stock-buying teams travelled to distant fairs and markets, particularly those on the fringes of arable and pastoral zones, where the best young animals from the hills of Wales and northern England might be on offer. And as the cost of transport was low in proportion to the animals' value, the bailiffs could go to fairs and markets without much heed to the droving costs involved – provided the route did not take the beasts through towns which charged transit tolls or across bridges where pontage or other dues might be levied.

The early Winchester pipe rolls show that Wales was a useful source of horses by the early thirteenth century. In 1210–11 Twyford had among its stock seven foals from Wales, Bishopstoke twenty-three forest horses, and Taunton twenty-five mares which William Cok had bought there for £12 10s. By the middle of the century, the cattle trade from Wales was powerful enough to make Newent and unmake Dymock, as the drovers bringing cattle through Ross-on-Wye found the former a better halting place on their way to Gloucester and Newnham.[172] Tidenham (Glos.) in 1272–3 bought cows from Monmouth, as well as from Magot the dairymaid and others who were

[170] *Pipe Roll of Winchester*, ed. Holt, pp. 57, 115, 131, 144.
[171] WPR 159321, 159377, 159395.
[172] *Pipe Roll of Winchester*, ed. Holt, pp. 15, 30, 96; Finberg, 'Welsh cattle trade', pp. 12–13.

probably also villagers, and in 1289–90 it bought in Monmouth ten head of cattle. By the end of the century the Tidenham bailiff was buying oxen also at Cardiff, Caerleon, and Chepstow. The horses bought by Merton College manors at Winchcomb and Chipping Campden fairs may also have come from Wales, on the first stage of journeys which took them as far as the coast of Kent.[173] So may the six oxen which Knowle (War.) bought at Wenlock in 1301–2, and possibly the three it purchased in Birmingham the same year, or the ox which Woolford bought there in 1352–3, though by that time dealers from midland towns like Tipton and Wednesbury were also prominent. Demesne lords like the Catesbys and the Beauchamps in the midlands stocked their manors with Welsh cattle bought in the markets of Bromyard and Worcester, as well as with local beasts bought at Chesterfield. Maldon (Surrey) bought four oxen in 1353–4 from a William Walshman, who may later have abandoned droving for milling, as in 1359–60 the manor leased the mill to William Walisch, and charged him 12d. for the summer agistment of his mare.[174]

Some of the cattle offered at Birmingham had probably come from north-west England, on the roads south through Preston and Wigan, supplied by fairs like Bolton's. There is more evidence for a cross-Pennine trade, such as that which took wool for shipment from York or Newcastle, for fairs and markets appeared early on the roads to the north-east. Corbridge, where an important road from Scotland crossed the routes in the valley of the north Tyne, had a major cattle fair: the bursar of Durham Cathedral priory bought twenty-six oxen there in 1338–9, and others at Hexham, specifically for the plough and not for the larder. In 1343 the Durham instaurer travelled 70 miles to the Tweed to buy ten horses from Sir Robert Manners, after buying the previous year four colts which that breeder had sent for sale in Yorkshire. In other years the priory bought its horses at Ripon fair, and its oxen at Darlington, Durham itself, Barnard Castle, Morpeth, Newcastle, and even Penrith and Kendal; the old Roman road over Stainmore seems to have carried a lot of livestock.[175] York in 1304 had three butchers named Scot, and three others with names suggesting origins in Carlisle, Ulverston, and "Brakonthwayt" – surely a Lake District name.[176] But the north-east was well supplied with cattle and

[173] PRO SC 6/859/18, 21, 27, 29; MCR 4394, 4517, 5257.

[174] WAM 27700; MCR 4410; R. Holt, *The Early History of the Town of Birmingham 1166–1600*, Dugdale Soc. Occasional Papers, no. 30, 1985, p. 10; A. Watkins, 'Cattle grazing in the forest of Arden in the later middle ages', *AHR*, xxxvii, 1989, p. 13.

[175] Fraser, 'Trade in the north-east', pp. 49–50.

[176] M. Prestwich, *York Civic Ordinances, 1301*, St Anthony's Hall Publications, no. 49, 1976, p. 24.

sheep-rearing areas of its own – the Pennine uplands, the Cheviots, and the Yorkshire Wolds – and may not have needed in normal years to buy in working or breeding animals from outside. Some of the Yorkshire fairs seem of exceptional importance as sources of livestock. The bishop of Durham's Candlemas fair at Northallerton was noted for its horses and cattle, and was visited by horse dealers from all parts of England and also from the continent. At times it lasted the whole month of February. A later fair at Bartholomew-tide specialized in horned cattle on the first day, and in sheep on the second. The bishop of Durham's fair at Howden became famous for horses, and, according to one writer, in the later middle ages "was probably the largest in Europe".[177] The archbishop of York also had a notable collection of fairs at Beverley, Ripon (where fair and market tolls were worth £40 annually in 1341), and at York itself, which was probably a source of fit animals as well as fattened beasts on their way to the shambles, as the archbishop collected tolls on animals leaving the city after sale as well as those driven to it. He also had fairs on several manors, such as Otley, Kilham, and Pateley Bridge; their location suggests that they, like Bolton priory's fairs at Embsay and Appletreewick, were also mainly for livestock.[178] This was true of Wakefield's fairs at midsummer and All Saints, of Malton fair, and perhaps also of Bradford's.

These fairs seem not to have supplied many animals for the agrarian areas of the midlands and south. Merton College, while willing to send its bailiffs and sometimes its fellows to Winchcomb and Chipping Campden, made little or no use for stockbuying of their regular visits to its northern manors. Holywell received a mare from Northumberland in 1333–4 and sent it to Maldon (Surrey), but it may have been a transfer from Embleton rather than a market purchase, and it seems to be the only such movement recorded.[179] Durham priory had extensive business at Boston fair, selling its wool there and, at the beginning of the fourteenth century, using it for over a third of its purchases; it did not, however, use its officials' visits to the south to sell any of its livestock. The only Yorkshiremen to appear before the St Ives courts were dealers in wool or cloth, not in livestock. Stamford, on the main road south towards London, may have had some larger part in marketing animals driven from the north. Henry III in 1247 ordered that £26 13s. 4d. from the profits of Stamford fair should be spent on horses for himself – but these might easily have come from neigh-

[177] K. L. MacCutcheon, 'Yorkshire fairs and markets to the end of the eighteenth century', Thoresby Soc., XXXIX, 1940, pp. 45, 127.
[178] Kershaw, Bolton Priory, pp. 26, 29–30; MacCutcheon, 'Yorkshire fairs and markets', pp. 33, 101, 102, 106, 128.   [179] MCR 4494.

bouring parts rather than from the north. The obedientiaries of Peterborough abbey also bought horses at Stamford fair, but went to nearby Market Deeping for oxen. The East Anglian manors went no further than Wisbech or Bedford for their animals. When the Westminster abbey cellarer began speculating in livestock, it was to the Cotswold fairs that he turned when he could not meet his needs from the abbey's own manors.[180]

The implication of these records, therefore, is that the north-east and Scotland played little part in supplying midland and southern England with livestock. The evidence of the manorial accounts is that bailiffs made their more urgent purchases at market towns within ten miles or so, and also visited in due season such of the annual fairs as were likely to offer more animals, or better ones, than could be expected locally. In the middle Thames area, Abingdon was the outstanding source for livestock: Basingstoke (Hants.) and Cuxham bought cart horses there, West Wycombe and Holywell plough horses, Cheddington and the Westminster cellarer oxen, West Wycombe and Cuxham sheep. Holywell bought steel and iron there, Steventon (Berks.) slates, tiles, and lime for building repairs. Holywell, Cuxham, and Basingstoke sent animals there for sale.[181] Of the transactions at Abingdon, many were made at the regular Monday markets, not at the annual seven-day fair at the Nativity of the Virgin. Among the items needed by medieval manors, only millstones seem not to have been available there, perhaps because of Henry II's ban (to appease Oxford and Wallingford) on its river-borne traffic.[182] Its rivals Thame and Aylesbury also had a lot of the Merton manors' business for both horses and oxen. Again, the millstones had to come from afar – Cuxham fetched them from Oxford and London, Cheddington from Stony Stratford, Holywell from Brackley and Southampton. The college's Surrey manors of Maldon, Leatherhead, and Thorncroft did most of their livestock trading at Croydon, Dorking, and Kingston-on-Thames, and bought their farming gear in Guildford or London. Stratton St Margaret (Wilts.) bought riding horses at Malmesbury and as far away as Winchcomb and Aylesbury. In 1354–5 the bailiff of Stratton used the warden's money to buy a bay palfrey at Malmesbury for 100s., with 1d. *pro argento dei* to seal the contract, 2d. in toll, and 3d. *pro carite*. But the horse proved unsatisfactory: the bailiff then took it to Winchcomb

---

[180] Moore, *Fairs*, pp. 13, 56–7n, 60–2, 83; *Account Rolls of Peterborough*, ed. Greatrex, pp. 121, 129; WAM 18865, 18873.

[181] MCR 4354, 5856; WPR 159380; MCR 4491; MCR 5546, WAM 18865; WPR 159327, MCR 5836, 4494; WAM 7449; MCR 4493, 5846, 5531.

[182] *VCH Berks.*, II, p. 53; III, p. 533.

and exchanged it for a chestnut palfrey, paying an additional 26s. 8d., and a further 1d. *in argento dei*, 2d. *pro carite*, and 4d. in toll (probably 2d. for the horse he brought to the fair and 2d. for the one he took away), and he incurred a further 18d. in expenses while there.[183]

More remarkable is the long-distance trade in horses which Merton College developed, rather unprofitably, between Winchcomb and Elham (near Folkestone). Many years the Elham bailiff travelled to Winchcomb, and often to Chipping Campden as well; sometimes he bought surplus stock from the college's other manors, or at the fairs at Crowmarsh, Reading, Windsor, Smithfield, Ashstead, and Godstone. Some accounts describe the horses – a four-toothed ruby foal with a few white hairs on its forehead, bought at Winchcomb for 23s 2¼d., or the black foal *cum auricula sinistra scissa* purchased at Chipping Campden for 26s. 0¼d. In 1326–7 Elham paid £21 8s. 7¼d. to buy fourteen horses at Winchcomb and seven at Abingdon, including tolls and other costs. But this was not the end of the expenses, for the horses still had to be led or ridden to Kent. In 1340–1, after buying twenty-six horseshoes at Oxford, three lads and five horses ran up bills of 4d. at Henley, 6d. at "Colbroc", 7d. at Otford, 1½d. at "Gilleford", 6d. at Hollingbourne, 3d. at Charing, and 2d. at Wye. Next year a party of two men with six horses went by way of Henley, "Colbrook", Kingston, Otford, Maidstone, and Wye. There are gaps in the middle of these itineraries, probably filled by overnight rests on the college's Surrey manors. Even so, the costs mounted: in 1317–18 the bailiff travelled from Oxford to Elham with the lads and sixteen horses, and the party spent 10s. 10¼d. And, at the end of this splendid enterprise, the horses fetched little more than the bailiff had paid for them. The twelve sold in the summer of 1298 realized £9 1s. 8d.; the bailiff had bought them, on the other side of England, for £7 18s. 9d. A few Elham accounts name the buyers – Thomas the Baker, John Clerk, Thomas the Forester, William Packham, and the smith of Ottinge – the villagers of Elham and Lyminge. Sometimes the bailiff varied the pattern. In 1320–1 he sold horses in Canterbury, and in 1329–30 in Maldon and Farnborough, but most of them usually went to the villagers. Often the bailiff had to provide them with credit into the bargain: in the autumn of 1328 Thomas atte Sole bought a black horse for 22s., paying 4s. down and promising the balance at Ascension-tide the next year, and William Packer a bay with a white star on its head for 26s. 8d., 6s. 8d. down and 20s. next Ascension Day.[184] One wonders why the college and the bailiff bothered to serve so unrewarding a market, buying the horses at the major Cotswold fairs,

[183] MCR 5841, 5853, 5875, 5546, 4491, 5690, 5819, 5752, 5753, 4317.
[184] MCR 5257, 5293, 5294, 5275, 5262, 5278, 5283, 5284; but see below, p. 459.

leading them past urban centres like Oxford, Reading, and Maidstone, avoiding London, and delivering the animals on credit to the people in the hamlets at the head of the Nail Bourne valley.

So peculiar a trade was not typical. This may also be true of the variety of sources recorded for Holywell's purchases from July 1360 to July 1361. The manor bought six oxen at Chipping Campden, three at Woodstock, two at North Hinksey, and two at Standlake; it purchased two new ploughs at West Wittenham and one at Water Eaton, yokes at Water Eaton and goads at Abingdon and Appleton, two pairs of cart wheels at Stokenchurch, and a further two at Woodstock fair. It bought an iron chain from Thomas de Bugworth, and fifteen rods of steel from John atte Yate. And it spent 4s. 6d. on hiring three horses to go to Stourbridge fair and back, with a further 3s. 6d. for horsebread and hay. Such a diversity of sources had precedents (though never so many in one year): in 1330–1 Holywell had bought livestock, hay and farming gear in London, Abingdon, Banbury, Brackley, Bicester, and Eynsham, and in other years it purchased things at Binsey and Godstow fair, at Cowley and Beckley, Wallingford and Witney. This diversity contrasts, however, with the very conservative nature of Holywell's grain marketing: the accounts, surviving for about forty years, show it sending wheat only once to Henley, and once to Reading, and, possibly, barley once to Evesham.[185]

This contrast is repeated in other areas where the markets were not dominated by the halls and cook-shops of a university town. Longbridge Deverill and Monkton Deverill again provide excellent examples. Binegar fair, seventeen miles away, provided the Deverills with oxen in 1332–3, horses in 1341–2, and lambs in 1458–9. Monkton Deverill bought lambs at Castle Cary in 1418–19, 1424–5, and 1457–8. The bailiffs made a few purchases at much nearer places like Maiden Bradley, Horningsham, and Bishopstrow; among the more distant fairs where they bought stock were Sturminster Newton, Somerton, Evercreech, Priddy, Glastonbury, and Yarlington, the last an unlikely place granted in 1314 a Tuesday market and a three-day Assumption-tide fair, apparently still held in 1460–1.[186] In contrast to the wide distribution of their sources, the bailiffs sold almost all their stock at Hindon, usually sending their sheep to the St Luke's fair around 18 October, and escorting them with a complement of bailiff, reeve, and two or three shepherds. In 1472–3 the bailiff of Monkton Deverill took a horse to Warminster and then to Shaftesbury to sell it, but this was a rare exception. Surprisingly, the accounts record no purchases or sales of stock at the important Heytesbury fair (four miles from Longbridge

---

[185] MCR 4474, 4503. The latter roll is defective: Evesham may be the buyer's surname.
[186] GAD 9730, 9622, 9794, 9720, 9698, 9998, 9795; CChR, III, p. 241.

Deverill), at Wells, or even at Salisbury and Winchester, which the Glastonbury abbey chamberlain regularly visited at fair-time, charging Longbridge Deverill with part of his expenses. Bishopric of Winchester manors sold pigs at Priddy in 1304–5, and bought others there the next year; and bought sheep at Hindon and Heytesbury. Hindon was the most convenient market for East Knoyle and perhaps others of the bishop's manors, and so may have been used far more than the pipe rolls record.[187]

The East Anglian evidence confirms that manors bought livestock at places further away than the towns and villages in which they commonly sold their grain. Birdbrook purchased plough horses at Newmarket and Haverhill, and cows at Great Bardfield and Hedingham, an average distance of eight miles. It sold cattle at Hedingham and Haverhill, and sheep at Hadstock fair, and livestock of all varieties to people who were probably villagers of Birdbrook. In a few years, such as 1384–5, the manor also bought some cows and calves from local persons, thereby reducing somewhat the average distance travelled to make the purchase. Feering bought horses at the fairs of Maldon (Essex) and Colchester, in Bishop's Stortford, and from a Coggeshall man, in places which were an average distance of eleven miles away. Hargrave sent sixteen miles to buy sheep at Thetford in 1369–70, Bircham twenty-four miles to buy plough horses at Wisbech in 1322–3, and Fornham twenty-six miles to buy the same at Ely fair in 1400–1. The Hinderclay bailiff crossed Norfolk in 1309–10 to buy four foals at North Walsham. Gamlingay bought sheep at Royston (ten miles away) and at Hitchin (fifteen), but as it regularly sold stock and grain at Baldock (eleven) and Cambridge (thirteen) its sales were almost as far removed as its purchases. Harston (Cambs.) in the 1310s also commonly bought sheep at Royston, and sometimes in Cambridge and at Barnwell fair, or from individuals like Henry Lucas of Harston, or a man at Hadstock nine miles away. It bought fresh horses from William Goding, and sold him its old ones. Its cattle it sold at Barnwell fair, and its sheep directly to butchers.[188]

Whereas most manors preferred to buy their livestock at fairs, or in reliable markets like Abingdon's, many of them, as we have seen, were also trading with their own tenants and other villagers. For some manors this may have been the dominant practice, rather than a supplementary one. The Sussex manors of Battle abbey, for example, almost never dealt at fairs – even though Battle itself had an important

---

[187] GAD 9880, 9825, 9803; WPR 159408, 159321, 159294, 159322; see also Fig. 4.2, above.

[188] WAM 25480, 24727, 25691, 25732; Suffolk RO, E3/15.10/2.16; PRO SC 6/930/3; Suffolk RO, E3/15.6/2.38; Regenstein Library, Chicago, Bacon Mss. 444; MCR 5388, 5409, 5378, 5344; BL Add. Roll 18522. I owe this last reference to Edward Miller.

one; its bailiffs bought and sold *in patria*, or, less commonly *in foro*, or obtained and despatched their livestock by inter-manorial transfer, or sent them to Battle to feed the monks. A Barnhorne account for 1414–15 records the purchase of a cow and calf at Lewes, and one for 1417–18 that of two oxen and seventy-two lambs at Selmeston fair, but otherwise the manor relied on the district for its stock – three plough horses one year, three foals and twelve calves in another, two plough horses, two oxen, and three cows in a third. Apuldram and Lullington also bought and sold chiefly in their districts. From the prices, most of the cattle seem good quality beasts sold to villagers for stock, not fattened cattle released for slaughter. Its isolation may have made Sussex depend on locally raised livestock more than most areas. These later Battle abbey accounts, like the later Durham ones showing more trade between lord and tenant, suggest the narrowing of the economic gap separating them, as the lords divested themselves of their demesnes and as the survivors of the plague increased the size of their holdings. Other accounts from post-Black Death years show the same thing: at Chevington in the 1390s it was no longer the abbot of Bury St Edmunds who dominated the market, but livestock dealers like John Aleyn and Walter Boon.[189]

Another occasional source of manorial livestock was heriot, the surrender to the lord of a dead peasant's best animal. Although inconsistent in practice, this was a heavy burden for widow or son, and may have been a reason why manors often forbade their villeins to sell their animals without the lord's leave. On the Ely estates the common provision was that villeins might not sell male colts or oxen of their own rearing without the lord's or bailiff's leave, perhaps to safeguard heriot rights or, maybe, simply to give the lord a right of pre-emption.[190] Manors receiving horses or cattle in this way, or occasionally smaller animals, usually sold them again within the year – very often, one suspects, to the families which had just surrendered them to the lord. Heriots were more a source of income than a source of animals the bailiff would want to match with the lord's in the demesne ploughteams.

The medieval treatises on estate management gave more attention to

---

[189] Suffolk RO, E3/15.3/2.19, 2.20a, 2.21.

[190] This common incident of villeinage is occasionally named as one of the purposes of an inquiry, as on the St Paul's manors *c.* 1320 (*Domesday of St Paul's*, ed. Hale, p. 157) and at Cuxham in 1310 (*Records of Cuxham*, ed. Harvey, p. 632). The fee charged for the licence to sell was only 1d. or 2d. (see *The Register of Worcester Priory*, ed. W. H. Hale, Camden Soc., XCI, 1865, p. 15a; PRO SC 6/859/18, 19, 22), and I have never noticed this as the reason for a prosecution in a manorial court. For the Ely information I am again indebted to Edward Miller.

culling animals for slaughter than to any other aspect of marketing. The *Seneschaucy* demanded the culling of the sheep in May, at Lammas, and again at Michaelmas, and the culling of the oxen, cows, and young cattle after midsummer, so that the poorer ones could be fattened for market. Walter of Henley urged inspection of both plough animals and sheep between Easter and Whitsun, the defective stock to be set aside and fattened.[191] Accounts of the fourteenth century usually reckon the sheep sold before shearing separately from those sold after shearing (to enable the fleece account to be balanced), and show that the late spring and early summer were busy times for sheep dealers. Barren cows often went to market at the same time. Some oxen went to graziers in the fairs around St Bartholomew's day, but many manors kept them until later in the year, getting a final summer's work and perhaps a few weeks of autumn ploughing out of them before having them fattened for slaughter for the lord's larder, or for sale in some market or fair. Whether they were sold early or late might depend on the extent and condition of the manorial pastures, or how distant the manor was from a major urban centre – oxen would not make good carcases if slaughtered immediately after a long drove, without a week or two to put on weight again, and they might not be ready for the Christmas trade if they had been kept back until Martinmas.

The manorial accounts sometimes show very large numbers of animals despatched for slaughter. In 1218–19 Taunton sent 181 oxen and 693 pigs to Winchester, though how many were used by the bishop's household and how many were sold at the fair or in the city's markets is not recorded. Two years later, the bishop ordered Taunton to buy pigs for him, and men from the manor thereafter drove 734 of them eastwards on their way towards Winchester.[192] This did not become a regular practice, as the bishop found alternative sources closer to his city. Though the accountants' inconsistencies make it hard to be exact, even a generation after the Black Death the bishop's Hampshire and Thames valley manors seem to have despatched most of their fat oxen and pigs to the lord's household, those sent to the market frequently being described as useless, unhealthy, putrid, or almost dead. These, probably, were animals which had fallen sick between the regular inspections and which the bailiff or reeve had hurried to market to have them "killed to save them". On the other hand, the bishop's Somerset and Wiltshire manors (if the silences in the accounts are not deceptive) supplied the lord's household only rarely, and sent their slaughter stock routinely to the local markets in Taunton and Hindon and Downton, and perhaps elsewhere.

The other account series are generally more informative than the

---

[191] *Walter of Henley*, ed. Oschinsky, pp. 275, 331, 337.   [192] WPR 159275, 159277.

Winchester pipe rolls, and often record some extended journeys to slaughter, almost rivalling the horse trade from Winchcomb to Elham. Many of these travels were *ad hospicium domini*, however, not for sale in market or fair. Oakham in 1338–9 paid 2s. 3d. to a man for leading a boar to Westminster – certainly a heroic experience. Tidenham, which itself bought stock as far west as Cardiff, sent six oxen, seven bullocks, twenty-six cows and seven heifers to Hampstead in June 1295.[193] Turweston paid two lads 20d. for driving fifty-one sheep for sale in London in October 1339, and another lad 12d. for driving five oxen there. Westminster's Severn-side manor of Hardwicke despatched oxen and pigs eastwards on the first stage of journeys which would take them to Islip and Denham and to the abbey kitchens: one man in 1372/3 drove a boar and twenty-four pigs from there to Islip for 10d., some forty-five miles as the crow flies, and probably rather more by trotter. In the one year 1346–7 Islip sent to Denham one deer and two fawns – apparently alive, as the carters bought milk and peas for their needs on the journey – and also three oxen; to Eybury it sent a boar and twenty pigs; it despatched to Pyrford forty-three cocks and hens in December, and capons, doves, and eggs in May; to *La Neyte* a boar in April, and straight to Westminster six pigs to help the monks to celebrate Easter. Pershore also served Westminster as a place for assembling its meat supply: in 1343–4 it forwarded to Knightsbridge twenty head of cattle and forty-eight pigs from Pershore itself, Hardwicke, Longdon (Worcs.), and Bourton-on-the-Hill (Glos.), at a total cost in four men's wages and animal fodder of 10s. 2d. In 1302–3, Knowle had sent thirty-four oxen, cows and young cattle to the abbey a hundred miles away.[194] In the cattle trade, distance was no obstacle if the lord wanted to eat the beef he had raised. After the Black Death, the abbey cellarers themselves became cattle wholesalers: John de Lakingheath and Richard Honington bought oxen "up country" at Kingston, Abingdon, and Woodstock as well as from abbey manors like Staines, Kelvedon, and Westerham (Kent), or from other traders like John Kent the butcher and Peter Cok the drover, or at Smithfield market. They fattened them in pens near the abbey and sold them in large numbers – thirty to Eli de Weston in 1388–9, thirty more to Henry Bocher the next year.[195] By that time the butchery business around London was almost out of control, the northern suburbs having something of the atmosphere and all too much of the smell of a cattle town in the nineteenth-century U.S.A., London butchers went to Stratford and Stepney to intercept the droves from the eastern counties, to buy the best beasts and to fatten them on the marshland east of the

[193] WAM 20254; PRO SC 6/859/24.
[194] WAM 7790, 8444, 14794, 22121, 27701.
[195] WAM 18865, 18867, 18871, 18873.

city, or, illegally, on the common pastures of Tottenham. Among the London craft gild members who bought land at Tottenham between 1413 and 1450, there were ten butchers, and only one baker; there was also among the residents a Warwickshire drover named Holder, who had purchased some twenty acres of enclosed land there, presumably for fattening up his beasts after their journey from the midlands. A taste for lamb encouraged some Canterbury Cathedral priory manors after the Black Death to produce for the table as well as for the loom; in the late 1450s the victualler of the English garrison in Calais bought all his sheep in Kent, but had to get most of his beef cattle from Coventry and Hertfordshire.[196]

Although the trade in slaughter cattle had something in common with the grain trade, the drovers and butchers never became as powerful as the bladers had been. Only one London butcher became an alderman in the fourteenth century, and none thereafter until the nineteenth. To some extent the regulations and restrictions on the butchers, far more limiting than those on other trades and crafts, may reflect their lack of political influence. Much more, though, they show civic awareness of the dangers of tainted meat and the nuisance caused by slaughtering within the town, in London and elsewhere. The London court rolls are predictably full of the butchers' misdemeanours. In 1350 the jurors presented Thomas Austyn as a common forestaller, as he had gone out to Iseldon in Middlesex and bought 80 sheep from John le Rous, and then to Highgate, where he had bought 120 pigs from Walter de Baldeswell, before the drovers had brought them to the city. Robert Dru was sent to prison in 1306 because he had slaughtered 60 lambs before he had fully paid for them; in 1345 butchers William Lemman and William de Herlawe were gaoled for not paying the same day for the cows they had bought from John Cok, drover, at West Smithfield. In 1366 another drover recovered substantial debts from butchers John and Henry Cornwaille.[197]

The most serious problem, though, was that caused by the mess and smell. In 1361 London banned slaughtering from the city, and it may have been this which led Westminster's cellarer to encourage the trade by the abbey. But the butchers moved back into London, and in 1368 a jury found that

the butchers of St Nicholas Shambles and their servants were in the habit of carrying the said offal and filth to the bridge called "*Bochersbregg*" near Castle

[196] D. Moss, 'The economic development of a Middlesex village', *AHR*, XXIX, 1980, pp.109, 114; Mate, 'Agrarian economy after the Black Death', p. 345; *idem*, 'Pastoral farming in south-east England', p. 527.

[197] *Cal. Plea and Memo. Rolls 1323–1364*, ed. Thomas, pp. 217, 235; *Cal. Early Mayor's Court Rolls*, ed. Thomas, p. 237; *Cal. Plea and Memo. Rolls 1364–1381*, ed. Thomas, p. 20.

Baynard, and there casting it into the Thames, making the water foul, that in its passage through the streets some of the offal fell from the vessels in which it was carried, and that the blood of the animals slaughtered in the Shambles aforesaid found its way down the streets and lanes to the Thames, making a foul corruption and abominable sight and nuisance to all dwelling near or using those streets and lanes.[198]

Then the bishop of London and two earls petitioned against the butchers leaving the offal of slaughtered beasts on land by the Thames near the Dominican friary, "to the grievous corruption of the water".[199] Moving part of the trade to Westminster merely transferred the nuisance. Following the cellarer's example, the residents also began to fatten stock for the market; in 1407 nineteen people were charged with owning stray pigs – 20 of them, in one case. King Street was a confusion of pigs, prostitutes, and pie-stalls, serving the assorted needs of the ecclesiastical and administrative communities of Westminster. Cok or Cook is so frequent a name among the drovers and butchers that it suggests a chain of supply, stretching at times from manor to cooked-meat stall. And supplementing the Westminster meat market was that at Southwark, which offered as well as slaughter houses the hopped beer of Flemish brewers and the well-regulated stews of Bankside.[200]

Many English towns reproduced the conditions of the London meat trade, albeit on a smaller scale. Winchester had eight butchers, all in the northern part of the High Street, as early as 1110; the occupations nearest them in numbers were the complementary ones of the tanners and cooks, with three each. In the thirteenth century Winchester was already famous for its butchers. The number of resident butchers stayed around a dozen during the fourteenth and fifteenth centuries, but by the early fifteenth century they were joined by butchers from outside. The mayor regulated the price at which meat was sold, trying to hold the profit margin to a penny in the shilling, and in 1413 the butchers were forbidden to charge more than 10d. for 12 lb of rough tallow sold to chandlers. They persisted, though, in throwing the offal into the cathedral cemetery.[201] The butchers in Exeter appeared before the city courts in cases of debt (whether as debtors or creditors) more often than any group except the rich merchants of the civic oligarchy, and the city

[198] *Ibid.*, p. 93.   [199] *Ibid.*, p. 94.

[200] A. G. Rosser, 'The essence of medieval urban communities: the vill of Westminster 1200–1500', *RHS*, 5th ser. xxxiv, 1984, pp. 99–100; *VCH Surrey*, ii, pp. 250–1; J. B. Post, 'A fifteenth-century customary of the Southwark stews', *J. of the Soc. of Archivists*, v, 1974–7, pp. 418–28.

[201] *Winchester in the Early Middle Ages*, ed. Biddle, p. 429; *English Historical Documents 1189–1327*, ed. Rothwell, p. 822; Keene, *Medieval Winchester*, i, pp. 256, 258, 264.

regulated and supervised them more closely than the other trades. Their shops were in the covered Fleshfold, watched over by the two wardens they elected every Michaelmas to regulate slaughtering and inspect meat – an unpopular office sometimes evaded by those chosen. In Exeter, as in London and Winchester, bulls had to be baited with dogs before being slaughtered, a practice intended to make the meat more tender, though a jury of London butchers in 1349 avowed that it did nothing of the sort.[202] By 1311 Colchester also had two meat wardens, to oversee the resident butchers (twenty-one by 1400) and also the others who came in to the Saturday market, and to enforce the rules against selling stale meat as fresh, or selling dog meat from the same stalls as meat for human consumption.[203] In Bristol the butchers had to buy their slaughter cattle in the "Brodemede" or outside the Dominican friary – except at Martinmas, when the throng of animals from the autumn cull could be bought and sold anywhere in the city; any cook or butcher who sold diseased meat (*carnes porcinas super seminatas vel carnes de morina*) – or who bought from Jews – would be fined the first time, pilloried the second, gaoled the third, and expelled on the fourth offence.[204] Those at Leicester had no second chance: by the ordinance of 1467, any butcher selling meat "with any manner of sickness" was to be imprisoned during the mayor's pleasure, and so was any butcher trading in his house or shop rather than in the shambles or market place. Northampton, however, decreed that all rotten meat should be given to the sick (*infirmis*).[205] Rents from butchers' stalls provided York with over 5 per cent of its civic revenues in 1292–3. Edward III thought the city stank worse than any other in the kingdom, and even the Franciscans complained of the smell from offal tipped into the Ouse near their church. Though it tried to attract more butchers in the hope of lowering the price of meat, the city also compelled them to remove the offal across the Ouse so that the countrymen could cart it away for manure – an interesting variation on the nitrogen cycle.[206] Reading had a public abattoir in the street appropriately named Gutter, and in 1464 the mayor and burgesses organized a boycott to make the butchers "sclee theyre flessche in the sleynng house", and nowhere else.[207]

Smaller towns needed fewer regulations. Henley merely forbade slaughtering near the market cross. High Wycombe, where there were

---

[202] Kowaleski, 'Local markets and merchants', pp. 186, 239–40; *Cal. Plea and Memo. Rolls 1323–1364*, ed. Thomas, p. 228.

[203] Britnell, *Growth and Decline in Colchester*, pp. 131, 138.

[204] *The Little Red Book of Bristol*, ed. F. B. Bickley, Bristol, 1900, II, pp. 218, 230–1.

[205] *English Historical Documents, IV, 1327–1485*, ed. A. R. Myers, London, 1969, pp. 576, 578.

[206] *VCH Yorks., City of York*, pp. 35, 99, 107–8. [207] *VCH Berks.*, III, p. 350.

at least fourteen butchers, decreed in 1362 that there should be no live cattle or pigs within the borough, but soon made exceptions to let first Walter Chapman, and then Richard Donne, chaplain, have cattle pens alongside their shops. A rule which may have been better kept required butchers to bring the hides and skins to the market as well as the carcases, to allow the local leatherworkers a chance to buy them before outside purchasers forestalled them for the London trade.[208] The butchering business reached into hamlets as well. John Gouffe, *carnifex* of Brightwell Baldwin, bought four head of cattle from Cuxham in 1309–10. Turweston in the 1390s sold cattle and pigs to John Bocher of Brackley and a boar to William Bocher of Banbury. Birdbrook had several regular customers, possibly drovers buying for a distant market but as likely to be village butchers, such as William Coplyng of Haverhill, William Capold of Stoke-by-Clare, and John Bocher of Horseheath.[209] Twenty-one men purchased butchering licences at Broughton (Hunts.) between 1288 and 1340; at least two of them – John Tabbard and Thomas de Wendale – stayed in the business for twenty years.[210] Feering in 1393–4 sold cows and sheep to two men from Coggeshall and one from Kelvedon, and a calf, three "soklynges" lambs, and sixteen pigs to John Bocher (of unstated provenance). The dealings of Chevington with Walter Boon extended over many years: in 1394–5 it sold him a weak cart horse, two oxen, and five cows, in 1395–6 a plough horse, two bulls, two oxen, six cows, and a boar, and in 1396–7 a bull, and a part-share in six rams and 119 sheep. In this last year Simon Smyth bought from the same manor two horses and forty-eight head of cattle for £16 17s. 4d., at least one of the purchases being made at a fair, not directly from the bailiff. In 1421–2 Walter Boon appeared again, buying ten acres of *grossi bosci*; perhaps he was more a general dealer than someone trying to corner the Suffolk meat trade.[211] Some of the dealers operated on the grand scale: in 1401 three men were accused in Birmingham of evading tolls on 300 head of cattle they had brought to sell there, and in 1404 a fourth was presented for evading tolls of £10 on cattle sold in the town's fair and markets, the dues on a thousand beasts or more. Two midland peasant families who rose to prosperity through fattening cattle for the market were the Deys of Drakenage and the Baillys of Middleton. Others were humbler and poorer; when Walter Baldeswell, a Bedfordshire drover, and possibly the man who had sold pigs to a forestaller at Highgate in 1350,

[208] *Henley Borough Records, 1395–1543*, ed. Briers, p. 124; *The First Ledger Book of High Wycombe*, ed. R. W. Greaves, Bucks. Rec. Soc., II, 1956, pp. 6, 23, 32, 34.
[209] MCR 5834; WAM 7832, 7834, 25476, 25477, 25479, 25450.
[210] E. Britton, *The Community of the Vill*, Toronto, 1977, p. 89.
[211] WAM 25727; Suffolk RO, E3/15.3/2.19, 2.20a, 2.21, 2.31.

failed to pay £24 in debts to a London merchant, the jury in 1374 found that his only assets were 1½ acres of arable land, worth 10d. a year, and carrying a crop of dredge worth only 5s. 3d. So many were active in the livestock trade that even local monopolies would have been impossible, especially as butchers could obtain their needs from a wide area if necessary: the Colchester butcher Richard Petrisburgh normally got his beasts from the villages within six or seven miles, but might occasionally buy as far away as Ely fair. Then, in Colchester's Saturday market, Petrisburgh and the other butchers of the town would have to compete with "outside" butchers from nearby villages like Lawford and Manningtree. At the retail level, there were few fortunes to be made. Those who gained most were the great grazier-butchers, such as Wolsey *père* in Suffolk, and John Spencer and Benedict Lee in Warwickshire, who were able to pay high rents for the enclosed pastures of villages deserted in the upheavals of the later middle ages.[212]

Occasionally an estate sent to market some of its surplus stock of birds, and, increasingly, rabbits. Bishops Sutton (Hants.) in 1388–9, for example, recorded £7 17s. 11d. for 530 *cuniculis* sold to the lord's hospice at 2½d. each and 190 sold *in foro* at 3d.; Overton (Hants.) in 1402–3 sold *in foro* 250, 144 of which were taken by the king's purveyors. More frequently the accounts mention poultry sent for the use of lord and household. Chevington in 1347–8 sent to London, for the needs of the abbot of Bury St Edmunds, 10 swans valued at 3s. each, 12 pheasants at 2d., 43 rabbits at 2½d., 50 partridges at 2d., 89 geese at 3d., and 209 hens at 2d., and the manor had to pay R. le Foulere and W. le Hunte 3s. 3d. for catching the game. Islip in 1328–9 had geese carted to Laleham, and partridges carried there, and Denham in 1387–8 forwarded to Westminster abbey 11 swans (worth 3s. 4d. each) as well as 19 geese and 558 doves.[213] "A fat swan loved he best of any roost," wrote Chaucer – who knew Westminster abbey well – of his gluttonous monk.[214] In the 1390s the bishop of Winchester had about two hundred swans at Downton alone.

But marketing the poultry of the villagers, and such wildfowl as could be netted in the fens and marshes, was primarily for the humblest of the traders. In 1306 eleven poulterers accused the sheriff of London of seizing from them 51 pigeons, 7 hens, 6 capons, 8 pullets, 250 eggs,

---

[212] Holt, *Early History of Birmingham*, p. 10; A. Watkins, 'Cattle grazing in the forest of Arden', pp. 18–19; PRO C 131/21; Britnell, *Growth and Decline in Colchester*, p. 142; C. Dyer, 'Deserted medieval villages in the West Midlands', p. 30.

[213] WPR 159395, 159407; Suffolk RO, E3/15.3/2.7; WAM 14788, 3412.

[214] *Complete Works of Geoffrey Chaucer*, ed. F. N. Robinson, London, 1957, p. 19 (General Prologue, line 206).

and 5 cheeses; in the end, the sheriff kept the poultry and the poulterers went to prison "because the plaintiffs were common forestallers who forestalled poultry both in the lodgings of poulterers and by meeting foreigners coming to the City". At a generous valuation, the stock of the average poulterer in this group cannot have been worth more than 14d. before the sheriff seized it. Later that same year five others were attached "for buying poultry within the city to sell it outside, as though they were freemen, thus producing a scarcity of poultry to the damage of the citizens".[215] These were luckier: they pleaded that they had bought the poultry in the markets of Kingston, Barking, and St Albans, paying tolls there, and also murage dues on bringing it to London, and, after paying fines, they were admitted to the burgess freedom of the city. Like the butchers, the poulterers could cause a nuisance. In 1345, after complaints that the road between the Stocks and the Conduit in Cheap had been blocked by their stalls in the highway, the city ordered them to sell their goods only from their shops and regular stalls. In the troubles following the Black Death, London pilloried or imprisoned many poulterers for forestalling. In 1355 it swore in certain of them to supervise the trade, ensure fair prices, and compel poulterers from outside the city to sell their wares openly in Leadenhall (in aula plumba) market.[216] London juries kept up the pressure in the 1360s, accusing John Stukle for selling poultry to a cook at the latter's lodgings, and John Cokhow and John Stylle for keeping a stall in the Poultry where they had sold the goods of outside poulterers "as though they were the goods of freemen, thus defrauding the Sheriff of his customs". When ordered to name those who had sold poultry at illegally high prices, the jurors produced a long list, with their own names included on it. A cook, Edmund Cadon, went to prison for forestalling the market by buying geese at Leadenhall before the hour of prime. Others the city punished for trading outside the market, by forfeiting the items in question – the 400 eggs which Hugh Stag of Towcester had sold to John Yue in the street outside Cheap, and the four mallard, four teal, two woodcock and one partridge which John Clerk had bought improperly outside the Poultry.[217]

In such cases the arm of civic authority seems unnecessarily long. In many towns, though, the poulterers seem to have had one small advantage: they paid no tolls on what they brought to market, perhaps because direct sales from producers to consumers were usually toll-free. None of the thirteen schedules of northern towns' charges which C. M. Fraser printed mentions dues on poultry, and this seems true of Oxford

[215] Cal. Early Mayor's Court Rolls, ed. Thomas, pp. 241, 246.
[216] Cal. Plea and Memo. Rolls 1323–1364, ed. Thomas, pp. 222–3, 232–3, 250.
[217] Cal. Plea and Memo. Rolls 1364–1381, ed. Thomas, pp. 7, 8, 66, 164, 165.

as well.[218] Instead, the town might control prices, and other aspects of the trade. York's Civic Ordinance of 1301 insisted that poultry be sold only on the bridge over the Ouse (probably to facilitate disposal of the waste), and at prescribed prices – 3d. for a goose, 5d. for a brace of mallard, plovers and woodcocks for 1d. each, blackbirds and thrushes at six for a penny. A rabbit, though, would cost 5d. In York the trade seems to have been dominated by men. Of the thirty-seven York poulterers indicted in 1304 for breaking the rules, only five were women. In contrast, two-thirds of those charged there for regrating were female. Of those poulterers charged, only one achieved freeman status, whereas twenty-one of the forty-nine butchers indicted then were either burgesses already, or soon became so. This confirms the lowly status of the poulterers among the victualling tradesmen of the city. Most seem not to have been active in other trades: of the thirty-seven, two at most were also named as regrators, and a third may have been the husband of a woman accused of both hostelling and brewing offences; three others had surnames suggesting other occupations – Adam Candeler, John le Chaundeler, and Letitia le Cornemanger. At Exeter, in contrast, the trade was mainly in the hands of women, and there may have been less specialization in this smaller city; John Somerford sold poultry as well as meat and dairy products, and worked also as a fuller and hide dealer. Of the eight poulterers presented for offences in Winchester in 1299, six were women; few of the city's medieval poulterers were ever listed among the owners of property there.[219]

Mainly it was a trade in which the poor could participate, and in which the wives of villagers could bring to the town markets the hens and eggs from their crofts and gardens, albeit for only small rewards. Manors were generally content to leave the poultry business to the villagers, sometimes receiving hen and egg rents from their customary tenants, sometimes buying in what they needed for the table or breeding stock from the ample supplies available locally. Barnhorne, for example, bought forty geese in patria in 1386–7, and thirty-two the next year – to learn before long the perils of poultry keeping, for in 1396–7 it lost ten of its geese to foxes. Only the rabbit trade was an exception, as the lords exploited their rights of warren in the years after the Black Death, and even here the legal market was probably supplemented from the fruits of poaching. Wilton abbey's purchases in 1299 show that, even when Wilton's markets had been overshadowed

---

[218] Fraser, 'Trade in the north-east', App. facing p. 66; Oxford City Documents 1268–1665, ed. J. E. Thorold Rogers, Oxford Hist. Soc., XVIII, 1891, pp. 304–6.

[219] Prestwich, York Civic Ordinances, 1301, pp. 14, 24, 27–8; Kowaleski, 'Local markets and merchants', p. 171; Keene, Medieval Winchester, I, pp. 261, 262.

by Salisbury's, the nuns were able to buy geese and doves, hens and eggs, as well as salmon and trout and mackerel, on any day of the week, including Sundays.[220] So, while bailiffs might send swans and geese to feed their lords afar off – as they did with beef and bacon and grain – the market trade in poultry seems to have been local, and amply supplied even so, without the participation of wholesalers like the bladers, or the drovers and graziers who dealt in the large animals.

E. MARKETING WOOL, CHEESE, AND HIDES

By 1200 the wool trade was already the most famous and sophisticated part of the English economy. The thirteenth and fourteenth centuries also proved it the most vulnerable to disease and royal interference. It nourished meanwhile the fairs and ports of eastern England, and provided the raw material for the industry which ultimately supplanted it in importance. In practice, there were two wool trades. One, very visible, took high-quality wool to the eager looms of Flanders and France and Italy; this was a commerce which foreigners dominated well into the fourteenth century. The other was a quieter trade by which native merchants took wool to the combers and carders, the weavers and fullers of the English towns and villages. When the Plantagenets had largely broken the first by burdening it with war taxation, many of the better wools moved from the foreign looms to the domestic.

In marketing wool, the Cistercians set the pace. The monks of Rievaulx, "holy men who glorified God in the practice of poverty", showed some worldly wisdom as well by getting Henry I to exempt them from tolls throughout England, and at least twenty-two other Cistercian houses had followed their prudent example by 1200. As this privilege applied only while the wool was in monastic hands, the abbeys arranged their own transport to the delivery points, thus saving the buyers both inconvenience and tolls. With their lay-brothers or *conversi* to do the work, they also became pre-eminent in the dressing and other preparation of wool for the buyer – washing, stretching, drying, sorting, and packing into sacks and canvas sarplars for carting to the places assigned. As the Cistercians could get better prices than other producers, they bought up the wool of other growers, preparing and packing it themselves, and marketing it as *lana collecta*, even though their General Chapter had prohibited this as early as 1157. Henry III in 1237 forbade both monks and *conversi* to traffic in wool and hides produced by others. When Bolton Priory traded in *collecta* at the end

---

[220] Crittall, 'Account of the cellaress of Wilton', pp. 147–56.

of the thirteenth century, it made net profits of 37 to 57 per cent by acting as middleman, and the Cistercians probably found it at least as lucrative.[221] The Cistercians developed, and may have pioneered, many of the trade routes which persisted through the middle ages, even though they shifted as the Cotswold wools later gained in favour at the expense of the northern. In the twelfth and thirteenth centuries the wool travelled from Yorkshire and Lincolnshire to Boston, from the north-west across the Pennines to Newcastle and then by ship to Boston or London, and from the midlands and the Welsh borders to London or Southampton. In later years much English wool would go through Hull, and a few hundred sacks through King's Lynn, Ipswich, Yarmouth, and Hartlepool in the east, and Chichester, Sandwich, and Melcombe in the south. A little trickled through Bristol and Exeter, but the dominant ports remained those of the east coast and, in years of peace, Southampton. And it may have been their continental links which led the Cistercians to rely almost entirely on foreign merchants to take their wool abroad, at least until the fourteenth century, and which trapped them in practices which proved ruinous for many of their monasteries.[222]

By the middle of the twelfth century, the monks were making long-term contracts with buyers keen to commandeer the Cistercian wool-clip for their customers. With ambitious buildings to finance, abbeys took money for the fleeces of sheep yet unborn, and merchants like William Cade of St Omer used such contracts both as a guarantee of supply and as a cloak for usury. When Cade died about 1166, Louth Park abbey owed him £46 13s. 4d. for wool not yet delivered, and Roche abbey 22 weys of wool and 2,200 fleeces for which he had already paid. Despite another prohibition by the General Chapter in 1181, some Cistercian houses continued to pledge their wool ten years or more in advance. Short-sighted at best, as such contracts prevented producers benefiting from a rising market, the practice proved disastrous when epidemics of murrain and sheep scab ravaged the flocks and ruined the fleeces in the later thirteenth century. Many abbeys were put at the mercy of their creditors. In 1291 Pipewell abbey (Lincs.) had to commit itself for thirteen years to supply John de Redole and other Cahorsin merchants with the best of the clip, prepared under the merchants' supervision at the abbey's expense, at pre-determined prices, and to pledge the church and "all their goods, moveable and

---

[221] English Historical Documents 1042–1189, eds. Douglas and Greenaway, p. 692; Donkin, Cistercians, pp. 68, 91, 141; Lloyd, The English Wool Trade, p. 295; CCR, 1234–1237, p. 352; Kershaw, Bolton Priory, pp. 85–7.

[222] Carus-Wilson and Coleman, England's Export Trade, pp. 36–69; Donkin, op. cit., p. 148.

immoveable, ecclesiastical and secular, present and future".[223] Kirkstall abbey was bankrupt in 1276, and Rievaulx in 1288, while Flaxley fell into receivership three times between those dates. Pipewell's monks, after further disasters in the 1310s, were so ruined that they had to live on black bread and pottage.[224] Despite such experiences – it was hard to get off the back of the tiger – for two hundred years almost all the Cistercian wool dealings were with foreign merchants: first those of France and Flanders, taking their wool to the fairs of Flanders and Champagne and ultimately to Ghent and Ypres and Bruges, then the Cahorsins, offering links to southern Europe, and the Italians, whose galleys then reopened by the end of the thirteenth century the sea-routes through the Straits of Gibraltar to the weavers of Florence and its rivals.

Stewards on other estates, less dependent on wool, borrowed many of the Cistercian practices without stumbling into comparable economic disaster after the epidemics. Most of them came to use central bargaining for their wool sales: bishopric of Winchester manors made the change in the mid-thirteenth century, and Canterbury Cathedral priory followed suit in 1289. Westminster abbey entrusted the bargaining to its treasurer in the wake of the Black Death. On the Glastonbury abbey manors, it was often the chamberlain who handled the wool sales. St Swithun's priory in Winchester, and Bolton priory and the Aumale estates in Yorkshire all used central negotiations. Crowland abbey did the same, usually bargaining with merchants or middlemen at King's Lynn, but at least once sending its agent across the Channel. Battle abbey usually left it to the bailiffs to sell the wool *in patria*, but even there an abbey official might order it to be delivered to a London merchant, as in 1321–2.[225] The other estates imitated the Cistercians also in using carts, not pack-horses, in attending the same fairs, and in shipping from the same ports. Perhaps because their wool was generally of less value, the buyers were less likely to trap them with over-generous credit. Most of the other estates did not deal in *lana collecta* (Bolton was an exception; its profits were noted above), perhaps because the areas where the great Benedictine abbeys had their manors did not produce wool as highly prized as that of Kirkstead, Bruern, or Tintern. They were also more likely to sell to English merchants, even

---

[223] Lloyd, *op. cit.*, pp. 289–90; *CCR, 1288–1296*, pp. 192–5 (the contract is discussed more fully in Lloyd, *op cit.*, pp. 296–8, and in Salzman, *English Trade*, pp. 304–6).

[224] Power, *The Wool Trade*, pp. 43–4.

[225] T. H. Lloyd, *Movement of Wool Prices*, pp. 6, 35, 37; Page, 'Bidentes Hoylandie', pp. 606–7; PRO SC 6/1016/6 (the grain prices show that this must be for 15/16 Edward II, not (as listed) 15/16 Edward III).

if the latter subsequently re-sold to aliens. The Winchester clip of 1251–2 had gone mainly to Bernard Prosperin of Florence, and that of 1254–5 to Walter of Flanders, but the buyers named in subsequent years were Alice Hachard and Jordan the Draper, Adam Thormund, Simon Draper of Winchester, Thomas of Micheldever, Thomas Cok of Abingdon, and, in the 1310s, the great John of Burford, burgess of London. Under the arrangement known as an *arra*, Eynsham abbey in 1268 committed its wool-clip to the Witney merchant Roger Harang until it had paid off his advance of £160 10s. In the early 1270s, forty Winchester merchants had been active in the export of wool, but by the 1330s their number may have fallen as low as fifteen.[226] Glastonbury's customers in the early fourteenth century included Thomas Selide of Andover, Robert Cnoel and several others from Salisbury, Stephen Russel of Winchester, John Pew of Frome – who defaulted on his payment – and an unnamed merchant of Bristol. Combe dealt with a wool buyer from Wantage. Birdbrook sold its 1381–2 wool to John Deighstere of Halstead; in the middle of the following century Longbridge Deverill sold one year to a Glastonbury man, and the next to one from Wells.[227] In these last cases, however, the wool was probably spun, woven, and finished within England. In later years, too, when credit was extended, it was likely to be from the estate to the buyer, and not from the purchaser to the grower. The bishops of Winchester, and doubtless many others, found great difficulty in selling their clip speedily on what had become a buyer's market. Other producers, even those operating on a similar scale, did not blindly follow the Cistercian examples.

The small producer – the lord with a single manor, the villager with a share of common pasture and the duty to fold his sheep on the lord's land – is almost invisible in the manorial records as the great estates which kept their records of arable husbandry had no reason to buy wool unless they dealt in *collecta*. Dealers in wool seldom appear before the courts of manor or borough, and, unlike their social betters before the Exchequer courts, almost never for debt. The Wakefield court rolls for 1348–50 record some exceptions, perhaps as a consequence of the disasters of those years, and show a number of small debts incurred over wool sales for sums like 4s. 8d., 4s. 3d., and 7s. 6d. In wool, as in many other products of the countryside, there was probably a lot of informal,

[226] WPR 159447, 159291B, 159292, 159294, 159300, 159306, 159325, 159327; D. Postles, 'Markets for rural produce in Oxfordshire, 1086–1350', *Mid. Hist.*, XII, 1987, p. 20; Keene, *Medieval Winchester*, I, p. 293.

[227] GAD 11272, 11215, 11216, 8074, 9643, 9624; *Documents of the English Lands of Bec*, ed. Chibnall, pp. 150, 168; WAM 25477; GAD 9838, 9839.

small-scale trading among the members of village and family groups. A sheep-rearing peasant, with a weaving wife and a "spinster" daughter, had within his tenement the essential ingredients of cloth production. Even in a city like Winchester, spinning "was perhaps the most characteristic means of livelihood for respectable women living alone". In a village community, the carders and combers and spinners obviously knew which peasants kept sheep; they may have helped to wash and shear them (as they were commonly obliged to with the demesne flocks). And there were, by the thirteenth century, plenty of fairs and town markets where they could buy what additional fleeces they needed. In the finished cloths, too, much of the trade was in small quantities: the cloth vendors of Coventry in 1397–8 sold an average of 10.7 cloths each, but those in other Warwickshire areas many fewer – 1.4 cloths in Warwick, 1.3 cloths in Stratford-upon-Avon.[228] Bargaining over the wool crop might take place, sight unseen, in London or at Boston fair, the buyer trusting the reputation of the producer and knowing the price that wool from that area normally fetched abroad. A detailed contract (insisting that, for example, the fleeces include no wool from belly or breech, or locks discoloured or torn), and specifying the dates for payment, confirmed the deal. A list like Pegolotti's, prepared in the early fourteenth century for the Bardi, might accelerate the negotiations. It stated the prices appropriate for the best, the middling, and the inferior wools of each abbey, and how many sacks it normally produced. Or the bargain might be struck on the manor, and the costs of hospitality to ease negotiations recorded on the manorial expense account – Longbridge Deverill spent 4s. 9¾d. in 1311–12 on entertaining Stephen Russel when he came *pro lana emenda*, and also supplied cheese for his men and oats for their horses. Or the exporter might buy from a dealer, perhaps using the same one over many years, as Richard Cely did in buying "in Cottyswolde" from William Midsummer of Northleach. Or it might be the lord who travelled to meet the buyers, as the fellows of Merton did when at Newcastle in 1337–8.[229] In the bishopric of Winchester the practice varied. In the early thirteenth century it was the bailiff who sold the clip locally. Then the central authority – probably the steward – negotiated the sales, after the buyer had inspected the wool of each manor or group of manors. The Somersetshire and Oxfordshire manors often stayed outside these central negotiations, because of their remoteness

---

[228] *Wakefield Court Rolls, 1348–50*, ed. Jewell, pp. 2, 60, 63; Keene, *Medieval Winchester*, I, p. 300; R. A. Pelham, 'The cloth markets of Warwickshire during the later middle ages', *Birmingham Arch. Soc.*, LXVI, 1945–6, p. 135 (my calculations).

[229] Lloyd, *Movement of Wool Prices*, pp. 52–61; GAD 9643; *The Cely Papers*, ed. H. E. Malden, Camden 3rd ser., I, 1900, p. 21 *et passim*; *History of Oxford*, ed. Catto, I, p. 341.

and the chance of a local market for their wool, or because the steward hoped they would do better separately. In the fourteenth century the manors usually sent their wool straight to Wolvesey Castle, there to disappear from the records except for the credit allowed to the bailiffs or reeves for its value. Probably it was sold, eventually, directly to a merchant or consortium buying directly from bishop or steward. The lack of income from the "great beam" at the St Giles's fair makes it unlikely that much wool was sold at the fair after the early 1320s. When John of Burford bought most of the bishopric's clip in 1314–15, it was weighed at Alresford, the reeve being allowed four shillings "for the expenses of the merchants weighing the lord's wool there".[230]

The hundred years beginning around 1270 proved the most difficult century for the English wool-grower, at least before Victorian times. Sheep scab, which had been widespread since the early thirteenth century, became much more serious in the 1270s. Heavy mortality among the flocks accompanied it. In September 1269 there had been 14,983 sheep on the bishopric of Winchester manors; in September 1286 there were only 9,338. Two-thirds of the lambs born in 1286 at Crawley, Bishops's Waltham, and East Meon manor died before weaning; at Twyford 441 died out of 453. In some areas the diseases of the 1310s were even more devastating: Crowland abbey virtually stopped keeping sheep, and at Bolton the numbers dropped to a third of what they had been. The wool-growers at least got higher prices in those awful years, for wool which had averaged 3s. 6d. a stone in 1268 was fetching about 5s. 9d. at the end of the 1270s and, after a period of lower prices, reached 6s. 9d. in 1321.[231] But the grower had no such compensation for the other curse, the taxes and controls placed on trade which had formerly been unregulated and duty-free. Merchants had tolerated the "Great and Ancient Custom" of 6s. 8d. a sack imposed on wool exports in 1275, but the 40s. a sack *maltote* of 1294, and the forced loans of 1294 and 1297, came at a time of low prices and pushed them even lower. So did the revived 40s. *maltote* of 1336 (soon to become a regular parliamentary subsidy), more loans and taxes on wool in 1337, and Edward III's cynical seizure and sale of the English merchants' wool at Dordrecht in 1338 (in return for credits to be applied against duties payable on their subsequent exports). Even the most skilful merchants could not make profits to cover such extra charges, except by forcing down the price they paid the growers. The bailiff or steward trying to market export-quality wool in the mid-fourteenth century had to contend with low prices, frequent interruptions to trade during the Hundred Years War, and monopolistic groups of financier-merchants

---

[230] WPR 159329.
[231] WPR 159450A, 159307; Page, 'Bidentes Hoylandie', p. 608; Kershaw, *Bolton Priory*, p. 80.

like the de la Poles of Hull and the Goldbeters of York to whom the
king had virtually sold control of the trade. The 1353 Ordinance of the
Staple, which parliament confirmed as a statute in 1354, regulated the
market more equitably, and, aided by low prices, wool exports held up
reasonably well in the 1350s and 1360s. But thereafter, with prices fairly
firm, exports tailed off – from a high level of perhaps 40,000 sacks a
year to about 20,000 in the 1380s, and to about 10,000 for most of the
fifteenth century. In nearly half of the years between 1400 and 1500
growers averaged no more than 3s. a stone for their wool.[232] This
period of prolonged low prices gave the English cloth industry the
chance to recover from a long domination by foreign textiles. The
weavers of Coggeshall and Lavenham, Frome and Stroud, Totnes and
Exeter, provided the English sheep farmer – most likely by now to be
a *firmarius* renting the demesnes and pastures the lords no longer
bothered to work directly – with local markets for the fleeces, for
making into cloths which suited the characteristics of the local wool.
But, even with lower marketing costs, the producers' margins were too
tight for inefficiency or sentiment on the sheep farms where, as the
Tudor moralists put it, "sheep ate up men".

Two other aspects of animal husbandry were the marketing of dairy
products, and of skins and hides. Its keeping qualities made cheese much
the most important of the former; butter and milk were sold
infrequently and in small quantities. Cheese sales boomed in the early
thirteenth century: in 1210–11 the bishopric of Winchester manors
received about £49 for their cheese, in 1252–3 over £136 (equivalent
to about 40 per cent of the £340 they obtained that year from wool
sales).[233] The manors selling cheese were the manors with flocks of ewes,
for most of the Winchester cheese at that time came from the milk of
sheep, not cows. The purchasers of the cheese were often the buyers of
the wool, in the same or subsequent years. In 1251–2 most manors sold
their cheese to Nicholas Hachard and Jordan the Draper, and in 1254–5
to Nicholas Hachard and Adam Thormund. A few years later, Alice
Hachard and Jordan the Draper, and then Adam Thormund, took over
from the continentals as wool buyers. In the 1270s Simon Draper of
Winchester bought both cheese and wool. Thomas of Micheldever
bought much of the cheese in 1282–3, and most of the wool-clip two
years later.[234] The place most celebrated for cheese in the thirteenth
century was Jervaulx, by the foot of Wensleydale; according to

[232] Fryde, *Wool Accounts of de la Pole*, p. 14; Lloyd, *The English Wool Trade*, pp. 204–7; Lloyd,
Movement of Wool Prices, pp. 41–4.
[233] *Pipe Roll of Winchester 1210–11*, ed. Holt, *passim*; WPR 159291A.
[234] WPR 159447, 159291B, 159292, 159294, 159300, 159305, 159306.

Pegolotti, it also offered for sale more wool than any other Yorkshire abbey except Rievaulx and Fountains.[235] At least two of the Norman abbeys with lands in England had a taste for English ewes' milk cheese, for they listed the duty of carrying cheese to Southampton among the obligations of their tenants at Minchinhampton and Avening (Glos.), Combe and Brixton Deverill (Wilts.), while those at Povington (Dorset) had to carry both cheese and wool to Wareham for shipment to the mother house. One of the bishop's tenants at Crawley had the duty of transporting wool and cheese to Winchester, Southampton, or Bitterne (Hants.), and the obligations of the virgaters at North Waltham and Ecchinswell (Hants.) to carry wool and cheese anywhere within the county could easily have included journeys to the ports.[236] But the production of ewes'-milk cheese inevitably suffered from the sheep disease of later years: at Mere (Wilts.) in 1296–7 the bailiff blamed the poor price of cheese on the weakness of the ewes – *precii nimis modici propter infirmitatem verobarum quam habebant oues matrices*. Flocks much reduced in size obviously produced less milk, and the high mortality among the lambs suggests that the milk may have been inferior. Other regions used cows' milk for cheese, and this probably became more common as the fourteenth century advanced. Richer pastures, and a longer lactation period, often allowed cheese production on a limited scale to continue through the whole year. Combe had made cheese from ewes' milk only between St George's day and Michaelmas, with full production only between 14 May and 14 September. Using cows' milk, Baltonsborough, an abbey manor a few miles south of Glastonbury, made two cheeses a day in June and July, one a day from August to early November, and again from the New Year to the beginning of June, and one every two days in November and December. On poorer pastures, however, and in a more hostile climate, the cows might have adequate milk for only five months or so. On the Bolton priory lands the season lasted only from early May until Michaelmas; with disappointing yields, all the cheese and butter were consumed by the canons and the priory's household until the 1320s.[237]

By the early fourteenth century the marketing of cheese seems to have separated from the marketing of wool, and even on the Winchester manors cows' milk became a more important component. When the policy of leasing cows (and sometimes ewes) to the cowman or

---

[235] *English Historical Documents 1189–1327*, ed. Rothwell, p. 883; Lloyd, *Movement of Wool Prices*, p. 59.

[236] *Charters and Custumals of the Abbey of Holy Trinity, Caen*, ed. M. Chibnall, London, 1982, pp. 72, 84; *Documents of the English Lands of Bec*, ed. Chibnall, pp. 42, 63, 70.

[237] *Accounts of the Earldom of Cornwall*, ed. Midgley, p. 56; *Documents of the English Lands of Bec*, ed. Chibnall, p. 156; GAD 11246; Kershaw, *Bolton Priory*, pp. 101–3.

dairymaid became almost universal, manorial accounts ceased to record cheese sales at all. Only a few Winchester manors sold demesne cheese after the Black Death, and the only good series of cheese prices for the fifteenth century are from Alton Barnes (Wilts.) in the early years and from Alciston (Sussex) in the remainder. Their price levels are so stable that they may be sales *ad hospicium domini*, not market sales. Yet the export trade in cheese continued, even on a large scale, perhaps because the farmers of the cows were selling to wholesalers. A Flemish ship was exporting from London a hundred weys of cheese belonging to English merchants when challenged in 1361, and in 1386 Richard II authorized a serjeant-at-arms and an Ipswich merchant to buy sixty weys of cheese in Essex and Suffolk to send to the Calais garrison. Bristol sometimes shipped it: cheese worth £1 was apparently the only cargo of the *Godhale* of Swinefleet when it left the port in 1324, and an alien merchant, Peter Durant, exported a similar amount with some cloth the next year. But the next record is of a hogshead of cheese worth 13s. 4d. shipped with cloths and two horses to Bordeaux in 1461. From Bristol, clearly, the trade was neither regular nor substantial.[238]

Within England, leasing the cows to *firmarii* swiftly broke up the earlier practices of central bargaining by the great estates. The *firmarius* or *daie* could not easily attend distant markets or fairs unless there was someone else to milk the cows. The trade therefore became more localized. A dairyman might contract at quiet periods to supply at a later date, as John le Herde did on 21 March 1339 for delivery of twelve cheeses to a Colchester man on Midsummer's day, or sell to itinerant cheesemongers or, perhaps, to poulterers who marketed cheese with their other wares in London. Some of those who bought butter and cheese at Writtle were apparently middlemen making purchases for re-sale in the village's market or at Chelmsford fair. This trade was not so insignificant as to escape tolls, such as the ½d. a wey levied at Corbridge and Haydon in the 1330s, or the heavier toll of ¼d. a stone for murage at Durham. A 1430 London ordinance tried to fix the price of butter: eight ounces for a halfpenny from the beginning of May to the beginning of October, six ounces for a halfpenny for the rest of the year. At Exeter, fines for forestalling and regrating dairy products were much more common than for similar offences with poultry: between 1378 and 1388, the mayor's tourn fined 168 persons for the former, and only 45 for the latter.[239] The number was still small, though, in

---

[238] *CCR, 1360–1364*, pp. 215–16; *CCR, 1389–1392*, p. 56; Carus-Wilson, *The Overseas Trade of Bristol*, pp. 169, 170, 216.

[239] Britnell, *Growth and Decline in Colchester*, p. 45; Clark, 'Debt litigation', p. 258; Fraser, 'Trade in the north-east', App. following p. 66; *Cal. London Letter-Book K*, ed. Sharpe, p. 101; Kowaleski, 'Local markets and merchants', p. 204.

comparison with the total fined for brewing offences, or the five or six hundred punished for selling oats by false measure, or for improper dealing in hides and woolfells. None the less, the cheese trade was an important one, and perhaps changed more than most in the fourteenth century when the manors leased their dairy herds and flocks to entrepreneurial *daies* and cowmen.

Britons wore skins before they wove cloth. The leather industries were vital to England and Wales from pre-Roman days until the time of Victoria. Saxon Winchester had named its *Tænnerstret*, like its *Flæscmangerestraete*, before the end of the tenth century, but the distinctions between the butchers and the leatherworkers were not always clear-cut.[240] The relationship between the manorial bailiffs and the tanners was also complicated, for the raw materials reached the eventual consumers by a number of routes. There were three separate leather-making techniques, and they were organized in two distinctive ways.

The bailiff on a manor with mixed husbandry might well have a dozen hides and one or two hundred sheep and lamb skins to sell each year. The thirty-five bishopric of Winchester manors sold in 1210–11 242 hides of large animals, and 4,276 sheep and lamb skins, at prices as high as 2s. for a single oxhide at Woodhay (Hants.).[241] Very nearly all were the skins of animals which had died of disease, not of those slaughtered for the table. Tanners of later years apparently preferred to get their hides from the butchers, but much of the thirteenth-century industry depended on the hides flayed from beasts dead from natural causes. This was certainly the case with the sheep skins, for too few muttons and ewes were sent for slaughter for their skins to satisfy demands for light leathers and for parchment. Manors selling a lot of hides *in grosso*, or disposing of very large numbers at identical prices, were probably selling to wholesalers, or even to tanners with capital coming "up country" looking for hides to keep their pits and tanks busy. According to one scholar, however, most of the trade was in the hands of wholesalers who obtained almost all their hides directly from butchers. Sales of oak bark might be profitable for the lords, and sometimes manors sold tallow and lime as well. If, however, the manor sold its fattened animals alive, whether to butchers directly, or indirectly through drovers and graziers, town and market officials regulated what happened to the hides after slaughter. The butcher usually had to offer the hide or skin for sale as well as the carcase. Most towns forbade him any part in leather-making beyond flaying the hide.

---

[240] *Winchester in the Early Middle Ages*, ed. Biddle, pp. 234, 235.
[241] *Pipe Roll of Winchester 1210–11*, ed. Holt, pp. 99, 101.

At markets and fairs the hide trade could be hotly contested: to protect the local industry, the king granted to the burgesses of Montgomery that the burgesses of Shrewsbury and Ludlow should not be allowed to buy hides there. Even within a city there might be discrimination: Newcastle allowed its poorer burgesses to buy only the hides of young animals whose ears were longer than their horns. In Winchester only freemen could buy undressed hides or skins, and they were forbidden to take them out of the city. In the early fifteenth century the butcher Richard Hunte had difficulty collecting debts incurred by a tanner and a parchment-maker who had bought their raw materials from him, and the leather trades of Winchester were facing illegal competition from tanners of Overton and St Mary Bourne, who were selling hides secretly in inns.[242]

The *Seneschaucy* urged that the skins of dead sheep should be sold along with the wool, the same buyer taking both. Manorial accounts do not show whether this practice was widespread in earlier years, but the Celys were certainly buying both through their dealers in the fifteenth century. A few accounts are more specific: Harston in the 1310s, with a lot of woolfells from sheep which had died of murrain, sold the skins at Royston or to a Haverhill man, perhaps a chandler.[243] Sometimes accounts list small transactions alongside much larger ones; perhaps the buyers were villagers working part-time at making leather by the simpler processes. These were relatively cheap and speedy, needing little more than a vessel large enough to hold the skins while they were soaked in whale and fish oils, and even that tank was not required if the worker "tawed" the skins by rubbing them repeatedly with a mixture of alum, salt, flour, and egg yolk. Normally the person who tawed or oil-dressed the skin would also complete the subsequent stages of manufacture – into gloves, or purses, or the supple "uppers" for shoes, and so might be the only intermediary between the bailiff or shepherd and the buyer of the finished product.

The heavy leather industry was very different. Having purchased their cattle and horse hides, the tanners soaked them in solutions of lime to loosen the hair and to make the fibres absorb the tanning liquids better. Having scraped the hides clear of hair and fat, the tanners "bated" them by soaking in mixtures of bird or dog excrement and

---

[242] M. Kowaleski, 'Town and country in late medieval Exeter: the hide and leather trade', in *Work in Towns, 800–1800*, ed. P. Corfield and D. Keene, Leicester, forthcoming; *Select Cases concerning the Law Merchant*, III, ed. Hall, p. 142; C. M. Fraser, 'Medieval trading restrictions in the north-east', *AA*, 4th. ser. XXXIX, 1961, p. 139; Keene, *Medieval Winchester*, I, pp. 288, 289.

[243] *Walter of Henley*, ed. Oschinsky, p. 273; *Cely Papers*, ed. Malden, pp. 8, 12–13, 31–2; BL Add. Roll 18522.

water (to soften them), and then immersed them for months or even years in oak-bark solutions.[244] The equipment might be expensive – a 1340 valuation reckoned one tanner's equipment as worth £8 9s. 2d. – and the tanner had to wait a long time for any return on what he had spent on buying the hides.[245] Needing a regular cash-flow, the tanner tried to purchase hides at various seasons through the year (though, of course, the beasts were sent to market at irregular intervals and seasons), so that there should always be some ready for sale. This made necessary several pits or tanks for the soaking processes, and made the large tanneries more likely to be profitable. The tanner needed skill and experience, for the leather could be ruined if left too long in any of the liming, bating, or tanning liquids. The tanner sold his product as "crust" leather; then it would go to curriers for them to soften it with oil and waterproof it with tallow, shave it to the thickness needed for a specific purpose, and perhaps stain it and grain it. Again, this was a skilled craft.[246] In later times, at least, much of this was run on the "putting-out" system, by middlemen who were in effect leather merchants, and in some places it was the tanners themselves who were the middlemen. Town regulations normally forbade tanners to be curriers, or curriers to be saddlers or cordwainers.

The interdependence of the stages of the heavy leather industry made it appropriate for urban communities, or preferably their outskirts, with a river for water and a wind to disperse the smells. Colchester seemingly had thirteen tanners in 1301, including the town's most heavily taxed resident, and there were several others in associated crafts. There were also a few in nearby villages, threatening competition. In many places bark supply could be a serious problem, and it could be easier to take the hides to the bark than transport the bark to the hides. In a later period, tanning 1 lb of leather needed 4 or 5 lb of oak bark (taken normally from trees already felled, though in Yorkshire the barkers stripped the bark from living trees).[247] The Glastonbury abbey tannery in 1274–5 bought sixty-eight hides, for a total of £7 11s., and had to spend 41s. 3d. on buying bark to process them – fourteen cart loads, two *plaustrum* loads, and twenty-one *summs* – and a further 5s. 8d. on carrying the bark to the tanner. When the hides were ready, Osmund the tanner hired a horse and took the "crust" leather to fairs

---

[244] A Norwich tanner, Richard de Stalham, was fined in 1289 and again in 1291 for tanning with ash-tree bark (*Leet Jurisdiction at Norwich*, ed. W. Hudson, Selden Soc., v, 1891, pp. 28, 39).

[245] Thrupp, *Merchant Class*, p. 111.

[246] This summary is based on the description by L. A. Clarkson, 'The organization of the English leather trade in the late sixteenth and seventeenth centuries', *EcHR*, 2nd ser. XIII, 1960, pp. 246–7.   [247] Faull and Moorhouse, eds., *West Yorkshire*, III, p. 688.

some distance away – to *Homedene* in May, Sherborne (seventeen miles) and Tintinhull (twelve miles) in July, and Ilchester (ten miles) in August. During the year he sold sixty hides for £10 4s. 9d., having bought them for £6 17s. 8d. A third batch, of eight hides, remained unsold at the end of the account, and would add a little surplus, but the profits on the first sixty were almost entirely consumed by the cost of bark, by Osmund's salary of 10s. a year and his lad's of 4s., and by small expenses such as wax for his candles, and his travels to the four fairs.[248] Battle abbey seems to have run its Marley tannery more profitably, for it yielded up to £20 net in a single year. This tannery bought hides on the open market, as well as those "sold" to it by the larderer from the animals slaughtered for the monastery and its guests.[249]

The best evidence for the hide trade in operation again comes from Exeter, where the market courts regularly listed those who bought and sold hides and woolfells outside the market place, or without being freemen of the city. Over a quarter of the offenders were not Exeter residents, though most of these outsiders lived within five miles of the city. Some came from further afield – Christopher Tanner and John Ivoun of Tiverton (the latter active in Exeter's hide market for over fourteen years), Hugh Tanner of Ottery St Mary, Roger Tanner of Bradninch. In the Exeter region the tanners were prominent as middlemen, buying from the bailiffs and villagers and rural butchers of east Devon, processing the hides, and selling the "crust" leather to the cordwainers and saddlers, who then hired curriers to finish it to their requirements. In other cases the cordwainers seem to have bought raw hides and skins directly from the butchers, and they probably then hired tanners to prepare the leather for them.[250] And alongside this heavy-leather industry there were the other craftsmen, buying skins from the manors or wholesalers, tawing with alum or dressing with oil, and producing on the same premises the gloves and purses for the townsmen of Exeter and the villagers of the region. Around York, though, the interaction between town and country was somewhat different: hides tanned elsewhere were brought into the city for sale, but tanners from the region came to the city market to buy untanned hides for dressing outside – perhaps because there were so many York butchers with skins for sale. The city's tanners and glovers and

---

[248] Britnell, *Growth and Decline in Colchester*, p. 14; L. A. Clarkson, 'The English bark trade, 1660–1830', *AHR*, XXII, 1974, pp. 136–7; GAD 11244 m. 35.

[249] Searle, *Lordship and Community*, p. 310. Searle regarded the Marley tannery as evidence of the industry's rural nature; it was, however, less than a mile downwind of a major town. There are many instances of tanners working within towns, or on the fringes of them.

[250] Kowaleski, 'Local markets and merchants', pp. 346–9. Maryanne Kowaleski kindly supplied me with additional information.

parchment-makers and cordwainers acted together to ensure that only good hides were brought into York. Despite, or perhaps because of, such restrictions, the number of leatherworkers among the city's freemen declined by some 40 per cent in the fifteenth century.[251]

Some of the hides and skins sold in York's market went to exporters. Edward III lumped this export trade together with that in wool and woolfells under the various Staple ordinances, channelling it through Calais even though this Staple town was not near a traditional market for hides from the British Isles. Ireland was a major source. In 1390 one Bristol merchant bought 12 lasts (that is, 240 hides) in Limerick and Galway to ship to Calais, and two Drogheda burgesses sent a shipload to Picardy in *La Marie Welfare* of Dartmouth; the following year, Drogheda sent hides to Gascony in *Le Pietre* of Furness and *La Marie* of Milford, and *La Margarete* of Dartmouth carried a load to Westminster. Four ships which docked in Bristol between 16 and 18 August 1437 carried hides and skins from Ireland. Norman and other foreign merchants were probably among the leather-buyers at Battle's fairs. The three identified fairs at which Osmund sold Glastonbury's hides were all on the roads to the south coast. The Southampton brokage books record a large trade through the port, with calf and lamb skins shipped out by the thousand, and an even larger import trade including the hides of exotic animals as well.[252] But the history of hide exports is too remote from agrarian marketing for further discussion here.

F. MARKETING THE PRODUCE OF WOODLAND AND PASTURE

Woodland supplied the lord with timber for his buildings, fuel for his fires, wood for his ploughs and carts, bark for his tannery, rough pasture for his cattle, and mast for his pigs. The lord's woods also had to meet the kindred needs of villagers and nearby townsmen as well. Mature trees had high capital value: selling the timber became a quick way to pay the debts awaiting a new bishop, or the costs of a campaign. In the first year of Bishop Raleigh, fourteen of the Winchester manors each sold timber worth £10 or more, a sum recorded only twice in the seventeen surviving pipe rolls of his predecessor Peter des Roches (once at Wargrave and once at Woodhay).[253] War expenses in 1301–2 may

---

[251] *VCH Yorks., City of York*, pp. 90–1.

[252] *CCR, 1389–1392*, pp. 33, 195, 258, 270; Carus-Wilson, *The Overseas Trade of Bristol*, pp. 204–5; *Brokage Book, 1439–40*, ed. Bunyard, *passim*; *Brokage book, 1443–44*, ed. Coleman, *passim*.

[253] WPR 159287. Details of timber sales were collected during a sabbatical leave from St Thomas More College, University of Saskatchewan, with the aid of a grant from the Social Sciences and Humanities Research Council of Canada; this help is gratefully acknowledged.

have been the reason why Chesterford (Essex) sold thirty-seven acres of underwood for £18 10s., *per brevem Comitis.*[254]

With low labour costs and self-renewing soil, mature timber rewarded its owner richly. South Frith (Kent) earned for Elizabeth de Burgh some £390 from timber in 1333–4, £149 in 1334–5, £66 in 1340–1, £156 in 1341–2, £142 in 1342–3, and £212 in 1345–6. Hindolveston (Norfolk) sold timber for £213 in 1272–3 to help repair Norwich Cathedral priory after a riot.[255] Bungay (Suffolk) sold timber for £114 in 1300–1, Chepstow for £71 in 1303–4, and Ivinghoe for £84 in 1309–10. Knowle in 1302–3 made £90 for Westminster abbey by selling *in grosso* 414 small oaks. Selling trees from an assart brought Downton £52 in 1251–2, and clearing the Chiltern woodlands gave Ivinghoe £10 or more in most of the years between 1305–6 and the Black Death. Peterborough abbey sold two acres of *grossi bosci* in 1404–5 for £20. Weston (Herts.) obtained £6 for one acre of *bosci* in 1396–7, Hendon (Middx) 43s. 4d. per acre in 1372–3, and Stevenage (Herts.) £3 an acre in 1377–8 for timber it sold to Carmelite friars.[256] Birchanger (Essex) sold four acres of *bosci* for £7 6s. 8d. in 1400–1; two years later its neighbour Takeley sold four acres for £10 to Robert Cokerton and Thomas Flemyng. These were all genuine sales, not transfers *ad hospicium domini*, but only rarely do the accounts name these wholesale purchasers – men such as that versatile dealer Walter Boon, who bought ten acres from Chevington in 1421–2 for £16 13s. 4d. Richard Syward, another general dealer who sold wine, tar, and oats to Peterborough, also purchased timber from it; so did John Paris of Rockingham (for £30), the bailiff of Oundle (for £40), and Robert Dyghton, merchant of Lincoln (for £90).[257] But many of the transactions were very modest bargains between the lord and the villagers. West Wycombe recorded eighteen deals in 1388–9, worth £6 8s. 0d. in all, for sums varying from 20d. for one beech tree to 20s. for seven. In the same year, fifteen different men bought wood from Billingbear for a total of only £1 15s. 4d., and twenty-six bought beech trees from Ivinghoe for £4 5s. 3d. between them; two years later, thirty-seven buyers together paid Ivinghoe £8 8s. 7d. for more of the same.[258]

As well as these sales to outsiders and the local villagers, estates used their woodlands to supply the needs of the co-manors. The woods near

---

[254] PRO SC 6/827/24.

[255] PRO SC 6/890/26, 27; 891/5, 6, 7, 8; Rackham, *Ancient Woodland*, pp. 157–8.

[256] PRO SC 6/991/26, 992/8; WPR 159325; WAM 27701; WPR 159447; *Account Rolls of Peterborough*, ed. Greatrex, p. 114; PRO SC 6/873/25; WAM 32588, 26352.

[257] New College, Oxford, 5581, 7011; Suffolk RO, E3/15.3/2.30; *Account Rolls of Peterborough*, ed. Greatrex, p. 177.   [258] WPR 159395, 159398.

Highclere, particularly the tract known as *La Wasshe*, sent timber to bishopric of Winchester manors as distant as Witney and Adderbury, some 40 and 53 miles away; even the Merton manor of Cuxham bought shingles there in 1297–8, though it more commonly fetched its wood from Ibstone, a co-manor a few miles away on the Chiltern ridge. Winchester's Chiltern manors of Ivinghoe and West Wycombe, and its Thames-side manor of Wargrave, furnished the bishop's needs down-river at Southwark; the first two shipped through Marlow, while Wargrave loaded firewood at its river bank as early as 1210–11. The Farley woods supplied not only Merton's other Surrey manors but even Elham in Kent: having borrowed carts from as far away as Cuxham, the Elham bailiff in 1344 carted the timber for a new grange from Farley to Greenwich, paid 3s. 4d. for a place there to store it, then £8 for its shipment around the coast to Folkestone, 11s. 7d. for unloading it there, and 4s. 4d. for hiring a watchman to guard it for twenty-six days while the Elham carts moved it to its destination six miles inland. This odyssey was all the more remarkable as Elham lay alongside Lyminge Forest in a county still well-wooded. Some of the crown's gifts of timber seem equally illogical – from Cumberland to Bury St Edmunds, for example – but these may have been outsize trees begged for major building projects.[259] Possibly Merton found it easier to pay for the transport than to purchase standing trees in Kent, or possibly the county had no timber of appropriate species or maturity, or possibly the college knew of no estate selling timber; more likely, Merton used the Farley woods so that the Elham bailiff and carpenter could select and fell the trees best suited to their plans. The payment Harwell made to a carpenter in 1378–9 specifically included the cost of selecting the trees at Billingbear, some twenty-five miles away.[260] Whatever the reason, these long inter-manorial transfers of timber warn one not to take massive sales of timber as evidence of a plentiful supply everywhere at every time.

Where beechwoods predominated, manors often bought the oak timbers preferred for major construction, not only for great beams but even for laths. Bishops Sutton in 1355–6 paid £20 for 366 oaks, and in the same year West Wycombe spent nearly £7 on buying oak and ash. In 1377–8 Rimpton, to build a new oxshed, bought oaks from Roger Dene and Thomas Knoel for £5 6s. 8d., and elms from Thomas Burch for 11s. 10d. In 1309–10 Ivinghoe – despite sales of dead wood and hawthorns for over £84 – spent £33 1s. 3d. net for new timber, after selling the loppings and bark from it for £6 4s. 7d., and also bought laths at St Albans and Dunstable. In 1362–3 Witney made £11 10s.

[259] MCR 5814; *Pipe Roll of Winchester 1210–11*, ed. Holt, p. 85; MCR 5298, 5300; Rackham, *Ancient Woodland*, pp. 152–3.   [260] WPR 159386.

from the sale of trimmings and bark from timber it had bought for new buildings. Sometimes manors purchased young trees for planting – such as the 700 poplars Bishopstoke bought in 1327–8 – but more commonly paid for the digging up and replanting of self-sown seedlings: poplars, hawthorns, and willows along the banks of ditches, or young ash to create what Highclere was calling by 1390–1 *la asshpark*.[261]

The cash market for timber, though, passed quickly from scarcity to surplus, either through the collapse of demand or sudden over-supply. The bishopric of Winchester manors together averaged some £80 a year in the fourteenth century from the sale of trees, underwood, loppings, firewood, and bark, but this dropped to about £7 in 1348–9 and an average of around £13 a year over the first six years following the plague's arrival. The great storm of 1361–2 blew down trees on almost all the bishop's manors: Bishop's Waltham, Farnham, Marwell, Culham, West Wycombe, and Ivinghoe were still selling off the trees in 1366–7, and Ivinghoe did not complete the task until 1369–70, even though its fallen beeches must have been thoroughly rotten by then.[262]

By the fourteenth century, with the assarting movement almost over, selling *subboscum* or underwood provided more income for most manors than the occasional sale of great trees. Coppiced woodland or alder thickets provided poles for fences and hurdles, laths for buildings, and most of the fuel for heating and cooking. Between 1270 and 1360 underwood in eastern England increased in value by about 6d. per acre per year, and perhaps rather more thereafter.[263] Early records show it sold by the cart-load – Twyford in 1225–6 took 8s. for forty-eight cart-loads of *subbosci* – but manors later sold it by the acre, the sales by Cheriton (Hants.) in 1245–6 at 2s., 2s. 6d., and 3s. per acre being probably the earliest whose records have survived. Sometimes the prices were very much higher. The £56 13s. 4d. taken by Wabridge and Sapley (Hunts.) in 1439 for thirty acres of *subbosci* suggest either some very old underwood or else a scribal error, but Ditchingham (Norfolk) in 1268–9 sold 65 acres for £20 12s. 2d., Lopham (Norfolk) 48 acres in 1270–1 for nearly £23, Merdon 27 acres in 1388–9 for 10s. an acre, and Monkleigh (Devon) one acre for 20s. in 1393–4.[264] The buyers were villagers, often by the dozen. Bourton-on-the-Hill in 1356–7 sold 13¼ acres and two "angles" of *subbosci* to twenty-eight different men for a total of 62s. 8d., and Stevenage in 1377–8 sold 2

[261] WPR 159366, 159385, 159325, 159373, 159340, 159398.

[262] WPR 159372, 159377, 159379.   [263] Rackham, *Ancient Woodland*, pp. 166–7.

[264] WPR 159280, 159288; PRO SC 6/885/28, 933/20, 937/29; WPR 159395; Dean & Chapter Archives, Exeter, 1133.

acres to ten different buyers for 19s. 3d. The Bury St Edmunds manor
of Rickinghall (Suffolk) was particularly careful in recording how its
underwood was used – that the *subboscum* cut in 1336–7 excluded that
from 4½ acres used for the hedges in the wood and on the manor, and
¼ acre given to the *famuli*, while the 31 acres sold in 1338–9 for
£7 11s. 7d. left out one acre allowed for the roads and marshland in the
area felled, and also the acres cut for the manor's own needs. The
1400–1 account records a payment of 8d. to John Bradynham for
measuring the underwood sold, and several accounts have full lists of
purchasers. Of the eighteen who bought *subboscum* in 1384–5, seven
were repeat buyers or tenants of Rickinghall, and eleven were
apparently outsiders. Sibton abbey also sold underwood both to locals
and also to outsiders: thirteen of those who bought in 1363–4 did so
again at least once in the next eight years, whereas twelve did not.
Among Sibton's regular customers were local craftsmen – John le
Tyler, William le Smyth, William le Masoun, and William le Mellere.
Occasionally a manor had to buy an acre or so of underwood, as
Bishopstone regularly did in Cranborne Chase to get sticks for hurdles
and fencing.[265]

While underwood provided raw materials for many of the rural
artisans, another important use was as fuel. Here it supplemented and
partly replaced the trimmings of the great trees, the branches blown
down by the wind, and the other casual sources. Where a lot of mature
timber had been felled, even the *escheats* could reach a valuable total –
£12 16s. 4d. at Kelsale (Suffolk) in 1293–4, £14 2s. 2d. at Lopham two
years later. In the fourteenth century, more commonly, bailiffs and
woodwards had these trimmings and much of the *subbosci* made into
faggots, for transport *ad hospicium domini*, for sale in the market town,
or for sale in the woods or parks where they were cut and bound
together. Selling on the site became more common after the Black
Death as transport costs increased. Chevington in 1347–8 received 15d.
a hundred for faggots sold in the woods, and 20d. a hundred for those
sold in Bury St Edmunds; by 1386–7 those sold in Outwood *sine
cariagio* fetched 18d., while those delivered *cum cariagio* cost 3s. a
hundred.[266]

The numbers could be high. Bearpark (Durham) made 53,000
faggots for 64s. 3d. in 1302–3. Hendon (Middx) made 12,475 faggots
and 45,725 "baneyns" in 1346–7, Hampstead (Middx) 13,500
"baneyns" and 837 faggots in 1375–6; for both, making faggots for
Westminster abbey's brewery and bakehouse was a major part of their

[265] WAM 8285, 26352; BL Add. Roll 63515, 63517, 63567, 63553, 63555, 63556, 63557, BL
Add. Ms. 34560; WPR 159388, 159389.
[266] PRO SC 6/1000/18, 938/9; Suffolk RO, E3/13.3/2.7, 2.16.

economic activities. Earnwood (Salop) made 60,000 "*talwode*" in 1386–7 for £9, spent a further £5 12s. 6d. in carrying them to the Severn, and sold them there for £36. As well as faggots, "baneyns" or "bavins", and "talwode", the bundles might be called "astells", "tosards", "splints", "fardels", "billets", or "kidells". Heckley (Hants.) called them *focalia*, or, confusingly, *lignis*; an early Winchester account called them *busci*.[267] Some terms, such as "talwode", more properly belong to logs, but manors were often inconsistent in labelling them: Leatherhead (Surrey) in 1345, for example, sold *faggotti vocantur banayne*. As with the underwood sold by the quarter-acre, many of the buyers were among the humblest of householders. Claret in 1347–9 sold 700 faggots to the miller, and 150 to Alice Klipping, but the other villagers bought only 25 each, or at most 50.[268]

A few manors sold laths for wattle-and-daub construction, and a smaller number produced sawn timber. Heckfield (Hants.) supplied oak boards for New College and for some of the college's manors in nearby counties. Islip (much nearer to Oxford than Heckfield) sent oak boards to the other Westminster manors of Todenham (Glos.) and Sutton-under-Brailes (Glos.). Far more commonly, though, manors bought the sawn timber they needed, particularly the *estrichbords* from the Baltic. Some fetched them from King's Lynn or other east-coast ports, or bought them at Stourbridge fair; most probably got them from timber dealers in the market towns, who were themselves likely to be supplied through the networks which also handled grain and fish traffic. King's Lynn was so much the centre of the timber trade that South Frith in 1332–3 shipped beech boards there from Kent, rather than to London. Inland, Reading, and Stratford-upon-Avon were frequent sources of sawn timber: Heyford (Oxon.) bought 92 oak boards at Stratford in 1382–3, and paid 32s. 7½d. for rafters there in 1428–9. Woolford bought a cart body there for 18d. in 1327–8, and allowed the bailiff and carter a further 9d. in expenses; the bailiff returned in 1329–30 to buy hurdles, and in 1343–4 for timber for house repairs, paying 39s. for the wood and 12d. in toll. Monkton Deverill bought laths at Shaftesbury in 1412–13 and in 1434–5, on the latter occasion paying 5s. for 525 and 8d. for their carriage over nine miles.[269] For building a new grange in 1295–6, Holywell bought boards and other timber in Oxford, Woodstock, and Wallingford, in thirty-two separate transactions. In other years it bought boards at Bradfield (Berks.); Cuxham also made timber purchases there, and at Aldermaston,

---

[267] The Prior's Kitchen, Durham, Dean & Chapter Enrolled Accounts, 1302–3; WAM 32559, 32497; PRO SC 6/967/8; Bodleian Library, Queen's College Rolls 215, 228; WPR 159277 (West Wycombe).   [268] MCR 5725; PRO SC 6/838/23.

[269] New College, Oxford, 6288, 6329; MCR 4386, 4388, 4400; GAD 9695, 9705.

Wallingford, and Reading.[270] Other manors bought sawn wood from village sawyers, or hired them by the day to cut up demesne timber for the manor's needs.

Woodland also supplied charcoal and bark from the trees felled for other purposes, or, very occasionally, in order to provide charcoal for the forges of the Weald or the Forest of Dean, as probably with the £139 received by Trelleck (Mon.) in 1328–9, £18 by Chepstow in 1292–3, and £11 by South Frith in 1350–1. After 1356–7 South Frith leased its smithy at *Tendele* to Richard Colpeper, with the right to make 50 "dozens" of charcoal, for £13 6s. 8d. a year. As "sea-coal" became used more widely even by blacksmiths, and as iron from Spain displaced the local product even around Durham, the references to charcoal grow rarer in the manorial accounts. In 1408–9, though, the Canterbury Cathedral priory treasurer spent over £95 on making and transporting from the priory's own woods 77,000 faggots and "talwode", 332 cart-loads of firewood, and 140 qr of charcoal – not for sale but for the monks' own use.[271]

Despite its importance for tanning, bark seldom earned much in return for the cost of stripping it. Trelleck, in the year of its record charcoal income, made £10 1s. by selling bark to the abbot of Tintern (who must have been in the tanning trade, like other Cistercians at Fountains and Beaulieu). Castle Rising (Norfolk) in 1452–3 sold six cart-loads of bark, stripped from 61 oaks, to Thomas Sherman of King's Lynn for 28s., and Earnwood sold eight loads for 20s. in 1373–4. The bark of 40 oaks felled for Westminster abbey at Claygate (Surrey) in 1320–1 fetched 13s. 4d., that of 35 oaks cut at Bearpark in 1340–1, 11s. 8d.[272] When lords or bailiffs sold tracts of timber by the parcel or by the acre, the buyers of course had the bark rights, but often sold them to the specialist "barkers", who stripped the trunks and supplied the tanners.

All this evidence (which could be multiplied many times) leaves several questions unanswered. One cannot safely extrapolate from the marketing arrangements for other products. Great timber, with a growth cycle of eighty or a hundred years, was not a regular crop; even the underwood and coppices (at least after 1300) were seldom cut at less than five-year intervals. A 1374 jury investigating the assets of Walter of Myldercombe, in debt for £500, reported that he owned ten acres of great timber, but because it was not mature its only value that year was 10d. for pannage.[273] Heavy trunks could hardly be carried from

[270] MCR 4467, 4496, 5830, 5836, 5840, 5842.
[271] PRO SC 6/926/8, 922/5, 891/10, 14; Cathedral Library, Canterbury, Obedientiaries T1.
[272] PRO SC 6/933/5, 967/3; WAM 27204; Durham Enrolled Accounts, 1340–1.
[273] Rackham, *Ancient Woodland*, p. 141; PRO C 131/21.

market to market in search of buyers. Major sales of capital assets would not be left to the discretion of a local bailiff or reeve or woodward, yet one does not find much evidence for the participation by lord or steward in arranging the transactions, or of the payment of purchase money to anyone but the local official. How did the sellers of timber contact the buyers, and who made the first move, particularly for the large transactions? Probably bailiffs or woodwards could use local markets to make it known that a few trees blown down or branches broken by storms were for sale in the demesne woods, but this could not have sufficed for major sales. If the lord needed money urgently, and was selling from several woods at once, the difficulties must have increased, especially in the thirteenth century while assarting was still widespread. Possibly the social activities of the lords – at the king's court, at tournaments, in parliaments, or county courts – might have passed the word among landholders. Bishops or deans with building projects in hand might have used the consecration of a new bishop to make him an offer he could not refuse. But this is only speculation. Even with more modest sums one cannot know whether it was the buyer or the seller who made the first approach, as, for example, when the manor of Oldington (Worcs.) in 1284–5 sold timber worth in all £19 3s. 4d. to the cellarers of Worcester Cathedral priory and of Tewkesbury abbey; what had they in common, and where did they meet? When John Sadeler of Watlington in 1390–1 bought nineteen beech trees for £3 from West Wycombe, nine miles away, did he know that they were for sale, or did he seek out the bailiff to persuade him to sell? Or was his family, despite the surname, in the timber business? A William Sadeler of Watlington had joined in 1366–7 with a man from Ibstone and another from Medmenham to buy 331 beeches from Merton's manor at Ibstone, but the price – £12 in all, payable in three instalments – suggests a rather modest operation.[274]

Selling firewood and faggots was easier, for these could be carted to market instead of being sold in the woods where they had been cut. Woodwards could leave the *subboscum* uncut, to gather value, until buyers came along (though this might disrupt a cropping cycle). One would expect the same buyers to come back season after season to purchase an area of underwood in the source nearest to their homes; the few surviving lists of buyers, as at Rickinghall and on the Sibton abbey estates, suggest that the trade was divided fairly evenly between regular and casual customers.

Again, while some of the timber buyers made purchases worth scores or even hundreds of pounds, one knows little about them or the

[274] PRO SC 6/1070/6; WPR 159398; MCR 5112, 5114, 5115.

chains of supply they forged. The frequent sales *in grosso* imply that many were wholesalers or middlemen, yet not so wealthy that they could always pay spot cash. Sibton abbey in 1363–4 specifically recorded that W. le Rede and his companions had paid in full the £11 16s. 8d. they had promised, and that Robert Roliolp paid £10 in part-settlement of a timber deal listed in the previous account. The Peterborough receiver's account for 1504–5 includes payments for six pieces of woodland, at contracted prices ranging from £20 to £90; only one of the purchases was paid in full, and two of the others remained unsettled at the end of the following year. At humbler levels the trade kept largely out of sight. Wood sellers were not prominent at fairs: St Ives in 1278 had only two, paying 1s. each towards the total stall rent of £7 11s. 8d.[275] The London court records barely notice them – some Thames Street dwellers of the craft of *buscariorum* in 1300, a Cornhill man forestalling timber in Kingston and Southwark on its way to London in 1306, a carter warned in 1375 for using an iron-shod cart to bring a load into the city, contrary to a 1277 ordinance. Winchester, though, had more difficulty in obtaining its wood supplies, which came from further afield than the grain or livestock sold there. There were attempts to regulate the firewood market (which until the Black Death had been held inside the cathedral cemetery), but forestalling was common in the 1360s, especially by bakers and cooks and perhaps also dyers; apparently they bought in bulk outside the city to heat their ovens and vats, and sold the surplus from their houses. Smiths, cooks, and innkeepers – who ran a brisk retail trade in it – were among those whom Winchester prosecuted for forestalling charcoal. Bristol forbade strangers to leave timber "in the common places next the Quay" for more than five days, and ordered that firewood, like coal, straw, and hay, should be sold by the load only in "St Mary Port Street, the street before St Peter's church, Winch Street beyond the Pillory, and St Thomas Street". Leicester merely regulated the price at which charcoal might be sold – 7d. a sack in winter, and 6d. in summer.[276] Perhaps the unhurried and predictable nature of the trade (except in an abnormally long or cold winter) allowed most townsmen to buy their fuel supplies from nearby woods, without paying more dearly in a local market. For woodland products more than most commodities, direct sales offered advantages. Carpenters, turners, wheelwrights, and other craftsmen could select their trees and cut and

[275] *The Sibton Abbey Estates*, ed. Denney, p. 113; *Account Rolls of Peterborough*, ed. Greatrex, pp. 177, 191; Moore, *Fairs*, p. 147.

[276] *Cal. Early Mayor's Court Rolls*, ed. Thomas, pp. 85, 245; *Cal. Plea and Memo. Rolls 1364–1381*, ed. Thomas, p. 186; Keene, *Medieval Winchester*, I, pp. 265, 270; *Little Red Book of Bristol*, ed. Bickley, II, pp. 28–9, 54–5; *English Historical Documents 1327–1485*, ed. Myers, p. 579.

trim them to their needs, while villagers who bought and cut parcels of underwood, or who bought faggots in the woods, saved many of the labour and transport costs, and the market tolls as well.

Apart from small occasional revenues, for wild honey, or for a good crop of nuts like that which earned Bitterne (Hants.) 20s. 6d. in 1223–4, the woods also provided the manors with rough pasture. Domesday Book had assessed woodland by the number of pigs that could be pannaged there, but this underestimated the value. At irregular intervals, oak and beech produced heavy crops of acorns and beech-mast, and for a few weeks the woods fed hundreds of pigs where there were usually only a few dozen. Instead of a small sum, levied from the customary tenants at the rate of a penny or two per pig for the autumn, woodwards might collect windfall sums like the £14 6s. 9d. paid by "outsiders" at Bishops Sutton in 1312–13, the £15 16s. 5d. collected by Weston before tithe in 1297–8, £26 13s. 4d. at Petworth (Sussex) in 1347–8, and £29 7s. 9d. at South Frith in 1332–3. A lower total, the £11 3s. collected by Lopham in 1270–1, included 479 pigs at 3d., 316 hogs at 2d., and 207 piglets at 1d.[277] Where did they all come from, especially as mast-years tended to occur simultaneously on many manors in the same region (as on the Winchester manors in 1312–13 and 1347–8)? Peasants could not multiply their pigs overnight. The extra pigs can only have come from beyond the village or even the region. Local markets may have spread the news of mast, but sometimes this was not enough: Bishops Sutton in 1326–7, while taking £9 4s. 5d. for pannage, noted that it received no more because of the lack of buyers. Wellow (Somerset) took nothing in pannage in 1351–2 *quia custumarii non habent porcos.* Unassisted, news of mast might spread too slowly; Adderbury therefore fairly regularly sent a lad to Ivinghoe, thirty-three miles away, to ask if there were any pannage there.[278]

Tenants' pigs thus provided a small regular income, which sometimes (as on Winchester's Taunton manors) turned into a customary rent, and occasional mast-years brought much larger sums from pig-owning outsiders fattening their animals before the November killing. Some manors varied this pattern: Damerham (Hants.) allowed oxen and sheep to be pannaged as well as pigs, and Crawley in 1406–7 took 14s. in pannage for 23 cows and 15 *boviculi*, at 6d. per cow and 2d. per bullock for the Hokeday term. Some manors sold the mast itself, rather than the permission to put the pigs in the woodland: Bishop's Waltham

---

[277] WPR 159278; 159327; PRO SC 6/873/19; *Ministers' Accounts of the Manor of Petworth, 1347–1353*, ed. L. F. Salzman, Sussex Rec. Soc., LV, 1955, p. 3; PRO SC 6/890/25, 937/29.
[278] WPR 159339; PRO SC 6/974/23; WPR 159353.

frequently did this when the mast came from the trees in the bishop's park, as in 1318–19, 1320–1, 1324–5, 1325–6, and 1327–8. In every case the Bishop's Waltham figures are "round", suggesting a wholesale transaction, and the bailiff specifically described the 1325–6 sale as *in grosso*. Occasionally manors sold acorns instead of beech-mast, as Wargrave did in 1220–1 and again in 1235–6, when it received 7s. 6d. for 18 qr of *glandarum*. Hampton Lucy (War.) had no pannage money in 1371–2 *quia null' glandes*.[279]

Woodland and parkland formed much of a manor's reserve of grazing land, able to earn agistment money if the trees were pollarded or mature enough not to be harmed by beasts eating the leaves and young shoots they could reach. Agistment incomes on many manors declined first when the old woodlands were cleared by assarting, again when demesnes built up their own herds, and again, as Glynde (Sussex) reported in 1368–9, *pro defectu emptorum* – a phrase echoed hundreds of times in the accounts after the Black Death. Even in years when grass and hay were scarce, as in 1388–9, bailiffs had trouble finding buyers. That year, the forty-eight Winchester manors still in hand collected only £55 15s. from agistments in meadow, park, pasture, and stubble, and from the sale of hay and herbage, yet Alresford, North Waltham, and Waltham St Lawrence all noted the lack of buyers.[280] But, in other years and on other manors, hay and herbage could provide much of a manor's revenues: in 1374–5 Lydden (Kent) obtained from herbage sales £25 16s. 6d. of its total income of £40 10s. 8d. Appledore (Kent), another Canterbury Cathedral priory manor, averaged herbage sales of almost £20 a year between 1304–5 and 1336–7. Several Westminster abbey manors found hay profitable: Bourton-on-the-Hill took £14 3s. in 1313–14, Hardwicke £11 7s. 10d. in 1325–6, Pershore £4 6s. 8d. in 1345–6, and Deerhurst £5 16s. 6d. in 1365–6. Westminster's cellarer in the 1380s leased herbage outside the abbey in *Marketmede* to Peter Bocher for 30s. a year. Steventon "sold" some of its meadows and pastures in 1401–2 for £5 2s., but could not lease the others *pro defectu conductorum*. Glastonbury abbey's manor of Brent (Somerset) got much of its early income from meadow and pasture: £15 14s. 5½d. in 1257–8, £16 0s. 5½d. in 1274–5, £16 16s. 2d. in 1281–2, but only £3 12s. 1½d. in 1300–1 and £5 2s. 6d. in 1312–13. In that last year, agistments and the sale of pasture at *Gavenhulle* at Badbury earned the abbey over £10. In Devon, the hay harvest at Bishop's Clyst sometimes yielded over

[279] GAD 11244; WPR 159410, 159333, 159334, 159337, 159338, 159340, 159277, 159284; Worcs. RO, BA 2636/009:1/163/92, 160.

[280] East Sussex RO, Glynde Ms. 1073; WPR 159394 (the figure cited includes £4 15s. 8d. for hay sold *ad hospicium domini* or to other Winchester manors).

ninety loads, valued at £23 5s. in 1430–1 and £23 10s. in 1443–4.[281] In the north, Durham's manors of Ketton and Bewley were able to get £10 or £11 for their herbage in the 1370s. Herbage and agistment revenues fluctuated, though not as much as those from "outsiders'" pannage, as the lords often found it hard to lease their grazing. Near towns, though, pasture was especially valuable. Holywell was able to rent out thirty acres of meadow in 1299–1300 for £7 2s. 6d., and the following year thirty-six acres for £9.[282] Chaucer's Clerk of Oxenford may have had a horse "as leene … as is a rake", but there were others nearby who could afford to feed their mounts properly.

Town markets and fairs, of course, generated a local demand for hay and other fodder for visitors' horses and for the livestock offered for sale. Early Winchester had its *fenarius* or haymonger; York's shambles were by its Haymongergate, and the name Haymarket still survives in London, Newcastle upon Tyne, and other ancient cities. Some of the hay bought by the load in market towns went to innkeepers, who retailed it for their lodgers' horses. Much of it, however, passed out of the town and back to manors in need. Longbridge Deverill, for example, bought nine cart-loads of hay in Frome in 1342–3, but in later years Longbridge and Monkton Deverill either bought local tithe hay, or purchased it at West Knoyle manor, *Merewodelond*, or *in parochia Gillyngham*, some eight miles away. This was obviously more convenient than buying in a town, saving both tolls and carting costs. Oakington (Cambs.) sold its demesne hay *in tasso in prato* in 1363–4 and 1378–9, to local buyers like William Cheyne, knight, William West of Histon, and John Withobbe of Cambridge.[283] Turweston in 1329–30 sold one load in the meadow to John Deistere for 10d., but charged 2s. 6d. a load for the hay it delivered to Thomas Leedbetere and Robert Smyth. Some manors even bought hay by the truss from villagers, as Tidenham did around 1300 from Sarra *le Fox* (alias *le Waleys*), Robert Silveyn, and Robert Jordan, *ad affros et boues sustinendos*.[284] With hay, as with timber products, grain, and livestock, manors could be buyers as well as sellers, and learned to trade without passing through formal markets or fairs.

[281] Cathedral Library, Canterbury, Bedell's Rolls, Lydden and Appledore; WAM 8260, 8432, 22122, 8450, 18867, 7450; GAD 10762, 11244, 11273, 11216; Dean and Chapter Archives, Exeter, G3/4.
[282] The Prior's Kitchen, Durham, Dean and Chapter, Ketton, Bewley; MCR 4476, 4477.
[283] GAD 10604, 9795, 9692; Cambridge Univ. Library, QCR 6/2, 6/4.
[284] WAM 7833; PRO SC 6/959/25, 26, 28.

G. BARGAINING FACILITIES AND RESTRICTIONS

So far, this chapter has examined some of the ways in which produce of the countryside moved to the consumer. As we have seen, the largest sales needed the authority and bargaining skills of a great estate's central administration – to sell the Winchester wool sent to Wolvesey or the Glastonbury fleeces collected at Damerham, the standing timber for money to pay a new bishop's debts, as at Winchester and Worcester, or even for the grain. Islip, for example, in 1346–7 sold 27 qr of wheat *per litteras domini*; in 1332–3 Monkton Deverill distinguished between grain sales made *per litteras domini* and those made *sine Warento*, and the next year it made all its sales by warrants, six for the wheat and five for the barley.[285] To sell the wool from their northern manors, the fellows of Merton might journey to Newcastle; to sell the clip from their southern properties, some of them might go to Dunstable or Stokenchurch to meet the buyers. Even the warden might ride out to Ibstone, as in 1358–9, to choose timber for a new mill. Monastic obedientiaries like the Westminster abbey cellarer might join vigorously in the capital's fatstock market, despatch monks as in 1302–3 to supervise the sale of Knowle's oaks for £90, or send Thomas de Laleham to inspect the livestock at Birdbrook in November 1345 and cull and sell the old sheep. Sometimes several men shared the responsibility for buying and selling: Leatherhead in 1282–3 bought oxen *per visum* of Simon the reeve, sold calves and bought sheep and geese *per visum* of the shepherd, sold wethers *per visum* of John of Abingdon, and sold pigs and capons, and bought barley and oats, *per visum* of Richard Tannere. At Cuxham in 1357–8 *dominus* Henry Hedecrone arranged the sale of the wheat *in grosso* and authorized the delivery of 21 qr for the price of 20 qr (as the familiar allowance *in avantagio mercatorum*).[286] Oakington sold large quantities of barley and dredge *per preceptum senescalli*. At Claret it was the constables of the castle who sold off the old cattle, bought new plough beasts, and sold the surplus grain. Sometimes there might be confusion, as at Chesterford in 1296–7 when *magister* Thomas de Sodington sold the barley in a heap to John le Dancere, who then paid the money directly to the Bigods at Framlingham (Suffolk) without the reeve's knowledge. But the advantages of using an expert or trusted agent, rather than the average bailiff or reeve, outweighed such occasional inconveniences; so it was that Henry Baret, bailiff of Crawley and instaurer, bought livestock for Winchester manors as far away as Adderbury. Peter-

---

[285] Dyer, *Lords and Peasants*, p. 176; WAM 14794; GAD 9730, 10617.

[286] MCR 5586, 5886, 5104; WAM 27701, 25442; MCR 5694; *Manorial Records of Cuxham*, ed. Harvey, pp. 573, 581.

borough abbey in 1404–5 not only bought wheat *de* Thomas Peer but also *per* him, pigs both *de* and *per* William Sampson, bulls from Robert Bulwer and sheep at Whittlesey through him.[287] Central bargaining, especially for wholesale transactions, thus reduced both the reeve's responsibilities and his temptations.

On the other hand, I have also argued that most of the trading was local, within a radius of six or seven miles, or about two hours' walking distance. Livestock, though, moved further than grain, and fairs attracted customers from a wider area than did weekly markets. Even so, large towns like Exeter and Colchester got most of their victuals and other supplies from the villages and manors close at hand. A few cities – London certainly, Bristol and York, perhaps Norwich and Coventry – needed longer lines of supply, and even villages like Elham (for no convincing economic reason) brought horses and timber from afar. Even great estates channelled much of their produce to local consumers, as Winchester did with grain sales to its captive customary tenants on the Taunton manors and its extensive sales *per mutuum* and *in foro* elsewhere, or Battle abbey's sales *in patria*, or Glastonbury's sales of grain in the unlicensed markets of hamlets near its eastern manors, or the Bury St Edmunds manors with the sales of faggots in their woods. At this modest level the manors were competing with the produce offered for sale by the more fortunate of their own tenants. On a larger scale, of course, only the manors, or the farmers of tithes or demesne herds and flocks, could supply wholesalers in grain or cheese, or the more discriminating wool buyers; as we have seen, the small producers often sold their fleeces to the great monasteries, which could then market the wool as *collecta* at a healthy profit for themselves. At both levels, a high and probably increasing proportion of the produce of the countryside evaded altogether the tolls and other restrictions imposed in formal markets and fairs; hence much of the decline in urban revenues in the fourteenth century. Of the 282 qr of wheat bought by Peterborough abbey in 1404–5, only 4 qr (bought at Stourbridge fair) seem to have been purchased publicly; in 1433–4, 360 qr out of a total of 378 qr came from a single dealer, Nicholas Othehill, none at all being bought at market or fair.[288]

Some formalities were not so easily avoided. Every sale was a form of contract; how could it be made binding? At one time a hand-shake would suffice to confirm a deal; by 1259, though, Grimsby's charter decreed that only burgesses of the town should "make bargains by hand-clasp for herring, or other fish, or for corn", though such

---

[287] PRO SC 6/838/22, 30; 839/4; 837/22; *Account Rolls of Peterborough*, ed. Greatrex, pp. 118–19, 121.   [288] *Ibid.*, p. 165.

bargains must hold unless the goods delivered were of worse quality than those over which the hands had been shaken. Elsewhere, and perhaps more commonly, the buyer confirmed the bargain by giving a coin to the vendor in front of witnesses, or by placing it on the article. Preston in the twelfth century had decreed that a seller regretting the bargain thus struck should pay back double the earnest-money; Berwick in 1249 permitted no alteration once the money had been exchanged *in argento dei*; Northampton about 1260 warned buyers not to place the penny on the merchandise until the vendor had agreed to the bargain. In practice, sealing a bargain by exchanging a coin proved an adaptable custom: many a hapless drinker in later centuries found himself in the army after a recruiting sergeant had slipped the King's Shilling into his ale-pot. At St Ives fair, for example, money *in argento dei* served to bind a man to carry a bundle to London, to seal a partnership between two men travelling to trade together in Scotland, and to confirm the lease on a house for the coming Boston fair, as well as for purchases as varied as a pair of tongs and two barrels of salt haddock. A 1295 debt case, complaining that the prior of Swavesey had bought two pieces of frieze cloth for 5s. 4d. and had paid only *argentum dei et iiij d. in arris*, made some distinction between "God's silver" and the earnest-money, which here seems to be a part-payment rather than a demonstration of contract.[289] The Merton manorial accounts fairly often record that the odd penny or halfpenny added to the price of a horse or ox was *in argento dei*, and these payments are so frequent, even when not specifically explained, that they seem the usual practice with stock purchases in the thirteenth and early fourteenth centuries. When Cuxham paid £15 16s. 8d. for five millstones in London in 1330-1, it spent 1d. *in argento dei* and a further 2s. 1d. for five gallons of wine to celebrate; money spent *in beueragio* as well as *in argento dei* doubtless added to the pleasures of marketing and the profits of inn-keepers. Such explicit references become rare as the decades pass, probably because enrolled recognizances became more common, though in 1346-7 Gussage All Saints (Dorset) bought two oxen at Shaftesbury for 25s. 1d. *cum argento dei et Beueragio*. One must guess from the prices whether the practice continued. In 1378 the reeve of Hampton Episcopi (Worcs.) claimed 16s. 1d. as the cost of an ox bought, the final penny probably being *in argento dei*; the auditor refused the claim, and cut the allowance to 15s. 6d., perhaps in a deliberate attempt to suppress the custom. The Westminster auditors in 1384 refused the Kelvedon reeve the final penny on the prices of a cart horse for which he claimed

[289] *Borough Customs*, II, ed. M. Bateson, Selden Soc., XXI, 1906, p. 182; *Borough Customs*, I, ed. M. Bateson, Selden Soc., XVIII, 1904, pp. 217-18; *Select Cases concerning the Law Merchant 1270-1638*, I, ed. C. Gross, Selden Soc., XXIII, 1908, pp. 43, 47, 50, 68, 75, 77.

26s. 1d. and two plough horses which he claimed to have bought for 24s. 1d. and 13s. 5d. The great majority of livestock prices recorded for horses and cattle between 1350 and 1400 are for exact numbers of shillings, or for multiples or fractions of the mark (13s. 4d.), and seem to exclude "God's silver" and celebratory tippling. But extra pennies reappear in the accounts of many manors at the very end of the century – at Feering in 1397–8, Gussage in 1399–1400, Birdbrook in 1400–1, and Alton Barnes in 1403–4, for example – and suggest a revival of the old practice.[290]

Whether confirmed by hand-shake, or coin, or drink, or some formal document, the bargain was usually a contract requiring payment for goods handed over, or the delivery of goods for which payment was made in advance. It needed some process for enforcement. Hence the proliferation of debt litigation, which proved so fertile a field for studies of Exeter markets and the trading links at Writtle. By the early fifteenth century the villagers of Writtle, a large royal manor in Essex, had evolved a complicated system of credits and loans – deferred payment for goods taken, advance payment for goods promised, peasants lending seed-corn or livestock to each other, or loaning money against promises of later work in return. Butchers supplied meat and skins to their customers on credit. Herdsmen, dairymen, and poulterers likewise extended credit to each other. Some of them were middlemen intending to retail butter and cheese in Writtle market or at Chelmsford fair. Nearly half the debt disputes to reach the Writtle court were disputes over sales, most commonly the sales of livestock. In about one-fifth of the cases, debts had been made payable on demand, but creditors often let them continue indefinitely until they needed the money. More than half the cases which cited the date of the original agreement were for debts incurred at least four years before, and 18 per cent were over ten years old. It was not the very poor who obtained credit: two-fifths of the debtors who appeared before the court were tradesmen or peasants prosperous enough to own their own ploughs, and about two-fifths of the debtors also appeared before the court as creditors.[291]

Such a network of lending and borrowing among acquaintances, mainly for small amounts, could well strengthen the social fabric of a village with a fairly static population. It could not serve in the same way an international fair, a port, or even a major market town, where

[290] MCR 5853; Bodleian Library, Queen's College Roll 22; Worcs. RO, BA 2636/009: 1/163/92, 162; WAM 25845, 25735, 25496; Bodleian Library, Queen's College Roll 42; New College, Oxford, 5830.
[291] Clark, 'Debt litigation', pp. 247–79. Some of the calculations are mine, based on data in this article.

litigants could not wait for the next regular borough court to press their pleas. The crown had long recognized the need for procedures which would settle swiftly disputes involving visiting traders – "before the third tide", as the early twelfth-century Customs of Newcastle prescribed. Merchants who had advanced money to Cistercian abbeys against a future wool-clip expected royal aid even in Richard I's reign. Kings who hoped to expand trade and to be able to borrow from merchants had to make it easy for them to recover money from other debtors. It was equally essential for towns or their lords to provide summary jurisdiction to settle arguments over debts or contracts, in a manner which ensured fair treatment for the trader from outside; otherwise, there would be no visiting merchants. Some towns, like York, Hereford, and Chichester, lost their normal courts at fair-time altogether. At Winchester the bishop's officials took control of the city gates and had *custodiam totius civitatis predicte et cognitionem omnium placitorum*; by the fifteenth century, most of the revenues from St Giles's fair came from the pie-powder court held in the Pavilion.[292] At Bristol and Gloucester the fair courts were integrated with the civic courts: pleas begun in the pie-powder courts could be continued in the tolsey courts during the rest of the year. But speed was usually the essence of pie-powder jurisdiction. At Colchester in 1458, for example, the plaintiff sued at 8 a.m. for the recovery of a debt; the defendant failed to answer the court's summons at 9 a.m., 10 a.m., and 11 a.m.; at noon, the court ordered his goods to be seized and valued; the appraisers made their report at 4 p.m. and the court thereupon delivered the goods to the plaintiff. The 1426 pie-powder court in Winchester took a little longer – about two days in difficult cases – but was still impressively fast by the standards of the central courts.[293]

The economic conditions of the later thirteenth century made it a time of rapid developments in recording and recovering debts. The great fairs, assembling in a regular cycle, allowed merchants to incur a debt at one fair and pay it off at the next: thus three Frenchmen who bought woolfells from a Leicester man at Boston fair in 1285 undertook to pay the purchase price in equal parts at the coming Winchester and Northampton fairs. A borrower had to establish his creditworthiness: a Northampton rule of about 1260 ordered that no credit be given to a knight or any other, unless the lender first found out how he had left his previous creditor – that is, whether he had paid off his earlier debts. Until 1275, when the First Statute of Westminster ended the practice

[292] *English Historical Documents 1042–1189*, eds., Douglas and Greenaway, p. 971; Lloyd. *The English Wool Trade*, p. 289; Table 4.3, above.
[293] *Select Cases concerning the Law Merchant*, i, ed. Gross, pp. xxi, xxii, xxvi; *English Historical Documents 1327–1485*, ed. Myers, pp. 564–5.

(for English denizens), all the members of a town's gild-merchant were jointly liable for debts incurred by individuals belonging to it. Eight years later, the Statute of Acton Burnell ordered that debts should be formally enrolled by the mayors of London, York, or Bristol, and the bonds between debtor and creditor confirmed with a royal seal (perhaps in imitation of earlier arrangements by which the king had helped Jews recover their debts). If the debtor defaulted, the mayor of the appropriate city could seize his chattels, sell them, and reimburse the creditor out of the proceeds, with the help of Chancery and the sheriffs if the debtor did not have sufficient assets within the mayor's jurisdiction. If his assets still proved insufficient, the debtor would go to prison (with bread and water at the creditor's expense) until the debtor's friends settled the account.[294] Then the 1285 Statute of Merchants amended this radically, multiplying the number of towns where debts might be enrolled and decreeing immediate imprisonment for the defaulter. The debtor now had three months to sell his assets; if he failed to realize enough, the creditor seized his chattels and took over his lands until their revenues had paid the debt in full. In some ways ironic, for the crown was the most shameless of debtors and still out of its creditors' reach, the system of enrolment and sealed bonds gave merchants documents which were binding and immediately enforceable against lesser defaulters.[295] The threat that their lands might be seized for debt led the Ordainers in 1311 to order that no land other than burgage tenements might be seized by creditors, but Edward II restored the statute's power over freeholds in 1322.

After the Black Death, Edward III's Statute of the Staple introduced in 1353 an even simpler and cheaper process, which charged only $\frac{1}{2}$d. in the £1 for enrolling recognizances for sums up to £100, and $\frac{1}{4}$d. thereafter, in contrast to the Statute Merchant's fees of 1d. in the £1 at markets and $1\frac{1}{2}$d. at fairs. In the later fourteenth century, convenient devices such as the bill of exchange and the promissory note also gained wide circulation. So did the sealed tally which, according to the *Liber Albus* in the early fifteenth century, was by London custom as strong as a bond: *un taillé de dette ensealé par usage de la citée est auxi fort come une obligacioun*. It was still no guarantee when the crown was the debtor, and many account rolls record the waste of time and money as reeves rode around carrying their tallies and trying to get payment for what the king had commandeered. In 1347–8, for example, Cuxham spent 2s. o$\frac{1}{2}$d. on the reeve's expenses at Reading trying to get money for wheat taken by the queen the year before, 1s. 4d. on journeys to

[294] Moore, *Fairs*, pp. 117–18; *Borough Customs*, I, ed. Bateson, p. 209; *Select Cases concerning the Law Merchant*, III, ed. Hall, pp. xix, xxiv, xxv.

[295] T. F. T. Plucknett, *Legislation of Edward I*, Oxford, 1949, pp. 138, 144.

Guildford, Henley, and Maldon (Surrey) seeking money for wheat sold to the king, and 2d. on a ride to Oxford begging payment for hay eaten by the king's oxen – and that after paying at least 3s. 4d. on various occasions to bribe the king's men to take the royal horses and cattle away from Cuxham.[296]

Manorial accounts seldom mention any of these formal methods of debt registration and collection. For the accounting official, the tally was a receipt, acknowledging that the bailiff or reeve had handed over to the lord's treasurer or steward some part of the manorial revenues, or perhaps a record of grain discharged from the granary. At the end of the account year, the balance owed by the bailiff to the lord might include some rents or purchase money not yet collected from the villagers, but essentially the arrears to be paid off the next year represented a cash balance left in the official's hands. It is rare to find a note such as that in the 1334–5 Turweston account recording that the Brother Simon de Hirchesdon had a *scriptum obligatorium* for £4 3s. 4d. from William Squier for 25 qr of dredge sold to him, or that in the Longbridge Deverill account for 1342–3, noting that John Park had stood surety when John Pew of Frome bought more of the Glastonbury wool than he could afford. When a peasant purchased something from his lord, as when the Elham villagers bought their horses in the autumn with a small deposit, a promise to pay the balance at Ascension day, and a friend to stand pledge, further formalities seemed hardly necessary. Yet an Elham roll includes two lists of debts owed to the bailiff in July 1331, the one naming fourteen people who owed the manor for horses, the other listing thirty-two persons who owed for a variety of debts; seven or eight individuals appear in both lists.[297] Such indebtedness may have been atypical, but, as with the dealings at Writtle, it suggests that access to credit could be very important in the normal operation of village life.

As well as the statutes which made the existing urban arrangements for recording and collecting debts into a national system, Edward I's reign saw an almost accidental extension of the local rules against unfair market practices. In the *Leges Henrici Primi*, "forestalling" had meant a surprise attack on someone on the highway, one of the pleas reserved to the crown.[298] By the 1260s, several towns had rules forbidding middlemen to buy up goods on their way to market, and in 1268

---

[296] *Select Cases concerning the Law Merchant*, III, ed. Hall, pp. xxxiv, lxxxv; *Borough Customs*, I, ed. Bateson, p. 204; *Manorial Records of Cuxham*, ed. Harvey, p. 436.

[297] WAM 7787; GAD 10604; MCR 5285.

[298] R. H. Britnell, 'Forstall, forestalling and the statute of forestallers'. *EHR*, CII, 1987, pp. 89–102. This paragraph is entirely based on this article which the author kindly sent me in advance of publication.

Henry III granted London a charter threatening forfeiture and imprisonment for anyone "intercepting" merchants travelling to the city to buy or re-sell.[299] London ordinances introduced by Mayor Henry le Waleys between 1281 and 1283 applied the old name of "forestalling" to those activities in the fish trade which violated the 1268 charter. In 1285, with the city in the king's hands, Edward I's Statute of London extended these rules to include all kinds of merchandise coming to the markets there. This principle was applauded in obscure and unofficial works like the *Judicium Pillorie* and the *Composicio ad puniendum infringentes assisam panis et cervisie, forestallarios, cocos, etc.*, the latter using language echoing canon law. Then the legal handbook *Fleta* in the 1290s inserted the London rules against forestalling alongside Magna Carta and the more formal Edwardian statutes of the previous decades, giving them an authority the king could hardly have foreseen. In 1304, though, Edward I sent a commission of *oyer and terminer* to investigate complaints against forestallers in some East Anglian towns, and before the end of 1307 his son appointed another commission to enforce generally the laws against forestalling and breaches of the assize of weights and measures.[300] The justices on the 1321 London eyre agreed in defining forestalling as a collusive action between buyer and seller, an offence committed by middlemen intending to re-sell what they had intercepted on the way to market (it being no offence to buy such goods for personal consumption), and they confirmed that the rules against it were intended to prevent unfair profits.

In earlier parts of this chapter I cited some prosecutions for forestalling, usually of items of modest value. Some cases, though, were for much larger amounts. The Norwich courts in 1375 charged Geoffrey de Bixton and William the Blackamoor with forestalling 400 qr of grain, Roger de Bergham with forestalling 300 qr of wheat, 60 qr of rye, and 200 qr of barley and oats, having gone out to meet it "in streets and lanes, at gates and bridges", and John de Gaywood with forestalling so many eggs that he filled twenty-eight barrels and exported them out of the kingdom.[301] In times of economic difficulty, as in London in the spring of 1350, forestallers might go to prison or the pillory, but at other times the punishments were minimal, hardly more severe than for offences against the assizes of bread and ale or for prostitution – in effect, licences to go on sinning. The harvest surpluses in most years after 1375, and the greater quantities of meat reaching the market in later years, were probably more effective than legislation in

[299] Or, perhaps, "merchants travelling to buy or sell goods in the city".
[300] *English Historical Documents 1189–1327*, ed. Rothwell, p. 524.
[301] *Leet Jurisdiction in Norwich*, ed. Hudson, pp., 61, 63.

restraining profiteering by forestallers in a population thinned by plague and partly dispersed from towns into villages. And if an increasing proportion of trade was by-passing markets and fairs altogether, there would be fewer breaches of the forestalling laws.

The fate of the assizes of weights and measures shows how ineffective national economic legislation could be, especially amid the fierce local traditions and decaying central authority of the later middle ages. Magna Carta, in this respect much more specific than the *Articuli Baronum*, had boldly demanded "one measure for wine throughout our kingdom, and one measure for ale, and one measure for corn, namely 'the London quarter'; and one width for cloths whether dyed, russet or halberget, namely two ells within the selvedges", and similar consistency with weights. With what Hubert Hall called a "monotonous series of statutes and ordinances", Edward I and his successors strove for a single standard, but in vain. On grounds of cost the crown ignored parliament's preferred remedy, that justices be appointed for the special supervision of weights and measures, and that the Treasury despatch sets of standard metal measures to every county.[302] Kings preferred to send the royal Clerk of the Market or his deputy on occasional forays of inspection (for the clerk's authority extended for twelve miles from wherever the royal household was), together with pack-horses carrying the standard measures. Witney in 1336–7 paid 6s. 8d. *de fine coram Clerico Mercati Hospicii Domini Regis*, probably compounding for possible breaches of the assize, and hurrying the hated official on to his next destination. After the Black Death, Edward III gave some of the justices enforcing the Statute of Labourers the responsibility for the assize of weights and measures too, but in 1361 he transferred both charges to the regular J.Ps. Still lacking standard measures against which to check those in local use, the justices had an impossible task. Explicit references to abnormal measures – measures of the market, measures of the *patria*, great measures, old measures, and so on – seem at least as common after the Black Death as before it. In this respect the mayors and towns successfully resisted centralization according to the London standard. And even at London's Queenhithe, probably the busiest grain market in England, the five senior cornmeters were arrested in 1375 because they had measured corn "by false and deceptive... measures which were lower at the top in one part than the rest... and... had done so for three years past".[303]

Like the rules against false measures, penalties against bad ale were ancient; the Customs of Chester recorded in Domesday Book had

---

[302] Magna Carta c. 35, in *English Historical Documents 1189–1327*, ed. Rothwell, p. 320.

[303] *Select Cases concerning the Law Merchant*, II, ed. H. Hall, Selden Soc., XLVI, 1929, pp. xlv, xlviii; 1: WPR 159348; *Cal. Plea and Memo. Rolls 1364–1381*, ed. Thomas, pp. 189–90.

prescribed the same four-shilling fine for both offences. But control of brewers and bakers rested almost entirely with the local authorities, with no support from the crown except for exhortations such as that from John in 1202 ordering that the assizes of bread and ale be observed, or judicial pronouncements such as Chief Justice Scrope's when on the 1329–30 Northamptonshire eyre. Scrope confiscated the market charter of a man who had no tumbrel, on the grounds that "a market cannot be held unless the assize of bread and ale is duly enforced, and that cannot be if the corporal penalties cannot be imposed." Even the non-parliamentary statutes of the later thirteenth century, decreeing the weight of the farthing loaf and the price of ale, assumed that local self-interest would ensure enforcement without further effort by the government. The 1318 Statute of York forbade active members of the victualling trades to be appointed to enforce the assizes; it failed, for dealers in foodstuffs were already dominant in many towns, and when the statute was repealed in 1512 it was on the pretext that towns had "few or none persons of substance" who were not in those trades.[304] Normally the assizes of bread and ale were little more than routine procedures for collecting modest business fees from small traders, rather than punitive measures to regulate the economy. Even the ale-tasters often lacked enthusiasm: the Crowland abbey courts fined them for neglecting their duties almost as regularly as they amerced the brewers for contravening the assize. In times of dearth and high grain prices, however, some officials tried to keep the weight of the farthing loaf so high that there was no profit left for the baker. The bakers of Coventry went on strike in December 1483 against such treatment.[305] Despite such temporary injustices, medieval England generated profits enough to support large numbers of bakers and encourage a multitude of ale-wives to put their surpluses on sale.

A few other royal and parliamentary attempts to control bargaining and marketing need only the briefest mention here, as they are considered more fully in the next chapter. The Statutes of Labourers at first tried to restore the price of labour to what it had been in 1346; they failed, but probably kept wages lower than they would have been otherwise. Later statutes conceded higher wages. The crown kept the value of English currency high – making profits from seignorage dues and recoinages, not by debasements – until the Tudors came to the throne, despite Edward III's changes in the mid-fourteenth century. But the government's occasional efforts to control prices nationally

---

[304] *English Historical Documents 1042–1189*, ed. Douglas and Greenaway, p. 869; M. Paris, *Chronica Majora*, RS, II, p. 480; SR, I, pp. 178, 199; III, p. 30.
[305] Page, *Crowland Abbey*, pp. 338, 342, 348, 352, 353, 360, 364, 376, 378; *The Coventry Leet Book*, ed. Harris, II, p. 518.

were a total failure, as after the disastrous harvests of the mid-1310s. And when a city or town tried unreasonably to hold prices down during a famine, the reeves and villagers could use that most basic marketing trick of withholding supplies, to sell their produce from granary or shed for whatever hungry townsmen would pay. "God send me a good market for our horse and you a good market for our fells", Richard Cely wrote to his brother George in 1479, but the Celys and all other dealers in the produce of the countryside had found marketing techniques which required divine aid no more than they needed formal markets or fairs.[306]

[306] *The Cely Papers*, ed. Malden, p. 15.

CHAPTER 5

PRICES AND WAGES, 1350–1500

A. INTRODUCTION

Abundant before the Black Death, the manorial evidence on prices and wages withers away in the century after it. For many years in the reigns of Edward I and Edward II there is material from a hundred or more well-filled account rolls; by the reign of Edward IV all that survives may be skimpy records from a couple of Battle abbey manors. The student may lightly discard doubtful material from the earlier period, even though the process of averaging it with more reliable figures would have removed most of the dangers of incorporating it. He cannot be so selective with evidence for the later fifteenth century, for there may be no alternative sources at all. The geographical distribution of the material also changes for the worse. For the fourteenth century, evidence is available from most areas of England south of a line between the Severn and the Wash; by the 1440s, however, almost all the manorial sources are from Hampshire and Sussex alone. Fortunately, better institutional records atone in part for the dearth of manorial accounts in the later years. The prices and wages paid, for example, by Exeter Cathedral and King's College, Cambridge, are consistent with those recorded elsewhere in their geographical areas, and have therefore been included in the figures presented here. Both manorial and institutional records are generally silent on prices and wages in Wales throughout this period. Almost the only guide to price levels in the principality is found in valuations made for the central government.

The statistics in this study are as consistent as possible with those published for the period 1000–1350 in volume II of this *Agrarian History*. They are not entirely compatible with those calculated by Professor Bowden for volume IV.[1] In one respect, too, my calculations in this volume differ from those in its predecessor: the wage series printed here exclude entries from the London area. London wages had

---

[1] D. L. Farmer, *AHEW*, II, pp. 716–817; P. J Bowden, *AHEW*, IV, pp. 593–695, 814–70.

been somewhat higher than those elsewhere before the Black Death, but the gap widened greatly after 1348. Had it been included, the London-area wage material from the manorial and obedientiary accounts of Westminster abbey would have distorted all calculations of "national wage levels", particularly for the fifteenth century[2] when other sources are irregular. On the other hand, London prices were not consistently dearer than those elsewhere. They are particularly useful when other information is scarce, and have therefore been incorporated with other price material in the tables which follow.[3]

B. PRICE AND WAGE TRENDS

Oxen remained the most important demesne plough beasts in late medieval England, and their purchase was regular wherever arable farming persisted. Save for temporary disturbances, when oxen were

[2] The main explanation of statistical method is in the appendix on pp. 495–7, but some definitions are necessary at this stage.

Dates. Manorial and other accounts usually ran from Michaelmas (29 September) in one calendar year to Michaelmas eve (28 September) in the next. To minimize confusion, dates in this chapter usually show both calendar years: thus a price or wage entry dated 1365–6 is taken from an account roll for the period 29 September 1365 to 28 September 1366. Each account records what was done with the harvest *gathered before the account commenced* (in this case, in the summer of 1365), and what was spent on gathering the next harvest (that of 1366). As one usually does not know in what part of the account year the transaction took place, 1365–6 has to be given as the date for all prices, for all building wages, and for threshing and winnowing wages. But as all payments for mowing and harvesting were made in the summer of the second year, mowers' and reapers' wages could be safely assigned to the calendar year 1366. By the harvest of 1366 I mean the crop produced from grain sown in the autumn of 1365 and spring of 1366, reaped in the summer of 1366, and threshed in the autumn of 1366 or winter of 1366–7 for subsequent internal use or sale. This information has to be extracted from two successive account rolls, those for 1365–6 and 1366–7.

National price level. This is the (unweighted) mean of the (unweighted) regional means of the (weighted) average prices paid or received by manors within each region. The method of calculation is described more fully in the appendix. Unless the context clearly shows otherwise, a statement that "the price of wheat in 1365–6 was 6s. a quarter" refers to the "national price level".

Decennial price. This is the (unweighted) mean of the "national price levels" in that decade. A statement that "the price of wheat in the 1360s was 8s. 2d. a quarter" indicates that this figure is the mean of the "national price levels" of the ten account years from 1360–1 to 1369–70 inclusive.

National wage level and *decennial wage.* These are calculated as for prices, except that figures from the Lower Thames/London region are excluded.

Prices and wages before the Black Death. Unless the context clearly shows otherwise, whenever this chapter or the statistical appendix discusses levels "before the Black Death", it refers to the mean of the "national price levels" or "national wage levels" in the seventeen account years from 1330–1 to 1346–7, calculated as above, save for the inclusion of the Lower Thames/London figures in the wage series.

[3] I have to acknowledge permission to use and reproduce copyright material from the Beveridge Collection in the British Library of Political and Economic Science, from the Battle

scarce and expensive following outbreaks of cattle disease around 1320, or when their price dropped during the two years of minimal investment immediately after the Black Death, their cost was a remarkably reliable pointer to economic trends. Moreover, as the prices of the other large animals – plough horses, cart horses, and cows – remained in fairly steady ratios to the cost of oxen, oxen prices are broadly representative of other livestock prices as well. Wheat prices are likewise representative of grain prices in general. As a poor wheat harvest led to increased demand for substitute grains, the prices of rye and barley often reflected the success of the wheat crop rather than the yields of the other grains themselves. With the level of demand fairly steady (apart from interruptions caused by outbreaks of plague and occasional exports), and with relatively little grain stored from one year to the next, wheat prices were very sensitive to the fate of the harvest, and consequently fluctuated more sharply than those of any other major commodity. As a result, while changes in the cost of oxen best demonstrate long-term price movements, short-term fluctuations are most obvious in the variations in wheat prices.

Before the Black Death oxen had cost manors about 12s. 6d. Their price fell to 8s. or so immediately after the onset of the plague, but recovered to 12s. after the harvest of 1350. During the next dozen years oxen prices fluctuated between about 12s. and 14s. Subsequently manors had to pay rather more, with prices exceeding 17s. between 1364–5 and 1373–4. The cost then dropped, to 13s. or less, for most of the 1380s and 1390s. After a few years of higher prices – of 15s. or more between 1398–9 and 1405–6 – prices fell back and remained steady for the first half of the fifteenth century, with oxen seldom costing less than 12s. or more than 14s. In the second half of the century prices were slightly higher, and occasionally exceeded 16s. After 1450 their prices appear to fluctuate more sharply from year to year than in earlier periods; this is probably just the result of unrepresentative figures occurring in the much smaller sample of material surviving for the later years. The only period of sustained high prices in the later middle ages was that between 1364–5 and 1373–4, when oxen cost about 30 per cent

abbey collection in the Huntington Library, and from the Martin A. Ryerson Collection of Court and Manorial Documents from the Estate of Sir Nicholas Bacon, in the Joseph Regenstein Library, Chicago. I am grateful for help received from the PRO, the Devon, East Sussex, Norfolk, Plymouth, Salop, and Worcs. ROs, and the Archivists of Westminster abbey, Exeter Cathedral, and New College, Oxford. I am especially grateful to the Hants. RO for completing the major task of photographing the later Winchester pipe rolls for me. I am glad to record the financial aid granted by the Canada Council, St Thomas More College, and the University of Saskatchewan's President's fund. This study was completed during sabbatical leave from St Thomas More College, and was assisted by the hospitality of the Department of Agricultural Economics in the University of Reading.

more than in the expensive years of the mid-1350s and late 1380s. During the short period of high prices around 1400 their cost was about 15 per cent above that "floor" price.

Wheat prices show many of the characteristics of oxen prices, at least for the first hundred years after the Black Death, though the year-by-year fluctuations were inevitably much more acute. In the seventeen harvests before the plague, wheat prices had averaged a little over 5s. a quarter. After two particularly cheap years, the cost rose to about 7s. a quarter in the two account years immediately prior to the onslaught. But the Black Death so reduced demand that, even with much of the crop left standing in the fields, the price fell below 5s. in 1348–9. In 1351 there was an exceptionally bad harvest, ruined by weather rather than by shortage of labourers, and the price soared to nearly 12s. as a result. An excellent crop in 1352 and a good one in 1353 reversed this, and prices again sank below 5s. The 1360s saw two years of very high prices, 1363–4 and 1369–70, the 17s. a quarter after the 1369 harvest being much the highest price of the later middle ages. Following a few years with prices exceeding 8s., there began in 1376–7 a remarkable period of low prices. In all but four of the next twenty-four years, wheat cost less than 6s. a quarter. The price in 1392–3 was the lowest for over a century, and it was never as low again. The early fifteenth century began with higher prices for wheat as well as for oxen, the peak being a little over 10s. in 1401–2. In the first half of the fifteenth century the price was usually under 6s. a quarter, though there were interruptions of much higher prices after the bad harvests of 1437, 1438, and 1439. The only high prices in the second half of the century were in 1481–2, 1482–3, and 1483–4, and even in the worst of those years wheat still cost under 10s. a quarter. Prices were particularly steady in the middle of the century: between 1440–1 and 1480–1 wheat only once cost as much as 8s. Showing no warning of the inflation which was soon to follow, the 1490s saw wheat prices at almost their lowest for two centuries. These developments are demonstrated in Fig. 5.1.

In general, the movements of oxen and wheat prices tell similar stories: prices high in the 1360s and early 1370s, low in the 1380s and 1390s, fairly high around 1400, and (except for dear grain in the late 1430s and early 1480s) relatively low for the rest of the century. This is not to say that the prices of oxen and wheat always moved upwards or downwards together. In short-term fluctuations, changes in the cost of oxen followed, rather than accompanied, changes in the price of wheat. This is clear in the rise after the Black Death, the fall in the later 1350s, the rise in the 1360s, and especially during the period of declining prices after the mid-1370s. The time-lag is easily explained. Two or three years of good prices would be needed to encourage manors and

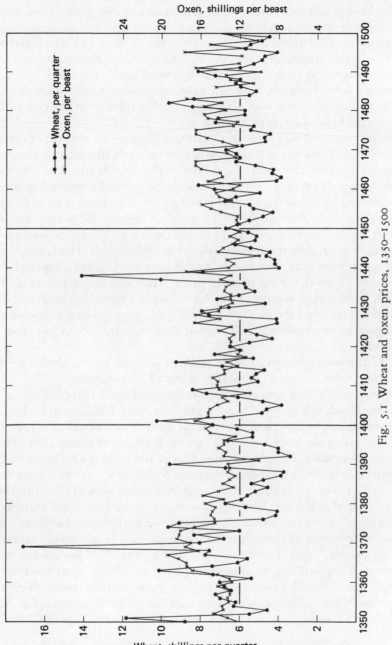

Fig. 5.1 Wheat and oxen prices, 1350–1500

enable peasants to improve their ploughteams by competitive purchasing, and only after two or three years of low grain prices would slackening demand depress the market for oxen and plough horses. Even so, the relationship between the costs of oxen and wheat did not stay constant throughout the later middle ages. In the period 1270–1300, on average, less than 2 qr of wheat would have purchased an ox. A century later, between 1370 and 1400, 2½ qr would have been needed. The main cereal crop was declining in value relative to the cost of the principal beast used in producing it.

This was even more true of the cost of labour – or, at least, of certain types of it. The average price of wheat in the early fifteenth century was almost exactly the same as in the early fourteenth, but by then harvesting cost 60 per cent more and threshing and winnowing 70 per cent more.[4] Thatchers cost an extra 98 per cent, carpenters an additional 58 per cent. By the middle of the fifteenth century the wages paid for most types of agricultural and building work purchased at least twice as much grain as in the first decades of the fourteenth. The labour costs of agriculture thus rose steeply in the later middle ages, especially in relation to the declining price of grain. They did so, moreover, in the teeth of repeated legislation and a rigorous accounting and auditing system. Figure 5.2 shows (by means of seven-year moving averages) the long-term movements in the costs of oxen, wheat, and certain types of labour.

As the consequences of these changes provide a main theme of this volume, their causes naturally demand investigation. The most fundamental factor was probably demographic. Whether the 1348–9 Black Death killed only the 27 per cent postulated by J. C. Russell (from among the atypical ranks of the heirs of tenants-in-chief), or the 65 per cent calculated by J. Z. Titow at Bishop's Waltham, the effects were profound.[5] The plague wiped away the surplus of labourers. On most manors the vacant holdings soon found new tenants – according to A. E. Levett's calculations, by 1354 there were only 233 holdings still empty on the eighteen Winchester manors she studied – and acute local shortages of labour attracted migrant workers from elsewhere, but there was never in the next century or so that "countryside teeming with people" that Titow detected before 1348.[6] Many of the new tenants were widows, or young people, or men with other holdings as well; they would often need to hire help at busy times. For the landlords the consequences may not have been catastrophic immediately; indeed, it has been argued that there was an "Indian

---

[4] The comparisons here are made between 1300/1–1346/7 and 1400/1–1449/50.

[5] Russell, *British Medieval Population*, p. 216; J. Z. Titow, *English Rural Society*, London, 1969, p. 70.   [6] Levett, *The Black Death*, p. 82; Titow, *op. cit.*, p. 71.

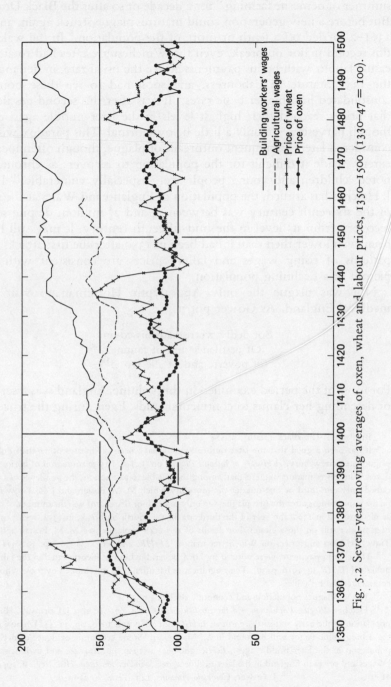

Fig. 5.2 Seven-year moving averages of oxen, wheat and labour prices, 1350–1500 (1330–47 = 100).

summer of demesne farming " for a decade or so after the Black Death.[7]
But before a new generation could mature, plague struck again, and in
1361–2 carried off a tenth or more of the population.[8] In the wake of
this second major outbreak, even the Winchester estates had to attract
casual labour with bonus payments above the usual rate, in defiance of
the 1351 Statute of Labourers, and soon had to see these bonuses
consolidated into higher basic rates.[9] It was after this second pestilence
that prices reached their highest levels in the later middle ages, even
though harvests were only a little below normal. This paradox will be
considered later. Subsequent outbreaks of plague, though often local in
extent, made it difficult for the population to recover; as chroniclers
noted, children and young people were especially vulnerable.[10] If, as
J. Hatcher has argued, the population of England and Wales at the start
of the sixteenth century was between $2\frac{1}{4}$ and $2\frac{3}{4}$ million, despite some
recovery from its level in the mid-fifteenth century, it may still have
been even lower then than it had been in 1350 after the first attack. The
patterns of rising wages and falling prices are consistent with this
picture of a declining population.[11]

Nor was plague the only Apocalyptic Horseman to visit late
medieval England. As Gower put it,

> Bot dedly werre hath his covine
> Of pestilence and of famine,
> Of poverte and of alle wo…[12]

For most of the period examined in this volume, England was asserting
or defending her claims to continental lands. Even during the truces in

---

[7] Bridbury, 'The Black Death', p. 584.

[8] It has been argued that the later outbreaks may have been of diseases other than bubonic
plague. See Shrewsbury, A History of Bubonic Plague, pp. 127–8. My examination of heriots on a
dozen Winchester manors suggests that, among those liable to pay heriots, the pestilence of 1361–2
caused only one-third or one-quarter the mortality which M. M. Postan and J. Z. Titow found
on the same manors after the first plague. On only one manor (Fareham) was the number of deaths
at all abnormal in 1369, the year of the third attack; the fourth outbreak, in 1374, seems to have
been milder still on those estates. For details of the 1348–9 plague, see M. M. Postan and J. Z.
Titow, 'Heriots and prices on Winchester manors', EcHR, 2nd ser. XI, 1959, pp. 392–411.

[9] These extra payments were noticed by Lord Beveridge but not incorporated in the tables he
published (EcHR, III, 1936, p. 37). Their significance has often been overlooked by those who have
commented on his tables.

[10] Bean, 'Plague, population and economic decline', p. 431.

[11] Hatcher, Plague, Population and the English Economy, p. 69; see also J. Cornwall, 'English
population in the early sixteenth century', EcHR, 2nd ser. XXIII, 1970, pp. 32–44. Discussions of
the demographic factor will be found in M. M. Postan, 'Some economic evidence of declining
population in the later middle ages', EcHR, 2nd ser. II, 1950, pp. 221–46, and in J. Schreiner,
'Wages and prices in England in the later middle ages', Scandinavian Econ. Hist. Rev., II, 1954, pp.
61–73.   [12] J. Gower, Confessio Amantis, Lib. Terc., ll. 2267–9.

the Hundred Years War, the "Free Companies" attracted the footloose to lives which, if not solitary, were certainly brutish and usually short. The rebellions and dynastic wars of the fifteenth century also trimmed back the numbers of men of breeding age. Famine, however, was much less prevalent in this period than in the overcrowded century which preceded it. Only rarely do the later chroniclers hint at hunger. According to Stow, in 1391 men were so hungry that they ate too much fruit and died of "the Flixe", while in 1439 "breadcorne was so scarce in England that poore people made them bread of forne roots".[13] Another London chronicler, copied in part by Fabyan, recorded that in the latter year Londoners had to make bread of barley, beans, peas, and vetches; in earlier times the peasantry at least would have reckoned this no hardship.[14] There seems little evidence that famine directly reduced the population in this period (as it certainly had done in 1315–17), though in bad years undernourishment may have made diseases more deadly.[15]

Had the production of grain dropped as sharply as the population, its price would have remained high. This did not happen, partly because most arable land stayed under the plough and, at least on the Winchester estates, was soon producing higher yields than before the Black Death.[16] The improvement in grain productivity came with a bumper harvest in 1376, and the Winchester manors produced better-than-average yields in all but three of the eighteen crop-returns recorded between then and 1395. To these good harvests obviously belongs much of the credit for the low grain prices of the last quarter of the fourteenth century. On the Winchester manors the crops benefited from the larger number of manure-depositing livestock on the demesnes and from the frequent dry summers. The yields (as multiples of the quantity of seed sown) may also have been improved by scattering the seed more thinly. Some credit may also be due to more vigorous auditing of the accounts, but there is little evidence of major change in arable management on the estates examined in this chapter.

Both in England and on the continent, a more kindly climate in the later fourteenth century probably helped to keep grain prices low. As

[13] J. Stow, *The Annales of England*, London, 1601, pp. 491, 627.

[14] *Fabyan's Chronicles*, ed. H. Ellis, London, 1811, p. 612; *Chronicles of London*, ed. C. L. Kingsford, Oxford, 1905, p. 146.

[15] I. Kershaw, 'The great famine and agrarian crisis in England, 1315–1322', *PP*, no. 59, 1973, *passim*; J. M. W. Bean, 'Plague, population and economic decline', p. 429.

[16] Farmer, 'Grain yields on the Winchester manors', pp. 555–66. Despite the questions posed by A. R. Bridbury ('The Black Death', p. 590), I see no reason to doubt the competence of the new tenants, who had grown up in an agricultural society and gained experience through casual work on the demesne, for other peasants, or for their own husbands.

Titow has shown, the years of particularly cheap grain after 1375 were years when dry summers predominated, occasionally interrupted by cold winters. Similar combinations had produced the best Winchester harvests before 1350 as well.[17] In the later fourteenth and early fifteenth centuries the Alpine glaciers ceased to advance. In Germany tree-growth showed the effects of warmer weather, and the tree-ring evidence from southern England suggests that the climate became less damp there.[18] The chroniclers also point to weather in the later middle ages being warmer than in the period before 1350 or in the "little Ice Age" which began in the seventeenth century. Although Professor Lamb has argued that the years between about 1419 and 1459 were climatically "stressful", only in the late 1430s do the grain prices denote crop failure and hunger.[19]

Although they had powerfully influenced price changes in the two centuries before the Black Death, short-term currency fluctuations had less effect after 1350. The later middle ages saw no re-minting of the currency, such as had been ordered on eight occasions in the twelfth and thirteenth centuries. But the crown progressively reduced the weight of silver in the penny, from about 22 grains in 1334 to 20 in 1344, 18 in 1351, 15 in 1411, and 12 in 1464. The changes made by Edward III in 1344 and 1351, to meet the need for new coins and to increase the crown's profit in minting them, were followed by livestock prices slightly higher than usual for a year or two after each devaluation. After the first, grain prices were high despite a good harvest; after the second, which accompanied a disastrous harvest, they were exceptionally high. But later changes in the weight of silver in the penny seem to have had little effect on prices. The pennies introduced in 1411 and 1464 were struck with about the same silver content as the old coins currently in circulation, for the latter had lost much of their weight through wear and tear, as well as from deliberate clipping. If anything, prices were lower than usual in the account years after the

[17] J. Titow, 'Evidence of weather in the account rolls of the bishopric of Winchester, 1209–1350', EcHR, 2nd ser. XI, 1960, pp. 360–407; idem, 'Le climat à travers les rôles de comptabilité de l'évêché de Winchester, 1350–1450', Annales ESC, 25, 1970, pp. 312–50.

[18] I am grateful to J. Fletcher of the Oxford Research Laboratory for Archaeology and the History of Art for advice on the interpretation of tree-ring evidence. See also H. H. Lamb, The English Climate, London, 1964, p. 165; idem, Climate: Present, Past and Future, London, I, 1972, and II, 1977; E. Hollstein, 'Jahrrings-chronologische Datierung von Eichenholzen ohne Wald Kante', Bonner Jahrbücher 165, pp. 1–27; E. Le Roy Ladurie, Times of Feast, Times of Famine, New York, 1972; F. Sandon, 'A millennium of west European climate – a cu-sum look at dendroclimatology', Weather, 29, 1974, pp. 162–6.

[19] Lamb, Climate, II, pp. 458, 459. While the historian must be overawed by Lamb's accumulation of material from arcane sciences, he may feel that some historical studies (e.g. Titow's 'Le climat') have been unjustly overlooked.

later changes. Wheat remained around 5s. a quarter for several years
after 1411, and the cost of oxen fell. In the 1460s both oxen and wheat
prices rose a little, but these increases were neither at the same time nor
at the same rate, and it would be rash to blame Edward IV's devaluation
for the modest levels they reached.[20]

On the other hand, the money supply increased both absolutely and
per capita in the 1350s and 1360s. This was probably the principal reason
for the continued high prices of the two decades after the Black Death,
a period when the collapse of domestic demand would otherwise have
made them tumble. During the first half of the fourteenth century
English silver stocks had contracted to half their former volume.[21] In
the 1350s and early 1360s, according to T. H. Lloyd's calculations,
England had a favourable annual trade balance, averaging about
£150,000, available for overseas expenditure by the crown or others,
or for repatriation as specie.[22] Consequently between 1351 and 1358
Edward III minted gold nobles worth over £1,250,000. Much went
overseas to pay war costs; much disappeared into private hoards, thus
releasing silver into circulation.[23] The return of plague in 1361–2 and
in 1369 helped to keep *per capita* stocks high for a while, even though
the balance of trade narrowed after 1363 and fell to an annual average
of little more than £50,000 between 1386 and 1399. In the last quarter
of the century the export market for English wool contracted, and that
for cloth failed to expand. Moreover, grain exports – which had helped
raise domestic prices in the 1350s – could no longer compete in
European markets with cheap Hanseatic rye from Russia and Poland,
or wheat brought by the Genoese from Sicily and North Africa.[24]
Between 1373 and 1384 the annual average value of money minted was
back to the level of the depressed early 1340s; even in the 1390s minting
activity was less than in any period between 1344 and 1373. The money
supply in England was almost certainly contracting, both absolutely
and *per capita* in the absence of any major recurrence of plague. War
expenditures and incidentals like papal taxes drained away more than

[20] I have not followed J. E. T. Rogers and others in attempting to express medieval prices in
terms of constant weights of silver. Such exercises ignore the value of silver relative to the stock
in the economy in which it circulates.

[21] D. Metcalfe in *Edwardian Monetary Affairs 1279–1343*, ed. N. J. Mayhew, British Archaeological Reports, 36, 1977, p. 9, summarizing N. J. Mayhew's 'Numismatic evidence and falling
prices in the fourteenth century', *EcHR*, 2nd ser. xxvii, 1974, pp. 1–15.

[22] In *Edwardian Monetary Affairs*, p. 106.

[23] M. Mate, 'The role of gold coinage in the English economy, 1338–1400', *Numismatic
Chronicle*, 7th ser. xviii, 1978, p. 135.

[24] *Ibid.*, p. 140. The European crisis is examined by J. Day, 'The great bullion famine of the
fifteenth century', *PP*, no. 79, 1978, pp. 3–54.

the traders could earn. From the continent, too, bullion was sucked eastwards in exchange for luxuries from the Arab world. Europe's own silver production was in decline, with the accessible lodes exhausted and the deeper lodes unworkable until pumping machinery was developed.[25]

In this period of continent-wide contraction, England's bumper harvests and the loss of some export markets contributed to low agricultural prices. There were profound consequences for the manorial system. The accounts demonstrate a fall in economic activity (at least on the demesnes), with agricultural profits eroded by higher wages and reduced returns, and most people short of ready money. The Peasants' Revolt itself was partly the result of unprecedented taxes intensifying the cash-flow problems of the peasantry. An increase in the velocity of currency circulation might have compensated for a fall in the volume of currency, but none seems to have occurred. The most visible benefits of the weaving industry were not national but local, in the great Perpendicular churches of East Anglia and the Cotswolds. The general stability of fifteenth-century commodity prices strongly suggests that the economy was stagnant.

Direct attempts to limit prices and wages also had some effect. The medieval economy was subject to restraints by the crown and parliament, by towns and gilds, by the lords of fairs and markets, and by the officials serving the great landholders. The accounting and auditing procedures on the manors made the reeves and bailiffs responsible for the lord's loss if the crop fell below expectation, if they accepted too little money for the demesne grain or paid too much for the purchase of seed-corn or livestock, and if they hired workers at rates the auditors thought excessive. The alterations made by the auditors – raising sale prices and cutting wages and purchase prices – appear in almost every series of manorial accounts, the only major exception being the Winchester pipe rolls.[26] These, as "fair copies", show only the sums approved by the auditors, and not the figures originally submitted by the reeves and bailiffs. Indeed, the relatively modest wage payments recorded on the Winchester estates in the 1350s may show the toughness of the auditors in penalizing the bailiffs more than they show the passivity of the peasantry.

In the wake of the Black Death, the civic and manorial authorities were especially zealous to enforce the 1349 royal proclamation

---

[25] Day, loc. cit., p. 35; J. U. Nef in CEcH, 2nd edn, II, pp. 723–7.

[26] The pipe rolls do however record the oneratio charges imposed on the reeve whenever the crop fell short of expectations. By the end of the fourteenth century these penalties were imposed more often than not.

forbidding increases in prices or wages. The city of London, for example, had to arbitrate when the saddlers accused the fusters of demanding 2s. or 30d. for a wooden saddle-tree instead of the former 6d. or 7d., and it also punished forestallers and brewers who charged for ale as much as 2d. a gallon.[27] More powerfully, the members of the commons petitioned the king in 1351 against the "malice of Servants, which were idle, and not willing to serve after the Pestilence, without taking excessive Wages", and secured the Statute of Labourers to try to push wages back to the levels of 1346–7.[28] While it is not easy to disentangle the effects of this and subsequent legislation from the consequences of the other factors, B. H. Putnam's verdict may well stand: "Wages were not kept at the statutory level, but they were kept...at a lower level than would have resulted from a regime of free competition."[29] And, if one may trust the manorial evidence, they did not rise as much as critics of social change and disorder, like the poet John Gower or the monastic chronicler Henry of Knighton, claimed they did.[30]

C. GRAIN PRICES

In the thirteenth and fourteenth centuries the prices of all the grains and legumes had normally risen and fallen together, usually guided by the success of the wheat harvest. If wheat had done badly the cost of barley rose, even if its own crop had been good, for in those circumstances barley was bought as a substitute for wheat. The price of rye, peas, and oats also rose for the same reason: if barley was expensive because it was being used in place of wheat, more oats would be bought for brewing and more peas for livestock.[31] This practice of substitution was less common in the later middle ages, as famines were rarer, and some long-term changes in the relative values of the different grains make occasional substitutions less obvious. In the later thirteenth century and until the end of the 1310s, the decennial values of the other grains and peas relative to wheat had remained fairly constant, with rye costing about 80 per cent, barley and peas about 70 per cent, and oats about 40 per cent of the price of wheat. The gap widened a little, both before and

---

[27] Cal. Plea and Memo. Rolls 1323–1364, ed. Thomas, I, pp. 233, 235, 238–9.

[28] SR, I, p. 311.

[29] Putnam, The Enforcement of the Statutes of Labourers, p. 221.

[30] J. Gower, Mirour de l'Omme, lines 26434–46, in The Complete Works of John Gower, ed. G. C. Macaulay, Oxford, 1899–1902; Chronicon Henrici Knighton, RS, 1889–95, II, pp. 58–65, translated in The Peasants' Revolt of 1381, ed. R. B. Dobson, pp. 59–63.

[31] D. L. Farmer, 'Some grain price movements in thirteenth-century England', EcHR, 2nd ser. X, 1957, pp. 213–15, 218–19; AHEW, II, pp. 716ff.

Table 5.1. *Grain sale prices by decades, 1300–1500, in shillings per quarter*

	Wheat	Rye	Barley	Oats	Peas
1300–10[a]	5.37	4.18	3.94	2.30	3.68
1310–20	7.94	6.23	5.67	3.18	5.22
1320–30	6.90	5.02	4.68	2.76	4.35
1330–40	5.24	4.22	3.92	2.29	3.79
1340–7	4.88	3.81	3.57	2.19	3.24
1350–60	7.05	4.89	5.18	3.15	4.41
1360–70	8.16	5.43	5.82	3.13	4.94
1370–80	6.67	4.57	4.73	2.60	3.87
1380–90	5.25	3.60	3.52	2.22	3.30
1390–1400	5.46	4.11	4.08	2.49	3.69
1400–10	6.47	4.24	4.24	2.44	3.64
1410–20	6.01	4.15	3.89	2.34	3.67
1420–30	5.57	4.45	3.51	2.10	3.38
1430–40	7.33	5.47	3.84	2.23	4.20
1440–50	4.93	3.36	2.73	1.83	2.74
1450–60	5.63	4.04	2.97	1.74	2.67
1460–70	5.60	4.10	3.39	1.77	3.00
1470–80	5.76	4.30	3.01	1.68	3.18
1480–90	6.85	4.22	3.60	1.85	4.61
1490–1500	5.39	4.67	3.33	1.67	2.59

[a] Each period extends from 29 September in the first-named year to 28 September in the second-named year.

after the Black Death: by the 1370s rye cost less than 70 per cent and peas less than 60 per cent of the price of wheat. The 1390s interrupted the decline of the other grain and legume prices relative to the cost of wheat, but by the middle of the fifteenth century peas and barley cost only half, and oats only a third, of the price of wheat. After the sequence of Winchester pipe rolls ends in 1453–4 the different geographical distribution of the material makes further comparisons unreliable, but rye and barley possibly recovered something of their relative value towards the end of the century. Apart from changes relative to the cost of wheat, the prices of the other grains moved somewhat in relation to each other. In the middle of the thirteenth century, rye had cost nearly a third more than barley. In the third quarter of the fourteenth century, however, it cost less than barley; in the fourth quarter it cost about the same. In the thirteenth century peas had cost almost exactly the same as barley; in the fourteenth they cost less, the difference being particularly marked in the 1360s and 1370s.

Relative to the other cereals, oats cost most in the 1350s, when their harvest suffered as manors used their depleted labour forces to gather first the more valuable grains.

Short-term price fluctuations also suggest a marked consumer preference for wheat rather than the other grains, and show that many purchasers were willing and able to pay high prices for it rather than make do with substitutes. In 1369–70 wheat prices were 125 per cent higher than in the previous account year, whereas the costs of the others rose much less – barley by 93 per cent, rye by 87 per cent, peas by 67 per cent, and oats by 48 per cent. In the extended period of bad harvests in the late 1430s, the sharp rise in wheat prices between 1436–7 and 1437–8 had little immediate effect on the cost of barley or peas; it was only after the second successive year of high wheat prices that the cost of the substitutes rose above 7s. a quarter. It was then that Londoners had "to eat beans, pease and barley more then in a hundred yeeres before".[32] This reluctance to accept substitutes for wheat seems to confirm that for craftsmen and city-dwellers it had become the principal – almost the only – breadcorn. The cheapness of peas relative to barley shows the importance of the latter as the main cereal for brewing.

Although more stable than in the thirteenth and early fourteenth centuries, grain prices in the later middle ages were thus far from static. Sometimes having to sell wheat for less than 4s. a quarter, the bishop of Winchester's Hampshire manors were able to get at least 10s. a quarter for it in twelve years during the century after the Black Death. In two account years a few prices exceeded 20s. a quarter – in 1369–70 on some Winchester manors and on the Westminster abbey manors of Hyde in London and Feering in Essex, and in 1438–9, when the abbey treasurer had to pay as much as 24s. a quarter to buy wheat for the Westminster monks. The "national price level" calculated for wheat doubles from one year to the next on only one occasion in this period (between 1368–9 and 1369–70), and rises by 50 per cent at only three other times; on the other hand, it falls with comparable swiftness on two and eight occasions respectively.[33] Replenished granaries, therefore, lowered wheat prices faster than empty ones encouraged them to rise. The cost of the other grains changed less than that of wheat; on only three occasions, for example, did the price of barley fall by a third from one year to the next. The highest barley prices to survive from the later middle ages are 14s. at Ashmansworth and 13s. 4d. a quarter on some other Hampshire manors in 1369–70; the lowest are 2s. or less a quarter at Stoke Bishop, West Wycombe, and Hyde in 1387–8, West

---

[32] Stow, *Annales*, p. 627. [33] i.e., by 50 per cent and $33\frac{1}{3}$ per cent respectively.

Wycombe and Hindolveston in 1388–9, North Elmham in 1404–5 and 1406–7, Alton Barnes in 1431–2, Coleshill in 1444–5 and 1445–6, and Witney in 1446–7.[34] At Hampton Episcopi in 1389–90 the bishop of Worcester's auditors refused to accept that 2s. was the rate at which the reeve had sold the manor's barley, altered the price to 2s. 8d., and forced him to pay the difference. Several manors obtained 13s. 4d. a quarter for rye in 1369–70, and Droxford got 12s. in 1438–9. In southern England rye seldom fetched less than 3s. 4d., though the price was sometimes lower at Adderbury and Stert, and on East Anglian manors such as Hinderclay, Redgrave, and Plumstead. Oats were of course the cheapest cereal, but the comparison of individual entries may be misleading because the accounts seldom distinguish between "great" oats and the less valuable "small" oats. Moreover, the most complete series of oats prices in the fifteenth century comes from the north-east, and one should not pay much attention to an apparent steep rise in the price of oats in 1488–9 when the only evidence for it comes from Finchale and Jarrow. On the Winchester manors, for oats as for the other grains, 1369–70 was the most expensive year, with a rate of 5s. 4d. established almost universally, in contrast to a price of between 2s. and 3s. 4d. in the previous year and a fairly general 3s. 4d. a quarter in 1370–1. In the fifteenth century the oats prices on the Winchester manors were particularly low, and commonly exceeded 2s. a quarter in only four of the twenty-two years for which the pipe rolls survive between 1420–1 and 1453–4. These lower prices were probably partly the result of the marked improvement in the yield of oats on the Winchester manors in the later middle ages.

Peas and other legumes served some of the purposes of the cheaper grains, especially for fattening livestock, food deliveries, and pottage for the manorial servants. The cost of peas fluctuated very much as grain prices did. Again, the highest prices were in 1369–70 (10s. to 13s. 4d. a quarter on the Winchester Hampshire manors) and in 1438–9. At the other extreme, in 1386–7 peas cost only 2s. a quarter on some manors in Hampshire and even less on the Winchester manors in Somerset and the Chilterns. These lower prices are the more surprising because in the second half of the fourteenth century most of the Winchester demesnes reduced the proportions of arable given to peas, although they retained about the same number of *famuli* and increased sharply the number of livestock.

Prices were normally highest in those areas with urban markets of their own or inexpensive access to London, but there were some

[34] I exclude from this list some unverified entries given in J. E. T. Rogers, *History of Agriculture and Prices*.

Table 5.2. *Grain price ratios, 1350–1500*

	Wheat	Rye	Barley	Peas	Oats
1350–60*a*	100	69	73	63	45
1360–70	100	67	71	61	38
1370–80	100	69	71	58	39
1380–90	100	69	67	63	42
1390–1400	100	75	75	68	46
1400–10	100	66	66	56	38
1410–20	100	69	65	61	39
1420–30	100	80	63	61	38
1430–40	100	75	52	57	30
1440–50	100	68	55	56	37
1450–60	100	72	53	47	31
1460–70	100	73	61	54	32
1470–80	100	75	52	55	29
1480–90	100	62	53	67	27
1490–1500	100	87	62	48	31

a Each period extends from 29 September in the first-named year to 28 September in the second-named year.

inconsistencies in the regional distribution of prices. Hampshire wheat prices were higher than average after the Black Death, while barley prices were close to the "national price level" and oats prices slightly below it. Wheat prices in the Upper Thames region were below the national level both before and after 1350, but barley and oats prices dropped from substantially higher to substantially lower than the national level by the early fifteenth century. In the London area, wheat prices were marginally above the "national price level" both before and after the Black Death. Whereas the cost of barley there dropped down to the national level, the cost of oats in London rose well above it by the 1410s. In the Chilterns in the 1360s, wheat was fairly cheap, barley and oats rather dear. Wheat in Essex was of average price, but barley and oats there cost more than the "national price level". Wheat and oats remained a little on the dear side in Norfolk and Suffolk both before and after the Black Death, but barley changed from being very dear before 1350 to being very cheap afterwards. In Durham and Northumberland wheat and barley were dear, but oats were cheap.

These regional variations were often most marked in years of good harvests. After the bad harvest of 1369, the most northerly Winchester manors – Adderbury, Witney, and Harwell – sold their wheat at 20s. a quarter, as did most of the bishop's other manors, but their prices in the

Table 5.3. *Regional grain prices as percentages of national price levels*[a]

	Wheat			Barley			Oats		
	1299–1303	1360–70	1410–20	1299–1303	1360–70	1410–20	1299–1303	1360–70	1410–20
South Hants.	118	108	106	115	99	107	123	95	104
North Downs	112	105	100	100	103	99	116	98	93
Upper Thames	99	92	94	113	96	82	112	104	83
Lower Thames	113	112	112	113	106	101	93	101	119
Cotswolds	79	82		75	89		103	100	
Chilterns	94	92	86	100	108		101	115	91
Wilts.	105	109	99	100	97	98	116	108	106
Somerset & Devon	121	104	111	83	104	107	105	92	87
Kent & Sussex	102	99	100	100	88	107	113	94	
Essex	96	94	103	110	111	108	124	108	116
Norfolk & Suffolk	105	102	108	115	90	77	110	101	114
Durham & Northumb.		102	109		110	110		94	82
Cambs.	89		78	118		76	85		84

[a] Each period extends from 29 September in the first-named year to 28 September in the second-named year.

preceding and succeeding years of good harvest were much lower in the north than in the south and west. This was also true of the prices of other grains. Like the Hampshire manors, Adderbury received 13s. 4d. a quarter for rye in 1369–70, but got only 2s. in 1365–6 and 3s. 8d. in 1372–3, in contrast to the 4s. 2d. and 7s. respectively averaged in Hampshire in those years. On manors nearer London the price fluctuated less: whereas the 1369–70 Adderbury wheat price was nearly seven times the 1365–6 price, the cost of wheat on the Canterbury manor of Great Chart in the former year was only 75 per cent higher than in the latter. Monkton, the only Canterbury manor regularly selling it, received 5s. a quarter for rye in 1365–6, less than 7s. 6d. in the famine year 1369–70, and 5s. 6d. in 1372–3, variations insignificant in comparison with those at Adderbury. On the other hand, the high prices for Hampshire barley in 1369–70 were not reflected further north. Whereas barley fetched 13s. 4d. in Hampshire, prices elsewhere – on the Winchester manors in the Chilterns and the Thames valley, on the Westminster manors of Islip, Feering, and Birdbrook, at Blakemere in Shropshire – were around 10s. a quarter, and a few manors (such as Plumstead, Hinderclay, and Monkton) got only 7s. or 8s. Oats prices in the eastern counties similarly failed to rise in 1369–70 in the way they did in Hampshire. These examples suggest that in years of high prices it was worth moving the more costly grains, especially those used for making bread, from the remoter manors on to national markets.[35] In years of relative plenty, transport costs would make such movements uneconomic. It is possible, therefore, that the period of good yields and low prices made marketing arrangements more local or regional than hitherto.

The principal factor determining grain prices was of course the adequacy of the previous harvest. It is possible to calculate the yields on the Winchester estates for over eighty harvests following the Black Death, and for nearly half those years crop returns may be calculated from at least forty manors.[36] Even though the bishop's manors were all in southern England, there is a close correlation between the "national price levels" and the success of the harvests recorded on the Winchester estates. This is particularly clear when the Winchester evidence is most plentiful. But as yields differed greatly in the same year even on adjacent manors, there were few harvests which were everywhere either bountiful or disastrous. In the majority of years the Winchester manors brought in crops which were within 10 per cent of the normal for the estate as a whole. If one excludes the few harvests immediately after the Black Death and those for which returns can be calculated from fewer than twenty manors, the pattern is clear: in a total of sixty-one harvests, the wheat yield rose above 110 per cent of the long-term mean only sixteen times, and fell below 90 per cent of the mean only fourteen times. After the sixteen unusually good harvests, the price of wheat averaged only 5s. a quarter, and in only one of these better years, following the high-price year of 1369–70, did its cost exceed 7s. On the other hand, the fourteen unusually poor wheat harvests were followed by prices averaging 9s.; in only one year, 1406–7, was a poor Winchester harvest followed by a "national price level" of less than 6s. a quarter. The barley and oats prices also show the consequences of the harvest, but rather less clearly because of the practice of substituting these grains for wheat when the latter cropped badly. After the seventeen harvests when barley yields exceeded 110 per cent of the

[35] D. L. Farmer, 'Two Wiltshire manors and their markets', *AHR*, XXXVII, 1989, p. 7.
[36] Farmer, 'Grain yields on the Winchester manors', p. 555, J. Z. Titow, 'Le climat', p. 312. It should be noted that Dr Titow under each year quotes the price of wheat at Merdon and Ecchinswell in the account year *before* the harvest; this practice to some extent masks the connection between crop yields and subsequent prices (though obviously prices would rise somewhat during a summer in anticipation of a bad crop). There are many misprints in the *Annales* paper.

long-term mean, the price averaged less than 3s. 9d. a quarter, in
contrast to an average of 5s. 5d. after the ten harvests when yields were
less than 90 per cent of the long-term level on the Winchester manors.
Eleven abnormally poor oats harvests were followed by prices
averaging 3s. 3d. a quarter, the fourteen unusually good harvests by
prices around 2s. 2d.

A few comments are necessary. The yields of barley and oats were
much higher on the Winchester estates in the fourth quarter of the
fourteenth century than in the third quarter, and thus coincided with
the period when almost all prices were particularly low. This was also
the case on the manors of Westminster abbey.[37] In the years
immediately after the Black Death wheat had taken priority, and much
of the barley and oats had been left standing in the fields because of the
lack of labourers; this problem persisted into the 1360s and helps
explain why barley and oats prices were fairly high even though wheat
yields had improved. For the most part though, as has been said, the
success or failure of the wheat crop affected the prices of the other
grains as well as the price of wheat. All grains were more expensive
after the harvests of 1379 and 1389, even though the barley and oats
crops on the Winchester manors were unusually good. The 1361 barley
harvest was very poor, but wheat did rather well and the prices of both
grains fell. The 1384 oats crop was worse than the previous year's, but
wheat did better than in 1383; the cost of oats, like the prices of barley
and wheat, fell in the subsequent account year. After 1350, in the
eighty-four years for which Winchester crop returns can be calculated,
wheat prices increased nationally between one year and the next on
thirty-seven occasions; in only eight of these cases did higher prices
coincide with better wheat yields on the Winchester estates. Incomplete
though the material is, it shows how close was the relationship between
yield and price, and how the practice of substituting an inferior grain
for wheat recurred in years of high prices.

One must wonder why prices stayed firm at all. If plague had carried
off a third or a half of the population, why was demand so buoyant?
Some demesne arable, certainly, was put to sheep pasture, and some
was leased out to tenants – but on the Winchester manors and many
others the changes were not dramatic. In the 1370s the Winchester
estates were still cultivating about 85 per cent of their pre-Black Death
area of arable, and in the 1410s still nearly three-quarters of it.[38]
Moreover, much of the land leased to tenants must have remained as
ploughland. But though grain production remained high, prices were

---

[37] Farmer, 'Grain yields on Westminster Abbey manors', pp. 344–6.
[38] Farmer, 'Grain yields on the Winchester manors', pp. 561–3.

still sensitive to harvest fluctuations despite the contraction of the market. If the peasants' strips grew heavy crops in the years when the demesnes did so, the tenants would have less need to purchase any demesne grain in just those years when the manors had most for sale. On the other hand, if the crops of both the peasants and their lords did badly, the countrymen would have to compete with the townsmen for whatever grain was available for purchase. The presence of the great mass of countrymen on the fringe of the market – sellers in good years, buyers in bad – therefore multiplied the effects of harvest variations. Secondly, all classes seem to have had expectations of a higher standard of living after the Black Death, and many people were prosperous enough not to cut back their consumption in years when grain was scarce and expensive. Furthermore, as Sir Michael Postan pointed out, farmers sometimes respond to periods of high prices by reducing the acreages they work, and to periods of low prices by increasing the acreages (to limit the amount of hard physical labour to that needed to pay their rent and purchase basic necessities).[39] Thus the high taxes, good harvests, and low prices of the last quarter of the fourteenth century may have driven peasants to grow more grain for sale, and may explain why estate auditors were so harsh in penalizing reeves who failed to get into the demesne granaries as much grain as had been expected.

Although the better returns for seed sown, especially marked on Winchester's Hampshire manors, resulted from heavier manuring of the demesne arable, more favourable weather, and perhaps a reduction in the density of sowing, they may also bear witness to this more vigorous supervision by the auditors. At Winchester as on other estates, the reeve was liable to be charged with the value of the quantity of grain by which the crop had fallen short of expectations. For example, the 1413–14 pipe roll shows the reeve at Ivinghoe being "charged" with 12 qr of wheat (because the crop of some 27 qr had not reached the target of four and a half times what had been sown), 30 qr of barley and 18 qr of oats. A year later the same official was "charged" with nearly 8 qr of wheat, 20 qr of barley, and 24 qr of oats. Westminster abbey in 1370–1 held the reeve of Feering responsible for 42 qr of wheat, 2 qr of barley, and 32 qr of oats. At Henbury, a small manor belonging to the bishop of Worcester, the *oneratio* in the 1382–3 account totalled nearly 26 qr, the grain actually harvested barely 70 qr. The reeve at Plumstead in 1415–16 had to compensate Norwich Cathedral priory for a shortfall of 3 qr of wheat, 11 qr of oats, and no less than 39 qr of barley.

Some auditors were also aggressive in rejecting the prices which the

[39] M. M. Postan, *The Medieval Economy and Society*, London, 1972, p. 260.

reeves claimed to have paid or received for demesne grain. At Apuldram they rejected the account of wheat sales submitted by the reeve for 1363–4 and raised the price of some from 8s. a quarter to 10s., and the rest from 6s. 8d. to 8s. Other auditors refused to believe that Monkleigh had sold wheat at 9s. 4d. in the hungry year of 1369–70, and forced the reeve to find an extra 4s. a quarter. At Stoke Bishop in 1389–90 the wheat sale price was raised from 5s. 4d. to 6s. a quarter because it was *sic apud Hembury*.[40] At Hampton Episcopi, another Worcester manor, the price the reeve claimed for the purchase of oats in 1381–2 was cut from 2s. 4d. to 2s. a quarter, apparently because it was at this lower rate that the reeve had sold the manor's oats that year.

These alterations present a problem: should the historian accept the rate claimed by the reeve, or should he assume that the auditors' changes were justified? There are several other pitfalls for the unwary. The accounts seldom state at what time in the year the sale was made. In the course of an account year, the price might rise steeply as the old grain ran out and a poor crop seemed likely. In 1407–8, for example, Westminster abbey bought most of its wheat at 5s. 4d. or less, but in August and September 1408 had to pay 9s. 6d. a quarter. As the fears of a poor harvest proved justified, in the following account year most of Westminster's wheat cost 10s. a quarter. Uncertainty about the date of a transaction is therefore one reason why one must hesitate before drawing conclusions from price levels on different manors or in different areas.

There are several other reasons for caution. Was the grain of consistent quality? On the whole, wheat probably was, for it was the standard practice to sort the inferior grain from the rest, and to sell it at a lower price as curall or give it to the manorial *famuli* as part of their grain delivery. Sometimes the reeve added a note about the condition of the grain: Meopham in 1394–5 sold wheat at 4s. 4d. and 4s. 2d. a quarter, and then some at 3s. 8d. *propter le melledew*. Occasionally one meets curall barley: Egloshayle sold it in 1399–1400 at less than half the price of the other barley. Later accounts often record the sale of barley malt, at a higher price than unmalted barley; was the barley malted more often than the accounts tell? Peas might be white peas, grey peas, green peas, pottage peas, or, most common of all, peas unlabelled. Oats might be "great" oats or "small" oats; the accounts seldom say which.[41]

How accurate or consistent were the bushels used to measure grain? Lord Beveridge long ago detected a change in the size of wheat

[40] Worcs. RO, BA 2636/171/92415 – 1/8.
[41] The introduction to the statistical appendix (below, p. 496) explains my treatment of these problems.

measures used at Exeter, and later argued that in the 1350s many of the Winchester manors abandoned the use of abnormally large bushels. One need not accept all his conclusions to be aware that a major problem exists.[42] The Battle abbey accounts, as P. F. Brandon has shown, record the adoption by several manors of large local measures around the end of the fourteenth century, in defiance of repeated legislation trying to make the small "standard" bushel universal.[43] Many estates, like those of Battle abbey, New College, and the bishopric of Worcester, sold the quarter of grain by measuring out seven levelled bushels and then one heaped bushel. While one may readily adjust figures to compensate for this last practice, the survival of abnormal local measures compels one to be cautious before comparing prices in different regions. This factor may explain some of the variations displayed in Table 5.3 (above, p. 448).

Further problems arise from the use of different marketing techniques. The later Winchester rolls frequently state that a manor's grain was sold *per mutuum, ad hospicium domini* or *in foro*. Sometimes the grain sold was tenants' grain surrendered to the demesne mill in multure, or, as at East Meon church, paid in tithe. Sometimes, especially on the manors around Taunton, the sales were described as having been made to the customary tenants; at Bishop's Waltham in 1427–8 and 1432–3, the wheat was sold "to the poor tenants of the lord" (though at prices higher than the general local levels). Occasionally the range of prices was quite wide: at Ecchinswell and East Meon in 1357–8 wheat was sold *per mutuum* at 9s., *in foro* at 7s., and *ad hospicium domini* at 6s. a quarter. The lowest rate was for the credit allowed the reeve for grain "bought" from the manor by the bishop's household. The middle rate, the market price, explains itself. The meaning of *per mutuum*, though, is far from clear. Beveridge thought that the term "might indicate either a credit transaction or an exchange".[44] Paying for purchases by bills of exchange or credit notes (if this is what Beveridge meant) rather than cash would have been a logical development in an age short of coins, but why these transactions should usually be measured in abnormally large bushels (as Beveridge also argued) is less obvious. Moreover, the money transfer paragraphs in the account rolls seem to count the revenues from *per mutuum* sales as cash, rather than credit notes. Possibly *per mutuum* meant a sale by contract at a price negotiated in advance, or perhaps an arrangement by which the purchaser had first choice of the grain offered. Either of these

---

[42] W. H. Beveridge, 'A statistical crime of the seventeenth century', *J. of Business Admin. and Hist.*, I, 1929, pp. 503–33; idem, 'Wheat measures in the Winchester rolls', *Econ. Hist.*, v, 1930, pp. 19–44.   [43] Brandon, 'Cereal yields', pp. 415–17.

[44] Beveridge, 'Wheat measures', p. 41; see also above, pp. 360–2.

would help to explain why *per mutuum* sales were often at prices slightly higher than sales not so described, although the pattern was far from consistent.

The market price of grain, of course, had to cover the cost of getting it to the market place. The rates at which the abbey treasurer bought wheat frequently included the cost of carriage to Westminster from such manors as Harpenden and Sawbridgeworth. Transport charges were usually quite modest, particularly where the journey could be made by water; wherever the cost would have been otherwise, of course, the grain was not moved. It cost only 4s. in 1395–6 to transport 43½ qr of grain from Bredon to Tewkesbury by water – though Battle abbey had to pay 26s. 8d. in 1423–4 for a ship to carry 34¼ qr of wheat and barley from Apuldram to Hastings. As demonstrated elsewhere in this volume, overland transport facilities were extensive, even though they became more costly in the later fourteenth century. The Thames, the Severn, and the sluggish waters of eastern England helped carry grain in bulk to the major centres of consumption. Even imports from overseas could be justified whenever domestic prices rose steeply. London annalists commended their mayors for organizing grain imports (usually rye from Prussia) in years such as 1391–2 and 1438–9 when London prices were relatively high.[45]

Although English towns other than London did not maintain municipal granaries – a practice widespread on the European continent – civic intervention helped stabilize prices in several ways. Justices or aldermen enforcing the assize of bread and ale determined what a loaf of bread should weigh: when a quarter of wheat was sold for 4s., a standard loaf (*wastellus de quadrante*) must weigh as much as 456 silver pennies, but when the quarter cost 8s. the loaf need balance only 204.[46] Magistrates tried to protect the consumer through firm interpretation of statute law, and this duty remained a prominent part of their responsibilities, especially after the Black Death. Of the 485 separate offences considered by some Lincolnshire justices in 1373–5, 31 were for having charged excessive prices.[47] Later in the century the Warwickshire and Coventry sessions tried 73 indictments for forestalling and regrating, breaking the assizes of bread and ale, using false weights, or selling shoddy goods, but only 43 cases where workers

[45] Stow, *Annales*, pp. 491, 621; *The Great Chronicle of London*, ed. A. H. Thomas and I. D. Thornley, London and Aylesbury, 1938, p. 84.

[46] *The Mediaeval Archives of the University of Oxford*, ed. H. E. Salter, II, Oxford Hist. Soc., LXXIII, 1921, pp. 130–1. The most complete records of the operation of the assize of bread are probably those for Exeter; the practice there is described in Beveridge, 'A statistical crime', pp. 503–7.

[47] *Records of some Sessions of the Peace in Lincolnshire, 1360–1375*, ed. R. Sillem, Lincs. Rec. Soc., 30, 1936, p. xlvi.

were accused of taking excessive wages or in other ways violating the
Statute of Labourers.[48] The Cheltenham J.Ps in 1422 tried twenty-eight
traders and craftsmen for over-charging, but only one man from the
whole lordship for taking illegally high wages.[49]

One must not exaggerate the significance of individual price entries,
liable to distortion from such a variety of causes. But the general picture
remains clear, at least for the period up to 1453–4 while the Winchester
records provide sufficient entries to permit representative averages. In
short, once the manors had recovered from the immediate shock of the
Black Death, an inflated money supply, and the high costs of the 1360s,
there were only a few years of unsuccessful harvests and dear grain
prices. The buyers' preference for wheat kept its price fairly high – in
relation to the cost of the other major grains – in the later middle ages.
The success of the wheat harvest affected the price of all grains, not
merely that of wheat. Although a deterrent to national marketing
when prices were low, transport costs were cheap enough to allow
grain to be distributed fairly widely whenever prices were higher. The
spectre of famine, common in the first quarter of the fourteenth
century, was a relatively rare visitor in the later middle ages.

D. LIVESTOCK PRICES

The evidence on late medieval livestock prices is much less complete
than on grain prices. The only series worthy of much confidence is that
provided by oxen purchases, and even these appear less frequently after
the Winchester pipe rolls end in 1453–4. For cart horses, and even for
plough horses, there are only a few reliable entries for each decade in
the later fifteenth century, and none at all for the 1490s. There is slightly
better material on cow and sheep purchases, and on pig sales, but for
most animals the sum of the evidence for later fifteenth-century prices
is less than for a decade in the early fifteenth century, or for some single
years in the early fourteenth century. The problem derives in part from
the need to compare like with like. Grain bought by manors was very
much the same as grain sold by manors, but it was not so with
livestock. Most animals were purchased at the beginning of their useful
working or breeding lives. Most of those sold were sent for slaughter,
usually at only a fraction of the cost of healthy replacements. Except for
pigs, where sale prices are used because manors almost never bought
castrated *porci* for fattening, this chapter therefore considers only
purchase prices. Any survey which counted together livestock purchase
and sale prices would show serious distortions. Minor distortions arise

---

[48] *Rolls of the Warwickshire and Coventry Sessions of the Peace, 1377–97*, ed. E. G. Kimball,
Dugdale Soc., XVI, 1939, pp. lxiv–lxv.   [49] Hilton, *English Peasantry*, p. 83.

from listing together the purchase of cows, cows-in-calf, and cows
with calves, and by not distinguishing between sheep bought before or
after shearing, but the errors thus introduced are not serious. Major and
unacceptable distortions would result from counting together all the
horses, even though the "Livestock Purchases" paragraphs of manorial
accounts sometimes call them all *equi*; one must look elsewhere in the
account to see whether they were plough horses, cart horses, or riding
horses. As cart horses typically cost at least 50 per cent more than
plough horses, and riding horses a lot more, their prices must be kept
separate.[50]

An earlier part of this chapter examined ox-price movements as
guides to the general long-term price changes in the later middle ages.
In brief, oxen cost about 13s. in the 1350s, between 16s. and 19s. for
most of the 1360s and early 1370s, about 13s. or 14s. for the rest of the
fourteenth century, slightly more at the start of the fifteenth century,
and anything between 12s. and 16s. thereafter. Of the other large
animals, cart horses had cost about a third more than oxen before the
Black Death. The gap subsequently widened: from the 1360s to the
1440s (and the end of reliable statistics on horse prices), cart horses cost
at least half as much again as oxen. In the 1390s and 1400s their price
was over 70 per cent higher than that of oxen. Plough horses also
became more expensive in relation to oxen. Before the Black Death,
their price had been less than 80 per cent of that of oxen, but by the
1370s and 1380s they were nearly as expensive. At the end of the
century they cost about 10 per cent more than oxen. Their price later
steadied at about 90 per cent of the cost of oxen, but (if one may trust
very slender evidence) dropped sharply at the end of the fifteenth
century. There was no obvious reason for this willingness to pay more
for horses (or, in effect, less for oxen) at the end of the fourteenth
century and the beginning of the fifteenth – no great scourge of
murrain such as had ravaged cattle in the late 1310s, no widespread
seizures of horses for wars foreign or domestic.[51] Possibly the higher
yield and lower cost of oats then made it less expensive and more
attractive than usual to keep horses. Perhaps the horses, adaptable to
some extent for plough, cart, or pannier bags, had some advantages
which made them more attractive then for the village tenants, with the
result that the lords also had to pay more to buy them. Certainly there
was no general replacement of oxen by plough horses, which in
England as a whole at the start of the fifteenth century supplied only

---

[50] These two errors are weaknesses in the statistics in Rogers's *History of Agriculture and Prices*,
and in certain studies based on his work.

[51] Hornchurch in 1445–6 bought 23 cows to replace those killed by murrain, but this seems an
isolated case.

Table 5.4. *Livestock prices, 1300–1500, in shillings per animal*

	Oxen (bought)	Plough horses (bought)	Cart horses (bought)	Cows (bought)	Wethers (bought)	Pigs (sold)
1300–10[a]	12.73	11.56	19.75	9.36	1.41	2.99
1310–20	15.99	14.50	23.41	11.52	1.29	3.32
1320–30	15.38	11.81	18.28	11.72	1.63	2.98
1330–40	12.61	10.26	17.51	9.60	1.12	2.81
1340–7	12.14	9.45	14.65	9.32	1.11	2.23
1350–60	13.41	10.34	17.95	9.75	1.43	2.82
1360–70	16.31	13.50	25.58	11.55	1.85	3.09
1370–80	16.15	15.72	25.76	11.50	2.25	3.28
1380–90	13.76	13.54	22.36	10.34	1.66	2.66
1390–1400	13.47	14.89	23.01	10.64	1.63	2.80
1400–10	14.31	16.42	24.30	10.50	1.83	2.82
1410–20	13.19	14.37	21.94	8.92	1.80	2.85
1420–30	14.05	12.51	20.37	8.37	1.43	2.57
1430–40	13.72	12.62	21.46	8.25	1.64	2.81
1440–50	12.74	12.04	18.92	7.76	1.59	2.80
1450–60	13.67	9.20	18.65	7.24	1.24	2.74
1460–70	14.28	8.00	28.33	9.26	1.70	2.66
1470–80	14.73	10.00	13.79	8.81	1.73	2.69
1480–90	14.01	10.00	16.36	9.56	1.92	2.71
1490–1500	12.96			7.48	1.86	2.75

[a] Each period extends from 29 September in the first-named year to 28 September in the second-named year. It must be noted that after 1450 there are very few entries for animals other than oxen. The abnormal decennial price for cart horses in the 1460s, for example, is calculated from the purchase of only two beasts.

about 30 per cent of demesne draught animals (though the leasing of some demesne lands to tenants perhaps transferred a larger share of cereal production to smallholders and others who were more likely to use horses than oxen).[52] In 1347, 14 per cent of the animals in the Winchester ploughteams were horses, but in 1395 less than 12 per cent. Examination of a random sample of manors inspected by royal escheators suggests that demesne oxen outnumbered plough horses by about seven to one.[53]

The prices of the other animals behaved more predictably. Throughout the fourteenth century cows cost about three-quarters of

[52] J. Langdon, *Horses, Oxen and Technological Innovation*, pp. 170, 218, 252.
[53] *Cal. Inq. Misc.*, IV (1377–88), V (1387–93), VII (1399–1422).

the price of oxen, but their relative value declined thereafter: from the 1420s onwards, the decennial price of cows was about three-fifths that of oxen. By then almost every manor had abandoned the dairy business, and demesnes owned cows merely to lease them out to the *daie* or the *vaccarius*, in return for six shillings or so in lactage every year. In the 1440s manors bought their cows for about 7s. 6d., rather than the 11s. 6d. of the 1360s and 1370s. By the mid-fifteenth century, then, a cow cost the lord little more than he could expect to receive in one year's rent for the beast and the right to graze it on demesne pasture.

Sheep prices were sensitive to changes in the value of wool. Sheep cost most – relative to the price of oxen – during those decades when the price of wool was highest. Between the 1360s and 1430s the decennial price of wool remained above 3s. 5d. a stone; in all but one of those decades a wether cost at least 12 per cent of the cost of an ox. The 1370s saw the highest decennial wool price of the later middle ages; the same decade saw the cost of wethers reach 14 per cent of the price of oxen. Thereafter the price of wethers declined from 2s. 3d. each to a mere 1s. 3d. in the 1450s, but it subsequently recovered to 1s. 11d. in the 1480s, a decade when wool prices improved as cloth exports increased.

Although *porci* were produced only for domestic consumption or sale as food, pig prices did not follow the year-by-year fluctuations in the price of grain but remained relatively stable. Their cost dropped from a maximum of 3s. 3d. in the 1370s to a minimum of 2s. 7d. in the 1430s. When grain was dear, as in the 1360s and 1430s, a pig cost about 38 per cent of the price of a quarter of wheat. When grain was cheap, as in the 1380s, 1390s, and 1440s, pigs cost more than half the price of a quarter of wheat. The amount of pork reaching the market was probably too small for it to be in any way a substitute for bread when grain was dear. On the other hand, pig prices kept a steady relationship to the cost of oxen: in the period 1350–1500, the decennial price of *porci* was never less than 18 per cent of that of oxen, and never more than 22 per cent.

Livestock prices varied from region to region as much as grain prices did. In the fourteenth century, oxen bought in the London area cost a fifth more than the national average, those in Essex a quarter more, and those in Somerset and Devon almost a third more. In south Hampshire, by contrast, their price was only 88 per cent of the "national price level", and in the Cotswolds only 75 per cent. These disparities occur even in the purchases made by a single estate. Forty-eight of their individual accounts between 1363–4 and 1379–80 show the Winchester manors in Somerset paying 20s. or more each for oxen, while only nine record purchases averaging less than 20s. Only fourteen accounts from

Table 5.5. *Regional livestock prices, as percentages of "national price levels"*[a]

	Oxen			Plough horses			Wethers		
	1356–80	1380–1400	1400–25	1356–80	1380–1400	1400–25	1356–80	1380–1400	1400–25
South Hants.	99	88	94	100	98	92	88	87	90
North Downs	88	92	99	96	107	116	93	90	97
Upper Thames	96	95	101	87	85	88	109	113	97
Lower Thames	105	119					103	95	
Cotswolds	98	75	96	81	90		102	121	120
Chilterns	94	98	93	89	77	91	102	100	106
Wiltshire	87	100	100	98	63		97	109	92
Somerset & Devon	126	131	131	79	116	119	87	107	88
Kent & Sussex	112	99	105	153[b]	161	89	69	79	78
Essex	126	126	108					91	116
Norfolk & Suffolk	98	89					93	82	
Durham & Northumb.	89	93	76						80

[a] Each period extends from 29 September in the first-named year to 28 September in the second-named year.
[b] Almost all entries before 1400 come from the estates of Canterbury Cathedral priory; almost all those after 1400 come from the Battle abbey manors.

Winchester's more numerous south Hampshire manors record prices of 20s. or over in that period, whereas ninety of them show oxen bought for less than that. But Somerset and Devon were not the most expensive areas for other livestock. Plough horses were particularly dear in Kent, where their price in the 1380s and 1390s was two and a half times that in Wiltshire, more than twice that in the Chilterns, and almost twice that in the Upper Thames area. In this period prices paid for wethers in the Cotswolds were half as much again as those paid in Kent and Norfolk. As animals were relatively mobile and therefore cheap to drive to the best markets, these differences are rather surprising. Perhaps Somerset oxen and Kent plough horses, like Cotswold sheep, were so much better than beasts bought elsewhere that one should regard them as superior breeds. But even in the same area widely different prices demonstrate variations in quality. Hindolveston in 1358–9 paid 14s. for one plough horse and 24s. for another. Taverham in 1369–70 bought three plough horses, one for 14s., one for 15s., and one for 23s. 1d. Apuldram gave 13s. 4d. for a cart horse in 1356–7; next year it paid 28s. 1d. for another. On the other hand, the prices might be fairly consistent, even in a large number of purchases: Birchanger in 1394–5 bought cows in eleven separate deals, never paying more than 12s. 10d. or less than 9s. 3d.

Livestock transactions in the accounts also show some of the marketing techniques recorded for grain sales. Pigs were often "sold" *ad hospicium domini*. Highclere in 1400–1 "sold" some pigs to the lord's household at 2s. 8d., and disposed of worse ones *in foro* at 3s. The 1370–1 Winchester pipe roll lists large transfers of sheep and pigs to the bishop's household, though this time the reeves were credited with "sales" at higher prices than the real sales in the markets. The 1351–2 cellarer's roll shows that Battle abbey also allowed its reeves fair prices for the oxen and wethers "bought" from its manors. But the sceptical pen of the auditor appears among the livestock prices as well as elsewhere. At Alton Barnes in 1400–1 the reeve's claim for the purchase of two oxen was cut by two shillings. At Hampton Episcopi in 1377–8 the reeve was allowed 7s. less than he claimed for buying an ox, and at Stoke Bishop in 1386–7 the auditors cut the payment expected for buying five cows from 55s. to 44s. The auditors at Gussage in 1364–5 insisted that the manor's pigs had been sold at 3s. 6d., not the 3s. 4d. reported by the reeve.

Occasionally the accounts record other types of payment. Some Westminster abbey manors bought by part-exchange. Feering in 1353–4 paid 3s. for "changing" four cows. Birdbrook in 1376–7 paid 3s. 4d. for "changing" three cows, and in 1393–4 gave 10s. and an old cart horse in return for a new one. Sometimes the lord shared with the tenant farmer the cost of replacing livestock; this was so, for example, at Wargrave in 1423–4.

Although they are relatively few, the surviving formal valuations of livestock in this period provide some useful information on prices in regions from which there are no manorial accounts. When the crown's escheators carefully assessed the possessions of Alice Perrers, the victims of the Merciless Parliament, and sundry other unfortunates, their reports amplify the evidence from other sources. Alice Perrers's oxen in 1377 were valued at around 10s., her plough horses at 5s., her cart horses at 10s., and her cows at 6s. 8d.[54] In 1388, after the Merciless Parliament, the escheators found in Devon, Leicestershire, and Yorkshire oxen worth about 7s. 2d., plough horses in Northampton-

[54] *Cal. Inq. Misc.*, IV, pp. 3, 5, 8, 11, 13.

shire and Kent worth about 5s. 5d., cart horses worth 4s. in Leicestershire and 6s. 8d. in Northamptonshire, and cows varying from 5s. in Yorkshire to 8s. in Kent.[55] These valuations are of course much lower than the purchase prices recorded in the manorial accounts, for the escheators were estimating what the animals would fetch if sold, presumably for immediate slaughter; moreover, in the 1380s the prices of most things were abnormally low. In 1397, after William Hampteshire of Great Marlow had drowned himself in the Thames, the escheators reported among his possessions eight sheep worth 12d. each, four pigs worth 3s. 4d. each, £6 3s. in coin, six bunches of garlic worth 4d. a bunch, a cow worth 8s., six quarters and three bushels of wheat worth 34s., a silver spoon worth 9d., a brass pot worth 4s. 9d., and a red horse worth 10s.[56] In 1400, when grain prices were higher, the escheators recorded higher assessments – oxen worth between 8s. and 13s. 4d., plough horses worth 6s. 8d., cows between 6s. and 10s., and sheep varying from 4d. (for 420 "stinking" sheep at Down Ampney) to 1s. 4d. at Cirencester and Richmond.[57] Other valuations suggest that prices in the Welsh marches were as high as in England. The earl of Warwick's oxen in Radnor and Montgomery were valued at 8s., 8s. 4d., and 9s. in the autumn of 1397, his cows at 6s. 8d., and his sheep at 12d. His wheat there was worth 6s. or 6s. 8d., his rye 5s., his barley 4s., his peas 6s., and his oats 3s. or 4s. a quarter. Warwick's sheep and oxen at Kirtling in Cambridgeshire were then valued a little higher, his cows there a little lower. But all the grains at Kirtling were substantially cheaper than those in Wales – wheat at 4s., barley at 3s. 4d., peas at 4s., and oats at 2s. 4d. a quarter. On the duke of Gloucester's Yorkshire manors the escheators found oxen worth 12s., 14s., or 16s. a head, and cows worth the remarkable price of 20s., dearer than anywhere else in the country. On the other hand, the wheat was cheap at 4s. a quarter, while peas were worth as little as 2s. 6d.[58] In short, the escheators' assessments, like the manorial accounts, record substantial regional differences in both livestock and grain prices.

E. SOME DEADSTOCK PRICES

During the fourteenth century the production of wool became the principal economic activity on an increasing number of manors. Yet it often proved unprofitable. As T. H. Lloyd has shown, English wool prices were depressed throughout the later middle ages, and sagged

[55] *Cal. Inq. Misc.*, v, pp. 1, 6, 9, 10, 21, 31.   [56] *Cal. Inq. Misc.*, vi, p. 95.
[57] *Cal. Inq. Misc.*, vii, pp. 26–7, 29–30, 44–5, 65–6, 71, 89.
[58] *Cal. Inq. Misc.*, vi, pp. 107–8, 121, 202. The grain measures used in these areas may not have been of the same capacity.

even in comparison with grain prices (which, it has been argued here, were themselves lower in relation to livestock prices). Lloyd has demonstrated that both the Duchy of Lancaster and Bruton priory failed to make true profits from sheep farming in the fifteenth century.[59] In the first thirty years of the fourteenth century the price of wool had averaged nearly five shillings a stone. In only one subsequent medieval decade – the 1370s – did wool prices again approach that level. Many factors combined to drive down the price of wool: heavy government taxation, damage to fleeces by scab disease, Edward III's interference with the wool trade for strategic and economic reasons during the Hundred Years War, the Burgundian bans on English cloth exports imposed in 1434 and 1447, and competition from peasants who (as Lloyd has argued) were able to produce wool more cheaply than demesne lords could.[60] Just as arable farmers continued to produce a lot of grain during periods of low grain prices, wool growers may also have been unwilling or unable to change their ways. The response to low wool prices might well have been for both landlords and tenants to try to get more money by sending even more fleeces to market. Wool prices, it is true, were high in the 1370s when most other farm prices were falling; this probably reflects both the demands of the domestic cloth industry and the consequences of a wool shortage caused by heavy sheep losses from murrain during the previous decade. The high prices of the 1370s probably played some part in encouraging lords and peasants to transfer some investment from arable farming to sheep raising, and thereby deepened the depression of wool prices in subsequent years.

The slump was severe indeed. The price of wool in the last two decades of the century was only 71 per cent of the price in the 1370s, when it had fetched nearly 5s. a stone. The price recovered to nearly 4s. 3d. at the beginning of the fifteenth century, but then dropped progressively to only 2s. 4d. in the 1450s, less than half the price of the 1370s. In the 1460s and 1480s the price improved slightly, helped by expanding cloth exports, but for the rest of the later fifteenth century it fetched only a few pennies above 2s. a stone. In proportion to the cost of sheep, the price of wool fell by more than a half between the first half of the fourteenth century and the second half of the fifteenth, as Table 5.6 shows.

In the fifteenth century manors clearly found it hard to dispose of their wool at acceptable prices. They frequently kept it in store for many years. Duchy of Lancaster wool grown in 1444 was not sold until

[59] Lloyd, *Movement of Wool Prices*, esp. pp. 25–6.
[60] J. H. Munro, *Wool, Cloth, and Gold: the Struggle for Anglo-Burgundian Trade*, Toronto, 1972, pp. 106, 134; Lloyd, *op. cit.*, p. 28.

Table 5.6. *Purchase price of wethers and sale price of wool*

	Wethers s. each	Wool s. per stn	Wool price as percentage of wether price
1300–1347[a]	1.31	4.40	336
1350–1400	1.76	3.78	215
1400–1450	1.66	3.57	215
1450–1500	1.69	2.69	159

[a] Each period runs from 20 September in the first-named year to 28 September in the second-named year.

1447, and the 1452 clip apparently not until 1456.[61] On two occasions eight years supply accumulated at Wargrave and Witney before the bishop of Winchester was able to sell it.[62] Whereas large estates might be able to wait for better prices, their tenants could not hold back in the same way. The peasant producer probably had to sell his fleeces at prices below those obtained by the major landlords, and may have had to turn to producing sheep for sale to large estates as the latter developed the practice of sterilizing their ewes rather than breeding from them. This would have been to the advantage of the tenants, for the price of sheep stayed much firmer than that of wool.

Even though many estates were rash to invest so heavily in wool production, the prices they paid for sheep reflected to some degree the value of the fleeces in that region. Between 1350 and 1400, the highest prices for wethers were paid in the Cotswolds and Upper Thames area, an average of 2s. each; these areas also obtained the best prices for wool, averaging between 4s. 7d. and 6s. 4d. per stone in that period.[63] Sheep prices were lowest in Essex, Kent and Sussex, Norfolk and Suffolk, and, after 1400, Northumberland and Durham; all of these except Essex had wool prices averaging less than 2s. 11d. a stone between 1350 and 1400. In Somerset, Wiltshire, and the Chilterns wethers averaged 1s. 9d. or 1s. 10d., close to the national level; these were also areas of middling wool prices – 3s. 6d. in Somerset, 3s. 10d. in the Chilterns, and 3s. 11d. in Wiltshire in the second half of the fourteenth century. The premium prices attracted by the best wool of the Cotswolds and the Welsh

[61] Lloyd, *op. cit.*, p. 26.

[62] I owe to T. H. Lloyd this information and the suggestions in the following sentences.

[63] My comments are necessarily limited to those areas from which sufficient information has survived on the price of sheep. Exact comparisons are impossible, as Lloyd's regional boundaries differ from mine. His districts numbered 10, 11, and 12 correspond closely to my Cotswold and Upper Thames areas.

borders enhanced the value of the local sheep, while the low wether prices in the east and south-east confirm the prejudice against the wool of Sussex, Kent, East Anglia, and the north-eastern counties.[64]

During the thirteenth century the price of cheese had changed less than that of any other major commodity: in the 1290s its cost was only 19 per cent higher than in the 1200s. Increasingly, though, demesnes made their cheese from the milk of cows rather than ewes. After averaging 12s. 4d. a wey during the 1310s, the price subsequently dropped to 9s. 7d. in the years before the Black Death. During the 1350s cheese prices rose to the level of the 1310s, but fell back during the next decade (even when other prices were rising) to little more than 9s. by the end of the century. In the early fifteenth century the decennial price varied between 9s. and 10s. a wey, apart from a sharp rise in the 1430s when, like many other commodities, cheese cost more. The price then declined to a level below 7s. a wey in the second half of the century. But one should not make much of these later cheese prices. After the Black Death almost all manors rapidly abandoned the production of cheese for sale, and even the Winchester manors rarely sold it after 1365. As a result, there are very few entries in manorial accounts. Most of the late fourteenth-century prices come from Sharpness and Wolricheston, the early fifteenth-century ones from Hornchurch and Alton Barnes, and the later entries from Alciston. The lack of evidence results not from the absence of cows – the Winchester manors had about 70 per cent more in 1396 than in 1347 – but from the practice of leasing them out to a dairymaid or cowman at an annual rent for lactage of five or six shillings (or rather less if the lord took the calves produced). For the lord this was a remarkably good bargain. In return for pasture and the modest capital cost and low depreciation of the cows, he had an assured cash income and manure for his fields. The gross income from renting out a single cow might well exceed that from two acres of demesne wheat, while the cost of sowing, cultivating, weeding, reaping, and threshing the wheat (and of leaving the arable fallow in rotation) would have been much greater than that of maintaining the dairy herd – for the lessee dairymaid or cowman had to do all the work. It is surprising to find the humble *daie*, normally paid only a few shillings a year and a bushel of barley a fortnight as a member of the manorial *famuli*, able to lease twenty or thirty cows from the demesne, manage them herself, and make a sufficient living from the sale of their milk, butter, and cheese – especially with salt dearer. The volume of dairy produce reaching the market probably explains why cheese was so cheap in later years. Sometimes the manor

[64] See Lloyd, *op. cit.*, pp. 52–61, 70–1, for assessments of relative regional values of the wool crop.

also farmed out its ewes: Middleton in 1364–5 charged 6s. a year for each cow and 6d. a year for each ewe. Monks Eleigh too in 1359–60 charged 6s. a cow for lactage, and also rented out its cockerels and hens as well for 6d. each.[65]

Almost all manors had to purchase salt, essential for food and for preserving meat. In the dairy a pound of salt might be needed for every ten pounds of butter or cheese.[66] Its cost rose more steeply than that of grain in the years immediately following the Black Death: in the 1350s its price was nearly two and a half times that in the 1340s, and it was slow to fall thereafter. In only one decade before the plague had its price exceeded 3s. 6d. a quarter; in no decade after it did its price drop more than a fraction below 4s. Using figures printed by Thorold Rogers, A. R. Bridbury argued that salt prices dropped sharply in the later fourteenth century as imports from the Bay of Bourgneuf took an increasing share of the English market.[67] The more comprehensive material now available does not support this case; salt stayed expensive. In the 1330s and 1340s, a quarter of salt had cost only 25 per cent of the price of an ox. After the abnormal figures of the 1350s, the ratio remained steady at about 40 per cent until the 1390s, and then around 33 per cent until the end of the fifteenth century. Between 1300 and 1347, the cost of a bushel of salt averaged 58 per cent of the price of a bushel of wheat; in the fifteenth century it averaged 75 per cent of the price of the latter. In the 1380s and 1440s salt cost more than wheat, the only decades in the thirteenth, fourteenth, or fifteenth centuries when this was so. One may guess at some reasons for the continued high price of salt, despite the growth of Bourgneuf supplies and the series of warm summers which should have reduced the costs of evaporation. Salt production and subsequent transportation were labour intensive and therefore more costly after the Black Death, and many salters may have abandoned their unpleasant work to return to agriculture when more land became available after 1350. Firewood and peat for heating the salt-pans became scarcer, and had to be supplemented with coal in later years. Moreover, salt-pans were taxed, the *salsae* levy at Droitwich rising from 2s. 4d. in 1347 to 4s. by the beginning and 5s. 6d. by the middle of the fifteenth century.[68] The continuing demand for salt on the dairy and stock farms also helped to keep its price high in the later middle ages.

[65] This was more than they usually cost to buy, but presumably the payment also included the right to have the poultry feed on demesne land.

[66] A. R. Bridbury, *England and the Salt Trade in the Later Middle Ages*, Oxford, 1955, p. xv.

[67] *Ibid.*, pp. 151–2.

[68] E. K. Berry, 'Medieval Droitwich and the salt trade', in *Salt: The Study of an Ancient Industry*, ed. K. W. de Brisay and K. A. Evans, Colchester, 1975, p. 80.

There were marked regional variations in the price of salt. In general, it was cheapest near coastal salt-pans and dearest away from them. The lowest prices between 1355 and 1400 were in Durham and Northumberland, where salt cost on average 4s. 7d. a quarter, and in south Hampshire, where it cost 4s. 9d. A day's ride away from the latter, it cost 5s. 3d. The dearest areas in the later fourteenth century were the Upper Thames and the Cotswolds (about 7s. a quarter) and the Chilterns (about 7s. 3d.). These last regions probably got their salt from the saline springs of the Droitwich area, not from imported or domestic coastal supplies, and paid rather more for it even at source. The bishop of Worcester's manors, not far from Droitwich, paid slightly more than the "national price level" during the last thirty years of the fourteenth century. Those areas served by the ancient saltways radiating from Droitwich – Birmingham, Hereford, Lechlade, Princes Risborough – obviously had to pay even more than the bishop's properties.[69]

Nails were among the most important of the building materials bought by manors, for they were essential to construction work and, unlike timber or thatch, could not normally be made from local products. Before the Black Death lath-nails had cost about 9d. a thousand. In the 1350s their price averaged more than twice as much. At Oxford their cost rose from 8d. a thousand in 1346–7 to 2s. 8d. in 1352–3, though entries for the intervening years suggest that the price had remained low immediately after the plague, perhaps because existing stocks were enough for the very limited building operations of those years. Later, the usual price of lath-nails dropped back from almost 20d. a thousand in the 1350s to some 16d. by the end of the fourteenth century, 14d. in the mid-fifteenth century, and 12d. or less in the 1470s and thereafter. Save for some discrepancies in the later fifteenth century (when the evidence on both is flimsy), the movements of salt and nail prices were curiously similar: in most decades one could have bought a quarter of salt for almost exactly what it cost to buy four thousand lath-nails. This coincidence may be accidental, of course, but it may perhaps indicate the long-term trend of prices of important high labour-cost, non-agricultural commodities which had to be bought by lord, tenant, and townsman alike, for some other items of deadstock also doubled in price. The heavy cart wheels the Winchester manors called "briddes" cost the bishop's reeves about 3s. 6d. a pair in the second quarter of the fourteenth century, but from the mid-1350s until well into the fifteenth century his manors almost invariably paid between 6s. and 7s. The *ligatura* for the cart, needing about 250 lb of

[69] *Ibid.*

Table 5.7. *Prices of miscellaneous commodities in shillings, 1300–1500*

	Wool[a] per stone	Cheese per wey	Salt per qr	Lath-nails per 1,000	Oxen each	Wheat per qr
1300–10[b]	4.83	10.25	2.60	0.76	12.73	5.37
1310–20	4.81	12.32	5.47	0.82	15.99	7.94
1320–30	5.26	11.85	3.48	0.79	15.38	6.90
1330–40	3.57	10.68	3.30	0.76	12.61	5.24
1340–7	3.55	9.59	2.81	0.71	12.15	4.88
1350–60	3.04	12.47	6.84	1.62	12.41	7.05
1360–70	3.97	10.43	6.61	1.52	16.31	8.16
1370–80	4.91	9.31	6.43	1.48	16.51	6.67
1380–90	3.41	9.06	5.55	1.36	13.76	5.25
1390–1400	3.59	9.47	4.68	1.31	13.47	5.46
1400–10	4.20	9.13	5.48	1.25	14.31	6.47
1410–20	3.66	9.68	4.29	1.21	13.19	6.01
1420–30	3.42	9.99	4.41	1.14	14.05	5.57
1430–40	3.48	12.33	4.54	1.17	13.72	7.33
1440–50	3.10	9.99	5.11	1.14	12.74	4.93
1450–60	2.32	8.44	4.16	1.03	13.67	5.63
1460–70	3.28	6.62	3.90	1.09	14.28	5.60
1470–80	2.39	6.72	4.24	0.99	14.73	5.76
1480–90	3.21	6.81	5.29	1.04	14.01	6.85
1490–1500	2.26	7.56	3.98	0.88	12.96	5.39

[a] Calculated from the "Annual means" in Lloyd, *Movement of Wool Prices*, pp. 41–4.
[b] Each period runs from 29 September in the first-named year to 28 September in the second-named year.

iron, cost 11s. or 12s. before the Black Death, but 24s. to 30s. in the succeeding years of high metal prices.

F. WAGES

Land and food, not money wages, remained the principal rewards for work on many demesnes in the later middle ages. While most of the manorial accounts record a fair number of money wages, relatively few of these entries can be used by the historian. It may be rash, therefore, to draw general conclusions from any of the money-wage series which can be calculated. For agricultural work, the best series are the payments for harvesting the grain in the late summer and for threshing and winnowing it thereafter. Payments for mowing the meadows, though frequently recorded in the accounts, are unsatisfactory as indications of current economic forces because mowing wages were much influenced by manorial traditions and because the work was done at a quiet time in the agricultural year. There are copious records of wages paid by the manors to certain craftsmen, in particular carpenters, masons, slaters, and thatchers. Unlike the entries on payments for agricultural work, which fade out quickly after 1450 with the disappearance of demesne farming, wage series for building workers can be continued satisfactorily until 1500 or later with information from institutional records. But none of these money-payment wage series was necessarily typical. When the accounts fell silent as the demesnes were gradually leased out in the later fourteenth and early fifteenth centuries, most of the work in this labour-intensive industry was still being done by the full-time members of the manorial staff or by customary tenants, even if the latter had to be enticed to work with money payments or – as at Apuldram – with a Christmas party to encourage them to come the more willingly to reap the lord's grain the next summer. Whereas the wage-earner ultimately did better after the Black Death, the customary tenant might be in serious difficulties if the lord demanded that he pay to be excused the labour services no longer needed on the demesne, especially in times of low produce prices and shortage of coin. By the 1360s Westminster abbey had reimposed labour services on the abbot's customary tenants at Islip and Hardwicke – and continued to collect the additional money rent demanded in place of those services immediately after the Black Death.[70] The *famuli*, too, did less well than the day-wage or piece-rate workers after the plague. On most Winchester manors, the *famuli* in the 1390s got no more money, and perhaps received less grain, than they had been given fifty years before. Only rarely in the accounts is there any hint, as at West Wycombe in 1401–2, that higher prices justified higher agricultural wages *propter caristiam victualium*.

Threshing and winnowing were not operations which had to be carried out urgently, unless to prepare wheat or winter barley for autumn sowing (as at Feering in 1368) or to take advantage of good prices for the new harvest if the previous crop had been exhausted. At Gussage, for example, the bulk of the threshing seems to have been left until February or later. Threshing and winnowing payments are therefore useful guides to the general movement of agricultural wages, though they still present some problems. Many manors had much of the threshing done by the customary tenants, or required the resident dairymaid to winnow half or more of the total threshed; such manors

---

[70] Harvey, *Westminster Abbey and its Estates*, p. 259.

had to hire threshers only in years when the harvest was exceptionally heavy. Some Winchester manors, and most Battle abbey manors, paid the threshers with a part of the grain they threshed. Those manors which paid their threshers in cash did so in a variety of ways. The Winchester manors used a number of different formulae to calculate the threshing and winnowing wages – even though the totals were often identical. Some Winchester manors openly paid higher wages immediately after the Black Death, giving in 1348–9 4d. rather than 2d. or 2½d. for threshing a quarter of wheat *pro defectu trituratorum*. Others in the same year added a bonus of a few shillings for the job as a whole.[71] This practice was soon to be revived.

During the early fourteenth century, threshing prices had risen modestly. In the years before the Black Death, manors paid about 5⅓d. on average for threshing and winnowing three quarters of grain, one each of wheat, barley, and oats.[72] In the 1350s, away from London, auditors allowed the reeves to pay about 6d. for the same task. The rate rose to 7½d. in the 1370s, more than 8d. in the early fifteenth century, and more than 9d. by the mid-fifteenth century. A few late entries from the 1460s suggest that threshing wages then were twice what they had been before the Black Death. In contrast, most of the grains threshed were worth less in the later period than in the earlier. Threshing rates did not rise simultaneously on all manors: wages clearly varied more from place to place than did grain prices. By 1356–7 the Winchester manors were paying less than immediately after the plague, and for several years gave almost everywhere a standard 5¼d. for threshing and winnowing the three mixed quarters. Battle abbey, which paid its threshers with grain, raised their payment between 1356 and 1357 from 4 or 5 per cent of what they threshed to 6 or 7 per cent.[73] Other estates were more generous (that is, more desperate for workers). For threshing and winnowing three quarters, the West-minster abbey almoner paid 13d. in 1356–7, 1359–60, and 1365–6, and a remarkable 19½d. in 1374–5. For the work of threshing alone, Knightsbridge's payment rose from 5⅓d. in 1348–9 to 18d. in 1349–50, dropped back to 9d. in 1352–3 after the Statute of Labourers, and then rose again to 12d. in 1356–7. Eybury, also in the London area, had paid 7d. for threshing and winnowing three mixed quarters in the autumn of 1348; the following year it paid over 26d. Although the Eybury rate dropped to 10½d. immediately after the statute, it rose again to 13d. in

[71] WPR 159358. Downton, East Knoyle, and Bentley provide examples of the first method, East Meon and Hambledon of the second.

[72] This formula is a statistical convenience; it never appeared in the accounts in this manner. Unless otherwise specified, all the rates discussed here are for this composite task.

[73] Searle, *Lordship and Community*, p. 313.

1356–7, and to 16d. in 1362–3 after the second outbreak of plague. These last rates all come from the London area, but abnormal (and illegal) payments are also recorded elsewhere. Monkleigh in Devon in 1363–4 allowed 6d. for threshing, and in 1393–4 paid 8d. for threshing and 1d. for winnowing, a single quarter of wheat. Plumstead in Norfolk paid 5d. and 6d. a quarter for threshing wheat in 1353–4; even in 1370–1 it was paying 14d. for threshing and winnowing three mixed quarters. By that time even the Winchester manors had increased their payments. In 1363–4 they resumed their old practice of giving presents or tips to the threshers, either in cash or in grain, *ratione pestilencie et paucitate operariorum*, as a later Burghclere account put it.[74] Witney, for example, paid its threshers and winnowers 58s. 2½d. (calculated at the earlier rate of 5¼d. for three mixed quarters), and also gave them curall wheat worth 30s. Fareham did something similar. Next year Witney paid the workers 27s. 10½d. at the old basic rate, but added a tip of 11s. 11½d.; this curious sum was clearly calculated to raise the effective rate to 7½d. for three quarters. Likewise, a tip at Ashmansworth raised the effective rate from 5¼d. to exactly 6¾d.[75] Within a few years the bonuses were consolidated, and 7½d. was established as the new basic rate at Witney and on many other Winchester manors. But not everywhere: it was not until the early fifteenth century that Bishop's Waltham paid more than 6d. for the same work, and the bishop's Somerset manors were still paying threshers the pre-Black Death rate when the demesnes were leased out in the fifteenth century. In the middle of the fifteenth century, among the last Winchester manors in hand, Bishopstone, Overton, and Ecchinswell paid 7¼d. for threshing and winnowing the three mixed quarters, while Meon church gave 8d. or 8½d. for the same. Records from other estates show the same diversity of payment. The Apuldram bailiff allowed 11d. for the same task in 1354–5 and 1355–6, but only 9½d. a hundred years later. In the 1390s the bishop of Worcester's auditors permitted payments ranging from 7½d. at Bibury to 10d. at Henbury. At Gussage the reeve had paid just over 6d. for the same work before the Black Death; by 1357–8 the rate had risen to 8d. and so remained (apart from two years at 7½d.) until the manor was leased out after 1415. In short, although the weight of the evidence shows that wages for threshing and winnowing roughly doubled between the 1340s and the 1450s, the increases did not occur simultaneously in all regions or on all manors, and were sometimes interrupted by local regressions to lower payments.

[74] WPR 159378.
[75] My tables exclude the value of the tips, which are not always expressed in cash. Had tips been included, the effect would have been to show wages rising more swiftly in the 1360s and more slowly in the 1370s.

Table 5.8. *Wages, 1300–1500, in pence*

	Carpenter (solo), per day	Thatcher and helper, per day	Slater/tiler and helper, per day	Mason (solo), per day	Reaping & binding, per acre	Threshing & winnowing 3 mixed qr	Mowing, per acre
1300–10[a]	2.89	3.55	5.17		5.45	4.73	4.97
1310–20	3.10	4.06	5.82		6.65	4.82	5.46
1320–30	3.12	3.70	5.04		6.40	5.27	5.82
1330–40	3.20	3.83	5.38		6.16	5.32	5.56
1340–7	3.03	3.60	5.22		5.87	5.38	4.95
1350–60	3.74	4.64	6.05	3.97	7.22	6.00	6.32
1360–70	4.26	5.51	6.77	4.27	8.17	6.46	6.96
1370–80	4.20	5.98	7.36	4.60	9.22	7.56	7.58
1380–90	4.26	6.15	7.50	4.50	9.14	7.77	7.60
1390–1400	4.27	6.28	7.28	4.46	8.73	7.69	6.79
1400–10	4.69	6.70	7.93	4.80	9.54	8.59	7.04
1410–20	4.47	6.72	8.06	5.08	9.95	8.37	6.85
1420–30	4.82	6.92	8.30	5.37	9.21	8.27	6.95
1430–40	5.11	8.10	7.72	5.24	9.48	9.16	6.46
1440–50	5.17	8.74	8.23	5.38	10.45	9.16	6.35
1450–60	5.45	9.41	9.63	5.54	9.93	9.95	6.72
1460–70	5.42	9.00	9.75	5.73	10.00	10.59	6.58
1470–80	5.83	8.92	9.82	5.92		10.92	6.25
1480–90	5.71	10.00	9.17	5.49	10.00		6.13
1490–1500	5.25	9.58	9.00	5.64			

[a] Each period extends from 29 September in the first-named year to 28 September in the second-named year. Decennial means before 1347 include wages from the London area; those after 1350 do not. There are very few agricultural piece-rate entries after the 1450s. In none of the tasks listed above were the workers given food in addition to money wages.

Harvesters' wages increased rather less than threshing wages during the century after the Black Death. In the 1330s and early 1340s, the normal payment had been about 6d. for reaping and binding a measured acre of grain, though even in those years harvesting wages had fluctuated more than threshing wages because the reeves sometimes had to pay more to get the workers needed to finish a late harvest or to get in one threatened by bad weather. In the first harvest after the plague struck, manors paid about 10½d. an acre on average, but the three succeeding harvests were cut for around 8d. an acre, either in partial deference to the ordinance and Statute of Labourers, or because the reeves concentrated on getting in the wheat and bothered less about the other grains (as the Winchester records suggest). The second major outbreak of plague brought higher wages, even on some of the Winchester manors: Farnham had to pay 12d. an acre in the summers of 1361 and 1362, in contrast to 8d. in 1360 and 9½d. in 1363. More manors now had to hire harvesters when there were insufficient customary tenants owing labour services and boon-works. Again, wages were much higher in the London area. Eybury paid reapers 9d. an acre in the summer of 1346, 18d. in 1349, and 22½d. in 1354; in the 1370s it again gave 18d., though the level fell back to 14d. in the 1390s. Hyde hired harvesters by the day rather than on contract by the acre and (perhaps surprisingly) usually had the work done more cheaply than Eybury. Halliford, a Westminster manor further out than Eybury or Hyde, paid about 16d. in the 1370s and 14d. in the 1390s. Away from London such rates were seldom paid. In Kent, Monkton paid 18d. an acre in 1411 and Eastry 16d. in 1428, but in Essex the Canterbury manors gave much less. When the reeve of Bocking paid 8d. an acre in 1375 he apologized for it *pro defectu operariorum*. A shilling an acre at Wargrave in 1391 and West Wycombe in 1402 had to be excused *propter caristiam victualium*, and even in 1416 the reeve at North Waltham had to justify the modest payment of 8d. *propter caristiam victualium et paucitatem laborariorum*.[76] Alton Barnes had to pay 13d. an acre in 1380, but got the rate down to 6d. in the 1390s. In the next decade it saved even more money by hiring men by the day and paying for their food: the cost varied from about 4.8d. in 1407 to 5.7d. in 1444. Hampton Episcopi paid for reaping, binding, and stooking 12½d. an acre in 1378, but only 10d. in 1382 and 7½d. in 1389. On other bishopric of Worcester manors the auditors usually kept the payment (for reaping and binding alone) down to 8d. an acre or less. At Gussage the customary tenants were required to do the harvesting for only 4d. an acre. When the reeve in 1364 had to hire additional harvesters at 7d. an acre, the auditors refused to allow him more than the 4d. permitted the customary tenants. The auditors were more lenient in 1365, justifying the 7d. rate because some customary tenancies had lapsed into the lord's hand, and again in 1366, when the excuse was that the weather was rainy. A few years later, the additional money for the outside harvesters appears to have been provided as "expenses"; later still, the pretences were dropped and almost all the grain was cut by contract at 7d. an acre. The labour shortage continued in the fifteenth century. Battle abbey's Sussex manors had to attract reapers from ten or fifteen miles away, pay them in sheaves of grain, and supply them with carts to carry their allowances home. When wheat prices were low, the harvesters could compel the abbey to substitute generous board *ad mensam domini* for their grain allowances. C. Dyer has shown how many lords had to provide harvest workers with better food in the fourteenth and fifteenth centuries to recruit enough of them.[77]

[76] WPR 159398, 159405, 159418.
[77] P. F. Brandon, 'Demesne arable farming in coastal Sussex during the later middle ages', *AHR*, XIX, 1971, pp. 118–19; C. Dyer, 'Changes in diet in the late middle ages: the case of harvest workers', *AHR*, xxxvi, 1988, pp. 21–37.

Although most harvesting contracts did not discriminate between
the various types of grain, a substantial minority paid more for some
than for others. Barley, the most unpleasant of the grains to handle,
sometimes attracted a premium wage, as at Middleton in 1389, when
the bailiff gave 12d. an acre for cutting barley but only half as much for
harvesting wheat and oats. Maristowe in 1398 paid 9d. an acre for
wheat, rye, and barley, but only 7d. for oats. Feering often paid 6d. and
a loaf of bread for cutting an acre of wheat, 5d. and a loaf for an acre
of oats, and 10d. without bread for an acre of barley. Despite these local
variations, it is clear that the rate of payment for harvesting increased
by slightly more than half between the Black Death and the early
fifteenth century. Thereafter it was probably fairly stable at about 10d.
an acre, though the sources after 1450 are too few for confident
calculations.

Mowing wages rose much less – indeed, the decennial rates declined
after the 1370s and 1380s, and did not thereafter recover. Many manors
continued to have the work done by customary mowing services as
long as there were demesne meadows to be cut. Those estates which
hired mowers seldom had to pay high wages before the Black Death
because there was less urgency in mowing than in harvesting, and the
areas were much smaller. Some Winchester manors had paid 8d. or so
an acre in the troubled 1310s, but wages thereafter dropped to about 5d.
an acre in the 1340s. It was this rate which the 1351 Statute of Labourers
prescribed as the maximum. In 1350 Knightsbridge paid 12d. an acre
for cutting the first crop and 10d. for the second, twice as much as in
the summer of 1348, but by 1354 the rates fell to 8d. for the first and
6d. for the second mowing. Eybury paid 8d. an acre in the late 1350s,
but had to go up to 10d. in 1362 and again in the 1370s and 1380s for
the first crop. Hyde paid 12d. in 1363, 8d. later in that decade, and 10d.
or $10\frac{1}{2}$d. in the 1370s. Southwark paid 12d. in 1375, 1377, and 1384, but
only 9d. in the 1410s. These high London-area payments were seldom
repeated elsewhere. Monkton in Kent occasionally paid a shilling, but
the other Canterbury manors gave less. The Battle abbey manors of
Apuldram and Lullington usually paid 8d. an acre, but the abbey's
manor of Barnhorne cut its payment from 10d. in the 1370s to 8d. in
the early 1400s and 7d. for most of the fifteenth century.[78] The
decennial rates in the fifteenth century average between 6d. and 7d. an
acre, roughly the same as in the 1350s and 1360s, and about a penny less
than in the 1370s and 1380s. One must be cautious in studying this
evidence that mowing wages were falling. The entries are relatively

[78] In 1473 Barnhorne paid only 4d. for the mowing, but gave an extra 8d. for the further
operations of spreading, lifting, collecting, and "making" each acre.

infrequent, and it is not always clear how many operations the payment covered. In more cases than the accounts record, the meadows may have been reckoned "as they lie", *sicut jacentes*, rather than in measured acres; some of the rates may have been for work performed by customary tenants under compulsion, and some manors probably gave unrecorded food and drink as well as money. The first two of these factors probably tend to underestimate the fall in mowing wages, as it became more usual to reckon in the larger measured acres and harder to extract services from customary tenants. The general picture is certainly one of stable or declining remuneration, and it warns one against accepting either threshing or reaping payments as necessarily typical of agricultural wages in the later middle ages.

Day-wages paid for building work were relatively free from the shadow of manorial custom, but were still subject to practices which make difficult the tasks of calculating and interpreting them. Day-workers were often hired *ad mensam domini* or *cum cibo*; their food might be worth the 2d. a day claimed by the Battle abbey reeves, or the mere farthing or so allowed for the masons employed by the Exeter city receiver.[79] Sometimes an unusually low wage-rate makes one suspect that the worker was given food, even though the account does not record it. Often a man was paid more for a day's work in the summer than he received for work on a short winter's day – as indeed the Statute of Labourers and its subsequent revisions required. Islip, for example, paid a thatcher 3d. in December 1362, but gave him 4d. a day the following April. Exeter Cathedral in the 1420s and 1430s also paid its carpenters and plumbers a penny a day less in the winter months. When men were hired by the week, one can seldom tell how many days' work they did.[80] Building workers, no less than farm labourers, expected higher wages in the London area, as Table 5.9 shows. The value of these figures must not be exaggerated; most are calculated from very few entries. They suggest, however, that for a century after the Black Death London wages were half as high again as those in other regions, but the differential narrowed in the later fifteenth century.

Payments to carpenters provide the best series of day-wages in the middle ages, for both manors and institutions needed them for repairs as well as for new construction work. The Statute of Labourers allowed master carpenters 4d., and other carpenters 3d. a day in summer, provided they did not get food or drink as well. These had in fact been the usual rates – almost the traditional rates – before the Black Death.

[79] Calculations suggest, however, that the true value of the *mensa domini* was about 1d., not 2d. See below, p. 482.

[80] B. Harvey, 'Work and *festa ferianda* in medieval England', *Jnl of Ecclesiastical Hist.*, XXIII, 1972, pp. 300–1.

Table 5.9. *London wage differentials, 1350–1500 (National decennial wage for each worker or task in decade = 100)*

	Carpenter	Thatcher & mate	Slater or tiler & mate	Mason	Threshing & winnowing	Reaping & binding	Mowing	Mean of other columns
1350–60ᵃ	151	142	166	126	196	180	133	156
1360–70	139	132	121	117	193	169	132	143
1370–80	144	155	137	121	164	208	133	152
1380–90	142	131	119	133	141	211	123	143
1390–1400	123		142	179	125	180	128	146
1400–10	148		152	167			142	152
1410–20	179		143	118	155		131	145
1420–30	154		151		121			142
1430–40	146		173	143				154
1440–50	160		164	154				159
1450–60	147		130	153				143
1460–70	148		135	143				142
1470–80	128		132					130
1480–90	125		136	148				136
1490–1500	126		128					127

ᵃ Each period runs from 29 September in the first-named year to 28 September in the second-named year.

Although Knightsbridge paid only 4d. a day in 1353–4, after the plague Westminster abbey and its manors around London normally paid at least 5d., usually 6d., and occasionally more. The abbey's sacrist, for example, paid carpenters 6d. or more in the 1350s, 8d. in 1361–2, and more than 8d. in the 1440s. Elsewhere, of course, rates were lower. Eastry, Monkton, and Meopham (Kent) sometimes had to pay 6d. in the later fourteenth century, but 5d. was more common, and in the 1390s they could get carpenters for as little as 4d. The Battle abbey manors in Sussex seldom paid more than 4d. a day in the fourteenth century, but by the 1450s it was usual at Apuldram and Lullington to pay 5d. *sine mensa* or 3d. *ad mensam domini*; Barnhorne in 1467–8 paid 4d. *ad mensam*. The Winchester manors in Hampshire normally paid 4d. a day in the later fourteenth century, though there were higher payments at Wolvesey and Highclere and, across the Surrey border, at Farnham (usually for work on the castle by a master carpenter). The Winchester manors in the Thames valley gave their carpenters 3d. or 4d. a day in the 1360s and 1370s, though Wargrave had to pay 6d. in 1361–2 for repairs after storm damage. By the fifteenth century 5d. was common and 6d. sometimes necessary. In Oxford itself, carpenters' wages in the late fourteenth century were only a little higher than in the countryside around; in the fifteenth century, however, 6d. was the rule rather than the exception (though a man employed by Lincoln College in 1476–7 received only 5d. because he lived in a college house). Further west, and well into the fifteenth century, the Winchester manors consistently paid only 4d. a day without food. Obedient at first to the statute, Exeter paid its carpenters only 3d. a day in 1351–2, but soon advanced to 4d. and, by the late 1370s, to 5d. This remained the prevailing rate in the fifteenth century, though occasionally 6d. was given, and in 1474–5 the city hired a master carpenter at 8d. and his assistant at 6d. a day to repair a fulling mill. The usual rate was also 5d. on the manors of Monkleigh and Sidbury in Devon, and at Egloshayle and Ruan Lanihorne in Cornwall. In eastern England, Monks Eleigh increased carpenters' pay from 3½d. in 1359–60 to 6d. in 1401–2. Bocking paid 6d. in the months after it had witnessed the outbreak of the Peasants' Revolt. Plumstead, which had paid over 6d. a day in 1351–2, gave as little as 4d. even in the 1410s. Apart from a few payments of 3d., both Redgrave and Hinderclay kept steadfastly to 4d. in the later fourteenth century. Birdbrook in the 1390s regularly employed the same carpenter, John Packgate, for 4d. a day, though it sometimes paid other men 5d. or even 6d. Steeple Morden in 1438–9 had to give 7d., but four years later hired a carpenter for only 4d. a day. Hornchurch usually paid 6d., or, as in 1474–5, 5d. *cum cibo et potu.*[81] Receiving about 5½d. a day in the later fifteenth century, carpenters outside London were getting then about three-quarters more than they had before the Black Death.

Masons' wages also improved, though less substantially: in the later fifteenth century masons received about two-thirds more than before the Black Death. Unlike the carpenter (who could sometimes demand high wages for repairing storm damage) the mason was usually employed on new construction, work which might be delayed if labour costs seemed too high. In the decades before the Black Death, the mason's pay had averaged between 3¼d. and 3½d. a day, about a farthing more than the carpenter's. There are few records of high wages immediately after the first plague: the Winchester and Westminster manors employed very few masons in the 1350s, and seem to have avoided paying more than 4d. Westminster abbey, however, like the Exeter city receiver, had to pay 6d. a day in that decade. Elsewhere, the payments gradually crept up. Occasional entries record much higher wages, such as the 8d. a day paid in 1373–4 by Taunton, normally the most miserly of the Winchester estates. By the 1370s wages of 4½d. or 5d. had become general outside London, with most manors paying masons the same as carpenters and a few slightly more. By the early fifteenth century masons were averaging about 5d. a day, a level not

---

[81] New College, Oxford, 6469.

attained by the carpenters until a generation later. In the 1470s both masons and carpenters were usually getting 6d. a day, the rate confirmed by the 1495 revision of the Statute of Labourers.

Unlike carpenters and masons, who were usually hired as individuals, thatchers, slaters, and tilers were usually employed in teams of master and boy. Like carpenters, however, these roofing workers were often needed for emergency repairs to buildings damaged by storms, and were thus occasionally able to bargain for better pay. Slaters and tilers and their mates secured by the end of the fifteenth century wages which were better by three-quarters than before the Black Death. Thatchers and their helpers may have obtained even larger increases, possibly of 150 per cent, but the evidence is scanty and unreliable. Before the plague the thatcher had normally received 3d. a day and his helper 1d. or 1½d., though the Winchester manors often gave less. Cheriton in 1347–8 had hired a team for 3d. a day without food, but a year later, after the plague had struck, nearby Merdon had to give twice as much. After some years when the wages prescribed by the Statute seem to have been enforced, many Winchester manors had to increase their payment to 6d. a day for the team when the second plague brought a new labour shortage. The bishop's Hampshire manors kept the rate down to 5d. in the 1390s, but higher wages came with the new century. Between 1405 and 1420, most teams were employed at 6d. a day, and over a quarter of the entries record a rate of 7d. After 1429, 7d. was the prevailing wage, with 8d. or even 9d. sometimes given. The Winchester manors in the Upper Thames, Cotswold, and Chiltern areas paid 6d. a day to each team in almost all cases from the 1360s to the 1420s, after which 7d. or more became usual. In Kent, the thatching team's wages rose from the legal 4½d. a day in the 1350s to 5d. or 6d. in the 1360s, 7d. occasionally in the 1370s, and 8d. as often as not in the 1400s. Rates in the west country rose more slowly than in most regions, but by the 1390s 6d. or more had become established. By the 1430s Alton Barnes was giving 10d., and in the hungry year of 1438–9 Dawlish paid 11d., 2d. more than was usual in Devon in that decade. In East Anglia wages rose faster. Feering paid 7d. and Redgrave 9d. a day for thatching teams in the 1370s. Hindolveston in 1373–4 paid 5s. a week (that is, at least 10d. a day) for a reed-thatcher and his helper, and Monks Eleigh apparently gave 13d. in 1401–2. Hornchurch, able to hire a team for as little as 6d. as late as 1421–2, had to pay 9d. in 1428–9, 10d. in 1438–9, and 11d. in 1450–1. Even if the highest rates were not always maintained, thatchers and their mates were getting in the mid-fifteenth century very much more than in the early fourteenth.

Slaters and tilers also achieved large wage increases; not many of them shared the piety of John Asppeschaw, slater at Newark, who

worked with his son on the chapel roof *ex devocione*.[82] But slaters' pay
rose less than thatchers'. In the later fifteenth century both workers
received about 9½d. a day with their helpers, whereas before the Black
Death the slater or tiler and his mate had received over 40 per cent more
than the thatching team. On the Winchester estates after 1350, slaters
or tilers and their mates seldom had to take less than 6d. a day. Witney
kept the wage down to 4½d. as late as 1359–60, but had to pay 7½d. in
1361–2. By 1450 the bishop's manors were paying 9d. or 10d. to the
team. The Canterbury manors in Kent paid slaters and their mates 8d.
a day in the 1350s, but very seldom gave more in the succeeding
decades. In Devon the rates remained close to the legal maximum of
4½d. even in the 1360s, but by the end of the next decade the Exeter
receiver had to pay twice as much. A full century later, tilers working
on Exeter Cathedral received the same pay, 9d. a day for craftsman and
helper together. London wages were again much higher: Westminster
abbey paid slaters and their helpers 13d. a day for the greater part of the
fifteenth century, though rather less before 1420 and again after 1478.
It is possible, of course, that London workers were more skilled. When
Exeter Cathedral hired "William Plumber of London" in 1442–3 it
paid him 10d. a day, not the 6d. usually given to the cathedral's
plumbers.

For most of the later middle ages, the plumber remained the best
paid of the itinerant building workers, for his skills were in short supply
even then. In 1378–9 Farnham spent 20d. on sending a man and horse
to look for the plumber at Windsor and bring him back; thereafter
Farnham hired him at 10s. for three weeks' work. Later, in 1402–3,
Farnham paid its plumber (apparently working alone) as much as 12d.
a day. Blakemere and Doddington, remote in Shropshire, had to pay
a plumber 8d. a day in 1426–7, twice the wage given to the thatcher.
But the plumber's advantage gradually dwindled. By the end of the
fifteenth century, thatchers', slaters' and tilers', and plumbers' wages –
very different in the 1340s – had become almost the same. The 1495
revision of the Statute of Labourers prescribed 6d. a day as the wage for
all of them.

This was not the only differential to narrow. Before the Black Death,
craftsmen had received at least twice as much as their helpers, and the
immediate consequence of plague mortality was to put an extra
premium on the skill of the former. In subsequent years the helper's
wage increased faster than his master's. This may have been partly
because unskilled workers were also in short supply, but this does not
explain why the change became more marked in the fifteenth century.
Perhaps the skill and status of the assistant improved as time went on.

[82] *The Book of William Morton*, ed. P. I. King, Northants. Rec. Soc., XVI, 1954, p. 66.

Table 5.10. *The day-wages of craftsmen and their helpers*

	Craftsmen[a]	Helpers[b]
1300–10[c]	227	100
1310–20	243	100
1320–30	229	100
1330–40	225	100
1340–7	210	100
1347–56	245	100
1356–60	196	100
1360–70	190	100
1370–80	193	100
1380–90	188	100
1390–1400	184	100
1400–10	173	100
1410–20	187	100
1420–30	173	100
1430–40	157	100
1440–50	145	100
1450–60	149	100
1460–70	140	100
1470–80	140	100
1480–90	144	100
1490–1500	140	100

[a] Thatchers, slaters, tilers, masons, and plumbers. The ratio given is the mean of all the ratios observed in the stated period for craftsmen and their own helpers.
[b] No distinction is made between helpers of different status.
[c] Each period extends from 29 September in the first-named year to 28 September in the second-named year. The figures for the period before 1356 appeared also in *AHEW*, II.

The fifteenth-century thatchers may have been served by experienced helpers with skills comparable to those of a journeyman qualified in a craft. The team therefore may have accomplished more in a day than when the thatcher had been helped by women, customary tenants, or manorial *famuli* (as had been common previously). The accounts sometimes speak of a triple hierarchy – the master, his *socius*, and his *servus* – with wages reflecting those distinctions. As Table 5.10 shows, by the beginning of the fifteenth century the craftsman's wage averaged only 70 per cent more than his helper's, and this lead shrank to less than 50 per cent by the 1440s.

Of the seven piece-rate and day-wage series examined in this chapter, six increased substantially after the Black Death. As we have seen, wages for thatching rose most, followed by those for threshing and winnowing, for carpenters, for slaters and tilers, for harvesters, and for masons. In contrast, mowing wages rose only a little, and did not maintain even the rates of the 1370s and 1380s. Although agricultural workers sometimes fared better – in 1371–2 Bibury gave its harvesters 5d. a day, its thatcher only 4d. – payments to building workers generally increased more than those to farm labourers. This reversed the trend during the century or so before the Black Death, when craftsmen's wages had risen even more slowly than those of farm workers. Moreover, if the development of sheep rearing and cattle ranching made English farming less labour-intensive in the later middle ages (as is indeed probable), it was the ploughman or reaper, not the carpenter or thatcher, who was most likely to lose his job.

Payments to the manorial *famuli* confirm that many peasants did not prosper greatly after the Black Death. Some parts of their remuneration were static and hard to assess – the value of the lord's possible ploughing of their smallholdings if they had any, the customary gifts of food or money at Christmas and Easter, produce from their own plots, extra food and drink during the autumn boon-works, oatmeal pottage at other times. The remainder of their pay, partly in cash but mainly in grain, was very slow to improve. Although the labour shortage after the Black Death gave them a brief chance to do better, the Statute of Labourers grasped them even more tightly than piece-rate and day-workers. On most of the Winchester manors, their money incomes were no higher at the end of the fourteenth century than on the eve of the Black Death: the typical carter or shepherd got 4s. a year, the ploughman 3s. or 4s., the *daie* only 2s. At Bishopstone, Cheriton, and Ivinghoe there were minor improvements for some of the *famuli* by the 1390s, but not elsewhere.[83] About half the Winchester manors raised cash wages between the 1390s and the 1410s, but usually only by small amounts: Overton, for example, gave each *famulus* an extra shilling a year. Even after further increases during the next twenty years the Winchester *famuli* remained poorly paid. By 1432 carters were getting 5s., 6s., 6s. 8d. or, at Droxford, 10s. a year. Ploughmen at Knoyle and Overton received 13s. 4d., but those at Hull and Staplegrove only 2s. 6d. Knoyle paid one shepherd 13s. 4d., but Fareham gave another only 4s. a year. Brightwell and East Meon still paid their dairymaids only 2s., the same rate as two hundred years earlier. In contrast, the Ramsey abbey *famuli* received more cash, and won it sooner. Before the Black Death most had been paid 3s. 6d. a year, but the rate for the majority rose to 6s. a year by 1351 at Slepe, and by the 1360s at Houghton and Abbots Ripton. By 1396 the Abbots

---

[83] This survey is limited to twenty manors which remained in demesne well into the fifteenth century.

Ripton *famuli* got 10s. a year, though those at Slepe and Holywell had to be content with 6s. well into the fifteenth century.[84] The Durham priory manor of Pittington increased the money payments to the carters and ploughmen from 5s. in 1310 to 14s. in 1379 and 17s. or 18s. in 1410.[85] On the Battle abbey manors, the stipends of the Apuldram ploughman and carter rose from 6s. and 6s. 6d. respectively before the Black Death to 7s. and 8s. by 1352–3 and 8s. and 10s. by the mid-1380s. By the 1420s the ploughmen were getting 13s. 4d., and after 1450 16s. a year *ad mensam domini*. At Lullington the ploughman's stipend rose from 6s. in the 1380s to 8s. in the late 1410s, while the shepherd in charge of the Clopham flock received at about the same time a pay increase from 5s. to 8s. a year, and a further 2s. extra later when he lost the right to have sheep of his own on the lord's pasture. At Barnhorne the ploughman's cash wage with grain deliveries rose to 13s. in the mid-1350s and 14s. in the 1380s; by the 1450s it had risen to 20s. a year *ad mensam*.

On these estates, of course, the *famuli*'s food deliveries were worth more – often much more – than their cash wages. The deliveries increased little in quantity or quality after the Black Death, and ultimately declined in money value as grain became cheaper. Both before and after the first plague, most Winchester manors gave identical food liveries: a quarter of barley every ten weeks for the ploughmen, carters, and senior shepherds, a quarter every twelve weeks for any assistant shepherds, pigmen, or cowmen, and a quarter every sixteen weeks for the wretched dairymaid. The Taunton *famuli*, never getting more than 2s. 6d. in money a year, had to stretch their food liveries (half rye, half peas) over twelve weeks. The true value of the *famulus*'s income, therefore, depended largely on the current price of cereals, though the Statute of Labourers protected the lord from having to be too generous in times of high prices by allowing him discretion to give money in place of grain. It is certainly possible that the amount of grain given at Winchester actually declined after the Black Death: if, as Lord Beveridge argued, the size of the Winchester bushel commonly used in Hampshire was reduced from 10 gallons to 8 gallons in the mid-1350s, and remained at the lower capacity thereafter, the *famuli* would have been much worse off, for there was no increase in the number of bushels of grain given them. Even without this possible reduction, the increase in money wages between the 1340s and the 1440s hardly compensated for the fall in the value of the barley they were given. The Ramsey abbey *famuli*, despite their higher money wages, may have fared no better in real terms, for after the middle of

---

[84] Raftis, *Estates of Ramsey Abbey*, pp. 202–4.

[85] R. A. Lomas, 'The priory of Durham and its demesnes in the fourteenth and fifteenth centuries', *EcHR*, 2nd. ser. XXXI, 1978, p. 345.

the fourteenth century the proportion of wheat in their livery was cut and the proportion of peas increased.[86] The Gussage *fugator* received 4s. in cash in the 1340s, 5s. in the 1350s, and 10s. by the end of the century, but as his grain livery remained unchanged at a quarter of barley every twelve weeks the money increase was almost exactly balanced by the fall in the value of his food. These changes were obviously not to the disadvantage of the lord.

Elsewhere the *famuli* may have been more fortunate, especially in the fifteenth century. At Alton Barnes in 1399–1400, carters received 12s. or 10s., shepherds the same, and ploughmen 8s. or 7s. a year, each with a quarter of grain (about one-fourth of it wheat) every ten weeks. By 1430–1 the manor paid its carter 30s., its ploughman 23s. 4d., its *fugatores* 23s. 4d. and 20s., and its shepherds 16s. and 13s. 4d. a year, with a quarter of mixed grain (half wheat, half barley) every ten weeks. With the grain valued at its current prices, the senior *fugator* would have been about 17 shillings better off in 1430–1 than in the earlier year. On some Battle manors, among the last to be kept in demesne, the fifteenth-century *famuli* were fed *ad mensam domini*. The accounts assert that the value of the *mensa* for the craftsman was 2d. a day, a rate which would have made the annual value of the food and drink supplied to the *famulus* more than 60s. But the details in the accounts suggest strongly that the money spent on the purchase of meat and fish, and the value of the grain, meat, and poultry from the manor's own stocks, amounted to much less than this. At Barnhorne the value of the food and drink supplied to the *famulus* was almost certainly less than one penny a day, and at Apuldram it was only slightly more. In the 1340s the Apuldram ploughman had received 6s. in money and about 18s. 7d. worth of barley; by the 1380s the stipend was worth 8s. and the grain about 23s. In the 1420s his stipend was 13s. 4d., with food worth about 21s., and in the 1450s he received 16s. in money, 4s. for his clothes, and food and drink *ad mensam*, worth around 30s. His income, therefore, had roughly doubled in the century after the Black Death. At Barnhorne, though, the total value of food purchased or transferred from manorial stocks each year in the later fifteenth century was less than the total cash wages paid to the *famuli*, even though some of the food was given to craftsmen hired *ad mensam* and to additional workers brought in at harvest-time. The Barnhorne ploughman, who had received 12s. in cash and grain worth around 22s. 8d. in the 1360s, and 14s. and grain worth about 17s. 8d. in the 1380s, might not have been much better off with his stipend of 20s. *ad mensam* in the 1460s. On the adjacent manor of Lullington, the ploughman certainly did not benefit.

[86] Raftis, *op. cit.*, p. 205.

Given *vadia* of a penny a day from Hokeday to Michaelmas, and a bushel of barley a week from Michaelmas to Hokeday, in addition to a stipend of 6s. or 8s., his income in the 1460s was worth only about 33s. a year, as it had been both in the 1380s and 1410s. At Alciston, too, the *famuli* seem not to have improved their conditions in the later middle ages; their income also came mainly from the weekly bushel of barley.

It is surprising to find such disparities on manors only a few miles apart, and all of them properties of the same abbey. It is also surprising to find the practice of grain deliveries persisting so long on most mid-fifteenth century manors, for a statute of 1446 apparently assumed that the *famuli* would all be *ad mensam* when it laid down maximum stipends of 20s. a year and clothing worth 4s. for the shepherd or carter and rather less for the other manorial servants. In fact, *famuli* permanently *ad mensam* never appear in the Winchester pipe rolls, or in the other late series examined in this study except at Apuldram and Barnhorne. The evidence from these two manors does not make it clear whether they retained the perquisites of some of the early medieval *famuli*, such as smallholdings and perhaps the right to the lord's ploughteams to help cultivate them.[87] The material is quite insufficient to allow one to draw general conclusions. The strongest hint that the *famuli*'s remuneration might be improving is to be found, curiously enough, in the 1446 and 1495 revisions of the Statute of Labourers.

G. THE STATUTES OF LABOURERS

Although the best known, the 1351 Statute of Labourers was only one of many attempts to regulate and control the medieval economy. Edward III's first response to the Black Death had been by proclamation in June 1349, "considering the grievous incommodities, which of the lack especially of Ploughmen and such Labourers may hereafter come". He forbade the payment of wages higher than those of 1346–7, insisted that workers remain in their existing employments, and required that the mayors and bailiffs should compel all "Sellers of all manner of Victual... to sell the same Victual for a reasonable price".[88] London, at least, tried to enforce the proclamation. Several bakers' servants were indicted in July 1349 for forming a conspiracy not to work for their masters except at double or treble the wages formerly given, and one William Amery was sent to prison for having demanded 5s. for some work which another mason then did for 12d.[89]

---

[87] M. M. Postan, *The Famulus: The Estate Labourer in the Twelfth and Thirteenth Centuries*, *EcHR*, supplement 2, Cambridge, 1954, p. 21.   [88] *SR*, I, pp. 307–8.

[89] *Cal. Plea and Memo. Rolls 1323–1364*, ed. Thomas, pp. 225, 231.

Elsewhere the proclamation fell flat, and in 1351 the commons, full of men who were themselves employers, petitioned the crown for firmer action. Complaining that "servants completely disregard the said [1349] ordinance in the interests of their own ease and greed, and...refuse their service to magnates and others unless they have payments of food and money two or three times as great as they used to have", the statute prescribed the maximum rates for various categories of workers. No one might pay or receive more than 5d. a day or 5d. an acre for mowing meadows, 3d. a day for harvesting, 2½d. for threshing a quarter of wheat or rye, or 1½d. for threshing a quarter of barley, peas, or oats. Master masons could get 4d. a day, but other masons – like thatchers and tilers – were limited to 3d. a day for themselves and 1½d. for their helpers. Master carpenters might not take more than 3d. a day, or other carpenters more than 2d. All these rates were to be paid without food, and in summertime only. The *famuli* were to receive no more money or grain than in 1346–7, had to be employed by the year, and hired openly in market towns. The lord had the right to substitute money payments, at a maximum of 10d. a bushel, in place of their former grain deliveries. Those workers who refused to swear obedience to the statute were to be put in the stocks and then sent to the nearest gaol. Having commanded the building of stocks in every village, the statute ordered the appointment of justices of labourers to "enquire and make due punishment...of Hostlers, Harbergers, and of those that sell Victual by Retail".[90]

The chronicler Henry Knighton thought the policy too feeble. Afterwards, he wrote, the labourers "served their masters worse from day to day than they had done previously".[91] But the evidence shows that the authorities tried hard to enforce the statute. The justices (of whom over 600 were appointed during the 1350s) were certainly very active. In addition to the large number of violations punished locally, B. H. Putnam estimated that nearly 9,000 cases, each involving up to five or six individuals, came before the central courts during the reign of Edward III alone.[92] By 1354–5 the "national wage levels" for all the seven wage series examined in this chapter were lower than in the previous years. Except in the London area, most wages recorded in the mid-1350s were close to the maxima laid down by the statute. The accounts show the thatcher and his mate averaging the legal 4½d. a day.

[90] *SR*, I, pp. 311–13. At Knightsbridge the carpenter who made the stocks was paid the illegal rate of 5½d. a day.

[91] *Chronicon Henrici Knighton*, ed. J. R. Lumly, RS, 1895, II, p. 74 ("ab eo die pejus servierunt magistris suis de die in diem quam ante fecerant").

[92] Putnam, *The Enforcement of the Statute of Labourers*, p. 173. The details in this study are still essential for understanding the working of the statute.

The carpenter, with $3\frac{1}{2}$d., was only $\frac{1}{2}$d. over the daily limit for a master carpenter, and the mason at $3\frac{3}{4}$d. was below the maximum permitted for a "master mason of freestone". The threshing and winnowing payments were also within the legal limits. By 1359, even though some wages had increased a little, the crisis seemed over. The justices of labourers were therefore disbanded, with some of their duties (such as the supervision of weights and measures) being transferred to the regular justices of the peace. Although the enforcement of the 1351 statute was temporarily in abeyance, new wage legislation continued: in 1360 a new law ordered craftsmen to be employed by the day, not by the week (to deprive them of the paid holidays provided by a weekly rate calculated without regard to feast days), and prohibited "all Alliances and Covines of Masons and Carpenters".[93] The first of these orders, at least, had little success: weekly contracts seem as common after 1360 as before it.

A more serious challenge came with the return of pestilence in the summer of 1361. Again manors had to bid against each other to attract workers. Harvesting cost $2\frac{1}{2}$d. an acre more in 1362 than in 1360. Slaters and their helpers took home in 1362–3 $1\frac{1}{4}$d. a day more than in 1360–1. As was mentioned earlier, even the Winchester manors had to break rank and custom by giving bribes and presents. Parliament now compelled the justices to hold their sessions more frequently, and the crown authorized them to enforce the old labour laws. Nor was price control ignored: in 1363 a statute forbade the sale of hens for more than 2d.[94]

Many parts of the country saw vigorous action by the justices in the 1360s and 1370s. Some Lincolnshire justices in 1373–5 tried 485 separate offences, 152 of them being violations of the labour laws. Most common among the charges were refusal to take employment as the statute directed, and giving or receiving excessive wages. Most violations were fairly trivial. A thatcher at Partney had taken 4d. a day with food, and mowers at Halton 5d. an acre with food. Rather than serve at the statutory wage, a woman had left Saxby *pro excessiuo salario capiendo*, and the *famuli* of the rector of Hougham had taken deliveries of wheat and rye, not the customary peas.[95] Similar offences appear in the records of Essex magistrates a few years later, with 170 prosecutions for breach of contract, vagabondage, and giving or receiving excessive wages; only seven of the indictments were for over-charging. John Underwood of Littlebury was charged not only with taking 30s. a year for his work as a shepherd, but also with enticing away another man's servant by offering him illegal wages. At Dunmow it was the

---

[93] *SR*, I, p. 367.   [94] *SR*, I, pp. 374, 378.
[95] *Sessions of the Peace in Lincolnshire, 1360–1375*, ed. Sillem, pp. 18–19, 33, 173.

constables themselves who were in trouble, for having failed to make the labourers swear to work and take wages according to the statute.[96] In contrast, the Warwickshire and Coventry justices tried more indictments for forestalling and regrating than for any other types of economic offences. Even though the Stratford-upon-Avon building wages paid throughout the second half of the fourteenth century were all higher than the statutory rates, the Warwickshire justices tried nearly as many presentments for breaches of the assize of bread and ale as for taking excessive wages.[97] This was also the case at Oxford, where an occasional fine of 8d. or 12d. for having taken illegally high wages was almost a craftsman's annual licence fee – just as a small fine for breaking the assize of bread and ale was often no more than a licence for home-brewing.[98] A hardened offender like Nicholas Carpenter cannot have been troubled by the fines of 8d. imposed on him in March 1391, March 1392, and November 1392.[99] Yet the Oxford magistrates were undoubtedly making a vigorous effort to control both wages and prices in accordance with a new statute of 1390, which obliged them both to proclaim each year what wages would be permitted according to the local price of food, and also to limit the sellers of food to taking only reasonable profits.[100] In general the justices' efforts to control wages in the 1360s and later seem to have been less successful than in the 1350s. Six out of the seven wage series examined here climbed after 1361–2, with only the mason's wages lagging behind. By the early fifteenth century, as we have seen, most workers were getting at least 50 per cent more than the payments stipulated in 1351, and in most cases their wages continued to rise thereafter.

Yet parliament kept its faith in legislative restrictions. In 1368 it was a matter of routine for parliament to reaffirm the "Statute and Ordinance made of Labourers and Artificers" alongside Magna Carta and the Forest Charter.[101] Richard II's second parliament, rather belatedly, conferred on the 1349 proclamation the full authority of a statute.[102] In 1383 parliament ordered the justices and sheriffs to examine vagabonds, "and upon them to do that which the law demandeth".[103] A comprehensive statute in 1388 tried to limit wandering by workers at the end of their contracts, required craftsmen

---

[96] *Essex Sessions of the Peace, 1351, 1377–9*, ed. E. C. Furber, Colchester, 1953, pp. 47–8, 161–2, 169.

[97] *Warwickshire and Coventry Sessions of the Peace, 1377–97*, ed. Kimball, pp. lxiv–lxv, 27–8; T. H. Lloyd, *Some Aspects of the Building Industry in Medieval Stratford-upon-Avon*, Oxford, 1961, p. 13.   [98] Hilton, *English Peasantry*, p. 45.

[99] E. A. Gee, 'Oxford Carpenters, 1370–1530', in *Oxoniensia*, XVII, 1952, p. 160.

[100] B. H. Putnam in *Medieval Archives of the University of Oxford*, ed. H. E. Salter, II, pp. ix–xv; *SR*, II, p. 63.   [101] *SR*, I, p. 388.

[102] *Soit affermez et tenuz pur estatut* – *SR*, II, p. 11.   [103] *SR*, II, p. 32.

and gild members as well as servants and apprentices to assist with harvesting, and compelled children who had worked in agriculture before the age of twelve to remain for ever "at the same labour, without being put to any Mystery or Handicraft". It also laid down for the first time the maximum stipends for the *famuli* – 10s. a year for the carter or shepherd, 7s. for the ploughman, and 6s. for the swineherd or dairymaid – rates which were higher than had been usual before the Black Death, and which were more than twice as much as the Winchester manors were paying in 1383.[104] In 1390 came a more liberal law requiring the justices to

make Proclamation by their Discretion according to the Dearth of Victuals, how much every Mason, Carpenter, Tiler, and other Craftsmen, Workmen, and other Labourers by the Day, as well in Harvest as in other Times of the Year, after their Degree, shall take by the Day with Meat and Drink, or without Meat and Drink...notwithstanding the Statutes thereof heretofore made.[105]

A law of 1414 emphasized that masters, no less than workers, were to be held responsible if payments exceeded those authorized. Another in 1423 reminded justices to regulate prices as well as wages, and led to reductions in the payments made to masons working on London Bridge.[106] In 1446 a further statute attempted to return to fixed maximum rates for day-wages, piece-rates and the *famuli* alike, removing the discretionary powers of the local magistrates. But this law acknowledged that the price of labour had risen irreversibly: the carter or shepherd could now get yearly 20s. in money, and 4s. worth of clothing, together with his food and drink, while the "common servant in Husbandry" might receive 15s. in cash and 3s. 4d. worth of clothes. A master tiler, ordinary mason, or carpenter might take $4\frac{1}{2}$d. daily and other labourers $3\frac{1}{2}$d. in the summer months, but less in winter or when food was supplied. A "master mason of freestone" or master carpenter was allowed $5\frac{1}{2}$d. a day between Easter and Michaelmas without food. Mowers might receive 4d. a day with food, or 6d. without it, while reapers were limited to 3d. and 5d. respectively.[107] These levels are close to the wages recorded (except in London) in the modest number of accounts surviving from this late period. These legal wage levels also confirm the account roll evidence that the mowers gained least after the Black Death, for even the 1351 statute had allowed the mower 5d. a day without food. The last wage legislation of the middle ages came in 1495, confirming the piece-rates authorized in 1446, allowing a little more for some members of the *famuli*, and

---

[104] *SR*, II, pp. 56–8.   [105] *SR*, II, p. 63.
[106] *SR*, II, pp. 176–7, 225; L. F. Salzman, *Building in England down to 1540*, p. 75.
[107] *SR*, II, p. 338.

permitting the "Freemason maister Carpenter Rough Mason Brick-
leyer maister Tyler Plommer Glazier Kerver nor Joyner" 4d. a day
with food, or 6d. without it.[108] These maxima were somewhat more
generous than the wages usually paid at the end of the fifteenth century
anywhere except in London.

The Statutes of Labourers were not the only forces at work to
restrain wage inflation in the later middle ages. The manorial lords
were helped by their own auditing systems, which made it easy for
them to transfer the responsibility to their own officials. As we have
seen, if the reeve had to pay high wages to recruit harvesters, the
auditors could refuse part of his claim for reimbursement. If the reeve
failed to recruit the harvesters needed, the auditors could hold him
responsible for the loss if the crop fell below expectations. Evidence of
such auditors' activities appears fairly often in the accounts before the
Black Death, and much more frequently after it. At Hendon they cut
the money paid for threshing wheat in the summer of 1350 from 8d.
for nine bushels to 6d. for eight. At Harpenden the reeve in 1351–2 was
allowed ½d. less than he claimed for threshing each quarter of wheat and
barley. The reeve of Bircham in 1352–3 claimed that he had paid
threshers 4d. a quarter for rye, 3d. for barley, and 1½d. for oats; the
auditors allowed him 2½d., 1½d., and 1d. respectively, less for oats than
the statute permitted. In 1353–4 the Knightsbridge bailiff claimed to
have paid threshers 6d. a quarter for wheat and 4d. a quarter for barley
and oats; the auditors allowed 4d. and 3d. respectively, but even these
rates were well above those paid there in 1346–7 (for quarters of nine
bushels, 3d. for wheat, 2d. for barley, and 1d. for oats). These auditors'
reductions continued after the second pestilence. At Islip in 1362–3 the
reeve claimed 11½d. for threshing and winnowing three mixed quarters;
the auditors allowed him 9½d., still well above the legal rate. The
Monkleigh reeve in 1363–4 claimed 8d. an acre for mowing, and got
6d.; the statute permitted only 5d. In 1376–7 the Gussage bailiff claimed
7s. each in yearly stipends for the carter and oxherd; he was granted 5s.,
a shilling more than in 1346–7. The Worcester auditors cut the 1385–6
Bibury reeve's claim for the ploughman's stipend from 13s. 4d. to 10s.,
and for the harvesting wages from 10d. an acre to 8½d. Disagreements
persisted even after the 1390 statute had made the rules more flexible.
The bailiff of Alton Barnes claimed 13s. 4d. each for the two carters in
1399–1400; he was allowed 12s. for one and 10s. for the other. The
1407 North Elmham reeve had his claim for threshing payments cut by
a penny a quarter. As late as 1447–8 and 1450–1, after the further
revision of the statutes, the Hornchurch bailiff was refused part of his
payments to building workers.

[108] SR, II, p. 585.

While the statutes probably strengthened the hand of the auditor in supervising the reeve, and that of the reeve in dealing with the labourer, it is clear that there was no general or concerted drive to force payments down to precisely the levels specified by law. Many manors paid wages higher than the statutes permitted; many paid less. Neither statutes nor auditors could isolate manorial wage bills from the general economic pressures of the time. Some of these pressures were local, rather than national, and help to explain the variations in the cost of labour even on the manors belonging to a single estate. Even the first outbreak of the Black Death had affected some areas less than others. The 1351 statute, although trying to prevent vagabondage, accepted that many areas had surplus workers who would have to travel to other counties to help with the harvest. Within a few years the economy had partly adjusted to the shrunken population: widows and landless peasants took over vacant holdings, and craftsmen moved to the areas most needing their skills. By the late 1350s regional wage differences had narrowed somewhat from what they had been immediately after the plague; labour costs had become lower in high-wage areas like London, and higher in low-wage areas like the Upper Thames. But the 1361–2 pestilence upset this new balance, even though the mortality was less. The result was a sharp climb in the cost of labour and, after some bad harvests, in the cost of food as well. In the last quarter of the fourteenth century wage rates were fairly stable again, but may show simply that there was less upward pressure on wages when good harvests and the end of monetary inflation brought cheap grain. Higher grain prices in the early fifteenth century, especially in the 1430s, perhaps explain the rise of wages then – though it is not clear from the evidence which change happened first, nor is it obvious why building workers should have benefited more than agricultural labourers. The manorial lords, after all, were not always blind to market forces: Westminster abbey, for example, accepted that threshing would cost more at Knightsbridge and Eybury than at Islip. While produce prices remained high, the cost of labour was not ruinous; A. E. Levett long ago concluded that in the years immediately after the plague the bishop of Winchester "could have paid double or treble the current rate of wages without converting his profit to a loss – in some cases without any serious diminution of his profits..."[109] In contrast, it was during the later decades when grain was plentiful and cheap that the justices in many counties were most vigorous in enforcing the labour laws, the parliaments particularly determined to affirm them, and the results the least successful. By the end of the fourteenth century the profitability of medieval agriculture had been undermined by the continued low

---

[109] Levett, *The Black Death*, p. 60.

prices for grain and wool, and by labour costs which the combined powers of legislation, stringent auditing, and market forces could not push back to the pre-Black Death levels. The new statutes of 1390, and even more those of 1446 and 1495, confirmed these changes. But one should not dismiss the laws as failures because they did not restore the wages of 1346–7. The 1351 statute almost certainly helped to keep wages lower than they would otherwise have been. The additional aims of getting the unemployed into agricultural service and reducing vagabondage were equally important, and may have been achieved more completely. The great Elizabethan law of 1563 was the lineal descendant of the fourteenth-century legislation.

H. THE STANDARD OF LIVING

The payments recorded in manorial accounts give a very imperfect indication of living standards: even in the fifteenth century, relatively few households outside the towns or the rural centres of cloth production obtained their principal income from money wages. The details of the medieval peasant's diet remain uncertain. We can have little idea how much he bought from neighbours owning or leasing cows and sheep, what vegetables he grew in his garden, or how much poaching of fish, rabbits, or larger game he might accomplish. Were the grain deliveries to the *famuli* ever intended to feed whole households, or merely unmarried demesne employees? Could many peasants hope to get as much food as the soldiers in Edward I's army, for whom food and drink containing over 5,000 calories a day were apparently provided?[110] By how much did the average tenant's land increase in size after the Black Death had carried off so many of his fellows? Did the thatchers and masons hired by the manors have plots of land as well? Was the number of days a year worked by casual farm labourers and building craftsmen greater after the plague than before it? What contribution to peasant prosperity was made by domestic weaving as the cloth industry developed in the fourteenth century?[111] Did the larger number of cattle and sheep bring more meat into the labourer's diet? Or was undernourishment partly the reason why Englishmen remained so vulnerable to the plague and other diseases?

As so few of these basic questions can be answered adequately from

---

[110] M. Prestwich, 'Victualling estimates for English garrisons in Scotland during the early fourteenth century', *EHR*, LXXXII, 1967, p. 538.

[111] A fairly generous guess, based on the production and price of cloth, suggests that the value of the weaving industry may not have exceeded 6d. per head of population even in a good year.

Table 5.11. *The labour cost of consumables, 1300–1500*

	Cost of purchases (shillings)	Units of agricultural work needed	Units of building work needed
1300–10[a]	34.45	27	35
1310–20	45.70	32	42
1320–30	39.74	27	40
1330–40	33.16	23	32
1340–7	30.12	22	30
1350–60	39.84	24	33
1360–70	44.19	25	32
1370–80	39.03	19	27
1380–90	30.69	15	21
1390–1400	33.57	17	23
1400–10	34.77	17	22
1410–20	33.27	16	21
1420–30	30.53	15	18
1430–40	34.52	17	20
1440–50	26.44	12	14
1450–60	25.49	11	12
1460–70	28.02	12	14
1470–80	26.49		13
1480–90	32.31		16
1490–1500	26.60		13

[a] Each period extends from 29 September in the first-named year to 28 September in the second-named year. No calculations for agricultural work units are offered for the decades after 1470 as there is insufficient information on farm wages then. The purchases listed are described, and units of work are defined, in n. 115.

the manorial sources, it may seem a little incautious to hail the fifteenth century as "the golden age of the English labourer", or write of the "time of much greater prosperity from 1380 to 1510".[112] Low prices for agricultural produce undoubtedly increased the purchasing power of building workers in regular employment, but they certainly did not help those who produced food and had to sell their surpluses to buy farming equipment, clothes and salt, and to pay rent and taxes. Changes in the purchasing power of building workers – a relatively small part

[112] J. E. T. Rogers, *Six Centuries of Work and Wages*, London, 1886, p. 326; E. H. Phelps Brown and S. Hopkins, 'Seven centuries of the prices of consumables compared with builders' wage-rates', *Economica*, NS XXIII, 1956, p. 306.

of the community – do not necessarily point to changes in the prosperity of the country as a whole. As we have seen, building wages almost doubled between the Black Death and the end of the fifteenth century, but agricultural wages rose less.[113] The scanty evidence on cash and food payments to the remaining *famuli* suggests that their incomes rose less than those of casual farm labourers. If the fifteenth-century farm worker was not as prosperous as some have thought, the deterioration in his lot under the Tudors would also have been less marked. But it is beyond doubt that the people of the countryside were generally better off in the fifteenth century: at the end of the middle ages the peasants were better fed, housed, clothed and equipped than their ancestors had been.[114]

The changes in the purchasing power of building and agricultural workers may be demonstrated in several ways, though none of them eliminates the problems posed at the beginning of this section. As Table 5.11 shows, to buy a standard "shopping basket" of consumables had required 32 units of agricultural work, or 42 units of building work, in the hungry 1310s.[115] In the 1340s, before the Black Death, the same basket required 22 units of the former or 30 of the latter. In the 1350s and 1360s slightly more work was needed: about $24\frac{1}{2}$ units of agricultural or $32\frac{1}{2}$ units of building work. From the 1370s, however, purchasing power improved rapidly. To buy the same "shopping basket", agricultural labourers had to work 19 units in the 1370s, 16 in the 1410s, and 12 in the 1440s. Building workers had to perform 27 units in the 1370s, 21 in the 1410s, 14 in the 1440s, and 13 in the 1470s. These figures probably underestimate the gains by the building craftsmen, many of whom were in full-time employment, in contrast to the farm labourers whose casual work was inevitably seasonal and intermittent. These figures are for a "basket" with a large cereal and pea content. E. H. Phelps-Brown and Sheila Hopkins calculated the changes in the cost of a "basket" holding a lot of meat and fish, and

[113] Building wages: unweighted mean of indices of day-wage payments to carpenter, mason, thatcher and mate, and slater or tiler and mate. Agricultural wages: mean of indices of piece-rate payments for threshing and winnowing, reaping and binding, and mowing and spreading.

[114] Dyer, *Standards of Living*, pp. 157–77.

[115] The "shopping basket" used here (as in vol. II of *AHEW*) comprises 4 qr barley, 2 qr peas, one-tenth of an ox, half a wether, half a pig, a quarter of a wey of cheese, one stone of wool, and one-tenth of a quarter of salt. A "unit of agricultural work" is taken as the work required to thresh and winnow one quarter each of wheat, barley, and oats, to reap and bind one measured acre of grain, and to mow and spread one measured acre of meadow. A "unit of building work" is taken as one day's work as a carpenter (unaided), one day's work as a thatcher (with helper), and one day's work as a slater or tiler (with helper). In all cases the work is valued without food or drink being given.

Table 5.12. *Calculations of building wages and the cost of consumables*

	Phelps-Brown and Hopkins (100 = 1450–99)		Farmer (100 = 1330–47)	
	Consumables	Building wages	Consumables	Building wages
1330s	106.7	60.1	104.0	101.0
1360s	141.5	59.0	138.5	133.7
1390s	108.6	77.2	105.0	143.4
1430s	115.1	88.9	108.2	176.7
1470s	94.3	106.6	81.1	191.1

demonstrated a similar if slightly less pronounced improvement in the spending power of building workers, as Table 5.12 shows.

The calculations of Phelps-Brown and Hopkins suggest that building-workers could buy exactly twice as many meat- and fish-laden "shopping baskets" in the 1470s as they could in the 1330s. My figures indicate that their ability to purchase a cereal-based diet had risen by as much as 137 per cent.

This improvement is shown even more clearly by examining changes in the amount of work required to purchase a single commodity such as barley, the most versatile of the cereals. As Table 5.13 makes clear, threshers in the fifteenth century had to do only one-third of the work that had been required of them in the 1310s to earn the cost of a quarter of barley. On the other hand, the labour required from mowers and harvesters fell only to one-half for the same purchase. In the 1310s a carpenter had to work for 22 days to earn the cost of a quarter of barley; by the early fifteenth century the number of days had halved, and by the end of the century 8 days or less were enough. A mason's purchasing power improved similarly. In the later fifteenth century, a thatcher and his helper needed to work only a quarter as long as in the 1310s, and a tiler and his mate for only one-third of the time formerly needed to buy the same.

Although the benefits were not equitably distributed, for some workers the fifteenth century was a fortunate time. The exceptional advantage enjoyed by the lucky was the result not only of higher wages but also of lower prices. To take an extreme example: between the 1360s and the 1440s a carpenter's wage rose by only 21 per cent, but the price of wheat fell by 40 per cent. After bad harvests, such as those of 1401, 1438, and 1482, the building worker would still be able to buy

Table 5.13. *The purchasing power of wages, 1300–1500: units of work needed to buy barley*[116]

	Barley, pence per quarter	Threshing and winnowing units[b]	Reaping and binding units[c]	Mowing and spreading units[d]	Carpenter (solo)[e]	Thatcher and helper[e]	Slater/ tiler and helper[e]	Mason (solo)[e]
1300–10[a]	46.8	10	9	9	16	13	9	
1310–20	68.0	14	10	13	22	17	12	
1320–30	56.0	11	9	10	18	15	11	
1330–40	47.0	9	8	8	15	12	9	
1340–7	43.0	8	7	9	14	8		
1350–60	62.2	10	9	10	17	13	10	16
1360–70	69.8	11	9	10	16	13	10	16
1370–80	56.8	8	6	7	14	9	8	12
1380–90	42.2	5	5	6	10	7	6	9
1390–1400	49.0	6	6	7	11	8	7	11
1400–10	50.9	6	5	7	11	8	6	11
1410–20	46.7	6	5	7	10	7	6	9
1420–30	42.1	5	5	6	9	6	5	8
1430–40	46.1	5	5	7	9	6	6	9
1440–50	32.8	4	3	5	6	4	4	6
1450–60	35.6	4	4	5	7	4	4	6
1460–70	40.7	4	4	6	8	5	4	7
1470–80	36.1	3		6	6	4	4	6
1480–90	43.2		4	7	8	4	5	8
1490–1500	40.0				8	4	4	7

[a] Each period extends from 29 September in the first-named year to 28 September in the second-named year.
[b] Threshing and winnowing one quarter each of wheat, barley, and oats.
[c] Reaping and binding one measured acre of grain.
[d] Mowing and spreading one measured acre of meadow.
[e] Number of days' work required from individual or team.

as much as his ancestor in an average year before the Black Death. For the tenant who could still produce a small surplus, such poor harvests offered the chance of better grain prices, but for his neighbour who had to buy food or seed-corn the crisis might be very serious. In such a year the *famulus* living *ad mensam domini* might still be among the most fortunate of the villagers. After all, there are limits to what calculations of prices and wages can reveal of the day-to-day conditions of rural life. No hungry man is appeased by learning that his decennial average wage is 50 per cent higher than his grandfather's. The only bellies statistics fill are those of statisticians.

[116] For calculations of the units of labour needed to buy wheat as well as barley, see D. L. Farmer, 'Crop yields, prices and wages', pp. 146–7.

I. STATISTICAL SUPPLEMENT

The statistical material on prices and wages here is as consistent as possible with that presented in volume II of this *History*, in a form which was itself based on an earlier thesis on price movements.[117] Lacking computer assistance, I was unable to attempt the more sophisticated statistical approach used in volume IV by P. J. Bowden, who multiplied every entry by a factor determined by the long-term ratio between the price from that source and the price series chosen as the standard – wheat at Exeter, barley at Cambridge, beans at Oxford, wool at Durham, and so on.[118] The survival of long continuous price and wage series, especially for the Winchester and Battle abbey manors, and for institutions like Westminster abbey, made this procedure less necessary for the period before 1450 or 1500. This present study therefore attempts to collate several hundred thousand pieces of information (many of them hard to read in the manuscript) by means of a million or so simple calculations. Undoubtedly many errors in transcription and arithmetic have found their way into my totals. Wherever a price or wage is given correct to two decimal places, the final digit is virtually meaningless. In preparing the indices which follow, I have used the same base $(1330/1–1346/7 = 100)$ as I used for the Price and Wages Indices in volume II. These indices are therefore fairly continuous from 1208–9 to 1499–1500, though they are much more reliable for the middle period (about 1270–1 to 1450–1) than for the extremities.

I prepared this study principally from the original account rolls or microfilms of them, and also used some of the extracts made for Lord Beveridge's International Committee on Wages and Prices, and certain of the figures published by J. E. T. Rogers and P. J. Bowden, where examination showed that they could safely be incorporated with those from my own researches. These sources are listed in Appendix A below. All doubtful entries were discarded. In the time available it was not possible to make a double-check of my sources or my calculations (except when a figure was unusual enough to make me suspicious). Limitations imposed by time and distance compelled me to calculate the "national price levels" and "national wage levels" before I had completed my study of the sources. As a result, a few manors (notably those of the bishopric of Worcester) did not contribute price and wage information to the general calculations even though I discuss their entries in the text.

These optimistically labelled "national price" and "national wage"

---

[117] *AHEW*, II, pp. 779–817; D. L. Farmer, 'An examination of price fluctuations in certain articles in the twelfth, thirteenth and early fourteenth centuries', Oxford Univ. D.Phil. thesis, 1958.   [118] *AHEW*, IV, pp. 865–70.

levels were obtained in the following way. I calculated first the average
(i.e. weighted) price received, or wage paid, on each manor in a single
account year. I then calculated the regional (unweighted) mean from
the manorial averages worked out for all the manors in that area. The
mean of the regional means then provided the "national price level"
for that commodity, or "national wage level" for that type of work.

Grain, pea, and cheese prices came mainly from records of manorial
sales, supplemented by cereal purchases by institutions like Westminster
abbey throughout the period, and by manorial purchases after 1430
whenever there was no entry for the sale of that commodity by the
manor in that year. I always excluded prices for grain described as
"curall", "weak", or otherwise inferior. All the barley was spring
barley (not mancorn), but prices for peas and oats include all varieties
of both. Salt prices were calculated solely from purchases, by both
manors and institutions, and include both coarse and fine salt. Wool
prices were taken directly from T. H. Lloyd's study (and are more truly
"national" than the other prices given here).[119]

Most of these articles were bought or sold by the bushel.
Unfortunately, repeated legislation failed to make universal the use of
"standard" measures. Where it has been shown clearly that dealers
used bushels of abnormal size (as did many Battle abbey manors and the
city of Exeter), and whenever grain was sold with "the eighth bushel
heaped", I have adjusted the prices to make them correspond to what
would have been paid for the quarter of eight standard levelled bushels.
I have also adjusted the prices recorded on the manors around Taunton,
but not the other Winchester manors; this problem is examined in
Appendix B below.

All but one of the livestock price series were calculated for the
purchase of adult animals in good condition. The exception, for pig
prices, was calculated from the sale of *porci* for slaughter. I kept separate
the costs of plough horses and of cart horses, and ignored riding horses
altogether. I made no distinction, however, between the prices of cows,
cows-in-calf, and cows with calves, or between the costs of sheep
bought before and after shearing.

The wage series also presented some problems, as it was often
uncertain how many operations were included in piece-rates or
whether food and drink were provided. The figures used are for wages
paid to workers to whom no food was given (as far as one can tell),
irrespective of the time of year or the length of the working day. When
a craftsman was employed by the week, I assumed that he worked a full
week of six days – though over an extended period his toils would have

---

[119] Lloyd, *Movement of Wool Prices*, pp. 38–44.

been interrupted by occasional feast days which thus became holidays with pay. Agricultural wages were calculated from payments to threshers who carried out the threshing and either winnowing or fanning, for mowers who cut and spread the hay but did nothing else, and for harvesters who did the reaping and binding, but not the stooking, carrying, or stacking. The building wages are for craftsmen who worked with materials provided by the employer, and include master masons and master carpenters along with the others (for the accounts seldom record the individual's status). As the name *cooperator* was often used for all three, the only guide to whether a roofing worker was a thatcher, a tiler, or a carpenter working on the rafters may come from details of the building materials purchased for his use. Errors of interpretation may therefore have blurred a little the distinctions between these craftsmen and their pay.

London wages posed a special problem. Before the Black Death agricultural workers in the London area had received about a quarter more than those elsewhere, and building workers about a third more. These differentials have little effects on the "national wage levels"when averaged with the wages from a dozen other regions. But in the fifteenth century the London differential was around 50 per cent, and there often survive entries from only one or two other regions to balance the London figures. To have included the London figures would have produced violent year-by-year wage fluctuations, quite inconsistent with the general stability over long periods recorded by each separate source. After experimenting with other procedures, I decided to ignore the London wages altogether in calculating the "national wage levels" after 1350. Because London labour costs were included in the statistics in volume II of this *Agrarian History*, the earlier series may be inflated by up to 3 per cent as a result. This factor must be remembered before making comparisons of wages before and after the Black Death.

Despite different solutions to the problems of statistical method and interpretation, there is a high degree of consistency between the calculations of Thorold Rogers, Lord Beveridge, and P. J. Bowden, and those presented here. This is demonstrated by Appendix C. It should be noted, though, that Rogers changed his statistical method for livestock prices after 1400, and thereafter based his calculations on the highest prices recorded, rather than on a mean or average.

Appendix E expresses in two ways the grain yields calculated from the Winchester pipe rolls. The first figures show harvest successes as percentages of the long-term yields, the second the gross yield of each grain (as a multiple of what had been sown). Appendix J offers a rough comparison between decennial wheat prices in England, the Low

Countries, Spain and central Germany. The Low Countries, like England, experienced high grain prices in the 1360s, 1430s, and 1480s. The 1430s and possibly the 1480s were expensive in Germany too, but the Spanish prices were somewhat below average in those decades.

APPENDIX A. REGIONAL MARKETING AREAS AND SOURCE MATERIAL

The price and wage material from the sources was arranged in the following regional groups:

SOUTH HAMPSHIRE: Alresford[w], Beauworth[w], Bishopstoke[w], Bishop's Waltham[w], Bitterne[w], Cheriton[w], Crawley[w], Droxford[w], East Meon[w], East Meon church[w], Fareham[w], Havant (Brockhampton)[2], Merdon[w], Marwell[w], *Padwell*[d], Bishops Sutton[w], Twyford[w], Wield[w], and Wolvesey[w].

NORTH DOWNS: Ashmansworth[w], Bentley[w], Burghclere[w], Ecchinswell (Itchenswell)[w], Farnham[w], Highclere[w], Leatherhead[t], North Waltham[w], Overton[w], and Woodhay[w].

UPPER THAMES: Billingbear[w], Brightwell[w], Coleshill[p], Culham[w], Harwell[w], Holywell[t], Islip[a], Moreton[w], Oxford (including Oriel, Magdalen, and New Colleges)[t], Waltham St Lawrence[w], Wargrave[w], and Windsor[t].

LOWER THAMES: Ashford[a], Esher[w], Eybury[av], Halliford[av], *Hendon*[a], Hyde[av], Knightsbridge[av], Sion[pv], the Wardrobe[v], Westminster abbey almoner[v], sacrist[v], keeper of new works[v], and treasurer[a].

COTSWOLDS: Adderbury[w], *Bibury*[g], Deddington[t], Heyford[t], Witney[w], Woolford[t], and Woodstock[t].

CHILTERNS: *Harpenden* (*Kenesbarne*)[a], Ibstone[t], Ivinghoe[w], Radclive[k], Weedon[t], and West Wycombe[w].

WILTSHIRE AND DORSET: Alton Barnes[k], Bishopstone (Ebbesborne)[w], Bromham[b], Downton[w], Fonthill[w], *Gussage All Saints*[d], East Knoyle[w], Stert[k], and Upton[w].

SOMERSET, DEVON AND CORNWALL: Cockington[y], Dawlish[x], Egloshayle (Burneir)[y], Exeter Cathedral fabric[x], Exeter City market[v], Exeter City receiver[y], Holway[w], Hull[w], Maristowe[r], Monkleigh[y], Otterton[t], Poundisford[w], Rimpton[w], Ruan Lanihorne (Tregear)[y], St Sidwell's[x], Sidbury[x], Staplegrove[w], Taunton[w], Wellow[t], and Yarcombe[y].

KENT AND SUSSEX: Adisham[c], Alciston[bv], Apuldram[p], Barnhorne[hv], Battle abbey almoner and treasurer[v], Beeding[t], Eastry[c], Ebony[c], Great Chart[c], Lullington[p], Meopham[c], and Monkton[c].

SEVERN: Blakemore and Dodington[s], *Bredon*[g], *Hampton Episcopi*[g], *Henbury*[g], and *Stoke Bishop*[g].

ESSEX: Birchanger[k], Birdbrook[a], Bocking[c], Feering[a], and Hornchurch[k].

NORFOLK AND SUFFOLK: Bircham[p], Caldecotes[t], Heveningland[t], Hinder-clay[jv], Hindolveston[n], Middleton[c], Monks Eleigh[c], North Elmham[n], Plumstead[n], Redgrave[jv], Sedgeford[n], Spitling[t], Taverham[n], and Wymondham[t].

CAMBRIDGESHIRE: Cambridge (including Peterhouse and King's College)[t], Gamlingay[t], Hinton[t], and Steeple Morden[k].

NORTHUMBERLAND AND DURHAM: Durham almoner, bursar, and cellarer[v], Finchale[tv], Jarrow[tv], and Wearmouth[tv].

EAST MIDLANDS: Kibworth[t], Ormsby[t], and Stamford[t].

The source or sources used are indicated by the supralineated letters as follows: a, Westminster abbey; b, Battle abbey (Gage Collection, Lewes); c, Canterbury Cathedral priory; d, Domus Dei, Southampton (Queen's College rolls in Bodleian Library, Oxford); g, Bishopric of Worcester (Worcs. RO); h, Huntington Library, California; j, Bacon Collection, Joseph Regenstein Library, Chicago; k, New College, Oxford; n, Norwich Cathedral priory (Norfolk RO); p, PRO, London; r, Roborough accounts (Plymouth City archives); s, Bridgewater Papers (Salop RO); t, printed in Rogers, *Agriculture and Prices*, II and III; v, transcript in Beveridge collection (LSE); w, Winchester pipe roll (Hants. RO); x, Exeter Cathedral fabric rolls; y, Exeter City (Devon RO). Manors in italics are mentioned in the text, but their data are not included in the calculations.

Some material was taken from more than one source: the Knightsbridge figures were obtained partly from the manuscripts in Westminster abbey, partly from the extracts made from them for the Beveridge collection. Alternative sources were available in some cases: the Apuldram evidence, which might have been copied from the Beveridge extracts or from the pages of Thorold Rogers, was in fact taken from the originals in the PRO. The greater part of the material taken from Rogers was for day-wages paid to building workers, as these entries were relatively uncomplicated; very little use was made of his figures for grain or livestock prices, or for agricultural wages, though the cost of lath-nails was calculated partly from his material.

APPENDIX B. THE WINCHESTER BUSHEL

Lord Beveridge first advanced the argument that most Winchester manors prior to 1354 used abnormally large bushel measures (ranging in capacity from $8\frac{1}{2}$ gallons in Wiltshire to 10 gallons in some parts of Hampshire and 11 gallons in Somerset), and that during the 1350s almost all changed to the "standard" 8-gallon bushel.[120] His assistants had found evidence for the change in several references in the

---

[120] Beveridge, 'Wheat measures', pp. 31–8.

Winchester pipe rolls (especially that for 1354–5) to the use of measures of different capacity, in an increase (consistent with a change to smaller measures) in the number of bushels of seed sown to the acre, and in a reduction of the margin by which wheat prices in Hampshire and Wiltshire exceeded the national average. P. F. Brandon has argued that the price of wheat on the Winchester manors in central Hampshire after the 1350s was virtually the same as on nearby Battle abbey manors during the time that the latter used what their accounts specifically described as "small" measures.[121]

Beveridge also claimed from separate evidence that abnormal measures had been in use on many Winchester manors in 1318, though the degree by which these bushels differed from the standard was usually not the same as in 1350. I have elsewhere given my reasons for questioning his conclusions on the evidence in the 1318–19 pipe roll, though my doubts (like Beveridge's arguments) had little to do with the case advanced for changes in the 1350s.[122] When I prepared the statistics for volume II of this History I was puzzled by the absence of any direct evidence in the accounts for the introduction of larger measures between 1318–19 and 1354–5, and also by observing that by 1358 seed rates (for virtually all grains on all manors) had returned to exactly the level used before 1354. This suggested strongly that whatever new measures had been introduced in the mid-1350s were abandoned before the end of the decade. For these reasons I decided not to alter the Winchester grain prices or threshing wages to make them correspond to what would have been paid for quarters measured by the standard. The statistics in volumes II and III of this History therefore incorporate the Winchester prices and wages unadjusted except at Taunton, where the evidence for change is somewhat different and relatively clear-cut.

Some further considerations appeared in the course of my research. The prices on the Winchester manors (especially in Hampshire) are more consistent with each other after 1360 than before 1350; this may reflect the standardization of measures, the frequency of sales *per mutuum* and *ad hospicium domini*, or all of these. If the changes in sowing rates about 1357–8 had cut the number of bushels per acre to the pre-1354 levels while retaining the smaller measures, the reduced density of seed might help to explain why grain yields per seed increased in the later fourteenth century (though the improvement was delayed for nearly twenty years). On the other hand, the number of bushels of barley given to the Winchester *famuli* in the later fourteenth century was the same as before the Black Death; it would be rather surprising

[121] Brandon, 'Cereal yields', p. 416.
[122] Farmer, 'Grain price movements', pp. 208–10.

if the bishop paid these workers less grain in the labour-short 1350s than in earlier decades, for even the 1351 statute did not try to reduce grain deliveries *below* the level in 1346–7. Moreover, while the Battle abbey accounts take great pains to make it clear whether the manors are using the *mensura parua*, the *mensura rasa*, or the *mensura patrie*, and other estate accounts explicitly record when the grain was sold with the eighth bushel heaped, there appears a conspiracy of silence throughout the sequence of Winchester pipe rolls, interrupted only by the somewhat cryptic hints in 1318–19 and 1354–5. With the matter thus in doubt, I left the figures unaltered.

If the Winchester measures used in the fourteenth and fifteenth centuries had remained large throughout, the "national price levels" for grain are too high, and the threshing wages too low, by 2 or 3 per cent in the fourteenth century and by rather more in the early fifteenth century when most of the material comes from Winchester's southern manors. If there was a change from abnormally large measures to standard ones in the 1350s, "national price levels" of grain are too high, and "national wage levels" for threshing are too low, by the same factor of 2 or 3 per cent up to the mid-1350s, but are correct thereafter. In this case the change would distort the continuous price and wage indices by the same degree. If the Winchester measures remained constant and standard throughout, there is of course no problem.

Appendix C. *Prices calculated by different authors*

(a) *Wheat, shillings per quarter*

	Rogers	Beveridge	Bowden	Farmer
1350–1400	6.13	6.89	—	6.52
1400–1450	5.77	6.34	—	6.06
1450–1500	5.53	—	6.32	5.85

(b) *Oxen, shillings per beast*

	Rogers	Beveridge	Bowden	Farmer
1350–1400	14.87	14.92	—	14.62
1400–1450	18.45[a]	14.19	—	13.60
1450–1500	17.79[a]	—	13.77	13.93

(c) *Wethers, shillings per beast*

	Rogers	Beveridge	Bowden	Farmer
1350–1400	2.06	1.79	—	1.76
1400–1450	2.11[a]	1.71	—	1.66
1450–1500	1.87[a]	—	1.72	1.69

Appendix C. (cont.)

(d) Salt, shillings per quarter

	Rogers	Beveridge	Bowden	Farmer
1350–1400	6.40	6.05	—	6.02
1400–1450	4.82	4.68	—	4.77
1450–1500	4.10	—	—	4.31

[a] Rogers's livestock prices after 1400 are the highest prices recorded, not means or averages.

Sources: Rogers, Agriculture and Prices, IV, pp. 292, 355–6, 410; W. H. Beveridge, 'The yield and price of corn in the middle ages', in E. M. Carus-Wilson, ed., Essays in Economic History, I, p. 20; P. J. Bowden in AHEW, IV, pp. 857–8.

Appendix D. Sale prices of major grains and legumes (1330/1–1346/7 = 100)

100 =	Wheat 5.09s.	Rye 4.05s.	Barley 3.78s.	Oats 2.25s.	Peas 3.55s.	Mean
1350–1	172	150	176	189	151	168
1351–2	232	215	202	201	165	203
1352–3	107	120	151	180	159	143
1353–4	90	72	101	102	76	88
1354–5	124	85	101	107	84	100
1355–6	122	89	101	109	106	105
1356–7	137	116	136	142	171	140
1357–8	141	131	142	144	134	138
1358–9	125	105	132	119	103	117
1359–60	134	123	129	106	92	117
1360–1	137	116	130	129	126	128
1361–2	106	87	137	137	129	119
1362–3	145	125	144	148	158	144
1363–4	199	165	159	134	133	158
1364–5	145	104	132	117	103	120
1365–6	119	98	131	112	92	110
1366–7	114	118	143	131	132	128
1367–8	153	120	140	136	138	137
1368–9	149	139	148	140	143	144
1369–70	336	269	276	207	238	265
1370–1	158	162	187	148	140	159
1371–2	133	114	124	105	86	112
1372–3	163	133	142	123	116	135

Appendix D. (*cont.*)

100 =	Wheat 5.09s.	Rye 4.05s.	Barley 3.78s.	Oats 2.25s.	Peas 3.55s.	Mean
1373–4	118	98	111	106	105	108
1374–5	190	151	149	141	135	153
1375–6	179	140	159	150	155	157
1376–7	94	89	116	103	94	99
1377–8	82	77	90	90	87	85
1378–9	80	77	79	90	86	82
1379–80	113	87	97	101	88	97
1380–1	132	82	102	111	91	104
1381–2	117	94	98	101	93	101
1382–3	110	113	96	95	83	99
1383–4	102	74	114	119	110	104
1384–5	89	84	96	105	102	95
1385–6	106	98	100	114	134	110
1386–7	94	79	89	81	72	83
1387–8	76	73	71	76	71	73
1388–9	72	69	66	77	77	72
1389–90	132	123	100	108	96	112
1390–1	188	186	168	151	163	171
1391–2	106	84	102	102	85	96
1392–3	66	56	79	94	83	76
1393–4	79	72	83	96	81	82
1394–5	79	83	99	99	93	91
1395–6	93	95	95	97	102	96
1396–7	129	118	114	115	114	118
1397–8	105	113	133	143	117	122
1398–9	105	94	100	100	105	101
1399–1400	120	112	108	109	99	110
1400–1	145	120	110	108	103	117
1401–2	201	181	162	138	123	161
1402–3	133	106	127	116	130	122
1403–4	96	71	104	98	79	90
1404–5	90	60	90	86	79	81
1405–6	76	67	85	88	90	81
1406–7	94	77	78	85	81	83
1407–8	120	100	97	94	92	101
1408–9	151	124	117	137	101	126
1409–10	166	141	151	133	147	148
1410–11	118	114	119	103	125	116
1411–12	99	86	96	110	96	97
1412–13	106	89	84	87	81	89
1413–14	102	86	91	109	98	97
1414–15	93	85	98	104	108	98

Appendix D. (*cont.*)

100 =	Wheat 5.09s.	Rye 4.05s.	Barley 3.78s.	Oats 2.25s.	Peas 3.55s.	Mean
1415–16	135	110	123	116	119	121
1416–17	183	130	137	113	110	135
1417–18	105	124	95	87	132	109
1418–19	143	105	92	89	57	97
1419–20	96	95	105	122	109	105
1420–1	127	91	96	92	106	102
1421–2	108	111	85	86	75	93
1422–3	85	91	100	92	75	89
1423–4	101	101	86	85	108	96
1424–5	112	117	84	93	82	98
1425–6	95	91	88	81	88	89
1426–7	80	86	84	87	73	82
1427–8	81	91	84	88	72	83
1428–9	149	148	107	113	88	121
1429–30	157	173	114	116	186	149
1430–1	129	122	85	97	89	104
1431–2	92	99	79	78	132	96
1432–3	139	151	100	111	136	127
1433–4	118	139	107	101	109	115
1434–5	104	103	80	82	94	93
1435–6	113	91	65	78	94	88
1436–7	115	85	73	80	87	88
1437–8	198	192	107	129	110	147
1438–9	278	224	192	144	202	208
1439–40	155	143	127	89	131	129
1440–1	78	76	68	68	83	75
1441–2	83	76	67	68	65	72
1442–3	83	67	79	111	94	87
1443–4	92	62	70	84	83	78
1444–5	87	66	65	79	67	73
1445–6	107	81	65	88	—	85
1446–7	123	115	74	85	94	98
1447–8	104	93	78	76	70	84
1448–9	101	96	78	76	77	86
1449–50	110	99	77	77	63	85
1450–1	132	126	87	77	85	101
1451–2	121	120	76	74	60	90
1452–3	108	104	78	73	63	85
1453–4	95	89	87	84	94	90
1454–5	85	93	71	76	75	80
1455–6	105	95	78	82	—	90
1456–7	108	71	71	65	80	79
1457–8	133	119	79	76	65	94

Appendix D. (*cont.*)

100 =	Wheat 5.09s.	Rye 4.05s.	Barley 3.78s.	Oats 2.25s.	Peas 3.55s.	Mean
1458–9	122	99	81	81	65	90
1459–60	98	82	79	85	92	87
1460–1	144	123	106	82	103	112
1461–2	161	—	97	96	75	107
1462–3	82	103	92	59	75	82
1463–4	77	62	59	62	75	67
1464–5	86	91	121	89	70	91
1465–6	85	123	102	85	150	109
1466–7	103	87	90	85	66	86
1467–8	122	110	82	74	86	95
1468–9	118	107	76	73	70	89
1469–70	122	104	72	81	75	91
1470–1	132	148	84	77	113	111
1471–2	116	132	97	87	103	107
1472–3	93	99	84	77	80	87
1473–4	94	82	84	87	70	83
1474–5	88	107	76	62	75	82
1475–6	107	93	67	61	74	80
1476–7	105	99	76	80	94	91
1477–8	142	—	77	67	—	95
1478–9	141	103	68	84	94	98
1479–80	114	92	84	65	103	92
1480–1	113	104	80	67	113	95
1481–2	166	121	144	117	188	147
1482–3	190	—	135	106	221	163
1483–4	165	—	78	70	150	116
1484–5	109	99	95	72	89	93
1485–6	102	82	72	65	89	82
1486–7	118	—	92	76	113	100
1487–8	123	148	80	72	75	100
1488–9	118	148	90	106	—	116
1489–90	143	132	87	73	—	109
1490–1	160	—	103	78	—	114
1491–2	118	115	104	82	—	105
1492–3	105	—	85	65	—	85
1493–4	97	115	78	59	75	85
1494–5	93	99	70	63	56	76
1495–6	80	99	70	72	66	77
1496–7	113	165	88	84	53	101
1497–8	108	132	107	89	92	106
1498–9	97	99	84	78	113	94
1499–1500	88	99	91	71	56	81

Appendix E. *Harvest successes[a] and the yield of grain[b] on the Winchester manors*

	Wheat	Barley	Oats
1350	72.5 (2.71)	72.6 (2.69)	51.6 (1.35)
1351	65.3 (2.55)	85.9 (3.56)	82.4 (2.43)
1352	136.1 (5.23)	50.4 (2.37)	51.6 (1.31)
1353	100.0 (4.01)	82.5 (3.31)	93.8 (2.33)
1354	104.2 (3.92)	97.8 (3.67)	92.0 (2.43)
1355	100.2 (3.63)	95.4 (3.92)	94.1 (2.64)
1356	99.1 (3.66)	63.4 (2.72)	59.6 (1.72)
1357	98.1 (3.56)	80.0 (3.37)	88.3 (2.35)
1358	111.4 (4.29)	94.7 (3.57)	103.8 (2.76)
1359	95.7 (3.42)	96.9 (4.00)	88.4 (2.44)
1360	110.5 (4.01)	93.7 (3.51)	97.3 (2.36)
1361	117.6 (4.23)	80.2 (3.28)	71.0 (1.94)
1362	79.9 (3.28)	70.8 (2.95)	104.3 (2.86)
1363	80.1 (2.96)	97.2 (3.85)	104.5 (2.86)
1364	96.8 (3.49)	104.5 (4.23)	98.3 (2.45)
1365	107.2 (3.92)	105.1 (3.86)	101.1 (2.54)
1366			
1367	76.9 (2.73)	85.0 (3.02)	86.4 (2.35)
1368	97.4 (3.51)	95.1 (3.38)	92.3 (2.21)
1369	79.6 (2.76)	92.8 (3.42)	95.3 (2.36)
1370	110.7 (3.69)	110.5 (3.87)	99.4 (2.57)
1371			
1372	96.7 (3.55)	95.2 (3.80)	88.3 (2.30)
1373	122.5 (4.40)	140.4 (5.60)	118.0 (3.11)
1374	80.2 (2.97)	109.6 (3.79)	102.1 (2.66)
1375	90.0 (2.96)	106.1 (3.52)	96.8 (2.42)
1376	125.2 (4.77)	115.3 (4.32)	107.9 (2.84)
1377	119.5 (4.26)	117.3 (4.55)	117.6 (3.13)
1378	132.7 (4.61)	127.7 (4.77)	109.6 (2.91)
1379	90.9 (3.29)	109.7 (4.05)	106.1 (2.79)
1380			
1381	105.2 (3.68)	124.1 (4.52)	116.4 (3.11)
1382	107.3 (3.74)	121.7 (4.50)	117.5 (3.24)
1383	116.2 (4.30)	117.9 (4.36)	118.3 (3.38)
1384	125.0 (4.72)	118.6 (4.65)	98.9 (2.70)
1385	104.3 (3.97)	114.3 (3.74)	115.7 (3.05)
1386	109.0 (4.25)	119.9 (4.03)	138.2 (3.82)
1387	126.1 (4.84)	121.2 (4.54)	123.8 (3.47)
1388	129.2 (4.81)	133.2 (4.68)	120.0 (3.14)
1389	98.3 (3.68)	114.9 (4.16)	108.7 (2.95)
1390	88.4 (3.25)	102.0 (3.75)	92.9 (2.55)
1391			

Appendix E. (*cont.*)

	Wheat	Barley	Oats
1392	120.0 (4.21)	105.9 (4.10)	101.2 (2.82)
1393	110.8 (4.14)	112.7 (4.11)	116.9 (3.25)
1394	122.6 (4.43)	92.3 (3.69)	101.3 (2.79)
1395	103.0 (3.98)	111.4 (4.25)	110.1 (2.95)
1396	83.6 (3.09)	105.5 (4.28)	99.1 (2.85)
1397			
1398	98.4 (3.68)	94.8 (3.15)	97.8 (2.64)
1399	105.3 (4.36)	102.9 (4.15)	103.1 (2.69)
1400	95.3 (3.69)	102.4 (4.26)	109.9 (2.74)
1401	70.7 (2.66)	103.2 (3.72)	100.8 (2.66)
1402	93.3 (3.50)	102.6 (3.85)	113.1 (3.13)
1405	127.9 (5.26)	92.9 (4.15)	82.3 (2.15)
1406	80.7 (3.18)	96.6 (4.80)	97.7 (2.80)
1407			
1408	90.3 (3.74)	90.6 (3.73)	95.0 (2.58)
1409	90.4 (3.45)	99.0 (3.84)	97.9 (2.61)
1410	94.3 (3.89)	98.2 (4.46)	99.0 (2.84)
1411	94.9 (3.67)	105.2 (4.33)	108.9 (3.07)
1412	100.9 (3.90)	114.5 (4.66)	119.6 (3.25)
1413	102.3 (4.03)	98.3 (3.96)	102.6 (2.78)
1414	101.1 (4.23)	99.0 (4.00)	104.3 (2.42)
1415	96.9 (3.68)	94.9 (3.90)	111.3 (3.08)
1416	86.2 (3.32)	94.9 (3.60)	106.6 (2.85)
1417			
1418	83.3 (3.44)	94.0 (4.10)	107.6 (2.91)
1419	111.4 (4.65)	97.5 (4.37)	91.7 (2.30)
1420	79.9 (3.19)	101.0 (4.05)	108.9 (2.95)
1421	94.0 (4.33)	103.6 (4.19)	104.7 (3.03)
1422	101.6 (4.48)	65.9 (3.59)	80.0 (1.96)
1423	103.7 (4.16)	103.4 (4.30)	113.0 (3.18)
1424			
1425	97.4 (3.82)	97.1 (3.54)	109.6 (3.31)
1426			
1427	99.0 (4.25)	97.6 (4.11)	120.5 (3.72)
1428			
1429	95.8 (4.07)	97.3 (3.79)	106.0 (2.63)
1430	91.6 (3.90)	101.1 (4.20)	112.5 (3.40)
1431	98.5 (4.32)	106.5 (4.54)	115.9 (3.46)
1432	86.2 (3.45)	88.7 (3.63)	98.3 (2.62)
1433	92.2 (4.20)	79.9 (3.74)	106.5 (3.29)
1434	100.6 (4.53)	105.7 (4.61)	120.3 (3.69)
1438	55.5 (1.89)	91.4 (3.81)	102.6 (2.93)
1439			

Appendix E. (*cont.*)

	Wheat	Barley	Oats
1440	107.8 (4.97)	96.5 (4.18)	109.7 (3.17)
1441	89.7 (3.99)	91.4 (4.02)	126.3 (3.68)
1447	81.4 (3.43)	83.3 (3.84)	111.4 (3.14)
1448	96.8 (4.04)	98.1 (3.94)	121.2 (3.50)
1449	86.3 (3.49)	77.5 (3.24)	101.0 (2.98)
1450			
1451	87.0 (3.42)	83.3 (3.28)	126.3 (3.68)
1452	92.3 (3.66)	84.3 (3.24)	117.8 (3.37)
1453	104.7 (4.22)	92.7 (3.42)	142.0 (3.84)

[a] This is a percentage. I calculated each manor's crop (expressed as gross yield less tithe, divided by seed sown previously) as a percentage of the average for that grain on that manor 1350–1453. The mean of the manorial yield percentages (irrespective of regional grouping) provided the Index of Harvest Success.

[b] Gross yield less tithe, divided by seed sown previously. These figures are printed in parentheses in the table. To reduce domination by the Hampshire manors, I first worked out the yields for the regions used for the National Price and Wage levels (see Appendix A above), and then calculated the mean of these regional yields. This same method was used to calculate the figures printed in *AHEW*, II, pp. 796–8.

Appendix F. *Prices of livestock* (*1330/1–1346/7 = 100*)

100 =	Oxen bt 12.42s.	Affers bt 9.99s.	Cart horses bt 16.35s.	Cows bt 9.48s.	Wethers bt 1.37s.	Pigs sd 2.57s.	Mean
1350–1	98	83	87	95	98	98	93
1351–2	107	107	105	102	93	131	107
1352–3	118	100	80	105	103	135	107
1353–4	110	89	112	110	107	134	110
1354–5	111	104	108	109	107	120	110
1355–6	105	101	103	100	102	106	103
1356–7	106	120	100	96	104	111	106
1357–8	104	95	137	100	104	119	110
1358–9	105	96	138	103	111	100	109
1359–60	114	141	128	108	110	116	119
1360–1	103	92	121	127	95	118	109
1361–2	105	91	118	90	116	91	102
1362–3	115	109	142	115	126	103	118
1363–4	135	114	157	115	130	131	130

Appendix F. (*cont.*)

100 =	Oxen bt 12.42s.	Affers bt 9.99s.	Cart horses bt 16.35s.	Cows bt 9.48s.	Wethers bt 1.37s.	Pigs sd 2.57s.	Mean
1364–5	140	125	164	131	138	133	138
1365–6	140	153	155	129	144	127	141
1366–7	147	175	171	128	155	111	148
1367–8	155	160	187	126	144	126	150
1368–9	131	169	168	130	138	123	143
1369–70	141	162	182	128	164	137	152
1370–1	137	186	217	141	162	179	170
1371–2	148	206	170	140	185	133	164
1372–3	146	178	180	132	172	133	157
1373–4	145	164	169	120	171	120	148
1374–5	133	136	163	116	159	132	140
1375–6	117	129	120	108	169	123	128
1376–7	118	156	160	103	134	124	132
1377–8	120	121	152	108	164	122	131
1378–9	119	131	107	116	160	111	124
1379–80	117	166	137	129	166	100	136
1380–1	126	170	140	130	140	111	136
1381–2	110	174	137	114	141	111	131
1382–3	128	155	134	107	124	111	126
1383–4	114	138	129	102	142	110	122
1384–5	102	121	145	103	128	100	116
1385–6	110	119	127	103	108	96	110
1386–7	105	122	151	106	97	106	114
1387–8	100	109	137	111	110	106	112
1388–9	107	126	128	102	115	87	111
1389–90	105	121	138	113	108	99	114
1390–1	107	148	133	114	120	91	119
1391–2	80	—	151	119	93	114	111
1392–3	110	121	144	97	112	113	116
1393–4	108	137	139	110	122	109	121
1394–5	114	127	127	103	118	97	114
1395–6	109	153	128	108	118	101	119
1396–7	110	141	154	113	123	105	124
1397–8	100	160	144	123	—	131	132
1398–9	121	191	144	112	120	107	132
1399–1400	125	161	143	123	147	122	137
1400–1	119	195	168	124	139	118	144
1401–2	134	161	159	134	153	116	143
1402–3	122	166	163	118	122	125	136
1403–4	123	211	—	109	146	106	139
1404–5	121	133	147	121	97	111	122

Appendix F. (*cont.*)

100 =	Oxen bt 12.42s.	Affers bt 9.99s.	Cart horses bt 16.35s.	Cows bt 9.48s.	Wethers bt 1.37s.	Pigs sd 2.57s.	Mean
1405–6	115	—	136	125	141	107	125
1406–7	106	168	141	98	142	99	126
1407–8	111	140	140	90	117	105	117
1408–9	88	—	—	73	—	98	86
1409–10	114	140	134	115	146	114	127
1410–11	115	170	159	102	160	124	138
1411–12	115	182	147	112	139	119	136
1412–13	119	—	144	105	136	115	124
1413–14	110	113	140	99	134	107	117
1414–15	110	140	119	98	130	101	116
1415–16	98	95	122	90	126	94	104
1416–17	108	147	141	94	114	112	119
1417–18	91	150	—	84	—	126	113
1418–19	99	150	133	87	—	115	117
1419–20	96	147	102	69	112	95	103
1420–1	106	123	115	—	119	102	117
1421–2	104	96	123	77	101	90	98
1422–3	106	129	128	86	107	99	109
1423–4	102	120	151	94	105	105	113
1424–5	114	—	84	80	94	112	97
1425–6	104	138	122	98	108	110	113
1426–7	135	117	—	—	86	97	109
1427–8	113	105	146	84	104	94	108
1428–9	134	180	122	100	110	82	121
1429–30	114	118	131	91	109	107	112
1430–1	113	147	117	88	110	97	112
1431–2	103	113	148	101	135	108	118
1432–3	105	129	143	79	126	101	114
1433–4	105	101	110	72	111	114	102
1434–5	110	127	125	78	134	115	115
1435–6	108	—	—	82	97	94	95
1436–7	103	—	—	86	122	91	100
1437–8	113	—	—	72	108	102	99
1438–9	104	133	144	86	120	156	124
1439–40	141	133	—	127	131	117	130
1440–1	106	119	106	105	139	116	115
1441–2	102	133	156	84	115	104	116
1442–3	107	—	—	96	111	130	111
1443–4	81	110	—	63	131	108	99
1444–5	115	—	—	70	—	101	95
1445–6	111	127	—	82	—	90	102

Appendix F. (cont.)

100 =	Oxen bt 12.42s.	Affers bt 9.99s.	Cart horses bt 16.35s.	Cows bt 9.48s.	Wethers bt 1.37s.	Pigs sd 2.57s.	Mean
1446–7	100	124	112	77	119	111	107
1447–8	99	103	116	—	114	114	109
1448–9	105	87	110	75	103	100	97
1449–50	97	160	93	84	94	117	107
1450–1	107	—	69	—	85	97	89
1451–2	97	107	128	—	97	112	108
1452–3	100	92	112	72	94	115	97
1453–4	99	114	122	74	93	104	101
1454–5	113	85	156	70	92	110	104
1455–6	121	—	67	—	76	100	91
1456–7	128	—	—	—	91	—	109
1457–8	104	67	143	74	82	107	96
1458–9	114	—	—	85	92	106	99
1459–60	117	89	—	82	101	107	99
1460–1	102	—	—	95	119	107	106
1461–2	97	80	—	—	—	97	91
1462–3	123	—	—	87	—	91	100
1463–4	111	—	—	100	135	97	111
1464–5	113	—	—	98	122	117	112
1465–6	129	—	—	—	138	97	121
1466–7	133	—	183	84	115	123	128
1467–8	133	—	—	105	153	—	130
1468–9	101	—	163	114	103	—	120
1469–70	108	—	—	—	110	97	105
1470–1	134	—	—	—	—	—	134
1471–2	99	—	—	101	146	108	113
1472–3	112	—	101	—	137	113	116
1473–4	123	—	—	98	147	129	124
1474–5	134	—	68	—	115	91	102
1475–6	133	—	—	93	132	89	112
1476–7	103	100	—	94	108	96	100
1477–8	99	100	—	—	105	104	102
1478–9	123	—	—	99	121	98	110
1479–80	126	—	—	73	—	115	105
1480–1	109	—	—	85	79	118	98
1481–2	126	—	—	78	156	130	122
1482–3	112	—	119	99	195	122	129
1483–4	141	—	—	116	185	—	147
1484–5	—	—	—	140	158	106	135
1485–6	—	—	—	103	123	85	104
1486–7	116	—	82	—	142	112	113

Appendix F. *(cont.)*

100 =	Oxen bt 12.42s.	Affers bt 9.99s.	Cart horses bt 16.35s.	Cows bt 9.48s.	Wethers bt 1.37s.	Pigs sd 2.57s.	Mean
1487–8	86	—	—	94	126	73	95
1488–9	105	—	—	93	123	106	107
1489–90	108	100	—	—	115	98	105
1490–1	80	—	—	79	141	124	106
1491–2	133	—	—	—	145	116	131
1492–3	98	—	—	72	—	118	96
1493–4	—	—	—	89	—	—	89
1494–5	96	—	—	100	153	91	110
1495–6	142	—	—	60	142	124	117
1496–7	92	—	—	72	151	87	100
1497–8	121	—	—	72	115	115	106
1498–9	82	—	—	91	127	65	91
1499–1500	96	—	—	—	115	125	112

Appendix G. *Prices of miscellaneous commodities (1330/1–1346/7 = 100)*

100 =	Cheese 10.21s. per wey	Wool 3.56s. per stone	Salt 3.07s. per qr	Nails 8.90d. per thousand
1350–1	113	82	308	230
1351–2	146	87	323	235
1352–3	114	80	203	232
1353–4	111	83	181	211
1354–5	113	92	238	215
1355–6	141	84	219	207
1356–7	116	90	206	212
1357–8	128	93	163	217
1358–9	108	73	161	212
1359–60	132	97	227	209
1360–1	137	86	179	201
1361–2	114	96	187	214
1362–3	88	84	195	217
1363–4	96	87	211	219
1364–5	106	113	187	206
1365–6	88	113	178	210
1366–7	—	130	282	201
1367–8	106	127	255	196

Appendix G. (*cont.*)

100 =	Cheese 10.21s. per wey	Wool 3.56s. per stone	Salt 3.07s. per qr	Nails 8.90d. per thousand
1368–9	88	110	223	190
1369–70	95	128	256	197
1370–1	91	126	232	202
1371–2	98	134	221	197
1372–3	88	138	206	210
1373–4	98	149	215	211
1374–5	100	146	217	197
1375–6	78	143	200	187
1376–7	91	164	187	187
1377–8	91	140	189	208
1378–9	88	135	193	196
1379–80	88	129	236	193
1380–1	88	99	223	169
1381–2	88	97	186	181
1382–3	98	111	170	181
1383–4	98	109	165	182
1384–5	78	125	158	185
1385–6	88	95	177	200
1386–7	91	91	180	188
1387–8	89	84	181	194
1388–9	78	87	186	179
1389–90	91	88	180	175
1390–1	78	72	164	190
1391–2	98	93	164	159
1392–3	88	105	150	169
1393–4	101	101	155	176
1394–5	98	91	154	184
1395–6	88	100	156	182
1396–7	103	99	158	179
1397–8	91	113	141	171
1398–9	93	107	129	176
1399–1400	88	101	152	177
1400–1	82	99	166	173
1401–2	90	103	167	161
1402–3	108	110	229	162
1403–4	82	133	135	191
1404–5	93	102	—	163
1405–6	83	101	203	166
1406–7	91	124	194	174
1407–8	85	121	185	152
1408–9	93	114	170	173

Appendix G. (cont.)

100 =	Cheese 10.21s. per wey	Wool 3.56s. per stone	Salt 3.07s. per qr	Nails 8.90d. per thousand
1409–10	88	141	157	169
1410–11	88	131	158	170
1411–12	88	117	150	169
1412–13	118	132	133	158
1413–14	98	107	126	167
1414–15	111	99	146	161
1415–16	104	105	161	148
1416–17	69	93	149	155
1417–18	91	81	111	167
1418–19	83	82	135	172
1419–20	98	88	128	163
1420–1	75	125	126	158
1421–2	101	91	196	141
1422–3	91	79	144	146
1423–4	90	85	159	158
1424–5	109	95	121	149
1425–6	107	81	146	161
1426–7	99	89	108	153
1427–8	91	87	120	152
1428–9	98	106	180	161
1429–30	117	135	136	155
1430–1	114	111	116	158
1431–2	91	108	109	156
1432–3	114	109	151	161
1433–4	—	85	131	154
1434–5	137	94	140	157
1435–6	137	102	144	150
1436–7	—	84	117	176
1437–8	114	83	186	153
1438–9	137	110	177	151
1439–40	—	100	207	—
1440–1	—	101	150	152
1441–2	—	99	132	164
1442–3	—	86	151	183
1443–4	—	92	129	150
1444–5	114	75	117	140
1445–6	91	86	107	—
1446–7	101	109	145	146
1447–8	73	87	120	164
1448–9	106	88	144	129
1449–50	101	77	143	154

Appendix G. (*cont.*)

100 =	Cheese 10.21s. per wey	Wool 3.56s. per stone	Salt 3.07s. per qr	Nails 8.90d. per thousand
1450–1	65	75	142	140
1451–2	102	74	150	144
1452–3	126	47	136	145
1453–4	90	79	136	149
1454–5	—	69	123	135
1455–6	—	56	130	142
1456–7	65	59	114	127
1457–8	65	74	121	138
1458–9	65	70	123	—
1459–60	—	56	179	135
1460–1	65	66	174	112
1461–2	65	76	113	169
1462–3	52	80	108	—
1463–4	65	87	109	166
1464–5	75	128	87	118
1465–6	—	122	116	169
1466–7	65	122	131	157
1467–8	65	78	126	107
1468–9	65	66	161	177
1469–70	—	87	145	—
1470–1	—	76	179	157
1471–2	—	64	163	—
1472–3	65	63	125	94
1473–4	65	58	87	—
1474–5	66	53	147	135
1475–6	59	50	134	148
1476–7	65	46	134	135
1477–8	75	94	—	124
1478–9	65	54	124	124
1479–80	65	78	152	152
1480–1	65	112	185	121
1481–2	65	153	164	—
1482–3	76	75	163	157
1483–4	65	124	—	140
1484–5	65	126	163	—
1485–6	—	83	130	146
1486–7	65	69	179	157
1487–8	65	69	178	—
1488–9	—	81	184	135
1489–90	65	62	204	129
1490–1	74	58	174	112

Appendix G. (cont.)

100 =	Cheese 10.21s. per wey	Wool 3.56s. per stone	Salt 3.07s. per qr	Nails 8.90d. per thousand
1491–2	—	81	143	—
1492–3	—	76	107	124
1493–4	—	76	179	129
1494–5	—	58	146	—
1495–6	—	89	98	107
1496–7	—	84	98	112
1497–8	—	54	123	112
1498–9	—	84	97	112
1499–1500	—	53	130	139

Appendix H. *Piece-rates and day-wages (1330/1–1346/7 = 100)*

100 =	Threshing & winnowing 5.38d.	Reaping & binding 6.04d.	Mowing & spreading 5.66d.	Carpenter (solo) 3.13d.	Thatcher & helper 3.74d.	Slater & helper 5.31d.	Mason (solo) 3.41d.
1350–1[a]	148	119	114	118	129	121	108
1351–2[a]	98	130	126	102	124	119	117
1352–3[a]	105	140	106	113	125	108	117
1353–4[a]	119	125	124	118	128	104	118
1354–5[a]	112	138	100	112	120	114	112
1355–6[a]	91	113	106	115	111	118	125
1356–7	106	107	121	132	124	114	111
1357–8	109	114	97	130	124	115	117
1358–9	117	104	106	129	116	118	117
1359–60	111	106	116	126	141	111	121
1360–1	113	129	103	130	139	111	117
1361–2	111	148	102	130	137	122	124
1362–3	110	125	106	135	140	134	140
1363–4	119	132	121	137	150	123	130
1364–5	128	131	127	137	147	122	124
1365–6	139	140	152	143	152	130	117
1366–7	116	142	118	134	145	130	136
1367–8	135	141	127	137	144	124	133
1368–9	112	131	145	133	161	128	108
1369–70	118	133	131	145	158	151	124
1370–1	121	147	125	127	156	124	119
1371–2	166	110	147	137	166	182	110

Appendix H. (*cont.*)

100 =	Threshing & winnowing 5.38d.	Reaping & binding 6.04d.	Mowing & spreading 5.66d.	Carpenter (solo) 3.13d.	Thatcher & helper 3.74d.	Slater & helper 5.31d.	Mason (solo) 3.41d.
1372–3	130	152	136	142	158	146	145
1373–4	139	148	123	130	152	135	152
1374–5	133	145	144	134	155	135	132
1375–6	137	165	134	134	170	137	139
1376–7	143	166	137	139	161	129	140
1377–8	141	162	138	131	155	139	134
1378–9	143	159	123	134	157	127	141
1379–80	152	172	131	132	168	132	137
1380–1	177	116	141	128	187	151	—
1381–2	148	159	136	146	155	125	147
1382–3	142	163	140	138	155	133	117
1383–4	143	162	145	138	168	139	148
1384–5	137	151	128	140	160	160	148
1385–6	142	156	135	131	164	139	117
1386–7	133	157	126	141	176	151	117
1387–8	140	155	127	132	166	137	117
1388–9	141	147	124	134	155	137	133
1389–90	141	147	141	134	157	—	142
1390–1	136	153	121	134	157	146	123
1391–2	139	116	133	140	185	141	161
1392–3	134	150	124	135	165	139	135
1393–4	136	151	106	133	166	129	123
1394–5	144	153	124	140	171	122	—
1395–6	141	150	124	133	170	132	121
1396–7	135	140	121	133	165	141	121
1397–8	170	120	115	147	167	152	147
1398–9	142	154	119	134	172	138	128
1399–1400	152	159	115	136	162	132	117
1400–1	149	157	110	148	180	151	125
1401–2	129	159	—	148	157	151	147
1402–3	142	167	117	145	180	153	126
1403–4	200	138	124	157	187	—	147
1404–5	164	144	133	143	174	151	137
1405–6	162	157	124	141	175	127	117
1406–7	151	169	133	131	176	146	156
1407–8	146	164	—	148	157	158	147
1408–9	195	—	124	192	214	153	—
1409–10	157	166	133	144	191	155	165
1410–11	142	160	133	134	184	132	154
1411–12	140	158	141	148	163	157	147

Appendix H. *(cont.)*

100 =	Threshing & winnowing 5.38d.	Reaping & binding 6.04d.	Mowing & spreading 5.66d.	Carpenter (solo) 3.13d.	Thatcher & helper 3.74d.	Slater & helper 5.31d.	Mason (solo) 3.41d.
1412–13	148	170	102	138	190	144	117
1413–14	147	172	115	139	178	165	132
1414–15	149	171	124	135	161	138	161
1415–16	157	167	128	147	177	151	—
1416–17	157	157	113	146	185	173	132
1417–18	204	162	119	160	196	174	156
1418–19	156	160	124	146	183	154	176
1419–20	155	170	111	133	179	132	166
1420–1	157	174	131	154	174	151	176
1421–2	159	155	133	147	175	155	161
1422–3	151	151	126	143	163	153	147
1423–4	148	145	122	141	153	159	165
1424–5	158	—	124	159	160	169	147
1425–6	157	155	122	155	200	153	154
1426–7	139	—	—	164	214	169	176
1427–8	138	155	117	149	188	151	136
1428–9	173	132	115	164	229	—	166
1429–30	157	152	117	162	194	147	147
1430–1	148	155	113	139	187	144	147
1431–2	154	156	108	162	195	164	149
1432–3	148	163	108	160	203	163	117
1433–4	145	151	106	158	203	163	162
1434–5	155	152	115	152	207	162	155
1435–6	184	—	124	166	214	—	—
1436–7	195	154	—	175	264	—	174
1437–8	221	—	115	166	227	174	170
1438–9	150	167	124	182	233	162	154
1439–40	203	157	115	173	235	176	154
1440–1	150	171	115	166	218	165	136
1441–2	164	178	115	161	206	165	151
1442–3	188	196	115	165	267	169	170
1443–4	196	182	115	160	214	188	161
1444–5	177	182	106	157	267	169	148
1445–6	190	157	115	177	—	198	163
1446–7	177	166	106	166	227	158	171
1447–8	160	168	115	165	241	163	169
1448–9	153	166	115	164	235	171	154
1449–50	149	166	106	172	227	172	154
1450–1	212	—	115	173	294	193	167
1451–2	160	166	106	168	243	168	150

Appendix H. (*cont.*)

	Threshing & winnowing 5.38d.	Reaping & binding 6.04d.	Mowing & spreading 5.66d.	Carpenter (solo) 3.13d.	Thatcher & helper 3.74d.	Slater & helper 5.31d.	Mason (solo) 3.41d.
100 =							
1452–3	158	166	133	170	241	181	169
1453–4	158	166	115	169	259	178	173
1454–5	190	149	124	170	201	179	161
1455–6	194	—	133	172	—	169	158
1456–7	212	177	115	188	267	179	167
1457–8	194	—	106	172	—	179	171
1458–9	194	—	124	177	267	207	161
1459–60	177	—	—	184	241	179	148
1460–1	203	—	115	179	241	192	191
1461–2	203	—	124	174	—	182	167
1462–3	180	166	115	180	—	188	128
1463–4	203	166	115	156	—	160	155
1464–5	203	—	124	172	—	169	—
1465–6	203	—	133	160	—	207	172
1466–7	176	—	106	176	—	169	181
1467–8	—	—	106	182	241	192	168
1468–9	—	—	115	172	241	188	176
1469–70	203	—	110	180	—	188	176
1470–1	203	—	—	192	—	188	174
1471–2	—	—	—	192	241	188	163
1472–3	—	—	115	189	214	188	196
1473–4	203	—	106	176	254	—	168
1474–5	—	—	124	176	214	174	—
1475–6	—	—	—	189	—	—	176
1476–7	—	—	—	208	—	198	169
1477–8	—	—	106	189	—	—	176
1478–9	—	—	106	181	267	188	176
1479–80	—	—	106	172	241	169	166
1480–1	—	166	106	176	—	169	176
1481–2	—	—	—	170	—	169	161
1482–3	—	—	106	172	—	169	161
1483–4	—	—	115	192	—	179	152
1484–5	—	—	106	182	—	179	132
1485–6	—	—	—	192	—	—	153
1486–7	—	—	106	192	—	—	176
1487–8	—	—	106	176	—	—	147
1488–9	—	—	115	180	—	—	176
1489–90	—	—	106	192	267	169	176
1490–1	—	—	—	182	—	179	172
1491–2	—	—	—	188	241	148	—

Appendix H. (cont.)

100 =	Threshing & winnowing 5.38d.	Reaping & binding 6.04d.	Mowing & spreading 5.66d.	Carpenter (solo) 3.13d.	Thatcher & helper 3.74d.	Slater & helper 5.31d.	Mason (solo) 3.41d.
1492–3	—	—	—	190	294	165	—
1493–4	—	—	—	174	267	169	165
1494–5	—	—	—	204	—	188	176
1495–6	—	—	—	177	—	159	—
1496–7	—	—	—	192	—	179	169
1497–8	—	—	—	181	254	188	154
1498–9	—	—	—	160	241	—	161
1499–1500	—	—	—	192	241	151	161

^a The figures for these years differ slightly from those published for the same years in *AHEW*, II, p. 817. Those given in this volume are calculated from more extensive material, but include no data from the London area for the reason explained above (p. 497).

Appendix I. *Prices of consumables and labour*

	Basket of consumables		Wages	
	Cost^a (shillings)	Index (100 = 31.91s.)	Agricultural^b	Building^c
1350–1	46.62	146	127	119
1351–2	53.31	167	118	115
1352–3	44.36	139	117	116
1353–4	30.84	97	123	117
1354–5	32.00	100	117	114
1355–6	33.60	105	103	117
1356–7	42.72	149	111	120
1357–8	41.40	130	107	121
1358–9	37.22	117	109	120
1359–60	36.30	114	111	125
1360–1	39.55	124	115	124
1361–2	39.68	124	120	128
1362–3	42.86	134	114	137
1363–4	43.78	137	124	135
1364–5	38.01	119	129	132
1365–6	37.55	118	144	135
1366–7	43.70	137	125	136

Appendix I. (cont.)

	Basket of consumables		Wages	
	Cost[a] (shillings)	Index (100 = 31.91s.)	Agricultural[b]	Building[c]
1367–8	43.51	136	134	135
1368–9	44.54	140	134	134
1369–70	70.51	221	129	132
1370–1	50.85	159	127	144
1371–2	37.37	117	131	131
1372–3	42.03	132	139	148
1373–4	36.75	115	137	142
1374–5	45.08	141	141	139
1375–6	47.00	147	145	145
1376–7	36.16	113	149	142
1377–8	32.70	102	147	140
1378–9	29.91	94	142	140
1379–80	32.47	102	152	142
1380–1	33.26	104	145	155
1381–2	31.49	99	144	143
1382–3	30.73	96	148	136
1383–4	35.79	112	150	148
1384–5	31.59	99	139	152
1385–6	35.21	110	144	138
1386–7	28.20	88	139	146
1387–8	25.17	79	141	138
1388–9	24.17	76	137	140
1389–90	31.22	98	143	144
1390–1	45.94	143	137	140
1391–2	30.03	94	129	157
1392–3	27.48	86	136	143
1393–4	28.59	90	131	138
1394–5	31.56	99	140	144
1395–6	31.06	97	138	139
1396–7	35.56	111	132	140
1397–8	38.45	120	135	153
1398–9	33.08	104	138	143
1399–1400	33.96	106	142	137
1400–1	34.09	107	139	151
1401–2	43.76	137	144	151
1402–3	39.51	124	142	151
1403–4	31.59	99	154	164
1404–5	30.46	95	147	151
1405–6	29.58	93	148	140
1406–7	27.69	87	151	152

Appendix I. (*cont.*)

	Basket of consumables		Wages	
	Cost[a] (shillings)	Index (100 = 31.91s.)	Agricultural[b]	Building[c]
1407–8	31.92	100	155	152
1408–9	35.24	110	159	186
1409–10	43.88	138	152	164
1410–11	38.69	121	145	151
1411–12	31.12	98	146	154
1412–13	29.92	94	140	147
1413–14	31.94	100	145	153
1414–15	33.21	104	148	149
1415–16	37.18	117	151	158
1416–17	38.03	119	142	159
1417–18	33.19	104	162	171
1418–19	28.86	84	147	165
1419–20	32.60	102	145	152
1420–1	30.83	97	154	164
1421–2	29.00	91	149	159
1422–3	29.77	93	143	151
1423–4	29.64	93	138	154
1424–5	28.28	89	141	159
1425–6	29.49	92	145	165
1426–7	27.05	85	139	181
1427–8	26.96	84	137	156
1428–9	32.16	101	140	186
1429–30	42.11	132	142	162
1430–1	30.10	94	139	154
1431–2	31.51	99	139	167
1432–3	35.49	111	140	161
1433–4	34.97	110	134	171
1434–5	29.43	92	141	169
1435–6	27.01	85	154	190
1436–7	27.73	87	174	204
1437–8	33.98	106	168	184
1438–9	54.53	171	147	183
1439–40	40.44	127	158	184
1440–1	27.16	85	145	171
1441–2	25.34	79	152	171
1442–3	29.62	93	166	193
1443–4	26.50	83	164	181
1444–5	24.70	77	155	185
1445–6	24.29	76	154	179

Appendix I. (cont.)

| | Basket of consumables | | Wages | |
	Cost^a (shillings)	Index (100 = 31.91s.)	Agricultural^b	Building^c
1446–7	27.51	86	150	180
1447–8	26.39	83	148	184
1448–9	27.29	86	145	181
1449–50	25.60	80	140	181
1450–1	27.18	85	163	207
1451–2	24.75	78	144	182
1452–3	25.82	81	152	190
1453–4	27.56	86	146	195
1454–5	24.71	77	154	178
1455–6	25.37	80	163	166
1456–7	24.04	75	168	200
1457–8	23.91	75	150	174
1458–9	24.87	78	159	203
1459–60	26.68	84	177	188
1460–1	30.99	97	159	201
1461–2	27.75	87	163	174
1462–3	23.24	73	154	165
1463–4	22.63	71	161	157
1464–5	32.20	101	164	170
1465–6	36.58	115	168	180
1466–7	28.71	90		175
1467–8	29.07	91		196
1468–9	24.88	78		194
1469–70	24.13	76		181
1470–1	29.91	94		185
1471–2	30.51	96		196
1472–3	26.45	83		197
1473–4	26.10	82		199
1474–5	24.39	76		188
1475–6	22.82	72		182
1476–7	25.27	79		192
1477–8	25.61	80		182
1478–9	26.07	82		203
1479–80	27.77	87		187
1480–1	28.55	89		174
1481–2	45.54	143		167
1482–3	48.28	151		167
1483–4	31.75	99		174
1484–5	31.27	98		164

Appendix I. (*cont.*)

	Basket of consumables		Wages	
	Cost*a* (shillings)	Index (100 = 31.91s.)	Agricultural*b*	Building*c*
1485–6	27.34	86		172
1486–7	30.98	97		184
1487–8	24.96	78		161
1488–9	27.20	85		178
1489–90	27.25	85		201
1490–1	29.03	91		178
1491–2	29.62	93		192
1492–3	27.10	85		216
1493–4	25.85	81		194
1494–5	23.02	72		189
1495–6	23.79	75		168
1496–7	25.75	81		180
1497–8	27.66	87		194
1498–9	27.55	86		187
1499–1500	26.60	83		186

The agricultural wages series is fragmentary and unreliable, 1466–1500

a See n. 107. This "basket" includes a lot of grain. There is some reason to believe, however, that by the fifteenth century the labourer's diet included more meat and fish than hitherto.
b Mean of the Indices for Threshing and Winnowing, Reaping and Binding, and Mowing and Spreading.
c Mean of the Indices for Carpenters, Thatchers and helpers, and Slaters and helpers.

Appendix J. *Some English and continental decennial wheat prices*
$(1450/1–1459/60 = 100)$

	England[1]	Bruges[2]	Ghent[3]	Quesnoy[4]	Antwerp[5]	Aragon[6]	Valencia[7]	Vienna[8]	Augsburg[9]
1350–60[10]	125	72		107					
1360–70	145	103		164					
1370–80	118	97		83				33	
1380–90	93	102		69		105		39	
1390–1400	97	69		83		69		54	
1400–10	115	95	87	94		118		30	
1410–20	107	84	90	107		111	95	86	
1420–30	99	97	102	94	102	107	92	98	45
1430–40	130	129	137		123	93	104	164	179
1440–50	88	91	110	108	95	96	97	92	110
1450–60	100	100	100	100	100	100	100	100	100
1460–70	99	76	81	69		100	92		83
1470–80	102	97	125	127		129	104	89	92
1480–90	122	160	190	193	193	97	94	118	102
1490–1500	96	97	108	97	184	105	88	130	133

[1] Calculated from the National Price Levels in this volume.
[2] *Dokumenten voor de Geschiedenis van Prijzen en Lonen in Vlaanderen en Brabant*, ed. C. Verlinden, II, Bruges, 1965, pp. 33 *et seq.*
[3] *Dokumenten*, 1959, I, pp. 37 *et seq.*
[4] G. Sivéry, 'Les profits agricoles au Bas Moyen Age', *Annales ESC*, XXXI, 1976, p. 626.
[5] *Dokumenten*, 1959, I, pp. 253 *et seq.*
[6] E. J. Hamilton, *Money, Prices and Wages in Valencia, Aragon, and Navarre, 1351–1500*, Cambridge, Mass., 1936, pp. 223 *et seq.*
[7] *Ibid.*, pp. 213 *et seq.*
[8] A. F. Pribram, *Materialien zur Geschichte der Preise und Löhne in Österreich*, Vienna, 1938, I, pp. 447–9.
[9] M. J. Elsas, *Umriss einer Geschichte der Preise und Löhne in Deutschland*, Leiden, 1936, I, p. 593.
[10] Each period extends from 29 September in the first-named year to 28 September in the second-named year.

CHAPTER 6

LANDLORDS

A. THE STRUCTURE OF LANDED SOCIETY

(i) *Nobility and gentry*

Contemporary descriptions of the general levels of lay landed society
are not lacking for England in the late middle ages. Models of the
household economies of the major levels of status in lay society have
come down to us in *The Black Book* of the royal household, where it
is assumed that a duke enjoyed a clear annual income from lands of
£4,000 a year, a marquis one of £3,000, an earl one of £2,000, a
viscount one of £1,000, a baron one of £500 and a knight banneret one
of £200. A landed income of £100 was assigned to a knight who was
one of the "sufficient and valiant men" of that order.[1] But these details
tell us nothing of those below this knight in wealth and status – that is,
the untitled members of the group of landowners to whom historians
have attached the label "gentry", who formed the largest group of the
kingdom's landowners in terms of numbers. Indeed, the description
attached to the knight with £100 a year suggests that he is at the
pinnacle of the shire's knights, a conclusion that fits the view that £40
a year was required to maintain the status of a knight. In contrast, for
Sir John Fortescue in the third quarter of the fifteenth century a net
income of £5 a year provided a good living for a yeoman.[2] This
certainly fits Bishop Latimer's description of his upbringing in the
household of his yeoman father in the late fifteenth century: "My
father was a yeoman, and had no lands of his own: only he had a farm
of three or four pounds by the year at the uttermost and hereupon he
tilled so much as kept half a dozen men."[3]

The problem is to produce a definition of what lay between an
important knight, who occupied a dominant position in shire society,

---

[1] A. R. Myers, ed., *The Household of Edward IV: the Black Book and the Ordinance of 1478*,
Manchester, 1959, pp. 95–6, 97, 99–100, 102–5, 109–10.

[2] Sir John Fortescue, *The Governance of England*, ed. C. Plummer, p. 151.

[3] Quoted, e.g., in W. G. Hoskins, *Essays in Leicestershire History*, Liverpool, 1950, p. 152.

and the peasant proprietor, whose prosperity distinguished him from his fellows to the extent that by the mid-fifteenth century it had earned him a special social status. The only reliable guide is to be found in a parliamentary statute of 1439 which laid down that a minimum net income for appointment as a justice of the peace was £20.[4] The assumption embedded in this requirement was that an income at this level guaranteed a solid position in local society that secured respect from neighbours. It is safe to assume that there was a lower level of gentry, for example, the sons and heirs of such £20 landowners who might not yet enjoy an income at this level but whose expectation of it put them in the same status group. But in any analysis of social structure it makes sense to proceed from hard data that are warranted by contemporary evidence. We cannot analyse the structure of landed society without the use of the term gentry: there can be no doubt that someone who was not a knight but enjoyed a net income of £20 a year could be so described.

The essential element in any such structural study must be a body of evidence that provides some sort of overall view of conditions at a specific point in time. At several points in English medieval history these exist, the most famous being Domesday Book and, to a lesser extent because the geographical coverage is limited, the hundred rolls of 1279–80. For the years 1350–1500 we have at our disposal the surviving records of the income taxes imposed by crown and parliament in the fifteenth century, in the form of both enrolled summary statements and various kinds of detailed returns sent to the exchequer from the localities. The gross unreliability of the last of these taxes for which records have survived – that of 1450 – has recently been demonstrated.[5] That of 1436 was the subject of an important study by H. L. Gray over fifty years ago;[6] and his conclusions have attracted a great deal of attention from those interested in both long-term and short-term problems in the history of English landownership, some building general conclusions partly on its basis. Despite this interest, however, there are strong grounds for distrusting the surviving records of this tax as a source of information on the structure of landed wealth. Quite apart from geographical limitations and proven inaccuracies in the treatment of individuals,[7] the taxpayers' assessments were based on declarations made under oath before commissioners. It is not surprising, therefore, that even some peers and peers' dowagers

---

[4] 18 Henry VI, c. 11.

[5] R. Virgoe, 'The parliamentary subsidy of 1450', *Bull. IHR*, LV, 1982.

[6] H. L. Gray, 'Incomes from land in England in 1436', *EHR*, XLIX, 1934.

[7] C. D. Ross and T. B. Pugh, 'The English baronage and the income tax of 1436', *Bull. IHR*, XXVI, 1953.

Table 6.1. *Total assessments by county for the income taxes of 1404 and 1412 (totals to the nearest £)*

(a) Counties

	1404	1412
	500 marks or above	£20 units
Berkshire	166	1,280
Cornwall	480	missing
Derbyshire	106	2,660
Devon	2,416	3,920
Essex	869	6,840
Gloucestershire	1,188	3,320
Hampshire	535	4,740
Herefordshire	151	missing
Hertfordshire	143	1,260
Kent	445	6,280
Lincolnshire		
Holland	510	
Kesteven	367	
Lindsey	517	
	1,394	missing
Middlesex	146	760
Norfolk	1,113	9,040
Northamptonshire	367	missing
Nottinghamshire	93	2,580
Oxfordshire	465	missing
Rutland	322	540
Shropshire	229	missing
Staffordshire	191	missing
Suffolk	871	4,600
Wiltshire	missing	4,240
Worcestershire	374	missing
Yorkshire		
East Riding	1,426	
North Riding	1,208	
West Riding	382	
	3,016	missing
Bedfordshire	345	} 3,120
Buckinghamshire	338	
Cambridgeshire	313	} 3,560
Huntingdonshire	240	
Somerset	762	11,000
Dorset	367	
Surrey	163	} 6,100
Sussex	347	
Warwickshire	223	} 6,100
Leicestershire	756	
Cumberland	missing	missing
Lancashire	missing	missing
Northumberland	missing	missing
Westmorland	missing	missing
Total	17,934	81,940

Table 6.1 (cont.)

(b) Cities and towns

	1404	1412
London	456	4,220
Bristol	100	660
Coventry	missing	640
Lincoln	missing	140
Norwich	0	400
York	6	620
Total	562	6,680

are missing from the returns. A more serious weakness from the standpoint of the social and economic historian, however, is the fact that the individual assessments that survive for a number of counties provide only summary totals applying often to holdings in several counties, sometimes not even mentioning the other counties by name or even giving their number.

For these reasons the records of the earlier income tax of 1412 deserve serious attention. Their great advantage as evidence is that both the parliamentary peerage and the non-peers, including the dowagers of both, were generally assessed in each county for their holdings within it. To be sure, the enrolled statements which are all we have for many counties were based on units of £20 net annual income – £20, £40 and upwards – the margin between the steps of payment being untaxed. But there survives a substantial number of original returns that provide details of actual incomes, sometimes extending below the £20 level. While caution must always be used and scepticism held at the ready in studying evidence of this kind, it is also clear that within the limits of the income levels they cover both the surviving detailed returns and the final assessments of 1412 were much closer to reality than those of 1436. The major merit of our information about income levels in 1412 is that they generally deal with all the landowners within a single county. And the use of the £20 unit of assessment has the advantage that it accords with a separate and roughly contemporary assessment of clear gentry status in the statute of 1439.[8]

Table 6.1 summarizes the details of total values of the incomes assessed in 37 counties for taxation in 1412. In addition, it provides similar information for a more limited income tax levied in 1404 in which total incomes of 500 marks (£333 13s. 4d.) or above were taxed. Totals are also provided for both years for cities and towns for purposes of comparison.

[8] For a full discussion of all these issues see J. M. W. Bean, 'The English income taxes, 1404–50', forthcoming.

The totals set out in Table 6.1 for 1412 include, it must be said, a small amount of land belonging to the Church, since the income tax was levied on those lands acquired by ecclesiastics since the Statute of Mortmain (1279). But they do provide a picture of the range of landed wealth presented by the kingdom's counties. Table 6.1, however, does not assist in the analysis of the structure of landed society. For this purpose it is necessary to turn to those detailed county returns that have survived which all provide income totals for individual landowners. Table 6.2, excluding the lands of the Church, sets out the available information. It includes in a number of cases incomes below the £20 level, since the commissioners appear to have made an effort to investigate incomes below the level of payment and some of the resulting returns have survived.[9]

In every county listed in Table 6.2 the number of landowners, the Church apart, with incomes ranging from £20 and £40 was substantially in excess of the total of all those with incomes above this level. Table 6.2 contains nothing to suggest that landed society in each of the counties concerned was dominated by a small group of great landowners. Further investigation into this is best handled by means of the conventional approach of dividing landowners, including the respective dowagers, into those who belonged to the parliamentary peerage and the gentry. Table 6.3 provides an analysis of the surviving returns for individual counties along these lines. It shows that in most of these the holdings of individual peers must, in terms of value, have been indistinguishable from those of many gentry.

Out of seventeen counties, in only four (Berkshire, Essex, Huntingdonshire, and Sussex) did the proportion of the landed values held by the peerage exceed 25 per cent and in none of these did it reach 30 per cent. In the case of three counties (Derbyshire, Dorset, and Surrey) it was, in contrast, below 10 per cent. Over all the counties listed in Table 6.3 as a whole the proportion held by the peerage amounted to 17.8 per cent. Moreover, if we look at the average value of the county holdings of the peerage and gentry we find that there were eight counties in which the gentry figure was the higher one (Berkshire, Cambridgeshire, Derbyshire, Dorset, Hampshire, Huntingdonshire, Middlesex, Surrey). There are, to be sure, strong grounds for suggesting that the proportion held by the peerage over the kingdom as a whole must have been somewhat higher than 18.2 per cent, since the counties for which we have no returns include Cumberland, Northumberland, and Yorkshire, where there was a high

---

[9] It includes, mainly in the counties close to London, lands held by London merchants. But it is impossible to separate these from other landowners, since we cannot be sure that all of them are identified as merchants.

Table 6.2. *Distribution of incomes in county returns in 1412 (excluding the Church)*

(Figures in square brackets indicate number of landowners in the category)

County	£5–19	£20–39	£40–99	£100–99	£200–99	£300–99	£400+
Bedfordshire	346 [34]	778 [33]	522 [10]	168 [1]	0	0	0
Berkshire	289 [41]	710 [32]	526 [9]	0	0	0	0
Cambridgeshire	531 [50]	1,269 [53]	1,229 [22]	0	0	0	0
Derbyshire	126 [14]	907 [41]	1,415 [278]	574 [5]	0	0	0
Devon		1,470 [72]	1,648 [38]	300 [3]	0	0	400 [1]
Dorset	305 [30]	1,424 [58]	1,570 [29]	601 [5]	732 [3]	0	0
Essex	267 [24]	2,421 [106]	2,894 [56]	525 [4]	217 [1]	613 [2]	0
Hampshire	437 [44]	1,607 [70]	1,866 [36]	321 [3]	775 [3]	0	0
Huntingdonshire	317 [32]	251 [10]	445 [8]	211 [2]	0	0	0
Kent	22 [3]	2,347 [94]	2,734 [51]	1,142 [9]	0	0	0
Middlesex	358 [42]	324 [14]	239 [5]	100 [1]	0	0	0
Nottinghamshire	360 [38]	1,324 [57]	1,303 [19]	0	0	0	0
Somerset	22 [3]	2,355 [105]	2,953 [64]	1,062 [8]	432 [2]	301 [1]	0
Surrey	25 [2]	1,097 [53]	627 [13]	0	0	0	0
Sussex	189 [20]	1,251 [52]	1,295 [24]	1,154 [10]	228 [1]	0	546 [1]
Wiltshire	957 [91]	1,846 [77]	2,086 [36]	740 [6]	231 [1]	0	0

concentration of magnate holdings. Even so, if we take into consideration the absorption of the highest county totals in Table 6.3, it is impossible to believe that a country-wide peerage percentage would have much exceeded 20 per cent.

The difficulty of venturing further on the basis of Table 6.3 is that landed assets were not confined to a single county, especially in the case of families whose heads attended the lords in time of parliament. For this reason Table 6.4 adopts a regional approach, providing results over eight southern counties at the respective levels of dukes and earls, barons, and those outside those ranks. In effect, with the exception of Cornwall, the results provide a picture of the structure of lay

Table 6.3. *Total incomes of peerage and gentry in 1412 ($\pounds$)*
() = number in category
[ ] = average value

County	Total	Peerage, including dowagers		Gentry and others, including dowagers		Peerage incomes as per cent of total
Bedfordshire	1,814		294		1,520	16.2
		(6)	[49]	(38)	[40]	
Berkshire	1,465		368		1,097	25.1
		(13)	[28.3]	(26)	[42.2]	
Cambridgeshire	2,929		371		2,558	12.7
		(10)	[37.1]	(64)	[40]	
Derbyshire	2,975		290		2,685	9.8
		(8)	[36.3]	(64)	[42]	
Devon	3,718		766		2,952	20.6
		(9)	[85.1]	(104)	[28.4]	
Dorset	4,225		275		3,950	6.5
		(10)	[27.5]	(83)	[47.6]	
Essex	6,887		2,060		4,827	29.9
		(25)	[82.4]	(142)	[34]	
Hampshire	4,640		675		3,965	14.6
		(18)	[37.5]	(92)	[43.1]	
Hertfordshire	1,302		243		1,059	23.0
		(8)	[30.4]	(39)	[27.2]	
Huntingdonshire	1,138		320		818	28.1
		(7)	[45.7]	(12)	[68.2]	
Kent	6,223		814		5,409	15.1
		(13)	[62.6]	(141)	[38.4]	
Middlesex	921		140		781	15.2
		(7)	[20]	(13)	[60]	
Nottinghamshire	2,987		324		2,663	10.9
		(11)	[24.5]	(113)	[23.6]	
Somerset	7,125		1,393		5,732	19.6
		(17)	[81.9]	(163)	[35.2]	
Surrey	1,729		160		1,569	9.3
		(6)	[26.7]	(63)	[27.4]	
Sussex	4,653		1,387		3,266	29.8
		(12)	[115.6]	(75)	[43.6]	
Wiltshire	5,710		903		4,807	15.8
		(16)	[56.4]	(103)	[46.7]	
Total	60,441		10,783		49,658	17.8

landowning society south of the Thames. The impressions developed on the basis of Table 6.3 are markedly deepened. The great majority of landowners belonged to the £20–39 category, most of these holding lands confined to a single county.

Three main conclusions about the structure of landed society south of the Thames emerge from Table 6.4. First, there was a distinct tendency for those with incomes above £40 to hold land outside a single county. Second, many barons and some earls, including dowagers at both levels, held total holdings south of the Thames that were no more lucrative than those of non-peers. And, third, there were several non-peers who enjoyed incomes in the region superior to those of some peers. Two counties provide exceptions to this general pattern – Devon and Sussex, where the earls of Devon (£400) and Arundel (£548) respectively held conglomerations of land that placed them in dominant positions.

It is unfortunate that the information provided in Table 6.4 is confined to the south of the Thames and we possess no equivalent details for the north and substantial portions of the midlands. But support for the suggestion that the general picture displayed in Table 6.4 can be applied to the rest of England can be obtained from two other sources. First, Table 6.3 supplies data for six counties north of the Thames, involving different regions – two, Essex and Middlesex, close to London, two, Cambridgeshire and Essex, on the fringes of East Anglia, two, Bedfordshire and Huntingdonshire, on the edge of the East Midlands, and two, Derbyshire and Nottinghamshire, in the north midlands. In all these counties the structure of landownership was not remarkably different from that displayed in Table 6.4. Second, there is the record of the limited income tax paid in 1404 and summarized in Table 6.1.

It is certainly unlikely that the totals for 1404 in themselves give an accurate picture of the peers and the most wealthy of the gentry: the few returns that have survived for single counties provide totals for individuals that are suspiciously round. At the same time the totals for 1412 underrate real incomes, providing only obligations in terms of £20 units of assessment. To be sure, the contrast between peers and non-peers exhibited in Tables 6.1 and 6.2 has to be injected into our appreciation of the totals of Table 6.4. But, if this is done, there is good reason to apply to the whole of England a pattern of landownership in which most landowners belonged to the £20–39 category and those families that belonged to the parliamentary peerage did not enjoy a dominant share of the kingdom's landed wealth. It is fair to state on the basis of other knowledge that three counties missing from the

Table 6.4. *Distribution of incomes in eight southern counties in 1412 (totals to nearest £)*

[ ] = number of individual assessments

[F] = number of holdings held by females

F = total value of holdings held by females

The counties are: Berkshire, Devon, Dorset, Hampshire, Kent, Surrey, Sussex and Wiltshire

	£20–39	£40–99	£100–99	£200–99	£300–99	£400+	Total
(a) Non-peerage holdings							
In one county only	9,763 [418] 1,006 F [44 F]	6,994 [144] 521 F [10 F]	1,729 [15] 100 F [1 F]	238 [1]	—		
In two counties	702 [24] 67 F [2 F]	3,396 [54] 312 F [4 F]	1,282 [10]	—			
In three counties	176 [5]	1,004 [15] 52 F [1 F]	2,078 [14] 113 F [1 F]	466 [2]	674 [2]	—	
In four counties	—	—	776 [5] 157 F [1 F]	269 [1]	—	500 [1]	
In five or more counties	—	—	195 [1]			460 [1]	
(b) Baronial holdings							
In one county only							
In two counties	61 [2] 31 F [1 F]	200 [3] 70 F [1 F]	715 [5] 112 F [1 F]	—			
In three counties	—	—	449 [3] 170 F [1 F]	—	—	—	
In four counties	—	—	191 [1]			479 [1]	
In five or more counties	—	—	327 [2]				
(c) Comital and ducal holdings							
In one county only	—	—	—	—	—	—	
In two counties	—	117 [2]	118 [1] 118 F [1 F]	—	324 [1] 324 F [1 F]		
In three counties	—	—	—				
In four counties	—	—	—	252 [1] 252 F [1 F]	—	1,885 [4]	

Table 6.4 (cont.)

	£20–39	£40–99	£100–99	£200–99	£300–99	£400+	Total
In five or more counties	—	—	—	—	—	609 [1]	
(d) Totals							
Non-peerage	10,641 [447]	11,394 [213]	6,060 [44]	973 [3]	674 [2]	960 [2]	30,702 [711]
	1,073 F [46 F]	885 F [15 F]	370 F [3 F]				2,328 F [64 F]
Barons	61 [2]	200 [3]	1,682 [11]			479 [1]	2,422 [17]
	31 F [1 F]	70 F [1 F]	282 F [2 F]	—	—		383 F [4 F]
Dukes and earls	—	117 [2]	118 [1]	252 [1]	324 [1]	2,494 [5]	3,305 [10]
			118 F [1 F]	252 F [1 F]	324 F [1 F]		576 F [2 F]
Total	10,702 [449]	11,711 [218]	7,860 [56]	1,225 [4]	998 [3]	3,933 [8]	36,429 [738]
	1,104 F [47 F]	955 F [16 F]	652 F [5 F]	252 F [1 F]	324 F [1 F]		3,287 F [70 F]

returns of 1412 – Cumberland, Northumberland, and Westmorland – replicated what we see in Devon and Sussex, since the Percy inheritance (its earl was in fact restored in 1416 after his father's and grandfather's rebellions in the years 1403–5) dominated both Northumberland and Cumberland.

It must also be emphasized that the position was different prior to 1399. At that time the duke of Lancaster had dominated the county palatine of Lancaster and enjoyed the highest incomes from land in both Yorkshire and the north midlands, with substantial holdings also in Lincolnshire and parts of the south. The seizure of the crown by Henry of Lancaster in 1399, however, had transformed the situation, enlarging the territorial holdings of the crown and reducing proportionately those of its subjects. In the early fifteenth century only four counties – Northumberland and Cumberland in the north, Sussex in the south and Devon in the west – contained the holdings of powerful magnates whose landed wealth within their boundaries placed them in positions of dominance.

Taken as a whole, the evidence of Tables 6.1–6.4 fits remarkably well with assumptions about gradations of landed wealth contained in *The Black Book* of the royal household. Those who administered the income tax of 1412 found no difficulty in searching out those with net incomes of £20 or more. Although not all those at this level were accorded knightly rank, the figure of £100 does make sense as an indication of the level of wealth of a leading knight: among those who held land in several counties in Tables 6.3 and 6.4 there were non-baronial taxpayers whose incomes must have given them positions of leadership in at least one county. But the mass of gentry were not in this category. If on the basis of the gradations of landed wealth exposed in Tables 6.3 and 6.4 we try to develop a picture of divisions within the gentry class it makes sense to distinguish between, on the one hand, local gentry, those in the £20–39 category and, on the other hand, their superiors in landed wealth who were county, and in a few cases, regional gentry.

But what of those below the £20 level? In real economic terms and also in terms of the relationships of local society the range between the £20 landowner and the yeoman with £5 a year was substantial, the one who was barely within the gentry by the higher figure enjoying an income almost four times that of his social and financial inferior. On this point the returns of 1412 give little help. To be sure, there are a number of detailed returns in which individuals are assigned incomes below £20, but this did not happen in all the surviving returns and it is difficult to avoid the conclusion that much depended on the zeal of local commissioners and that, even when this had some effect, many with incomes below £20 were left out. On this point, indeed, despite their deficiencies, it may be useful to turn to the surviving records of the income tax of 1436, since these began at the £5 level. The available information is summarized in Table 6.5. The numbers are far in excess of those we have for 1412; but they must be treated with care. It is all too likely that, since the first level of assessment began at £5 and went up to £100, there was a tendency to declare incomes within this range as low as possible, so that some that were in reality somewhat above the £20 level were pushed unduly low. All in all, however, the numbers are impressive and certainly suggest a sizeable population with incomes below £20 but above £5.

The evidence of Table 6.5 contains, indeed, a warning not to assume that those whom contemporaries would have regarded as gentry invariably had incomes of £20 or more. In practice in some years a temporary crisis in local farming might depress an individual's income below the £20 level. Some below this level may have been the sons and heirs of gentry whose incomes were substantially above the £20 level. Those with incomes in the £5–19 range must have been proportionately more difficult to define in terms of social status the higher they moved towards the top level of this group.

It is, in fact, important to bear in mind that the term that defines the lower level of this group – the yeoman – emerged from the usages of the great lord's household and was still not free of such associations.

Table 6.5. *Yeoman incomes in 1436 (totals to nearest £)*

	£5–9		£10–14		£15–19	
County	Total value	Number of holdings	Total value	Number of holdings	Total value	Number of holdings
Cambs.	291	51	232	22	36	2
Cumb.	157	26	77	7	0	0
Derbs.	307	52	225	20	65	4
Essex	1,194	216	535	52	227	12
Hants.	330	58	330	30	124	8
Herts.	333	59	275	24	31	2
Hunts.	94	18	60	6	0	0
Leics.	313	57	173	16	33	2
Lincs.	1,236	216	836	75	182	11
Notts.	332	59	327	29	125	8

The term (Latin: *vallettus*) was applied there to those who performed duties superior to those of the groom and below those of one who was apprenticed for knighthood – the squire (*armiger*), whose status was bound up with the original duty of bearing his lord's arms when in attendance on him on campaign or in tournaments. By the middle of the fifteenth century it was inevitable that contemporaries would seek a term to define a well-to-do peasant who occupied a position of some importance below the lord of the manor. But the term in its original meaning was still to be found in the noble household.

These comments are important because they underline both the amorphous character of the £5–19 income group and the inclusion in it of some who were indistinguishable from those with £20 a year or more in terms of local standing as distinct from wealth. Historians have emphasized the extent to which many manors had no resident lord, a situation that must have enhanced the capacity of lesser gentry to participate in leadership of the local community. Many of them, indeed, may have been "parish gentry" in the sense which some historians of Tudor England have argued.[10] These arguments are strengthened by attention to what we know of the economic situation of the lord's squire attending in his household and sometimes recruited by indenture of retinue. An examination of such indentures and the financial records of great lords suggests that the annual fee for a squire

[10] E.g., J. Cornwall, 'The early Tudor gentry', *EcHR*, 2nd ser. XVII, 1964–5.

was generally either £5 or £6 13s. 4d. (£10 being infrequent). This was not the full extent of his income: he usually received both wages and board. If we assume that he served his lord in the household for two-thirds of the year, his total emoluments must in most cases have been double his annual fee and would have put him well into the middle range of the £5–19 group.[11] Yet in terms of social status a squire belonged to the class of landowners above this level. Some squires might, indeed, succeed to an inheritance in the gentry class or marry within it. All these considerations point to the conclusion that some landowners who fell below the £20 level in terms of income nevertheless deserve to be classed as gentry purely in terms of social status. But the difficulty is that it is impossible to draw a clear line of demarcation that separated them from yeomen. At least in the case of a line of division at £20 for those who were clearly gentry we are on solid ground.

These uncertainties may help to explain the difficulties that historians have encountered in interpreting the precise social status of the "franklin" described in Chaucer's Prologue to *The Canterbury Tales*. The word itself suggests a social position equivalent to that of the yeoman; but Chaucer's franklin was more than that, even apparently serving as knight of the shire on several occasions. The employment of an annual income of more than £20 as the lowest limit for the gentry class is safe. It can be justified by stressing an important difference between the gentry and those below them in rural society. It is a reasonable assumption that a landowner with a net income of £20 a year drew a substantial part of it from rents and farms of tenants, whereas a yeoman, while he might be a freeholder and also engage in subletting to other peasants, was generally a tenant of a manorial lord. There remained, however, a greater difference between the man with an income of £15 and a yeoman with £5 than between the former and one with £20. If we are to place a figure on the income of Chaucer's franklin, it would be in the upper reaches of the £5–20 group, perhaps even slightly above the higher limit, a circumstance which may explain his serving as a knight of the shire.

While this discussion illuminates the structure of rural landowning within the shires of England, it provides an imperfect account of the total landed wealth of peerage and gentry. None of the income taxes discussed gave attention to incomes from land within Wales and the marches. While there is no reason to believe that many gentry enjoyed substantial portions of income from these regions, this is not true of a number of leading English landowners. On this point we have to rely on the surviving financial records of this group and, to a lesser extent, surveys carried out after forfeitures through rebellion and treason. As

---

[11] For a discussion of these issues see J. M. W. Bean, *From Lord to Patron*, pp. 154–74.

sources of income, holdings in the marches of Wales could be substantial. In the middle of the fifteenth century Richard, duke of York (d. 1460) drew roughly two-thirds of his landed income from this area, a proportion that would have to be raised for his maternal ancestors, the Mortimer earls of March. Richard, earl of Arundel (d. 1397) and his son and heir similarly drew two-thirds of their landed income from marcher lordships. In 1448–9 Humphrey Stafford, duke of Buckingham (d. 1460) held the lordships of Brecon, Hay, Huntingdon, Talgarth, Newport, and Caus, which brought in 30 per cent of his net income. The proportion of the total net income of the Mowbray dukes of Norfolk in the fifteenth century contributed by their lordship of Gower must have been in the same range. The number of magnates in this position had in fact been larger in the fourteenth century when the Bohun earls of Hereford and Essex still survived in the male line and the dukes of Lancaster held substantial Welsh lordships. But in 1399 the Lancastrian lordships, together with a half-share of the Bohun holdings that came through Henry of Bolingbroke's first marriage, were attached to those of the crown descending to Henry V.

In terms of the total number of dukes, earls, and barons this group of substantial marcher lords was never a large one. But it contained most of the wealthiest magnates. Between 1350 and the seizures of the throne by the house of Lancaster in 1399 and by the son and heir of Richard, duke of York, in 1461, it was their Welsh holdings that put some of the leading magnates into the top category of landed wealth.[12] The Percy earls of Northumberland did not belong to this group; but their northern rivals the Nevilles did after Richard Neville, the son and heir of Richard, earl of Salisbury (d. 1460), became through his marriage to the Beauchamp heiress not merely earl of Warwick but also lord of Glamorgan. Most of the leaders of landed society in England in the late fourteenth and fifteenth centuries were thus the eventual beneficiaries of Norman colonialism.

In the last resort any analysis of landed income must address itself to an examination of its component elements. To what extent do the various statistics derived from the income tax of 1412 cover agrarian, as distinct from other sources? Grants of lands, offices and fees, and annuities, from the crown as well as from other landowners, could all contribute to total income; and the commissioners of 1412 were explicitly charged with assessing these, provided they were freehold, a term of tenure that included holdings for life. There can be no doubt that some part of the charges summarized in the budget of 1433 went into the pockets of courtiers and officials by way of fees and annuities.

---

[12] For further details, see R. R. Davies, *Lordship and Society*, pp. 188–9.

And income from such sources is certainly reflected in the totals returned in 1412. Just how large an item they formed it is difficult to say. Moreover, such patronage was not the sole prerogative of the crown. Great landowners paid out annual fees to the knights and squires they had retained for service in peace and had also granted annuities for past and future services. If these payments were for life, they were treated as part of the landowner's permanent charges and deducted before the declaration of net income. Fees from offices in the administration of a great lord could also form a sizeable element in the incomes of some gentry. It was not unusual, for example, for the steward of a great lord to receive 20 marks or £20 a year. The scale of such disbursements can best be assessed by looking at two examples. Both are important because the bulk of the landed holdings concerned were concentrated within a limited number of shires, and must have exercised a powerful influence on the financial situations of local gentry. The Percy earls of Northumberland in the fifteenth century could bestow offices with fees totalling £600 a year. John of Gaunt, duke of Lancaster from 1361 to 1399, although in a wider group of counties, could bestow similar patronage to the extent of £2,000 a year.

But what of fees and annuities that were granted for services unconnected with administrative office? The returns of 1412 provide us with one body of remarkable insight into the extent to which gentry in the neighbourhood of a great estate could derive financial advantage from its service. Out of 64 gentry listed in the Derbyshire returns, 21 held annuities from the king as duke of Lancaster. The total of the declared incomes of all of them was £853 and of this annuities totalled £513. This is a rare survival.[13] It is fair to point out that the gentry of Derbyshire were in terms of landed resources many of them among the poorest in the kingdom and therefore especially prone to seek and to accept such grants, while the Duchy of Lancaster enjoyed territorial wealth to an extent far in excess of any other landowner. And Henry IV was exploiting this situation to an extent greater than his father.

It is a pity that the returns of 1412 do not tell in similar detail about other counties where the Duchy of Lancaster was the dominant landowner.[14] But were local gentry dependent to a similar extent on resources supplied by other great landowners? The available evidence suggests that this was not the case. A recent examination of the surviving

---

[13] One peer also held an annuity of £20 out of a total of £40.

[14] An inspection of the valors surviving from the first decade of the fifteenth century suggests that the duchy contributed substantially to the incomes of many gentry in the West Riding of Yorkshire (e.g. PRO DL 29/728/11988).

financial records of English magnates in this period reveals that in the late fourteenth and fifteenth centuries John of Gaunt, duke of Lancaster, at the close of the fourteenth century and the Percy earls of Northumberland in the mid- and late fifteenth century dispensed fees and annuities over and above those for administrative duties on a substantial scale, Gaunt paying out a total of more than 25 per cent of his gross income, and the Percies doing so at very near this level.[15] It may well be that the scale of such disbursements was equalled by the Neville earls of Salisbury and Warwick within the limits of their Yorkshire estates alone in the 1450s and 60s. But the records of all other magnates that have come down to us reveal nothing on a similar scale. In the light of this information we cannot exclude the possibility that in 1412 in some counties the revenues of the Duchy of Lancaster contributed appreciably to gentry incomes; but throughout England in the years 1350–1500 as a whole, fees and annuities paid for services to the king and the magnates contributed to the incomes of no more than a minority of gentry.

Another possible source of non-agrarian income was, of course, rents from urban property. In view of the economic character of many cities and towns, to be sure, the distinction between such revenues and those from manorial rents was in practice a somewhat unreal one, even though burgage holdings were markedly different in terms of legal character from feudal or manorial tenures. Table 6.1(a) does provide totals of £20 units for cities and towns where they have survived. One member of the peerage – Michael de la Pole, earl of Suffolk – had a substantial estate worth £133 in Kingston-upon-Hull,[16] built up three generations earlier by the merchant founder of his family's fortunes. In contrast, however, the detailed returns that have survived for non-merchant holdings of laity in the city of London provide totals as follows: 13 dukes and earls, £140; 17 barons, £106; 35 knights, £483; and 41 squires, £199.[17] A comparison of the information with the details assembled in Tables 6.1–6.4 indicates that non-agrarian sources could not have played an appreciable role in the fortunes of most peers and gentry.

In the light of this discussion and the statistics assembled in Tables 6.1–6.4, it is worthwhile to attempt an estimate of the total wealth of the English peerage and gentry at the beginning of the fifteenth century, even though the gaps in our sources permit only approximate calculations. The total value of the holdings listed in Table 6.1(a) is £81,940. It is necessary to add to this a total representing the counties

---

[15] See Bean, *From Lord to Patron*, pp. 158–65.   [16] *Feudal Aids*, VI, p. 546.

[17] J. C. L. Stahlschmidt, 'Lay subsidy *temp*, Henry IV', *Arch. J.*, XLIV, 1887, pp. 56–82.

missing from the records of the income tax of 1412. Unfortunately, these include the largest county of all – Yorkshire – and one of the largest – Lincolnshire; but for the purpose of a rough estimate it is enough to assume that these equalled a number of counties, three in the case of Yorkshire and two in that of Lincolnshire. If we multiply the resulting total – 17 – by the average of the known county totals of 1412 and add the result to the total in Table 6.1(a), we achieve a total of almost £140,000. This, of course, represents £20 unit totals, not declared values. And to obtain the latter we have to add 12.5 per cent – that is, the average margin between the unit assessments in Table 6.1(a) and the declared values in those counties where the latter are available. We also have to take into account the reality that the declared values fell short of actual net incomes. An examination of those cases where a comparison between declared values and other evidence relating to income is available suggests that it is wise to add another 40 per cent. We thus reach a total of £220,500. This includes lands acquired by the Church since 1279; but it is also necessary to add to it the property held by the peerage and gentry in cities and towns. Accordingly it is fair to suggest that the total wealth of peerage and gentry – that is, all lay landowners with incomes in excess of £20 a year – amounted to approximately £220,000 a year.

(ii) *The crown*

The crown's share of the lands of its kingdom was not a constant in the years 1350–1500 but changed with political circumstances. It is best to begin the discussion of this problem roughly one-third through this period, when, with the Lancastrian usurpation of 1399, the estates of the Duchy of Lancaster were added to those of the crown. On the face of it this was an important strengthening of the crown's landed resources, since it added an inheritance worth £12–13,000 a year. But the net financial gain was less: the value of the inheritance was reduced by the lavish disbursements on fees and annuities for life made by John of Gaunt, by further such expenditure on the part of his son and heir to strengthen support for his seizure of the throne, and the dispositions made by Gaunt for his children by Katherine Swynford, his third wife. But for the crown, as for any great landowner, the advantages of landownership were not confined to the actual revenues it received, but also embraced sources of patronage, in the case of the Lancastrian inheritance disseminated through most of the counties of the kingdom. The new king also brought with him to the throne his first wife's half-share of the Bohun inheritance, in due course handed on to his son and heir Henry V.

An exceptional opportunity to assess the extent of the crown's landed resources is provided by the well-known budget that Ralph, Lord Cromwell, presented to parliament in 1433.[18] According to this the Duchy of Cornwall brought in £2,789 gross, lands in south Wales £1,140, those in north Wales £1,098, the principality of Chester £765 and Windsor Castle £208, all gross figures. These totals, in fact, give a misleading impression: according to this budget statement charges on all these items of revenue amounted to £4,814, leaving a net total of £1,183.

These figures alone give a distorted picture. Like any other landowner, the king at any time might be burdened with responsibilities to dowagers. In 1433 there were two queens dowager, each holding a dower of 10,000 marks a year, making a total of £13,333. In addition, the Duchy of Lancaster did not figure in the budget of 1433; its yield was approximately £12,000. In theory, therefore, without taking into account the charges described in 1433, the estates that belonged to the crown were worth roughly £30,500 a year.

The vicissitudes that afflicted these resources down to 1500 have received a great deal of attention, especially from students of royal finances. There can be no doubt that, with the accession of a vigorous and militarily successful king in the person of Edward IV, a tendency to dissipation began to be reversed, especially after his return to power in 1471; and, in addition, he enjoyed the great inheritance that came to him from his father Richard, duke of York. The victory of Henry Tudor over Richard III brought him not only the landed inheritance of the house of York but also control of that which had once belonged to Richard, earl of Warwick. It has been customary among historians in recent generations to play down the effects of the "Wars of the Roses" and to emphasize that this period of intermittent civil war did not destroy the English nobility. At one level this is true enough. But it should not disguise the fact that the development of the struggle over the throne in the years 1455–85 and the eventual total success of Henry VII resulted in powerful additions to the territorial resources of the crown. In addition to what it had held in 1433, it now controlled estates that had once belonged to the two wealthiest magnates of the middle years of the fifteenth century – those of Richard, duke of York (d. 1460) and Richard Neville, earl of Warwick (d. 1471). Moreover, these included a substantial body of lordships in the marches of Wales.

In the light of approximate calculations of the total wealth of peerage and gentry that have been made, it is worthwhile attempting a

[18] For a summary and discussion see B. P. Wolffe, *The Royal Demesne in English History: the Crown Estate in the Governance of the Realm from the Conquest to 1509*, London, 1971, pp. 89–96.

comparison of the landed wealth of the crown with that of its subjects. It is best to do so on the basis of the budget of 1433, provided it is borne in mind that the crown's base of territorial wealth expanded by the end of the century, and a comparison with the total assembled on the basis of the income tax of 1412 is feasible, since this was only twenty years earlier. Although agrarian decline may have affected the revenues of some landowners in the intervening years, this must have been slight in terms of an approximate comparison. The available information thus suggests that in the early fifteenth century the total landed wealth of lay society in England amounted to roughly £250,000; and of this approximately 15 per cent was held by the crown.

(iii) The Church

The effort to assess the share of the kingdom's landed wealth held by the Church requires the study of a different body of evidence. The researches of R. V. Lennard into the statistics of the Domesday survey produced the conclusion that in 1086 the Church held 26 per cent of the land in England.[19] According to E. A. Kosminsky, on the basis of his study of the hundred rolls of 1279–80, the proportion in the area these records covered was one-third.[20] If we accept both these totals, the apparent increase over a period of two centuries is not surprising. The Cistercians and other new orders appeared in the course of the twelfth century. Kings, barons and knights had continued to invest in the spiritual welfare of themselves and their ancestors by endowments to the older Benedictine foundations as well as to the new ones. And the Church, partly because it did not have to face the perils of rebellion and forfeiture and the risks of relief and wardship, probably had more capital than laymen for the purchase of new properties.

The problem is to discover the situation at the end of the middle ages. The obvious source is the *Valor Ecclesiasticus*, the great survey of Church holdings engineered by Thomas Cromwell in 1535. Its value as a source of social and economic data has been understood for generations. And the researches of A. Savine at the beginning of this century showed that, although it is possible to query particular totals and there is not total consistency in the ways the survey handles information, the evidence of the *Valor* does provide a reasonably firm foundation for an overall assessment of the Church's wealth. Furthermore, a recent study of those portions of the *Valor* that deal

[19] R. V. Lennard, *Rural England, 1086–1135*, Oxford, 1959, p. 25.
[20] E. A. Kosminsky, *Studies in the Agrarian History of England in the Thirteenth Century*, Oxford, 1956, p. 109.

with episcopal estates in the light of their surviving financial records of the early sixteenth century has also produced an impression of general reliability.[21]

The total net value of the temporal possessions of all English monasteries – that is, all direct incomes from land, tithes being excluded – amounted to £100,700. The equivalent total for bishops' temporalities was £25,000. The total for all the landed revenues of the Church (excluding tithes) was thus about £126,000. It is possible to make a comparison, albeit impressionistic, between this and the total wealth of lay landowners on the basis of the preceding discussion of the information contained in the records of the income tax of 1412 and the budget of 1433. To be sure, land values had begun to rise by 1535; but there is reason to believe that monastic landowners at least had made no serious effort to boost their revenues since the end of the fifteenth century. For the purpose of a rough comparison it is sufficient to assume that the annual value of all lay estates, including those of the crown, in the first half of the fifteenth century amounted to £250,000. Crown, nobility and gentry all made some successful efforts to boost revenues in the first three decades of the sixteenth century, so that the equivalent figure for 1535 must have been higher. Crude though the resulting totals may be, they are useful in suggesting that we take seriously the view of Kosminsky that the Church held one-third of the kingdom's landed wealth. Indeed, the margin between the two totals and the certainty that the Church had increased its landed holdings since the late thirteenth century together suggest that the Church's share may have been a little larger than one-third.

How much of this was achieved in the years 1350–1500? At first sight it is tempting to seek assistance in answering this question from the series of licences to alienate in mortmain that were enrolled on the patent rolls of the royal Chancery. The practices involved in the granting of such licences by the crown have recently been examined by S. Raban.[22] In the light of these researches there can be no doubt that the Church continued to acquire land from the late thirteenth century onwards; but it is quite impossible on the basis of the details in the licences, or even the occasional valuations they contain or the amounts of the fines demanded, to produce reliable totals for the Church's acquisitions or any sort of assessment of the stages of growth in quantitative terms.[23] The best approach is once again to proceed on the basis of the income tax of 1412, which was exacted from the holdings

---

[21] F. Heal, *Prelates and Princes: a Study of the Economic and Social Position of the Tudor Episcopate,* Cambridge, 1980, p. 31.

[22] S. Raban, *Mortmain Legislation and the English Church 1279–1500,* pp. 153–7.

[23] See especially *ibid.,* pp. 153–7.

the Church had acquired since the promulgation of the Statute of Mortmain in 1279 (excluding those held in frankalmoign). Valuations are to be found in the detailed returns from sixteen counties. The total is £4,822. If we assume that the proportion this forms of the total wealth of the landed peerage and gentry in the counties concerned can be applied to the whole of England, we obtain a total of £16,800.

This consisted of clear values; and, of course, we have to take into account the likelihood of under-assessment. Even so, this total is roughly 13.5 per cent of the Church's net temporal wealth in the *Valor Ecclesiasticus*. And it is a total that covers the years 1279–1412 and needs to be reduced if we are to form an assessment applying to the period 1350–1500. The overall impression from S. Raban's researches must be that the Church's acquisitions were larger in the years 1279–1350 than in 1412–1535. Like the calculations relating to lay society, these omit Wales and the marches. But these, if known, would hardly affect the conclusion that the expansion of the Church's landed holdings in the years 1350–1500 was in no sense remarkable.

The contents of the *Valor Ecclesiasticus* reveal a structure of Church wealth that replicates that of lay society to a remarkable degree.[24] There was a total of 554 monastic houses in England. Of these 168 had incomes below £50 a year; and 79 of these were below £20. In other words, just over 14 per cent of the monasteries did not even possess incomes that would have put them in the gentry category of lay wealth. At the other extreme, there were certainly great houses with incomes that placed them on a level equivalent to that of the parliamentary baronage or higher. Fifteen monasteries, mainly Benedictine houses with some endowments that went back to Anglo-Saxon times, including the cathedral priories, enjoyed net revenues within the range of £1,000–1,999 a year. And five, including one cathedral priory – Canterbury – and the order of St John of Jerusalem, possessed incomes of over £2,000 a year, putting them in the same range as the comital class. The remaining foundations thus enjoyed incomes that placed them on a level with the upper gentry. All the English bishops possessed incomes that placed them at levels equivalent to those of the parliamentary peerage. Five – the two archbishops, Winchester (the wealthiest), Durham and Ely – were clearly at the level of the kingdom's earls and were magnates in terms of landed wealth, Lincoln and Bath and Wells falling not far short of this level.

[24] These details are based on A. Savine, *The English Monasteries on the Eve of the Dissolution*, pp. 270–88.

B. TENURE AND INHERITANCE

(i) *The framework of tenure*

The fortunes of the lay landowners of England were inseparable from the body of rules that governed the descent of their inheritances and their incapacity at law to provide for their families. Indeed, this was probably more true of the years 1350–1500 than at any time before or since in English history, because the legal situation was so complicated. In a sense there were two systems existing concurrently, one a body of rules based on feudal tenure, the other a body of practices that arose in reaction to this.

Feudal tenure was an integral part of landownership throughout this period. Indeed, the classical statement of the rule of feudal land tenure – the treatise *On Tenures* by Thomas Littleton, a common lawyer who became a judge of the Court of Common Pleas and a knight – was written in the third quarter of the fifteenth century. Its author, in fact, became a prominent member of the West Midlands gentry.[25] Occasionally even the nobility might hold lands under tenures that were non-feudal – in socage, in burgage tenure or gavelkind. But it is fair to say that all those landowners who enjoyed net incomes of £20 a year or more held most of their lands by feudal tenure. Thus the bulk of the land of the kingdom's nobility and gentry were held of one or more feudal lords in return for the performance of military service (when required by the crown, an obligation that was virtually defunct by 1350 and definitely so after 1385). There was an obligation to assist the lord financially on certain occasions – at the knighting of his eldest son, the marriage of his eldest daughter and in the event of his being ransomed. Certainly the first two occasions were exploited by the crown as sources of revenue in these years; and there are occasional references to magnates and even gentry exercising these rights. However, by 1350 the most important consequences of feudal tenure appeared on the death of a landowner. If he left more than one son, the rule of primogeniture was enforced, all his holdings going to the eldest. If he left only daughters as issue, the inheritance was divided equally between them. If the heir or heirs were over age, a relief (for mesne tenants £5 per knight's fee) was paid. If under age, the feudal lord exercised the right of wardship of the lands until the age of majority was reached – twenty-one for a male, fourteen for a daughter not betrothed at the time of her father's death. In addition, there was the right to the wardship of the body of an heir and also his or her marriage to a person of the lord's choice. It is in connection with this last right

[25] C. Carpenter, 'The fifteenth-century English gentry', p. 45.

that the situation could be especially complicated in the late middle ages, since there was a difference between that of the tenant-in-chief holding of the crown and those landowners who held only of mesne lords. The lands held of lords other than the king by a tenant-in-chief were subject to "prerogative wardship" – that is, all those held by feudal tenure went into royal wardship. But in the case of mesne tenants each lord held the wardship of the lands held of him and the issue of the wardship of the body and marriage was decided by the principle of "priority of enfeoffment" – that is, which of the tenures was of the greatest antiquity.

The situation could be further complicated by two other rules. If a wife survived her husband, she had the right to a life interest in one-third of his lands. And this was entirely unaffected by any subsequent remarriage. The other rule – "tenure by courtesy" – is encountered less frequently. It applied when a wife who had brought an inheritance into her marriage died before her husband. He then secured a life interest in these lands if issue had been born of the marriage, even though it had died in the meanwhile.

Legal and constitutional historians have long stressed the importance of these rules; but their role in landownership still needs emphasis. They gave opportunities of financial advantage to lords; but they were a source of tension between them and their tenants, partly because a tendency to dispute was built into them. Three centuries or more after feudal tenures had emerged the identities of lords might be difficult to discover. Moreover, the tensions were not totally on one side: mesne lords were tenants of other lords. Only the landowner who was a tenant-in-chief of the crown was in a clear-cut situation. The king held of no lord; and there was no doubt that he would exercise his rights, since the crown had at its disposal administrative resources created in the late thirteenth and early fourteenth centuries for this purpose – an escheator in each shire, and a body of writs and inquisitions *post mortem* to investigate its rights. In one respect, however, tenants-in-chief and all other feudal tenants shared a disability in common. Primogeniture and the other rules governing the descent of feudal holdings had a corollary in the total prohibition of testamentary bequests of lands held under feudal tenure. A few landowners who held by burgage tenure or in gavelkind would be able to make directions concerning these in their testaments. But the nobility and gentry were, these slight exceptions apart, in effect forbidden to make in their lifetimes arrangements for the benefit of younger sons or daughters or to pay debts if these were to take effect after death. Arrangements that took effect in a landowner's lifetime were feasible; but they would deplete the revenues he could enjoy from his inheritance.

It is not surprising that a body of practice developed that enabled landowners to circumvent the rules of feudal tenure. They had their origins in the century preceding 1350. What made all of them ultimately possible were changes that occurred in the thirteenth century, giving freedom of alienation of their holdings to all feudal tenants.[26] The basic principle was laid down in the Statute of *Quia Emptores* (1290) which abolished subinfeudation, effectively granting freedom of alienation on condition that, when land was conveyed in fee simple, the donee was substituted for the donor in the latter's tenure from his feudal lord. The position in the case of tenants-in-chief was not absolutely settled until 1327, when a statute regulated the application of the royal right to license all alienations by tenants-in-chief. It was laid down that, if land held in chief was alienated without licence, a pardon would be granted on payment of a reasonable fine. It is no coincidence that by 1350 a number of devices were in place that gave landowners a freedom of disposal over their inheritance unknown a century before.

The term "entail" embraces a number of such devices. Entailed lands (*in feodo talliato*) were settled in ways that cut them off from the normal rules of descent. Land was given to an individual and the heirs born of his body, it being possible to limit such issue to males or females. By the early fifteenth century the doctrine had appeared that such entails endured as long as there were heirs of the prescribed class: the occupant of the inheritance in any generation held only a life interest.

Neither this simple definition nor what we read in the writings of legal historians gives an adequate account of the complexities of the entail's origins or its employment. The beginnings of such arrangements are to be found in the *maritagium*, a conveyance in which a father granted land to a daughter on her marriage. In this, as in grants to younger sons, the assumption was that the lands concerned were still part of the family inheritance and would in due course revert to the main line. The attempt to ensure by the statute *De Donis Conditionalibus* (1285) that such intentions would be respected did not work out. By the middle of the fourteenth century it was clear enough that for some generations at least entailed lands were inalienable; but how many generations were involved was far from certain. It is ironic that within two generations of the case of 1410, in which the court adopted the position that entails were inalienable as long as there were heirs of the prescribed class, lawyers had developed in the common recovery a method of breaking entails, this being in place by 1472 and probably employed before then.

[26] J. M. W. Bean, *The Decline of English Feudalism, 1215–1540*, ch. 2.

One of the most remarkable features of the ways in which landowners handled their inheritances in the years 1349–1500 is the extent to which entails were used despite the substantial legal uncertainties surrounding them. The explanation for this situation involves several influences. One lies in the development of the entail for a particular purpose that, in fact, harked back to the thirteenth-century *maritagium*. This means of settlement was still conceivable to lawyers and the subject of discussion into the fifteenth century. But in reality, as a means of settling land on a daughter at the time of her marriage, it virtually disappeared in the early fourteenth century. In part, the reform of 1285 had come too late. The obvious disadvantage of the *maritagium* was that, even if it returned in due course to the main (donor's) line, it did so only after it had reduced the value of the inheritance for some generations to come. Landowners, therefore, began to provide instead a sum of money when arrangements were made for a daughter's marriage. In return, the father of the husband-to-be settled land in tail on his son and daughter-in-law. It is easy enough to explain the substitution of a lump sum of money for land. But under the previous practice land had always been granted by the bride's father, not the husband's. On this point it is worth noting that the known examples, at least in the fourteenth century, involved eldest sons. The most likely explanation is that the bride's father was thinking of the possibility of a situation in which the marriage produced only daughters and the risk that in these circumstances the husband's father would make arrangements for the devolution of the inheritance in the male line, especially if the son and heir died. By the end of the fourteenth century this form of marriage settlement was certainly a very frequent practice, providing a wife with what became known as a jointure. An inspection of royal licences and pardons and of the feet of fines shows that it can be encountered at every level of landed society. And several types of approach were available: sometimes only a joint tenancy by husband and wife was created, sometimes the settlement would be on male issue alone.

But this is only one aspect of the development of the entail. Increasingly in the course of the fourteenth century settlements in tail were quite deliberately created by the heads of families. Since under the common law a man could not convey lands to himself, the practice developed whereby landowners conveyed lands to one or more trusted individuals who then settled the lands concerned on the grantor in the terms he requested. With this there entered on the scene of landowning practices the device known as the contingent remainder – that is, sons could be listed in turn, together with their sisters, followed, or even interspersed with, collateral heirs, each person named being given an interest in tail contingent on failure of issue in the preceding entail.

The motives behind this practice can only be conjectured. Historians have stressed the desire to avoid forfeiture in the event of treason or felony, a view supported by the fact that, concurrently with the employment of such entails, there appeared in the late fourteenth century the doctrine that entailed lands were immune from forfeiture. Even so, the actual employment of these devices by landowners does not quite fit this interpretation. Although several of the leading nobles who effected such settlements in the middle years of the century – the earl of Arundel, for example – belonged to families that had forfeited inheritances in the troubled years of the 1320s, entailed lands had also been involved in these forfeitures; and the entails made in the next generation occurred in a period of peace and co-operation with the crown. For an explanation we should probably turn to the particular circumstances of each of the families concerned. For example, Henry, Lord Percy executed an entailment of his inheritance in 1334, because he had been granted large holdings in Northumberland in tail by Edward III a few years previously and it made sense to put the whole inheritance on the same basis. Settlements in tail male created by Richard Beauchamp, earl of Warwick, followed quickly on the death of his eldest son and heir, without a male heir. Richard, earl of Arundel, made three separate entailments of different portions of his estates – one at the time of his second marriage, one when this produced a son, and the third when he secured the Warenne inheritance.

It is worth noting that these examples are drawn from the ranks of leading families. And it is quite likely that their actions were encouraged by the policy of the crown regarding earldoms which were invariably granted in tail male. The motives behind the deliberate creation of entails must, however, be considered in the light of the contemporary state of legal doctrines. It is easy to assume that these arrangements were intended to control the devolution of inheritances for as many generations as possible. But, in view of the uncertainty regarding the meaning of entails, this would have been groping in the dark. It is likely that the landowners concerned, even in the latter half of the fourteenth century, thought in terms of no more than the next generation or two. It is equally true that entails that could endure as long as there were heirs of the prescribed class were effective for little more than the half century that separated the appearance of the necessary doctrine and the discovery of means of breaking them.

The other device available to landowners by 1350 was the "use" – the practice of conveying land to feoffees who thus became seised at common law while their feoffor continued to occupy the land concerned and enjoy its profits. Uses could be created for specific purposes – for example, to provide security for the repayment of a loan. But their main advantages came into play at the death of the

original feoffor (the *cestui que use*) when his feoffees continued to be
seised at common law. The land concerned was not then subject to the
incidents of feudal tenure. More important, the feoffees could carry out
directions made by their feoffor before his death. In effect, a device was
available that permitted those who held lands under feudal tenure to
devise them by will. The origins of the practice go back to the late
thirteenth century, the rise of the office of executor acting as a catalyst
to give coherence to tendencies that go back to Anglo-Saxon times.
The available evidence indicates that uses first appeared in the lower
reaches of feudal tenure. The device was taken up by leading
landowners during the generation following 1350, great feudal lords
emulating the example of their tenants and their tenants' tenants.[27]

There is no simple or single explanation for the growing popularity
of the device. The argument that the motive was to evade the rule that
lands held by feudal tenure could not be left by will begs the question
why it was necessary to evade that rule. How far evasion of the rights
of the feudal lord *per se* was a motive it is difficult to say. A distinction
must be drawn between those who held in chief of the crown and those
who were mesne tenants. A landowner who sought to evade royal
rights of wardship and marriage took on a formidable opponent in the
form of a local official – the escheator – and a body of investigatory
procedures all of which could be set in motion by those who sought the
wardship of the heir. In fact, it was rare for the crown's rights to be
totally evaded, it generally securing the wardship of the body and of
some lands. In contrast, the feoffees of mesne tenants were often in a
position to play off against one another the lords of whom they held;
and, while the courts of common law developed a definition of
collusion, mesne lords made little effort to protect their interests,
presumably because they were benefiting themselves as mesne tenants
from the practice. It is occasionally possible to point to circumstances
that explain the creation of uses by individuals – service in the French
wars, or late fourteenth-century crusades, that necessitated arrangements
to protect the interests of a family in the event of the feoffor's death
overseas.[28] But to construe feoffors' motivations simply in terms of the
evasion of lords' rights is to look at consequences rather than causes. In
the case of an heir who was over age, the avoidance of the relief was
hardly an important financial consideration, since it was only £5 per
knight's fee. In the case of an heir who was under age what happened
was that revenues that would otherwise have accrued to a feudal lord
were used for the payment of the deceased tenant's debts and the
payment of testamentary bequests and provision for younger children.

[27] Bean, *Decline of English Feudalism*, ch. 3.
[28] N. Saul, *Scenes from Provincial Life: Knightly Families in Sussex, 1280–1400*, pp. 174–5.

An examination of testaments and wills of land in the latter half of the fourteenth century shows that these concerns were important from the beginning. In addition, landowners often made provision, sometimes quite lavish, that gave widows more than they would have secured through dower.[29] Generally, however, such arrangements were conditional on a widow's not remarrying.

The full consequences of the existence of uses for the development of English property law lay well beyond 1500. But already there are indications in the fifteenth century that they had created a dimension of family practices that lay outside the framework of feudal rules. A landowner who held only of mesne lords avoided, if he had conveyed all his lands to feoffees, not only his lords' rights of wardship of his lands but also those of wardship of the body and marriage of his heir that belonged to one of them. He thus enjoyed opportunities similar to those available after the final abolition of feudal tenures in 1660.

In the years 1350–1500 landowners thus enjoyed a freedom in the disposition of their inheritances that was denied to their thirteenth-century ancestors. In any effort to understand their emergence, uses are best viewed as a long-term reaction to the imposition in the late twelfth century of the rule that prohibited the devising by will of lands held by feudal tenure. A landowner could now engage in one, or both, of two kinds of arrangements for the disposition of his lands after his death. He could execute a settlement, an entail, or a joint enfeoffment in fee simple, that gave him a life-interest, the lands concerned going to a person of his choice after his death. Or he could convey all or a portion of his lands to feoffees to his use, thus enabling him both to employ their revenues after his death for various purposes and also to direct the feoffees to settle them according to his wishes.

The relationship between entails and uses presents a complicated problem that requires further research. Even a cursory inspection of the body of directions to feoffees that has survived, mainly attached to, or included in, testaments, shows that entailed lands were often conveyed to feoffees to uses and, even if the rights of the heirs were eventually respected, the interest of the life-tenant did not terminate with his death. The problem is further complicated by the history of the entail in the fifteenth century, since the doctrine that an entail was inviolable as long as heirs of the prescribed class endured became at risk in the courts of law within a generation of its appearance. On this point it is necessary to distinguish between legal doctrine and actual practice. Efforts were made to employ procedures of warranty as a means of

---

[29] For a correction of the view that uses eroded widows' rights to dower, see Bean, *Decline of English Feudalism*, pp. 136–7.

breaking entails. In theory they could not have this effect; but the effort was nevertheless made. The sources contain many examples of purchases made in spite of, or in ignorance of, entails. And these efforts occurred without employing the device – the common recovery – which, even if it had been in use for some years, did not appear in the Year Books until 1472. Uses, indeed, had provided an additional means of avoiding the consequences of entails, a series of barriers in the form of successive conveyances to separate groups of feoffees being set up between the heir under the entail and the eventual *cestui que use*. This is not to say that the existence of entails was invariably treated with cynicism or contempt. It is possible to encounter testators who expressed concern in this area – Richard Neville, earl of Salisbury in 1460, for example[30] – or those who warned executors or feoffees that their directions involved lands that might be entailed. Even so, such details are an illustration of the extent to which entails had been merged within, and were being eroded by, the freedom to devise.

It is unfortunate that we cannot produce a clear statistical picture of the balance between entails and uses in landowners' dispositions. There are two fundamental deficiencies in the information available. One is that we know much less about mesne tenants than about tenants-in-chief, since for the latter licences and pardons relating to their arrangements are to be found on the Chancery patent rolls. The other is that the surviving testamentary documents do not always contain directions to feoffees. Even so, the patent rolls' information covers members of the gentry as well as the nobility and provides some suggestive statistics. The total number of entails revealed in this source in the years 1361–80 was 200. It may be unwise to place great emphasis on the fact that the equivalent figure for the years 1421–40 was 107, since this may reflect the limitations imposed by existing entails on the creation of new ones. What are impressive are the totals for enfeoffments to uses – 133 in 1361–80, and 177 in 1421–40. There can be no doubt that in the earlier period enfeoffments to uses were becoming popular; by the later period they had become a fully accepted means of arranging landowners' affairs.

(ii) *Family and inheritance*

What effects did entails and uses have on attitudes towards the family inheritance among English landowners? The results of any investigation into this are inevitably impressionistic. There is a remarkable gulf between the size of the group for which we have information and the

---

[30] *Testamenta Eboracensia*, ed. J. Raine, II, pp. 142–3.

total number of landowners in the gentry class and above. And the available evidence is disproportionately informative about the higher nobility.

The issue is the extent to which the application of entails and uses eroded the principle of primogeniture which had dominated the evolution of concepts of landed inheritance in the two centuries preceding 1350. Landowners had always been able to make arrangements for the future of younger children. But the new devices meant that these could now be made in ways that took effect after a father's death, there being no diminution of the revenues available to him in his lifetime. On this point it is necessary to distinguish between daughters and younger sons. Daughters in the years 1350–1500 were provided for by means of money portions which generally purchased not only a marriage but also a settlement on the husband and wife that guaranteed her a portion of land for life. When such arrangements were made, the husband's father did part with some of his landed holdings. But he did receive a sum of money that might be invested in a fresh purchase. And, when the husband was his son and heir, the detachment of land from the inheritance was a temporary affair.

The real risk to the maintenance of the inheritance as a unit through the generations in fact came from two other kinds of arrangement. One was provision for younger sons if there were one or more surviving the father. The other was a situation in which a landowner had no lawful issue. He could then pass lands to individuals of his choice, within or outside blood relationships, thus depriving those who were collateral heirs at common law.

The period 1350–1500 does provide some impressive examples of efforts to deprive those who would succeed by the normal rules of inheritance. John, Lord Mohun of Dunster (d. 1376) conveyed the bulk of his inheritance to his widow, who then sold the reversion after her death, thus depriving three female issue.[31] John Hastings, earl of Pembroke (d. 1375) made arrangements that, if he died without issue or his issue died, a substantial portion of his inheritance was to go to Sir William Beauchamp, and in the event that he refused or could not fulfil the conditions imposed, his feoffees were to settle the lands on Sir William Clinton on the same conditions.[32] In 1381 Maud, the heir to the honour of Cockermouth in Cumberland, on the occasion of her marriage to Henry Percy, earl of Northumberland, settled this, the major portion of her inheritance, on her husband and herself in tail, with successive remainders in tail on his eldest son by his first

[31] Maxwell Lyte, *History of Dunster*, I, 49–53.
[32] *CCR, 1374–7*, pp. 286–8; R. I. Jack, 'Entail and descent: the Hastings inheritance, 1370 to 1436', *Bull. IHR*, XXXVIII, 1965.

marriage, on the earl's brother and on his two younger sons.[33] In 1389 Ralph, Lord Basset of Drayton, left his lands to his nephew, Sir Hugh Shirley, in tail male, thus depriving the heir general, the earl of Stafford.[34] The most impressive of such cases is that of Ralph Neville, earl of Westmorland (d. 1425) who made arrangements, employing both entails and enfeoffments to uses, under which the bulk of his inheritance went to his eldest son by his second marriage, thus depriving the son and heir who inherited the earldom of Westmorland. All these cases, to be sure, come from the ranks of the nobility. But it is possible to point to a remarkable case – that of the Swillington inheritance – within the ranks of the gentry.[35]

The way these landowners exploited the freedom to dispose of their lands needs, however, to be put in perspective. Special circumstances applied to most of them. Lord Mohun could salve his conscience, as could his widow, with the thought that his three daughters were all married to magnates. The second wife of the earl of Westmorland was a Beaufort: it is not surprising that the king's cousins should be preferred over the heir by a first marriage. In the case of the earl of Pembroke, the Lucy heiress and Lord Basset, conditions were imposed that reveal a form of desire for the perpetuation of the inheritance and the family's fame. Sir William Beauchamp, or alternatively Sir William Clinton, was to bear the deceased earl's arms and persuade the king to make him earl of Pembroke. In the Lucy and Basset cases the beneficiary of the settlement was under similar conditions – in the former case to quarter the Lucy arms, and in the latter to bear the deceased's name and arms. The preference given to a bastard in the settlement of the Swillington inheritance is exceptional: the known dispositions of both the nobility and the gentry reveal no tendency to endow illegitimate children with any portion of a family's inheritance.

The acid test of the attitude to primogeniture is, of course, the extent to which provision was made for younger sons.[36] It is certainly possible to compile a list of settlements of land, generally in the form of directions to feoffees, to illustrate the practice. Out of a sample of seventeen in the years 1350–1500, fourteen provided for younger sons in tail.[37] Two provided grants for life only. But these details must also be put in their proper perspective. Henry Percy, earl of Northumber-

[33] Bean, *Estates of the Percy Family*, pp. 8–9.   [34] *Complete Peerage*, II, pp. 3–4.
[35] Ross and Pugh, 'English baronage and the income tax of 1436', pp. 7–8.
[36] Richmond, *John Hopton*, ch. 1.
[37] To be found in J. P. Cooper, 'Patterns of inheritance and settlement by great landowners from the fifteenth to the eighteenth centuries, App. 2', in *Family and Inheritance: Rural Society in Western Europe, 1200–1800*, ed. J. Goody, J. Thirsk and E. P. Thompson, Cambridge, 1976. For a somewhat different perspective on what follows, showing changes in attitude, see K. B. McFarlane, *The Nobility of Later Medieval England*, pp. 61–82, 268–79.

land (d. 1489), did provide substantially for his younger sons, giving his second son 1,000 marks a year. But his inheritance had been greatly expanded through his mother by the acquisition of the Poynings and Brian inheritances. Moreover, the grants were for life only. By his dispositions John of Gaunt founded the fortunes of the Beaufort family in the fifteenth century; but he did so in the knowledge that his son and heir had married, and had issue by, the heir to half the great Bohun inheritance. William, Lord Lovel (d. 1455) left substantial holdings to all his younger sons; but he had married a baronial heiress all of whose holdings went to his eldest son and heir. Above all, none of the arrangements made by these landowners for the benefit of younger sons conveyed an inheritance in fee simple, the most given being an inheritance in tail male or general. There were also other limits. None of the inheritances conveyed would have put the sons concerned within the upper gentry or, in the case of the higher nobility, within the baronage. These conclusions are supported by a rough quantitative assessment based on those testaments and directions to feoffees left by baronial landowners and those above them in the years between 1360 and 1500. About 10 per cent of these left lands in inheritance to younger sons. In two-thirds of these cases, either the father or the eldest son and heir had married an heiress, so that the size of the estate that went to the heir was not less than his father's.

Although the nature of our evidence and the absence of data about most gentry families warn against firm conclusions, there is good reason to believe that the same picture is true of the gentry. A recent study of the gentry of Derbyshire in the fifteenth century has delineated two prominent features of their treatment of younger sons – the use of entails to secure continuance of the inheritance in the male line and a tendency to make no more than life arrangements for younger sons.[38] The annual incomes provided for them were remarkably low, sometimes not even amounting to the traditional yeoman's £5 a year. A search of the surviving testamentary materials for the archdiocese of York and the diocese of Norwich produces no serious conflict with the picture for Derbyshire,[39] though in these regions, when provision was made for younger sons, it was at a higher level than we see in Derbyshire, a fact that is hardly surprising in the light of the comparative poverty of the latter county. What emerges especially from the Yorkshire and the East Anglian evidence is the testator's sense at one and the same time both of a total family inheritance and of the opportunities provided by enfeoffments to uses, a reasonable balance

[38] S. M. Wright, *The Derbyshire Gentry in the Fifteenth Century*, pp. 48–9.

[39] *Testamenta Eboracensia*, ed. Raine, I–III, *passim*; Norfolk RO, Consistory Court of Norwich, Probate Registers.

being kept between them. In both these regions, however, there is no decisive indication of a preference for grants in tail male to younger sons. This impression is certainly markedly strengthened by an examination of the series of feet of fines for a number of counties in the south, south-east and the midlands – Dorset, Essex, Somerset, Sussex, and Staffordshire. In this evidence, the middling and lower gentry of these areas did not display much interest in the maintenance of the inheritance by means of entailments in the male line. It was the nobility and upper gentry who displayed an interest in this form of settlement. This is not surprising. The role of the nobility in the kingdom's affairs and the ambitions of the upper gentry were predicated on the permanence of the inheritance; and the best guarantee of this was its preservation in the male line. Middling and lesser gentry were not concerned to the same degree with the retention of a family's power and influence.

It is difficult to estimate the effects of these phenomena on the financial position of the landowning classes. In the twelfth and thirteenth centuries the rules of feudal landholding might impose consequences that afflicted a family for generations to come. While after 1215 the payment of relief was not a serious hardship, wardship could last for twenty years, with some risk of physical damage to the resources of the inheritance, while the choice of spouse for the heir would not be in the hands of his or her kin. There can be no doubt that this situation was considerably mitigated by the development of the jointure, the entail, and the use. The development of marriage settlements encouraged landowners to make arrangements for the marriage of heirs during their lifetime, while landowners who had enfeoffed to uses had the satisfaction of knowing that the portion of the inheritance concerned would, if the heir was under age, be in the hands of persons of their choice.

But the new ways of handling land did nothing to mitigate one aspect of feudal land law – the widow's dower, since she had an absolute right to this, even against those to whom her husband had conveyed a portion of his lands. Widows could survive many years. Firm statistics are possible only in the case of the parliamentary peerage. Over the period 1361–1460, twenty-five widows survived their husbands for 6-10 years, twenty-two for 11-15 years, twenty for 16-20 years, fifteen for 21-25 years, thirty-three for 26-40 years, and twelve for more than 40 years. But from the standpoint of the financial position of the landed classes, this is only one side of the picture. In fact, most widows remarried and his wife's dower was a source of additional income for the occupant of a landed inheritance. How far landowners in general compensated for losses incurred through their mothers' dowers by marrying widows it is impossible to say. But a perusal of *The Complete Peerage* shows that this was a frequent occurrence. It must also be stressed that landowners showed no concern about this aspect of feudal land law. Indeed, some gave directions to feoffees that gave their widows more than they were entitled to by way of dower.

But there is a more fundamental issue in which a consideration of the financial effects of the new devices involves also the structure of landed society. There is no doubt that the years 1350–1500 saw fathers sometimes making a deliberate and substantial effort to provide for younger sons; and, even when such arrangements were limited to the lives of the beneficiaries, they depleted the landed income of heirs. But the extent to which this occurred depended on other elements in a family's fortunes – whether a father had increased the inheritance by marriage or purchase and whether the eldest son made a good marriage. In fact, though, the cases where heirs, eldest sons as well as collaterals, and their issue enjoyed a reduced inheritance as a result of an ancestor's dispositions were rare.

To what extent, then, did the treatment accorded to younger sons increase the size of the ranks of landowners below the nobility? Those who received inheritances, whether in fee simple or in tail, joined the ranks of the gentry. But the available information indicates that their number was slight; and the positions in local society achieved by many of the younger sons of middling gentry must have been indistinguishable from those of many yeomen. There are, for example, remarkably few younger sons to be found with incomes above £20 a year in the surviving returns of the income tax of 1412.[40]

(iii) *Marriage and politics*

It is, of course, a truism in the history of English landownership that families were constantly rising and falling, partly through the vicissitudes of life and death, partly through changes in economic fortunes even when families survived. To this the years 1350–1500 are no exception. One in four of all peerage families failed in the direct male line every twenty-five years.[41] Sometimes there were daughters to inherit, sometimes collaterals consisting of a mixture of male and female heirs, so that the death of a landowner could result in the fragmentation of his inheritance. It is quite true that the landowners of the years

[40] Of the names of all the male landowners in the counties listed in Table 6.3, a total of 220 out of 1,211 (18 per cent) included those of two or more individuals. The actual proportion of gentry holdings created by settlements on younger sons must have been lower since (1) this is a gross total, including those with lands in more than one county; (2) it contains a number of peerage families; and (3) it also includes cases of fathers and their heirs.

[41] McFarlane, *Nobility of Later Medieval England*, pp. 172–6.

1350–1500 had at their disposal, in the entail and the use, methods of avoiding these particular consequences of the hazards of life and death. And they were used. But their employment did not destroy or warp a pattern in which the major means of expanding an inheritance was deliberately through marriage or by means of fortuitous accident resulting from the effects of a marriage in future generations. We can illustrate this situation through a calculation of the number of families of parliamentary nobility that gained in this way. In the years 1360–81 the total was twelve, in 1381–1400 thirteen, in 1401–20 nine, in 1421–40 thirteen, and two in 1441–60. But these figures illustrate only one side of the picture. The very families that gained inheritances in one generation could die out in the next in the male line. For example, two earls of Arundel in the last sixty years of the fourteenth century made great gains, including the estates of the earls of Warenne; but the earl who was their son and grandson respectively died without issue in 1415. Similarly, the family of the Mortimer earls of March made what was probably the most spectacular marriage for a comital family in fourteenth-century England when Earl Roger married the daughter and eventual sole heir of the king's son, the duke of Clarence, her mother being the sole heir to the great de Burgh inheritance. But the Mortimers died out in the male line in 1425. The result, however, was the creation of the greatest conglomeration of lands in the hands of one person in fifteenth-century England, Richard, duke of York being the heir not only of his father but also of his mother, the sole Mortimer heir. In discussing these phenomena the historian cannot avoid being dependent on illustrations drawn from the ranks of the parliamentary peerage, since it is for this group that the necessary genealogical information is available. But the failure to beget issue, or its premature death, can be found at every level of landed society. Viewed from the standpoint of families and their occupation of land, English landed society was a changing kaleidoscope of wealth and power.

The effects of two elements injected into this situation require examination. One consists of the vicissitudes of political life, which of course only had an effect in times of political crisis. These occurred off and on in the years 1350–1500, largely in the reign of Richard II and in the period of intermittent conflict called the "Wars of the Roses", best defined as covering the years 1455–97, and ending with the achievement of security for his dynasty by the Tudor Henry VII. During these events the hold of families upon their inheritances was certainly disturbed from time to time. But the record shows that few families suffered permanent loss. Two forces endemic in English politics served to save families from total and enduring disaster. One was the growth of the doctrine that entailed estates were immune from forfeiture for treason or felony. This was invoked to ensure the eventual restoration of heirs. To be sure, even when such restoration occurred, protracted efforts might have to be pursued to ensure the total restoration of all the entailed estates.[42] There were clearly elements of self-interest in the support and acceptance respectively that the lords and commons in parliament gave to this principle, since all were well aware of the possibility that circumstances might arise in which they themselves might be subject to forfeiture.

The other influence on the situation was the crown's perception of its ultimate self-interest. Political conditions might change quite rapidly: a family that had suffered forfeiture might in a few years' time deserve restoration as a means of gaining support in a region of the kingdom in which it was powerful, a motive that explains, for example, the acts of patent leniency on the part of Edward IV after he gained the throne in 1461. In the course of the fifteenth century royal government employed an effective weapon against opponents in the parliamentary act of attainder which had the special advantáge of providing in explicit terms for the forfeiture of estates entailed on, and held to the use of, the attainted person. Even so, a detailed examination of the attainders and forfeitures of the "Wars of the Roses" has shown that of 397 attainders between 1453 and 1504, 256 (possibly 265) of the families concerned – about 64 per cent – were ultimately restored. Some families, it must be said, did not secure complete restoration: the Staffords of Grafton, for example, never recovered their paternal, as distinct from maternal, inheritance completely. And there were certainly those whose attainders were never reversed.[43] There are indications that Henry VII was less lenient than his predecessors in the treatment of his enemies.[44] A recent study has drawn attention to the effects in the West Midlands of the redistribution of forfeited lands in his reign. But, taken as a whole, the record indicates that forfeiture for treason did not have important effects in the long term on the structure of English landed society. The permanently unfortunate tended to be at the lower levels of landowning society: only nine of the permanent forfeitures under Edward IV affected persons above the rank of squire, the equivalent total under Henry VII being thirteen. Five noble families that were never restored ended in the male line anyway. Most of the estates that were never restored were those of squires or lesser men. In strict terms, to be sure, treason and rebellion were not the only routes to forfeiture, since a felony in the courts of common law carried the penalties of death and forfeiture respectively for the felon and his heirs.

---

[42] E.g., Bean, *Estates of the Percy Family*, pp. 60–80, 109–11.
[43] J. R. Lander, *Crown and Nobility, 1450–1509*, London, 1976, pp. 150–7.
[44] Carpenter, 'The fifteenth-century English gentry', p. 44.

Detailed work on the functioning of criminal justice in these years has yet to be done; but it is difficult to believe that the gentry could not, if indicted, in most cases secure a favourable verdict or, if necessary, a pardon. And uses provided protection against forfeiture in the courts of common law.

(iv) The market for land

The most important influence, of course, on the rise and fall of inheritances, the consequences of marriage apart, was the purchasing and selling of land. This is an extremely complicated problem in terms of the issues involved in the study of the evidence. The sources – the records of the courts of common law and thousands of deeds involving the conveyance of land – provide abundant confirmation of the existence of a land market. But no collection of deeds, even if there is a fair degree of information about its provenance, can provide totally sure ground in tracing the history of an estate, since there is always the possibility that a document of crucial importance is missing. Even if this weakness in the evidence did not exist, there would be no guarantee that a single estate was typical. At first sight late medieval England yields a collection of conveyances that is quite remarkable in the number of transactions it reveals – the series of feet of fines preserved in the records of the Court of Common Pleas. But the number of these documents diminished markedly during the course of the fifteenth century, probably because the execution of a fine was a cumbrous and expensive process and the proliferation of uses, each original conveyance to feoffees involving a train of deeds, ultimately made such expense prohibitive. A further complication is produced by the existence of uses. When we encounter a deed in which land is conveyed, we cannot be certain that the grantee was not acting as a feoffee to the grantor's use. In the case of an inheritance for which we possess financial records doubts can generally be removed; but such opportunities are rare, and in other cases it is sometimes a single document that might easily have disappeared that provides the essential clue.[45]

For these reasons any sort of quantitative assessment of the conditions of the market for land in this period is out of the question. Nevertheless, it is possible to delineate several features of the land market. One was the remarkable range of purchases in both the size and the value of the holdings involved. Historians who study the rise and fall of landed families are necessarily dependent on the guidance of county histories,

---

[45] See *The Tropenell Cartulary*, ed. J. S. Davies, 2 vols., Wilts. Arch. and N.H. Soc., 1908, I, p. xiv; II, pp. 130–2, where the deeds in a cartulary identify as a feoffee of the purchaser an individual whom the editor identified as the seller.

both those of the late seventeenth and eighteenth centuries and the volumes of the *Victoria County History*. All these train our sights on the descent of manors. But if serious scholars have learned by now not to "count" manors, there still remains a further danger in investigating the land market from the standpoint of the units of ownership called "manors". There is abundant evidence to point to the existence of sales and purchases below the level of manorial ownership. The extent to which this situation existed may have varied from region to region. What we know of variations in manorial structure suggests that purchasers with the same amount of money might have been able to buy a small manor in, for example, East Anglia, whereas in other regions such purchases were not as available, and a purchaser might instead have to buy lands and tenements held of the lord of a manor. Impressionistic though this conclusion must be, it was at this level of land purchase that the yeomen must have been active, together with others in the £20–39 range shown in Tables 6.1–6.4. Occasionally we secure light at this level of activity. A study of *The Book of Bartholomew Bolney*, a compilation of evidences relating to his holdings compiled by a Sussex gentleman in the mid-fifteenth century,[46] reveals the extent to which an original inheritance, apparently of no more than one manor, had been expanded by small transactions, sometimes by purchasing lands and tenements held of Bolney as lord of the manor, on other occasions involving the purchase of tenants' interests within other lords' manors. The same pattern can be observed, though to a less pronounced degree, in cartularies drawn up for the holdings of gentry in other shires in the fifteenth century – Robert Hylle in the west country[47] and Thomas Tropenell in Wiltshire.[48] One interesting feature of these lucky survivals of collections of evidence is what these three gentry had in common: all had a legal background and had served important landowners in administrative duties, which probably brought opportunities of purchase to their attention. Hylle and, perhaps, Tropenell were at a higher level of income than Bolney. But they all invested in the land market at a level below that of manorial units.

A second feature of the land market is the extent to which it did not involve purchases that took immediate effect, the purchase being that of a reversion. There was definitely an element of speculation in this in that a purchaser might have to wait many years for his acquisition to take effect. Perhaps the most telling illustration is that of the sale by Lady Mohun of the castle, manor, and barony of Dunster in Somerset

---

[46] *The Book of Bartholomew Bolney*, ed. M. Clough, Sussex Rec. Soc., LXIII, 1964.
[47] *The Hylle Cartulary*, ed. R. W. Dunning, Somerset Rec. Soc., LXVIII, 1968.
[48] *Tropenell Cartulary*, ed. Davies.

to Lady Elizabeth Luttrell. The sale took place in 1376; but it was almost thirty years before the purchaser's son and heir, Sir Hugh Luttrell, secured the estates.[49]

Investment in the purchase of land was also speculative in another sense. The development of entails and uses had greatly complicated the problems facing would-be purchasers. A seller might not reveal the existence of an entail that gave him no more than a life-interest, while enfeoffments to uses might have created other interests disguised during negotiations.

The last main feature of the land market is that capital for purchases might not be readily available. It is a fair assumption that landowners who were dependent solely on their landed revenues would rarely build up a substantial surplus. Certainly the models of household economies at the main levels of landed society set out in *The Black Book* of the royal household assumed that landed revenues of the seven levels of landed society would be consumed by the maintenance of the household. It is this scarcity of capital in the hand of individual landowners that explains the interest in reversions. There is also reason to believe that purchase prices were often spread out in instalments. This could even occur in the case of a purchaser whose resources transcended those of competitors in the land market. Two illustrations are provided by the sale of two manors that had belonged to Ralph, Lord Cromwell (d. 1456). Richard Neville, earl of Warwick, promised to pay for the manor of Collyweston on an instalment plan.[50] And Edmund, Lord Grey of Ruthin (later made earl of Kent) purchased the manor of Ampthill and all Cromwell's lands in Bedfordshire through payments spread over sixteen years.[51]

These features of the land market were not peculiar to the period 1350–1500 but must have been present, at least to some degree, in the preceding two centuries. There is good reason to believe that one of them – the complexities of the land law – was aggravated by the growth of enfeoffments to uses. One aspect of the activities of the landed classes in these years, however, did provide opportunities for windfall profits that might alleviate a scarcity of capital for individuals. This aspect – the French wars that began before 1350 and continued to dominate the policies of the crown in varying degrees through the fifteenth century – has attracted much attention from historians in recent years. English landowners who fought for their king in France were well aware of the profits they could gain through the winning of booty and ransoms. And following Henry V's conquest of Normandy

[49] Maxwell-Lyte, *History of Dunster*, 1, p. 80.
[50] HMC, *Report on the Mss. of Lord De l'Isle and Dudley*, 1, pp. 188–9.
[51] *The Grey of Ruthin Valor*, ed. Jack, pp. 34–5.

and then his heir's succession to the throne of France and lasting until 1450, there was a period in which a substantial number of English nobles and gentry also held lands in France.

To what extent, then, were their profits channelled into the purchase of land in England? It is certainly possible to quote examples of remarkable profits made by English captains and their men through booty and ransoms. It is, of course, true that Englishmen lost when they themselves had to be ransomed. But there are grounds for thinking that in this area of gains and losses the balance was in favour of England. There were two families that had to pay heavy ransoms for which some documentation exists. John Talbot, earl of Shrewsbury (d. 1453) and the Hungerfords do not appear to have suffered any lasting crisis.[52] And there is only one case of a baron – William, Lord Say and Sele (d. 1471), who had to sell substantial amounts of land to pay a ransom.[53]

More important as a source of profits were the grants of lordships in the conquered areas of France which English lords and gentry received at the hands of Henry V and, after his death, from the government of Henry VI, covering large portions of Normandy, Maine, and Anjou. The career of one of these beneficiaries has been studied by the late K. B. McFarlane who showed that Sir John Fastolf, who entered into an inheritance of £46 a year in 1404, was able to increase this to £775 a year by means of the gains he made in France and can be shown to have channelled most of his profits back into the land market in East Anglia.[54]

It is necessary, however, to put these issues in perspective. First, recent scholarship has indicated that only a minority of gentry took part in the French wars.[55] Second, it is wrong to assume that large profits were inevitably channelled into the purchase of land in England. The largest fortune in cash we know of in late medieval England was that left by Richard, earl of Arundel (d. 1376) amounting to £72,250. He had certainly purchased lands in Sussex; but obviously most of the fortune he had amassed had not been used for this purpose.[56] It may be that he was a discriminating purchaser, interested only in acquiring lands that would strengthen his territorial ascendancy in Sussex, and such property was in limited supply. Among those who purchased property out of the profits of war there are good grounds for believing

[52] A. J. Pollard, *John Talbot and the War in France, 1427–1453*, pp. 113–18; McFarlane, *Nobility of Later Medieval England*, pp. 126–8.   [53] *Complete Peerage*, XI, p. 482, n.c.

[54] K. B. McFarlane, 'The investment of Sir John Fastolf's profits of war', in *idem, England in the Fifteenth Century*.

[55] E.g., N. Saul, *Knights and Esquires: The Gloucestershire Gentry in the Fourteenth Century*, Oxford, 1981, pp. 50–6; Lander, *Crown and Nobility*, p. 56.

[56] L. F. Salzman, 'The property of the earl of Arundel, 1397', *Sussex Arch. Colls.*, 91, 1953.

that Sir John Fastolf was a special case. His determination to gain landed wealth, putting him within the baronial class in terms of income, was remarkably obsessive. But, more important, in terms of the volume of lands gained in France by Englishmen, at least down to 1435, his gains were exceeded by those of only two of the leading magnates – John, duke of Bedford, the regent after Henry V's death, and Thomas Montague, earl of Salisbury (d. 1429), the leading commander.

The third, and most important, point arises from the need to obtain some sort of calculation of the total profits that were made. A rough estimate is possible in the case of the lands gained in France, since the majority of the grants conferred, at least to 1437, provide details of values as they were in 1410. Those made by Henry V in Normandy must have totalled £22–22,300 a year.[57] If we accept the statement of William Worcester that the duke of Bedford granted lands to his English followers in Maine and Anjou to a total of 10,000 marks a year, we obtain a grand total of under £30,000 a year.[58] This is no more than 14 per cent of the landed incomes of the English nobility and gentry in 1412 as suggested in Tables 6.1–6.4. To assess the effects on the land market in England it is useful to proceed from the assumption that the holdings in France yielded for English nobles and gentry a total amount equal to fifteen years' income at the levels mentioned in the grants. If we convert this on the basis of twenty years' purchase, we obtain a figure of just under £22,500 a year. In fact, of course, there could never have been channelled into England enough to buy lands to this extent. The dislocation and devastation caused by warfare must have seriously reduced the net worth of the French holdings. At least some, if not many, of the English owners must have seen a large portion of their net profits disappear in the form of ransoms and other losses. Accordingly it is difficult to believe that landed holdings in France overall produced a total capital sum sufficient to purchase as much as one-twentieth of the landed resources of the nobility and gentry in England. And to achieve this all those involved would have had to have displayed the single-minded acquisitiveness of Sir John Fastolf.

It cannot be denied that financial gains from the French wars played a role in the land market. But it is difficult to believe that the effects were substantial. This conclusion gains support from the cases of two leading landowners. Humphrey Stafford, duke of Buckingham (d.

[57] Based on R. A. Newhall, *The English Conquest of Normandy, 1416–1424*, New Haven, Conn., 1924, p. 167, at a conversion rate of 1l.t = £1. The total has been revised upward to take into account omissions and grants of land vacated through death. The conclusions argued above are supported by the implications of C. T. Allmand, *Lancastrian Normandy, 1415–1450*, Oxford, 1983, pp. 50–80.

[58] William Worcester, *The Boke of Noblesse*, ed. J. G. Nichols, Roxburgh Club, no. 77, London, 1860, p. 32.

1460) held the county of Perche, listed in valors of his estates as producing 400 marks a year in 1441–2, with a valuation of 800 marks a year in time of peace in 1447–8, totals that were no more than 5 and 10 per cent of his income from England and Wales.[59] In fifteenth-century England the most remarkable case of a nobleman who expanded his inheritance by land purchases is provided by Ralph, Lord Cromwell (d. 1456). He did, it is true, buy the manor of Ampthill in Bedfordshire from John Cornwall, Lord Fanhope (d. 1443), who had originally bought it through the investment of his gains in France. But Cromwell himself had not served in France since 1422 and had gained only a little urban property in Harfleur. In his case the circumstantial evidence suggests that the major source of his purchases was the profits of office: the greater part of them were made while he held the treasurership of England (1433–43).[60]

There is, however, one distinct indication that the demand for land by would-be purchasers was increasing in the period 1350–1500. In the middle of the thirteenth century the current rate of purchase was ten years' annual value. Two centuries later it had risen to twenty years. These rates, it must be emphasized, were standards applied by seller and purchaser, and actual prices were not invariably at the current rate. It is not easy to chart the chronology of the rise that occurred. In 1375 the testament of Richard, earl of Arundel, directed the purchase of land at a rate of 13.33 years' purchase.[61] Twelve years later a range of rates was employed in the sale of the lands of those who forfeited in the Merciless Parliament of 1387–8. But two of the sales were at twenty years' income, a fact suggesting that twenty years had already entered on the scene.[62] And there is solid evidence that it was generally accepted by the middle of the fifteenth century.[63]

There are two elements in the explanation for this phenomenon. One was the absence of a substantial amount of land for sale. As the head of a family acting in the interests of his issue a landowner made every effort to keep the inheritance intact. And the development of uses made this easier. Purchasers on their side preferred to buy land close to existing holdings since distant acquisitions could present administrative problems that might ultimately depreciate their value.[64] John Carpenter, bishop of Worcester, had to range over the whole of his diocese in search of suitable properties.[65] And, when a substantial and

---

[59] Staffs. RO, D641/1/2/17; Longleat House Ms. 6410.

[60] Rhoda L. Friedrichs, 'The Career and Influence of Ralph, Lord Cromwell, 1393–1456', Columbia Univ. Ph.D. thesis, 1974, ch. 6.   [61] Salzman, 'Earl of Arundel', p. 35.

[62] CPR, 1388–92, pp. 100, 194–6.

[63] McFarlane, Nobility of Later Medieval England, pp. 56–7. Other evidence, e.g. Dyer, Lords and Peasants, p. 205, does not support the caution of Raban, Mortmain Legislation, pp. 178–9.

[64] See Carpenter, 'The fifteenth-century English gentry', p. 39, for comment on this point.

[65] Dyer, Lords and Peasants, p. 205.

important property, for example, Sir John Fastolf's manor of Caister came on the market, there was great competition for it. But part of the explanation is also to be found in an increase in the amount of capital available for the purchase of land. It is impossible to quantify this. Certainly the French wars resulted in increased demand. But the increase in years' purchase was under way before the end of the fourteenth century: although some profits must already have been made from the campaigns of 1337–60, those from the occupation of lands in France were yet to come. It is more reasonable to assign a major role to the effects of uses which provided capital for the future of younger sons and daughters. Attention should also be given to two other influences. One was investment by those who had done well in the law and in commerce, especially London merchants. It is reasonable to assume that the expansion of England's cloth industry from the mid-fourteenth century onwards improved the financial resources of all those in control of production and export. At the same time within the agrarian economy itself the fortunes of those who had come to be known as yeomen by the mid-fifteenth century were based not merely on direct agricultural management but also on the piecemeal purchase of small properties.

C. LANDED REVENUES

The way landlords exploited the revenues from their landed holdings is at once the most fundamental and the most difficult of the problems encountered in the study of late medieval landed society. At first sight the task seems straightforward enough, since substantial information has survived in the form of manorial accounts, rentals, court rolls, and other records of estate management. But these belong almost entirely to the level of the great landowners. Comparatively little has survived of the records of the gentry and virtually none from the lowest levels of landowning. The serious implications of the gaps in our knowledge can best be appreciated in the light of the details assembled in Tables 6.1–6.4. In effect, we know very little of the vast mass of England's landowners' estate management. And those of Wales below the levels of the great marcher lords present an even more misty area. We are confronted with no more than the fragmented tip of a missing iceberg.

(i) *The structure of landed revenues*

The major items in a landowner's revenues are in basic terms easily defined – rents of various kinds, including those from villeins, labour services, either performed on the lord's demesne or rendered in kind, or commuted for money, the revenues obtained through direct involvement in farming activities, mills and the profits of manorial and other types of jurisdiction. Each of these general categories of revenue itself presents a range of types. Rents could be received from one or more kinds of tenant – freeholders, villeins, and cottars, sometimes also forms of tenancy with origins in Anglo-Saxon times – sokemen in Lincolnshire and Yorkshire or cornage tenants on the Scottish border.

To understand the considerations that influenced landowners in handling whatever complex of revenues they owned, it is important to reach beyond the definitions of tenant status and the legal character of other seigneurial rights. At the heart of the economics of landowning there was a fundamental dichotomy between revenues that were not the product of market forces and those that at any point in time were at the mercy of economic conditions.

The rents received from tenants had their origins centuries before 1350. On large manors in the late fourteenth and fifteenth centuries, manorial accounts and surveys still laid out the separate categories. But more frequently we encounter the all-embracing definition of "Rents of Assise" (*Redditus Assise*). The assumption of stewards and other manorial officials was that these were controlled by manorial custom. And the language of definition employed also reveals the principle that the amount paid by each tenant was fixed by that custom. In the years 1350–1500 "Rents of Assise" were not totally immune from economic forces. On some manors the depopulation created by the Black Death and the plagues that followed it could lead to vacant holdings and a reduction in "Rents of Assise". If demand for holdings locally was weak, that reduction could be permanent. There are, however, manors where deaths of tenants without issue or other heirs, giving the lord freedom under manorial custom to negotiate a new rent, could result in a higher annual payment, since the old one might have been set generations before when monetary values were lower. In contrast, if a landowner decided to lease his demesne meadows and pastures, a prospective tenant would pay only what was feasible in terms of potential profit. Lords, tenants, and manorial officials, in fact, recognized the contrast between the two main types of revenue by calling the latter a "farm" (*firma*), not "rent".

From these comments must emerge the conclusion that the state of a lord's revenues at any point in time, and the capacity of a manorial economy to weather the economic blizzards unleashed by disasters such as pestilence and bad harvests, depended on the balance between the two types of revenue. Where the lord had farmed out his demesnes and mills and the total revenues produced by these were low in comparison with "Rents of Assize", the effects of disaster or depression would be mitigated. Tenants would encounter difficulties; but customary rents cut much less deeply into gross farming profits than annual dues negotiated under market conditions.

The problem of the balance between rents and the size of demesne lands was investigated over fifty years ago by Kosminsky in his study of the hundred rolls of 1279–80. He argued that the proportion involved was a basic element in the economy of small estates, since gentry must have derived a markedly higher proportion of their income from their demesnes than great proprietors did. These conclusions were based on substantial areas of the West and East Midlands; but recent work on gentry holdings in the fourteenth century suggests that similar conditions can be found outside this region.[66] To what extent such conclusions can be applied to the whole of England it is impossible to say. A priori, it is not difficult to understand the possible validity of this interpretation for the twelfth and thirteenth centuries. Rents in varying degrees originated in a seigneurial authority which went back to the Norman Conquest and beyond, whereas gentry holdings were originally knights' fees or portions thereof. When creating them these great lords must have thought primarily of providing land for the maintenance of a knight and his family.

There is, however, an important qualification to be imposed if we are to apply such conclusions to the years 1350–1500. It is unwise to underrate the extent to which rents bulked large in some gentry incomes. For example, rents formed the dominant part of the income of the Filliol family in Dorset in the late fourteenth and fifteenth centuries.[67] An examination of the land-purchases made by Bartholomew Bolney in Sussex, Thomas Tropenell in Wiltshire, or the tenants of the new manor of Knole in Kent shows gentry and yeomen buying up holdings simply as rent-paying investments.[68]

There can, however, be no doubt that rents dominated the revenues of great landowners. The point is best illustrated from the great lay estates, since these have left valors that summarize the separate items of revenue over the whole of an inheritance. In the case of the Duchy of Lancaster's lordship of Pontefract at the close of the fourteenth century, the farm of demesne lands brought in a mere 9 per cent of revenues, the same percentage being true of the farm of the mills. It can be argued that this is a special case, since this was a lordship that had remained

[66] R. H. Britnell, 'Production for the market'; idem, 'Minor landlords in England and medieval agrarian capitalism', PP, no. 89, 1980.

[67] Nottingham Univ. Library, Middleton Mss. Mi 6/170/17.

[68] F. R. H. Du Boulay, 'The assembling of an estate: Knole in Sevenoaks, c. 1275 to c. 1525', Arch. Cant., LXXXIX, 1974.

intact for centuries so that the effects of an ancient seigneurial authority and the dues associated with it were very powerful. But, if we move south on the duchy estates, the farm of demesne lands produced less than one-fifth of the total gross revenues of the Northamptonshire manor of Higham Ferrers.[69] In the case of four of the duchy's large manors in Dorset and Wiltshire, the percentage that demesne lands provided of total revenues amounted to 25, 10, 6 and 3 per cent respectively. An inspection of the valors of two great estates – those of the duke of Buckingham and the earl of Northumberland[70] – in the middle of the fifteenth century shows that the revenues produced by the farms of demesne lands and mills had been absorbed within the category of rents and farms as a whole on most manors, rarely being listed separately.

It is much more difficult to provide such illustrations in the case of the great ecclesiastical estates, partly because they showed less concern with drawing up valors of all their holdings, partly because they had always engaged themselves in agricultural activities to an extent markedly greater than lay magnates. Recent studies of some of these indicate that demesne revenues bulked larger than on the great secular holdings. Nor is this surprising. The endowments of the great Benedictine houses had always been intended to provide for the maintenance of large monastic communities. Even so, the proportion occupied by demesne revenues exhibits marked variations. For example, in the case of five manors of the bishop of Worcester under direct management in the years 1370–1400, the proportions ranged from 21 to 65 per cent.[71]

How important were revenues derived from jurisdictional and other seigneurial rights, as distinct from those from tenants' rents and demesne lands and mills? On this issue it is important to draw a contrast between the revenues from great marcher lordships enjoyed by some English lay magnates and their revenues in England. Within their marcher lordships they enjoyed incomes analogous to those of the crown within the kingdom of England. For this reason perquisites of courts of various kinds bulked large. Above all, an important source of revenue resulted from their total responsibility for the exercise of justice within the lordship concerned. The right to hold a general eyre presented both a formidable administrative undertaking for the lord and a source of fear for his tenants. The practice, therefore, developed of imposing a system of virtual ransom, the tenants compounding with

[69] PRO DL 29/787/11975–87.
[70] Buckingham: Staffs. RO, D641/1/2/17; Longleat House Ms. 6410; Northumberland: Petworth House Mss. D.9.3.   [71] Dyer, Lords and Peasants, p. 119.

a large sum to avoid the imposition of an eyre. On several occasions documented before 1400 large sums were paid by way of *dona* for such redemption. The practice seems to have become stronger in the aftermath of the rebellion of Owain Glyndŵr, providing a lucrative source of revenue in dealing with tenants who were now less subservient. It is difficult to be certain that all the marcher lordships were subject to this practice, but those of the Duchy of Lancaster, the Stafford earls (later dukes) of Buckingham, the Mortimer family and the lordship of Glamorgan were.[72]

Within England such lords, like all other manorial landowners, great and small, enjoyed no equivalent source of manorial profits. It is difficult to generalize about the volume of the revenues generated by manorial jurisdiction, since to do so would require substantial series of court rolls. But some solid conclusions are possible. The evidence that has survived for other holdings provides no reason to doubt that the results of an analysis for the estates of the bishops of Worcester in the fifteenth century can be applied generally. On these estates the perquisites of courts were a low source of income, providing about 6 per cent of total revenues in 1419–20 and about 4 per cent in 1506–7.[73] There is every reason to believe that such revenues were higher in the years 1350–1400. Two elements were especially important in the decline – resentment against the disabilities of villeinage and the collapse of a system of manorial discipline as a result of the commutation of labour services, this becoming a permanent feature of the manorial landscape because of the abandonment of demesne farming by the lord. It is clear that in the light of this situation in the course of the fifteenth century lords began to realize the importance of entry fines, and to distinguish between them and other perquisites of courts. For the full effects of this perception, however, we have to wait until the close of the century when the demand for tenancies began to rise.[74]

Great landowners, lay and ecclesiastical, drew revenues from two other seigneurial sources – rights of delegated royal jurisdiction such as private hundred courts and those of feudal lordship. The former were a small source of revenue by 1350. The latter, however, could be more substantial, because occasionally they yielded rights of wardship and marriage. Feudal lords, however, were effectively helpless to prevent the growth of uses, even though they remained conscious of their legal rights. The great landowners maintained feodaries within the lordships in which they were tenants-in-chief. Even so, an examination of the surviving financial records of the leading lay magnates of the period –

---

[72] Davies, *Lordship and Society*, pp. 183–4; *Marcher Lordships of South Wales*, ed. Pugh, pp. 36–40.   [73] Dyer, *Lords and Peasants*, p. 163.

[74] E.g. Bean, *Estates of the Percy Family*, pp. 51–66.

the duke of Lancaster in the late fourteenth century and the Staffords and the Percies in the fifteenth – shows that feudal revenues were slight in comparison even with perquisites of manorial courts.[75]

In terms of the sources of their revenues the various levels of English landed society during the period 1350–1500 thus present a complex picture. It is quite clear that a monolithic approach to the problems involved is not appropriate. To stress that demesne revenues were probably more important in the case of the gentry than in that of those above them in lay society overlooks the importance of rents to this group. For example, the revenue from the manor of Baddesley belonging to the Warwickshire squire John Brome contained little by way of rent; but, if his revenues from all his holdings are calculated, roughly half came from this source.[76] It is also important to bear in mind that the variation in the size of monastic estates we see in the *Valor Ecclesiasticus* has its counterpart in the structure of their respective economies. Two recent studies have shown that the holdings of small monastic houses must have presented problems of management totally different from those of the great houses. The economies of Austin houses of canons were dominated by small properties – glebe demesnes – that contained no rent component.[77] Haughmond abbey in Shropshire had built up a group of small pieces of land in the administration of which leasehold policies were always an integral part.[78]

(ii) Direct management and leasing

The history of the great landed estates of late medieval England reveals a profound change in policy – the abandonment of direct management of demesne lands, meadows, and pastures which were then leased to tenants. There is a consensus that the crucial years in this process were between 1380 and 1420, though it had begun, partly in the form of piecemeal leasing, before the former date. It is a pattern that has been thoroughly traced for some of the leading ecclesiastical estates – notably those of Westminster abbey, Canterbury Cathedral priory, Ramsey abbey, Durham Cathedral priory and the bishops of Worcester. It is, however, important to bear in mind that the process was uneven and sometimes not complete. The abandonment of pastoral activities

---

[75] The office of feodary in the south parts of the Duchy of Lancaster in 1393–4 produced a mere 2.6 per cent of the gross receipts (PRO DL 29/728/11981). The equivalent percentage for the Yorkshire estates of the Percy earl of Northumberland in 1442–3 was 2.14 (Petworth House Mss. D.9.3). [76] Dyer, 'A small landowner'.

[77] D. Postles, 'Problems in the administration of small manors; three Oxfordshire glebe-demesnes, 1278–1345', *Mid. Hist.*, IV, 1977.

[78] U. Rees, 'The leases of Haughmond abbey', *ibid.*, VIII, 1983.

occurred later than that of arable farming. And Canterbury Cathedral priory, for example, maintained sheep flocks as well as lands in hand for the subsistence of the monastic community through the fifteenth century.[79]

In this area as well as others a distinction must be drawn between lay landowners and those of the Church. The lay magnates had never been involved in demesne farming to the same extent as the bishops and great religious houses. This is not surprising. Their lives were peripatetic, sometimes involving them in missions or warfare outside the kingdom, whereas great monastic communities required regular provisions, especially grain, for their maintenance. A bishop's life, it is true, was closer to that of the magnate; but, while it might be peripatetic within his diocese, outside it tended to be limited to Westminster.

But the contrast between lay magnates and the great ecclesiastical landowners was not a total one, since there remained resemblances in the chronological pattern of change. By 1420 the great laymen had withdrawn from the cultivation of grain on their demesnes. The classic description of the process is that given by John Smyth of Nibley in the seventeenth century, describing the management policies of the lords Berkeley;[80] but a similar pattern can be demonstrated from the surviving records of the Duchy of Lancaster, the Stafford earls (later dukes) of Buckingham, the Fitzalan earls of Arundel and the Percy earls of Northumberland. As in the case of the great Church estates, the changeover to *rentier* status was not always total by 1420. The crown as duke of Lancaster in the 1440s still engaged in a little arable cultivation on one of its manors in the south,[81] as did the duke of Buckingham in his lordship of Holderness in Yorkshire.[82] The explanation in both these cases may well be the continued maintenance of sheep farming, which meant that estate officials and their underlings required liveries of grain.

In the case of pastoral farming, some lay magnates continued to maintain large flocks of sheep beyond 1420 – for example, the duke of Buckingham in the lordship of Holderness or Ralph, Lord Cromwell at his manor of Tattersall.[83] Involvement in pastoral farming at this level, however, seems to have ended by 1450 or so. It was in the early 1440s that the Duchy of Lancaster gave up its sheep flock in the lordship of Pickering. The explanation for its abandonment can probably be found in the experience of the duchy administrators on its manors in

[79] M. Mate, 'Pastoral farming in south-east England', p. 530.
[80] John Smyth of Nibley, *The Lives of the Berkeleys*, ed. Sir J. Maclean, II, p. 6.
[81] PRO DL 29/683, *passim*.   [82] Staffs. RO, D64/1/12/17.
[83] For Cromwell, see PRO SC 11/822.

Wiltshire and Dorset, where large sheep flocks were maintained beyond 1440 and not totally abandoned for twenty years or so. The substantial body of manorial accounts that has survived for these estates documents the crisis that occurred in the 1440s because of the fall in wool prices, the clip being kept in storage and not sold in many years.[84]

Recent scholarship, notably Dyer's work on the estates of the bishops of Worcester,[85] has delineated the reasons for the abandonment of direct management. It took a generation after the impact of the Black Death for landowners to realize the full nature of their economic situation. By 1370 or so wage costs had risen and were cutting into profits; but grain prices had remained buoyant. It was only after 1380 that a collapse in grain prices drove home the difficulties of selling grain at a price that would ensure even a slight profit, and demonstrated, where direct management of the arable was for the maintenance of a community or a household, that the necessary provisions could be bought in the market at prices below the cost of production on their own estates.

But this is a picture that cannot be applied at every level of landowning. Much less information has survived for the gentry than for the great landowners, lay or ecclesiastical. But what we have demonstrates that they often retained methods of direct management, both of arable and of pastoral, through the fifteenth century. Within East Anglia this can be seen in the case of Sir George Felbrigg,[86] Lady Alice Brian[87] and the Clere family.[88] In the case of the Catesby family in Warwickshire, the demesne of one manor served as a home farm, another maintaining a large flock of sheep. The accounts of the manor of Baddesley, the main holdings of John Brome, a Warwickshire squire, show that the grain produced there was consumed mainly in his household, market sales playing no part in manorial profits. There is good reason to believe that he never expected to buy grain on the market.[89] In the case of Derbyshire the Vernon family as well as other gentry maintained home farms as well as sheep flocks.[90] Where manorial accounts survive for these landowners, they show the greater part of the grain produced in their demesnes being consumed in their households, and in the case of their sheep flocks, while the wool-clips were sold, sheep and sometimes cattle were also consumed by the lord and his household. The details contained in the testaments of gentry in

[84] PRO DL 29/683, *passim*.
[85] See especially Dyer, *Lords and Peasants*, pp. 113–52.
[86] Norfolk RO, WKC/2/24–8, 40–6, 82–5, etc.   [87] PRO SC 6/989/3–990/1.
[88] Britnell, *Growth and Decline in Colchester*, p. 246.
[89] C. Dyer, *Warwickshire Farming*, p. 18; *idem*, 'A small landowner'.
[90] Wright, *Derbyshire Gentry*, p. 16.

this period suggest that this picture should not be limited to those whose records of estate management have survived, since bequests of sheep and sometimes grain are to be found in these probate materials.

How do we explain the contrast with the great landed estates these details present? There were several elements in the situation. One was the fact that a gentry life-style generally involved substantial stays, if not the whole year, at one residence, so that an integration of farming of the arable demesne and of household management was feasible. This appears in the case of Lady Alice Brian, where we are fortunate in having not merely a number of accounts for one of the manors concerned but also the accounts of the steward of her household for 1411–12.[91] This shows that the household's needs for grain and meat were supplied from her two manors of Acton and Foxheard. In some years at least, the steward of the household also acted as receiver and supervisor. In the case of Sir George Felbrigg at least part of the needs of his household were supplied from his main manor.

Embedded in these details is an explanation for the retention of sheep flocks by these gentry. The purpose of this was not merely to provide wool for sale but also meat for the household. Indeed, in these cases manorial accounts, even if they provide details of the size of a clip and the price at which it was sold, inevitably fail to provide a complete picture of the profitability of sheep farming, partly because sheep were consumed in the household, partly because the steward then sold woolfells and skins on the market. In a gentry economy the household was in some respects a trading enterprise. Barley from Felbrigg and other manors in the area belonging to Sir George Felbrigg was delivered to his household. The quantity received by his "maltster" amounted to five times or so what we encounter in the case of Lady Alice Brian. Her household's consumption of beer may have been less than Felbrigg's; but it could not have been substantially smaller. The Felbrigg household must have been selling a large quantity of malt on the market. The fact that the area was primarily a barley-growing one, together with our knowledge of the export trade in malt from the ports of East Anglia, lead to the conclusion that, like Sir George Felbrigg, many East Anglian gentry must have derived additional income from the sale of malt manufactured in their households.[92]

[91] *The Household Book of Dame Alice de Bryene*, ed. V. B. Redstone, Ipswich, 1931.

[92] For Fastolf, see McFarlane, *England in the Fifteenth Century*, p. 196. For the export trade in malt, see Britnell, *Growth and Decline in Colchester*, pp. 246–7.

D. THE FORTUNES OF LANDLORDS

(i) *The administrative background*

Any effort to offer a general assessment of the economic situation of English landlords in the years 1350–1500 is fraught with difficulties. For most of them we have no information: and there are obvious risks in applying to other landowners conclusions derived from the holdings of a minority of lay magnates, leading monasteries, and bishops.

On one point there can be certainty. It is clear enough that landlords in general possessed the administrative resources to chart the effects of economic trends on their financial situation. On the great lay estates the structure of the collection and administration of revenues has long been understood – the payment of manorial revenues from reeves and bailiffs to receivers who exercised such responsibility for all a lord's manors within a shire or larger region and then, after the deduction of the payments for which he was responsible, the transference of his remaining revenues to a receiver-general or direct to the lord's household. Overall supervision was exercised by a council that included the leading officials – the receiver-general, the chief steward and auditors, together with the leading household officials and important retainers. The most important function of the council must have been the review of the annual audits that took place at the end of the financial year. And it was this that gave rise to the practice of making valors – in effect, budgets summarizing the state of the lord's landed revenues. There are marked variations in the approaches followed in the compilation of valors. Some might give details of the cash actually received as well as unpaid arrears, others might be concerned with providing a summary of the respective items of revenue due from manorial officials as well as their disbursements; and some provided details of the payments for which receivers were responsible. Those of the Duchy of Lancaster in the late fourteenth century are unique in providing auditors' comments on the condition of certain items of revenue. It is obvious that valors, as well as providing enlightenment for the lord's council, also armed the auditors with information they could use in future years in examining manorial officials' accounts. Auditors, receivers and other members of the lord's council were, it must be stressed, faced with a difficulty that the historian of landed estates in this period also encounters – the fact that the accounts presented by manorial officials and receivers were statements of an individual's personal indebtedness. Though the methods employed in constructing valors varied, and none that have survived give a complete picture of both the actual as well as the expected revenues of an estate, this form of document does reveal the existence of efforts to press beyond limits of personal accountability. At the very least they did provide an approximate sense of the fortunes of an estate at the time of compilation.

There are also indications in this period of improvements in the administration of landed revenues. In the late fourteenth century, the earliest appearance being on the estates of the Courtenay earl of Devon in Devon and Cornwall in 1383–4,[93] there appeared the new office of supervisor (or surveyor), who generally had responsibility for the estates within the area of a receiver's financial administration. There is no surviving description of the functions of this office. While it was an independent one on some estates – for example, on those of the bishop of Worcester in the early fifteenth century – it was often combined with other offices, especially that of receiver. Even so, its existence, even when amalgamated with another office, reveals an awareness of problems that could not be handled by officials whose responsibilities were defined in terms of the collection and spending of revenues.

Even deeper concerns in this area are revealed by a development on some great estates in the late fifteenth century – the appearance of groups of itinerant commissioners, especially well documented on the estates of the Stafford dukes of Buckingham and the Percy earls of Northumberland.[94] The most important task entrusted to such commissioners was the acceptance of new tenancies, the granting of leases and the assessment of entry fines. Their appearance revealed a realization that the profits of manorial courts had been eroded by a weakening of seigneurial authority, and that it was in consequence desirable to disentangle matters that bore directly on the level of landed revenues from the rest of manorial jurisdiction. It is no mere coincidence that commissioners appeared at a point when the demand for tenancies on great estates was beginning to improve.

Most of the estates of the Church present a different administrative picture. The bishops appear to have had a bureaucracy on the same lines as lay magnates, revenues being handled by receivers: in the case of at least one bishop – Worcester – the office of supervisor appeared. Monastic holdings present a different picture with considerable variation, because the structure of estate administration was part and parcel of that of the community. But valors make their appearance in the case of both bishops and the leading monasteries.[95] Of course, in the last resort the effectiveness of any administrative resources depended on the degree of commitment to efficiency displayed by the landowner,

---

[93] BL Add. Roll 64319. For other details see Dyer, *Lords and Peasants*, p. 155.
[94] Bean, *Estates of the Percy Family*, pp. 48–9; McFarlane, *Nobility*, p. 216.
[95] E.g., Du Boulay, *The Lordship of Canterbury*, p. 243.

much depending on the personality of the lay lord, bishop, or abbot. In the case of a duke, earl, or baron, absence on the king's wars in France might have some effect on the quality of his administration, and, in that of the bishop, stays at Westminster could be protracted, especially if the bishop held an office in the royal administration. Even so, the affairs of such lords would continue to be handled by many experienced and trusted officials. Indeed, biographical data assembled for many of these in several recent studies reveals a group of personnel whose involvement in the administrations of great landowners constituted a career.

In the case of the gentry estates for which information has survived, lords seem to have been involved directly in their administration. There was often a close connection between the household and nearby manors, and in some household and manorial administration dovetailed. Although such estates generally maintained a receiver, manorial issues in substantial amounts were often paid direct to the lord or his lady. At the same time there were those small gentry estates where the lord himself performed the functions exercised by the receivers and the council on the estates of his social superiors.[96]

(ii) Crisis or stability?

A precise chronological outline of fluctuations in landed revenues in the whole period 1350–1500 is not possible. The available results of research into those records that have survived do, however, justify a tentative division of these years into four approximate periods – 1350–80, the aftermath of the Black Death and the plagues of the next twenty years; 1380–1420, the abandonment of direct management of arable farming on the estates of lay magnates and leading ecclesiastical landowners; 1420–70, a period in which there was a marked fall in landed revenues on many estates; and 1470–1500, years of recovery.

For the earliest of these periods a detailed overall view is difficult, partly because the survival of evidence is so sporadic, partly because when it has survived it reveals considerable variations in the incidence of the depopulation caused by plague. It is, however, clear that these years were by no means ones of unmitigated disaster. In 1916 A. E. Levett demonstrated that on a number of manors of the bishop of Winchester windfall profits from heriots and entry fines during the Black Death and its immediate aftermath more than compensated for

---

[96] See, e.g., the accounts of the small estate of the west country knight, Sir John Burwash (Somerset RO, DD/WO).

the collapse of other revenues caused by the enormous death rates of tenants.[97] But the simultaneous publication of similar investigations into other Winchester manors, confirmed by later research, showed that on these a net loss of revenues occurred.[98] As the wealthiest of the bishops, enjoying a landed income at the level of a leading earl, the bishop of Winchester held landed holdings that provide a rough sample of the manors of southern England. There can be no doubt that other landowners fared as he did on his most prosperous manors. Indeed, this can be seen in the surviving manorial accounts of the East Anglian manors of the Clare family.[99] Existing knowledge, therefore, indicates that the fortunes of landowners during the Black Death and its immediate aftermath depended partly on the incidence of plague and the resulting loss of tenants, partly on the extent to which there existed a high density of population within a manor, since if there was a substantial cottar or landless group there might be no serious difficulty in letting vacant holdings.

In this situation fortunes must have varied considerably. But recent scholarship has brought to light another aspect of the economic situation of landowners in this period which must have played a role in the phenomena depicted by Levett: the period was one of buoyant grain prices. In this situation a landlord who could command adequate supplies of labour, whether through labour services and the payment of wages or through wages alone, encountered no serious difficulties in maintaining the direct farming of his arable demesnes. There are strong indications, clearly demonstrated in the case of manors of the bishop of Worcester, for example, that the maintenance of arable farming at a profit served to disguise the long-term consequences of the Black Death and other plagues on the demand for grain.[100] At the same time continued prosperity could not have been universal. A landowner's capacity to benefit from buoyant grain prices depended on the supply of labour available to him; and there must have been manors where this was seriously depleted.

The abandonment of direct management of arable farming in the years 1380–1420 needs to be put into a proper perspective. In simple terms it can be attributed to a crisis caused by the effects of rising labour costs and falling grain prices. But it would be wrong to assume that there was an accompanying crisis in the level of landlords' revenues. Direct management continued on the estates of the gentry through the

[97] A. E. Levett, *The Black Death*.

[98] *Ibid.*, chapter by A. Ballard on 'The manors of Witney, Brightwell and Downton'; Postan, 'Economic evidence of declining population', reprinted in his *Essays on Medieval Agriculture*, pp. 208–9.   [99] Holmes, *Estates of the Higher Nobility*, pp. 90, 114–15.

[100] Dyer, *Lords and Peasants*, pp. 113–50.

next century. The process of abandonment was a phenomenon encountered at the level of the lay magnates and the great ecclesiastical landowners. And even within their ranks the process of abandonment at least maintained and in some cases actually boosted revenues.

There are two grounds for this conclusion. First, there is a number of cases in which it is possible to demonstrate that the leasing of demesnes produced farms that were higher than the net profits of direct management in recent years. In the west country the demesne lands of at least two manors of the Courtenay earl of Devon yielded more when farmed out in 1421–2 than they had under direct management in 1382–3.[101] Though the chronological gap is longer, the demesne lands of the Percy manors in Sussex in 1426–7 yielded markedly higher amounts in the form of farms than they had from direct management fifty years previously.[102] On the manor of Dorking in Surrey, belonging to the earl of Arundel, the arable demesne produced a loss in 1391–2 but a farm of £6 13s. 4d. in 1406–7.[103] When a Warwickshire squire, Richard Verney, leased most of his manor of Kingston to a Coventry butcher in 1437, the farm agreed on was 60 per cent higher than the net receipts of the whole manor in 1395.[104] The records of the Duchy of Lancaster provide the cases of two contiguous manors, Higham Ferrers and Raunds in Northamptonshire. In the mid-1380s the auditors drew attention to the fact that direct management of the arable demesnes of both was operating at a loss. In contrast, twenty years later they were yielding farms totalling £9 a year.[105] It is difficult to believe that these are isolated or unusual cases, since they come from different areas of southern England. To be sure, those of Dorking, Higham Ferrers, and Raunds raise the question why the lords concerned persisted in direct management as long as they did. The reason must lie in a tendency to cling to a policy in which direct management was integrated with the provision of grain for the maintenance of the household. All, it should be noted, were near a place at which the lord had kept his household, or provided a point at which he might spend some time when travelling from distant estates to Westminster. In these circumstances it may for some years have seemed worthwhile to continue direct management even though it was producing a loss.

In the second place, it is important to place both these details and the general practice of rendering farms for demesne lands in their proper context. When a tenant agreed to pay an annual amount for a lease of

[101] Devon RO, CR 584; PRO SC 6/1118/6. The manors were Plympton and Sandford Courtenay.

[102] Petworth House Ms. MAC/2; Bean, Estates of the Percy Family, pp. 16–20.

[103] Arundel Castle Mss. A.1783, 1791.   [104] Hilton, English Peasantry, pp. 169–70.

[105] PRO DL 29/728/11975 – 729/12002.

demesne lands, he was incurring an annual obligation that would form one of several major items, albeit probably the largest, in his own costs of farming operations. Information that has survived from the fifteenth century relating to the lordship of Ellesmere in the marches of Wales and manors in Bedfordshire and Northamptonshire indicates that lords and tenants generally operated on the assumption that the annual farm paid for the lease of demesne lands amounted to one-third of the value of the grain produced.[106] In this light there can be no doubt that, when tenants took over leases of demesne lands in the years 1380–1420, they were confident that they could make farming operations pay more successfully than their lords could. It was certainly clear to lords of great estates that, in the economic climate of the times, to maintain direct management would be to risk financial loss or at best a marginal profit. What made the abandonment of direct management by great lords an inevitable decision was a mixture of considerations. In the case of a lay magnate whose way of life was peripatetic, partly because of the needs of service to the crown, especially in war, partly because of the wide distribution of his holdings, there was no guarantee that in any year it would be possible to consume in the household the bulk of the grain produced, while the alternative of market sales promised lower prices than in previous years, perhaps, indeed, difficulties in finding purchasers. Bishops found themselves in a similar situation. That of the leading monasteries is more complex, because in some cases there was not a total abandonment of direct management. But they too often had widely distributed estates; and the risks of market sales were especially apparent in the case of manors distant from the monastic house.

For these reasons it is unwise to regard the abandonment of direct management of the arable demesne as simply a response to a crisis in the market for grain and in labour costs. It was a policy both limited and governed by the extent to which a lord was engaged in such farming in 1380: and in the case of lay magnates this was small in proportion to their estates as a whole. The comparisons that can be made between the net profits of direct management and the farms later paid by tenants for the same lands have, of course, implications for our understanding of the continuance of direct management on the estates of the gentry and their willingness, at least in parts of the south, to take on leases of episcopal and monastic demesnes. In their case, as in the case of other lessees, the production of grain continued to be worthwhile.

The years 1420–70 witnessed two separate agrarian phenomena. One was a strong tendency for great landowners to abandon sheep farming. It was not universal even among this group – for example, Canterbury

---

[106] Pollard, 'Estate management in the later middle ages', *EcHR*, 2nd ser. xxv, 1971–2, p. 560; *Grey of Ruthin Valor*, ed. Jack, pp. 71, 79.

Cathedral priory did not abandon pastoral activities.[107] And there are strong indications that gentry continued to maintain flocks and herds. It is clear, however, that, when great landlords pulled out of sheep farming, they were doing so in response to market conditions to an extent that cannot be found in their abandonment of arable farming. The governing consideration was not a rise in labour costs, imperceptible in the case of pastoral agriculture, but the fall in wool prices that was a pronounced feature of the years 1440–60. This, to be sure, affected the gentry as well; but their methods of estate management were directed partly towards the production of meat for the household.

The second phenomenon – falling rents and farms – can be found throughout England. Even so, caution must be exercised in delineating the details of this situation, since its incidence varied both from region to region and within a region from manor to manor. Not all items of manorial revenue were affected equally. In Cumberland and Northumberland, for example, customary rents fell, sometimes drastically, whereas elsewhere it was the farms paid for leases of demesne lands and mills that bore the brunt of the decline. In any manor much depended on the balance between customary rents and the farms of demesne lands and mills. A manor in which "Rents of Assize" and other customary payments formed a high proportion of the total might well enjoy a degree of insulation from the worst ravages of decline. Behind the decline in the value of rents and farms there were, in fact, two separate forces at work. One consisted of the effects of depopulation, whether caused by plague and other epidemics or by the effects of peasant migration. The other was the role of market forces – demand for grain and wool – that could reduce the prosperity of peasant farming and thus lead to pressures for reductions in the farms paid for demesne lands and mills. It is unfortunate that no direct evidence exists to throw light on the condition of peasant farming. But it is a reasonable assumption that, especially in the highland zone and in other areas dominated by pastoral agriculture, lords' tenants must have suffered seriously in the years 1440–60 from the collapse in wool prices.

There is some reason to believe that the incomes of great landlords from some manors were also affected by a formidable increase in arrears. The appearance of arrears on a manorial account is not in itself proof of the existence of difficulties encountered by tenants. In some cases the debtors were important tenants who could not have lacked the resources to pay their rents. Another element in the situation was the

[107] Mate, 'Pastoral farming in south-east England', pp. 529–30, 534.

role of fines and amercements imposed in the manorial court, which often formed a substantial proportion of accountants' arrears. Even so, there are indications from some estates that arrears were at their worst at the point when any difficulties on the part of tenants would also have been at their worst, especially in the 1450s.[108] There were thus occasions when landlords encountered not merely a fall in rents and farms but also difficulties in collecting already depleted revenues.

It is difficult to decide the extent to which the years 1470–1500 witnessed a general recovery of rents and farms, as distinct from a cessation of the previous decline. On many estates, particularly in the south, there was some recovery in the farms paid for demesne lands and mills. There are also indications that the farms paid for pasture rose at a higher rate than those paid for arable. The explanation must lie in the growing demand for wool as the kingdom's cloth exports rose from the mid-70s onwards. At worst, then, on the holdings of the great landowners, the years 1470–1500 were ones of stability on some of their manors, while on others there was a limited increase in total revenues from rents and farms.

This rough pattern of fluctuations in landed revenues in the years 1350–1500 constitutes by itself a warning against generalizations about the fortunes of landlords in terms that embrace the whole of England. There is certainly good reason to believe that troubles afflicted many landlords in two periods – 1350–70 and 1420–70. But there is equally reason to believe that difficulties were more widespread and cut deeper into incomes in the latter period. In the earlier period landlords derived some relief from buoyant grain prices; and those whose holdings lay in the more densely populated areas secured additional revenue from heriots and entry fines. In the years 1420–70 these forms of relief were absent, landlords being exposed to a slack, and sometimes declining, market for tenancies, while grain prices lacked buoyancy and after 1440 wool prices fell.

This is a picture, however, that rests primarily on the evidence of developments on great estates. Despite the enormous gaps in our knowledge, we know of cases of prosperity among the gentry. In Warwickshire John Brome exploited the market for his livestock as well as that for stone and tiles. He managed to buy additional property. In the west country the Luttrell family enjoyed the benefits of comparatively stable rents and farms on their Somerset holdings. In Norfolk Sir George Felbrigg produced malt from his household for the market to an extent that more than compensated for any diminution in manorial revenues.

These examples, it must be said, come from the south of England.

---

[108] For a recent discussion, see Dyer, *Lords and Peasants*, pp. 179–83.

But they must also be viewed against the background of the gentry's continued involvement in direct management of demesne farming. Even on those estates where there was some decline in rents and farms, the continued organization of their demesne resources for the purpose of provisioning their households insulated them in some measure from the consequences of an often poor market for their grain and, for twenty years or so, falling wool prices. The evidence of Tables 6.2–6.4 demonstrates that it is the levels of landowning society to which these arguments apply that possessed the greater part of the kingdom's landed wealth.

In the light of all these details and arguments two conclusions are possible. One is that there was a reduction in the revenues received from most, if not all, manors in the years 1350–1500. The other is that it was the highest levels of landed society, lay and ecclesiastical, that were worst affected. It would be wrong to conclude, however, that the resulting decline in net income was always large. Much depended on the location of individual manors and the structure of revenues within them. Estimates covering the whole period are extraordinarily difficult in the case of lay landowners, partly because of the paucity of evidence, partly because many of the families for which information exists died out in the male line within the period, and inheritances were broken up or transferred to other families. But we possess totals for the archbishopric of Canterbury and the bishopric of Worcester during the fifteenth century; and these do not indicate any remarkable fluctuations.[109]

The location of these two episcopal estates must, of course, have put them in a better position than many others. But even the situation of lay magnates and gentry with estates in more depressed areas of the agrarian economy must be placed in a wider perspective. Unlike the bishops and the great monasteries, this group enjoyed sources of financial gain denied to Church landowners. A lay landlord who married a widow enjoyed during her lifetime the income from her dower. If, as often happened, a landowner married a widow as his second wife, having fathered heirs by a deceased first wife, he must have secured a source of income that more than compensated for the effects of agrarian decline. More important overall than this element in the situation of landlords was the role of the marriage market. A landowner who married an heiress secured the income from her lands during her lifetime (and even during his if she gave birth to live issue but died before him); and if a male heir survived the father, the family inheritance was enlarged. Nor was the role of the marriage market confined to the marriage of heiresses. At every level of lay landed

---

[109] Du Boulay, *The Lordship of Canterbury*, p. 243; Dyer, *Lords and Peasants*, pp. 163, 177.

society the practice whereby a bride brought a sum of money with her under the terms of a marriage settlement increased the financial resource of her husband's family.

Another form of compensation for the effects of agrarian decline was to be found in the opportunities presented by the development of uses. The pressures of indebtedness during a landowner's lifetime were reduced; and, although arrangements for the payment of his debts by his feoffees might reduce his heir's income for a time, at least indebtedness did not result in the erosion of the inheritance. Uses also facilitated the development of marriage settlements, making it possible to raise sums for this purpose after a father's death, and in his lifetime providing through conveyances to feoffees guarantees for the settlement of lands by him on his son and daughter-in-law.

There can thus be no doubt that opportunities existed for the amelioration of the financial situation of those landlords whose manorial revenues were subject to decline. Even so, such opportunities required efforts at exploitation. Two features of this situation of lay landlords require emphasis. One was the role of personal competence. The effects of personal ambition and efficiency in the conduct of business have always received attention from historians of the rise and fall of landed families. Those studying the years 1350–1500 do not possess the detailed evidence about personalities available in later centuries. But a perusal of, for example, the correspondence of the Paston family reveals the range of business capacity that could be encountered. The other feature of landed society certainly emerges strongly from the records of the courts of law and the vicissitudes of individual families – the competition for inheritances or shares of them, encouraged by the obscure technicalities of the land law. It is reasonable to assume that litigation, despite its costs, was encouraged in many cases by the effort to compensate for declining revenues.

In the last resort the success or failure achieved by a family in avoiding a crisis in its fortunes depended on a complex of influences. What we know of the incidence of agrarian decline suggests that careful management both of the various sources of income and of expenditure could prevent disaster, even if a family's holdings did not increase in size. There is, indeed, no evidence that lands were sold to any marked extent because of indebtedness. If we are to provide a summary description of landlords' fortunes in the years 1350–1500, it must be one of uneven stability.

CHAPTER 7

TENANT FARMING AND TENANT FARMERS

A. THE NORTHERN BORDERS

The Durham land surveys provide a convenient starting point for a discussion of peasant farming in the northern region in the late middle ages. Bishop Hatfield's Survey, probably compiled between 1377 and 1382, and Bishop Langley's Survey, made in 1418, give details of the various categories of land in each of the bishop's vills, the tenants who held the land, and the rents and services due from each tenant. These surveys divide the bishop's land into various categories: demesne land, tenant land, exchequer land, land held by the bond tenants, by cottagers, by freemen and by drengs; but this classification was maintained for record purposes and for the assessment of the obligations due from the tenants rather than as a real distinction between classes of men. The character of peasant farming was rather different from that suggested by the rigid categories of the surveys, and on the bishop of Durham's lands, as on other great estates in the northern region, the direct exploitation of the demesne and the liability of the unfree tenants to labour services had all but vanished by 1400, and the evolution of a copyholding peasantry was well advanced.[1]

By the early fifteenth century landlords throughout the northern region had ceased to cultivate their demesnes, but this generalization conceals much variation in the pace and timing of the abandonment of demesne farming. On the Lucy honour of Cockermouth and the Percy barony of Alnwick the leasing of the demesne appears to have been complete by 1314. On the lands of the great religious houses, however, the demesne was kept in hand longer. The bishop of Durham had leased his demesnes by 1387, but on the prior's estates the change took more time, and although most demesnes were leased by the end of the century some were still in hand as late as 1416. By the fifteenth century the priors of Tynemouth had abandoned all their demesnes to their

---

[1] Langley's Survey is unpublished: PRO SC 12/21/29.

tenants except at Tynemouth itself and at Preston; and the priors of Hexham retained only Anick by 1479.[2]

In the northern region, as elsewhere in England, the demesnes were farmed by men varying widely in wealth and status, and on terms that differed from estate to estate. Most commonly, the demesnes were farmed to groups of tenants in the vill where the demesne lay. On the Lucy lands in Cumberland this appears to have been the normal practice in the fourteenth century; in the vills of the Eden valley the demesnes were in the hands of groups of tenants by 1371; and on the lands of the barony of Alnwick the demesnes were usually farmed to the tenants-at-will. The priors of Tynemouth and Hexham farmed their demesnes to their tenants, and some of the demesne lands of the bishop of Durham had been in the hands of the tenants since the twelfth century. But this was not the universal practice. On the former Umfraville lands in Northumberland, the earl of Northumberland farmed his demesne at Prudhoe to one tenant only, and on the lands of Durham priory practice varied. Some demesnes were leased to the whole vill, some to groups of tenants, and some to gentry or to wealthy individuals such as Roger Thornton, a merchant of Newcastle-upon-Tyne. For the most part, however, the demesnes on estates for which evidence survives were farmed by groups of tenants, separately or together; on few manorial demesnes did one farmer take all the lands, and thus in the northern region the class of well-to-do tenant farmers did not emerge in quite the way it did further south. Again, one reason for this may have been the war with Scotland: in Northumberland and Cumberland, the danger of Scottish raids made profitable demesne farming more hazardous than it was elsewhere and militated against the willingness of one man to risk his money in taking a long-term lease. In 1427, for example, the receiver of the Duchy of Lancaster lordship of Dunstanburgh was unable to lease the demesnes of Embleton, and the king, concerned at the lack of revenue from the demesnes, instructed the receiver to attempt to lease them to a tenant for three years at 20 marks a year; if he could not do this, he was to lease them for a year at the highest obtainable rent. Unfortunately the outcome is unknown. Almost certainly one reason for the reluctance of any tenant to farm the Embleton demesne was its vulnerability to attack from north of the border. The uncertainty and danger, rather than actual raiding, tended to depress agricultural activity and diminish men's willingness to take land and property at farm. Perhaps, too, men who might in other parts

---

[2] Bean, *Estates of the Percy Family*, p. 12; Dobson, *Durham Priory*, p. 272; T. Lomas, 'South-east Durham', pp. 302–3; E. M. Halcrow, 'The decline of demesne farming on the estates of Durham Cathedral priory', *EcHR*, 2nd ser. VII, 1955, pp. 345–56; cf. R. A. Lomas, 'The priory of Durham and its demesnes', pp. 339–53; *NCH*, VIII, p. 229; *Priory of Hexham*, ed. Raine, II, pp. 3–5.

of England have established their prosperity by taking leases of demesne land were here attracted to a military career and the pursuit of reward in the service of the king or the border magnates.[3]

The length of leases of demesne land varied substantially. On the Duchy of Lancaster lands in Northumberland it was policy to try to secure three-year leases, though the difficulty in finding farmers meant that the receiver might have to settle for annual leases. At Bamburgh leases ran for three years, but on the Percy lands in the fifteenth century 21-year leases were usual, though shorter leases were not unknown, while in the late fourteenth century Durham priory preferred leases of 15 years. Neither the prior of Durham nor the earl of Northumberland appears to have experienced much difficulty in leasing their demesnes to groups of tenants for long periods, and it may be that the Duchy of Lancaster's problems were caused not merely by the danger from the Scots but by its preference for a single tenant and, perhaps, by its insistence on too high a rent.[4]

By the beginning of the fifteenth century, therefore, the tenants farmed the demesnes in many vills in the northern region, and thus the distinction between demesne land and tenant land became blurred so far as farming practice is concerned. From the tenurial point of view, however, the distinction remained important on most estates through-out the fifteenth century, for a tenant's own holding was subject to substantially different customs. On the Percy lands by the late fifteenth century the tenants held for the lives of themselves and their lord, and thus they had substantial security, though no formal hereditary right. A similar development took place on the lands of Tynemouth priory. On the lands of Durham priory, however, the position of the tenants was more complex, and, ultimately, less advantageous. In the later fourteenth century holdings were usually demised to tenants for life, though some tenancies at will were still being created. The assumption that a *nativus* could hold only at the will of the lord still survived, though some bondages were in fact demised to *nativi* for life. Other tenancies were created to last "until another shall pay more", an event which can seldom have occurred in the period of land surplus which followed the plagues, and these tenancies must have amounted in

---

[3] R. A. Lomas, 'The priory of Durham and its demesnes', esp. p. 347; PRO C 135/185, 202; SC 11/155, 12/13/61; *NCH*, II, p. 33; VIII, p. 229; *Priory of Hexham*, ed. Raine, II, pp. 5–8; *VCH Durham*, II, p. 184; *Percy Bailiff's Rolls of the Fifteenth Century*, ed. J. C. Hodgson, Surtees Soc., CXXXIV, 1921, p. 63; *Feodarium Prioratus Dunelmensis*, ed. Greenwell, pp. 98–206. For the distraction war presented to one of Durham priory's leaseholders, see J. L. Drury, 'Early settlement in Stanhope park, Weardale', *AA*, 5th ser. IV, 1976, pp. 139–49.

[4] PRO SC 2/195/1100; Bean, *Estates of the Percy Family*, p. 56; *Halmota Prioratus Dunelmensis*, ed. Longstaff and Booth, pp. 100, 120; R. A. Lomas, 'Developments in land tenure on the prior of Durham's estate in the later middle ages', *North. Hist.*, XIII, 1977, pp. 27–43, esp. p. 36.

practice to life holdings. By the middle of the fifteenth century, however, Durham priory's policy of demising tenant land for life had been halted and reversed. The blurring of the distinction between demesne and tenant land was recognized by the priors by 1430, when they began to lease blocks of land, including both demesne and tenant land, to tenants for a term of years. The leases were usually short – often three, six, or nine years, and this development meant that by the mid-fifteenth century the priory's tenants had less security than the tenants on other estates, though there is some evidence that similar developments were taking place on the lands of the bishop of Durham. This policy built up for the prior's successors, the Dean and Chapter of the refounded cathedral, a tenurial problem which was not finally settled until Elizabeth's reign.[5]

By the sixteenth century, many tenants in the northern counties held their land by what was known as "tenant-right", a heritable estate in land which was usually considered to be bound up with the obligation to perform military service on the border. Recent work has, however, cast doubt on the view that the heritable nature of the tenancy was the defining characteristic of tenant-right. Its essence was rather, it is suggested, the right of the tenant to alienate his holding without licence from his lord, and the right of the lord to exact a fine from the tenant at the change of lord as well as the change of tenant, as in copyhold tenure. The principle that a fine should be levied on tenants at the lord's death was established on the Percy lands in Northumberland and Cumberland by the late fifteenth century, but, as R. W. Hoyle has pointed out, tenant-right thus defined could only develop on estates such as those of the Percies, where the prevailing custom was to demise lands for life, and thus tenant-right did not exist uniformly throughout the northern counties. On the estates of Durham priory, for example, the development of leasehold tenures in the fifteenth century marked a step down a quite different road.[6]

The abandonment of direct demesne farming, and the surplus of bondage holdings which followed the plagues of the fourteenth century, produced on many estates in the region a lively land market and a substantial differentiation of wealth and status within the village community. In the years immediately after the Black Death, for example, Roger de Tykhill took advantage of the deaths of many of his

[5] Bean, *Estates of the Percy Family*, p. 57; R. A. Lomas, 'The priory of Durham and its demesnes', pp. 37–8; *Halmota Prioratus Dunelmensis*, ed. Longstaff and Booth, pp. xxxvi–xlii; Dobson, *Durham Priory*, p. 272.

[6] R. A. Lomas, 'Developments in land tenure', pp. 37–9; R. W. Hoyle, 'Lords, tenants and tenant right in the sixteenth century: four studies', *North. Hist.*, xx, 1984, pp. 38–63; *idem*, 'Tenant right in north-western England in the sixteenth century', *PP*, no. 116, 1987, pp. 24–55.

neighbours to build up a substantial holding of bondage lands in the Bishop Auckland area. In the vill of Salkeld in the Eden valley in 1371, eight tenants farmed the demesne land, and of these eight Roger de Salkeld was indisputably the wealthiest, holding 4 bovates of demesne, 10 bovates of tenant land, 5 purprestures and 2½ acres of land called Gresland. Similarly, at Sandhoe on the lands of Hexham abbey there were 13 husbandlands each having 24 acres of arable and meadow, but the grouping of husbandlands had created substantial differences of wealth. Simon de Sandhoe, described as *nativus domini*, held at least 48 acres of land and meadow, whereas William and Robert de Matfen, also described as *nativi domini*, held a cottage each and one acre and half an acre respectively. The same inequalities developed on the bishop of Durham's lands, and at Newbottle 320 acres of demesne land were divided amongst the tenants in such a way that, although most of the holdings consisted of 19–26 acres, there was one of 35 acres and one of 43, and three of 10 acres or less. In the vill of Easington, according to Bishop Hatfield's survey, the average size of a holding was 24.8 acres, but there were five tenants with over 45 acres, and thirteen with 10 or less. In the more upland vills holdings tended to be smaller, though, for many tenants, livestock grazed on common pasture was a more important source of wealth than arable land. At North Auckland, two-thirds of the tenants had 10 acres or less, and there were only eight tenants with more than 30 acres. At Wolsingham three-quarters of the tenants were smallholders, and there were only five with 30 acres or more. Thus, although the substantial farmer holding all the demesne in a vill was something of a rarity in the northern region, a group of peasant farmers appreciably wealthier than their neighbours had emerged by the beginning of the fifteenth century, and the numerous smallholders characteristic of northern rural society in the thirteenth century survived into the later middle ages. These marked variations in the size of peasant holdings imply a freedom in peasant land transactions that was limited only by the inheritance customs of the manor and by the obligation to record such transactions in the manorial court and pay the appropriate fine. On the lands of Durham priory entry fines continued to be levied on most transactions until the 1370s, but over the next fifty years they gradually declined to the point of extinction. The abandonment of entry fines on the prior's estates does not, however, seem to have been paralleled on other estates in the north. On the bishop of Durham's lands entry fines were commonly levied in the fifteenth century; on the Percy lands they were systematically imposed throughout the century, though it was not until the early sixteenth century that the earl of Northumberland sought to increase them and develop them as a source of revenue. On the Durham priory lands subletting (*tabernatio*) was regularly allowed on payment of the appropriate fine, though if a tenement was sublet without licence it was liable to be taken into the lord's hand. Apart from safeguarding the rights of the heir, the manorial court, in Durham at least, seems to have been concerned to register rather than control peasant land transactions, and bondage holdings frequently changed hands in the late fourteenth and fifteenth centuries. In particular, there was an increasing tendency for land to pass away from the blood. The decline of family continuity in holdings at this period has been remarked upon elsewhere in England, and Durham is no exception. At Haughton not a single family holding a bondage in 1380 was still in possession of it in 1418; at Easington only two out of the thirty-one bondages remained in the hands of the same families during this period; and in other vills the same family names occur but they hold different bondages. The descent of holdings in the blood of the tenant seems the exception rather than the rule by the early fifteenth century, though there is some evidence that family inheritance was once again becoming common by the end of the century.[7]

Where a holding was transmitted in the blood, one son might normally expect to inherit in the Durham vills, and in view of the limited geographical occurrence of ultimogeniture or Borough English it seems safe to assume that this son was the eldest. On the Durham lands partibility was very uncommon, though not unknown: at South Shields in 1345 a toft was divided into two for the benefit of William and John, the sons of William de Blenkowe; but both in this instance and in the few instances known from the bishop's estates it may be that special factors were at work, and these isolated examples should not be taken as evidence for the survival of an earlier, more widespread, custom of partibility. In Westmorland, particularly in those districts where the cloth industry established itself in the fifteenth century, the previously widespread custom of partible inheritance seems to have survived into the sixteenth century, but with the exception of Bewcastle impartibility seems to have prevailed elsewhere in the north-west by *c.* 1500.[8]

In the upland districts of Tynedale, Bewcastle, and Redesdale, on the other hand, there is little doubt that partible inheritance was the rule. The evidence comes entirely from sixteenth- or early seventeenth-

[7] PRO Dur. 3/12, ff.18v, 19r, 28r; SC 11/156, 12/21/29, ff.11, 86, 117; *Bishop Hatfield's Survey*, ed. Greenwell, pp. 7–8, 33–41, 60–7, 127–32; *Halmota Prioratus Dunelmensis*, ed. Longstaff and Booth, pp. 81–4; Bean, *Estates of the Percy Family*, pp. 51–67; Faith, 'Peasant families and inheritance customs', pp. 77–95; T. Lomas, 'South-east Durham', pp. 296–301.

[8] *Halmota Prioratus Dunelmensis*, ed. Longstaff and Booth, p. 18; T. Lomas, 'South-east Durham', pp. 300–1; A. B. Appleby, *Famine in Tudor and Stuart England*, Liverpool, 1978, pp. 51–4.

century sources, and it is of course possible that partibility replaced primogeniture in these valleys in the late middle ages. If this was the case, however, it would have been a development unique in medieval England, and it is more likely that partibility was an ancient, though unrecorded, custom in these upland districts. In Elizabeth's reign it was stated that the tenants of north and south Tynedale "have ever had a custom, if a man have issue ten sons, eight, six, five or four and sits on a holding of but 6s. rent, every son shall have a piece of his father's holding", and the 1604 Survey of the Border recorded that in Redesdale "the Tenement after the death of the Tennant is parted equally among his sonnes". The evidence suggests that the system of inheritance was one of genuine partition rather than joint family ownership, under which a man's heirs lived close together and farmed their land in common. The emphasis in the sixteenth century on the poverty of the tenants of Tynedale, Bewcastle, and Redesdale, and the belief of contemporaries that their poverty arose from the practice of partible inheritance, makes it almost certain that the holdings were physically divided.[9]

Although the peasants in the arable vills of the eastern coastal plain enjoyed considerable freedom in the disposal of their land, serfdom had not entirely disappeared by the beginning of the fifteenth century. On the Percy estates, labour services had been commuted with the cessation of demesne farming in the early fourteenth century, and by 1498, when Cartington's rental was compiled, the tenants are described as tenants-at-will: *nativi* seem to have disappeared. The prior of Durham's *nativi*, however, make their appearance in the Halmote rolls throughout the fourteenth and early fifteenth centuries. In the 1350s there were disputes about their labour services in some of the prior's west Durham vills, and they displayed a certain sensitivity about their status: in 1365, for instance, the Halmote court had to issue orders forbidding the tenants from calling anyone *rusticum*. From time to time the prior's court held inquiries into the number and whereabouts of his *nativi*, but more with a view to exacting the payment for non-residence (*albinaria*) than the imposition of other burdens. Inquiries of this kind continued into the fifteenth century, the last one occurring in 1460 when thirty-two villeins were enumerated, all living in the arable vills of south-east Durham. On the lands of Hexham priory, too, villein status survived well into the fifteenth century. At Sandhoe in 1469 there were four men described as *nativi domini*, but their services were the same as those of the free husbandmen and consisted merely of the obligation to maintain the mill at Anick. At Anick itself there were three *nativi*, all cottagers; two at Dotland; two at Kirkheaton; one at Bingfield and

---

[9] J. Thirsk, in *AHEW*, IV, pp. 23–5; *Cal. Border Papers*, I, no. 50; *Survey of the Debateable and Border Lands, AD 1604*, ed. R. P. Sanderson, Alnwick, 1891, p. 85.

one at Eachwick. On the Hexham lands, as on those of Durham priory, villeinage was a vestigial survival by the middle of the fifteenth century, and the villein's terms of tenure differed little, if at all, from those of the freemen who surrounded him.[10]

The legal and tenurial position of the northern peasantry in the later middle ages is well illuminated from the Durham records and, to a lesser degree, from the records of the other great estates of the region; but the size and structure of the peasant family is a much more elusive subject. The poll-tax returns for 1377, many of which list each taxpayer separately, are of course wholly lacking for the bishopric of Durham, but fortunately they survive for the western, or upper, part of Coquetdale ward in Northumberland, a district where arable farming and upland grazing existed in close association. These returns make possible some analysis of the peasant family in that district, and they have been used in studies of marriage patterns amongst the English population generally. Evasion and under-enumeration make the returns hazardous as a source for the total size of the population, but they may be less inaccurate in their indication of the proportion of the population who were married.[11]

The names of individual taxpayers are listed for thirty-five out of forty-five vills in the ward, and the total number of taxpayers listed is 1,155: 866 of these were married men and women, 58 were single men, 64 were single women, 56 were sons over 14, 28 daughters over 14, and 83 were domestic servants, sex often unspecified. Thus 75.5 per cent of the population was married, a figure which is very close to the national percentage of married couples in vills with less than fifty inhabitants, as calculated by Professor Russell, though rather higher than the figures for Rutland calculated by R. M. Smith. Amongst the single persons, men and women are almost equally represented: 5 per cent men, 5.5 per cent women. Some of the women are described as widows, and the slightly higher percentage of single women is no more than would be expected in any community, bearing in mind their longer expectation of life. In all probability, therefore, the sporadic warfare on the border was not at all costly of life in these communities.[12]

The most striking characteristic of the population of upper

[10] Bean, *Estates of the Percy Family*, p. 57; *VCH Durham*, ii, pp. 214–17, 220–2; *Bishop Hatfield's Survey*, ed. Greenwell, p. 11; *Halmota Prioratus Dunelmensis*, ed. Longstaff and Booth, pp. 40–1, 136; *Priory of Hexham*, ed. Raine, ii, pp. 4–6, 10, 36, 45.

[11] Russell, *British Medieval Population*, pp. 124–30; J. Hajnal, 'European marriage patterns in perspective', in *Population in History: Essays in Historical Demography*, ed. D. V. Glass and D. E. C. Eversley, London, 1965, pp. 101–43; R. M. Smith, 'Hypothèses sur la nuptialité en Angleterre aux XIIIe–XIVe siècles', *Annales ESC*, 38, 1983, pp. 107–36.

[12] Russell, *British Medieval Population*, pp. 154–6; this discussion is based on an analysis of the returns in PRO E 179/158/29.

Coquetdale, however, is the very low proportion of unmarried sons and daughters over the age of fourteen: 4.75 per cent sons, and only 2.5 per cent daughters. There may, of course, have been widespread evasion of the tax due from such persons, but another hypothesis is possible. It is unlikely that the ordinary peasant household in upper Coquetdale could afford to maintain children within the household once they had reached the age at which they could work. Daughters might be boarded out as servants, both within the district and outside it, while sons might have sought work as agricultural labourers, entered the households of gentry or great lords, or migrated to the towns. Some of those described as servants may well have been the sons and daughters of other taxpayers in the district. Furthermore, few of the households could afford to maintain servants: only 7.25 per cent of the population was described as servants, and although widespread evasion is possible, it is unlikely that households which were unable to maintain their own children of working age could afford large numbers of servants. The size of the peasant household is a matter of some controversy, and the poll-tax returns leave many questions unanswered. It is impossible, for instance, to discover whether three generations normally dwelt together, or how many children under fourteen there were in each household. Allowing for these deficiencies, however, one may cautiously suggest that the peasant family in this part of Northumberland was small in size, that few servants were kept, and that children tended to leave home once they had reached working age.[13]

It is, of course, questionable how far these conclusions apply to other parts of the region. The larger, more prosperous vills of south-east Durham may have supported more substantial peasant families, and in the urban community of Carlisle the structure of the population in 1377 was very different, with married couples a smaller proportion of the population and many more servants kept. At the opposite extreme, in the upland districts of Tynedale and Redesdale, the custom of partible inheritance may have discouraged emigration by sons and perhaps contributed to the chronic disorder noted by later observers. The evidence from the northern region is too sparse to make an important contribution to the controversy over the size of the peasant family in medieval England, but it does suggest that the arable east may have been broadly similar in its social structure to arable areas further south. In this, as in so many other respects, the north was not distinctly

[13] Russell, op. cit., pp. 124–30; J. Krause, 'The medieval household: large or small?', EcHR, 2nd ser. IX, 1956–7, pp. 420–32; H. E. Hallam, 'Some thirteenth-century censuses', EcHR, 2nd ser. X, 1957–8, pp. 340–61; R. A. Houlbrooke, The English Family, 1450–1700, London, 1984, pp. 171–8.

different in its agrarian and social structure from the rest of late medieval England: the real distinction lay between the settled arable lands of the region and the upland border valleys, where a society which differed radically from that of the lowland parts of the north as well as from the rest of England evolved in the later middle ages and received the interested, if surprised, attention of the sixteenth-century commentators.[14]

B. YORKSHIRE AND LANCASHIRE

In Yorkshire and Lancashire, as elsewhere during the late middle ages, circumstances tended to favour tenants as a reduced population, and the abandonment of demesne cultivation by landlords, increased the supply of land relative to demand and made easier the terms on which it was available to tenants. These circumstances may have encouraged a more appropriate use of land in some cases, some increase of stock farming in parts of lowland Lancashire being a case in point; and they also weakened the force of lordship which, even if it had never dominated agricultural routines in the northern countryside to quite the same extent as in some other parts of the country, had still moulded the patterns of society. The changes which ensued are often masked by the conservative terminology of the records. In the mid-fourteenth century it is not surprising to find in Yorkshire bondage tenants at Grewelthorpe, *nativi* and *native* at Wheldrake, or a serf being solemnly manumitted with all his progeny born or to be born at Muston; but these old categories survived on the Duchy of Lancaster manors in the 1380s and later, on the prebendary's estate at Riccall in 1400, and on the Hexham lands at Salton and Brawby well into the fifteenth century, while at Hemingbrough in 1430 there were still "ancient bovates of ancient bondage". Traditional attitudes, too, were resistant to change. Lessees on the Fountains estate, even into the sixteenth century, were expected to show a decent deference. A tenant of part of Trenhouses (in Malham, Yorks.) in 1514 was required to be "of good demeanour to the above-named abbot and convent ... and he shall be ready at all times when the [abbey's] officers come into the country to watch upon them if he be called upon". Failure to display this courtesy could entail the forfeiture of his farmhold.[15]

The realities underlying these conservative appearances, however,

[14] PRO E 179/158/28; J. L. and A. D. Kirby, 'The poll tax of 1377 for Carlisle', *CWAAS*, NS LVIII, 1959, pp. 110–17; Bowes and Ellerker, 'Survey of the Border, 1542', in J. Hodgson, *History of Northumberland*, III(2), pp. 171–248.

[15] BL Add. Ms. 40010, ff.9–9d, 14, 20d, 28d; *Yorks. Deeds*, IX, no. 231; PRO DL 29/465/7604, 507/8228; *VCH East Riding*, III, pp. 49, 85; *Priory of Hexham*, ed. Raine, II, pp. 72–9; *Fountains Abbey Lease Book*, ed. Michelmore, no. 54.

were often somewhat different. Customary tenants listed in manorial documents as *bondi*, *nativi* or tenants-at-will in many cases had their titles to their holdings validated and made specific by the receipt of a copy of the entry on the roll of the manor court, recording their assumption of their tenement and the terms on which they had taken it. Even tenancies-at-will might be held "freely" or for specific terms of years and, while at Ackworth (Yorks.) a bond holding reverted to the lord when its tenant died, it did so only until the latter's nearest heir in blood (or failing an heir someone else) paid an entry fine to have it. The expectations of heirs were put even more categorically at Wincobank (Yorks.) when John Combe's holding passed to his son: the latter was to hold according to the custom of the manor "for ever". Tenures that might appear precarious, moreover, might be made less so in order to secure a tenant at a time when tenants were sometimes scarce: thus one holding at Yeadon (Yorks.), previously held at will, was in 1382 conceded for life. The difference might be more apparent than real, but some strengthening of the tenant's hold on the land was entailed.[16]

In addition to customary holdings of these types, however, there were others (and especially demesne lands conceded to tenants) subject to specific leasehold bargains. The dispersal of demesnes to tenants, in fact, involved a considerable diversity of arrangements as a few details relating to the Yorkshire manors of the honour of Pontefract make clear. In 1399 the Ackworth demesne was demised to divers tenants in parcels on 15-year terms, while that at Altofts was leased to only two men for ten years; and in 1425 the Tanshelf demesne was partitioned among some fifty tenants, that at Elmsall was held by *bondi* on 50-year leases, Warmfield demesne was divided among the *nativi* to hold with their oxgangs (and perhaps by contagion was held by copy of court roll), and at Barwick-in-Elmet the "ancient demesne" was leased to divers men while the "new demesne" (after being let earlier to sixteen *nativi*) was in the hands of a single leaseholder. A similar variety of arrangements is evident elsewhere, but what is clear is that the dispersal of demesnes might offer opportunities both for small men seeking a modest increase of their resources and for entrepreneurs operating on a much larger scale.[17]

Leaseholds, or at least tenures for a specific term, were not restricted

---

[16] T. W. Hall, *Descriptive Catalogue of Sheffield Manorial Records*, I, pp. 40, 61–195; PRO DL 42/106, f.19; PRO SC 6/1085/18; *A Transcript of the Court Rolls of Yeadon, 1361–1476*, ed. G. R. Price, p. 74 (this edition is less than satisfactory, but so long a run of rolls needs to be used wherever that is possible).

[17] PRO DL 29/507/8229, DL 42/106, ff.14–15, 22, 38; *Miscellanea*, IX, Thoresby Soc., XXVIII, 1928, pp. 238–43.

to demesne arable. In Yorkshire Fountains abbey and in Lancashire the Duchy of Lancaster leased their stock farms; at Bowes and in Arkengarthdale mills, vaccaries, common rights and a quarry were "farmed", as were meadows, crofts, the tenteryard and the common oven at Snape; but so were bond holdings at Forcett, the customary holdings at Yeadon increasingly were let for a fixed number of years, and tenants at will at Ashton-under-Lyne held for a term of twenty years. The duration of leases or quasi-leases was very various. Leases for life or lives, or for thirty years or even more, were by no means unknown, but shorter terms were commoner still. On the Whitby estate in the 1390s most lettings were for three, six, nine, or twelve years and, in the second half of the fourteenth century, customary holdings at Yeadon were conceded for terms which ranged from three years to life. By the third quarter of the fifteenth century, however, virtually all Yeadon lettings were for ten years, as the leases of the Blackburnshire vaccaries had been in 1417. By the end of the fifteenth century, on the other hand, the term for Blackburnshire leases was creeping up to twenty years, although it was still a real concession to the tenants when Henry VII in 1507 decreed that henceforth the vaccaries might be held by copyhold for life or lives. At the same time, of course, the finality of even shorter terms should not be exaggerated, since leases could be renewed and their provisions varied in order to enable sons to become co-tenants with their fathers. Such arrangements on the Fountains estate enabled the Todds to keep their hands on Halton Gill from 1457 to the Dissolution, save for a 12-year gap when a Todd widow took it temporarily to a second husband; and the Bucks similarly retained possession of a moiety of Darnbrook House even though they subdivided it still further between members of the family. Customary tenants at Yeadon achieved continuity of tenure by similar devices, renewing their 10-year leases as they expired (as no less than nine of them did in 1472), or by a father surrendering his holding to his son, a surrender that would become effective after the father's death.[18]

Tenurial distinctions, in other words, were becoming increasingly blurred, a tendency furthered by the fact that many individuals held land by a variety of titles. At Oulton (Yorks.), for instance, Richard Batell had an acre of freehold, $1\frac{1}{2}$ acres of leasehold and a bond oxgang, and at Wawne the four demesne lessees were also tenants of customary arable and meadow. Further, the conditions under which customary

---

[18] *Three Lancs. Documents*, ed. Harland, p. 108; *Memorials of Fountains*, III, ed. J. T. Fowler, p. 244; PRO SC 6/1085/18; Ashcroft, 'Snape account rolls', p. 33; PRO DL 29/76/1498, 1500; *Cartularium Abbathiae de Whitby*, ed. J. C. Atkinson, II, pp. 559–63; Cunliffe Shaw, *Royal Forest of Lancaster*, pp. 256, 474–5; *Fountains Abbey Lease Book*, ed. Michelmore, nos. 33, 57; *Court Rolls of Yeadon*, ed. Price, *passim* and pp. 153, 188–9.

and leasehold tenants held land were often broadly similar: thus, in Lancashire, both were under an equal obligation to keep houses, fences, barns and even a turf-cote in good repair. What probably mattered in practice was not so much how a man held his land, but rather the common estimate of his substance and standing. That is the sort of impression which is conveyed by the witness lists of many fifteenth-century charters, which go far to suggest that all villagers of any consequence, save for the occasional esquire or gentleman, might be subsumed under the titles of yeomen or husbandmen.[19]

Yeomen and husbandmen, of course, do not in fact exhaust the ranks of villagers. In 1379, 4 per cent of West Riding taxpayers were servants. Many of them were doubtless domestics, but others were probably servants in husbandry who often lived in the households of their employers, like the four menservants called "hynes" for whom the keeper of the Fountains grange at Haddockstones had to find bed and board. Besides such full-time workers, however, there were clearly others who took employment on a less continuous basis, and both seem clearly to have been scarcer in the circumstances prevailing in the generations after 1349. These same circumstances encouraged a greater mobility on the part of labourers seeking better wages, something already evident in the Wakefield townships in June 1352 when seventeen men and women were reported as having "gone away against the ordinance"; and the ruling at Stainburn (Yorks.) that *operarii* ought first to work for wages for the lord, and then for the tenants of the manor if they needed workers, was doubtless no more effective than national legislation in preventing movement. Lords themselves often cast their net widely to get servants, as the prior of Watton seems to have done in 1370 when he had in his service at Watton men from the surrounding villages of Kilnwick, Cranswick and Rotsea. Doubtless, too, one result of competition for labour was payment by some employers of wages higher than the law prescribed, something which in turn might encourage still greater labour mobility.[20]

Not all villagers, furthermore, relied solely upon agriculture for their livelihood. Woollen manufacture was established in Blackburnshire by the fifteenth century, even though it had not yet developed far, and

[19] *Miscellanea*, VII, Thoresby Soc., XXIV, 1919, pp. 295–9; BL Egerton Ms. 1141, ff.183d–8; *Court Rolls of the Honour of Clitheroe*, ed. Farrer, I, pp. 2, 4–5, 7; *York. Deeds*, IV, nos. 391–2.

[20] The 1379 poll-tax returns for the West Riding are in *Yorks. Arch. J.*, V–VII, 1879–82; for labourers: *Fountains Abbey Lease Book*, ed. Michelmore, no. 227; BL Add. Ms. 40010, f.7d; PRO DL 30/128/1925; *Wakefield Court Rolls, 1350–1352*, ed. Habberjam et al., pp. 91–2; *Notes on the Religious and Secular Houses of Yorkshire*, ed. W. P. Baildon, II, Yorks. Arch. Soc. Rec. Ser. LXXXI, 1931, p. 50.

village craftsmen were a significant element among West Riding taxpayers in 1379. Even in the early 1350s there were ironworkers, coalminers and clothworkers in the townships of the manor of Wakefield; iron smelting, as well as cloth-making, continued to be much in evidence in the countryside around Leeds, Wakefield, and Bradford, as well as around Sheffield and Rotherham; and at Kippax in 1399 "sea-coal pits" paid rents totalling 46s. annually. The textile industry in the fifteenth century developed westwards around Halifax and Huddersfield, and to the north there may have been some expansion of mining, for royalties from the Arkengarthdale lead mines were leased for as much as £20 yearly at the opening of the sixteenth century. At least in some parts, therefore, there were growing opportunities for farmer-craftsmen and for countryfolk to acquire skills which could be put to urban use. This may have been true of those Bradford villeins who were said in 1360 to have made their way to Pontefract, Selby, and York.[21]

The majority of countrymen, however, continued to get their living from the land and even village craftsmen were often part-time farmers. How land was distributed amongst them is not easily determined from the surviving records: they seldom deal with all the land in a village, they use customary measures of doubtful and varying dimensions, and they rarely indicate the ways in which sub-tenancies distort the picture they present. At least in Yorkshire, on the other hand, there is some evidence to suggest that the spread of arable holdings did not differ significantly in essentials from what it had been before 1349. At Barwick-in-Elmet, Scholes, and Rothwell in 1425, for instance, nearly one-third of holdings were in the 10–30 acre range, nearly half were under 10 acres, and less than a fifth were over 30 acres. These proportions cannot be taken as typical, but there are many signs that middling and smallholding farmers were still the characteristic villagers. There is, at the same time, some evidence for a reduction of the number of tenants with the very smallest holdings. At Salton (Yorks.), only seventeen dwellings survived on thirty-nine cotlands; and in the same county, at Brawby, five cottages were waste and in the hands of tenants of oxgangs, at Bowes in 1436 three cottages were waste and three more were at least temporarily in the hands of the lord, and at West Gilling vacant cottages accounted for a large part of the "decayed" rents. Possibly an increasing proportion of cottage holdings were being occupied by the widows or other dependants of the more substantial

[21] Above, p. 52; *VCH Lancs.*, II, pp. 295–6; *Wakefield Court Rolls, 1350–1352*, ed. Habberjam et al., pp. 75, 81, 96; PRO DL 29/507/8229; Faull and Moorhouse, eds., *West Yorkshire*, III, pp. 592–3, 775–80; R. Fieldhouse and B. Jennings, *A History of Richmond and Swaledale*, London, 1978, p. 63.

tenants: thus, at East Heslerton (Yorks.) in 1369, two tenants each with two oxgangs also held additional cottages, and eight out of the fourteen cottages were held by women.[22]

If smallholdings apparently became less numerous, there were still opportunities for tenants to acquire more land, and sometimes much more land, at a time when landlords were only too anxious to welcome offers for tenancies and when demesne lands were being let. In these circumstances tenants had to be allowed a good deal of freedom to deal in the land market, provided at least that their dealings took place through the manorial court. One consequence was that some customary holdings disintegrated, as Walkeroxgang at Rothwell had done by 1425 into twelve fragments, many of them enlarging other holdings. There was also some accumulation of standard holdings. A modest instance can be seen at Cridling, where earlier a dozen tenants (with one exception) had each held one oxgang or less: by 1425 the number of tenants had been reduced to eight, of whom five had between $1\frac{1}{4}$ and 2 oxgangs each. Some accumulators went a good deal further. At Yeadon (Yorks.) by 1440 Robert de Yedon and his son held three and two oxgangs respectively, and in 1445 they arranged through the manor court that their combined holdings should pass to the son after Robert's death. Another tenant, at Chatburn (Lancs.), constructed a fair-sized farm out of more miscellaneous constituents, for there, in 1496, Nicholas Robinson left to his heir the tenancy of a messuage and garden, an acre of waste, $20\frac{1}{2}$ acres of arable, 4 tofts, 14 acres of arable and meadow, half an acre of demesne arable and a small assart. Nicholas Robinson looks like a man who had exploited the land market astutely, but plague mortality might also be some men's opportunity. At Woodhouse (Yorks.) in 1399 ten oxgangs, "formerly in the hands of bond tenants, now dead", had been demised to a single tenant.[23]

By one means or another some quite considerable agricultural holdings were constructed during the late middle ages. Some demesne leases may have had the effect of creating new, intermediate lordships, like the leases of Lancashire vaccaries to Sir John Biron in 1422 or, later in the century, to the busy duchy official, William Leyland. Lessees of this standing normally sublet their acquisitions to one or more husbandmen.[24] Many of the men who took up or accumulated substantial holdings, however, did so in order to cultivate all or much

[22] *Miscellanea*, VII, Thoresby Soc., pp. 287–92 and IX, pp. 238–54; *Priory of Hexham*, ed. Raine, II, pp. 75, 77; PRO SC 6/1085/18; *Yorks. Deeds*, II, no. 183.

[23] *Miscellanea*, VII, Thoresby Soc., pp. 288–9; PRO DL 42/106, ff.50d–1d, DL 29/507/8229; *Court Rolls of Yeadon*, ed. Price, pp. 145, 153; *Court Rolls of the Honour of Clitheroe*, ed. Farrer, I, p. 16.

[24] PRO DL 29/76/1498; Cunliffe Shaw, *Royal Forest of Lancaster*, pp. 471, 489–90.

of them; and, especially in the case of demesne leaseholders, they might be assisted to embark on operations on this scale by the willingness of some landlords to provide part of the working capital. When John Bacon, for example, took over the Sewerby demesne in 1377, he received the carts, ploughs, livestock, and other equipment with the land; and the lessees of part of Thorp grange got from Selby abbey seed corn, implements, two cows, and two carts. Not all of the larger agricultural units which appeared in the late middle ages survived intact. Robert Wood used his holding of $7\frac{1}{2}$ messuages and 66 forest acres (each of four statute acres) in Knaresborough Forest to provide for four grandchildren; but Ralph Pollan passed on his little estate of 13 messuages and 100 forest acres to his son. Many of the families which leased the Fountains dairy farms, like the Todds at Halton Gill or the Beckwiths at Swinton, remained in possession over several generations; and some of the husbandmen who took over the Blackburnshire vaccaries, like the Harleys of Wycollar, fathered yeoman families.[25]

Only very occasionally is it possible to invest our knowledge of tenant farms with much in the way of detail, although one exception to that rule has been more than once mentioned. The fact that Thomas de Westhorpe fell foul of the law in 1366 has preserved more information about his farming than is commonly available. He had nearly 240 acres under grain crops on the north side of the Vale of Pickering; he was a sheep farmer on a larger scale than Whitby or Meaux abbey at that time; he had a herd of 152 cows as well as calves and store oxen, and 135 pigs of various sorts. He was, in other words, a mixed farmer evidently producing mainly for the market, and indeed it is known that he sold both his own wool and wool he collected from others to merchants of York or Beverley. Information of this sort, however, is quite unusual and all too often all that is known is the size of a tenant's arable holding. Some arable farming, of course, was carried on by most tenant farmers. Even the keeper of the Fountains "dairyhouse" at Lofthouse, in the upper reaches of Nidderdale, enjoyed as part of his perquisites "all such corn as groweth within the bounds of the said grounds", and arable was doubtless much more prominent in less hilly districts. The needs of arable farming may explain the willingness of Snape tenants to pay their lord around 10s. per head for oxen, although at Wetwang in the wolds the arable husbandry of both lord and tenants seems to have relied solely on horses. Debt litigation involving small amounts of grain also suggests the existence of a local market for small arable surpluses as well as the

[25] *Yorks. Deeds*, VI, no. 422; G. S. Haslop, 'The abbot of Selby's financial statement, 1348', *Yorks. Arch. J.*, XLIV, 1972, pp. 166–7; Jennings, ed., *History of Nidderdale*, pp. 92–3; *Fountains Abbey Lease Book*, ed. Michelmore, no. 152.

wider markets that were available to men farming on the scale of Thomas de Westhorpe; but the Yeadon tenant with $2\frac{3}{4}$ acres under rye and 9 acres under oats in 1365 is unlikely to have had more than the most modest of surpluses for sale.[26]

This same Yeadon tenant, on the other hand, was not only a cereal grower, for he also had a pair of horses (presumably his draught animals) and two cows; and at Brandwood in Castleton (Lancs.) in the early sixteenth century arable land was only about 38 per cent of tenant holdings. Throughout Yorkshire and Lancashire livestock represented some part of the resources of tenants and sometimes was their principal resource. The tithes paid from Whitgift and Reedness in the Humberhead lowlands point to tenants there with 1,000 lambs, 300 young pigs and enough hens to lay 12,000 eggs; and court rolls everywhere are full of references to straying beasts belonging to manorial tenantry, to unringed pigs, and sometimes to troublesome geese that had to be barred from arable and meadow during the growing season. Individual flocks and herds were probably usually small, but some were large enough to have real commercial significance. The grange keeper at Haddockstones, close to Fountains abbey, was allowed grazing for two horses for harrowing and three pigs for his own larder, but also for a mare and a foal, eight cows and their calves, and forty ewes and their lambs. In Lancashire, too, in the fifteenth century there were men overcharging Burnley common with 40 sheep, or Padiham common with 80 sheep and 30 cattle, or Ightenhill common with 60 cattle. More typically, at Yeadon in the 1390s, John de Yedon had 11 straying pigs as well as geese and sheep, Adam Walker had 4 heifers and 3 cows with their calves, and John Pye had 6 cows and 8 other beasts; later, in the mid-fifteenth century, John Pykard's strays numbered 40 sheep, 4 bullocks, 5 heifers and 2 horses, and a year later he had at least 80 sheep. Many of these flocks and herds were clearly not mainly designed, like the keeper's pigs at Haddockstone, as provision for their owner's larder; and the rule that dwellers in the townships of Knaresborough Forest might have eight pigs or more going in the forest suggests that some pigs might even be bred for sale.[27]

Rights to and in land, of course, whether for livestock or for arable

---

[26] Above, p. 190; Waites, 'A Yorkshire farmer in the memoranda rolls', pp. 445–6; *Fountains Abbey Lease Book*, ed. Michelmore, p. 295; Ashcroft, 'Snape account rolls', p. 44; PRO SC 6/1144/10; *Court Rolls of Yeadon*, ed. Price, p. 20.

[27] *Coucher Book of Whalley Abbey*, ed. W. A. Hulton, Chetham Soc., os xx, 1849, IV, pp. 1128–31; *Miscellanea*, VI, ed. C. E. Whiting, Yorks. Arch. Soc. Rec. Ser., CXVIII, 1953, pp. 47–52; *Fountains Abbey Lease Book*, ed. Michelmore, nos. 227, 275; *Court Rolls of the Honour of Clitheroe*, ed. Farrer, II, pp. 4, 12; *Court Rolls of Yeadon*, ed. Price, pp. 98, 177, 181; PRO DL 30/128/1915.

farming, had to be paid for, but on the whole the terms on which land was let were becoming more favourable to the tenant. Lords did their best to preserve antique obligations, like the requirement that one customary tenant at Flaxton (Yorks.) should provide for the prior of Hexham and his *familia*, when they came to the village, a "competent" chamber, candles, straw for their beds, and hay for their horses, although there is nothing to tell us how often this service was demanded. An equal concern was shown, however, to register the modest labour services which were the norm in northern England. In Lancashire the claim to a few boon services was carefully recorded well into the fifteenth century at Dilworth, Speke, and Ashton-under-Lyne. In Yorkshire, too, the ploughing, hay, and harvest boons owed in principle on the manors of the honour of Pontefract were no less carefully recorded in 1425, and thirty years earlier two men were amerced at Yeadon for failing to perform their harvest boons.[28] At Cockerham (Lancs.), on the other hand, the boon services set out in the 1326 custumal were omitted from the customs of 1483, although the memory of them is probably preserved in the provision that a tenant "warnt to do the lord servys for his place…sall com the same day that he hys warnt, or ells on the morn, payn ijs.". In Yorkshire, too, the Tinsley boon-works were mostly commuted by 1374; at Rothwell they were said to have been "anciently farmed" in 1357; and at Carlton in 1485 the rent and the value of the works for each holding were combined into a single figure. The conversion of works into cash payments might at first be concessionary and temporary. Thus at Beverley and Bishop Wilton in 1352 the works due were being "sold" on an annual basis; but in fact they were all "sold", a practice hardening into a custom. Land, more and more, was coming to be held almost exclusively for cash.[29]

To this rule there is a partial exception in the terms on which some demesnes were leased. The lessee of Wawne, for instance, had to pay annually to Meaux abbey 10 qr wheat, 40 qr drage, 20 qr oats, 8 pigs, 12 capons, 12 geese and 3 cartloads of straw, thus preserving for the monks some of the returns they might have expected when they had the grange in hand. Fifteenth-century leases of the Fountains dairy farms also looked to returns in kind: Lofthouse *logia*, for example, was let in 1454 with its 40 cows for an annual livery of stirks, cheese and butter

---

[28] *Priory of Hexham*, ed. Raine, II, pp. 80–1; *Cal. of Deeds and Papers in the Possession of Sir James de Hoghton*, ed. J. H. Lumby, Lancs. and Cheshire Rec. Soc., LXXXVIII, 1936, no. 506; *Three Lancs. Documents*, ed. Harland, pp. 94–5; *Cal. of Norris Deeds*, ed. J. H. Lumby, Lancs. and Cheshire Rec. Soc., XCIII, 1939, no. 75; PRO DL 42/106, *passim*; *Court Rolls of Yeadon*, ed. Price, p. 100.

[29] 'Two custumals of the manor of Cockerham', ed. France, pp. 44, 51; D. Postles, 'Tinsley "rentals", 1336–1514', *Yorks. Arch. J.*, LI, 1979, pp. 52–3, 57; PRO DL 29/507/8226, 511/8265; SC 6/1144/7.

according to the custom of the dale. That custom prescribed that the Lofthouse lessee should hand over each year one stirk for every two of the abbey's cows in his charge, 28 stones of butter and 56 stones of cheese.[30]

Straightforward money rents, however, were commoner than this sort of arrangement. How accurately they reflected the economic value of holdings is not easily determined. In the case of some freeholdings clearly they did not do so: at West Rounton (Yorks.) two oxgangs were held freely for knight service and 3s. 4d. yearly, but a like tenement held by a tenant at will paid 16s. 4d. Some leaseholders and customary tenants, too, apparently held on beneficial terms. The lessees of Lancashire vaccaries who then sublet them doubtless did not do so at a loss, and certainly the customary rent of 6d. a forest acre in Knaresborough Forest enabled tenants to sublet at a profit. Many rents, on the other hand, do appear to have responded to market forces; and especially in Yorkshire a reduced demand for land exercised a depressing influence on rents. At Scalby, for instance, one oxgang was let in 1400 for 5s. 6d. a year, but another similarly let in 1401 brought in only 5s. The old uniformity of customary rents was breaking down, and in many places there was something like a general downward trend. At Yeadon in 1365 three holdings which had been in the lord's hand for over two years could only be relet by cutting their rents by nearly a quarter; and among the properties dependant upon Bowes Castle in 1436 the farms paid by Kexwith, Easthorpe, and Eskerleth vaccaries had all been steeply reduced. It was the same in somewhat less remote places, for the rents paid for arable oxgangs had been cut at Forcett and Gilling, near Richmond; and at Danby Wiske near Northallerton the rent per acre of land "in the further part of the field" had fallen from 6d. to $4\frac{1}{2}$d., while the rents for demesne arable and meadow had been more than halved. In these places rents for customary land had fallen by around 35 per cent from their levels in 1299, and those for "foreland" (more marginal assart land) by over 50 per cent. On the other hand, at least in some townships, the downward movement may have been checked by around the mid-fifteenth century, giving way to a period of stability. At Yeadon, for instance, the rent paid for an enclosed holding called Norcroft fell from 26s. 8d. in 1370 to 25s. in 1390 and then to 20s. by 1443, but thereafter it seems (like other holdings in the manor) to have been let at each change of occupancy at the "customary rent".[31]

[30] BL Egerton Ms. 1141, f.183d; *Memorials of Fountains*, III, ed. Fowler, p. 244; *Fountains Abbey Rental of 1495–1496*, ed. Michelmore, Leeds, 1974, p. 7.

[31] *Yorks. Deeds*, II, no. 421; PRO DL 30/128/1925, SC 6/1085/18; *Court Rolls of Yeadon*, ed. Price, pp. 11, 96, 150, 175, 230; *Yorkshire Inquisitions*, II, ed. W. Brown, Yorks. Arch. Soc. Rec. Ser. XXIII, 1898, no. 32.

Other payments were due from tenants in addition to rents. Free tenants paid relief on succeeding to their inheritances, often fixed at double the annual rent; but the entry fines paid by customary or leasehold tenants at the commencement or renewal of their tenancies were usually assumed to be negotiable. Generally, however, fines do not appear to have been excessively high. A Burnley man did pay £3 6s. 8d. (about three times the annual rent) for an enclosed farm and £4 was paid for a somewhat larger farm at Haslington, but enclosed properties of this sort were perhaps especially desirable. By contrast the fines for 71 acres at Huncotes and for 2½ oxgangs at Pendleton were only 3s. 4d. In Yorkshire, too, a Worsborough heiress paid a fine of 13s. 4d. for an oxgang, less than its annual rent, and at Scalby some oxgangs passed from one tenant to another for as little as 6d. Some entry fines were pardoned or reduced to nominal sums to secure tenants for holdings which had been for some time in the lord's hand, or because rents had been modestly raised, or because the incoming tenant agreed to repair the buildings on the holding. Other theoretically negotiable fines fell under the sway of custom and became fines certain. An entry fine of 20d. was paid in 1469 for a tenancy in Fulwood (Yorks.) held for an annual rent of 5s. 10d. Thereafter it passed for the same fine from heir to heir until, in 1594, 20d. was said to be "according to the ancient custom".[32]

Custom, of course, could preserve as well as limit obligations. It had been a common rule that, when a customary tenant died, heriot was due: his best beast in the townships of Knaresborough Forest, 20s. if he had held an oxgang at Thorner, his second-best beast at Ashton-under-Lyne (the best went to "holy kirk"). At Cockerham, however, where the best beast had been owed in 1326, this obligation was not mentioned in the 1483 customs: it looks as though the charge had been abandoned. Similarly, the customary right of some Lancashire lords to receive a share of the goods of their dead *nativi* was also being modified: at Chatburn by 1425 the family could buy off this right and at Woolton some families were able to compound by doubling their rent in the year a tenant died. The traditional obligation of tenants to keep in repair or even to provide the buildings on their holdings may sometimes have proved more onerous, but in this connection too passive resistance by tenants produced concessions. On composite holdings it was often tacitly accepted that not all buildings should be

[32] *Court Rolls of the Honour of Clitheroe*, ed. Farrer, I, p. 18; II, p. 6; III, pp. 1–3; *Chartularies of the Priory of Monk Bretton*, ed. J. W. Walker, nos. 423–30; PRO DL 30/128/1925; *Court Rolls of Yeadon*, ed. Price, pp. 39, 135, 141; T. W. Hall, *Descriptive Catalogue of Sheffield Manorial Records*, I, pp. 24, 154–5.

preserved, so that when Adam Walker took up two messuages and two oxgangs at Yeadon in 1368 he was required to provide one new dwelling only. Increasingly, too, tenants were helped by grants of timber or of thatching straw or even of money to carry out necessary repairs.[33]

Other traditional charges of a more personal character were being similarly modified. In Knaresborough Forest customary tenants still owed tallage in the fifteenth century, but the rate was fixed and not very onerous by 1380, and it had been further reduced before 1426 *de gratia regis et regine*. Merchet was still payable when a villein woman married at Ackworth in 1425 and at Worsborough in 1432, and the bond tenants of the honour of Pontefract in 1425 had to fine for a son to be tonsured or if a daughter was discovered in fornication. Merchet, however, disappeared in Knaresborough Forest in the fifteenth century and everywhere these remnants of an older servility were falling into desuetude. Even in the 1350s the abbot of Meaux seemed to be fighting a losing battle when he tried to insist that his *nativi* at Wawne and Beeford were born to the yoke of servitude.[34] A few seigneurial rights did prove rather more enduring, and especially the right of lords to insist that their tenants used (and paid for using) monopolies like mills and ovens. There were still appreciable receipts from these sources at Snape in the 1450s; and at Cockerham in 1485 tenants who used an "out-mill" incurred a fine. When they used the lord's mill they paid a sixteenth of the grain milled if it was of their own growing, but only a twentieth if it had been "bought without the lordship". In many places, however, income from mills fell markedly and some mills were derelict, while common ovens were probably even more vulnerable. That at Lytham, which in 1400 had produced an annual revenue of 4s. 8d., was overblown with sand a century later.[35]

Medieval countrymen, of course, were family men as well as tenants and many of the affairs of families also continued to be governed by customary rules inherited from the past. These rules, among other things, prescribed the rights of a surviving widow in her husband's

[33] PRO DL 30/128/1915; *Miscellanea*, v, Thoresby Soc., xv, 1909, p. 166; *Three Lancs. Documents*, ed. Harland, pp. 94–5; 'Two custumals of the manor of Cockerham', ed. France, p. 44; *Court Rolls of the Honour of Clitheroe*, ed. Farrer, i, pp. 11–12; *Cal. of Norris Deeds*, ed. Lumby, no. 674; *Court Rolls of Yeadon*, ed. Price, pp. 24, 62, 96, 107–8.

[34] PRO DL 29/465/7604, 465/7607, 507/8228, DL 42/106, ff.19, 42; *Chartularies of the Priory of Monk Bretton*, ed. Walker, no. 423; Jennings, *History of Nidderdale*, p. 55; *Miscellanea*, vii, Thoresby Soc., pp. 12–13; *Chronica Monasterii de Melsa*, ed. Bond, iii, pp. 126–33, 141–2.

[35] Ashcroft, 'Snape account rolls', p. 34; 'Two custumals of the manor of Cockerham', ed. France, p. 51; *Priory of Hexham*, ed. Raine, ii, p. 144; H. Fishwick, *History of the Parish of Lytham*, Chetham Soc., NS LX, 1907, pp. 85, 90–1.

holding: in a few places she was entitled to continue in occupation of the whole of it, but more commonly her share was one-third, although only one-quarter at Colne and in a few other Lancashire townships. Widows had similar rights in leaseholds on the Fountains estate, their portion sometimes being half the holding. It was also a common, but not a universal, rule that the widow's entitlement lapsed if she remarried.[36] Ultimately, however, it was assumed that a man's free or customary holding would pass to his heir or heirs by blood, and powerful influences were at work making many leaseholds heritable in fact. Who the heir by blood was depended upon circumstances: sometimes a brother was next in line, once an aunt made good a claim to be her nephew's heir, and Jennett Clerke of Ightenhill claimed to be heiress to her father's sister's son. The accepted norm, on the other hand, was succession by the oldest surviving son; but if male heirs failed the holding was generally divided between daughters, although at Hemingbrough (Yorks.) the claim of the oldest daughter was preferred. Family arrangements might both buttress or modify these expectations. Some fathers transferred inheritances in their lifetime, thus smoothing the way of the heir, or added sons to their leases, thus turning holdings for a term effectively into hereditaments. Others detached some part of their land to provide for children other than the heir: this was probably the intention of Nicholas del Bothe of Colne in surrendering a messuage and 30 acres of "rodeland" to one (presumably his eldest) son and half a messuage and 15 acres to each of two other sons.[37]

That particular arrangement in fact broke down, but had it been implemented the outcome would have been similar to that arising from a custom of partible inheritance. Clear evidence for such a custom is anything but plentiful, but it does appear to have prevailed on the Rievaulx lands in Swaledale in the sixteenth century, and the joint tenure of Booze vaccary by five members of the Colyns family in 1436 may indicate its prevalence in this district at an earlier date. There may also be indications of its existence in those places in Lancashire where tenancies were in the hands of a number of representatives of a small group of families, like the four branches of the Plombe family holding at Garston in 1468, or the six Ashworths, four Brierleys, three Warlands and three Schofields among the twenty-eight Brandwood tenants in the 1530s. The fact that Nicholas Bothe had to make special

[36] *Court Rolls of the Honour of Clitheroe*, ed. Farrer, I, pp. 16, 24, 223–6; III, p. 4; *Fountains Abbey Lease Book*, ed. Michelmore, p. lxxiv.

[37] *Chartularies of the Priory of Monk Bretton*, ed. Walker, no. 423; *Court Rolls of the Honour of Clitheroe*, ed. Farrer, I, pp. 220–1; II, pp. 6, 8; *Yorks. Deeds*, X, no. 260; *Cal. of Norris Deeds*, ed. Lumby, no. 678; T. W. Hall, *Sheffield Manorial Records*, I, pp. 12, 24, 61.

provision for his younger sons at Colne, however, may suggest the possibility that partible inheritance was a custom only coming into being in the late middle ages in areas where land and grazing were in plentiful supply, as the great cattle farms of the landlords were released to tenants.[38]

At the same time, despite the strength of the hereditary principle, there does seem to have been some weakening of the ties between particular families and particular holdings, especially in the two or three generations after 1349. The Tanshelf rental of 1425, for instance, records the "previous" as well as the current holders of tenements, and sometimes also the predecessors of the "previous" tenants. The time scale involved is not absolutely clear; but, since some of the "previous" tenants were the fathers of the tenants in 1425, it cannot be excessively long. This information suggests that only about one in five of the 1425 tenants had secured their holdings by succession, and that only about one in eight of the "previous" tenants were certainly the heirs by blood of their predecessors. There are similar apparent discontinuities on other manors of the honour of Pontefract, which suggest that, when every allowance is made for the deficiencies of rentals as evidence for the descent of holdings, tenements passed relatively frequently out of the hands of the families which held them.[39]

One reason may have been high levels of mortality. At Wakefield the immediate effects of plague in 1349 were clear enough: for some holdings no claimant appeared and, even when an heir was found, he or she was often more remote than had been usual earlier. In 1331–3, 87 per cent of heirs taking up customary holdings had been the sons or daughters of the previous tenants. That proportion fell to 52 per cent in 1349–50 and to 58 per cent in 1350–2. At Tanshelf, on the other hand, there were Rayners, Bubwiths, Bennets and Silkstones holding both in 1425 and earlier, but different holdings were involved. One explanation may be that, with land in easier supply, young men were able to obtain a holding before the time came for them to succeed to their patrimony. Some heirs might then combine their inheritance with their earlier acquisitions, as the Yedon family seems to have intended in 1445. William Watson, however, exchanged the oxgang on which he was already settled at Yeadon for his father's two oxgangs as the latter grew old; while others, perhaps content with what they had, may have allowed the family holding to pass to someone else. The hereditary principle was strongly entrenched in rural custom, but in fact the link between heir and inheritance seems often to have been

---

[38] Fieldhouse and Jennings, *History of Richmond and Swaledale*, pp. 60–2; PRO SC 6/1085/18; *Cal. of Norris Deeds*, ed. Lumby, no. 223; *Coucher Book of Whalley Abbey*, ed. Hulton, IV, pp. 1128–31. [39] PRO DL 42/106, ff.11–15.

weakened during the late middle ages even though, towards the end of the fifteenth century, there are some signs that this link was once more gaining strength.[40]

There may have been during the later middle ages some widening of the social divisions between labourers grasping for higher rewards, husbandmen with their smallish or middling holdings and their modest flocks and herds, and the minority of ruthless entrepreneurs who seized the opportunities offered by the greater availability of land to let, its falling price, and the existence of markets to be conquered as the demesnes of landlords ceased to supply them. The solidarity of families, as well as social tensions, might threaten the peace of communities. This appears to have been the case at Yeadon in 1452 when at least two Watsons and two Walkers on the one hand, and three Rawdons on the other, were involved in a complicated series of interlocking affrays. There were, on the other, also many influences making for cohesion in townships where much land lay in intermixed holdings in common fields and much grazing was on common land. Cohesion might go so far as to permit a group of tenants at Ovenden (Yorks.) in 1483 (including "all ther childer that are waxyn and comyn to aghe") to reach a formal agreement to redistribute lands in the town field and to embody that agreement in writing; but in a more routine and continuous way villagers had to accept common responsibilities and to eschew anti-social behaviour. Each had to share in fencing the arable and meadows in the growing season; each helped to make the common way from the common pasture to the township; no-one was to keep pigs unringed or allow stock to stray onto the corn fields or the hay meadow; and between February and the end of harvest the movement of geese was strictly controlled. In such matters individual and family interests had to be accommodated to the interests of the community.[41]

Accommodation, of course, might involve strain, which was one reason for laying down formally the rules to achieve it. These rules sometimes took the form of by-laws enforced by, and probably promulgated by, the manorial court, a source which enabled regulations favouring the interests of landlords (as in the Cockerham customs of 1326) to be embodied in them. The Yeadon by-laws, however, were also concerned with villagers who assaulted each other or called each other outrageous names, and with men who made enclosures in the common fields to the detriment of the common rights of their

[40] Entries in the Wakefield court rolls for 1349–50 (ed. Jewell) and 1350–2 (eds. Habberjam et al.) compared with those in Wakefield Court Rolls, 1331–1333, ed. S. S. Walker, Yorks. Arch. Soc., Leeds, 1983; also Court Rolls of Yeadon, ed. Price, pp. 149, 153.

[41] Ibid., pp. 164–5; Yorks. Deeds, VII, no. 442; Court Rolls of the Honour of Clitheroe, ed. Farrer, I, pp. 7–13; BL Add. Ms. 40010, ff.15, 23d, 28–8d, 34.

neighbours. Not only that, but four keepers of the by-law were appointed by the manor court, who reported infractions of it, and sometimes penalties incurred by stock which strayed contrary to the by-law were apparently shared between the lord and the landholders who had suffered damage. Similar regulations in some of the townships of the Fountains estate emphasize their communal character even more clearly. They were called *statuta plebescite* and belonged to a category of *ordinaciones communes vicinorum*. The lord got a share of the penalties for breaches of them, but the major part went to the "reeve of the plebiscite". At Litton the plebiscite was held on Saturdays and absence incurred a fine. These meetings appear to be distinct from meetings of the manor court and at Aldfield, among other things, they determined the wages of the "common shepherd" to which every tenant contributed. These arrangements may have been exceptional, but at least they illustrate a capacity for common action amongst neighbours. That communal capacity, as well as the force of lordship and the bonds of family, provide a part of the framework within which the farmers of the later middle ages cultivated their land.[42] There is nothing to suggest, of course, that this capacity was something new; for "non-manorial gatherings of villagers" in west Yorkshire seem to be implied by references to "the community of the plebiscite" and the consideration "of the whole bylaw" (or perhaps more accurately *byrlaw*) in Wakefield court rolls at the end of the thirteenth century. It was, on the other hand, a capacity likely to have been strengthened by some weakening of the power of landlords in the circumstances of the late middle ages.[43]

C. EASTERN ENGLAND

After 1349 eastern England still included some of the most populous parts of the country, but numbers remained smaller than they had been in the earlier fourteenth century, and fell rather than increased until at least the 1470s. The villages in Essex studied by L. R. Poos lost nearly half their inhabitants in the Black Death and, despite partial recovery between 1350 and 1380, experienced new disasters in the period 1380–1420; in 1500 their population was still only half what it had been in the 1340s. A more extreme case is that of Spalding (Lincs.), where

[42] *Ibid.*, ff.13, 23d, 31; Ault, 'Open-field husbandry and the village community', p. 34; *Court Rolls of Yeadon*, ed. Price, pp. 12, 62, 118–19, 124.

[43] W. O. Ault, 'Village assemblies in medieval England', *Album Helen Maud Cam*, I, Studies Presented to the International Commission for the History of Representative and Parliamentary Institutions, XXIII, Louvain, 1960, p. 16; and cf. G. C. Homans, *English Villagers of the Thirteenth Century*, Cambridge, Mass., 1942, p. 104.

the population in about 1485 seems to have been less than one-third of its level in 1287. Eastern ports without specialized industry, especially Lincoln, Boston, and Lynn, decayed with the decline in the population of their hinterlands. Most inland market towns lost trade and some disappeared altogether. Even some cloth-making towns, like Bury St Edmunds and Clare, remained smaller than they had been before the Black Death.[44] Until the early fifteenth century general contraction of population was partly offset by industrial growth in a few more fortunate centres. Colchester (Essex), Hadleigh (Suffolk), Norwich, and some smaller market towns grew as a result of the increased production of woollen cloth. Thaxted (Essex) had an expanding cutlery trade. But any resulting local increase in urban demand was insufficient to offset the effects of rural contraction. After the early fifteenth century migration into the towns slowed down and disease reduced the size even of towns which had so far been growing.[45] The contraction of population permitted some increases in consumption *per capita*, but this did not compensate for the smaller number of consumers. Grain output never recovered its early fourteenth-century level, and the production of wool and meat, though at times they enjoyed higher profits in response to rising demand, and sometimes offered a use for land which it was no longer profitable to plough, did not save the fortunes of demesne husbandry nor enable landlords to maintain the former level of rents (see below, p. 619).

Though the rising cost of labour obliged landlords to reduce their involvement in supplying local markets, the scope for commercial agriculture by peasant farmers was less adversely affected. Even where agricultural techniques were most complex, small farmers possessed as much technical knowledge as the administrators of manorial demesne lands; on some manors the lord's officers were regularly drawn from among the bond tenants. And though small farmers were themselves often dependent upon wage-labour, and so had an interest in the enforcement of the Statute of Labourers, their dependence was less than that of the great estates. They were prepared to work hard on their own holdings, harder than they would do on their lord's land, so that the tasks of manuring, weeding, harvesting, and carting, which cost lords

[44] PRO SC 6/840/15r, 16r (Dunmow, Essex); Britnell, *Growth and Decline in Colchester*, pp. 83–5, 190, 250–1; Campbell, 'Population pressure, inheritance and the land market', pp. 95–101; Davenport, *Norfolk Manor*, p. 105; R. S. Gottfried, *Bury St Edmunds and the Urban Crisis, 1290–1539*, p. 54; idem, *Epidemic Disease in Fifteenth-Century England*, p. 206; Hallam, 'Agrarian economy of south Lincolnshire', p. 94; W. O. Massingberd, 'Social and economic history', in *VCH Lincs.*, II, pp. 319–21; Newton, *Writtle*, pp. 17, 79–81; Platts, *Land and People*, pp. 218–29; Poos, 'The rural population of Essex', pp. 515–30.

[45] Britnell, *Growth and Decline in Colchester*, pp. 86–97, 193–205; Mate, 'Agrarian economy after the Black Death', p. 351; K. C. Newton, *Thaxted in the Fourteenth Century*, pp. 26–7.

more and more to have discharged, were more thoroughly performed on the properties of their tenants. For these reasons the advantages of smaller units rose relatively to those of large ones. The individual enterprise of which small farmers were capable is well illustrated by the royal manor of Havering, where, besides an exceptional freedom from seigneurial constraints, the tenants also had the advantage of proximity to London.[46]

Economic individualism in the countryside was facilitated in many parts of eastern England by the nature of pasturing and cropping arrangements. Normally, it is true, villagers had rights of common in some woodlands, heathlands, or marshes. Larger areas of natural pasture, like Tiptree Heath, Epping Forest (both in Essex), the Essex marshes and the fenland marshes, were intercommoned by men from several villages.[47] In this respect communal organization was as developed in eastern England as in the rest of the kingdom. Commoning on arable lands was also normal in many parts, especially within the large area of open-field farming in northern Lincolnshire. The pastoral regime of East Anglia allowed manorial lords to regulate the sheep flocks of their tenants. Even the East Anglian system, however, left plenty of scope for individuality in cropping routines. And in most of Essex and Suffolk and in parts of the fenlands common rights on arable land were few; here individual farmers managed their crop rotations and pasturing without reference to any overriding constraints of village organization (see pp. 201–2).

Areas with few or no common fields often had many ancient enclosures, and new enclosure in the fifteenth century accompanied both the accumulation of former tenements by wealthy individuals and the break-up of demesne lands for incorporation into tenant farms. Around Witham (Essex), where common fields were probably non-existent and enclosures numerous, the late middle ages brought little new. Sometimes, however, particularly from the 1450s, the reorganization of estates brought about the subdivision and enclosure of fields

---

[46] BL Add. Rolls 10508, 10510 (Snape, Suffolk); PRO SC 2/174/10, m.4r (Wickham Bishop), SC 11/489 (Little Walsingham); S. Andrews and L. J. Redstone, 'Suffolk courts in English', *Suffolk Inst. of Arch. and N.H.*, XXII, 1929, pp. 205, 206; Campbell, 'Arable productivity', pp. 397–8; *idem*, 'Agricultural progress in medieval England', pp. 37–40; B. Dodwell, 'Holdings and inheritance in medieval East Anglia', *EcHR*, 2nd ser. XX, 1967, p. 66; Hoare, *History of an East Anglian Soke*, p. 133; N. Kenyon, 'Labour conditions in Essex in the reign of Richard II', *EcHR*, IV, 1934; McIntosh, *Autonomy and Community*, pp. 136–78, 223–35; L. R. Poos, 'The social context of Statute of Labourers enforcement', *Law and History Review*, I, 1983, pp. 35–7.

[47] *A Terrier of Fleet, Lincs.*, ed. Neilson, pp. v–lviii and map by p. 214; H. C. Darby, *The Medieval Fenland*, pp. 67–73; W. R. Fisher, *The Forest of Essex*, London, 1887, pp. 274–6, 289; P. Morant, *The History and Antiquities of the County of Essex*, London, 1768, II, p. 141, note N; *VCH Essex*, I, pp. 369–71.

Table 7.1. *Estimated size of individual tenants' holdings on some manors of eastern England*

Location of manor	Number of tenants			
	under 10 ac.	10–30 ac.	30 ac. and over	unclassified
Great Leighs (Essex), mid-fifteenth century	21	8	5	3
Bawdsey (Suffolk), 1437–8	51	7	0	9
Hollesley (Suffolk), 1501	41	11	6	2
Gimingham (Norfolk), 1484–5	58	14	5	7
Little Walsingham (Norfolk), 1481–2	60	15	0	2
Chatteris (Cambs.), 1472	14	7	0	0
Knapwell (Cambs.), 1448–9[a]	3	4	11	0
Moulton (Lincs.), 1506[b]	23	5	23	0
Thoresby (Lincs.), mid-fifteenth century[c]	16	20	12	0
Waddington (Lincs.), 1491–2[c]	3	13	18	0

[a] "xl acre faciunt virgatam", noted at the head of the rental
[b] assuming 30 acres to the virgate
[c] assuming 15 acres to the bovate
Sources: Hoare, *History of an East Anglian Soke*, pp. 207–12; BL Add. Mss. 23949, ff.2r–19v, 28165, ff.5r–14v; PRO DL 43/3/8, DL 43/6/31, DL 43/6/35, DL 43/6/37; SC 11/91, SC 11/96.

and pastures formerly subject to common rights. On occasion, as at Malton in Orwell (Cambs.), this was in response to depopulation and the abandonment of land by tenant farmers. The reduced demand for land lowered the value of the older rights of common and made it easier for landlords to ignore them. Conversion of land to severalty for the benefit of individual tenants provoked little opposition where older common rights were no longer exercised.[48]

The advantages of smaller farming units were partly realized by the splitting up of former manorial demesnes. The leasing of demesnes increased from the 1350s until by 1400 this was the normal mode of management for large estates and many small ones. Even where direct demesne management lasted longer, beside towns or on good lines of communication, often some parcels were leased. At Grantchester

[48] Britnell, 'Agriculture in a region of ancient enclosure', pp. 42–4; Britnell, *Growth and Decline in Colchester*, pp. 255–6; B. M. S. Campbell, 'Population change and the genesis of common fields on a Norfolk manor', *EcHR*, 2nd ser. XXXIII, 1980, p. 190; *VCH Cambs.*, v, p. 245.

Table 7.2. *Estimated size of individual tenants' holdings on the manors of Mettingham College*

Location of Manor	under 10 ac.	10–30 ac.	30 ac. and over	unclassified
Suffolk				
Mettingham (1485–6)	59	15	4	0
Shipmeadow (1491)	22	9	1	0
Ilketshall (1482–3)	40	13	9	0
Bramfield (1478–9)	34	14	33	3
Mellis (1483–4)	26	11	6	2
Norfolk				
Howe Hall (1483–4)	39	14	4	0
Howe Boyland (1485)	21	9	1	2
Lyng (1481–2)	22	6	4	0
Hudeston in Bunwell (1482–3)	71	17	4	0
Raveningham with Norton Sutcourse (1483)	33	0	3	0

Source: BL Stowe Ms. 934.

(Cambs.) in the 1430s Henry Somer had 280–90 acres under seed each year, but in 1437 there were also 186 acres of demesne on lease to over forty tenants. Where such leases were for short terms the area of demesne cultivated by the lord and his servants fluctuated rapidly, as on the bishop of Ely's manor of Wisbech Barton (Cambs.). Demesne leases did not greatly affect manorial structures where a landlord's personal preference, or the nature of the demesne (fenland granges, for example) determined that lands should be leased in one or two large blocks. But many demesnes were broken up, and often lords leased out tenements which came into their hands for want of a tenant who would take them on the old terms, so that leasehold tenures became very numerous.[49] In the long run a large number of small leases was unsatisfactory to both landlords and tenants, since they implied uncertainty and administrative complexity. So after the rapid expansion of leasehold, especially between about 1390 and 1420, its importance waned; many leaseholds

[49] BL Harl. 144 (granges of Kirkstead Abbey); *Brandon Manor Account Roll, 1386–7*, trans. J. T. Munday (duplicated), Lakenheath, 1971; Britnell, *Growth and Decline in Colchester*, pp. 146–7, 252; Davenport, *Norfolk Manor*, pp. 51–3, 57, 76; Holmes, *Estates of the Higher Nobility*, p. 92; F. W. Maitland, 'The history of a Cambridgeshire Manor', *EHR*, IX, 1894, pp. 428, 432–3; Massingberd, in *VCH Lincs.*, II, pp. 317–18; J. F. Nichols, *Custodia Essexae*, London Univ. Ph.D. thesis, 1930, p. 301; Page, *Crowland Abbey*, pp. 114, 129, 154, 169, 438–40; L. F. Salzman, 'Social and economic history: medieval Cambridgeshire', *VCH Cambs.*, II, pp. 71–2; *VCH Cambs.*, IV, p. 224; V, pp. 10, 76, 92, 102, 152, 168, 191–2, 206; VI, pp. 119, 210, 268.

Table 7.3. *Tenants of bond tenements on Mettingham College's manor of Shipmeadow (Suffolk), 1491*

	In Shipmeadow manor			In Mettingham manor			In Ilketshall manor		
	bond ac.	copyhold ac.	free ac.	bond ac.	copyhold ac.	free ac.	bond ac.	copyhold ac.	free ac.
William Hyrde	$4\frac{5}{8}$	$9\frac{5}{8}$	$14\frac{3}{4}$	—	—	—	$1\frac{3}{4}$	—	1
William Bryggez	$3\frac{1}{4}$	8	$3\frac{1}{2}$	—	—	—	—	—	—
William Goldsmyth	$24\frac{3}{8}$	5	—	$1\frac{1}{3}$	—	$32\frac{1}{4}+$	5	—	—
Robert Fowler	7	$3\frac{1}{2}$	—	$\frac{1}{2}$	$3\frac{1}{4}$	—	$\frac{1}{2}$	—	—
Villata de Mettyngham	5	—	—	$3\frac{1}{2}$	8	—	—	—	—
Robert Girlyng	16	—	—	—	18	—	$\frac{1}{2}$	100	—
John Wode	?	?	1	—	—	—	—	—	—
William Bedyngfeld, rector of Shipmeadow	2	—	$\frac{1}{2}$	—	—	—	—	—	—
Richard Caryon	1	8	$7\frac{1}{4}$	—	—	—	—	—	—
Richard Cappe	—	5	—	—	—	—	—	—	—
Robert Turnour	$\frac{3}{4}$	—	—	—	$1\frac{1}{4}+$	—	—	—	—

Source: BL Stowe Ms. 934, ff.5r–42v. The dates of the three rentals are indicated in Table 7.2.

were converted to copyholds, feefarms, bond feefarms, or simply rent-paying tenures which no one presumed to define too closely.[50] Some manors, particularly in Lincolnshire, were wholly converted to hereditary tenures by 1500.

Not all tenants benefited from these opportunities. Smallholdings remained conspicuous in parts of eastern England as they were before 1350. In the Lincolnshire fenlands, despite heavy losses of population, evidence from Spalding (*c.* 1485), Holbeach (1476–9), and Gedney (*c.* 1460) suggests that 68 per cent of tenants held fewer than 5 acres from any one manor. In Spalding the percentage was as high as in the late thirteenth century. Estimates from other manorial rentals are shown in Tables 7.1 and 7.2 to illustrate the large proportion of families holding fewer than ten acres from a single manor. The implications of these figures are not exactly what they seem; tenants in East Anglia often held land from more than one manor (Table 7.3). Even allowing for this, though, the figures suggest marked differences between the more populous parts of the region (East Anglia, central Essex) where there were many smallholdings, and the less populated parts (Cambridgeshire, much of Lincolnshire) where tenures of 30 acres or more were more usual. One reason for this is that some soils were exceptionally

[50] BL Stowe 934, ff.99v (Lyng, Norfolk), 109r–128v (Hudeston in Bunwell, Norfolk), Add. Ms. 32948, ff.9v, 13r (Bawdsey, Suffolk); PRO SC 2/171/80, mm.16d, 17d (Feering); *The Sibton Abbey Estates*, ed. Denney, pp. 78, 81, 83, etc.; Davenport, *Norfolk Manor*, p. 57; *VCH Cambs.*, VI, p. 91.

fertile, and capable of being cultivated more intensively than those elsewhere. In parts of the region, too, the availability of employment in manufacturing was greater than in the midland counties of England. In Hadleigh (Suffolk), for example, the number of smallholdings increased during the later fourteenth century as a result of the growth of the woollen industry there. Neither of these explanations will account for the large proportion of wage-earners and smallholders in villages like Great Waltham and High Easter (Essex), whose low level of fertility checked the recovery of population after the Black Death.[51]

The proportion of smallholders is not the most important statistic when it comes to examining the changing features of peasant agriculture. Since the total number of tenants, both free and unfree, was declining, and since the total amount of land they occupied was increasing, the average amount of land per tenant increased. Even supposing the proportion of smallholders had remained constant throughout the region, there would have been considerable changes in the distribution of property. In fact, in almost every village there was an increase in the number of large peasant farms producing a surplus for the market, taking over the commercial role which had previously belonged to manorial demesne farming. At Martham (Norfolk) in 1292 there were 376 landholdings, mostly under ten acres; there was only one holding of over fifteen acres, which occupied only 2 per cent of the total tenanted area. In 1497, by contrast, there were 77 holdings altogether, and 14 of these were over fifteen acres, together occupying 49.6 of the total area of tenant land. Such growing concentration was especially characteristic of the century after 1390.[52] An increase in the scale of peasant operations affected pastoral farming too; the great days of demesne sheep flocks were over even before the Black Death, and the production of wool for the English cloth industry during the Hundred Years' War and after was more dependent upon tenant farmers. Sheep had been very unequally distributed between villagers even before the Black Death, and after it inequality was even greater. The largest recorded sheep flocks found trespassing or abusing common

[51] Campbell, 'Agricultural progress in medieval England', p. 39; idem, 'The complexity of manorial structure', pp. 243–4; idem, 'Population pressure, inheritance and the land market', pp. 102–6; Davenport, Norfolk Manor, pp. 18–19; Dyer, 'Social and economic background', pp. 20–2; Hallam, 'Agrarian economy of South Lincolnshire', pp. 92–3; Mate, 'Agrarian economy after the Black Death', p. 351; E. Miller and J. Hatcher, Medieval England: Rural Society and Economic Change, 1086–1348, London, 1978, p. 144; L. R. Poos, 'Population and resources in two fourteenth-century communities: Great Waltham and High Easter, 1327–1389', Cambridge Univ. Ph.D. thesis, 1983, pp. 187–9, 292–4.

[52] B. M. S. Campbell, 'The extent and layout of common fields in eastern Norfolk', Norfolk Archaeology, XXXVIII, 1981, pp. 26–9; idem, 'Population change', p. 190; idem, 'Population pressure, inheritance and the land market', pp. 125–7.

rights increased between the mid-fourteenth century and the early fifteenth.[53] Agglomerations of property and livestock were often short-lived, since accidents of family history caused the splitting up of farms previously expanded parcel by parcel. But so many families enlarged their holdings rapidly that the engrossment of lands preponderated over their dispersal. The most successfully acquisitive families, including some of servile origin, became recognized as yeomen or gentry. Such were the Pastons, who already before 1419 owned about a hundred acres in Paston (Norfolk) and rapidly improved their fortune thereafter.[54]

The profitability of farming the larger tenant holdings depended in part upon the falling capacity of landlords to exact rents and other dues at their former levels. The rents of free lands, which were exceptionally numerous in East Anglia and Lincolnshire, were traditionally fixed, and were usually so low relative to the market value of the land that they did not fluctuate with changes in market conditions; many of these tenures were held on the same terms in 1500 as in 1350.[55] But the tenants of these lands resisted all obligations other than a fixed rent, and often landlords had difficulty in persuading them to perform fealty where this implied liability for an entry fine.[56]

Similar resistance was eventually possible for customary tenants. It is true that during the third quarter of the fourteenth century landlords recovered much of the ground lost after the Black Death. At Hutton (Essex) Battle abbey was temporarily successful after 1355 in restoring the former level of rents. In the bailiwick of Clare, too, the old rent roll was restored within a generation of the first plague epidemic. Conditions were particularly favourable to landlords in the 1370s. Such recovery did not imply that the demand for land was as great as before 1349. It sometimes involved the use of seigneurial authority over unfree tenants to obstruct the operations of the land market. Elsewhere recovery was facilitated by a gap between customary and market evaluations of land; for where rents were artificially low before 1349 they were more easily restored once normal patterns of trade reasserted themselves. Some rent increases reflected a response to local increases of demand for particular types of land; the rent of a pasture called Dagefen in Langenhoe (Essex) near Colchester rose by a third between

[53] Britnell, *Growth and Decline in Colchester*, p. 146; Davenport, *Norfolk Manor*, pp. 80–1; Postan, *Essays on Medieval Agriculture*, pp. 243–6; Ravensdale, *Liable to Floods*, pp. 75–8.

[54] *Court Rolls of Ingoldmells*, trans. Massingberd, p. xxix; *The Sibton Abbey Estates*, ed. Denney, pp. 20–1; *Paston Letters*, ed. Davis, I, pp. xli–xlii; Davenport, *Norfolk Manor*, p. 83; Page, *Crowland Abbey*, pp. 152–3; *VCH Cambs.*, VI, p. 268.

[55] As at Gibcracks in Great Totham (Essex), PRO SC 12/1/5.

[56] PRO SC 2/171/34, mm.1r, 2r (New Hall in Boreham), SC 2/171/81, mm.18r, 19r, 20r, 21r (Feering).

1387–8 and 1409–10.[57] However, recovery of rents was not universal even in the third quarter of the fourteenth century, and increases were unusual after the 1370s. By the 1420s falling rents were commonplace. At Forncett (Norfolk) the average annual rent per acre in leasehold contracts fell from about $10\frac{3}{4}$d. in 1376–8 to 9d. in 1401–10 and to about $7\frac{3}{4}$d. in 1422–30, and it remained at this lower level throughout the fifteenth century. At Hardwick (Cambs.) the rent from a villein holding fell from 17s. to 15s. during the episcopate of John Fordham of Ely (1388–1425). Moreover, though the generations after the 1420s enjoyed greater economic stability, there were further rent reductions in the mid-fifteenth century, as at Wilburton. Even at Newmarket (Suffolk), despite commercial expansion during the fifteenth century, the annual rent of an acre of demesne on lease fell from 10d. in 1428 to 8d. in 1472. Landlords demanding excessive rents risked resistance from tenants, arrears of rent and vacant holdings. Accounts from Takeley (Essex) from 1473 to 1475 show a string of arrears from the incumbent rent collector and his predecessors. On many estates, including those of the Pastons, arrears became a serious problem about this time. During the 1460s and 1470s the consequences of declining population were compounded by the problem of low prices for agricultural produce.[58]

The development of commercial farming by tenants would have been impeded had the distinction between free and unfree lands been rigorously maintained. But this distinction had already weakened before 1350 and did so more rapidly thereafter. Men of distinguished birth still usually acquired only free lands. But free men and townsmen became more willing to hold bond land. The choice between free and unfree lands depended upon practical considerations, and East Anglian families combined the two more commonly than those in other parts of England. The extension of leasehold introduced a new area of dissociation between tenure and personal status, since it affected all ranks of rural society; landlords often favoured existing tenants, whether free or bond, as potential lessees.[59] Some landlords, it is true,

---

[57] Essex RO, D/DEl M226, 227, D/DC 2/16; Britnell, *Growth and Decline in Colchester*, pp. 151–2; Davenport, *Norfolk Manor*, p. 55; Dyer, 'Social and economic background', pp. 23–8; K. G. Feiling, 'An Essex manor in the fourteenth century', *EHR*, XXVI, 1911, p. 335; Holmes, *Estates of the Higher Nobility*, p. 90; Maitland, 'Cambridgeshire manor', pp. 424–7; J. R. Ravensdale, 'Population change and the transfer of customary land on a Cambridgeshire manor in the fourteenth century', in R. M. Smith, ed., *Land, Kinship and Life-Cycle*, pp. 217, 219–23.

[58] Britnell, 'The Pastons', pp. 140–1; idem, *Growth and Decline in Colchester*, p. 257; Davenport, *Norfolk Manor*, p. 78; Maitland, 'Cambridgeshire manor', p. 434; Massingberd, in *VCH Lincs.*, II, pp. 317, 321; P. May, 'Newmarket 500 years ago', *Proc. of the Suffolk Inst. of Arch.*, XXXIII, 1975, p. 263; Rogers, *History of Agriculture and Prices*, III, pp. 714–15; *VCH Cambs.*, V, pp. 102, 168.

[59] *Court Rolls of Ingoldmells*, trans. Massingberd, p. xxix; H. L. Bradfer-Lawrence, 'Gaywood Dragge, 1486–7', *Norfolk Archaeology*, XXIV, 1932, pp. 153–83; Britnell, *Growth and Decline in*

attempted to regulate the commercial initiative of their bondmen by insisting that free land acquired by serfs had to be surrendered into the lord's hands to be taken up again as "soiled land", or as customary land held by copy of court roll. Even leases were sometimes made "by copy" to inhibit the development of personal freedom; the demesne of Popenhoe manor in Walsoken (Norfolk) was leased for ten years by copy from Michaelmas 1412.[60] But consistent policing of the land market was a task beyond the capacity of most estate managements, and even where it was effective it seems not to have greatly inhibited the ambitions of families wanting to accumulate.

This greater flexibility in the land market was made possible by changes in the character of customary tenure. Even before the 1390s landlords often took money from customary tenures instead of labour. During the fifteenth century they universally lost the power to opt for labour services, except in the case of some ploughing and harvesting works.[61] To a lesser extent they abandoned the right to exact labour services altogether. This was not because such services would not have been useful. Nor was it a consequence of demesne leases; where demesnes were leased intact it was normal for labour services to be made available to the lessee, and on many manors labour services were still the formal basis for some rents in the sixteenth century.[62] The fact was that landlords had to make concessions to get tenants, either by extending the scope of leasehold or by permanently altering individual rents. So everywhere the number of holdings owing labour services shrank. Occasionally the tenants as a body negotiated an alteration or commutation of services. Overhauling the structure of rents resulted in greater standardization of unfree tenancies and their closer assimilation to contractual ones.[63] Departures from custom after the Black Death

Colchester, pp. 259–60; Davenport, Norfolk Manor, p. 88; R. H. Tawney, The Agrarian Problem in the Sixteenth Century, London, 1912, pp. 23–4.

[60] For "soiled land", see BL Stowe 934, ff.62v, 102r (Wenhaston, Suffolk and Lyng, Norfolk), Add. Ms. 23948, ff.21v, 22v (Bawdsey, Suffolk); A. Clark, 'Serfdom on an Essex Manor', EHR, xx, 1905, p. 483; Davenport, Norfolk Manor, p. 70; Dyer, 'Social and economic background', pp. 24–5; Hoare, History of an East Anglian Soke, p. 135. For free lands held by copy, see PRO SC 2/171/27, mm.10d, 11r, SC 2/171/28, m.1r (New Hall in Boreham); Feiling, 'An Essex manor', p. 336; PRO SC 6/942/19r (Popenhoe).

[61] H. L. Gray, 'The commutation of villein services in England before the Black Death', EHR, xxix, 1914, pp. 644–5; Maitland, 'Cambridgeshire manor', pp. 419–20; Page, Crowland Abbey, pp. 101–3; VCH Cambs., iv, p. 104; v, p. 152; VCH Essex, v, pp. 216, 282; vi, p. 265.

[62] PRO DL 29/275/4380, m.1r (Long Bennington, Lincs.), SC 6/767/3d (Elsworth, Cambs.), SC 6/769/10d (Knapwell, Cambs.), SC 6/1008/17r (Woodhall, Suffolk); Maitland, 'Cambridgeshire manor', p. 432; Newton, Writtle, pp. 72, 74.

[63] PRO SC 6/767/2d, 3d, 4d (Elsworth); Davenport, Norfolk Manor, p. 58; Feiling, 'An Essex manor', pp. 336–7; Maitland, 'Cambridgeshire manor', pp. 433–4; Massingberd, in VCH Lincs.,

encouraged the practice of allowing tenants to possess copies of the court roll entries recording their conditions of tenure. Early examples often mention special terms of inheritance or liability for rent which could not be known from custom. Frequent changes of tenant weakened the ability of manor courts to depend upon the memories of witnesses and suitors, so for this reason, too, there were advantages in issuing copies of court roll entries. Some landlords systematically gave such copies to incoming tenants of customary land. This was policy on Westminster abbey's manor of Feering (Essex) by 1410, and in 1481 the bailiff had instructions to seize lands whose tenants had no copy. By 1450 tenure by copy or with copy was well established in eastern England. But this development was as yet simply a matter of convenience for lords and tenants, and did not affect the status of unfree tenures. On many manors tenure "by the rod" was more common even in 1500, and it remained normal to speak of native or bond lands even where the tenant held a copy.[64]

These developments owed much to the frequent movement of families from village to village. It is not known whether mobility was in fact greater than it had been before the Black Death, but its capacity to bring about social change was increased. The movement of villagers away from their family lands to bargain for higher incomes or freer status was especially noticeable at the end of the fourteenth century and the beginning of the fifteenth, when manorial custom was crumbling rapidly. This was also a period when transfers of land were numerous. Subsequently the level of migration fell, but frequent removals and frequent recontracting of tenures remained characteristic of the fifteenth century. If families had been content to stay put and stay together in this period, changes in terms of tenure could never have proceeded so far.[65]

Geographical mobility by tenant families was the chief cause of the decline of personal bondage during the fifteenth century. Some tenants bought their freedom, but lords usually held on to their serfs, and kept track of them so long as they remained on the manor. In 1444 bond tenants of the prior of Spalding still had to swear to be servile:

II, p. 319; M. Spufford, *A Cambridgeshire Community: Chippenham from Settlement to Enclosure*, Leicester, 1965, pp. 32–4; *VCH Cambs.*, v, pp. 92, 102; VI, p. 268.

[64] PRO SC 2/171/15, m.3r (Little Baddow), SC 2/171/27, m.10r (New Hall in Boreham), SC 2/171/79, mm.5d, 6d, 7d, etc., SC 2/171/81, m.21r, d (Feering); Essex RO, D/DBw M99, m.5r (Witham); *The Sibton Abbey Estates*, ed. Denney, pp. 91, 99–100; Feiling, 'An Essex manor', p. 337; Maitland, 'Cambridgeshire manor', p. 438; A. Savine, 'Copyhold cases in the early Chancery proceedings', *EHR*, XVII, 1902, pp. 296–303; Spufford, *Cambridgeshire Community*, p. 36.

[65] Britnell, *Growth and Decline in Colchester*, pp. 149, 158; Davenport, *Norfolk Manor*, p. 79; Campbell, 'Population change', pp. 188–90; A. McFarlane, *The Origins of English Individualism*, Oxford, 1978, pp. 98–9; Raftis, *Tenure and Mobility*, p. 153; Page, *Crowland Abbey*, pp. 149, 152–3.

I xall fayth bere to the lord of this lordeschep and justifyable be in body, godys and in catell as his oune mann att his oune wylle, so help me God att the holy dome and be this boke.

Personal villeinage survived long after 1500 – at Forncett until about 1575, at Gimingham until 1599, and at Ingoldmells (Lincs.) until the seventeenth century, but the numbers involved shrank considerably during the fifteenth century through the migration of bond families and the failure of heirs. On some estates the distinction between free and unfree families had disappeared by 1500. Where serfdom survived it was compatible with wealth and independence among villeins. Those who wanted to escape from serfdom, evidently the majority, had opportunities to do so.[66]

For all the contraction of direct demesne management, the decline of rents and the decay of serfdom, landlords maintained a dominant position in the countryside. They and their families remained powerful within village societies, and by the pattern of their expenditure they continued to influence the prosperity of smaller households. Landed magnates created the dominant political structure of the counties and often swayed even the activities of leading townsmen. To serve a major landlord as steward was a ready way to property and power; for example, the Audleys of Earls Colne (Essex) rose in the service of the earls of Oxford. Despite some disintegration and restructuring of manors, which was hardly a new feature of country life, the main institutions of lordship survived.[67] At village level, however, the ability of lords to profit from their seigneurial authority was adversely affected by changing tenurial relationships. Defiance of lords by individual tenants was an everyday matter, and sometimes whole communities resisted their lord when the burden of obligations was felt to be wrong. Landlords were unable to maintain court perquisites at the high level attained during the decades immediately following the Black Death. They could not go on using their powers of jurisdiction to compensate for falling rents, and during the fifteenth century the profits of manorial justice characteristically fell. Some courts then brought in so little that

---

[66] *Court Rolls of Ingoldmells*, trans. Massingberd, pp. xxix–xxxi; *The Sibton Abbey Estates*, ed. Denney, p. 19; Davenport, *Norfolk Manor*, pp. 88, 92, 96; Hoare, *History of an East Anglian Soke*, pp. 172, 310; Maitland, 'Cambridgeshire manor', pp. 436–9; Massingberd, in *VCH Lincs.*, II, p. 319; Page, *Crowland Abbey*, pp. 135, 138.

[67] Britnell, *Growth and Decline in Colchester*, pp. 252–3, 259; W. I. Haward, 'Economic aspects of the Wars of the Roses in East Anglia', *EHR*, XLI, 1926, pp. 178–84; R. Virgoe, 'The crown, magnates and local government in fifteenth-century East Anglia', in J. R. L. Highfield and R. Jeffs, eds., *The Crown and Local Communities in England and France in the Fifteenth Century*, Gloucester, 1981, pp. 83–4.

their lords reduced their frequency and scope.[68] The weight of court business shifted more towards the needs of tenants, especially those of the wealthier ones. Manor leet courts retained a policing function valued by village communities; a court leet at Wix (Essex) in 1500 concerned itself with the maintenance of ditches, watercourses and tenements, the prohibition of an illegal footway, and the amercement of an innkeeper for breach of statute. In more commercially active communities such economic regulation could be extensive. Manorial courts also retained their role as courts for cheap private litigation concerning land, personal assault, debt, and breach of contract.[69]

Despite a high turnover of families and the growth of inequality, villagers continued to work together for certain political, economic, and cultural ends. In 1381 the villagers of eastern England had been better able to organize resistance to the government than those in other parts of the kingdom. Often village communities appear in rentals as tenants of lands, pastures, or fisheries, and these tenancies suggest in some cases that village communities had committed themselves to new joint responsibilities.[70] The capacity of village societies to create new forms of communal activity is best demonstrated by the history of village gilds, which existed to further various pious and practical objectives. Some of their members were able to endow them with property, so that their wealth increased during the fifteenth century; their frequent occurrence in rentals as tenants is a new feature of the period. Village gilds were not peculiar to eastern England, but they flourished there – particularly in Lincolnshire, Cambridgeshire, and Norfolk – in greater numbers than elsewhere in England.[71]

However, eastern England under Henry VII was radically changed from what it had been under Edward III, and its society was

[68] BL Harl. Rolls D27, 29–34 (Donnington, Lincs.); Dyer, 'Social and economic background', pp. 30–4; CPR, 1401–5, p. 437; E. B. Burstall, 'A monastic agreement of the fourteenth century', Norfolk Archaeology, XXXI, 1957, pp. 211–18; Massingberd, in VCH Lincs., II, pp. 317–18, 321, 323; Page, Crowland Abbey, pp. 147–9, 154–5.

[69] PRO DL 29/243/3912, mm.1r, 2r, 3r, etc. (Lancaster manors, Lincs.), SC 2/174/28, m.6r (Wix); H. S. Bennett, The Pastons and their England, 2nd edn, Cambridge, 1932, pp. 253–7; E. Clark, 'Debt litigation in a late medieval English vill', in J. A. Raftis, ed., Pathways to Medieval Peasants, Toronto, 1981; McIntosh, Autonomy and Community, pp. 181–220; May, 'Newmarket', p. 267; Newton, Writtle, pp. 93–4.

[70] BL Stowe 934, ff.8v, 28v ("villata de Metyngham"); Add. Ms. 21034, f.1r ("villata de Walsham"); PRO SC 12/10/55 ("villata dicte ville de Lytylburgh"); The Sibton Abbey Estates, ed. Denney, p. 100 ("villata de Yoxford").

[71] C. B. Firth, 'Village gilds of Norfolk in the fifteenth century', Norfolk Archaeology, XVIII, 1914, pp. 188–90, 196; D. M. Owen, Church and Society in Medieval Lincolnshire, Lincoln, 1971, pp. 127–31; W. M. Palmer, 'The village gilds of Cambridgeshire', Cambs. and Hunts. Arch. Soc., I, 1902, pp. 343–6; H. F. Westlake, The Parish Gilds of Medieval England, London, 1919, pp. 138–238.

recognizably closer to that of modern times. Because of its many commercial opportunities, the freedom of its tenants, and the restricted scope of arbitrary constraints upon agricultural practice, eastern England in the later middle ages was outstanding among the regions of England for its commercialism and economic individualism.

D. THE EAST MIDLANDS

The ways in which the peasantry of the East Midland counties were affected by the changes in settlement and land use during the later middle ages were determined in some measure by the constraints upon them of lordship. It is therefore important to see how the landlords were affected by those changes, and how they viewed them. Much will hang here on the landlords' perception of change, and how it affected their interests. One man with a clear perception of his own interests was William of Thorpe, sometime chief justice of king's bench, who was disgraced in 1350 for corruption but thereafter pardoned. A single account roll survives from Marholm near Peterborough for the year 1377–8, just after William's death.[72] The reeve's charge was based on a tenurial structure of twenty-two virgates. In the time of William of Thorpe, and presumably after the Black Death, six and a half of those virgates had been divided amongst ten villeins, and a further virgate amongst four. In each case it was stated that this was done "to improve their position" (*ad emendacionem status eorundem*). Two and a half virgates were leased out to various tenants in small parcels (*per acram*). Set against this single snapshot, the Ramsey abbey account rolls offer a veritable kaleidoscope for about sixty years after the Black Death. In that time the pattern of landholding changed from year to year. To show and in a measure to simplify the change, Table 7.4 identifies in the village of Upwood all those holding at least half a virgate of arable land. The men and women in this category are taken as being the core of the resident farming community. It will be seen that just twenty years after the plague their number had fallen by about 40 per cent from the pre-plague level. At Warboys on the same estate the number of tenants with a half-virgate and more varied in the 1370s between 28 and 33; in the 1440s there was a lower figure, and a narrower range, of 24 or 25 people. This compares with 51 in the 1252 extent or 50 in the 1279 hundred rolls. Here the number of farmers has halved over the two centuries. As to the number of those holding more than a virgate, this varied between 5 and 8 in the 1370s, and was either 4 or 5 in the 1440s, a time when the tenurial structure seems again very stable.[73] To isolate

[72] Northants. RO, Fitzwilliam/Milton roll no. 194.
[73] J. A. Raftis, *Warboys*, pp. 175–6; *idem*, 'Changes in an English village after the Black Death', *Medieval Studies*, XXIX, 1967, pp. 158–77.

Table 7.4. *Tenants of half a virgate and more, Upwood (Hunts.),*
1251–1413

Date	More than a virgate	A virgate	Half a virgate – under a virgate	Total
1251	—	20	18	38
1371–2	11	5	7	23
1385–8	11	5	9	25
1392–3	9	8	7	24
1401–2	12	7	7	26
1406–7	9	3	12	24
1411–12	10	3	10	23
1412–13	10	1	11	22

Source: J. A. Raftis, 'Changes in an English village after the Black Death',
Medieval Studies, XXIX, 1967, pp. 168–72.

those with half-virgates and more is only one approach to the material,
but it can hardly be an arbitrary one, when it gives figures that reflect
so clearly the estimates that we have for population decline over the
same period. There were fewer people. Anything that is said on peasant
farming in the late middle ages must be said with reference to
population decline.

There survives from a few well-documented villages information on
the continuity of individual families. At Warboys there were 107
families in 1330; in 1360 there were 80, as there were in 1400. After this
there was a "drastic decline", with 71 families in 1410, 61 families in
1430 and 51 families in 1450. At Kibworth Harcourt, similarly, the
years from 1410 to 1440 saw the most rapid turnover of families. At
Holywell-cum-Needingworth, returning to the Ramsey estate, the
period of most rapid decline was from 1390 to 1410. The figures,
presented in Table 7.5, give an indication of the turnover of families.
They show that more families were lost to the village in the 1390s than
in the three preceding decades taken together. The comparatively poor
documentation surviving from Ramsey for the immediate post-plague
years is unfortunate. It is none the less clear that these years are not the
years which see the most rapid turnover of families.[74]

In the twenty years or so immediately after the Black Death the
landlords were living off their capital, nowhere more so than in the
capital represented by manpower. A little of the continuity in family

[74] Raftis, *Warboys*, p. 121; Howell, *Kibworth Harcourt*, pp. 47–8, 240–2; DeWindt, *Holywell-cum-Needingworth*, pp. 166–71.

Table 7.5. *Number of families in Holywell-cum-Needingworth (Hunts.),*
1300–1450

Year	Old	New	Disappeared	Total
1300	66	—	—	66
1310	58	15	8	73
1320	61	6	12	67
1330	59	6	8	65
1340	56	5	9	61
1360	46	6	15	52
1370	48	5	4	53
1380	47	12	6	59
1390	57	4	2	61
1400	46	4	15	50
1410	40	1	10	41
1420	35	3	6	38
1430	33	3	5	36
1440	31	2	5	33
1450	30	2	3	32

Source: DeWindt, *Holywell-cum-Needingworth*, p. 167.

tenure in the 1350s was born of compulsion; men "of the blood" of the
previous tenant could be, and were, compelled to take up his holding.
There were reserves of men in villages before the Black Death, men
with a place in the tenurial structure, which thereafter they were called
upon to fill. In a few decades, which were those of successive
revisitations of the plague, the reserves were exhausted. In the dramatic
year of 1381, Merton College, Oxford, undramatically abandoned the
idea that for every vacant holding there was an heir to be found.
Previously the reeve had been charged for any vacancy: thereafter he
was not.[75] This is an important change of attitude on the part of the
landlord, and we can see behind it a no less important social change. It
is the same change which can be looked at through another lens in the
account rolls of Ramsey abbey, when in the 1370s they begin to list
individually the different tenants and the terms of their tenure. The old
rental, and the reeve's memory, were no longer sufficient guides. The
pattern of landholding fluctuated from year to year.

With the concern for the individuals holding land, there came at the
same time an interest in recording the whereabouts of those men who
had moved away. Efforts were made to keep track of those tied to the
manor by blood. The effort is an important part of the story of the

[75] Howell, *Kibworth Harcourt*, pp. 48–50.

decline of villeinage, and as such it will be necessary to return to it. Here it is recorded as a further element of change. In villages of the Soke of Peterborough in 1391 the court officials, inquiring about migration, elicited an interesting set of replies. Two ladies from Peterborough, members of good families, were then in Ireland; another man was overseas. Two people were at King's Lynn. Several had moved no further than neighbouring villages, and they had not moved to escape the abbey's lordship, though that would have been easy enough. Villagers from Glinton and Longthorpe had gone to Eye and to Peterborough itself. A little learning provided a passport to wider horizons. The sub-dean of Salisbury, a *nativus domini* like the rest, had taken a couple of friends and relations with him to Wessex. Herbert Rythe was with the bishop of Winchester, and a son of Richard at the Green was with the Lord Willoughby of Eresby, Lincs.[76] The characteristic pattern of migration was one to neighbouring villages and towns.[77]

If the courts were at times concerned with absentees, they maintained a continuous interest in the proper upkeep of peasant buildings. At times the interest seems almost obsessive. Surveys would note those tenancies that were in decay. Men taking up land would undertake to make repairs, or to build anew. The entry which follows is from Castor, in 1366:

John Nichols gives 4 hens for entry into one built-up messuage and one messuage not built upon, and two virgates which John Reve, formerly a villein, held of the lord in Ailsworth... And he shall maintain at his cost whenever there shall be need upon the built-up messuage the chief house with the buildings (*cameris*) annexed to it and one barn, as they now stand upon the same messuage.

The empty messuage here was the result of the amalgamation of two holdings. Whether through amalgamation or fragmentation the result was the same. The link was broken between the house-site and the land. "Robert Wodereve has a half-virgate which pertains to the bond toft formerly that of Bartholomew Denis." Robert's holding here was made up of three messuages, one of them built upon, together with a half-virgate and six acres from two distinct virgates. Elsewhere the link between the house and the land was put another way. "Richard Walkelyn held a messuage with a virgate of land attached to it"; *adiacente*, suggesting that in the mind's eye the house and the land

[76] Northants. RO, PDC court rolls, box 1 no. 9. The most distinguished of these absent *nativi* can be traced. William Tuk, who occurs in the Glinton roll of this year, was indeed sub-dean of Salisbury. He appears there as William of Glinton, and held office from 1362 to 1396: J. Le Neve, *Fasti Ecclesiae Anglicanae, 1300–1541*, III, *Salisbury Diocese*, ed. J. M. Horn, London, 1962, p. 6.

[77] A similar impression is given for Warboys by the sketch-maps in Raftis, *Warboys*, pp. 264–5.

appeared together. These entries start with the tofts, and move from them to the land in the fields attached to the tofts. The symmetry of the old surveys reflected a symmetry in landholding in which this was the key link. After the Black Death it was broken. This can be seen very clearly in a series of surveys made for the demesne manors of the abbot of Peterborough in the years around 1400. Some of these were in the standard form, listing freeholders, virgaters, cottars, and so forth. In some cases, though, the old pattern was abandoned as unworkable, and the survey was made geographically, going from toft to toft along the village streets, and listing the arable which was attached to each toft. The following entry comes from the survey of Kettering, Northants.

Next to this cottage, Hugh Tresham and Simon Deye hold two-thirds of a messuage pertaining to the virgate which John Brown and John Wythie hold below, for 4d. The executors of Henry Richer hold the other third of the said messuage, which was formerly a barn and is now falling to ruin, for 2d. John Brown and John Wythie hold a virgate which once belonged to John Brown, which pertains to the messuage...[as above], for 20s. a year and the services which John Richer does. [The services amount to 3 days' ploughing and 2 days' work at the harvest.]

Not only had the toft become separated from its arable in this instance, but within the toft the house-site had become separate from the barn. The ruined barn is an appropriate symbol of the breaking of the link between the house and the land.[78]

While the landlords' concern about dilapidation is plain to see, and the nature of their worry not difficult to isolate, it is more difficult to establish a chronology. At Kibworth Harcourt, between the first plague of 1349 and the second of 1361, timber from old houses was reused in building new with the ready co-operation of the lord. That attitude did not last. In 1391 responsibility for the upkeep of the housing stock was placed in the hands of a group of "supervisors" (*supervisores terre et tenementorum*), who might distrain tenants to make them repair their houses. Elsewhere lords took the responsibility on themselves. For over a century after the Black Death, Ramsey abbey spent substantial sums on repairing buildings not taken up by the peasantry. The monks looked for a restoration of the old order, but that was not to come. Fewer families had no need and no incentive to maintain the stock of building inherited from a more populous age. The effect on the village plan can be seen at Kibworth Harcourt, as holdings were amalgamated. Two adjacent half-virgates were amalgamated and held by the Saunders family from 1358 to 1500. There were larger units formed also. Four half-virgate messuages were

[78] Northants. RO, Fitzwilliam/Milton roll no. 141; PDC a/c rolls, box 2 no. 18; BL Cott. Nero C VII, ff.85r–141r, 165r–208r (quotations from f.122r–v).

brought together by Richard Wynlyf in the early fifteenth century to form a single holding, now known as Paddock Farm. Such a survival is not unusual in the village; most of the holdings in the 1484 extent can be traced on the modern map. The houses here that had been built in the twelfth and thirteenth centuries on waste ground were no longer needed. Many of them were demolished, and the sites on which they had stood remained free pasture closes. When the map of the village in 1484 is compared with that in 1340 it shows in a striking manner the gaps between the houses along the main street.[79]

It is as well to have considered the falling numbers, the ruined houses, and the absent villeins, before looking at the changes in terms of tenure after the Black Death, the best known of which is the slow dissolution of villeinage. The main line of development in what had in 1349 been customary land is not difficult to isolate. For the estates of Leicester abbey surveys survive from 1341 and 1477. In the earlier survey the virgaters held in villeinage; over a century later their successors held at will. Over such a time span the change is simple, and it is abrupt. Where fuller records are available, they show that the pace of change was slow, and that the two forms of tenure would often exist side by side. At Kibworth Harcourt the last reference to land held in villeinage (*in bondagio*) came in 1439–40, in circumstances which will be considered below. But references occur to land held at will (*ad voluntatem domini*) soon after the Black Death, and from the 1390s onwards they become more frequent than references to villeinage.[80] Villeinage here had not been preserved for the needs of demesne agriculture, for this manor was peripheral on the Merton College estate, and its demesnes had always been leased out.

It is not surprising that the Ramsey abbey estate exhibited a more tenacious lordship. Here several demesnes were cultivated directly by the abbey until well into the fifteenth century. Customary services were performed on those demesnes at very much the same level as a century earlier. The virgaters at Broughton each owed 179 works a year in 1314, and 177 in 1392. The total number of works performed in the year was 2,667 in 1314–15 and 2,709 in 1392–3. A lot of clerical work went into achieving such stability. At Wistow the days of the week on which service was owed were specified, and a check was made to ensure that feast-days allowed fell on days on which service was due. The figures for works performed on this manor show more variation than those from Broughton. The low figure for 1368 (Table 7.6) resulted from the sale of all the autumn works due. A number of the Ramsey demesnes were leased in the years around 1410. A reorganiz-

[79] Howell, *Kibworth Harcourt*, pp. 55–6 and ch. 7; Raftis, *Tenure and Mobility*, pp. 190–8.
[80] Hilton, *Leicestershire Estates*, pp. 94–105; Howell, *Kibworth Harcourt*, pp. 50–2.

Table 7.6. *Villein services on the demesne of Wistow (Hunts.), 1335–94*

	Works due	Works performed	Percentage of works performed
1335	4,859	3,976	82
1351	4,116	3,084	75
1352	4,230	2,887	62
1368	3,626	1,924	50
1379	3,428	2,782	81
1389	3,667	2,580	71
1393	3,450	2,451	71
1394	3,466	2,471	71

Source: Hogan, 'Wistow', pp. 308–13.

ation of the terms of tenure naturally followed. Thus at Holywell-cum-Needingworth *ad opus* tenure was eliminated in 1409, and by 1412 a new level of rent (*novum censum*) had been introduced, which brought rents to the level of 1s. an acre.[81] It may be suspected that Ramsey abbey was unusual in maintaining into the fifteenth century the customary services of villeins. Certainly it was possible to maintain demesne farming without week-work. Peterborough abbey in the years around 1400 was still cultivating its demesnes in the Soke of Peterborough, but the surveys of this time contain no mention of week-work. What were retained, wherever the demesnes were retained, were ploughing services and boon-works. In the fenland manors there was more emphasis put on maintaining some help with the hay-making, and less on the ploughing services.[82]

The records of the great estates do much to conceal the difficulties that they, along with all lords, experienced after the Black Death. The records of lesser lords show these a good deal more clearly. The village of Woodford by Thrapston lies only a few miles away from Irthlingborough, one of the manors surveyed topographically by Peterborough abbey *c.* 1400. It shows a very different world. In February 1351 the court rolls contain the first entry of a kind that was to become plentiful.

Henry of Walcot and Agnes his wife came into court and recognized that they

---

[81] J. A. Raftis, 'The structure of commutation in a fourteenth-century village', *Essays in Medieval History presented to Bertie Wilkinson*, ed. T. A. Sandquist *et al.*, Toronto, 1969, pp. 282–300; Mary P. Hogan, 'Wistow: a social and economic reconstitution in the fourteenth century', Univ. of Toronto Ph.D. thesis, 1971, pp. 308–13; BL Add. Ch. 39897–39900; DeWindt, *Holywell-cum-Needingworth*, pp. 144–5.

[82] Peterborough abbey surveys, as cited in n. 78.

held of the lord, but they did not know which tenements they held; and so they were given a day at the next court [to find out].

At Michaelmas 1357 another man only marginally more convincingly acknowledged that he held *diversa tenementa*, but said that he did not know the terms on which he held (*sed nescit que tenura*). Margery of Aldwincle recognized that she held a messuage of the Maufe fee and other tenancies of which she was ignorant. Several people paid 4d. each every year to buy out their obligation to attend the court. The rental that so clearly was needed was made in 1387; it is not an impressive document. It lists individuals and the sums that they owed at the four terms of the year. The tenants then had to change their tune just a little. In 1400:

Thomas Benyll came into court and did homage and recognized that he held of the lord various lands and tenements by the service of 2s. 2d. a year, but he did not know the terms of his tenure (*sed ignoratur tenura*); and so he was given a day at the next court to show his charters and muniments.

The lord here, a member of a minor gentry family, was continuing to farm a demesne, but he was struggling to preserve even the most nominal control over his tenants.[83]

The advantageous benefits of a poor memory can be seen displayed also by the villagers of Maidwell, Northants, faced with their lord's efforts to track down fugitive villeins. Earlier courts had not displayed any interest in the matter, but in 1387 (a year for which a detailed account roll survives also) a list was given of those living away from the manor. In most cases it was stated where they lived. Members of the Carter family were at Clipston; one of them was a priest, ordained without the lord's licence. Richard Gibon was at Godmanchester. Sarra the daughter of Geoffrey Hochun used to live at Rushton. All of these were *nativi domini de sanguine*. A year later there was none of this detail. The memory of Sarra's good looks survived – she is Fayr Sare or Pulchra Sarra in later entries – but her whereabouts, and those of her fellows, were not known. Inquiries continued throughout the 1390s, but met with no success. A court of 1402 shows an attempt to bring some pressure. The next of kin were to bring the missing persons, if they were alive, from wherever they lived, under penalty of 40d. But who were the next of kin? It turned out – so at least it was stated in 1415 – that the villagers did not know who the next of kin were. Shortly thereafter, around 30 years after this group of villagers was first identified and presented as absent, any mention of them disappears from the rolls.[84]

[83] Northants. RO, St John (Melchbourne) Mss. 59–60.
[84] Northants. RO, Finch Hatton Mss. 418, 537, 463, 465, 527.

At Kibworth Harcourt the villagers were more direct in their opposition to seigneurial demands. In 1407 they refused to present the names of those living away from the manor, and demanded a reduction of rent and the abandonment of villein tenure and villein disabilities. The lead was taken by newcomers to the village. In 1401 they had, as a first shot in the campaign, surrendered thirteen tenements, comprising ten messuages, one cottage, seven bond and four demesne virgates. The land was not abandoned, and the rent continued to be paid; but in the end they, or their successors, carried the day. In 1427 the lord, Merton College, accepted that thereafter the eighteen customary virgates would be held "at the will of the lord according to the custom of the manor" and not *in bondagio*. The rent of these virgates was reduced by 3s. 4d. a year. Between 1439, when these changes were finalized, and 1594 the court at Kibworth Harcourt ceased to record the transfer of land. This action shows not only the abandonment of villeinage, but reflects a new stability in tenurial structure, replacing that so abruptly broken nearly a century before.[85]

To produce a single date at which the last reference to servility is found in any village is not of itself very helpful. The Kibworth Harcourt example makes this clear. It is not just that there are a number of words and phrases which go out of currency at different times. There is the further point that the words represent patterns of thought just as much as they stand for social conditions. This was true both for lords and tenants. An element of face-saving was involved. At Elton (Hunts.) the villeins refused to pay chevage immediately after the Black Death: the reeve argued that he could not levy it (*ut dicit*, said the auditors), and alternatively that all those who owed chevage were dead. The abbey refused to abandon the idea of chevage for those living away, but the resident villagers were allowed to pay a lump sum, "that they should not be called customary tenants". When the same Ramsey administration allowed a *nativus* of Barton in Bedfordshire to take orders in 1400, it was on condition that he should know his place and should not denigrate the abbey. He had licence to leave, but was not manumitted. Those who were manumitted at the same time were told that they were not to be "ungrateful". What was being said was not very precise, but the landlords' fears were no less real for being difficult to put into words.[86]

[85] Howell, *Kibworth Harcourt*, pp. 50–2.

[86] *Elton Manorial Records*, ed. Ratcliff, pp. 360, 383, 390; BL Add. Ch. 34370 (the entry in 1350 is "13s. 4d. de toto homagio ne vocentur per capita", in 1428 "6s. 8d. de toto homagio pro avantagio ne custumarii vocentur"); *Liber Gersumarum*, ed. DeWindt, no. 191; Raftis, *Tenure and Mobility*, pp. 186–7, 276–7.

To distinguish between manors principally in terms of the strength of lordship over them is to understate the variety of social structure within villages, and in particular to give too little weight to villages in those areas weighted to pastoral farming. There are some records to help right this balance, notably those of the highly idiosyncratic lordship which was that of the crown itself. At Brigstock in Rockingham Forest the standard tenancies were first a messuage and half-virgate, comprising 15 acres of arable and 3 acres of meadow, and secondly a cotsettle, which was a messuage without land. In 1416 the structure of tenure on this manor was as follows: 6 virgates, 18 half-virgates, 4 quarter lands, 4 half-quarter lands and 28 cotsettle-lands. There had, however, been a measure of consolidation of holdings. Six persons held two half-virgates each, one of whom had one and a half cottages also. Five of the half-virgates had cottages attached to them. With some amalgamation, the total number of tenants found in 1416 was 49. Almost identical figures are provided by records of 1596, when there were fifty tenants holding 31 messuages and 33 cottages. Such uniformity arouses suspicion, which up to a point is justified. The uniformity is provided by the "suit-houses"; it was to specified messuages and houses that the obligation of suit of court was attached. The king was not a demanding lord. Rent was at 4s. for 18 acres of land, and the standard fine for the descent of a socage tenure was 16s. But he was tenacious of the rights he held, chief among them the obligation of those with suit-houses to come to court every three weeks.[87]

The court records show that the uniformity of tenurial structure was combined with, and clearly was compatible with, an open market in land, subject only to registration of the transfer. Transfer was by surrender and admittance. The rolls show an active market in small parcels of land, and the custumals make it clear that these might be fragments of customary holdings. "He that hath the hearthstone shall gather the rent of all the lands so sold, for every rod $\frac{1}{2}$d., and shall answer it to the lord for all his parceners of the same land." The only restraints on alienation of any kind were the provision that the heir should have certain chattels that were "rootfast", and that the stepmother of the heir could not alienate chattels after her husband's death. The custom in Brigstock was Borough English. The very existence of suit-houses without land presumes pastoral farming, and it is clear in the Brigstock rolls that the pasture land was regarded as of the essence of the holding in a way that the arable was not. The question was asked

[87] Northants. RO, box X361 (rental of 1416); Misc. Ledger 141, ff.52–8 (survey of 1440); P. A. J. Pettit, *The Royal Forests of Northamptonshire 1558–1714*, Northants Rec. Soc., XXIII, 1968, pp. 164–82.

in the custumal whether the man who sold all the pasture away from his holding thereby escaped obligation to suit of court. It was found that he did not, but evidently the question was well put. With that pasture, and with the other resources of the forest, the cottage economy of this area of Northamptonshire was well developed.[88]

A land market in some respects similar can be seen in the records of another royal manor, that of Kingsthorpe, on the outskirts of (and now a suburb of) Northampton. Land here also was freely transferable, subject to procedures for registration which gave rights to kin over non-kin, and to men of the township over foreigners. Such foreigners might come from no farther away than Northampton itself. The custumal is concerned to stop the reception of such men into village houses, and to regulate the number of beasts that might be pastured from them. There are numerous examples in the rolls of tenements being transferred with half-acres of arable attached to them. The suburban nature of this "town", for as such it is described in the custumal of 1484, explains a number of its distinctive features. It does not explain them all. Kingsthorpe was held at fee-farm from the crown. Land was surrendered not before agents of the king, but "before the bailiff and the whole community of the village". It had its own seal, which bore the legend *Sigillum Commune de Kyngesthorp*. A striking feature of the records is the registration of peasant wills, and the references to land being bought from executors. Transfer by will was not the prerogative of the great men. In 1375 Isabella Webster bequeathed half a tenement, which she in turn had been given by her mother, to her father and step-mother and their children. The beneficiaries were named as executors. The clergy, who wrote the wills, were active in the land market of the township. The evidence is all of a piece. And the most remarkable feature of Kingsthorpe is the very existence of its records, surviving from 1350 as the records not of lordship but of the village community.[89]

Another kind of cottage economy may be looked for on the edges of the fenland. The Peterborough abbey manor of Eye had 15 virgated holdings, 10 "old" cottages and 19 other cottages in the early fourteenth century. Those cottages and a number of others are found listed in the survey of Eye made in 1399–1400. It shows the resources on which a cottage holder might draw. Margery Rote had a built-up cottage, two butts of land enclosed in a toft, a holm adjacent to this and some meadowland in le Harp. While the cottages at Brigstock had predominantly been held by smallholders, the cottages at Eye were not.

[88] Northants. RO, Misc. Ledger 141, ff.93–106 (custumal of 1391).

[89] Kingsthorpe parish records, memoranda rolls 1350–1418, court rolls 1372–1502, seal matrix c. 1396; J. H. Glover, *Kingsthorpiana*, London, 1883, pp. 38–45 (custumal).

There were eighty-nine tenancies listed in the survey. They were held by 38 people. Sixty-one cottages and tofts were listed, but only 16 people in Eye may be accounted cottagers. Some sites had been amalgamated, and some were in the lord's hand, but the greater number of them (25) were amalgamated with the tenancies of those holding parts of the virgated structure. Of the 22 people in this category, 16 had acquired cottage holdings also. The tenants' ranks shrank further in the course of the fifteenth century, for in the account roll of 1482–3 the same lands were held by 32 people. In 1300–1, 148 people had appeared at a harvest boon. These figures cannot be directly compared. It does seem, however, that the demand for smallholdings in Eye did not match similar demand in the forest area, nor that to be expected in the neighbourhood of a large town.[90]

The changes in peasant land-occupancy and in the terms of peasant tenure in the later middle ages have to be identified through the documents of the landowning class, which for much of the period felt itself threatened by the changes which were taking place. In the landlords' view the capital of the manor in terms of men was being dissipated. Much of the building stock was in decay. They could make no simple distinction between "abandoned" and "shrunken" settlements and those which survived. In the second half of the fourteenth century, it must have appeared that any settlement might go the same way. But by the 1440s, nearly a century after the Black Death, there were signs of stability. The village centre had a new layout, with gaps between houses, and some areas of colonization abandoned. The layout reflected in its turn a different pattern of landholding, the result of the demand for land expressed by a smaller number of peasant farmers. If their holdings were still expressed in terms of fractions of virgates, this was because of the pasture land attached to the houses, and the rights of commoning sheep and cattle that went with the pasture. New farming conditions established a new basis of custom, and with it changes in the terms of customary tenure. The lords could accommodate themselves to these changes. Their rights over their men were more clearly than ever expressed in economic terms. By the end of the fifteenth century villeinage was a matter of antiquarian interest.[91]

[90] Northants. RO, Fitzwilliam/Milton roll no. 2388; PDC a/c rolls, box 2 no. 18; BL Cott. Nero C vii, ff.167v–171v.

[91] Dating from c. 1470 there is in the Ramsey abbey Liber Gersumarum what amounts to an index of the villeins mentioned in it: Liber Gersumarum, ed. DeWindt, pp. 43–9.

E. THE WEST MIDLANDS

The epidemic of 1348–9 seems to have caused mortality in West Midland villages in excess of 40 per cent. Although a flurry of marriages – and presumably births – followed the catastrophe, successive lesser epidemics combined with changes in fertility led to a long-term decline in population. These demographic movements were not reflected immediately in changes in the numbers of tenants and in the size of holdings. Rentals and accounts compiled in the decades immediately after 1349, as on the Duchy of Lancaster's manors in Derbyshire and Staffordshire, show little decline in tenant numbers or rent income. The smallholdings of Halesowen (Worcs.) declined only from 43 per cent of the total to 35 per cent in the late fourteenth century, indicating that such tenements had a considerable capacity for survival, and on the Stoneleigh abbey (War.) estate in 1392 those with holdings below seven acres still accounted for 46 per cent of the tenants, compared with 62 per cent a hundred years earlier.[92]

An increase in the size of holdings became more marked in the fifteenth century. On the manors of Westminster abbey and Worcester Cathedral priory the development of individual holdings in excess of 60 acres, or changes in the distribution of land among tenants so that a majority held a yardland (30 acres) or more, are most often encountered after 1400, or even towards the middle of the fifteenth century. From about 1470 new houses were being built on the wastes in woodland districts, but there was no marked proliferation of smallholdings, in spite of other evidence for a modest growth in population.[93]

The size of holdings varied markedly from district to district. In south Warwickshire and the Cotswolds, where half-yardlands and full yardlands had been especially frequent before 1349, tenements expanded until accumulations of two or three yardlands are commonly found in the fifteenth century, and multiple tenements as large as five yardlands are known. In the woodland districts, or on the outskirts of towns, or in areas of industrial activity, smallholdings persisted, presumably because their tenants had two occupations, both as small-scale cultivators and as craftsmen or wage-earners. The contrast between holdings on champion and woodland manors is well-illustrated by a survey of the estates of Coventry priory in 1411. In the

---

[92] Birrell, 'The honour of Tutbury', pp. 72–81; Razi, *Life, Marriage and Death*, pp. 114–51; Z. Razi, 'Family, land and the village community in later medieval England', *PP*, no. 93, 1981, pp. 3–36; *Stoneleigh Leger Book*, ed. R. H. Hilton, Dugdale Soc., XXIV, 1960, pp. xxxix–xl.

[93] Harvey, *Westminster Abbey and its Estates*, pp. 266–7, 288–9; E. K. Vose, 'Estates of Worcester Cathedral Priory', chapter on development of manorial social structure, typescript, University of Birmingham; Blanchard, 'Economic change in Derbyshire', pp. 108–9.

champion south Warwickshire districts, 60 per cent of the tenants held 30 acres or above, and only a fifth of them had fewer than 15 acres. The manors in the wooded country around the then prosperous city of Coventry contained a majority of smallholders (60 per cent), and a mere 13 per cent of tenants had 30 acres or above. Such large numbers of smallholdings were unusual, but substantial minorities of them are found in the woodland village of Abbot's Bromley (Staffs.) in 1416, and in the cloth-making and market centre of Painswick (Glos.) in 1496. Local variations in the size of holdings are more difficult to explain, for example in the Severn valley in Worcestershire; here Ombersley adhered to the general pattern of the locality by retaining many quarter- and half-yardlands, and tenants with a yardland or above increased only gradually from 14 to 21 per cent of the total between 1400 and 1473, while on the neighbouring manor of Hartlebury in the 1470s two-thirds of holdings were of 30 acres or above.[94]

The mechanisms that lay behind the redistribution of land among tenants are still not fully understood. Sometimes the balance between holdings of different size was changed because holdings were simply abandoned, and either incorporated into the demesne or left to lie waste. The most frequent route to change lay through the land market, by which tenants could create multiple holdings by taking over land vacated by neighbours, or more commonly by acquiring holdings from sitting tenants. There are examples of this being done by enterprising smallholders, or even those without land, notably in the aftermath of the fourteenth-century epidemics. More often the better-off villagers, those with the resources to buy land and to equip it with stock and implements, gained extra holdings for themselves or for their children. This did not necessarily lead to the rise of long-lived dynasties of yeomen, for the new accumulations of land tended to be fragile, and might be broken up on the death of the tenant. Among the peasantry there may have been some prejudice against multiple holdings, expressed at Ombersley in 1415 in a decision of the homage to split a triple holding among the heirs, although primogeniture was the inheritance custom. A custom was declared at Bishop's Itchington (War.) in 1354 that no customary tenant should hold land in two villages.[95] Landlords disliked the engrossing of holdings, because many

[94] D. Greenblatt, 'The suburban manors of Coventry, 1279–1411', Cornell Univ. Ph.D. thesis, 1967, pp. 27–30; Staffs. RO, D1734/2/3/1; St Clair Baddeley, *A Cotteswold Manor*, Gloucester, 1907, pp. 126–34; Worcs. RO, ref. 705:56 BA 3910/24; Dyer, *Lords and Peasants*, pp. 299–301.

[95] Harvey, *op. cit.*, pp. 266–7; Razi, 'Family, land and the village community', p. 31; Dyer, *op. cit.*, pp. 308–10; Hilton, *English Peasantry*, p. 41; Shakespeare's Birthplace Trust RO, DR10/2594.

separate smallholdings generated more rent than a few large ones. Accordingly the lords campaigned for the repair of buildings which would make each tenement viable on its own, and the estate record-keepers maintained the memory of the separate identity of each holding, to which were attached the surnames of extinct tenant families. In the long run even the most conservative landlords came to accept the disappearance of many of their holdings as separate entities, and in the late fifteenth century gave up their claim to take heriots from each ancient tenement, but accepted a single beast or money payment on the death of a tenant of a multiple holding.[96]

An important qualification must be made to any generalization about holding size. We use, from necessity, documents which are likely to contain elements of fiction. Court records occasionally reveal the unofficial or illicit arrangements among tenants that could mean that the real distribution of land differed markedly from that recorded in the rentals or court rolls. For example, an inquiry at Twyning (Glos.) in 1358 disclosed the names of seven tenants who had sublet their holdings, and in 1482 eight Sambourn (War.) tenants were said to have let their lands and not to be resident within the manor. An accident of documentation for Alrewas (Staffs.) shows the frequency of mortgages, which must have existed elsewhere; again this may have led to subletting.[97] The hidden substratum of illicit or unnoticed tenures is likely to have been increasing during our period as the effectiveness of seigneurial control was diminishing. Indeed references to subletting become more frequent in late fifteenth-century court rolls in the form of licences to sublet, often granted at the beginning of a tenancy, but the extent to which tenants took advantage of them is not known.[98]

The relative shortage of tenants helped them to win for themselves improved conditions of tenure. The majority of West Midland tenants – perhaps as many as 60 per cent – held by customary tenures. The large numbers of free tenants concentrated in the north and west of the region were outnumbered by the customary tenants, who predominated in the more densely populated south and east. Free tenants, who already enjoyed relatively light obligations, were able to employ devices such as enfeoffment to uses to avoid heriots and other payments. The customary tenants, with their much more substantial rents and services, had a harder task to gain the advantage in their relationship

---

[96] Harvey, *op. cit.*, p. 287; Dyer, *op. cit.*, pp. 285–7.

[97] Glos. RO, D678/65; Shakespeare's Birthplace Trust RO, DR5/2357; Hilton, *English Peasantry*, pp. 39–40, 47.

[98] E.g. Worcs. Cathedral Library, E78, court roll of the Worcester priory estate, 1491, where licences to sublet were given "on condition that the sub-tenant is well-behaved".

with their lords. Many customary tenants suffered the disabilities of hereditary serfdom, and were called *nativi de sanguine*. Throughout the late fourteenth and early fifteenth century they appear not infrequently in court records being subjected to payments of personal dues, *merchet*, *leyrwite*, and chevage. In their landholding they were, with varying degrees of efficiency, prevented from holding by free tenure any free land that they might have acquired by marriage, inheritance, or purchase, but were required to surrender such land to their lord for regrant on customary terms. Serfs might also be ordered to take over vacant holdings. All the disabilities of serfdom are less frequently mentioned in court records after about 1420, and at the end of the fifteenth century the most prominent relics of unfree status were the lists of absent serfs, which seem to have been largely ineffective as a means of preserving seigneurial controls.[99]

Labour services ceased to form a major element in the obligations of tenants in the late fourteenth century, although commutation moved at varying speeds and a few lords were still using customary labour in quantity in the 1390s. Everywhere after 1400, however, the assize rent in cash became the main charge on customary holdings. The median level of rent for the region seems to have been 20s. per yardland per annum, the highest rents at 30s. or 40s. per yardland being found in the Vale of Berkeley and in the vicinity of Bristol, while the lowest, 10s. per yardland or below, predominated in south Staffordshire and south Warwickshire. Yardlands tended to be large in Gloucestershire, as much as 40 acres in the Vale, but the high rents of the area are still apparent if they are calculated per acre. These contrasts between different districts were very old by 1349, reflecting burdens of services and rents fixed in the early middle ages.

The "sticky" nature of rents meant that adjustments in their levels occurred slowly, usually downwards in the fifteenth century, through the process known to contemporary administrators as the "decay of

---

[99] The fullest series of court rolls from which these generalizations derive are: Berkeley Castle muniments (Berkeley manors, and St Augustine's, Bristol manors, both Glos.); Birmingham Reference Library, 167901-3, 168022, 168025-7, 168115, 168198 (Brailes, War.); 422734-422756 (Elmley Lovett, Worcs.); Glos. RO, D678/61, 62, 65, 94, 95, 98, 99 (Winchcomb abbey manors, Glos. and War.); D936a/M2, M5 (Gloucester abbey manors, Glos.); D621/M1 (Archbishopric of York manors, Glos.); Shakespeare's Birthplace Trust RO, DR18/3-33 (Stoneleigh, War., also PRO SC 2/207/79); DR 5/2357-8 (Sambourn, War.); Staffs. RO, D1734/2/1/102-3 (Burton abbey manors, Staffs.); Worcs. Cathedral Library, E16, E17, E20, E30, E46, E53, E54, E56, E59, E61, E64, E65, E69, E70, E78, E80, E83, E84 (Worcester Cathedral priory manors, War. and Worcs.); Worcs. RO, ref. 009:1 BA 2636/157-69; 173-6; 192-3; ref. 705:4 BA 54 (bishopric of Worcester manors, Glos., War. and Worcs.); ref. 705:56 BA 3910/22, 24, 39, 40 (Ombersley, Worcs.); ref. 899:95 BA 989/1/2-3 (Elmley Castle, Worcs.).

rent". A more decisive reduction involved the removal of the extra customary payments, such as tallages and common fines. These might be maintained in the late fourteenth century at their pre-plague levels, but were often abandoned in the fifteenth, under pressure from tenants who refused to pay.[100] So most payments made by tenants moved slowly to meet new circumstances; only entry fines changed rapidly and flexibly. Although it is possible to find individuals paying fines in the late fourteenth century at the pre-1350 rates of £2 or £3 per yardland, and occasionally as much as £10 per yardland, less attractive holdings could be had for little or nothing, the average fine on most estates sinking to less than a pound for a yardland. These modest fines slumped further in the first half of the fifteenth century until a tenancy of a yardland could be commonly acquired for a few capons. A recovery in the rate of fine, apparent as early as c. 1460 on the Worcester Cathedral priory estate, indicates a rising demand for land towards the end of our period, though even then there were few manors where fines were being paid above £1 per yardland.[101]

Innovations in the forms of tenure, notably the growth of various types of leasehold, began well before 1349. After that date the drop in population created an uncertain and unstable economic climate in which leases, often for terms of twelve years or less, or a single life, became common. Even more short-term were the many holdings held "at the will of the lord", or "sold" by a reeve or bailiff for a year at a time because they "lay in the lord's hands". Such arrangements, which allowed both lords and tenants the chance of adjusting to short-term changes, were especially prevalent in the late fourteenth and early fifteenth century. Some large manors in the west Cotswolds, Bisley, Hawkesbury, and Horsley, went over almost entirely to tenures for lives, while on the manors of Westminster abbey and the bishopric of Worcester hereditary customary tenures, copyholds held *sibi et suis*, returned to predominate in the fifteenth century. An increasingly common practice, even in manors with hereditary copyholds, was for a tenant to receive a tenement, often immediately after he had surrendered it to the lord, for three lives, usually naming his wife as the second life and a son as the third. Three-life leases were especially numerous in the mid- and late fifteenth century on the Stoneleigh abbey (War.) estate, sometimes being extended to include the lives of

---

[100] C. Dyer, 'A redistribution of incomes in fifteenth-century England?', in *Peasants, Knights and Heretics*, ed. R. H. Hilton, pp. 192–215; *Accounts of the Obedientars of Abingdon Abbey*, ed. R. E. G. Kirk, Camden NS LI, 1892, pp. 153–5, 162–3; Hilton, *English Peasantry*, pp. 65–9.

[101] These generalizations are based on the records of the manors of the Berkeley family, St Augustine's Bristol, Winchcomb abbey, Worcester Cathedral priory, and the bishopric of Worcester, cited in n. 99 above.

all of the children. On manors which retained leaseholds for terms of years, such as Lidney (Glos.), the length of the terms in the fifteenth century became as long as seventy years.[102] Everywhere in the southern counties of the region the amount of land held on lease was increased around 1400 through the widespread letting of demesnes to farmers. A substantial minority of demesnes, especially in the woodland districts, were leased in parcels, and so added to the land available to the peasant community. In such villages as Westbury-on-Trym (Glos.), many peasants were able to combine a customary tenement on copyhold with a piece of demesne for a term of years. Similar arrangements may also have existed on manors where the demesne was apparently leased *en bloc* to a gentleman farmer, because a lessee of this sort could have sublet it to the local peasantry.[103]

The rents paid for leasehold land were supposedly more flexible and more readily changed than customary assize rents. However, after some initial sharp fluctuations in the uncertain times around 1400, most leasehold rents became relatively sluggish, with a tendency to decline. Important exceptions are found in the leases of pastures, such as those of north Derbyshire, which were in sufficient demand after a brief mid-fifteenth-century slump for increases in rents to be paid.[104]

The waning authority of the landlords is indicated in letting agreements by the frequent rehearsal of the obligations of tenants, and in court-roll presentments of the neglect of both written and unwritten rules. Non-payment of rent, failure to cultivate land, illicit subletting, and the unlicensed felling of trees, were all offences frequently committed, but none are mentioned so often in the records as the failure to keep buildings in repair, especially after about 1370. Building clauses, requiring a new tenant to put up a house or a barn, are found in quantity in the century 1380–1480. Their disappearance from the records in the late fifteenth century reflects the weariness of landlords, who came to realize that tenants could not be forced to erect buildings that they did not need, because the collapsed buildings often belonged to holdings that had been incorporated into a multiple tenement. As well as their attempts to compel tenants to maintain their buildings, lords carried out repairs at their own expense, especially in the early fifteenth century. They also sought to maintain the attractiveness of holdings for prospective tenants by drawing up inventories of major

[102] Harvey, *Westminster Abbey and its Estates*, pp. 244–93; Dyer, *Lords and Peasants*, pp. 292–7; PRO SC 2/175/10; 175/46; 175/63; 207/79 (Bisley, Hawkesbury, Horsley); Shakespeare's Birthplace Trust RO, DR18/7–33 (Stoneleigh); Glos. RO, D421/M19 (Lidney).

[103] Dyer, *op. cit.*, pp. 209–17.

[104] *The Duchy of Lancaster's Estates in Derbyshire, 1485–1540*, ed. I. S. W. Blanchard, Derbs. Arch. Soc. Rec. Ser. III, 1971, pp. 1–13.

chattels (*principalia*) to be passed from one tenant to another. On the Winchcomb abbey (Glos.) estate new tenants were occasionally encouraged with gifts of draught animals.[105]

Falling rents and an erosion of control by lords can be taken to reflect the internal economy of the peasant holding in two ways. The tenants benefited from the reduction in the lord's demands on their resources. They were gradually relieved of irregular and unexpected payments, like the *merchet* of £4 taken from a Honeybourne (Worcs.) serf in 1405.[106] So the peasants' savings were less vulnerable to arbitrary expropriation, and more money was available for investment, indicated by increasing flocks and herds, and the peasant enclosure movement documented above (Chapter 3, E). On the other hand, the lower rents may indicate some of the problems facing the peasant in the context of the generally depressed prices for agricultural produce and the labour shortage. Peasants did not suffer from these adverse developments as much as a large-scale farmer would have done, because of the elements of auto-consumption and family labour in the peasants' economy. They still found it difficult to make large cash profits to pay the rent and to invest in such expensive items as buildings.

These problems help to explain the paradox that tenants of relatively large holdings could be afflicted by extreme poverty, like a serf of Admington (War.) in 1452, Thomas Roberts, who, although he held a yardland, was judged too poor to keep his tenement. He could neither pay his rent nor repair his buildings, so he was sent to live on another manor on the Winchcomb estate.[107] Not infrequently large holdings were surrendered into the hands of the lord, and vacant large tenements were not always quickly taken by new tenants. These cases are usually found in champion, open-field villages, where the problems of low grain prices and scarce labour must have been felt most acutely. From the woodland districts we hear less frequently reports of ruinous buildings, to take one characteristic problem of the period. In the Arden woodland of north Warwickshire, there seems to have been a good deal of prosperity, judging from the quantity of parish church building in the area, and the relative increase in its tax payments between 1327 and 1524, both changes being indicative of the rising wealth of the upper ranks of the peasantry. The woodlands had the advantage of having a good deal of enclosed land from assarting before 1349, an already existing pastoral element in the economy, and weak social controls, whether from landlords or village communities. Consequently the innovations needed to increase peasant farm

---

[105] Field, 'Worcestershire peasant buildings, household goods and farming equipment', pp. 105–45; Hilton, *English Peasantry*, pp. 191–3; *VCH Staffs.*, vi, p. 40; Glos. RO, D678/94, 99.
[106] Glos. RO, D678/61.   [107] Glos. RO, D678/62.

efficiency, such as consolidation, enclosure, and the extension of grazing land, would have been much more easily accomplished in the woodlands than in the open-field villages. Much of the evidence for rapid change in peasant agriculture comes from the areas of dispersed settlement and old enclosure. To take a Staffordshire example, Thomas Halsey's holding at Cannock, recorded in 1467, consisting of three adjacent enclosed crofts in a consolidated block, would be inconceivable outside a woodland environment.[108]

Most peasant farms were directed towards satisfying the food needs of the household, as is suggested by the continuation of some arable cultivation in pastoral areas in spite of the general moves towards greater agricultural specialization. However, no peasant holding was an island of self-sufficiency, and larger holdings of a yardland or above would be capable of producing sizeable saleable surpluses. The management of a holding involved complex decisions on the degree of market orientation, the balance between arable and pasture, and the extent to which the holding would be managed directly or rented out. The last practice might lead to disputes, revealing the contractual arrangements, like the *champart* tenures by which better-off Halesowen tenants let parts of their holdings to poorer neighbours. Animals too were often leased out, as at Harvington (Worcs.) in the 1370s, where twelve ewes were let for four years, and at Stoneleigh (War.), where a cow was hired out just before 1493 for four years in return for a half of its "increase", with the lessee agreeing to replace with females any male calves born. These contracts are only recorded because they were broken; they were probably representative of a normally hidden labyrinth of leasing of land and resources in each village. The sale of produce need not have been simple either. The aptly named John Deye of Ombersley attempted to recover his debts in 1377, revealing that he had sold cheese to thirteen villagers on credit. Sales outside the village to butchers or cornmongers no doubt involved cash advances by the buyers.[109] Many villagers disposed of some of their surplus produce by selling bread, ale, or meat retail to their neighbours, but increasingly through our period the selling of ale became a specialized preserve of smallholders who gained the bulk of their livelihood from the trade. Peasants would also involve themselves in the extraction of raw

[108] L. J. Proudfoot, 'The extension of parish churches in medieval Warwickshire', *J. of Historical Geography*, 9, 1983, pp. 231–46, esp. table 2; M. J. Stanley, 'Medieval tax returns as source material', in *Field and Forest, an Historical Geography of Warwickshire and Worcestershire*, ed. T. R. Slater and P. J. Jarvis, Norwich, 1982, pp. 231–56, esp. maps 10.3 and 10.5, and Table 10.4; Staffs. RO, D1734/2/1/176.

[109] Razi, 'Family, land, and village community', pp. 32–3; Worcs. Cathedral Library, E30; Shakespeare's Birthplace Trust RO, DR18/32; Worcs. RO, ref. 705: 56 BA 3910/39; Hilton, *English Peasantry*, pp. 42–53.

materials or the manufacture of industrial goods. Some crafts, like linen weaving, would use materials produced on the holding; metal- and woodworkers, potters and tilers, would all have been able to obtain raw materials or fuel from woods and wastes. Smiths and clothworkers often depended on supplies from further afield, in the latter case provided by entrepreneurs. Many industrial processes were fitted into the slack seasons of the agricultural year, like lead mining in Derbyshire, where peasants apparently used their earnings from mining as a source of rent-money.[110]

If the peasant holding was a "family farm" in the sense that one of its main functions was to supply the subsistence requirements of the household, was it also regarded as family property, to be passed down from generation to generation? Courts rolls show a constant traffic in land, its passage from tenant to tenant suggesting a decline in family links with their holdings. In spite of this, it has been shown at Halesowen (Worcs.) in the period 1351–1430 that 57 per cent of transfers of land were between relatives, including such comparatively remote kin as cousins and in-laws. Peasant communities valued hereditary succession by far-flung relatives, and enshrined this prejudice in declarations of custom, like those at Thornbury (Glos.) in 1486, and at Painswick (Glos.) in c. 1490, and put their ideas into practice in making difficult judgements in manor courts over the rival claims of heirs to customary holdings.[111] However, it would be dangerous to generalize from a few examples, as clearly the net outward migration from unattractive champion villages shows that in adverse circumstances the link between a family and its land could be broken. A tenant who fled at night from his derelict tenement, a not uncommon occurrence, was clearly not motivated by a strong attachment to his family's land. Also, in the case of those places where a great deal of inheritance continued, such as Halesowen, the necessity of recognizing remote kin, including people living at some distance from their ancestors' village, indicates the decline of the nuclear family as a group within which property was transmitted, often simply because direct male heirs were lacking.

The frequency with which land passed by inheritance also changed over time. Succession to holdings within the nuclear family was evidently more common in the late fourteenth century than after 1400.

---

[110] Hilton, *English Peasantry*, pp. 45–6; Dyer, *op. cit.*, pp. 344–9; Carus-Wilson, 'Evidences of industrial growth', pp. 190–205; J. R. Birrell, 'Peasant craftsmen in the medieval forest', *AHR*, XVII, 1969, pp. 91–107; I. S. W. Blanchard, 'The miner and the agricultural community in late medieval England', *AHR*, xx, 1972, pp. 93–106.

[111] Razi, 'Family, land and the village community', p. 17; St Clair Baddeley, *A Cotteswold Manor*, pp. 135–40; Gloucester Public Library, RQ303.2.

In the middle of the fifteenth century at Kempsey (Worcs.) peasants, who were presumably much affected by the shortage of hired labour, bought and sold land in order to adjust the size of the holding to suit their needs as their families grew and then became smaller. A substantial minority of better-off peasants, perhaps disturbed by the rapidity of the transfer of land, arranged three-life tenures so as to make the eventual succession of their sons more certain, or they sold the reversion of the holding to a son. Still, as before the plague, the older generation might retire to a corner of the messuage to make way for a younger successor. All of these measures might still fail to secure the succession of heirs, either because the heirs themselves died, or because young men might see better opportunities elsewhere.[112]

The family's role as a labour force may lie behind many inheritance arrangements. A son (not necessarily the eldest) worked on his parents' holding in expectation of taking over the tenancy. The 1381 poll-tax returns for Staffordshire make the position of children clear by describing them as "son and servant" or "daughter and servant". Children could provide only part of the necessary labour force, especially for larger holdings, and in the demographic circumstances of the later middle ages many peasant households would lack mature offspring. In its labour supply, as in much else, the household formed an "incomplete" economic unit, dependent on exchange of labour for cash and goods with its neighbours.

Wage-labour came from two main sources, smallholders and others working part-time, hired by the day, and resident servants who were employed full-time on annual contracts. The former type of workers included quarter-yardlanders; six of these at Willoughby (War.) in 1359 refused to accept wage-work when offered, presumably in order to gain higher wages. Even tenants with considerably larger holdings than a quarter-yardland might be available for hire, like Simon Medowe of Baddesley Clinton (War.), who ploughed and carted for wages in the 1440s. The proportion of wage-earners should not be under-estimated. In the records of the 1381 poll tax for Gloucestershire about 40 per cent of the adult male population were described either as labourers or servants, the former term sometimes implying that the wage-worker had a household, and perhaps a smallholding, of his own. In contemporary south Staffordshire out of a total of 2,312 people paying tax in rural settlements 7 per cent (165) were described as labourers, cottars or workmen, and another 10 per cent (231) were called servants. There were also 9 per cent (203) listed under some craft occupation. The overall proportion of wage-earners must have been

---

[112] Dyer, op. cit., pp. 305–15; Hilton, English Peasantry, pp. 28–30.

well in excess of 30 per cent, because many of the women, sons, or daughters, and the 363 (16 per cent) of unknown status or occupation doubtless should be included in the part-time labour force.

The full-time living-in servants were more likely than any other social group to evade the poll tax. Even so, in eight north Derbyshire villages in 1381 almost a half of the *cultores* or peasants (46 per cent) are recorded as employing at least one servant, and 7 per cent had at least three. In Gloucestershire many substantial peasants were recorded as having one or two servants, and one exceptional household is found with five and another with seven. No doubt the servants were often young people who were earning wages at the first stage of their working lives. They were paid in kind, in food and clothing, with only sums of a shilling or two in cash mentioned in occasional litigation over non-payment. In spite of these disputes, the relationship between employer and employee could be so close as to blur the distinction between children and servants. A striking example of the virtual adoption of a servant as a child-substitute comes from Thornbury (Glos.) in 1439 when Richard and Joan Brocke named Alice their servant as the third life to follow them in a three-life lease.[113] The precise number of wage-earners employed in the peasant community must remain obscure because of the lack of high-quality evidence. The generally high level of daily wage rates must reflect an overall shortage of labour, but within this context any changes in the structure of the labour force are uncertain. On the one hand the evidence of disputes recorded in both royal and seigneurial courts points to a growing importance of short-term employment; on the other, the reduction in the numbers of smallholders and the growth of pastoral farming, with its special labour needs, may have led to a relative expansion of full-time service. These ambiguities of the evidence can only be resolved by further research.[114]

The village acted as an important recruiting ground for wage-labour, and the village notables were conscious of the need to maintain labour discipline, notably through by-laws which sought to compel local wage-earners to accept employment within the village at harvest time. Individual villages could rarely be self-sufficient in labour, and

[113] *The Poll Tax of 2–4 Richard II, AD 1379–81*, ed. W. Boyd and G. Wrottesley, Staffs. Rec. Soc., XVII, 1896, pp. 157–205; L. M. Midgley, 'Some Staffordshire poll tax returns', Staffs. Rec. Soc., 4th ser. VI, 1970, pp. 1–25; Hilton, *English Peasantry*, pp. 34–5, 51–2; Putnam, *The Enforcement of the Statutes of Labourers*, p. 224; Dyer, 'A small landowner, p. 13; R. H. Hilton, 'Some social and economic evidence in late medieval English tax returns', in *Spoleczenstwo, gospodarka, kultura. Studia ofiarowane Marianowi Maliowistowi*, ed. S. Herbst, Warsaw, 1974, pp. 111–28; Blanchard, 'Economic change in Derbyshire', pp. 496–500; Staffs. RO D641/1/4c/7.

[114] Razi, 'Family, land, and the village community', pp. 31–2; A. Kussmaul, *Servants in Husbandry in Early Modern England*, Cambridge, 1981, p. 101.

workers of all kinds travelled long distances to find employment. Notable among them were those possessing specialist skills, such as building workers. Unskilled labour came from the reservoir of manpower to the west, and gangs of Welsh harvest workers moved through the region; at other seasons the heavy labour of digging ditches and ponds was done by itinerant groups of Welsh "dikers".[115]

Such problems as labour shortage and the decline in direct hereditary succession to holdings can be seen as weakening the cohesion of village communities. They resulted in rapid migration, so that it became unusual for a family in the direct male line to be traceable in one place for more than three generations. At Ladbroke (War.), for example, only four of the thirty-two surnames listed in a rental of 1374 appear in a comparable document of 1457. However, the discontinuities created by migration ought not to be exaggerated. In north Worcestershire in the late fifteenth century newcomers were assimilated with ease, and recent immigrants played a full part in the economy and government of their villages within a few years of their arrival.[116] The vital force that kept the village inhabitants together was their common interest in their fields and pastures, together with a need to maintain good order against various types of anti-social behaviour. Newcomers and older inhabitants alike would appreciate the collective controls that helped to protect their way of life, and this feeling is most clearly visible in the numerous by-laws that were announced and enforced in the seigneurial courts. The fullest series of by-laws is found in the records of such courts as that held at Elmley Castle (Worcs.), a nucleated, open-field settlement, but they are also found in dispersed, woodland landscapes which might be expected to have had less concern with common fields.[117] The by-laws provide us with ambiguous evidence. They are proof of the continued existence of the village community; the need to repeat and revise the rules indicates the tensions that threatened the future of the close-knit village. The real enemies of the village community were not so much the poor, against whose idle, feckless, and criminal behaviour many by-laws were aimed, but the members of the village elite who pursued their own economic interests by enclosure or overstocking to the detriment of the long-term future of the common fields.

[115] Worcs. RO, ref 009:1 BA 2636/173; T. H. Lloyd, *Some Aspects of the Building Industry in Medieval Stratford-upon-Avon*, Dugdale Soc., Occ. Paper no. 14, 1961, p. 11; *Proceedings before the Justices of the Peace in the Fourteenth and Fifteenth Centuries*, ed. B. H. Putnam, London, 1938, pp. 410–11; Shakespeare's Birthplace Trust RO, Ferrers Mss., 801–2.

[116] Dyer, *Lords and Peasants*, pp. 355–72; PRO SC 12/16/27, SC 12/16/30; R. K. Field, 'Migration in the later middle ages: the case of the Hampton Lovett villeins', *Mid. Hist.*, VIII, 1983, pp. 29–48.   [117] Ault, *Open-Field Farming*, pp. 106, 110–13, 118–22, 125–36.

F. WALES AND THE MARCHES

The social structure in many localities of Wales and the marches in the later middle ages was subjected to considerable and various pressures. A noteworthy feature was the emergence, from the social flux, of the *uchelwyr*, a native Welsh squirearchy characterized by noble descent, social status, and personal wealth. The acquisition of lands, consolidation of estates, and tenure of offices are recorded in official and estate collections of documents, and a significant corpus of poetry was composed in praise of the *uchelwyr*. The surviving evidence from this period confirms not only the increasing predominance of an emergent gentry class but also the continued vitality of social groupings whose distinctive features conformed in several respects to those identified in a comparatively recent definition of the late medieval peasantry. Possession was normally exerted over the means of agricultural production. Holdings were worked on a family basis although the peasants were frequently associated with a more extensive unit which involved the exercise of collective rights. Artisans and craftsmen involved in non-agrarian pursuits formed an integral part of the peasant community. Moreover, the production of commodities which were surplus to their own subsistence requirements enabled the peasants to fulfil extraneous obligations, such as those imposed by seigneurial and commercial authorities.[118]

Distinctions within peasant communities included those based upon personal status and tenurial arrangements. On the manors freemen held land by a variety of military and socage tenures, whilst villein tenants who resided in nucleated villages occupied customary lands which were cultivated in conjunction with the demesne. They were protected by the "custom of the manor" but were subject to numerous renders and labour services, which by the mid-fourteenth century had been largely commuted to cash payments. Labour services imposed on customary tenants occasionally survived the termination of demesne-based operations, and at Condover in 1422 the labour services were defined as "moweing, casting abrode and gathering together" the hay.[119] The customary holding was the lord's property, and his permission was

---

[118] Hilton, *English Peasantry*, p. 13; C. Thomas, 'Peasant agriculture in medieval Gwynedd', *Folk Life*, 13, 1975, pp. 28–9, also considers various concepts of the peasantry and these again may be related to communal arrangements in Wales at this period. These two works are valuable sources for the themes considered in this chapter, together with the works cited above in ch. 2, n. 124, and ch. 3, n. 119.

[119] Rees, *South Wales and the March*, pp. 144–51, 173–83; W. J. Slack, 'The Condover extents, 1283–1500', *Shropshire Arch. Soc.*, L, 1940, p. 130.

therefore required for the acquisition or disposal of land. The occupants of customary land comprised a variety of tenurial groupings and in one locality of south-west Wales there were two main categories of customary tenants. The *coloni* or husbandmen occupied on a hereditary basis land formerly held by villein tenants and represented the most significant class of tenants at the episcopal manor of Lamphey in 1326. The second category included the *censarii* or censory tenants, who held lands such as the demesne or escheated plots which had formerly been in the lord's hands; their position was often that of tenants for life.[120]

Tenurial forms which resembled customary tenure were found in some parts of north-west Wales towards the middle of the fourteenth century. Bond tenants continued in certain localities to hold their lands by *tref gyfrif* tenure, which involved the recurrent partition and allocation of equal shares of arable land. Grazing rights were also exercised in the waste land which surrounded the arable *tir cyfrif* holdings. The agrarian activities of the bondmen were carefully regulated by the *maer biswail*, or land mayor, and his main settlement, the *maerdref*, contained the *llys*, or local court, and a large area of *tir bwrdd*, or demesne land, on which the bondmen were traditionally required to perform labour services.[121] Groups of bondmen in Anglesey in 1352 held land by *tref gyfrif* tenure and also in townships which contained *gwelyau*. These occupants of *gwelyau* were of bond personal status: they were bound to the soil and were required to undertake various communal obligations. Their tenurial position, however, corresponded to that of their free *tir gwelyawg* counterparts and similar regulations related to the succession and partition of bond and free *gwelyau*.[122]

The establishment of bond *gwelyau* may well have resulted from a conscious and deliberate administrative policy aimed at the colonization of marginal territory, with the bondmen encouraged to vacate their lands by the grant of a more favourable *tir gwelyawg* status. The distinctive agrarian and tenurial arrangements of the *gwely*, with its

---

[120] B. E. Howells, 'Pembrokeshire farming, *circa* 1580–1620', *NLW Jnl.*, IX, 1955–6, pp. 414–17; *idem*, 'Open fields and farmsteads in Pembrokeshire', *The Pembrokeshire Historian*, 3, 1971, pp. 16–20.

[121] G. R. J. Jones, 'The tribal system in Wales', pp. 119–20; *idem*, 'Field systems of North Wales', pp. 434, 460–71.

[122] G. R. J. Jones, 'The distribution of medieval settlement in Anglesey', *Anglesey Antiq. Soc.*, 1955, pp. 54–7, 75–84; H. Ellis, ed., *The Record of Caernarvon*, Rec. Comm., 1838, pp. 49–50, 54, 60–1, 65–6; A. D. Carr, 'The extent of Anglesey, 1352', *Anglesey Antiq. Soc.*, 1971–2, pp. 173–6, 187–9, 204, 217, 219; *idem*, *Medieval Anglesey*, pp. 29–35; Jones Pierce, *MWS*, pp. 274–5 refers to the distinction in size between a free and a bond *gwely* township with the smaller bond *gwely* township often corresponding to a hamlet.

incorporated share-lands, were particularly associated with free communities. Clan-land, designated either as *gwely* or as *gafael*, was occupied by members of the *gwelygordd*, or free agnatic kindred. The *priodor* (free clansman) exercised hereditary proprietary rights in the pasture, wood, and waste land and *tir priod* (the appropriated land), which usually consisted of a *tyddyn* (homestead) and *tir gwasgar* (scattered arable plots). Restrictions were placed upon the *priodor*'s ability to dispose of his property and also upon the redistribution of appropriated land.[123] The inheritance of proprietary rights was based upon the principle of *cyfran* (partible succession), but whereas the original homestead of the *gwely*-founder was reserved for the youngest son, the partition of appropriated land could only be effected on three occasions. Following *gorffenran* (final partition), involving members of the *gwelygordd* linked at least by a second-cousin relationship, only the waste unappropriated land of the *gwely* could be divided among the free clansmen.[124]

The tenurial systems based upon the direct cultivation of the demesne and on clan holdings were both subject to dislocation and disruption in the later middle ages (see above, pp. 96–106). Customary tenure, a distinctive feature of the manorial system, was inevitably modified as a result of the leasing of demesne lands and increasingly gave way to a variety of tenurial forms. Copyholders, who were frequently in a powerful tenurial position in the fifteenth century, occupied customary holdings and portions of demesne lands in various localities of south Wales and the border shires.[125] Tenants-at-will, who were frequently indistinguishable from copyholders, occupied bond-lands formerly attached to the *maerdref* of Hendwr, in the barony of Edeirnion, in 1390, and also appeared among the landholders on the monastic estates of Aberconway and Strata Florida.[126] Towards the end of the fifteenth century tenures at will tended to be converted to

[123] G. R. J. Jones, 'The distribution of medieval settlement in Anglesey', pp. 56–7; *idem*, 'The tribal system in Wales', pp. 114–18; *idem*, 'Field systems of North Wales', pp. 432–3; T. Jones Pierce, in *AHEW*, IV, pp. 363–6; *idem*, *MWS*, 334–5.

[124] G. R. J. Jones, 'Field systems of North Wales', p. 433; *Llyfr Colan*, ed. D. Jenkins, Cardiff, 1963, pp. 35–6, 149–50. For further discussion of *tref gyfrif*, *gwely* and *gafael* holdings, see above pp. 95–7, 249–51.

[125] I. S. Leadam, 'The security of copyholders in the fifteenth and sixteenth centuries', *EHR*, VIII, 1893, pp. 684–96; R. H. Hilton, *The Decline of Serfdom in Medieval England*, London, 1969, p. 58; Rees, *South Wales and the March*, pp. 261–2; R. R. Davies, 'The lordship of Ogmore', pp. 309–10; Slack, 'The Condover extents', pp. 117–18, 130–1; C. S. Davies, *A History of Macclesfield*, Manchester, 1961, p. 28.

[126] A. D. Carr, 'An Edeyrnion inquisition, 1390', *JMHRS*, VI, 1969, p. 2; R. W. Hays, *The History of the Abbey of Aberconway, 1187–1537*, Cardiff, 1963, pp. 163–4; G. D. Owen, 'Agrarian conditions and changes in West Wales during the sixteenth century', Univ. of Wales Ph.D. thesis, 1935, pp. 171–3.

leasehold tenure, with leases being drawn up for a specific number of lives or a period of time. Tenants sought greater security whilst landlords were eager both to ensure stable profits and to exert a more stringent control over their territory in a period of falling rents. Long-term leases, in particular, fulfilled these conditions and a period of 99 years was frequently stipulated. The substantial sums of money involved in these transactions resulted in the leases being held by the more prominent individuals of the locality. Short-term leases, obtained for small sums for money, represented an increasingly popular proposition for members of the peasant community, whilst the opportunity of regaining control within a shorter period of time was also welcomed by the landowner. The occupation of small portions of escheated lands on short-term leases involving limited capital outlay particularly appealed to peasant proprietors at a time of political disturbance and social dislocation. The leases were normally subject to an annual rent and obligations relating to the maintenance of buildings were occasionally imposed. Tenants who leased in 1470 portions of the Hafod y Porth grange, which belonged to the Cistercian abbey of Margam, thus received timber so that the property was kept in a state of good repair.[127] An even more striking change involving customary tenements was the adoption of freehold tenure. The charter-lands recorded on a rental compiled for Senghennydd in 1450 represented customary holdings which had been converted into freehold by the lord's grant of a charter.[128]

Those lands which had been removed from the communal authority of kindred groupings were held on individualist terms by tenants required to pay a cash rent for each property held. One of the agencies responsible for this transition was the process of escheat. Territory thus involved was "extended" or valued by royal or seigneurial officials and was therefore described in contemporary financial documents as "extent-lands" or *Tir Stent*. The size and value of these lands are frequently recorded and a specific official, the escheator, was responsible for the maintenance of renders from this source. The occupants of escheated lands in north-west Wales were tenants at will of the crown and were subject to "extended" or "improved" rents. Their status had

---

[127] Halcrow, 'The decline of demesne farming', pp. 352–3; G. A. Holmes, *Estates of the Higher Nobility*, pp. 114–16; Glanmor Williams, *The Welsh Church*, p. 169; numerous examples of long leases include NLW, The Mynde Park Deeds and Documents 160, and Pitchford Hall Deeds and Documents 299,190 and 558,133; Pugh, *Marcher Lordships of South Wales*, pp. 165–6; Duby, *Rural Economy and Country Life*, pp. 323–4; above, pp. 97, 103–4; W. de Gray Birch, *A History of Margam Abbey*, London, 1887, p. 348.

[128] J. Beverley Smith, 'The lordship of Senghennydd', pp. 320–1; NLW, Plymouth Deeds and Documents 412.

been recognized as inferior to that of the *tir gwelyawg* tenants and early
in the fourteenth century petitions had been submitted against the
original imposition of escheat.[129]

The opportunity of acquiring vacated holdings formerly attached to
the demesne or the property of kindred groupings was seized by
ambitious elements active in Wales and the borderlands. Settler English
families introduced into Wales immediately after the Edwardian
conquest acted as a stimulus to the process of social change. Colonies
established in various parts of Wales were inhabited by English families
induced to settle in them by the grants of property on favourable
conditions. In the neighbourhood of Denbigh, territory formerly
occupied by clan groupings was secured as a result of the operation of
escheat and the resettlement of native inhabitants. The land was then
divided into individual plots and offered to immigrant English families
on attractive tenurial terms.[130] The burgesses of Oswestry and the
residents of the plantation boroughs founded in north-west Wales were
actively involved in the acquisition of small clan-holdings located in the
adjacent rural hinterlands. Bondlands especially attracted the attention
of acquisitive burgesses and the boundaries of the boroughs of Conway
and Beaumaris were extended, in 1355 and 1366 respectively, by the
addition of lands formerly subject to bond tenurial status.[131] Native
Welshmen also exploited the available opportunities and, like their
counterparts among the settler families, laid the foundations for the
large freehold estates which were appearing by the early sixteenth
century. Some enterprising *priodorion*, or members of free kindred
groupings, succeeded, by propitious participation in an active and
flourishing land market, in establishing themselves as *uchelwyr*. Estate
consolidation, in the late fourteenth and again in the fifteenth century,
was partially effected by the acquisition of property rights in the
territories of several clans.[132]

Most members of the peasant community suffered from the various
economic and political pressures which were responsible for the
disruption of the basic tenurial systems. A symptom of difficulties

[129] E. A. Lewis, 'The decay of tribalism in North Wales', *Hon. Soc. Cymmr.*, 1902–3, pp. 32–3;
J. Beverley Smith, 'The lordship of Senghennydd', pp. 318–21; *Cal. of Ancient Petitions relating
to Wales*, ed. W. Rees, Cardiff, 1975, pp. 64, 164.

[130] Lewis, *Medieval Boroughs of Snowdonia*, p. 58; D. Huw Owen, 'The Englishry of Denbigh:
an English colony in medieval Wales', *Hon. Soc. Cymmr.*, 1974–5, pp. 57–76.

[131] Slack, *The Lordship of Oswestry*, pp. 142–3; L. O. W. Smith, 'The lordships of Chirk and
Oswestry', pp. 314–17; Jones Pierce, *MWS*, pp. 196–8; Lewis, *Medieval Boroughs of Snowdonia*,
pp. 46, 50.

[132] Jones Pierce, *MWS*, pp. 236–7, 239–40; C. Thomas, 'Patterns and processes of estate
expansion in the fifteenth and sixteenth centuries', *JMHRS*, VI, 1972, pp. 335–7; C. A. Gresham,
Eifionydd, pp. 9–11, 82–3, 102–5, 204–5.

encountered by peasants was the increased morcellation of holdings which may be observed towards the middle of the fourteenth century. The size of each holding was naturally influenced by the labour force employed on it, and a combination of the effects of demographic pressures and of partible inheritance explains the reduction in the average size of holdings. A rental of the lordship of Hay, compiled in 1340, recorded that only 4 of the 119 tenants in the Welshry held properties of more than ten acres and that 79 individuals, representing two-thirds of the total tenantry, occupied holdings of less than five acres each. In the lordship of Monmouth two-thirds of the tenants at Whitecastle held in 1386 properties of under ten acres, and at Hadnock 48 of the 100 tenants occupied, again in the late fourteenth century, holdings of under fifteen acres.[133] The majority of free clansmen in the fourteenth century are believed to have held between six and ten acres of arable land. The size of the average property accounted for in the escheators' accounts of the commote of Arllechwedd Uchaf (Caerns.) in the period 1300 to 1400 amounted to six acres of arable land. The extent of morcellation in this locality is further emphasized in the mid-fifteenth-century rental prepared for the Conway burgess, Bartholo-mew Bolde, who acquired, during the years 1420 to 1453, hundreds of small properties in the commote. This rental reveals that approximately 375 statute acres in the hamlet of Llwydfaen were occupied by at least sixty-nine tenants. Gafael Rhys ap Bleddyn, a kindred grouping which occupied 50 acres in the hamlet, included nineteen dispersed holdings of one, two, or three acres. Following the purchase of most of these units, together with that of other small adjacent lands, the territorial consolidation of Llwydfaen by the Bulkeley family had been completed by 1462–3, and the accumulated lands, forming a substantial estate, comprised the Caernarfonshire lands of the Bulkeley of Beaumaris family. A number of the holdings recorded in the Bolde rental had been formed as a result of consolidation, and it is therefore probable that plots of land in an earlier period had been of an even smaller size. The extreme partition of proprietary rights by the mid-fifteenth century is illustrated by the calculation that the proprietary share of one clansman in Melin Castell, a mill which had once belonged to the clan, was worth $\frac{1}{2}$d.: "the profit of one day's multure".[134]

[133] Above, pp. 96, 250 for discussion on the effects of Welsh inheritance law; G. L. Fairs, *A History of the Hay*, Chichester, 1972, p. 41; Glamorgan RO, the former Cardiff Library Collection, C.L./Manorial box 3, Extent of the Manor of Hay, 1340; R. R. Davies, 'The Bohun and Lancaster lordships in Wales in the fourteenth and early fifteenth centuries', Univ. of Oxford D. Phil. thesis, 1965, p. 212; PRO DL 43/13/7–8.

[134] Jones Pierce, in *AHEW*, IV, p. 360; *idem*, *MWS*, pp. 195–217; C. A. Gresham, 'The Bolde rental (Bangor Ms. 1939)', *Caerns. Hist. Soc.*, XXVI, 1965, pp. 31–49; D. C. Jones, 'The Bulkeleys of Beaumaris, 1440–1547', *Anglesey Antiq. Soc.*, 1961, pp. 1–4.

Small parcels of land, formerly associated with the demesne or kindred systems, appear frequently in the extant conveyances of the later middle ages.[135] Caution should certainly be exercised in assessing the nature of some plots of land whose size was apparently restricted. Extensive rights of pasturing on the *cytir* (common) were occasionally attached to certain holdings occupying a small territorial area. The dispersed and fragmented nature of many holdings, however, served to encourage both the depressed element among the peasantry to dispose of uneconomic units and also the more ambitious individuals who sought to create viable estates. These complementary trends were achieved despite the operation of traditional restrictions. Court rolls record payments associated with the transfer of customary lands and these included renders of a heriot on leaving the property, and an entry fine on taking possession of it.[136] Entry fines frequently represented a high proportion of the profits of manorial courts, and in the lordship of Newport in 1434–5 they amounted to over 85 per cent of the total manorial income. Fines were also paid for licences to alienate land and again small properties were often involved. Entries in the court rolls for the manors of Hadnock and Monmouth in the first half of the fifteenth century refer to the payment of fines of 1d. and 3d. for licences to surrender units of 1, $2\frac{1}{2}$, and 4 acres of land.[137]

Licences were also issued which provided for the transfer of territory formerly subject to the control of kindred groupings. Fines paid for these licences, which ensured that the lands would be held in fee, often represented substantial sums of money, and transactions frequently involved members of the more prominent native families. Some of the licences stipulated that the lands to be held in fee had formerly been occupied by means of a *prid* transaction. The process of *prid*, a perpetual mortgage or vifgage, constituted the most common form of clan-land alienation in the period.[138] Welsh land law restricted the transfer of real property and sought to safeguard the integrity of clan-holdings. The financial benefits accruing from a carefully regulated land market would seem to have been appreciated by the native thirteenth-century

[135] Numerous examples include NLW, Bronwydd Deeds and Documents 1348, 828, 810, and Mynde Park Deeds and Documents 347(xv), 83, 22, 34.

[136] Rees, *South Wales and the March*, pp. 151–2; NLW, Badminton Deeds and Documents 1089 illustrates this form of payment recorded on a court roll of the lordship of Usk compiled in 1438.

[137] Pugh, *Marcher Lordships of South Wales*, p. 173; NLW, Milborne Family Papers and Documents 118, 115, 114, 161, 162, 119.

[138] J. Beverley Smith, 'Crown and community in the principality of North Wales', pp. 150–1; Jones Pierce, *MWS*, pp. 364–6, 384–6. A comprehensive and penetrating study of *prid* transactions appears in Llinos Beverley Smith, 'The gage and the land market in late medieval Wales', *EcHR*, 2nd ser. xxxix, 1976, pp. 537–50; *idem*, 'Tir prid: deeds of gage of land in late medieval Wales', *Bull. BCS*, xxvii, 1977, pp. 263–77.

rulers of Gwynedd. The extensive use of the *prid* diploma in the tenurial transactions of the fourteenth and fifteenth centuries suggests that the controls and restraints thereby imposed on the alienation of clan-lands were motivated by seigneurial pressure. The *prid* constituted a lease for a term of years and the *priodor* was allowed to transfer his property for a consideration. The lease might be renewed perpetually, but as the property was liable to redemption by the *priodor* or his heirs, tenure of the *prid*-lands was regarded as a form of temporary possession. The purchase of licences ensured the evasion of restrictions inherent in the occupation of both clan-lands and *prid*-lands and also proved to be a lucrative source of seigneurial income. Surviving estate and county records reveal the successful attempts made by the *uchelwyr* to utilize the *prid* deed as a means of circumventing traditional and seigneurial regulations. Studies of the formation of estates in north-west Wales illustrate the prevalence and significance of *prid* transactions in the acquisition and consolidation of landed property. The tenurial device of *prid* was also employed by those members of the peasant community who, although able to defend and promote their own interests in this period, did not attain the territorial influence and social status achieved by the *uchelwyr*. Prosperous peasants, therefore, who included tenants in the upland areas of the lordship of Oswestry and in the commote of Nanconwy in Caernarfonshire, succeeded in obtaining possession of small dispersed holdings by means of the *prid* device.[139]

The acquisition of fragmented holdings was accompanied by efforts to consolidate the scattered properties. An examination of the incidence of consolidation shows that greater frequency was evident in those lands subject to bond *tref gyfrif* tenure. On the demesne lands prosperous peasants were increasingly able to acquire strips of land which were adjacent to their own in the open fields and thus form consolidated arable holdings. Extant deeds record agreements made to exchange and consolidate strips in the common fields of Shropshire. In Herefordshire, the acquisition by purchase or exchange of strips by wealthier tenants resulted in the formation of compact blocks of territory in the open fields, a reduction in the number of landholders and a consequent increase in the size of the holdings.[140] The

---

[139] C. Thomas, 'Patterns and processes of estate expansion in the fifteenth and sixteenth centuries', pp. 335–7; Gresham, *Eifionydd*, pp. 9–10, 83, 104–5, 205; Llinos Beverley Smith, 'The gage and the land market in late medieval Wales', pp. 546–7 for the accumulation of lands by means of *prid* transactions in north-west and north-east Wales; Slack, *Lordship of Oswestry*, pp. 170–1; Jones Pierce, *MWS*, p. 52; PRO Wales 20/1.

[140] G. R. J. Jones, 'Rural settlement in Anglesey', p. 224; Davies, *History of Macclesfield*, pp. 12–13; J. Thirsk, in *AHEW*, IV, p. 246; NLW, Pitchford Hall Deeds and Documents 2434, 2029; A. J. Roderick, 'Open-field agriculture in Herefordshire in the later middle ages', *WNFC*, XXXIII, 1949, pp. 66–7.

redistribution of land, which together with the enlargement of individual holdings resulted from the consolidation of clan-lands and of parcels of the demesne, in turn led to an increased stratification within the peasant community. An examination of the financial accounts compiled for the lordship of Denbigh in the period 1397–1402 reveals that Welsh landholders may be divided into two distinct groups: a group containing those who held official posts in the commotes and possessed sufficient resources to occupy lands by means of the payment of fines, and a second, more numerous group comprising individuals who leased small portions of escheated lands on short-term leases.[141]

Many peasant farmers succeeded in maintaining and improving their positions. The freehold estates which were in process of formation contained lands farmed by groups of comparatively affluent and prosperous tenants. A rental of the Penrhyn estate compiled in 1413 records that a small group of prosperous tenants farmed Penwynllys in Anglesey, whilst six tenants in Cororion (Caerns.) occupied between them a total of seventeen holdings and paid as rent sums ranging from 6s. to 14s. per annum.[142] The availability of land in the early fifteenth century placed the tenant in an advantageous position *vis-à-vis* his lord. Tenants were often prepared to move to another locality to take advantage of improved agrarian and tenurial conditions. A rental of the customary lands of St Florence in south-west Wales reveals that in 1424 only a small minority of tenants, recorded in five out of 28 entries, had inherited their holdings. Many supporters of Owain Glyndŵr's rebellion in Wales and in the marches were soon able to regain control of confiscated lands. The lordship of Mawddwy thus seems to have constituted an exception to the general trend, and in this locality few heirs of Glyndŵr's supporters were able to recover their family lands.[143] In the lordship of Senghennydd in south-east Wales fairly substantial holdings in 1450 were vested in the hands of a large number of free proprietors who held their lands directly of their lord. A group of small proprietors still survived in the hamlet of Clenennau at the end of the fifteenth century despite the vigorous efforts of the family of John ap Maredudd, a *priodor*, to acquire proprietary rights and

---

[141] Duby, *Rural Economy and Country Life*, pp. 326, 337–41; D. Huw Owen, 'The Lordship of Denbigh, 1282–1425', Univ. of Wales Ph.D. thesis, 1967, pp. 269–71; PRO SC 6/1233/8, 1184/22, 1185/4.

[142] J. R. Jones, 'The development of the Penrhyn estate up to 1431', Univ. of Wales M.A. thesis, 1955, pp. 169, 204; UCNW, Penrhyn Coll. 1599.

[143] B. E. Howells, 'Studies in the social and agrarian history of medieval and early modern Pembrokeshire', Univ. of Wales M.A. thesis, 1956, pp. 119–20; *Cal. of the Public Records relating to Pembrokeshire*, ed. H. Owen, III, pp. 107–9; R. A. Griffiths, 'The Glyn Dwr rebellion in North Wales through the eyes of an Englishman', *Bull. BCS*, xx, 1967, pp. 152–3; K. Williams-Jones, 'A Mawddwy court roll, 1415–16', *ibid.*, xxiii, 1970, pp. 329–45.

consolidate scattered holdings within the commote of Eifionydd in Caernarfonshire.[144]

Individual bondmen appeared occasionally as participants in commercial transactions. In 1440 Dafydd ap Gwilym Selff leased for a term of 40 years two mills in the manor of Dowlais, in the lordship of Newport, for an annual rent of 33s. 4d. Some bondmen also secured their enfranchisement, and instances of this process are recorded in north-east Wales in the second half of the fourteenth century.[145] Flexibility may be observed in tenurial arrangements in that descendants of villeins often held freehold tenements whilst freeholders occupied customary lands. Free peasant proprietors also increasingly encroached upon those bond townships which were subject to depopulation and to heavy financial pressures. The acquisition of bond lands was frequently achieved despite the efforts of royal officials to protect and even in some cases repatriate the bondmen. In the lordship of Chirk, *prid* conveyances constituted a method of encroachment. A charter granted to the tenants of the lordship in 1355 contained a provision which attempted to regulate this process and also derive revenue from the sale of licences.[146]

These trends, combined with the consequences of almost total commutation of dues, contributed to the blurring, in some localities, of traditional differences between free and bond tenures. The distinction became increasingly a purely financial one, with tenants distinguished by their wealth and territorial possessions rather than by their social status. The 1494 rental of the manor of Whitbourne records that thirty-one tenants held their land of the bishop of Hereford, but does not distinguish between free and customary tenure.[147] The survival of bond obligations, however, including the payment of the heriot and entry fine as integral elements in the transfer of customary lands, ensured that distinctions between freemen and bondmen would continue to be observed. In north-west Wales the perpetuation of these differences contributed to the tensions which characterized relations between royal

[144] J. Beverley Smith, 'The Lordship of Senghennydd', pp. 323–6; Jones Pierce, *MWS*, pp. 234–9; Gresham, *Eifionydd*, pp. 102–3.

[145] Pugh, *Marcher Lordships of South Wales*, pp. 168, 200; G. R. J. Jones, 'The tribal system in Wales', pp. 125–7; NLW, Wigfair Deeds and Documents 8 (a transcript of this document is in F. Seebohm, *The Tribal System in Wales*, London, 1904, App. E).

[146] J. Beverley Smith, 'Crown and community in the principality of North Wales', pp. 152–5; Llinos B. Smith, 'The Arundel charters to the lordship of Chirk in the fourteenth century', *Bull. BCS*, XXIII, 1969, pp. 157–9, 165; *The Extent of Chirkland, 1391–3*, ed. G. P. Jones, p. 13.

[147] C. Thomas, 'The social and economic geography of rural Merioneth', in *Merioneth County History*, II (forthcoming: see above, ch. 2, n. 153); R. R. Davies, 'The lordship of Ogmore', pp. 308–11; Phyllis Williams, 'Land tenure on the bishop's manor of Whitbourne', *WNFC*, XL, 1972, pp. 342–3.

officials and those prominent freemen anxious to exert their influence over the bond townships.[148]

The other main grievance of the free community of north Wales concerned disabilities imposed upon them on account of their nationality.[149] Petitions submitted in 1305 to the prince of Wales on behalf of Welsh communities indicated an awareness of the restrictive nature of Welsh land law. The irritation caused by the rejection of demands such as the freedom to purchase and sell lands according to English legal practice was accentuated by the privileged position of English colonists and burgesses in Wales. A clear distinction was drawn between English and Welsh tenurial forms, and the court rolls of the lordship of Ruthin illustrate the strenuous efforts made to maintain the differences and prevent the transfer of land between Englishmen and Welshmen. Additional tenurial disabilities were experienced as a result of the national rebellion led by Owain Glyndŵr in the early fifteenth century. The penal legislation of 1401 included restrictions on the acquisition of lands in England and in the English boroughs of Wales. Despite these provisions, Welshmen succeeded both in securing the status of English tenure and in acquiring lands in England and in the boroughs of Wales. Emancipation from these legal prohibitions was achieved by prominent individuals such as Gwilym ap Gwilym ap Gruffudd, who in 1439 petitioned parliament to be "made English", and letters of denizenship were granted to those Welshmen who had distinguished themselves by administrative and military service.[150]

English tenurial procedures enjoyed similar prestige among the more ambitious and successful members of the Welsh peasantry, and they were undoubtedly represented in those free communities which were granted charters of liberties in the early sixteenth century. Memoranda relating to conversion of Welsh tenure to English tenure are contained in a court roll of the lordship of Ruthin dated 1426 and emphasis was placed on the payments of a fine and relief.[151] In the borderlands Welsh peasant farmers were able to participate in the commercial life of boroughs such as Welshpool and Oswestry and the records of estates located in Cheshire, Shropshire, and Herefordshire illustrated the active

---

[148] NLW, Badminton Deeds and Documents 342, 1098, 1487; J. Beverley Smith, 'Crown and community in the principality of North Wales', pp. 145–7.

[149] ibid., p. 156 for reference to the central administration, the colonists and the indigenous community as "the three essential elements of the classical colonial situation".

[150] H. Ellis, ed., Record of Caernarvon, pp. 212–14; above, pp. 99–102; R. R. Davies, 'Race relations in post-conquest Wales: confrontation and compromise', Hon. Soc. Cymmr., 1974–5, p. 42; I. Bowen, ed., The Statutes of Wales, London, 1908, pp. 33–4; Rot. Parl., v, p. 16; R. A. Griffiths, 'Gruffydd ap Nicholas and the rise of the house of Dinefwr', NLW Jnl., XIII, 1963–4, p. 258.

[151] CPR, 1494–1509, pp. 434, 464–5, 471, 523–4, 586–7; NLW, Lleweni Coll. 470.

involvement of members of Welsh communities in tenurial transactions.[152] An examination of two financial documents compiled by officials of the lordship of Denbigh, a 1334 survey and a 1437 rental, indicates the success of Welsh tenants in obtaining lands in townships from which they had been excluded in 1334 and in consolidating their position where a minority had formerly settled. Whereas 91 plots in the Park of Segrwyd had all been held by Englishmen in 1334, the 108 holdings in 1437 were occupied by 74 Englishmen and 34 Welshmen. Furthermore, in Sgeibion, whose tenants in 1334 consisted of 52 Welshmen and 46 Englishmen, the ratio in favour of the Welshmen had been radically modified by 1437 to 137:22. In the older lordships of the southern and middle march, whose administrative divisions of Englishry and Welshry were variously based on economy, race, and tenure, Welshmen were able to penetrate the fertile lowland Englishries. The availability of cheap land in the period which followed the Glyndŵr rebellion may well have been responsible for this migration, and Welshmen constituted a substantial number of householders in the lowland Englishry of the lordship of Ogmore.[153]

Despite the attraction of novel tenurial practices there was a considerable survival of traditional landholding customs. The application of the feudal incident of escheat met with some resistance in Wales, and the right of the community to control escheated lands was stressed in several cases recorded in accounts compiled after the outbreak of pestilence. The community of the Welshry of Llangeinor, in the lordship of Ogmore, prevented the local lord, the duke of Lancaster, from gaining possession of escheated lands which they claimed and had occupied. Welsh land law survived in the later middle ages and its capability of adapting to changing circumstances is illustrated by the widespread use of *prid* transactions. The inheritance rights of illegitimate children, a feature of Welsh land law, continued to be safeguarded, and *cynnwys* licences were obtained whereby illegitimate children could acquire and hold hereditary lands. Arbitrators, or official Welsh judges, were also frequently employed to resolve

---

[152] B. G. Charles, 'The Welsh, their language and place-names in Archenfield and Oswestry', in *Angles and Britons*, O'Donnell Lectures, Cardiff, 1963, pp. 105–6; J. Gwynfor Jones, 'Government and the Welsh community: the north-east borderland in the fifteenth century', in H. Hearder and H. R. Loyn, eds., *British Government and Administration: Studies presented to S. B. Chrimes*, Cardiff, 1974, pp. 59–60; M. Richards, 'The population of the Welsh border', *Hon. Soc. Cymmr.*, 1971, pp. 86–92; Hewitt, *Medieval Cheshire*, pp. 150–1; NLW, Aston Hall Deeds and Documents 2222, and Mynde Park Deeds and Documents 87, 180.

[153] D. Huw Owen, 'The lordship of Denbigh, 1282–1425', p. 255; Vinogradoff and Morgan, eds., *Survey of the Honour of Denbigh*, pp. 12–17, 27–33; NLW, Wynnstay Manuscripts and Documents 86; Rees, *South Wales and the March*, pp. 27–31, 199; R. R. Davies, 'The lordship of Ogmore', p. 310.

disputes involving the occupation and ownership of land.[154] Evidence of the strong and continuing hold of Welsh tenurial law is provided by the partition of an estate in Caernarfonshire in 1463 according to *cyfran*, the Welsh law of partible inheritance. John ap Maredudd had inherited a substantial estate consisting of many scattered holdings of land, but his right to the property was challenged by his ward, Ifan ap Robert. The case proceeded according to Welsh custom and, following the appointment of arbitrators and an umpire, and the preparation of legal documents, the lands in question were divided between the two contestants. Native tenurial customs continued to be practised in the early sixteenth century and in some recorded instances even survived the Union legislation of 1536–43.[155]

The defence and protection of traditional rights contributed to the tensions experienced during this period in Wales and the borderlands. In Cheshire the efforts of the administration of the Black Prince to extract as much revenue as possible from the forests of Delamere, Macclesfield, and Wirral resulted in the outbreak of a revolt in 1353 and the submission of a petition in 1376 by the commonalty of the Wirral.[156] A series of charters granted in 1324, 1334, and 1355 by the earls of Arundel, as lords of Chirk, conferred on their tenants a number of concessions, and these charters may be regarded as a compromise between seigneurial demands and traditional privileges. A conservative resistance to change was accompanied by the desire of some prosperous tenants to exploit to their own advantage the opportunities presented by novel tenurial conditions. In Wales attempts to secure the benefits of the prestigious English tenure by the evasion of prohibitions and restraints were resented by English colonists. The racial tensions consequently aroused were reflected in the body of prophetic poetry produced and also in occasional outbursts of violence, culminating in the Owain Glyndŵr rebellion. Peasant discontent, compounded by racial hostility, found expression in the revolt. Welsh labourers returning from England were among the earliest recorded supporters of Glyndŵr, whilst numerous attacks were launched by his forces on boroughs and manors. Racial friction was again exhibited during the

---

[154] Rees, *South Wales and the March*, p. 212; above, p. 655; R. R. Davies, 'The twilight of Welsh law, 1284–1536', *History*, LI, 1966, pp. 158–9; Vinogradoff and Morgan, eds., *Survey of the Honour of Denbigh*, pp. 285–6, 290–1; G. P. Jones, ed., *The Extent of Chirkland*, p. 61; UCNW, Mostyn Coll. 785; NLW, Bronwydd Deeds and Documents 972.

[155] Jones Pierce, *MWS*, pp. 233–6, 369–89; Gresham, *Eifionydd*, pp. 20–2, 82; R. R. Davies, 'The twilight of Welsh law', p. 164.

[156] J. J. Bagley, *Life in Medieval England*, London, 1960, pp. 43–4; Hewitt, *Medieval Cheshire*, pp. 12, 15–17, 42–4, 152; R. Stewart-Brown, 'The disafforestation of Wirral', *Lancs. and Cheshire Hist. Soc.*, LIX, 1907, pp. 165–80 and 'Further notes on the disafforestation of Wirral', *ibid.*, LXXXIX, 1937, pp. 23–7.

fifteenth century. The inhabitants of the city of Chester adopted an exceptionally hostile attitude towards Welshmen and the prevalence of cattle stealing in the border shires undoubtedly hardened anti-Welsh sentiments.[157]

Animosity based on racial considerations exacerbated tensions created by cataclysmic social and tenurial changes. Difficult living conditions were accentuated by seasonal factors, such as the adverse effects of a poor harvest on the production of corn in Cheshire in 1437. Interruptions to the regular agrarian activities of the peasantry were caused by the perpetual demands on human and financial resources necessitated by the military involvements of the English monarchy. Wales and the border shires produced regular and substantial supplies of troops for the French wars and constant attempts were made to raise revenue for military purposes. The numerous campaigns actually waged in Wales and the marches also left their physical imprint on the countryside. An examination of the causes of the Cheshire rising of 1400 emphasizes the resentment caused by compulsory military service and the devastation of localities situated near to the Welsh border.[158] Whereas many peasants suffered from the imposition of military and seigneurial pressures at a time of financial difficulties and of demographic collapse, others succeeded in safeguarding and consolidating their holdings. The consequent stratification of the peasant community, together with the erosion of kindred and customary tenurial procedures, thus prepared the way for the distinctive landlord–tenant relationships which may be observed on the freehold estates of the sixteenth century.[159]

[157] Llinos B. Smith, 'The Arundel charters to the lordship of Chirk', pp. 153–66; Glanmor Williams, 'Prophecy, poetry and politics in medieval and Tudor Wales', in Hearder and Loyn, eds., *British Government and Administration*, pp. 104–16; idem, *Owen Glendower*, London, 1966, pp. 5–17, 22–9; J. G. Jones, 'Government and the Welsh community', pp. 60–5; Kimball, ed., *The Shropshire Peace Roll*, p. 46.

[158] J. T. Driver, *Cheshire in the Later Middle Ages*, Chester, 1971, p. 96; Duby, *Rural Economy and Country Life*, pp. 332–3 for discussion of the effects of military requirements upon peasant communities; A. D. Carr, 'Welshmen and the Hundred Years' War', *Welsh Hist. Rev.*, IV, 1968, pp. 21–46; D. L. Evans, 'Some notes on the history of the principality in the time of the Black Prince', *Hon. Soc. Cymmr.*, 1925–6, pp. 45–7; G. Barraclough, *The Earldom and County Palatine of Chester*, Oxford, 1953, pp. 23–4; P. McNiven, 'The Cheshire rising of 1400', *Bull. JRL*, 52, 1970, p. 394.

[159] B. G. Charles, *George Owen of Henllys: a Welsh Elizabethan*, pp. 31–42; G. Dyfnallt Owen, *Elizabethan Wales: the Social Scene*, Cardiff, 1964, pp. 75–9; Glanmor Williams, 'The economic life of Glamorgan, 1536–1542', pp. 9–42; W. Ogwen Williams, *Tudor Gwynedd: the Tudor Age in the Principality of North Wales*, Caernarvon, 1958, pp. 37–57.

G. THE HOME COUNTIES

One characteristic of peasant farming in late medieval England can be illustrated from all parts of this region. This is an increasing variation in the size of holdings. Holdings tended to be enlarged or combined, more by the larger tenants than by the smaller ones – the virgaters rather than the cottagers. The result was a markedly greater difference than before between the largest peasant farms and the smallest ones, with an overall increase in their average size. The phenomenon appears so frequently that it seems to have been the norm. R. J. Faith found it in at least seven of the eight places she investigated in Berkshire, A. C. Jones in at least four of five places in Bedfordshire, and D. Roden in at least three of four places in the Chilterns.[160] There are many clear examples elsewhere in the region, as at Haversham (Bucks.), Wormley (Herts.), and Banbury (Oxon.). On the other hand there are a few equally clear examples of places scarcely affected by it, such as Merton or Great and Little Milton or Stonesfield (all Oxon.).[161]

This peasant engrossment was brought about by three causes, operating singly or together. One was the need for manorial lords to find occupants for vacant holdings, which were often offered on more or less favourable terms to those who were already their tenants. Thus at Codicote (Herts.) tenants for holdings made vacant by the Black Death were found mostly from within the manor; at Arlesey (Beds.) holdings that could not be let out in the ordinary way came to form a reserve of land on which the manor's fifteenth-century internal land market was based, being taken up piecemeal or for short periods by tenants in the village who wished to supplement their existing holdings. This factor operated particularly in the early part of the period, and in the late fourteenth century the extent of peasant engrossment may even serve as an index to the loss of population in the plague; thus in north-east Oxfordshire Charlton-on-Otmoor, which was relatively lightly hit by the Black Death, had no peasant engrossment by 1390, whereas at Hethe, where plague deaths were heavy, holdings had been reduced in number and increased in size by 1371.[162] The second cause was the decline in demesne farming; manorial lords often leased part or all of their demesne lands piecemeal to their peasant tenants, either as a prelude to leasing the demesne *en bloc*

---

[160] Harvey, ed., *The Peasant Land Market*, pp. 107–251 *passim*; D. Roden, 'Studies in Chiltern field systems', London Univ. Ph.D. thesis, 1965. The exceptions are, respectively, Brightwalton (Berks.), Willington (Beds.), and Berkhamsted (Herts.).

[161] *VCH Bucks.*, II, p. 62; *VCH Herts.*, IV, p. 212; *VCH Oxon.*, V, pp. 225–6; VII, p. 131; X, p. 53; XI, p. 187.

[162] Roden, 'Studies', p. 163; Harvey, ed., *The Peasant Land Market*, pp. 217–20; *VCH Oxon.*, VI, pp. 84, 177.

to a single farmer or as a permanent arrangement. At Brightwalton (Berks.) in 1393 six tenants held, in all, 77 acres of demesne on leases of from seven to ten years; at Shillington (Beds.) the amounts of demesne similarly leased out were 66 or 67 acres from 1368 to 1381, 218 acres from 1381 to about 1400, 458 acres (nearly the whole demesne) from then on; at Wymondley (Herts.) parcels of demesne were being leased from the 1350s, and by 1411 a farmer had taken over the whole of the demesne not already let out; at Cogges (Oxon.) the demesne arable, 75 acres in 1387, had by 1412 been divided into customary holdings.[163]

The third cause of peasant engrossment was the deliberate aim – the ambition even – of particular families which set out to build up accumulations of lands, often acquired in small units over a generation or more and held in various ways. Thus at Woolstone (Berks.) William at Hulle inherited one virgate, leased another and a further 4 acres from his fellow tenants, leased 2 acres more from the manorial demesne, and took over a further half-virgate, two cottages, and a curtilage when they fell vacant. Piecemeal accumulation of holdings had, of course, occurred earlier; the Smith (later Gamage) family at Littlemore (Oxon.) had begun in the late thirteenth century the process of acquisition which continued to the early fifteenth. But the reduced demand for land and the new availability of customary and demesne lands drastically changed the situation in the mid-fourteenth century; in much of Hertfordshire, for example, the change was marked by a new emphasis on the transfer of larger units than before. It was now easy to form composite holdings of very varied components. Occasionally this was on a scale to make a particular family pre-eminent in a village, as at Englefield (Berks.), where by 1474 Thomas Tovy had formed a composite holding that was by far the largest on the manor, or at Shirburn (Oxon.), where three members of the Frankleyn family paid £7 10s. of the village's £8 12s. 2d. assessment for the 1523–4 subsidy, sixteen other villagers the rest. Even without accumulating holdings a local tenant might achieve pre-eminence by taking a lease of the demesne; at Launton (Oxon.) in the mid-fifteenth century the only tenant with more than about 45 acres was a cottager who farmed the demesne, perhaps some 300 acres.[164] But more often

[163] L. C. Latham, 'The decay of the manorial system, during the first half of the fifteenth century, with special reference to manorial jurisdiction and the decline of villeinage', London Univ. M.A. thesis, 1928, p. 150; Harvey, ed., The Peasant Land Market, p. 206 (other Bedfordshire examples of piecemeal leases of demesnes to local tenants are given ibid., pp. 182, 197–200, 228); F. B. Stitt, 'Manors of Great and Little Wymondley in the later middle ages', Oxford Univ. B.Litt. thesis, 1951, pp. 82–4; J. Blair and J. M. Steane, 'Investigations at Cogges, Oxfordshire, 1978–81: the priory and parish church', Oxoniensia, XLVIII, 1982, p. 105.

[164] Harvey, ed., The Peasant Land Market, pp. 128, 151, 152; VCH Oxon., v, p. 209; VIII, p. 189; P. D. Glennie, 'A commercializing agrarian region: late medieval and early modern Hertford-

the enlargement of holdings was on a modest scale, serving merely to differentiate their tenants more sharply than their thirteenth-century predecessors from the cottagers who formed the unchanging lowest stratum of rural landholders.[165]

Although it is easy to show that these changes took place, it is practically impossible to assess precisely their extent or significance. One reason is the difficulty of tracing or comparing holdings at different times. Tenements were often broken up, sometimes overtly, sometimes while superficially maintaining the existing pattern. Thus at Woolstone (Berks.) after the Black Death ten vacant holdings were split between two or more tenants; although they were to be held thus only "until anyone shall come to claim the whole tenement", some remained permanently divided. At Blunham (Beds.) the earl of Kent in 1471 tried to curb the fragmentation of tenements by a charter which allowed his customary tenants to alienate parts of their holdings provided that a nucleus remained intact: 6 acres in a 14-acre half-virgate, 3 acres in a 7-acre quarterland.[166] No similar regulation is known elsewhere in the region, but there is no lack of examples of the practice it was designed to check. Thus at King's Walden (Herts.) and Leighton Buzzard (Beds.) traffic in small pieces of customary land throughout the period meant that by the end of the fifteenth century all traces of the standard units of the former villein tenure had disappeared.[167] Again, the nomenclature of holdings sometimes varied; on the Merton College manors of Cuxham (Oxon.) and Ibstone (Bucks.) we find uncertainty whether particular holdings were virgates or half-virgates.[168] A further difficulty is that the newly formed large peasant holdings were often very short-lived and seldom held together

shire', Cambridge Univ. Ph.D. thesis, 1983, pp. 39–40 (cf. for King's Walden: Roden, 'Studies', pp. 115, 117); Harvey, *Westminster Abbey and its Estates*, p. 289.

[165] Detailed illustrations of the developments described in this paragraph can be found in the many case studies of individual peasant families that have been set out for Coleshill (Berks.), Arlesey and Leighton Buzzard (both Beds.), and Wymondley (Herts.): R. J. Faith, 'The peasant land-market in Berkshire during the later middle ages', Leicester Univ. Ph.D. thesis, 1962, pp. 149–90; A. C. Jones, 'The customary land market in Bedfordshire in the fifteenth century', Southampton Univ. Ph.D. thesis, 1975, pp. 111–23, 174–94; Stitt, 'Manors of Great and Little Wymondley', pp. 142–54.

[166] Harvey, ed., *The Peasant Land Market*, pp. 124, 198; Godber, *History of Bedfordshire*, pp. 143–4.

[167] Roden, 'Studies', p. 390; Harvey, ed., *The Peasant Land Market*, p. 234. Harvey, *Westminster Abbey and its Estates*, pp. 286–7, suggests that this occurred particularly on "semi-urbanized manors" and contrasts Denham (Bucks.) with Turweston (Bucks.), Islip, and Launton (both Oxon.).

[168] Harvey, *Medieval Oxfordshire Village*, p. 139; D. Roden, 'Field systems in Ibstone', *Records of Bucks.*, XVIII, 1966–70, p. 51.

for more than a generation or so. Very occasionally the substantial yeoman farms of the sixteenth century and later had a fifteenth-century origin; the holding of the Pope family of Sotwell Stonor (Berks.), built up over the century before 1510, is a case in point.[169] But far more often the families that became large peasant proprietors in the later middle ages failed to maintain their position, and the holdings that they had brought together were as rapidly dispersed.[170] Moreover, even while it lasted, the composition of a single large holding was flexible and fluid: lands would be taken on leases of varying lengths, lands bought might be sold after a few years and others might or might not be bought in their place. It is very difficult to build up a true picture of peasant landholding in the period even for a single parish.

The difficulty is increased by the problem of what allowance to make for subletting. Inter-peasant leases of both free and customary land were certainly not unknown, though references to them are rare. Subletting clearly occurred among Westminster abbey's customary tenants in Hertfordshire and Oxfordshire, though in the fourteenth century they were allowed to sublet only for short terms and later they probably seldom sublet for more than a few years. In Bedfordshire, the customary tenants of Ramsey abbey had to pay for permission to sublet for more than three years but not for a shorter period, while at Leighton Buzzard pleas of debt refer to a man who in 1468 was renting from a fellow tenant small pieces of land adjacent to his own holding, and a woman who in 1471 was letting out lands to other tenants probably because, having been widowed two years before, she was unable to work them herself.[171] Manorial court rolls occasionally record permission to sublet customary lands or the amercement of those who had done so illicitly, and the chronological pattern of such cases at Woolstone (Berks.) is of some interest: one in 1339, three in 1341, ten in 1346–7, and one each in 1385, 1396, 1399, and 1414. This may mean that leasing of this sort declined at Woolstone after the Black Death because it was so much easier than before to rent small pieces of land direct from the lord of the manor; alternatively it may be that inter-peasant leasing continued as in the 1340s, but moved outside the lord's surveillance with the relaxing of customary control and the introduction of new forms of tenure.[172] Certainly we cannot assume that subletting did not occur – either generally or in any particular place – because it is seldom mentioned on surviving manorial court

---

[169] Harvey, ed., *The Peasant Land Market*, pp. 141, 168.

[170] Thus, e.g., *ibid.*, pp. 157–8, 167–8, 351; *VCH Oxon.*, VI, pp. 214, 226; Glennie, 'Commercializing agrarian region', pp. 39–40.

[171] Harvey, *Westminster Abbey and its Estates*, pp. 309–11, 321; Harvey, ed., *The Peasant Land Market*, pp. 193, 242–3. [172] Harvey, ed., *The Peasant Land Market*, pp. 124–7.

rolls. On certain manors, as we shall see, holdings came to be acquired either by local town dwellers or by complete outsiders; the former must very often have done this simply in order to sublet, the latter always. Thus at Speenhamland (Berks.) the richest tenant in 1376, William Wode, held some twenty urban and rural holdings which he let out to eight sub-tenants. At Chalfont St Peter (Bucks.) in the mid-fifteenth century we find two cottages and gardens held, clearly for subletting, by William Whaplode, who had held local office under the crown and the Duchy of Lancaster, and who was one of the more important people in the area. At Cheshunt (Herts.) in about 1500 Henry Coote had holdings for which he paid the manor £4 12s. 6d. rent, but from the sub-tenants to whom he let them out he received £31 10s. 10d., giving him a clear annual profit of £26 18s. 4d.; here too local custom left copyholders free to let out their holdings for up to three years.[173] The existence of subletting makes it even harder for us to be sure exactly what lands were actually worked by a particular peasant tenant, what was the effective division of a vill's lands among the tillers of its soil at any one time.

Sometimes the enlargement of an individual's holding of land, combined with subletting, produced an estate that came to be called a manor. The properties originally built up by John Windbush at Tetsworth (Oxon.) in the reign of Edward III were referred to as a manor in 1471, when they consisted of not more than eight messuages and 260 acres of land. At Wymondley (Herts.) the principal free tenant of the Argentein family's manors in the mid-fourteenth century was Nicholas de la Mare, who held some 90 acres of which probably very little was sublet; his death in 1361 extinguished the male line of the family, but the property continued as a unit, was augmented about twenty years later by a further 90 acres, of which much was sublet, and by 1419 was being called the manor of Delameres. Some of these new manors were very small; one that appeared at Berkhamsted in the fifteenth century may have been little more than 50 acres. At Longworth (Berks.) a new manor took its origin in 1467 from a copyhold tenement sold by the abbot of Abingdon after he had evicted its tenants (who, however, were of sufficient standing to complain in a petition to the court of Chancery). New manors appeared in this period in most parts of the region, but there seem to have been none in central and northern Bedfordshire, eastern Berkshire, and the Berkshire Downs, while the phenomenon is most marked in and around the Chilterns and, especially, in east Hertfordshire. Arguably this suggests

[173] *Ibid.*, p. 144; E. M. Elvey, 'The abbot of Missenden's estates in Chalfont St. Peter', *Records of Bucks.*, XVII, 1961–5, p. 36; R. Somerville, *History of the Duchy of Lancaster*, I, London, 1953, p. 591; Glennie, 'Commercializing agrarian region', pp. 325–6.

that in these areas tenants were building up estates that were larger and more permanent than elsewhere, and were more likely to have sub-tenants of their own.[174]

Even as early as the 1340s labour services in the form of week-work seem to have been almost unknown in the region except in Berkshire and Oxfordshire, and there too there must have been many manors where they had already disappeared, such as Charlton-on-Otmoor and Lower Heyford (both Oxon.).[175] Where week-work remained, it often vanished in the Black Death and its aftermath. At Wood Eaton (Oxon.) we are told that after the plague of 1349 there remained barely two tenants, and they would have left if the abbot of Eynsham had not negotiated new terms with them; the old terms had included week-work or an alternative money rent, the new were based on money rent and boon-works alone. In this case we cannot be sure how far this meant a change in practice, as we do not know which alternative, week-work or money rent, had been the norm before; but at Cuxham (Oxon.) the changes of the 1350s ended the obligation to week-works which had been almost fully enforced, and at Launton (Oxon.) the old-fashioned system of service-holdings for the demesne ploughmen finally ended in 1351. At Islip (Oxon.) week-works were commuted immediately after the Black Death, but they had reappeared for the harvest season by 1357, and probably were finally commuted only in 1386. A similar pattern appears at Brightwalton and Woolstone (both Berks.), where sales of works rose sharply in the 1350s but then fell once more.[176] However, by the end of the fourteenth century it must have been exceptional to find a manor where there remained even a theoretical obligation to do week-work.

On the other hand there is no difficulty in finding places throughout the region where boon-works survived well into the fifteenth or even the sixteenth century. They appear for instance at Souldrop (Beds.) in 1530, Sandhurst (Berks.) in 1498, Essendon (Herts.) in 1468, Cowley

[174] *VCH Oxon.*, VII, p. 151 (the description of the property, taken from a final concord, may not be accurate but it was at least no larger than this); Stitt, 'Manors of Great and Little Wymondley', pp. 143–7; Roden, 'Studies', p. 206; *VCH Berks.*, IV, p. 469. Another example of a copyhold tenement that became known as a manor had occurred at Rickmansworth (Herts.) by the mid-sixteenth century (*VCH Herts.*, IV, pp. 213–14). Some other new manors in west Berkshire in the fifteenth century are noted by P. J. Jefferies, 'A consideration of some aspects of landholding in medieval Berkshire', Reading Univ. Ph.D. thesis, 1972, p. 392.

[175] *VCH Oxon.*, VI, pp. 84, 187. At Meesden (Herts.) week-works were due in the 1340s but at least in 1346 many were sold (*VCH Herts.*, IV, p. 196); at Kinsbourne (Herts.) some week-works were still rendered in 1352–3, though more were sold or lost through vacancies (D. V. Stern, 'A Hertfordshire manor of Westminster Abbey', London Univ. Ph.D. thesis, 1978, p. 300).

[176] *Eynsham Cartulary*, ed. H. E. Salter, Oxford Hist. Soc., OS XLIX, LI, 1907–8, II, pp. 19–20; Harvey, *Medieval Oxfordshire Village*, pp. 82, 138–9; *VCH Oxon.*, VI, pp. 213 (cf. Harvey, *Westminster Abbey and its Estates*, pp. 257–9), 237; *VCH Berks.*, II, pp. 185–7.

(Oxon.) in 1512.[177] Everywhere, however, they tended to decline in the course of the period. Typical evidence comes from Islip (Oxon.), where in 1349 boon-works had been demanded in full but where they were finally commuted in 1433, over a quarter having already been lost by 1390 through leasing holdings on new terms; from West Hendred (Berks.), where in 1381 a messuage and virgate were leased for a term of lives at 11s. a year, being 4s. "for the old rent" and 7s. in place of listed boon-works and customary rents; from King's Walden (Herts.), where the last record of labour services was the presentment of arrears of five harvest works at the manorial court in 1431; and from Toddington (Beds.), where in 1485 five tenants were paying fines of 4d. or 8d. for non-performance of boon-works, sums less than the normal rate of commutation would have been.[178] It is probably true to say that whereas in 1350 most peasant holdings owed at least some boon-works by 1500 most did not.

Perhaps for this reason records of refusals to do labour services date mostly from the earlier part of the period. Some cases were local difficulties recorded simply on the manorial court rolls; they might be temporary, as at Blunham (Beds.) in 1417, or more persistent, as at Bletchley and Fenny Stratford (Bucks.), and Coleshill (Berks.) in the 1370s and 1380s. But in some places they formed part of a larger pattern of discontent. Withdrawals of men from boon-works at Tyttenhanger (in Ridge, Herts.) in 1357 and 1366 may reflect longer retention of labour services on the St Albans abbey estates than elsewhere in the area; freedom from services was included (though not very prominently) among the demands made by the abbey's tenant in the Peasants' Revolt of 1381, and again at Barnet in 1417, when the abbey's copyholders claimed to hold their land freely, but at both dates the protest was against a wide variety of irksome restrictions and obligations, of which services were only one element. The same was probably the case on the estates of Abingdon abbey, where there was concerted withdrawal of services at Hurst and Winkfield (both Berks.) in 1393–4 and again in 1485.[179]

Even where boon-works remained, the disappearance of week-work meant that money rents were the principal receipts of manorial lords

[177] *VCH Beds.*, II, p. 90; G. A. Kempthorne, 'Sandhurst, Berks.', *Berks., Bucks. and Oxon. Arch. J.*, XXI, 1915–16, p. 21; K. R. Davis, 'An account of the excavations at Coldharbour Moat, in Friday Field, Essendon, Herts.', *East Herts. Arch. Soc.*, XI, 1940–4, pp. 22–5; *VCH Oxon.*, V, p. 86.

[178] *VCH Oxon.*, VI, p. 213; Harvey, *Westminster Abbey and its Estates*, p. 270; J. G. Milne, 'Muniments of Holy Trinity Priory, Wallingford', *Oxoniensia*, V, 1940, pp. 69–70; Roden, 'Studies', pp. 383–4; Godber, *History of Bedfordshire*, pp. 141–2.

[179] Jones, 'Customary land market', p. 70n; W. Bradbrook, 'Manor court rolls of Fenny Stratford and Etone (Bletchley)', *Records of Bucks.*, XI, 1920–6, p. 306; Harvey, ed., *The Peasant Land Market*, p. 164; *VCH Herts.*, II, p. 366; IV, pp. 195–6, 206; *CPR, 1391–6*, pp. 294, 444; *CPR, 1476–85*, p. 552.

from their tenants. Although customary levels of rent may have exerted some influence, the amounts paid seem to have depended generally on local supply and demand. To take two examples from north Oxfordshire, we find that at Upper Heyford, following heavy mortality in the Black Death, virgate holdings in 1357 were being let out for 5s. a year for all services, but by 1375 one virgater was paying 14s. and also owed heriot; while at Brookend rents were being reduced to attract newcomers and arrest the village's slow decline, so that by 1441–2 lands which had formerly produced rents of £3 13s. 0½d. were being let out for short terms for £2 9s. 11d. Also in north Oxfordshire we find a less usual phenomenon at Broughton, where in 1444 former demesne lands were being let out for rents of corn and straw.[180] Meaningful comparison of rent levels throughout the region is practically impossible, as we have no way of knowing the area or quality of land that went to make up the holdings called virgates or half-virgates in different places. Moreover, the once-for-all payment on entry may often have affected the level of rent; this appears clearly in the early fifteenth century in Bedfordshire, where at Blunham the annual rent for a half-virgate might be no more than 2s. with an entry-fine of 20s., while at Willington, a couple of miles away, the half-virgate paid 13s. 4d. a year in rent but an entry-fine usually of only 8d. or 1s. But it would be wrong to see a consistent pattern in this; at Leighton Buzzard (Beds.) and elsewhere in Bedfordshire entry-fines in the fifteenth century show so much apparently random variation that they must have been fixed simply by bargaining with the individual tenant.[181] Entry-fines, like rents, were probably determined principally by what the tenant was prepared to pay. In Berkshire and Oxfordshire entry-fines apparently tended to fall in the course of the period, and both here and in Buckinghamshire we find some being paid wholly or partly in kind, in the form of from one to twelve capons. In Bedfordshire, on the other hand, their general level remained stable, or tended to rise, and they were paid only in money.[182]

The disappearance of unspecified labour services did not mean the end of villeinage. Cases of imprisonment of alleged villeins, which hinged on the legal status of the plaintiffs, were brought against manorial lords of Launton (Oxon.) in 1372, Dorton (Bucks.) in 1491–2, and Whitchurch (Bucks.) in 1508.[183] The various liabilities of servile

[180] VCH Oxon., VI, p. 199; IX, p. 93; T. H. Lloyd, 'Some documentary sidelights on the deserted Oxfordshire village of Brookend', Oxoniensia, XXIX/XXX, 1964–5, p. 125.

[181] Harvey, ed., The Peasant Land Market, pp. 201, 204, 211–12, 220, 244; A. Jones, 'Land and people at Leighton Buzzard in the later 15th century', EcHR, 2nd ser. XXV, 1972, p. 24.

[182] Harvey, ed., The Peasant Land Market, pp. 114, 115–18, 212, 220; VCH Oxon., VI, p. 214; Harvey, Westminster Abbey and its Estates, pp. 271–2; Harvey, Medieval Oxfordshire Village, p. 139; VCH Bucks., III, p. 40.

[183] VCH Oxon., VI, p. 236; VCH Bucks., III, p. 446; IV, p. 47.

status – merchet, leyrwite, tallage, and so on – seem to have been generally enforced to the end of the fourteenth century, and to have then fallen mostly into disuse.[184] The lord's monopoly of milling, which was the greatest cause of contention between St Albans abbey and its tenants in 1381, was still being insisted on by the abbey in the mid-fifteenth century, when it stopped the construction of a horse-mill at Watford (Herts.); and the lord of Lower Heyford (Oxon.) was still enforcing his milling rights in 1548.[185] Heriots tended to be fixed in advance either with a cash alternative to the tenant's best beast or as a simple money payment. At Wheathampstead with Harpenden (Herts.), Islip and Launton (both Oxon.), all Westminster abbey manors, the first record of this occurs in 1395, 1416, and 1427 respectively.[186] Changes in forms of tenure probably contributed a lot to the disappearance of servile disabilities, as some at least may have been seen as attaching to the tenure rather than to the person of the tenant. Cases of personal manumission are rare and, although in the early part of the period we find grants being made by lay lords, those that occur in the fifteenth century come mostly from the records of the great ecclesiastical landholders: the bishopric of Winchester, St Albans abbey, Ramsey abbey, Reading abbey. This may be an accident of archive survival; but it may reflect the insistence of these landlords on the formal maintenance of personal servility that others had allowed to lapse. By 1500, however, the concept of villeinage was certainly still alive in the region; in the archdeacon's court at Brill (Bucks.) in 1492 a man was accused of defamation for saying to another, "avaunte chorle and I wolde preve the a chorle of condicione".[187]

In the course of the period the unfree tenures of the 1340s took on a bewildering variety of forms and inconsistency of nomenclature, and often they came to have little in common beyond being administered in and through the manorial court. They are most simply classified by their length: they might be indefinite and hereditary (whether specifically or not), or they might be limited to a term of one or more lives or a fixed number of years. The early part of the period saw a great

---

[184] Thus, e.g., Jones, 'Customary land market', p. 87; Latham, 'Decay of the manorial system', pp. 82–3, 85–7, 93–4; VCH Oxon., VI, p. 84 (Charlton-on-Otmoor: merchet and tallage owed, 1390), 214 (Islip: tallage assimilated with assessed rents, 1433).

[185] VCH Herts., II, p. 452; VCH Oxon., VI, p. 191.

[186] Harvey, Westminster Abbey and its Estates, p. 272. At South Moreton (Berks.) in the 1430s partial exemption from heriot could be bought by a high entry-fine (Harvey, ed., The Peasant Land Market, p. 138).

[187] G. R. Elvey, 'Medieval charters at Claydon House', Records of Bucks., XVII, 1961–5, pp. 192–3; ibid., XIII, 1934–40, p. 244; H. C. Andrews and E. E. Squires, 'Codicote past and present', East Herts. Arch. Soc., V, 1912–14, p. 50; Godber, History of Bedfordshire, p. 144; VCH Berks., II, pp. 67–8; F. W. Ragg, 'Fragment of folio M.S. of archdeaconry courts of Buckinghamshire, 1491–1495', Records of Bucks., XI, 1920–6, p. 32.

many tenements formerly held on normal customary terms being let out on fixed leases, presumably so as to attract tenants by offering more favourable terms but without prejudicing a future return to the old form. Thus at Islip (Oxon.), former customary holdings were leased out for money rents and light services "until someone else comes who will hold the said tenement according to the custom of the manor", and similarly at Arlesey (Beds.) we find a tenement leased out in 1379 "because no heir wished to take it at the old rent and custom".[188] This replacement of indefinite tenure by temporary leasing seems to have occurred throughout the second half of the fourteenth century, and probably became increasingly common from the 1370s; we find entire customary holdings being leased for terms of years at Wymondley (Herts.) from 1351, at Woolstone (Berks.) from the 1390s, and at Fawley (Bucks.) in 1397, for instance, and for terms of lives at Coleshill (Berks.), Codicote (Herts.), and Shirburn (Oxon.). On some manors all tenure came to be for fixed terms, as at Willington (Beds.) and Englefield (Berks.). But on others indefinite hereditary tenure continued side by side with tenure for fixed terms, as at Wymondley (Herts.) and Brightwalton (Berks.); on Westminster abbey's manors those who held by lease seem normally to have held more cheaply than those with hereditary tenure.[189]

Imposed on this basically simple structure of development were two complicating features, tenure by copy and tenure at will. Supplying the tenant with a copy of the court-roll entry of his tenure was known in the region by the mid-fourteenth century: it appears at Newland (Herts.) in 1311–12, at Woolstone (Berks.) in 1372 (for an admission in 1349), and at Willington (Beds.) in 1383. Copies could perfectly well be supplied for tenure for fixed terms; but as the practice spread in the region – probably rather slowly – it was often restricted to those who held hereditary tenures, and on some manors to certain groups of these.[190] Tenure at will in the thirteenth century was a distinctive if obscure form of tenure, but in the present period "to be held at the will of the lord" was often no more than a phrase included in some or all court-roll entries of tenure on certain manors in order to emphasize the limited rights of the tenant. Thus in Berkshire it was applied at Brightwalton in the 1420s and 1430s both to fixed and to hereditary tenures, and at Coleshill it formed a regular part of the formula for

[188] VCH Oxon., VI, p. 214; Godber, History of Bedfordshire, p. 101. Cf. Harvey, Westminster Abbey and its Estates, pp. 244–5.

[189] Stitt, 'Manors of Great and Little Wymondley', pp. 130–2, 133, 136; Harvey, ed., The Peasant Land Market, pp. 125, 133, 151, 156–7, 203; VCH Bucks., III, p. 40; Roden, 'Studies', p. 400; VCH Oxon., VIII, p. 188; Harvey, Westminster Abbey and its Estates, pp. 263–4 (Islip (Oxon.); Harpenden, Stevenage, Wheathampstead (all Herts.)).

[190] Levett, Studies in Manorial History, p. 139n; Harvey, ed., The Peasant Land Market, pp. 130, 203, 338; VCH Oxon., VI, p. 226.

leases for lives from 1428 on.[191] Copyhold and tenure at will were not mutually exclusive: thus tenure by copy at the will of the lord occurred, by implication or explicitly, at Mackney in Brightwell (Berks.) and at Cuxham (Oxon.).[192] But because both terms were often applied selectively to restricted groups we sometimes find the tenants of a particular manor divided into copyholders and tenants at will, or classified in other anomalous terms; thus at Lilley (Herts.) in 1359 tenants held either in bondage or at will or in fee, and at Tilsworth (Beds.) in 1472 either freely or at will.[193]

Free tenure, determined outside the manorial court and often by charter, was likewise either indefinite or for a fixed term, and where permanent customary tenure was replaced by one of limited duration this sometimes took the form of free leasehold. At South Moreton (Berks.) in 1361 four tenants each paid £1 to hold a virgate, formerly in villeinage, for a life term; at Kempston Drayton (Beds.) in 1434 some forty holdings of all sizes were being held on twenty-year leases by charter, suggesting a general conversion to this system. Such tenures might perfectly well include boon-works – at King's Walden (Herts.) in 1359, for instance, $4\frac{1}{2}$ acres of free land were leased for 2s. 10d. rent and two harvest works – and the precise nature of a particular tenure, whether free or customary, could well be in doubt; at Coldrop (Berks.) in 1424 it was questioned whether a particular tenant held by free or villein tenure, and at Willington (Beds.) in 1383 copyholders of fixed term were described as holding freely (*libere*). In tenures the only general trend in the region seems to have been away from indefinite customary tenure and towards fixed leases of whatever legal status.[194]

Where customary land was held by permanent, hereditary tenure the local inheritance custom continued to operate; this was usually primogeniture, with life-estate to the widow. However, as land now could usually be acquired without difficulty these customs were far less rigorously insisted on than in earlier periods. Thus at Ibstone (Bucks.) the local rules were applied only in cases of intestacy, and at Sotwell Stonor (Berks.) in the fifteenth century only to inheritance by

---

[191] Harvey, ed., *The Peasant Land Market*, pp. 134, 156–7.

[192] *Ibid.*, p. 142; at Cuxham tenure that is specifically both "per Copiam Rotuli Curie" and "ad voluntatem domini" occurs in 1488 (Merton College, Oxford, muniments 5940) but is implied earlier by references to the customary tenants in general holding by copy (in 1398: *ibid.* 5923, mem. 7) and at will (as in 1458, 1475: *ibid.* 5932, 5935).

[193] *VCH Herts.*, III, p. 37; Godber, *History of Bedfordshire*, p. 139. General discussion of tenure by copy and tenure at will, with some particular references to evidence from this region, is in Harvey, *Westminster Abbey and its Estates*, pp. 246–8, 280n, 284–5, and in Harvey, ed., *The Peasant Land Market*, pp. 335–8.

[194] *Ibid.*, p. 137; Godber, *History of Bedfordshire*, p. 139; Roden, 'Studies', pp. 383–4; Latham, 'Decay of the manorial system', p. 138n; Jones, 'Customary land market', p. 72n.

widows.[195] Also such devices as joint tenure, or surrender while retaining a life interest, might be used to evade strict inheritance custom.[196] Adding to this the trend towards non-inheritable tenures of fixed term, we find a general decline in the importance of inheritance in peasant landholding. Detailed studies in Berkshire and Bedfordshire show this very clearly in both counties. Thus at Brightwalton (Berks.) the proportion of all movements of land entered on the court rolls dealing with transfers within the family fell dramatically in the late fourteenth century: 37 per cent in 1300–40, 40 per cent in 1341–62, 34 per cent in 1363–82, 13 per cent in 1383–1402, 19 per cent in 1403–9. At Arlesey Bury manor in Arlesey (Beds.), of transfers of customary land (all held by inheritable tenure) recorded between 1377 and 1536, 10 per cent were within the family during the tenant's lifetime, 21 per cent within the family on death, 64 per cent outside the family during life, and 5 per cent outside the family on death. At Chalfont St Peter (Bucks.) all copyhold tenements vacated after the mid-fifteenth century had been surrendered to use.[197] Before the mid-fourteenth century the growth of a peasant land market in the area may have owed a lot to the need to acquire non-customary land in order to provide for daughters and younger sons.[198] With the decline of inheritance custom, however, this need became far less pressing, and it may have played little part in the land market in the present period.

But this did not mean that the decay of inheritance custom diminished the peasant land market. On the contrary, it augmented it. Buying, selling, and subletting of lands between manorial tenants now extended to parcels of demesne that had been leased out and, ever increasingly, to customary lands as well. Surrender to use was well established before the mid-fourteenth century, and, as we have seen, attempts in the present period to restrict either alienation or subletting of customary lands were few and limited. In the 1380s and 1390s the formula admitting a customary tenant at Great Amwell (Herts.) and Launton (Oxon.) began to mention his assigns as well as his heirs, and at Brightwalton (Berks.) in 1435 we even find that the fiction of surrender to use was forgotten, and a new tenant was said to have

[195] Roden, 'Field systems in Ibstone', p. 44; Harvey, ed., *The Peasant Land Market*, pp. 139–40 (cf. p. 156: in the Berkshire manors that R. J. Faith studied the right of the widow was normally the rule of customary inheritance that survived longest).

[196] Roden found this occurring very widely in the Chilterns: 'Studies', pp. 167–8, 239–40, 285–6.

[197] Harvey, ed., *The Peasant Land Market*, pp. 132, 217; Elvey, 'The abbot of Missenden's estates', p. 34.

[198] Thus Roden, 'Studies', pp. 166–7; D. Roden, 'Inheritance customs and succession to land in the Chiltern Hills in the thirteenth and early fourteenth centuries', *J. of British Studies*, VII, 1967, pp. 6–7; Stitt, 'Manors of Great and Little Wymondley', p. 154; *VCH Oxon.*, VIII, p. 188.

bought a customary holding.[199] The payments due on each transaction could of course make this very profitable to manorial lords, giving them an interest in maintaining a high level of sales. In fact the exact pattern of the land market differed a good deal in the various places where it has been studied in detail. At King's Walden (Herts.) the mid-fourteenth century saw a change in the character of the market in freehold land, which started to change hands in larger units than before, often (from 1404 on) being acquired by groups of three or four tenants; this may reflect the fact that a busier market in customary land had developed, dealing in smaller pieces than the freehold. On Westminster abbey's two Oxfordshire manors there were relatively few sales of land between tenants, but more at Launton, where most tenants held by hereditary tenure, than at Islip, where tenure for life was more usual. In Berkshire we see a clear contrast, probably reflecting varying demand for land, between Woolstone and Brightwalton: at Woolstone sales and leases between peasants were very few, presumably because it was possible and preferable to get land direct from the lord, whereas at Brightwalton a similar situation from the 1350s was succeeded first, in the 1380s and 1390s, by an increasing entry of new tenants, and then, in the fifteenth century, by a high rate of sales between tenants. In Bedfordshire we find similar contrasts. At Willington (where demand for land was demonstrably low) and on the Ramsey abbey manors of Barton, Cranfield, and Shillington, there was little traffic in small parcels of land; at Blunham the market was likewise at a low level, then suddenly developed in the second half of the fifteenth century; at Arlesey Bury manor there was a fairly steady low traffic, mostly in very small pieces of land; at Leighton Buzzard, too, there was a steady market, far more active than elsewhere, in small pieces of land, declining a little at the end of the period, with a market in larger parcels developing in the fifteenth century. There is a further interesting contrast between Arlesey and Leighton Buzzard: the land involved at Arlesey came from a limited number of tenements which, coming into the lord's hands, had been broken up and formed a kind of reserve of land available in small pieces while the other tenements remained intact, whereas at Leighton Buzzard holdings tended much more to fragment, so that the virgates and half-virgates there had wholly disappeared in the second half of the fifteenth century.[200] These variations probably all spring from differences in demand for land, and

[199] Harvey, *Westminster Abbey and its Estates*, p. 305; Harvey, ed., *The Peasant Land Market*, p. 134.

[200] Roden, 'Studies', pp. 115, 117, 389–90; Harvey, *Westminster Abbey and its Estates*, pp. 323–7; Harvey, ed., *The Peasant Land Market*, pp. 125–7, 132–3, 134, 200–1, 203, 211, 217, 219–20, 238–40; Jones, 'Land and people at Leighton Buzzard', p. 23.

factors affecting this demand must have included the location of the manor, local population pressures (with, at Leighton Buzzard, the special attraction of an urban centre), and varying forms of tenure and manorial administration.

Manorial lords as well as manorial tenants might be involved in the market in small parcels of land. The Pusey family, lords of Pusey (Berks.), had in the thirteenth century acquired many single tenements and small pieces of land in other manors, but from the middle of the fourteenth century they sold or leased out many of the more distant ones. Before the mid-fourteenth century manorial tenants who participated in the land market likewise did not confine themselves to their own manor or parish, and it is normal to find them taking up lands elsewhere in the neighbourhood.[201] However, the growth of the inter-peasant land market in the present period was mostly very local, confined to the particular vill and its immediate surroundings. At the same time, three groups of outsiders were involved in the market in peasant land. First were townsmen who invested in lands in the rural manors of the district; thus we find men of Oxford holding lands at Cowley and Iffley or men of Hitchin at Arlesey, Knebworth, and Offley.[202] Second – the same phenomenon on a larger scale and at longer range – Londoners from the early fifteenth century appear as purchasers of smallholdings, free and customary, in centres with links of trade or communication with London, such as Leighton Buzzard (Beds.) or Stevenage (Herts.); by the late fifteenth century most tenants of more than fifty acres in the Lea valley were Londoners.[203] Third, a few men invested on a large scale in peasant holdings and other small properties over wide districts. An example is John Olney of Weston Underwood, who in the mid-fifteenth century held two free yardlands and thirteen tenements in Banbury (Oxon.) and its hamlet Neithrop.[204]

Migration from villages in the region, recorded in court-roll references to absent villeins and abandoned holdings, had begun in a small way before the mid-fourteenth century.[205] An immediate consequence of the Black Death was that people left at least some

[201] Jefferies, 'Some aspects of landholding in medieval Berkshire', pp. 23–5, 28–9; Harvey, *Medieval Oxfordshire Village*, pp. 115–16; Roden, 'Studies', pp. 162–3.

[202] *VCH Oxon.*, v, pp. 86, 200; Harvey, ed., *The Peasant Land Market*, p. 221; Roden, 'Studies', p. 276.

[203] Harvey, ed., *The Peasant Land Market*, pp. 234–5; *VCH Herts.*, III, p. 140; Glennie, 'Commercializing agrarian region', p. 335.

[204] *VCH Oxon.*, x, p. 56. For the Olneys see *VCH Bucks.*, IV, p. 498, and Chibnall, *Sherington*, p. 135.

[205] Thus Roden, 'Studies', p. 163 (Codicote, Herts.); Raftis, *Tenure and Mobility*, pp. 146, 149 (Shillington and Cranfield, both Beds.); J. M. Bennett, *Women in the Medieval English Countryside*, New York, 1987, pp. 52, 224–5 (Iver, Bucks.).

villages to take advantage of greater opportunities offered elsewhere. The lord of Sharpenhoe (Beds.) in 1352 brought back to his manor four of his villeins who had been working as labourers at Caddington, Luton, and Streatley (all within 7 miles of Sharpenhoe) and one who had been helping a merchant at St Albans; all five belonged to a single family. At Codicote (Herts.) in 1351 four missing villeins were at Baldock, Knebworth, Weston (all within 11 miles), and London.[206] In their destinations these two groups of migrants were typical of the whole period. Most movement seems to have occurred within the immediate neighbourhood; thus, hardly any of those taking up land on Arlesey Bury manor (Beds.) in the fifteenth century came from more than 5 or 6 miles away. But certain towns had a wider circle of attraction; surnames at Banbury (Oxon.) in the late fourteenth century, as in the previous 150 years, show immigration from all directions within a radius of 10 miles, but more selectively beyond that, coming from areas north-east of the town up to 20 miles away and from areas to the west between 20 and 50 miles distant, presumably reflecting the town's trading contacts. Carpenters and other woodworkers employed in Oxford colleges were drawn from a number of Oxfordshire villages and from as far away as Burford, Henley-on-Thames, and Newbury.[207] London had a still wider catchment area, drawing people especially from Bedfordshire and Hertfordshire. John atte Lee of King's Walden (Herts.) had worked in the kitchen of the manor house there, then in the kitchen of a house near Chelsfield (Kent), and by 1413, established as a chandler in London, had no wish to return to King's Walden as heir to his brother's holding; he may well have typified many who found their way to London after a series of moves. Other more distant migration was rare, though we find that of four villeins missing from Tyttenhanger (Herts.) in 1369 one was on the neighbouring manor of Mimms, but two were in Kent and the fourth was overseas.[208] It may well be that Bedfordshire and Hertfordshire were the counties where there was most mobility in general. It would be wrong to attach much importance to a simple lack of evidence, but there certainly seem to be fewer references to migration in the western counties of the region; thus, presentments of fugitive villeins are relatively rare in the court

[206] *VCH Beds.*, II, p. 89; *VCH Herts.*, IV, p. 195.

[207] Harvey, ed., *The Peasant Land Market*, p. 221; *VCH Oxon.*, X, p. 61; E. A. Gee, 'Oxford carpenters, 1370–1530', *Oxoniensia*, XVII/XVIII, 1952–3, pp. 146–68. Places occurring as surnames in Bedford and Dunstable in the fourteenth century are listed in Godber, *History of Bedfordshire*, pp. 117, 119.

[208] Roden, 'Studies', pp. 384–5; *VCH Herts.*, IV, p. 195. The east midlands in general, and Bedfordshire in particular, were the origin of a disproportionately large number of immigrants in fourteenth-century London (E. Ekwall, *Studies on the Population of Medieval London*, Stockholm, 1956, pp. xliii, l).

rolls of Berkshire manors. It is likely that throughout the region migration was patchy and spasmodic. Thus in Hertfordshire there was no early migration from Standon or Stevenage, while at Codicote and King's Walden we find it developing in the early fifteenth century; similarly at Islip (Oxon.) migration of villeins was recorded in the early fifteenth century while at Coleshill (Berks.) seven migrations were recorded in the late 1420s and early 1430s, then only a further four down to 1520. Even in the years immediately after the Black Death it was unusual for migrants, albeit recorded as fugitive villeins, to be brought back by their manorial lords; exceptionally, in 1395, one was returned from London to the manor of the canons of Windsor at Deddington (Oxon.) at a cost of 20s.[209]

We know little about the composition of the individual peasant's holding, what lands it contained at any time and how these were held; but we know even less about how he made a living from it. How the changes that have been described affected the peasant agrarian economy can only be surmised. We have seen that over the region as a whole the proportion of permanent pasture to ploughed land increased in the course of the period, and that not only manorial lords and demesne farmers but also tenants of smaller holdings maintained substantial flocks of sheep (see Chapter 2, G). Among manorial tenants in the region, however, there is no sign of any specialist pastoral farmers, and it seems most likely that the peasant holding would typically be run as a mixed farm, with perhaps greater emphasis on sheep farming among the larger peasant proprietors. Those with smallholdings, which may have done no more than supplement the profits from a craft or the wages from an employer, are unlikely to have produced with a view to the market. But we can be more confident than in earlier periods that most manorial tenants will have sold some part of their produce. The demands of London probably affected marketing throughout much of the region and it is interesting that compared with the north of the county the south of Hertfordshire gained between 1334 and 1524 in wealth per acre as assessed for taxation.[210]

Nor can we draw any but the most general conclusions about the social structure of the rural community resulting from these developments. Clearly places differed from each other in many ways. It does seem, however, to have been a period of increasing differentiation among manorial tenants: village aristocracies became more prominent than before, and in some places one or two families attained very

---

[209] Latham, 'Decay of the manorial system', p. 88; *VCH Herts.*, IV, p. 195; Roden, 'Studies', pp. 384–5; *VCH Oxon.*, VI, p. 215; Harvey, ed., *The Peasant Land Market*, p. 157; H. M. Colvin, *A History of Deddington, Oxfordshire*, London, 1963, p. 84.

[210] Glennie, 'Commercializing agrarian region', pp. 8–11.

dominant positions. R. J. Faith, working on Berkshire, suggests that the opportunities given by taking leases of manorial demesnes, by accumulating holdings of land, by enclosure, and by sheep farming, all played their part in this.[211] It is more doubtful, however, whether the rural community as a whole covered a wider economic and social spectrum than before: the landless, the largely unrecorded pool of labour which had formed the lowest stratum of rural society in the days before the Black Death, were much diminished in number and in a far stronger economic position than before. There is evidence that rural communities now included an increasing number of craftsmen, who were less concentrated than before in local market centres.[212] Many of those who worked for others within the village seem now to have been those with smallholdings rather than the completely landless; for the first time a substantial number of the poorest people in a village fall within the purview of the written record.[213] At the same time the withdrawal of manorial lords from direct exploitation of their demesne lands, and thereby from much direct intervention in the village, must have produced changes that are difficult for us to appreciate. In the background of the developments that have been discussed was the silent revolution by which the administrative initiative in the vill passed from the manor to the parish. It is only occasionally that we get any hint of this – as at Brightwalton (Berks.) in 1427 and 1434, when it was ruled that of the penalties collected for breaches of by-laws half should go to the manorial lord and half to the churchwardens for the use of the parish church, or at Shillington (Beds.) in 1472, when a copyhold tenement was surrendered to use in the church "before Matthew Chaumbre the lord's bailiff and all the parishioners present there".[214]

In some villages in the region there was a craft or industrial activity of more than merely local importance. The stone quarried at Totternhoe (Beds.) was used over a wide area, particularly in Hertfordshire, and the pottery of Brill and Boarstall (both Bucks.) was distributed within a twenty-mile radius.[215] Some of these industries,

---

[211] Harvey, ed., *The Peasant Land Market*, pp. 165–77.

[212] Some evidence from Oxfordshire is set out in P. D. A. Harvey, 'Non-agrarian activities in the rural communities of late-medieval England', in the proceedings of the 14th Settimana di Studio (1982), Istituto Internazionale di Storia Economica Francesco Datini, Prato (in press).

[213] Harvey, ed., *The Peasant Land Market*, pp. 163–4; Harvey, *Medieval Oxfordshire Village*, pp. 79–80, 139–40; Stitt, 'Manors of Great and Little Wymondley', pp. 142–3.

[214] Latham, 'Decay of the manorial system', p. 60; Raftis, *Tenure and Mobility*, p. 201n.

[215] E. Roberts, 'Totternhoe stone and flint in Hertfordshire churches', *Med. Arch.*, XVIII, 1974, pp. 66–89; E. M. Jope, 'Recent mediaeval finds in the Oxford area', *Oxoniensia*, X, 1945, p. 96; E. M. Jope, 'Medieval pottery kilns at Brill, Buckinghamshire', *Records of Bucks.*, XVI, 1953–60, pp. 39–42; H. E. J. Le Patourel, 'Documentary evidence and the medieval pottery industry', *Med. Arch.*, XII, 1968, pp. 108–24 *passim*; M. Farley, 'A medieval pottery industry at Boarstall,

while important, were relatively short-lived; our period saw the beginnings of significant stone-quarrying at Headington (Oxon.) at the end of the fourteenth century, but also, at just about the same time, the collapse of the tile-making industry of Penn (Bucks.), where production apparently outran demand. Other short-lived industrial activities were less important, but no less distinctive, such as the bell-founding at Toddington (Beds.) and Wokingham (Berks.).[216] Local centres of marketing and general country crafts also underwent varied fortunes during the period. Throughout the region we find small towns of this sort turning back into simple agrarian villages: Aldermaston (Berks.) and Denham (Bucks.) are among a number that stopped being called boroughs, Odell (Beds.), Datchet (Bucks.), and Markyate (Herts.) among others that lost their fairs or markets.[217] Some declined, but recovered in the course of the fifteenth or sixteenth century: Lambourn (Berks.) and Hertford are examples.[218] Where a local centre flourished or expanded in this period it very often owed this either to a growing specialized industry, such as the cloth-making of East Hendred and Wantage (both Berks.), or to its position on a long-distance route, such as Sawbridgeworth and Ware (both Herts.), or Abingdon and Maidenhead (both Berks.) – but not always, as witness Finchampstead (Berks.), to which a three-day fair was granted in 1458.[219] On the whole, however, the small centres of marketing and country crafts were in decline. Possibly the crafts rather than the marketing had been their *raison d'être*, so that their decline resulted from the dispersal of craftsmen into rural villages.[220] But for whatever reasons, the changes in agrarian economy and society in this period demanded fewer, more widely separated, local centres of this sort than had been required by earlier conditions.

Buckinghamshire', *Records of Bucks.*, XXIV, 1982, pp. 107–17. D. F. Renn, *Potters and Kilns in Medieval Hertfordshire*, Hitchin, 1964, provides a survey of the pottery industry in another county.

[216] *VCH Oxon.*, V, p. 163; C. Hohler, 'Medieval paving tiles in Buckinghamshire', *Records of Bucks.*, XIV, 1941–6, pp. 5–13; *VCH Beds.*, III, p. 439; *VCH Berks.*, I, pp. 412–15.

[217] *VCH Berks.*, III, p. 388; *VCH Bucks.*, III, pp. 252, 255; *VCH Beds.*, III, p. 69; *VCH Herts.*, IV, p. 207. The Buckinghamshire evidence is fully set out by M. Reed, 'Markets and fairs in medieval Buckinghamshire', *Records of Bucks.*, XX, 1975–8, pp. 563–85. In Hertfordshire some three-fifths of the local markets disappeared between 1349 and 1500, losses being especially heavy in the centre and north-east of the county (Glennie, 'Commercializing agrarian region', pp. 44–6).

[218] *VCH Berks.*, IV, p. 251; *VCH Herts.*, III, p. 500.

[219] *VCH Berks.*, I, pp. 376–7; III, pp. 97–9, 242, 244; IV, pp. 294, 321, 439; *VCH Herts.*, III, pp. 336, 382–4.   [220] As suggested by Harvey, 'Non-agrarian activities'.

H. KENT AND SUSSEX

The late middle ages in England are frequently described both as a time of economic decline and as the "golden age" of the English peasant.[221] The reasons seem obvious. Land was plentiful: rents dropped in many parts of the country and entry-fines were frequently minimal or non-existent. A much smaller percentage of the peasant's income than in the past went to the lord in the form of rent or judicial fines, and capital was released to invest in land and livestock.[222] An active land market gave the enterprising an opportunity to expand their holdings into farms of fifty or more acres. In addition the lowest categories of villagers, the landless or cottagers, with less than an acre, were able to acquire land of their own and build up a smallholding.[223] For many peasants their standard of living improved and they ate less bread and more fresh beef and mutton.[224] Agricultural labourers and small craftsmen – the tiler, thatcher, or carpenter – especially benefited from higher money wages at a time when food prices were stable or falling. Their real wages thus increased significantly.[225] Yet Marx, Brenner, and others have long insisted that it is a mistake to look at economic forces in isolation from class structure. For, in Brenner's words, "it is the structure of class relations, of class power, which will determine the manner and the degree to which particular demographic and commercial change will affect long-term trends in the distribution of income and economic growth, and not vice-versa".[226] Brenner certainly seems to be right

[221] I wish gratefully to acknowledge the receipt of a NEH Travel to Collections grant that made possible some of the research on which this chapter is based. The term "golden age" for the peasant was first coined by J. E. Thorold Rogers, *History of Agriculture and Prices*, I, *1259–1400*, pp. 252–325; IV, *1401–1582*, pp. 489–525. It is used by J. R. Lander in *Conflict and Stability in Fifteenth Century England*, London, 1969, pp. 27–8, and in *Government and Community: England 1450–1509*, Cambridge, Mass., 1980, pp. 2, 11. See also M. M. Postan, *The Medieval Economy and Society*, London, 1972, p. 142 and Hatcher, *Plague, Population and the English Economy*, pp. 31–5, 47–54.   [222] Dyer, 'A redistribution of incomes', p. 33.

[223] For good studies of the late medieval land market see Harvey, ed., *The Peasant Land Market*, and Richard M. Smith, ed., *Land, Kinship and Life Cycle*.

[224] Christopher Dyer, 'Changes in nutrition and standards of living in England, 1200–1500', pp. 35–45 in R. W. Fogel, ed. *Long-term Changes in Nutrition and the Standard of Living* (papers presented at the ninth international economic history congress, Berne, 1986). See also Christopher Dyer, 'Changes in diet in the late middle ages: the case of harvest workers', *AHR*, XXXVI, 1988, pp. 21–37.

[225] Phelps Brown and Hopkins, 'Seven centuries of the prices of consumables' (*Economica*, NS XXIII, 1956), reprinted in Peter H. Ramsay, ed., *The Price Revolution in Sixteenth-Century England*, London, 1971, pp. 18–41. Although the Phelps Brown–Hopkins index deals only with the wages of building labourers, it is generally assumed that it is fairly representative of wages received by other craftsmen.

[226] Robert Brenner, 'Agrarian class structure and economic development in pre-industrial Europe', p. 11 in T. H. Aston and C. H. E. Philpin, eds., *The Brenner Debate*, Cambridge, 1985.

when one compares the differing fortunes of peasants in areas of Kent and Sussex, where seigneurial power was relatively light, with those in areas where it remained strong.

Most Kentish gavelmen were legally free, whereas a number of tenants in Sussex were not. This distinction between freedom and bondage affected the amount of dues owed to the lord. Thus, while lords in both Kent and Sussex frequently sought to collect rents in kind, labour services and ancient dues such as common fines and pannage, only in Sussex could they demand the payment of merchet and chevage. Furthermore in Sussex lords successfully insisted that all transfers of bondland, whether by inheritance, marriage or sale, be recognized in their courts, and the appropriate payments made. Unauthorized transfers could be voided and the land forfeited. In contrast a Kentish tenant in gavelkind could freely sell or give his lands to whom he wished during his lifetime. Although when he acquired land he was supposed to do fealty for it and pay the lord a relief, these payments were quite small – usually about a quarter of the annual rent – whereas the entry-fines paid in Sussex rose and fell in accordance with the demand for land, and, in some areas, in the early fifteenth century, were exceedingly high. These differences markedly affected the land market in each area. In Kent men were willing to buy, sell, or exchange small units of land – half an acre to three acres – for the costs were low. But this factor, coupled with partible inheritance, encouraged the fragmentation of holdings and prepared the way for a growing division among the peasantry between the very wealthy and the very poor. Moreover the absence in Kent of any clear distinction between freeland and bondland, beyond, perhaps, a slightly higher rent, facilitated the entry into the land market of outsiders – merchants from London and elsewhere, and gentry. In Sussex land was usually inherited by a single heir, and bought or sold in the form of an integral holding, including pasture rights. Thus the differentiation between large and small holdings tended to be less than in Kent. Furthermore the legal disabilities attached to bondland discouraged its acquisition by gentry and it remained primarily in the hands of peasants.

Lords, from the thirteenth century onwards, frequently found themselves in a dilemma: should they commute rents in kind or labour services into money payments and risk lessening their authority, or should they continue to exact them and risk losing many of their tenants? One way out of the difficulty was to make partial concessions that could be reversed when circumstances changed. On the archiepiscopal lands, tenants in Kent owed ploughing, sowing, harrowing, and reaping services, with amounts varying from manor to manor. In Sussex tenants living in the Weald owed works of hedging, fencing, carrying wood, making wooden objects: those living outside the woodland area owed works of ploughing, manuring, and threshing. On the Pagham estates all the major tasks including carting, hedging, ditching, ploughing, and harvesting were, in the thirteenth century, regularly performed by villein services.[227] But, as land became more plentiful after 1348, tenants often refused to take tenements burdened with labour services. By the 1430s, if not before, most of these works, together with rents in kind, had been commuted into money payments. But the commutation was at the will of the lord and when a whole manor was farmed out it was generally handed over "with the works and boons of villeinage". Usually there is no record of whether or not the farmer exacted these services, but in the early 1420s the serjeant at Framfield noted that some of these works were carried out. In 1420–1 tenants reaped 128 acres, in 1423–4 they reaped 73 acres, and in 1424–5 they reaped 100 acres. Similarly the manor of Ouleburgh (in Maidstone) was handed over to Richard Woodville, Lord Rivers, together with the right to have 30 acres ploughed, 49 acres reaped, and the hay of 15 acres of meadow raised. These services appear to have been regularly performed throughout most of the fifteenth century, and it is not until the account of 1488–9 that there is a reference to their final commutation. In the mid-fifteenth century, however, when tenants on the archiepiscopal lands became very assertive, it is likely that not all services were actually performed. But the archbishop clearly did not give up his right to exact them. Tenants on a number of Kent estates were refusing to carry out services in the 1460s and 1470s. In other years, on other manors, they may have been less recalcitrant.[228] A similar situation appears to have existed on the estates of the cathedral priory of Christ Church, Canterbury. Despite the technical commutation of services since the late thirteenth century, the carriage of grain from the east Kent manors was regularly performed so long as the manors were in hand. When the manors were leased, the labour services on the priory estates went to the lessee. In 1399–1400, however, discord arose between the lessee of the manor of Hollingbourne and the tenants there "concerning their customs", and the prior was forced to visit the manor to negotiate (*ad tractandum*) with the tenants.[229]

[227] For further details see F. R. H. Du Boulay, 'The Pagham estates of the Archbishop of Canterbury during the fifteenth century', *History*, NS XXXVIII, 1953, pp. 201–18 and *idem, Lordship of Canterbury*, London, 1966, pp. 164–76. See also B. C. Redwood and A. E. Wilson, eds., *Custumals of the Sussex Manors of the Archbishop of Canterbury*, Sussex Rec. Soc. 57, 1958.

[228] Du Boulay, *The Lordship of Canterbury*, p. 175. The labour services on the archiepiscopal manor of Ringmer had been commuted by John Darell, steward from 1423–37, at the rate of 15s. a virgate: Lambeth Palace Library, ED 930, 454, 455, 456, 1224, 1234; Kent AO U409/M3.

[229] Cathedral Archives and Library, Canterbury, Beadle's rolls, Hollingbourne. See also M. Mate, 'Labour and labour services on the estates of Canterbury cathedral priory in the fourteenth century', *Southern History*, VII, 1985, pp. 55–68.

Hollingbourne was one of the few manors where the labour services were rarely performed. Thus the discord may have arisen because the lessee went against past practice and tried to demand labour from the tenants. But there are no other records of confrontation so it is quite possible that tenants on at least some of the east Kent manors continued to work for the lessees as they had done for the priory.

Other lords, both lay and ecclesiastical, clearly continued to exact labour services throughout much of the fifteenth century. On the Battle abbey estates, although commutation spread rapidly in the early fifteenth century, it was, as elsewhere, always at the will of the lord. When the monks had need of labour, they could usually insist that the works actually be done. Tenants on the Kent manor of Wye, for example, owed 553 carrying services, the ploughing of 97 acres, the mowing of 33 acres, and the reaping of 50 acres of wheat. In most years of the mid-fifteenth century, some of the carrying services were performed, since tenants are known to have carted wheat and barley from the rectory at Wye to the house at Battle, but the other works were commuted. In 1464–5, however, the tenants also ploughed 51 acres and reaped 18 acres.[230] Thereafter there is no record of works being done, so the abbey appears to have given up utilizing tenant labour. Some lay lords, however, demanded more work from their tenants and for a longer period. When the Duchy of Lancaster manor of Harting was in hand in 1426–7 tenants spent two days washing and shearing sheep and fourteen days carrying manure. In addition all the work of weeding the grain, mowing, making and carrying the hay, and leading the grain after the harvest, was carried out by tenant labour.[231] Similarly on the manor of Laughton, belonging to the Pelhams, the customary tenants continued to perform some labour services and provide both hens and eggs for the household throughout the fifteenth century. The system, however, was inherently flexible, and the number of works sold or performed depended on the needs of any one year. Yet, as late as 1512–13 tenants supplied the household with 91 hens and 638 eggs and carried out 40 works of harrowing, 44 works of reaping, and small amounts of other services, including weeding. Services did not finally cease until the 1520s.[232] Although these works usually consumed just a small fraction of a tenant's time in any one year, they were still regarded as irksome. Many fifteenth-century court rolls contain references to individual tenants who refused to do one or more services: to come to the weeding, to collect and turn the hay, to carry wood, etc. Above all labour services symbolized lack of personal freedom: one's time was not one's own.

[230] PRO SC 6/902/32, 904/19–22, 905/23, 905/30.   [231] PRO DL 29/442/7113.
[232] BL Add. Roll 32339.

Seigneurial power made itself felt in a variety of other ways as well. On Wealden manors such as Laughton, pannage dues continued to be collected throughout the fifteenth century. In 1504, for example, forty-four people paid dues, some for as many as thirty pigs or piglets.[233] In addition, throughout the fourteenth century, harvesters were generally paid, as they had been in the past, with a grant of the tenth sheaf.[234] During the early fifteenth century, however, both the archbishop of Canterbury and the monks of Christ Church priory started paying harvesters with money. The monks of Battle abbey followed suit on their Kent manor of Wye, but on their Sussex estates retained the old system of payment. At Alciston the number of reapers fluctuated from a low of twenty-two to a high of forty-four, and most years they appear to have had no objection to receiving their payment in kind. But in 1462–4, when grain prices were at their lowest (barley, for example, was selling for 2s. and 2s. 8d. a quarter) many reapers refused to reap for the customary sheaf "because of the low value of the grain". After that the monks moved back and forth between paying money wages and granting payment by the tenth sheaf. It was not until the 1490s, however, that money payments became the general practice.[235] In contrast, the Sackvilles, at Chalvington, switched to money payments in the 1430s. It is not clear, in most of these changes, whether the initiative came from the peasants or the lords, but since the money wages were often high – 16d. an acre on the Christ Church manor of Barton – it is quite likely that their adoption was with the agreement, if not at the insistence, of the tenants.

In mid-century tenants throughout south-east England became more assertive, as traditional collective dues became increasingly burdensome with the continued drop in population. But, although they demanded a reduction in the rate, they frequently continued to meet their obligation. In 1445–6, on the manor of Lamport, in Eastbourne, the chief pledge paid 12d. of common fine and no more because, as he explained, different lands and tenements accustomed to pay the old assessment remained in the hands of the lord for lack of tenants, so that

[233] BL Add. Roll 32058. At Laughton the payment was 2d. for a pig more than one year old and 1d. for a piglet more than six months old: A. E. Wilson, ed., *Custumals of the manors of Laughton, Willingdon and Goring*, Sussex Rec. Soc., LX, 1961, p. xxxix.

[234] On the Battle abbey estates the tenants were obliged either to find two men for each half-hide to reap in the lord's fields, or, if the lord preferred, each hide could reap in one day an acre of wheat or oats or half an acre of barley or vetches with as many men as they chose. In either case the reapers were paid with a grant of every tenth sheaf: S. R. Scargill-Bird, ed., *Custumals of Battle Abbey in the Reigns of Edward I and Edward II*, Camden Soc., NS XLI, 1887, pp. xix, 28.

[235] East Sussex RO SAS G44/111. The change brought about a great increase in expenditure. At Alciston in 1399–1400 (SAS G44/54) the monks paid just 22s. 10d. on food for harvest boons and in 1492–3 (SAS G44/138) they paid £12 7s. 4d.

it was not possible to levy the ancient sum of 5s. 4d.[236] Tenants of the
Duchy of Lancaster in a number of villages and small towns around
Pevensey also complained in the 1440s about the burden of paying the
common fine or tithing penny. These payments had become fixed sums
paid annually by the community as a whole. According to the tenants,
when the area had been teeming with people they had had no trouble
in paying. But in the early fifteenth century the region had become
depopulated, as men were continually withdrawing from the royal
lands into those of the archbishop to escape the necessity of paying the
fines. The remaining inhabitants, therefore, demanded that henceforth
the fine should be levied at the old rate of 1d. for every male over the
age of twelve.[237] Their request was granted. A similar concession was
made by the Pelhams for their Sussex Wealden manors. But on the
Battle abbey estates the common fines had not been so high and
therefore so burdensome, and they continued to be paid. Even so, in
1450, at the time of Cade's rebellion, nothing was received on any of
the Sussex manors "on account of the insurrections and disobedience of
the people rebelling against such customs".[238] The rebellion, however
was short-lived and by the next court the fine was paid once more.
Tenants on the archiepiscopal lands began refusing to pay their
common fines in the 1460s. Arrears mounted up year by year until
1468. Then on some manors the debt was paid. On the other manors
the arrears were not paid, but they did not increase either.[239] This could
either mean that tenants were now paying their full yearly dues or that
the archbishop had ceased to exact them. In view of the widespread
continuance of common fine payments, however, the former
explanation seems the more likely. Tenants also resisted paying the
customary recognition – palfrey money – on the appointment of a
new archbishop. In the early fifteenth century just a few tenants were
rebellious, but, after the accession of Thomas Bourgchier, the refusal to
pay was universal. Each year these payments were carried forward as
debts, but not one of the manors appears to have met its obligations.
The loss of revenue to the archbishop was substantial.[240] Yet, on the
appointment of the next archbishop there is no record of any refusal to
pay. As with the common fine, this could mean either that the tenants
did pay, or that the archbishop did not try to collect it. Certainly other
ecclesiastical lords continued to exact similar payments. In 1491–2 the

---

[236] East Sussex RO CP4.   [237] PRO DL 29/442/7117.
[238] East Sussex RO SAS G18/46.   [239] PRO SC 6/1130/1.
[240] Lambeth Palace Library. Bailiwick of Otford (ED 1241) £40; bailiwick of Maidstone (ED
1223) £38 6s. 8d.; bailiwick of Croydon (ED 1213) £10; bailiwick of Aldington (ED 1193A)
£41 13s. 4d; bailiwick of Pagham (ED 1262) £36 10s.; bailiwick of South Malling (ED 1302)
£20.

abbot of Battle returned 30s. to his tenants at Blatchington after they had "well and faithfully, by ancient custom" paid £3 6s. 8d. for palfrey money.[241]

These struggles between lords and tenants resemble a tug-of-war with neither side a clear victor. In some years lords successfully reasserted their authority, and in other years tenants gained a few concessions. But lords were reluctant to admit ultimate defeat and give up their rights altogether. This was particularly true with regard to the right to collect merchet and chevage. In the early years of the fifteenth century, merchet, one of the surest tests of villein status, was still paid in Sussex fairly regularly. By mid-century, however, it had become a rare, rather than a common, occurrence. Yet it was still paid. In 1467, at the manor court of Bishopstone, William Petman paid 5s. to marry his four daughters to whomsoever he pleased. One daughter was already married and her father had not felt it necessary to obtain a licence before the marriage took place.[242] For, although no one seems to have challenged the lord's right to collect merchet, villeins did not always volunteer payment, nor did local officials strictly enforce the lord's claim. Thus a large number of unauthorized marriages could take place before a more zealous official caught up with them, if he ever did. On the Battle abbey manor of Alciston, in 1511, it was discovered that the five daughters of Giles Page (bondman) had each married without a licence. In addition the two daughters of Richard Page, and the daughters of Dennis and William Page, had likewise married without licence. This, however, was not an idle discovery. Within the next few years six of the husbands came to court and each paid 12d. fine "to put himself in grace" for his misdemeanour.[243] Even in the early sixteenth century seigneurial authority over marriage was still intact, whether or not it was always exercised.

It was far harder for lords to collect chevage – the payments that authorized villeins to leave their home manor and dwell apart from the lordship. The need for labour, as the population fell after 1348, pulled villeins as well as others away from their ancestral homes. They ended up in London, in other towns, and on neighbouring estates working for other lords. Their local court might order them to return home, but they rarely did. In 1471, for example, the manor court of Heighton noted that the three sons of William Brightrich dwelt outside the lordship without paying chevage. Two of the sons lived elsewhere in Sussex – one at Ringmer and the other in Framfield – but the third son

---

[241] East Sussex RO SAS G18/52.

[242] BL Add. Roll 31279. A very good discussion of the legal aspects of villeinage in the twelfth and thirteenth centuries can be found in Paul R. Hyams, *King, Lords and Peasants in Medieval England*, Oxford, 1980.   [243] East Sussex RO SAS G18/55.

had moved to Canterbury in Kent. Nine years later they were still away and the court again ordered their bodies to be seized.[244] They never did come back or make chevage payments. They maintained their freedom, but the cost was the break-up of the family unit. The lure of an inheritance, however, did sometimes persuade an absentee villein both to return and to pay chevage. In 1479 Juliana Upton, on the death of her parents, returned home so that she could be admitted to the family holding. Having done so, she gave the lord 12d. chevage that she could live outside the lordship for one year.[245] But it is not clear whether she paid it again when the year was up. Thus the ability to go away and find work without difficulty was a powerful force dissolving the ties of personal bondage. But not everyone was willing to leave home and family in order to become free. For those who wished to remain on the family land, the only route to freedom was through manumission. At least two villeins belonging to Battle abbey were manumitted – one in 1448 and the other in 1512. In each case the abbot promised that neither he nor his successors from henceforth could collect payments by reason of villeinage. The amounts paid for merchet and chevage were usually not a major financial burden, but were undoubtedly psychologically burdensome, signifying as they did "the yoke of servitude".[246]

Rents and entry-fines, on the other hand, in parts of south-east England, could consume a large portion of tenant resources. For although some landlords, like the nuns of Syon abbey, did significantly reduce rents in the course of the fifteenth century, others did not. In 1436–7, at Ickham, the Christ Church monks renegotiated the rents, but they charged 2s. 6d. an acre for the eighty acres of cotland. When the monks of Battle abbey commuted labour services into a money rent, they did so at the rate of 1s. an acre. Thus William Alman, who held a messuage and 27 acres in the common fields of Alciston, owed 27s. of annual rent. Tenants who enjoyed pasture rights sometimes paid even more. John Syger, for example, at Alfriston, held 8½ acres of arable, ½ acre of meadow and the right to pasture 26 sheep on the common pasture and he owed 11s. annual rent.[247] In most cases these rents remained unchanged until the end of the fifteenth century. But if rents were stable, entry-fines were not and seem to have fairly accurately reflected the demand for land. In the early fifteenth century at Lullington entry-fines were high and could equal five times the annual rent. A tenant, for example, paid 20s. fine for a cottage and 4½ acres (with an annual rent of 4s.), and another paid 13s. 4d. for a cottage

[244] East Sussex RO SAS G1/25, G1/36.   [245] BL Add. Roll 32495.
[246] East Sussex RO SAS G1, Charters 267, 317. The latter charter included the words "made free from all yoke of servitude and bondage".   [247] PRO E 315/56 ff.239, 249v.

and a garden. By the mid-fifteenth century the bottom had fallen out of the land market and tenants were scarce. The abbey drastically reduced its entry-fines. When half a wist (c. 10 acres) which had remained in the abbey's hands for lack of tenants was finally rented out, the fine was just 3s. – a third of the annual rent of 9s. The larger the holding, the harder it was to find takers and the lower proportionately the entry-fine. The new owner of a tenement of 40 acres, for example, paid six capons entry-fine and no more "because of the scarcity of tenants to take the great burden of the said tenement". By the late 1460s the population and the market had improved slightly and entry-fines stabilized at approximately one year's rent. But in the 1490s land and cottages were once more remaining in the hands of the lord for long periods. The new tenants, when they were found, paid exceedingly low entry-fines – 12d. for a cottage and $5\frac{1}{2}$ acres, and 20d. for a wist of 23 acres.[248] Even lords as powerful as Battle abbey, while they might maintain rents at the customary level, could not insist on high entry-fines in the face of a slump in demand.

High rents, however, did not prevail everywhere. Free land normally rented for less than bondland. Thus assart land in the Sussex Weald rented for 2d. and 4d. an acre. Elsewhere in parts of east and north Kent the difference in rent between free land and bondland was slight and in such places the distinction between the two tenures became blurred. With the relief for new acquisitions in Kent often as low as 1d. an acre, men who were not peasants saw little disadvantage in acquiring bondland and built up significant holdings. The process is very clear on the Christ Church manor of Eastry. In 1475 all the lands were measured and new rents were established at the rate of 2d. an acre for free land and 5d. an acre for land subjected to carrying service (bondland). By 1481, at the time of a new rental, all the larger tenants held both free land and bondland. Moreover, much of the land was held by men who were neither peasants nor local inhabitants. Richard Catour of London, for example, held 105 acres; the chantry established by Thomas Ely in the town of Sandwich held 177 acres and the Hospital of St Bartholomew held $30\frac{1}{2}$ acres. Eight other men from Sandwich also held land within the manor. Over the next thirty years much of this land changed hands, but outsiders continued to form a significant portion of the tenantry. In 1511–12 tenants included one Londoner, and six inhabitants of Sandwich. The gentry had also moved into the land market. Sir Thomas Lovel (knight) who had owned no land in 1481, had built up a holding of 224 acres.[249] This, however, was not an

---

[248] East Sussex RO SAS G18/43, 46, 47, 51.

[249] Cathedral Archives and Library, Canterbury, Misc. accounts 31, ff. 13–22; Misc. accounts 33. Eastry contained $151\frac{1}{2}$ acres of free land and 856 acres of *averland*.

isolated example. Local gentlemen and townsmen abounded on other
Christ Church manors. The situation was no different on the Battle
abbey manor of Wye. In mid-century the larger tenants there included
Sir George Browne, the College of Wye, Thomas Kempe, bishop of
London, and Walter Moyle, king's serjeant at law and steward of the
abbey. In north Kent, with its closer proximity to the metropolis, the
proportion of Londoners was naturally higher.[250] In most instances
these men probably did not cultivate these lands directly by their own
servants, but let them in much smaller parcels to sub-tenants.

Tenants who wanted to enlarge their holdings as the size of their
family increased did not have to buy land. They could usually rent or
lease some from the lord or from fellow tenants for a term of years. In
this way they saved themselves both the purchase price and the entry-
fine (or the relief in Kent), but did not, of course, acquire any
permanent assets that they could then sell in their turn. Even when
demesnes were kept in hand, as at Alciston, some of the unused
demesne fields were leased out, usually in small plots of half an acre or
an acre. So too, in many places, even where the manor was leased out
to a single taker, a few acres were separately rented to individual
tenants. In years when it was impossible to find a demesne lessee, a
larger area was rented. The amount of rent paid, however, varied
considerably. At Alciston the normal rate was 1s. an acre. In Kent at
Charing, in 1467–8, 38 acres of demesne were leased for ninety-nine
years at 4d. an acre. At Gillingham 295 acres of arable land were
temporarily rented to tenants at 6d. an acre. At Teynham, in 1457–8,
126 acres of arable land, lying in the fields, were rented to different
tenants at 20d. an acre and it was noted that they used to rent for four
bushels of barley. By the time of the next account (1461–2) the rent for
67 of these acres had gone up to 2s. an acre. In the 1470s, however, all
the rents were re-negotiated and they ranged from 1s. to 2s. an acre.[251]
Rents for subleased tenant land were undoubtedly equally diverse and
in most cases must surely have been higher than the rent owed by the
tenant to the lord. Widows and elderly tenants frequently found leasing
a useful way to keep their holdings intact when they could not or did
not want to work them themselves. But subleasing was such a
widespread phenomenon that some men at least must have acquired

---

[250] Mary Norah Carlin, 'Christ Church, Canterbury and its lands from the beginning of the
priorate of Thomas Chillenden to the Dissolution', Oxford Univ. D. Phil. thesis, 1970, p. 142.
At Chartham the outsiders included Elizabeth, Lady Bergavenny (the widow of Sir George
Neville) and citizens of Canterbury: Angela Langridge, 'The population of Chartham from 1086
to 1600', *Archaeologia Cantiana*, CI, 1984, p. 238. Helen Elizabeth Muhlfeld, *A Survey of the Manor
of Wye*, New York, 1933; PRO E 315/56; Anne Brown, 'London and north-west Kent in the
later Middle Ages: the development of a land market', *Archaeologia Cantiana*, XCII, 1976, p. 150.

[251] Lambeth Palace Library, ED 1223, 1226.

new land with the express purpose of renting it out again. Thus families who had a temporary need for a few more acres would have had no trouble finding land.

The Potman family at Alciston provides a good example of men who combined demesne work with farming their own smallholding and who were willing to lease land as well as own it. Early in the fifteenth century, John Potman worked as a shepherd and supplemented his income with brewing. At his death in 1432 he held a cottage and messuage, and leased 15 acres of bondland. His son, William Potman, took over the holding and the leasehold land, and may well have taken over his father's job, for in 1435–6 he is clearly working as a shepherd. He also had a flock of his own, for he pastured his ewes with the ewes of the lord and paid for the pasture rights by giving up half his lambs. In the 1440s he was still working as a shepherd and may have been working part-time as a carpenter, for someone bearing that name was frequently hired by the day. In the 1450s, however, nearly all the land he and his father had been leasing was given up and he kept just 3 acres. It is possible that, in accordance with the Chayanov model, he shed land as familial responsibilities diminished. For, by the time of his own death, in 1465, his wife and his son, John, had already died and he left his cottage and garden to the use of his daughter-in-law, Joanna.[252]

Nearly all men who worked full-time as *famuli* received an increase in their money wages during the course of the fifteenth century, but the rise was far steeper in Kent than in parts of Sussex. On the Battle abbey manor of Wye the ploughman who had been earning 8s. 4d. a year in 1393–4 was being paid 26s. 8d. in 1410–11, and the shepherd, who in 1393–4 had been paid 10s., was earning double in 1413–14. Such high money wages may not have been uncommon, for at Cobham, in 1402–3, a ploughman was being paid 26s. 8d. and a carter 20s. When the Christ Church manor of Monkton was taken in hand in 1410–11 the eight *famuli* were receiving 20s. each for their yearly wages (*stipendiis*).[253] On the archiepiscopal manor of Otford and the Christ Church manor of Barton the wages rose a little more slowly (see Tables 7.7 and 7.8), but by the early 1430s skilled labourers – carters and ploughmen – were earning more than twice what they had been given in the late fourteenth century and even the unskilled pigman had received a considerable increase. Meanwhile their grain liveries had

[252] East Sussex RO SAS G18/44, G44/88. In 1435–6 he handed over 30 new-born lambs: SAS G18/48. For a good critique of the Chayanov analysis see R. M. Smith, 'Some issues concerning families and their property in rural England, 1250–1800', in Smith, ed., *Land, Kinship and Life-Cycle*, pp. 6–21.

[253] PRO SC 6/902/3, 902/27, 902/33; BL Harl. Ms. C22; Cathedral Archives and Library, Canterbury, Beadle's rolls, Monkton.

Table 7.7. *Wage rates for* famuli *on the archiepiscopal manor of Otford (Kent), 1391–1444*

Year	Carter	Ploughman	Shepherd
1391–2	10s. 0d.	10s. 0d.	10s. 0d.
1410–11	13s. 4d.	13s. 4d./10s. 0d.	10s. 0d.
1418–19	20s. 0d.	13s. 4d./10s. 0d.	10s. 0d.
1427–8	26s. 8d.	20s. 0d./16s. 0d.	13s. 4d.
1431–2	26s. 8d.	20s. 0d./16s. 8d.	16s. 0d.
1437–8	26s. 8d.	23s. 4d./20s. 0d.	16s. 0d.
1443–4	26s. 8d.	18s. 0d.[a]/16s. 0d.[a]	16s. 0d.

[a] employed part of the year

Table 7.8. *Wage rates for* famuli *on the Christ Church manor of Barton (Kent), 1406–39*

Year	Ploughman	Shepherd	Pigman
1406–7	11s. 0d.	11s. 0d.	11s. 0d.
1413–14	15s. 0d.	11s. 0d.	11s. 0d.
1417–18	15s. 0d.	14s. 0d.	12s. 8d.
1419–20	15s. 0d.	14s. 0d.	12s. 8d.
1422–3	15s. 0d.	14s. 0d.	12s. 8d.
1431–2	20s. 0d.	20s. 0d.	14s. 2d.
1434–5	26s. 8d.	20s. 0d.	15s. 8d.
1438–9	26s. 8d.	20s. 0d.	15s. 8d.

remained unchanged. In contrast on the Battle abbey manors of Lullington and Alciston the money wages being paid to ploughmen and shepherds merely went up from 6s. to 8s. by the 1420s, and they stayed at that level for the great part of the century. These low rates, however, were by no means atypical for the county, for on the Syon abbey manor of Hampton in 1420–1 the ploughmen, carter, and shepherds were each being paid 10s. a year and the pigman 8s. Similarly on the Duchy of Lancaster manor of Harting in 1426–7, the shepherd, ploughman, and the pigman were each paid 7s. a year and on the archiepiscopal manor of Pagham the year before the *famuli* were earning 8s. each.[254]

What can account for such a great disparity in wage levels? Nigel Saul has suggested that the wages and stipends entered in the discharge

[254] PRO SC 6/1032/5; DL 29/442; Lambeth Palace Library, ED 959.

section were not necessarily the actual sums paid by the serjeant to his workers. "They were simply the amounts that the auditors allowed him for that purpose, and whatever he had to pay in excess in order to retain staff he was expected to meet out of his own pocket."[255] If the low wages occurred on just one or two manors, then such an explanation might well be correct. But as the recorded payments to *famuli* on so many Sussex estates, both lay and ecclesiastical, in the early fifteenth century were only a half to one-third of the wages of similar workers in Kent, it is hard to imagine that all these bailiffs were willing to make up the difference out of their own resources, especially on large manors when the total sum involved would have been enormous. Moreover, if Battle abbey auditors were indeed taking such a strict line for some of the Sussex estates, why did they not take a similar hard line on the Kent manor of Wye? Saul's explanation thus raises more problems than it solves. There are, however, other possible explanations.

First, Sussex *famuli* often enjoyed non-monetary privileges. On the bishop of Chichester's manor of Ferring, for example, in the thirteenth century, a shepherd could keep one or two cows in the fallow before the lord's fold and one horse tethered after the fold. He could also keep twenty-five ewes and one wether with the lord's ewes. Finally, and perhaps most importantly, he had the use of the eleventh acre of the fallow, and on it could pitch the lord's fold on the eve of St Thomas day (21 December) and keep it there until 6 January, and then sow the land with his own grain and have the yield. Ploughmen at Laughton traditionally enjoyed the use of the lord's plough on Saturday; could put two beasts on the lord's pasture for the whole summer quit of herbage; could pasture one pig free of pannage; and were granted one log each year for their hearth.[256] Such rights could well have lasted into the fifteenth century and help to account for some of the disparity in money wages. *Famuli* whose money wages were higher may well have lost or given up their pasture and other rights. The clearest evidence in support of this hypothesis comes from the manor of Lullington. In the late 1420s one shepherd there was paid 10s. and his three fellows were paid 8s; the bailiff explained that the higher wage was because "he did not have any sheep at pasture with the sheep of the lord".[257] Second, wage-rates may have been more highly localized than historians have assumed. Even in the early fourteenth century annual wages paid to plough holders on the Christ Church estates varied from 5s. 2d. on the Surrey manor of Merstham to 9s. 6d. on the Kent marsh manor of

[255] Saul, *Scenes from Provincial Life*, p. 126.

[256] W. D. Peckham, *Thirteen custumals of the Sussex manors of the Bishop of Chichester*, Sussex Rec. Soc., XXXI, 1925, p. 73; Wilson, ed., *Custumals*, p. 21.   [257] PRO SC 6/1026/11.

Elvington.[258] Customary rates were thus clearly lower in some places than in others. Third, the growing shortage of population, as the fifteenth century progressed, may have forced some lords to pay, not the customary rate, but a rate that reflected the actual balance existing in a particular area between the demand for labour and its supply. In Kent, with its close proximity to London and the continent, a work force, reduced by death and emigration, and faced with competing demands for its labour, may have been able to secure higher wages than the work force in Sussex, where the demand for labour was less acute and seigneurial power was stronger.

On a few Sussex manors, where labour appears to have been scarce, wages did approximate to those in Kent. Lords, however, clearly sought to return to lower wage-rates as soon as possible. On the Pelham manor of Laughton, in 1412–13, three *famuli* were hired for 13s. 4d. each. In 1415–16 just one man was employed but he was paid 20s. a year. In this instance there may have been a temporary, but acute, shortage of labour in the area as a result of the renewal of the Hundred Years War. By the following year, however, the lord was able to hire his workers for less, and paid one man 13s. 4d. a year and another one 10s.[259] Similarly on the Battle abbey manor of Apuldram, in the early 1420s, the *famuli* were earning 20s. a year, but by 1428–9 the wages had been cut to 13s. 4d. a year, although they climbed back again during the bad weather of the 1430s. Men at Apuldram may have enjoyed fewer non-monetary privileges than *famuli* employed on the other Battle abbey Sussex manors, but they may also have been able to force a higher money wage on the abbey by virtue of a superior bargaining position. For Apuldram is situated on an inlet fairly close to Chichester, and it is quite likely that its inhabitants were continually lured there. In 1422–3, for example, the rent-collector could not collect 18s. of the assessed amercements "because men had left the neighbourhood and could not be distrained".[260] If the area was suffering from an acute shortage of manpower, as a result of both death and migration, the abbey may have had no option but to pay high money wages.

The wages paid to building and other part-time workers employed on demesnes also increased significantly in the first two decades of the fifteenth century. The average rate for mowing, which had been 7d. an acre in the late fourteenth century, reached 8d. an acre almost everywhere in both Kent and Sussex. But, as was the case with yearly wages, workers in Kent frequently received far greater increases than

---

[258] M. Mate, 'Labour and labour services', p. 65.

[259] BL Add. Rolls 32147, 32148, 32149.

[260] PRO SC 6/1017/17, 18, 25. In 1436–7 the master ploughman was paid 20s., but the two other ploughmen were paid 16s. each: SC 6/1018/9.

their counterparts in Sussex. On the Battle abbey Sussex estates and on lay manors such as Chalvington, tilers and carpenters generally received 4d. a day and their helper, if they had one, received 2d. In contrast, on the archiepiscopal manor of Maidstone, in 1408–9 a tiler with helper was making 10d. a day. In this instance Maidstone, with its proximity to London, may have been affected by the outbreak of plague in 1408, producing a dearth in the neighbourhood. For by the time of the next account, in 1414–15, the wage had been cut to 9d. a day.[261] Perhaps by then the population had been replenished by immigration from the countryside. At Otford, in north Kent, a carpenter in 1402 was being paid 4d. or 5d. a day and by 1427–8 was receiving 6d. a day, while a tiler with boy was being paid 7d. a day in 1402–3 and 8d. a day in 1427–8. The high wages commanded by tilers may have resulted from the strains imposed by the war effort. For, after the capture of Harfleur, tile-makers, stone-cutters, and tilers were sent to mend the houses and other buildings of the captured city. As a result the countryside was sometimes denuded of necessary personnel. At Otford, in 1418–19 the serjeant was unable to make any tiles at all "for lack of workers".[262] But the Kent rate for carpenters was also higher than in other parts of the country, perhaps because its workers were being attracted not only abroad, but to the London metropolis.[263]

Wages were also influenced by prices, although they did not always move in tandem with them. The late 1430s were years of poor harvests. Although grain prices did not rise as high in Sussex as they did in London and other towns, they almost doubled. Wheat, for example, which was valued at 5s. 4d. a quarter in 1424–5 was selling for 10s. 10d. a quarter in 1437–8, and the value of barley had gone up from 3s. 4d. to 5s. 4d. Thus even though the carpenter and roofer at Lullington were paid 5d. a day, instead of 4d. a day as earlier, the increased wage in no way compensated for the rise in grain prices. On the Sussex archiepiscopal estates the workers did a little better. At Mayfield a tiler and helper were paid 10d. a day. Carpenters were generally earning 6d. a day. At Tarring, however, one man was paid 5d. a day and given his food. In view of the high cost of food, his real wage was probably higher than elsewhere. Similar high wages prevailed on the other archiepiscopal estates. At Otford two tilers were earning 9d. and 10d.

[261] Lambeth Palace Library, ED 670, 672.　　　[262] Ibid., ED 838, 853, 858.

[263] The average wage paid to carpenters on the Winchester manors in 1401–10 was 4.64d., in 1411–20 4.51d., and in 1421–30 4.52d. W. H. Beveridge, 'Wages on the Winchester manors', EcHR, VII, 1936–7, p. 40. On just a few manors carpenters were earning 5d. a day; none was earning 6d. At Stratford-upon-Avon, before 1411, some carpenters were paid 5d. a day, although 4d. was the more usual rate. By 1427–8, 5d. had become the normal rate: T. H. Lloyd, Some Aspects of the Building Industry in Medieval Stratford-upon-Avon, Dugdale Soc. Occasional Paper, no. 14, Oxford, 1961.

a day and at Lambeth, on the outskirts of London, one tiler was paid 14d. a day.[264] Once the danger of famine was over, wages might be expected to fall, especially since the 1440s and 1450s were a time of deflation. In many places wages, particularly for agricultural workers, did fall. South-east England shared in the general trend. At Barton the rate for mowing, which had remained at 8d. an acre in the early years of the century and risen to 10d. in the crisis years of 1434–5, dropped back to 7d. an acre and stayed there for the next three decades. At Lambeth, in Surrey, the exceedingly high wages paid in 1437–8 were reduced to the early fifteenth-century levels. At Hollingbourne, in the 1460s, a common labourer was paid 2d. a day, a carpenter 5d., and a tiler and his son 7d. a day, all without food.[265] But not all wages dropped. At Barton a tiler and boy were paid 10d. a day in the mid-1440s. At Otford and some other places in Kent carpenters continued to receive 6d. a day. At Lullington and Alciston in Sussex carpenters were paid 5d. a day in the early 1440s, but at the end of the decade some men were being paid 4d. a day (the level of the 1420s). Even so, since grain prices, in mid-century, were generally below the level of the 1420s, their real wage had almost certainly increased.

Lords, however, did not make any more concessions than they had to. As in the past, they frequently paid labourers, such as carpenters, less in the winter months and more during the peak summer months, when the working day was longer and the demand for labour was at its highest.[266] In addition, in the mid-1440s, as food prices dropped, it became increasingly common in Sussex to feed such workers "at the table of the lord". When that happened, their money wage was reduced. On the lay manor of Chalvington, for example, mowers were paid 4d. an acre with their food, and carpenters and roofers received $2\frac{1}{2}$d. a day, plus food. On the Battle abbey manor of Alciston a carpenter was paid 3d. a day with food and 4d. a day without food. These Alciston rates remained virtually unchanged until the end of the

---

[264] Lambeth Palace Library, ED 706, 1064, 863, 566.

[265] Lambeth Palace Library, ED 513. In a detailed study based on forty wage series, J. H. Munro concludes that in the period 1440s to 1480s the agricultural wage index declined by 21 per cent, whereas the industrial wage index fell by just 7.6 per cent: Munro, 'The behaviour of wages during deflation in late medieval England and the Low Countries', paper presented at the ninth international economic history congress (Berne, 1986).

[266] The Statute of Labourers in 1351 laid down that masons, carpenters, and plasterers should take no more than 6d. without food for the working day in summer (from Easter to Michaelmas), and 5d. in winter. The statute of 1446 fixed the following rates: a master carpenter, 4d. with food or $5\frac{1}{2}$d. without food in summer and 3d. or $4\frac{1}{2}$d. in winter; an ordinary carpenter, 3d. or 4d. in summer and $1\frac{1}{2}$d. or 3d. in winter; a common labourer, 2d. or $3\frac{1}{2}$d. in summer and $1\frac{1}{2}$d. or 3d. in winter. The reduction in the winter months, however, was not invariable: Salzman, *Building in England*, pp. 68–75.

century. In 1490–1 a roofer there was still paid 3d. a day, plus food, but in 1492–3 (the last surviving account) both the roofer and tiler were paid just 2d. a day with their food.[267] These men may have eaten well themselves, but they had less money to take home to their families, and so less control over their own lives. Moreover, in years when grain prices were exceedingly low, it is likely that the cost of the food provided by the lord was less than the alternative money wage. The failure of many Sussex wages to follow the steady progression so familiar from the Winchester data makes one realize that neither were all labourers so well provided for, nor lords so burdened as hitherto thought.

Most years, however, a carpenter or tiler could not expect to be employed full-time on the demesne and had to supplement his income in other ways. He almost certainly found additional work repairing the buildings and implements of his fellow villagers and he probably migrated to neighbouring villages, when extensive building works were undertaken.[268] In addition, most craftsmen worked their own land, as well as brewing occasionally. At Alciston, for example, in 1432, a roofer, John atte Nasshe, paid 7s. a year for a messuage, curtilage, garden, and six acres and he leased another acre for 1s. The major carpenter on the estate, John Thatcher, paid 8s. for a garden, croft, and seven acres in the common fields, together with the right to put one ox and two cows in the common pasture. At that time he or his wife was brewing once or twice a year. In the 1440s he was working fairly regularly for the abbey as a carpenter, being paid 3d. a day at table. In 1449–50, in addition to his meals, the monks paid him 4s. 6d. and the following year he took on the additional responsibility of repairing the abbey carts, ploughs, harrows, and wagons for an annual wage of 6s. 8d. During these years the family continued to brew, but only occasionally. Farming was clearly an important part of their life, for in the late 1450s, Thatcher was leasing an additional five acres. Unfortunately he had no heir to succeed him. When he died his land passed to his widow, and, on her death, the holding was surrendered to others.[269] Craftsmen like these were clearly not solely dependent on their wages but, like their fellows in the sixteenth century, relied partly on the fruits of their agricultural activities.[270] With land readily

---

[267] East Sussex RO SAS G44/136, 138.

[268] Christopher Dyer, 'English peasant buildings in the later Middle Ages', *Med. Arch.*, xxx, 1986, pp. 19–43 provides evidence for the existence of well-built peasant houses, using the services of skilled craftsmen.

[269] PRO E 315/56; East Sussex RO SAS G44/98–9, G44/102–3.

[270] Donald Woodward found that for many sixteenth-century carpenters "farming did not simply provide a useful supplement to the family diet, but yielded extra income to enhance the family's capacity to purchase goods and services": 'Wage rates and living standards in pre-industrial England', *PP*, no. 91, 1981, p. 41.

available, few men had to be content with just a cottage and its garden. A family with a holding around seven acres, where the husband worked as carpenter, tiler, or *famulus*, and the wife brewed occasionally and helped at the harvest, or haymaking, could quite successfully combine their paid employment with keeping a few animals and growing a few crops to feed both the family and the animals. They may even have sold some of their produce in the local market, although the low price level for agricultural goods must have reduced profits. None the less with this kind of occupational flexibility such families, despite the smallness of their holding, may have had a relatively stable existence. It is important to remember that no clear-cut demarcation existed between agricultural and other forms of work. Many peasants were jacks of all trades and would help out with the tiling and carpentry as required. Moreover, there was no demarcation between the paid labourer and the independent farmer. Even men with fifteen acres were willing to work for a lord part-time, as the need arose.

Unfortunately there is very little evidence about the actual farming methods utilized on either small or large holdings. Tenants working their own land may have worked harder than they did when working for others, and so the tasks of manuring, weeding, ploughing, etc. may have been carried out more thoroughly and efficiently than they were on demesne estates, but this is impossible to prove. Certainly some tenants were interested in increasing the productivity of their land, for, throughout the fifteenth century, men paid fines for the privilege of marling small patches. Moreover, on one occasion at least, a shepherd relinquished some of his grain livery in return for the compost of the lord's fold.[271] On another occasion a sub-tenant agreed to compost one acre of the land he was renting each year of the lease.[272] Such arrangements may have occurred fairly often. On the other hand, although tenants clearly grew wheat, barley, and occasionally oats, there is little evidence for any widespread cultivation of legumes. But if they were consumed by animals in the fields, as they were on so many demesne estates, they may have been exempt from paying tithes and so have escaped detection. In addition tenants could fold their own stock on their own land and utilize any compost collected in their barns. This is particularly important, since by the fifteenth century there appears to have been no shortage of tenant livestock. On the contrary, men frequently complained that their fellows failed to keep their closes in good repair so that stock escaped and encroached on the land of others. So, too, lords routinely cited tenants for trespassing on demesne fields and pasture. Such complaints encompassed a wide range of beasts – pigs, mares, foals, cows, bullocks, oxen, and flocks of sheep from 40 to

---

[271] East Sussex RO SAS G1/46.　　　　[272] *Ibid.*, SAS G1/24.

400 animals. Heriots in Sussex, however, in the early fifteenth century, were generally paid in oxen or cows and very rarely in horses. For peasant farmers in Sussex appear to have followed the practice of lords in the area and continued to use oxen for most of their hauling and ploughing. Men hired to carry grain or hay did so with ox-drawn wagons, even when they provided their own equipment. Pasture was plentiful and an ox had one great advantage over a horse: it could be eaten when its useful life was over. Moreover, tenants who did not own oxen of their own or at least not enough for a ploughteam, could easily rent them from those who did.[273] On downland manors, where arable husbandry continued, nothing appears to have changed during the course of the century. Although horses were clearly being bred, they seem to have been kept in addition to and not at the expense of oxen. In much of the Sussex Weald, however, as pastoral husbandry became more important, the use of oxen appears to have diminished. By the end of the century heriots were most often paid with cows and bullocks, sometimes with mares and rarely with oxen. But unfortunately there is so little information about the actual amount of stock kept on any one holding that it is impossible to say for sure whether practices differed markedly between large and small holdings.

It is equally hard to determine the relative proportion of large and small holdings. Rentals of individual manors may show a preponderance of families with a holding of under 20 acres, but there is usually no means of knowing how many of these families held from other lords.[274] But, on the death of John Rolf, in 1508, the local court inquired into his landholdings elsewhere. Although a bondman he held on his home manor of Heighton two cottages, a tenement, and five wists (c. 75 acres). In addition he held freely two tenements in Firle, plus 30 acres by copy of the court roll of the manor of Laughton from Thomas Pelham. At the same time he held from Lord la Warr a tenement and 4 acres at Selmeston, and 19 acres at Sherrington. Thus altogether he held at least 128 acres, but if one had access only to the rental of Selmeston, he would be classified as a smallholder.[275] Similarly the village of Hoathly was controlled by two families – the Pelhams and the Gages – and many tenants held land from both. Thus the bondman, Hugh Brightrich, held 2 acres from the Pelhams and 24 acres

[273] William Lulham agreed to pay 8s. for the use of four oxen, but failed to pay on time: BL Add. Roll 31955.

[274] See Anne Reiber DeWindt, 'Redefining the peasant community in medieval England: the regional perspective', *J. of British Studies*, 26, 1987, pp. 163–207 for evidence of peasants holding property in more than one village.

[275] East Sussex RO SAS G1/29. According to an inventory of his goods, he possessed at Selmeston 9 oxen, 2 bullocks, 7 cows, 5 calves, 1 mare, 8 pigs, and 8 piglets.

from the Gages. On his death, his son John sold the 2 acres to Laurence Salmon, who already held 80 acres from the Gages.[276]

Nonetheless a broad gulf clearly separated the most successful tenants – the men who usually took on the demesne leases – and the landless and those who worked for wages and farmed a few acres. The lessees of the Romney marshes, for example, were substantial landholders, frequently leasing several demesnes either from the same lord or from different lords. Richard Tylly, in 1474–5, farmed the archiepiscopal marsh manor of Willop, paying part of his farm in kind, providing wethers and oxen for the archiepiscopal household. In 1480 he took over the Christ Church marsh manors of Orgarswick, Gokyhall and Lyddcourt. There, too, he paid part of his farm in kind, supplying victuals to the cellarer.[277] Another important family who rented land from both the archbishop and the priory was the Brockhills. In the late fourteenth century John Brockhill farmed the archiepiscopal manor of Northfleet, and in the early fifteenth century Thomas Brockhill farmed the Christ Church manor of Small Chart. In 1477 William Brockhill took over the archiepiscopal manor of Cheyne Court with 800 ewes supplied by the archbishop. Like Tylly he paid part of his farm in stock, supplying 13 oxen and 441 wethers. By the 1490s he was leasing, in addition to Cheyne Court, a further 300 acres newly enclosed within the marsh. His total rent came to £116 19s., but he had no difficulty paying it all in money. In 1501–2 he served as serjeant at Aldington and deputy for Sir Thomas Etchingham, the supervisor of the archiepiscopal lands.[278] Meanwhile the Knatchbulls had replaced the Brockhills as the principal lessees of the archbishop's marsh manors.[279] They paid the archbishop in cash and sent at least some of their stock to the garrison and burghers of Calais. In 1488–90 John Knatchbull shipped 90 live sheep to Calais, and in 1513–14 Richard Knatchbull shipped 116 unshorn sheep to Calais from Sandwich and William Knatchbull shipped 210 live sheep from Dover.[280] Clearly such men were geared more to supplying the needs of the market than their own households.

[276] East Sussex RO SAS G1/25; BL Add. Roll 31987.

[277] Lambeth Palace Library, ED 1198; Cathedral Archives and Library, Canterbury, Misc. accounts 6, ff.89–120.

[278] Lambeth Palace Library, ED 1199, 1201, 1202. Later in 1513 he leased the Christ Church marsh manor of Appledore, where his rent was £46 14s. 9d. for the first seven years and £50 13s. for the last three years: Cathedral Archives and Library, Canterbury, Register T, f.109. William Brockhill also leased small parcels of land for 6s. 8d. and 3s. 4d. on the Christ Church manor of Hollingbourne: Lambeth Palace Library, ED 504, 506.

[279] In 1490–1 Richard and John Knatchbull were leasing respectively the Christ Church manors of Mersham and Adisham. In 1504 Richard and Thomas Knatchbull began to lease the archiepiscopal manor of Willop, and in 1525 John Knatchbull took over the lease of Cheyne Court: Lambeth Palace Library, ED 1203–8. [280] PRO E 122/130/2.

At the other end of the spectrum lived Nicholas Fener, who primarily made his presence felt through his anti-social behaviour. Although he married a widow and took over the 5½ acres belonging to her former husband at Telton (in Sussex), he later forfeited that land for waste and for not repairing the buildings. He probably had some land at Waldron, for in the 1460s the jury there accused him of assaulting his neighbours, of eavesdropping, of playing at kailes (casting the stone) and other illegal games, and enticing the servants of different men out at night to do harm. He also appears to have resented the prosperity of one of the wealthiest men in the village, Thomas Frankewelle, a tanner, for he unjustly took tanned hides out of Frankewelle's house and hired certain strangers to abuse and kill him. For a few years after this Fener was quiet, or at least his activities were unrecorded by the court rolls. Then in 1473 he was accused of breaking and entering a house, having first placed a pile of lit straw in the doorway, so that the house owner, for fear of death, was forced to relinquish his chamber. Over the next six years he continued to assault and fight his neighbours, play at cards, and, in 1479, entice the servant of a widow to leave her service. Then again he is lost from sight until in 1487 a jury complained that Nicholas Fener is "not a good compatriot: he does badly: he does suspectly and he does not work".[281] Yet he did survive. For nearly thirty years he lived in the same place and by fair means and foul acquired enough to feed, clothe, and shelter himself.

Far more common, of course, were the carpenters and roofers, like those at Alciston, and the butchers and bakers who catered to the needs of local communities. Often these latter businesses were family affairs, with two brothers or a father and son working together. Moreover, butchers sometimes worked as tanners as well, and a baker and his wife would brew regularly. Although the evidence is limited, it would seem that, as in other parts of the country, a butcher or tanner was quite likely to become one of the wealthier men in the community, building up a holding of 30 to 50 acres or more, whereas a baker was likely to hold half that amount.[282] On the Battle abbey manor of Wye (in Kent) various members of the German family worked either as butchers or tanners. In the rental of 1452 one member held 37 acres, one held 58 acres and the third (Hamo, a butcher) held 85 acres. Much of this land, however, was leased out to others and not cultivated directly. The Herts were an equally successful family. Early in the fifteenth century

---

[281] East Sussex RO SAS G18/48 (1404); BL Add. Rolls 32458, 32487, 32488, 32492, 32493, 32495, 32503.

[282] At Chartham in Kent the Bolles, who were demesne farmers in the mid-fifteenth century, were involved in tanning: Angela Langridge, 'The population of Chartham', p. 236. On the royal manor of Havering, Essex, the tanners were the leaders of political life in the fifteenth century: McIntosh, *Autonomy and Community*, p. 154.

Thomas and John Hert were working as butchers in Wye. After 1426 Thomas was no longer cited and he may have died or retired. But by the 1440s another Thomas, perhaps a son or nephew, had joined the family business and was leasing pasture from the lord. In the mid-1450s he held a messuage and $33\frac{1}{2}$ acres and John Hert (tanner), son of Thomas Hert, held $77\frac{1}{2}$ acres.[283]

Some Sussex butchers were equally successful. The Haywards first arrived in Lullington in mid-century, when John Hayward acquired a cottage and an acre previously owned by a butcher, Thomas Haselwood. In 1477 John was joined by his son Richard and for a while the two men both worked as butchers. By 1491 John has disappeared (presumably dead) and Richard Hayward has taken over as one of the principal butchers in the village. In addition, the family income is clearly being augmented by the work of Richard's wife, Marion, who is regularly cited as a "common brewer" and sometimes is also referred to as a huckster and baker. Before his death Richard divided his property in Lullington between his two sons, Thomas and Richard (jnr). Both young men worked for a while as butchers, but in 1521 Thomas died leaving a 7-year-old son. Richard, however, continued to work as a butcher. This was now the third generation working as butchers, and he almost certainly owned property elsewhere, for in the 1524 subsidy roll his worth was assessed at £8, one of the highest assessments in the village.[284]

The fifteenth century, however, may not have been such a "golden age" for the vast majority of Sussex peasantry. Many men did not receive high money wages. Even carpenters and roofers frequently received nearly half their wages in the form of food. So too ploughmen and shepherds were often partly compensated with grain liveries and special privileges, such as pasture rights. Although labour services had been generally commuted into money payments, in a few places some of the works were still being performed, and elsewhere the commutation payments made the rents high. Land may have been readily available, but on only a few manors had rents fallen drastically. On manors like Alciston a high money rent could consume a large portion of someone's yearly earnings. In the 1480s, for example, a cottage and three acres rented for 4s. a year and another cottage and five acres rented for 8s. a year, yet the yearly money wage for the *famulus* was just 8s. a year.[285] Seigneurial power was still largely intact. Lords demanded heriots, entry-fines and other customary payments such as pannage,

---

[283] For details of holdings at Wye see Muhlfeld, *Survey of Wye*, and for citations of butchers, PRO SC 2/182/26–52.

[284] East Sussex RO, SAS G18/46–55; *Lay Subsidy Rolls for the County of Sussex, 1524–5*, ed. Julian Cornwall, Sussex Rec. Soc., LVI, 1956, p. 117.

[285] For a rental of the 1480s, see PRO SC 12/15/64.

common fines and the palfrey money paid to each new archbishop or abbot, as well as those traditional symbols of bondage – merchet and chevage. Furthermore, in a few places, harvesters continued to be paid throughout most of the fifteenth century by being granted the tenth sheaf. Customary tenants in Sussex were thus likely to be more heavily burdened than their counterparts in Kent. There money wages were higher, rents usually lower and payments such as heriots, entry-fines, merchet and chevage either non-existent or minimal. In addition rural industrial growth in Kent, with the expansion of the cloth industry, had opened up greater opportunities for small producers to supplement their income. Yet, even in Kent some customary works were still being performed: harvesters were paid by the tenth sheaf until the early fifteenth century, and common fines were collected until mid-century, and perhaps even later.

In addition economic forces were working both for and against the peasant farmer. The general shortage of labour allowed men to leave their homes and seek work elsewhere and lords could neither force their return nor collect chevage payments. The difficulty in finding tenants persuaded some lords, like the nuns of Syon abbey, to reduce rents, and others, like the monks of Battle abbey, to cut back on entry-fines. Everywhere the burden of common fines was reduced, even if it was not eliminated, as the population fell. Above all the general low level of prices in mid-century meant purchases taking a smaller bite out of peasant budgets. For many families a combination of activities – brewing, wage labour, and farming – allowed them to survive in an economy that was still depressed. The smallholders in particular – those who farmed between 5 and 15 acres – could use up most of the grain and animals they produced for their family's needs. But the low prices also meant that any surplus goods sold on the market produced low revenues. The collapse of the overseas market for wool in mid-century may have affected the small producer more than the demesne farmer, for he may have reared sheep primarily for their wool, not their meat. Low grain prices may also have hurt the peasants more than the lords. Large-scale farmers could produce high yields by sowing crops on land that had been sown with legumes, or well composted, or left fallow for long periods of time. Such methods were not always available to the small farmer. He simply did not have enough land to leave it fallow for three or more years. If yields were low, then he had less to sell and, with low prices, a smaller income. Few of the tilers, thatchers, or carpenters prospered enough to move up into the yeoman class. It was not until the end of the century, with the development of new markets and the general improvement in the economy, that large-scale land accumulation became common.

By the early sixteenth century the agrarian economy of south-east

England was changing radically. In Kent partible inheritance and a fluid land market had encouraged the proliferation of smallholdings. Within the Weald an expanding cloth industry allowed the growing number of inhabitants to maintain themselves on a few acres, but elsewhere smallholders found it harder to survive, especially when prices began to rise. Land turned over rapidly and men and women sought employment and new lives within the towns.[286] The holdings of former peasants were then picked up by wealthy yeomen, the gentry, or merchants, who either subleased them or produced for the market. Tenants like the Knatchbulls, who maintained large sheep flocks, were keeping them as much for their meat as for their wool. Such men, who leased demesnes in addition to their own land, occupied a middle position between the lord on the one hand and the smallholder on the other. Within Sussex, for most of the century, the disparities in wealth among the tenants was less marked. But there too, by the 1520s, some men had been able to accumulate holdings of over 250 acres, and reared cattle and sheep for the market, in addition to producing grain. The foundation for the farms of the future had been laid.

I. THE SOUTHERN COUNTIES

On the eve of the Black Death most tenants in southern England, as elsewhere, had relatively small holdings and some had holdings that were very small indeed; and, although there were isolated farms in some places, most holdings were interlocked with others in hamlet or village territories and their tenants were members of a manorial group owing various obligations to its lord. At Castle Combe in 1340, for instance, before the industrial development of that village had gone very far, irrespective of status the majority of the forty-four customary and ten free tenants were either modest virgate or half-virgate holders (29) or were smallholding cottagers (21). Only four tenants had two virgates or more, and the customary tenants owed labour services as well as other dues. This old world survived intact, at least theoretically, on Frampton priory's manor at Bincombe (Dorset) a generation later. The typical tenants were half-virgaters, each with 11 customary acres, owing labour services which included five days of work each week in harvest, although they got occasional bonuses like the two loaves, the dish of beef and mutton, the quarter goose, and the cheese for each plough furnished for the lord's ploughing. On the other hand they could not put their sons to learning, or marry their daughters outside

---

[286] By 1500 it was becoming harder to find work in places like Romney and the migrant was faced with harsh and repressive legislation against beggars, vagabonds, and the unemployed: A. F. Butcher, 'The origins of Romney freemen, 1433–1523', *EcHR*, 2nd ser. xxvii, 1974, pp. 16–27.

the manor, without permission. There were also smaller holders at Bincombe – *operarii* and cottagers – and it was the latter's duty to milk the lord's ewes. The old world could hardly be more perfectly preserved.[287]

In fact, of course, that world was changing. Its recovery from plague mortality after 1349 showed its remarkable resilience, but in the absence of significant industrial development the long-term tendency was often for tenant numbers to fall. Downton, with *c.* 175 tenants in the early thirteenth century, had only *c.* 150 in 1377 and probably fewer in the fifteenth century; Badbury (Wilts.) had only about half as many tenants in 1518 as in the late twelfth century, and there was a similar reduction at Martin (Hants.). This is no more than might be expected, given the many records of tenants abandoning their holdings and of tenancies which no kinsman, and perhaps no one at all, appeared to claim.[288] As a result holdings sometimes had to be "improved" before they could be re-let. Margaret Pipelas's cotland at Winfrith (Dorset) was let in 1398 only after 4 acres of demesne arable, and possibly more generous common rights (including pasture for 100 sheep), were added to it *in emendacionem tenure predicte*, and it was also conceded that the grantee's widow might hold for life if she outlived her husband. The Dean and Chapter of Wells in 1452 went further than an individual bargain. Previously the dean had been unable to "better" tenements by joining parcels of demesne to them for a term longer than his own life: it was now agreed that such grants should be effective in perpetuity.[289]

Holdings might be "bettered", in other words, because there was less competition for land and because demesnes were being dissipated. Letting parcels of demesne, of course, was not something new in the late middle ages: most Downton customary tenants, for example, had plots of *bordland* (discarded demesne) attached to their holdings in 1349, and on the Winchester estate generally demesne had long been shrinking. That tendency, however, was checked in many places during the generation after 1349 and systematic leasing of demesnes had made little progress in the Wiltshire chalklands by 1380, but thereafter it became common on lay estates by 1400 and general even on Church lands after 1430, although many sheep flocks were still kept in hand. The dissipation of demesnes in the Hampshire chalklands seems scarcely earlier. By the end of the fifteenth century, on the other hand, most

[287] G. P. Scrope, *History of the Manor and Barony of Castle Combe in the County of Wiltshire*, pp. 146–50; Carus-Wilson, 'Evidences of industrial growth', p. 198; *Somerset and Dorset N. & Q.*, X, 1906–7, pp. 42–8, 89–90.

[288] *VCH Wilts.*, IX, p. 16; XI, p. 36; E. H. Lane Poole, *Damerham and Martin*, Tisbury, 1976, p. 187; *Wilts. N. & Q.*, IV, 1902–4, pp. 442, 446; WPR 159388, 159412 (1381–2, 1409–10).

[289] PRO SC 2/170/59; *Cal. of the Mss. of the Dean and Chapter of Wells*, I, HMC, 1907, p. 455.

demesnes were in the hands of tenants, significantly augmenting the resources at their disposal. At Downton in the early sixteenth century 509 acres of *bordland* had been added to 156 acres of customary bondland; at West Lydford (Somerset) in 1433 the rents from demesne arable, meadow, and pasture exceeded by one-third the traditional assized rents; and at Crawley in 1487 the demesne lessee had pasture for 10 horses, 20 oxen, and 1,300 sheep, a scale of tenant farming that had barely existed two centuries earlier.[290]

Larger holdings, with larger surpluses above household needs, were likely to be more responsive to market forces. The export market for wool, especially in the 1350s and 1360s, offered expanding opportunities to tenant as well as to landlord flockmasters. Still more important, expanding cloth manufacture in southern England, much of it in villages and small towns, opened up markets near at hand (and not only markets for wool) for small as well as for large farmers. Industrial development at Castle Combe, for example, generated a demand for foodstuffs of all sorts which its own fields could not fully satisfy. Industrialization in southern and western Wiltshire in the late fourteenth and early fifteenth centuries kept rents for holdings relatively high, and probably delayed the withdrawal of landlords from demesne cultivation, in the prosperous chalklands from which industrial communities drew supplies. Industrial depression in the mid-fifteenth century had correspondingly serious consequences for a time for Wiltshire agriculture. Industrial development in Somerset and elsewhere must have had similar effects. The fact that so much of it took place in centres of modest size meant that much of the demand generated could be met by relatively small producers, while at the same time it provided incentives for the more enterprising among them to add to their acres, their flocks, and their herds.[291]

The results are apparent in the records. The neat subdivision of tenants into a few well-defined grades, so often found in early surveys, was probably always something of an optical illusion, distorted in practice by adding *bordland* to bondland and by inter-peasant transactions. The early sixteenth-century picture, however, was often very different. At Porlock, for instance, three-quarters of the tenants had quite small holdings of individually held arable, meadow, and pasture: four of them, indeed, had no land at all, nineteen had under 5

---

[290] Above, pp. 143–4; *VCH Wilts.*, XI, pp. 35, 37; Hare, 'Demesne lessees', pp. 1–2; J. N. Hare, 'Change and continuity in Wiltshire agriculture in the later middle ages', in *Agricultural Improvement: Medieval and Modern*, ed. W. Minchinton, pp. 9–10; PRO SC 6/972/1; Gras, *English Village*, pp. 466–8.

[291] Above, pp. 150–1; Carus-Wilson, 'Evidences of industrial growth', pp. 203–4; Hare, 'Demesne lessees', p. 2; *idem*, 'The Wiltshire rising of 1450', pp. 16–19.

acres and nine between 5 and 10 acres. Common rights, however, might compensate for these modest holdings of land. William Erle, with only 2 acres of pasture of his own, had common for 100 sheep and 6 cows; seven of the tenants with 5–10 acres had between them common for 600 sheep and 34 cows, and thirteen holders of less than 5 acres in total had common for 480 sheep and 33 cattle. A few tenants, too, were markedly better endowed. Walter Popham, the demesne leaseholder, was in a class of his own with 435 acres of arable, meadow, pasture, and heath, and with common for 240 sheep and 12 cattle; but the six tenants with 10–25 acres and the three with 25–50 acres, with one exception, were also notable graziers, enjoying common between them for 1,700 sheep and 111 cattle. The contrast with the regularities of the 1306 survey of this same manor is striking.[292]

There were much larger individual holdings where arable farming was more important than at Porlock, but similar tendencies were at work. At Grittleton on Glastonbury's Wiltshire estate in 1518 two tenants each had over 100 acres of arable through adding parcels of demesne to half-hide tenements; three had 75–100 acres, mainly by accumulating customary holdings; four had 50–75 acres, either by accumulation or by taking up plots of demesne; and seven tenants with less than 50 acres mostly had traditional holdings only slightly modified. No one at all had less than 10 acres. Combined arable, meadow, and pasture holdings at Nettleton display a similar diversity: seven out of 34 tenants held less than 25 acres, ten had 25–50 acres, ten 50–75 acres, five 75–100 acres and two above 100 acres. Much of these holdings was open-field arable, but most included some enclosed land, and the smallholding cotlands had either vanished or been absorbed into the larger holdings. This last development was already taking place at Enford in 1403. The messuages of some of the cotlands in the lord's hand were let separately from the scraps of land once pertaining to them, and for lower rents than they had once commanded; and four cotlands were let together with a messuage and a half-virgate to a single individual "because the cottages are not built and the messuage is in decay". Where larger tenancies occur they often represent the engrossing of customary holdings or the addition to them of parcels of demesne land or both. At South Damerham in 1518 John Atteford had both a virgate and a half-virgate, but 20 acres of demesne land made up his total holding to 75 acres, and 25 acres of demesne made up Joan Moreys's virgate to 58½ acres. The engrossing of holdings, too, was very common by the late fifteenth century. John Aldriche held a virgate, two half-virgates and a cotland at Wilsford (Wilts.) in 1499; the four ferlings John Mille held at Crawley in 1503 had been in the

---

[292] Chadwyck Healey, *West Somerset*, pp. 409–22.

hands of four different tenants in the 1440s; and at Beechingstoke (Wilts.) there were only eight tenants of the 23 copyholds and John Adams had five of them, the nucleus of one of the principal farms of the village in the future.[293]

The terms on which land was held were also being revised, for the reduced demand for land forced lords into concessions, going so far as to make Boscombe (Wilts.) a community of free tenants only, since "no one there will hold land in bondage". This pressure was the more effective because individuals, as they had always done, escaped conditions they thought intolerable by flight, but now with better chances than in the past of finding elsewhere land or employment on better terms. John Selwyn of Castle Combe took this course in 1365, taking with him a pheasant from the warren for immediate sustenance; and John Spondel, another *nativus* from the same manor, showed that there were other than agricultural opportunities available. He left Castle Combe in 1354 and efforts to reclaim him to assume a vacant holding were unavailing. He soon appeared across the county boundary, now described as flaxmonger, at Tetbury; and he was still there in 1386, by then regularly known as John Flaxman. Lords were increasingly compelled to compromise with the increased mobility of customary tenants. Even the Duchy of Lancaster in the 1430s had to permit, for annual payments of between 4d. and 12d. each, some eleven Shapwick villeins to reside elsewhere; in 1468 Shapwick customers were to be found at Cranborne, Kingston Lacy, one of the Tarrents, Pimperne, and Charlton; in 1472 the annual payments they made were never higher than 6d. and there were other *nativi domini de sanguine* living outside the manor without payment or licence.[294]

In these circumstances the modification of traditional terms of tenure proceeded steadily even in the face of the reluctance of some landlords to make concessions. Some Glastonbury tenants in Wiltshire were still listed as *nativi* in 1518, and John Wrotte of Idmiston was said to owe sheep-shearing services as well as heriots for each of his two virgates. An ox was still paid as heriot at Urchfont in 1498, although by then this was a levy often commuted into a cash payment; and payments of eggs and fowls for rent or as church scot survived at Muchelney throughout the fifteenth century, although by the end of it the reeve of Wilsford professed his total inability to levy fowl rents.[295] Rents of fixed quantities of produce paid by some demesne lessees also survived until

---

[293] BL Harl. Ms. 3961, ff.5–15d, 17d–38d, 151, 153; BL Harl. Roll X7; *Wilts. N & Q.*, VIII, 1914–16, pp. 352–4; Gras, *English Village*, pp. 491–2; *VCH Wilts.*, x, p. 16.

[294] *Abstracts of Wilts. i.p.m. ....1327–77*, ed. E. Stokes, p. 315; Scrope, *History of the Manor and Barony of Castle Combe*, pp. 160–4; PRO DL 29/683/11062, DL 30/57/707.

[295] BL Harl. Ms. 3961, f.144d; *Wilts. N. & Q.*, v, 1905–7, pp. 164, 167; VIII, 1914–16, p. 357; *VCH Somerset*, III, p. 43.

relatively late in some places: at Enford in the 1430s, at Pawlett c. 1440, at Urchfont in 1460, at Abbotsleigh even in 1492, making the lessee half tenant and half manager. By the late fifteenth century, however, the Enford and Pawlett lessees, like most lessees, paid only money rents. Again, although some vestiges of labour services survived even into the sixteenth century, most of them had gone by then, and the majority of tenants owed a straightforward money rent, paid a fine to take up a holding or vary its terms of tenure, and possibly (if they were customary tenants) a heriot in cash or kind as a sort of death duty.[296]

A straightforward cash relationship between landlord and tenant favoured the increased diversification of holdings. If some of them were engrossed, others disintegrated and their fragments were combined with other lands. In the case of two half-virgates at Heytesbury in 1392, for instance, one was leased for 5s., but its croft had been demised to a different tenant for 2s. 6d. The other was farmed jointly by four men (an arrangement very likely to lead to its complete disintegration), and its messuage and curtilage had been detached and let separately. An increased diversity and instability of tenements make it much more difficult to determine the trends over time in what tenants paid for land, particularly when these trends were neither continuous nor everywhere the same. Rent totals, for instance, were maintained or even rose in the early fifteenth century in industrial western Wiltshire and the fertile chalkland which supplied it, but fell in the north and the less fertile parts of the county, only for these positions to be reversed when hard times came for clothworkers in the mid-century.[297] Over the long term, however, rents tended to fall. We hear, time and time again, of "tenements demised at lower rents than they used to pay", and of lands that at least for the time no one would take at all, or which no kinsman claimed, or which a tenant refused to hold any longer, or which could not be let at the old rent.[298] At Aldbourne customary tenants, who had once paid 8s. to 9s. per virgate for rent and works, by 1426 paid only a flat rate of 6s.; and some demesne leasehold rents followed a similar course, falling at Manningford Bohun (Wilts.) from £20 in 1412 to £12 towards the end of the century and at Westwood (Wilts.) from £7 in 1365 to £5 in 1469. The rents of the Wiltshire demesnes of the bishop of Winchester, on the other hand, with the exception of

---

[296] BL Harl. Rolls X8–9; *Manorial Accounts of St Augustine's Abbey*, ed. Sabin, pp. 10–11, 35–8, 46–53; *Wilts. N. & Q.*, IV, 1902–4, pp. 546–51; V, 1905–7, pp. 9–16; and for labour services, above, pp. 142–3.

[297] PRO SC 6/1053/7; Hare, 'The Wiltshire rising of 1450', pp. 17–19.

[298] *Manorial Accounts of St Augustine's Abbey*, ed. Sabin, pp. 182–9; WPR 159412; PRO DL 30/57/707.

Downton, rose slightly between the early and middle years of the fifteenth century; but in Hampshire, with a few exceptions, the tendency was the other way and was particularly marked at Benstead, where the rent paid in 1440 was less than half of what had perhaps been a too optimistic figure in 1400. A downward tendency was also evident at Rimpton in Somerset, and in Hampshire where the demesne was let piecemeal as at Droxford Philip. Some rent reductions may have been regarded as temporary "until better tenants come"; but a new rent, once established, easily became customary even if it could be maintained. This was all the more likely to happen when tenancies, like some at Holway in 1409, were let for a term of twenty years or even life: the qualification, *nisi infra tempus predictum carius posset dimitti*, is unlikely often to have been a realistic aspiration.[299]

Increasingly, therefore, more and more land was held not on traditional terms but for a price governed by its quality, the demand for it, and the economic prospects at a particular moment. What that price was is not easily determined, since many holdings were measured in customary acres which might vary in size from place to place. If the available figures can be taken at their face value, however, parcels of demesne were let at Nunton in Downton for about 7d. per acre in 1360 (but only for about half that sum in 1400), for $7\frac{1}{2}$d. to 1s. per acre at Holway in 1378 and 1409, for 6d. to 1s. 3d. per acre at Rimpton in 1400 and 1440, and from 1s. 1d. to 1s. 3d. per acre at Droxford Philip, before rents there were reduced to around 7d. an acre at the beginning of the fifteenth century. Most of these figures are relatively high when they are compared with the rents paid by some of the customary tenants on the Glastonbury manors in Wiltshire in 1518: about 4d. an acre at Grittleton, 3d. to 4d. at Nettleton, $3\frac{1}{2}$d. to $5\frac{1}{2}$d. at Kington and 3d. to $4\frac{1}{4}$d. at Damerham. Most of these tenants, it is true, in addition to their rents were liable for heriots at death; at Nettleton and Badbury they contributed to a common fine, at Kington they paid for pasture rights and at Damerham for pannage, at Badbury and Idmiston hay and clipping services were still owed (or money in lieu), and Easter eggs had still to be delivered at Badbury or three gallons of best ale when a tenant brewed at Damerham. Most of these charges (except perhaps for heriot) were not particularly heavy, but in aggregate they added to the price payable for customary land.[300]

Fines to take up or to vary the terms of a tenancy might occasionally be a heavier burden. Industrialization at Castle Combe enabled Sir John

[299] PRO DL 29/682/11058; *VCH Wilts.*, x, pp. 209–10; xi, p. 229; *VCH Somerset*, iii, p. 171; WPR 159405, 159412; details of demesne leases on the Winchester estates communicated by David Farmer.

[300] WPR 159371, 159388, 159405, 159412, 159436; BL Harl. Ms. 3961, *passim*.

Fastolf to order his steward to inquire "what man will give most" for
a vacant holding, and some fines paid at Urchfont in 1490 were as high
as those paid a century earlier. In Dorset, too, William Mantell in 1393
paid a fine amounting to nearly seven years' rent for a cotland with a
little additional arable and some grazing rights, and at Brockhampton
(Hants.) about the same time fines of £4 and even £8 were offered for
two-virgate holdings, prices perhaps inflated by urban development at
Havant. In many places, however, there was downward pressure on
fines as well as rents. When tenants had to be dragooned to take up
virgate or two-virgate holdings at Marwell in 1412–13 fines as low as
12d. were accepted, and only 6d. was asked of a man taking up a ferling
at Crawley in like circumstances. Similarly, at Overton in the 1430s, a
fine of only 3s. 4d. was charged for 1½ virgates combined with a cotland
abandoned by their tenants; and at Downton, while heirs paid fines of
6s. 8d. for half-virgate holdings, only 2s. was charged when no heir
appeared. In either case, moreover, these fines were much lower than
the 30s. to 40s. their half-virgates had commanded in the 1340s. There
were, as a result, wide disparities between individuals and between
manors in the levels of fines for land. On the Glastonbury estate in 1518
fines averaged about half a year's rent at Damerham, about a year's rent
at Grittleton, twice the annual rent at Kington and more than three
times the annual rent at Nettleton. Averages, of course, conceal
individual disparities: at Nettleton William Bullock paid only 1s. fine
for his half hide of about 50 acres, 7 per cent of his annual rent; but Paul
Crase (perhaps because he was *nativus domini*) paid £5 for his half hide
of around 84 acres, more than five times his rent. In general, however,
fines like rents were apt to be lower than they had been before 1349.[301]

The changes of the late middle ages were social as well as economic.
In the mid-fourteenth century a high proportion of tenants in the
region were bondmen, villeins, *nativi* (about 70 per cent of those whose
status is specified in Wiltshire inquisitions in the period 1349–75), a fact
with personal as well as tenurial implications. The tenant of two
virgates at Great Burton (Dorset) in 1378, for instance, owed rents,
labour services, heriot, and similar charges for his holding, but he was
also obliged to take a forced loan of wheat from the lord each year and
pay for it at the highest summer price current in the neighbourhood;
he needed permission to marry his daughter, send his son to school, or
sell a foal or bull calf; and he had to serve as reeve or hayward if the
lord required it. No doubt, like an Evercreech tenant about the same
time, he might have been described as *nativus domini de sanguine* whose

301 Carus-Wilson, 'Evidences of industrial growth', p. 204; *Wilts. N. & Q.*, IV, 1902–4, pp.
443, 447; V, 1905–7, pp. 115, 164, 200–4; WPR 159388, 159403, 159415, 159430; BL Harl. Ms.
3961, ff.19d, 25.

servitude embraced all his family, one reason why a list of the earl of Pembroke's *nativi* at Odcombe (Somerset) included a note of what sons and daughters they had.[302] *Nativi* and "bondmen by blood", moreover, survived long after 1378: at Kilton (Somerset) in 1448, at Dunster in 1449, at Urchfont and Wilsford in 1499, and on the Glastonbury manors in 1518. A petitioner in chancery alleged that a gentleman had seized his muniments, spoons, rings, and other jewellery on the grounds that he was a villein; St Swithun's priory in the fifteenth century spent money on lawyers to assess the adequacy of evidence that a man was a villein; and a Burton Stacey (Hants.) villein paid the large sum of £10 for general acquittance of all actions against him.[303] Similarly, in the 1480s villeins on the Athelney estate at Lyng (Somerset) and Reginald Pope at Bishop's Caundle (Dorset) sought formal manumission, no doubt at a price; and even a villein's daughter at Shapwick paid a fine "from that day forward to be free for ever". By 1518, however, *nativi* were exceptional among the Glastonbury tenants: six members of two families at Idmiston, for instance, or eleven members of five families among the numerous tenants at Damerham and its hamlets. Nor were they necessarily among the poorer villagers. Four *nativi* of the Wrotte family held at Idmiston. William, the least well endowed, had a 27-acre virgate and pasture for 66 sheep; John had more than twice as much land and pasture for nearly 200 sheep; Nicholas had 120 acres of land and grazing for 300 wethers; and Robert was farmer of the demesne and had over 500 acres of arable in the fields of Gomeldon. For all their "nativity" the Wrottes were on their way to becoming farmers in the modern sense of that word.[304]

At the end of the middle ages there continued to be a minority of tenants holding freely, in perpetuity, and under legal protection; but the great majority held by customary titles, the variety of which was often more apparent than real. Much land, for instance, was said to be held at will, and might literally be so held: thus at Porlock parcels of the demesne demised at will in 1419 had been resumed by the lady of the manor by 1424. On the other hand, tenants at will at Porlock in the early sixteenth century included some holding for lives, and at Urchfont in 1498 there were tenants holding for life at the lady's will according to the custom of the manor. Custom, in fact, was usually the

---

[302] *Abstracts of Wilts. i.p.m. ....1327–77*, ed. Stokes, pp. 199–392; *Somerset and Dorset N. & Q.,* VIII, 1902–3, p. 170, XII, 1910–11, pp. 341–2; PRO DL 43/14/3, f.72.

[303] *Wilts. N. & Q.,* V, 1905–7, p. 164; VIII, 1914–16, pp. 352–4; *VCH Somerset,* V, p. 93; H. C. Maxwell Lyte, *History of Dunster and the Families of Mohun and Luttrell,* I, pp. 319–20; *Somerset and Dorset N. & Q.,* X, 1906–7, p. 201; *Compotus Rolls of the Obedientiaries of St Swithun's Priory, Winchester,* ed. G. W. Kitchin, Hants. Rec. Soc., 1892, pp. 285, 378.

[304] *Somerset and Dorset N. & Q.,* II, 1890–1, pp. 4–5; VIII, 1902–3, p. 111; PRO DL 30/57/707; BL Harl. Ms. 3961, ff.138, 140–6.

regulator, and it was buttressed for many tenants by a copy of the entry in the manorial court roll recording their assumption of a tenement. Wherever tenants were scarce, moreover, custom was likely to favour security of tenure even for villeins by blood: thus John Tullock of Heytesbury in 1392 held 2 acres at farm for life *non obstante quin ipse nativus domini est*. Tenure for life by copy of court roll was common by the fifteenth century, as at Cricket St Thomas (Somerset); and a Lacock copyhold early in the sixteenth century was conceded for three lives (husband, wife, and son), a term that became very common in Dorset later in that century.[305] Demesne leases, by contrast, were often for much shorter terms. On the Winchester estate down to the mid-fifteenth century they were usually for periods of 6 to 12 years, although at Wield (Hants.), where the demesne had been broken up and let out by fields, there were some twenty-year leases in 1453, and at Otterford (Somerset) the demesne was leased for life by 1430. Possibly, at least initially, landlords were very slow to accept the option of abandoning direct cultivation as something permanent.[306]

A high proportion of tenants, even at the end of the middle ages, had middling holdings at best, commonly dispersed in open fields and cultivated at least in part for self-supply. Even mere husbandmen, however, might enjoy a modest prosperity. John Bedill of Portbury (Somerset), for instance, was able in 1457 to leave bequests of farm animals and bushels of barley, as well as 6s. 8d. to provide a chalice for the parish church; and John Jenes of Milborne Port (Somerset) left silver spoons, 12 platters and a mazer, as well as 20 ewes for his daughter and 30d. for his confessor. Testators described as yeomen were possibly rather better off, although one yeoman's widow provided less money to support a chaplain celebrating for her own and her husband's souls than a Chew Magna husbandman did for a like purpose.[307] Some tenants, on the other hand, had clearly emerged from the ruck, especially some demesne lessees already anticipating the rich farmers of the demesnes of gentlemen, observed later by Thomas Gerard, who "begin much to encroach upon the gentry". These men were in a different way of business from most of their neighbours. Walter Popham at Porlock had $52\frac{1}{2}$ acres of enclosed arable, 72 acres of enclosed meadow, 98 acres of several pasture, and 204 acres of heath as well as much common for cattle and sheep; Robert Wrotte at Idmiston had a 4-acre close, $15\frac{1}{2}$ acres of common meadow and 529 acres of open-

[305] Chadwyck Healey, *West Somerset*, pp. 413, 422, 434; *Wilts. N. & Q.*, v, 1905–7, p. 201; PRO SC 6/1053/7; *VCH Somerset*, IV, p. 136; *Lacock Abbey Charters*, ed. K. H. Rogers, Wilts. Rec. Soc., XXXIV, 1979, no. 218; J. H. Bettey, 'Land tenure and manorial custom in Dorset, 1570–1670', *Southern Hist.*, IV, 1982, p. 33.   [306] WPR 159429, 159436, 159444.
[307] *Somerset Medieval Wills*, ed. Weaver, pp. 172–3, 295, 336–7, 355–6.

field arable; the lessee of the demesne land and rents at Stockton in 1399 paid £24 a year for them, and the lessee of both the land and the sheep at Crawley a century later paid £22 a year. Some lessees operated on an even grander scale. John Stannford, as well as leasing the large Duchy of Lancaster demesnes at Collingbourne and Everleigh, also had interests in Upavon, Charlton, and Rushall; and various Goddards leased demesnes at Hinton, Mildenhall, Eaton, Overton, Aldbourne, and Ogbourne (Wilts.). Some of these larger entrepreneurs grouped lands previously in the hands of different occupants in a way that might favour more efficient management; but even the lessee of a single demesne was likely to be farming on a larger scale than the traditional manorial tenant.[308]

The origins of leaseholders were very diverse. In Wiltshire, John Stannford had been a duchy official and Sir Walter Hungerford was both gentleman and official; a few were merchants or butchers whose business careers might bring them into regular contact with farming; but most seem to have been drawn from the ranks of the leading customary families in the villages. It seems to have been rare, however, for serf-lessees to continue far into the fifteenth century, although Robert Wrotte, lessee of Idmiston, was still described as *nativus* in 1518. Leaseholding, in fact, might offer an avenue for social promotion. The Goddards, who leased Ogbourne for all or most of the century after 1445, were called husbandmen in the fifteenth century, but gentlemen by 1510; and the Harvests at Urchfont enjoyed a not dissimilar advancement. They were probably descended from a family of customary tenants playing a prominent part in the manor in the late fourteenth century; but in the second half of the fifteenth century it provided most of the demesne lessees at Urchfont as well as a lessee of All Cannings and a receiver of St Mary's abbey. Not surprisingly, when William Harvest made his will in 1502, he could be described as a yeoman and had £6 to leave for a priest to sing for his soul and the souls of his kindred.[309]

How leaseholders acquired the capital to take up demesnes is seldom clear. The resources needed might be considerable: when John Stannford took Collingbourne and Everleigh in the mid-fifteenth century, he had to find around £77 to buy the sheep flock as well as whatever working capital he required. Some of the capital lessees

---

[308] G. E. Fussell, 'Four centuries of farming systems in Dorset, 1500–1900', *Dorset N.H. and Arch. Soc.*, LXXIII, 1951, pp. 119–20; Chadwyck Healey, *West Somerset*, pp. 412, 415–21; BL Harl. Ms. 3961, f.138; BL Add. Rolls 24395–8; Gras, *English Village*, pp. 466–8, 493; J. N. Hare, 'Change and continuity in Wilts. agriculture', pp. 12–16; idem, 'Demesne lessees', pp. 1–14.

[309] Hare, 'Demesne lessees', pp. 3–11; *Wilts. N. & Q.*, IV, 1902–4, p. 546; V, 1905–7, pp. 115, 157–8, 165, 165n., 199.

required may have come from the profits of office or trade or butchering, but even more may have been provided by landlords withdrawing from direct cultivation. The terms on which John Gervays held Enford in the 1430s come near to one type of share-cropping arrangement. He probably started off with so much land sown (or he was provided with the seed to sow it) and with a stock of pigs and poultry, enabling him to pay his rent in the form of liveries of grain, pigs, geese and capons: in effect, he had been given a long-term loan in kind by his landlord. Similar arrangements are found when only a cash rent was envisaged. This seems to be the case at Fifehead Magdalen in the 1490s, where the lessee had apparently been provided with seed-corn, oxen, 20 cows and a bull, poultry, 30 wagon loads of hay to see the stock through the first winter, and the implements and other "dead stock" needed to work the manor. At Fifehead responsibility for the upkeep of the buildings was placed upon the lessee, but even in this respect some landlords were willing to help. When John Couper leased Crawley in 1487 he undertook to maintain the buildings with thatched roofs and earthen walls, but the bishop of Winchester undertook responsibility for those with tiled roofs and walls of stone.[310]

By the end of the middle ages, then, there were rather more men cultivating on a scale which had been rare among earlier villagers: demesne leaseholders, engrossers of manorial tenements, possibly some isolated farmers on the frontiers of medieval cultivation from which other settlers had withdrawn. The Stradlings of Water Farm and the Steynings of Grimesland, descendants of medieval free tenants who down to the seventeenth century held farms on the margins of Crowcombe (Somerset), were perhaps examples of this last category, or Joan Moreys who in 1518 held the mainly enclosed outlying farm of Damerham at Stapleton. Many others, however, continued to live within the confines of village communities, and were perhaps responsible for the conversion of some of the traditional village long-houses into farm houses with added farm buildings of the kind archaeologists have revealed, for instance at Gomeldon. At the same time, by no means everyone was willing to accept responsibility for an above-average holding. In 1430–1 one son and heir refused to take a Highclere holding consisting of 2 tofts, 2 messuages, a virgate, 2 cotlands, 9 acres of land, and 33 acres of purpresture; and at Overton a tenant abandoned another combining a virgate, a half-virgate, a toft, and a cotland, a generously low fine of 3s. 4d. being accepted to secure a successor. This attitude may provide one of the reasons why middling

---

[310] Hare, 'Demesne lessees', pp. 8–9; BL Harl. Rolls X8–9; *Some Manorial Accounts of St Augustine's Abbey*, ed. Sabin, pp. 68, 70–3; Gras, *English Village*, pp. 466–8.

holders were still the typical tenants at the end of the middle ages, even though in most places a few tenants had appeared operating on an altogether larger scale.[311]

These substantial farmers, like manorial demesnes so long as they were kept in hand, needed labourers, both full-time and part-time, of the sorts that demanded excess wages in Wiltshire in the 1350s. Some had been taken on for particular tasks: threshers, harvest workers, day labourers, the men who mowed the meadow at Upavon; but others were hired by the year, like a shepherd in Kinwardstone hundred or Roger Dounton who left Walter Wormerigge's service when another employer offered him better pay and subsistence. Some at least of these latter workers were probably "servants in husbandry", living in their employer's household – perhaps like the manservant and maidservant to whom Henry Vincent, *ruralis homo* of Frome Selwood, left a cow apiece in 1487; and they may well have been the type of labour preferred by employers in the post-1349 circumstances when wages were rising and living costs falling. Certainly available labourers were eagerly snapped up, like two fugitive Somerset *nativi* found wandering in Devon in 1373, although in this instance their lord discovered them and brought them back to Huish Champflour. Full-time labourers, however, were never more than a small part of the labour force in late medieval villages, just as *famuli* had never provided more than a proportion of the labour needs of manorial demesnes. The seasonal character of agricultural operations itself ensured the importance of part-time employment; and it may well be that, as part-time villein labour progressively disappeared, the demand for part-time wage labour actually increased.[312]

Given the scarcity of labourers, especially in the later fourteenth century when gleaners, even women gleaners, were carefully scrutinized as potential harvest workers, the inevitable tendency was for wages to rise. By 1450 the bishops of Winchester were paying substantially more than they had a century earlier for threshing and similar tasks, although in the second half of the fourteenth century they had more success in avoiding significant increases in the wages in cash and kind they paid to full-time workers. Not all landlords were as successful. In the 1350s and 1360s the cash wages paid to shepherds at

[311] *VCH Somerset*, v, p. 59; R. C. Hoare, *Modern History of South Wilts.*, IV(2), p. 43; WPR 159449; J. Musty and D. Algar, 'Excavations at the deserted medieval village of Gomeldon', *Wilts. Arch. Magazine*, 80, 1986, p. 145.

[312] E. M. Thompson, 'Offenders against the Statute of Labourers in Wilts.', *Wilts. Arch. and N.H. Magazine*, XXXIII, 1904, pp. 386–408; *Somerset Medieval Wills*, ed. Weaver, pp. 266–7; *Land, Kinship and Life-Cycle*, ed. R. M. Smith, pp. 35–7; B. H. Putnam, *The Enforcement of the Statute of Labourers* App., pp. 460–3.

Heytesbury, Crawley, and Wellow were 4s. to 5s. per year; towards the end of the century, with very similar supplementary grain liveries as earlier, they were 6s. to 6s. 8d. at Evercreech, Farleigh Hungerford, Sandford Orcas, and Enford and as high as 10s. to 12s. at Heytesbury, possibly reflecting the special role of Heytesbury in Hungerford sheep farming. At Aldbourne in the 1420s and at Urchfont in the 1460s shepherds were also paid 10s., but only 5s. at Kingston Lacy as they had been in 1390. There, on the other hand, the wages of carters and ploughmen, who had also been paid 5s. in 1390, rose to 10s. and 8s. respectively by 1429. There is, by contrast, less indication of improvement in the liveries in kind which normally supplemented cash wages and which were usually more valuable than the money income which workers earned. To this extent the gains of full-time workers were somewhat less than might at first sight appear: but that they made some gains, as did part-time workers, seems clear.[313]

Improvements in the lot of villagers during the late middle ages derived from a combination of circumstances: improved employment prospects, rather better wages, greater access to land on easier terms and for somewhat lower rents. The more enterprising amongst them were also enabled to undertake production on a much larger scale than their neighbours, generating new demands for labour. The labourers themselves leave few memorials; some of them, however, no doubt continued to be drawn from the ranks of cottagers, even though those ranks in many places were much thinner than they had been in the opening decades of the fourteenth century. On the other hand it is probably incorrect to draw too sharp a line between labourers and tenant farmers. While the tenant family provided much or most of the labour needed by most tenant family farms, it might often have some to spare for others to hire; and younger sons and daughters, even sons and heirs before they stepped into a holding, might work as labourers to earn a living or obtain some modest initial capital. The improved rewards of labour during the late middle ages may have been sufficient to make this phase in the life-cycle of many villagers rather more attractive.

Medieval villagers, of course, cannot merely be regarded as tenants or employees. Individuals were also members of family groups, and

---

[313] Scrope, *History of the Manor and Barony of Castle Combe*, p. 161; Ault, 'Open-field husbandry and the village community', p. 14; D. H. Farmer, above, pp. 479–81; *idem*, 'Crop yields, prices and wages', pp. 114–18; Gras, *English Village*, pp. 172, 175; PRO SC 6/970/21–2, 974/24, 1052/17, 1053/6; BL Harl. Roll X7; *Somerset and Dorset N. & Q.*, III, 1892–3, pp. 315–16; XI, 1908–9, pp. 236–8; PRO DL 29/682/11046, 11051, 11058; *Wilts. N. & Q.*, V, 1905–7, pp. 10, 13; BL Add. Roll 66603.

even customary holdings were assumed to descend within the family, so that problems only arose when there was no one of the "blood" to claim them. Normally a single son succeeded, often the oldest (at Twyford in 1394–5 a younger son got a half-virgate only when his older brother refused it); but succession by the youngest son was the custom at, among other places, Fonthill Bishop, East Knoyle, and Crawley. Only when there was no son to succeed did the holding pass to a daughter, at Crawley by analogy with the rule for male succession to the youngest daughter. The operation of these rules was subject to two qualifications. In many places a tenant's surviving widow had a right to occupy the holding: at Winfrith, Urchfont, and Wellow, for instance, so long as she remained single and chaste; or without restriction at Bishop's Waltham, where a widow could take the tenement to a second husband who in turn could keep it for life after her death provided he did not re-marry. Secondly, some provision might be made for children other than the heir in portions of the holding or on parcels of acquired land. At Fordington (Dorset) in 1352 a father and his son and heir appear to have made joint provision in this way for a younger son when he married; John Hickes of Yatton (Somerset), on the other hand, bequeathed £5 to his younger son for his marriage, the holding and everything pertaining to husbandry going to his older brother.[314]

Sometimes, of course, there were no surviving sons or daughters, or they might reject their inheritance, in which case the claims of more distant kin might be entertained. On the Winchester estates grand-children succeeded grandparents, nephews and nieces uncles and aunts, a stepchild a stepfather; and very often the relationship between predecessor and successor was indirect enough to make its precise nature difficult to establish. The bond between family and holding continued to be very strong to the extent that a family name often remained attached to a holding, as in the case of "Vaynes" at Crawley, long after the family ceased to occupy it. On the other hand, the rupture of this bond does appear to have become commoner during the later middle ages, even though the instability of surnames makes them a less than adequate measure of the continuity of family tenure. The Winchester evidence, however, does strongly suggest the weakening of continuity. In 1341–3 over 75 per cent of tenants taking up standard holdings were widows succeeding husbands or children succeeding parents, with less than 20 per cent having no apparent relationship to

[314] WPR 159401; VCH Wilts., XI, pp. 79, 90; Gras, English Village, p. 56; PRO SC 2/169/29, 170/58, 200/46; Wilts. N. & Q., v, 1905–7, pp. 62–4, 114, 202; J. Z. Titow, English Rural Society, 1200–1350, London, 1969, p. 187; Somerset Medieval Wills, ed. Weaver, p. 359.

their predecessors. By contrast, in selected years in the period 1353–1432, only 12 per cent were widows succeeding husbands, 25 per cent children following parents, and 55 per cent were apparently unrelated to their predecessors. Lists of the tenants of twelve customary ferlings at Crawley in the century before 1503 carry a similar implication: continuity of family tenure is clear in only two between 1410 and 1448 and in only three between 1448 and 1503. These figures may exaggerate discontinuities, but it is difficult to deny some weakening of the tie between family and holding: that much is also implied by the many records of tenements which no one of the "blood" appeared to claim.[315]

It is much more difficult to look at these holdings from within. It is merely an inference, although a reasonable one, to suppose that the larger tenancies were farmed much more for the market than smaller or middling holdings. Their basic structure, like that of demesnes, was governed by location and terrain. At Porlock, on the edge of Exmoor, George Almysewurthe's moorland common for 240 sheep, 20 cattle, and a couple of horses was probably more important to him than his 10 acres of ploughland; but in most of southern England arable land was the core of holdings. A Lacock copyhold in 1523, for example, consisted of 8 acres of open-field arable and about an acre of meadow and, in 1351, the beadle of the Wiltshire hundred of Kinwardstone held a messuage, 56 acres of arable, 2 acres of pasture, and 3 acres of underwood. In some places pasture rights assumed a greater importance: at Amesbury in 1379 pasture for 31 sheep went with a toft, $11\frac{1}{2}$ acres of arable and a little meadow; in 1497 for a horse, 5 oxen, 50 sheep, 2 rams, and 10 pigs with a half-virgate; and in 1474 for 170 sheep with a cottage, $70\frac{1}{2}$ acres of open-field arable and $3\frac{1}{2}$ acres of meadow. Holdings like this reflect the traditional mixed farming of the medieval peasantry, with its base in arable production but expanding into animal husbandry to the extent that pastoral resources permitted. Those resources may have become more generously available as tenant numbers dwindled and landlords gave up even their sheep farming. To that extent smaller producers may have been able significantly to expand their role in farming for the market.[316]

[315] Data relating to the tenants taking up standard holdings on the Winchester estates in Wilts. and Hants., as recorded in the Winchester pipe rolls, communicated by David Farmer; Z. Razi, 'Family, land and village community in later medieval England', in Landlords, Peasants and Politics in Medieval England, ed. T. H. Aston, Cambridge, 1987, pp. 376–84; Gras, English Village, pp. 305, 477, 491–2.

[316] Chadwyck Healey, West Somerset, p. 413; Lacock Abbey Charters, ed. Rogers, no. 218; Wilts. Extents for Debt, Edward I–Elizabeth I, ed. A. Conyers, Wilts. Rec. Soc., XXVIII, 1973, no. 10; Cal. of Antrobus Deeds, ed. R. B. Pugh, Wilts. Rec. Soc., III, 1947, nos. 28, 71, 75.

Tenancies, and especially customary tenancies, were subject to a variety of conditions. Landlords tried to insist that the buildings and equipment of holdings were maintained, with forfeiture as the ultimate sanction, although one that was only reluctantly invoked when tenants were hard to get. Conversely, an Urchfont tenant was excused all but 2s. of a £5 entry-fine provided he rebuilt the house and repaired other buildings on the holding. Tenants were also forbidden to denude their tenements of trees or to leave their closes unfenced; and a Reybridge (Wilts.) cottager was required to use all the manure from his messuage on his land. That injunction may hardly have been necessary, for both at Aldbourne and at Longbridge and Monkton Deverill tenants were willing to pay good money to have the lord's sheep folded on the *terra villanorum*.[317] Occasionally tithe data provide a few indications of the crops which tenants grew. At East Meon, during selected years in the period 1350–1441, the bishop of Winchester and his villagers harvested more or less identical proportions of wheat (37 per cent) and pulses (4 per cent); but the tenants harvested more barley (25 per cent) than the bishop (16 per cent), and the bishop more oats (43 per cent) than the tenants (34 per cent). One explanation may be that the bishop had more livestock and fed them better (with oats especially) and that, as in the eighteenth century, barley was an important breadgrain for southern English villagers. Certainly all or most of the liveries given to full-time workers at Urchfont, Enford, and Crawley were of barley.[318]

Tenants needed some access to grazing if only to feed their draught animals, even a Winfrith cottager having common for one affer. He was perhaps one of those not infrequent smallholders, especially in Wiltshire and Hampshire, whose only working livestock were horses; but in most places oxen seem to have been the commoner plough beasts, as they were assumed to be at Sherborne and in the neighbouring villages in 1378 (although one Long Burton tenant had a mixed team of oxen and affers). Many tenants, however, must have had horses as well as oxen since they were very regularly required to bring horses to harrow the lord's land. In general, none the less, the dominance of oxen as draught animals on demesnes is reproduced on tenant holdings.[319]

---

[317] *Wilts. N. & Q.*, v, 1905–7, p. 65; *Somerset and Dorset N. & Q.*, VIII, 1902–3, pp. 171, 210; PRO DL 29/682/11058; information relating to the Deverills from GAD 9702, 9837, 9883, 9945, provided by David Farmer.

[318] East Meon harvest data, as recorded in the Winchester pipe rolls, communicated by David Farmer; Ashley, *The Bread of our Forefathers*, pp. 6–8, 24–5; *Wilts. N. & Q.*, v, 1905–7, pp. 10, 13; BL Add. Roll 66603; Gras, *English Village*, p. 275.

[319] PRO SC 2/170/58; Langdon, *Horses, Oxen and Technological Innovation*, pp. 198, 200–1; *Somerset and Dorset N. & Q.*, x, 1905–7, pp. 43–4; XII, 1910–11, pp. 255, 311, 341–2.

Other tenant livestock tends to reflect the self-supplying character of much small-scale farming. The Winfrith cottager mentioned above had pasture, as well as for his horse, for a single pig and a single cow. Pannage payments for pigs (often at the rate of 1d. for a full-grown animal and half that for young beasts) totalled 17s. 8d. at Crawley in 1355 and the very high figure of £6 12s. at Kingston Lacy in 1429, but in most places payments were much more modest and they yielded no more than 4d. or 5d. a year at Stockton in 1399–1403. Pigs, in brief, were usually domestic rather than commercial animals. Many cows, too, must have been kept principally to provide dairy produce for the tenant's household and periodic replacements for his plough beasts and cow-byre. Even on so pastoral a manor as Porlock, where sales of meadow and payments for agistment raised not insignificant sums, only 29 of the 42 tenants c. 1525 had common rights for cattle, and of these seven could pasture only a single cow or other beast, and eight more had pasture for no more than 2–5 beasts. Only seven tenants had common for 6–10 beasts and seven more for up to 20 cattle, sufficient to suggest that their objectives were more commercial. There were probably others like them in the Somerset Levels and even in the wood-pasture districts further east. Henry Vincent of Frome Selwood left a cow and a calf for each of the two lights in the parish church, a cow to each of his two servants, his two best cows to his executors, and still had livestock to bequeath to his nephew and heir.[320]

For most tenants, however, sheep were more important than cattle. In Somerset, at Porlock, there was common for 3,000 sheep as against 187 cattle, and one man with no arable and a single cow had grazing for 40 sheep; at Evercreech in 1379 one commoner was illegitimately feeding 200 sheep; at Cricket St Thomas each copyholder had common for 42 sheep and at Wellow tenants around 1400 were paying to pasture anything up to 40 sheep. In Dorset, too, one Winfrith cottager had pasture for 40 wethers and another grazing for 100 sheep, and in the 1390s tenants were overloading the common with flocks of 50, 80, 140, 150 and 200 sheep; while at Shapwick in 1433 there were customers possessing their own folds and flocks of 150 sheep, and at East and West Stour three Gillingham tenants each claimed to have pasture for 300 sheep.[321] Tenant sheep flocks appear to have been larger still in

<hr/>

[320] Gras, *English Village*, pp. 270, 278; PRO DL 29/682/11051; BL Add. Rolls 24395, 24398; Chadwyck Healey, *West Somerset*, pp. 412–22, 428, 434; *Somerset Medieval Wills*, ed. Weaver, pp. 266–7.

[321] Chadwyck Healey, *op. cit.*, pp. 412–22; *Somerset and Dorset N. & Q.*, VIII, 1902–3, p. 172; *VCH Somerset*, IV, p. 136; PRO SC 2/170/58–9, 200/45–6, SC 6/974/25; *Cal. Inq. Misc.*, IV, no. 264; PRO DL 29/683/11066.

Wiltshire and Hampshire. In the former county even the rector of Edington had 300 sheep, twice his entitlement, on the town fields in 1502; William Long of Trowbridge had 1,000 sheep at West Ashton; the principal free tenants at Warminster had pasture for nearly 2,000 sheep and around 1380 were paying for 1,080 lambs to feed on the lord's down; while at All Cannings tenants pastured 1,260 sheep on the down and at West Amesbury one virgater had common for 200 sheep. In Hampshire, at Crawley, where the tenants possibly had about 1,250 sheep in the thirteenth century, no customer had more than the authorized 25 sheep on the common in the 1350s, but in the fifteenth century John Wayte paid 3s. 4d. a year to pasture 50 sheep with the lord's wethers. John, however, was a two-ferling holder, and probably a member of what became a yeoman family which survived in the village until 1879. Sheep may have contributed as much as arable to its advancement.[322]

Many of the tenants in the southern counties, therefore, were in some degree sheep farmers. Most, like the majority of Crawley tenants, probably had modest flocks, but even a few cottagers, to say nothing of thriving entrepreneurs adding acre to acre and many farmers of demesnes, operated on a very much larger scale. When John Couper leased the Crawley demesne in 1487, he offered an annual rent of £6 13s. 4d. for all the lands, meadows, and pastures pertaining to husbandry; but he also took over 950 sheep (and it was envisaged that he might keep up to 1,300) for an additional rent of £15 3s. 4d. Clearly he was first and foremost a sheep farmer. Sheep, moreover, were kept mainly with an eye to the market. Their main product was their wool, with expanding outlets in the textile industry of the region; but tenants as well as lords must have sold discarded stock to butchers and those of them, like one Winfrith cottager, who had little flocks of wethers, must have been able to rely upon a stores market to replace them. The ewes of tenants, too, perhaps made some contribution to cheese and butter production, although probably mainly for domestic consumption; but, generally speaking, sheep may well have been the most important commercial resource of most tenant farmers in the region, the more particularly when demesne flocks were dispersed to leaseholders.[323]

Medieval villagers, of course, were more than merely tenants and family men concerned about their landholding and the obligations it entailed, and for wives, children, and servants. They were also

---

[322] VCH Wilts., VIII, pp. 107, 207, 243–4; X, p. 26; Cal. of Antrobus Deeds, ed. Pugh, no. 45; Gras, English Village, pp. 45, 236, 270, 297.
[323] Gras, English Village, pp. 466–8; PRO SC 2/170/58.

members of local communities and parishioners; and in their wills they made bequests to their parish church, its lights and its altars, to their god-children and perhaps to neighbours, and for the repair of the local roads. At the same time some landlords, in their wills, remembered their tenants as well as family, friends, and churches. William Carent remitted a quarter's rent to each of his customary or copyhold tenants; and Sir Thomas Brooke left money for his poor tenants in Dorset and Devon who rendered him capons, bedrepes, and ploughings, with an extra sum to make amends to any he had oppressed or wronged. If the tenant farmer's context extended beyond manor and family, perhaps the relationship between landlord and tenant needs also to be regarded as one which was not inevitably a battleground.[324]

J. DEVON AND CORNWALL

Neither its peninsular shape nor a predominantly dispersed settlement pattern served to lessen the impact on the south-west of the great plague of 1348 and its successors.[325] A petition, calamitous in tone, from the keepers of the temporalities of Bishop Grandisson, who died in 1369, blamed plague (perhaps the severe outbreak that year)[326] for a fall in rents, services, and customary payments from peasant farmers on episcopal manors throughout the length and breadth of the south-west, and from other estates there is evidence for similar short-term disruptions of rural life.[327] Dislocation of commerce in the immediate aftermath of each outbreak of plague in the late fourteenth century shows in sharp falls in the output of the Cornish stannaries, decline in fishing, and depletion of population in the boroughs of Truro, Penryn, Helston, and Bodmin.[328] All of this is to be expected in two counties

---

[324] *Somerset Medieval Wills*, ed. Weaver, pp. 22–3, 68–9, 172–3, 266–7; for Sir Thomas Brooke, *Somerset Arch. and N.H. Soc.*, XLIV, 1898, pp. 9–18.

[325] For a very early date for the arrival of plague in Devon (before 16 June 1348) see M. Prestwich, *The Three Edwards*, London, 1980, p. 255. Plague reached Bodmin before Christmas 1348, and affected other Cornish manors shortly thereafter: *William Worcestre, Itineraries*, ed. Harvey, pp. 94–5; Duchy of Cornwall Archives, roll 4.

[326] PRO SC 6/1138/2. For the outbreak of 1369 on another Devon manor, Werrington, see Devon RO, W1258M/D/70.

[327] For example, PRO SC 6/828/21 and Duchy of Cornwall Archives, roll 4, for mortality among "the greatest part" of landless tenants, suitors to a mill (at Lydford) and tenants alike in 1348–9; C 135/164/11, 145/169/4; Hatcher, *Duchy of Cornwall*, p. 105 n.1 for a rough estimate of mortality in 1348–9.

[328] Hatcher, *Duchy of Cornwall*, p. 103, *CCR, 1360–64*, p. 220, *Register of the Black Prince*, II, p. 158 and Lewis, *The Stannaries*, p. 40 for the stannaries; Duchy of Cornwall Archives, Haveners' accounts (e.g. roll 13, which refers to reduced rents paid by users of Cornish fishing coves "because no boats can be furnished…on account of pestilence"), and Arundell Mss. at Hook

whose rural and industrial economies necessitated many movements of people with livestock and merchandise, movements which doubtless helped to spread the disease into the remotest corners and coombes of the peninsula.[329] During the first three-quarters of the fifteenth century the evidence for recurring outbreaks of heavy mortality is obviously patchy and incomplete, for they were less widespread than those of earlier years, but it is nevertheless unequivocal.[330] Some regions became very sparsely populated, particularly mid-Devon and the environs of Bodmin Moor, which went over to extensive livestock rearing; almost all of the Devon parishes exempted from the subsidy of 1428 on account of having populations of less than ten were in mid-Devon.[331] Here mortality, emigration from the least attractive holdings, and, perhaps, the maintenance of unmarried servants in husbandry on the large surviving pastoral tenancies all probably combined to give the landscape the empty air which it still wears today.[332]

As numbers of tenant farmers dwindled, the size of tenures increased through engrossing. Accounts and other documents contain numerous references to two or more holdings now occupied *sub una tenura*,[333] but the true extent of engrossing may be accurately measured only through nominal analysis of rentals as shown in Table 7.9. On all the manors represented in the table, numbers of smallholdings declined significantly and on some farms of below 16 acres were eliminated altogether. Within the great manor of Hartland, for example, the old pre-plague structure of inter-related smallholders (typically farming 15 acres or less), their land intermixed within the territories of their hamlet, had become unrecognizable by the sixteenth century, replaced by large

Manor, MA 225, a/c of 1383–4; *CCR, 1377–81*, pp. 54–5; PRO SC 6/1138/2; *Register of the Black Prince*, II, pp. 63–4; *William Worcestre, Itineraries*, ed. Harvey, pp. 94–5.

[329] For an example of "commercial" movements – to and from Dartmoor – see above, ch. 2; for livestock movements, ch. 3.

[330] Examples are: Hatcher, *Duchy of Cornwall*, p. 154; *Register of Edmund Lacy*, ed. Dunstan, III, pp. 91, 256–66, 272–3, 315–19. The national outbreaks of 1427 and 1437 are witnessed in local sources for the south-west: Devon RO, CR 436 and Hatcher, *English Tin Production*, p. 157; Dean and Chapter Archives, Exeter, 4807.

[331] *Feudal Aids*, I, pp. 473–5. Several mid-Devon parishes and parishes around Bodmin Moor recorded populations of under about 80 (indicating about 30 families or less) in 1377, which suggests that population decline in these poorly endowed regions may have been quite severe even in the third quarter of the fourteenth century: PRO E 179/95/40, 45; J. Maclean, 'Poll tax account for the county of Cornwall', *Roy. Inst. Cornwall*, IV, 1871–3, pp. 27–41 (Warleggan, St Clether, Otterham, and Michaelstow). See also *Register of Edmund Lacy*, ed. Dunstan, II, pp. 146–8 and N. J. G. Pounds, 'Taxation and wealth in late medieval Cornwall', *Roy. Inst. Cornwall*, NS VI, 1971, p. 166.

[332] Above, chs. 2 and 3 for desertion of settlement and extensive livestock rearing in these regions; below, pp. 736–7 for servants in husbandry.

[333] For example, PRO SC 6/822/16 and Arundell Mss. R&S 8, 14.

Table 7.9. *Sizes of holdings on five south-western manors*

	No. of tenants	Mean size of holdings (acres)	Percentage of holdings in size groups (acres)			
			6–15	16–25	26–35	36+
Hartland						
1301	128	13.9	99.2	0.8	—	—
c. 1365	64	25.5	43.8	4.7	28.1	23.4
1566	19	46.3	—	—	47.4	52.6
Helston-in-Kirrier						
1337	86	41.3	15.3	20.0	17.6	47.1
1371	46	52.3	7.6	18.2	21.2	53.0
1486	34	71.1	—	9.5	4.8	85.7
Stokenham						
c. 1347	147	30.6	4.1	6.1	81.6	8.2
c. 1360	120	44.9	0.8	—	64.2	35.0
1548–9	87	54.4	7.1	—	30.6	62.3
Tybesta						
1337	47	20.7	25.5	59.6	6.4	8.5
1406	45	24.1	22.3	40.0	20.0	17.7
1497	27	40.1	—	33.3	7.4	59.3
Helstone-in-Trigg						
1337	85	16.7	38.8	55.3	5.9	—
1371	74	21.5	20.3	56.7	12.2	10.8
1497	57	26.3	10.5	47.4	19.3	22.8

Notes: 1. For Hartland sizes of holdings in parts of the manor lying outside the parish, and in areas for which the rental of *c.* 1365 is missing, are not included in the calculations. 2. Holdings of less than 5 ac. – very few on some manors and non-existent on others – are not included. 3. Free-holdings, whose size is often not stated in the documents, are not included. *Sources*: As for Table 2.18.

compact farms such as John Atkyn's customary holdings of 90 acres, which he occupied together with a further 36 acres of demesne land. At Tybesta and elsewhere on the Duchy of Cornwall's estate amal-gamation of tenures, beginning in the later middle ages and continuing into the sixteenth century, produced "a small group of kulaks" whose farmsteads, in place of groups of smallholders' messuages, are in some cases now marked as "mansion" on the 1-inch map.[334]

[334] Sources as for Table 7.9; G. Haslam, 'An administrative study of the Duchy of Cornwall', Louisiana State Univ. Ph.D. thesis, 1980, p. 113.

The reduction in numbers of smallholders and growth in numbers of tenants with substantial acreages suggest that the ambitious and resourceful, and lucky, tenant could promote himself into a higher stratum of landholding under the less competitive conditions of the late middle ages. In 1393 John Colen of Culmstock entered into two cottages, perhaps now to be physically united as one farmhouse, and took at the same time a piece of demesne; John Fowlesdon of Sidbury surrendered a cottage on which the entry fine was 6s. 8d. and simultaneously took up a full holding clearly of some size, for the fine was 40s., which he was allowed to pay in instalments. Cottagers on Stokenham manor who promoted themselves to become occupiers of full holdings are revealed by the family names of Chaunte, Viel, and Stede, among others, borne only by cottagers in a pre-plague rental, but by occupiers of farm holdings about thirty years later.[335] If cottagers were able to break into the ranks of holders of more than a few acres, accumulation of holdings must have been even easier for tenants already in possession of some farmland: Henry Gartha of Liskeard manor, for example, who began as an occupier of a holding of 22 acres but who had by 1427 acquired seven others amounting in all to nearly 200 acres.[336] The results of promotion of landholding on some scale are abundantly clear from Table 7.9. Under the prevailing south-western system of convertible husbandry, to acquire an additional holding did not mean expensive investment in additional seed-corn, plough beasts and granaries; flocks and herds could be expanded slowly to fill the new closes, and maintenance of more hedges – an obligation often neglected – would be the only major new item of running costs. The building up of large multiple tenancies was also made easy in the south-west by a land market in which the units circulating were whole peasant tenures or sizeable blocks of demesne rather than parcels of an acre or so. The absence from Devon and Cornwall of that very active market in small pieces to be found in some parts of later medieval England, particularly the east, will only be fully explained after detailed examination of earlier periods, for where it existed its origins undoubtedly lay largely in the fragmentation of holdings under population pressure.[337] But whatever the ultimate

[335] Dean and Chapter Archives, 4936; *ibid.*, 4834; PRO SC 11/765 and Huntington Library, San Marino, HAM box 64, rental of "1577".

[336] Hatcher, *Duchy of Cornwall*, p. 250 and also pp. 230–1, 251. Examples elsewhere are the huge holdings (150 and 180 acres respectively) of John Poope and William Pynwill of Stokenham manor in 1548 or the ten ferlings (approximately 300 acres in all) held by William Whitchurch of Werrington manor in 1491: PRO SC 11/168 and Devon RO, W1258M/D/70, court before St Thomas the Apostle, 7 Henry VII.

[337] Court rolls from Devon and Cornwall normally record transfers of odd acres or half acres at a rate of far *less* than one per year. Holdings did not fragment into many small pieces, perhaps

Table 7.10. *The turnover of tenants' surnames on some south-western manors*

Manor	Period of turnover	Turnover of surnames (percentage)
Dean Prior	Between the holder previous to the tenant in 1408 and the tenant in 1408	86
Newton St Cyres	Between the holder previous to the tenant in 1408 and the tenant in 1408	90
Axmouth	Between the holder previous to the tenant in 1463 and the tenant in 1463	82
Helstone-in-Trigg	1356–71	· 61
Tybesta	1356–71	74

Sources: BL Harl. Ms. 4766 (for Dean Prior and Newton); PRO SC 11/163 (for Axmouth); PRO E 306/2/1, 2 and Duchy of Cornwall Archives, 475 (for Helstone and Tybesta).

reasons for a land market dominated by whole peasant tenures, it meant that, during a period when land was relatively freely available, holdings could be easily expanded not little by little but by leaps and bounds.[338]

Acquisition of land and the building up of multiple tenures were assisted, too, by the ease with which holdings could be obtained outside the family. Neither lords nor tenants seemed much concerned to record in court rolls the details of hereditary descent of holdings. At Sidbury between 1421 and 1500, about 89 per cent of all transactions in customary tenures involved holdings passing from tenants with one family name to tenants with another, and percentages are rarely much lower in series of court rolls from other manors.[339] Rentals which name

because of lack of partible inheritance, because of ample opportunities for earning a living away from the land, and because convertible husbandry set the minimum size of holdings rather high. An underworld market in small sublet parcels did exist, though to only a limited degree. But see Hatcher, *Duchy of Cornwall*, pp. 232–5.

[338] As reported from manors elsewhere in England: Harvey, ed., *The Peasant Land Market*, p. 344.

[339] Dean and Chapter Archives, 4798–4835 (Sidbury); 4927–4950 (Culmstock); Devon RO, 902M/M/2–30 and 55/13/2 (Stoke Fleming); CR 14–30 (Waddeton); Longleat House Mss., Uplyme court rolls for the years 1351–1407. See also B. E. Morris, 'The south-western estates of Syon monastery in the later middle ages', Univ. of Kent MA thesis, 1977, pp. 100–4. In these calculations free tenures, on which hereditary principles of succession were more closely adhered to, are not included; the passing of land from a husband to his widow on death is not included as a "transaction".

former (*nuper*) holders of land and successive listings of tenants likewise reveal high levels of apparently extra-familial transactions (Table 7.10). Figures such as these, based largely on surnames, are bound slightly to underestimate hereditary descent of holdings, for descent to distantly related kin is misclassified. A case can, however, be made for the approximate validity of figures derived in this way.[340] Moreover, the very fact that so few sons claimed their fathers' holdings (the proportion is so low that lack of sons cannot be responsible in all cases) makes it unlikely that more distant kin were frequent claimants.

The wandering of families between holdings, attested by many cases of tenants who "relinquished" their land to the lord, is well illustrated by an example from the manor of Helstone-in-Trigg, where a messuage and 15 acres in Fentonadle passed from Warin Dirman to Richard Harry, to Christopher Fentonadle, to John Berman in the space of twenty-four years between 1347 and 1371. On the Duchy of Cornwall's estate as a whole, it was rare indeed for a farm to be associated in the late fourteenth century with the same family name as in the years immediately after the Black Death.[341] Elsewhere it is not unusual to find a tenant giving up one holding in favour of another on the same manor, as when Geoffrey Gibbe of Waddeton in 1376 relinquished his holding to the lord but simultaneously took up a tenure once Nicholas Twyman's.[342] Movement between manors in order to take up land is seldom directly revealed by the sources: the case of Richard Hollway, who gave up a holding in Salcombe Regis to take another at Sidbury, two miles away, is known to us only because of a chance note by the steward in a court roll. But movements of this kind must have been very common to judge from turnover rates in the names of tenants, which can indicate the arrival of an almost completely new set of farming families during the course of the later middle ages.[343]

---

[340] Dyer, 'Changes in the link between families and land in the West Midlands', pp. 305–11.

[341] PRO E 306/2/1 and Duchy of Cornwall Archives, 475.

[342] Devon RO, CR 16. Among other examples of the same thing is a case of the exchange of tenures between apparently unrelated families at Culmstock in 1393: Dean and Chapter Archives, 4936.

[343] Dean and Chapter Archives, 4834. An example from Waddeton manor is "the man of unknown name" (probably an outsider) who took up a smallholding there in 1437: Devon RO, CR 29. Examples of high turnover rates in names of customary tenants are: only 11 per cent of the names of farming families (excluding cottagers and free tenants) at Stokenham in c. 1347 were still present on the manor in 1548; 9 per cent at Ashwater, 1346–1523, 16 per cent at Yarcombe, c. 1300–1445, 9 per cent at Dawlish, c. 1385–1513: PRO SC 11/765 and 168; Devon RO, Cary Mss., Ashwater rental of 1346 and survey of 1523; PRO SC 11/171 and 172; Dean and Chapter Archives, 2937 and 3684. It should be noted that a degree of fluidity in surnames may slightly deflate these figures.

Rapid circulation of holdings among families in the south-west may be explained in part by circumstances which brought hereditary succession to a low ebb in most parts of later medieval England. Greater availability of vacant land meant that sons could take their pick without having to wait for succession to the patrimonial holding. At Sidbury in 1454 John Knoll junior took a tenure formerly of Henry White, and at Trewalder in the 1350s John son of Warin Wape took up a holding formerly of John Trevellok; in both cases their fathers were still alive.[344] In addition, there must have been many instances in which no close kin survived to inherit. A number of distinctive features of the land market in the south-west also encouraged transfer of holdings outside the family. First, on many manors large numbers of occupiers were *conventionarii*, holding under a system of regularly re-negotiated leases which, in its most highly developed form, meant that all tenants simultaneously surrendered their holdings at an "assession" held every seven years, each to be bargained for anew and leased to the highest bidder, with no allowance at all for hereditary descent of land.[345] The presence of such tenures on one manor in a neighbourhood must have stimulated the land market of the whole district.[346] Second, it was unusual in the south-west for demesnes to be leased *en bloc* and to fall into the hands of substantial families for several generations; instead we find the almost ubiquitous practice of dividing demesnes into a number of medium-sized units leased and re-leased at regular intervals, such as the eleven demesne "tenures" at Connerton in 1464 or the closes, pieces, and meadows of the Stonor demesne at Ermington, let to twenty or so tenants.[347] An active market in these attractive new demesne tenures, leased according to competitive not hereditary principles, must have quickened the pace of non-hereditary land

---

[344] Dean and Chapter Archives, 4819; PRO E 306/2/1.

[345] Tenants could be ousted by whoever "would give most", and if a holding was considered to be attractive it was only the occasionally lucky tenant who could remain on it without an increased fine "because no other man came": J. Hatcher, 'Non-manorialism in medieval Cornwall', *AHR*, xviii, 1970, p. 8; Devon RO, W1258M/E/24 (conventionary fines). The system may have originated in order to facilitate movement of tenants to and from other occupations, e.g. mining, at regular intervals and to the regular profit of lords.

[346] The conventionary *system* was widespread in Cornwall on estates other than the duchy's: BL Add. Rolls 64391, 64534; PRO E 306/2/6 and SC 11/151; Devon RO, CR 435, 470, W1258M/E/24 (bishopric estate); Arundell Mss. MA 34; PRO SC 6/822/17 (Hylle estate); *The Cartulary of Launceston Priory*, ed. P. L. Hull, Devon and Cornwall Rec. Soc., NS xxx, 1987, pp. xxiv, xxxix, xl. "Conventionary" tenants were to be found on very many other manors, both in Devon and Cornwall, but the term does not always seem to imply regularly re-negotiated leases.

[347] Arundell Mss., R&S 8; PRO SC 12/1/1. The usual wording in accounts is that the demesne was let "to diverse tenants" or "to diverse persons".

transactions in general. Thirdly, the many opportunities which existed
in the south-west for sons to accumulate capital in non-agricultural
occupations, and then to enter into vacant holdings perhaps more
attractive than the patrimony, no doubt contributed to the circulation
of land among families.[348]

Acquisitions of multiple holdings were also made easier by relatively
modest outgoings. It is impossible to generalize about levels of rents
and fines in the south-west, except perhaps to say that they were on the
low side. Examples from late fourteenth-century Devon (all for
standard holdings of about 30 acres, and all including commuted
works) are annual rents of 13s. 4d. at Sidbury, 4s. and a few hens at
Stoke Fleming, 3s. 4d. plus 1s. 9d. aid at Stokenham, 6s. 8d. and 2s. aid
at Hartland. On the Arundell estate in Cornwall, 13s. 4d. was a high
level of rent, even for substantial holdings, in the 1460s; on the duchy
estate rents for holdings of around 30 acres varied from between 3s. 8d.
and 13s. 4d.[349] The generally low level of rent meant that increases,
when and where they were made, still left the tenant with relatively
low outgoings. Variability of entry-fines around a low mean can be
illustrated by 30-acre holdings at Stoke Fleming where, between the
1460s and the 1490s, fines were remitted altogether in three cases and
in others varied between 5s. and 33s. To take another example, the
Duchy of Cornwall regularly used small increases in fines in order to
reassess the financial burden on holdings, yet even by the 1490s few
fines on individual tenures on the attractive manor of Climsland were
above £2, and none at Helstone-in-Trigg was above 23s.[350] Nor were
a tenant's outgoings much increased by commutation, simply because
the burden of works was very light throughout the south-west, and
their value correspondingly low. Typical were the works owed by
tenants of the Earl of Devon at Okehampton, ploughing, harrowing,
mowing, and reaping for one day *per annum* at each task, valued for
each tenant at 5d. To these light tasks in husbandry might be added, on
some manors, a few works reflecting the south-west's diversity of
resources – working in the woods at Kingskerswell, for example, or
watching for the approach of mullet on the shore of Stokenham.
Week-works were very rare. On most of the manors of the Duchy of

[348] As very plausibly suggested for another mining district by I. Blanchard, 'Industrial
employment and the rural land market, 1380–1520', in *Land, Kinship and Life-cycle*, ed. Smith, pp.
259–60.
[349] Dean and Chapter Archives, 2945; Devon RO, 902M/E/5; Huntington Library, San
Marino, HAM box 64, rental of "1577"; Arundell Mss., R&S 5, 8; Hatcher, *Duchy of Cornwall*,
pp. 278–85.
[350] Devon RO, 902M/M/15–28; Hatcher, *Duchy of Cornwall*, pp. 278–9, 282–3. It should be
noted that the duchy entry-fines were paid every 7, 14, and 21 years.

Cornwall tenants owed no agricultural services at all.[351] A tenant's total outgoings of a "manorial" kind were further reduced by the infrequency of merchet and leyrwite; moreover, it was rare for *post mortem* duties to be anything more than the best beast.[352] Under all of these circumstances, it is not surprising to find that, whatever news of the rising of 1381 reached Exeter and beyond, it did not ignite any popular movement against the landlords of Devon and Cornwall.[353]

It was during the fifteenth century that the most impressive gains were made in the transformation from small to larger farms. On some of the Duchy of Cornwall's manors and on the east Devon estate of Syon abbey there was a down-turn in income from rents and fines at some time in the 1420s or 1430s, as tenants in a "buyers' market" were able to bargain for reductions in payments for some holdings. At Sidbury from the late 1420s and at Stoke Fleming in the 1430s the "pool" of holdings lying vacant for a short time grew in size, giving greater scope to the acquisitive.[354] Several circumstances converged to encourage growth of larger holdings during the fifteenth century. A flood of attractive demesne tenancies became available in the early decades of the century, probably resulting in growth in the pool of less desirable holdings lying vacant before eventually being taken up by engrossing tenants.[355] Population declined to levels lower than those of the late fourteenth century: counts of tenants are no sure indicators of the extent of demographic decline, but severe reductions in numbers of tenants during much of the fifteenth century (as in Table 7.9) must to a degree reflect smaller rural populations. At certain places, reluctance to stay on the land on the part of some tenants presented further opportunity for engrossing among those who remained: when Bishop Lacy wrote in 1446 of "the land ravished by pestilence and the sword", this was no mere formula, for we hear of his own tenants at Clyst, in the 1450s, who "dared not occupy the land" on account of "the

[351] BL Add. Roll 64663; Arundell Mss. MA 251; Huntington Library, San Marino, HAM box 64, rental of "1577"; Hatcher, 'Non-manorialism in medieval Cornwall', pp. 10–13. For a rare example of week-work see Devon RO, CR 496 (Plympton).

[352] Appropriation of villeins' other chattels has been noted only at Werrington and on the duchy estate: Devon RO, W1258M/D/70; *Cal. Inq. Misc.*, IV, pp. 107–8.

[353] The sheriff of Devon dared not levy estreats within his county in 1381; in Cornwall it was claimed that Sir William Bottreaux attacked the property of a neighbour with eighty followers, an example probably of use of knowledge of the revolt to further a family feud by genuine violence or false indictment; news of the revolt may have emboldened the tenants of Clayhidon to present grievances against their reeve at the Michaelmas manorial court of 1381: C. J. Tyldesley, 'The Crown and the local communities in Devon and Cornwall from 1377 to 1422', Univ. of Exeter Ph.D. thesis, 1978, pp. 22–3, 133; Arundell Mss. MA 246.

[354] Hatcher, *Duchy of Cornwall*, pp. 158–9; Morris, 'The south-western estates of Syon', pp. 109–13; sources for Sidbury and Stoke Fleming as in n. 339 above.

[355] Above, ch. 2 for demesne leasing.

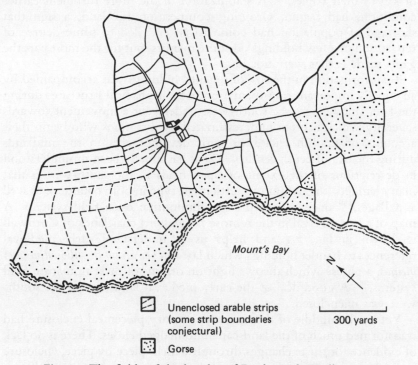

Mount's Bay

N

▨ Unenclosed arable strips
(some strip boundaries
conjectural)

300 yards

▨ Gorse

Fig. 7.1 The fields of the hamlet of Predannack Wollas, 1695
Source: The Lanhydrock Atlas at Lanhydrock House

quarrel between the Earl of Devon and Lord Bonville", and of attacks
on coastal manors by the French and Bretons.[356] Growth of larger
holdings was not necessarily accompanied by the establishment of long-
lived, stable dynasties of substantial tenants; for example, Henry
Gartha's large collection of holdings on Liskeard manor, assembled in
the 1420s, had passed to another family by 1448, while the evidence of
much turnover in local surnames points in the same direction.[357] It is
only towards the end of the fifteenth century that some contrary signs
– of reduced availability of land and greater stability in landholding –
become apparent. At Stoke Fleming the pool of vacant holdings
diminished from the 1470s, and at Sidbury from the 1480s. From both
manors there are also signs of greater competition for land in the last
decades of the fifteenth century and first decades of the sixteenth: of
tenants anxious to acquire reversions of holdings or to add the names

[356] *Register of Edmund Lacy*, ed. Dunstan, III, pp. 259, 316; Alcock, 'An East Devon manor', II,
pp. 150–1; above, ch. 2, nn. 331 and 350. For parliament's view of the disruption caused by civil
war see *Rot. Parl.*, v, p. 285.   [357] Hatcher, *Duchy of Cornwall*, p. 250; above, n. 343.

of kin to their copies.[358] A stabilization of the more turbulent earlier conditions had begun. Growing competition for land, a sign that shortage of population had come to an end, led to some degree of repartition of a few holdings on some manors, but for the most part the gains made earlier were not lost.

Transformation in the size of tenants' holdings was accompanied by an equally important transformation in their physical structure: during the later middle ages the south-west underwent a movement towards severalty which is often underestimated by historians who begin their accounts of English enclosure with developments in the midlands during the late fifteenth century. What has usually been misunderstood in descriptions of the extent of open fields in the south-west is that many hamlets (the ubiquitous settlement type in both counties), as well as villages,[359] once had their own diminutive open-field systems. A map of a late survival in the remote far western coastlands of Cornwall is shown in Fig. 7.1 and helps us to understand early medieval references to hamlet holdings which lay *acra per acram* or *sullonatim inter vicinos*, a phrase which throws light on origins of these miniature field systems.[360] A good deal of the early medieval landscape of the south-west was unenclosed.

Yet by the middle of the sixteenth century piecemeal enclosure had transformed much of the landscape into hedged closes. There is no lack of evidence for the exchanges through which, piece by piece, enclosure was achieved: in 1357, for example, two Cornish tenants urged that an exchange between them would be "for the profit and convenience" of their lord, and in 1415 five tenants of Stoke Fleming paid capons for permission to exchange strips "in order to improve their holdings" (*ad meliorandum tenuras*).[361] Piecemeal enclosure was rendered easy and

---

[358] Sources as in n. 339 above. At Werrington the first recorded reversion was in 1491 and at Wreyland after 1480 a good proportion of land transactions involved reversions: Devon RO, W1258M/D/70; *Wreyland Documents*, ed. C. Torr, Cambridge, 1910, pp. 23–68. On the Duchy of Cornwall's estate a degree of stabilization of landholding came somewhat earlier in the fifteenth century, and after about 1470 there was little further growth in numbers of tenants with multiple holdings: Hatcher, *Duchy of Cornwall*, pp. 220, 226–8.

[359] H. P. R. Finberg, 'The open field in Devon', in W. G. Hoskins and H. P. R. Finberg, *Devonshire Studies*, pp. 265–88; Fox, 'Chronology of enclosure', pp. 183–4; Fox, 'Field systems: East Devon', pp. 94–7.

[360] Royal Institution of Cornwall, Henderson transcripts, vol. 19, no. 314, and vol. 26, no. 67 (Trevellion in Luxulyan); Cornwall RO, DDME, Treworyan Deeds no. 1 (Treworyan in Probus); *ibid.*, DD Carlyon, Lantyan Deeds (Little Lantyan in Lostwithiel); Devon RO, Z1/10/26 (Brownstone in Morchard Bishop); *Cornwall Feet of Fines*, ed. J. H. Rowe, 2 vols, Exeter, 1914–1950, I, p. 48 (Boduel in Liskeard); *Register of Edmund Lacy*, ed. Dunstan, III, p. 289 (Uton in Crediton).

[361] *Register of the Black Prince*, II, p. 129; Devon RO, 902M/M/13. For other examples: Fox 'Chronology of enclosure', pp. 186–7, 189, 192–3; Cornwall RO, DDR 2068–9 (Trevollard in

uncontentious by an absence of rigidly controlled fallowing systems and common rights in the open fields, and by relaxation during the later middle ages of pressure on wastes which, earlier, had often been used as periodically cultivated outfields, but could now be used exclusively as common pastures in place of the arable core.[362] Moreover, a farmer who had added two or more holdings together might often find that a whole block of strips fell to him, naturally as it were, by "unity of possession". There can be little doubt, given the findings of earlier chapters on trends in land use, that enclosure was designed in many cases for the more careful management of animals, perhaps especially of their breeding. A sixteenth-century survey of Tinten on the flanks of Bodmin Moor, looking back perhaps to the reign of Henry VIII, described how "the landes were of late in common feilds, and nowe all inclosed and converted much into pasture and...gresing of cattle", while the Devonian John Hooker realized that holdings divided by "mightie greate hedges and dytches" into small closes (the typical products of piecemeal enclosure) allowed livestock "by theire often chaunges...[to] feede styll as it were upon a new springnynge grasse".[363] Regional variation in the chronology of the movement, too, suggests a close relationship with trends towards pasture. It was largely completed by 1500 in the most strongly pastoral regions, including much (except the south) of Devon, a county which Leland saw in the 1530s, later describing enclosure in progress on Anglesey as "after Devonshire fascion". It proceeded more slowly and with less thrust, leaving some open fields intact into the sixteenth century in the more arable regions, including the coastlands of Cornwall to which Carew's observation (c. 1600) on survival of open-field husbandry "in times not past the remembrance of some yet living" is most relevant.[364]

It is to be expected that an increase in the size of holdings, and improvements in the structure of their fields, were associated in the long term with improvements to tenants' buildings. Excavations show

Lanreath); BL Egerton Ms. 3671, f.30v. (Rowden in Brentor); PRO SC 2/167/46 (Otterton); Dean and Chapter Archives, 4807 (Sidbury); Devon RO, 1334M/M/1 (Sidmouth); *ibid.*, Z1/10/26 (Brownstone in Morchard Bishop); A. M. Erskine, 'Evidence of open field cultivation in Culmstock', *Devon and Cornwall N. & Q.*, xxxii, 1971–3, pp. 161–3.

[362] H. S. A. Fox, 'Outfield cultivation in Devon and Cornwall: a reinterpretation', in M. Havinden, ed., *Husbandry and Marketing in the South-West 1500–1800*, Exeter, 1973, pp. 32–3.

[363] BL Harl. Ms. 71, f.63v.; W. J. Blake, 'Hooker's Synopsis Chorographical of Devonshire', *Devon. Assoc.*, xlvii, 1915, p. 344.

[364] Fox, 'Chronology of enclosure', pp. 194–6; Leland, *Itinerary*, iii, p. 90; Carew, *Survey of Cornwall*, ed. Halliday, p. 138 and the related text 'Of measuring land in Cornwayl', BL Cott. Ms. Faust. E. V. A few examples of late surviving hamlet open-field systems on the coastlands of Cornwall are: Cornwall RO, DDME, Landrake survey (Blarrick); PRO E 315/388 (Tregurrian); Arundell Mss., R&S 12 and 42 (Bedrugga and Bosoughan in Colan, Porth Veor and Trebelsne in Newquay, Tolcarne in St Mawgan).

that a typical peasant house in the south-west in the thirteenth and early fourteenth centuries might have an internal length of about 50 ft and a width of about $13\frac{1}{2}$ ft.[365] The average dimensions of surviving later medieval farmhouses (mostly from the late fifteenth century) which have been examined in detail are 53 ft by 18 ft, representing a good gain in area, the more so when it is realized that all of the earlier buildings were long-houses which included accommodation for animals, while many of the later houses had separate byres and barns for the more elaborate agricultural activities which larger holdings supported.[366] The sophisticated surviving roofing of these later houses, suggesting local schools of carpenters, is matched by documentary references to employment of specialists to work on roofs.[367] The documents also allow us to see a proliferation of farmyard buildings associated with the partial phasing out of long-houses: a barn 53 ft long built for a tenant on the manor of Cargoll in 1403–4, a barn of two bays at Sidbury in 1461, and separate stables, cowhouses and carthouses elsewhere.[368] It is possible to write of a "great rebuilding" of farmhouses, in Devon at least, during the later middle ages; the houses of this movement were substantial and have proved to be durable; they were in some cases soon given interior modifications which allowed for a good deal of comfort, but which were less sophisticated than the changes wrought by the better-known phase of rebuilding of the late sixteenth century.[369] It is noteworthy that a significant proportion of surviving later medieval buildings are now being attributed to the generations immediately before and after 1500: their construction, in other words, can probably be linked to the stabilization of landholding which took place at about this time, rather than to the early fifteenth century when a more fluid market in holdings was not conducive, as presentments for dilapidations show, to any great investment in buildings.

Many tenant farmers at the close of the later middle ages were not

---

[365] Based on D. Austin, 'Dartmoor and the upland village of the South-West of England', in D. Hooke, ed., *Medieval Villages: a Review of Current Work*, Oxford, 1985, p. 74, and excluding obvious cottages and seigneurial buildings.

[366] Based upon surveys of later medieval farmhouses in Devon, by N. W. Alcock, S. R. Jones and C. Hulland in *Devon. Assoc.*, C, 1968 – CXVI, 1984. For some reason the chronology of rebuilding appears to have been different in Cornwall, and few smaller houses of this date have yet been identified there.

[367] C. Hulland, 'Devonshire farmhouses', pts v and vi, *Devon. Assoc.*, CXII, 1980, p. 168 and CXVI, 1984, p. 60; Dean and Chapter Archives, 5055–6; N. W. Alcock, 'The medieval cottages of Bishops Clyst, Devon', *Med. Arch.*, IX, 1965, pp. 151–3.

[368] Devon RO, W1258M/E/24; Dean and Chapter Archives, 4823; *ibid.*, 4829; PRO C 116/37, m.1; Devon RO, Cary Mss., Ashwater court after the Invention of the Holy Cross, 6 Edward IV.

[369] N. W. Alcock and M. Laithwaite, 'Medieval houses in Devon and their modernization', *Med. Arch.*, XVII, 1973, pp. 100–25.

only occupiers of larger holdings and more substantial farmsteads than those of their now distant predecessors of the thirteenth century, but were also more specialist in their farming enterprises. In Devon and Cornwall farming regions were already well developed by the end of the fifteenth century; this applied not only to minor agricultural practices and products – the very pronounced regionalization in the use of marl and in cider production, for example – but also, as Chapters 2 and 3 make clear, to basic emphases between grain and livestock production and within those sectors. Regional specialisms were not so well developed that many farmers were reliant on intra-regional "imports" for subsistence, as they came to be in later centuries, but the seeds of such developments were already deeply sown. One explanation which has been put forward for agricultural specialization in later medieval England at large is that tenant farmers sank back into a kind of lethargic subsistence economy, concentrating on producing for their own households those items which their lands yielded best.[370] But one may also argue that specialization was a more vigorous reaction to market demands more sophisticated in their structure than those of the thirteenth century. In these last paragraphs we examine the nature of such demands.

The market among landless cottagers and other agricultural labourers by no means disappeared during the course of the later middle ages. At many places in the later fourteenth century there are, of course, references to unoccupied and decayed cottages. Here are a few examples from among many: at Fremington in 1326 there were 39 holdings comprising "a cottage, a yard, and certain pieces of land", but "divers destroyed cottages" by 1388; seven cottages at Lanherne in 1343 had all disappeared by the fifteenth century; at Tregaire in 1396–7 several cottages were "prostrate", later to be described as "totally destroyed for many years"; an account for Holcombe Rogus in 1405–6 records a decayed cottage, doubtless a cavernous place, which is graphically called "Prothole".[371] A sharp decline – not everywhere, but in many places – of independent cottage holdings is to be expected when promotion to full landholding became more feasible and when demesnes were contracting.[372] But did the food market among agricultural labourers decline to the same degree as the decline in independent cottage holdings? The new, larger farms of the fifteenth

---

[370] W. G. Hoskins, 'Regional farming in England', *AHR*, II, 1954, p. 7.

[371] PRO C 134/99 and *Cal. Inq. Misc.*, v, p. 89; Arundell Mss., R&S 1 and 8; BL Add. Rolls 64534 and 64546; Devon RO, DD 54916. See also N. W. Alcock, 'An East Devon manor', II, pp. 158–9.

[372] Some cottagers seem originally to have been given their holdings specifically in return for services: PRO C 133/2/7, 134/93/13, SC 6/830/29.

century, despite their generally more pastoral orientation, must, after all, have been dependent to some extent on labour drawn from outside the family,[373] yet the farm labourer in the later middle ages is a rather shadowy figure where poll-tax returns from 1381 have not survived. The best statistical guide comes, in fact, from the end of the period: the lay subsidy returns for 1524–5 show that 36 per cent of those taxed in Devon and 30 per cent in Cornwall were assessed at £1. A good proportion of these men, particularly in parishes with little non-agricultural employment, must have been farm labourers.[374]

A considerable body of labourers, combined with a decline in cottage holdings rented directly from lords by cottagers, indicates without doubt that some farmworkers during the later middle ages were being provided with accommodation by their employers. In the mid-Devon parish of Ashwater no cottagers are recorded in a survey of 1523, yet the lay subsidy of 1524 lists 29 men assessed at £1, many of whom may therefore have been living-in servants in husbandry employed upon large pastoral holdings which were the products of much engrossing during the fifteenth century; employment of labourers on yearly terms was especially suited to pastoral farming and to dispersed settlement. Again, a rental of Trelawne in 1523–4 lists no cottagers, but the subsidy reveals twelve labourers who are also likely to have been living-in servants in husbandry.[375] The Cornish bondman who left his manor to join a Devonshire farmer, to be apprenticed *ad artem suam de husbondrye*, was doubtless a servant in husbandry, as probably were some of the Cornish servants whose masters were named before the justices of labourers in 1358.[376]

Living-in servants of husbandry made no demands upon the market for agricultural produce, but another category of farmworkers, provided with a different type of arrangement for accommodation and more independent from his employer in terms of subsistence, did. By this arrangement, also suited to periods of high real wages, cottages were rented at nominal rents by large tenant farmers and presumably used as "tied cottages" to house labourers with accommodation provided in part payment of wages. A rental of Stokenham made *c.* 1347 lists many independent cottagers, yet by *c.* 1360 59 per cent of

---

[373] This is clear from a comparison with demesne labour requirements.

[374] *Devon Lay Subsidy Rolls 1524–7*, ed. T. L. Stoate, Almondsbury, 1979, p.x, and *Cornwall Subsidies in the Reign of Henry VIII*, ed. T. L. Stoate, Almondsbury, 1985, p. vii.

[375] Devon RO, Cary Mss., survey of Ashwater, and *Devon Lay Subsidy Rolls*, ed. Stoate, p. 134; above, ch. 2, for engrossing; A. Kussmaul, *Servants in Husbandry in Early Modern England*, Cambridge, 1981, p. 23 and L. Poos, 'The social context of Statute of Labourers enforcement', *Law and History Review*, I, 1983, p. 49; PRO E 315/385, and *Cornwall Subsidies*, ed. Stoate, p. 107.

[376] BL Add. Roll 64453; B. H. Putnam, *The Enforcement of the Statutes of Labourers*, App., pp. 152–7.

cottages were attached to farm-holdings; some of the larger tenant farmers, such as John Shath with a farm of 180 acres, rented (in addition to a farmhouse) two cottages, for which they paid small rents of 8d. or 4d. Comparable figures are 80 per cent of cottages "tied" to farm-holdings at Axmouth in 1483, 75 per cent at Yarcombe in 1445, 29 per cent at Stoke Fleming in 1523, and 24 per cent at Newton St Cyres in 1408.[377] Such arrangements can be seen, from the viewpoint of employers, as a way of saving on labour charges, as an inducement to labourers and perhaps as a means of extending service in husbandry to married couples. It could be argued that their introduction led to some degree of debasement of the condition of some labourers in the so-called "Golden Age" of labour.[378]

There remained, of course, many independent labourers without the ties which came with provision of accommodation by an employer, who found daily and seasonal employment in a variety of tasks. One could speculate that this semi-itinerant and least secure class of labourer was by no means unimportant during the later middle ages: because of high wages, there were incentives for large farmers to employ "disposable" labour at times of peak demand in the farming year. Many of the "poor" to whom lords made occasional payments, sanctioned in accounts, were presumably available when needed as farm labourers, as were men known as *censarii* taxed, in the words of the Duchy of Cornwall's accounts, *pro libertate manerii habenda*. We hear too of labourers, clearly not in regular employment, who slept by day at Blackawton; of those men from Ashwater in pastoral mid-Devon who in autumn 1436 made their way, to earn harvest wages, for over 25 miles *usque lez Southammys*; of Sidbury men who sought harvest work "in eastern parts", presumably the more arable regions of Somerset.[379] Many of those Cornishmen who were prosecuted by the justices of labourers in 1358 for taking excessive wages appear to have had no master.[380]

---

[377] PRO SC 11/765 and Huntington Library, San Marino, HAM box 64, rental of "1577"; PRO SC 11/163; SC 11/172; Devon RO, Cary Mss., Stoke Fleming rental of *c.* 1523; BL Harl. Ms. 4766. For possible examples of farmers adding cottage holdings to their tenures, see Somerset RO, DDWO 47/3, a/c of 1438–9 and Royal Institution of Cornwall, HB/20/12 (Heanton Punchardon).

[378] For the origin of such arrangements, after 1348, see Huntington Library, San Marino, HAM box 64, rental of "1577" and PRO SC 6/1118/6 (Sampford Courtenay).

[379] PRO SC 6/823/28, Arundell Mss. MA 61 (Lanherne and St Columb), Devon RO, W1258M/D/38/15 (Leigh) for payments to paupers; Hatcher, *Duchy of Cornwall*, p. 219 and Morris, 'The south-western estates of Syon', pp. 198–201, for some buoyancy in numbers of landless *censarii*, even in the fifteenth century; Devon RO, W1258M/G/1/39; *ibid.*, Cary Mss., Ashwater court of Oct. 1436; Dean and Chapter Archives, 4802, 3, 10. See also Devon RO, 314M/M/2.   [380] Putnam, *op. cit.*, App., pp. 152–7.

Food markets among agricultural labourers were not, therefore, as restricted during the later middle ages as might at first sight be supposed. Further markets, vigorous enough to encourage regional specialization in tenant farming, were to be found among populations dependent largely or partly upon non-agrarian sources of income. Almost everywhere in the south-west the sources present a diverse, lively scene in the non-agrarian sector. It is interesting to find landlords, perhaps especially smaller landlords, investing in "alternative" sources of income as demesne production declined, just as they did in other periods when agricultural prices were uncertain. At Clayhidon the lord retained a team of oxen and had a waggon newly built in order to carry away the output of a charcoal-burning industry which he had established there.[381] At Halton on the Cornish side of the Tamar the Hylles owned a quay yielding keyage on imports of "wine, sand, iron, and other necessities" and also, no doubt, useful for shipping out the products of industrial enterprises on the manor and its members: from tinworks and fulling mills which were common enough in certain parts of the south-west, and from two less widespread but locally important industries, quarrying and lime burning in which the family invested over 100s. for a new kiln in 1411.[382] But for every act of investment by a landlord there were many others by craftsmen, merchants, and other speculators. In the stannaries merchant tinners and others opened up tinworks. Tuckers and other tradesmen and craftsmen – cornmillers and tailors for example – constructed or rented fulling mills.[383] Consortia of countrymen invested in non-agrarian enterprises, such as the twenty tenants of Yarcombe who built a fulling mill in the 1440s, or those who responded to the indulgence granted by Bishop Lacy for the building of a new quay to protect fishing boats at Newquay in 1440.[384] The presence of numerous artisans and non-agricultural workers in the later medieval countryside and its petty country boroughs is clear from some unusual sources: from a list of the followers of the earl of Devon in his campaigns against Lord Bonville

[381] Arundell Mss., CR 447, a/c of 12–13 Henry IV and MA 247, a/c of 1420–1.

[382] PRO SC 6/822/15–24, 823/3–4; *The Hylle Cartulary*, ed. R. W. Dunning, Somerset Rec. Soc., LXVIII, 1968, p. 90. For other references to burning of lime, one only of numerous types of stone quarried in the south-west, see Longleat House Mss. 10654 (Uplyme); Dean and Chapter Archives, 2857 (Staverton); Huntington Library, San Marino, HAM box 74, a/c of "Salisburysland" (Yealmpton); Cambridge University Library, Add. Ms. 3298; *Trevelyan Papers*, ed. J. P. Collier, Camden Soc. OS LXVII, 1857, p. 13.

[383] Hatcher, *English Tin Production*, pp. 60–2; BL Harl. Ms. 4766, f.13v.; Royal Institution of Cornwall, HB/20/12 (Beaford); PRO SC 6/1118/6 (Chulmleigh).

[384] Morris, 'The south-western estates of Syon', p. 170; *Register of Edmund Lacy*, ed. Dunstan, II, p. 176.

in 1455, in which such workers comprised a large element; from a long list of the names of those accused by Thomas Stonor of trespass in his several ground at Ermington; from the passages on Cornwall in Leland's *Genethliacon*, written to celebrate the birth of a new duke in 1537; from a genealogy of two Cornish bond families whose sons found employment as apprentices to a waxmaker, a webber, a merchant, a mariner, and to two masters working in another significant south-western industry, that of tanning.[385]

Mining provided income for many countrymen. In the royal lead and silver mines near the Tamar a capitalist organization of mining flourished; here the crown and its lessees employed a large work force of labourers, some on a full-time basis, who must have been significant consumers of farm produce.[386] But tin mining – practised on all of the Cornish moors and on Dartmoor – was not constrained for technological reasons to follow this type of capitalistic organization, for "streaming" of alluvial deposits predominated over shaft mining, and could theoretically have been the province of the lone tinner or small consortium. Some tinworkers, as Ian Blanchard has argued, were undoubtedly farmers who worked in the tin fields as a by-employment, such as the "sturdy farmer-miner" John Symon with about 25 acres, or John Kendal with 7 acres in the vicinity of Blackmoor Stannary in the early years of Richard II's reign.[387] The fact that output in the stannaries was seasonal, with a peak in the months following the end of lambing, calving, and hay-making on pastoral farms, and the fact that the average annual output per tinner was very low, both further suggest some degree of association between farming and mining.[388] But they can be attributed in part, too, to the presence of labourer-tinners who combined tinning not with the working of a farm-holding but with other labouring or craft occupations, and who supplemented their incomes from the diverse resources of the moors.[389] The listings of

---

[385] M. Cherry, 'The struggle for power in mid-fifteenth-century Devonshire', in R. A. Griffiths, ed., *Patronage, the Crown, and the Provinces in Later Medieval England*, Gloucester, 1981, p. 137; *Stonor Letters and Papers*, ed. Kingsford, I, pp. 63–5; *Itinerary of John Leland*, ed. T. Hearne, London, 3rd edn, 1768–9, IX, pp. xxi–xxii; BL Add. Roll 64453.

[386] L. F. Salzman, 'Mines and stannaries', in J. F. Willard, W. A. Morris and W. H. Dunham, eds., *The English Government at Work, 1327–1336*, III, Cambridge, Mass., 1950, pp. 71–5; PRO E 101/266/25.

[387] I. Blanchard, 'Rejoinder: stannator fabulosus', *AHR*, XXII, 1974, p. 71.

[388] For seasonality, T. A. P. Greeves, 'The Devon tin industry 1450–1750: an archaeological and historical survey', Univ. of Exeter Ph.D. thesis, 1981, p. 289; Hatcher, *English Tin Production*, p. 78 and 'Myths, miners and agricultural communities', *AHR*, XXII, 1974, pp. 58–9. For low output per miner, Blanchard, 'Rejoinder', p. 74 and Finberg, *Tavistock Abbey*, p. 191.

[389] For example, Richard French, cobbler, of Buckfastleigh, a taverner of Crediton, and John Tucker of Lewtrenchard: PRO E 179/12, 15, 33. It should be noted that the source used here, lists

Devonshire tinners wrongly taxed (despite their supposed exemption) by collectors of the lay subsidies include some men, probably itinerants, who had since "departed from the stannary", others from tithings so far from Dartmoor that they are more likely to have been itinerant labourers than more stable farmer-miners.[390] In Cornwall, penetration of the stannaries by large-scale capitalist ventures and by usury, which made many tinners virtually the labourers of the merchants who advanced them income, meant that the independent farmer-miner may not have been the typical figure, as John Hatcher has stressed. We hear too of turf diggers who migrated, perhaps seasonally, from the Cornish stannaries to Devon in order to dig on Dartmoor and who are unlikely, because of the distances involved, to have been occupiers of farm holdings.[391] The trend towards larger farm-holdings during the later middle ages must have meant that to combine tinning with farming was more difficult, and less necessary, than it once had been; the basic tasks of winning and smelting ore must have become more and more the province of increasingly proletarianized landless labourers.[392] It will never be possible to estimate the proportion of landless among the 3,000 tinners estimated to have been working on one alone of the four Cornish stannaries in 1404, or the 1,150 alleged tinners of Dartmoor counted in 1373, but the number of such men cannot have been inconsiderable and cannot have failed to encourage the development of local food markets.[393]

Clothworkers provided further markets. The beginnings of the industry were modest, for the reliable aulnage figures from the last decade of the fourteenth century indicate that cloth production in the south-west was then dwarfed by the output of other woollen districts in Wiltshire and the Mendips, while of the 120 or so fulling mills recorded in Devon and Cornwall during the period covered in this volume, only one-quarter are known to have existed before 1400. But by the last decade of the fifteenth century the number of cloths exported from Exeter exceeded those from any other provincial port

of those claiming exemption from taxation on account of being "miners", may include some whose involvement in the industry was very slight: for example, CCR, 1374–7, pp. 380–1 and PRO E 179/95/31, m.6. See also H. P. R. Finberg, 'The stannary of Tavistock', Devon. Assoc., LXXXI, 1949, pp. 172–84. For diverse resources, above, ch. 2.

[390] For example, PRO E 179/95/12, 14, 15, 33.

[391] Hatcher, English Tin Production, pp. 51–79, and 'Myths, miners and agricultural communities', p. 59; CPR, 1461–7, p. 482.

[392] After the first pestilence, the Black Prince, as controller of the stannaries, attempted to prevent the abandonment of tin-works by tinners, and there was probably a "large-scale migration from mining into farming": Lewis, The Stannaries, p. 40, and Hatcher, Duchy of Cornwall, p. 120. Thereafter tinning may have been the province of the most needy among labourers.   [393] Hatcher, Duchy of Cornwall, pp. 31–2; PRO E 179/95/28–9, 30, 32.

except Bristol and Southampton.[394] This remarkable fifteenth-century expansion in cloth production was no doubt linked with the overall pastoral trend in land use experienced in both counties, graphically illustrated by examples of the conversion of corn mills to fulling mills, as at Botelet in the early fifteenth century.[395] The first signs of growth were in the 1430s and 1440s when, according to the evidence presented by the distribution of fulling mills, a concentration of the industry took place in south-east Cornwall, south of Foweymoor Stannary and around the borders of Dartmoor, where rough "Tavistocks" were produced.[396] Output from the Cornish stannaries, and to a lesser extent the stannary of Dartmoor, declined significantly during those decades,[397] and it is tempting to see a link between the two developments, as labourers in the tin-fields of necessity took more and more to weaving. According to the export figures another and more dramatic phase of expansion took place in the 1480s and 1490s, when a third regional concentration emerged, in the vales of east Devon. Exeter and its surroundings had boasted a clothing trade for some time, but now the industry expanded remarkably both in the city and in the boroughs and rural parishes of the region. East Devon, far from the stannaries, was already a well-developed pastoral region, with much emphasis on dairying, where tenements tended to be smaller in size than the engrossed rearing farms of some other parts of Devon, and it is on these smallholdings that the rural roots of the industry may initially have grown;[398] the timing of the expansion here may well have been related to the beginnings of recovery of population, resulting in a growth in numbers of people dependent upon craft work.

Within east Devon and elsewhere in the south-west it is notoriously difficult, as researchers on other parts of England have found, to

[394] H. L. Gray, 'The production and exportation of English woollens in the fourteenth century', *EHR*, XXXIX, 1924, p. 34; maps of the distribution of fulling mills in H. S. A. Fox, 'Medieval rural industry and mining', in *An Historical Atlas of South-West England*, ed. R. J. P. Kain and W. Ravenhill, forthcoming; Carus-Wilson and Coleman, *England's Export Trade*, p. 145, and for exports from the port of "Plymouth" (which included the Cornish ports), p. 155.

[395] BL Add. Roll 64348. For other similar references, Devon RO and Cary Mss., Luffincott rental at end of Ashwater rental of 1464–5; Finberg, *Tavistock Abbey*, p. 151.

[396] Maps of fulling mills as in n. 394 above; *Rot. Parl.*, V, p. 621. The smaller-scale earlier industry had been concentrated in east Devon and around Barnstaple.

[397] Hatcher, *English Tin Production*, pp. 157–8. Expansion in cloth exports at this time is noticeable both at the port of "Exeter" (which included Dartmouth, whence cloths from the borders of Dartmoor were shipped) and Plymouth (cloths from the Tavistock vicinity and eastern Cornwall).

[398] Below, n. 400 for examples of east Devon manors with fulling mills; E. M. Carus-Wilson, *The Expansion of Exeter at the Close of the Middle Ages*, 1963, pp. 9, 17–19; above, ch. 3, for dairying. Standard 5-acre tenements, relatively unusual in Devon, were to be found in a number of manors in the region.

pin-point precisely the labour force upon which the whole industry was founded. When we read of thefts of cloths or dyed wool from houses on completely rural manors, or of syndicates of tenants who built or leased fulling mills near Yarcombe and at Trembleathe, we come close to glimpsing the industry in the countryside but not quite close enough to be sure of the status of workers in wool and cloth.[399] It may be significant that some rural places with, or near to, fulling mills, such as Uffculme, Newton St Cyres, and Sidbury in east Devon, or Menheniot in south-east Cornwall, also had relatively large populations of independent rather than "tied" cottagers,[400] suggesting that spinning and weaving were by-employments among some farm labourers, while mills close to the mining districts may indicate a joint interest in tinning and clothmaking among a certain element in the population. With urban places we can be a little surer of concentrations of workers in cloth. Numbers of petty seigneurial boroughs were greater (per land area) in Devon and Cornwall than in any other county, yet, despite this, relatively few declined to insignificance during the later middle ages. Some, such as Liskeard and Saltash in the textile region of eastern Cornwall, or Tiverton and Ottery St Mary – two of a network of towns which grew in wealth as Exeter's size and cloth exports expanded – were exceedingly flourishing little places at the end of the fifteenth century and beginning of the sixteenth.[401] Other boroughs lost any serious claims to burgality during the later middle ages, yet survived as physical settlements which may best be described as "industrial villages". Such was the petty planted borough of South Zeal on the northern flank of Dartmoor, with a fulling mill by 1445 and a significant concentration of tuckers and weavers (and tanners too) in the third decade of the sixteenth century.[402] Here, in

[399] PRO SC 2/168/61, court of Sept. 1486, Devon RO, 902M/M/3, CR 1446, Dean and Chapter Archives 4835 for theft; Devon RO, CR 97 for a plea of debt, probably concerning fulling, between an urban fuller and a Callington man; Morris, 'The south-western estates of Syon', p. 170, and Arundell Mss. MA 34.

[400] PRO C 138/52, 139/51; BL Harl. Ms. 4766; Dean and Chapter Archives, 2945, 4798–4835; BL Add. Roll 40730.

[401] Leland, *Itinerary*, I, pp. 208, 210 and, for some hints of migration into, and textile-related occupations within, these Cornish towns, BL Add. Roll 64453, Devon RO, CR 97, Hatcher, *Duchy of Cornwall*, p. 222; Carus-Wilson, *op. cit.*, pp. 18–19 for Tiverton; BL Add. Roll 13975, which gives a lively picture of the cloth industry at Ottery St Mary, five fulling mills, places for washing, stacking, and stretching cloth, the occupations of webber, dyer, and tailor.

[402] PRO C 139/123; *Devon Lay Subsidy Rolls*, ed. Stoate, p. 63. Although a minute town, South Zeal was one of the places visited by the aulnager in 1395–6; its heavy involvement in the cloth industry continued until the late eighteenth century: PRO E 101/338/11; F. M. Eden, *The State of the Poor*, London, 1928 edn, p. 174 (S. Tawton). From Colyford, another decayed petty borough, there is evidence for fulling in the fifteenth century and tanning in the sixteenth: BL Add. Roll 13776 and Devon RO, 123M/E/77.

these humble "towns", as well as in the more flourishing country boroughs and ports, and in the countryside itself, were significant concentrations of industrial population and wealth which cannot have failed to stimulate regional specialization in agriculture among tenant farmers.

CHAPTER 8

PEASANT REBELLION AND PEASANT DISCONTENTS

A. INTRODUCTION

The three centuries between the Peasants' Revolt of 1381 and Monmouth's rebellion of 1685 are distinguished from other periods of English history by the recurrence of regional revolts. Many of these risings secured such wide popular support that the royal government was initially quite unable to resist them. In 1381 and 1450 the rebels from Essex and Kent were able to enter London. In 1489 the Yorkshire rebels occupied York. In 1497 the Cornishmen traversed without hindrance the whole of southern England and were rounded up only within sight of London.

The earlier series of these risings, down to 1497, had one main cause in common. They all represented, in one way or another, reactions to the worst deterioration in the quality of internal government that England had experienced since the civil wars of the thirteenth century. At least three of the risings, in 1381, 1489, and 1497, were triggered off by new taxes. But resentment at taxation was only a symptom of the popular exasperation against official corruption and oppression and the breakdown of justice. These things were a perennial cause of misery for the bulk of the population. In the words of the late-thirteenth-century English poem, the "Song of the Husbandman", the royal officials with their cheating and bullying "hunted the poor man as a hound hunts a hare on the hill".[1] These evils were inordinately aggravated in the late middle ages by an unexpected collapse of law and order. The surprising thing is not that popular risings occurred, but that there were not more of them.

The rising of 1381 marked also the culmination of widespread economic and social unrest, that can be traced back, in its more acute manifestations, at least, to the plague epidemic of 1348–9. The first thirty years after this first onset of plague were a time of exceptional

[1] T. Wright, ed., *Political Songs of England*, Camden OS VI, 1839, p. 152; Natalie Fryde (now von Stromer) gave much assistance with research for this chapter, which is gratefully acknowledged.

upheaval in the English countryside. The long-term effect of it all was to persuade the English landowners that direct exploitation of their estates was becoming too troublesome and risky. Between about 1380 and 1450 most of them pulled out of the direct management of their properties, leased the manorial demesnes for rents, and abandoned most of the demands on the labour of their servile tenants. Personal serfdom gradually dwindled and the restrictions on the migration of the former bondmen away from their native manors were eased. While these changes may have offered chances of economic improvement to some peasants, they were also very unsettling for society generally. The great increase in the number of uprooted and disoriented men searching for a living in new ways and in unfamiliar places increased the likelihood of popular tumults. It is no accident that the most important risings occurred in areas of fastest economic change like East Anglia, Kent, Essex, and other districts around London.

B. LANDLORDS AND TENANTS AFTER THE BLACK DEATH

Bubonic plague reached England through harbours in Dorset in early June 1348 and was causing havoc in Devon by the middle of that month.[2] It spread to most of the country during the next twenty months. In many localities the plague killed on average at least a third of their inhabitants, though some places lost twice as many, and a small minority of villages was even entirely depopulated. It is probable that the widespread poverty and habitual undernourishment of much of the population contributed to the high mortality from the plague. Equally serious was the further history of this disease. It became endemic in England, as in the rest of western Europe, especially in the towns, and its recurrent visitations continued to diminish still further the already shrunken population. These recurrent outbreaks had possibly a more demoralizing and disheartening effect on people than did the first visitation. Furthermore, in many localities the reserves of surplus manpower had been largely swept away by the first plague. Any further losses of inhabitants in subsequent epidemics were likely to damage the productive capacity of local communities so much that the survivors ceased to be able to raise sufficient crops. This appears to have happened in England in 1361–2. The second plague in those years apparently did not cause as many deaths as the first epidemic, but in 1362–4 prices of corn rose more considerably than in 1349–51. There was also a more marked increase in friction between landlords and their tenants and employees. A study of these developments in Essex suggests

[2] On 15 June the sheriff of Devon and his entire staff were all desperately ill and only the sheriff survived: PRO E 13/77, m.40.

that in that county "the plague of 1360–1 had more disturbing results than the more famous outbreak of 1349". The bishops of Worcester were forced into more decisive concessions to their tenants in 1362–4 than they had been obliged to make in 1349–53.[3]

Two more general outbreaks of plague in 1369 and 1374–5, together with a severe famine in 1370, brought the English population to its lowest point in the late 1370s. In a preamble to one of their petitions, the commons in the Good Parliament of 1376 claimed that "there is not a third part of the people or of the other things there used to be".[4] We know now that they were exaggerating, but they clearly did not think so. This is the background to the exceptional turbulence in the years immediately preceding the Great Revolt of 1381.

The statement about the lamentable decline in population formed part of the commons' general claim that the country was greatly "impoverished and destroyed". Our understanding of the causes and extent of popular discontent after 1348 must depend on an estimate of how far this was true. A comparison between England and France might be instructive. One way of testing the state of the English and French economies after 1349 is to ask whether the labour of the shrunken population was in fuller demand than before. In France the plague was followed by an initial jump in the wages of agricultural labourers, but the long-term decline of the French economy apparently tended to annul this. The fall in the productive capacity was so great that the main "result was a marked growth of poverty. Fiscal documents testify almost everywhere to an increase in the number of the poor."[5]

The English economy, though also hard hit, appears to have been undermined less severely. Unlike France, England was noted after 1349 for the attempts at a vigorous enforcement of the "freezing" of wages which were supposed to remain at a pre-plague level. This did not prove very effective, though it caused a vast amount of discontent among the labouring population. The long persistence of this policy, as well as its relative failure, reflect the relatively greater buoyancy of the English economy. But, as in France, the plague did not end widespread poverty and may even have increased it, because productive capacity

[3] N. Ritchie (née Kenyon), 'Labour conditions in Essex in the reign of Richard II', in E. M. Carus-Wilson, ed., *Essays in Economic History*, II, p. 103; E. B. Fryde, 'The tenants of the bishops of Coventry and Lichfield and of Worcester after the plague of 1348–9', in R. F. Hunnisett and J. B. Post, eds., *Medieval Legal Records edited in Memory of C. A. F. Meekings*, London, 1978, pp. 224–66, for this and subsequent references to the estates of the bishops of Worcester.

[4] Cited by G. A. Holmes, *The Good Parliament*, Oxford, 1975, p. 145.

[5] H. Dubois, 'Peste noire et viticulture en Bourgogne et Chablis', *Économies et Sociétés au Moyen Age. Mélanges offerts à Edouard Perroy*, Paris, 1973, pp. 428–38; M. Mollat and P. Wolff, *The Popular Revolutions of the Late Middle Ages*, London, 1973, p. 112.

declined, especially in districts which had always been poorer and less densely populated. This was particularly true of the northern counties. The revenues of Durham Cathedral priory derived from tithes in widely scattered villages in Northumberland, the Palatinate of Durham and Yorkshire, fell sharply between 1348 and 1350 by over £200, mainly because of a decline in the production of corn. Much of the loss was never made good in subsequent years.[6]

It must not be assumed that a considerable proportion of the surviving landless men and smallholders managed after the plague to improve substantially their economic position by taking over the larger holdings of their dead richer neighbours. For example, on the estates of the bishops of Worcester, who lost in 1348–9 about 36 per cent of their tenants, only the smallholdings were soon filled up. Few new tenants could be found for the larger holdings and the majority of those remained vacant. It is true that the rents and services demanded for them may have deterred some prospective takers. But the large amount of land that remained untenanted suggests that we must look for some more fundamental explanations. Presumably the bulk of the peasantry was too poor and too lacking in necessary animals and equipment to embark on such large ventures.

It remains true that the difficulties experienced by the bishops of Worcester, as by many other landowners, sprang to some extent from their reluctance to offer sufficiently far-reaching concessions to new tenants. The society in which they had grown up was used to occasional upheavals caused by war, famine, or epidemics among men or domestic animals. But the basic pattern of fairly stable prices and wages was not usually seriously disturbed for long by such disasters. Even after the exceptional catastrophe of 1348–9 the members of the landowning class were inclined to assume that values of all things would soon revert to roughly the levels of the years before the Black Death and that no economic changes would be allowed to alter the established social hierarchy. The idea that far-reaching and irreversible social and economic changes were henceforth inevitable was contrary to their past experience and profoundly repugnant to them. As was to be expected, the temptation to behave as if nothing decisive or enduring had happened was strongest among the officials of the royal exchequer, but similar conservative assumptions coloured the outlook of most members of the aristocracy and of the officials maintained by them.

Faced with the disaster of the plague, the exchequer officials continued in most cases to enforce the normal exchequer rules. They continued to assume that economic values did not alter over long

[6] Dobson, *Durham Priory*, p. 271.

periods, and that it was quite practicable to charge accountants after the disaster of 1348–9 "according to the ancient accounts before the pestilence", to quote the complaint of the exasperated custodian of the vacant bishopric of Norwich in 1355.[7]

Where, in the years after the first plague, custodies of vacant bishoprics were entrusted to experienced local officials, these men knew that they would be courting disaster if they tried to fulfil the expectations of the exchequer. At Worcester in 1349 and 1353, the local escheator from the start prudently claimed allowance for revenues that had been lost through the plague, knowing that the local juries would in every case uphold his statements. Where the custodians had no such connections with local interests, disasters befell the manorial officials and other tenants of the vacant episcopal estates. After the vacancy at York, lasting from July 1352 to February 1353, fourteen different manorial reeves and rent collectors from eleven estates were menaced with imprisonment by the custodian, William Kellesey, a veteran exchequer official. They were rescued by the new archbishop, John Thoresby, who became a surety on their behalf for debts totalling £48 6s. 4d., "in order to save the said tenants from imprisonment".[8]

Worse things happened on the Canterbury estates after the death from plague in May 1349 of Archbishop John Offord.[9] The royal custodian, William Epworth, was both unscrupulous and inefficient. His total claims against various manorial officials amounted initially to £264. Some of the officials were imprisoned for lengthy periods in 1353–5. At Charing and Maidstone the liabilities of the reeves were extended to all the tenants (the "homage") who had elected these men at the height of the epidemic, after the deaths of former archiepiscopal reeves. The main point at issue was Epworth's demand that the entire "homage" at each of these manors should be held liable for the debts of the deceased reeves, though according to the tenants this was contrary to the custom of the archiepiscopal estates in Kent. The "homage" at Maidstone, charged with £51, did not consist merely of humble peasants. It comprised the prior of Leeds, the master of the school at Maidstone, and members of some prosperous landed families, including at least one knight. In the summer of 1353 the sheriff of Kent seized the goods of tenants of Maidstone worth £30, but could find no buyers for them.

These events may have left lasting and bitter memories. Some of Epworth's most unjust demands had been made at Otford. He had been

---

[7] PRO SC 6/1297/26.

[8] PRO E 368/124, mm.256–9; E 368/126, St. Vis. Comp., Mich., mm.10–11, 19–23; E 136/12/10 and 13/25A.

[9] PRO E 368/122, m.260; E 368/125, mm.265–6; E 13/76–8, *passim*.

trying to exact amercements imposed on men who had failed to attend the lord's court at the height of the epidemic, rents due from holdings which had in fact lapsed into the lord's hands through deaths of tenants, and revenues from deserted mills that could not be leased. It is not, perhaps, surprising that during another archiepiscopal vacancy, after the murder of Archbishop Sudbury by the Kentish rebels in June 1381, the men of Otford should have again defied royal custodians and should have refused to perform customary services.[10]

Most private landlords could not afford to behave quite so intransigently as did the exchequer and some of its agents. In 1349 vacant land was much more plentiful and labourers scarcer than at any time that men could remember. The majority of landlords found it prudent, therefore, to make some concessions to their tenants. We have for this the testimony of the Leicester chronicler, Henry Knighton. "The great men of the land, and other lesser lords who had tenants, remitted the payment of their rents, lest their tenants should go away on account of the scarcity of servants and the high price of all things – some half their rents, some more, some less, some for one, two, or three years according as they could come to an agreement with them."[11] Knighton is describing temporary relaxations of demands, which the landlords were hoping soon to reverse. Modern studies of particular estates confirm that several major landowners did this successfully, like, for example, the abbot of Battle at Hutton in Essex and, more speedily, on his most efficiently exploited estate of Alciston in Sussex. On the Black Prince's properties in the Duchy of Cornwall a large proportion of the revenue came from contractual 7-year leases, which could be flexibly modified, and the prince's council ordered considerable remissions of payments until 1356 because "the surviving tenants were so impoverished that they would relinquish their holdings if the fines and tallages were not remitted".[12]

Knighton goes on to list other concessions by landlords. "Similarly, those who had let lands on yearly labour-services to tenants, as is the custom in the case of villeins, were obliged to relieve and remit these services, either excusing them entirely, or taking them on easier terms, in the form of a small rent, lest their houses should be irreparably ruined and the land should remain completely uncultivated."[13] He does not treat any of these concessions as irrevocable, but it would have been, for instance, very difficult to revive labour services after they had been entirely suspended. In the years immediately after the first plague major English landowners were still trying to avoid far-reaching and virtually

[10] A. Réville and C. Petit-Dutaillis, Le Soulèvement des Travailleurs d'Angleterre en 1381, p. 222.
[11] Dobson, Peasants' Revolt, p. 63.   [12] Hatcher, Duchy of Cornwall, p. 104.
[13] Dobson, Peasants' Revolt, p. 63.

irreversible concessions to their villeins. Local conditions determined in each case what bargains they were able to strike. The great divergences in the nature and size of concessions wrung from unwilling landlords was in itself a very disorganizing feature of the years after the first plague. Different solutions might be forced on neighbouring lords and even the same landowner might be compelled to treat differently estates within easy reach of each other. Peasants everywhere came to learn that changes were occurring all around them and this was most potent knowledge, weakening the power of the landlords to deal with their dependent men.

At this stage, as indeed at all subsequent stages, the gradual collapse of the manorial type of estate was mostly brought about not by organized violence but through an accumulation of petty acts of obstruction and insubordination on the part of the peasantry. They were refusing to take up vacant holdings except on their own terms. They were managing to make less use of various services provided by their lords and constituting seigneurial monopolies, such as the compulsory use of the seigneurial mill or the pasturing of animals on the lord's meadows. There was a sharp rise in the number of minor delinquencies in the performance of customary labour services. On the estates of the abbey of Ramsey "the court rolls reveal fines for such wholesale non-performance of certain work over the two decades after the Black Death that it may be logical to consider the lord's acceptance of these fines as another form of commutation".[14] There was much piecemeal withholding of rents and of other customary payments, and, especially, of any amercements that might be imposed by the lords' courts. Fear of desertion by tenants formed the ultimate sanction that persuaded many landowners into prudent compromises, though flights of villeins were apparently less common at first than they were destined to become after the two further plagues of 1361–2 and 1369 and the famine of 1370.

The great variety of concessions forced upon major landowners in the first decade after the Black Death can be illustrated from the estates of the two adjoining bishoprics of Worcester and of Coventry and Lichfield. By the autumn of 1349 the plague had produced extreme demoralization on the estates of the bishops of Worcester. Bishop Wolstan's death on 6 August 1349 was followed, while the plague was still raging, by widespread plunder of animals and other goods from the episcopal estates. Such things were always likely to occur on the deaths of bishops, and of secular lords as well, unless a powerful adult heir was able to intervene. But the depredations on the Worcester estates reached a colossal scale in 1349, the plundered goods that could not be

---

[14] Raftis, *Estates of Ramsey Abbey*, p. 257, n.15.

recovered being appraised by outside arbitrators at £766 13s. 4d. Though Wolstan's successor, John Thoresby, was the king's chancellor, he could do nothing to trace most of the offenders and was reduced merely to ordering that "certain sons of perdition whose names we do not know" were to be solemnly excommunicated on Sundays after Mass in all the parish churches of the diocese.[15]

Thoresby's brief episcopate of less than three years produced some general concessions to the episcopal tenants. Each new bishop was entitled to a "recognition" from his servile tenants. During the vacancy of 1302–3 the royal custodians had collected £40 7s. 4d. Thoresby appears to have carried out a revision of the quotas due from each village. During the vacancy of 1352–3, after Thoresby's translation to York, the royal custodians put into operation this reduced scale of payments and collected £3. Thereafter the size of recognition fluctuated somewhat, reaching £5 again by 1364. Seventy years later, during the vacancy of 1433, the royal custodians, acting perhaps at the instigation of the royal exchequer, tried to restore the recognition to its 1302 level. This provoked the concerted refusal of the tenants on all the episcopal estates to pay anything at all. Their successful resistance ruined this source of income for ever, not only for custodians during subsequent vacancies but for the bishops as well. Bishop Carpenter tried to collect it in 1444, but received nothing. The reduction of the annual tallage raised from all the servile tenants also probably went back to Thoresby's time. At Bredon, in eastern Worcestershire, it was being levied in 1375–6 at the rate of 6d. per virgate, instead of its pre-plague level of 2s. per virgate, though in that year the bishop's auditors tried to challenge this reduction.[16]

The great majority of the bishop's estates remained as going concerns. On most of them there is no evidence of deliberate immediate conversions of villein tenements into rent-paying holdings, though all manner of piecemeal concessions had to be made to face up to the brute fact that a part of the tenantry had vanished for the time being. One of the few exceptions was the formerly flourishing manor of Hanbury by Droitwich. Out of the 38 holders of half-virgates in 1299 only 4 tenants remained at the end of 1349, holding between them four virgates. By the end of the reign of Edward III the bishop gave up altogether the direct exploitation of his demesnes on this estate. Fladbury in the valley of the Avon was particularly crippled by the plague, as were other villages along the river.[17] Of all the bishop's Worcestershire estates it secured the highest remission of a royal tax in 1353. It is not surprising that by 1353 the bishop's surviving tenants at

[15] Thoresby's episcopal register: Worcs. RO, BA 2648/3(11), pp. 11, 49, 51.
[16] Worcs. RO, BA 2636/158/92014–15.
[17] Worcs. RO, BA 705/7; PRO E 13/82B, mm.32v., 73.

Fladbury were freed from the duty of ploughing and harrowing their lord's demesne in Lent "because their tenure has been changed into a different service", which points to a permanent commutation. The only recorded instance of violent resistance to the continuation of labour services comes, characteristically enough, from the wealthiest and most populous of all the episcopal estates, Henbury Saltmarsh, lying just outside Bristol. Some time in 1351 strangers from outside the manor plundered the bishop's goods, seriously injured one of his servants and "by conspiracy procured his bondmen and other tenants of the same town to refuse to do their services due to him and so he had to expend a great sum before he could compel them by law to do the said services".[18] As in 1381, the men of the most prosperous parts of the country were the most restless and most ready to resort to violence, attacking in this instance even the Lord Chancellor of England.

Bishop Roger Northburgh of Coventry and Lichfield, who held that see from 1322 to 1358, fared worse than his neighbour of Worcester. He was an experienced administrator, who had been keeper of the king's wardrobe throughout the civil war of 1321–2, and had subsequently served twice as the king's treasurer. Though he lost far fewer tenants he was forced into much more far-reaching surrenders of authority over his villeins.[19] On his four Warwickshire estates none of the vacated $12\frac{3}{4}$ virgates was ever reoccupied in his lifetime, because nobody else wanted "to perform the services which the previous tenants had been accustomed to render before the pestilence". Elsewhere, he was able to fill many of the vacant holdings, but only at the cost of a permanent remission of all servile burdens to the new tenants, even if the newcomers were heirs or close relatives of the previous holders. One main group of his properties lay in south-eastern Staffordshire, several adjoining Cannock forest. The presence of ample woodland pastures, the scattering of some of the tenants in small hamlets, the abundant possibilities of reclaiming new land within the forest area,[20] were all factors encouraging the bishop's unfree men to assert a measure of independence in the decade after 1348. Brewood was one of the most important episcopal manors, where the bishop owned in 1358 four carucates of demesne arable, an unusually large amount of land. In 1377, there were as many as 280 "adults" at Brewood, so that it is reasonable to conjecture that quite a considerable population existed there in 1358.[21] Yet in the place of twenty holders of servile half-virgates who had died in 1349, only ten new tenants

[18] CPR, 1350–4, p. 275.
[19] PRO E 368/132, St. Vis. Comp. Pascha mm.15–21 and 368/133, St. Vis. Comp., Mich., mm.10–14; SC 6/1132/7; BL Add. Ms. 6165, pp. 189–206.
[20] Hilton, English Peasantry, p. 230.   [21] PRO E 179/177/20.

could be found in Bishop Northburgh's lifetime, and these were now all rent-paying tenants, freed from servile tallage and all labour services. The bishop badly missed the labour of the new tenants as well as the services due from the nine half-virgates that could not be filled. He had to demand instead more labour from his remaining twenty-nine tenants, who had again to perform some services that had been normally commuted in the past.

C. EMPLOYERS, LABOURERS, AND THE LABOUR LAWS AFTER THE BLACK DEATH

On 18 June 1349, while the plague was still raging and no parliament could be convened safely, the royal council issued an ordinance regulating prices, wages, and conditions of employment of servile dependants and of other labourers and servants. Its most important objective was to "freeze" wages at a low, pre-plague level. This ordinance remained in force, with some alterations, for the remainder of the reign of Edward III. The first parliament held after the plague, early in 1351, enacted a Statute of Labourers, but this merely clarified and amended some of the provisions of the conciliar ordinance. During the next twenty-five years there was a number of further alterations, brought about mostly by the petitions of the landowning interests in the house of commons. "It was the ordinance, not the statute that was enforced in the courts until the reign of Richard II," when it was at long last put on a statutory basis in November 1378. With further re-enactments in 1388 and during the fifteenth century, necessitated above all by a need to revise upwards the scales of permitted wages, this legislation remained in force until 1497 when it was abruptly rescinded.[22]

The Ordinance of Labourers was an attempt to regulate on a national scale matters which, in a much less uniform way, were the subject of local restrictions on numerous manors. Long before 1348 inhabitants of English villages were used to elaborate regulation of agricultural practices. This was particularly essential in villages which practised open-field agriculture. Over and above this, landlords as a matter of course minutely regulated the conduct of their villein tenants and other servile dependants. It was the essence of servile tenure and status that anything that suited the lord's interests might be demanded of his bondmen and anything that hurt the lord was sure to be prohibited. The study of any long series of manorial court rolls brings out the oppressive interference of the lords with the lives and conduct

[22] S. B. Chrimes, *English Constitutional Ideas in the XV Century*, Cambridge, 1936, p. 235, n.4; *SR*, II, pp. 11 (2 Richard II, c. 8), 637 (12 Henry VII, c. 3).

of their servile dependants. For example, in the reign of Elizabeth an official of the bishop of Hereford compiled from the medieval court rolls of his master a digest of regulations applied in the past on the episcopal estates. One of the most striking features is the great number and variety of offences, some of them seemingly quite trivial, for which servile tenants had been deprived of their tenements.[23] As long as land was scarce, and peasants competed fiercely with each other for such tenements as lords were willing to concede to them, men with holdings would not lightly disobey and there was little danger that many of them would flee. While labourers were plentiful, under-employment the common lot of many, and wages correspondingly low, landless men could be kept on the manors of their birth by fear that there might be even less employment outside them. It is probably no accident that the Statute of Labourers treated the wage-rates around 1346 as the norm because this was a time of economic recession, when wages were depressed.

The recession in the decade before the Black Death had been aggravated by the outbreak of the Hundred Years' War in 1337. Even before the war had begun, some parts of England were experiencing a long-term economic depression which wartime taxation turned into acute distress. When things were at their worst, in 1339–40, contemporaries feared a popular uprising. But there was as yet no widespread withdrawal by landlords from direct exploitation of their domanial estates. Without the catastrophe of the plague the structure of seigneurial regulations on which it rested could have been maintained a good deal longer, though even before 1348 landlords would have liked to strengthen their legal powers still further by getting more support from the royal courts. One of the drawbacks of their position was that manorial courts of different lords did not co-operate, and fugitives from seigneurial jurisdiction were usually immune from molestation outside the lordship of their master. Lords could seek royal support to recover fugitive villeins, but seldom did so as this involved much cost and trouble. Just before 1348 some lords were seeking an improvement in their legal position against fugitive villeins. In 1347 Edward III consented to a parliamentary petition demanding that in future all contested cases of villein status should be tried in the county of the alleged serf's birth. This seemed a reasonable procedure for ascertaining the true facts, but a counter-petition complained in vain that leading lords would completely dominate the local juries.[24]

It was a symptom of the new situation created by the plague that in 1349 landowners needed royal intervention over a much wider range

[23] A. T. Bannister, 'Manorial customs on the Hereford bishopric estates', *EHR*, XLIII, 1928, pp. 218–30.   [24] *Rot. Parl.*, II, pp. 173 (no. 66), 180 (no. 21), 193 (no. 73).

of conflicts with their dependants. Their grip over their servile tenants and other labouring employees was clearly loosening, and the royal government had to help them over matters that had hitherto been fairly adequately regulated by the manorial courts or the councils of individual landlords. In France, a royal ordinance of February 1351, exactly contemporary with the first English Statute of Labourers, tried to deal with a similar situation by allowing the moderate increase in prices and wages that seemed unavoidable. The English regulations were far more drastic. As has been stressed before, the chief aim of the new legislation was to "freeze" wages and prices at the level around 1346. In practice, the justices enforcing this new legislation were above all concerned with wages. A large part of the English landowning class still exploited their demesnes directly. Since the disaster of the plague the demands of their servants, and of agricultural labourers in general, for higher wages threatened to curtail drastically the profits of large-scale farming. The incomes of moderately wealthy and especially of the lesser landowners were particularly menaced. As a parliamentary petition of 1368 reminds us, they included people who were not lords of manors and did not possess any villeins of their own, but farmed substantial properties using only personal servants and hired labourers. Hence the fierce demand by this group of petitioners that fines imposed on delinquent labourers should be doubled.[25]

From this class of moderately wealthy landowners were recruited the men who ran the local government for the king and represented their shires in the house of commons. Their need for cheaper labour demanded, and of course received, a speedy recognition. Lionel Bradenham, owner of the single village of Langenhoe, four miles south of Colchester which he continuously supplied with food, provides a good example of a local squire who would be sure to enforce zealously the Ordinance of Labourers, as he himself relied entirely on hired labour. He acted as a justice of labourers for Essex from 1355 to 1362, abused his authority and extorted money from his neighbours. He was finally removed after complaints from Colchester which he had been terrorizing with armed gangs.[26]

Unlike most medieval English enactments, which nobody intended to observe seriously, the wage regulations of 1349–51 continued for several decades to be enthusiastically applied. It was, perhaps, the most zealously enforced ordinance in medieval English history. Some of the provisions of the royal ordinance of 1349 tried to apply uniformly to the whole country regulations that some manorial lords were habitually enforcing on their own manors. On the estates of the abbey of Ramsey

[25] *Ibid.*, p. 296 (no. 15).   [26] Britnell, 'Production for the market', p. 385.

(Hunts.) since at least 1299 a succession of manorial ordinances had tried to keep down the price of ale.[27] This subject looms large in 1352 in the earliest surviving roll of the justices enforcing the Ordinance of Labourers in Wiltshire. To come to graver matters, landlords were trying to stop labourers from leaving their native villages during harvest. This seems to have been a fairly common manorial regulation and there is one printed instance of it as early as 1340. It reappears in the Statute of Labourers of 1351.

Some of the provisions of the ordinance of 1349 resulted in numerous prosecutions: the receiving of excessive wages was the offence most frequently mentioned in indictments and most of the accused were members of the labouring classes. These cases were relatively uncomplicated, except for the computation of the exact amounts received in excess of the permitted wages, and because of this the resultant fines fluctuated erratically. An important clause of the ordinance insisted that servants should undertake to remain in the employment of the same master for at least a year. They could be prosecuted for an earlier withdrawal from service, though the employers could dismiss them at any time. In practice the justices found these cases of alleged breach of contract very troublesome and frequently adjourned them. The ordinance also gave the lords the first claim on the labour of their bondmen. The need for such a provision illustrates the weakening of the lords' grip over their serfs; it produced some very awkward cases where lords claimed the labour of men who had entered into regular yearly contracts with other employers. An oft-quoted, though presumably exceptional case, concerned the claim of the Cistercian abbot of Meaux in Yorkshire that a family of particularly wealthy villeins of the abbey had suborned some of his other serfs into contracts of annual service.[28] The abbot won, and most such cases were similarly decided in favour of the lord. Lastly, the ordinance gave to the justices the power of compelling able-bodied labourers without regular employment to enter into the service of employers chosen for them. This was specifically intended to increase the supply of agricultural labour. Prosecutions under this clause produced some very interesting evidence of the drifting of former agricultural workers into a great variety of other occupations.

The fiscal preoccupations of Sir William Shareshull, the chief justice of the king's bench from 1350 to 1361, were probably an important force behind the vigorous enforcement of the labour legislation in the first decade after the Black Death. Shareshull was a great believer in using the judicial machinery to raise revenue. In the case of the labour

---

[27] Raftis, *Tenure and Mobility*, pp. 112, 126.
[28] *Chronica Monasterii de Melsa*, ed. Bond, III, p. 128.

legislation, it was probably Shareshull's idea that the revenue from the fines might be used to reduce the burden of ordinary direct taxation.[29] In order to finance the war with France the direct taxes (lay fifteenths and tenths) went on being collected during most of the decade after 1348. Since 1334, the royal government had given up its previous attempts to base these taxes on new assessments and agreed to a fixed yield of slightly under £38,000. Each county contributed henceforth its accustomed quota and the contribution of every locality within each shire was also fairly stable. With the passage of time this arrangement became increasingly unpopular, as the fixed assessment was becoming progressively obsolescent, but it was politically dangerous to devise a satisfactory alternative. It was in order to escape from this particular straitjacket that the English crown ultimately resorted to poll taxes in 1377–81, thus provoking the Great Revolt of 1381.

Nothing so radical was attempted in 1349. The heavy mortality from the plague had made the fixed assessment of taxes absurdly out of date, and it was felt that something must be done to alleviate the worst injustices caused by it. As a concession to his impoverished subjects, the king authorized in November 1349 an arrangement under which the fines from the breaches of the labour legislation in each shire should be deducted from its accustomed quota of taxation. The new scheme was put into operation in connection with the three-fifteenths and tenths levied in 1352–4. In each county the revenue from fines was to be used to alleviate the tax burden of localities most impoverished by the plague. The scheme was certain to stimulate still further the zeal of the special justices of labourers commissioned to enforce this new legislation. It is impossible to calculate exactly the revenue from the fines and the amounts deducted from taxes, but in 1352–4 the latter came to at least £8,371 or $7\frac{1}{3}$ per cent of the total assessment of three-fifteenths and tenths levied in those years. In a few shires the proportion of tax remitted on account of fines was very high. It rose in 1352 to 58 per cent in Essex, which seems always to have attracted a record number of prosecutions for the breaches of the labour laws. The proportion in Buckinghamshire was 50 per cent, and it amounted to around one-third in Berkshire, Cambridgeshire, and the Parts of Lindsey in Lincolnshire.[30]

Writing of the first decade after the Black Death, B. H. Putnam was convinced that "regulations as efficiently carried out as these were, for a short period", were bound to have some effect. She concluded that

[29] B. H. Putnam, 'Chief Justice Shareshull and the economic and legal code of 1351–52', *Univ. of Toronto Law J.*, v, 1944, pp. 251–81.

[30] Figures based upon Putnam, *The Enforcement of the Statutes of Labourers*, with supplementary material from various classes of exchequer records.

758   PEASANT REBELLION AND DISCONTENTS

"wages were not kept at the statutory level, but they were kept for ten years at a lower level than would have resulted from a régime of free competition".[31] She may be right. The labour legislation strengthened the hands of those employers who, because they managed to preserve their authority over their bondmen or were able for local reasons to secure sufficient labour, remained in any case in a strong position. On the manor of Alciston in Sussex, an exceptionally well-managed estate of the abbot of Battle, wages soared in 1349–50. But in the following year wages of the *famuli*, the permanent agricultural servants, were reduced again to the level of 1347 in accordance with the ordinance, and stayed there for some years, while the wages of temporarily hired labour also declined. In this, as in most other respects, at Alciston "the plague caused only a slight and temporary dislocation" and the area of demesne under crops reached its highest extension, of 475 acres, in the year of the Peasants' Revolt.[32]

The number of people prosecuted under the labour legislation, however, seems to have represented only a small proportion of all the offenders. Many of the employers were among the worst culprits, but there is no evidence that people of higher social rank were prosecuted for paying excessive wages. The labour legislation was fairly ineffective, especially in the more developed areas of the country, because many employers found it to their advantage to ignore it and could afford to do so. For example, the estate officials of the bishops of Worcester habitually broke the wage regulations. At the Warwickshire judicial sessions at Stratford in 1357 the justices treated 3d. as the lawful daily wage for reaping corn and several labourers were fined for receiving 6d. a day. Yet in August 1372 the reeve of the bishop's manor of Hampton, very near Stratford, paid 6½d. a day to over thirty men employed in gathering harvest over a period of nearly two weeks. That autumn the harvesting of corn on 172 acres of the bishop's demesne at Hampton worked out at 12½d. per acre and the same thing happened again in 1378.[33] These were rates far in excess of lawful limits and, to find parallels for them on other major estates, one would have to go back to the properties of the bishop of Winchester at the height of the disaster of 1349, before the ordinance had begun to be enforced.

Some men appear to have acted habitually as agents for procuring labour for others. At the Suffolk sessions of June 1361 a man described as a weaver was accused of being a "common procurator of agricultural *famuli* for taking them outside their vill in the autumn".[34] At the

---

[31] Putnam, *op. cit.*, p. 221.   [32] Brent, 'Alciston manor', p. 95.

[33] Putnam, *op. cit.*, p. 226; Worcs. RO, BA 2636/163/92160, 92162.

[34] B. H. Putnam, ed., *Proceedings before the Justices of the Peace in the Fourteenth and Fifteenth Centuries, Edward III to Richard III*, London, 1938, p. 343.

Norfolk manor of Forncett, belonging to the countess of Norfolk, a man was indicted for leading each autumn six or eight others outside the manor to work at higher wages. This is not surprising, as by 1378 the countess had leased most of her demesne at Forncett and had largely lost control over her servile tenantry of disgruntled smallholders. Another Norfolk man was indicted in 1378 for suborning labourers of various people and then hiring them out to others. At the bishop of Worcester's manor of Bibury, in south-eastern Gloucestershire, on a single day in the autumn of 1372, the reeve brought from outside as many as 127 men, hired at the illegal wage of 5d. a day, to gather and bind the lord's corn, in addition to employing all the bishop's tenants from Bibury.[35]

The prosecutions before the king's bench in Essex in 1389–90, during which 791 persons were indicted for offences under the Statute of Labourers, reveal a very ambiguous pattern of proceedings. Some of the accused were hardened offenders, for whom fines were simply a part of anticipated business expenses. It is noticeable that the men who are known to have been taking up leases of manorial demesnes do not appear as prosecutors of their employees; presumably their profits depended not on economies over wages but on other factors. A few of these enterprising farmers, however, saw their labourers prosecuted at the behest of the local manorial lords, as happened for example at Thaxted, where the lord apparently wanted to put pressure upon them shortly before their leases were due for renewal. Some of the proceedings were obviously part of an obscure local pattern of economic rivalries, feuds, and jealousies, and we are watching only a small tip of the iceberg of delinquency, where it suited someone's interest to prosecute.

The labour legislation stirred popular hatred out of all proportion to any economic effectiveness that it might have achieved. It led to numerous outlawries of men who refused to face trial. A petition of the commons in the Good Parliament of 1376 claimed that this was no hardship for men who had no intention of returning to their counties of origin and were never likely to be tracked down in other parts of the country. This might be true as far as their chances of finding new, gainful employment were concerned, but meant painful losses of contact with relatives and friends.[36]

The statute of 1351 was followed during the next thirty years by several petitions from the commons demanding still sterner measures. Most of them, including some that were highly impracticable, were rejected by the royal government. We lack the roll of the parliament

[35] Worcs. RO, BA 2636/160/92051.   [36] Rot. Parl., II, pp. 340–1 (no. 116).

of 1361 and cannot be sure that the exceptionally vicious statute of that year originated in a petition from the commons, but it probably did. The statute included a provision that labourers who had escaped from their masters and had been outlawed for not standing trial were, on recapture and conviction, to be branded on the forehead with the letter F, for falsehood, if their accusers insisted on this. The final section of this clause of the statute included various regulations which were likely in practice to diminish the number of occasions on which this barbarous penalty would be applied. They read like practical safeguards tacked on to the original petition by the royal judges.[37]

The enforcement of the Ordinance of Labourers with its various subsequent "enlargements" increased the perennial popular hostility towards the local agents of the king, and the justices of labourers became the special target of popular hatred. Their activities constitute one of the most important causes of the revolts of 1381. It is no accident that "the area of the greatest intensity of the revolt coincides with the area for which there is definite evidence of the greatest efforts at enforcement of the labour laws". Langland, in a version of his poem dating from around 1377, makes Piers the Plowman curse "the kynge and al his conseille after, Suche lawes to loke laborers to greve".[38]

D. LORDS, SERFS, AND SERFDOM

In granting, late in 1381, a pardon to nobles and others who had taken the law into their own hands in suppressing the revolts in the summer and autumn, the royal government described the rebels as "villeins and other malefactors". The rebellion was clearly regarded as, above all, a rising of the villeins. This is also what John Gower thought of it: in his terrifying description of the rising, which for a few days drove him into hiding in the forests, he speaks of it as a rebellion of "servile peasants against nobles and gentlefolk".[39]

The eyewitness account of the irruption of the rebels into London in the *Anonimalle Chronicle*, probably written by William Pakington, the keeper of the king's wardrobe, assumes that "the supreme and overriding purpose of the revolt was the abolition of villeinage and all that went with it. This was the heart of the matter."[40] "Nede they fre be most" is the summing up of the anonymous writer of the hostile

[37] *SR*, I, p. 367.

[38] Putnam, ed., *Proceedings before the Justices of the Peace*, p. cxxiii; W. W. Skeat, ed., *The Vision of William concerning Piers the Plowman*, Oxford, 1886, I, pp. 222–3.

[39] *Rot. Parl.*, III, p. 103 (no. 30); the original preface to Gower's *Vox Clamantis*, in G. C. Macaulay, *The Complete Works of John Gower*, IV, Oxford, 1902, p. xxxi.

[40] V. H. Galbraith, 'Thoughts about the Peasants' Revolt', in F. R. H. Du Boulay and C. M. Barron, eds., *The Reign of Richard II: Essays in Honour of May McKisack*, London, 1971, p. 53.

poem, "The Rebellion of Jack Straw", and it was the keynote of the rising to most of the contemporary chroniclers. The demand for freedom from serfdom was certainly "the one most persistently presented when the rebels were directly negotiating with the king".[41] Villeins hated their servile tenure and status because it made them rightless in their relations with their lords. As the court book of Ramsey abbey put it, their holdings were "servile tenements held in bondage at the will of the lord for customary services and obligations".[42] But the terms of their tenure only remained customary as long as it suited the lord and he could, and did, change them at his will. The limits of how far he could do so were purely practical, not legal.

In the years 1349–81, on a larger scale than ever before, lords were being forced into reconsidering drastically by what methods they might maintain the profitability of their estates. Whatever they did, the customary position of their tenants was bound to be modified and in most places this was likely to create new causes of friction between lords and their bondmen. Some historians have used the term "seigneurial reaction" to describe some of the efforts of lords to cope with rising costs, more fluctuating profits, and difficulties of securing enough labour, as well as with a fall in some of the traditional sources of revenue. Such a description may be appropriate to cover what happened on some estates, but it does suggest a picture of concerted seigneurial pressure in the country as a whole which obscures the great diversity of problems facing different landlords and the corresponding variety of their responses to this disturbing situation.

Where direct management of manorial demesnes by their lords persisted for several years after 1349, as it apparently did on the majority of manors, this did frequently result in the more vigorous exaction of the customary labour services. They were demanded more frequently from the surviving servile tenants while the number of services temporarily commuted for annual payments declined markedly. Great Shelford, a Cambridgeshire manor of the bishop of Ely, does not appear to have been seriously affected by the first plague: there was only a slight decline in the number of servile tenements occupied by tenants.[43] Yet a comparison between the manorial accounts for 1346–8 and those for 1350–2 shows that the bishop's revenue from the commutation of services was halved in the years immediately after the plague. There was a corresponding fall in the number of services that the bishop's officials still continued to commute.[44]

---

[41] T. Wright, ed., *Political Poems and Songs relating to English History*, RS, 1859, I, p. 225; R. H. Hilton, *Bond Men Made Free*, p. 224.   [42] Raftis, *Tenure and Mobility*, p. 201.
[43] Based on a comparison of the pre-plague accounts, PRO SC 6/1133/2, mm.1–2, with a royal survey, BL Add. Ms. 6165, pp. 263–4.   [44] PRO SC 6/1133/2, mm.1–6.

There are some well-documented examples of other kinds of intensified seigneurial pressures on servile tenants and of determined efforts to step up the collection of arrears. One such occurred in the 1360s at Hutton in Essex, a manor of the abbot of Battle, lying only three miles from Brentwood, where violent resistance to the royal poll-tax commissioners in May 1381 triggered off the Great Revolt. On the properties of the abbey of St Albans, after a long period of slack management before the Black Death, a vigorous attempt at recovering arrears and at enforcing the abbey's domanial claims occurred between 1353 and 1374, when John Mote was the abbey's cellarer. This may help to explain the hatred felt towards him in 1381 by the rebels from the town of St Albans and from the abbey's manors.

After the first plague of 1348–9 a large proportion of the manorial lords still tried hard to preserve their traditional arrangement of direct domanial exploitation. After three more plagues and a major famine, between 1361 and 1375, this determination to avoid drastic changes began to crumble. Instances of partial or total leasing of demesnes multiply from the late 1360s onwards. This might have removed one cause of potential friction between servile peasants and their lords, but because of the continued legal rightlessness of the villeins it could not end their resentments and their fears. The reserve of powers retained by the lords over their serfs could be put to all sorts of novel uses. One simple example comes from the estates of the cathedral priory of Durham. After the priory had leased some of its demesnes around 1370, it tried to compensate for the loss of corn from these properties by imposing new obligations on its servile tenants. Henceforth the priory had the first claim on the surplus corn of these tenants and they could sell it to others only by permission of the priory's officials.

Where demesnes had been leased completely by lords, this was usually followed by a fairly complete commutation of the labour services of the tenants into rent charges. For many serfs their villein tenure was thus becoming changed into something more fixed and less burdensome; but as long as their servile status remained unaltered, these changes could be reversed. Any concessions that the lord had made to his villeins could be revoked as long as they remained his bondmen.

We know now that most of the leases of manorial demesnes became permanent, but contemporaries had no such certainty. The early leases were often made in a manner suggesting that this might be a temporary expedient. Besides, there was no assurance that a succession of farmers could be found who would be prepared to take up leases of demesnes on the terms acceptable to the lords. Though the lords' preference for farming out demesnes became more manifest as time went on, their ability to do so lagged behind. On 1 December 1374 the council of the earl of Warwick deliberated about the leasing of the manor of Flamstead in Hertfordshire. Its previous farmer, a member of a prominent London mercantile family, was replaced by one of the earl's own serfs, but the latter only agreed to take up the lease on condition that he would be excused £3 for each of the first two years of his contract out of the annual rent of 40 marks.[45] A report of the auditors of John of Gaunt, duke of Lancaster, in 1388, revealed a still more disturbing situation. The manors of Methwold and Snettisham in Norfolk, which used to yield £166 when farmed, had reverted to the duke's direct management for "improvement". Presumably they had deteriorated in the hands of the farmers, but the costs of direct exploitation were so high that they now yielded only £78.[46]

Though demesnes might be leased and labour services commuted, the lord's bondmen had every reason to remain insecure in their new way of life. Many of them were turning to industrial employment or were taking advantage of the diminution of their seigneurial burdens to develop and increase their holdings. This helps to explain why the demand for the abolition of serfdom was very widespread and vociferous in the regions, like East Anglia and Essex, where servile tenure was being commuted rapidly and rural industries were growing most prosperously. Thaxted in Essex provides a model example of such a village. Its demesnes had been leased for some twenty years before the Great Revolt of 1381 and almost all the labour services had been commuted. Over half its population in 1381 practised various crafts, including about a hundred metal workers, mostly cutlers. Yet during the rising of 1381 the inhabitants destroyed the manorial custumal recording their servile charges and disabilities. An unofficial copy of it was being secretly preserved in the village by some of the lord's tenants, but they refused to show it to the lord's council when a new seigneurial survey of Thaxted was being drawn up in 1393. They clearly wanted to keep the lord in the dark about his previous claims and dreaded, presumably, that he might restore these older arrangements.[47]

In a large and prosperous village the villeins collectively often held considerable possessions which were deemed, of course, to belong legally to their lord. At Michaelmas 1340 the goods held by the villeins of William de la Pole in the great lordship of Burstwick were valued by the royal commissioners. Burstwick lay in the East Riding of Yorkshire, the most prosperous region of northern England, and in the following year, when resumed into the king's hands, it produced an annual income of £989, out of which £851 was actually paid out in

---

[45] BL Add. Ms. 28024, f.189v.
[46] Holmes, *Estates of the Higher Nobility*, pp. 127–8.
[47] Newton, *Thaxted*, pp. 31, 58.

cash to the central royal receivers. It was one of the most valuable blocks of property in the country, yet the collective value of the goods of the villeins, assessed at £2,561, was three times greater than the net yearly income from Burstwick. The assets of Burstwick's villeins, distributed between sixteen different villages and hamlets, were being estimated in 1340 as part of a reassessment of the price which William de la Pole should have paid to the king on his purchase of Burstwick in 1338. They formed part of the assets of the estate, just like the animals in his domanial flocks.[48]

A directive sent in 1391 by the council of the earl of March to the earl's reeve at Odcombe in Somerset brings out the concern of the manorial lords that their servile population should be preserved intact. The reeve was ordered to cancel the demise of a free tenement to a free man, and was forbidden to allow this to happen if servile tenants could be found, especially when they could be made to pay higher rents, as in this particular case, where a prospective bond tenant was available who would pay annually 26s. 8d. more. There followed a further general instruction that no serf of the lord "by blood", male or female, was to be allowed to leave the manor as long as some sort of livelihood could be found for him or her.[49]

Theoretically the villeins were supposed to derive their goods entirely from the lord or his ancestors, though there is little historical justification for this. Some contemporaries were prepared to regard as extortion the seizure by a lord of any goods which his villeins had acquired by their own efforts. In the "Parson's Tale" Chaucer condemns this in a passage on avarice and "covetise" that may, in its original form, date from before 1381. He identifies such conduct with "harde lordshipes", and denounces the "distraining" of tenants by tallages, customs, and carriage services "more than hire dutee or resoun is". The amercements taken from bondmen "myghten more reasonably ben clepen extorcions than amercimentz". After citing the opinion of some stewards of certain lords that all this was legitimate because the "cherl" had nothing that did not belong to his lord, he bursts out: "But certes thise lordshipes doon wrong that birewen hire bondefolk thynges that they nevere yave hem." Chaucer was no radical and he was, presumably, voicing here an opinion shared by other more charitably minded and thoughtful contemporaries.[50]

The seigneurial extortions from serfs could assume really outrageous proportions. In 1382 the bondmen of the two Cornish manors of Climsland and Liskeard, held of the royal Duchy of Cornwall,

[48] E. B. Fryde, 'The last trials of William de la Pole', *EcHR*, 2nd ser. xv, 1962, p. 21 and n.9; PRO E 142/49.   [49] Holmes, *Estates of the Higher Nobility*, pp. 128–9.
[50] F. N. Robinson, ed., *The Works of Geoffrey Chaucer*, 2nd edn, Oxford, 1957, pp. 252, 766.

petitioned their royal master for the abrogation of the local custom under which on a tenant's death all his chattels lapsed to the lord. They alleged that their children, in order to escape utter impoverishment, on the death of their fathers were migrating to other places. According to the tenants their position was exceptionally wretched. They named other duchy manors where no such custom existed. A royal inquiry confirmed that on these other named properties, which included the Cornish estates of the bishops of Exeter and of the earls of Stafford and Warwick, the successors of the deceased bondmen owed only their best beast as a heriot.[51]

The oft-cited case of William Heyne's family at Castle Combe in Wiltshire shows how a particularly grasping lord, Sir John Fastolf, a veteran of the French wars, could squeeze a fortune out of his richest villeins by merely enforcing his customary rights over them. William Heyne, starting from very little, had built up a prosperous business as a woollen manufacturer. At his death in 1435, Fastolf's council chose to pretend that Heyne's goods alone were worth £2,000. The local jury scaled this down to the net value of £200. His widow had to pay £40 for permission to remain in her main dwelling and for the recovery of personal chattels. In 1437 she had to offer £100 for a permission to remarry and to re-enter her late husband's remaining properties. These included valuable industrial installations comprising not only a fulling mill but also a gig mill, the earliest on record in this country. Fastolf had to allow her to spread repayments over the next six years. On her death in 1455 only £4 was exacted from her son for permission to recover his share of the inheritance, but in 1463 he was mulcted of a further £20 as a price of his manumission from serfdom. In the space of twenty-eight years Fastolf had extorted £164 from this one family, apart from the annual rents that he was receiving from their tenements, which certainly surpassed £1 a year.[52] It is not surprising that in the more prosperous parts of England like East Anglia, Essex, and Kent the persistence of villeinage was regarded with particular abhorrence by the more prosperous bondmen and in communities that were undergoing rapid industrialization.

During the turbulent decades after the Black Death the main targets for the resentment of the servile part of the peasantry were the ordinary "incidents" of their servile tenure and status. To enumerate them all would be difficult as this collection of customary exactions bristles with eccentric peculiarities, some of the oddest being of great antiquity. The most important were the high rents from servile holdings, always

---

[51] *Cal. Inq. Misc.*, IV, no. 190; *Register of the Black Prince*, II, pp. 215–16.

[52] A. Savine, 'Bondmen under the Tudors', *RHS*, NS XVII, 1903, p. 278; Carus-Wilson, 'Evidences of industrial growth', pp. 200–1.

considerably above the rents due from free tenants, the heriots, consisting of the best beast or chattel due whenever a tenement was surrendered into the lord's hands, the fines of merchet for permission to marry outside the lordship, the annual seigneurial tallages, and the multitude of fines and amercements imposed under one pretext or another in the lord's court. Even the catastrophe of the Black Death did not stop the exaction of heriots. In 1348–9 heriots partly compensated the lords of numerous deceased tenants, such as the bishop of Winchester, or the abbots of St Albans and of Crowland, for other losses of revenue.

Long before the fourteenth century men regarded subjection to serfdom as something degrading and a matter of shame. In the second half of the fourteenth century, as servile tenure was in many places becoming an economic anachronism, the conviction that bondage ought to be abolished altogether became widespread among the servile peasantry. The hostility towards the maintenance of serfdom had its counterpart in a contemptuous attitude towards serfs among some members of the propertied classes, which exacerbated the exasperation of the servile peasants. A petition of the commons in 1391, demanding that sons of villeins should not be allowed to go to school lest they become clergymen, justified this by the need to maintain "the honour of all the freemen of the kingdom".[53]

An incident in 1390 at Wingham in Kent highlights the readiness of some lords to humiliate their serfs as part of what they regarded as the maintenance of their rights and of the proper social hierarchy, but it also brings out how ashamed some serfs were of their bond status. Six customary tenants of Archbishop Courtenay of Canterbury, instead of driving cartloads of hay and litter to his palace of Canterbury, as they were obliged to do by custom, brought it all secretly and on foot, so that they should be less conspicuous while performing this shameful obligation, which otherwise was not particularly arduous. They were sentenced for contempt of the archbishop and ordered to parade like penitents round Wingham church, each carrying on his shoulders a sack of hay and straw. Courtenay, a younger son of the earl of Devon, commemorated his triumph by recording the sentence in his register with a picture of a penitent villein in the margin.[54]

One way to escape from all this was to flee from the manor. If a man was prepared to work as a labourer elsewhere he was sure of employment at any time after 1348. His new employers would not inquire about his personal status. Holdings, too, could be secured from other lords, though lack of animals and equipment could be an obstacle,

[53] *Rot. Parl.*, III, p. 294 (no. 39).
[54] Du Boulay, *The Lordship of Canterbury*, p. 189 and frontispiece.

unless the new lord was prepared to help a stranger tenant. Sometimes whole families decamped secretly and by night after having denuded their holdings of possessions and taken away all that could be moved. Surreptitious flight had the further advantage of avoiding the payment of a heriot demanded by lords when a tenement was surrendered openly. An illegal fugitive also escaped the lord's claims to compensation for any alleged damage to the buildings and lands of the abandoned tenement.

A statute of 1352 made it much easier for lords to recapture legally their fugitive villeins.[55] Hitherto, a man claimed by a lord as his bondman could secure a temporary respite from all danger of arrest by procuring a royal writ *de libertate probanda*. This enabled him to have his status settled by a jury verdict in the king's court and placed him under the king's protection pending such a trial. The action had been in frequent use since the late twelfth century. The petition of the commons that led to the change of the law in 1352 claimed that fugitive villeins had abused this remedy to the detriment of their lords. There was some justification for this complaint, but the upshot of the petition was to deprive the writ of *de libertate probanda* of much of its practical usefulness, so that it virtually fell into disuse. Henceforth, a lord could recapture his fugitive villein even if the latter had procured a royal writ for proving his freedom, and detain him until the time of the trial. This strengthening of the lord's position led to some appalling abuses where free men were falsely detained as serfs in private prisons and could secure no effective redress. But it did not much help most lords, who either lost track of their fugitive villeins or could not afford the trouble and the cost of capturing and bringing them back.

From the late 1360s onwards there was a notable increase in such illegal withdrawals of tenants in most parts of the country. In the manorial court rolls the record of flights is usually followed by drastic orders to compel the return of the fugitives, to secure all their belongings, and to put pressure on their relatives. There is a good deal of talk about capturing the fugitives, though usually nothing seems to come of it. Obviously quite often the manorial officers could not be depended upon to execute the lord's orders in such matters.[56] Certainly, on the estates of Ramsey abbey, "usually the lord was able to exert no coercive pressure through the courts for the recovery of a villager".[57]

In 1381 occurred the extraordinary bid for the outright abolition of villeinage by the king's order. The men of Essex, Hertfordshire, and Kent secured this at the meeting with Richard II at Mile End on 14 June for all the bondmen in their shires, and it is possible that similar

[55] *Rot. Parl.*, II, p. 242 (no. 48) and *SR*, I, p. 323.
[56] F. G. Davenport, *Norfolk Manor*, p. 74.   [57] Raftis, *Tenure and Mobility*, p. 168.

collective remissions of serfdom were also extorted by men of some other counties. They were all inevitably annulled on 2 July, though the young king seems to have been somewhat reluctant to go back upon his word. This is suggested by the curious form of words used in submitting the repeal of his charters of manumission for parliamentary confirmation in November 1381. The king intimated that he was prepared to maintain the manumissions if parliament so desired, "as it has been reported to him that some of you wish" to accept them. A few days later came the unanimous rejection of the king's suggestion. "The prelates and temporal lords as well as the knights, citizens and burgesses replied with one voice that this repeal was well done. They added that such a manumission and enfranchisement of the villeins could not be made without their assent, who had the greatest interest in the matter. And they had never agreed to it...nor would they ever do so, even if it were their dying day."[58]

But things could never be the same again: for "what the state denied was silently achieved, though not till villeinage became economically unprofitable by the land-owning class. Villeinage was not abolished; it just faded away...and the complicated process by which this happened owed much, perhaps everything, to the Revolt."[59] Henceforth the villeins refused more and more "to accept the implications of serfdom", and all the burdens that specifically arose out of their servile tenure and status met with special resistance for that very reason.[60] In the course of roughly a century after 1381 the servile peasantry, by persistent nibbling at the whole structure of servile exactions, greatly reduced its profitability to the lords until the point was reached when it became wiser not to mention serfdom at all.

E. TAXATION AND THE IMMEDIATE BACKGROUND OF 1381

The renewal of the Anglo-French war in 1369 was bound to provoke serious internal troubles in both countries as heavy taxes were piled up on their shrunken populations. Members of the propertied classes in both France and England voiced fears of social upheaval. In France at this period "chroniclers, moralists and judges seem to have experienced a panic fear of total subversion". In England the poet John Gower in his *Mirrour de l'Omme*, written in the last years of Edward III's reign, urged "la seignourie" to face up to the growing insubordination and assertiveness of the villeins and warned of the danger of a sudden popular uprising. His fears were shared by the drafters of a commons'

[58] *Rot. Parl.*, III, pp. 99 (no. 8) and 100 (nos. 12–13), translated by Dobson, *Peasants' Revolt*, pp. 327–9.   [59] Galbraith, 'Thoughts about the Peasants' Revolt', p. 56.
[60] R. H. Hilton, *The Decline of Serfdom in Medieval England*, London, 1969, p. 57.

petition in the first parliament of King Richard II, in the autumn of 1377. They warned that England might become the scene of troubles comparable to the rebellion and confederacy of the French villeins against their lords. They were presumably referring to the "jacquerie" of 1358 in the region around Paris. They also added the gratuitous charge that in order to avenge themselves against their lords they might ally themselves with the enemies of the kingdom if there should be a sudden French raid.[61] This last accusation completely misrepresented the real state of mind of the population of southern England. In reality the rebels of 1381 expressly prohibited the inhabitants of the coastal districts to join in their march on London lest this should weaken the coastal defences against the French. Members of parliament failed to anticipate that this dreaded rising was going to be precipitated by the taxes that they themselves were piling upon the English people.

The renewal of the war was followed by a reintroduction of unusually heavy and continuous direct taxation. Yet there was nothing to show for this; most of the English territories in France were rapidly lost. The coasts of southern England and English shipping in the Channel suffered severely from a series of raids by strong Franco-Castilian fleets and lived in constant dread of more disasters. The first notable expression of mounting exasperation with the conduct of the war occurred in the so-called "Good Parliament" in the spring of 1376. It is important to stress that its members were extremely hostile to some of the most important aspirations of the rebels of 1381. One of the commons' petitions in the Good Parliament demanded that all strangers seeking labour outside their native localities should be temporarily imprisoned until it was discovered whether they had absconded from the service of their lawful masters.[62] Yet there is a direct connection between the protests voiced in the Good Parliament against the mismanagement of the war and the rebellion of 1381. In 1376 the opposition to the royal government popularized the belief that the war was being lost through treachery and corruption in the king's entourage, a belief that would inspire in 1381 one of the main demands of the Kentish and Essex rebels for the execution of the "traitors" among the king's ministers and councillors. Richard Lyons, the most unpopular of the financiers impeached by the commons in 1376, was thereby designated for popular vengeance and was murdered by the rebels in 1381.

The king's ordinary annual revenue may have averaged in the 1370s around £100,000. Between June 1371 and the outbreak of revolts in

---

[61] Mollat and Wolff, *Popular Revolutions in the Late Middle Ages*, p. 178; G. C. Macaulay, ed., *The Complete Works of John Gower*, I, Oxford, 1899, pp. 293–4; *Rot. Parl.*, III, p. 21 (no. 88).

[62] *Ibid.*, II, pp. 340–1 (nos. 116–17).

late May 1381 a further £382,000 was assessed on the lay population as the result of eight separate parliamentary grants, 57 per cent of this total in the period 1377–81, that is, in the years immediately preceding the Great Revolt.[63] In view of the growing obsolescence of the traditional fifteenths and tenths, the government began in 1371 a series of experiments with new taxes which were not assessed on property but on people. These new taxes caused a partial shift in the burden of taxation to the least depopulated parts of the country. If comparison is made with the yield of the traditional tenths and fifteenths, in the first of these experiments, the parish tax of 1371, the assessment of Norfolk was increased by a third, that of Essex by four-fifths, and the charge on Suffolk more than doubled. All these shires were in the forefront of the revolt in 1381. The last and most fatal of the financial experiments, the third poll tax imposed in December 1380, was expected to yield 100,000 marks (£66,666 13s. 4d.), nearly twice as much as a conventional fifteenth and tenth. Its effect on the same relatively well-populated counties would have been even more crushing than the burdens imposed by the tax of 1371 if widespread evasion had not occurred in the early months of 1381. The government's attempts to recover the missing money precipitated the general uprising.

The increased fiscal pressures contributed to the growth of agrarian unrest. As has been already noted, in the years 1369–75 England experienced two further epidemics of plague and a major famine. The years 1369–81 were certainly a time of mounting tension in the relations between landlords and peasants. On several estates manorial court rolls reveal an increase in the number of fugitive villeins. The number of labour cases tried by the justices of the peace mounted in the decade before 1381: in Essex in 1378 and in Norfolk in 1372 and 1375–9 they constituted more than half the total number of offences tried.[64] A petition of the commons in the last parliament of 1377 prefaced its already quoted prophetic forecasts of a forthcoming peasant rebellion with a gloomy picture of widespread troubles. According to the petitioners resistance by villeins was greatly impoverishing many landlords. Villeins were accused of forming confederacies and of setting up common funds to finance their activities. Seigneurial officials were being intimidated so that they dared not distrain tenants to render accustomed services for fear of being murdered. It was alleged that in many parts of the country corn was not being harvested because of the impossibility of finding men willing to reap it. The resultant statute authorized the arrest of any villeins that

[63] For this and much of what follows, see E. B. Fryde's introduction and App. II to the 1969 edn of C. Oman, *The Great Revolt of 1381*.

[64] Putnam, *Proceedings before the Justices of the Peace*, p. cxxii.

their lords denounced as rebellious and of their confederates. They were not to be freed until they had been tried by the justices and, if convicted, they were not to be liberated without the permission of their lords. Other petitions of the commons in the same parliament demanded desperate remedies to assure a satisfactory supply of agricultural labour at statutory wages. This included a demand that no labourer should be excused from being compelled to work for employers designated for him by the justices on the ground that he possessed some smallholding of his own or practised a craft. The government wisely refused in this case to add any further to the existing laws. On the eve of the revolts a section of the landed class was clearly displaying a truculence that matched the violence of the discontented peasantry.[65]

The ensuing rising was caused, however, not by the initial parliamentary grant of December 1380, but by the unwise manner of its collection in the early months of 1381. The 100,000 marks that it was supposed to yield had to be gathered in unusual haste. It was needed to finance three different military expeditions, though only one had been publicly disclosed to the parliament that made the grant. Hence the government's panic when its financial experts realized in the course of February and March 1381 that the high rate of tax was causing widespread evasion which was going to diminish its yield cata-strophically. In nineteen shires and seventeen towns for which we have the initial returns, 46,700 taxpayers were "rediscovered" after fresh inquiries. This was only the tip of the concealed iceberg of evasion. No exact comparison is possible between the poll tax of 1377, when the minimum age limit was fourteen, and the final returns for 1381 when it was raised to fifteen. But this slight difference cannot account for the "disappearance" within four years, during which there is no record of any serious epidemic, of 458,356 taxpayers, constituting a third of the contributors of 1377. Some 102,500 were missing in London and nine shires of the south-east adjoining the capital, where the rising was chiefly concentrated. The highest rates of evasion occurred, however, in the particularly impoverished areas of the country. Some 115,000 taxpayers were "concealed" in the six south-western counties, representing 43 per cent of the contributors of 1377 in those shires. This proportion rose to 47 per cent in the exceptionally impoverished northern region of Cumberland, Westmorland, and the West and North Ridings of Yorkshire. The final net yield of the tax fell short of the government's target of 100,000 marks by some £22,700, amounting to a third of the expected total.

[65] Rot. Parl., III, pp. 17 (no. 54), 21–2 (no. 88).

New special commissioners were appointed in March 1381 to search out the missing taxpayers. In many localities the inhabitants regarded their receipts for their local quotas of tax as acquitting them once and for all, and met with angry refusal all further demands. Some of the original tax collectors dared not levy the additional surcharges indicated to them by the new commissioners. The collectors in Suffolk refused to collect £184 of such arrears and dared not levy these sums even after the revolt was over in the autumn of 1381. Subsequently, in response to a parliamentary petition, the king had to acquit all collectors of all such surcharges, unless it could be proved that they had actually levied these additional amounts.[66]

A clash between the Essex commissioner of inquiry and the men of Fobbing and two adjoining villages on 30 May 1381 sparked off the rebellion. The commissioner, Thomas Bampton, and his little party of clerks and sergeants were beaten up and driven out. If the royal government had acted coolly at this point there might still have been no general rising. Instead, Chief Justice Belknap was sent at once to the disaffected district to seek out and punish the rioters. The government was acting unwisely in sending a man of his importance and yet not providing him with any special armed escort. His appearance at Brentwood on 2 June provoked a riot and, though the justice escaped with his life, some of his assistants were put to death. The men of Fobbing and their associates now felt that they had gone too far and that their salvation lay in raising the other villages of Essex. Within a few days the whole county was in revolt and a parallel rising started simultaneously in Kent.

F. THE REVOLTS OF 1381 AND THEIR AFTERMATH

Two of the most notable features of the uprising of June 1381 are the extraordinary speed with which it spread and the remarkable cohesion of the main rebel groups of Kent and Essex as they converged on London on 11 and 12 June. Both are more readily explicable if the attitudes of the local communities to the outside world are scrutinized. In an England where lawlessness was growing, and the royal government was increasingly ineffective in stemming the tide of corruption and oppression by the local notables and the officials associated with them, the humbler part of the population sought security in acting collectively against all outsiders, as well as against the more influential and powerful landowners in their own midst.

This sums up much of what happened in June 1381. The manor

---

[66] *Ibid.*, III, p. 116 (no. 83); PRO E 368/154, recorda, Pascha, m.14.

houses of many richer landowners were attacked and their estate records burnt, amidst a widespread peasant strike as customary rents and services were being withheld. Numerous attacks occurred in all the shires of south-eastern England on the local tax collectors, justices of the peace and their underlings, as well as the sheriffs, coroners, escheators, and their subordinates. Their official records were singled out for destruction. Local fury was especially directed against local officials and notables who were outsiders or recent newcomers. Over and above these outbursts, a formidable demonstration occurred against the traitors who were believed to be dooming the kingdom to defeat. This largely inspired the march of Kentishmen and of the men of Essex on London to demand from the king that these traitorous royal councillors should be handed over for punishment. Only after the news of the successful entry of these rebels into London had spread to the surrounding counties did serious troubles erupt in Cambridgeshire and East Anglia.

An anonymous poem of "the Yorkshire partisans" dating from c. 1392 gives a glimpse of humble men organized locally against a hostile outside world. After complaining of their extreme poverty, which compelled them to feed on shrews, the poet exhorted fellow Yorkshiremen "to meynteyne him als his brother *both in wrong and right*" and also to "mayntayn our neighbour with all our might". An indictment of 1387 against the fraternity of the Holy Trinity at Chipping Campden (Glos.) accused its members of being similarly bound "by oath to maintain each other against other persons in pleas whether true or false." The gild was alleged to number a hundred members not only from Chipping Campden but from the villages around.[67] Strong feelings of local solidarity promoted the speedy spread of the risings in June 1381 and some of the local officials assumed the lead in their native localities. The royal bailiff of the hundred of Tendring in Essex was accused of organizing a march on Colchester and of being assisted by the constable of the village of Manningtree, whose men subsequently killed a Fleming. In Kent an official of the hundred of Wye made a proclamation that all its men should assemble in arms to assist the rebels.[68] One suspects that constables of other Kentish hundreds may have played a prominent part in arraying the rebels, as their successors certainly did during the subsequent Kentish rising of 1450. In all the main areas of the revolt, from Norfolk to Kent, several of the local organizers were men of some substance, rich

[67] R. H. Robbins, ed., *Historical Poems of the Fourteenth and Fifteenth Centuries*, New York, 1959, p. 60; Hilton, *English Peasantry*, pp. 92–3.

[68] Réville and Petit-Dutaillis, *Le Soulèvement des Travailleurs*, pp. 216–17; Hilton, *Bond Men Made Free*, p. 217.

peasants or craftsmen, who presumably owed their position to being the accepted leaders of their communities in expressing their discontents. It was symptomatic of the sense of separate identity of the rebels from each county that, instead of procuring a general abolition of serfdom, the men of Essex and Hertfordshire should have sought separate county charters from the king, as probably did the peasants of some other shires.[69]

As late as the seventeenth century the men of Kent had a particular reputation for clannishness and hostility to outsiders. After three major rebellions in 1381, 1450, and 1471, besides several more localized tumults, the Kentishmen justifiably earned the reputation of being most impatient of injuries and of being restless seekers of novelties. Polydore Vergil thus described them at the beginning of the sixteenth century.[70]

Kent was one of the wealthiest counties, but this only exacerbated social inequalities. The Kentish custom of "gavelkind", or partible inheritance, encouraged men to remain in their native communities, as they could all look forward to receiving a share of their family holdings, but it also led to excessive subdivision of land. In the words of a royal charter of 1276 freeing the land of John Cobham from this custom, "Gavelkind...causes the division into small parcels of land, which, if undivided, would...provide decent victuals for many, but which when divided, cannot provide for any."[71] In some of the most overcrowded districts of Kent men could only survive by practising a great variety of crafts, and the Kentish rebels of 1381 included men of most varied occupations. The proximity of the London market and the export of foodstuffs by sea to the continent made food more expensive in Kent than in most other parts of England. Its geographic position made it particularly vulnerable to the hazards and miseries of war. Its coasts were raided by the French, the royal purveyors often seized supplies of food and military stores, and it was frequently traversed by mutinous bands of soldiers and sailors. As recently as July 1380 deserting shire levies were causing disorders at Maidstone and Rochester.[72] The advanced level of Kent's economy created an exceptionally large gentry divided by a multitude of feuds. It also seems to have encouraged a peculiarly sophisticated body of abuses and corruption in local government and justice. The poet John Gower was almost certainly speaking of his native Kent at the end of the reign of

[69] Thomas Walsingham, *Chronicon Angliae*, ed. E. M. Thompson, RS, 1874, pp. 298–9 (Herts.); J. A. Sparvel-Bayly, 'Essex in insurrection', *The Antiquary*, XIX, 1889, p. 69 (Essex); a draft charter for Somerset is published by B. Harvey in *EHR*, LXXX, 1965, p. 91.

[70] A. Everitt, *The Community of Kent and the Great Rebellion, 1640–1660*, Leicester, 1973, pp. 14–16; Du Boulay, *Lordship of Canterbury*, p. 186.   [71] *CChR, 1257–1300*, p. 198.

[72] Réville and Petit-Dutaillis, *op. cit.*, p. lxxiii, n.4.

Edward III when he described "a regularly established class of men whose occupation it was to arrange for the due packing and bribery of juries" and the terrible abuses that had been caused by their activities.[73]

The economic prosperity of Essex grew strikingly during the later middle ages and this process was already well under way in the decades preceding the Great Revolt. The proximity of London encouraged diverse industries: textile workers and various skilled craftsmen in metals and leather were present in 1381 in large numbers in the villages and small towns of the county. As far as can be judged from the surviving fragments of poll-tax returns, in some districts craftsmen and small traders actually outnumbered landholding peasants and agricultural labourers.[74] The high wages enjoyed by the industrial workers inevitably raised the wages of agricultural labourers and servants. Dissatisfied employees had exceptional opportunities for changing jobs in breach of their annual contracts. Hence prosecutions for breaches of the labour legislation were exceptionally numerous in Essex and agricultural labourers were being enticed away by a most varied assortment of trading and industrial employers. The remnants of serfdom were turning into an exceptional anachronism in many villages of Essex. As has been noted above, the fear of serfdom's return rather than the oppressiveness of its survivals may have inspired the destruction of manorial records at places in Essex where the old manorial organization was a thing of the past. This may also help to explain why, at their meeting with King Richard II at Mile End on 14 June, the men of Essex were so eager to secure a charter abolishing serfdom throughout their county and obtained such a document bearing the date of 15 June.

In Norfolk and Suffolk many manorial lords still exploited their demesnes directly in 1381 and bonfires of their records occurred on an exceptionally large number of East Anglian manors, hampering the enforcement of seigneurial rights for many years thereafter. As late as 1388 the estate auditors of John of Gaunt, duke of Lancaster, ascribed the decline in the revenue from his manor of Methwold in Norfolk partly to the destruction of the rentals, extents, custumals, and other evidences "burnt by the rebels in the time of the Rumour" (of 1381).[75] But, as in Essex, in many localities of Norfolk and Suffolk, craftsmen, chiefly textile workers, outnumbered the men living mainly by agriculture. This was notably so around North Walsham in north-eastern Norfolk, which formed the "cradle" of the revolt in that county on 16 June and where the rebels took their last desperate stand

[73] G. C. Macaulay, ed., *Complete Works of John Gower*, I, pp. lxviii, 277.

[74] Statistics of occupations in Essex and East Anglia are summarized in Hilton, *Bond Men Made Free*, pp. 170–4.   [75] Holmes, *Estates of the Higher Nobility*, pp. 127–8.

ten days later.[76] In Norfolk, as in the other principal areas of the rising, the revolt was clearly as much a movement of rural industrial workers as of mere peasants. It was the first manifestation of a new kind of internal threat that the rulers of Tudor England would particularly dread. As Sir William Cecil warned in 1564, "the people that depend upon the making of cloth ar of wors condition to be quyetly governed than the husband men".[77]

The main events of the revolt need not be recounted here in detail as they belong to the general history of England and form one of its most familiar stories. Amidst general panic that disarmed resistance the rebels from Kent and Essex forced their way into London on the night of 12 June. The next day, the "Savoy", the magnificent London palace of Duke John of Gaunt, the *bête noire* of the rebels, went up in flames and hated officials, lawyers, and Flemings were murdered with impunity. On 14 June, while Richard II was parleying with some of the rebels at Mile End, their principal leaders broke into the Tower of London, again without any resistance, and murdered the king's two principal ministers, Chancellor Sudbury, who was also archbishop of Canterbury, and Treasurer Hales, the prior of the Hospitallers in England. The next day Richard again met the rebels at Smithfield. Their Kentish leader, Wat Tyler, behaved in an exceptionally offensive manner, probably because he dreaded the disbandment of his followers if an agreement was reached, as had happened the previous day at Mile End. His insulting behaviour brought about his death at the hands of the lord mayor of London, William Walworth, and his bewildered followers were soon rounded up by the organized forces of the richer London citizens. Troubles continued for several more weeks throughout south-eastern England and there were some isolated risings in more distant parts of the country, but a mortal threat to the country's capital and the government of England was over by the night of 15 June.

The risings of the Kentishmen and the men of Essex triggered off a multitude of localized movements only loosely connected with the main revolt. Because of the special interests of the monastic chroniclers, attacks on religious houses are particularly well documented. As is usually the case with corporate landlords, they tended to be particularly conservative in the treatment of their tenantry and stubbornly tenacious in enforcing their rights, though with this often went much inefficiency.

Attacks on the abbeys of Bury St Edmunds and of St Albans are amongst the best-known incidents of the revolt. Both the abbeys had a long history of troubles with the quite sizeable towns that had grown

---

[76] Hilton, *Bond Men Made Free*, pp. 173–4.

[77] R. H. Tawney and E. Power, *Tudor Economic Documents*, II, London, 1924, p. 45.

around them, because they persisted in treating their townsmen as if they were rightless manorial tenants. This was particularly anomalous in the case of Bury, which, according to the poll tax of 1377, was the fifteenth most populous town in England. In each case the townsmen were the ringleaders but were supported by the villages belonging to their monastic masters. The rebels at St Albans boasted that they were allied with thirty-two localities in the abbey's liberty. The outbreak at Bury was the more savage of the two and amongst the monks who had to be surrendered for instant execution was the keeper of the abbey's barony. At St Albans the most unpopular monks fled in time, including the former cellarer, John Mote, whose vigorous enforcement of the abbey's rights and claims against its peasantry has been noted earlier. The rebellion on the abbey's estates was not "an outburst born of economic misery", but a rising "against the inescapable seigneurial pressure of the abbey's administration". The tenants did not suffer from particularly galling labour services but they "objected to their unfree status, their suit at the lord's mill; to the strictness with which warrens and hunting and fishing rights were preserved". Their "discontent was enhanced by their proximity to London and by the consequent influences of migration and the sharper demand for wealth".[78] On several manors there occurred a wholesale destruction of the abbey's estate records, but the monks could accept this with equanimity as all the essential information had always been copied into its special estate registers safely preserved at the abbey itself.

While in most areas there were no indiscriminate personal assaults on the lay landlords and their families, the destruction of manorial records was very widespread and it was normally followed by temporary refusals of the tenants to render customary services. In the weeks after the revolt several special commissions had to be appointed by the king to aid particular landlords in recovering control over their dependants. Strikes of tenants spread to districts outside the main area of the revolt. It is not surprising that troubles should have occurred on the estates of the prior of Worcester. Already in 1379 he had seized all the chattels of his serfs into his hands. On 5 July 1381 he felt unable to travel to the chapter-general of the Benedictines at Northampton because the priory's tenants "on the pretext of their claim to have a certain manumission...refuse to do and perform the services they owe us, services on which a large part of our and our chapter's sustenance relies". This was but one incident in a prolonged conflict. In 1385 the prior was again seizing all the chattels of these rebellious tenants.[79]

[78] Levett, *Studies in Manorial History*, p. 179.
[79] Dobson, *Peasants' Revolt*, pp. 299–300; Hilton, *English Peasantry*, pp. 61–2.

The records of the first sessions of the manorial courts held after the revolt deserve systematic study. For example, the court roll of Moze in Essex bears the heading: "The first court held after the rebellion and the burning of the court rolls."[80] This is mentioned as the sole crime of the manor's servile tenants and their other associates. For this outrage all the servile tenements were resumed into the hands of the lady of the manor and regranted to their former holders only on the payment of fines. It should be noted that these servile holdings were surrendered back to these *nativi* and to "their heirs and assigns", which shows that at Moze the servile tenants already enjoyed in practice a virtually hereditary tenure, though this had not restrained them from violence. As one moves to outlying parts of England some faint echoes of the main revolt can still be found in surprisingly remote places. At Aston, under the Wrekin, a Shropshire property of Shrewsbury abbey, the court roll of 20 July, the first after the revolt, differs from the preceding rolls in revealing some slight infringements of the abbot's rights. Fourteen men were fined for trespasses in his woods.[81]

Destruction of manorial records took place even on several estates belonging to the king's mother in Essex and on at least one royal manor, Kennington in Surrey. Here the manorial custumal and other documents were burnt on 14 June by men of Lambeth in conjunction with local tenants. A month later Richard ordered the arrest of all his tenants at Kennington for their participation in this outrage and prohibited the release of any of them on bail. The worst disaster befell the records of John of Gaunt. As late as 1388 bailiffs of his franchises in south-eastern England, responsible for the levying of his judicial income, could not be brought to account because all the "remembrances" concerning their accounts had been destroyed on 13 June 1381 in the burning of the Savoy, John's splendid palace in London.[82]

The demands of the two main rebel armies which entered London must be pieced together from what happened at their two meetings with the king on successive days at Mile End and at Smithfield. We may not have a complete list of these demands. The royal proclamation of 2 July, revoking all the concessions previously made to the rebels, is more precise than all the other sources, but it only mentions the promises made at Mile End and actually embodied in royal letters patent.[83] For the rest we have to turn to chroniclers whose statements

[80] G. A. Holmes, *The Later Middle Ages, 1278–1485*, Edinburgh, 1962, photostat facing p. 132.

[81] NLW, Aston Hall Ms. 5340.

[82] Réville and Petit-Dutaillis, *Le Soulèvement des Travailleurs*, pp. 213–14, 220; Holmes, *Estates of the Higher Nobility*, p. 126.

[83] *Rymer's Foedera*, ed. A. Clarke *et al.*, Rec. Comm., 1816–69, IV, p. 126.

are often regrettably vague. Only the *Anonimalle Chronicle*, easily the best of our narrative sources, gives a lengthy but apparently not an exhaustive list of Wat Tyler's demands at Smithfield.

As has been already stressed, at every stage in the negotiations between Richard II and the rebels the complete abolition of serfdom was in the forefront of their demands. All the royal letters patent granted to various communities after the meeting at Mile End included this concession, coupled with a general pardon for all felonies and trespasses and the abrogation of all subsequent outlawries. At Smithfield Richard reiterated his promise to give similar letters to all who still required them.

The royal proclamation of 2 July, besides abrogating these concessions, also revoked two other promises extorted from Richard at Mile End. They concerned the renting of servile land and restrictions on internal trade. The *Anonimalle Chronicle* mentions the demand that land should not be rented at more than 4d. an acre. The proclamation of 2 July makes it clear that this was meant to apply only to *servile* tenements, which, of course, bore other charges besides rents.[84] The king was also made to promise that the rents of servile tenants who were paying less than 4d. per acre were not to be increased. This last proviso suggests that the rent of 4d. per acre for servile land was not absurdly low. This is also confirmed by the valuations in 1378 of some of the confiscated lands of Alice Perrers, the former mistress of Edward III. On some of her estates in Hertfordshire and Middlesex arable without crops was valued at between 1½d. and 4d. an acre.[85] These were the counties from which came some of the rebels who parleyed with Richard at Mile End.

Conflicts between town and country were less acute in fourteenth-century England than in parts of the Netherlands and in some other continental regions. Some friction was inevitable. At Mile End the rebels secured the promise that all the king's subjects should be allowed to buy and sell freely in all the cities, boroughs, and market places, and everywhere else in the kingdom. If enforced, this would have abrogated the main trading privileges of towns. Recent conflicts in East Anglia may have sharpened the desire for this concession. In the Good Parliament of 1376 the commons had impeached William Elys, a member of the ruling merchant oligarchy of Yarmouth in Norfolk, and this had led to a temporary revocation of the town's recent charter assuring to it a monopoly of trading within the radius of seven miles. It was claimed that Yarmouth was using this to monopolize the trade

---

[84] *Ibid.*, "quod nulla acra terrae…quae in bondagio vel in servitio tenetur".
[85] *Cal. Inq. Misc.*, IV, pp. 11–12 (nos. 15–16).

in herrings and to raise the price of fish and other victuals destined for the surrounding countryside. Yarmouth soon regained its privileges. This provoked a fresh petition by the communities of Norfolk and Suffolk and of all the other counties in the parliament that preceded the Great Revolt, but they only achieved the setting up of yet another royal inquiry.[86] Six months later the Norfolk rebels occupied both Norwich and Yarmouth on two successive days (17–18 June). There was no resistance as the ruling rich merchants dreaded general uprisings of the poorer townsmen. Not surprisingly the rebels marching on Yarmouth were also joined by the men of lesser towns and villages of Suffolk who had been the main victims of Yarmouth's privileges. On entering Yarmouth on 18 June the rebels tore up its hated charter and sacked the houses of Elys and other ruling oligarchs.

Besides the concessions to the rebels annulled in the royal proclamation of 2 July, chroniclers also credit the rebel leaders at Mile End with some further demands. According to the *Anonimalle Chronicle* they stipulated that nobody should render any service to a lord or should be obliged to work for others except of his own free will, and then by contract.[87] This would have spelt the end of all seigneurial claims to the labour of their tenants and would have also consigned to oblivion some of the most crucial provisions of the Statutes of Labourers.

Taken together, the demands put forward at Mile End came from rebels who were not devoid of some property and who had hopes of improving their condition still further. The peasants among them appear to have been predominantly, not landless men, "but rather tenants wishing to be rid of the irksome burdens of villeinage and the manor". They were moved by rising expectations and there seems to be an element of truth in Froissart's famous comment attributing the risings in south-eastern England to "the ease and riches that the common people were of".[88]

"The shocked imagination of the upper classes credited the rebels of 1381 with all kinds of extravagant aims, such as to divide the kingdom into provinces with rulers of their own appointment and to put every member of the aristocracy to the sword." The absurd demands attributed by the *Anonimalle Chronicle* to Wat Tyler at his meeting with King Richard at Smithfield lent credence to these fears, though, as has been already suggested, they were probably put forward merely in order to kill off all further negotiations. These enormities included the demands "that there was to be no law in future save that of Winchester,

[86] Holmes, *The Good Parliament*, pp. 114–18; *Rot. Parl.*, III, pp. 94–5 (no. 39).
[87] V. H. Galbraith, *The Anonimalle Chronicle, 1333 to 1381*, Manchester, 1927, pp. 144–5.
[88] Holmes, *The Later Middle Ages*, p. 143; Dobson, *Peasants' Revolt*, p. 370.

that all lordship should be abolished except that of the king, that the goods of the church should be given to the parishioners and that there was to be no bishop except one".[89] Mixed with these fantastic articles were some other demands, equally inadmissible but more realistic and more akin to the practical concessions wrested from the king at Mile End. The demand for the abolition of serfdom was reiterated. Outlawry was to be abolished. Its frequent use against fugitive labourers must have added to the detestation with which it was regarded. According to Knighton's chronicle, Tyler also demanded that "all warrens, as well in fisheries as in parks and woods, should be common to all; so that throughout the realm, in the waters, ponds, fisheries, woods and forests, poor as well as rich might take the venison and hunt the hare in the fields". Under the existing restrictions poaching was "perhaps the most widespread and most natural of all country sports",[90] but the penalties for being caught could be grim. Hence, as the medieval popular ballads make it abundantly clear, foresters were the most hated of all royal and seigneurial officials and fair game for the poachers' arrows. The achievement of the freedom to fish and hunt would have fulfilled one of the most cherished dreams of the English peasantry.

A presentment against the rebels in Essex before the court of King's Bench in the autumn of 1381 ascribed the rising to "the instigation of the Devil".[91] This was also the view of the St Albans monk, Thomas Walsingham, one of the most detailed contemporary chroniclers of the revolt. Among its other instigators he lumped together the mendicant friars and John Wycliffe. Quite gratuitously, he made John Ball into one of Wycliffe's disciples. This radical priest, who during the first days of the rising had been released by the Kentish rebels from the archbishop's prison, certainly preached highly incendiary sermons to the rebel host. Walsingham ascribes to him the unusual doctrine that servitude had been introduced into the world not as a punishment for man's original sin but against the will of God.[92] Most of Ball's other alleged sayings could be echoed from countless fourteenth-century sermons foretelling the dreadful punishments awaiting after death the men and women who had acquired power and riches through iniquitous oppression of others. This gave encouragement to his fellow

---

[89] B. Wilkinson, 'The peasants' revolt of 1381', *Speculum*, xv, 1940, p. 27, summarizing *The Anonimalle Chronicle*, ed. Galbraith, p. 147.

[90] M. Keen, *The Outlaws of Medieval Legend*, London, 1961, p. 166; G. G. Coulton, *Chaucer and his England*, London, 1950, p. 280.

[91] J. A. Sparvel-Bayly, 'Essex in insurrection', pp. 70–1.

[92] Dobson, *Peasants' Revolt*, pp. 364, 375.

rebels but cannot provide the main explanation for the spreading of the revolt. Reports of a breakdown of law and order were quite sufficient to induce most men to rise.

For Walsingham and Knighton, as for some other members of the higher clergy, the rebellion could only be explained as the outcome of a vast conspiracy of heretics and itinerant preachers. This myth of Wycliffe's influence on the revolt added in subsequent years a further justification for the persecution of his Lollard followers. By the last decade of the fourteenth century a forged confession of John Ball, incorporated into a Carmelite tract against the Lollards, assured its readers that the sole hidden purpose of the revolt of 1381 was to impose Wycliffe's teachings on the entire kingdom.[93] A generation later resentment at religious persecution did ultimately make some Lollards ripe for revolt. In January 1414 hundreds of them answered the call of Sir John Oldcastle, a personal enemy of Henry V, to congregate in London and capture the king. The plot was betrayed before the rebels could strike. The subsequent trials show that most of Oldcastle's followers could not in any sense be described as peasants and the conspiracy had nothing to do with any peasant aspirations.

In his opening speech to the parliament of October 1383 the chancellor, Michael de la Pole, attributed the rising of 1381 to the hostility felt towards the local royal officials. He was one of the wealthiest magnates and had himself suffered losses as a landlord. His family records had been destroyed in the rebellion. But he accepted that exasperation against the lesser royal officials was the most immediate cause of the rising. As he put it, "the acts of disobedience and rebellion which men have recently committed and which continue from one day to another towards the lesser servants of the king, such as the sheriffs, escheators, collectors of the subsidies and others of the same type, were the source and chief cause of the treasonable insurrection recently made by the commune of England...This insurrection...was firstly a rebellion against the said lesser servants, then against the great officers of the kingdom and finally against the king himself."[94]

A similar realistic analysis of the causes of the rebellion is to be found in a speech of Sir Richard Waldegrave, the speaker for the commons in the first parliament after the Great Rebellion, assembled in November 1381. Waldegrave, knight of the shire for Suffolk, seems to have provided Chaucer with his model for the "veray parfit gentile knight" of the prologue to the *Canterbury Tales*. He was a king's knight and a very experienced soldier. Waldegrave had been one of the commissioners appointed in March 1381 to inquire into the evading of the poll tax in Essex, but he had never filled any local offices either in

[93] *Ibid.*, pp. 377–8.
[94] *CPR, 1381–5*, p. 75; Dobson, *op. cit.*, p. 362, translating *Rot. Parl.*, III, p. 150 (no. 6).

Suffolk or any other county. Perhaps he secured in 1377 an exemption from having to hold any such posts against his will because he felt distaste for the malpractices inherent in local government. This may account for the truthful realism with which, as speaker, he castigated the abuses of royal and magnate officials.[95]

The most remarkable feature of Waldegrave's speech is his recognition that the "outrages...which have lately been done to the poor commons, more generally than ever before, made the said poor commons feel so hardly oppressed that they caused the said lesser commons to rise". Like speaker Peter de la Mare in the Good Parliament of 1376, he expressed the general exasperation at the lack of effective defence against the French raids, despite the "great treasure" that had been granted to the government for this purpose. He was putting his finger here on one of the major causes of the rising in Kent and Sussex. He complained of the perennial abuses of the royal purveyors, "who pay nothing to the commons for the victuals and carriage taken from them", the heavy taxes levied by the king and of "other grievous and outrageous oppressions done...by various servants of our lord the king and other lords of the realm". He particularly blamed the lords for the perversions of justice and spoke of the outrageous multitude of embracers of quarrels and maintainers, "who act like kings in the country, so that justice and law are scarcely administered to anybody". He warned that still worse troubles were to be feared "if good and proper remedy is not provided in time for the above-mentioned outrageous oppressions and mischiefs".[96]

Waldegrave was not isolated in his fear. The poet Gower, writing perhaps in 1382, dreaded the resentment of the defeated peasants and warned of the continuous danger of further troubles.[97] Henceforth the upper classes lived in dread of another general upheaval and saw its coming in every more serious manifestation of local unrest. The writer of *Annales Ricardi Secundi*, in recording the troubles in Cheshire early in 1393, remarked "that men all over England were sure another general insurrection was at hand".[98] In this atmosphere of frequent local disorders and of continuous tension between lords and tenants, the domanial type of estate largely disappeared from England in the forty years after the Great Revolt.

---

[95] J. S. Roskell, 'Sir Richard de Waldegrave of Bures St Mary, Speaker in the parliament of 1381–2', *Proc. of the Suffolk Inst. of Arch.*, XXVII, 1957, pp. 154–75.

[96] *Rot. Parl.*, III, p. 100 (no. 17), translated Dobson, *op. cit.*, pp. 330–1; cf. E. Searle and R. Burghart, 'The defence of England and the Peasants' Revolt', *Viator*, 3, 1972.

[97] *Vox Clamantis*, in Macaulay, ed., *Complete Works of John Gower*, IV, pp. 79–80.

[98] J. G. Bellamy, 'The northern rebellions in the later years of Richard II', *Bull. JRL*, XLVII, 1965, p. 264.

G. PEASANT DISCONTENTS AFTER 1381

The period stretching from 1381 to the last popular rebellion of the fifteenth century in 1497 is still a very obscure age in the history of the English countryside. We have to deal with the interplay of economic stresses, a partial dislocation of village communities as personal serfdom largely disappeared, and with the consequences of the recurrent breakdowns of effective royal government. The relative importance of these factors at different times is still very imperfectly understood. One has an impression of growing disunity in the country and contrasts between different regions seem to have been particularly marked. Every new monograph reminds us of the fragility of our generalizations about this period and many more detailed studies are clearly needed. At present it is possible to say what some of the main trends were and to identify the principal problems, but it is far more difficult to offer convincing explanations.

The speedy collapse of the revolts in June 1381 did not disarm the peasantry, and the memory of this upheaval encouraged further disorders. "Concerted action by peasants of particular villages to withdraw their services from the local landlord or destroy his manorial records was a common feature of the English social scene after 1381."[99] There are repeated echoes of these disturbances in the records of successive parliaments. For example, in 1390 parliament imagined that it could check this persistent violence by again prohibiting labourers and "artificers" to hunt or to keep hunting dogs or other equipment that could be used to catch wild animals. The preamble to that statute alleged that these prohibited activities allowed such people "at these times their meetings for debate, covin and conspiracy in order to stir up riot and sedition". It is undoubtedly true that many a wild venture originated from a poaching expedition. Some of the alleged peasant conspiracies during the disorders of 1450 were apparently preceded by suspicious gatherings in secluded woods.[100]

Some startlingly oppressive provisions were added to the labour laws, including the introduction in 1388 of a scheme for issuing special passes under the seals of local justices to all labourers travelling away from their native districts. The same statute also prohibited the apprenticing to crafts of sons of poorer peasants in order to keep them on the land as agricultural labourers.[101] There is no evidence that these additional restrictions were effectively enforced and the rest of the labour legislation, while constituting a constant irritant in the eyes of the peasantry, was certainly not solving the problems of landowners.

---

[99] Dobson, *Peasants' Revolt*, p. 334.
[100] Keen, *Outlaws*, p. 166, translating *Rot. Parl.*, III, p. 273 (no. 58); PRO KB 9/262, nos. 56–8.
[101] *SR*, II, pp. 56–7, 77.

This continuous background of tension and unrest cannot by itself explain why the leasing of manorial demesnes became more widespread from about 1390 onwards. Fluctuations in corn prices may have broadly determined the chronology of this change. A decline in corn prices in the last decade of the fourteenth century may have influenced some landowners to give up direct exploitation on most estates by about 1420. But rising wages and other difficulties of the landlords with their peasants may often have played an important part in forcing upon them the actual decision to give up direct farming. Such a change ensured a considerable reduction of costs. In some particularly prosperous areas such as the Kentish estates of the cathedral priory of Canterbury in the 1390s, it could even yield, at first, revenues from rents substantially higher than the profits of direct farming. Once leasing had been completed, there came a prolonged effort by the landlords to maintain any improvements in their income that they had been able to achieve, or at least to stabilize it at a fairly high level and to prevent any serious decline in the future. The wave of demesne leasing was followed, however, by a prolonged period of fresh difficulties for landlords. Some of them sprang from the very nature of these changes. Village communities had been profoundly disorganized and there was much more social and economic instability. Large-scale migration of peasants away from their native manors became easier, and often inevitable. During most of the fifteenth century landlords continued to be at a disadvantage, because vacant arable land remained abundant while men who could till it continued to be relatively scarce. It seems almost certain that population was still falling during the first half of the fifteenth century, and that it may have continued to decline quite markedly in some parts of the country. There were some further national outbreaks of plague and several more local ones. There were particularly numerous epidemics in the 1430s, including a fairly generalized outbreak of plague and other illnesses following in the wake of a famine in 1438–9. This was happening at the very time when the problems of landlords were also aggravated by the disordered condition of the kingdom. A deterioration in the maintenance of law and internal peace had set in long before the fifteenth century, but a particularly serious breakdown of effective government occurred under Henry VI. This was a new development which nobody could have foreseen before the death of Henry V in 1422. It added to the difficulties of landlords in all sorts of ways. For this and other reasons, in the middle decades of the fifteenth century many of them were fighting, for the time being, a losing battle in trying to avert a further decline in their incomes.[102]

[102] R. A. L. Smith, *Canterbury Cathedral Priory*, pp. 191–4; Hatcher, *Plague, Population and the English Economy, passim*.

The lack of "good governance" of which the subjects of Henry VI complained with good reason was depressing the economy and intensifying general insecurity and lawlessness. It affected adversely the capacity of the landlords to cope with the rebelliousness, or at least the passive resistance, of their tenants, and to assure the obedience of their officials. "The maintenance of order in England had always depended on co-operation between the central government and the landed classes and this partnership was dissolving."[103] Powerful lay magnates could still manage to protect their interests reasonably well by brute force. One is not surprised to find that an intelligent and brutal ruffian like Edmund, Lord Grey of Ruthin, who controlled his estates from 1440 to 1490, should have preserved the stability of his income and made sure that none of his servants defrauded him. Some magnates, like Humphrey, the first duke of Buckingham, seem to have appreciably increased the revenues from their properties even in the 1440s, when the majority of landowners were particularly embarrassed.[104] Weaker people, and especially ecclesiastics, who depended much more on the help of their more powerful neighbours and the protection of the crown, were at a serious disadvantage in that disordered age. On the Gloucestershire property of the nuns of Syon at Cheltenham the tenants refused for seven years, from 1445 to 1452, to pay a yearly render of £10 0s. 7¼d. for commutation of their labour service. It required two visits of a magnate arbitrator, Lord Sudeley, before a settlement could be reached. Violence may have been expected because on the first occasion he brought with him twenty-four mounted attendants and for the final arbitration, in September 1452, he was followed by as many as forty-six horsemen. The obnoxious annual payment was reduced to 10 marks (£6 13s. 4d.), but "the expenses of the arbitration amounted to four times the amount by which the payment was relaxed".[105]

In studying the management of certain great ecclesiastical estates in the fifteenth century, such as the properties of the abbots of Westminster or of the bishops of Worcester, one is particularly struck by their persistent anxiety to humour local notables. Estates were leased to them for long periods in order to retain their goodwill. These influential leaseholders and important free tenants defaulted for long periods over their obligations and could apparently do so with impunity. Late in the fifteenth century the abbot of Westminster complained of one such over-mighty farmer, John Cassy, who had run up large arrears on his lease of the manor of Deerhurst in Gloucestershire, that "there was no remedy to be had against him in the ordinary course of the law 'by cause of his grete myght, kynne and alyaunce'".[106]

---

[103] R. L. Storey, *Thomas Langley and the Bishopric of Durham, 1405–1437*, London, 1961, p. 113.
[104] McFarlane, *Nobility*, pp. 205–6.   [105] Hilton, *English Peasantry*, pp. 67–8.
[106] Harvey, 'The leasing of the Abbot of Westminster's demesnes', pp. 21–2.

As will be illustrated in more detail later, peasant resistance to the demands of their landlords was also persistent in the fifteenth century and, especially during its middle decades, fairly effective. The leasing of manorial demesnes and the commutation of labour services had removed only some of the causes of friction between landlords and their tenants, and there were still plenty of reasons for discontent among the peasantry. The commuted labour services were replaced by additional rent charges and this added to the burden of rents in money and kind due from servile holdings. Tenants were frequently unwilling to spend as much as their lords expected on the upkeep of the buildings and other assets attached to their tenements. The successors of former villeins were particularly irritated by the persistence of various seigneurial rights which served as perpetual reminders of serfdom. In an age when men could readily expect to find better conditions of employment and even fresh arable holdings outside their native manors, the continuing efforts of the lords to restrict the migration of their serfs aroused much hostility.

Manorial officials were intimidated by the passive resistance of the tenantry backed up by threats of violence and even occasional physical attacks. Even more demoralizing to the lords' agents was the threat of financial ruin hanging over them, as they were usually held liable for the mounting arrears of debt from rents and seigneurial dues withheld by the fractious peasantry. The private seigneurial courts were ceasing to be dependable instruments for enforcing the will of their lords. Landlords were becoming less sure of having all their orders carried out by frightened and demoralized officials. In the routine matter of stopping the peasants' illicit migration from their manors, lords were certainly becoming less able to control the movements of their servile dependants as their manorial officials were increasingly unwilling or unable to enforce the customary restrictions. One strange case should be mentioned where a lord may have been openly defied in his own court. A receiver of John Talbot at Whitchurch in Shropshire, put on trial in 1433 before the court leet of his master, was acquitted of corruptly enjoying certain "profettes" at his master's expense, which were set at just under £15.[107] This may have been a piece of blackmail to force him into some private settlement with his master, but lords did not normally put their agents on trial by a jury of their own tenants unless they were counting on a conviction and it is possible that Lord Talbot's normal expectations were frustrated in this case. The inability of the royal law courts to function expeditiously or impartially, which was becoming a public scandal under Henry VI, made increasingly problematic the enforcement of lords' legal claims against their

---

[107] Pollard, 'Estate management in the later middle ages', pp. 560–1.

dishonest or fugitive officials or against their more powerful free tenants.

H. LORDS AND THE PEASANTRY AFTER 1381

One of the most striking features of English peasant society in the late fourteenth and the fifteenth centuries was the unprecedented mobility of the population. This caused in turn a much quicker turnover in landholding. The authority of the manorial lords had been sustained in the past by the absence of rapid changes and this new situation undermined their control over the persons, labour, and rents of their dependants.

People moved much more freely in search of higher wages and better conditions of landholding. Away from their native villages they would rank in practice as freemen. This could even mean higher wages. At the abbot of Ramsey's manor of Warboys (Hunts.) a carter and a ploughman each received an additional yearly bonus of 8s. because they were free, presumably to ensure that they did not wander away.[108] But it must be stressed that the striking increases in the number of migrants were not simply a response to the existence of better opportunities elsewhere. Only a general deterioration in conditions of life and economic prospects can explain why the movement extended, in some localities at least, to men with substantial holdings, belonging to families long established in their native villages. This certainly happened on the estates of the abbots of Ramsey. While some regions of the country maintained, or even increased, their prosperity, England had also in the first half of the fifteenth century its full share of depressed areas. This was certainly true of the north-eastern region where lay the estates of the bishops and of the cathedral priory of Durham.[109] The history of peasant migrations from the manors of the abbeys of Crowland and Ramsey strongly suggests that economic conditions were also deteriorating in parts of south-eastern Lincolnshire, Cambridgeshire, and Huntingdonshire.

On the Cambridgeshire estates of the abbots of Crowland illicit flights of villeins, numerous since 1350, became a flood from around 1395 onwards. In 1396 slips of parchment began to be attached to the manorial account rolls recording the debts owed by the fugitives. As vacant holdings accumulated in the abbot's hands, he tried to force the remaining villagers to designate new tenants, but he had to abandon all claims to fines for entry from these reluctant nominees of their

---

[108] Raftis, *Estates of Ramsey Abbey*, p. 201.
[109] Dobson, *Durham Priory*, ch. 8; Storey, *Thomas Langley and the Bishopric of Durham*, p. 70.

communities. The abandoned tenements were increasingly left in a state of serious disrepair. After 1394 the abbot's officials had to spend money on the restoring of almost every vacated tenement.[110]

In near-by Huntingdonshire, similar villein flights began around 1400 on the properties of the abbey of Ramsey. It coincided here with the leasing of the remaining portions of the abbot's demesnes. Hitherto the gradual leasing by the abbot of some bits of demesnes may have helped to retain some of the peasantry in the village. Once their chances of getting more of the lord's land had gone, a larger exodus began. Throughout the first half of the fifteenth century the abbot did everything in his power to stop the flight of his villeins, but he was largely helpless. Detailed records were kept of the whereabouts of the fugitives and of their descendants in the hope that this might somehow profit the abbot. Concessions were made to the remaining tenants to retain them on Ramsey properties. In 1452 William Wattes was freed by the abbot from serfdom at Abbots Ripton on condition that he should continue to live there for the rest of his life, maintaining the tenement held of the abbot in good repair and "paying the rents at the usual times as well as all the other obligations". This was probably not an isolated case. From the time that William Wattes gained his independence there was a decided fall in the number of tenements left unoccupied in Ramsey villages.[111]

The threat to leave could be the ultimate argument in the resistance of the tenants to seigneurial demands. When during the vacancy of the bishopric of Worcester in 1433–5 the royal custodians tried to reimpose obsolete exactions, they were assured that an exodus of tenants would ensue. This was the end of the attempt to collect a "recognition" from the tenants at the original high rate, current in 1302, but much reduced after 1349. A recent outbreak of plague in 1434 had increased local depopulation and the ability of the tenants to settle elsewhere was not in doubt. Nor was this an idle threat. On two of the bishop's estates, Alvechurch (Worcs.) and Blockley (Glos.), some of the peasants did migrate in order to escape paying rents and other dues to the custodians. Because of this, the reeves and rent-collecting beadles incurred arrears amounting to £12 16s. 2½d., and these debts had to be written off as the fugitives had removed all their chattels.[112]

Flight had always been the last resort of ruined officials. After about 1400 this became a frequent occurrence on the estates of Ramsey abbey. As the tenants proved increasingly unable or unwilling to discharge their obligations, arrears of rents and other dues grew apace and many

---

[110] Page, *Crowland Abbey*, pp. 148–9, 153.
[111] Raftis, *Estates of Ramsey Abbey*, pp. 282–4; *idem, Tenure and Mobility*, pp. 152–78, 189.
[112] Worcs. RO, BA 2636/174/92465.

of the abbey's manorial officials were trapped in a deteriorating situation. At Upwood in 1407 ten acting or former officials owed between them £17 9s. 7d. The liabilities of the beadles, who were the collectors of rents, accounted for a large part of this total. This may be the reason why a good many members of the leading Upwood families left the village about this time. The abbots of Ramsey do not appear to have tried to seize the goods of their defaulting officials unless they had fled or died, but several of their agents were ruined. A survey of the arrears due at the manor of Slepe in 1419 revealed that sixteen men owed £108 2s. 6d. A previous farmer of the manor, who by himself owed £59 8s. 6d., was devoid of any assets as were two former beadles. A former reeve who owed £7 had fled, and the majority of the debtors were dead.[113] Even superior officials could be reduced to a hopeless situation. Thomas Lawson, the bursar of Durham Cathedral priory from 1432 to 1438, was admittedly an inadequate man, but it was his fate to be in charge of the priory's revenues at a time of agrarian depression. It was later alleged that he had piled up debts of over £1,210, "concealed from the prior and convent". Lawson was touring the convent's estates when news reached him that the full extent of his mismanagement had been uncovered. He fled in the middle of the night and disappeared into hiding. A special tax had to be imposed on all the dependencies of the priory to cover the losses thus incurred.[114]

Flights of villeins played their part in the initial undermining of the manorial organization that ultimately led to the leasing of the seigneurial demesnes and the commutation of labour services. These changes disrupted traditional village society and obviously, as on Ramsey estates, they might aggravate the economic decline. "The increasing indebtedness on the manorial accounts, the disrepair and dilapidation of properties, the under-capitalisation of demesne" in the hands of impoverished farmers "reduced opportunities for the villager in his home manor". All this in turn led to still larger migrations. A chain of events was set in motion which could lead to a virtual depopulation of some localities. On the estates of the cathedral priory of Durham, at the height of the economic depression in the years before 1446, the reluctance of peasants to take up available leases on terms acceptable to the monks led to widespread neglect of cultivable land: "In South Shields most of the vill lay waste and completely depopulated."[115]

At least fifteen families lived in 1363 at Brookend, an Oxfordshire manor of the abbots of Oseney. Flights of villeins first became a serious

[113] Raftis, 'Changes in an English village' p. 175; *idem, Estates of Ramsey Abbey*, p. 294.
[114] Dobson, *Durham Priory*, pp. 285–8.
[115] *Ibid.*, pp. 284–5; Raftis, *Tenure and Mobility*, p. 170 n.11.

problem in 1381. During the subsequent years the abbots tried to check this by imposing collective fines on the whole population in order to compel the return of the fugitives. This had the opposite effect of stimulating further flights. The vacated holdings were engrossed by a few richer tenants. "When a tenant engrossed several holdings the lord tried to insist that he keep all the buildings in good repair. This was very unpopular with the tenants. Many of those who left Brookend did so because they were harrassed by the lord to carry out repairs." The abbot was fighting a losing battle and once the vacated homesteads fell into ruin it became certain that they would never attract new settlers. By 1441 only three landholders remained permanently, of whom two held between them $5\frac{1}{2}$ virgates, while the abbot had on his hands a further $7\frac{1}{2}$ virgates which no one was willing to lease for long periods. By 1469 the abbot had ceased to exploit any land at Brookend, which was now split up among four tenants, the wealthiest of whom held $8\frac{1}{8}$ virgates.[116] Brookend was depopulated against the wishes of its lord. Deliberate depopulation of hamlets, or even populous villages, by landlords was also occurring in the fifteenth century and, especially in parts of the midlands, was beginning to become a major cause of misery and anxiety among the peasantry. More detailed attention will be given to these disturbing innovations in studying the particularly disordered decades after 1450. A chronic shortage of dependable labour would by itself explain why wages continued to rise throughout the late fourteenth and fifteenth centuries. However, the wanderings of a large group of uprooted, restless, migratory labourers tended to raise wages still further. It would be a mistake to regard the rises in the wages of agricultural employees as invariably a sign of friction between agricultural labourers and their masters. A desire to reward fairly satisfactory labourers or to give added incentives for good work presumably lies behind some deliberate awards of higher wages to permanent employees, such as occurred in 1401 on the Kentish manor of Wrotham belonging to Archbishop Arundel of Canterbury. Wages of all the agricultural servants were raised "so that they should conduct themselves better in the lord's service". A glance at the movement of wages of a particular type of labourer or at the oscillations in differentials between workmen of unequal skills, as they can be studied for example on the estates of Crowland abbey between 1381 and 1417, reveals puzzling fluctuations that cannot be fitted into any intelligible pattern. In order to explain them we would have to know a good deal about each of these labourers.[117]

[116] T. H. Lloyd, 'Some documentary sidelights on the deserted Oxfordshire village of Brookend', *Oxoniensia*, XXIX–XXX, 1964–5, pp. 123–8.

[117] Du Boulay, 'Demesne farming at Otford', p. 123 n.3; Page, *Crowland Abbey*, pp. 315–16.

The enforcement of the regulations about wages and prices was significantly reformed in 1389. Justices of the peace and of labourers in each county were ordered to promulgate twice a year local schedules of lawful wages which were to be related to the current prices of victuals.[118] This new flexibility meant, in practice, that an element of uncertainty was introduced that boded ill for the enforcement of these rules in the future. The proceedings at Oxford in the last decade of the fourteenth century show that many of the alleged offenders were really unsure whether they had broken any regulations.[119] The statute of 1389 specifically enacted that the schedules of wages promulgated by the justices were to be enforced as if they had been laid down in the statute itself. Subsequent legislation in the first decade of Henry VI's reign shows, however, that as no specific penalties were mentioned in the enactment of 1389 for the infringement of the orders of the justices, this often became an excuse for not punishing offenders. There was also a marked reluctance to convict because employers might have to be punished as well as their labourers. A new addition to the existing legislation, early in the reign of Henry IV, introducing fines on labourers who had drawn wages for feast days, expressly exempted their masters from any punishment. The statute of 1427 extended this exemption to all breaches of the labour legislation on the ground that otherwise it was quite unenforceable, "because the punishment...is too hard upon the masters of such servants, forasmuch as they shall be destitute of servants if they do not want to bypass the ordinance of the statute." This concession was rescinded in a new statute of 1445, at a time when there were again particularly widespread rises in wages. The preamble explained that the justices were inflicting derisorily small fines and a minimum amercement of 3s. 4d. was enjoined. This statute of 1445 reintroduced a national schedule of lawful wages. In cases where comparisons are possible, these were now roughly twice as high as the rates permitted in 1351 and marked also a significant advance on the wages sanctioned in 1388. Though obviously incapable of stemming the rises in wages, the labour legislation still remained enough of an irritant to appear in the articles of the Kentish rebels of 1450. In the "requests by the Captaine...in Kent" the Statute of Labourers is mentioned among the things "they may no longer beare".[120]

Individual employers tried to counter the rises in wages by employing fewer permanent agricultural servants and expecting them to work longer hours. Two exceptionally well-managed estates provide

[118] *Rot. Parl.*, III, pp. 268–9 (no. 38); *SR*, II, p. 63 (13 Richard II, St. 1, c. 8).

[119] H. E. Salter, ed., *Medieval Archives of the University of Oxford*, II, Oxford Hist. Soc., LXXIII, 1921, p. x.

[120] *SR*, II, pp. 233–5 (6 Henry VI, c. 3), 337–9 (23 Henry VI, c. 12); *Rot. Parl.*, III, pp. 501–2 (nos. 59–60); v, p. 113; Dobson, *Peasants' Revolt*, p. 342.

instructive examples of this, though in both cases an excessive rise in wages could not be avoided in the long run. Otford in Kent was the last of the home farms retained in direct cultivation by the archbishops of Canterbury. From the late fourteenth century until 1428 the annual labour bill rarely reached £10 and was maintained at that level partly through cuts in the labour force. In 1393 the number of permanent ploughmen was reduced from six to four. After 1428 the £10 annual limit began to be breached regularly. In 1443, the year of the death of Archbishop Chichele, the expenditure on wages rose to £23. In 1443–4 a new agreement had to be reached with the manorial staff, commuting the corn liveries annually made to them into money payments at a rate favourable to them. In that year Otford was being run at a loss and in 1444 Chichele's successor understandably decided to lease it.

Alciston in Sussex, belonging to the abbey of Battle, was exploited with exceptional efficiency. The use of tenant labour had caused problems in the fourteenth century and, at the time of the Peasants' Revolt, a large amount of hired labour had to be used, because of a temporary strike of the abbey's villeins. Some twenty-three agricultural servants were employed in the decade after the revolt, and by 1408–9 the use of tenant labour had been virtually given up. For most of the fifteenth century the abbey continued to manage Alciston with the labour of its permanent servants, though cutting down on their numbers and increasing the amount of work demanded of them. There were periodic rises in wages, but differentials between labourers of differing skills were sharply maintained. Between 1445 and 1487–8 the abbey managed to maintain an almost identical wage bill. But by the last quarter of the fifteenth century the area under cultivation had shrunk to less than half of what it was a century earlier. This, and the rising costs finally led to the leasing of Alciston in 1496.[121]

If attention is confined to the period from c. 1400 to 1460, two types of happenings provide the main evidence for the existence of chronic friction between some landlords and their tenants: the persistent flights of peasants from their native villages, and the "rent strikes", which have received considerable recent attention. But we must not confuse two different sets of circumstances that might lie behind the refusal of tenants to pay their dues. Resistance to seigneurial demands sprang in many cases from real impoverishment of the tenants. In some parts of England they were hit even harder by the general agrarian depression than were their lords. This is a very different matter from movements organized by relatively prosperous tenantry who were trying merely to profit from their lords' embarrassments to improve still further their own position.

---

[121] Brent, 'Alciston manor', pp. 95–102.

One suspects that impoverishment was the main driving force behind the failure of the tenantry of the abbots of Ramsey to fulfil their obligations. Reductions of customary rents from holdings mounted, reaching a climax about the middle of the century. They either took the form of outright rebates, or else of reductions in the first years of tenure of a new tenant "for repairs" or "for recovery". Debts of officials increased apace. Some were pardoned because nothing could be levied from the tenants, or, as the accounts put it, "they do not know where they are able to raise them". Arrears, usually slight before 1400, started increasing fast in the first decade of the fifteenth century. At Houghton, a particularly depressed manor, they reached £48 in 1408. Much worse was yet to come. By 1452 arrears climbed to £170 15s. and attained £261 in 1456. Here, as on other estates, all this accumulated mass of irrecoverable debts had simply to be written off a few years later.[122]

The "rent strike" on the estates of the bishops of Worcester also reached a climax in the episcopate of Bishop Carpenter between 1444 and the early 1460s.[123] Much of the most determined resistance to seigneurial dues was confined to a group of episcopal estates in eastern Gloucestershire and properties closely adjoining them. The Cotswolds appear to have been particularly prone to popular disturbances in that period. The abbot of Gloucester seized all the chattels of his bondmen on two of his Cotswold estates in 1412. In 1449 another abbot of Gloucester provoked a violent assault on the estates of the abbey by his friendship with the royal court. The attack occurred after he had returned from an embassy to the German emperor.[124] The success of the tenantry at Cheltenham in reducing between 1445 and 1453 the size of their annual payments for the commuted labour services has also been noted above. This parallels the same kind of opposition to seigneurial dues on Bishop Carpenter's properties at Bibury, Withington, Blockley, and Bishop's Cleve (Glos.), as well as Cleeve's near neighbour, the manor of Bredon, just across the border into Worcestershire.

On these episcopal estates the most tenacious opposition occurred against renders originally arising out of serfdom and against seigneurial exactions other than rents paid directly in return for land. Bredon and Bishop's Cleeve formed the most obdurate core of resistance. According to Bishop Carpenter's roll of arrears drawn up in 1462, since

---

[122] Raftis, *Estates of Ramsey Abbey*, pp. 288, 292, 298.

[123] Dyer, 'A redistribution of incomes', pp. 11–33, supplemented with further evidence from the PRO and Worcs. RO.

[124] Hilton, *English Peasantry*, p. 62; 'Gloucester Annals' in C. L. Kingsford, *English Historical Literature in the Fifteenth Century*, Oxford, 1913, pp. 355–6.

the time of his accession in 1444 these manors had entirely failed to pay both "worksilver" in commutation of labour services and the annual common fine due in recognition of the lord's right to hold the view of frankpledge over his villein tenants. At Bibury the same payments began to be discontinued in 1450. No annual tallage could be levied at Withington under Bishop Carpenter, the tenants alleging that it had been relaxed by the bishop's predecessors. The bishop claimed that on these four estates the non-payment of these seigneurial dues had caused him a loss of at least £59 7s. The reeve's account for Bredon in 1455–6 shows that in that year only about one-eighth of the fines imposed by the manorial court could be collected. Of particular interest is the refusal of several villages to continue to pay "churchscot", an ancient due dating from before the time of the Norman Conquest. This was withheld at Bibury and a few other places, as was "woodsilver", an annual payment for the right to use the lord's woods, which since 1444 had not been paid at Tredington; and the annual render of £1 for the fisheries at Bredon, which could not be raised from 1458 onwards. Some of this resistance was undoubtedly encouraged by important free tenants at odds with the bishop. Thomas Throckmorton, a member of a thriving family closely connected with the earls of Warwick, was himself withholding from Bishop Carpenter rents from his freeholds, amounting between 1444 and 1462 to £180. He was also responsible for the refusal of the tenants at Fladbury (Worcs.) to contribute 3s. of the annual common fine, while the lordly family of the Botelers were similarly behind the loss of 4s. a year from the common fine due from two dependencies of Bishop's Cleeve.[125]

A poem written in 1401 in the dialect of that area of the south-western midlands complained that lords would never take any notice of what grieved the "comouns" unless payments of rents ceased. The withholding of rents was clearly something quite familiar to landholders in that part of the country. It was more widespread than other forms of tenant resistance on the episcopal estates of Worcester. As R. H. Hilton observed, "at what stage the normal medieval dilatoriness in making any cash payment on time merges with what could be called a 'rent strike' is impossible to say". In this view "that stage seems to have been passed" on these estates by the middle of the fifteenth century.[126]

[125] The chief sources are Worcs. RO BA 2636/176/92488 (a roll of arrears on the bishop's estates in 1462) and 193/92627/10/12 (a roll recording measures taken to deal with the arrears, which C. Dyer dates around 1450).

[126] J. Kail, ed., *Twenty Six Political and other Poems*, EETS, CXXIV, 1904, pp. ix–xi, 12; Hilton, *English Peasantry*, p. 65.

One must not ignore the allegations of poverty as an important reason for the refusal of many tenants to pay their rents in full. At Lighthorne (War.), an estate of the earls of Warwick, Richard Beauchamp (the richest earl of his house) ordered his stewards in 1437 to "moderate" the rents levied from the villein holdings "because the tenants had complained that the rents were so heavy that they could not keep alive". In the earl's opinion this was the reason why so many holdings were in the hands of his officials for lack of tenants. We have already seen that similar allegations of poverty secured concessions over rents on some of the properties of the bishops of Worcester during the episcopal vacancy of 1433–5. On the other hand, some of the episcopal tenants were certainly well above the poverty line and were exploiting the eagerness of their poorer neighbours to support them in their resistance to their common masters. To quote a complaint against tenants that a Tudor pamphleteer of 1550 put into the mouths of the landlords, "they will appoint us what rent we shall take for our groundes".[127]

Peasant tenants did not as a rule default completely on their rents. That was the privilege of people much higher up on the social scale, like the Throckmortons or the Vampages, another family of influential gentlemen among the free tenants of the bishops of Worcester. Lesser men could not risk going that far, but merely claimed that they ought to be paying less. Some of the peasant tenants alleged concessions by the previous bishops or else asserted, in spite of contrary evidence, that they were personally free and therefore only liable to smaller fixed payments. Prolonged refusals to pay more than a part of their rents were likely, in the conditions prevailing in the middle of the fifteenth century, to force the bishops to accept the tenants' offer sooner or later, as representing the best that could be got out of them. One of the most striking features of the whole situation was the reluctance of the bishops' officials to take any measures more drastic than imposing fines on the recalcitrant tenants, knowing full well that even these might not be paid. Orders to tenants to carry out repairs on their buildings were ignored for years with impunity. The whereabouts of the bishop's former officials, who had fled from his estates, were perfectly well known, but nothing could seemingly be done to bring them back.

If the rents withheld by the Throckmortons and the Vampages and other debts not connected with the peasantry are put aside, the remaining arrears due to Bishop Carpenter amounted in 1462 to some £930, corresponding to about a year's revenue. If particular estates are examined, one discovers arrears amounting to more than a year's

[127] Ibid., p. 67; J. M. Cowper, ed., The Select Works of Robert Crowley, EETS, xv, 1872, p. xxi; Tawney and Power, Tudor Economic Documents, III, pp. 57–8.

income on eleven properties, that is on more than half the bishop's manors. This was very embarrassing, but the bishop was far from being ruined. His situation closely resembled that of the majority of the major landowners in the middle decades of the century. Even the rents for leased demesnes tended to decline and, where they had been leased collectively to the entire peasantry of the manor, arrears could become quite considerable. However, it is difficult to generalize about the level of rents for leases unless enough is known about the entry-fines paid on their renewal. Unfortunately, fines for larger leases were being collected not by manorial officials but directly by the lord's trusted servants, and are likely to have been recorded only in their household accounts, which are mostly lost.

Allowing for this gap in our information, it does appear that in the middle decades of the fifteenth century the incomes of the majority of major landlords had declined by some hundreds of pounds and a large proportion of accumulated arrears could not be recovered. But they still controlled viable properties and, on most of these, the situation improved somewhat in the last thirty years of the fifteenth century. The richer section of the peasantry was prospering. The labourers were enjoying for the time being higher real wages than was usual in the middle ages, but there were fewer of them and they had to work exceedingly long hours.[128]

I. POPULAR REVOLTS AFTER 1381

Between 1381 and 1405 at least five more popular revolts broke out, or were averted only at the last moment. They were mostly confined to a fairly limited area and only the Cheshire rising of 1403 merged into a major civil war. There were troubles in Kent and the adjoining counties in 1388 and in Yorkshire and Cheshire in 1391–3. The deposition of Richard II in 1399 provoked a series of attempts to overthrow his usurping successor, Henry IV. In one way or another, these conspiracies were responsible for popular movements in Essex and Cheshire in 1400, again in Cheshire and other adjoining districts in 1403, and, lastly, in and around York in 1405. Like the Great Revolt of 1381, all these risings were triggered off by political events and grievances, but one suspects that the existence of widespread agrarian discontent made it easier to rouse the peasantry of particularly disaffected regions.

In 1388 there was a threat of a particularly dangerous crisis, which might have resembled the revolts of 1381. The population of Kent and

---

[128] For the hours required of workmen in the later middle ages, see D. Knoop and G. P. Jones, 'Masons' wages in medieval England', *Econ. Hist.*, II, 1933, pp. 492–4.

of the other south-eastern counties had been gravely disturbed by the menace of a French invasion in the summer and autumn of 1386. The government's defensive measures had been singularly oppressive and inept, and the forcible evacuation of the inhabitants of some of the coastal areas of Kent caused particular outrage. The king's chamberlain, Sir Simon Burley, who as warden of the Cinque Ports had been in charge of these preventive measures, became the most hated man in Kent. When in the spring of 1388 he was being prosecuted by his political enemies in the "Merciless Parliament", disorders broke out in Kent and the adjoining counties to enforce demands for his execution. A petition presented by the commons in the second session of that parliament (April–May, 1388) shows that there was also vast discontent at the lack of justice and at the high taxes for the war, which seemed utterly wasted. The fear of a general revolt silenced the last attempts to secure Burley's reprieve.[129]

The political causes of the disorders in Yorkshire and Cheshire in 1391–3 remain mysterious.[130] The troubles in Yorkshire, especially around Knaresborough and Doncaster, were stirred by enemies of John of Gaunt and of the violent and corrupt officials whom he maintained in power. The malcontents were recruited almost entirely from the poorer classes and included numerous outlaws. When a small army of rebels briefly occupied Doncaster on 27 January 1392 they prohibited the townsmen to levy tolls on the inhabitants of the surrounding countryside. The much more serious rising in Cheshire in the early months of 1393 was likewise directed against John of Gaunt and his younger brother, Thomas, duke of Gloucester. As a justice of Chester, but also a man unfriendly to Richard II, Gloucester was particularly hated in Cheshire. The revolt against him was but one of a long series of disturbances that recurred there between 1353 and 1403. The county had a well-justified reputation of being one of the most lawless regions of England. In the second half of the fourteenth century it was thinly populated and relatively poor. Service as mercenaries in the Welsh, Scottish, and French wars had for centuries provided one of the main sources of livelihood of the inhabitants of certain districts. From 1356 onwards this violent and hardy population of military veterans turned to raiding the neighbouring English counties, and the special legal immunities of the royal Palatinate of Chester allowed them to do so, with virtual impunity. Its officialdom was notoriously violent,

---

[129] J. J. Palmer, *England, France and Christendom, 1377–99*, London, 1972, pp. 74–6, 136–7, 237–8; J. A. Tuck, *Richard II and the English Nobility*, London, 1973, pp. 75–6, 126.

[130] The best account is Bellamy, 'The northern rebellions in the later years of Richard II', pp. 254–74.

oppressive, and corrupt. The county had suffered from excessive financial exploitation by Edward, the Black Prince, which had caused a sort of rising in 1353. Edward's son, Richard II, was unable in 1389 to levy a subsidy of £2,000 and in 1391 the sheriff was robbed of such part of it as he had finally collected. The rebels of 1393 seem to have been largely recruited from unemployed former soldiers and the revolt ended without much bloodshed when they were enrolled in an army destined for Gascony.

In his later years Richard II treated Cheshire with exceptional favour and recruited there his lawless and universally detested bodyguard of "Cheshire archers". It was inevitable that a conspiracy of some of Richard's friends to assassinate Henry IV at Windsor, early in January 1400, should have had ramifications in Cheshire. The rising started on 10 January in the city of Chester itself, but the rebels also sought reinforcements from the surrounding countryside. The arrival of the news that the main conspiracy had been betrayed put a speedy end to the revolt.[131]

A very different sort of movement occurred in January 1400 in Essex. Thousands of peasants flocked together to lynch John, earl of Huntingdon, Richard's half-brother and one of the leading conspirators against Henry IV. Many of them were former tenants of Thomas, duke of Gloucester, whom Huntingdon had helped to seize at Pleshey in Essex in 1397 and whose subsequent murder they were thus avenging. Huntingdon, though a traitorous rebel, was also Henry IV's brother-in-law, and his execution by Essex peasants was condemned by the king's council, which recorded that "the commons...have become so overbearing that they have not desisted from wilfully killing many of the king's lieges without any process of the law".[132]

The inquiry into the causes of the Cheshire rising of January 1400 was entrusted by Henry IV to his new justice of Chester, Henry ("Hotspur") Percy. What Percy thus learnt about the widespread hostility of the men of Cheshire to the new Lancastrian regime seems to have encouraged him in the summer of 1403 to use the Palatinate of Chester as the base for his own revolt against Henry IV. Cheshire contributed a large contingent to Hotspur's army which was defeated on 21 July at Shrewsbury. Two years later, in May 1405, the Percies instigated yet another rising against Henry IV. The movement was speedily suppressed before the rebels from the northern border, led by

---

[131] In addition to Bellamy, *op. cit.*, see H. J. Hewitt, *Medieval Cheshire*; P. H. W. Booth, 'Taxation and public order in Cheshire', *North. Hist.*, XII, 1976; P. McNiven, 'The Cheshire rising of 1400', *Bull. JRL*, LII, 1970.

[132] A. Goodman, 'The countess and the rebels. Essex and a crisis in English society (1400)', *Essex Arch. Soc.*, 3rd ser. II, 1970, p. 273.

the earl of Northumberland, could combine with a large crowd of townsmen and peasants which Archbishop Scrope of York had assembled near the city of York. His manifesto protested against "the unbearable taxes, subsidies, extortions and oppressions which were ruining the king's subjects", but it is impossible to discover what part these grievances played in rousing his supporters.[133]

While there was plenty of lawlessness in Lancastrian England, no sizeable regional risings occurred again until 1450. In the meantime, the domanial type of estate largely disappeared and with it vanished many of the older grievances of the peasantry. If we are to judge by their manifestos, the rebels of 1450 were moved almost exclusively by political discontents. In this their rising differed considerably from the movements of 1381, but they were clearly inspired by the memories of that Great Revolt: the Kentish leaders of 1450 closely imitated the strategy of Wat Tyler in 1381. In his *Henry VI, Part II*, Shakespeare deemed it quite appropriate to adapt passages from Holinshed's account of the events of 1381 to the doings of Jack Cade in 1450.[134]

On both occasions the population had been exasperated by defeats in France and the waste of the taxes that had been granted to finance the war. Both risings occurred in counties most exposed to French naval raids. After a five years' truce the war had re-started in the summer of 1449 and most of Normandy was lost by the end of that year. A grave shortage of money, inept defensive measures, and rapid desertion of the Norman population combine to explain this stunning débâcle, but the baffled Englishmen at home were prone to ascribe it to treachery within the royal government. In the twelve months after 29 September 1448 English exports of cloth slumped by about 35 per cent below the figures of the previous year and they remained at this low level during 1449–50.[135] This may help to account for the widespread participation of textile workers in the risings in the summer of 1450 and, in particular, for the extension of the original Kentish revolt into the textile areas of Hampshire and Wiltshire.

The taxes levied in the autumn of 1449 were heavier than the usual fiscal burdens of recent years. Half a fifteenth and tenth was collected in November 1449, twice as much as was usually collected at any one time in this period. When in May–June 1450 parliament granted a new, more fairly distributed tax on incomes, it coupled with it a request to the king "to consider the universale poverte and penurie of yowre liege people ... so that we canne, may, ne darr not in eny wyse charge youre seid people with such usuell charges as afore this tyme to yowe have

---

[133] P. McNiven, 'The betrayal of Archbishop Scrope', *Bull. JRL*, LIV, 1971–2, p. 182.

[134] Cf. A. and J. Nicoll, *Holinshed's Chronicle as used in Shakespeare's Plays*, London, 1927, p. 115.

[135] Calculated from Carus-Wilson and Coleman, *England's Export Trade*, pp. 96–7.

been graunted in yowre Parlements". This grant coincided with the outbreak of the revolt in Kent and one of the complaints of the rebels seems to refer to the arrangements for its collection.[136]

It was inevitable that Henry VI's principal minister, William, duke of Suffolk, should have become the scapegoat for the disasters in France. But Suffolk's extreme unpopularity had deeper causes: by exploiting the obvious incapacity of Henry VI to govern effectively, he had by 1447 achieved a virtual monopoly of power. Because he "had no rival in the manipulation of crown patronage", Suffolk was able to misuse his position in ways that outraged even his demoralized contemporaries. "Of all his malpractices in office none was more damaging ... than his perversion of legal processes in favour of his local interests and those of his clients."[137] The Kentish rebels were above all incensed at the exactions and oppressions of Suffolk's underlings in their native county. They demanded the surrender to them for punishment as traitors of a Kentish escheator and four successive sheriffs of the county, one of whom, Lord Saye and Sele, had become by 1450 the king's treasurer. Saye and his son-in-law, William Cromer, who was the sheriff of Kent at the start of the rising, were executed by the rebels after their entry into London.

Suffolk was widely credited with the responsibility for the death, in 1447, while under arrest, of Humphrey, duke of Gloucester, the king's uncle and heir. In June 1450 the Kentish rebels reiterated this charge, coupling with it some further, less justified allegations of other political murders. But during the parliamentary session in November 1449 Suffolk's underlings, within Westminster Palace, certainly tried to kill Ralph, Lord Cromwell, a veteran royal councillor. Thereafter Cromwell became the main instigator of the impeachment of Suffolk by the house of commons when parliament reassembled late in January 1450. Earlier that month, Suffolk's leading associate, the former keeper of the privy seal, Bishop Moleyns of Chichester, had been murdered at Portsmouth by mutinous sailors and soldiers awaiting shipment to Normandy. Their pay had been long in arrears and they accused Moleyns of withholding some of it. One is not surprised to find that this undisciplined force proved worthless in Normandy and was largely massacred by the French on 15 April. The last remaining outposts in Normandy had to surrender within the next two months. The news of these disasters prompted the Kentish risings at the end of May to remove once and for all from the king's entourage the "traitors" who were blamed for the loss of Normandy.

[136] Rot. Parl., v, pp. 142–4, 173; art. 14 of the 'Complaint of the Commons of Kent' in Dobson, Peasants' Revolt, p. 340.

[137] R. L. Storey, The End of the House of Lancaster, London, 1966, p. 59.

These risings in south-eastern England were preceded in the early months of 1450 by a spate of abortive conspiracies or of rumours of them. They are of interest as the forerunners of serious rebellions and because they reveal a strain of virulent anti-clericalism. Kent was one of the centres of Lollardy, and the extreme hatred of beneficed clergy that crops up repeatedly during the troubles in the 1450s seems to have come from men permanently estranged from the established church.[138] A conspiracy of some quite obscure people at Westminster was being investigated in late January 1450: they had allegedly plotted to murder various people close to the king, including the treasurer, Lord Saye, the future victim of the Kentishmen, and Bishop Ayscough of Salisbury, destined to be murdered in Wiltshire in June 1450. A few days later inquiries were afoot into an alleged conspiracy of some 200 men who were said to have gathered on 24 January at Eastry in Kent. Their leader, Thomas Cheyne, yeoman, styled himself "Bluebeard" and distributed among his "captains" titles like the king and queen of the fairies, Robin Hood, and other such fanciful names. But grim intentions were attributed to them, of demanding the surrender of the "traitors" around the king, who were to be executed, and of intending to despoil and kill prelates, monks, and beneficed clergy. Cheyne was executed in February at Canterbury.[139]

The parliamentary proceedings against Suffolk gave wide publicity to his alleged treasons, quite imaginary, of course, as well as to the well-justified charges of corruption, extortion, and perversion of justice. In order to save him the king on 19 March 1450 decreed his exile. A London mob manhandled Suffolk and his servants on their way out of the city. His departure abroad on 30 April gave a signal for attacks on some of the men whom he had sheltered in his days of power. It must be stressed however that some of the people who now took this opportunity to avenge old wrongs had otherwise nothing in common with the popular rebels. On 2 May Sir Humphrey Stafford of Grafton tried to kill, inside the church of Stanton Harcourt in Oxfordshire, the lord of that village, Sir Robert Harcourt, who two years earlier had murdered Stafford's eldest son. Harcourt was personally connected with Suffolk and this probably explains why neither he nor his servants had been previously tried for the murder. Yet Sir Humphrey Stafford was otherwise a loyal supporter of the king and was killed by Cade's men on 18 June, while leading the advance-guard of the king's army.[140]

---

[138] R. Virgoe, 'Some ancient indictments in the King's Bench referring to Kent, 1450–52', in *Kent Records*, ed. F. R. H. Du Boulay, Kent Arch. Soc. Records Branch, XVIII, 1964, p. 218. In 1456 a group of conspirators in Kent, expressly denounced as Lollards, were accused of intending to kill pluralists and men of evil conduct among the beneficed Kentish clergy, and to mutilate the rest: PRO KB 9/288, nos. 58–9.   [139] PRO KB 9/263, nos. 56–8, 64.

[140] Storey, *End of the House of Lancaster*, pp. 57–8.

Suffolk was intercepted on his way abroad by English sailors, who executed him on 2 May and threw his body ashore near Dover. It was soon rumoured in Kent that the king would avenge the murder by devastating the whole county; Lord Saye was quoted as making such threats. It is probable that this fear actually sparked off the general Kentish uprising in the last days of May. The "Complaint of the Commons of Kent", submitted by the rebels to the king in mid-June 1450, starts by explaining that "it is openly voysed that Kent should be destroyed with a royale power, and made a wilde Forest, for the death of the Duke of Suffolke".[141]

Some of the king's intimate entourage was eager to instil in the mind of their suspicious and credulous master the conviction that the Kentish rising was instigated by Richard, duke of York, the principal political rival of Suffolk. The king distrusted York and had relegated him since 1449 to a virtual exile in Ireland as the king's lieutenant there. The claim of the Kentish leader, Jack Cade, that his real name was Mortimer, which would suggest that he was the duke's relative, gave support to the suspicion that he was York's agent. It was obviously to Cade's advantage to make such claims. Some of the men implicated in his rising were later on important supporters of York. By September 1450 the duke was himself sufficiently encouraged by disorders in England to return to this country at the head of an army, in defiance of the king's wishes. But no convincing evidence has hitherto come to light to prove that he had originally instigated the first risings in May–June 1450.

We have the names of over 2,200 people in Kent and Sussex who were pardoned subsequently. They included a substantial group of at least 108 squires and gentlemen and of over 300 yeomen, who were presumably prosperous peasants. Of special interest is the presence among the pardoned of 98 constables of vills and hundreds. Clearly in many communities the ordinary machinery of array was used to send forth contingents under their accustomed local leaders. These were not risings of the discontented poor but formidable general demonstrations by large bodies of men of substance and of some local standing. They were protesting against what they regarded as the betrayal of the country's defences by the "traitors" around the king and against the oppressions and injustices committed by the local underlings of these corrupt royal advisers. It was a rebellion of men who were, or felt themselves to be, outside the charmed circle of major notables and of the corrupt officialdom allied with this top group.

This interpretation of the rising helps to account for the peculiar case of Robert Poynings, member of a local lordly family, who acted as a standard bearer to Cade. He had been deprived of most of his

---

[141] Dobson, *Peasants' Revolt*, p. 338.

inheritance by one of the king's magnate supporters with the complicity of his detested stepmother and of her son by a former marriage, William Cromer, the unpopular sheriff of Kent. Poynings profited from the rising to remove from Cromer's house belongings worth 100 marks which the latter had illegally appropriated after the death of Poynings' father. After the rebellion was over, Poynings apparently did not bother to seek a pardon and remained sufficiently influential in Sussex to be returned as one of that county's shire knights in the parliament of October 1450.[142]

The demands put forward by Jack Cade and his chief supporters further confirm the predominantly political nature of the revolt. The early proclamation of 4 June, specifically Kentish in many of its details,[143] was followed by a fuller and more generalized statement of similar complaints in the documents submitted to Henry VI during the abortive parleys between the king and the rebels in the middle of June.[144] That last document, after protesting that the commons "may no longer beare" the purveyances for the king "of wheat and other graines, beef, mutton and all other victuall", adds that the Statute of Labourers is similarly insupportable. But this "proletarian" complaint is quite isolated. These documents constitute chiefly a skilfully worded programme of political demands, interspersed with protests at fiscal exactions and legal injustices. The need for the protection of property owners who have "great right, truth and perfect Title to their land" against fraudulent deprivation is the subject of one of the clauses. This was clearly concerned only with the rights of freeholders. The inquiries held in Kent in August and September 1450 by a commission headed by Cardinal Kemp amply confirmed the truth of these and other complaints against the malpractices of the Kentish officialdom.[145]

This is not the place for a detailed account of Cade's revolt, and only certain features of it require a further comment. After Henry VI on 18 June dismissed out of hand Cade's demands presented to him in the royal camp on Blackheath, his advisers showed further their contempt for the rebels by confidently sending ahead a small advance party under Sir Humphrey Stafford, which was promptly massacred at Sevenoaks. At the news of this the followers of some of the great lords who

---

[142] R. Jeffs, 'The Poynings–Percy dispute: an example of the interplay of open strife and legal action in the fifteenth century', *Bull. IHR*, xxxvi, 1961.

[143] Published as an appendix to *Three Fifteenth-Century Chronicles*, ed. J. Gairdner, Camden NS xxviii, 1880, pp. 94–9.

[144] Dobson, *Peasants' Revolt*, pp. 338–42. Another somewhat different text is partly printed in Kingsford, *English Historical Literature*, pp. 360–2; and there is yet another, significantly different, version in Magdalen College, Oxford, Ms. Cartae Misc. 306, published in HMC, *8th Report*, 1881, App. I, pp. 266–7.

[145] Cf. Virgoe, 'Some ancient indictments in the King's Bench', pp. 220–41.

followed the king unexpectedly mutinied and the entire royal army suddenly became quite unreliable. Many of its members obviously sympathized with the general political programme of the rebels and especially the demand for the punishment of "traitors". Lord Saye and William Cromer, the *bêtes noires* of the Kentish rebels, were seized in the king's presence and he agreed that they should be dispatched to the Tower of London. Henry himself now fled there and subsequently, despite entreaties from the leading citizens, he abandoned the city to its fate and withdrew to the Lancastrian strongholds in the midlands. He still left Saye and Cromer in the Tower, thus condemning them to murder by the rebels after they had entered London. The inquiries of Cardinal Kemp's commission show that some of the king's leading followers, in retreating through Kent, treated its inhabitants as if this was some foreign enemy country.[146]

The bulk of London's population openly sympathized with the rebels and they were admitted across London Bridge on 3 July without any serious resistance. In addition to Kentishmen, Cade also had followers from Sussex and Surrey, while a substantial Essex contingent entered London from the east. Some plundering occurred and this convinced the richer citizens that Cade must be barred from the city, but they waited until the evening of 5 July for fear that in daylight the London populace might have intervened to help the rebels. A general royal pardon, valid until 8 July, led to the rapid disbandment of the rebel army, but disorders continued for many months in Kent and Sussex. Cade was killed on 12 July by the new sheriff of Kent.

In contrast to what happened in 1381, Cade's followers do not appear to have massacred Flemings or other aliens. Cade made some financial demands on the Italian merchants in London, but did not otherwise molest them. It is clear, however, that in the summer and autumn of 1450 Italians dared not travel through England. Only four sacks of wool were exported that year by aliens in place of the usual hundreds or even thousands. One anti-alien rising occurred in July at Romsey, near Southampton, but this arose out of stresses peculiar to the cloth-manufacturing regions of south-western England. For many years Genoese and other Italian merchants had been in the habit of importing through Southampton unfinished cloth from the Netherlands, dispatching it to various Hampshire villages where labour was particularly cheap, and then re-exporting the finished textiles to the Mediterranean. Romsey formed the main centre of this finishing industry and its men obviously detested their Italian employers. They marched into

[146] See also a statement that Thomas Daniel was killing people in Kent in G. L. Harriss and M. A. Harriss, eds., 'John Benet's Chronicle for the years 1400 to 1462', *Camden Miscellany*, XXIV, Camden 4th ser. IX, 1972, pp. 164, 199.

Southampton "for to have robbyd the lumbardes". The town authorities successfully intervened to protect the Italians, who were the mainstay of Southampton's prosperity.[147]

The disturbances in counties of southern and south-western England had their chief centre in Wiltshire and in the adjoining districts of Berkshire, Dorset, and Hampshire. The risings in Wiltshire are particularly well documented through the survival of a complete file of indictments for that county.[148] A serious revolt began here nearly a month after the outbreak of the Kentish risings, with the murder on 29 June of Bishop Ayscough of Salisbury, the extremely unpopular confessor of Henry VI. His assassins shouted that he was a traitor and deliberately put him to death in the presence of a large crowd. Ayscough had a reputation of being very greedy and large amounts of valuables and other possessions were carried off from his episcopal palace at Salisbury and his various other residences. There were attacks on his properties in different parts of his diocese. This wave of troubles persisted until the first days of August. A new series of risings restarted at the end of that month with an abortive attempt to assassinate the sheriff of Wiltshire. Disturbances continued for some six weeks, ending with a riot on 10 October at Salisbury itself.

The Wiltshire risings seem to have been chiefly confined to textile workers and peasants. Indictments mention very few rebels of a higher social status, and at least one indictment, perhaps truthfully, speaks of a rising designed to destroy all magnates and gentlemen. The presence of all kinds of textile workers, both skilled and unskilled, from every corner of Wiltshire, is particularly noticeable. So is the pronounced hostility to the clergy: Bishop Ayscough was seized while celebrating Mass in the church of Edington. On the day of his murder a large crowd, led by a smith, gathered at Salisbury proclaiming that they intended to destroy all the religious houses in Wiltshire. All manner of religious establishments in various parts of the diocese of Salisbury suffered from attacks. Troubles spread to the neighbouring diocese of Winchester, where Bishop Waynflete's episcopal palace was assaulted.

The exile and death of Suffolk, followed by the murder of other "traitors" such as Lord Saye and Bishop Ayscough, encouraged in other parts of England similar attacks on prominent members of the ruling group and their henchmen. Where there was a powerful group of Suffolk's opponents among the county notables, they took charge of

---

[147] Carus-Wilson and Coleman, *England's Export Trade*, pp. 60–2; O. Coleman, ed., *The Brokage Book of Southampton, 1443–4*, I, Southampton Records Ser. IV, 1960, pp. xxv–xxvi; A. A. Ruddock, *Italian Merchants and Shipping in Southampton, 1270–1600*, Southampton, 1951, pp. 166–7 (although Dr Ruddock was unaware of the main causes of the rising at Romsey).

[148] PRO KB 9/133.

proceeding against his underlings using the established legal machinery, and they restrained the rest of the population from revolting. This would help to explain why no widespread risings occurred in Suffolk's native region of East Anglia, though there were a few scattered outbreaks of violence. The rector of Alderton, who was Suffolk's chaplain, was murdered and there was an assault on the episcopal palace of Bishop Lyhert of Norwich, the confessor of the unpopular Queen Margaret. The sheriff of Worcestershire was assaulted and lost an arm. The people of Gloucestershire ravaged the properties of the abbot of Gloucester, one of Suffolk's prominent supporters. John Brome, an important supplier of meat for the king's household, and a Warwickshire justice of the peace since 1449, endured a series of tribulations in July and August 1450. His house at Warwick was sacked and his store of wine was carried away. The labourers on his estates were so intimidated that they refused to work for him.[149]

Cade's death did not end disturbances in Kent and Sussex. For months rumours persisted that he was still alive. A "second captain" of Kent arose in August 1450 at Faversham; after he had been rounded up and executed a "third captain" appeared, though he too was captured by 30 October. The commission of inquiry into official misdeeds, which started its activities at the end of August under the chairmanship of Cardinal Kemp, included fewer judges than was usual, because some of the justices allegedly did not dare appear in Kent.[150] In January 1451 the king himself visited the county to stop these endemic troubles and several men were executed, but this did not prevent yet another fairly widespread uprising both in Kent and in Sussex in April 1451. Its leader, Robert Haseldene, was executed at Lewes (Sussex) in the middle of May. In contrast to Cade's revolt, all these disturbances involved almost exclusively only craftsmen and peasants.

While Cade's associates had included some people who were well-disposed towards the duke of York, this element rapidly dwindled in the subsequent Kentish disturbances. York himself was included in a Kentish commission appointed in December 1450 to try rebels and this may have helped to destroy popular trust in him. When in February 1452 he was trying to organize risings in various parts of England and moved with an army into Kent, the Kentishmen sullenly kept aloof. His army, encamped at Dartford, was probably smaller than the king's forces and York's only chance of success lay in rousing the Kentishmen. Their refusal to stir forced the duke to surrender to Henry VI.

Between 1452 and 1485 the majority of Englishmen tried as far as possible to avoid being too directly involved in the internal struggles

[149] Kingsford, *English Historical Literature*, pp. 355–6, 366; Dyer, 'A small landowner'.
[150] 'John Benet's Chronicle', eds. Harriss and Harriss, p. 202.

of the Wars of the Roses. The warring princes and magnates preferred to fill their armies with professional military retainers or with the well-trained dependants of the country gentlemen who usually followed one or another of these noble patrons. But nobles might need to inflate their armies by pressing into service the tenantry from their estates. John, Lord Howard, appears to have done so on his properties in East Anglia. One of the earliest known cases of an intervention by the Lord Chancellor to protect the rights of an heir to a small servile holding concerns a copyholder from Toyfield Hall in Middlesex. When his father died, leaving a messuage and $5\frac{1}{2}$ acres of meadow, his son was wrongly rumoured to have been killed while serving in Edward IV's army in Yorkshire, and the lord admitted someone else into the tenement.[151]

These were the first prolonged civil wars in English history where most leading protagonists used propaganda to enlist popular support. They all promised a more effective government and better justice. The ordinary population desperately wanted these things; they turned hopefully to each successive victor in the civil wars, only to be each time more disappointed. In K. B. McFarlane's words, "inevitably they were disposed to regard whoever was in power as responsible for the evils they suffered. Some of them could usually be relied upon to join in any attempt to turn out the existing government."[152] But until the fiscal risings against Henry VII there were no further independent, popular revolts and it is worth stressing that none of the main protagonists in the Wars of the Roses seem to have feared that by rousing popular support they were likely to provoke serious social upheavals.

The last two popular risings of the fifteenth century, in Yorkshire in 1489 and in the south-western shires in 1497, arose out of resistance to taxation. The Yorkshire rising remains a mysterious affair.[153] It is possible that Henry VII secretly desired it in order to increase his grip on the north and to end the predominance of the Percies there. The Yorkshiremen resented their liability to fifteenths and tenths while their northern neighbours on the Scottish border were exempted. The double fifteenth and tenth, granted to Henry VII in November 1487, and used by him to pay the expenses of a campaign in Brittany, was encountering exceptional opposition in Yorkshire. As late as April 1489 most of it still remained unpaid there. Henry Percy, earl of Northumberland, who was the king's chief representative in those

[151] W. I. Haward, 'Economic aspects of the Wars of the Roses in East Anglia', *EHR*, XLI, 1926, pp. 188–9; PRO C 1/31, nos. 342–5.

[152] K. B. McFarlane, 'The Wars of the Roses', *Proc. B. Acad.*, L, 1964, p. 113.

[153] The following account is chiefly based on M. E. James, 'The murder at Cocklodge, 28th April 1489', *Durham Univ. J.*, NS XXVI, 1965, pp. 80–7.

parts, had warned Henry VII that concessions were necessary, but had received in reply peremptory orders to enforce collection. It looks as if the king deliberately wanted to provoke a showdown. Yorkshiremen blamed Northumberland for failing to protect their interests, and, at the news that collection was to continue, a rebel party made their way to Northumberland's home and killed him with several of his servants on 24 April. One of the suspicious features of this affair was the presence of a royal forest official at the head of the rebels. The rising now grew in size, and leadership was assumed by a cousin of Northumberland, whom Henry subsequently treated with suspicious leniency. The rebels briefly occupied York, but were dispersed within a month after a mere skirmish with a royal army.

The Cornishmen revolted in 1497 to resist taxes for a war with Scotland. A subsidy and two fifteenths and tenths, conceded by parliament in January of that year, constituted the heaviest tax grant of the whole reign. The Cornishmen were allegedly assured by one of their leaders, to quote Francis Bacon, that "subsidies were not to be granted nor levied for wars of Scotland", because the feudal duty of military service or its substitute of scutage should have provided for that and "much less when all was quiet and war was made but a pretence to poll and pill the people".[154] The rising started in Cornwall as soon as the collection of the first instalment of these taxes began in May. It was directed against the king's "evil councillors", who were blamed for the imposition of these burdens. One of the main leaders was a blacksmith named Joseph, but members of the lesser gentry joined the movement. The rebels marched east towards London, keeping strict discipline and abstaining from pillage. On the way they even picked up a disgruntled peer, Lord Audley, and appointed him one of their leaders. They were making for Kent, expecting help there, but found none. Entrenched in Cade's former encampment on Blackheath, they were reduced by a much larger royal army after a brisk fight on 17 June. Only the leaders were executed. But the west country was still seething with discontent, and when a Yorkist pretender, Perkin Warbeck, landed in Cornwall on 7 September, another formidable rising flared up. This time the nobility and the gentry of Cornwall and Devon stood mostly by the king and many of them withdrew into Exeter, where the rebels besieged them in vain. The hatred of tax collectors still persisted and some were brutally killed. Warbeck realized by 21 September that all was lost and deserted his men, who soon surrendered. Fines of over £15,000 were collected by Henry VII from the western counties, teaching them a lesson that they did not easily forget. There were no more western risings until 1549.

---

[154] Cited in A. J. Fletcher, *Tudor Rebellions*, 2nd edn, London, 1968, p. 15.

J. ENCLOSURE, DEPOPULATION, AND ENCLOSURE RIOTS

Rural depopulation was one of the most intractable social problems inherited by Tudor statesmen. Cardinal Wolsey started an inquiry into this matter in 1517 and several of his ablest successors tried to tackle it in one way or another. They all assumed that depopulation was being caused by the deliberate action of landlords, by what a Warwickshire chantry priest, John Rous, writing about 1486 called "the plague of avarice",[155] and was therefore capable of being checked by governmental intervention. It was assumed that depopulation resulted from combining smaller farms into larger units, the eviction of tenants, and sometimes the conversion of the depopulated arable land into pasture for cattle or sheep, especially the latter. The large pasture farms had, of course, to be fenced in, and hence the custom had sprung up of summing up all these changes under the single term of enclosure, though this does not always appropriately describe them.

Mention has already been made of examples of depopulation over periods of many years, as one tenant after another withdrew from shrunken villages to more attractive places. Sometimes, as at Brookend in the Cotswolds, this had happened despite all the efforts of the lord to arrest such ruinous desertion of his properties. The village of Woollashill (Worcs.) belonged until 1436 to a family of that name, who owned very little else and had concentrated all their serfs on this one manor. Before 1348 there were twenty-two tenants, of whom as many as twenty were servile villeins. This, and the relatively high level of rents, may explain the gradual drift away of the population, especially as the soil was also not very fertile. By 1442 the village's new lord, John Vampage, the royal attorney-general, was left with only nine tenants and several vacant holdings. At some date during the next hundred years the Vampages "found so many holdings on their hands that pasture farming seemed the most profitable way of exploiting both demesne and vacant tenant land".[156]

But destruction could come to a village suddenly and brutally. According to the Leicestershire returns to Wolsey's inquiry of 1517 and the subsequent judicial proceedings, on 2 October 1494 the earl of Shrewsbury had evicted sixty people at Bittesby. On 10 November 1495 Sir Ralph Shirley drove out thirty people from Willowes who, according to the jurors, "departed weeping and probably perished". Sir Robert Brudenell, the new owner of Holyoak, and later chief justice of common pleas, on 2 December 1496 turned adrift thirty people who

---

[155] Beresford, 'The lost villages of Yorkshire', Part II, *Yorks. Arch. J.*, XXXVIII, 1952, p. 48.

[156] C. Dyer, 'The deserted medieval village of Woollashill', *Worcs. Arch. Soc.*, 3rd ser. I, 1965–7, pp. 55–61.

were allegedly "killed or perished". Sir John Villiers was accused of evicting twenty-four people from Brooksby on 6 December 1492, though this charge was denied by his successors in 1545. One striking feature of all these examples of mass eviction is that they took place in the autumn or early winter, after the last harvest had been cleared and in good time to prepare the conversion to pasture, in utter disregard of the dangers threatening the hapless victims during the most inhospitable part of the year.

These inhuman proceedings may have been exceptional and there has been a tendency among historians to minimize the extent of forcible depopulation. Most of the statistics published so far seem to be incomplete and to underestimate the amount of dislocation that may have occurred in certain midland districts, especially in south Warwickshire and Leicestershire, where much land was equally suitable for arable or for pasture. Nor can this merely be treated as a matter of statistics. These proceedings must have sent shudders of fear and insecurity through the entire countryside of the midland counties most affected. On a smaller scale depopulation was occurring also in the fifteenth century in Lincolnshire and the East Riding of Yorkshire.

Because Wolsey was the first minister to start official inquiries into depopulation, we know far more about what was happening after 1485 than about the much more obscure period of the reigns of Henry VI and the Yorkist kings. A survey of deserted villages in Leicestershire records some twenty localities wholly or partly depopulated under Henry VII, as against only about five cases between 1450 and 1485. Yet John Hales, who in the 1540s was an expert on the subject of "enclosures", firmly believed that "the chief destruction of towns and decay of houses was before the beginning of the reign of Henry VII". Hales was employed in 1547–9 by Protector Somerset to hold inquiries into depopulation and to devise remedial legislation, and there is every reason to assume that this particular comment was based upon correct information.[157]

Hales's statement is borne out by the activity and writings of John Rous. This chantry priest in the service of successive earls of Warwick was particularly interested in the antiquities of his native Warwickshire, and shocked by its gradual depopulation in the course of the fifteenth century. He presented a petition against it, now lost, during the Coventry parliament of 1459. Presumably he wanted some specific royal intervention and must have been petitioning against deliberate depopulation by landlords. Nearly thirty years later, in his *Historia Regum Angliae*, when describing the wasting of Yorkshire by William

[157] J. Thirsk, in *VCH Leics.*, II, pp. 254–64; E. Lamond, ed., *A Discourse of the Common Weal of this Realm of England*, Cambridge, 1929, p. lxiii.

the Conqueror, he inserted a passage on what he regarded as a comparable destruction of parts of his own native district in his own time. Rous wrote this passage about 1486 and there is no evidence that Hales knew it.[158] He listed fifty-eight localities partly or wholly depopulated within the radius of about twelve miles round Warwick, mostly in southern Warwickshire but including a few in Gloucestershire and Worcestershire. He was a serious investigator: in the case of eleven villages he compares their much larger population in the hundred rolls of 1279 with the situation in his own day. His statements inspire confidence. Only twice does he say explicitly that the expulsion of tenants caused depopulation: at Billesley Trussell, where after turning out the tenants (*omnibus expulsis*) only the manor house remained; and at Fulbrook where John, duke of Bedford, created a park in 1421 after first, according to Rous, driving out all the villeins (*villanis effugatis*). Clearly, however, he regarded depopulation as due largely to greedy landlords (*per tales cupidos*) and he hoped that God would avenge this "nefarious slaughter of villages".

Using chiefly the lists of Rous and of William Dugdale, a seventeenth-century historian of Warwickshire, at least seventy-four localities in that county have been identified which were wholly or partly depopulated in the fifteenth century, mostly by 1485. Rous stressed the decline of trade resulting from depopulation at that time, but he deplored above all the increase of insecurity. Because of the destruction of Church Charwelton, where travellers from Warwick to London sought refuge in the past, they now deviated from the route they once had followed. Causton-over-Dunnismore, bereft of its inhabitants, was now a hide-out for robbers and murderers, and the ordinary road from Coventry to London had become hazardous. Rous concludes that "if such destruction took place in other parts of the kingdom, it would be a danger to the whole country". It must certainly have increased the insecurity of peasant communities in the midlands.[159]

Directly or by implication Rous provides the most detailed body of evidence for assuming that, before 1485, many landlords were responsible for deliberate depopulation of settlements. The exceptional lawlessness prevalent under Henry VI and the Yorkist kings may have facilitated the forcible evictions of "inconvenient" tenantry, a suggestion which requires more detailed confirmation from future

---

[158] W. E. Tate, 'Enclosure acts and awards relating to Warwickshire', *Birmingham Arch. Soc.*, LXV for 1943–5 (publ. 1949), pp. 58–61; M. W. Beresford, 'The deserted villages of Warwickshire', *ibid.*, LXVI for 1945–6 (publ. 1950), p. 55.

[159] Cited in Beresford, 'Deserted villages of Warwickshire', p. 54. Rous may have been wrong about Fulbrook: Dyer, 'Deserted medieval villages in the West Midlands', p. 25.

research. Modern scholars, tempted by the much more abundant evidence after 1485, have done little to explore the possible connections between lawlessness in the age of the Wars of the Roses and an increase in the frequency of deliberate acts of depopulation by landlords.

The civil wars led to numerous confiscations of estates, followed by their re-grant to new owners who might be more likely to have recourse to radical innovation. Wormleighton (War.) was confiscated in 1495 when its hereditary lord, Sir Simon Montfort, was executed for alleged complicity in the conspiracy of Sir William Stanley. It was regranted to a leading household official of Henry VII who, in 1499, proceeded to depopulate it, turning sixty people adrift. Acquisition of an estate by an enriched former native of a village could be equally disturbing. Henry Weaver, who originated from Cestersover in Warwickshire, had prospered as a London draper, becoming one of the city's sheriffs. His native village was granted to him by Edward IV between 1462 and 1467, whereupon he enclosed some 500 acres, turning most of them into pasture.[160]

Violent attacks by peasants on enclosed land raises a presumption that they were avenging wrongs suffered previously. In 1448 a husbandman of Hoton (Leics.) was charged with breaking down the enclosure of Richard Neel, a justice of common pleas, and ploughing up his pastures. In 1463, in the same county, four husbandmen allied with a merchant of Leicester were accused of invading the enclosed pasture of the lord of Frisby and pasturing their own animals on it. A man who had leased 360 acres of pasture from the abbey of Garendon at Eastwell (Leics.) complained in 1490 that this land had been forcibly ploughed up by a number of people.[161] One suspects that many other rural riots of this period likewise arose out of previous conversions of arable to pasture.

K. CONCLUSION

As we have just seen, in the second half of the fifteenth century some lords were able to turn to more profitable uses the vacant holdings of their serfs after having first expelled these "inconvenient" tenants. But, except in certain regions particularly suited for conversion to pasture, the majority of lords continued to depend upon their tenants' rents, which they were anxious to retain. We have already traced some of the concessions over services and rents which landlords were being forced to make in the later fourteenth and fifteenth centuries. Equally far-reaching, but much less obvious, were the gradual changes in ideas about the conditions on which the former servile tenantry held their

[160] Thorpe, 'The lord and the landscape', p. 51; Beresford, 'Deserted villages of Warwickshire', p. 89. [161] R. H. Hilton in *VCH Leics.*, II, p. 193.

lands. Here, too, passive resistance by the peasantry, together with the very real threat that they might migrate elsewhere, forced lords into making gradual concessions. In practice servile dependants had increasingly to be treated as hereditary tenants and seigneurial controls over their right to sublet land were silently abandoned. It became wiser for lords to attenuate and ultimately to omit altogether all references to serfdom. These shifts in ideas about what was practicable were reflected in gradual changes in the words used in the manorial court rolls. The resultant evolution of nomenclature is very significant and deserves much more systematic study than it has received hitherto. The pace of change might be different even on the estates of the same landlord, as is certainly true of the properties of the abbots of Ramsey. The ultimate consequence was the consolidation in the course of the fifteenth century of a new legal terminology. By 1500 lawyers assumed that peasants who were not freeholders held by copyhold tenure, based on the record of the tenant's admission to his holding in the lord's manorial court roll. A tenant who had paid his entry-fine for admission to the holding received a copy of the entry in the court roll.

Once tenants were recognized to enjoy in practice an effective security of tenure, the entries in the court rolls recording the terms on which they had been admitted to their tenements acquired a new and greater legal importance. The courts of common law were debarred in the fifteenth century from paying much notice to these changes, but from the reign of Henry VI onwards we begin to find petitions to the Lord Chancellor asking him to enforce legal claims based on manorial court rolls. In a case that dates from the 1450s a man complained that he had not been allowed to inherit a copyhold tenement held by his mother from the abbot of St Albans because the clerk of the abbot's manorial court had denied that his mother's tenure was recorded in the manorial court roll. A jury of other tenants upheld the plaintiff's claim and the clerk's evasive replies suggest that he had tried to suppress vital evidence.[162]

According to the strict interpretation of the common law, contracts about land between the lords and their servile tenants were not legally enforceable as they could at any moment be broken by the lord. In practice such contracts were being made with increasing frequency from the thirteenth century onwards, though their wording might send shivers through the spine of a common lawyer. Leases of manorial demesne to servile tenants produced some particularly striking "deviations" of nomenclature from an early date. In 1368 the council of John of Gaunt, duke of Lancaster, leased collectively to all the servile peasantry (the "homage") of Long Sutton (Lincs.), for an

[162] Savine, 'Copyhold cases', p. 300.

annual rent of £162 4s. 5d., the duke's entire demesne containing a thousand acres of land with the demesne flocks and herds. The lease was made to the "aforesaid homage and their *heirs in bondage*". Legally bondmen could have no heirs and this choice of words constituted a legal monstrosity, but seventy-one years later the contract still remained in force, though by 1439 the tenantry had managed to reduce their annual rent to £128 6s. 8d.[163]

Occasionally, a particularly explicit entry in a court roll shows how the difficulties experienced by landlords were forcing them into concessions that were gradually modifying servile land tenure. On 10 November 1394, at Cottenham (Cambs.), a tenement of an unusually wealthy deceased man was surrendered into the hands of the abbot of Crowland. It comprised ten virgates and the tenant's widow could not cope with it. Nobody else came forward to take it up, and the abbot finally forced the whole of the servile group ("homage") to designate three men who would hold it. They were not required to pay entry-fines as the tenement had been forced upon them and it was conceded in hereditary tenure, though the abbot carefully avoided in this instance the word "heirs" and used instead the specifically servile term of *sequela* (their brood).[164]

As is to be expected, F. W. Maitland was a pioneer in tracing the changes in tenurial nomenclature. He devoted to them a section of his study of the Cambridgeshire manor of Wilburton belonging to the bishop of Ely. Significant changes in terminology, as in eastern England generally, were first noted by him in the reign of Richard II. At Wilburton their first appearance antedated by several years the leasing of the manorial demesne. Maitland noted that a hereditary grant combined with a servile wording first occurred in 1389, when two different grants were made to two men and their *sequela*, and such concessions multiplied thenceforward. This was a transitional form, replaced later on by grants to a man, his heirs and assigns, the last term recognizing the full freedom to lease or otherwise alienate to all other persons. This new formula first appears at Wilburton in the last years of Richard's reign but the servile nature of the tenement is still safeguarded by the statement that it is held "at the will of the lord". In the first half of the fifteenth century grants to a man and his *sequela* persisted side by side with grants to a tenant and his heirs and assigns.[165]

While landlords were increasingly forced to tolerate a virtually hereditary tenure of servile holdings, some of them were under-standably reluctant to accept the full consequences of this. An illuminating petition to the Lord Chancellor dates from the early 1450s: the plaintiff was a cousin and the next heir of a deceased

[163] Power, *The Wool Trade*, pp. 38–9.   [164] Page, *Crowland Abbey*, p. 418.
[165] F. W. Maitland, *Collected Papers*, ed. H. A. L. Fisher, Cambridge, 1911, II, pp. 400–2.

copyholder at Melksham in Wiltshire. The lord's steward had refused to accept from him the customary entry-fine of one year's rent because a stranger, who apparently had no hereditary claim, had been admitted to the holding on paying a larger fine.[166]

The estates of the abbots of Ramsey supply an exceptional wealth of evidence about the changes in conditions of servile tenure and the consequent evolution of nomenclature. In addition to numerous court rolls from particular manors we have the abbey's court book containing a chronological digest of the admissions of new servile tenants on all his properties between 1397 and 1457. When it begins there is virtually no suggestion of any limitation on the lord's absolute control. A typical grant of 1397 speaks of a grant "in bondage at the will of the lord according to the custom of the manor for the term of the tenant's life rendering annually all services and customary dues entirely as the previous tenant had held it".[167] By 1457 there is an interesting variety of entries which defy any neat summary, with elements of servility often still very much in evidence. This does not entirely support some of the generalizations of J. A. Raftis, whose discussion of the Ramsey evidence is too preoccupied with manors like Lawshall, where exceptionally precocious changes took place in the first half of the fifteenth century.[168]

At Lawshall the manorial court rolls mention no hereditary concessions of holdings between 1392 and 1401, but they constituted the great majority of concessions between 1402 and 1456 (119 out of 139 entries). After 1456 all the holdings without exception were conceded to tenants with their heirs and assigns. But, to judge by the Ramsey court book, as late as the 1450s concessions of holdings for only one life still predominated on the other manors of the abbey. Some of the grants for life specifically prohibited subletting without the abbot's licence. When hereditary concessions were made, the older servile wording was still recurrently used, granting a holding to a tenant and his *sequela* in bondage at the will of the lord.[169]

Maitland noted that at Wilburton it became common in the middle of the fifteenth century to describe the servile tenants as holding *per copiam*. They had received copies of entries on the manorial court rolls recording their admission to their holdings. On the estates of Ramsey abbey mentions of these "copies" creep in more gradually and do not appear to be in general use until the later years of the reign of Edward IV. The term "copy" first appears in the accounting records of the abbey's chamberlain in 1450–1. In the Ramsey court book the earliest

[166] PRO C 1/19/162; Savine, 'Copyhold cases', pp. 299–300.
[167] BL Harl. Ms. 445, f.1r.   [168] Raftis, *Tenure and Mobility*, pp. 202–3.
[169] E.g. BL Harl. Ms. 445, ff.225v (Dec. 1448), 246v (Dec. 1453), 255r (Sept. 1456).

mentions of tenure "by copy" are normally accompanied by a peculiar security clause specifying that if the tenant should default on the payment of rent the lord had the right to reoccupy the holding "notwithstanding this copy" or "notwithstanding the payment of the entry fine". The abbot was clearly uneasy that the possession by the tenants of "copies" might somehow curtail his power to re-enter their holdings. These security clauses suggest that we are watching here early experiments with tenure "by copy". The impression of novelty is reinforced by an entry of 20 September 1456. It specifically mentions that the abbot had re-entered a tenement held by copy after its tenant had fallen in arrears with rent for two years, and had then re-granted it to a new tenant for life only, without any mention this time of tenure "by copy".[170]

One of the principal nightmares of the abbots of Ramsey in the fifteenth century was the fear of accumulating vacant holdings through the loss of tenants. There was no point in evicting new tenants who had failed to pay the promised entry-fines. The abbots allowed them to continue in occupation subject to the payment of tiny amercements of 2d. or 1d. per year, a sort of recognition of lordship. On the margin of the court rolls there appear against these people in the first half of the century notes like "land without fine" or "not fined for". Once tenure "by copy" became the norm these defaulting tenants were denied their copies and came to be labelled in the court rolls as "without copy" (*sine copia*), though in practice they continued to enjoy tranquil possession.[171]

By the end of the fifteenth century "tenure by copy" was widely prevalent, though one suspects that even then it was not universally accepted by all landlords. Where servile tenants enjoyed a virtual heredity of tenure combined with freedom to sublet and alienate, it also became possible for them to devise their holdings by will. In this respect they were freer than the owners of freeholds. In the reign of Henry VII tenants of the manor of Forncett in Norfolk, who are specifically described as of "servile blood" (*nativi de sanguine*), were freely bequeathing to their widows or leaving to their executors their entire holdings.[172]

During most of the fifteenth century copyholders normally recognized that they were not entitled to any protection of their tenure by the courts of common law. In 1440 two daughters of a Southwark grocer, who had been denied their claim to inherit lands at Dulwich held "by copie", petitioned the chancellor for redress because they "be withoute remedie at the common lawe". However, even this situation

---

[170] Raftis, *Tenure and Mobility*, p. 202 n.86; BL Harl. Ms.445, ff.231r (1449–50), 246v (Dec. 1453), 255r.   [171] Raftis, *op. cit.*, pp. 198–9.
[172] F. G. Davenport, *Norfolk Manor*, pp. lxxviii–lxxx.

began to change by the reign of Edward IV at the latest. In two cases, in 1467 and 1481, two different justices of the common pleas expressly affirmed that a customary tenant who had paid his fine for entry and had not defaulted on rents or other services ought to have a right to undisturbed possession. Both justices recognized that no possessory action was available to such tenants, but on both occasions they upheld the validity of an action of trespass by a tenant against a lord who had wrongfully dispossessed him. A successful action of trespass would at least entitle a tenant to damages against his lord. In the case tried in 1481, when the landlord's attorney demurred that no action could be allowed at common law because a copyholder could not aver that he was seized of a freehold, Chief Justice Brian made the interesting distinction that though such a tenant could not indeed claim freehold tenure he could allege freehold *interest* created by his payment of an entry-fine and the due discharge of stipulated services. We are here at the beginning of reasoning that within another century will create an effective legal protection for copyholders through the extension of the action of trespass to their special needs.[173]

The extraordinary bid, by some of the rebels of 1381, for the outright abolition of serfdom was apparently never forgotten among the English peasantry. Henceforward the villeins refused, with ever increasing persistence, to accept that they were unfree. All the burdens that arose specifically out of servile status and tenure met with specially strong opposition for that very reason. It was, however, by piecemeal opposition and passive resistance, rather than by extensive rebellions, that the English peasantry between 1348 and 1500 assured the virtual disappearance of personal serfdom. The attitudes and behaviour of the peasantry contributed greatly to the leasing of manorial demesnes by landlords and to the consequent commutation of labour services. These were permanent changes. The pressure for the reduction of rents and entry-fines also achieved temporary concessions in the late middle ages; and labourers in towns and countryside alike were able to attenuate, and often even nullify altogether, the operation of the labour laws. The improvement in the purchasing power of the labourer's wage, on the other hand, was a temporary boon, soon destined to be reversed under the Tudors. Rents, too, again moved upwards in the sixteenth century, an age in which population once more began to grow, increasing pressure on resources and, consequently, renewing opportunities for highly profitable farming. By 1500 the servile tenantry had gained, at least in part, a species of hereditary tenure; but they remained without adequate protection against eviction by landlords whenever the latter

[173] PRO C 1/9/139; Savine, 'Copyhold cases', pp. 298–9; I. S. Leadam, 'The inquisition of 1517. Inclosures and evictions', *RHS*, NS VI, 1892, pp. 240–4.

were really determined to get rid of unwanted tenants. Legal protection for the titles to their copyholds was achieved by the descendants of the former serfs only after a century of bitterly resented enclosures and evictions. Their claims to unrestricted exploitation of common woodland, pasture and mineral deposits were unrecognized for much longer.

The one permanent result which the peasant revolts did help to achieve was to convince governments that in England it was dangerous to impose particularly oppressive taxes like the poll tax of 1381. England, unlike the kingdom of France, remained a country in which direct taxes were collected only occasionally. The tradition of popular "murmurs" against excessive or too frequent direct taxation persisted into the sixteenth century, and was one which even Henry VIII was unable to ignore.

CHAPTER 9
RURAL BUILDING IN ENGLAND AND WALES

ENGLAND

A. INTRODUCTION

(i) *Building materials*

Timber was the traditional building material of England and thatch the oldest roof covering. It was still possible near the end of the fifteenth century to build manor houses with very considerable timber elements, but it was out of fashion. Men of substance had seen no reason at an earlier date to use stone other than for their military castles unless it was cheap and handy, but by the later fourteenth century house building had become a matter of prestige, an outward sign of prosperity and success. Stone was more prestigious than timber, and where stone was by nature scarce, brick, a material that had been in use in east-coast towns for half a century and more, was eagerly taken up for new houses in the countryside nearby. Nevertheless both materials remained to some extent intrusive among a solid core of timber houses.

It is generally accepted that timber was in short supply in the later middle ages, and certainly the lords kept a tight hand on its felling. It was augmented by a flourishing import trade from the Baltic, especially of floor boards and wainscoting. There is no doubt that a certain amount of planting was going on and that existing woodland was carefully managed. But timber framing required a surprising number of trees – one house, for example, not even of manorial status, was estimated to have required some 300 small trees in its construction.[1] Most lords tended to take timber from their own estates, both for the manor house and its appurtenances, and for the houses of their tenants in places where custom decreed that the principal house timbers should be supplied.

Oak was the usual building timber. Other woods are found both in

[1] Rackham, *Ancient Woodland*, pp.137–40. See also his 'Grundle House: the quantities of timber in certain East Anglian buildings in relation to local supplies', *Vernacular Architecture*, III, 1972, pp. 3–7.

surviving buildings and in building accounts. Of these ash is perhaps the most frequent, but elm and alder are known, and seem to have lasted well, though all were in only occasional use. Oak is the timber normal in surviving manor houses and in barns, in small houses of less than manorial status, in such peasant houses as are still in use, and in building accounts where these are extant.

Amid this universal use of timber, stone building was something of an intrusion. The magnates had occasionally used stone as early as the eleventh century and by the mid-fourteenth most lords had turned to it at least for their more important manors. England produced much good building stone, but its carriage was costly. The wealthy transported it long distances and even brought it from overseas, but preferred to look near at hand for supplies, and first of all to their own estates.[2] They hired quarries or opened them *ad hoc*, only buying on the open market when other sources failed. There were areas too where it was in use even among the peasants, sometimes roughly squared, occasionally as reused ashlar, most frequently in the form of rubble. Small stone-built houses seem to have survived less well than their timber counterparts, perhaps because they were usually bonded with clay, as opposed to the lime mortar in use on larger buildings.[3]

By the late fourteenth century even peasant houses were rarely constructed with groundsills set directly on the bare earth. Sole-plates were generally raised onto low stone walls constructed, in the case of peasant houses, often from material quarried on the croft itself. Posts and crucks tended to be set on padstones, either set directly on the ground or more frequently within the walls. Such raising of the principal timbers has been seen by some as a response to climatic deterioration, but this is still a matter under discussion.[4] Early in the fifteenth century brick became popular for new manor houses, particularly among those investing the profits of the French wars in building, familiarized, perhaps, with its potential by what they had seen of the brickwork of north-west France and the Low Countries. It spread also during the fifteenth century to smaller manors along the lower reaches of the Humber river system, but this seems to have been an independent development. A steady trickle of imported brick can be

[2] A. Clifton Taylor, *The Pattern of English Building*, London, 1972, pp. 58ff for building stone in the regions.

[3] For quarrying practice, Salzman, *Building in England*, pp. 119–39. Lime mortar is not usually present when peasant houses are excavated, nor is it mentioned in the rare building accounts for such houses. Housebote, the right to timber for house building, appears to have extended to the use of stone in some areas: see J. Rawlinson Ford, 'The customary tenant right of the manors of Yealand', *Cumb. and Westmor. Antiq. and Arch. Soc.*, NS, 1909, p. 155.

[4] Wright, 'Barton Blount', pp. 148–52; M. L. Parry, *Climatic Change, Agriculture and Settlement*, pp. 135–46.

traced in the customs accounts, but there is no doubt that most bricks were made from clay dug and fired on the manor for whose house they were intended, by local men, working initially under the supervision of Dutch or German brick-makers. In the course of the century considerable skill was developed both in control of colour and in cutting and moulding brick to emulate stone carving.[5]

(ii) *Building methods*

The principal timbers of all buildings were those that supported the roof and there had long been two methods of construction in use. The first depended on the use of pairs of curved timbers which met at the roof ridge, known in antiquity by a variety of names, but nowadays universally termed crucks; the second dependent on trussed posts. Each had, by the later middle ages, developed a variety of forms. Recent intensive research on the distribution of the two traditions has not substantially altered the well-known pattern, in which crucks were favoured in the west country and post and truss construction preferred in the east, with a broad band in which both forms were in use between the two extremes. It has, however, gone far in refining the distribution of various forms of cruck, and of the methods of joining the crucks to the ridge piece that is an integral component of this method of building. It seems that at manorial level there was a preference for base crucks in the later middle ages, but that this form too was tending to give place to post and truss construction even in the cruck heartland. In those parts of the country where framing had been traditional, crown-post roofs were tending to replace other methods of support.[6]

Timber was rarely seasoned. The usual practice was for the carpenter concerned to select his trees and to oversee their felling. In the case of reconstruction or repair of the houses of customary tenants felling had to be approved and often overseen by a manorial official, even though the trees might be growing on the croft itself.[7] Once felled and rough trimmed, timbers were either taken straight to the building site or to a special framing-place equipped with a saw-pit, where most of the carpentry was done. The work was then dismantled, the timbers

---

[5] Repairs at Stonor (Oxon.) were in brick in 1430. Other manors followed. For brick building in England, see T. P. Smith, *The Medieval Brickmaking Industry*, British Archaeological Reports, British Series 138, Oxford, 1985.

[6] J. T. Smith, 'Cruck distributions: an interpretation of some recent maps', *Vernacular Architecture*, VI, 1975, pp. 3–17. For base crucks: N. W. Alcock and M. W. Barley, 'Medieval roofs with base crucks and short principals', *Antiquaries J.*, LII, 1972, pp. 132–68. The use of crown posts is discussed in E. Mercer, *English Vernacular Houses*, RCHM, London, 1975, pp. 82–8.

[7] For the occasional preference for seasoned timber, see Salzman, *op. cit*, p. 239.

numbered and then carted to the building site where they were
reassembled, pegged, and finally raised, an activity attended by
ceremony and free ale. By 1350 all the major building processes were
in the hands of professionals, though with help from unskilled labour,
including women.

Whatever the building material, the unit of construction in the later
middle ages was the bay, generally measuring 15 feet or more at
manorial level, nearer 10 or 12 feet at peasant level, each bay
terminating in a pair of principal posts or crucks.[8] All types of building
tended to be described in terms of the number of these bays or of the
number of large timbers required rather than in precise measurements.
It was only in the less thriving villages that this type of construction,
and indeed the setting of sole-plates on sill walls, was still unknown by
1350. An intermediate arrangement, the interrupted sill, whereby the
main roof supports were placed on padstones at ground level and
tenoned into a sole-plate placed on the sill wall, tended to be used
mainly at manorial level.

The walls themselves varied considerably: the principal timbers
could be embedded in a wall of thick cob; there could be vertical studs
between the main posts, close or wide-spaced, the intervals infilled with
wattle and daub, or daub strengthened with laths; sometimes there
were two rows of studs, one over the other, separated by a horizontal
rail; or there could be large or small rectangular timber panels,
similarly infilled and sometimes with either arch or tension bracing.
The method preferred was partly a matter of date, rather more a matter
of local custom. Continuous planking, either vertical or horizontal, was
rare but not unknown.

Small houses and the less important buildings of the manorial
complex were normally thatched, though in some parts of the country
thatch was replaced by stone roofing tiles (sclatts) even on peasant
houses. Reed thatch seems to have been more highly considered than
straw thatch, and wheat straw than that of other cereals. Accounts for
thatching indicate the use of considerable amounts of clay for
tempering; cresting, with straw, turf, or either plain or decorated
ceramic ridge tiles, was universal. Stone tiles became popular in the
period, but wooden shingles, in general use for manor-house roofs of
earlier date, seem to have gone out of fashion.

A fair number of manor houses included at least one room floored
with ceramic tiles, occasionally two-coloured and decorated, though
such tiles remained something of a luxury throughout the period.
There was some use of stone flooring, even among the peasantry, and

[8] Dyer, 'English peasant buildings', pp. 19–43.

plank flooring was to be expected in the larger houses, especially for upper rooms, though for these latter floors of plaster mixed with straw or hair were not uncommon. It is probable, however, that the floors of most small houses, as well as those of barns and manorial out-buildings, continued to be of beaten clay, carefully prepared with such inclusions as straw, lime, and even cinders.

B. MANOR HOUSES

(i) *General*

In 1350, though change was on its way, most manor houses retained the characteristics of the previous century. Typically they possessed a dual function, being both residence and farm, in the modern sense of that word, with the whole range of agricultural buildings required for working the demesne lands. The capital messuage, as it was usually called, was both house and farm. In the previous century, indeed, it would have been more appropriate to reverse the terms and say that the typical manor was both farm and house, for so the lords, whose peripatetic way of life did not anchor them exclusively to one residence or one locality, seem to have regarded it. Repairs to farm buildings in the great Bigod estates, for example, came under the heading *domus necessaria* in the accounts, and those to the dwelling house under that of *domus non necessaria*.[9] In a different vein, early leases of the Chapter manors of St Paul's gave precise measurements of barns and byres, while often merely itemizing the domestic buildings.[10] The balance had already begun to change at the beginning of our period; by its end it had been reversed. It will be convenient to consider these two aspects separately, confining this section to the residence, though glancing also at the physical relationship of house to farm.

The life-style of those who occupied manor houses throughout the country differed in degree rather than in kind, regional variation showing itself in carpentry tradition and to a lesser extent in room arrangement, and tending to be blunted in face of common custom. The house of the one-manor man, on the rare occasions when it can be identified, as, for example at Langenhoe, Essex, does not differ in its accommodation from manor houses in ampler estates.

The focal room of all manors, and the largest, was the hall, used for a multitude of purposes from ceremonial dining to the transaction of manorial business, and even to chopping wood, but seldom, contrary

---

[9] The form occurs in all medieval manorial accounts in which repairs are recorded for the Bigod estates in the PRO.

[10] Guildhall Library, St Paul's Cathedral Mss., box 32, no. 644.

to popular belief, for holding the manorial court. There were many variations in detail, but the common elements were opposed doors in the long sides towards the "low end", itself identified by the siting of the service rooms. There was a cross passage between the doors, separated from the body of the hall by either a temporary screen or a permanent wall, and beyond it were the buttery and pantry. At the opposite, or high end, were concentrated such features as dais, canopy, oriel, bay window or other adornment, as well as a door or doors for access to private rooms. Frequent alterations in our period were the raising of window height to give room for tapestries and benches below, and the removal of the old central hearth to a more convenient position, either on one of the long walls or against the wall of the cross passage (Pl. Ia). The hall remained open to the roof until near the end of the period, and even then ceiling was rare, nor is there much sign of a reduction in its size, perhaps because of the importance of ceremony among the seigneurial class. It was, indeed, during this period that the hammer-beam roof was developed, allowing aisle posts to be cleared even from halls of considerable breadth.

The needs of the lord and his family were met by a varying number of private rooms, whose differing disposition will be discussed. On the more important manors their number increased considerably and came to include both a room called a parlour and a dining room, for though it had been usual for the lord to dine in the hall, his presence there came increasingly to be confined to ceremonial occasions. The greater manor houses had long possessed a private chapel. Now a licence for a chapel or oratory was frequently acquired on one pretext or another, and it was usually sited either in the principal chamber or close beside it. A privy was mandatory even on the smallest manors, and usually within the house. The kitchen, by contrast, was nearly always detached, together with its ancillary buildings, the bakehouse, brewhouse, and sometimes a larder for preparing meat (Pl. Ib). Such was the standard manor of the period.

Major manor houses differed partly in the scale of the various apartments, partly in the elaboration of their enclosures and gatehouses, but chiefly in the presence of accommodation for retainers, which increased very considerably during the period. Earlier such manors had included a communal hall for knights, another for squires, and often a third for clerks. Now the demand for increased comfort and privacy prevalent among the lords extended to their followers, leading to the provision of private rooms in considerable numbers, sometimes arranged in one of the wings, sometimes occupying a whole court. Such manors were necessary for king and magnates, and were spreading down the hierarchy among those aspiring to higher status. It must be remembered, however, that the estates of the men who held them included also a stock of standard manors, sometimes leased, sometimes kept in hand.

Below both major and standard manors were what are generally called reeve's manors, on which was the whole run of agricultural buildings, and accommodation in the shape of a chamber for a visiting official, and sometimes a hall. Like all other manor houses they were surrounded by enclosures.

The site of a manor constituted a reserved area that was curiously persistent, its grazing often leased for centuries after the site had been emptied of buildings. Even when divided up and overbuilt it could be kept separate for accounting purposes. Its hedges, quick or dry, its thatched cob walls and its palings needed frequent repair. Stone walls, and the brick walls that were sometimes built towards the end of the period, were both more durable, but a limit was set to their height and solidity unless a licence to crenellate had been acquired. Wet moats on the other hand were cheap to make and easy to maintain, needed no licence, and offered a bonus in the shape of fish. The peak period of moat construction had been somewhat earlier, but where the terrain was suitable the period saw an increase in their numbers and complexity (Pl. IIa). Their distribution was mainly in lowland areas, and especially in the clay lands.[11]

Major manors had usually included a number of separate enclosed courts, and standard manors more than one. The tendency now was to increase the number and to specialize the function of each. Large manors developed separate courts for retainers and often for stabling, each with its gatehouse. Orchards and gardens had their own enclosures and so did the farm, which could sometimes be moved right away from the manor house. Finally, the main enclosure on major manors could itself be compartmentalized, with separate small courts for lord, for important guests, for officials, or for the kitchen and its offices.

Various pressures combined to separate the living quarters of late medieval manors from their farms. The demand for privacy required more rooms and more space; there was increasing interest in the appearance of the house; there was the leasing of arable and stock which meant that farm buildings were not needed by the lord. Nevertheless, in a surprising number of cases farm and manor house remained alongside one another, as they still do today.

Along with these changes went a reduction in the number of manors in regular use by any one family. An important factor here was the sheer expense of the prevailing fashion for ostentatious display, which

[11] H. E. Jean Le Patourel, 'Fortified and semi-fortified manor houses', *Château Gaillard*, IX–X, Caen, 1982, p. 194.

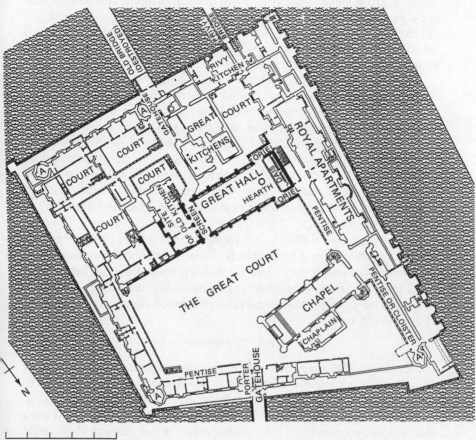

Fig. 9.1 Eltham, Kent, inner court (English Heritage)

spread to all who could afford it and many who could not. Another, important among the magnates, was the enormous amount of accommodation necessary to house their attendant trains. Life, too, was becoming more sedentary for many, with a single manor looked on as "home". Even the king was involved, living entirely in southern England except when military necessity sent him northward. The number of his chamber manors fell from about twenty-five to sixteen during the period and fewer hunting lodges were kept in repair.[12] The trend can be observed also among the major ecclesiastics and lay magnates. The number of Yorkshire houses kept up by the archbishop

[12] Numbers fluctuated somewhat during the period; see R. Allen Brown, H. M. Colvin and A. J. Taylor, *The History of the King's Works*, I, London, 1963, pp. 242–8.

dropped from eleven to seven, while the Staffords are said to have had only two manors that could accommodate their whole train in the fifteenth century. At a lower social level the Methums, who had moved among three Yorkshire houses late in the fourteenth century, were using only one a hundred years later.

When not needed for residence manor houses were usually leased, with the obligation to repair placed squarely on the tenant wherever possible. When the demesne was leased in parcels the agricultural buildings were often split, even into bay units, to go with the land. Both courses led to depreciation and decay. Otherwise buildings could be transferred to other manors on the same estate, or they could be sold off for what they would fetch.[13] Similar treatment was meted out to monastic granges. Empty sites were then either let for grazing, exploited for quarrying or other minor industrial use, or built over, all to provide extra rent.

Monastic granges will not be considered as a separate class, for by this time they differed little from standard manors in accommodation and arrangement, though they were more often stone-built, an inheritance from the past. Some were leased as manors to laymen, others were kept in hand, in which case house and farm continued alongside one another as a working unit.

(ii) The regions

Eastern England is a region where stone was scarce, timber building the norm, and brick eagerly embraced as the fifteenth century advanced. Moated enclosures were very common, especially in East Anglia.

The only royal manor kept in repair was Havering, Essex, and even this was not modernized. It is among other major manors that trends characteristic of the period are visible.[14] Sir John Fastolf rebuilt his house at Caister (Norfolk) in local brick, dressed with stone from France. Wet moats, brick revetted, segregated the two courts one from another and both from the outside world. The house on the principal island included both a hall and a "winter hall", and there was a tall, slender, chamber-tower. Fastolf had spent his working life in France, to which country these features, as well as the use of brick, may owe something. Lodgings for his retainers and servants were on the second island, and the farm lay beyond the moat. He built other houses but in his later years lived only at Caister (Fig. 9.2).[15]

Lord Cromwell's manor at Tattershall was also surrounded by a complex, brick-revetted moat system believed to be contemporary

---

[13] Timbers from Northolt, for example, were sold for use at Sutton, and a whole building moved from Byfleet to Sheen: *ibid.*, pp. 998, 1004.   [14] *Ibid.*, p. 958.

[15] W. D. Simpson and A. J. Barnes, 'Caister Castle', *Antiquaries J.*, XXXII, 1952, pp. 35–41.

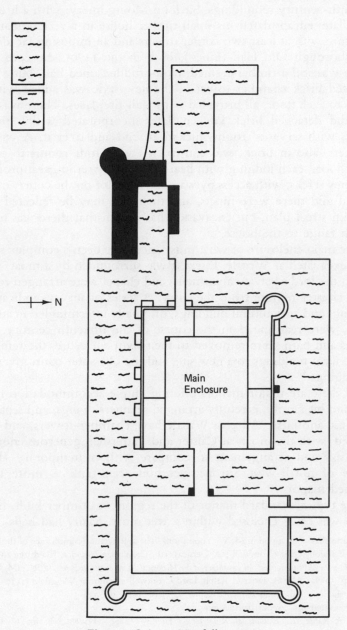

Fig. 9.2 Caister, Norfolk, 1780

with his sumptuous new brick chamber-tower. This was only one among a number of buildings in the principal enclosure, all the rest of which have disappeared. At Faulkbourne (Essex), another of these early fifteenth-century rebuildings, Sir John Montgomery, with a licence to crenellate, encapsulated his small timber house in a rectangular brick structure with at least two corner towers and an imposing façade.[16] At Gainsborough Old Hall (Lincs.), built in the 1470s, the core of the house was still a timber-framed, close-studded open hall, but a three-storeyed brick chamber-tower in the new style was added with one room to each floor, all provided with wall-fireplaces. There was also a splendid detached brick kitchen, later incorporated within the hall range, with servants' rooms tucked around and over it. A wing for retainers, also in brick, was constructed with four rooms to each of three floors, each lodging with hearth and privy set in great projecting chimney stacks, with access by way of a corridor on the courtyard side. Leland said there were moats, and their line may be reflected in the modern street plan, but excavation has shown that there was never a fourth range to the house.[17]

The main enclosure of what must once have been a complex site has been excavated at Writtle, Essex. It was surrounded by a moat, within which the lord's private apartments and chapel were arranged round a small cloister remote from the entry. A series of surveys indicate that lodgings and agricultural buildings, originally intermingled in an outer court, were rearranged in the course of the fifteenth century, when stables and barn were removed to their own enclosure, the remainder of the farm buildings to a new site, and the old outer court given over to lodgings.[18]

All these are major manors offering ample accommodation for the lord and his family, carefully arranged retainers' wings, and separation of house and farm. All save Writtle have chamber-towers, and all are moated, with the moats at Caister and Tattershall generous enough in their size and arrangement to compare with contemporary *Wasserburgen* of north-west Europe, yet none can rank as more than a fortified manor.

The typical standard manor of the region was timber built, though it too was often enclosed within a wet moat. Many had halls of two

---

[16] Tattershall is discussed in M. W. Thompson, 'The architectural significance of the building works of Ralph, Lord Cromwell', A. Detsicas, ed., *Collectanea Historica*, Maidstone, 1981, pp. 155–8. For Faulkbourne, see *An Inventory of the Historical Monuments in Essex*, II, RCHM, England, 1921, pp. 59–72; Also A. Emery, 'Ralph, Lord Cromwell's manor at Wingfield (1439–c. 1450): its construction, design and influence', *Arch. J.*, CXLII, 1985, pp. 332–3.

[17] Excavated 1984, report forthcoming.

[18] P. A. Rahtz, *Excavations at King John's Hunting Lodge, Writtle*, Soc. for Med. Arch., Monograph Ser., III, 1969, pp. 7–12, 24–5.

bays, rather fewer of three bays, with storeyed wings at either end, usually roofed at right-angles to the hall, and with upper floors jettied to give extra space to what were still the most important private rooms. The kitchen was as a rule detached, though it has been suggested that houses such as that at Croxton, Cambs. (Pl. IIb), where one of the wings was sufficiently elongated to dwarf the hall, may foreshadow its eventual inclusion within the house. Some of the older halls still retained their aisles, but new houses had aisleless halls open to a coupled-rafter roof, usually supported with crown posts and often thatched.[19] Houses of Wealden type spread into the region from the south-east, but these will be discussed later. All these manors must originally have possessed outer enclosures, farm buildings, and at least one gatehouse, but survival of such features has been rare. The prestigious gatehouses of the region belonged to large manors like Hadleigh (Essex) or Oxburgh (Norfolk), and were of brick.

The use of brick extended into the east midlands, though there stone was more readily available. The only royal manor to be repaired was at Clipstone (Notts.), and even that was neglected in the fifteenth century. Most of the larger medieval manors still standing had either originated at an earlier period, or have been too much modified by constant occupation to give reliable evidence of their original arrangement. Exceptions are the ruined Hastings manor at Ashby-de-la-Zouch and Kirby Muxloe, both in Leicestershire. Ashby, at first a very modest stone-built house, had grown by accretion, and in the fifteenth century a great stone chamber-tower was built, its principal rooms far above the ground, reached by an adjoining stair turret (Pl. IIIa). Kirby Muxloe, by contrast, was designed as an entity, intended completely to replace an earlier house. It was planned as a quadrangular building with corner towers and an imposing gatehouse, the whole in brick manufactured on the manor, its moat an integral part of the design. It was never finished and no trace remains of a possible base court or farm buildings.[20]

Scrooby (Notts.), a residential manor belonging to the archbishop of York, is now represented only by earthworks, but Leland, usually reliable, said it was of timber, apart from a brick front to the hall, which was approached by a flight of steps.[21] Both the upper-floor hall that this implies and renovation in brick are altogether in line with what was happening on the archbishop's manors further north.

---

[19] *An Inventory of the Historical Monuments in the County of Cambridge*, I, RCHM, England, London, 1968. For typology of medieval houses in the county, p. xlvii; for Croxton, p. 68.

[20] T. L. Jones, *Ashby de la Zouch Castle*, London, 1953, pp. 5–12, 20. For Kirby: A. Hamilton Thompson, 'The building accounts of Kirby Muxloe castle', *Leics. Arch. Soc.*, XI, 1913–20, pp. 193ff.   [21] Leland, *Itinerary*, p. 34.

A group of Lancastrian manors in the region are of interest because the survival of account rolls demonstrates the varied fates of redundant houses. They were grouped with Higham Ferrers (Northants.), where the castle was kept in repair and sometimes occupied, though its agricultural buildings were leased when tenants could be found. Rushden, a few miles away, with all the buildings of a standard manor, was repaired in the fourteenth century, but by 1429 the whole complex had been split among a number of tenants. At Raunds, also in the county, agricultural buildings, including a stable and a kiln, and a timber-framed building for the seneschal, were all repaired at much the same time but these must have been situated in subsidiary enclosures, for the enclosure adjoining the church, believed to be the site of the manor, proved, on excavation, to have always been empty of buildings. In 1444, when most of the agricultural buildings were separately leased, a man with the suggestive name of John Bullock was farming the grazing of the manorial site. Passenham, still within the county and in the same group, seems to have had some pretensions as a residence. There were six windows to its hall, an oriel, a porch, and at least three further chambers, including a white-washed guest chamber. The house was walled and roofed with stone, and most of its agricultural buildings were of the same material, so too were the walls surrounding the various courts. The whole manor was leased permanently to the bailiff early in the fifteenth century. Glatton (Hunts.) was altogether smaller, with a hall, chamber, and a workshop (*fabrica*), said to be dilapidated. Nothing appears to have survived beyond the early fifteenth century. Wardington (Oxon.) in 1447 had reached the final stage of disintegration, its site overbuilt with five cottages.[22]

Unwanted granges had similar fates, as a group belonging to Ramsey abbey demonstrates. Shillington (Beds.) was first split among those leasing portions of the demesne. In 1422 its buildings were back in the hands of a single tenant who agreed to house the seneschal when required, a frequent provision when granges were leased. It included all the accommodation of a standard manor as well as a chamber named the Abbot's Bower. Hunneye was leased to the bailiff, but seems to have had little beyond hall and chamber, while at Ellington (Hunts.) there were peasant houses on the site by the fifteenth century, of which one was reserved to the lord for holding a court if he needed it.[23]

In the south-east there were no less than fourteen royal chamber manors, though only Eltham (Kent) has any standing buildings. Access

---

[22] PRO DL 29/328/5364, 325/5321, 327/5353, 326/5335, 328/5370.

[23] DeWindt, *Liber Gersumarum*, pp. 171, 194, 235, 271. The manor of Hunneye was in Chatteris, Cambs.

by water was evidently considered desirable, for Gravesend and Greenwich in Kent and Rotherhithe and Sheen in Surrey all had riverside wharves as well as watergates to their moats. At Eltham the main enclosure was divided into two quadrangles by the great hall and its appurtenances, the northernmost further subdivided into little courts, each with its function and apartments. Herstmonceux (Sussex) was similarly arranged though there seems only to have been a single enclosure to this great, brick-built manor house, with everything planned around it.[24]

Gatehouse towers were more common in the region than other chamber towers. Examples in brick survive at Esher and Farnham (Surrey) and in stone at Knole (Kent), and Apuldram (Sussex), all properties of important prelates. Most standard manors have been replaced or very much modified, though it is possible to pick out some Sussex manors, like Brede Place or Filching, which include a good deal of early work; and although the manor house at Great Dixter, Northiam, was very much modified by Lutyens, its hall has an interesting roof with alternating hammer-beams and crown-post trusses.

A good picture of a working manor of the period may be built up from successive leases of the St Paul's manor at Barnes, Surrey. A lease of 1418 shows an establishment with two enclosures, one for the house, the other for the farm, the latter notable for still retaining its *domus* for servants. The house sounds as if it had grown piecemeal. There were five rooms grouped round a "great upper chamber", a chapel reached by a passage, with a small room above it, and at the low end of the hall, above the services, a room with a privy. All buildings, both residential and agricultural except the sheephouse, were roofed with ceramic tiles, though all were timber-framed.[25] It sounds substantial but somewhat old-fashioned in a region from which so many innovations sprang.

A well-designed timber-framed house specific to the region was the Wealden house, a plan originating, it is supposed, among the small manor houses of Kent. Though providing much the same accommodation as manors of similar size in eastern England, it differed in that the hall and its wings were roofed in a single great sweep, which necessitated sophisticated carpentry to carry the roof across the recessed hall. The roof was always hipped, thus making the upper rooms rather lower than their counterparts elsewhere, but the type was clearly successful as it spread in considerable numbers into Surrey and Sussex

---

[24] For plan see D. E. Strong, *Eltham Palace*, London, 1958, end-papers. For Herstmonceux, W. D. Simpson, 'Herstmonceux Castle', *Arch. J.*, XCIX, 1942, p. 121.

[25] Guildhall Library, St Paul's Cathedral Mss., box 32 nos. 646, 647.

and sporadically into eastern England and the home counties, and it continued to be built well into the post-medieval period.[26]

The home counties, which included buildings in the forefront of late medieval design, constituted also a region of mixed tradition. At magnate level, and among the new rich, stone and brick were in demand, while the considerable number of timber houses included both cruck and framed buildings.

To begin with the brick: Leland said that Stonor in Oxfordshire was of timber, brick, and flint, and Ewelme, in the same county, of timber, brick, and stone. A little medieval brickwork survives at Stonor, but Ewelme manor house has gone. A seventeenth-century drawing, however, shows what appears to be a free-standing lodgings wing, perhaps of brick. The new material played an important part within the region, where additions and alterations seem normally to have been of brick quite early in the fifteenth century, while by the mid-century houses such as Rye House, Hoddesdon (Herts.), and Someries (Beds.), were in process of construction, using elaborate moulded brick in the Flemish style, and by the end of the century the use of brick in contrasting colour was well established, as at Hatfield (Herts.) (see Pl. Ia).[27]

A good example of stone building, though in ruins, is the house at Minster Lovell (Oxon.) (Pl. IIIb). Like Gainsborough Old Hall, it had three wings only. The site sloped down to the river Windrush, and the farm was placed immediately alongside. Its most precocious feature was the arrangement of hall, chapel, chamber, and solar in a double pile at a time when it was still usual to link buildings in line rather than in depth (Pl. IV). William of Worcester's description of Hunsdon (Herts.) suggests another such, and recent excavations have tended to confirm his accuracy. A chamber-tower was added to Minster Lovell late in the century. The hall, here, like most southern halls, was at ground level, though excavation has shown that a hall as important as that of the Black Prince at Kennington (Surrey) could still be constructed on an undercroft, even in the south-east, possibly to allow for a ceremonial stairway.[28]

[26] S. E. Rigold, 'The distribution of the Wealden House', in I. Ll. Foster and L. Alcock, eds., *Culture and Environment*, London, 1963, pp. 351–4.

[27] The hall at Hatfield became the stable of the later house. For the early plan, *An Inventory of the Historical Monuments in Hertfordshire*, RCHM, England, London, 1910, p. 59. For Rye House: T. Garner and A. Stratton, *Domestic Architecture of England during the Tudor Period*, I, London, 1929, p. 121. For Someries Castle, T. P. Smith, 'The early brickwork of Someries Castle', *J. of the Brit. Arch. Assoc.*, CXXIX, 1976, pp. 42–58.

[28] For Hunsdon, C. P. Partridge, 'Excavations at Hunsdon House', *Hertfordshire's Past*, XVII, 1984, pp. 15ff and J. H. Harvey, ed., *William Worcestre, Itineraries*, p. 51. For Minster Lovell, A. J. Taylor, *Minster Lovell Hall*, London, 1958.

Ockwells manor (Berks.), while much restored, demonstrates that timber was not necessarily regarded as inferior material. The windows of the four-bay hall are fashionably high, its barge-boarding exquisite. It probably had service rooms in the usual position, but if so they have gone, and access from the kitchen is via a cloister rather than the usual passage.

In this populous part of England it is seldom possible to get much idea of the whole manor, but an early map shows Rye House, built by Andrew Ogard from French war profits, ranged round a corner of a large moated enclosure (Fig. 9.3). Neighbouring earthworks confirm the position of other buildings, but it is to two recent excavations that we have to turn to see the whole disposition of a late medieval manor house. Both manors still possessed the dual function of earlier days. At Chalgrove (Oxon.) there were three enclosures within a moat. The hall in the northernmost was provided with fixed benches, and an adjoining room was floored with decorated tiles (Fig. 9.4). It is not yet clear, in the absence of a final report, whether the middle court, into which the hall opened, was an extension of the house or part of the farm whose barn occupied the third enclosure, or whether, indeed, the buildings of both were intermingled in the old manner, as was still the case at Writtle early in the fifteenth century.[29]

The second large-scale excavation, at Leighton Grove (Beds.), demonstrates the enormous area that could be devoted to agricultural buildings as compared with the house, even when the latter was both important and well-built. Late in the period a stone-built house was replaced by timber construction, possibly reflecting a decline in the residential function of the manor, but not necessarily so, for good quality timberwork was acceptable in the region, as has been seen at Ockwells.[30]

In south-central England building in timber at manorial level was largely confined to Hampshire, where stone was scarce enough to restrict its use to such major manors as Bishop's Waltham and the like. The quality and quantity of stone elsewhere in the region has resulted in a very high survival rate for medieval manors, though they are often incorporated in a later shell. Pevsner estimated that there were over a hundred in Somerset alone, and this was before the current upsurge of interest in ancient buildings.

Because the life-style of their owners was similar, the standard manors were a version of the timber-framed houses of east and south-east England, so that, while not sharing the symmetry of the Wealden

---

[29] P. Page, 'Chalgrove, Harding's Field moated site', *The Moated Sites Research Group Annual Bulletin*, VIII, 1981, pp. 22–3.   [30] Excavated by E. Baker, report forthcoming.

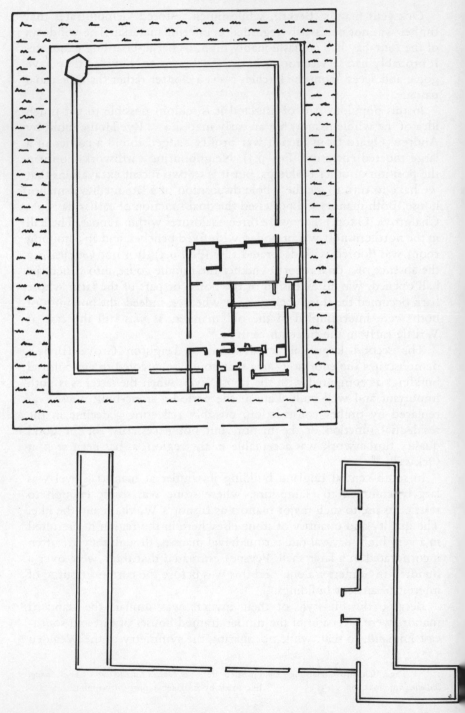

Fig. 9.3 Rye House, Hoddesdon, Herts., sixteenth-century plan. The relationship of the subsidiary buildings to the main enclosure, today represented by grass-covered banks, suggests a late addition

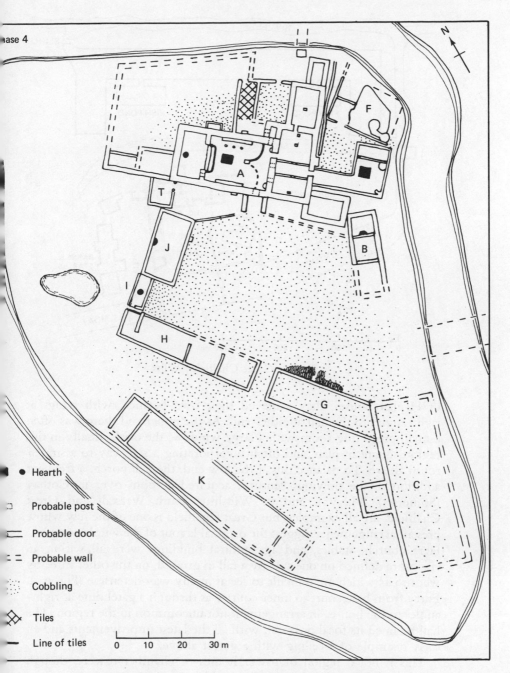

ase 4

N

F

A

T

J

I

B

H

G

K

C

• Hearth

Probable post

Probable door

Probable wall

Cobbling

Tiles

Line of tiles

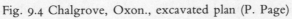
0   10   20   30 m

Fig. 9.4 Chalgrove, Oxon., excavated plan (P. Page)

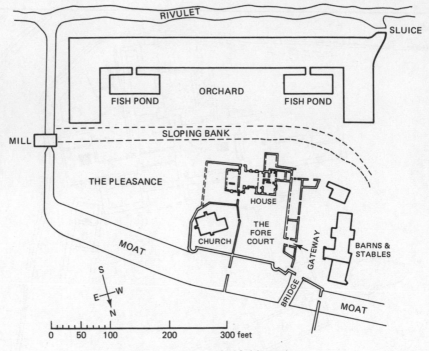

Fig. 9.5 Great Chalfield, Wilts.

or H-plan houses, they achieved their own balance, with wings at right-angles to the hall at either end. At the upper end there was often a small projecting room with a large window, the oriel, usually in this region square in plan, and often incorporating a stairway to a similar room above. To balance this at the low end, the hall porch, a frequent addition in the previous century, acquired a room over it. Cothay (Somerset) (Pl. Va), and in Wiltshire South Wraxall and Great Chalfield, are all examples, but Great Chalfield is one of the few whose present arrangements suggest the original layout of the whole complex. Here church, stables, and agricultural buildings were all within an enclosure defined on one side by a fall in ground, on the other three by wet moats which are difficult to see as in any way defensive (Fig. 9.5). Entry from base court to inner court was through a gatehouse at right-angles to the house, an arrangement not uncommon in the region. The hall retained its focal position, with all the latest improvements and an early example of a ceiling with a garret above.

This is not a region of tower houses or chamber-towers, though there are a few isolated examples, such as the three-storeyed porch at

Ia Hatfield, Herts., fifteenth-century hall, showing high windows.

b Gainsborough Old Hall, Lincs., showing kitchen, originally detached (NBR)

IIa Haddlesey, Yorks., complex moat system (Camb. Univ. Coll.,
Crown Copyright, henceforward CC)

b Manor House, Croxton, Cambs. (NBR)

IIIa Chamber tower, Ashby-de-la-Zouch, Leics. (NBR)

b Minster Lovell, Oxon., ruins of manor house (NBR)

IV Manor house, Ewelme, Oxon., lodgings wing (NBR)

Va Manor house, Cothay, Somerset (NBR)

b Littlehempston, Devon (*Country Life*)

VIa Tintagel, Cornwall, Trevera manor house (NBR)

b Wressel Castle, Yorks. (NBR)

VIIa Samlesbury, Lancs. (NBR)

b Ashleworth, Glos.

VIIIa Garmondsway, Durham, village tofts and crofts (CC)

b Duggleby, Yorks., medieval farmsteads (CC)

IXa Corbridge, Northumb., the Vicar's pele (NBR)

b One of a number of cruck-built cottages, Stoneleigh, War.

Xa Bradford-on-Avon, Wilts., granary and one of two barns (NBR)

b Little Wymondley, Herts., aisled timber barn (NBR)

XIa Ashleworth, Glos., cruck barn

b Shepherd's wheeled hut (BL)

XIIa Meare, Somerset, fish-house (NBR)

b Brandsby, Yorks., potter's croft and buildings at the end of the village, opposite modern
farm house (CC)

Birdcombe Court, Wraxall, and the ornamental gatehouse turrets at Durleigh, Somerset. Systematic study of priests' houses in the region has shown them to differ in their internal arrangements from the usual manor house, but this study has not yet been repeated in other parts of the country to show whether or not it is a general trend.[31]

In the south-west the surviving major manor houses owe little to regional tradition save their construction in local stone. Dartington Hall, Devon, was rebuilt late in the fourteenth century and though it belonged to John Holland, half-brother to Richard II, it seems to have lacked any defensive elements at all. The main buildings were arranged round three courts, of which two survive, separated, as at Eltham and Herstmonceux, by the hall, a spectacular building with a hammer-beam roof, the latest advance in roof construction. It still had the old long, narrow, low-set windows, but the hearth had been moved to the wall behind the dais, a more comfortable position. Some few of the lodgings survive in the outer court, sets of rooms on two floors, each with its privy, the upper floor sets approached by an external stair. Entry to the manor house was through an unpretentious opening between barn and stable.[32] No other gatehouse is known. Across the Tamar in Cornwall, Cotehele, as it stands today, includes a great deal of post-medieval date, but the plan, with its small lodgings court and its adjacent farm, reflects the early arrangement.[33]

Within the region are a number of unpretentious stone-built manor houses with more distinctively local features. Littlehempston (Devon) was probably preserved because it was taken over by the Canonsleigh nuns, so that its agricultural buildings remained in use (Pl. Vb). One of its barns still stands in the forecourt, and service buildings of a more domestic nature, the kitchen and dairy, are behind the house. What stands out in the region at this level, however, is the variety of plan among the standard manors, many of which had highly individual features. Ham Barton (Devon) has what is in effect a double hall, two hall-like rooms one over the other, a similar arrangement, though on a larger scale, to that found at Gothelney in neighbouring Somerset. Cornish Roswarne also has two halls, this time on either side of a gateway.[34] Whether such arrangements indicate joint occupation, whether one was in fact the chamber, or whether one indeed was a winter hall such as has been mentioned at Caister, would need

---

[31] W. A. Pantin, 'Medieval priests' houses in south-west England', *Med. Arch.*, I, 1957, pp. 118–46.   [32] A. Emery, *Dartington Hall*, Oxford, 1970, *passim*.

[33] S. E. Rigold, 'Cotehele', *Arch. J.*, cxxx, 1973, pp. 256–9.

[34] For plans of Ham Barton, Pantin, *op. cit.*, p. 142. For Roswarne, C. Thomas, 'Roswarne manor house', *Arch. J.*, cxxx, 1973, p. 260.

documentary evidence to decide. At Traymill (Devon), the hall bays were a mere 6 feet long at a time when the standard bay of even a peasant house was between 10 and 12 feet. The Cornish manors of Truthill and Trevera (modern Tintagel) (Pl. VIa) appear little more than peasant houses in their arrangements, though many of these small manors had their private chapel.[35] There must have been ancillary enclosures and agricultural buildings but they have seldom survived.

The six northern counties do not form a homogeneous region. The border counties stand apart because of the risks to which they were subjected, and by 1350 houses on the routes into England had either been strengthened or destroyed. New building was planned to resist assault and in the face of military threat it is noticeable that stone walls were preferred to wet moats, though some houses had both.

Standard manors like Burnside Hall, Strickland Roger, and Preston Patrick (Westmor.) are examples of adaptation of H-plan houses to the needs of defence (Fig. 9.6). One cross-wing at Burnside was massively walled, with two rooms and a dividing passage, each separately vaulted, and the stairs to upper floors so arranged as to be defensible. There was a strong enclosing wall of the kind known locally as a barmekin, and a further enclosure for cattle.[36]

An alternative arrangement was a thick-walled tower, often initially attached to a hall, as at Hazelslack (Westmor.), but eventually incorporating the whole dwelling house within the tower. The ground floor was vaulted to resist fire, the necessary rooms stacked one above the other, sometimes with small anterooms and privies in the wall thickness, sometimes in a corner turret. They could be quite small, like the Northumberland vicars' peles at Chatton and Corbridge, or of considerable size, like Belsay and Cocklaw in the same county, or the castle-like Dacre in Cumberland, this last within a moat that looks as though it were made for the tower's predecessor. The type spilled over into Yorkshire, and is found as far south as Paull Holme on the Humber coast, less for defence than for show.[37]

Major manors were often built in quadrangular fashion round a courtyard, usually moated. An excavated example at Rest Park in the West Riding was built for the archbishop, of stone, but with two half-timbered wings against the perimeter wall. More characteristic,

[35] For Traymill, see Hoskins and Finberg, *Devonshire Studies*, pp. 132–8. A plan and section of Truthill are in E. M. Jope, *Studies in Building History*, London, 1961, pp. 198–9. For Trevera, see S. E. Rigold, 'Tintagel old Post Office', *Arch. J.*, cxxx, 1973, pp. 247–8.

[36] *An Inventory of the Historical Monuments in Westmorland*, RCHM, England, London, 1936: Burnside Hall, p. 213, Preston Patrick, pp. 195–6.

[37] For Hazelslack Tower, *ibid.*, p. 41. For Dacre, J. H. Parker, *Some Account of Domestic Architecture in England*, II, Oxford, 1853, p. 214. For Paull Holme Tower, P. F. Ryder, *Medieval Buildings of Yorkshire*, Ashbourne, 1982, p. 117.

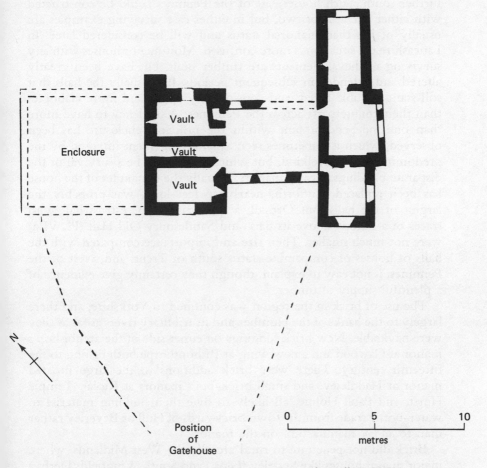

Fig. 9.6 Strickland Roger, Westmor., Burnside Hall (RCHM)

perhaps, were the Percy house at Wressel (Pl. VIb), now in ruins, and those whose moats survive at Leconfield and South Frodingham, all in the old East Riding.[38] The ultimate development of the plan came at Castle Bolton in the North Riding and Lumley in Co. Durham. All had upper floor halls, and chambers contrived in substantial corner towers, the latter with thick walls on the outer sides, but otherwise simply merging into the adjoining wings.

Towards the south of the region timber building remained common and traditional aisled halls survived long after aisles had been abandoned

[38] H. E. Jean Le Patourel, *The Moated Sites of Yorkshire*, Soc. for Med. Arch. Monograph Ser., v, 1973; for Rest Park, pp. 45–8; for Wressel, pp. 6, 117.

further south. Such houses east of the Pennines could be constructed with either one aisle or two, but in either case surviving examples are usually of less than manorial status and will be considered later. In Lancashire the situation is more confused. Most manor houses with any surviving medieval elements are timber built, but have been greatly altered and extended in subsequent periods. It is usually the halls that still stand, double-aisled, and considerably larger and more elaborate than their counterparts across the Pennines. A tendency to have more than one independent unit within the principal enclosure has been observed, which is sometimes seen as an arrangement imposed by the predominance of gavelkind, but which might also be a survival of the disparate buildings of early manors. Usually the remainder of the house has been replaced. Rufforth, nearly 50 feet long, was probably the largest of the halls, but Ordsall, a quasi-aisled, spere-truss hall with traces of a canopy above its dais, and Samlesbury Old Hall (Pl. VIIa) were not much smaller. Their size and importance compared with the halls of houses of comparable status south of Trent, and, west of the Pennines, is not easy to explain, though they certainly give evidence of a plentiful supply of timber.[39]

The use of brick in the region was confined to Yorkshire, and there largely to the banks of the Humber and its tributary rivers as far as they were navigable. New brick lodgings on either side of the archbishop's manor at Cawood and a new wing at Bishopthorpe both belong to the fifteenth century. There were brick additions to the large moated manor at Haddlesey, and small brick-built manors at Riccal, Temple Hurst, and Paull Holme, all likely to owe their building material to water-borne trade from the town brickyards of Hull or Beverley rather than to *ad hoc* manufacture on the manor.[40]

Brick did not penetrate to rural areas in the West Midlands, where major manor houses like Sudeley (Glos.) and South Wingfield (Derbs.) were stone-built. Both were of the double courtyard plan, but Sudeley is heavily restored and has been in continuous use. Original arrangements can be deduced from the ruins at Wingfield, another of the fifteenth-century buildings of Ralph, Lord Cromwell. Here the plan owes much to the lie of the land, a spur whose northern end is occupied by the great hall and the private apartments, looking out across a steep hillside. Though it was at ground-floor level within the courtyard, the

---

[39] The problem is discussed by J. T. Smith: 'Lancashire and Cheshire houses: some problems of architectural and social history'. *Arch. J.*, CXXVII, 1970, pp. 156–77.

[40] Le Patourel, *op. cit*, pp. 31–6 for Haddlesey. Brick making in Hull is discussed, with contemporary accounts, in F. W. Brooks, 'A medieval brick-yard in Hull', *J. of the Brit. Arch. Assoc.*, 3rd ser. IV, pp. 156–74. Kilns making both brick and tile have recently been excavated outside Beverley.

hall was nevertheless on an undercroft, with stairs to the garden level below from the northernmost of the two porches that terminated each end of the cross passage. The lord's apartments were arranged to take maximum advantage of the view from the hill as well as proximity to the hall. Both enclosures were lined with lodgings, including a chamber tower between the two, and to the south the present farm is likely to overlie a medieval predecessor.[41]

Warwickshire has as high an incidence of wet moats as any county in the country, and though many are believed to be associated with woodland assarts, some few, especially in the Felden, enclosed manor houses, usually at least partly timber-framed. Further south stone was the rule, though moats were still favoured where the terrain was suitable, as at Icomb Place (Glos.) or Harvington (Worcs.), the latter with an upper hall, rare in the region. Even in the Cotswolds, however, there were pockets of timber-framing, as Alderton and Brockworth demonstrate.[42]

Ashleworth Court (Glos.) belonged to the Augustinian Canons. It adjoins the church and seems to have been laid out in two adjacent courts for residence and farm respectively. It has all the appearance of a standard manor, with hall, services, and a cross-wing at the upper end, and an oriel and stair within the angle between hall and wing. It is interesting to compare this grange with the close-studded timber manor house in the same village, which is of roughly similar date (Pl. VIIb). It is possible that not enough is allowed for personal preference in areas where more than one type of building material is available.[43]

C. PEASANT AND OTHER SMALL HOUSES

(i) General

Below the manor house in size and status were the houses of the great majority of those who lived and worked in the countryside. The period with which we are concerned saw very great changes in the character of many peasant houses, and it saw also the emergence of substantial dwellings, the yeoman or gentry houses of the future, hardly yet numerous enough to rank as a separate class save possibly near the end of the period. They derive from manor houses rather than from those of the peasantry, and themselves represent, no doubt, the models at which the peasants were aiming.

[41] Thompson, 'Building works of Ralph, Lord Cromwell', pp. 161–2; A. Emery, 'Ralph, Lord Cromwell's manor at Wingfield', pp. 284ff.

[42] B. K. Roberts, 'Moated sites in Midland England', *Birmingham Arch. Soc.*, LXXX, 1965, p. 26.

[43] Platt, *Monastic Grange*, pp. 187–8.

Peasant houses of earlier centuries are known almost entirely from excavation, which has shown them with earth-fast posts, or with sills set directly on the ground or into shallow trenches. Flimsy and short-lived has been the verdict of the archaeologists, who judged them to have been rebuilt in each generation, often on new alignments within the toft. Their slightness was ascribed to the use of timbers of small scantling, a diagnosis which seemed to be substantiated by a reported lack of reused timbers in surviving houses of early post-medieval date. In an era when everything was reused that could be, even at royal level, such a lack would suggest that early peasant houses had included nothing worth salvaging.[44]

Recent work has, however, made it necessary to modify the picture as far as houses of the late medieval period are concerned, and this for a number of reasons. By the fifteenth century there were, over much of southern England and the West Midlands, a variety of small houses so well built that they are still in occupation today. They are sufficiently numerous to make it certain, even without further evidence, that many of them must have been used by the peasantry at some period, and stylistic evidence would suggest that this was in the later middle ages. Their distribution is patchy. Fewer have survived in the East Midlands and only a handful in the north, and these only at the upper end of the scale, but other evidence shows that there must have been many in these parts of England, sturdy and well-constructed even though they no longer stand. It must always be remembered, however, that in spite of the many hundred houses claimed to be of medieval date, and certainly medieval in tradition, very few have a hard and fast date based on dendrochronology, or other scientific technique, though a number can be linked with very suggestive documentary evidence.

There is in this period, for the first time, written evidence relating to houses of the customary tenants, houses which were the property of the manorial lord, even though custom gave the peasant reasonable security of tenure. It comes principally from court rolls, less frequently from manorial accounts, very occasionally from extents and surveys. These all present semantic problems, and there are always gaps in the available evidence; nevertheless, they do allow a few generalizations based on samples of reasonable size. Furthermore they do, as far as they go, seem to indicate that people had a reasonable amount of space, a supposition that is supported by the nature of those houses that survive. Most were of at least two, and often of three bays, each of between 10 and 15 feet long by some 14 to 16 feet wide. Some peasant houses were

---

[44] For the argument against reuse of timber, see Mercer, *English Vernacular Houses*, p. 4. C. R. J. Currie reported considerable reuse in Sussex: 'Timber supply and timber building in a Sussex parish', *Vernacular Architecture*, XIV, 1983, pp. 52–3.

considerably larger, with up to five bays in the West Midlands, and occasionally in the north; the additional length was replaced by a storeyed end in the south and south-east.[45] The change from earlier centuries is considerable, and it is necessary to try to see how it came about.

The permanence of a house depends on a number of factors: the materials used in its construction, the skill of those who built it, the continued usefulness of its design and accommodation to ensuing generations. In this period houses were built by professionals, masons, carpenters, daubers, and roofers, though minor repairs may perhaps have been undertaken by the peasants themselves. Manorial custom varied, but most customary tenants had the right to housebote, that is to timber and sometimes to stone, for building and repair of houses, and this could on some occasions be stretched to include barns. It is, however, an area where precise evidence is difficult to obtain. There is no doubt that the nature and quality of timber was very much at the discretion of the lord through his agents, and that the source from which it was drawn varied from manor to manor. Examples can be cited where it was felled on the peasant's own croft, of cases where he could fell a certain number of trees without authority, and of others where the timber had first to be viewed by the bailiff. Otherwise it came from woodland, waste or park. An example at Abbot's Ripton (Hunts.) shows that very considerable timbers might be available, for 400 sixty-year-old oaks growing on the site of the manor were said to be reserved for the farmer and the copyholders for their houses.[46] Assignments of "young" trees, oak, ash, or alder, are more frequently met.

The expense of carriage, when the timber had to be moved for some distance, could be greater than the cost of the material itself. Sometimes the lord took responsibility for transport as well as for provision, but there is no way of telling how frequently this occurred. Instances are recorded at Methley in the old West Riding, where the timber was carried in a manorial cart, and when, in 1471, 128 pairs of crucks were distributed among a number of Northumbrian settlements for house repair and their cost was entered on the Percy accounts, it presumably included transport. Otherwise the timber had to be collected by the householder, and an interesting glimpse of how things could work in practice is afforded by the chance survival of some slivers of parchment, addressed to a Yorkshire parker, directing him to allow, to the tenant

---

[45] Four- and five-bay houses in the West Midlands are listed in Field, 'Worcestershire peasant buildings, household goods and farming equipment', pp. 134–5.

[46] VCH Hunts., II, p. 102.

named in each, specified timbers for house repair. Such transactions would not normally come to light, for they do not appear in manorial documents relating to the manor concerned.[47]

It appears, too, that on some manors the lord expected to provide a house along with a customary holding. This is never spelled out, but it seems implicit in such cases as that at Little Raveley, where in 1428 a fire destroyed the buildings on three tofts, and it was the *firmarius*, as the lord's representative, who rebuilt house, barn, and bakehouse on each. A little later in the century a house at Thorner (Yorks.) was similarly rebuilt after a fire. In a slightly different vein, a lease of the manor of Birtley (Durham) made the farmer responsible for keeping the village houses in repair.[48]

In spite of such seigneurial activity, plenty of examples can be quoted of tenants taking up holdings and agreeing to build with or without help from the lord in cash or kind. Such cases have not yet been examined to see whether or not the men concerned were incomers to the manor, or were adding to existing holdings. It is possible that when there was no direct heir to a holding, or when the tenant had abandoned it, as so often happened in the period, an ensuing lease would not necessarily carry all the old rights. If this were so it would go a long way to explain the varying incidence of the right to free timber.

During the later middle ages the number of buildings within each toft tended to rise, and there is no doubt that this was a matter of seigneurial policy. This tendency will be considered in more detail in connection with farm buildings; here it is stressed as part of the improvements in housing being made on a number of estates in the early fifteenth century. A "well built-up toft", aimed at by many lords, was one that included three or even four buildings: the dwelling house, usually called the insethouse, a barn, and a bakehouse, are those most frequently recorded. To achieve the desired end permission was sometimes given to take a building from an empty toft for re-erection. In the rare cases when the addition of a solar is recorded, help from the lord's carpenter might be allowed. There were frequent and repeated injunctions to put to use timbers provided for repairs, and fines for failing to do so. All in all it seems that at this time it was the lord who wished to attract and keep tenants, and was therefore anxious to increase the attractiveness of a holding, while the peasants, who did not

---

[47] For the Northumberland crucks, J. C. Hodgson, ed., *Percy Bailiff's Rolls of the Fifteenth Century*, Surtees Soc., CXXXIV, 1921, *passim*. The Cridling Stubbs precepts are in BL Add. Ch. 17146.

[48] For Raveley, DeWindt, ed., *Liber Gersumarum*, p. 204. For Thorner, Leeds District Archives, Mexborough Coll., MD 10/13. For Birtley, J. C. Hodgson, *op. cit.*, p. 72.

own the houses they lived in, and might not wish to continue to occupy them, were not eager to undertake either building or repair. Nevertheless, increased prosperity among the peasantry, combined with the lords' need to keep their tenants, opened the way for considerable improvement in the quality of housing, and this is reflected in the quality of the houses that remain.

The lords were building new houses and cottages in the period over and above those on the regular village holdings. Some were cottages to replace the old communal halls for *famuli*, others were put up to bring in further rent. The practice was not new. Cottages had already been erected by Henry de Bray at Harlestone (Northants.), late in the thirteenth century. But either it increased, or accounts for such houses appear more frequently in the records. A terrace of four cottages at Bishops Clyst (Devon), houses built terrace-wise in Battle (Sussex) and others at Thorner (Yorks.), demonstrate that it was widespread in the fifteenth century. Similarly, instances of building on the site of a redundant manor as, for example, at Patrington (Yorks.), Ellington (Hunts.), or Wardington (Oxon.), seem to represent more speculative building, intended to bring in extra rent. In each case there were five houses recorded, their rent appearing as a separate item in the account. At Wharram Percy (Yorks.) excavation on what had once been a manorial site showed a succession of houses that differed from that excavated on one of the regular tofts.[49]

In general, it may be said that at this time the diversity of the available evidence gives a more rounded picture of the nature of peasant housing than is possible in a period when reliance has to be placed exclusively on excavation. As far as the arrangement of buildings within the tofts is concerned and the pattern of crofts within the settlement, however, it is still necessary to lean principally on excavation, though aerial photography and fieldwork offer supporting evidence (Pls. VIIIa, b).

There are houses built in the period which can be numbered neither among manor houses nor peasant houses. These sizeable dwellings, of which a considerable number survive, are those that in later times are known as "gentry houses", the homes of merchants, of lesser ecclesiastics, and of prospering freeholders, all men of substance. The margin between the smaller manors at one end of the spectrum, and the

---

[49] St Paul's Chapter manors and the Bigod manors in eastern England all included a building for servants within the manorial enclosure early in the fourteenth century. For Bishops Clyst see N. W. Alcock, 'The medieval cottages of Bishops Clyst', *Med. Arch.*, IX, 1965, pp. 146–53. For Harlestone, D. Willis, ed., *The Estate Book of Henry de Bray*, Camden 3rd ser. XXVII, 1916, pp. 49–51. For Wharram Percy, D. D. Andrews and G. Milne, eds., *Wharram, a Study of Settlement on the Yorkshire Wolds*, 1979, Medieval Archaeology Monograph Ser. VIII, pp. 39–41.

dwellings of the more prosperous copyholders at the other, tends to be blurred. For convenience, such houses will be considered in the regions among those of peasants and other smallholders.

(ii) *The regions*

Turning now to the regions, eastern England was the home of timber-framed buildings with rafter roofs and thatch, except in Lincolnshire where excavation has shown pockets of stone building in such deserted villages as Somerby and Kettleby Thorpe, but standing houses of medieval date in Lincolnshire are rare indeed.[50] Otherwise counties in the region all have houses of late medieval date still in use, modified to a greater or lesser extent by subsequent alterations and additions. At the top end of the scale are a scattering of Wealden-type houses, and hall houses with storeyed wings at either end, roofed at right-angles. This arrangement gave height to the prestigious upper rooms, which were often also jettied to give extra floor space and usually included a hearth. Because the hall was open to the roof each upper room required its separate stair, which would, if required, simplify multiple occupation. The hall usually retained its central hearth, and the regular arrangement of the houses gave no room for an internal kitchen. Nor did a privy seem to have been thought necessary, at least within doors, and everything beyond has gone.

Such houses are often described as "gentry houses", or "yeoman houses". Yet if we look at the arrangements made for old people, and for widows surrendering customary tenancies, we find provision made in upper rooms, and sometimes the use of what is called a hall, together with a barn, and outbuildings and even, in one case, of a "bedchamber".[51] As it has to be supposed that the incomers would also require living space, it seems likely that in eastern England, as in the south-east, some of these sizeable dwellings were in the hands of customary tenants. The gap between peasant houses and what later were to be termed yeoman or gentry houses was already somewhat blurred in the more prosperous parts of the country.

Timber-framed houses with a single wing, like Uphall farm, Garboldisham, Norfolk, were probably common in the region, and in Essex significant numbers of small, single-storey houses have survived, of a kind to have been inhabited by the majority of the peasants. To see

[50] An exception is the house at Coningsby: M. W. Barley, A. Rogers and P. Strange, 'The medieval parsonage house at Coningsby, Lincolnshire', *Antiquaries J.*, XLIX, 1969, pp. 346–66. For Somerby, see D. C. Mynard, 'Excavations at Somerby, Lincolnshire', *Lincs. History and Archaeology*, IV, 1969, pp. 63–91; for Kettleby, interim report in *Med. Arch.*, IX, 1965, p. 213.

[51] DeWindt, ed., *op. cit.*, pp. 279, 307.

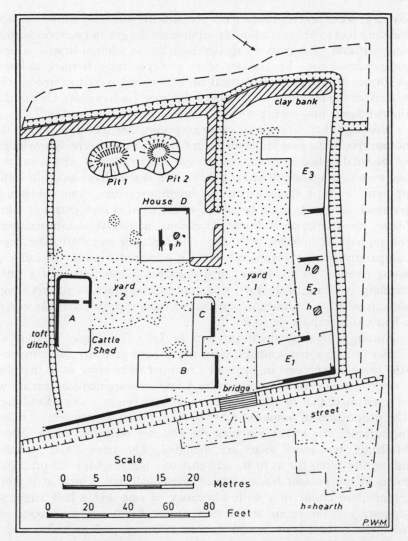

clay bank

Pit 1   Pit 2

House D

E_3

yard 1

yard 2

h

E_2

h

A

toft ditch

Cattle Shed

C

B

E_1

bridge

street

Scale

0   5   10   15   20
        Metres

0   20   40   60   80
        Feet

$h = hearth$

P.W.M.

Fig. 9.7 Grenstein, Norfolk, an excavated peasant toft (P. Wade-Martins)

the layout of a peasant toft we have to look at Grenstein, Norfolk (Fig. 9.7) where excavation showed boundary banks and ditches surrounding the whole area, and a bridge across the ditch to the village street. The dwelling house had its own banked enclosure, situated as far as possible from the entry, and its agricultural buildings were aligned along the boundary bank, the whole arrangement like a manor house in miniature, as no doubt it was intended to be. The walls, however, in this village, which was to be deserted soon after the mid-fourteenth century, were not yet raised onto groundsills, and the position of each building had to be worked out from differential ground surfaces within and without. Excavation at Goltho (Lincs.) demonstrated a less prosperous scene. The houses were not yet fully framed and the padstones on which their vertical timbers rested were too irregularly spaced for the buildings to have been designed for bay units. One of the slight houses, however, proved to include the village smithy.[52]

Although there are one or two exceptions, late medieval houses do not survive in the East Midlands except within a few towns. Knowledge of the smaller houses in the countryside has to depend on documents and excavation alone. Ramsey abbey's aim was to have its crofts built up with at least three structures, insethouse, barn, and bakehouse (*pistrina*), to which could be added where needed such extras as kiln-house, cart-house, an additional chamber, or, rarely, accommodation for animals. A holding with only one building seems to have been comparatively infrequent, and when it occurred it might be called a house (*domus*), an insethouse, or a chamber (*camera*), the last a free-standing building, it appears, that could be as much as 50 feet long, though whether its function was that of what is more normally called a house it is impossible to say.[53]

Among several hundred entries in the *Liber Gersumarum* relating to houses on the abbey's estates, only thirty-nine give any indication of size, usually expressed in terms of a number of binding studs that the context makes clear were bay posts. A few measurements in feet allow us to estimate that in this case a bay was between 10 and 12 feet long. The proportion of houses of three bays, just over 50 per cent of those measurable, was rather less than the number estimated in the West Midlands, but more solars are included. The term "hall" occurs sufficiently often for us to be sure that this was used for the principal room in the peasant house, while "gabylwall hall", used at Ripton (Hunts.), in connection with a tenancy of one and a half virgates, suggests a main room at the end of the house, as was found at Wythemail (Northants.), and "crosselar" may perhaps indicate the lower room of a two-storeyed end.[54]

The buildings were framed and could be transported from one tenancy to another and even from village to village. The walls were infilled with splinting and clay between studs, the floors rammed, the

---

[52] P. Wade-Martins, 'Village sites in Launditch Hundred, Norfolk', *East Anglian Archaeology*, x, 1980, pp. 118–24. For Goltho, see G. Beresford, *The Medieval Clayland Village*, pp. 26–34.

[53] DeWindt, ed., *op. cit.*, p. 283.

[54] *Ibid.*, p. 318. For Wythemail, D. G. and J. G. Hurst, 'Excavations at the medieval village of Wythemail, Northamptonshire', *Med. Arch.*, XIII, 1968, p. 176. The size of medieval houses is discussed in Dyer, 'English peasant buildings', pp. 19–54. For Ripton, see DeWindt, *op. cit.*, p. 318.

roofs thatched. Four cart-loads of straw were used for one house, an acre of straw for another, while a whole tenement required the straw from four acres. It does not sound as if these small East Midland houses differed greatly from those of eastern England, and bearing in mind the maturity of the oaks at Ripton reserved for peasant houses, and that Ripton was one of the abbey's manors, it is difficult to account for their disappearance. It might be argued that the apparent lack of stone foundations – there is no mention of any stone – could have made them vulnerable, but one of the few houses in the region still in use, Weavers, Wennington, seems to have had its main posts on padstones only, while excavated houses at Faxton and Lyveden (Northants.) were on stone sills, and another at Wythemail was thought to have been of stone throughout. It does not appear, therefore, that the type of wall foundation was crucial to survival. It has been suggested that perhaps the houses were too low for the convenient insertion of upper storeys, but this has been successfully achieved at Wennington (Fig. 9.8).[55]

Weavers in Wennington, the house that did stand the test of time, was a linear house of one storey, now with two rooms separated by what was once a through passage, and a single full-length aisle. No supporting buildings have survived, though it must surely have had at least a barn, like an excavated toft in the Northampton village of Faxton, where there was both a barn and a kiln, or another at Wythemail, where there were also subsidiary buildings across a yard. This last, like Weavers, had two rooms on the upper side of the central passage, and a couple of bays beyond it, though here the lower area was interpreted as a byre. Unusually, the only hearth in the house was in the end room, perhaps a "gabylwall hall" as at Ripton. It was, however, in the central position normal in peasant houses.

The south-east is the region with the greatest number of small medieval timber-built houses still in use. Though frequently of two bays only, all have at least one storeyed end. At the top of the scale is the Wealden house considered earlier (p. 833 above).[56] It is supposed that the plan originated at manorial level, on account of the sophistication of the carpentry, the occasional dais and the carved timbering on some examples. The problem such houses present is, however, more complex. Furthermore, their Kentish origin raises the

---

[55] E. M. Davies, 'Weepers [sic]; a small late medieval aisled hall in Cambridgeshire', *Med. Arch.*, XXVI, 1982, pp. 158–62. The present owner found padstones in position when underpinning. For Faxton, see *Current Archaeology*, VI, 1968, pp. 163–4. For Lyveden, G. F. Bryant and J. M. Steane, 'Excavation at the deserted settlement at Lyveden', *J. of the Northampton Museums*, IX, 1971, pp. 1–94.

[56] Rigold, 'Distribution of the Wealden House', in Foster and Alcock, eds., *Culture and Environment*, pp. 351–4.

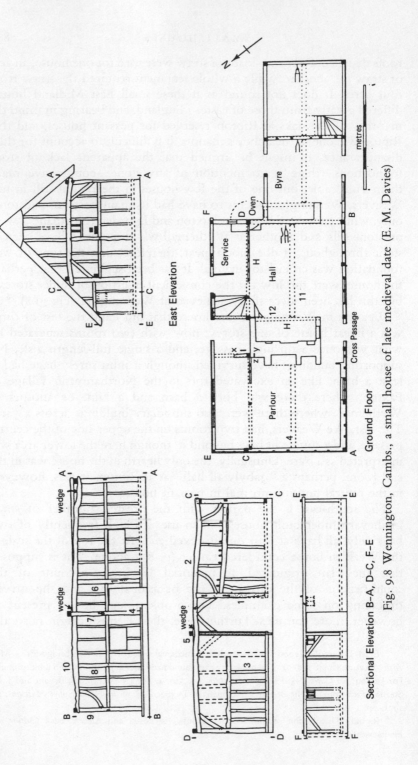

East Elevation

Byre

Oven

F

D

Service

H

Hall

B

11

12

H

Cross Passage

Parlour

4

Ground Floor

N

metres

Sectional Elevation B-A, D-C, F-E

A

wedge

wedge

10

6

7

4

8

9

B

B

A

wedge

5

2

1

3

C

C

D

D

E

E

F

F

Fig. 9.8 Wennington, Cambs., a small house of late medieval date (E. M. Davies)

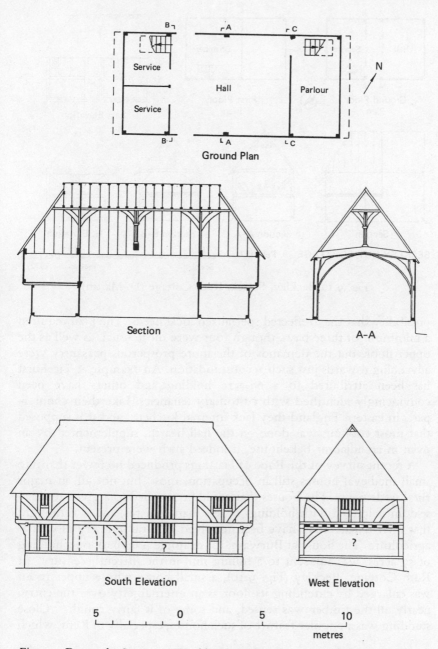

Fig. 9.9 Burwash, Sussex, a Wealden-type house associated with a 59-acre holding (D. Martin)

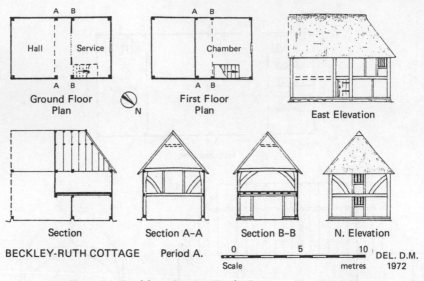

Fig. 9.10 Beckley, Sussex, Ruth Cottage (D. Martin)

possibility that they reflected specialized local needs. The plan required a minimum of three bays, though four were more usual, as well as the upper floor, but the demands of the more prosperous peasantry were advancing towards just such accommodation. An example at Ticehurst has been attributed to a 60-acre holding and others have been convincingly identified with customary tenancies. Like their counterparts in eastern England they lack internal kitchens, and it is supposed that most cooking was done on the hall hearth, supplemented by an oven in an adjacent bakehouse, if indeed such were present.

A recent survey of the Rape of Hastings produced no fewer than 110 small medieval houses still in occupation, most, but not all, in major rural settlements. The houses that could be assigned to a given tenancy seldom belonged with holdings of less than 50 acres, and it is thought that their tenants may have been involved in rural industry as well as agriculture. The house at Burwash, for example (Fig. 9.9), on a holding of 59 acres, was adjacent to a fulling mill in the fifteenth century. At Ruth Cottage, Beckley (Fig. 9.10), a small house whose upper room was enlarged by extending its floor as an internal jetty over the entry, nearly all the timber was reused, and some of it fairly rough.[57] Close studding was a popular feature of such houses, especially in Kent, which

[57] D. Martin, 'Housing in eastern Sussex in the late medieval period', in P. Drewett, ed., *Archaeology in Sussex to 1500*, CBA Research Report, XXIX, 1978, pp. 93–6.

does not suggest any great shortage of timber. Many of the Sussex houses possessed an adjacent barn, some few of which have survived. Although similar small houses are still in use in Surrey villages, notably Charlwood and Burstow, proximity to the capital has probably been responsible for the disappearance of many of those in northern Kent and Surrey. Such houses have not yet been found in Hampshire, but an excavation at Foxcott suggests the possibility that they extended further west than standing houses would suggest. The sill wall of this excavated house was of knapped flint, with corner-post emplacements that could well have borne the weight of a solar. More unusual, the room at the low end included an oven, and in a subsidiary building that was probably a brewhouse there was a further oven as well as several cisterns.[58]

Sussex was not without its small stone houses, though timber building predominated, as in most of the region. At the deserted medieval village of Hangleton the latest of the excavated buildings occupied the sites of four earlier dwellings. The house itself was a narrow, flint-walled building with a carefully levelled floor and a roof of Horsham stone. It was unusual in having a hearth against the side wall in one of its two rooms. Also within the toft were a thatched barn and a small bakehouse, its oven projecting beyond the rear wall (Fig. 9.11). One has the impression that such bakehouses could incorporate the functions of the manorial kitchen, bakehouse, and brewhouse all in one little building, and that the old communal village oven was in many places a thing of the past. Whether the Hangleton farm perished because the village itself was deserted, or whether there was something inherently unstable in small stone houses as they were built in this part of England, it is impossible to say, but certainly the timber-framed houses have proved the more durable.[59]

The home counties did not form a cultural unity as far as their buildings are concerned. East Hertfordshire had much in common with eastern England; Bedfordshire and Buckinghamshire belonged rather with the East Midlands; north Oxfordshire seems to have had no tradition of timber building at all, and there are no remaining stone houses from the period. Berkshire peasants could build in stone in the late fourteenth century, as the houses strung along both sides of the village street at Seacourt (Berks.) demonstrated when they were seen and planned on the occasion of the construction of a new road. In the south of the county timber building was in the tradition of the Upper

---

[58] F. J. Green, *Medieval Village Research Group Annual Report*, XXXVI, 1982, p. 12.

[59] D. G. and J. G. Hurst, 'Excavations at the deserted village of Hangleton, Part II', *Sussex Arch. Colls.*, CII, 1964, pp. 102–7.

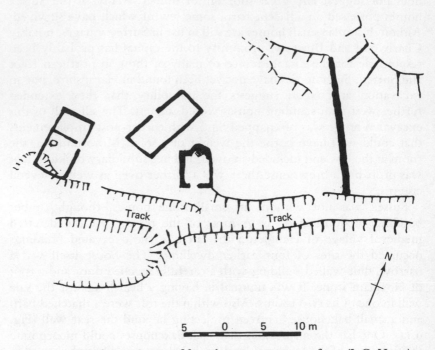

Fig. 9.11 Hangleton, Sussex, fifteenth-century peasant farm (J. G. Hurst)

Thames valley and cruck buildings mingled with framed houses even in the same village, as at Steventon, and small framing and close studding could exist alongside one another in apparently contemporary housing. It is only towards the west of the region, in Harwell, that single-storey, cruck-trussed houses have been recognized.[60]

Whole tofts have been excavated at Dornford (Oxon.), and at Great Linford and Woughton-on-the-Green (Bucks.), all of which had buildings arranged round cobbled yards, and in each case a separate kitchen or bakehouse (Fig. 9.12 (a) and (b)). These are the sort of tenements implied in arrangements made for old people on Ramsey abbey's properties in Bedfordshire: a room "below the principal chamber" for a widow at Cranfield, a holding of one and a quarter virgates; easement in hall, kitchen, and "other buildings" on two virgates at Shillington; or a room called "shepenende" and a garden on

---

[60] For a plan of Seacourt, Beresford and Hurst, *Deserted Medieval Villages*, p. 121. For Steventon, Berkshire, S. E. Rigold, 'The timber-framed buildings of Steventon and their regional significance', *Newbury District Field Club*, x, 1953, pp. 4–11.

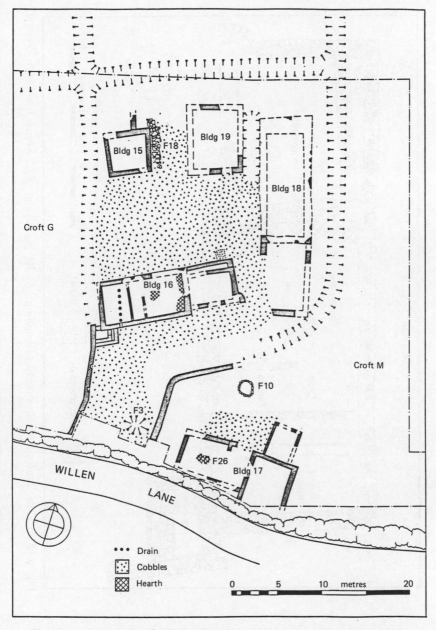

Fig. 9.12(a) Great Linford, Bucks. (By permission of C. Mynard and R. J. Zeepvat)

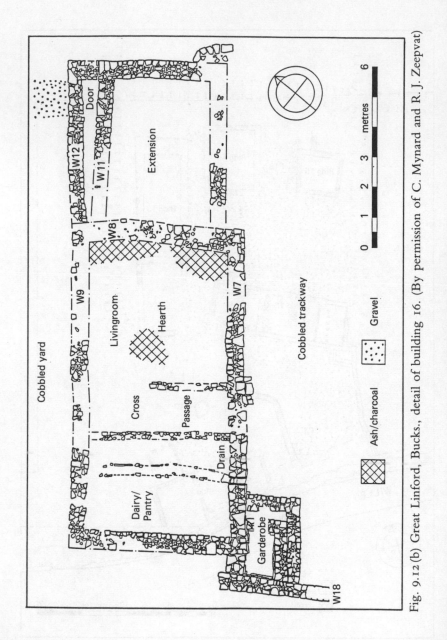

Fig. 9.12 (b) Great Linford, Bucks., detail of building 16. (By permission of C. Mynard and R. J. Zeepvat)

a single-virgate holding in the same village. Though all within the croft, such premises would doubtless rank as separate households for taxation purposes.[61]

Recent surveys of vernacular buildings in south-central England have brought to light a number of late medieval buildings still in occupation in Somerset, for the most part linear and of both two and three bays. Though naturally enough none survive in the original condition a number betray their origin by the length of the room below the cross passage, which is believed originally to have been used for some agricultural need.[62]

An excavated long-house at Barrow Mead, one of a score or so of deserted hamlets in north-east Somerset, had clay-bonded stone walls believed to have risen to full height. A thatched roof was inferred from the absence of roofing nails. The byre end was paved, the floors of the two living rooms above the cross passage were of straw-tempered and rammed clay. There was a hearth in the smaller room only. Improvement had begun before desertion of the hamlet, for the entry to the cross passage, once wide enough for cattle to enter, had been narrowed, and the yards on either side of the house cobbled. Houses in the same tradition are still extant, like a cruck house of five bays at Coombe Keynes, Dorset, believed originally to have been of chalk and cob.[63]

Excavation has demonstrated development towards peasant farms in the crofts such as has been seen elsewhere, but it would be premature to say how general the process was in this region.

In the south-west, hamlets in Cornwall and isolated farms in Devon were more common than nucleated villages in either county. It is a region where long-houses were general and an excavation in the upland hamlet of Garrow Tor, Cornwall, shows the long-house as it was in the mid-fourteenth century, just before the hamlet was deserted. House and barn were built of local granite on a platform levelled from the hillside. There was accommodation for cattle both in the low end of the house and in an extension of the barn. There was only one living room, with a central hearth backed by a granite slab. The contemporary form

[61] For Woughton, see D. Mynard, *Bucks. Arch. Report*, xx–xxi, 1974, p. 27; for Dornford, G. Cowling and E. J. Adnams, *Medieval Village Research Group Annual Report*, xii, 1968, p. 19; for Great Linford, *ibid*, xxv, 1977, p. 19 and xxiv, pp. 16–17; for arrangements at Cranfield and Shillington, DeWindt, ed., *op. cit.*, pp. 248, 293, and for shepenende, p. 143.

[62] L. J. Hall, *The Rural Houses of North Avon and South Gloucestershire*, City of Bristol, Museum and Art Gallery, 1983, *passim*.

[63] J. Woodhouse, *Barrow Mead, Bath, 1964 Excavations*, British Archaeological Reports, xxviii, 1976, pp. 19–20. For Coombe Keynes, P. M. Cunningham, *Dorset N.H. and Arch. Soc.*, xcviii, 1976, pp. 69–72.

of long-house in Devon may not have been very different. Almost all of those still standing belong to a later age, but Tor Farm, Widecombe-in-the-Moor, is thought to have been built originally of one storey only, and has the typical low end beyond a cross passage.[64]

In the south and east of the county small houses of substantial build were originally divided only by stud and panel partitions that were little more than 6 feet high, leaving the roof space undivided. Smoke-blackened roof timbers give evidence of a central hearth, later replaced by a wall fire. Where there was an inner room it was unheated. Both stone and cob walls were used, but the roof was always thatched and carried on crucks, often jointed, and tied only at collar level. Sometimes there were hip crucks, the end or gavil fork of northern documents. It is thought that well before the end of the period solars were added by inserting joists resting on the screens, laid to project into the hall to form a jetty. The type extends into western Somerset.[65]

More unusual in the region are a surviving farm at Neadon on the edge of Dartmoor, accepted as of medieval date, with two rooms on the upper floor and accommodation for animals below, and a terrace of cottages at Bishop's Clyst, known only from a manorial account, each unit of which measured some 25 by 15 feet internally, smaller than anything still standing.[66]

In the north several plans were in common use for houses of less than manorial status, each substantial of its kind. Near the Scottish border were a number of small peles with all the living accommodation within the tower, some of them occupied by parish priests (Pl. IXa). They stood originally within a stone-walled enclosure termed a barmekin, which may possibly have once held supporting buildings and must surely have been used for sheltering cattle.[67]

Further south on either side of the Pennine slopes there were substantial houses of less than manorial status. These have been studied in detail in Yorkshire where they were sometimes of close-studding on stone sill walls, occasionally of stone, more frequently of mixed construction. The king posts and roof ridges of the north were general, and the use of stone slates very common. They could be either linear, or with a single cross-wing, but in either case the open hall was separated by a stout stone wall from the cross passage at its low end, and

[64] D. Dudley and M. Minter, 'The medieval village at Garrow Tor, Bodmin Moor, Cornwall', *Med. Arch.*, VI–VII, 1962–3, pp. 272–8. For Tor Farm, Mercer, *English Vernacular Houses*, p. 151.
[65] N. W. Alcock and M. Laithwaite, 'Medieval houses in Devon and their modernization', *Med. Arch.*, XVII, 1973, pp. 100–5.
[66] W. G. Hoskins, 'Farmhouses and history', *History Today*, X, 1960, p. 339; Alcock, 'The medieval cottages of Bishop Clyst', pp. 146–53.
[67] An example is the Vicar's pele, Corbridge: F. Graham, *The Castles of Northumberland*, Gateshead, 1976, pp. 117–19.

against this was set the hearth. The hall itself could have one aisle or two. In spite of these old-fashioned aisles, they were comfortable and commodious, and their owners are likely to have been as much involved in rural industry as in agriculture.[68]

The houses of customary tenants have seldom survived in the north, save for one or two isolated examples which include an open-hall house at Scriven Green. Yet building and repair accounts frequently mention stone roofing in connection with the construction of such houses, which should indicate building of some solidity.

Excavation in the north has produced mostly long-houses, with a few exceptions which include a house representing one phase of the sequence on an old manor-house site at Wharram Percy, and another within a croft at Osgodby which, like the Wharram house, showed interrupted sill construction.[69]

The excavated long-houses at West Whelpington (Northumb.) were rather smaller than their counterparts at Wharram, possessing only one room above the cross passage as against Wharram's two, though each house was equipped with a hearth stone, and the byre end was drained. Moreover, some of the houses were of stone to eaves-level. An out-building was associated with the majority of houses, either a barn or a rectangular building with a single door. There was no decisive evidence for the use of crucks, but given the general use of such timbers further east in the county, suggested by the Percy bailiff's rolls, it is not unlikely.[70]

There were two rooms above the cross passage in the earlier of two consecutive long-houses on a village toft at Wharram Percy, which, though no sign of bay posts remained, would be the equivalent of three bays of approximately 13 feet or four of 10 feet – the upper range of house size suggested for the East and West Midlands. Its successor was larger still and with a good stone hearth and an open-ended building at right-angles to it, likely to have served some agricultural need.[71]

These relatively solid houses should be compared with the much slighter long-house excavated at Alnhamsheles (Fig. 9.13). It is known

[68] *Rural Houses in West Yorkshire*, West Yorkshire Metropolitan County Council and RCHM, England, Supplementary Ser. 8, London, 1986, pp. 27–32.

[69] P. G. Farmer, 'Excavations at the deserted village of Osgodby near Scarborough', *Scarborough and District Arch. Soc.*, IX, 1966, fig. 5, p. 48; D. D. Andrews and G. Milne, eds., *Wharram, a Study of Settlement on the Yorkshire Wolds*, I, *Domestic Settlement 1: Areas 10 and 6*, Soc. for Med. Arch., Monograph 8, London, 1979, pp. 38–41.

[70] D. H. Evans and M. G. Jarrett, 'The deserted village of West Whelpington, Northumberland', 3rd report, Part I, *AA.*, 5th ser. xv, 1987, pp. 209–20.

[71] Andrews and Milne, eds., *op. cit.*, pp. 28–54. For a revised interpretation, see S. Wrathmell, *Domestic Settlement 2: Medieval Peasant Farmsteads*, York Univ. Arch. Pubns., VIII, 1989.

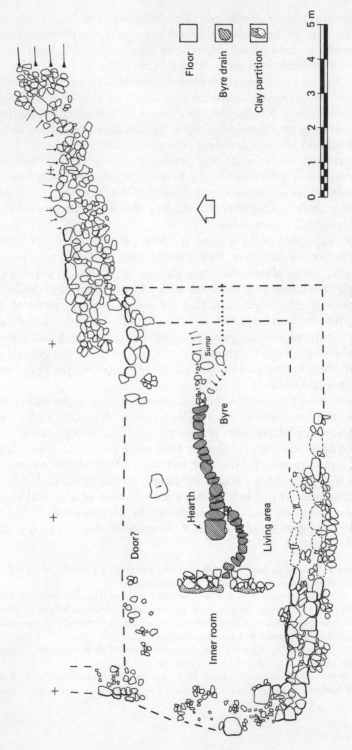

Fig. 9.13 Alnhamsheles, Northumb., long-house (P. Dixon)

5 m

4

3

2

1

0

Floor Byre drain Clay partition

Door?

Inner room

Hearth

Living area

Byre

Sump

that some houses in the north cost no more than 10s. to build, and that a house at Sowerby (Yorks.), blown down by the wind, could be carried off by a neighbour.[72]

Working on surviving accounts for fifteenth-century rebuilding and repair in the Vale of York, Harrison has shown interesting variations as between different manors within the same estate, with framed houses on stone sills in three Bedale villages on the west side of the vale, and flimsy building with no stonework a couple of miles to the south, while in a group of five on the other side of the vale, cruck and framed buildings were intermingled in two villages, but on three more northerly settlements only crucks were used. Repairs on the Percy estates in Northumberland, however, involved the use of crucks only, and of ten houses for which more than repair timber was required one was of at least five bays, five of at least two bays, and four of a single bay, unless the number of pairs of *syles* allowed to the tenant was intended for partial repair only. Direct comparison of building costs is hazardous, for different items tend to be omitted. On the half-dozen or so accounts that are available timber and stone were not costed, presumably because they were covered by housebote. At Thorner, a single house cost £4 8s. 3d., a house and barn within the same tenement £7 13s. 1d. The house was stone roofed, the barn thatched. The stone roofing slates, and the laths and moss on which they were bedded, were much the most expensive item. Accounts for two different houses in the vale were higher, one at £11 3s. 9d., the other at £4 15s. 6d., but in these cases carpentry costs were greater than those for the stone roofs.[73]

The evidence for medieval sheilings is as yet unsatisfactory. Such as it is, it will be considered, like other dwellings associated with outlying cattle and sheep runs, in connection with farm buildings. Some of the Durham villages, however, still seem to have been maintaining communal buildings, or at least buildings for whose repair the whole community was responsible, such as oven, forge, piggery, and sheephouse. The common oven at Leeds is known to have been within a building, a precaution against northern weather that could have been widespread.[74]

Small medieval houses are still occupied in the West Midlands except in the north of the region, where none has yet been identified in

[72] P. J. Dixon, 'Alnamsheles', *Med. Arch.*, xxv, 1981, p. 223. The Sowerby incident is from a Wakefield court roll, Yorkshire Arch. Soc., MD 223/1/76.

[73] For North Yorkshire, B. Harrison and B. Hutton, *Vernacular Houses in North Yorkshire and Cleveland*, Edinburgh, 1984, pp. 4–7. Northumberland repairs, Hodgson, ed., *Percy Bailiff's Rolls*, passim; Thorner houses are in Leeds District Archives, Mexborough Coll., MD 10/11 and /13.

[74] J. W. Kirby, ed., *The Manor and Borough of Leeds*, Thoresby Soc., LVII, no. 127, 1981, p. 6.

Derbyshire. At Ashleworth (Pl. VIIb) and Upton St Leonards (Glos.) there are houses of one and a half bays, astonishingly small for survival. In Cotswold regions there is a scattering of long-houses, and at Chew Stoke the byre end of one house has been turned into a dairy, a logical metamorphosis, though the original use of the area below the cross passage is always something of a problem unless there is a tell-tale drain. Both here and in Worcestershire there are cruck-built houses where the hall was originally open and the size of the room below the cross passage suggests long-house derivation. They were always thatched, but could be either stone or cob. The seventy or so houses belonging to the period identified by R. K. Field from Worcestershire court rolls seem to have included only one with an upper room, and very few long-houses. Over 67 per cent of them were of three bays or more, and a further 20 per cent were of two.[75]

By contrast, cross-passage plans are almost unknown in Warwick-shire, where small surviving cruck houses at Stoneleigh include both two- and three-bay houses (Pl. IXb), the latter with upper rooms, the former sometimes with a door on the gable end.[76]

Derbyshire has no extant small houses of medieval date, yet, as in the north, there were those that sound sturdy enough from their building accounts. Among the many settlements that figure in the Duchy of Lancaster account rolls for the fifteenth century, there are only two, Scropton and Brassington, where the lord can be seen to take responsibility for repairs and new building. He might make gifts of timber or cash in other places, but in Hartington it is at one point expressly stated that a tenant was bound to rebuild two bays of an insethouse as well as the supporting buildings. The contrast may be a matter of chance, or it may be simply a matter of differing custom as between manors. However that may be, the entries offer a certain amount of information for a district where there are no surviving houses. The most informative account is for work at Brassington, where a four-bay house and a three-bay barn were rebuilt for a customary tenant. Craftsmen were hired for the work: a carpenter, a mason, a dauber, a roofer, and an unskilled labourer to clear the site and lend a hand. The exterior walls of the house were of stone mortared with clay to full height, the interior walls, the *parcloses*, of wattle and daub. The barn, on the other hand, was to have stone walls only to half height. There is no hint of an upper floor to either. Both roofs were

---

[75] Field, 'Worcestershire peasant buildings, household goods and farming equipment', pp. 125–45.

[76] N. W. Alcock, J. C. Braithwaite and M. W. Jeffs, 'Timber building in Warwickshire', *Birmingham and War. Arch. Soc.*, LXXXV, 1973, pp. 125–45.

thatched and crested and the floor of the house tempered with clay and straw and rammed. The cost of the two buildings together, without timber and stone, was £8 9s. 2½d.[77]

By contrast, excavated buildings at Barton Blount, in the same county, were constructed on padstones too irregularly spaced to represent bay units. Here again the toft included both house and barn, the barn reported as larger and better built than the dwelling house, yet another example of the variety of small houses in contemporary use in any given region.[78]

D. FARM BUILDINGS

Just as on manorial sites dwelling houses had come to be regarded as entities rather than as separate units of accommodation connected by passages, and their arrangement had become important, so the agricultural buildings had very frequently been gathered into one or more tidy rectangles. The rearrangement was to some extent reflected in the village tofts, where a barn was becoming a common element in the holding. At this level accommodation specifically for stock is rarely mentioned. Where long-houses were still in use the low end was available for animals, at least in part, and excavated examples have shown the occasional extension, either to house or barn, probably for the same purpose. No doubt barns, too, were sometimes used to stall animals, as they were at a later date, though no stalling arrangements have been found during excavation. It has been supposed, rather, that cattle were kept during the winter in crew-yards, sheltered between house and barn.

Fieldwork and aerial photography have demonstrated the existence of small out-lying farms, particularly in upland areas and on the margins of cultivation. Surface indications suggest both long-houses and farmsteads with several buildings in addition to the dwelling house. Some, no doubt, belong to the later middle ages, but only excavation can show how many. Isolated buildings judged to be field barns, byres, sheephouses, or stables, all of whose existence is indicated by documentary allusions, seem to be mainly, but not exclusively, in upland regions. Finally, it must be remembered that on the manors buildings originally serving domestic purposes could be down-graded to farm use. Examples have been found of the use of old halls or chambers for storing grain or stabling horses.

[77] PRO, DL 29/369/6180.
[78] Beresford, *The Medieval Clayland Village*, pp. 27–31.

(i) Barns

The largest and most imposing of medieval farm buildings was the barn, the only agricultural building to survive in considerable numbers into modern times. Such survivals, however, represent only a tiny proportion of the original numbers. The ecclesiastical corporations in particular normally built several on each grange, because of the extent of their own estates and because by the later middle ages they had appropriated a very large number of rectories with their attendant tithes. It is not unusual to find three, four, or even five in surveys of ecclesiastical manors. The needs of the standard lay manors were more modest, though almost all possessed at least one large barn. Excavation at Whittonstall (Northumb.) produced only one, and so too at the Oxfordshire manor of Chalgrove, both instances where work was on a scale likely to show every building present (Fig. 9.4). Groups of manors sometimes shared storage space. Late thirteenth-century surveys of the Rabayne estates, for example, enumerated only four barns to serve the five Lincolnshire manors, though in Dorset there were five among four manors.[79]

The most striking characteristic of these barns is their huge size, a characteristic apparent in even the earliest records and among the earliest surviving buildings. They needed to be big because medieval corn was stored on the stalk until it was threshed, which, according to Walter of Henley, might not be until after Christmas. The use of aisles extended the space laterally, and aisles continued to be a feature of many of these buildings long after they had disappeared in dwelling houses. This may not have been only because farm buildings tended to lag behind domestic buildings in their style and carpentry, but also because the method of construction tended to compartmentalize the aisles, giving useful areas for stalling animals, storing carts, and other miscellaneous purposes if required.

The barns were not only long and wide, they were surprisingly high. A seventeenth-century farmer spoke of packing haybarns so tightly that a cat could hardly crawl between crop and ridge, an exaggeration perhaps, but the careful measurements of height sometimes given on the St Paul's manors, not only from floor to tie-beam but from tie to ridge, suggest that every bit of space might be needed.[80]

---

[79] Whittonstall, excavated by C. Mahany, report forthcoming; for Chalgrove, Page, 'Chalgrove, Harding's Field moated site', pp. 22–3. For a detailed survey of the manors of the Raybayne estates, PRO C 133/41/12.

[80] C. B. Robinson, ed., *Rural Economy in Yorkshire in 1641*, Surtees Soc., XXXIII, 1857, p. 36. For the Navestock measurements, Guildhall Library, St Paul's Cathedral Mss., Liber I, f.73.

Each barn may originally have been intended for a single crop, as contemporary references to "barley barn", "oat barn", or "wheat barn" imply, but such specialization seems to have been rather loosely adhered to, for when chance shows what was actually in a given barn, there were stacks of all kinds of grain and of peas and beans as well. Hay, on the other hand, was usually stored in a specific building, often kept in hand when other barns were leased. Where there was more than one barn there was usually a separate enclosure, the barn yard, hedged or walled, and gated, which could at times include such buildings as the manorial dovecote, henhouse, and granary.

There seems little doubt that the number of barns declined in the period, and that new barns when built were often considerably smaller than their predecessors. On the St Paul's estates in Essex, Herts., and Surrey, for example, a number of barns built in the thirteenth century were all in use early in the following century; by the 1490s the seventeen that were distributed among five manors had dropped to six, while two other barns had been truncated so that, of the original nineteen storage bays they could count between them, only twelve remained.[81]

By 1350 all the major structural improvements had already taken place. Opposed doors on the long sides had in most cases replaced the single door common at an earlier date, always on the long side, in contrast to continental practice which placed doors at the end. Thatch was general though stone slate, in spite of its enormous weight, was surprisingly common where the material was available locally; ceramic tile was relatively uncommon. Porches, or at least sheltering hoods, protected the doorway, and many of the large monastic barns had an upper room in the porch to accommodate an official. The barn floor was carefully prepared with rammed clay, and some building accounts indicate the presence of a hearth, whether for agricultural needs or for some quasi-domestic purpose is uncertain; for, once the crop was out, these great buildings were used for a variety of purposes, from the housing of servants to meetings of the manorial court.[82] Even parliament is known to have met in a barn. Occasionally part of the barn included an upper floor, a development more common at a later date.

Regional variation. As far as style and building method are concerned, the barns do not fit readily into anything but the loosest of regional

[81] *Ibid.*, box 32/644, 647; 35/950, 952; 36/1092, 1022, 1027; Liber I, f.80.

[82] An *astrum* is mentioned at Ditchingham and Little Framlingham, Norfolk, early in the fourteenth century and in 1379 one was put into a new barn at Forncett. Possible examples have been excavated at Whittonstall and Leighton Grove.

divisions. Aisled timber barns, some few of which were later clad in stone, are known across east and south-east England, and there is an outlying group in the north-east.[83] Unaisled barns, often stone-built, are occasional in most regions, but characteristic of western and south-western regions where crucks were usual.

Aisled timber barns characteristic of eastern England have survived in numbers, especially in Essex. They are often of no more than five bays, with hipped roofs usually supported on crown posts and principal posts braced with passing shores. Sometimes, as at Netteswellbury, the rafters are strengthened with wind braces. An exception was a barn at Belchamp St Pauls, lately destroyed, one of an original group of three, archaic in its carpentry though with a carbon date of around 1400.[84]

In the south east the barns of Kent have also been studied in considerable detail. Structurally they differ little from those of eastern England though some, like the group that survived until recently at Lenham, were of somewhat greater size.[85] The archbishop's barn in Maidstone is exceptional in that it was both stone-built and with an upper floor from the first, reached by an outside stair.

Barns in the home counties were more varied, reflecting the cultural traditions of the region. Late in the fourteenth century St Albans abbey built no less than five new barns on its manors, all aisled timber barns and four with crown-post roofs, but all roofed with ceramic tiles in place of the thatch of eastern England, as at Wymondley (Pl. Xb). None was very large, and only that at Radlett was equipped with a mid-stray for threshing. In strong contrast were the unaisled barns of Oxfordshire, stone-built and with stone roofs supported on raised crucks. These were sometimes also of considerable size, Swalcliffe, for example, being 128 feet long, and of ten bays. Church Enstone, of late fourteenth-century date, though smaller, was in the same tradition.[86]

In south-central England there already existed, in the mid-fifteenth century, a rich heritage of stone barns, often with elaborate roofs based on the cruck tradition (Pl. XIa). Recent work at Bradford-on-Avon has located a second large barn set at right-angles to the well-known

[83] S. E. Rigold, 'The distribution of aisled timber barns', *Vernacular Architecture*, II, 1971, pp. 20–1. For northern additions, see D. W. Clarke, 'Aisled timber barns in the Pennines', *Brigantian*, III, 1974, pp. 18–20.

[84] The Essex barns are discussed in C. A. Hewitt, *The Development of Carpentry*, Newton Abbot, 1969, pp. 111, 117, 124; the dating difficulties in 'The potential and limitations of radiocarbon dating', in R. Berger, ed., *Scientific Methods in Medieval Archaeology*, Berkeley, 1970, pp. 41–53.

[85] S. E. Rigold, 'Some major Kentish barns', *Arch. Cant.*, LXXXI, 1966, p. 20.

[86] The St Albans barns are published by J. H. Roberts, 'Five medieval barns in Hertfordshire', *Herts. Archaeology*, VII, pp. 159–80. For Swalcliffe and Church Enstone, R. B. Wood-Jones, *Traditional Domestic Architecture in the Banbury Region*, Manchester, 1963, pp. 21–2.

example that once served the Shaftesbury nuns, completing the conventional barn yard (Pl. Xa).[87]

Cargoll Farm (Cornwall) has the only surviving barn of the any size in the south-west, but in the north there are a few late medieval barns in use. Stank Hall barn, now in the outskirts of Leeds, and a very similar barn that belonged to Bolton priory, were both originally walled with wattle and daub, and both have the characteristic king posts and ridge pieces of the north. Their stone slates are in the tradition of the region.[88] An excavated barn at Whittonstall (Northumb.) indicates that, east of the Pennines, the aisled barn extended considerably further north than had been supposed. There is little evidence, however, of the position in the north-west, where small cruck barns appear to belong to a later period.

The traditions of south-central England extended northward into the West Midlands to produce such stone-built, unaisled buildings as Bredon barn (Worcs.), which has a dendrochronological date of around 1350, and a roof structure in the cruck tradition. Here very large barns were still built late in the period, as at Ashleworth, with its ten bays of limestone and stone slate roof, or at Grafton (Worcs.), where there was an agreement to build a ten-bay barn in the mid-fifteenth century.[89]

One or two peasant barns still stand in south-east England (Fig. 9.14). Otherwise such information as is available comes from excavation or documents. Excavated barns of which only the foundations remain are identified by their lack of hearth, for otherwise there is little to distinguish them from the adjoining house. There were at least two barns among the buildings round an excavated toft at Grenstein and Thuxton in eastern England, and at Markshall and Faxton in the East Midlands. Excavated tofts at Woughton-on-the-Green and Dornford each produced two barns in the home counties still in use in the fifteenth century in this village that was soon to be deserted. Excavated evidence is meagre in south-central England and the south-west, but the fact that long-houses had often been improved and their low ends converted to domestic use presupposes the addition of at least a barn to the peasant toft. In the north some of the houses at West Whelpington were associated with barns, but none has been recognized yet on village excavations in Yorkshire or in the West Midlands.

Nevertheless these regions were not lagging far behind in the general improvement of peasant tofts that was taking place in the period. At

[87] J. Haslam, 'Bradford on Avon, Barton Farm', Med. Arch., XXVIII, 1984, pp. 246–7.

[88] H. E. J. Le Patourel, ed., 'Stank Hall Barn, Leeds', Thoresby Soc. Miscellany, XVI, pt 3, pp. 237–46.

[89] It was to be 100 feet long: J. Harvey, English Medieval Architects, London, 1954. p. 293.

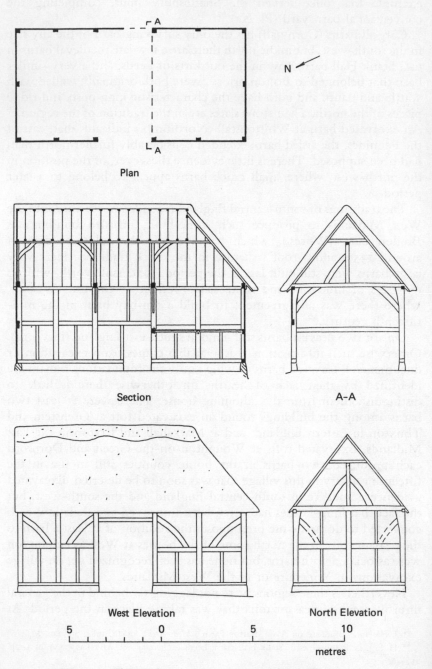

Fig. 9.14 Chittinghurst, Sussex, peasant barn (D. Martin)

Methley (W. Yorks.) manorial custom made the peasants responsible for repair of barn as well as house on the holding. At Thorner, in the same county, the construction of three peasant barns was accounted for in as many years. West of the Pennines a survey showed that in Orford, a hamlet of Warrington, five of a group of seven cottagers with 5-acre holdings held both house and barn, though one barn was situated beyond the croft. Of the buildings that occur in the published Halmote rolls of Durham Cathedral priory, it seems that about 40 per cent of the tenants, including cottagers, held a barn, a figure matched by the Warwickshire evidence published by Field.[90]

Most excavated barns differ little in size from the houses they accompany, and this similarity is reflected in the cost of their construction. At Thorner barns cost 63s. 5d., 63s. 10d., and 61s. 5d. respectively, figures that included carriage, nails, and labour only, for the stone for sill walls, slate stone for roofs, timber, wattle, clay and moss for bedding the slates, all came from the manor. A contemporary house built on the manor cost 89s., the difference partly made up by the cost of windows. A late fifteenth-century barn constructed for a customary tenant at Brassington was stone-built only up to half-height, unlike the contemporary house. Both buildings were thatched with straw from a neighbouring rectory. All these barns sound solid enough, but they do not give the whole story. A barn at Scropton, contemporary with the Brassington barn and on the same estate, was a two-bay timber-framed structure, costing only 20s. The roof of a barn on the manor of Wakefield was knocked off by a farm cart and carried away by the wife of another tenant, and even more flimsy must have been the barn at Fulwell in Co. Durham, built, apparently, with one pair of crucks and a couple of gavil forks. Neither example suggests anything very solid.[91]

In both Gloucestershire and Lincolnshire a substitute for the peasant barn was a helm, a platform constructed with solid timbers which stood, like many contemporary manorial granaries, on staddle-stones. Whether they were within the toft, like most contemporary barns, is uncertain, for they have not yet been recognized in excavation.[92] Late

[90] For Methley, H. S. Derbyshire and G. D. Lumb, eds., *The History of Methley*, Thoresby Soc., XXXV, 1937, p. 163. For Orford, W. Beaumont, ed., *Warrington as Described in a Contemporary Rent Roll*, Chetham Soc., OS XVII, 1849, pp. 124–33.

[91] The Thorner barns were built between 1422 and 1427: Leeds District Archives, MX MD 10/3/13. The Wakefield barn is in S. S. Walker, ed., *The Court Rolls of the Manor of Wakefield, 1331–3*, Yorks. Arch. Soc. Rec. Ser., 1983, p. 23. For the Fulwell barn, see Longstaffe and Booth, eds., *Halmota Prioratus Dunelmensis*, p. 111.

[92] C. Dyer, 'Evidence for helms in Gloucestershire', *Vernacular Architecture*, XV, 1984, PP. 42–6: S. Needham, 'Helms, hovels and belfreys: more evidence from probate inventories', *ibid.*, pp. 45–6.

manorial records, place names, and likely earthworks, all indicate that peasant barns were also situated on the open fields and on waste land away from the settlements. Shared barns, too, are recorded within the villages, and, after the demesne lands had been leased, storage bays in the manorial barns were sometimes let for peasant use.

(ii) *Granaries*

Even if grain were not threshed until the spring, it had eventually to be stored, and there were several different types of storage building in common use, though it is not easy to pin any one of them exclusively to a given region. The problem was to house a heavy but valuable commodity that would become mouldy in damp conditions, would germinate if the temperature were too high, and which was at risk from a whole range of predators, not excluding human ones.

One answer was to build a barn with an upper floor. An upper floor is reported for a Torre abbey barn at Shiphay (Devon), and another at Sudeley Castle farm (Glos.), this last with a chute, as there is for the purpose-built granary at Lypiatt (Glos.). These are west-country barns, but the archbishop's barn at Maidstone (Kent) also had an upper floor from the first, so if, as seems likely, these floors were for grain storage, it was not an exclusively regional type.

Another method was to erect a free-standing building of stone with a spine wall to carry weight. Such a building stood among the barns at South Witham (Lincs.), and another was excavated at Leighton Grove (Beds.). Whether these buildings were of stone throughout, or merely rested on a heavy stone base, is uncertain.[93]

Much the most widespread type, however, was a building raised above the ground on posts or staddle-stones. It is known to have been in use over eastern England, the south-east, the home counties, south-central England and the West Midlands, principally from repair accounts, for only one or two have survived from the middle ages, though a large number of post-medieval examples carry on the tradition. It is the only farm building whose repair demanded the use of planks for walling and timber for a stair and it was sometimes roofed with ceramic tiles at a time when the rest of the agricultural buildings were thatched. The interior was usually subdivided into at least four compartments for the various kinds of grain.

An example of this type of granary, of late fifteenth-century date, stood until recently at Tadlow (Cambs.) and has been re-erected (Fig. 9.15). It measured some 24 by 16 feet and 9 feet from floor to tie beam. No trace of internal arrangements remains, but the floor cants gently

[93] South Witham, excavated by P. Mayes, Leighton Grove by E. Baker, reports forthcoming.

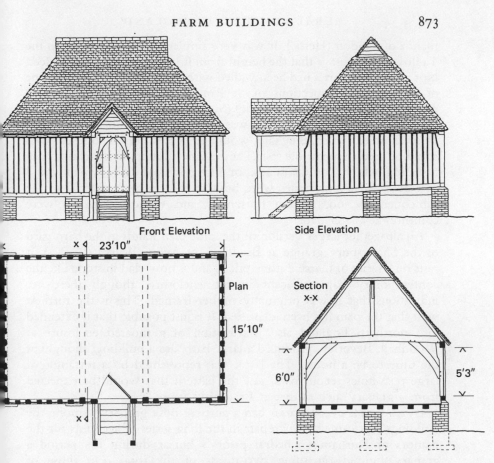

Front Elevation

Side Elevation

x 23'10"

Plan

Section
x-x

15'10"

6'0"

5'3"

x

Fig. 9.15 Tadlow, Cambs., granary (R. Harris)

forward to the door, which is centrally placed, sheltered by a hood, and approached by a flight of steps. The walls are of plank and muntin construction, the main timbers squared from the whole length of young trees. Its hipped roof, ventilated by gablets, was supported on crown posts and tiled. The granary had been threatened with destruction and was dismantled and eventually reconstructed. It now stands on brick posts but how it was originally supported is not known.[94]

A similar Essex granary at Navestock Hall could, perhaps, be that described in a survey of 1497 as having four compartments. Another which has not survived, was described in fourteen-century leases of the

[94] Re-erected at Wandlebury, Cambridgeshire; dendrochronology gives a felling date for the timbers of 1415. They were examined by O. Rackham, see his *Ancient Woodland*, p. 146 and G. Black *et al.*, 'The repair and dendrochronological dating of a medieval granary from Tadlow', *Cambridge Antiquarian Soc.*, LXXII, 1982–3, pp. 79–86.

manor of Sandon (Herts.). It was very similar in its dimensions to the Tadlow granary save that the height from floor to tie beam was 12 feet. Not all such granaries had been walled with plank, however, for on one of the periodic inspections of St Paul's Chapter manors the jury reported that the granary at Barnes (Surrey) was built of chalk-stone in very bad condition. They said it was too large and wanted it shortened by six couples, which, they said, would be 15 feet, and the timber saved could be used to repair the rest. They estimated it could be rebuilt with boarding, which would cost 40s., or with posts and daub, which would cost 20s.[95] Many granaries were built in the cheaper material in the subsequent period, though horizontal and vertical planking were common at a later date.

An altogether larger version of the same plan stands in the barn yard of the Shaftesbury grange at Bradford-on-Avon (Wilts.) (Pl. Xa). It rests on a series of massive stone pillars and is now clad in stone like the contemporary barn adjacent in the enclosure, though there are indications that it was originally timber-framed. This is the furthest west that the plan has been identified. It is just possible that it extended into northern England also. Excavation of a moated enclosure at Woodhall, Beverley, produced a large barn and a building, thought at the time to be a house. The latter was represented by a rectangle of large post-holes set in rows, just the pattern that would be expected from a granary such as that at Bradford.[96]

By no means every manor had a purpose-built granary. Among the buildings that came up for repair in the long series of accounts for the manors of Durham Cathedral priory's bursar during the period a granary figured on some two-thirds of the total. On those of Winchester Cathedral priory just before the mid-fourteenth century there were rather fewer, in contrast to the position on the Bigod manors in Norfolk or the St Paul's manors in Essex, Herts., and Surrey, where every manor had its granary. There is no evidence for the fate of the Bigod granaries in the later middle ages, but those of the St Paul's manors were all in disrepair by the end of the fifteenth century. Survival even in regions of stone building has been so rare, however, that it seems likely that a specialized building of this sort was something of a luxury. Certainly there is no sign of any such on the peasant holdings.

[95] Guildhall Library, St Pauls Cathedral Mss., Navestock, box 36/1042; Sandon, 38/1220; Barnes, 52/R 1.

[96] W. J. Varley, 'Excavations at Woodhall Manor, Beverley', East Yorks. Archaeology, II, 1975, p. 31.

(iii) *Kilns and kilnhouses*

Repair accounts on many manors refer to a kiln that is clearly within a building that required repairs to windows and door, and replacement of lost keys. Sometimes it looks as if this is to be equated with the manorial brew house, as, for example, at Sandon (Herts.), where it contained the kiln itself (*fornum*), an oven, two boilers, and five lead bowls. At other times it looks as though something rather different were intended.

Kilns have frequently been found in the course of archaeological excavation, but as free-standing structures, usually interpreted as corn-drying kilns. Corn was regularly dried in kilns in the post-medieval period, but it is very difficult to detect the practice in medieval England. Among many hundred manorial account rolls only one payment for drying corn has been found, and that for a paltry sum and in a very wet year.[97] Treatises on estate management do not mention the practice, nor was there any sight of it among the week-works which are accounted for in detail on the long run of Bigod rolls. It seems that normally sheaves were stacked straight into the barn. It is likely therefore that the primary purpose of most kilns was for malting, for ale was an important element in the diet of all classes, and malting a significant rural industry.

Two forms have been found, a rectangular sunken form with a rather long stoking pit, and a keyhole-shaped structure. The walls of both splayed outwards to carry some sort of frame for the hair blanket on which the sprouted grain was spread. Many of the kilnhouse roofs were thatched, so it must be supposed that they were either very high or that there was a substantial chimney, though only a slow fire would be required.[98]

(iv) *Byres*

Byres for plough oxen, and plough horses where they were used, were usually situated in the base court, occasionally on the fields, or even in the park. Manorial byres were solid, long-lasting structures which were still being put up late in the fifteenth century. At the top of the scale, a building account shows the bishop of Winchester's new byre at

[97] Between 1313 and 1314, 2s. was paid at Raunds for drying corn. PRO DL 29/1/3. The kiln at Elsworth (Cambs.) was enlarged by 20 feet between 1445 and 1446 on a half-virgate holding: DeWindt, ed., *Liber Gersumarum*, p. 307. Peasant kilns are also mentioned at Hemingford, Hurst, Ripton, and Upwood on the abbey's estates.

[98] For plans of medieval kilns, which are not known to alter during the whole period, see J. G. Hurst, *AHEW*, II, fig. 9.7, p. 874. A kiln within a building was found at Barrow: E. G. Bolton, 'Excavation of a house and malt kiln at Barrow, Rutland', *Med. Arch*, IV, 1950, pp. 128–31.

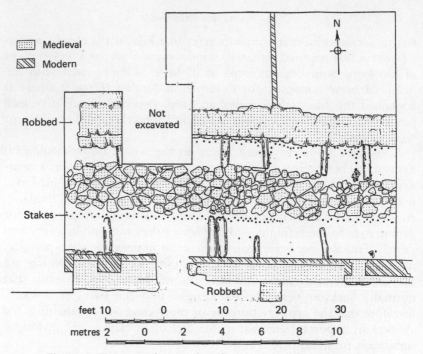

Fig. 9.16 Tynemouth, Northumb., excavated byre (G. Jobey)

Droxford (Hants.) in 1472, timber-framed and on sill walls of mortared flint. It required three carpenters with fourteen assistants to raise the frame, which was then infilled with wattle and daub, and thatched. It cost £4 2s. 6d., but its size was not mentioned. A contract for a combined byre and stable to be built at Elveden (Suffolk) a year later was more precise. It was to cost £5. Oak was to be used. It was to measure 51 by 19 feet and there was to be an internal wall between byre and stable. Each end was to have its own door, and the byre to have racks and mangers, but unlike the stable it had no windows. Nothing was said about stall partitions.[99]

The width tallies well with such information as is available on other byres. Fig. 9.16 shows an excavated example at Tynemouth. Its width was some 20 feet, allowing room for two rows of stalls each 5 feet wide on either side of its central drain. A couple at Navestock (Essex) were also 20 feet wide, one 48, the other 80 feet long. Another pair at Sandon are of interest because one was clearly cruck-built – its posts "met at

[99] For Droxford, Winchester Cathedral Records, Droxford Manorial Account, no. 102; for Elveden, D. Dymond, 'A fifteenth-century building contract', *Vernacular Architecture*, IX, 1978, pp. 10–11.

the top of the building ". It was smaller, 16 feet wide by 14 high, but solid, for it is identifiable a century earlier and just possibly as early as the mid-twelfth century. However, unlike its neighbour that was constructed with posts and a tie beam, it had disappeared by the middle of the fourteenth century.[100]

Confirmation of the long life of these buildings comes from two surveys of Heybridge, Essex. The first described a series of buildings straddling the gate of the manorial enclosure in 1301. Oxen and stotts were housed in a long building on one side, on the other was a room for the overseer, a cow byre, a stable for visitors' horses, a calf house, and a room for storing hay, all under one roof. In 1475, though other buildings had changed, the long range on either side of the gate was still there, though described as "ancient".[101]

On the peasant holdings tethering posts have been recognized in the low end of long-houses, and at Garrow there was accommodation for a beast at the end of a barn (above p. 858), an arrangement that emerges in one or two entries relating to Ramsey abbey tenements. Although a number of peasant barns have been excavated, there has been no report that any included either stalling arrangements or drains. It has been suggested rather that peasants were over-wintering their stock in crew-yards sited between barn and house.[102] Excavations that have demonstrated this practice have been on villages later deserted, and therefore perhaps not very prosperous, while such occasional records as have survived for arrangements for old people seem to suggest that at least in the East Midlands and eastern England their few animals required shelter.

A few buildings on specialized stock farms have been excavated and others recognized from earthwork. It is not easy to decide from either whether the buildings were for sheep or cattle. In Dundale, on the North Yorkshire Moors, there were at least three buildings within a large enclosure in an area where the Malton canons are known to have kept both sheep and cattle (Fig. 9.17). Not far away a building was excavated in another such complex in Ryedale (Fig. 9.18). It was a long narrow aisled building with end doors, one of which gave onto a yard with a small dwelling house at the far end, but whether for herdsman or shepherd it is impossible to say.[103]

---

[100] G. Jobey, 'Excavations at Tynemouth Priory and Castle', *AA*, 4th ser., XLV, 1967, pp. 58 and fig. 6. For Sandon, Guildhall Library, St Paul's Cathedral Mss., Liber I, 136, 178.

[101] *Ibid.*, box 36/1022, 1027.

[102] G. Beresford, *The Medieval Clayland Village*, pp. 13–18.

[103] The Dundale site was found by J. McDonnell and surveyed by S. Moorhouse. For the long building, see A. L. Pacitto, 'Rudland Close; site of a medieval aisled barn on the North York Moors', *Ryedale Historian*, II, 1966, pp. 20–43.

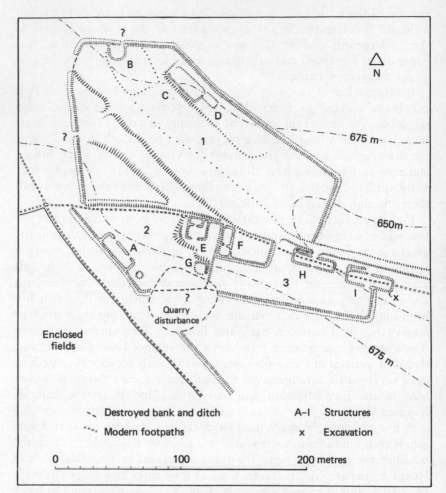

Fig. 9.17 Dundale, North Yorks. Moors, probable cattle ranch. (J. McDonnell and S. Moorhouse)

(v) *Sheephouses*

Three structures were used in the care of sheep, four if the essential dairy is included. The most ephemeral was a movable fold built with hurdles, occasionally with a corner roofed to shelter sheep or shepherd, though one manuscript shows the latter in a wheeled hut rather like a nineteenth-century bathing machine (Pl. XIb).

Sheephouses, by contrast, were permanent structures and one or more figured among the agricultural buildings of a great many manors, with some specialized manors having as many as five. The buildings

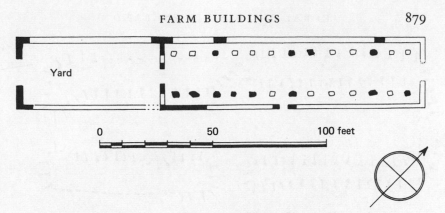

Fig. 9.18 Rudland Close, North Yorks. Moors, byre or sheephouse
(A. L. Pacitto)

were sometimes sited in the base court, sometimes beyond its gate, and
not infrequently well away from the manor house, especially in districts
where sheep were grazed on marsh or moorland. They always seem to
have been surrounded by an enclosure, when not actually in the base
court itself; hedges and ditches were usual in the lowlands, stone walls
on the hills.

Building and repair accounts indicate long narrow houses of timber
on stone sill walls – six cart-loads of ragstone were used for these at
Meon (Hants.) in 1402. Above the sills the wall timbers were infilled
with wattle and daub, the roof thatched. There are always exceptions:
a thousand boards were bought for a Yorkshire sheephouse, a
Winchester sheephouse was roofed with tile, a Gloucestershire
sheephouse had stone walls throughout. Length is the dimension that
stands out, for the houses are often well over 100 feet long,
exceptionally, as at Marlborough, over 200 feet. Even peasant
sheephouses, when recorded, were longer than the insethouse or byre
on the holding. No suggestions of windows appear in the accounts, but
the cost of hinges and locks for doors is frequently charged. Possibly
light and air entered through an open wall top, such as is sometimes
portrayed in illustrations, though it seems more probable that this is
simply a device to show the sheep within, for one pair of doors bought
for a sheephouse is described as "barn doors", which seems to indicate
a substantial building. Similarly an earthwork on the Wharram-le-
Street grange, which agrees precisely in size with a sheephouse said to
have been built late in the fourteenth century for overwintering the
ewes, also appears to represent a building of some substance (Fig.
9.19).[104]

[104] Winchester Cathedral RO, Manorial Documents for the Bishopric 44/1; Bitterne *bercaria*
was to have a great door made with two 'lefez vocatur berne dore'.

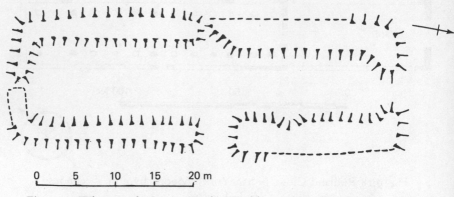

0   5   10   15   20 m

Fig. 9.19 Wharram-le-Street, Yorks. Wolds, earthworks of Meaux abbey
sheephouse

Specialized sheephouses in the hands of peasants must have been rare,
though all the tenants at Hartington (Derbs.) were supposed to erect
six-bay sheephouses on their holdings in addition to insethouse and
barn. Fountains abbey shepherds too kept quite sizeable personal flocks.
Tenants at West Rainton (Durham) seem by custom to have had a
common sheephouse, but they showed no great enthusiasm for keeping
it in repair.[105]

Priors Rakes on Malham Moor (Yorks.) should, from the place
name, be one of Bolton abbey's bercaries. The building excavated some
years ago was thought to have a lean-to against one of its long walls,
and a small room off-set from the main building, the whole enclosed
with walls and fencing (Fig. 9.20). It was situated in a south-facing
valley, sheltered from the wind on either side and set in an area covered
with small buildings and enclosures (Fig. 9.21). By contrast, an old
shepherd once employed by Fountains abbey spoke of his youth in a
communal lodge on the adjacent Fountains Fell, which must have been
a very different sort of establishment.[106]

Wool houses are known only on large manors. The ruins of a
substantial brick building between the moats at Tattershall traditionally
represent the wool house, and a number of scattered place names and
a few surviving leases suggest that such a building was not uncommon.

[105] For the Hartington tenants, PRO DL 29/369/6187; for West Rainton, W. H. Longstaffe
and J. Booth, eds., *Halmota Prioratus Dunelmensis*, p. 94.

[106] A. Raistrick and P. F. Holmes, 'Archaeology of Malham Moor', *Field Studies*, 1, no. 4,
1962, p. 23. The identification rests on entries in Bolton priory's accounts and rentals: Kershaw,
Bolton Priory, p. 81 and I. Kershaw, ed., *Bolton Abbey Rentals*, Yorks. Arch. Soc. Rec. Ser., CXXXII,
1970, p. 54. For the communal lodge, J. R. Walbran, ed., *Memorials of the Abbey of St Mary of
Fountains*, Surtees Soc., XLII, 1863, p. 310.

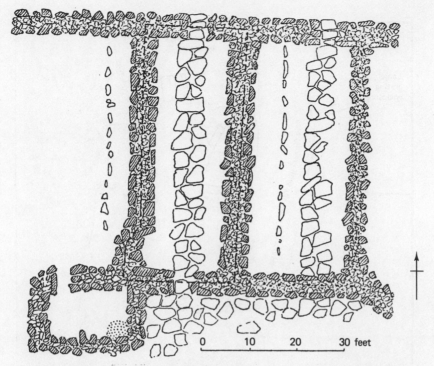

Fig. 9.20 Priors Rakes, Malham Moor, Yorks., excavated sheephouse
(A. Raistrick)

The chief requirement as laid down late in the thirteenth century was
for a clean place in which to pack the wool, and boards for both wall
and floor were recommended.[107]

Little is heard in this period of the dairies that had formerly been an
important adjunct to the sheephouse, though leases indicate that they
were still present on some manors. The dairy as a specialized room in
small houses was still a thing of the future.

(vi) Dovecotes

Dovecotes, originally a seigneurial monopoly, had usually been sited
near the dwelling house. Sometimes there were as many as three
attached to a single manor, for the squabs were a popular food. They
appear to have gone somewhat out of favour even before the mid-
fourteenth century, or at least the profits for many of them fell, but this
might have been due to the increase of their predators, the crows. Many

[107] R. A. Donkin, 'Bercaria and Lanaria', *Yorks. Arch. Jnl.*, XXXIX, 1958, p. 450.

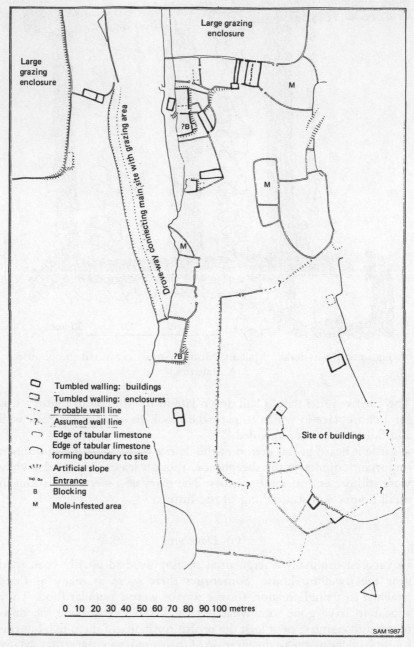

Large grazing
enclosure

Large
grazing
enclosure

M

?B

M

M

?B

☐   Tumbled walling: buildings
▱   Tumbled walling: enclosures
-- -   Probable wall line
--?--   Assumed wall line
⌒   Edge of tabular limestone
⌒   Edge of tabular limestone
    forming boundary to site
ᴠᴠᴠ   Artificial slope
═ᴅ ═   Entrance
B   Blocking
M   Mole-infested area

Drove-way connecting main site with grazing area

Site of buildings   ?

?

?

0 10 20 30 40 50 60 70 80 90 100 metres

SAM 1987

Fig. 9.21 Priors Rakes, earthworks associated with the sheephouse
(S. Moorhouse)

were leased in the course of the later middle ages, the reason, it must be supposed, for their occasional presence on peasant crofts. When kept in hand they tended to be moved to barn yard, orchard, park, or garden. Nevertheless it is still possible to point to many manors, like Minster Lovell, where the medieval dovecote remained near the principal enclosure, and to others, like Methley, where there were no less than three in the fifteenth century. Most of the enormous monastic dovecotes, too, remained in use until the Dissolution.

Cotes walled with cob and thatched and others timber-framed and infilled with clay are known, and they could be rectangular as well as circular, but the great majority were simple round stone structures with very thick walls to accommodate the nesting holes, usually L-shaped to give more shelter to the squabs. The birds entered through a central lantern above the roof and a single narrow door served for their keepers. Though sometimes thatched, the cotes were more often roofed with stone slate or ceramic tile because the birds tended to pick over thatch for seed and so to destroy it.

Early examples were equipped with a potence, an elaborate structure consisting of a central pole fitted at either end with an iron pin that rotated within a cup. Beams were attached at right-angles to the pole to carry a ladder, by means of which it was easy to extract the squabs from the nesting holes.[108] These were expensive contrivances, costing in some cases as much as 9 per cent of the whole building, and many late dovecotes, like those at Raunds (Northants.) or Newstead (Yorks.), were built without them.

(vii) Stables

Stabling on the manor was essential. Many lords liked to stable their own riding horses near the dwelling house or within one of its wings. One such stable was incorporated in a wing at Castle Bolton in north Yorkshire, but such stables have rarely survived, neither are there many excavated examples. A stable in one of the wings at Minster Lovell had a drainage channel in its cobbled floor, and is likely to have been for the lord's own horses, and there was probably another in a subsidiary range of the archbishop's moated manor at Rest Park in Yorkshire, its floor paved with edge-set limestone arranged in patterns.

On large manors a separate court for stabling was developing during the period, a court that included storage buildings for fodder and tack as well as accommodation for horses and grooms, though not stabling for the farm horses. Stabling was also required for manorial officials, for

[108] M. McCormick, *The Dunster Dovecote*, 1963; the mechanism was subjected to an x-ray.

members of the household, for visitors, and for the working horses needed for agriculture, horses which often shared a building with cows or oxen as in the combined stable and byre at Elveden, mentioned earlier.

There were also many peasants who used plough horses.[109] These are likely as a rule to have been stabled in a barn or shed on the croft, but occasional references to specialized buildings have been found. A man at Abbots Ripton in 1443 was allowed timber to rebuild a stable measuring some 21 by 13 feet, which might be expected to accommodate four horses; a peasant at Houghton (Durham) obtained permission to put up another in the waste measuring 30 by 20 feet; a stable at Holmfirth (Yorks.) of a mere 6 by 8 feet is likely to represent the stabling needed for a single animal. But it is impossible to know how representative such isolated instances are of the general position.[110].

(viii) *Miscellaneous buildings*

As long as the demesnes were cultivated directly, the manorial enclosures included a number of miscellaneous small buildings known mainly from repair accounts. They included cart sheds and buildings, sometimes free-standing, sometimes incorporated in a range, for storing such items as chaff, straw, turf, and timber. Pigs and poultry too had their accommodation, often timber-framed and, for the poultry, an upper area for roosting occasionally termed a solar.

Cider making had long been common in south-central England, the south-west, and parts of the West Midlands, but as the vines ceased to be productive it spread eastwards, and late in the thirteenth century a press house, and sometimes a cider mill were built on some manors. But such buildings were infrequent except in the south-west, and unheard of north of Trent. None of these smaller buildings is known to have survived.

(ix) *Park and woodland buildings*

There were buildings within the manorial park pale. Lodges for hunting parties, often moated, resembled small manor houses in their accommodation. Their service buildings included stables and a hay barn, used also for winter feed for the deer. Smaller lodges for parkers, foresters, and warreners were generally timber-framed, like a three-bay lodge erected in Roundhay Park (Yorks.) in 1442, but sometimes of stone as at Mildenhall and in Thetford Forest (Fig. 9.22a and b).

---

[109] Langdon, *Horses, Oxen and Technological Innovation*, pp. 172–253.
[110] For stabling at Holmfirth, PRO DL 29/560/8899; for Ripton, DeWindt, ed., *op. cit.*, p. 305.

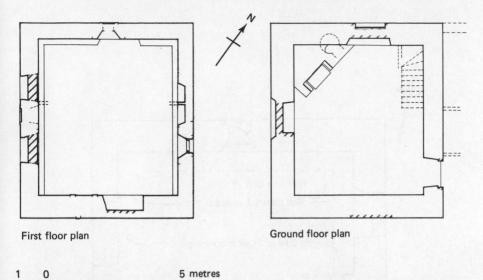

First floor plan Ground floor plan

1 0 5 metres

Fig. 9.22 (a) Mildenhall lodge, Suffolk (English Heritage)

Fishponds could also be sited within the park, but only monastic communities are known to have maintained fish houses, like the two-storied building at Meare (Somerset) (Pl. XIIa).[111]

E. RURAL INDUSTRIAL BUILDINGS

Many buildings in the countryside were associated with rural industry. Malting kilns have already been considered. Mills were usually sited away from the settlement because they needed either wind or water power. There were water mills both for corn grinding and for fulling. It is often possible to locate the sites of rural water mills, for their presence is betrayed by leets and dams adjacent to the course of streams or rivers, but without excavation it is impossible to assess their date. A wheel-pit lined with oak planks, however, was recently excavated at Batsford and this proved to belong to the medieval period. Windmills were very common, nearly always in the form of post-mills, as manuscript illumination, stained-glass representations, and wood-carving all show. The mill itself was small, its roof and walls both boarded. It rotated on a swivel on the post top, turned by a long tail-piece. It cannot have been very stable, but the lower part of the post, and the cross-trees that supported it, were usually set on stones and

[111] For Roundhay Park lodge, PRO DL 29/510/8251; for the Thetford Park lodge, S. E. Rigold, F. J. E. Raby and P. K. Baillie Reynolds, *Thetford Priory*, London, 1979, pp. 17–18.

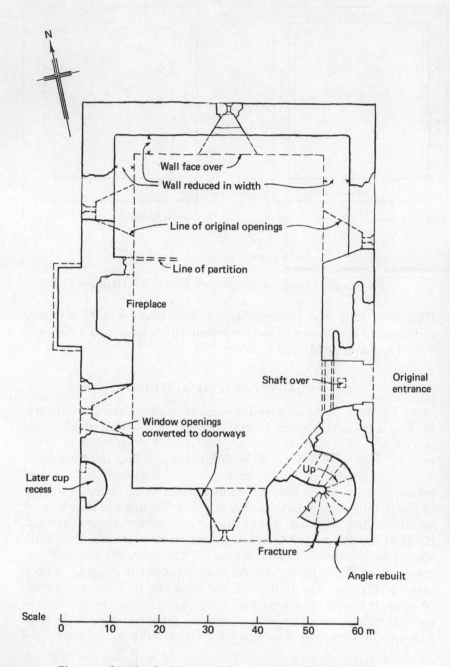

Fig. 9.22 (b) Thetford Forest lodge, Norfolk (English Heritage)

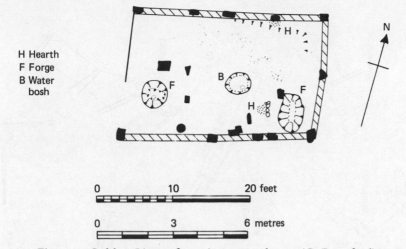

H Hearth
F Forge
B Water
  bosh

0   10   20 feet

0   3   6 metres

Fig. 9.23 Goltho, Lincs., forge in peasant house (G. Beresford)

covered by an earth mound, occasionally surrounded by a moat. Either its mechanism or its millstone seems to have required attention almost annually. The miller did not live in it, though his house is likely to have been nearby. Tower mills, where the cap alone rotated, were very rare.[112]

Villages of any size required a smithy. Excavation has shown it sited within the croft, at Goltho approached by paths of smithing slag, and at Somerby in a two-roomed house (Fig. 9.23). More unusual was a forge near the kitchen on what was probably a manorial site at Walsall. Some Durham villages maintained a communal forge for whose repair and manning the tenants were responsible.[113]

Fishponds, when not in the manorial park, could be very large indeed, evidence of an important rural industry. The Cistercians had sometimes dammed whole valleys, especially in the north, for what were reservoirs of very considerable size and depth, but more frequently there were a number of ponds of varying size for breeding and storing the fish. Manorial moats, particularly the complex moat systems

---

[112] For the Batsford wheel-pit, O. Bedwin, 'The excavation of Batsford Mill', *Med. Arch.*, XXIV, 1980, pp. 191–7. There is no general account of medieval windmills, though some representations of them are discussed in R. Wailes, *Windmills in England*, London, 1948, pp. 1–6. For the tower mill, see R. Allen Brown, H. M. Colvin and A. J. Taylor, *The History of the King's Works*, II, p. 638.

[113] For Goltho, Beresford, *The Medieval Clayland Village*, pp. 46–7; for Somerby, D. C. Mynard, 'Excavations at Somerby, Lincs', *Lincs. History and Archaeology*, IV, 1969, pp. 63ff; for Walsall, S. and S. P. Wrathmell, 'Excavations on the moat site, Walsall, 1972–4', *South Staffs. Arch. and Hist. Soc.*, XIV, 1974–5, pp. 25–9 and XVIII, 1976–7, p. 35.

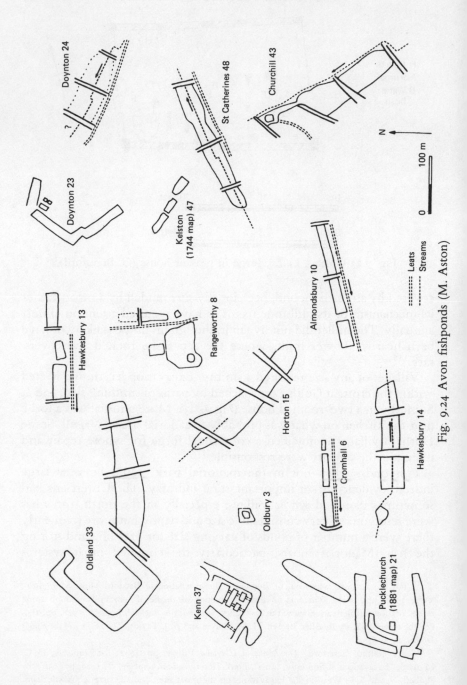

Fig. 9.24 Avon fishponds (M. Aston)

Doynton 24

St Catherines 48

Churchill 43

N

0   100 m

Doynton 23

Kelston
(1744 map) 47

Almondsbury 10

Hawkesbury 13

Rangeworthy 8

Horton 15

Hawkesbury 14

Cromhall 6

Oldland 33

Oldbury 3

Pucklechurch
(1881 map) 21

Kenn 37

········· Leats
- - - - - Streams

fashionable in the period, were also used for fish (Fig. 9.24). The hearth on the upper floor at Meare (Pl. XIIa), and another at the excavated fish-house near Redditch, suggest drying or smoking fish, a practice known also in connection with an earlier fish-house at Acle (Norfolk).[114]

Extraction of sea salt was an important rural industry along the coasts. That a salting required buildings is indicated by entries in the Durham halmote rolls, one of which shows the timbers of an unused salting annexed by a number of villagers at Cowpen Bewley (Durham). A recent excavation gave an indication of the nature of such buildings on a Lincolnshire salting (Fig. 9.25).[115]

Pottery, though also made in towns, was mainly a countryside industry. There were specialized hamlets like Potter Street, Harlow (Essex), others like West Cowick (Yorks.), where potters were only engaged part-time in potting, and villages like Brandsby (Yorks.), where a single potter's croft was sited at the end of a row of village tofts (Pl. XIIb). There were other groups still working in woodland, such as the Broyle potters in Sussex, while the very large number of pottery kilns found at Chilvers Coton (War.) suggest a specialized industrial site beyond the settlements. Besides the house and kiln a drying shed was needed for the pots.[116]

Decorated crests for house roofs were a potter's job, otherwise roofing tiles and bricks were generally made by townsmen. The only village tilery excavated, at Danbury (Essex), belonged to the early fourteenth century, but the workshop, kilns, drying shed, and living hut would hardly change.[117]

Excavation on a scale large enough to show the accommodation required in rural industries of this sort is a recent development, and it remains to be seen whether the extractive industries will produce similar industrial complexes.

[114] Fishponds south of Trent are discussed in M. Aston, ed., *Medieval Fish, Fisheries and Fishponds*, British Archaeological Reports, British Series, 182, 1988. For Yorkshire fishponds, see J. McDonnell, *Inland Fisheries in Medieval Yorkshire*, Borthwick Papers no. 60, 1981.

[115] R. H. Healey, 'A medieval salt-making site in Bicker Haven, Lincolnshire'; K. W. de Brisay and K. A. Ellers, eds., *Salt: the Study of an Ancient Industry*, 1975, p. 36.

[116] For pottery production, H. E. J. Le Patourel, 'Pots and potters', *Medieval Ceramics*, 10, 1986, pp. 3–16. For Chilvers Coton, P. Mayes and K. Scott, *Pottery Kilns at Chilvers Coton, Nuneaton*, Soc. For Med. Arch. Monograph Ser., 10, 1984.

[117] P. J. Drury and D. Pratt, 'A late thirteenth- and early fourteenth-century tile factory at Danbury, Essex', *Med. Arch.*, XIX, 1975, pp. 92–164.

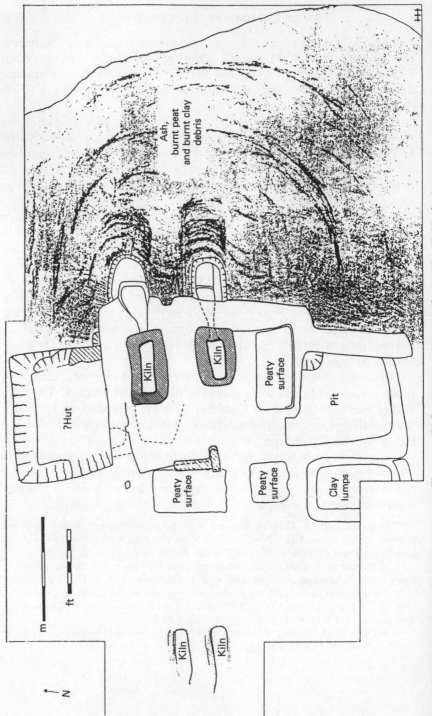

Ash, burnt peat and burnt clay debris

Kiln

Kiln

Peaty surface

Pit

?Hut

Peaty surface

Peaty surface

Clay lumps

Kiln

Kiln

N

m

ft

Fig. 9.25 Bicker Haven, Lincs, salterns (R. H. Healey)

WALES

Between the Black Death and the death of Prince Arthur in 1502 the land lying west of Offa's Dyke had been in the effective control of the English crown and the major barons. The death of Jasper Tudor in 1495 had brought the lordships of Pembroke, Glamorgan, Newport, Abergavenny, Haverfordwest, and Cilgerran directly under royal rule. Only the rebellion of Owain Glyndŵr and his ally Edmund Mortimer, earl of the March, had undermined that control early in the fifteenth century and sown a harvest of discontent which lingered on, exacerbated by family squabbles in the Wars of the Roses. Conversely, at the end of the same century the accession of Henry Tudor had offered an avenue to power and influence at court for many Welshmen. It was a path followed by the Cecils, the Vaughans of Golden Grove, the Meyrickes of Bodorgan, and the Prices of Plas Iolyn.

The political changes did little to alter the basic Celtic character of language, literature, and architecture within the greater part of Wales. The spirit of an independent principality achieved under Llywelyn ap Iorwerth between 1220 and 1240, and in a more limited fashion under his grandson Llywelyn ap Gruffydd between 1267 and 1277, lived on as a golden age to which bards, heralds, and lawyers looked back with nostalgia. The only areas which can be excluded from this pervading sense of Welshness were the "Englishry" coastlands stretching alongside the Bristol Channel from Chepstow Castle, rising above the Wye on the east, as far as Roch Castle standing above Broad Haven on the west. Here the influences of Norman and Fleming, settled in the twelfth century, remained strong and created an economic zone looking towards Bristol as its maritime metropolis. The influence of Chester upon the Dee estuary was less permanent, although the towns of the north Welsh coast from Flint to Harlech were English in creation and were peopled initially by English adventurers attracted there in the late thirteenth century. The impact of these political and economic changes upon rural life is uncertain. The continued existence and modification of the Welsh laws as a guide to manorial custom and tenurial practice for at least a century beyond the Black Death testifies to the traditional strength of their usage over much of Wales.

The territory under discussion includes all Wales west of Offa's Dyke and those marcher lordships which were not subject to shire authority until the Act of Union in 1536. This border zone included areas where Welsh speech and customs predominated. The district of Maelor fringing the Cheshire plain, the lordship of Oswestry in north-western Shropshire, and the district of Archenfield and part of Ewyas in south-western Herefordshire remained largely Welsh until the accession of the Tudor dynasty and even beyond. The hill country of the eastern border, from the Peckforton Hills to the heights of Wentwood above the Wye gorge, is one distinct geographical zone. The mountainous heartland of the central spine from Snowdonia to Blaenau Morgannwg is a second easily recognizable zone. The third, and by far the most fertile, area is the coastal plain, often little more than a narrow strip at the foot of the mountains. Only on the plain, in Anglesey and along the broad major river valleys, such as the Clwyd, Severn, and Towy, were conditions advantageous to permanent arable cultivation. The higher altitudes and the poorer soils dictated a mixed economy in which pastoralism prevailed.

The geological conditions have strongly influenced the choice of building materials. Slates and shales of the Cambrian series extend throughout western Wales in an arc from Conway to Cardigan with some less tractable volcanic rocks of the Harlech dome. Further east the Old Red Sandstone predominates, with a few areas of finer limestones in the Vale of Glamorgan and the coastlands of Gwent. These stones were all used in secular and ecclesiastical buildings of the highest quality, though augmented by finer grained stone for window tracery, door dressings, quoins and sculpture; the masons turned either to the limestones of Dundry and Bath or to the sandstones of Grinshill or Runcorn. In the middle and lower ranges of society, the domestic architecture was principally of timber. This is indicated both by the surviving buildings and by documentary evidence. Only at the lowest level of house and byre building was mud walling used; in parts of south-west Wales this was the usual material because of restricted access to better-quality stone and because of the limited availability of necessary timber. Roofing was also directly related to income and accessibility. At the highest social level, lead roofs and ceramic tiles were used; in the middle level the normal materials were freestone tiles in south Wales, wooden shingles in mid-Wales, and slates in the north. At the lowest social levels or for the meanest agrarian purposes there was the practice of covering roofs with a thatch of straw, reeds or heather, or of employing turf sods. The endemic warfare of the fifteenth century threatened all but the most substantial houses with destruction or decay, but positive evidence for a direct effect of warfare upon housing is hard to detect or substantiate.

Settlement and housing are discussed at the different social levels of ownership and occupation. At the highest level were the barons and bishops, who owned extensive tracts of territory and occupied a number of properties, often well defended. They travelled from one castle or palace to another, according to season and political priority. At the medium level were the gentry families, the *uchelwyr*, protective of their lineage and their own territorial rights, but normally possessing only one principal property where they resided at all times. At a parallel or slightly lower material level were the farms or granges of the monasteries and other corporate institutions; these were devoted entirely to agricultural and related industrial needs. At the lowest level were the peasant houses in nucleated villages, in hamlets or townships, and in dispersed settlement. The houses of the clergy can usually be equated with the more permanently-built peasant houses. The final category is industrial building, either serving communal agriculture or else processing an extracted mineral.

Only the most substantially built structures have survived later destruction and alteration. This inevitably tilts the evidence towards the middle and upper classes. The gaps must be filled by documentary sources and by archaeological excavation. Both have imperfections. Those documents prepared for taxation purposes and to assist land transfer are far more concerned with renders and boundaries than with house contents and appearances. The rate of documentary survival, particularly from episcopal visitations and from collegiate sources, is much lower than in England, thereby presenting an unbalanced view. However, the poetry of the Welsh bards sometimes conveys an impression of a building's splendour and novelty, together with its appropriateness as a setting for welcome civility and generous hospitality among the literate classes. By contrast the priorities of, and opportunities for, excavation have rarely focused on later medieval settlement; the record is correspondingly thin and erratic, concentrating upon individual houses rather than upon the totality of the farm or settlement complex. The material evidence is seldom more than a sample of the economy and cannot yet provide a reliable indicator of housing provision and development.[1]

[1] The general works are P. Smith, *Houses of the Welsh Countryside*, pp. 18–139, and (useful for methodology) E. Wiliam, *Traditional Farm Buildings in North-East Wales, 1550–1900*, Cardiff, 1982; also P. Smith in R. R. Davies, ed., *Welsh Society and Nationhood*, pp. 122–60.

There are three valuable regional studies in C. Fox and Lord Raglan, *Monmouthshire Houses*, I, Cardiff, 1951; S. Jones and J. T. Smith, 'The houses of Breconshire', *Brycheiniog*, IX, 1963; X, 1964; XI, 1965; XII, 1966–7; XIII, 1968–9; and H. Brooksby, 'The houses of Radnorshire', *Radnorshire Soc.*, XXXVIII, 1968, pp. 8–25; XXXIX, 1969, pp. 48–67.

The archaeological evidence for housing is reviewed in L. Butler, 'Deserted medieval settlements in Wales', in Beresford and Hurst, eds., *Deserted Medieval Villages*, pp. 249–76, and D. M. Robinson, 'Medieval vernacular buildings below the ground: a review and corpus for south-east Wales', *Glamorgan-Gwent Archaeological Trust: Annual report 1981–2*, Swansea, 1982, pp. 94–123.

A. THE ESTABLISHMENTS OF THE NOBILITY

Throughout the later middle ages the need for defence against civil unrest weighed heavily upon the minds of the baronial class. Castles were kept in good repair or, as at Croft, Raglan, and Treago, newly built. The episcopate also fortified their palaces with sufficiently deterrent walls and gates, as at St Davids and Mathern. Within these enclosures would stand a wide range of domestic buildings, including the provision for the storage of meat, corn, wine, and beer. Outside the enclosures would be situated the agrarian sheds for sheltering animals and for processing crops.

The evidence from the regulations for the bishop of St Asaph's household in the first decade of the fourteenth century indicates that as well as the thirteen named officials and their underlings, such as grooms, there were a considerable number of duties outside the court to be supervised by a steward of the manor.[2] Under his care was the judge (*iudex manerii*), the reeve, miller, granger, and hayward. These officials provided the legal and agricultural support for an essentially aristocratic household. The occasional mention of such officials in the court rolls and ministers' accounts indicates that for the next two centuries the great landowners maintained a similar arrangement.[3] The evidence for the tenurial obligations provided in the Welsh laws and in the manorial extents is at its fullest in the century before the Black Death, and has already been discussed.[4] However, the continued copying and amendment of the laws in the fourteenth and fifteenth centuries shows that they were the essential working foundation of manor courts in the Welshry.[5] They had not passed into the nostalgic care of heralds, antiquaries, and bibliophiles. Their use may also be inferred in some of the court rolls when carrying duties to the lord's mill or when repair obligations at the lord's court buildings had been neglected.[6] Although these repairs were principally upon the hall, chamber, and kitchen, they could include the stable, the lodges, the grange, or the cowsheds (*boveria*).

[2] NLW, Church in Wales Records, St. A./MB/1, ff.80–1; cf. Oschinsky, ed., *Walter of Henley*, 197–9, 387–409.

[3] G. P. Jones, *The Extent of Chirkland*, pp. xxx–xxxiv; A. D. Carr, *The Extent of Anglesey in 1352*, Anglesey Antiq. Soc., 1971–2, pp. 150–272.

[4] *AHEW*, II, pp. 933–5; L. A. S. Butler, 'Domestic building in Wales and the evidence of the Welsh laws', *Med. Arch.*, XXXI, 1987, pp. 47–58.

[5] D. Jenkins, *Llyfr Colan*, Cardiff, 1963; A. W. Wade-Evans, *Welsh Medieval Law*, Oxford, 1909, citing versions of c. 1350; see also R. R. Davies, 'The twilight of Welsh law 1284–1536', *History*, 51, 1966, pp. 143–64.

[6] Jones, *The Extent of Chirkland*, pp. xxxv–vi, 66, 67; Slack, *The Lordship of Oswestry*, pp. 22–9, 153–71, esp. 170–1.

The buildings required for agrarian purposes were normally situated in the outer bailey of the castle, as at Kilpeck or Whittington, or in the outer court of the bishop's palace, as at Llawhaden and Lamphey. Only at Tretower is it possible to see surviving buildings of these supporting ranges (see below p. 905). The domestic buildings within the walled enclosure or curtain wall often survive at castles and palaces. The impressive character of the halls, the decoration bestowed upon the chapels, and the strength of the gatehouses ensured that they have often survived and can be easily identified. These structures lie outside the scope of this survey.[7] The less substantial nature of the ancillary buildings, such as stabling and brewhouses, has resulted either in their disappearance or in their escaping recognition, as at the castles of Bronllys and Llansteffan. Only the substantially built circular dovecotes have remained as a prominent feature in some outer baileys. Without excavation the agricultural provision at the demesne farm will continue to remain unsubstantiated. Away from the outer bailey stood the lord's mill, a highly prized source of revenue whose structure is considered later (p. 917). Similarly the lord's lodges, which were constructed to assist the pursuit of deer and the capture of hawks and falcons in the protected forests and hays, are better known from documentary sources which record buildings distinct from the *llys* or lord's court. Although the forest boundaries and park pales can be identified on the ground, the locations of the lodges leave far more ephemeral remains and none has been excavated.

B. MANORS

In the late fourteenth century the tenurial term "manor" was often used in preference to the Welsh terms of landholding, the *gwely* and the *gafael*. The manor represented both the territorial unit of judicial control and the capital mansion from which that control was exercised. In assessing the status of manorial holders it is possible to discern a wide variation of income: those in the Englishry of Glamorgan or Gower might hold a manor nominally owing a quarter or a half of a knight's fee; those in the hill district of Merioneth might hold a dispersed manor indistinguishable from a "favoured tenancy", formerly owing service to the Welsh princes and now continuing to provide administrative and legal support for the new ruling class, either prince or baron. The Welsh landowners would act as deputy justiciar in the principality shires, as bailiff or steward in the baronial lordships, and as *rhaglaw* or *rhingill* in the hundreds or commotes (*cwmmwdau*). The houses of these royal and baronial servants would be little different in appearance and no different in their owners' aspirations from the halls and chambers of

---

[7] W. Rees, *South Wales and the March*, pp. 131–6.

the consolidated manor of the English settlers in the plain of Glamorgan or the coastlands of southern Pembrokeshire. The English might more often defend their homes with battlements and with moats in imitation of the baronial strongholds or of their gentry counterparts in Cheshire and Somerset.[8] For the Welsh the protection of a man's reputation, status, and lineage was more esteemed than the recourse to English manners.[9] Yet they did not spurn the opportunities to serve as royal squires, to fight in foreign wars, to hoard offices, or to dispense patronage. Their materialistic attitudes earned the criticism of Sion Cent.[10] The fifteenth-century poets were calling the freeholders on the Welsh lands by the title of "gentlemen" or "yeomen", thereby equating them in status with their English counterparts. This blurring of social distinctions was part of the decay of the manor as an institution in the decades after the Black Death. Indeed after Glyndŵr's rebellion the manor had ceased to be an active and definable economic unit, and had largely become a collection of customary rights whose enforcement depended upon political will and financial necessity.

The evidence of administrative documents is a valuable source of information about the range of buildings found within the manor and the limited amount of equipment and household stock contained in them. Although most documents tend to refer to the highest levels of society, the occasional inventory on the occasion of death or of confiscation for treason can be informative about gentry houses.[11] An example of this is the house of Rhys ap Roppert; at his death in 1377 he had occupied a house containing a hall, two chambers, a kitchen, and a small chamber.[12] Assuming all the rooms were under one roof (and the kitchen was not detached) this could easily describe the normal three-unit plan of a central hall flanked by two chambers at the dais (upper) end and by two chambers at the service (lower) end.

Another insight into the provision of housing for the gentry, the free men or uchelwyr, is given by the poetry composed by the bards, usually

---

[8] C. J. Spurgeon, 'Moated sites in Wales', in F. A. Aberg and A. E. Brown, *Medieval Moated Sites in North-west Europe*, British Archaeological Reports, International Series, S121, Oxford, 1981, pp. 19–70, esp. p. 53; A. H. A. Hogg and D. J. C. King, 'Masonry castles in Wales and the Marches: a list', *Arch. Camb.*, CXVI, 1967, pp. 71–132, esp. map 3 listing 25 towers and strong houses.

[9] Rhys Goch Eryri praises Gwilym ap Gruffydd's hall at Penrhyn, Llandegai: H. Lewis, T. Roberts and I. Williams, *Cywydau Iolo Goch ac eraill*, Cardiff, 1937, pp. 299–302.

[10] Sion Cent in G. Jones, ed., *Oxford Book of Welsh Verse in English*, London, 1977, pp. 54–8, part quoted in G. Williams, *Recovery, Re-orientation and Reformation. Wales c. 1415–1642*, Oxford, 1987, p. 110.   [11] Rees, *South Wales and the March*, pp. 135–6, 185.

[12] A. D. Carr, 'Rhys ap Roppert', *Denbs. Hist. Soc.*, xxv, 1976, pp. 155–70. Two rustic "architectural" poems, "The Leafy Hut" and "The Holly Grove", use either technical building terms or words newly introduced from French: R. Bromwich, *Dafydd ap Gwilym: a Selection of Poems*, Llandyssul, 1982, pp. 10–11, 16–17, 22, 24.

in praise of the hospitality lavished upon them by their hosts and patrons as they journeyed from one festive board to the next. Even though the reader now needs to make allowance for florid delivery and exaggerated sentiment, it is still possible to discern the grains of truth amid the chaff of verbiage and rustic metaphor. Although the generous gift and welcome hospitality were valued above all, the appearance of the house had to convey the status of the owner. Dafydd ap Gwilym, writing in the mid-fourteenth century, describes one such hall: "it was a fine place, no surly churl's home this".[13] The description provided of Sycharth, the home of Owain Glyndŵr, is one of the fullest in all Welsh medieval poetry. Its writer Iolo Goch, composing his verse in the last quarter of the fourteenth century, stresses both the architectural character of the hall and the hospitality of the owner; the two aspects are inextricably interlinked.

> Moated with water's gold round,
> Fine manor, bridge on the moat.
> . . . . .
> Close to heaven in his hall
> On each firm wooden pillar.
> A loft in the sturdy croft[14]

Elsewhere in the poem he speaks of "nine halls in matching pattern", "clean lime-white walls", and "fair glass windows", though this last item may be a flight of fancy as the poet's imagination takes him to London Cheapside. The "manor" of Sycharth has orchards and vineyards, a rabbit warren, a "fish-pond enclosed and deep", a "fine mill on a smooth-flowing stream", and a "dovecot [in] a bright stone tower"; in short it has all the gentry appurtenances which make it "a tent for bards from all regions". Less detailed is the description of the substantial stone-built house in Breconshire in a poem by Howel Davi in the early fifteenth century.[15]

The houses described in the poetry have all disappeared, but where it is possible to compare the poetry with the reality, like the poetry of Guto'r Glyn with the ruins of Neath abbey, then one can confirm the existence of decorated window glass and multi-patterned floor tiles. However, the comparison with Salisbury seems over-ambitious.[16] The

[13] J. P. Clancy, *Medieval Welsh Lyrics*, London, 1965, p. 43; R. G. Gruffydd, *Ysgrifau Beirniadol*, XI, 1979, pp. 109–15.

[14] Clancy, *op. cit.*, pp. 136–7; T. Parry, ed., *Oxford Book of Welsh Verse*, Oxford, 1962, pp. 80–3; D. B. Hague and C. Warhurst, 'Excavations at Sycharth Castle, 1962–63', *Arch. Camb.*, CXV, 1966, pp. 108–27, esp. 109–12.

[15] E. S. Roberts, *Peniarth MS. 67*, Cardiff, 1918, pp. 70–1, 99–101, quoted in I. C. Peate, *The Welsh House*, Liverpool, 1946, p. 131.

[16] Lewis Morgannwg, quoted in L. Butler, *Neath Abbey*, London, 1976, pp. 10–11.

poet might hope that his audience had heard of that distant cathedral but had not seen it; if his patron abbot had visited the cathedral, then he would be flattered by the grandeur of the comparison.

Another strand in understanding the gentry houses is the examination of the process whereby their families came to prominence. In the anglicized coastlands of south Wales the normal sequence of inheritance and the marriage of heiresses took place: families rose and fell; younger sons carved holdings out of the waste and eventually enclosed their manors with walls and ditches, as did the Stradlings at St Donats and the Bassets at Beaupré.[17] In the former principality of Gwynedd in north-west Wales the founding family might establish a holding on the margin of the cultivated land. The retention of such a unit undivided as a focal point for estate expansion would depend on a succession of single heirs over four or five generations. Conversely the fragmentation of holdings due to the operation of partible inheritance would result in a holding diminished to the point of non-viability. It is along these avenues that the gentry might rise to prominence: they might inherit an undivided property or apply for denizen rights to enjoy the English mode of primogeniture succession; they could consolidate the debris of many fragmentary inheritances by the application of *tir prid* rights of landholding. This process, as it operated in the mid-fifteenth century, has been studied in Arllechwedd by Jones Pierce, in Eifionydd by Gresham, in Ardudwy by Thomas and in Edeirnion and Tegeingl by Carr.[18] The verdict of Davies can be fully endorsed: "Multiple holdings and consolidated estates were being built out of the debris left by the plague mortality. This was a key period in the pre-history of many of the estate complexes of early modern Wales."[19]

The final avenue within the ranks of the gentry was the slow recovery from a depression in status after the loss of Welsh independence. Those who had served as officials at the prince's court, as had the sons of Ednyfed Fychan, retained only part of their former lands, and then in a few cases began a steady climb to a position of influence in the hundred or commote.[20] The rise of the gentry families of Nannau, Glynllifon, Peniarth, and Penrhyn starts with minor office

[17] R. A. Griffiths, 'The rise of the Stradlings of St Donats', *Morgannwg*, 7, 1963, pp. 15–47; D. B. Hague, *Beaupré Castle*, London, 1965; RCHM, Wales, *Glamorgan Inventory*, IV, i, 1981, pp. 46–63.

[18] T. Jones Pierce, 'The Clennenau estate', in *MWS*, 229–50; Gresham, *Eifionydd*, passim; A. D. Carr, 'The Barons of Edeyrnion, *JMHRS*, IV, 1961, pp. 187–93, 289–301; *idem*, 'The making of the Mostyns: the genesis of a landed family', *Hon. Soc. Cymmr.* 31, 1982, pp. 5–27.

[19] Davies, *Conquest, Coexistence and Change*, pp. 428–30.

[20] A. D. Carr, 'An aristocracy in decline: the native Welsh lords after the Edwardian conquest', *Welsh Hist. Rev.*, 5, 1970–1, pp. 103–29. G. Roberts, 'Wyrion Eden', *Anglesey Antiq. Soc.*, 1951, pp. 34–72.

holding as *rhaglaw* or *rhingill* in the fourteenth and fifteenth centuries. Only with the Herberts at Raglan in Gwent does the process accelerate through military service, so that this family attains the ranks of the nobility before 1500.

Wealth and social aspirations were chief ingredients in promoting house building, but the accessibility of materials, whether stone or timber, also determined their appearance and their rate of survival. The use of stone was predominant in the coastlands of Glamorgan, Carmarthen, and Pembroke, though it was also of more restricted occurrence on the fringes of Snowdonia; elsewhere timber was the more accessible material and it was fashioned into buildings that exhibited their owners' status and success.

The stone buildings represent three distinct yet related traditions: that of the tower house, the first-floor hall, and the hall-house at ground level. Few examples survive of the first type and it is preferable to regard them as modest attempts at castles rather than as upgraded manor houses. However, the appearance and circumstances of these houses shows well the diversity of their origins. On the shore of the Bristol Channel near Newton Nottage stands Candleston Castle, a small vaulted tower to which a (now ruined) first-floor hall was added. It was built by the minor gentry family of the Cantilupes.[21] On the north coast of Gower on a rocky hilltop overlooking the salt marshes of Llanrhidian stands Weobley Castle, described in 1410 as a fortified manor house. It was the home of the de la Beres, an Anglo-Norman minor gentry family. The main accommodation of hall and solar is on the first floor and the ancillary buildings, including a chapel, are grouped around a lightly defended courtyard.[22] A similar more compact castle dominates St Brides Bay in Pembrokeshire; Roche was the home of the family of that name. An equally impressive fortified house controls the coast road from Chepstow to Newport at Penhow; it contains a late medieval tower but was greatly altered by the Seymours and their successors. The tower house is rare in north Wales, probably because of the penal legislation of 1401–2 forbidding Welshmen to fortify their houses. Only two such houses now survive but both were built by native gentry families. The Tower at Barmouth ("Ty Gwyn yn Abermo"), built by Gruffydd Vychan between 1445 and 1485, still stands close to the shore. It is a rectangular two-storeyed house with a basement; it is entered at ground-floor level and has fireplaces in the end gable walls at both ground floor and first floor. Its rarity is shown in the begging poem (*cywydd*) by Tudor Penllyn, who likened its walls to those of Calais, a distant comparison but one likely

[21] *Arch. Camb.*, LXXXVIII, 1933, pp. 43, 44; *ibid.*, CI, 1950, pp. 74, 75; *Glamorgan Inventory*, IV, i, 1981, p. 348.   [22] W. G. Thomas, *Weobley Castle*, London, 1974.

to be appreciated by those who had served with the Lancastrians in France or had traded as wool merchants of the Staple. Its present state is undefended though it might once have had a crenellated parapet and a courtyard gatehouse.[23] The other tower is far more impressive. Rheinallt Gruffydd of Broncoed built his fortified residence in 1445 and used it as a base from which to terrorize the neighbourhood, particularly the inhabitants of Chester who supported the Yorkists. It also had a basement and two floors, but these were vaulted (unlike the timber floors at Barmouth). There was a two-storey chamber adjunct and a circular stair leading to a wall walk with machicolations and cruciform arrow slits.[24] Another fortification of similar character may have been added to Penrhyn in Llandegai (Caerns.), since there is documentary evidence of a licence to crenellate in 1438 and early pictorial evidence shows a tower with a circular stair adjoining the hall.[25]

The second main strand of gentry housing is the first-floor hall, which could both precede and succeed a tower house. However it is equally clear that it also occurred as an independent tradition, particularly in Pembrokeshire where it is also found in the towns of Tenby, Pembroke, and Haverfordwest. It is a rarity in north Wales and the only example is Llaneurgain, Northop (Flints.); it contains a vaulted basement running under part of the rectangular house, a vaulted ground floor and a spacious upper floor. There is an outside door and an internal stone stair to the basement. As at Barmouth, fireplaces serve the ground and first floor in one gable wall. An ornate arch-braced ceiling gives dignity to the upper room; this roof and the fine freestone details suggest a mid-fifteenth-century date.[26] By contrast the first-floor halls in south-west Wales are both modest in dimensions and coarser in stonework details. Above the vaulted basement was the main hall, while in an attached two-storey block were chamber and latrines. Examples have been discussed most recently by P. Smith, but dating can be problematical.[27] It is clear that the gentry families in Pembrokeshire, to a lesser extent in Glamorgan, and rarely in Carmarthen were prepared to live in first-floor halls over vaulted basements well into the sixteenth century, and that the impetus to change their mode of living only gathered momentum in the reign of Elizabeth Tudor. Some of these halls were served by lateral fireplaces with massive round chimneys, which imitated in roughly hewn stone

---

[23] Smith, *Houses*, pp. 609, 614.

[24] P. Smith and P. A. Hayes, 'Llyseurgain and the Tower', *Flints. Hist. Soc. Publ.*, XXII, 1965–6, pp. 1–8; Smith, *Houses*, pp. 135–9.

[25] D. B. Hague, 'Penrhyn Castle', *Caerns. Hist. Soc.*, XX, 1959, pp. 27–44, but see note by Smith, *Houses*, pp. 136 and 137 n.2.

[26] Smith and Hayes, 'Llyseurgain and the Tower', pp. 1–8.

[27] Smith, *Houses*, pp. 21–33b, 372–4.

the finely jointed freestone chimneys of earlier castles like Kidwelly and Skenfrith, and the poorly made chimneys at Manorbier and Pembroke. The service buildings within the courtyard adjoining these halls have long since disappeared.

The third tradition and the most popular one was the ground floor hall-house. It occurred where stone was the predominant material but was built in even greater numbers where timber was plentiful. Only in the poorest areas of Ceredigion and Merioneth is the hall-house a rarity, mainly because of the absence of well-formed mature oaks. Although the earliest gentry houses, as at Cefn-y-fan near Dolbenmaen and Gogarth near Llandudno, both in Gwynedd,[28] were two-unit hall and lower room, these represent an early fourteenth-century stage of development. The burning and abandonment of both houses in the Glyndŵr rebellion prevented them from receiving additional rooms and fireplaces.

The development typical of the fifteenth century is the three-unit plan with a large rectangular open hall set between a smaller room at the cross passage (lower) end and a parlour or withdrawing room at the dais (upper) end. The hall contained a hearth in the centre of the room, the smoke from which escaped through a specially constructed louvre in the roof ridge, as at Plas Uchaf, Llangar, Merioneth,[29] or found its way out through the open door or through the unglazed windows with shutters opened on the leeward side. The dais end, with the table set crossways and with side windows throwing light down upon it, was further emphasized by a coved wooden canopy set against the end wall of the hall. In the simplest arrangement, as at Neuadd, Patricio (Brecons.) or Ty Mawr, Beddgelert (Caerns.), the stone-walled hall had a roof of three bays, while both the upper and the lower ends were of one bay each. Timber partition walls divided the three units; the upper end had two rooms whose doorways were placed close to the side walls to avoid the dais table, while the lower end also had two rooms, but these were approached through doorways set close to the centre axis of the hall.

Other examples of stone-built houses vary the proportions of the ancillary rooms, but it is not until the late fifteenth century that one meets the storeyed upper rooms, reached by a ladder or wall stair, placed above the outer and inner rooms flanking a tall timber-roofed hall open to the rafters. The house at Ciliau, Llandeilo Graban (Radnors.), is a good example, though its lateral fireplace marks a later stage of domestic comfort. Among the stone-built houses this

---

[28] Specifically Smith, *Houses*, p. 41 and fig. 11, and, more generally, pp. 37–133; Smith, 'Welsh rural housing, 1500–1640' in *AHEW*, IV, pp. 767–88.

[29] P. Smith and F. Lloyd, 'Plas Ucha, Llangar, Corwen', *Ancient Monuments Soc.*, XII, 1964, pp. 97–112; Smith, *Houses*, figs. 49, 50.

sophistication can best be illustrated at Cochwillan, near Bangor, a house which was built by William Gruffydd probably in the closing decades of the fifteenth century. The hall plan is conservative but the side walls are pierced by three-light and two-light traceried windows and the hall roof has attractive hammer-beam trusses above a cornice rail decorated with flowing tracery. The rooms at both inner and outer end are two-storeyed and were probably fully domestic with the service functions being relegated to another building. This hall roof also marks the culmination of native roof development, since the earlier stone-built halls, such as Egryn, Llanaber (Mer.) and Penarth-fawr, Llanarmon (Caerns.) had aisle trusses usually erected by the screens passage, and collar-beam roofs employed as a decorative device.

The more ambitious gentry houses had the hall flanked by larger rooms which created an H-plan or a U-plan. Unfortunately most houses are now known only from fragmentary survivals or from antiquarian drawings. Hafoty, Llansadwrn (Anglesey) possessed a small central hall flanked by a kitchen wing of two rooms and a larger parlour wing also of two rooms. Both wings are of two storeys. A similar arrangement, though with the upper floor half-timbered, once existed at Hen Blas, Beaumaris (Anglesey). The grandest gentry houses were disposed around a courtyard where the hall was the focal point between elongated wings and where the opposing range contained a gatehouse. The best example is the extensive survival of the Vaughans' house at Tretower (Brecons.), where the hall with its collar-beam roof and elaborately cusped windbraces shows the pretensions of a major gentry family. At St Pierre, Gwent, the gatehouse and the adjacent servants' range is a similar indication of how the owners of the grander houses of south-east Wales aspired to impress those of equal rank from Somerset and the Vale of Severn.

All that has so far been discussed in relation to the stone-built houses is equally applicable to those of timber construction, namely the plan development, the cross passage, the abandonment of the open hearth, the introduction of the two-storey wing, and finally the expansion into a courtyard house. Three points need to be stressed: the first is the universality of timber construction throughout Wales, apart from the south-west, and the readiness to use timber at all gradations of gentry society; the second is that although the exterior may be plain with a simple box framing of wattle and daub panels, it could conceal an interior most sumptuously carved, especially in its roof details; and thirdly, the insertion of a chimney stack was often achieved by placing it within the hall against the cross passage, thereby diminishing the open space within the hall but increasing the sense of privacy. The rectangular outline of a cruck-framed or a box-framed house might act

as a hindrance to the construction of a solar wing or a service wing, but
it could assist in the horizontal partitioning to make two floors in those
bays flanking the hall; both these developments, however, seem to
belong principally to the sixteenth rather than to the fifteenth century.
The possibility of expanding the house by adding flanking wings, or
even of moving a box-framed house to a new site, was made easier by
the prefabricated nature of timber construction. In the Welsh laws the
house built of timber with auger holes was the most highly valued
asset.[30]

The three-unit plan is universally seen in the surviving houses. Most
stand on low sill walls, either on level ground or on an artificially
scooped platform set into the hillside. The cross-passage doorways
occur where the ground outside and the floor inside are at the same
level, though the lower-end room may be at a slightly lower level if it
had an agrarian use as a dairy or a byre. The latter use is rare and is
difficult to establish from surviving structures or from excavations. The
raised earth platform of the lower end did allow a drain to be
constructed below the floor level of the dairy or byre. A separate door
to allow cattle to be led into an undivided lower-end room with stalls
and a tethering rail has seldom survived. Hafod-yspyty, Ffestiniog
(Mer.) seems to be the most convincing example of a three-unit house
with a byre at the lower end. Sometimes the depth of the slope at the
lower end would allow for a cellar to be constructed, but at
Rhydycarw, Trefeglwys (Mont.) and at Cwm Nant Meichiad, Meifod
(Mont.) these occur beneath the parlour, perhaps as a treasury or as a
wine store only accessible to the householder and not to his servants.

In a timber-framed house the doorways are usually plain openings
but might be of arched or ogee form. The windows are similarly plain,
being square or rectangular spaces in the framing, usually with vertical
rods and external shutters capable of being secured from within the
house. The wall material is wattle and daub, limewashed or plastered,
usually in square panels but sometimes of close-studded narrow panels,
where the vertical stud and the intervening panel are of equal width.
The roofing material is frequently slate in Snowdonia but thatch was
common in the remainder of Wales, though not universal where tiles
of fissile sandstone were locally available. The restrained appearance of
the exterior was often disguising a more elaborate interior. The festive
hall was an owner's pride, a bard's joy, and a carpenter's masterpiece.
At either end was a timber-framed partition reaching to the full height
of the hall; it might echo the square framing of the outside walls, using
oak timbers and plastered wattles of hazel, or it might more elaborately

---

[30] Wade-Evans, *Welsh Medieval Law*, pp. 61 (lines 5–14), 214; Butler, 'Domestic building in
Wales', pp. 51, 52.

be of post and panel construction with vertical planking.[31] The dais-
end wall and the overhanging coved canopy were likely to be of oak
construction, whether built within a timber-framed house or in a stone-
walled structure.

The open hall enabled the roof structure to be admired. The
commoner type was the cruck frame found in every shire and lordship
east of a line drawn between Newport (Gwent) and Aberdyfi (Mer.),
though virtually absent in Lleyn and Anglesey. The space above the
collar could be decorated by cusped struts or arch braces; the collar
could carry an ornamental boss. Less usual within the fifteenth century
was the box frame, mainly found in north-east Wales. This type of
construction lent itself particularly well to the first-floor rooms at the
service and chamber ends, but gave added space and dignity to a
timber-built hall. However, its most impressive use was in the
composite aisled columns within a stone-walled or cruck-framed hall.
The examples of Penarth-fawr, Llanarmon (Caerns.), Egryn (Mer.),
and Plas Uchaf, Llangar (Mer.) show how effectively this device was
used to frame and define the entrance passage in a spere truss. Recent
detective work has shown eight surviving high-quality houses with
such aisle trusses, providing evidence of aristocratic pretensions.[32] At
Sycharth, Iolo Goch speaks of "each firm wooden pillar", either taken
literally to imply a fully aisled hall, as at Hafod, Llansilin, adjacent to
Sycharth,[33] or to be read impressionistically to record two pairs of
trusses in a four-bay hall. The roof timbers could also display
decoration with ornate moulding on the beams and cusped windbracing
between the roof members. The louvre truss above the open hearth
could additionally be cusped, as at Penarth-fawr, Egryn and Plas Uchaf
in Llangar. All three houses were built for gentry whose pedigrees were
later collected by the sixteenth-century heralds in their *cwrs clera*; these
were men of substance but their halls are still contained within the
traditional three-unit plan.

More ambitious were the H-plan houses as at Plas Newydd, Ruabon
(Denbs.), Upper House, Painscastle (Radnors.) and Althrey, Bangor
(Flints.), the last within a moated enclosure. The grandest of all the
surviving timber buildings was Bryndraenog, Bugeildy (Radnors.).[34]
This H-plan house contained two halls, the greater one resplendent
with moulded crucks and purlins, cusped bracing and a fretted arcade
between the truss and the collar. Windows with cusped heads in
Perpendicular style would have enhanced the impression of disposable
wealth created by its owner when he built in about 1460.

[31] Smith, *Houses*, p. 57, fig. 20b, p. 65a, fig. 28a.   [32] Smith, *Houses*, pp. 94–9.
[33] H. H. Hughes, 'Notes on the architecture of some old houses in the neighbourhood of
Llansilin, Denbighshire', *Arch. Camb.*, 5th ser. xv, 1898, pp. 154–79, esp. 158–62.
[34] Brooksby, 'The houses of Radnorshire', 1969, pp. 52–5; Smith, *Houses*, pp. 52–3.

The concentration of attention upon the great halls with their adjoining solar, parlour, or chamber at the dais end and their pantry and buttery at the service end obscures the fact that these houses did not stand alone but were accompanied by barns, stables, granaries, and dovecote.[35] Only in Iolo Goch's description of Sycharth and in the surviving complex of Sir Roger Vaughan's Tretower Court, the latter much rebuilt between 1457 and 1470, can one envisage the agrarian aspects of the manor. Yet every house of pretension would be served by bakehouse and brewhouse, stable, sties, and orchards. A varied diet would be provided by pigeons in the dovecotes and fish in the ponds and weirs.[36] Where the conditions were favourable, eels would be caught in the lakes and marshes and rabbits would be snared in the warrens on the coastal sand dunes.[37] The later manorial documents are less explicit about the lesser buildings of the manor but the grain barns and the oxhouses are the two buildings or complexes most often kept in good repair.[38] In considering the gentry society one can point to the blacker side of the great plague and its many recurrences, or to the resentments fostered in Glyndŵr's rebellion and its poisoned legacy, as evidence of a depressed countryside. On the other hand there is clear evidence for an expansion of agriculture, for domestic building activity, and for bardic optimism. The visible evidence of hall and chamber suggests a time of prosperity and hope.

C. GRANGES

The term *grangia* was an umbrella name for a self-contained agrarian establishment which functioned separately and usually at some distance from the major landholding administrative centre. This centre could be a lord's castle or his principal manor house, a Cistercian abbey or a Knights Hospitaller preceptory. In each case the provision of buildings would be similar on the fertile low-lying arable land with beast-houses, barns for the storage of grain and hay, and with mills powered either by water or by beast. Examples of this provision have been recorded on the lands of the secular lords, such as the Greys of Ruthin in Dyffryn Clwyd and the Fitzalans at Oswestry and Chirk. An example of a grange barn still stands at Wick on the lands of the lords of Ogmore,

[35] Poetry of Dafydd ap Gwilym, "The Holly Grove", or anon., "Love's Architect": Clancy, *Medieval Welsh Lyrics*, pp. 40–1, 161.

[36] Dovecotes: *Glamorgan Inventory*, III, ii, 1982, pp. 299–303, 362–3, 378–9; Rees, *South Wales and the March*, p. 252, n. 4.

[37] Rabbits: *Glamorgan Inventory*, III, ii, 1982, pp. 313–45; Rees, *op. cit.*, pp. 138–9; the creation of sand-dune encroachment on the coasts of Glamorgan, Kidwelly, and Llandanwg near Harlech and Newborough on the south coast of Anglesey in the later middle ages gave ideal conditions for rabbit warrens. For the repair of sea walls in Gwent: *ibid.*, pp. 66, 183.

[38] Rees, *South Wales and the March*, pp. 254–5.

Glamorgan: It stands up to 12 feet high, is externally buttressed at regular intervals and has a single entrance protected by a porch; it measures 80 feet by 28 feet.[39] The supervision of such granges would be in the care of a steward or reeve.

Ecclesiastical owners used the grange as an economic outstation to supply food to the main abbey. In the first century of Cistercian settlement in Wales each grange was set under the supervision of an experienced lay-brother as a granger and directly supported the monastic economy with supplies in kind. After the Black Death, with the decline of lay-brother recruitment, the grange became more secular in character and was often placed under the control of a lay bailiff. An example, drawn from the bailiff's accounts of 1387–9 relating to Merthyrgeryn, a grange of Tintern, shows the variety of buildings to be expected: specifically mentioned are the granary, stable, byres, cowhouse, sheepcote, henhouse, pig-sty, and garden.[40] A chapel and domestic accommodation would also be provided, as would mills, cart sheds, and a dovecote. Brigands and robbers would be deterred by the stone precinct wall and the two-storey gatehouse, as can still be seen at Ewenny (Glam.), but most of the interior buildings were of wood set on a stone base and thatch was the principal roofing material recorded.

In many cases the basic provision of building was made in the high summer of grange farming in the thirteenth century. The alterations in the later middle ages were new animal houses, when labour-intensive cereal production was replaced by animal husbandry: at Merthyrgeryn in 1387 there was built a new byre and a drover's chamber over one of the byres.[41] Another improvement replaced the fire hazard of thatch by a covering of Pennant stone or ceramic tiles, as at Woolaston in 1412 after a raid by supporters of Glyndŵr.[42] The third improvement was greater mechanization, replacing the manual labour of the lay-brothers, as is shown by the increasingly frequent mention of mills on abbey lands. Indeed one abbot of Basingwerk, Thomas Pennant (1481–1522), was praised by the poet Guttain Owain for his business acumen, since "with mills he has filled every available glen and hill".[43] Some of these would have been fulling mills in the Greenfield valley, while others must have been windmills turned by the onshore breezes of the Dee estuary.

The buildings which do survive are but ghosts of their former glory;

---

[39] *Glamorgan Inventory*, III, ii, 1982, pp. 370–1.

[40] Williams, *The Welsh Cistercians*, II, pp. 239–40, 256–7, 294–6.

[41] L. N. Parkes and P. V. Webster, 'Merthyrgeryn: a grange of Tintern', *Arch. Camb.*, CXXIII, 1974, pp. 140–54.

[42] NLW, Badminton Deeds and Documents, M. 1575, quoted in Williams, *The Welsh Cistercians*, I, p. 72.   [43] *Ibid.*, II, p. 286.

foundations lie under the turf at Merthyrgeryn, Monknash, and Marcross. The datable masonry fragments suggest thirteenth-century work with only minor additions of a later date. Similarly the surviving grange chapels tend to exhibit early architectural details from before the Black Death, apart from "Hen Eglwys" on the crag above Margam. Excavation, as on two granges of Neath and at Merthyrgeryn, has been on a restricted scale, and has failed to provide closely dated evidence for those buildings which continued in use throughout the monastic period. The conversion of the grange, either to a demised tenanted farm as at Sker (Glam.), held by the Loughor family from 1467, or into a multiplicity of copyhold tenancies as at Ardda near Maenan (Aberconwy II), has tended to obscure the basic grange building layout. Thorough surveys and selective excavation are still needed on the majority of granges in Wales and the marches.

The best group of field surveys has been that provided by the Royal Commission on Historical Monuments working in Glamorgan and recording fifty-three granges, mainly on the lands of the two Cistercian abbeys at Neath and Margam.[44] The field surveys at Marcross and Monknash have recorded a range of turf-covered foundations and isolated structures, set within an inner enclosure of 5 or 6 acres, but contained within an outer enclosure of 18–20 acres. Less extensive remains have survived at Gelligarn, Sker, St Michael's Grange, and Stormy. Excavation at Llandough near Cardiff has shown the foundations of a barn and a dovecote. On the Tewkesbury abbey grange of Llantwit Major an account roll of 1449–50 includes mention of the buildings of the rectory and in the enclosure are an oxhouse, granary, watermill, and dovecote. The enclosure bank is still visible, demarcating an area 270 by 80 yards, about 4 acres, with a predominantly thirteenth-century gatehouse, and the excavated remains of a dovecote 12 feet in diameter, a tithe barn measuring 115 feet by $27\frac{1}{2}$ feet with opposed porches, and domestic buildings.[45] The position of the watermill at Llantwit can be approximately identified, but is not so clear as the mill at Monknash, where a low mound stands beside the mill pond and mill-leats. Another aspect of the lowland granges was the need to protect the land from erosion and inundation by the building of sea walls, and the need to ensure a supply of fish by the construction of weir banks on shelving coasts and estuaries. The example of Llandrillo near Llandudno on the lands of Aberconway is a good example, though not capable of close dating.

[44] *Glamorgan Inventory*, III, ii, 1982, pp. 245–306.

[45] W. Rees, 'The possessions of the abbey of Tewkesbury in Glamorgan', *South Wales and Monmouthshire Rec. Soc.*, II, 1950, pp. 127–86, esp. 156–60, 174–7; V. E. Nash-Williams, 'The medieval settlement at Llantwit Major', *Bull. BCS*, XIV, 1950–2, pp. 313–33.

The upland granges have left far fewer physical remains, though names such as *hafod* (summer dairy house) and *bercaria* (sheephouse) indicate their primary economic role. On two Glamorgan granges, Resolven and Hafod-y-porth, house platforms still survive, though they are not necessarily monastic; at the latter site there is also a mill marked by a house mound, a pond, and a leat.[46] At Hen Ddinbych there are two long ranges set within a lightly embanked enclosure, and at Hen hafod, a grange of Strata Florida, there appears to be similar evidence; however in the absence of excavation their period of occupation is uncertain.[47]

D. PEASANT HOUSING

Any survey of peasant housing in Wales during the later middle ages must recognize the difficulties inherent in assessing the various types of evidence. The buildings occupied by the unfree or villeins seldom survive, and nearly every domestic structure now visible was occupied by freemen, yeomen, or landowners of higher social status. Similarly the documentary evidence is rarely explicit about buildings at the lower end of the social scale; the Welsh laws were still applied in the manorial courts but their appropriateness to the actual conditions of fifteenth-century Wales cannot be precisely established. The solution to these uncertainties should be resolved by recourse to the excavated material, but there are difficulties here, partly caused by the lack of recent excavations and by their uneven geographical coverage, partly by the absence of sound dating evidence from pottery or coinage, and partly by the extent of later site disturbance.

As with the gentry houses discussed above, the importance of building material and the limitations of access to supplies of stone and wood determine the stability and the survival of domestic and agricultural structures. The major zones are both geological and racial: the contrast between the slates and the freestones reflecting the contrast between the pure Welsh and the anglicized lands. In the anglicized coastlands alongside the Bristol Channel and beside the Dee estuary nucleated settlements are common. These may take the form of housing arranged around a green or else strung in linear fashion along a street or ridge. Although the earliest maps or surveys depicting such village layouts date from the late sixteenth or early seventeenth centuries, excavation at Barry and field surveys at Runston and Wilcrick suggest that this settlement pattern pre-dates the Black Death.

[46] *Glamorgan Inventory*, III, ii, 1982, pp. 266–7, 276–7.
[47] C. A. Gresham, W. J. Hemp and F. H. Thompson, 'Hen Ddinbych', *Arch. Camb.*, CVIII, 1959, pp. 72–80.

These examples, together with excavation at a hamlet site in Cwmcidy, are drawn from Glamorgan and Gwent.[48] However, in north Wales the linear settlement of "Hen Caerwys" provided some evidence of fifteenth-century occupation, while Ardda on the upper slopes of the Conway valley may well be late fifteenth-century in origin.[49]

The coastlands surrounding Cardigan Bay, sweeping from Bardsey southwards to St Davids, were practically immune to English influences and were for long hostile to such intrusions. The castle towns of Harlech, Aberystwyth, Cardigan, and Newport were pockets of intrusive alien settlers and had little impact on rural life. Dispersed settlements (*trefi*) were normal both in the fertile valleys and in the mountainous heartland. The reeve's township (*maerdref, vardre*) was a possible focus for nucleation within the hundred (*cantref, cwmmwd*), while an opposite factor was the tendency for further dispersion of settlement to spread onto the marginal lands newly won from the moors, or recently cleared from scrubland or forest.[50] These dispersed huts were randomly scattered, unlike the peasant holdings set in girdle fashion around the common field cultivated in strips or quillets. The principal method of gaining new land was for customary tenants to negotiate rights to a conditionally free landholding (*tir prid*). Many of the isolated rectangular huts visible in Snowdonia and on the western flanks of the Cambrian mountains may be units settled in this fashion.[51] The work of T. Jones Pierce and C. A. Gresham on the rental of Bartholomew Bolde has shown how such holdings were built up and exploited in the mid-fifteenth century.[52] Further south the study of Nannau in the Mawddach valley by Thomas[53] has shown the extreme

[48] R. Caple, P. H. Jarvis and P. V. Webster, 'The deserted village of Runston, Gwent: a field survey', *Bull. BCS*, XXVII, 1976–8, pp. 638–52; L. N. Parkes and P. V. Webster, 'The shrunken village of Wilcrick', *ibid.*, pp. 508–12; Robinson, 'Medieval vernacular buildings', pp. 94–7; *Glamorgan Inventory*, III, ii, 1982, pp. 215–17, 224–6; H. J. Thomas and G. Dowdell, 'A shrunken medieval village at Barry, South Glamorgan', *Arch. Camb.*, CXXXVI, 1987, pp. 94–137, esp. 97–102.

[49] T. Rogers, 'Excavations at Hen Caerwys, Clwyd, 1962', *Bull. BCS*, XXVIII, 1978–80, pp. 528–33; RCHM, Wales, *Caernarvonshire Inventory*, I, 1956, pp. 74–5, nos. 207–10, 215–17; also pp. 176–7, nos. 639–45.

[50] C. Thomas, 'Social organisation and rural settlement in medieval north Wales', *JMHRS*, VI, ii, 1970, pp. 121–31; *idem*, 'Patterns and processes of estate expansion in the 15th and 16th centuries', VI, iv, 1972, pp. 333–42.

[51] C. A. Gresham, 'Platform houses in north-west Wales', *Arch. Camb.*, CIII, 1954, pp. 18–53; *idem*, 'The interpretation of settlement patterns in north-west Wales' in I. L. Foster and L. Alcock, eds., *Culture and Environment*, London, 1963, pp. 263–79; RCHM, Wales, *Caernarvonshire Inventory*, III, 1964, p. clxxviii.

[52] T. Jones Pierce, 'The *Gafael* in Bangor MS. 1939', *Hon. Soc. Cymmr.*, 1942, pp. 158–88, esp. 162–77; C. A. Gresham, 'The Bolde Rental (Bangor Ms. 1939)', *Caerns. Hist. Soc.*, XXVI, 1965, pp. 31–49.

[53] C. Thomas, 'The township of Nannau, 1100–1600', *JMHRS*, V, 1960, pp. 98–104.

processes of fission among freeholdings, which gave ruthlessly determined operators such as Dafydd ap Meurig Vychan the opportunity to amalgamate non-viable units into gentry estates. In the aftermath of Glyndŵr's rebellion a combination of political volatility and aggressive land acquisition provided ideal conditions for some of the peasantry to climb in status at the expense of their less fortunate or less strongly motivated neighbours.

The social climbers would abandon or rebuild the simple long-huts, "the turf-roofed villein's house", set on its smallholding of a few acres.[54] Where manorial privilege was jealously guarded, as in the lordship of Hay, there was no opportunity to increase holdings beyond 5 acres, and even the free tenantry could be excluded from rights to woodland, pasture, mountain grazing, and ownership of mills. Where the reins of control were less tightly held, then larger holdings were possible. Houses such as Hendre'r ywydd, Llangynhafal (Denbs.) show an agglutinative house with byre, service area, hall, and parlour created in timber-framing on a stone-sill base.[55] Elsewhere in Radnorshire and Breconshire the use of cruck frames could provide one-bay or two-bay houses with possibilities for an added bay (of byre at the lower end or parlour at the upper end) when economic conditions permitted or social conditions dictated.[56] Modest living accommodation might give a false impression of a landholding. At Cil-eos-isaf, Llanrhaedr-ym-Mochnant, a bake house and brew house were contained in a separate out-building.[57] Documentary evidence makes it clear that byres and barns were often separate buildings "out in the butts" or "between garden and field".[58] Towards the end of the fifteenth century there are more frequent references to enclosed gardens (murdon), orchards, and hopyards at smallholdings below gentry level. Archaeological evidence

[54] "No old hut, rain thirsty room" (Dafydd ap Gwilym): Clancy, Medieval Welsh Lyrics, p. 31; "no churl's hut, no turf roof-top" (Llywelyn ab y Moel): ibid., p. 182. "The Ruin" by Dafydd ap Gwilym describes an abandoned house 'between pasture and moor' but it is probably of freeman status: Bromwich, Dafydd ap Gwilym, pp. 186–7, 200–1. The rights of landowners to transfer villeins (nativi) with their land (e.g. NLW, Sotheby Ms. 5 (of 1378) and 8 (of 1390–1)) was a disincentive for tenants wishing to improve their housing. However, there are occasional inventories of houses and their contents (e.g. at Bangor in Maelor Saesneg in 1434: NLW, Plymouth Ms. 70).

[55] I. C. Peate, 'Hendre'r ywydd Uchaf – a late 15th century house', Denbs. Hist. Soc., XI, 1962, pp. 12–27.

[56] Examples discussed by Brooksby, 'The houses of Radnorshire', and by S. Jones and J. T. Smith, 'The houses of Breconshire' cited in n.1 above.

[57] S. R. Jones, 'Cil-Eos Isaf; a late medieval Montgomeryshire long-house', Montgomeryshire Colls., 61, 1969–70, pp. 115–31.

[58] NLW, Aston Hall Ms. 2200 of 1485; Sotheby Ms. 36 of 1439; Llangibby Castle Ms. A1008 of 1487.

has shown barns, as at Cosmeston and Rhadyr, and corn-drying kilns, as at Collfryn and Cwm Fynhadog Uchaf.[59] One of the rectangular houses at Hen Caerwys appears to have been a smithy, despite the provision in the Welsh laws that the settlement smithy had to be built nine paces distant from the other houses of the settlement in order to minimize the risk of fire.[60]

High in the uplands were the summer dwellings, the temporary lodgings linked to a transhumance pastoralism. The isolated dairy houses amid the summer grazing were homes for five months of the year.[61] Small rectangular huts would be accompanied by or shared with a stone-flagged dairy (*lluesty*) or a cheese house (*ty caws*); nearby might be built a circle of stones to provide a stack stand for drying the hay or a field kiln to parch the barley. Life on the sheilings (*hafodau*) was spartan; few possessions were taken into the hills and all were returned to the home farm (*hendref*) when the September mists closed in. Excavation at an abandoned sheiling site yields little if any dating evidence: Bwlch-yr-hendre at the headwaters of the Rheidol produced none; houses at Ystradfellte (Brecs.) and rather later at Nantcriafolen in the Brenig headwaters on the Denbighshire moors were likewise sparse on datable evidence.[62]

Around the holdings there might be the clearance mounds of boulders where fields had been levelled to allow rye or barley to be planted; close to the house would be the decayed turf stack where a store of fuel had been abandoned. Some of these *hafodau* might become the location for permanent farms while still indicating by their names their transient origins: one such house is Hafod-yspyty in the hills above Ffestiniog, but the high quality of its cruck trusses suggests a more generous dwelling than the usual marginal sites.[63] Hafod in Llansilin (Denbs.) is another house rebuilt to a high standard in the fifteenth century; it has lost its peasant characteristics.[64]

[59] Gardens: NLW, Sotheby Ms. 21 of 1416, and Talbot of Hensol Ms. 225 of 1489; orchards and hopyards: Milborne Ms. 2140 of 1498; field kilns: W. Britnell, 'A 15th-century corn-drying kiln from Collfryn, Llansantffraid Deuddwr. Powys', *Med. Arch.*, XXVIII, 1984, pp. 190–4; RCHM, Wales, *Caernarvonshire Inventory*, I, 1956, p. 84 (no. 245) and p. 88 (no. 263); Thomas and Dowdell, 'A shrunken medieval village of Barry', pp. 112–14.

[60] Butler, 'Domestic building in Wales and the evidence of the Welsh Laws', pp. 50, 53.

[61] R. U. Sayce, 'The old summer pastures', *Montgomeryshire Colls.*, LIV, 1956, pp. 117–45; LV, 1957, pp. 37–86; C. Vaughan, 'Lluestau Blaenrheidol', *Ceredigion*, V, 1960, pp. 246–63.

[62] L. Butler, 'The excavation of a long hut near Bwlch-yr-hendre', *Ceredigion*, IV, 1963, pp. 450–7; C. Fox, 'A croft in the upper Nedd valley, Ystradfellte, Breconshire', *Antiquity*, XIV, 1940, pp. 363–76; D. Allen, 'Excavations at Hafod y Nant Criafolen, Brenig Valley', *Post-Medieval Archaeology*, XIII, 1979, pp. 51–7.

[63] Smith, *Houses*, p. 43, fig. 27; M. Richards, 'Hafod and hafoty in Welsh place-names', *Montgomeryshire Colls.*, LVI, 1959, pp. 13–20, 177–87.

[64] Hughes, 'Notes on the architecture of some old houses', pp. 158–62; Smith, in R. R. Davies,

E. HOUSES OF THE CLERGY

The wide variety in the levels of clergy income should be reflected by an equally wide variety of housing provision. However, many factors conspire against the survival of such housing except at deserted village sites where the buildings lie concealed by the turf of the churchyard. Because such sites represent village failures they may be an unfairly biased sample at the lower end of the social scale. The best example of this type of site is the partly excavated house and barn at Llanfrynach, near Cowbridge, Glamorgan.[65] What survived was part of a two-storeyed stone-built house of at least two rooms, with a clay floor and a stone-flagged hearth; Pennant tile and ceramic ridge tile covered the roof. Across a cobbled passage lay a barn with an internal corn-drying kiln. Although this complex may indicate the normal provision of a rectory and glebe barn, the appropriation of the living to the Cistercian abbey of Margam in 1384 might have been the occasion for new building and an extension to an existing farm range.

Elsewhere, as at Barry Island and Highlight, both in coastal Glamorgan, a single-roomed house sufficed into the late middle ages until such time as the chapels were abandoned. For churches which remained in use, the rectories and vicarages which continued to occupy their medieval sites were likely to be rebuilt in a more substantial form in the post-Reformation period. It is therefore of minimal help to search through the glebe terriers, the earliest of which date from the decade 1630–9. Usually these houses were catering for a married clergy, though the strictures issued in Archbishop Warham's visitation of Bangor diocese in 1504 show that lapses from strict celibacy did occur among forty-three of the clergy.[66]

The literary evidence may highlight the extravagant and the unusual rather than describe the commonplace. Dafydd ap Gwilym gives details of a Cardiganshire house with white lime-washed walls adorned with painted decoration and with a floor of "marble tiles", presumably highly polished slate.[67] More detailed and exuberant is Guto'r Glyn's poetic description of the house occupied by the vicar of Llandrinio in the mid-fifteenth century.[68]

ed., *Welsh Society and Nationhood*, p. 143; Smith, *Houses*, pp. 95–7, figs. 45, 55, 62. It would be very tempting to see this structure as timberwork transferred from Sycharth after 1420: the aisle posts are the 'four wondrous pillars' so admired by Iolo Goch.

[65] Glamorgan–Gwent Trust, *Annual report, 1981–2*, Swansea 1982, pp. 36–41.

[66] Glanmor Williams, *The Welsh Church*, pp. 394–5.

[67] T. Parry, *Gwaith Dafydd ap Gwilym*, Cardiff, 1979, pp. 132–3.

[68] I. Williams and J. L. Williams, *Gwaith Guto'r Glyn*, Cardiff, 1939, pp. 109–11, 132–4, 275–6; quoted in Peate, *The Welsh House*, p. 131. D. R. Thomas, 'Llandrinio in the sixteenth century – two poems by Gutto'r Glyn', *Montgomeryshire Colls.*, xxv, 1904, pp. 143–54.

A new long hall is this, nine houses in one and all white,
Corndon stone on its roof enclosing the nine houses.
A louvre prevents a downpour from the heavens
And a fair cross loft with a screen.
[It is] a tiled floored *plas*.

The nine houses is an allusion readily apparent to listeners and readers. Sion Mechain's hall is equated with the nine houses which the villeins had to build and maintain for their princes. The implication is clear that at Llandrinio under one roof was provided all that was necessary for civilized life. This vicarage obviously ranks among the gentry housing. The high quality of the surviving timberwork at the Old Vicarage, Glasbury-on-Wye, with ornate trusses and cusped windbracing to hall, passage, and parlour, marks this out as another gentry equivalent.[69]

The surviving clergy houses are indeed likely to be better built or more elaborately finished than those of their less sophisticated neighbours, which needed subsequent improvement or total rebuilding to bring them up to the fashionable standards required by the Georgian and Victorian parish clergy. This preponderance towards the upper end of the housing range is shown by the tower house, the Old Rectory at Angle (Pembs.), and the twin-vaulted rectory at Nolton (Pembs.). The rectories surviving at Llandow and St Donats, both in Glamorgan, are rectangular houses with a hall and service rooms on the ground floor, and two upper rooms linked by a mural stair. Stone detailing to the arched doorways and cusped window tracery emphasize their social standing.[70] They are closely comparable to the clergy houses across the Bristol Channel in Somerset and Devon.[71] Slightly smaller is the Chantry House in Llantwit Major, a single-unit building measuring 32 feet by 22 feet, with an end entry beside the fireplace in the hall and with a mural turning stair leading to a chamber provided with a fireplace and a latrine shoot at the upper level.[72] It may originally have been part of a larger structure but it seems more likely that the priest of the Raglan chantry had to be content with this modest accommodation.

F. INDUSTRIAL BUILDINGS

The natural resources of Wales in stone, coal, and mineral deposits were spasmodically exploited during the later middle ages. Documentary evidence of this exploitation and for the operation of rural industries is

---

[69] Brooksby, 'The houses of Radnorshire', 1969, pp. 48–51.

[70] *Glamorgan Inventory*, III, ii, 1982, pp. 136–7, 182–4.

[71] W. A. Pantin, 'Medieval priests' houses in south-west England', *Med. Arch.*, I, 1957, pp. 118–46.   [72] *Glamorgan Inventory*, III, ii, 1982, pp. 193–4.

slight in extent and erratic in occurrence. Archaeological work has tended to concentrate on the better-documented Elizabethan period and consequently has little to contribute to this period.

(i) Quarrying

Throughout Wales the slates were quarried as a valuable if intractable building material; they provided roofing for houses and churches.[73] Usually a quarry was opened as near as possible to the intended project, preferably on its uphill slope. In areas where the slate was of poor quality for external walling it was employed in the footing walls of half-timbered or mud-walled structures. Stone of better quality, derived from the lias limestones, the Wenlock series, and the Old Red sandstones, were increasingly used for houses of the gentry.[74] The finer details of window heads and door arches were carved in stone in south-east Wales and southern Pembrokeshire, reproducing the forms found in castles and churches. Elsewhere wood was the principal medium for door and window openings, screens and roofs. The use of thinly split roofing slates from the Pennant beds of the carboniferous limestones and from the fissile sandstones was also at a modest and localized level, but house names, such as "Ty slats", and poetic references show both its novelty and its social cachet. Lime was required for mortar, for agricultural use and for lime-washing upon the exterior and interior walls of houses, castles, and churches. Such lime-washing carried a gentry connotation. This practice has left some early kiln structures beside castles, but dating is imprecise.

(ii) Coal

This fuel continued to be mined in north-east Wales and in various lordships within south Wales.[75] Mines at Ewloe and Buckley near Chester and in the waste of Hopedale south of Caergwrle were worked at intervals throughout the fourteenth and fifteenth centuries, with additional sources from Faenol on the bishop of St Asaph's lands in 1397 and from Coedpoeth and Brymbo in the Arundel lordship of Bromfield and Yale in 1412. In south Wales pits at Machen and Caerphilly in east Glamorgan were still being worked during this period, as were drifts and shafts at Swansea, Neath, and Kilvey, in

[73] F. J. North, *The Slates of Wales*, Cardiff, 1946.

[74] E. Neaverson, 'Medieval quarrying in north-eastern Wales', *Flints. Hist. Soc. Pubs.*, XIV, 1953–4, pp. 1–21; R. Haslam, *The Buildings of Wales: Powys*, Harmondsworth, 1979, pp. 29–31; E. Hubbard, *The Buildings of Wales: Clwyd*, Harmondsworth, 1986, pp. 89–94.

[75] W. Rees, *Industry before the Industrial Revolution*, Cardiff, 1968, I, pp. 34–6, 70–2, 79–82; *idem*, 'Records of the lordship of Senghenydd', *South Wales and Mon. Rec. Soc.*, IV, 1957, p. 33.

Gower and west Glamorgan. The exploitation of coal at outcrops in southern Pembroke, particularly in the lordship of Haverfordwest between Roch and Kilgetty, commences in the late fourteenth century. It is difficult to determine whether any coal was used in domestic heating; it may have had an industrial use in metal processing but was more often restricted to assist agricultural lime-burning, where its fumes were readily dispersed. No pits or mine buildings of this date have been recognized and none has been investigated by excavation.

(iii) *Salt*

No satisfactory evidence has been found for the construction of salt-pans along the coast of Wales, even though many estuaries would have been suitable for this activity. Instead the Cheshire wiches and the industrial enterprise at Droitwich probably supplied the needs of castles and other households in Wales. Many tenants had carrying duties involving salt brought from port or market to the lord's castle or to an abbey.[76]

(iv) *Pottery*

The study of medieval pottery in Wales is still developing steadily.[77] It is likely that the two rural pottery centres of Ewloe near Chester and Ewenny near Bridgend continued in operation throughout the fourteenth and fifteenth centuries. However, the major supplier in mid-Wales appears to be the Malvern industry and no rural kiln sites are known.[78] The complete organization of the pottery kilns, the worksheds, and the potters' housing has still to be found at these three areas.

(v) *Glass*

Although it is evident that castles and churches were supplied with glazed windows and that a few gentry houses could expect similar refinement in the fifteenth century, no glasshouses are known in Wales.[79] Vessel glass was another imported commodity. Charcoal burning was an activity associated equally with glass-making and ironworking; it tends to be mentioned on the fringes of the Forest of Dean and at the margins of the Flintshire uplands. These are the two areas where late medieval forest glasshouses might be sought.

[76] *Denbs. Hist. Soc.*, XVII, 1968, p. 27.

[77] Since 1978 the annual reports of the Welsh Pottery Research Group have attempted to put the study of pottery on a firmer footing.

[78] A. Vince, 'The medieval and post-medieval ceramic industry of the Malvern region', in D. S. P. Peacock, ed., *Pottery and Early Commerce*, London, 1977, pp. 257–305.

[79] Sycharth had "fair glass windows": Clancy, *Medieval Welsh Lyrics*, pp. 136–7.

(vi) *Iron*

The mining of iron ores, mainly haematite, was confined to the Forest of Dean, the valleys of Glamorgan, especially the Neath and the Cynon, Wentwood from Trellech eastwards to Monmouth, and at Ewloe and Hopedale in Flintshire.[80] Documentary evidence identifies these areas as engaged in mining, smelting, and forging. Remains of a medieval furnace have been identified at Dol-y-clochydd near Dolgellau (Mer.), and it is claimed that it worked for the Cistercian abbey of Cymmer in the late fourteenth century.

Smithing was a necessary accompaniment to rural settlement, providing nails, staples, arrowheads, axes, plough furniture, bridle-bits, and horseshoes. An excavated house at Hen Caerwys had a smithy site across the slope: it was probably a late medieval addition.[81] Forges are recorded at Penmacho and at Dolbenmaen (Caerns.). The use of charcoal as a fuel for iron-smelting meant that negotiated access to the forests, woods, and wastes for the charcoal burners to pursue their trade is a supporting piece of evidence.

(vii) *Lead*

The working of lead and silver continued throughout the later middle ages.[82] It was undertaken at Minera and Erryris (Denbs.), Holywell and Hopedale (Flints.), Shelve and Minsterley (Salop.), Rudry, Pentyrch and Llangan (Glam.), and the Ystwyth valley (Cards.). There were short-lived attempts to mine lead in the lordships of Brecon and Builth and also near Llandovery. The principal use would be for roofing high-status castles and abbeys, the provision of water cisterns and underground pipes, such as those found at the abbeys of Tintern and Valle Crucis. Laws were made to regulate the mining process, smelting, stamping, and ore washing to ensure a good standard of lead purity and a reliable measure of weight. Additional inducements offered by manorial exploiters to attract miners were a plot for a house, with free timber to assist housebuilding, shelter and shuttering for the lead-workings, and charcoal for smelting.[83] A small amount of copper was mined at Dyserth and Talargoch at the north-eastern end of the Clwydian range. However, there are no certain remains of the medieval exploitation of lead or copper.

[80] Rees, *Industry before the Industrial Revolution*, I, pp. 36–42, 51–5. F. J. North, *Mining for Metals in Wales*, Cardiff, 1962.

[81] Rogers, 'Excavations at Hen Caerwys..., 1962', pp. 528–33.

[82] Rees, *Industry before the Industrial Revolution*, I, pp. 36–44.   [83] *Ibid.*, p. 55.

(viii) *Watermills – fulling*

In the century before the Black Death fulling mills were constructed by the manorial lords and the monastic landowners in the eastern half of Wales, but the rivers draining into Cardigan Bay were apparently not exploited for this purpose. A maximum of eighty houses existing before 1350 were listed by R. I. Jack in his comprehensive survey.[84] This number was reduced to an average of fifty in operation during the period 1350–1500, partly because these mills were frequently singled out as a target for destruction in Glyndŵr's revolt, as they represented an obvious sign of manorial exploitation. Mills were often repaired or newly built in the decades 1470–1500 when more peaceful conditions prevailed, and when private individuals were prepared to venture their capital into industrial enterprises.

Some structures contained a fulling mill and a grist mill combined under the same roof; near towns the fulling mill was usually separate from the grist mill but shared the same leat and mill-pond. The mill buildings were generally simple rectangular houses. If timber-built they could be dismantled and re-erected at a better site, as happened when a mill at Llangollen was transported to Chirk in 1339. The mill and the fuller's house might be thatched or tiled depending on local resources. The mill machinery comprised the mill wheel, the fulling stocks and the hammers; outside would be a tenter yard where space was available for stretching out the cloth on frames. The term *pandy* could refer to a fulling mill, a walk-mill or a tucking mill. Associated activities were the digging of fuller's earth and the extraction of dyestuffs for colouring the cloth. No site has been excavated, though the locations of many documented mills can be identified more or less precisely.

(ix) *Watermills – grinding*

Water-powered corn mills (*melin*) were frequent throughout Wales, and there are many references in manorial documents to the villeins' and tenants' duties to repair the lord's mills; these obligations include specifically the cleaning of the leats, the building of the dam walls, the provision of stone and timber for the mill building and, occasionally, the carting of the millstones. Good millstones were highly prized, as is shown by a *cywydd* written by Tudor Aled begging for millstones from Anglesey, presumably from Benllech.[85] The account of the keeper of

---

[84] R. I. Jack, 'Fulling mills in Wales and the March before 1547', *Arch. Camb.*, CXXX, 1981, pp. 70–127; NLW, Plymouth Ms. 7 (of 1416); Rees, *South Wales and the March*, p. 156, n.2.

[85] Tudor Aled *floruit* 1480–1526: quoted in R. O. Roberts, 'The mills of Anglesey', *Anglesey Antiq. Soc.*, 1958, pp. 6–7.

the mills at Sandford, near Oswestry (Salop.), between 1361 and 1365 shows the normal range of regular maintenance, including new stones and new ironwork.[86] The two excavated rural sites at Dixton near Monmouth and at Highlight near Barry have not provided conclusive evidence of date or of mode of operation, but both appear to h   ad overshot wheels. Many other mill sites have been identified l   ld survey in Glamorgan and Gwent.[87]

(x) *Windmills*

Late medieval references to windmills (*melin y wynt*) are rare, but field survey has identified earthen mounds on the edge of villages, as at Runston, or isolated stone bases, as at Marcross, Merthyr Mawr Warren, and Sully (Glam.).[88] The earthen mounds presumably held the cross trees for a vertical post to support a wooden mill house, but none has been excavated in Wales. The vertical-sided stone towers, in diameter between 18 and 23 feet, had a ground-level doorway into a basement store, and an upper-level doorway (formerly approached by steps or a ladder) into the grinding floor; early illustrations suggest that the sail-axle was at the top of the stonework protected by a cap of tile or thatch. Without excavation early stone mill towers may be identified as lime-kilns, beacons, dovecote, or watch-towers.

G. CONCLUSION

The character of rural housing and agrarian life in Wales in the century and a half after the Black Death can be understood best from the surviving gentry houses and the parallel strand of gentry-patronized literature. However, this corpus of gentry houses is not safe from deliberate or unwitting destruction, and the work of the Royal Commission on Ancient Monuments in the past forty years has been instrumental in raising an awareness of this threatened heritage. For all other types of building and industrial exploitation the standing structures are few and ruinous. For a better understanding of these aspects, a well-directed research programme is essential, but it must take into account the tenurial and documentary evidence, the considerations of geological resources, soil quality and climatic change, and the limitations of landscape exploitation. Rural housing represents

---

[86] NLW, Aston Hall Ms. 5793; also Mss. 5305, 5307–8 in same deposit.

[87] S. D. Coates and D. G. Tucker, *Watermills of the Monmow and the Trothy*, Monmouth, 1978; *Glamorgan Inventory*, III, ii, 1982, pp. 369–81.

[88] Caple, Jarvis and Webster, 'The deserted village of Runston, Gwent', pp. 638–52; *Glamorgan Inventory*, III, ii, 1982, pp. 367–8, 370, 378; Williams, *The Welsh Cistercians*, II, p. 291.

an alliance between what man could win from the land to make his livelihood and what man wished to display of his disposable wealth in order to impress his neighbours and protect his family.

SELECT BIBLIOGRAPHY

Alcock, N. W., 'An East Devon manor in the later middle ages', *Devonshire Association*, CII, 1970 and CV, 1973.

Allison, K. J., 'The lost villages of Norfolk', *Norfolk Archaeology*, XXXI, 1957. 'Flock management in the sixteenth and seventeenth centuries', *EcHR*, 2nd ser. XI, 1958.

Allison, K. J., Beresford, M. W. and Hurst, J. G., *The Deserted Villages of Oxfordshire*, Leicester Univ. Dept. of English Local History, Occ. Paper XVII, 1965.
The Deserted Villages of Northamptonshire, Leicester Univ. Dept. of English Local History, Occ. Paper XVIII, 1966.

Armitage Smith, S., ed., *John of Gaunt's Register, 1372–1376*, Camden 3rd ser. XX–XXI, 1911.

Ashcroft, M. Y., 'Snape in the fifteenth century: account rolls', *North Yorks. RO J.*, 5, 1977.

Ashley, W. J., *The Bread of our Forefathers*, Oxford, 1928.

Astill, G. and Grant, A., eds., *The Countryside of Medieval England*, Oxford, 1988.

Aston, T. H. and Hilton, R. H., eds., *The English Rising of 1381*, Cambridge, 1984.

Ault, W. O., 'Open-field husbandry and the village community: a study of agrarian by-laws in medieval England', *American Philosophical Society*, NS LV(7), 1965.
Open-Field Farming in Medieval England, London, 1972.

Bailey, M. D., *A Marginal Economy?: East Anglian Breckland in the Later Middle Ages*, Cambridge, 1989.

Baker, A. R. H., 'Evidence in the *Nonarum Inquisitiones* of contracting arable lands in England in the early fourteenth century', *EcHR*, 2nd ser. XIX, 1966.

Baker, A. R. H. and Butlin, R. A., eds., *Studies of Field Systems of the British Isles*, Cambridge, 1973.

Bateson, E., Hinds, A. B., Hodgson, J. C., Craster, H. H. E., Vickers, K. H. and Dodds, M. H., eds., *A History of Northumberland*, 15 volumes, Newcastle-upon-Tyne, 1893–1940.

Bean, J. M. W., *The Estates of the Percy Family, 1416–1537*, Oxford, 1958.
'Plague, population and economic decline in England in the later middle ages', *EcHR*, 2nd ser. XV, 1963.

The Decline of English Feudalism, 1215–1540, Manchester, 1967.
From Lord to Patron: Lordship in Later Medieval England, Manchester, 1989.
'The English income taxes, 1404–50', forthcoming.
Beresford, G., *The Medieval Clayland Village: Excavations at Goltho and Barton Blount*, Society for Medieval Archaeology, Monograph 6, 1975.
Beresford, M. W., 'The deserted villages of Warwickshire', *Birmingham Arch. Soc.*, LXVI, 1945 (publ. 1950).
'The lost villages of Yorkshire', *Yorks. Arch. J.*, XXXVII, 1951; XXXVIII, 1952–4.
The Lost Villages of England, London, 1954, repr. 1965.
Beresford, M. W. and Hurst, J. G., *Deserted Medieval Villages: Studies*, London, 1971.
Beresford, M. W. and St Joseph, J. K., *Medieval England: an Aerial Survey*, 2nd edn, Cambridge, 1979.
Beveridge, W. H., 'Wages on the Winchester Manors', *EcHR*, VII, 1936–7.
'The yield and price of corn in the middle ages', in E. M. Carus-Wilson, ed., *Essays in Economic History*, I, London, 1954.
Birrell, J. R., 'The forest economy of the honour of Tutbury in the fourteenth and fifteenth centuries', *Univ. of Birmingham Historical J.*, VIII, 1962.
'Peasant craftsmen in the medieval forest', *AHR*, XVII, 1969.
'Medieval agriculture', *VCH Staffs.*, VI, 1979.
Blanchard, I. S. W., 'Economic change in Derbyshire in the late middle ages', Univ. of London Ph.D. thesis, 1967.
'The miner and the agricultural community in late medieval England', *AHR*, XX, 1972.
Bond, E. A., ed., *Chronica Monasterii de Melsa ab anno 1150 usque ad annum 1506*, 3 vols., RS, 1866–8.
Brandon, P. F., 'Agriculture and the effects of floods and weather at Barnhorne in Sussex during the later middle ages', *Sussex Arch. Colls.*, CIX, 1971.
'Demesne arable farming in coastal Sussex during the later middle ages', *AHR*, XIX, 1971.
'Cereal yields on the Sussex estates of Battle abbey during the later middle ages', *EcHR*, 2nd ser. XXV, 1972.
Brent, J. A., 'Alciston manor in the later middle ages', *Sussex Arch. Colls.*, CVI, 1968.
Bridbury, A. R., 'The Black Death', *EcHR*, 2nd ser. XXVI, 1973.
Britnell, R. H., 'Production for the market on a small fourteenth-century estate', *EcHR*, 2nd ser. XIX, 1966.
'Agricultural technology and the margin of cultivation in the fourteenth century', *EcHR*, 2nd ser. XXX, 1977.
'Minor landlords in England and medieval agrarian capitalism', *PP*, no. 89, 1980.
'The proliferation of markets in England, 1200–1349', *EcHR*, 2nd ser. XXXIV, 1981.
'Agriculture in a region of ancient enclosure, 1185–1500', *Nottingham Medieval Studies*, XXVII, 1983.

Growth and Decline in Colchester, 1300–1525, Cambridge, 1986.

'The Pastons and their Norfolk', *AHR*, XXXVI, 1988.

Brooksby, H., 'The houses of Radnorshire', *Radnorshire Soc.* XXXVIII–IX, 1968–9.

Brown, W. *et al.*, *Yorkshire Deeds*, 10 vols., Yorks. Arch. Soc. Rec. Ser. XXXIX, L, LXII, LXV, LXIX, LXXVI, LXXXIII, CII, CXI, CXX, 1909–55.

Burleigh, G. R., 'An introduction to the deserted medieval villages in East Sussex', *Sussex Arch. Colls.*, CXI, 1973.

'Further notes on deserted and shrunken medieval villages in Sussex', *Sussex Arch. Colls.*, CXIV, 1976.

Butler, L. A. S., 'Domestic building in Wales and the evidence of the Welsh laws', *Med. Arch.*, XXI, 1987.

Butlin, R. A., 'Northumberland field systems', *AHR*, XII, 1964.

Campbell, B. M. S., 'Population change and the genesis of common fields on a Norfolk manor', *EcHR*, 2nd ser. XXXIII, 1980.

'The extent and layout of common fields in eastern Norfolk', *Norfolk Archaeology*, XXXVIII, 1981.

'The regional uniqueness of English field systems? Some evidence from eastern Norfolk', *AHR*, XXIX, 1981.

'Agricultural progress in medieval England: some evidence from eastern Norfolk', *EcHR*, 2nd ser. XXXVI, 1983.

'Arable productivity in medieval England: some evidence from Norfolk', *J. of Economic History*, XLIII, 1983.

'Population pressure, inheritance and the land market in a fourteenth-century peasant community', in R. M. Smith, ed., *Land, Kinship and Life-Cycle*, 1984.

'The complexity of manorial structure in medieval Norfolk: a case study', *Norfolk Archaeology*, XXXIX, 1986.

Carew, Richard, *The Survey of Cornwall*, ed. with notes added by Thomas Tonkin, London, 1811.

The Survey of Cornwall, ed. F. E. Halliday, London, 1953.

Carpenter, C., 'The fifteenth-century English gentry and their estates', in M. Jones, ed., *Gentry and Lesser Nobility in Late Medieval Europe*, London, 1986.

Carr, A. D., *Medieval Anglesey*, Llangefni, 1982.

Carus-Wilson, E. M., 'Evidence of industrial growth on some fifteenth-century manors', *EcHR*, 2nd ser. XII, 1959.

ed., *Essays in Economic History*, 2 vols., London, 1954–62.

'The woollen industry', in *CEcH*, II, ed. M. M. Postan and E. Miller, 1987.

Carus-Wilson, E. M. and Coleman, O., *England's Export Trade, 1275–1547*, Oxford, 1963.

Chadwyck Healey, C. E. H., *History of Part of West Somerset*, London, 1901.

Chibnall, A. C., *Sherington: Fiefs and Fields of a Buckinghamshire Village*, Cambridge, 1965.

Chibnall, M., ed., *Select Documents of the English Lands of the Abbey of Bec*, Camden 3rd ser., LXXIII, 1951.

Clarke, E., 'Medieval labour law and the English local courts', *American J. of Legal History*, XXVII, 1985.

Cokayne, G. E., *Complete Peerage of England, Scotland, Ireland, Great Britain and the United Kingdom*, revised edn by Vicary Gibbs *et al.*, 12 vols., London, 1910–59.

Cowley, F. G., *The Monastic Order in South Wales, 1066–1349*, Cardiff, 1977.

Cunliffe Shaw, R., *The Royal Forest of Lancaster*, Preston, 1956.

'The townfields of Lancashire', *Hist. Soc. of Lancs. and Cheshire*, CXIV, 1962.

Darby, H. C., *The Medieval Fenland*, Cambridge, 1940.

ed., *A New Historical Geography of England*, Cambridge, 1973.

Darby, H. C., Glasscock, R. E., Sheail, J., and Versey, G. R., 'The changing geographical distribution of wealth in England, 1086–1334–1525', *J. of Historical Geography*, 5, 1979.

Davenport, F. G., *The Economic Development of a Norfolk Manor, 1086–1565*, Cambridge, 1906.

Davies, M., 'Field systems of South Wales', in A. R. H. Baker and R. A. Butlin, eds., *Field Systems*, 1973.

Davies, R. R., 'The lordship of Ogmore', *Glamorgan County History*, III, ed. T. B. Pugh, 1971.

Lordship and Society in the March of Wales, 1282–1400, Oxford, 1978.

ed., *Welsh Society and Nationhood*, Cardiff, 1984.

Conquest, Coexistence and Change: Wales, 1063–1415, Oxford, 1987.

Davis, N., ed., *The Paston Letters and Other Letters and Papers of the Fifteenth Century*, I–II, Oxford, 1971–6.

Denney, A. H., ed., *The Sibton Abbey Estates: Select Documents, 1325–1509*, Suffolk Rec. Soc., 2, Ipswich, 1960.

DeWindt, E. B., *Land and People in Holywell-cum-Needingworth*, Toronto, 1972.

ed., *The Liber Gersumarum of Ramsey Abbey: a Calendar and Index*, Pontifical Institute of Medieval Studies, Subsidia Medievalia 7, Toronto, 1976.

Dobson, R. B., ed., *The Peasants' Revolt of 1381*, London, 1970.

Durham Priory, 1400–1450, Cambridge, 1973.

Du Boulay, F. R. H., 'Late continued demesne farming at Otford', *Arch. Cant.*, LXXIII, 1959.

'Who were farming the English demesnes at the end of the middle ages?', *EcHR*, 2nd ser. XVII, 1964–5.

The Lordship of Canterbury: an Essay on Medieval Society, London, 1966.

Duby, G., *Rural Economy and Country Life in the Medieval West*, trans. C. Postan, London, 1968.

Dunstan, G. R., ed., *The Register of Edmund Lacy, Bishop of Exeter, 1420–1455*, 5 vols., Canterbury and York Soc. and Devon and Cornwall Rec. Soc., 1963–72.

Dyer, C., 'A redistribution of incomes in fifteenth-century England', *PP*, no. 39, 1968.

'Population and agriculture on a Warwickshire manor in the later middle ages', *Univ. of Birmingham Hist. J.*, XI, 1968.

'A small landowner in the fifteenth century', *Mid. Hist.*, I, 1972.

Lords and Peasants in a Changing Society: the Estates of the Bishopric of Worcester, 680–1540, Cambridge, 1980.

Warwickshire Farming, 1249–c. 1520: Preparations for Agricultural Revolution, Dugdale Soc. Occ. Paper 27, 1981.

'Deserted medieval villages in the West Midlands', *EcHR*, 2nd ser. xxxv, 1982.

'The social and economic background of the rural revolt of 1381', in R. H. Hilton and T. H. Aston, eds., *The English Rising of 1381*, 1984.

'Changes in the link between families and land in the West Midlands in the fourteenth and fifteenth centuries', in R. M. Smith, ed., *Land, Kinship and Life-Cycle*, 1984.

'English peasant buildings in the later middle ages', *Med. Arch.*, xxx, 1986.

'Changes in diet in the later middle ages: the case of harvest workers', *AHR*, xxxvi, 1988.

Standards of Living in the Later Middle Ages: Social Change in England, c. 1200–1520, Cambridge, 1989.

Elliott, G., 'The system of cultivation and evidence of enclosure in the Cumberland open fields in the sixteenth century', *CWAAS*, ns LIX, 1959.

Faith, R., 'Peasant families and inheritance customs in medieval England', *AHR*, xiv, 1966.

'Berkshire: fourteenth and fifteenth centuries', in P. D. A. Harvey, ed., *The Peasant Land Market in Medieval England*, 1984.

Farmer, D. L., 'Some grain price movements in thirteenth-century England', *EcHR*, 2nd ser. x, 1957.

'Grain yields on the Winchester manors in the later middle ages', *EcHR*, 2nd ser. xxx, 1977.

'Crop yields, prices and wages in medieval England', *Studies in Medieval and Renaissance History*, ns vi, 1983.

'Grain yields on Westminster Abbey manors, 1271–1410', *Canadian J. of History*, xviii, 1983.

'Two Wiltshire manors and their markets', *AHR*, xxxvii, 1989.

Farrer, W., ed., *Court Rolls of the Honour of Clitheroe*, 3 vols., Manchester, 1897–1913.

Faull, M. L. and Moorhouse, S. A., eds., *West Yorkshire: an Archaeological Survey to AD 1500*, 4 vols., Wakefield, 1981.

Feiling, K. G., 'An Essex manor in the fourteenth century', *EHR*, xxvi, 1911.

Field, R. K., 'The Worcestershire peasantry in the later middle ages', Birmingham Univ. M.A. thesis, 1962.

'Worcestershire peasant buildings, household goods and farming equipment in the later middle ages', *Med. Arch.*, ix, 1965.

Finberg, H. P. R., *Tavistock Abbey: a Study in the Social and Economic History of Devon*, Cambridge, 1951.

Fox, H. S. A., 'Field systems of East and South Devon. Part I, East Devon', *Devonshire Association*, civ, 1972.

'The chronology of enclosure and economic development in medieval Devon', *EcHR*, 2nd ser. XXVIII, 1975.

'The alleged transformation from two-field to three-field systems in medieval England', *EcHR*, 2nd ser. XXXIX, 1986.

France, R. S., ed., 'Two custumals of the manor of Cockerham', *Lancs. and Cheshire Antiquarian Soc.*, LXIV, 1954.

Fraser, C. M., 'The pattern of trade in the north-east of England, 1265–1350', *North. Hist.*, IV, 1969.

Fryde, E. B., *The Wool Accounts of William de la Pole, a Study of some Aspects of the English Wool Trade at the Start of the Hundred Years War*, St Anthony's Hall Publications, no. 25, York, 1964.

'The tenants of the bishops of Coventry and Lichfield and of Worcester after the plague of 1348–9', in R. F. Hunnisett and J. B. Post, eds., *Medieval Legal Records edited in Memory of C. A. F. Meekings*, London, 1978.

Studies in Medieval Trade and Finance, London, 1983.

Godber, J., *History of Bedfordshire, 1066–1888*, Bedford, 1969.

Gottfried, R. S., *Epidemic Disease in Fifteenth-Century England*, Leicester, 1978.

Bury St Edmunds and the Urban Crisis, 1290–1539, Princeton, 1982.

Graham, T. H. B., 'The townfields of Cumberland', *CWAAS*, NS X, 1910.

Gras, N. S. B., *The Evolution of the English Corn Market*, Cambridge, Mass., 1926.

Gras, N. S. B. and Gras, E. C., *The Economic and Social History of an English Village: Crawley, Hampshire, AD 909–1928*, Cambridge, Mass., 1930.

Gray, H. L., *English Field Systems*, Cambridge, Mass., 1915.

'Incomes from land in England in 1436', *EHR*, XLIX, 1934.

Greatrex, J., ed., *Account Rolls of the Obedientiaries of Peterborough*, Northants. Rec. Soc., XXXIII, 1984.

Greenwell, W., ed., *Bishop Hatfield's Survey*, Surtees Soc., XXXII, 1857.

ed., *Feodarium Prioratus Dunelmensis*, Surtees Soc., LVIII, 1872.

Gresham, C. A., *Eifionydd: a Study of Landownership from the Medieval Period to the Present Day*, Cardiff, 1973.

Griffiths, R. A., ed., *Boroughs of Medieval Wales*, Cardiff, 1978.

Habberjam, M., O'Regan, M., and Hale, B., eds., *Court Rolls of the Manor of Wakefield, 1350–1352*, Yorks. Arch. Soc., Wakefield Court Rolls ser., VI, 1987.

Halcrow, E. M., 'The decline of demesne farming on the estates of Durham Cathedral Priory', *EcHR*, 2nd ser. VII, 1955.

Hallam, H. E., 'The agrarian economy of south Lincolnshire in the mid-fifteenth century', *Nottingham Medieval Studies*, XI, 1967.

ed., *The Agrarian History of England and Wales*, II, *1042–1350*, Cambridge, 1988.

Hamilton Thompson, A., 'The pestilences of the fourteenth century in the diocese of York', *Arch. J.*, LXXI, 1914.

Hare, J. N., 'Change and continuity in Wiltshire agriculture in the late middle ages', in W. Minchinton, ed., *Agricultural Improvement, Medieval and Modern*, Exeter, 1981.

'Demesne lessees of fifteenth-century Wiltshire', *AHR*, XXIX, 1981.

'The Wiltshire rising of 1450: political and economic discontent in mid-fifteenth century England', *Southern History*, IV, 1982.

Harland, J., ed., *Three Lancashire Documents of the Fourteenth and Fifteenth Centuries*, Chetham Soc., OS LXXIV, 1868.

Harvey, B. F., 'The leasing of the abbot of Westminster's demesnes in the later middle ages', *EcHR*, 2nd ser. XXII, 1969.

Westminster Abbey and its Estates in the Middle Ages, Oxford, 1977.

Harvey, J. H., ed., *William Worcestre, Itineraries*, Oxford, 1969.

Harvey, P. D. A., *A Medieval Oxfordshire Village: Cuxham, 1240–1400*, Oxford, 1965.

ed. *Manorial Records of Cuxham, Oxfordshire, c. 1200–1359*, Oxfordshire Rec. Soc., L, and HMC Joint Publications 23, London, 1976.

ed., *The Peasant Land Market in Medieval England*, Oxford, 1984.

Hatcher, J., *Rural Economy and Society in the Duchy of Cornwall, 1300–1500*, Cambridge, 1970.

English Tin Production and Trade before 1550, Oxford, 1973.

Plague, Population and the English Economy, 1348–1500, London, 1977.

'Mortality in the fifteenth century: some new evidence', *EcHR*, 2nd ser. XXXIX, 1986.

Hewitt, H. J., *Medieval Cheshire: an Economic and Social History of Cheshire in the Reigns of the Three Edwards*, Chetham Soc., NS LXXXVIII, 1929.

Hilton, R. H., *The Economic Development of some Leicestershire Estates in the 14th and 15th Centuries*, London, 1947.

'Peasant movements in England before 1381', *EcHR*, 2nd ser. II, 1949.

The English Peasantry in the Later Middle Ages, Oxford, 1975.

ed. *Peasants, Knights and Heretics: Studies in Medieval English Society*, Cambridge, 1976.

'Lords, burgesses and hucksters', *PP*, no. 97, 1982.

Class Conflict and the Crisis of Feudalism: Essays in Medieval Social History, London, 1985.

'Medieval market towns', *PP*, no. 109, 1985.

Hilton, R. H. and Aston, T. H., eds., *The English Rising of 1381*, Cambridge, 1984.

Hoare, C. M., *The History of an East Anglian Soke*, Bedford, 1918.

Hoare, R. C., *The Modern History of South Wiltshire*, 6 vols., London, 1822–44.

Holmes, G. A., *The Estates of the Higher Nobility in XIVth-Century England*, Cambridge, 1957.

Holt, N. R., ed., *The Pipe Roll of the Bishopric of Winchester, 1210–1211*, Manchester, 1964.

Hoskins, W. G., *The Midland Peasant: the Economic and Social History of a Leicestershire Village*, London, 1957.

Hoskins, W. G. and Finberg, H. P. R., eds., *Devonshire Studies*, London, 1952.

Howell, C., *Land, Family and Inheritance in Transition: Kibworth Harcourt, 1280–1700*, Cambridge, 1983.

Howells, B. E., ed., *Pembrokeshire County History*, III, *Early Modern Pembrokeshire, 1436–1815*, Haverfordwest, 1987.

Hull, P. L., ed., *The Caption of Seisin of the Duchy of Cornwall (1337)*, Devon and Cornwall Rec. Soc., NS 17, 1971.

Jack, R. I., ed., *The Grey of Ruthin Valor of 1467–8*, Sydney, 1965.

Jennings, B., ed., *A History of Nidderdale*, Huddersfield, 1967.

Jewell, H. M., ed., *Court Rolls of the Manor of Wakefield, September 1348 to September 1350*, Yorks. Arch. Soc., Wakefield Court Rolls ser., II, 1981.

Jones, G. P., ed., *The Extent of Chirkland, 1391–3*, Liverpool, 1933.

Jones, G. R. J., 'The tribal system in Wales: a reassessment in the light of settlement studies', *Welsh Hist. Rev.*, I, 1961–2.

'Rural settlement in Anglesey', in S. R. Eyre and G. R. J. Jones, eds., *Geography as Human Ecology*, London, 1966.

'Field systems of North Wales', in A. R. H. Baker and R. A. Butlin, eds., *Field Systems*, 1973.

Jones Pierce, T., 'Landlords in Wales: the nobility and the gentry', in J. Thirsk, ed., *AHEW*, IV, 1967.

Medieval Welsh Society: Selected Essays, ed. J. Beverley Smith, Cardiff, 1972.

Keene, D. J., *Survey of Medieval Winchester*, 2 vols., Oxford, 1985.

Keil, I., 'Farming on the Dorset estates of Glastonbury abbey in the early fourteenth century', *Dorset N.H. and Arch. Soc.*, LXXXVII, 1965.

Kenyon, N., 'Labour conditions in Essex in the reign of Richard II', *EcHR*, IV, 1934.

Kershaw, I., *Bolton Priory: the Economy of a Northern Monastery, 1286–1325*, Oxford, 1973.

Kimball, E. G., ed., *The Shropshire Peace Roll, 1400–1414*, Shrewsbury, 1959.

Kingsford, C. L., ed., *The Stonor Letters and Papers, 1290–1483*, Camden 3rd ser. XXIX–XXX, 1919.

Kitchin, G. W., ed., *The Manor of Manydown*, Hants. Rec. Soc., 1895.

Langdon, J., *Horses, Oxen and Technological Innovation: the Use of Draught Animals in English Farming from 1066 to 1500*, Cambridge, 1986.

Leadam, I. S., ed., *The Domesday of Inclosures, 1517–1518*, 2 vols., RHS, 1897.

Levett, A. E., *The Black Death on the Estates of the See of Winchester*, Oxford Studies in Social and Legal History, V, Oxford, 1916.

Studies in Manorial History, Oxford, 1938.

Lewis, E. A., *The Medieval Boroughs of Snowdonia*, London, 1912.

Lewis, G. R., *The Stannaries: a Study of the English Tin Miner*, Cambridge, Mass., 1924.

Lloyd, T. H., *The Movement of Wool Prices in Medieval England*, *EcHR*, Supplement no. 6, 1973.

The English Wool Trade in the Middle Ages, Cambridge, 1977.

Lodge, E. and Somerville, R., eds., *John of Gaunt's Register, 1379–83*, Camden 3rd ser. LVI–LVII, 1937.

Lomas, R. A., 'Developments in land tenure on the prior of Durham's estate in the later middle ages', *North. Hist.*, XIII, 1977.

'The priory of Durham and its demesnes in the fourteenth and fifteenth centuries', *EcHR*, 2nd ser. XXXI, 1978.

Lomas, T., 'South-east Durham: late fourteenth and fifteenth centuries', in P. D. A. Harvey, ed., *The Peasant Land Market in Medieval England*, 1984.

Longstaff, W. H. and Booth, J., eds., *Halmota Prioratus Dunelmensis*, Surtees Soc., LXXXII, 1889.

Luders, A. *et al.*, eds., *Statutes of the Realm (1101–1713)*, 11 vols., Rec. Comm., 1810–28.

McFarlane, K. B., *The Nobility of Later Medieval England*, Oxford, 1973.
England in the Fifteenth Century: Collected Essays, London, 1981.

McIntosh, M. K., *Autonomy and Community: the Royal Manor of Havering, 1200–1500*, Cambridge, 1986.

Maitland, F. W., 'The history of a Cambridgeshire manor', *EHR*, IX, 1894, repr. in H. A. L. Fisher, ed., *The Collected Papers of Frederic William Maitland*, II, Cambridge, 1911.

Martin, D., 'Housing in eastern Sussex in the late medieval period', in P. Drewett, ed., *Archaeology in Sussex to 1500*, CBA Research Report, XXIX, 1978.

Massingberd, W. O., trans., *Court Rolls of the Manor of Ingoldmells*, London, 1902.

Mate, M., 'Agrarian economy after the Black Death: the manors of Canterbury cathedral priory, 1348–91', *EcHR*, 2nd ser. XXXVII, 1984.
'Labour and labour services on the estates of Canterbury cathedral priory in the fourteenth century', *Southern History*, VII, 1985.
'Medieval agrarian practices: the determining factors', *AHR*, XXXIII, 1985.
'Pastoral farming in south-east England in the fifteenth century', *EcHR*, 2nd ser. XL, 1987.

Maxwell Lyte, H. C., *A History of the Castle, Manor and Barony of Dunster and of the Families of Mohun and Luttrell*, 2 vols., London, 1909.

Mercer, E., *English Vernacular Houses: a Study of Traditional Farmhouses and Cottages*, RCHM, England, London, 1975.

Michelmore, D. J. H., ed., *Fountains Abbey Lease Book*, Yorks. Arch. Soc. Rec. Ser. CXL, 1981.

Midgley, L. M., ed., *Ministers' Accounts of the Earldom of Cornwall, 1296–1297*, 2 vols., Camden 3rd ser. LXVI, LXVIII, 1942 and 1945.

Moore, E. Wedemeyer, *The Fairs of Medieval England*, Toronto, 1985.

Morris, B. E., 'The south-western estates of Syon monastery in the later middle ages', University of Kent M.A. thesis, 1977.

Neilson, N., ed., *A Terrier of Fleet, Lincolnshire*, B. Acad. Records of Social and Economic History, IV, London, 1920.

Newton, K. C., *Thaxted in the Fourteenth Century*, Chelmsford, 1960.
The Manor of Writtle, London, 1970.

Newton, R., *The Northumberland Landscape*, London, 1972.

Oman, C., *The Great Revolt of 1381*, new edn with introduction and notes by E. B. Fryde, Oxford, 1969.

Orwin, C. S. and Orwin, C. S., *The Open Fields*, 3rd edn, Oxford, 1967.

Oschinsky, D., ed., *Walter of Henley and other Treatises on Estate Management and Accounting*, Oxford, 1971.

Owen, D. H., ed., *Settlement and Society in Wales*, Cardiff, 1989.

Page, F. M., *The Estates of Crowland Abbey*, Cambridge, 1934.

Parry, M. L., *Climatic Change, Agriculture and Settlement*, London, 1978.

Payne, F. G., 'The Welsh plough-team to 1600', in J. G. Jenkins, ed., *Studies in Folk Life: Essays in Honour of Iorwerth C. Peate*, Cardiff, 1969.

Phelps Brown, E. H. and Hopkins, S., 'Seven centuries of the prices of consumables compared with builders' wage-rates', *Economica*, NS XXIII, 1956; repr. in E. M. Carus-Wilson, ed., *Essays in Economic History*, II, and in P. H. Ramsay, ed., *The Price Revolution in Sixteenth-Century England*, London, 1971.

Platt, C., *The Monastic Grange in Medieval England*, London, 1969.

Platts, G., *Land and People in Medieval Lincolnshire*, Lincoln, 1985.

Pollard, A. J., 'Estate management in the later middle ages: the Talbots and Whitchurch, 1383–1525', *EcHR*, 2nd ser. XXV, 1972.

John Talbot and the War in France, 1427–1453, London, 1983.

Poos, L. R., 'The rural population of Essex in the later middle ages', *EcHR*, 2nd ser. XXXVIII, 1985.

Postan, M. M., 'Some economic evidence of declining population in the later middle ages', *EcHR*, 2nd ser. II, 1950.

ed., *Cambridge Economic History of Europe*, I, *The Agrarian Life of the Middle Ages*, 2nd edn, Cambridge, 1966.

'Medieval agrarian society in its prime: England', in *CEcH*, I, 2nd edn, 1966.

Essays on Medieval Agriculture and General Problems of the Medieval Economy, Cambridge, 1973.

Postan, M. M. and Miller, E., eds., *Cambridge Economic History of Europe*, II, *Trade and Industry in the Middle Ages*, 2nd edn, Cambridge, 1987.

Postan, M. M. and Titow, J. Z., 'Heriots and prices on the Winchester manors', *EcHR*, 2nd ser. XI, 1959.

Power, E. E., *The Wool Trade in English Medieval History*, Oxford, 1941.

Price, G. R., ed., *A Transcript of the Court Rolls of Yeadon, 1361–1476*, Draughton, 1984.

Pugh, T. B., ed., *The Marcher Lordships of South Wales, 1415–1536: Select Documents*, Cardiff, 1963.

ed., *Glamorgan County History*, III, *The Middle Ages*, Cardiff, 1971.

Putnam, B. H., *The Enforcement of the Statutes of Labourers during the First Decade after the Black Death, 1349–1359*, New York, 1908.

Raban, S., *Mortmain Legislation and the English Church 1279–1500*, Cambridge, 1982.

Rackham, O., *Trees and Woodland in the British Landscape*, London, 1976.

Ancient Woodland: its History, Vegetation and Uses in England, London, 1980.

Raftis, J. A., *The Estates of Ramsey Abbey: a Study in Economic Growth and Organization*, Toronto, 1957.

Tenure and Mobility: Studies in the Social History of the Medieval English Village, Toronto, 1964.

'Changes in an English village after the Black Death', *Medieval Studies*, XXIX, 1967.

Warboys: Two Hundred Years in the Life of an English Medieval Village, Toronto, 1974.

Raine, J., ed., *Historiae Dunelmensis Scriptores Tres*, Surtees Soc., IX, 1839.

Testamenta Eboracensia, 3 vols., Surtees Soc., IV, 1836; XXX, 1855; XLV, 1865.

The Priory of Hexham, 2 vols., Surtees Soc., XLIV, 1864; XLVI, 1865.

Ramm, H. G., McDowell, R. W., and Mercer, E., *Shielings and Bastles*, RCHM, England, London, 1970.

Ratcliff, S. C., ed., *Elton Manorial Records, 1279–1351*, Roxburghe Club, 1946.

Ravensdale, J. R., *Liable to Floods: Village Landscapes on the edge of the Fens, AD 450–1850*, Cambridge, 1974.

Razi, Z., *Life, Marriage and Death in a Medieval Parish: Economy, Society and Demography in Halesowen, 1270–1400*, Cambridge, 1980.

'Family, land and the village community in later medieval England', *PP*, no. 93, 1981.

'The erosion of the family–land bond in the late fourteenth and fifteenth centuries', in R. M. Smith, ed., *Land, Kinship and Life-Cycle*, 1984.

Rees, W., 'The Black Death in Wales', *RHS*, 4th ser. III, 1920.

South Wales and the March, 1284–1415: a Social and Agrarian Study, Oxford, 1924.

Réville, A. and Petit-Dutaillis, C., *Le Soulèvement des Travailleurs d'Angleterre en 1381*, Paris, 1898.

Richmond, C., *John Hopton: a Fifteenth-Century Suffolk Gentleman*, Cambridge, 1981.

Roberts, B. K., 'Village plans in County Durham: a preliminary statement', *Med. Arch.*, XVI, 1972.

Rogers, J. E. Thorold, *A History of Agriculture and Prices in England, 1259–1793*, 7 vols., Oxford, 1866–1902.

Ross, C. D. and Pugh, T. B., 'The English baronage and the income tax of 1436', *Bull. IHR*, XXVI, 1953.

Russell, J. C., *British Medieval Population*, Albuquerque, 1948.

Ryder, M. L., 'The history of sheep breeds in Britain', *AHR*, XII, 1964.

Sabin, A., ed., *Some Manorial Accounts of St Augustine's Abbey, Bristol*, Bristol Rec. Soc., XXII, 1960.

Salzman, L. F., *Building in England down to 1540*, revised edn, Oxford, 1967.

Saul, N., *Scenes from Provincial Life: Knightly Families in Sussex, 1280–1400*, Oxford, 1986.

Savine, A., 'Copyhold cases in the early Chancery proceedings', *EHR*, XVII, 1902.

The English Monasteries on the Eve of the Dissolution, Oxford Studies in Social and Legal History, I, 1909.

Schofield, R. S., 'The geographical distribution of wealth in England, 1334–1649', *EcHR*, 2nd ser. XVIII, 1965.

Scrope, G. P., *History of the Manor and Barony of Castle Combe in the County of Wiltshire*, London, 1852.

Searle, E., *Lordship and Community: Battle Abbey and its Banlieu, 1066–1538*, Toronto, 1974.

Shrewsbury, J. F. D., *A History of Bubonic Plague in the British Isles*, Cambridge, 1970.

Skeel, C. A. J., 'The cattle trade between Wales and England from the fifteenth to the nineteenth centuries', *RHS*, 4th ser. IX, 1926.

Slack, W. J., *The Lordship of Oswestry, 1393–1607*, Shrewsbury, 1951.

Smith, J. Beverley, 'Crown and community in the principality of North Wales in the reign of Henry Tudor', *Welsh Hist. Rev.*, III, 1966.

'The lordship of Senghennydd', in T. B. Pugh, ed., *Glamorgan County History*, III, 1971.

Smith, J. T., 'Cruck distributions: an interpretation of some recent maps', *Vernacular Architecture*, VI, 1975.

Smith, L. O. W., 'The lordships of Chirk and Oswestry, 1281–1415', Univ. of London Ph.D. thesis, 1970.

Smith, P., *Houses of the Welsh Countryside*, 2nd edn, London, 1988.

Smith, R. A. L., *Canterbury Cathedral Priory*, Cambridge, 1943.

Smith, R. M., ed., *Land, Kinship and Life-Cycle*, Cambridge, 1984.

Smyth, J., of Nibley, *The Lives of the Berkeleys, Lords of the Manor of Berkeley*, ed. J. MacLean, 3 vols., Gloucester, 1883–5.

Stephenson, M. J., 'The productivity of medieval sheep on the great estates, 1100–1500', Cambridge Univ. Ph.D. thesis, 1986.

'Wool yields in the medieval economy', *EcHR*, 2nd ser. XLI, 1988.

Stokes, E., ed., *Abstracts of Wiltshire Inquisitions Post Mortem ... 1327–1377*, Index Library, XLVIII, 1914.

Sylvester, D., 'The open fields of Cheshire', *Hist. Soc. of Lancs. and Cheshire*, CVIII, 1956.

The Rural Landscape of the Welsh Borderland, London, 1969.

Taylor, C. C., 'Whiteparish: a study of the development of a forest-edge parish', *Wilts. Arch. and N.H. Magazine*, LXII, 1967.

'Three deserted medieval settlements in Whiteparish', *Wilts. Arch. and N.H. Magazine*, LXXIII, 1968.

The Making of the English Landscape: Dorset, London, 1970.

Fields in the English Landscape, London, 1975.

Thirsk, J., 'The common fields', *PP*, no. 29, 1964.

ed., *The Agrarian History of England and Wales*, IV, *1500–1640*, Cambridge, 1967; V, *1640–1750*, 2 vols., Cambridge, 1984–5.

Thomas, A. H., ed., *Calendar of Early Mayors' Court Rolls Preserved among the Archives of the Corporation of the City of London at the Guildhall, AD 1298–1307*, Cambridge, 1924.

Thomas, A. H. and Jones, P. E., eds., *Calendar of Plea and Memoranda Rolls Preserved among the Archives of the Corporation of the City of London at the Guildhall, AD 1323–1482*, 6 volumes, Cambridge, 1926–61.

Thomas, C., 'Peasant agriculture in medieval Gwynedd', *Folk Life*, 13, 1975.

Thorpe, H., 'The lord and the landscape', *Volume jubilaire offert à M. A. Lefèvre*, Louvain, 1964; repr. *Birmingham Arch. Soc.*, LXXX, 1965.

Titow, J. Z., *Winchester Yields: a Study in Medieval Agricultural Productivity*, Cambridge, 1972.

Toulmin Smith, L., ed., *The Itinerary of John Leland in or about the Years 1535–1543*, 5 vols., London, 1907–10, repr. 1964.

Trow-Smith, R., *A History of British Livestock Husbandry to 1700*, London, 1957.

Tupling, G. H., *The Economic History of Rossendale*, Chetham Soc., NS LXXXVI, 1927.

Vanderzee, G., ed., *Nonarum Inquisitiones in Curia Scaccarii*, Rec. Comm., London, 1807.

Vinogradoff, P. and Morgan, F., eds., *Survey of the Honour of Denbigh, 1334*, B. Acad. Records of Social and Economic History, I, London, 1914.

Waites, B., 'A Yorkshire farmer in the memoranda rolls', *Yorks. Arch. J.*, XLI, 1966.

　Moorland and Vale-land Farming in North-East Yorkshire: the Monastic Contribution to the Fourteenth and Fifteenth Centuries, Borthwick Papers, 32, York, 1967.

Weaver, F. W., ed., *Somerset Medieval Wills, 1383–1500*, Somerset Rec. Soc., XVI, 1901.

Whitfield, M., 'The medieval fields of south-east Somerset', *Somerset Arch. and N.H. Soc.*, CXXV, 1981.

Williams, D. H., *The Welsh Cistercians: Aspects of their Economic History*, Pontypool, 1969.

　The Welsh Cistercians, 2 vols., Caldey, 1982.

Williams, Glanmor, *The Welsh Church from Conquest to Reformation*, Cardiff, 1962.

　ed., *Glamorgan County History*, IV, *Early Modern Glamorgan*, Cardiff, 1974.

Williams, Gwyn A., *Medieval London: from Commune to Capital*, London, 1963.

Williams-Jones, K., ed., *The Merioneth Lay Subsidy Roll, 1292–3*, Cardiff, 1976.

Winchester, A. J. L., *Landscape and Society in Medieval Cumbria*, Edinburgh, 1987.

Wright, S. M., 'Barton Blount: climatic or economic change?', *Med. Arch.*, XX, 1976.

　The Derbyshire Gentry in the Fifteenth Century, Derbs. Rec. Soc., VIII, 1983.

Wynn, Sir John, *The History of the Gwydir Family*, ed. J. Ballinger, Cardiff, 1927.

INDEX

Note Counties are given in their pre-1974 form.